EVERY-DAY COOKERY

AND

HOUSEKEEPING BOOK.

This is a facsimile edition of the Victorian classic
Mrs Beeton's Everyday Cookery and Housekeeping Book
first published in London by Ward, Lock & Co. in 1893.
A short history of Mrs Beeton is included at the end of this book.

CONVERSIONS AND ABBREVIATIONS

WEIGHT
lb = pound; oz = ounce

1 ounce = 28.35 g
1 pound = 16 ounces = .454 kg
1 quatern = 3 pounds 8 ounces = 1.59 kg

VOLUME
1 gill = 5 fluid ounces = .14 L
1 pint = 20 fluid ounces = .57 L
1 quart (¼ of a gallon) = 2 pints = 1.14 L
1 gallon = 8 pints = 4.55 L
1 peck = ¼ bushel
1 bushel = 8 gallons = 36.4 L

TIME
h = hours; m = minutes

CURRENCY
£ = pound sterling
s = shilling
d = penny

e.g. £2 1s. 6d. = 2 pounds, 1 shilling and sixpence
    5s. = 5 shillings

1 guinea = 1 pound and 1 shilling
1 pound = 20 shillings
1 crown = 5 shillings
1 half crown = 2 shillings and sixpence
1 florin (2 bob bit) = 2 shillings
1 shilling = 12 pennies (a bob)
1 sixpence (a tanner) = 6 pennies
1 threepence (pronounced 'thruppence') = 3 pennies
1 penny = 2 halfpennies (pronounced ha'pny)
1 farthing = ¼ penny

The Five Mile Press Pty Ltd
Publishers of Rare & Unusual Books
1 Centre Road, Scoresby
Victoria 3179 Australia
www.fivemile.com.au

First published 1893 by Ward, Lock & Co., Limited
This edition published by The Five Mile Press, 2011

Printed in China

Cover design by Luke Causby, Blue Cork
Scanning, formatting and assembly by
The Small Back Room, Olinda, Victoria

National Library of Australia Cataloguing-in-Publication entry

Beeton, Mrs (Isabella Mary), 1836–1865

Mrs Beeton's everyday cookery & housekeeping book : a practical
and useful guide for all mistresses and servants / Isabella Beeton.

ISBN 9781742485812 (hbk.)

Recipes–England.
Cooking, English.
Home economics.

641.50942

In memory of Auntie Dot, and with thanks to Sue Gillies

LITH. IN HOLLAND BY EMRIK & BINGER, 379 STRAND, LONDON.

DINNER TABLE LAID FOR 12 PERSONS

BEETON'S
EVERY-DAY COOKERY
AND
HOUSEKEEPING BOOK.

𝕬 𝕻𝖗𝖆𝖈𝖙𝖎𝖈𝖆𝖑 𝖆𝖓𝖉 𝖀𝖘𝖊𝖋𝖚𝖑 𝕲𝖚𝖎𝖉𝖊
FOR ALL MISTRESSES AND SERVANTS.

ENTIRELY NEW EDITION,
REVISED AND GREATLY ENLARGED,
CONTAINING

NEW AND VALUABLE RECIPES, INCLUDING INSTRUCTIONS FOR FOREIGN AND VEGETARIAN COOKERY,

NEW FRENCH & ENGLISH MENUS FOR EVERY MONTH IN THE YEAR,

NEW MENUS FOR BREAKFAST, LUNCHEON, TEA, SUPPER & PICNICS, NEW TABLES OF HOUSEKEEPING ACCOUNTS AND HOUSEHOLD EXPENDITURE.

NEW COLOURED PLATES & FULL-PAGE & OTHER ENGRAVINGS.

WITH MUCH NEW AND VALUABLE INFORMATION WITH REGARD TO MODES OF COOKING, SCIENCE OF COOKERY, AND HOUSEHOLD ARRANGEMENTS.

LONDON :
WARD, LOCK & CO., LIMITED,
WARWICK HOUSE, SALISBURY SQUARE, E.C.
NEW YORK AND MELBOURNE.

PREFACE TO NEW EDITION.

N these days of progress in the culinary art, as well as in other arts and sciences, no matter how good a Cookery Book may be, or how replete with well-tried recipes and useful information, a time must come when a revised and improved edition will be needed.

The Editors feel that the time has arrived for bringing up to date " Mrs. Beeton's Everyday Cookery," a work that up to the present time has been considered only second to Mrs. Beeton's celebrated " Household Management." Within the last few years we have been driven to feel that for all girls in every station of life cookery should be a necessary part of education ; and that to cook without knowing anything about the constituents or properties of the various kinds of food used is a great mistake.

Within the last ten years there has been a great alteration in the prices of provisions, as well as an increase in the varieties at our disposal ; in most cases due to the greater facilities of importation and supply.

There is also a difference, and a very marked one, in the style of serving dinners and other meals ; while the decorations of the table are now considered almost as important as the dinner itself.

These reasons alone would be sufficient to render a new edition necessary in order that the book may retain its reputation of being thoroughly up to date, practical and complete.

The Editors have spared neither time nor pains to enable it to meet the requirements of the day, not only simply as a cookery book, but as a useful household guide in families, both large and small.

None of the old well-tried recipes have been taken away from "Mrs. Beeton's Every-day Cookery;" but all have been revised, and, where necessary, prices have been altered to the average ones of the present day.

But, while nothing has been taken away, much has been added, the new edition being increased by a very large number of New Recipes, and full Instructions are given in all the modern and approved Modes of Cookery, in accordance with the progressive improvements of the age.

We append a brief summary of the additional matter contained in the pages added to the work.

Practical Housekeeping: Housekeeping Accounts; Housekeeping Expenditure; Housekeeper's Table for Choosing and Buying all Fresh Provisions, showing their Seasons and Prices.

Serving of all Meals: Laying the Cloth for various meals; Folding of Serviettes; Waiting at Table.

Decorations for Tables for every Month in the Year.

Arrangement of Kitchen:—Lists of Articles required in those of various sizes.

The Science of Cookery.   Properties of Foods.

Cookery as an Education.   Various Modes of Cooking—Baking, Boiling, &c.

Trussing of Poultry and Game, fully Illustrated with Sketches from Nature.

New Menus in French and English, for every Month in the Year.

Menus for all Meals.

New Recipes, including Vegetarian Dishes.

New Full-page and other Illustrations.

Original Designs for Menu Cards for every Month in the Year.

New Coloured Plates specially prepared and designed for this work.

New Menus for every month in the year, written in both French and English, with charming designs for the cards upon which they may be printed.   These will be found of great value to dinner givers; while practical housewives will be glad to see that the cost of a large proportion of the dinners have been carefully calculated, showing at a glance the expense to be incurred.

Not only are there Menus for the chief meal of the day, but also for breakfast, luncheon, tea and supper.

A chapter that should be of extreme value to a good housewife is that devoted to the "Choosing and Buying all Fresh Provisions." The figures quoted are the average prices in large towns.

Tables showing the seasons when various provisions are obtainable and best are given, and no trouble has been spared to make these tables correct and reliable.

Another chapter is given to "Housekeeping Accounts and the Management of Housekeeping Expenses." In this, besides some useful advice to young housekeepers, is shown a simple yet good way of keeping accounts by week, month and year; also there are excellent tables of average household expenditure in families of from two to six persons, with incomes varying from £150 to £600 per annum.

Subjects accessory to cookery will be found thoroughly treated, as, for example, laying the cloth for the different meals, the manner in which they should be served, the folding of the serviettes, and the decorations.

In the folding of the serviettes many new and pretty ways are shown, by which they may be made an ornament to the table.

The hints upon table decorations will be found in a prettily-illustrated chapter, showing some receptacles for flowers and foliage which are of new and fashionable design; and besides this chapter, there are, in the dictionary itself, suggestions for seasonable decorations for every month in the year.

The "Science of Cookery" is treated of carefully; and it will interest many to know the constituents of all ordinary foods, as well as instruct them how best to combine them to form a good and healthy diet. The relative value of food is also an interesting subject to those who like to know the full value of all food prepared for the table; showing, as it does, not only what foods are the most economical, but by what process of cooking the best result is obtained.

Another useful table is "The Cook's Time Table," by consulting which the cook can see at a glance what time to allow for cooking all kinds of fish, meat, poultry, game and vegetables by the various modes of cooking. In the case of fish and meat, the tables show the time required for different weights.

"Trussing" forms a feature of the new book, and should prove invaluable to those who have to prepare poultry and game for the table; the illustrations, taken from nature, show the process at every stage, and teach, far more plainly than words could possibly do, how to accomplish what is always a difficult task to the inexperienced.

Chapters are added on the all-important subject of the proper management of servants and arrangement of their various work. The duties of the mistress towards her servants, as well as the duties of the servant towards her mistress, being fairly dealt with.

The book as now issued will, it is hoped, commend itself to all who can appreciate Good Cookery, alike to residents in England, America, in the Colonies or on the Continent; and all who have learned to value it in the old form will realise the great improvements made in the present edition.

" Mrs. Beeton's Every-Day Cookery " has always maintained the reputation of being the best Cookery Book issued at Three Shillings and Sixpence ; and the Publishers trust that in its Enlarged and Improved form, it may be still more acceptable and more firmly established as a never-failing guide in all English-speaking households. Infinite pains have been taken and great expense has been incurred in the preparation of this new edition. Every line has been re-composed, and two hundred pages are added, so that the work, it is hoped, may more than ever deserve the praise everywhere bestowed upon it, as being the Best and Cheapest, as well as the Most Complete and thorough Manual on Cookery and Housekeeping ever offered at the price to the English public.

PREFACE TO THE FIRST EDITION.

The reasons for the Publication of this Volume—the First of a Series of Practical Manuals which were to be called the " All About It" Books—were thus explained in a Prospectus issued a few months ago, and approved by the late Mrs. S. O. BEETON.

MANY wishes have been expressed to the Authoress of the "Book of Household Management" that a volume of Recipes in Cookery should be written which could be sold at a price somewhere between the seven-and-sixpenny "Household Management" and the Shilling Cookery Book. Accordingly Mrs. BEETON has prepared a Collection of Recipes, and of other Practical Information concerning the Dressing and Serving of Family Fare, which, when completed, will be published, in serviceable binding, at the price of Three Shillings and Sixpence.

As Mistress, Cook and Critic have declared that the details in Mrs. BEETON's larger work are *so easy to understand*, the Authoress has followed in every Recipe printed in the present Dictionary, the same simple plan she originally used. Regarding, however, the *arrangement* of the Recipes, the Authoress has chosen the Dictionary form, believing an alphabetical arrangement to be the best for a book that is being constantly referred to. By the adoption of a very intelligible system, all *cross* reference, and that very disagreeable parenthesis " (*See* So-and-so) " is avoided, except in a very few instances. Where any warning as to what should *not* be done is likely to be needed, it is given, as well as advice as to what ought to be done. No pains have been thought too great to make *little things* clearly understood. Trifles constitute perfection. It is just the knowledge or ignorance of little things that usually makes the difference between the success of the careful and experienced housewife or servant, and the failure of her who is careless and inexperienced. Mrs. BEETON has brought to her new offering to the Public a most anxious care to describe plainly and fully all the more difficult and recondite portions of Cookery, whilst the smallest items have not been " unconsidered trifles," but each Recipe and preparation have claimed minute attention.

CONTENTS.

COLOURED PLATES.

FULL-PAGE ILLUSTRATIONS.

ENTREES

PRACTICAL HOUSEKEEPING.

A GOOD HOUSEKEEPER.

In the fullest and best sense, how great is the significance in the term "a good housekeeper!" Whether she rule in mansion or cottage, her sway must be over a household in which the chief elements of a happy home will not be lacking.

Not everyone can realise what the work of a good housekeeper really is. We see in a well-ordered household everything neat, clean and comfortable, servants doing their work thoroughly, and meals well cooked and punctually served, and we take it far too much for granted that it should be so. Could we, however, look behind the scenes, we might be surprised at the method, care and labour needed to make and keep the wheels of domestic machinery running so smoothly.

We assert, and with reverence, that it could not be possible to over-rate the value of one who, by patience, energy and self-sacrifice, succeeds in making all around her contented and comfortable.

Praise is readily accorded to those whose province it seems is to shine in society, whose brilliant talents or accomplishments almost command admiration, while those who simply devote themselves to their home, to the comfort of their husbands and the care and culture of their children are, in comparison, but lightly esteemed; while in reality they should be more so. They often do a higher, nobler work than mere talents could effect, and seldom without self-sacrifice. These good women have their reward. If the works of their more gifted sisters find a place in the world, their deeds of forbearance, patience, and thoughtfulness live in the hearts of those they love; and they may be content in the knowledge that, in the truest meaning of the word, they are helpmeets to their husbands, and that hereafter "their children will rise up and call them blessed."

HOUSEKEEPING AS AN EDUCATION.

Housekeeping *should* be taught our young girls, but in these days of science and high-pressure education there is but little time they can spare for homely tasks. In many cases, at least, it is not till they marry and have to take upon themselves the guidance and responsibility of a household, that they realise (lacking a previous training) how hard that burden may be.

Far be it from us to detract from the value of the education that is daily a revelation of what good work the women of our day are capable, nor to assert, for one moment, that the highest culture is incompatible with good house-keeping. Yet it is a fact that, in many cases, young people are made to attempt too much, and there is not time enough to spare from study and gaiety to make a good knowledge of household matters other than a rare quality.

It seems a pity, particularly for the reasons that, when married, they so often give up their former occupations and amusements, but yet are not fitted to fulfil the duties then thrust upon them.

If the study must be accomplished, if it is thought necessary for so many young girls to learn a great deal that they will, in all probability, forget in the first years of married life, if not sooner, surely a little time might be spared from the gaiety and amusements of those emancipated from school life, to learn what in after years will be of essential value both to themselves and others. Learning need not be a toil. Take cookery for example, there are but few young people who cannot be interested in this ; and, beginning with the comparatively easy and pleasant task of making a cake or pudding, it would be thought no hardship to turn to more difficult branches of the art, nor to learn " the reason why " for everything.

In olden days notable housekeepers were notable women. In managing their homes and servants, training their daughters in homely fashion to bake and stew, spin and embroider, or concoct the herbal remedies needed for the relief of their poorer neighbours as well as themselves, the worthy dames seem to have found sufficient distinction as well as employment. They were proud of their housewifely skill, of their cookery, of the fair white linen their own hands had woven, and of their medicines, salves, and confections. No need was there then for cookery books or instructions in housekeeping, recipes and discipline were alike found at home. In these times it is hardly possible to do as they did, yet they may well teach us a lesson in the training of our girls to a liking for housewifely tasks and the realization of the fact that there are few stronger influences upon us than those brought to bear in our early home life.

There is an innate love for housekeeping in most girls, and it might so easily be cultivated.

Look at the tiny maiden with her dolls' house ; what pleasure she seems to find in making the little beds, sweeping the floors, and arranging and re-arranging the furniture, while, crowning delight of all, it is to her, to put some cookery of her own in its miniature saucepan over a real fire.

Abroad, both in France and Germany, toy kitchens are more common than here, and in the last named country girls soon learn household duties. It would be well if we also allowed our girls to make early attempts at cookery, as well as other household duties suited to their strength, teaching them then the never-too-soon-learnt lessons of cleanliness and economy.

HOME INFLUENCE.

How often is this underrated?

Not the higher moral influence of wife, mother, or mistress—that few would dispute—but the home *management*. Many would hardly believe that the making or marring of character could be due to such a homely influence, yet it is the case, and in even what would be called mere trivialities.

Take, for example, a child reared in a household where there is no regard for punctuality, and think how hard it will be for him or her in after years, when they come to the more important affairs of life, to forget their early training. They will be hampered at the onset. A late breakfast will make them late for school or office, while, if they bravely start without it, they will suffer, both in mind and body, from the loss of what should be one of the best meals of the day. Again, how does the same fault in housekeeping affect those older?

The tired man of business returing home after a harassing day, maybe one in which he has had no time to snatch a meal, sorely needs a pleasant, well-cooked, comfortable one to await him. If this be delayed, if hungry, and as a natural consequence (unless he be superior to masculine failings) cross, small wonder is it if he makes those around him suffer for the fault of the one whose duty it should have been to have provided for his needs.

Worse still, it often happens that a hardworking man thus tried goes from his home to his club, or, in a lower social scale, to a public-house, there to get what he should have had in comfort at home, only for the drawback of unpunctuality. A little fault it may be deemed, but oh, housewives, beware of it. Its approaches are so insidious that it forms a dangerous foe, and one that we should combat with at once and for ever.

Another drawback in a household is sometimes a lack of cleanliness and tidiness. Although the former as a virtue is supposed to rank next to Godliness, yet the want of it is not sufficiently condemned as a fault, while untidiness is often tolerated by even cleanly people.

Both, however, have the same root, and that is *laziness,* and it cannot be denied that it is one likely to be a drawback through life. Example is better (sometimes worse) than precept. Do the children and servants see the head of the household careless and untidy, it is an almost certainty that they will become the same ; nor can the mistress insist, with any justice, upon neatness and order in nursery and kitchen if she does not practise it herself.

A HAPPY HOME

Must be a well-managed one. It is impossible that where extravagance, disorder, or discomfort reign, there can be the same peace and content among the inmates as where a wisely-governing mind puts all her energies into making home comfortable and happy.

This should be the young housekeeper's first aim, but let her not imagine the details of her work to be so many sordid cares. Never let her lose the love of the beautiful in her anxiety to accomplish the practical. *After* cleanliness and comfort should come grace and beauty in the home, nor should they ever be lacking. It costs less *money* to make a house pretty and attractive than many people fancy, but it does cost time and trouble; still the housekeeper whose heart is in her work will not grudge the hours spent in making places look bright and pleasant, when she sees the result of her labour. A common error that the young housewife makes is to think it almost a necessity that, in her rôle of matron, she must lay aside, and thus lose, all the talents and accomplishments she has cultivated. How often we hear the cry of those whose singing or playing used to give us so much pleasure; " Oh, I gave up music when I married." What a pity it seems for them to have lost the power of giving enjoyment in this way, and why should they do so while still possessing youth and health ? They will say, in all probability, that they have not time for anything but the care of their home and visiting, but we venture to believe that they could, with good management, find, at any rate, an hour or two now and then ; and let us remind them, that, as time rolls on, their work and cares will probably increase and that they must not imagine it too heavy at the onset. To make home pleasant as well as comfortable should be the aim of all young married women, nor have they any right to lightly lay aside the accomplishments that give them additional charm in the eyes of their husbands.

The same girl who gives up her music when she marries is very likely the one who would grow careless in her attire, indifferent to her appearance when strictly in her home circle. Another and a still greater error. Remember, young matrons, *before* you were married you sang, played or dressed to please the one who is now your husband. Try to please him in these ways still. Wear suitable clothes, and dress well within your means, but make yourself as well as your home attractive, for his sake even more than for that of your friends.

We do not put these things before good management, for they should form a part of it. The more well-managed, the cleaner, tidier, and prettier, the more *refined* will be the home; therefore the better place for culture and study, and the more suitable a field for young minds and hands to be trained in knowledge and industry.

UNSELFISHNESS.

A good woman *should* be a good housekeeper, for the latter must possess one of the greatest of all virtues, namely, unselfishness. An utter abnegation of self is almost a necessity with the mistress of a household, for with her rests the question of the health and comfort, if not the happiness, of all its members.

A grave responsibility that it is only in human nature sometimes to shirk. It is so difficult to arrange for the best, so hard to plan things to give satisfaction to all, there is so much to be sacrificed. Yet, with one's heart in the work and one's shoulder to the wheel, there is no difficulty insurmountable if only *we think of others before ourselves.*

ENERGY AND INDUSTRY.

Although these qualities are seldom exalted to the place of virtues, they are yet some that might fairly rank with the lesser ones, good temper and good nature, and will be found invaluable qualifications for the housekeeper. In every-day affairs it is so easy to let things drift. So tiresome sometimes to leave an interesting book or study to fight out what is going wrong in kitchen or household, so trying to get at the bottom of the trouble, whatever it may be. Specially is it to one who has only lately taken upon herself the burden of household cares, to wrestle with them day by day. Yet it must be done, and only by energy and industry can we succeed in bringing a household into order and method. Servants need example in their mistress. If she makes a practice of being late in the morning she will find it one of the most difficult tasks to make them get up early, and the result may be that she will have her late breakfast served in a half swept, half dusted room, where reigns neither cleanliness nor comfort.

It has been truly said, "There is no work like morning work," and this applies equally to mistress and maid, and we know of no home that is really well kept where early rising is not the rule. A great part of a housewife's duties should be accomplished by ten o'clock in the day, and then there is a morning, not half a one, left for her own private occupations. The larder should have been inspected, the stores given out, the daily meals arranged by the time we have stated, and when these duties are done there is a certain sense of freedom for the housekeeper. It would not be possible to give any certain and fixed rules as to a housekeeper's or mistress' daily duties, for they would vary in every household. In some they would consist merely of giving orders and an occasional superintendence of the work, while in others she would have to give personal aid, and do many of the lighter parts of both cooking and housework herself, where only one servant was kept: but it would be hard to find the home where the two qualities of energy and industry would not be of value.

EXPERIENCE.

We all know that this alone brings perfection. However well fitted for a soldier a man may be by nature, it is only by hard drilling and discipline that he becomes able to do his duty.

So also it is with the housekeeper, although, fortunately for her, the weight of her cares fall gradually and slowly. If she has striven at their commencement to do her best, while the cares increase so do the difficulties proportionately lighten.

The experience of those who have had to learn the (sometimes) hard lesson of keeping house, should not be despised by the beginner; nor is it difficult to obtain. Helping hands are gladly held out to the young housekeeper, not only by friends who are competent to give advice, but by the many and useful books on the subject of housekeeping now published. In this one, we endeavour to be as *practical* as possible, and sincerely trust that our short summary of household duties, plans of work, relative duties of mistress and servants, time and seasons for various tasks, and the easiest and best way of keeping homes, large or small, in order and comfort, may be found of service.

KNOWLEDGE IS POWER.

We must know for ourselves how each household task must be done ; and furthermore, we must be able to perform them should occasion arise. Theory is all very well in housekeeping or cookery ; but it is not of much value when the housemaid is ill, or the cook has gone for a holiday. Better for us is it then to be able to cook a joint and boil a potato than to describe the process of making an elaborate entrée or soup, or to be able to sweep and dust a room thoroughly than to discourse upon the mode of sweeping carpets according to their kind, or the making of beds upon hygienic principles.

Only by actual knowledge, too, can we check waste or laziness in our servants. If we do not know that where four eggs have been used three would have been sufficient, we cannot blame the cook ; if we, by personal experience, do not know how long it takes to thoroughly clean a room, we cannot find fault if an hour more than it need have taken has been expended upon the task. Still more important is it to know when household work or cookery has been *properly* done and to be able to show the ignorant how each thing should be accomplished.

In no way is experience more valuable than by teaching us method in managing the work of a household. Whereas with this, a great deal of work may be got through with few hands ; without it, a houseful of servants will always be in a muddle. Bustle does not mean business, hurry is of no use in housework ; but only by a careful planning out of the work for each day, and by seeing that that work is accomplished, with nothing left undone to be thrust upon the next day's programme, can a household be kept in good order.

HEALTH IN THE HOUSEHOLD.

To a very great extent this lies in the hands of the housekeeper, for with her rests the responsibility of arranging : not only, as we have said, for clean rooms, comfortable beds, regular meals, &c., for the family, but that of providing the food for all, seeing that it is the best of its kind, suitable for various ages and constitutions, and that it is properly cooked and served.

It is often a very difficult matter, without attempting to please everybody's taste, to choose what is best for individual needs. The same food will not suit everyone—even children, brothers and sisters, will not thrive upon the same food ; and, without any pampering or pandering to the taste of a child, to keep it in health it must be fed with some wholesome kinds of which it is willing to take a sufficient quantity, even if it be not the one we have chosen to provide for the rest of the occupants of the nursery. Grown people are still more difficult to provide for ; and there are many who, caring little for eating, and not willing to give extra trouble, will cheerfully go without a meal rather than take anything they do not fancy. These have to be considered, and still more so those whose constitutions or digestions are delicate ; so that it is by no means an easy thing to arrange the daily meals.

FOOD FOR BOTH BRAIN AND BODY

is necessary ; and it would be well for those who buy or order food, as well as for those who prepare it, if they took the trouble to study its constituents, so that their own diet, as well as that of others, should contain the right elements.

As an aid to those who aspire to give and regulate a good and wholesome diet in their households, under the head of "Science of Cookery," will be found the tables of the "Constituent Parts of Food." These contain both the constituent parts in a lb., and also a lb. divided into a hundred parts, and a fair sample of every kind of food has been chosen, and carefully analysed, to make the tables a reliable guide.

Diet as a cure is now common, and in many cases does a great deal more than medicine in effecting the desired result.

In treating of the science of cookery we shall speak further on this subject; but while still offering advice to the young housekeeper, we would suggest her giving the question of food some thought, and realise how important it is that she provides what is most necessary for the tired man of business, the hard-working servant, or the delicate child ; being assured that it will not be labour or care wasted, while, in thus so greatly helping towards keeping her household in good health, she will reap her reward,

FRESH PROVISIONS.

CHOOSING AND BUYING PROVISIONS.

Iᴛ is too much the habit now, one which it is only natural that the young housekeeper should fall in with, that of ordering all they require from the tradespeople as they call, without every going near the shops or seeing what is sent in on its arrival. They deal, may be, with the best tradespeople in the neighbourhood, and they expect that what they order should be of the best. Far be it from us to say that it is *necessary* for the mistress to do her own daily shopping—in many cases it would not be possible for her to do so, and for this reason it is undoubtedly a convenience to be able to order what we require at our own doors; but we still think that an occasional visit paid to the shops would be as well. Then, if we only know how to choose fresh provisions, we can see for ourselves that we are being properly supplied. It is but human nature to give the best to those who can best appreciate it, and to pass off inferior articles upon those who do not know good from indifferent.

We were not surprised to hear the remark of a butcher, who, receiving a compliment from a customer on the quality of the meat he sold, said, "You see, ma'am, you *know* what meat should be and wouldn't have anything but the best." A sort of natural enquiry comes into one's mind as to how this man would treat those who hadn't the knowledge that this good housekeeper possessed—whether these unfortunates would not be the recipients, very often, of what was not good enough for her ?

How much better then is it to learn to distinguish, not good from *bad*, for that is easy, but good from *indifferent.* To those who have this still to learn, the following hints may be useful.

MEAT, TO CHOOSE AND KEEP.

Good raw meat is neither very pale nor very dark, it is a rich red, and (beef especially) has a marbled look given by the small veins of fat running through it. To the touch it is firm and elastic, and should scarcely wet the finger. When taken from a dish upon which it has been standing, little or no moisture should remain behind.

Bad or inferior meat is either lacking in colour or of a dark purply tint. It is wet or sodden to the touch, and if left standing will leave a pool of blood and water behind. Without having an actually tainted smell, it has often a very sickly one. The inside fat surrounding the kidneys and liver is often suffused with blood.

Keeping Meat in winter is comparatively easy, and it should always be hung till in good condition, it being better to trust this to our own cook than to the butcher. The larder is the one room in the house that should, if possible, face due north, so that the sun never comes in. Meat requires a dry, airy place, and should always be hung up, not laid upon a plate, or dish ; and before being hung up, it should be wiped ; and in summer, dredged with flour and pepper. The kernel in the round of beef and the marrow from the bone should always be taken out in hot weather before hanging. Veal keeps but badly at the best of times, and should not be hung long, if it cannot be cooked at once. Lamb also does not keep well, particularly in its proper season of hot weather. Should meat be tainted at all, it is best to wash it with vinegar and water or Condy's fluid, or powder it with charcoal and wash it off with water ; it is better roasted than boiled.

When it can be seen that the meat will not keep long, it is better to parboil or half roast it at once ; after which treatment when it is cooked it must be plunged, for boiling, into boiling water, or for roasting, put before a very hot fire to start.

POULTRY, TO CHOOSE AND KEEP.

There are three qualifications necessary, namely : that the birds should be *young, in good condition, fresh.* The first can be easily ascertained if sold in the feathers, for the plumage is half developed, the pen feathers are short; there is down under the wing. In towns, however, birds are generally sold ready plucked, when we must look for large soft feet and necks, and avoid the opposite as indicating age. The bones of all young things are soft and gelatinous, and it is easiest to test them by the pinions and breast bone. It is less easy to judge of *condition*, but it may be said that fat and firm flesh are good healthy signs; but excessively fat poultry should be avoided, as the fat so wastes in cooking. The freshness of a bird can be discovered more by smell than anything else ; and a good buyer would prefer to choose a bird untrussed. The feet should not be dry, nor the eyes sunken. Should there be any doubt about the freshness of a bird, it should be roasted, not boiled.

Poultry being always eaten fresh, does not require hanging; but birds, especially ducks and geese, may be kept in a good larder, if the feathers are left on and they are hung by their legs, for several days.

GAME, TO CHOOSE AND KEEP.

Early in the season it is not difficult to tell young birds or hares. The smoothness of the legs and the tenderness of the pinions show a young pheasant. A partridge may be known by the long feathers in the wing being pointed; in an old bird they are rounded. In all birds in good condition the breast should be thick and firm, while the feet being supple and moist will show that they are fresh. The ear of a young hare can be easily torn, its neck is stumpy and its joints long, so are those of a young rabbit; and there should be a small bony knob near the foot of a leveret.

Keeping game is more easy than keeping poultry, especially as it is not in season in the spring or summer; but it requires care and constant watching to hang it to bring it exactly into condition. No rules can be given as to how long game should hang, for not only does it depend upon the kind and the weather, but still more so upon the taste of the individuals who have to eat it. Some people like it almost putrid, others cannot touch it if at all high; but we may say that when the feathers come out very easily, a bird is *generally considered* fit for cooking. Old game will hang longer than young, and afterwards will require longer cooking.

GENERAL MARKETING.

Advice with regard to the purchase of such things as groceries—tinned provisions would be almost superfluous, yet we may suggest that these are cheapest when the best is bought. Of cheap tea for example, independent of its not being a pleasant drink, a greater quantity is required to make a strong cup than would be needed of a good one, so that the cost of the tea is after all much the same. In households where the servants have an allowance of tea and sugar, the former should certainly be good, though not costly, for their cup of tea often takes the place of our glasses of wine. In such items also as dried plums or currants, the best are invariably the cheapest, having so little waste, while eggs are not even guaranteed unless a certain price is given.

Economise, if necessary, rather in quantity than quality; and if you cannot afford a good kind of such luxuries as wine, for example, go without and take for stimulant (if necessary) some good ale or stout, rather than injure your constitution or that of your friends by having cheap champagne or inky claret at your table.

We all realise the mistake of buying cheap materials for clothing the outer man (or woman), why should we not be equally careful of the inner? We say it with emphasis, a glass of good wine may do us good, a glass of bad or inferior kind can scarcely fail to do us harm. In every household, however small, there should be some sort of store kept of such things as do not deteriorate by keeping. It saves a great deal of trouble to buy in what is needed for the week or month of such things, to say nothing of the convenience of having the materials at hand in case of emergency. Also, it to a certain extent regulates expenditure, and we know then so much better what is used than if we buy daily by giving our orders at the door.

In the country, when living some distance from the shops, it is absolutely necessary to keep a little stock of groceries and such like articles; and we think in town it would be equally convenient, even if it be not impossible to procure them at short notice. One word more upon the subject of buying, and that is, buy your coals if you can store them, in summer, when they are at their cheapest, and never let them run out so that you have to depend upon the nearest greengrocer for a sack, for which you will be charged a high price.

FRESH PROVISIONS.
TABLES OF SEASONS AND PRICES.

DIFFERENT KINDS OF FISH, PRICES AND SEASONS, WHEN BEST AND CHEAPEST.

Fish is always best when in full season. It greatly varies in price according to the supply, but the following are average prices in or near towns.

Name of Fish.	When in Full Season.	When Best & Cheapest.	Average Price.
Bloaters	September to April	September to February	1/0 to 2/0 per doz.
Bream	All the Year	Autumn	0/8 to 1/0 per lb.
Brill	All the Year	August to April	1/0 to 6/0 each.
Cod	October to March	December and January	0/4 to 1/0 per lb.
Crabs	April to October	Summer	0/6 to 4/0 each.
Crayfish	All the Year	Summer	1/0 to 3/0 per doz.
Dory	All the Year	Winter	2/0 to 5/0 each.
Eels	June to March	September to November	0/10 to 1/4 per lb.
Flounders	All the Year	August to November	0/1 to 0/3 each.
Haddocks	August to February	Winter	0/4 to 1/0 each.
Halibut	All the Year	November to June	0/4 to 1/0 per lb.
Herrings	May to January	June to September	1/0 to 2/0 per doz.
Lobsters	All the Year	Summer	0/6 to 4/0 each.
Mackerel	Nearly all the Year	April to July	0/4 to 0/8 each.
Mullet (Grey)	All the Year	Winter	0/6 to 1/6 each.
Mullet (Red)	All the Year	April to October	0/6 to 1/6 each.
Mussels	January to April	February and March	0/2 to 0/3 per qt.
Oysters	September to April	Winter	1/0 to 3/0 per doz.
Plaice	All the Year	May to November	0/6 to 1/0 per lb.
Prawns	All the Year	May to December	0/6 to 2/6 per doz.
Salmon	February to September	Summer	0/10 to 3/0 per lb.
Shad	February to September	Summer	0/6 to 0/10 per lb.
Shrimps	All the Year	April to November	0/3 to 0/6 per pint.
Scallops	January to June	March to May	0/6 to 1/0 per doz.
Smelts	October to May	Winter	0/6 to 1/6 per doz.
Soles	All the Year	April to July	1/0 to 2/0 per lb.
Sprats	November to March	November & December	0/1 to 0/3 per lb.
Sturgeon	April to September	Summer	0/9 to 1/6 per lb.
Trout	February to September	April to July	1/0 to 2/0 per lb.
Turbot	All the Year	Spring and Summer	1/0 to 2/0 per lb.
Whitebait	January to September	February to May	1/0 to 2/0 per pint.
Whitings	All the Year	Spring and Summer	0/3 to 1/0 each.

Different Joints and Parts of Beef, when in Season, Price.

Unlike any other fresh provisions, meat does not vary in price during the year, except in the case of early lamb. Beef is considered best in the depth of winter, and English Christmas beef is esteemed finer than any other, but by many this meat is preferred when less fat than that usually killed at that season. When bought in winter, beef should be hung for a certain time, but in summer, unless an exceptionally cool larder is available, it should only be purchased when required for table.

Joint or Part.	When in Season.	When Best.	Average Price.
Aitchbone	*All the Year.*	*During Winter.*	0/7 per lb.
Brisket................	,,	,, ,,	0/6 to 0/7 per lb.
Buttock (Steak)	,,	,, ,,	1/0 per lb.
Buttock	,,	,, ,,	0/9 per lb.
Flank	,,	,, ,,	0/6 per lb.
Leg-of-MuttonPiece	,,	,, ,,	0/9 per lb.
Neck...................	,,	,, ,,	0/6 per lb.
Ribs...................	,,	,, ,,	0/10 per lb.
Rump	,,	,, ,,	0/10 per lb.
Rump (in Steaks) ...	,,	,, ,,	1/2 per lb.
Shin	,,	,, ,,	0/6 per lb.
Silverside	,,	,, ,,	0/9 per lb.
Sirloin	,,	,, ,,	0/10 per lb.
Cheek	,.	,, ,,	0/5 per lb.
Heart	,,	,, ,,	2/0 each.
Kidney................	,,	,, ,,	0/10 per lb.
Tail	,,	,, ,,	3/0 each.
Tongue...............	,,	,, ,.	3/6 to 4/6 each.

Different Joints and Parts of Mutton, when in Season, Price.

Mutton varies but little in quality during the year, but it is best in winter and of least good quality when lamb is in full season. New Zealand and American mutton may be reckoned to cost quite 2*d.* to 3*d.* per lb. less than the prices quoted in the following table, but there is a certain amount of waste caused by the shrinking during cooking of American meat that renders it, by reason of the waste, not so much as 2*d.* or 3*d.* per lb. cheaper than the English mutton.

Joint or Part.	When in Season.	When Best.	Average Price.
Breast	*All the Year.*	*September to April.*	0/6 per lb.
Haunch	,,	,, ,,	0/11 per lb.
Leg	,,	,, ,,	0/10 per lb.
Loin	,,	,, ,,	0/9½ per lb.
Neck (best end)	,,	,, ,,	0/9½ per lb.
Neck (Scrag)	,,	,, ,,	0/7 per lb.
Saddle	,,	,, ,,	0/10 per lb.
Shoulder	,,	,, ,,	0/9 per lb.
Head................. ..	,,	,, ,,	1/0 each.
Heart	,,	,, ,,	0/4 each.
Kidney...............	,,	,, ,,	0/3 each.
Chops (Loin)	,,	,, ,,	1/2 per lb.
Chops (Chump)	,,	,, ,,	1/2 per lb.

DIFFERENT JOINTS AND PARTS OF LAMB, WHEN IN SEASON, PRICE.

This meat when it first comes in is usually dearer than when it is in full season, as in summer. As is the case with mutton, we receive much from America, but unlike the mutton—which approaches very nearly in good quality and flavour to our own—American lamb is decidedly inferior.

Joint or Part.	When in Season.	When Best.	Average Price.
Breast	*March to September.*	*May to July.*	0/9 per lb.
Fore-quarter	,, ,,	,, ,,	0/11 per lb.
Hind-quarter	,, ,,	,, ,,	1/0 per lb.
Leg	,, ,,	,, ,,	1/1 per lb.
Loin	,, ,,	,, ,,	1/0 per lb.
Neck (best end)......	,, ,,	,, ,,	0/11 per lb.
Neck (Scrag)	,, ,,	,, ,,	0/8 per lb.
Shoulder	,, ,,	,, ,,	0/11 per lb.
Fry	,, ,,	,, ,,	0/8 to 1/0.

DIFFERENT JOINTS AND PARTS OF VEAL, WHEN IN SEASON, PRICE.

Veal may be bought all the year round, but it is at its best in summer, when beef is not so good in quality. In buying veal it is important to note if it be perfectly fresh, as all young meat keeps less well than that obtained from the full-grown animal.

Joint or Part.	When in Season.	When Best.	Average Price.
Breast	*February to November.*	*In Summer.*	0/8 per lb.
Cutlet	,, ,,	,,	1/2 per lb.
Fillet	,, ,,	,,	1/0 per lb.
Knuckle	,, ,,	,,	0/6 per lb.
Loin	,, ,,	,,	0/9½ per lb.
Shoulder	,, ,,	,,	0/9 per lb.
Head....................	,, ,,	,,	5/0 to 6/0 each.
Heart	,, ,,	,,	0/6 to 0/9 each.
Liver	,, ,,	,,	0/10 per lb.
Sweetbread............	,, ,,	,,	From 1/0.

DIFFERENT JOINTS AND PARTS OF PORK, WHEN IN SEASON, PRICE.

Pork is out of season and generally considered unwholesome in summer, and at its best in the coldest weather. The fat of good pork should be very white, and the lean of a brownish tint, free from streaks and patches of colour. Small boned and lean pork is best for roasting.

Joint or Part.	When in Season.	When Best	Average Price.
Spring (generally pickled)	*September to April.*	*November to March.*	0/8 per lb.
Hand	,, ,,	,, ,,	0/7½ per lb.
Fore-loin	,, ,,	,, ,,	0/9 per lb.
Hind-loin..............	,, ,,	,, ,,	0/9 per lb.
Leg	,, ,,	,, ,,	0/8½ per lb.
Spare Ribs	,, ,,	,, ,,	0/8 per lb.

VARIOUS KINDS OF POULTRY, WHEN IN SEASON, PRICE.

The price of poultry varies greatly according to the season, and, in some cases, according to the demand. Thus, for example, turkeys can be bought cheaply in November, but are always dearer at Christmas time. Large fowls are cheaper to buy than smaller, thinner ones, as they can be carved with more regard to economy.

Poultry.	When in Season.	When Best.	Average Price.
Chickens	*February to October...*	*July to September......*	2/0 to 3/0 each.
Ducklings	*February to August...*	*May to July ....*	2/6 to 3/6 each.
Ducks	*August to February...*	*September and October*	3/0 to 4/0 each.
Fowls	*All the Year ....*	*June to October.........*	2/6 to 3/6 each.
Geese	*September to February*	*October and November*	0/7 to 0/10 per lb.
Green Geese	*May to August ....*	*June.......................*	6/0 to 10/0 each.
Guinea Fowl	*February to August...*	*Summer ....*	3/0 to 4/0 each.
Larks	*October to December...*	*November ....*	2/0 to 3/0 per doz.
Pigeons	*August to April.........*	*Winter.....................*	0/9 to 1/0 each.
Pigeons (Bordeaux)	*All the Year ....*	*Winter.....................*	1/0 to 1/4 each.
Rabbits	*All the Year ....*	*October to February...*	0/6 to 0/8 per lb.
Rabbits (Ostend) ...	*All the Year ....*	*October to February .*	0/7 to 0/8 per lb.
Turkeys	*October to March ......*	*November to January*	0/9 to 1/0 per lb.
Wheatears	*September to March...*	*September and October*	1/0 each.

VARIOUS KINDS OF GAME, WHEN IN SEASON, PRICE.

Game varies in price not only with the season but year by year, according to the scarcity or abundance of the birds; the prices quoted are, therefore, those of an average year. Our climate is too variable for any certain rules as to the keeping of game, but it should be remembered that whereas in winter or very cold weather it is not fit for eating unless well hung, it keeps no better than meat in damp or very mild weather. It may be generally ascertained when it is fit for cooking by the feathers coming out easily; but individual taste must decide the keeping of game, as some would consider it uneatable when others think it has arrived at perfection.

Game.	When in Season.	When Best.	Average Price.
Blackcock	*August to November...*	*September and October*	2/6 to 3/6 per brace.
Capercailzie	*September to April ...*	*January to March ...*	
Ducks (Wild).........	*October to September..*	*November & December*	2/0 to 3/0 per brace.
Grouse	*August to November...*	*September ....*	3/6 to 5/0 per brace.
Hares	*September to March...*	*October and November*	3/6 to 6/0 each.
Leverets	*August and September*	*August.....................*	3/0 to 4/0 each.
Partridges	*September to February*	*October and November*	4/0 to 5/0 per brace.
Pheasants	*October to February...*	*Winter.....................*	5/0 to 6/0 per brace.
Plovers..................	*October to February...*	*Winter ....*	1/0 to 1/6 each.
Ptarmigan	*September to April ...*	*September ....*	1/6 to 2/0 each.
Quail	*September to February*	*September and October*	1/0 to 1/6 each.
Snipe	*October to February...*	*October and November*	2/6 to 3/6 per brace.
Teal	*October to February...*	*October and November*	1/0 to 1/6 each.
Venison	*September to January*	*September and October*	1/0 to 2/0 per lb.
Widgeon...............	*October to February...*	*October and November*	1/0 to 1/6 each.
Woodcock	*October to February...*	*October and November*	3/6 to 5/6 per brace.

Turkey.

Pheasant.

Rabbit.

Woodcock.

Wild Duck.

Partridge.

Larks.

Hare.

Quails.

Snipe.

Golden Plover.

Widgeon.

Duck.

Fowl.

Teal.

Blackcock.

Pigeons

Ptarmigan.

Grouse.

Goose.

Poultry and Game.

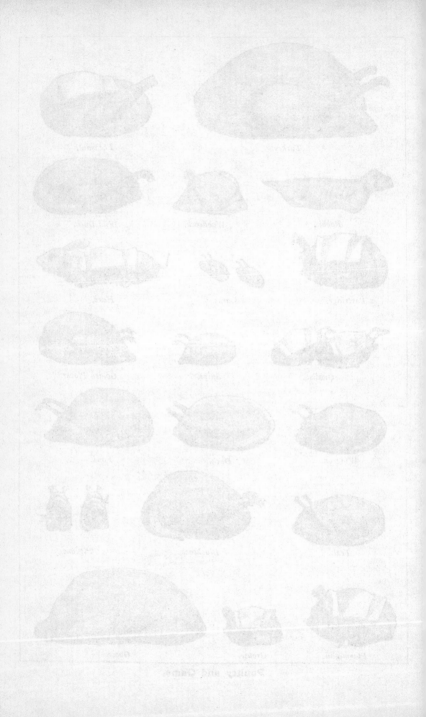

Poultry and Game.

DAIRY PRODUCE, HAM, BACON, &C., PRICE.

According to locality, dairy produce varies in price, but the quantities imported from other countries, combined with the increased railway facilities, have brought about a more uniform cost for it throughout this country. In the following tables will be found the prices of the best parts of bacon only, but it can be bought as low as 5d. per lb., only it must be remembered that to this is attached a large quantity of bone, and in consequence, waste.

Article.	Average Price.	Article.	Average Price.
Butter (Fresh)	1/6 to 1/10 per lb.	Bacon (best parts) ...	0/11 per lb.
,, (Dorset).........	1/2 to 1/6 per lb.	Eggs (Hens')	1/0 to 2/0 per doz.
,, (Salt)	1/0 to 1/2 per lb.	,, (Ducks')	1/0 to 2/0 per doz.
,, (Margarine) ...	0/10 per lb.	,, (Geese's)	3/0 to 4/0 per doz.
Cheese (American) ...	0/7 to 0/9 per lb.	,, (Guinea Fowls')	1/0 to 2/0 per doz.
,, (Cheddar)	0/10 to 1/0 per lb.	,, (Plovers')	3/0 to 5/0 per doz.
,, (Cheshire)	0/10 to 1/0 per lb.	,, (Turkeys').........	3/0 to 4/0 per doz.
,, (Cream)	0/6 to 1/0 each.	Milk	0/4 per quart.
,, (Dutch)	0/6 to 0/7 per lb.	,, (Separated)	0/2 per quart.
,, (Gorgonzola)...	1/0 per lb.	Cream	1/0 to 3/0 per pint.
,, (Gruyère)	0/11 per lb.	Whey	0/2 per pint.
,, (Stilton)..........	1/6 to 1/10 per lb.	Lard.........................	0/10 per lb.
Ham (English)	0/11 per lb.	Pickled Pork	0/8 per lb.
,, (American)	0/8 per lb.	Sausages	0/10 per lb.

VARIOUS KINDS OF FRUIT, WHEN IN SEASON, PRICE.

Fruit, like vegetables, varies considerably in price according to the supply of the season, this applying particularly to the wall fruits, such as peaches and apricots.

Fruit.	When in Season.	When Best.	Average Price.
Apples	October to March	October to December...	0/2 to 0/4 per lb.
Apricots	June to September ...	August......................	1/6 to 3/6 per doz.
Bullaces	Autumn	October	0/2 per lb.
Cherries	June to August	July	0/4 to 0/8 per lb.
Currants	July to September ...	August	0/3 to 0/6 per lb.
Damsons	September and October	October......................	0/1 to 0/3 per lb.
Figs	September and October	October......................	2/0 to 3/0 per doz.
Gooseberries(Green)	July to September......	August	0/4 to 0/8 per qt.
Grapes (Foreign) ...	All the Year	Autumn	0/4 to 0/10 per lb
Grapes (Hot-house)	September to December	October and November	2/0 and upwards.
Greengages............	August and September	August......................	0/3 to 0/8 per lb.
Medlars	October to January ...	October and November	0/4 to 0/8 per lb.
Melons..................	June to November......	October......................	1/0 to 5/0 each.
Nectarines	September and October	October......................	3/0 to 4/0 per doz.
Oranges	All the Year	Winter......................	From 0/4 per doz.
Peaches	September and October	October................. ..	3/0 to 6/0 per doz.
Pears	October to March	October and November	From 0/3 per doz.
Plums	August to October	September and October	0/2 to 0/6 per lb.
Quinces	September and October	October......................	2/0 to 3/0 per doz.
Rhubarb	January to May	March and April	0/3 to 0/8 bundle.
Strawberries	June to September ...	July	0/4 to 1/0 per lb.

VARIOUS KINDS OF VEGETABLES, WHEN IN SEASON, PRICE.

The prices quoted for these are the average ones that would have to be paid at green-grocers' in or near towns, but where vegetables are bought from farmers or other growers in the country their cost would almost invariably be considerably less. Vegetables vary also in price according to the scarcity or the abundance of the supplies obtainable.

Vegetable.	When in Season.	When Best.	Average Price.
Artichokes	*July to October*	*August*	0/4 to 0/6 each.
,, (Jerusalem)	*November to February*	*December*	0/2 per lb.
Asparagus	*January to July*	*April and May*	1/6 to 4/6 bunch.
Beans (French)	*May to November*	*September and October*	0/2 to 0/4 per lb.
Beans (Broad)	*July and August*	*August*	0/6 to 0/9 per peck.
Beans (Runners) ...	*July to October*	*August and September*	0/2 to 0/3 per lb.
Beetroot	*All the Year*	*Autumn*	0/1 to 0/2 each.
Brocoli.................	,, *(different kinds)*	*Autumn*	0/2 to 0/6 each.
Brocoli Sprouts......	*January to May*	*April*	0/1 to 0/2 per lb.
Cabbages..............	*All the Year*	*Spring and Summer*	0/1 to 0/2 each.
Cabbages (Red)......	*October to February*...	*November & December*	0/6 each.
Carrots.................	*All the Year*	*Autumn*	0/4 to 0/6 bunch.
Cauliflower......... ..	*April to July*............	*July*	0/2 to 0/6 each.
Celery	*October to March*	*November & December*	0/1 to 0/4 per stick.
Endive	*September to November*	*October*	0/1 to 0/6 each.
Horseradish	*All the Year*	*Winter*	0/1 to 0/2 per stick.
Leeks	*October to May*	*October and November*	0/4 to 0/6 bunch.
Lettuces	*June to November*......	*July and August*......	0/1 to 0/2 each.
Onions	*All the Year*	*Summer and Autumn*	0/1 to 0/2 per lb.
Parsnips	*October to April*........	*February and March*	0/1 to 0/2 each.
Peas	*June to September* ...	*July and August*	0/6 to 2/0 per peck.
Potatoes	*All the Year*	*Autumn*	0/1 per lb.
Potatoes (New)	*May to August*	*July*	0/3 to 0/8 per lb.
Radishes	*May to September*	*June to August*	0/1 per bunch.
Sea-kale	*January to May*	*February and March*	1/0 to 2/0 basket.
Savoys	*October to March*	*November to January*	0/1 to 0/3 each.
Spinach	*All the Year*	*Summer*	0/2 to 0/4 per lb.
Tomatoes...............	*June to December*	*September and October*	0/4 to 0/10 per lb.
Vegetable Marrow	*June to October*..........	*July and August*	0/1 to 0/6 each.
Watercress	*All the Year*	*Summer*	0/1 per bunch.

According to the weather so do vegetables come sooner or later into the market, but the above table shows them in average seasons.

HOUSEKEEPING ACCOUNTS.

"No man is rich whose expenditure exceeds his means, and no one is poor whose incomings exceed his outgoings." Unless household accounts are kept, the young mistress will very likely find that her expenditure *does* exceed her means, and that alone should be sufficient reason for keeping them carefully and regularly.

When at the end of a week one can look over every item of expenditure during the six days, it is easy to see if we have in any way been extravagant, if there has been too much meat or butter consumed, also if we have kept well within our means, and if we have laid aside sufficient for such extras as wages or coals, not paid weekly yet often included in the housekeeping money.

It gives but little trouble where orders are given by a servant daily to the tradespeople, to write down all that is required and then there is always a check upon the weekly bills. The weights of joints are usually sent by the butcher, and these should be saved till the end of the week, when the mistress should collect them, with the weekly bills and tradesman's book, and with her list of what has been paid for in ready money make up her account for the week. This should be done in a book where the separate items are put down; and the subjoined page of a weekly account will show the mode of entering not only what is paid but what has been received as housekeeping money, also that for extra moneys received and paid a separate account is made.

Independently of this housekeeping account, a young housekeeper should also keep separate ones of personal expenditure such as dress, cabs, &c., in fact enter everything as it is paid, or some items will be forgotten and, in reckoning up, some deficiency will be difficult to account for.

It is a useful plan to keep a tiny note book, with pencil, in the pocket, so that every shilling (or even penny) spent can be put down and afterwards, under its proper head, be entered in the housekeeping book.

EXPENDITURE.

To " cut our coat according to our cloth " is, in one case of small incomes, sometimes a difficult matter in keeping house ; and, to a certain extent, this is caused by the not knowing what we ought to spend upon the different items according to our family and our means.

There is only one way in which we can make a small income cover all our needs, and that is by making a plan of what we can afford to spend upon each thing. To do this we must first reckon up the cost of all *necessaries*, and it will not be difficult to apply the balance that remains.

The housekeeping allowance cannot be curtailed as other expenses such as rent, wages and dress may be, for we must have proper food, and if we can afford to live well, though not extravagantly, we need not grudge its cost.

A usual allowance for board in a family of more than two or three persons is ten shillings per head, upon which a very good table can be kept ; but in large families where there are young children it need not cost more than from six shillings to eight shillings per head.

Although every family has its own needs, and it would not be possible to make plans for imaginary ones with imaginary incomes that could be followed to the letter, yet those we give for different incomes, with their lists of what could be proportionately spent upon ordinary household requirements, may be useful to the young housekeeper.

Ere giving these may we venture to advise her if possible either to pay ready money or weekly bills for everything in the way of household expenses ? and the smaller the income the greater the necessity that this should be done, and the more necessary is it that some margin should be left.

It is far better to live in a small house that we can keep nicely in order, with service well within our means, than in a large one where the whole of our income is consumed and for which we can barely afford sufficient servants.

There are too many people who prefer to be grand than comfortable ; and still more who, without meaning to, spend a good deal more than they need or can afford upon unnecessary luxuries. Let our young housekeepers beware of falling into this grave error. Let them, whether their incomes be large or small, remember that it is their *duty* to live within their income and that extravagance is a vice, whether it is found in cottage or mansion. Let them also remember that though their incomes may not yearly increase, their expenses will, in all probability ; and, living in the present it is yet well to think of the future and its contingencies, with the happy conviction that there is something set aside for the "rainy day."

Nor should it be forgotten in health, that sickness *may* come, with its attendant expenses—in some cases heavy ones—and for such contingencies it is of all things most necessary to provide ; while there are always so many things that have to be paid for which do not come under any particular head and which in our tables we term "Sundries."

Housekeepers' Reckoner.

By consulting the following tables when it is wanted to know how much per day, week, month or quarter can be allowed out of incomes up to £500, much trouble may be saved. Above that sum it is very easy to reckon, by taking the excess in various sums, shown in the tables, and adding it to the £500. Thus, say it was £535, turning to £30 and £5 per annum and adding this to £500, a right result could be obtained.

The chief use of these tables is, however, to show the division of wages or salaries for servants or governesses, it being a common thing to reckon these by the year and yet pay by the month or quarter.

A large "ready reckoner" such as may be found in large houses of business is scarcely necessary for private accounts in a household, and we trust the one we give, a more complete one than is usually found in a cookery book, will be found by the housekeeper to be all that she requires.

Per Year.	Per Quarter.	Per Month.	Per Week.	Per Day.
£ *s.* *d.*	£ *s.* *d.*	£ *s.* *d.*	£ *s.* *d.*	£ *s.* *d*
1 0 0	- 5 0	- 1 8	- - 4½	- - 0¾
1 10 0	- 7 6	- 2 6	- - 7	- - 1
2 0 0	- 10 0	- 3 4	- - 9¼	- - 1¼
2 10 0	- 12 6	- 4 2	- - 11½	- - 1¾
3 0 0	- 15 0	- 5 0	- 1 1¾	- - 2
3 10 0	- 17 6	- 5 10	- 1 4¼	- - 2¼
4 0 0	1 0 0	- 6 8	- 1 6½	- - 2½
4 10 0	1 2 6	- 7 6	- 1 8¾	- - 3
5 0 0	1 5 0	- 8 4	- 1 11	- - 3¼
5 10 0	1 7 6	- 9 2	- 2 1½	- - 3¾
6 0 0	1 10 0	- 10 0	- 2 3¾	- - 4
6 10 0	1 12 6	- 10 10	- 2 6	- - 4¼
7 0 0	1 15 0	- 11 8	- 2 8¼	- - 4½
7 10 0	1 17 6	- 12 6	- 2 10½	- - 5
8 0 0	2 0 0	- 13 4	- 3 1	- - 5¼
8 10 0	2 2 6	- 14 2	- 3 3	- - 5½
9 0 0	2 5 0	- 15 0	- 3 5½	- - 6
10 0 0	2 10 0	- 16 8	- 3 10	- - 6½
11 0 0	2 15 0	- 18 4	- 4 3	- - 7¼
12 0 0	3 0 0	1 0 0	- 4 7½	- - 8
13 0 0	3 5 0	1 1 8	- 5 0	- - 8½
14 0 0	3 10 0	1 3 4	- 5 4½	- - 9¼
15 0 0	3 15 0	1 5 0	- 5 9	- - 10
16 0 0	4 0 0	1 6 8	- 6 2	- - 10½
17 0 0	4 5 0	1 8 4	- 6 6½	- - 11¼
18 0 0	4 10 0	1 10 0	- 6 11	- - 11¾
19 0 0	4 15 0	1 11 8	- 7 3½	- 1 0½
20 0 0	5 0 0	1 13 4	- 7 8	- 1 1¼
30 0 0	7 10 0	2 10 0	- 11 6	- 1 7¾
40 0 0	10 0 0	3 6 8	- 15 4½	- 2 2¼
50 0 0	12 10 0	4 3 4	- 19 3	- 2 9
60 0 0	15 0 0	5 0 0	1 3 0¾	- 3 3½
70 0 0	17 10 0	5 16 8	1 6 11	- 3 10
80 0 0	20 0 0	6 13 4	1 10 9	- 4 4½
90 0 0	22 10 0	7 10 0	1 14 7¾	- 4 11
100 0 0	25 0 0	8 6 8	1 18 5½	- 5 5¾
150 0 0	37 10 0	12 10 0	2 17 8	- 8 2¾
200 0 0	50 0 0	16 13 4	3 16 11	- 10 11¼
250 0 0	62 10 0	20 16 8	4 16 1¾	- 13 8¼
300 0 0	75 0 0	25 0 0	5 15 4¼	- 16 5¼
350 0 0	87 10 0	29 3 4	6 14 7	- 19 2¼
400 0 0	100 0 0	33 6 8	7 13 10¼	1 1 11
450 0 0	112 10 0	37 10 0	8 13 1	1 4 8
500 0 0	125 0 0	41 13 4	9 12 3¾	1 7 4¾

HOUSEKEEPING EXPENSES (WEEKLY).

	Monday.			Tuesday.			Wed'sday.			Thursday.			Friday.			Saturday.			TOTAL.		
	£	s.	d.	£	s.	d.	£	s.	d.	£	s.	d.	£	s.	d.	£	s.	d.	£	s.	d.
Baker	0	0	9	0	0	9	0	0	9	0	0	9	0	0	9	0	1	3	0	5	0
Butcher	0	2	0	0	5	7				0	3	6	0	2	4	0	4	8	0	18	1
Brewer										0	5	0							0	5	0
Charities	0	3	0	0	0	2							0	2	6	0	0	3	0	5	11
Coals	1	2	6																1	2	6
Dress				0	7	6	0	18	0				0	5	7				1	11	1
Fishmonger				0	3	6				0	7	0				0	1	4	0	11	10
Garden Expenses																0	4	0	0	4	0
Greengrocer				0	0	9	0	1	4	0	0	6				0	2	0	0	4	7
Grocer				0	4	8										0	6	0	0	10	8
Laundress																0	4	4	0	4	4
Milkman																0	4	9	0	4	9
Rates and Taxes										1	8	0							1	8	0
Rent				9	0	0													9	0	0
Sundries	0	2	7	0	5	1	0	3	9	0	4	8	0	1	2	0	5	6	1	2	9
Wages							1	6	8										1	6	8
Wine and Spirits				0	6	0							0	3	6				0	9	6
	1	10	10	10	14	0	2	10	6	2	9	5	0	15	10	1	14	1	19	14	8

The total of each week's expenses to be carried to the columns in the monthly account on the opposite page. This will give the total of the monthly expenditure. The weekly cash account must commence with the balance on hand from the previous week, and must show the balance left on hand at the end of each month.

It will be seen that both rates and taxes as well as rent and wages occur in this week's expenditure, which is reckoned as the first of the year.

Such household expenses as rent, rates and taxes, wages, coals, wines and spirits, are scarcely likely to be weekly ones, but they should all be set down in each week's list, so that no extra lines will be needed when they are paid.

Not to lose sight of the small sums spent during the day that come under no head but that of sundries, it is well to carry a pencil and card in the purse to jot them down as they occur.

HOUSEKEEPING EXPENSES (YEARLY).

	JANUARY.			FEBRUARY.			MARCH.			APRIL.			MAY.			JUNE.		
	£	s.	d.	£	s.	d.	£	s.	d.	£	s.	d.	£	s.	d.	£	s.	d.
Baker	1	1	6	2	0	0	1	3	9	1	6	4	1	3	0	1	7	6
Butcher	3	4	11	3	16	0	2	19	6	3	17	8	3	11	0	3	19	6
Brewer	1	0	0	1	5	0	1	0	0	1	0	0	1	0	0	1	0	0
Charities	0	19	5	1	2	0	0	12	8	2	0	6	0	10	0	0	7	6
Coals	1	2	6	1	15	6	1	2	6	0	15	0	0	15	0	0	12	6
Dress	4	15	9	3	19	0	2	17	0	5	9	3	1	16	0	3	1	7
Fishmonger	1	15	4	1	3	0	2	0	6	1	10	0	0	18	0	1	4	0
Garden Expenses	0	19	0	1	0	0	0	12	0	2	4	0	3	5	0	0	18	0
Greengrocer	0	16	9	0	15	0	0	14	8	1	0	4	0	14	0	0	13	2
Grocer	2	13	6	2	12	6	1	19	8	2	16	0	2	0	0	1	17	6
Laundress	0	19	6	1	2	0	0	18	6	1	4	0	1	5	0	1	10	0
Milkman	0	18	3	1	0	6	0	19	0	1	2	6	0	18	0	0	19	0
Rates and Taxes	1	8	0							1	11	8						
Rent	9	0	0							9	0	0						
Sundries	4	4	3	4	10	0	5	9	6	2	5	9	3	14	0	0	5	8
Wages	1	6	8	1	6	8	1	6	8	1	6	8	1	6	8	1	6	8
Wines and Spirits	1	11	6	1	8	0	0	19	7	1	2	0	1	0	0	0	18	0
	37	16	10	28	14	8	24	15	6	39	11	2	23	15	8	25	19	11

HOUSEKEEPING EXPENSES (MONTHLY).

	1st Week.			2nd Week.			3rd Week.			4th Week.			5th Week.			TOTAL.		
	£	s.	d.	£	s.	d.	£	s.	d.	£	s.	d.	£	s.	d.	£	s.	d.
Baker	0	5	0	0	5	6	0	5	0	0	4	9	0	1	3	1	1	6
Butcher	0	18	1	0	15	0	0	12	8	0	17	6	0	1	8	3	4	11
Brewer	0	5	0	0	5	0	0	5	0	0	5	0		......		1	0	0
Charities	0	5	11	0	4	8	0	6	4	0	2	6		......		0	19	5
Coals	1	2	6		......			......			......			......		1	2	6
Dress	1	11	1	2	4	0	0	3	8	0	17	0		......		4	15	9
Fishmonger	0	11	10	0	7	6	0	10	0	0	5	0	0	1	0	1	15	4
Garden Expenses	0	4	0	0	6	0	0	5	0	0	4	0		......		0	19	0
Greengrocer	0	4	7	0	3	2	0	5	0	0	4	0		......		0	16	9
Grocer	0	10	8	0	17	6	0	14	4	0	11	0		......		2	13	6
Laundress	0	4	4	0	5	0	0	6	2	0	4	0		......		0	19	6
Milkman	0	4	9	0	4	3	0	5	0	0	3	9	0	0	6	0	18	3
Rates and Taxes	1	8	0		......			......			......			......		1	8	0
Rent	9	0	0		......			......			......			......		9	0	0
Sundries	1	2	9	0	17	6	0	18	4	1	0	8	0	5	0	4	4	3
Wages	1	6	8		......			......			......			......		1	6	8
Wines and Spirits	0	9	6	0	7	0	0	5	0	0	10	0		......		1	11	6
	19	14	8	7	2	1	5	1	6	5	9	2	0	9	5	37	16	10

WEEKLY CASH ACCOUNT.

Receipts:—	£	s.	d.	Expenditure:—	£	s.	d.
Balance on hand	3	0	0	Cash spent	37	16	10
Cash received:—				Balance on hand	5	3	2
1st Week	20	0	0				
2nd Week	10	0	0				
3rd Week	5	0	0				
4th Week	5	0	0				
5th Week	0	0	0				
	£43	0	0		£43	0	0

HOUSEKEEPING EXPENSES (YEARLY)—continued.

JULY.			AUGUST.			SEPTEMBER.			OCTOBER.			NOVEMBER.			DECEMBER.			TOTAL.		
£	s.	d.	£	s.	d.	£	s.	d.	£	s.	d.	£	s.	d.	£	s.	d.	£	s.	d.
1	2	4	1	6	0	1	5	9	1	2	3	1	4	8	1	14	0	15	17	1
2	19	0	3	4	0	3	8	0	3	16	0	3	17	9	3	18	0	42	11	4
1	0	0	1	0	0	1	0	0	1	5	0	1	0	0	1	5	0	12	15	0
1	9	3	1	4	0	0	16	0	0	14	0	1	2	0	0	19	6	11	16	10
0	12	6	0	15	0	1	2	6	1	5	0	1	2	6	1	5	0	12	5	6
4	2	6	3	0	5	1	19	2	2	8	3	5	7	1	3	0	0	41	16	0
1	17	0	1	9	3	0	19	6	1	5	0	0	18	6	1	2	6	16	2	7
1	2	0	0	15	0	0	18	0	0	12	0	0	16	0	0	12	0	13	7	0
0	9	0	0	10	6	0	17	0	0	15	4	0	18	2	0	17	0	9	0	11
3	4	0	1	12	0	2	12	6	2	14	0	2	19	0	4	10	0	31	10	2
1	3	0	1	6	4	0	19	0	1	0	6	0	18	6	0	19	0	13	5	4
0	18	6	1	4	0	0	17	6	0	18	9	0	19	6	1	2	0	11	17	0
2	4	9		......			......		3	10	0		......			......		8	14	5
9	0	0		......			......		9	0	0		......			......		36	0	0
3	12	0	2	6	6	3	0	6	4	5	0	3	17	0	5	4	0	48	13	6
1	6	8	1	6	8	1	6	8	1	6	8	1	6	8	1	6	8	16	0	0
0	19	6	1	5	0	1	2	0	1	3	6	1	4	0	1	11	0	14	4	1
37	2	0	22	4	8	22	4	1	37	1	3	27	5	4	29	5	8	355	16	9

YEARLY CASH ACCOUNT.

Receipts :—	£	s.	d.	*Expenditure :—*	£	s.	d.
Balance in hand	3	0	0	January	37	16	0
January	40	0	0	February	28	14	8
February	25	0	0	March......	24	15	6
March..................	25	0	0	April	39	11	2
April	40	0	0	May..........................	23	15	8
May...................	25	0	0	June	25	19	11
June	25	0	0	July.............................	37	2	0
July.............................	40	0	0	August	22	4	8
August	25	0	0	September.....................	22	4	1
September.....................	25	0	0	October	37	1	3
October	40	0	0	November	27	5	4
November	25	0	0	December	29	5	8
December	25	0	0	Balance forward	7	3	3
	363	0	0		363	0	0

Balance forward, £7 3 3.

THE MANAGEMENT OF HOUSEKEEPING EXPENSES:

The following tables are intended to give a few suggestions to those inexperienced housekeepers who find it difficult to apportion small or moderate incomes so as to supply all the usual daily needs.

It has been well said that "no man is poor who spends less than his income, and none rich who exceeds it," but with means only sufficient for the necessaries of life, and very few of its luxuries, it is not always easy to do the former. In such cases the safe plan is first to make a list of what *must* be spent, and then to divide the surplus according to individual requirements.

TABLES OF COST OF HOUSEKEEPING,

With other Expenses, in Families of from Two to Six Persons with incomes of from £150 to £500.

COST OF LIVING OF TWO PERSONS WITH INCOME OF £150.

Weekly Expenditure :—	£	s.	d.	*Yearly Expenditure :—*	£	s.	d.
Butcher......................................	0	8	0	Butcher......................................	20	16	0
Baker..	0	1	6	Baker..	3	18	0
Grocery (including butter & eggs)	0	6	0	Grocery (including butter & eggs)	15	12	0
Fish	0	1	9	Fish	4	11	0
Milk	0	1	6	Milk	3	18	0
Vegetables	0	1	3	Vegetables	3	5	0
Rent	0	11	6	Rent	30	0	0
Rates and Taxes	0	3	10	Rates and Taxes................	10	0	0
Clothing	0	11	6	Clothing	30	0	0
Coals.....................................	0	2	0	Coals.....................................	5	4	0
Lighting	0	1	0	Lighting	2	12	0
Washing	0	2	0	Washing	5	4	0
Sundry Expenses	0	5	9	Sundry Expenses	15	0	0
	£2	17	7		£150	0	0

It will be seen that there is left a margin of £15 for sundry extra expenses. The 8s. allowed for butcher's meat will give 9½ lbs. of meat ; the 1s. 6d. for bread, 6 half-quartern loaves ; the same sum for milk, 1 pint per day and an extra quart for puddings ; and in the grocery is included bacon for breakfast, cheese, some rice or other grain, and dried fruit for puddings.

COST OF LIVING OF FOUR PERSONS WITH INCOME OF £200.

Weekly Expenditure :—	£	s.	d.	Yearly Expenditure:—	£	s.	d.
Butcher	0	11	0	Butcher	28	12	0
Baker	0	3	6	Baker	9	2	0
Grocery	0	7	0	Grocery	18	4	0
Fish	0	2	6	Fish	6	10	0
Milk	0	3	6	Milk	9	2	0
Vegetables	0	3	0	Vegetables	7	16	0
Rent	0	12	3¼	Rent	32	0	0
Rates and Taxes	0	2	9	Rates and Taxes	7	3	0
Lighting	0	1	6	Lighting	3	18	0
Coals	0	3	0	Coals	7	16	0
Washing	0	1	6	Washing	3	18	0
Clothing	0	15	0	Clothing	39	0	0
Extra Expenses	0	10	3¼	Extra Expenses	26	19	0
	£3	16	9½		£200	0	0

This imaginary family is supposed to consist of two adults and two children. It will be seen that of the £200 income £26 19s. is left for extra expenses, part of which would doubtless be paid in school fees. The washing is supposed to be done at home. No servant is included, but if the children were very young ones and would cost but little to keep or clothe, the income would warrant the wage and board of a girl as general servant or help.

COST OF LIVING FOR FOUR PERSONS WITH INCOME OF £300.

Weekly Expenditure :—	£	s.	d.	Yearly Expenditure:—	£	s.	d.
Baker	0	4	6	Baker	11	14	0
Butcher	0	16	0	Butcher	41	12	0
Grocery	0	10	0	Grocery	26	0	0
Fish and Poultry	0	4	6	Fish and Poultry	11	14	0
Milk	0	3	6	Milk	9	2	0
Vegetables	0	3	0	Vegetables	7	16	0
Wine, &c.	0	5	0	Wine, &c.	1}	0	0
Rent	0	15	4½	Rent	40	0	0
Rates and Taxes	0	3	10	Rates and Taxes	10	0	0
Lighting	0	2	0	Lighting	5	4	0
Coals	0	4	3	Coals	11	0	0
Washing	0	4	0	Washing	10	8	0
Wages	0	6	11	Wages	18	0	0
Schooling	0	5	0	Schooling	13	0	0
Clothing	0	17	6	Clothing	45	0	0
Extra Expenses	0	10	2	Extra Expenses	26	10	0
	£5	14	6½		£300	0	0

This family is also supposed to consist of two adults and two children, with the addition of a woman servant whose wages are shown. The 4s. allowed per week for washing is to represent it as put out to a laundress, if such things as kitchen towels were washed at home.

In households of moderate size it may be safely reckoned that each adult person's board, living well, should not exceed 10s. per week, and this should be sufficient for all except wine or spirit. In larger households the average board would be rather less, perhaps about 8s. The board of two young children may be reckoned as equivalent to that of one grown up person, that is, if they were fed upon the foods generally considered best for children and not given a quantity of meat.

COST OF LIVING OF SIX PERSONS WITH INCOME OF £500.

Weekly Expenditure:—	£	s.	d.	Yearly Expenditure:—	£	s.	d.
Baker	0	5	0	Baker	13	0	0
Butcher	1	5	0	Butcher	65	0	0
Grocery	0	15	0	Grocery	39	0	0
Fish and Poultry	0	7	0	Fish and Poultry	18	4	0
Milk	0	4	0	Milk	9	2	0
Vegetables	0	4	6	Vegetables	11	14	0
Wine, &c.	0	12	6	Wine, &c.	32	10	0
Rent	1	3	1	Rent	60	0	0
Rates and Taxes	0	5	0	Rates and Taxes	13	0	0
Lighting	0	3	6	Lighting	9	2	0
Coals	0	6	0	Coals	15	12	0
Washing	0	7	0	Washing	18	4	0
Wages	0	13	1	Wages	34	0	0
Schooling	0	10	0	Schooling	26	0	0
Clothing	1	10	0	Clothing	78	0	0
Extra Expenses	1	2	1¾	Extra Expenses	57	12	0
	£9	12	9¾		£500	0	0

It will be seen that more than one-sixth of this income is put down as extra expenses, these being intended to cover such ones as hire of horses and carriages, travelling, &c. School fees are reckoned, but if there were none in the family young enough for education, there would doubtless be other equal expenses. The wages of two women servants only are put down, but a family living in the country, where rent and many other things are less than in or near town, would probably require a gardener or useful man, who could attend upon a horse or pony if one were kept

COST OF LIVING OF SIX PERSONS WITH INCOME OF £600.

Weekly Expenditure:—	£	s.	d.	Yearly Expenditure:—	£	s.	d.
Baker	0	5	6	Baker	14	6	0
Butcher	1	6	0	Butcher	67	12	0
Grocery	0	15	0	Grocery	39	0	0
Fish and Poultry	0	10	0	Fish and Poultry	26	0	0
Milk	0	5	0	Milk	13	0	0
Vegetables	0	6	0	Vegetables	15	12	0
Wine, &c.	0	10	0	Wine, &c.	26	0	0
Rent	1	6	11	Rent	70	0	0
Rates and Taxes	0	6	2	Rates and Taxes	16	0	0
Lighting	0	4	3	Lighting	11	0	0
Coals	0	6	6	Coals	16	18	0
Washing	0	8	0	Washing	20	16	0
Wages	0	17	3½	Wages	45	0	0
Schooling	0	10	0	Schooling	26	0	0
Clothing	1	18	5½	Clothing	100	0	0
Extra Expenses	1	15	8¼	Extra Expenses	92	16	0
	£11	10	9¼		£600	0	0

Under the head of "extra expenses" should come insurance fees, for every household should insure against fire, if no life insurances be deemed necessary. Also there should be something put aside to defray such expenses as would be incurred in sea-side trips during the summer.

It is not supposed that taxes, rent, wages or schooling would be paid by the week, but to reckon the division of the income by the week it is necessary to divide what would in most cases be quarterly payments.

EVERY-DAY MEALS.

TIMES FOR MEALS.

ACCORDING to the occupations and ages of those for whom meals are prepared so must the hours for them be arranged; but there are two golden rules concerning them: namely, that there should be sufficient time allowed for them to be partaken of without hurry, and that they should be punctually served. Of little use is it having a dainty breakfast ready for the master of the house ten minutes before he has to start for business, or a well-cooked good dinner for the children when they have to hurry through it to be in time for afternoon school. Better is it to allow a little extra time than to run the risk of people having to bolt their food or go without it. There should always be a clear half-hour allowed for breakfast, and this should not be a meal that, as in many houses, runs on from eight to ten o'clock. This is fatal to the regular household routine; nor can breakfast be served comfortably and properly for different members keeping different times, unless it be in large households where there are many hands for the morning work.

The servants should be allowed time for their breakfast before that in the dining-room commences; and for them to do this it is absolutely necessary that they rise betimes. Children also should have an early breakfast, or there will be too long an interval between that and their tea of the day before. For master and mistress we cannot suggest a time, unless that it be not *later* than nine o'clock.

Where there are little ones and several servants, a dinner must be served in the middle of the day; but it is generally necessary to have some cooking done later when the master of the house returns. Most men who value their health prefer to have only a light luncheon during working hours and return to dinner late, and this is certainly more economical than dining away from home.

We would advise young housekeepers not to make a trouble of this meal, and to be ready to partake of it with their husbands. Many think it impossible with one or two servants to have a late dinner or what now often takes its place, a high tea; but in reality there is no more work attached to its preparation than that of an ordinary tea and its following supper, and the late dinner is served and cleared away long before a supper could be. If the latter meal be taken, it should be moderately early, and then we cannot see that it is more injurious than a very late dinner.

PUNCTUALITY AND REGULARITY.

Looking at punctuality and regularity from a health point of view, no one will deny that in the serving of our meals they are essential. To the healthy, irregularity is dangerous; to the delicate, it is absolutely injurious. It is known that a certain time should elapse, sufficient for digestive purposes, between our meals; but when that time has passed, and in waiting for a meal we lose the appetite for it we should have had, had it been served in time, so much good food is wasted, and a certain amount of harm done to our system.

It may take some time and trouble to so far plan out the time for meals so that, as far as possible, they are convenient and suitable for all; but when once this is done punctuality in serving them should be insisted upon, with a corresponding insistance on the punctuality of those for whom they are served. As a rule, it is no more trouble (nay, is less) to have regular meals than irregular ones; and where the latter exist, it is oftener the mistress to blame than the servants. If she does not make a point of punctuality with her children as well as the cook, and if she, above all, does not keep to times and hours *herself*, she can never expect either regular meals or regular work. Want of punctuality is more often than not an outcome of selfishness, for people with that bad quality naturally only think of their own comfort and convenience. It is nothing to them if they be not hungry that dinner waits also for half-a-dozen others, and it behoves housekeepers to make the tiresome ones suffer for their own fault, and not visit their sins upon those who have some consideration for the convenience of others.

Where there are but few servants, or it may be only one, an utter disarrangement of their duties is usually the result of lack of punctuality with regard to the time of meals; a d for their sake alone, it is essential that upon this point young housekeepers should be strict.

SERVING OF MEALS.

Whether we live plainly or upon every luxury to be obtained, the rule in serving our meals should be the same—to make them as attractive and as dainty as possible. When this is the case, not only does a good dinner taste the better, but a simple one is dignified and made a far more enjoyable meal than many a more costly one where the details are not perfect.

The damask may not be of the finest, the glass may not be costly, but the one can be white and the other bright. Make the best of everything. Let the

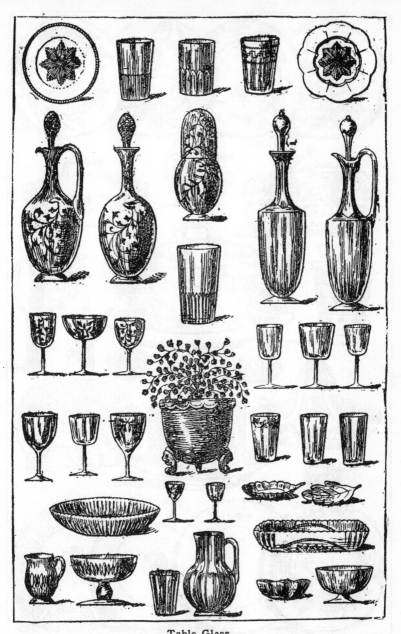

Table Glass.

3 Tumblers, 2 Glass Dishes, 2 Decanters, 2 Claret Jugs, Carafe, Water Jug and Glass,
9 Wine Glasses, 3 Champagne Tumblers, 1 Soda Glass, 1 Cream Ewer and Sugar Bowl,
2 Ice Plates, 2 Finger Basins, 1 Glass Centre Piece.

Dinner and Dessert China.

4 Dinner Plates, 4 Dessert Plates, 2 Vegetable Dishes, 1 Soup Tureen, 1 Jug, 1 Cheese Dish, 1 Ice Pail, 2 Salts, 1 Strawberry Dish, 1 Fruit Dish, 1 Spoon Warmer.

cloth be spotless, the glass polished, the knives bright and sharp, and the silver glistening, and always have some kind of decoration in the way of foliage plants or flowers. Let the viands if hot ones be served *really* hot and with *really* hot plates, and let there be as little delay as possible between the courses. Where it is not possible to serve as well as cook an elaborate meal, it is far better to have one of a few well-cooked dishes sent properly to table with their accompanying vegetables or sauces. Make whatever meal is served for the family or guests, however simple, as perfect as can be of its kind, and, as we have before said, let it look as attractive as possible.

LAYING THE CLOTH.

There is more art than people imagine in laying a cloth properly. Anyone can put a tablecloth over a table and add the necessary forks, knives, spoons, &c., but everyone cannot place these things neatly and accurately, cannot think of everything that will be required, nor dispose either silver, dishes, or other adjuncts to look pretty and tasteful.

A well laid table is one of the refining influences that home should bring to bear upon the young mind. Order, perfect cleanliness and good taste should be thought as essential at the table as in dress. Always have your table properly laid, and if it be done so every day, how much less the anxiety when guests are bidden to any meal. It is possible in many households where the service is not quite in proportion to the demand, that, for instance, in a house where only one general servant can be kept, that she has not always time to lay the cloth. Rather than let this be done in a slovenly hasty way, it is better to do it oneself. There is nothing hard nor derogatory in this task, nay, it would be more so to sit down to a meal

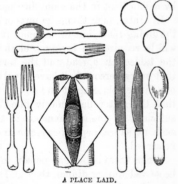

A PLACE LAID.

where everything was put upon the table with neither thought nor care except that of getting the table *laid* (?) in as short a time as possible.

We have later to speak of the preparation of the various articles used in setting a cloth, such as the burnishing of the silver, the folding of the napkins, and the arrangement of the flowers ; here we need only generalise ; but we must not forget a word, or rather a place, for the tablecloth. Let it be laid evenly, with the same quantity falling at the two ends and at the two sides, let it be refolded always in the same creases, and let it go in a press if possible. If there is no necessity for economy in laundry work, and a fresh tablecloth can be used for every meal, then, and only then, is it excusable to wisp it up when taking it off the table, instead of folding it neatly.

Even though both meals be served on the same table, it is best to have two tablecloths going for breakfast and dinner, and the one not in use in the press.

THE SIDEBOARD.

The sideboard for dinner (and for breakfast in large families) requires laying as well as the cloth ; and it should have its fancy cloth with fringed edges or its plain white one for the purpose.

On it should be laid at breakfast the spare plates, knives and forks, &c., the loaf and platter, and the large cold dishes, if any be served, such as a ham, pie, or cold joint.

At dinner it is usually the receptacle of the dessert plates, knives and forks, the spare bread or rolls, besides holding extra supplies of knives, forks, spoons and glasses. In ordinary family dinners, where dessert is not served, any cold sweets and their accompanying plates, as well as the materials for the cheese course, could be placed upon the sideboard. Some persons like to have the dessert laid out upon the sideboard, but this, in the case of strongly-scented fruit such as a pine or melon, is as great a mistake as putting it upon the table ; such fruits, too, as strawberries and other delicate kinds are not improved by being kept in the room during the time of serving a hot dinner.

In winter, such things as nuts or oranges cannot deteriorate by being kept in the dining-room, but the summer fruits almost invariably do. Everything that will be required in laying a cloth should first be brought into the room, then the tablecloth spread and the serviettes, neatly folded, placed equidistant so that every person shall have equal space. Lay the knives and forks the width of a dinner-plate apart and do not forget to put bread to each person, also see that the salt cellars, nicely filled with *dry* salt and with clean spoons, are sufficient for the requirements of the party ; and that there are condiments, such as sauce, pepper, cayenne and mustard at hand according to what is to be served.

When there is but one person to wait at table, if there be any cold dishes to be served during dinner they and their accompanying plates may be brought in and put upon the sideboard, for it should be the aim to save time and labour as much as possible and to avoid any waits during the meal, than which nothing can be more annoying.

A few plants when obtainable make the sideboard look a great deal nicer than without any decoration and they should be put in ornamental pots.

The old fashioned silver wine coolers make very handsome receptacles for pot plants and serve to brighten up the sideboard, which should be made to look as glittering and pretty as possible, particularly when laying it for dinner.

A short experience of cloth-laying will teach the beginner just what will be needed for individual meals; but we herewith give two lists that will show what would be required at an ordinary breakfast for eight persons and a dinner-party of twelve, independent of floral or other decorations.

BREAKFAST TABLE AND SIDEBOARD CLOTH

BREAKFAST FOR EIGHT PERSONS,

Consisting of tea, coffee, bread, rolls, toast, eggs, cutlets, ham,
coil pie, fruit, watercress.

The Table.

White cloth.

Plants or flowers in centre of table.

8 serviettes, very simply folded.

12 cups and saucers, 6 at each end, with spoons.

8 small plates and knives, one set at the left side of each person.

8 large hot plates placed before the cutlets, with knife and fork.

8 large knives and forks, one of each set to each person.

8 small plates, suitable for fruit, set at one corner.

2 breakfast cruets holding salt, pepper, and mustard, at corners, and 2 salts at other corners.

Watercress boat.

Egg stand, for 6 or 8, with spoons.

Butter dish, toast rack.

4 table spoons.

Coffee pot, crushed sugar, hot milk.

Tea pot, loaf sugar, cold milk.

The Sideboard.

Bread, platter and knife.

8 cold plates for ham and pie.

Knives and forks for ham and pie.

Carvers and helpers for both dishes.

3 or 4 each extra spoons, knives and forks.

To Lay the Table.

Put the serviettes in front of each person and a small plate and knife to the left. Set the cups and saucers in two semi-circles of six at each end of the table and the tea and coffee pot at either end flanked by milk and sugar.

In the centre of the table let there be a vase of flowers or plant and flank this with two dishes of fruit prettily arranged.

Set the hot dish at the centre of the side of the table and opposite to this put the hot rolls.

The toast, butter, eggs and watercresses will make four corner dishes, and fill up the remainder of the space on an ordinary breakfast table.

Let the toast be crisp and freshly made, the cold dishes nicely garnished with parsley, the butter in small rolls or balls, the plates and cutlets very hot, the tea and coffee good.

When fresh fruit is not obtainable a dish of stewed fruit, such as prunes or pippins, may take its place, or small dishes of marmalade and jam.

If the toast be buttered it should be placed either in a hot-water dish, or if that be not at hand, in a plate with a cover, set over a basin of hot water.

DINNER TABLE AND SIDEBOARD CLOTH.

DINNER FOR TWELVE PERSONS,

Consisting of soup, fish, two entrées (one hot, one cold), joint and vegetables, game, sweets, cheese, dessert, sherry, champagne, claret.

The Table.

12 prettily-folded serviettes.	12 fish eaters.
12 sherry, claret, and champagne glasses.	8 salt cellars.
	12 dessert forks.
12 soup spoons.	Soup ladle.
12 dessert spoons.	Fish carvers.
12 large forks.	8 table spoons.
12 large knives.	Water carafes and glasses.

The Sideboard.

3½ dozen large forks.	Biscuits, butter and pulled bread for cheese course.
3½ dozen large knives.	
12 small knives and plates, if cheese is to be served.	Cruets and sauces.
	Bread, cut, or rolls.
12 cold plates for cold entrées.	Some few spare knives, forks and spoons.
12 plates, if cold sweets.	
12 dessert plates, knives, forks, and finger glasses.	Glasses for whatever wines are to be served after dinner.
6 table spoons.	Ice in pails, if in summer.
Joint and poultry carvers.	Grape scissors, nutcrackers.
	Fruit spoons.

To each person place, as shown above, a serviette, a large knife and fork, a dessert spoon and fork, fish eaters, soup spoon, and three glasses, sherry, champagne and claret. To each also put a roll or thickly cut small piece of bread, and menu card if they are used.

Put carafes and glasses as there is room with reference to the decoration. Put salts and spoons at corners and sides of the table. Set the fish carvers and soup ladle at the head of the table, to be replaced, after using, with the meat carvers and poultry knife and fork.

The entrées, it is presumed, will be handed, when helpers according to what the dishes consist of should accompany them. Vegetables will also be handed, with their spoons, and in the case of asparagus, with tongs.

WAITING AT TABLE.

Those who wait at table should have for their qualifications, quickness, neatness and quietness, and they should be ready of eye to see where anything is wanting, where plates or glasses are empty, and watchful for summons from master or mistress.

SUPPER TABLE

In large establishments the butler would wait at table, supported by footmen and perhaps an under butler. In smaller ones a parlour maid is oftenest seen, helped when necessary by the housemaid, who takes the second place with regard to the former as a footman does with a butler. In still smaller households where but two servants are kept, all the waiting is done by the housemaid ; while where there is but one servant, it is unreasonable to expect any more attendance than the placing of the dishes upon the table and the changing of the plates, as, if she has the cooking to do, most of her time must perforce be spent in the kitchen during meals.

Still, whatever servants there be, if waiting is done certain rules apply, which we here give.

The attendance begins from the head of the table on the right side of the master of the house, where will be seated the chief lady guest, or if there be no guests the mistress of the house will be the first served. As plates are finished with they should be removed, as glasses are emptied they should be refilled, with permission of those using them. Everything is handed at the left side, but wine is poured out on the right.

At breakfast, luncheon or supper attendance is seldom exacted, and after the first course has been handed servant or servants are generally allowed to leave the room; and for this reason it behoves them to see that before doing so everything required for the meal is left upon the table or sideboard. At an elaborate luncheon with several hot courses, service would, of course, be required as at a dinner ; and at a ball supper, or even one with several guests, the servants would attend, but as the mode of waiting would be the same at all meals, we will confine ourselves to speaking of what would be required at a dinner.

Directly the soup is handed round in the order we have said, the sherry, or whatever wine is served first, is carried to each person. In serving the fish a plateful is taken to each person, the waiter or waitress having in the other hand the accompanying sauce, or being followed by a second servant with it and cruets if necessary.

For the entrées which—even where other dishes are put upon the table, are generally handed—plates replacing those used for fish are placed to each person, with clean knife and fork, and spoon if curry is served; the dishes are then handed round for every one to help themselves. The meat course is handed by the chief servant, the second following with the vegetables, and the game or poultry in like manner followed by its adjuncts.

The head servant also pours out the wine, going to the right hand, and, in the case of a choice, asking which will be taken. If beer is given the servant brings a small tray to the left side of each person, and on this they put their glass to be filled.

All plates, as we have said, should be carried away just as they are directly they are done with, but upon reaching the sideboard the servants must remove the knife and fork and put each into their proper receptacle, basket or tray which, to avoid scratching of silver or unnecessary noise, should have cloths at the bottoms, and the plates themselves should be put in a proper zinc-lined basket put for convenience near the door.

In the case of a good many courses it may be that the dinner service will be insufficient, and some plates will have to be washed during dinner, for which purpose a tub should be ready filled with very hot water and soda and the fish plates, if taken out directly after that course was finished and put into this, would be ready for a second entrée or for the joint, and, the tub being refilled, the plates used for the first entrée would be washed in time for the game.

After the game or last savoury course, plates for the sweets are put to each person and the dishes handed ; the same applies to a cheese course.

When the last is over, the table is completely cleared, slips if used are taken off, and the crumbs removed with scoop or brush and tray ; then the table is reset for dessert, with clean glasses according to the after-dinner wine, dessert plates, knives and forks and finger glasses, and the fruit and wine is placed upon the table.

Sometimes the servants hand round the principal dishes and pour out the wine, but after that their services are dispensed with.

Parlourmaid's or housemaid's dress for waiting at table, should be of black material, simply made, but brightened by smart and pretty caps and aprons ; and collar, cuffs and hands should be spotless. Good attendance is a very great comfort, both to mistress and guests ; it leaves the former free to entertain the latter, instead of having to devote herself to their wants, and it adds considerably to the enjoyment of a meal. Mistresses should make a point, if they have servants to wait at table, to have them, or train them to be, thoroughly competent, executing proper service, not only at a dinner party, but every day. If we have nothing glossed over when by ourselves at the family meal, either in the laying of the cloth or the waiting, there will always be a sense of security when we entertain, that the servants will do their duty.

INSTRUCTIONS FOR FOLDING OF SERVIETTES.

Without being as obtrusive as they often are at hotels or large public entertainments, these articles should still be part of the ornaments of the table. It used to be the fashion to have them only of plain damask ; but we now vary them with coloured borders and embroidered monograms. These are pretty enough in their way, but to be in good taste, the colour must be the one predominant in the decoration of the table ; and, therefore, unless one can have sets of serviettes with different-coloured ornamentation, if we want to vary our flowers or foliage, we had better be contented with the plain white ones, brightening them with a dainty little bouquet of two or three blossoms and foliage when using them for dinner or other entertainment.

For everyday family use an ornamental ring through which they are run is usual; but placed fresh for guests they should certainly be folded. For this

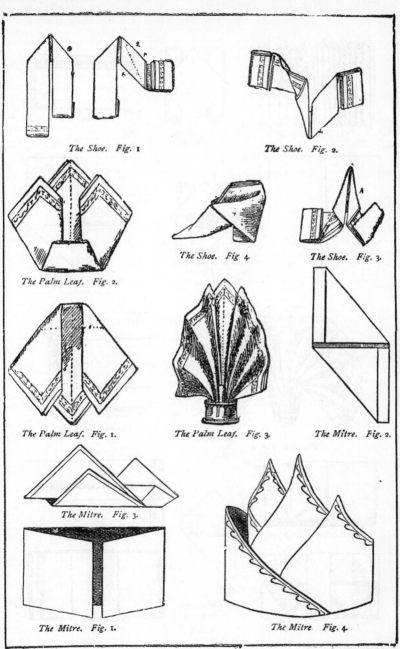

The Shoe. Fig. 1

The Shoe. Fig. 2.

The Palm Leaf. Fig. 2.

The Shoe. Fig 4.

The Shoe. Fig. 3.

The Palm Leaf. Fig. 1.

The Palm Leaf. Fig. 3.

The Mitre. Fig. 2.

The Mitre. Fig. 3.

The Mitre. Fig. 1.

The Mitre. Fig. 4.

Serviettes.

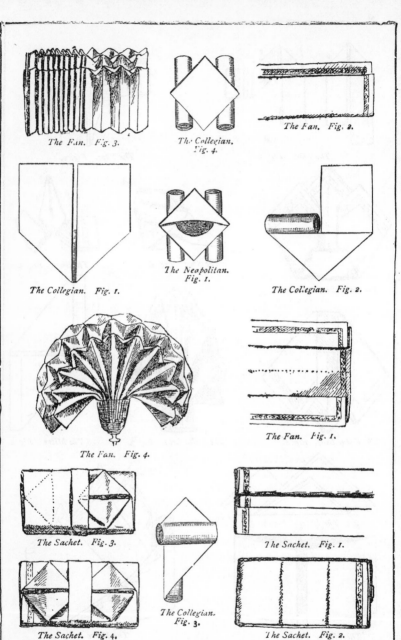

The Fan. Fig. 3.

The Collegian. Fig. 4.

The Fan. Fig. 2.

The Collegian. Fig. 1.

The Neopolitan. Fig. 1.

The Collegian. Fig. 2.

The Fan. Fig. 4.

The Fan. Fig. 1.

The Sachet. Fig. 3.

The Sachet. Fig. 1.

The Collegian. Fig. 3.

The Sachet. Fig. 4.

The Sachet. Fig. 2.

Serviettes.

purpose they should be slightly starched, but not stiff, and ironed in perfectly even folds.

We illustrate in different stages the folding of seven different patterns, of which the best known, the least trouble, and the most convenient is the "Mitre." There is a certain pretty neatness in this, and it is a handy recept-acle for the bread or roll.

The Mitre.—Fold the napkin in three to form a strip, then bring the two edges of this to the centre, as shown in fig. 1. Next fold down two corners as in fig. 2, and by doubling the folded napkin under lengthwise you will get fig. 3. Next bend the left-hand bottom corner towards the right hand, and slip it into the inner fold, as in fig. 4; and, turning the napkin, there will be a similar fold to receive the right-hand corner, with the result shown.

The Collegian.—Fold the serviette lengthwise into three, then turn over each side at the centre as shown in fig. 1. Turn over the serviette and roll up the ends as in fig. 2. Next fold these two rolls *under*, that the two rolls may lie side by side at the back of the square, as may be seen in fig. 3, with the result shown in fig. 4. Another way of folding this serviette is not to turn it before making the rolls, so that when they are put underneath, the napkin opens and gives space for the bread. This mode of folding is on page illustration.

The Neapolitan is folded like the Collegian, only that before turning down the serviette as in fig. 4, the topmost of the three folds is turned back half way, so that it opens as in fig. 1.

The Sachet.—This, like the Collegian or Neapolitan, is a neat, flat-lying serviette, suitable for breakfast or luncheon. It should first be folded in three and the centre fold rolled as a hem to the middle, as in fig. 1. Then, the napkin lying flat upon the table, hem uppermost, the two ends should be brought together, thus folding the strip in half and leaving the hem in the middle (see fig. 2). Next turn from the outer edge in three folds at dotted lines, then reverse the napkin and turn the other side in the same way. Now take the centre of each end, and, bending them back to take the form of the dotted lines, put the ends of the diamonds thus formed under the band which crosses the centre of the serviette, as shown in figs. 3 and 4.

The Fan.—Lay the serviette flat upon the table, and make a deep pleat in the centre, as shown in fig. 1; then fold the two edges together as in fig. 2. Now pleat in folds like a fan about an inch deep, backwards and forwards, as shown in fig. 3; then let it expand, and pinch down each fold till it presents the appearance shown in fig. 4, and put it either in a glass or napkin-ring. This style of folding a serviette is more suitable for the two ends than the sides of a table.

The Palm Leaf.—Fold the serviette diagonally across, and, if a very large one repeat the process, so that a triangular effect is the result. Next turn up the two ends so as to form three points, as shown in fig. 1, and fold up the lower edge as in fig. 2; then, having pleated up the serviette in regular folds as a fan, place it in a ring to stand up, as in fig. 3.

The Shoe —Fold the serviette in three, then again over, to make it half the width. Fold over at centre and turn up the ends, next *under* at the dotted lines, as in fig. 1. Again fold over at dotted line shown in fig. 1, at both sides (see fig. 2). Turn up the ends as shown on the right side, fig. 3; then fold forwards, bringing A to A, and set up the slipper as shown in fig. 4.

Table napkins for placing under a tart dish are usually folded in a square of four folds, and the corners turned under ; but a cut paper that effectually conceals the pie dish is a good substitute for the napkin.

For putting round a soufflé they are simply folded lengthwise and pinned round. For fish, they are folded to the shape of the dish ; but ornamental papers for both fish and pastry are now more often used than napkins.

MODERN TABLE DECORATION.

To most young housewives, this is quite one of the most attractive and pleasant of their duties. At the present time there is quite a furore for original designs for the ornamentation of our tables with flowers and foliage ; and fashionable dinner givers vie with each other in their floral arrangements, and the quaintness and beauty of the vases and other receptacles used for decoration. Fortunately, it is not always the costliness that enhances the beauty in these cases, for there are very many flowers which can be bought for a mere trifle (if not grown), that lend themselves perfectly for table decoration; while wild flowers have been found so pretty for this purpose that they have been used by professional artists in flowers at many grand dinners.

Field flowers mingled with grasses form a charming decoration in such blends as cornflowers lightly grouped with delicate brown grass, or poppies with lighter ones and marguerites ; buttercups also, if properly arranged to stand up well without any crowding, with plenty of feathery foliage, look extremely well; and one great charm that wild flowers for table use possess is, that they have so little scent. Some people cannot stand strongly-scented flowers in a room at all, and still more most strongly object to their being found upon a dinner table, where the heat too often makes them overpowering. The only perfumed flower that seems generally to find favour is the rose, and it is a lovely one for table decoration, if put into low bowls or baskets, or in single blooms in small glasses, with only their own foliage. Yellow being such a pretty, bright colour, and one that does not jar against surroundings in the way of other colours, is a very favourite one for dinner tables ; and if this colour, besides the roses named, small dwarf sunflowers, Alpine poppies, iris and marguerites are all effective. Apropos of iris, it forms a lovely decoration in pale mauve, yellow and white, with plenty of pale green as foliage. The darker shades of this flower are also beautiful ; but the deep blues are almost black by night, and should only be chosen to use by daylight.

Foliage alone can be used by those with taste and skill in arrangement to make a lovely table, quite as pretty as a floral one. We have seen this done,

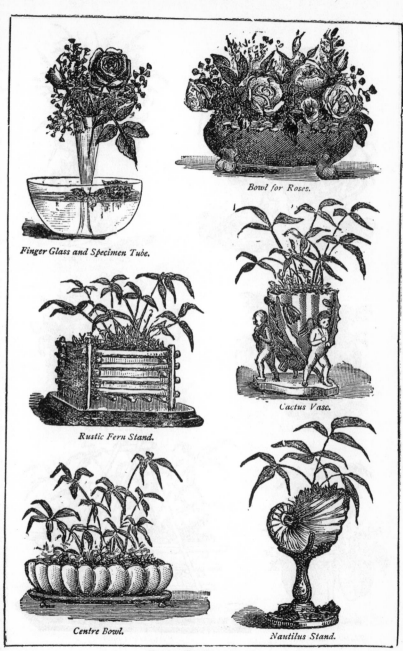

Finger Glass and Specimen Tube.

Bowl for Roses.

Rustic Fern Stand.

Cactus Vase.

Centre Bowl.

Nautilus Stand.

Table Decorations.

China Shell Vase.

Plain Glass Vase.

Nautilus Shell.

Specimen Tubes.

Tinted Glass Vase

Rustic Glass Basket.

Table Decorations.

both in hothouse foliage, in which the colours may be as rich as flowers, and equally well in the leaves and berries of ordinary hardy plants. In the country, in autumn, we have never far to seek for lovely-tinted leaves and bright-hued berries that cost only the trouble of picking ; and even in town, we can generally get some leaves and trails of Virginia creeper or sprays of the many-hued barberries.

BOHEMIAN GLASS.

The fashions in table decorations now change as often as those of our attire, that is, the different modes of arrangement and the vases in which the flowers are placed ; but two very good rules, that seem likely to hold good for a long time to come are, that they should be of one or two colours only, and that they shall not impede the view across the table.

It will be found easier to make a good effect with one colour in the flowers used and variety of the foliage than to blend a miscellaneous collection of blossoms.

The great aim of a good decorator is so to place the flowers that they look natural, and as if *growing*. Crowding them together takes away from the beauty of the flowers, which should stand clearly apart, their stems showing, with the grasses or fern with which they are intermingled veiling, but not hiding them, nor resting upon the blossoms.

This is neither the age of heavy dinners nor heavy decoration. Substantial entrées, immense joints and old port have departed with the solid masses of flowers that, filling the massive epergnes, hid host and hostess from view of most of their guests. The dinner tables of fashionable people are things of lightness and delicacy, and the menus to correspond.

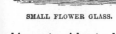

SMALL FLOWER GLASS.

Where time cannot be spared for decorating the table, plants may be used. Ferns especially look well, particularly in the rustic glass flower-stands (see page illustration). They also look very pretty in white china vases ; but these, to show up well upon the cloth, if not placed upon dessert centres of colour, should have velvet stands. One of the best lasting ferns we may mention, one that will bear exposure to gas, is the pteris, of which there are several varieties ; and experience goes to prove that they live better and longer in china pots without a hole for ventilation.

It has been now used so long that it is probable the dessert centre will go out of fashion before many seasons are over ; yet it is a useful feature on large tables, especially if flowers are not plentiful, there being only required with one of these two or three vases and a fringe of foliage and flowers. Prettier than the plain ones of plush or velvet, are those of soft silk, and even of such inexpensive materials as art muslin, puckered artistically, and with flowers introduced in the folds. Here is an example for a summer decoration: An oval table for twelve, covered (with but the space allowed for laying knives, forks, spoons and glasses) with pale pink silk laid on loosely and full, and gathered into innumerable folds. In the centre, a graceful vase, not more than eight inches high, of pink and white, the pink deeper than that of the silk, of cactus type, filled with white roses and foliage; six more corresponding vases, smaller than the centre one, also standing amongst the silken folds, and one tiny one, just a flower itself, holding a single white rosebud, set for each person. The silk also veiled by long trailing pieces of asparagus foliage, and with roses thrust into its folds here and there.

Another example is suitable for a spring decoration. The centre in this is of pale yellow, the colour of a daffodil. Upon it stands three delicate, feathery palms, the centre one a trifle higher than the rest, with at their bases only foliage of delicate tints and white. Fringing the cloth in irregular wreaths, small ivy and fronds of fern; down the sides, slender glass vases, holding daffodils, grasses and fern.

A looking-glass plateau with a border trough has a cool and pretty effect in summer, if arranged with a narrow-leaved green and white plant in the centre, with a base of yellow and white iris resting on the water, or rather glass. Round the plateau in the trough, should be placed wet moss, and, in this again, yellow and white iris and any water grasses. On the glass, and as it floating on the water, water lilies, either yellow or white.

Mountain ash berries, when ripe, set in richly-tinted autumn foliage, make a lovely decoration; and bracken, golden at that season, makes a charming contrast to green foliage or fern.

Upon very large tables, tall vases and high decorations are best ; and for this purpose, an excellent palm, whose stem is too fragile to intercept the view, and whose leaves are most delicate, is the Cocus Weddiliana.

Strewing the cloth with flowers or leaves, or laying upon it wreaths made lightly of suitable flowers and tied with ribbons, is a pretty fashion ; but for this purpose it must be remembered to choose such blooms and leaves as will stand heat and being out of water without flagging. Another way in which flowers are used without putting in water is, by setting them up in small sheaves (a few flowers and many grasses) arranged as sheaves of wheat would be, so as to stand upright, tied with ribbons to correspond in colour with the flowers.

THE KITCHEN DEPARTMENT.

A WELL-ORDERED KITCHEN.

To HAVE this in the best sense of the word, to know that the room in which the food for the household is prepared and cooked, and where servant or servants must spend a great part of their time is as neat, as nicely kept, and as clean as possible, is the ambition of all good housekeepers. It is an absolute comfort to feel that our meals are cooked in a proper and cleanly manner, and it is necessary for health's sake that they should be so.

In a disorderly kitchen, where utensils are allowed to get out of order, where oven is dirty, grate not properly cleaned, where such like slovenliness is tolerated, it is not possible to send food to the table fit to eat, nor equally is it so for the servants to sit down comfortably to their meals or evening's rest.

We hold it to be the duty of every mistress to have her kitchen not only provided with all necessary utensils for cooking, etc., and to insist on perfect cleanliness, but to make it, and have it kept a comfortable room in which it is no hardship for the servants to live.

On the Continent kitchens are prettier and brighter places than they are here, as a rule; but it is our own fault if ours are not attractive. A well-kept kitchen can be really pretty with its well-set dresser and its snowy cloth, its brilliant pots, pans and covers, its bright windows, highly polished grate, glittering fender, and well-scrubbed tables.

Of course it is not possible always to have everything in order, but even when there is litter there need be no muddle nor dirt.

Three golden rules for the kitchen are :

> "Keep everything in its proper place,"
> "Use every article for its proper purpose,"
> "Clear as you go."

The last rule is one of the most important to be followed. If the things used for the last meal be not cleared before the next one has to be prepared, a muddle must result ; and if dirty things are allowed to accumulate, ten to one when a pot or pan is wanted in haste it is sure to be unusable, without the

1

delay of washing. We should remember that the kitchen is the great laboratory of the household, and upon that which is prepared there depends greatly the health of the family ; and that the influence of a well-ordered one upon the members of a household, especially the servants, is great. That it should be of good size in comparison with the house, well lighted and well ventilated, and that there should be a plentiful water supply goes without saying.

And we now come to the subject of—

KITCHEN REQUISITES.

Under this heading would come not only the ordinary kitchen utensils but also its fittings and furniture, and of these we will first speak.

The *walls* of a kitchen should be covered with a varnished paper which can be washed, and it is well to have a wooden dado (also varnished), headed by a rail the height of the back of a chair, which will save much defacement, acting as a fender between the wall and any person or thing that may come into contact with it. All wood-work in a kitchen is better grained and varnished than painted, for the smooth glossy surface not only attracts less dirt than paint but is more easily cleaned than the latter.

The *floor* is usually covered with oil-cloth or linoleum, but this need not reach to the walls all round ; a border may be made by staining the floor about two feet in width and then varnishing, then all that will be necessary to keep both boards and covering clean will be to wipe them over, after sweeping, with a damp cloth, afterwards polishing them, for which purpose petroleum may be used to make them look bright.

The principal thing in the furnishing of a kitchen is its chief table, which should be sufficiently large, and very firm and substantial. The best kind is one with deal top, not less than $1\frac{1}{2}$ inch thick, with stained and varnished frame and legs. The deal should be constantly scrubbed and kept white, but there should be a table-cloth provided for covering it when work is over, as also a rug to lay down before the kitchen fender. Next in importance to a good table comes a clock, sufficiently large and of dependable make—want of punctuality cannot be condemned if there is no time-piece to guide the servants. The chairs should be firmly-made wooden ones, stained and polished ; the number would, of course, depend on the size of kitchen and the number of servants, but we may suggest that one of them should be an arm-chair. A linen press and a hall step-chair are both most useful things in a kitchen. Of the fixtures, the dresser is the most important. This has, as a rule, besides its racks for plates and dishes, its table-top and three drawers, and cupboards below ; but sometimes, instead of these cupboards there is a pot-board, which should be kept brightly black. The ledges should have hooks of different sizes, and different distances apart upon each ledge, for the hanging-up of cups, large and small, and jugs of various sizes. Cupboards in a kitchen are essential, and there are usually found one on either side of the fireplace. In most instances these are double ones, thus giving in all four

Boiling Pot.

Double Baking Pan and Stand.

Improved Tin Meat Screen.

Wooden Meat Screen.

Hanging Gridiron.

Groom's Registered Milk Saucepan.

American Grip Broiler and Toaster.

Dripping Pan and Ladle.

Iron Saucepan, with Steamer.

Kitchen Utensils.

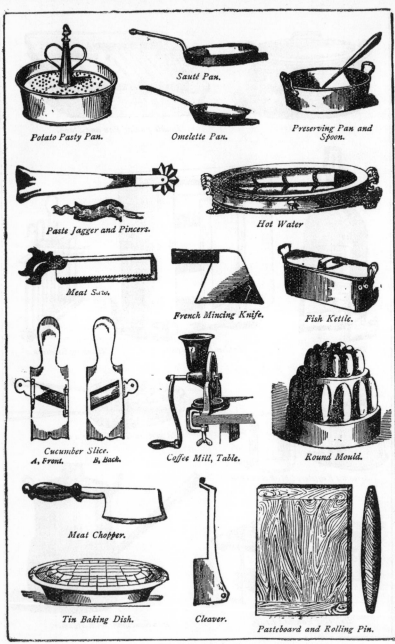

Potato Pasty Pan.

Sauté Pan.

Omelette Pan.

Preserving Pan and Spoon.

Paste Jagger and Pincers.

Hot Water

Meat Saw.

French Mincing Knife.

Fish Kettle.

Cucumber Slice.
A, Front.   B, Back.

Coffee Mill, Table.

Round Mould.

Meat Chopper.

Tin Baking Dish.

Cleaver.

Pasteboard and Rolling Pin.

Kitchen Utensils.

cupboards, which should each be devoted to a special purpose—to contain one kind of article. Thus one of the top ones might be used for the tea-things in use, and the other for the every-day glass; while one of the lower ones might serve for a receptacle for pie-dishes, and such like things; the other would be handy for keeping (not the stores of them, but just a little) wood and paper (the former dry and ready for use) for occasional use when the fire wants re-lighting. Upon the walls, we should not forget to mention, should be cover rails: one a straight one, with hooks for the covers to hang by, the other a sloped one—that is, put so as to take the lower edge of the largest cover at one end and of the smallest at the other, so as to keep them from touching the wall. Even when this precaution is taken, the covers should not be hung up if at all greasy at the edges, as they often are when taken off a hot dish.

KITCHEN RANGES.

There are now so many different kinds of kitcheners, stoves and ranges that it would be a difficult matter to say which, for economy, cleanliness and convenience, should take the palm. However, the choice of a range must necessarily depend upon several things—namely, the size of the kitchen, and the requirements of the family.

Besides the ordinary range or kitchener, it is well for a kitchen to be provided with some small stove, heated by gas or oil, that will be found most convenient in summer, or when hot water or some small cookery is needed in a hurry. If no larger one can be had, a small gas trivet and tube connected with a gas-burner is better than having to depend solely upon the kitchen fire for boiling a kettle.

UTENSILS FOR COOKING.

These may be divided into two classes, say those for boiling and those for roasting; these two classes having sub-divisions, such as stewing, steaming, baking, toasting, grilling and frying.

Under the first head comes, first, *boiling* pure and simple, in hot water, such as boiling a ham or a potato ; *stewing*, which is another kind of boiling by a more gradual heat and a longer process; *frying*, which is cooking in fat instead of water ; and *simmering*, which is a very modified kind of boiling.

Under the second head—that of roasting, come also several modifications of the same mode of cooking. *Roasting*, in its usual meaning, is cooking meat or other substances with heat that passes from its source through intervening and surrounding air—as, for example, a joint hung on a bottle-jack before the fire; *baking* may be termed roasting in an oven ; *broiling*, when the food is put close to the fire, either over it on a gridiron, or suspended before it ; and *toasting*, which is synonymous with broiling.

Under the head of utensils used in boiling there come also those for stewing and frying ; while under the head of utensils used in roasting come those for baking and broiling.

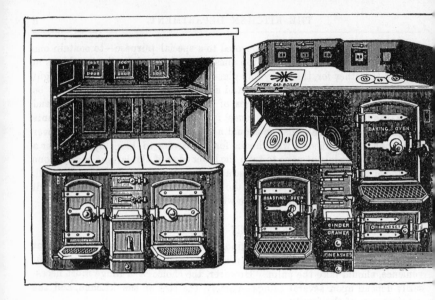

COOKING UTENSILS.

THE principal cooking utensils should be found in every house, be it cottage or mansion ; and by the term we mean a sufficient number of pots, pans, &c., to serve for the preparation of all ordinary meats and vegetables for the table.

We give below lists of articles usually needed in the kitchens of ordinary households, in which lists are included the brushes, brooms, &c., that are required for house-work.

In furnishing, it is often difficult to know what will be sufficient for our requirements in the kitchen. It is a far more easy thing to reckon up how many chairs and tables we may need than what we ought to buy for cooking our meals and for use below stairs.

In the following specifications we have named all that would be necessary in households of moderate requirements, and if the lists appear to be rather long ones for small families, it must be remembered that the same number of things would be required to cook a dinner for four as for one of twelve persons.

It is really economical to buy a good stock to start with, because if we are short of any articles, others not intended for the purpose are made to do duty and are often ruined in the process. Do not, however, have such a large stock that you tempt your servants to put away dirty pots and pans knowing they have more at hand to use.

The cost of the utensils in list No. 1 should, if bought of good quality at a good house, where the goods could be depended on for quality, be about £30 to £33; and for the list No. 2, it should not exceed the sum of £10 10s.

LIST No. 1, OF COOKING AND OTHER HOUSEHOLD UTENSILS REQUIRED IN HOUSES OF MODERATE SIZE.

	£	s.	d.
6 Wrought Iron Stewpans ...	2	1	0
6 Wrought Iron Saucepans ...	1	17	0
2 Block Tin Saucepans	0	4	6
1 Wrought Iron Boiling Pot ...	1	1	0
1 Wrought Iron Frying Pan ...	0	2	6
1 Tin Mackerel Saucepan and Plate	0	12	6
1 Wrought Iron Stock Pot and Ladle	1	0	0
1 Block Tin Fish Kettle	0	12	0
1 Copper Cutlet Pan	0	10	6
1 Copper Omelette Pan	0	5	0
1 Wrought Iron Bain Marie Pan, with Stock Pot, Glaze Pot and Stewpans	3	10	0
1 Block Tin Colander...	0	4	6
2 Block Tin Baking Sheets ...	0	7	0
1 Mincing Machine	0	15	0
2 Tin Jelly Moulds	0	5	0
1 Tin Pudding Mould	0	2	6
12 Tin Darioles	0	6	0
1 Copper Charlotte Russe Mould	0	6	0
2 Iron Ragout Spoons...	0	1	4
2 Table Spoons	0	2	0
1 Tin Seasoning Box	0	5	0
2 Boxes of Paste Cutters	0	6	0
6 Tartlette Pans	0	0	9
1 Set of Skewers	0	1	6
1 Bottle Jack...	0	15	0
1 Tin Dripping Pan	0	5	6
1 Stand and Ladle for Dripping Pan	0	5	6
1 Bread Grater	0	0	10
2 Gravy Strainers	0	3	0
1 Egg Whisk...	0	1	0
1 Egg Slice	0	0	10
1 Fish Slice	0	1	4
1 Fluted Bar Gridiron...	0	3	6
1 Flour Dredger	0	1	0
1 Sugar Dredger	0	1	4
1 Pepper Box...	0	0	6
1 Wrought Iron Tea Kettle ...	0	8	0
1 Tin Teapot...	0	3	9
1 Tin Coffee Pot	0	1	9
1 Tin Funnel	0	0	4
1 Spice Box	0	3	0
3 Canisters for Tea, Coffee and Sugar	0	5	0

	£	s.	d.
1 Chamber Pail	0	5	6
2 Larding and 1 Trussing Needles	0	3	0
1 Meat Saw	0	4	0
1 Meat Chopper	0	3	3
2 Cook's Knives	0	5	6
1 Weighing Machine and Weights	1	0	0
6 Kitchen Knives and Forks ...	0	6	3
1 Corkscrew	0	1	0
1 Coal Hammer	0	2	6
1 Coal Shovel	0	3	0
1 Cinder Shovel	0	2	0
6 Nickel Silver Tea Spoons ...	0	3	0
4 Nickel Silver Table Spoons ...	0	6	0
1 Wooden Meat Screen, with 2 Shelves	3	3	0
3 Cook's Sieves	0	2	2
4 Wooden Spoons...	0	1	4
1 Paste Board and Rolling Pin	0	4	6
1 Coffee Mill	0	4	6
1 Chopping Board and Knife ...	0	5	0
1 Flour Tub	0	3	0
1 Salt Box	0	2	6
1 Long Hair Broom	0	3	6
1 Carpet Broom	0	3	3
1 Mop	0	2	0
1 Area Broom	0	1	6
1 Banister Brush	0	2	0
1 Sweep's Brush	0	1	0
1 Dusting Brush	0	1	6
2 Scrubbing Brushes	0	4	0
1 Set of Shoe Brushes...	0	6	0
1 Housemaid's Tray, fitted with Brushes, Leathers, Cleaning Materials, &c.	0	17	6
1 Clothes Brush	0	4	6
1 Hat Brush	0	1	0
2 Hearth Brushes	0	3	0
1 Decanter Brush	0	1	6
1 Wooden Pail	0	2	3
2 Wooden Tubs	0	11	6
1 Patent Leather Knife Board...	0	13	6
1 Baize-lined Plate Basket ...	0	5	0
1 Linen Press	2	2	0
1 Clothes Horse	0	6	6
1 Pair of House Steps	0	8	6
1 Knife Tray...	0	3	0
TOTAL ...	£32	15	3

LIST NO. 2, OF COOKING AND OTHER UTENSILS REQUIRED IN SMALL HOUSES.

	£	s.	d.		£	s.	d.
3 Cast Iron Saucepans	0	5	0	1 Tea Canister	0	1	0
2 Enamelled Saucepans	0	3	3	1 Coffee Canister	0	1	6
1 Iron Boiling Pot	0	7	6	1 Coal Scoop	0	3	6
1 Iron Frying Pan	0	1	6	1 Stewpan	0	3	6
1 Tin Fish Kettle	0	5	0	1 Meat Saw	0	3	6
1 Tin Colander	0	1	6	6 Kitchen Knives and Forks	0	5	9
2 Tin Moulds	0	3	9	6 Tea Spoons	0	1	6
6 Tin Patty Pans	0	0	9	2 Tablespoons	0	0	8
2 Iron Table Spoons	0	0	8	1 Cinder Shovel	0	1	6
1 Set of Skewers	0	1	6	1 Hair Sieve	0	1	0
1 Tin Meat Screen, with Dripping				2 Wooden Spoons	0	0	8
Pan and Ladle	1	0	6	1 Paste Board and Rolling Pin	0	4	6
1 Egg Slice	0	0	10	1 Wooden Pail	0	2	3
1 Gridiron	0	1	6	1 Wooden Bowl	0	2	3
1 Flour Dredger	0	1	0	1 Wooden Tub	0	4	9
1 Pepper Box	0	0	6	1 Knife Board	0	5	0
1 Coffee Mill	0	4	0	1 Plate Basket	0	4	0
1 Mincing Machine	0	12	6	1 Knife Tray	0	1	6
1 Iron Tea Kettle	0	5	0	1 Clothes Horse	0	6	6
1 Bottle Jack	0	15	0	1 Long Hair Broom	0	3	6
2 Tin Candlesticks	0	4	0	1 Carpet Broom	0	3	0
1 Tea Pot	0	3	3	1 Banister Brush	0	2	0
1 Coffee Pot	0	1	6	1 Sweep's Brush	0	1	0
1 Gravy Strainer	0	1	4	1 Dusting Brush	0	1	6
1 Spice Box	0	3	0	1 Scrubbing Brush	0	1	6
1 Weighing Machine and				1 Set of Shoe Brushes	0	6	6
Weights	0	18	6				
1 Pair of Sugar Nippers	0	2	6	TOTAL	£10	11	8
1 Chamber Pail	0	5	0				

Should there be any washing done at home it would be as well to have a small washing machine or wringer in addition to the above kitchen requisites.

A small wringer, where there is not room for an ordinary washing machine, is a great help. It can be fitted on to the tub; and the clothes, &c., drawn through it will be found ready for the line, as it so thoroughly squeezes out the water, thus saving much labour. The prices of these range from £1 5s. to £2 5s.

A fluted washing-board, which costs but a mere trifle, on which the clothes should be rubbed, will be found a great help in washing clothes, &c.

The prices quoted in these lists are the highest given at good shops, where the quality of the goods is guaranteed. For cash, a discount varying from 2½ per cent. to 5 per cent. is always allowed, therefore this should be reckoned against the total cost in each list.

We append a list of some of the best manufacturers of these goods.

Adams and Son, 57, Haymarket, S.W.

Benetfink and Co., 89, Cheapside, E.C.

Benham and Sons, 50, 52 and 54, Wigmore Street, W.

Maple and Co., 141, Tottenham Court Road, W.C.

Oetzmann and Co., 67, Hampstead Road, N.W.

Wilson and Son, 7, King William Street, Strand, W.C.

SCIENCE OF COOKERY.

WHAT IS NEEDED FOR A HEALTHY DIET.

THERE are but few people who do not realise the fact so often stated by the highest medical authorities, that for invalids *food* is more important than medicine. Yet, when in health, how many of us are careless and indifferent about our diet, so long as we have what is pleasant to our individual taste.

It is well known that some of the most fatal diseases, such as consumption, are often brought on by poor food; and as equally well known is it that infectious complaints spread most quickly amongst the ill-fed; and these reasons alone should be sufficient for us to think it necessary to give some attention to the science and economy of food.

Appeal to a medical man as to the best means of avoiding illness, and one of his prescriptions will certainly be a good diet, one in which the constituents are those which, in their due proportions, go to make up a healthy frame and nourish a healthy body.

We assert that it is of vital importance for all who can to know what is necessary in the way of food to sustain and support the human frame in its full vigour; not only for their own sakes, but for those whom they may be called upon to provide for or advise.

It is undeniably a fact that a large number of the lower orders cannot have much variety or choice in their food, and a still greater number suffer from the poorness of its quality ; but in many homes where neither money, time nor knowledge should be lacking to ensure a perfect diet it is not found.

Many of the richest amongst us are no better fed or nourished than those who cannot afford good or varied food, simply because the former either do not know or do not care to take what alone can be a healthy diet.

Many physicians assert that amongst the large middle class of the population of this country, a far too great proportion of their food is drawn from the animal kingdom, especially in the diet of young people and children ; and that if they would diminish the quantity of the flesh foods, and in their place partake of a greater amount of vegetables, pulses and fruits, a better tone of health would be arrived at with the majority.

Vegetarians tell us that flesh foods are not necessary: that a hard-working man can be sustained upon a diet in which they find no place; yet, when we look at what should form the constituent parts of the food of a labouring man, carefully estimated by those who have made the science of food a study, we should find that, to obtain the desired result, a great deal too much in bulk of vegetable food would have to be taken. A happy mean between a vegetarian and animal diet is not difficult to arrive at when we know, not only a little about the human frame—what it wastes and what it needs to supply that daily waste—but the properties of the foods most common and most generally preferred.

COMPOSITION OF THE BODY.

The principal elements which enter into the composition of the human body are carbon, hydrogen, nitrogen and oxygen.

A human body weighing 154 lbs. is found to contain:—

	lbs.	oz.			lbs.	oz.
Oxygen	111	0	Carbon	21	0
Hydrogen	14	0	Nitrogen	3	10

The compounds of the body in which these organic elements exist, and their weights in a body, weighing 154 lbs., are:—

	lbs.	oz.
Water, containing oxygen and hydrogen	111	0
Gelatine, containing the four elements	16	0
Albumen ,, ,, ,, ...	4	3
Fibrine ,, ,, ,, ...	4	4
Fat, containing carbon and hydrogen	12	0

These compounds of the human body represent albumenoids or flesh-formers, heat-givers and mineral matters; and we may add that the ultimate elements of the food we take are precisely similar to the ultimate elements of the human body; therefore, we have now to consider the constituents of food so as best to know how to apportion the various kinds to supply the daily waste of the system.

QUANTITY OF FOOD NECESSARY.

Water passes away most quickly of all foods, then in order come fibrine and albumenoids, next gelatine and fat, and lastly mineral matters. Calculating the quantity of material removed daily, it appears that a period of forty days would suffice for removing the whole of the used material of the human body; thus, common sense would tell us that in forty days one must eat food equal in quantity to the weight of one's own body.

According to circumstances—work, digestion and weather—so may the daily ration of an adult vary, but the following is a fair average diet for a man of ordinary size, doing moderate work:—

A DAY'S RATIONS.

	In 100 parts.		In 24 hours.		
			lbs.	oz.	grs.
Water	81·5	...	5	8	320
Albumenoids	3·9	...	0	4	110
Starch, sugar, etc.	10·6	...	0	11	178
Fat	3·0	...	0	3	337
Mineral matter...	0·3	...	0	0	170
Common Salt	0·7	...	0	0	325

This table shows the actual aliment required per diem, and the following one will show an example of what common articles of food may be taken to furnish it:—

	oz.		oz.
Bread	18	Cheese	3½
Butter	1	Sugar	1
Milk	4	Salt	0¾
Bacon	2	Water alone, and in Tea, Coffee	
Potatoes	8	or Beer	66¼
Cabbage	6		

These quantities will weigh in all 6 lbs. 14½ oz., but they contain about 1 lb. 5¼ oz. of dry substance only.

PROPERTIES OF FOODS.

We have said that a perfect diet must consist of water, albumenoids or flesh-formers, starch and floury foods, and fat as heat-givers, and mineral matters, such as common salt, etc.; and, therefore, the following tables will show their own utility. By them, the constituents of all ordinary food being given, it will be easy to see how to combine them, in due proportion, to suit both our tastes and needs.

In a book of this kind it would not be possible to treat of such an important subject as Food in detail. We can only trust that what little has been said may induce our readers to search further for themselves, and that the following tables, being *reliable*, may be useful in enabling those who study them to approach nearer to a perfect diet.

In the case of young children the properties of the foods given require special consideration, many requiring those containing a large proportion of lime, which goes to form and strengthen the bones.

CONSTITUENT PARTS OF ALL KINDS OF FOOD, FLESH FORMERS, HEAT GIVERS, &c.

CONSTITUENTS IN 100 PARTS OF VARIOUS FOODS.

Name of Food.	Water.	Albume-noids.	Starch, Sugar, &c.	Fat.	Mineral Matter.	Total.
Bacon	22·3	8·1	—	65·2	4 4	100
Barley (Pearl)	14·6	6·2	76 8	1·3	1·1	,,
Beef	50·0	15·1	—	29·9	5 0	,,
Butter	10·0	1 0	0·3	87·7	1·0	,,
Cabbage	89·0	1·5	7·8	0·5	1·2	,,
Cheese	34·3	29·2	2·0	29·6	4·9	,,
Eggs	71·7	14·0	—	13·0	1 3	,,
Fowl	76·5	21·0	—	Traces.	2·5	,,
Lamb	50·6	10·9	—	35·0	3·5	,,
Maize Meal	14·5	9·0	69·5	5·0	2·0	,,
Milk	86·3	4·1	5·1	3·7	0·8	,,
Mutton	44·0	12·5	—	40 0	3·5	,,
Oatmeal	5·0	16·1	66·7	10·1	2·1	,,
Peas	14·3	22·4	57·8	2·5	3·0	,,
Pork	38·5	10·0	—	50·0	1·5	,,
Potatoes	75·0	2·3	21·4	0·3	1·0	,,
Rice	14·6	7·5	76·9	0·5	0·5	,,
Salmon	77·0	13·1	—	4·4	5·5	,,
Sole	86·6	11·2	—	0·2	2·0	,,
Veal	62·5	16·5	—	16·5	4·5	,,
Wheaten Flour	13·0	10·5	75·0	0·8	0·7	,,

CONSTITUENT PARTS IN 1 LB. OF VARIOUS FOODS.

Name of Food.	Water.		Albume-noids.		Starch, Sugar, &c.		Fat.		Mineral Matter.		Total.	
	oz.	grs.	oz.	grs.	oz.	grs.	oz.	grs.	oz.	grs.	oz.	grs.
Bacon	3	250	1	132	—	—	10	191	0	301	16	0
Barley (Pearl)	2	147	0	434	12	125	0	91	0	77	16	0
Beef	8	0	2	184	—	—	4	340	0	350	16	0
Butter	1	262	0	70	0	21	14	14	0	70	16	0
Cabbage	14	105	0	105	1	108	0	35	0	84	16	0
Cheese	5	214	4	294	0	140	4	322	0	341	16	0
Eggs	11	207	2	105	—	—	1	332	0	231	16	0
Fowl	12	107	3	156	—	—	Traces.		0	174	16	0
Lamb	8	44	1	323	—	—	5	263	0	244	16	0
Maize Meal	2	140	1	193	11	51	0	350	0	140	16	0
Milk	13	233	4	1	5	1	3	7	0	8	16	0
Mutton	7	16	2	0	—	—	6	176	0	245	16	0
Oatmeal	0	350	2	253	10	291	1	270	0	147	16	0
Peas	2	126	3	255	9	108	0	175	0	210	16	0
Pork	6	69	1	263	—	—	8	0	0	105	16	0
Potatoes	12	0	0	161	3	185	0	21	0	70	16	0
Rice	2	147	1	87	12	133	0	35	0	35	16	0
Salmon	12	143	2	43	—	—	0	301	0	387	16	0
Sole	13	374	1	350	—	—	0	14	0	136	16	0
Veal	10	0	2	281	—	—	2	281	0	312	16	0
Wheaten Flour	2	34	1	297	11	0	0	57	0	49	16	0

COOKERY.

NECESSITY FOR LEARNING.

As an education, cookery is happily becoming more common every day, and not only are we shown in the schools for the purpose how to bake, boil or stew various foods, but the *reasons why* for doing these things, how to combine the right kinds of food and how to prepare everything in the best and most economical manner.

Excellence in the art is of course attained only by practice, experience and skill; but we hold it the duty of all women of middle class to know practically how to cook plain ordinary dishes, whether or no they ever attempt anything more ambitious in the way of cookery.

It is a knowledge that gives power whether we have to use it or not, and it is scarcely possible in theory to direct those under our authority to make dishes exactly as we require them if we can never show them by ocular demonstration what may be amiss.

Seldom too does it happen that necessity does not arise, some time or other, for the mistress or the daughters of a household to either give assistance or have to do some cooking alone; and for these emergencies it is well to be prepared.

Another argument in favour of knowing how to cook is that we can check waste or extravagance in those who cook for us, which we could not do if we were not sure from personal experience that, for example, three eggs would serve for one kind of dish where four were used, or that less butter was needed than had been employed in the making of another. In such little matters even the best of servants are apt to be indifferent till, service over, they come to cook for themselves.

QUALIFICATIONS NECESSARY TO MAKE A GOOD COOK.

Those who aspire to success in cookery should first be sure of their qualifications; and for even the simplest of dishes, for those who have not had experience, care and patience are needed. But, when we hope to attain to be skilful cooks and to be able to make elaborate and dainty dishes, we must remember that the art cannot be learnt in a day, and that through many failures we may arrive at the desired end. Some cannot hope to be excellent cooks—they are too heavy-handed for pastry, not keen enough in the senses of smell and taste for flavouring, and have not the talent of blending with good effect the colours at command in various dishes, either savoury or sweet. Still for all it is possible to do plain and necessary cooking, such as roasting a joint or boiling a potato.

CLEANLINESS.

This in cookery is almost, if not quite, as essential as in dairy work. No one would dream of having good butter out of a dirty dairy; why should we expect good dishes from a dirty kitchen? It is far easier to prepare food in a clean and orderly room, with all utensils required for cooking ready for use; and no time is saved, in fact it is lost, by neglecting that time-honoured maxim in the kitchen of " clear as you go." By clearing we mean not only getting rid of litter, but washing and cleaning everything as it is used and returning them to their respective places. All vessels and utensils used in cooking should be delicately clean. If a saucepan be filled with water directly it is finished with, or knives are plunged in a jug of hot water after using, they will to a certain extent clean themselves.

Serious trouble too often arises by not having such things as pots and pans cleansed properly : food may be spoilt, and worse than that in the case of copper utensils, health may be injured. Saucepans, fish kettles, etc., after being well washed, should be dried before the fire before being put away.

Frying pans, if black inside, should be cleaned with a crust of bread and washed with hot soda-and-water.

Coppers should be cleaned with turpentine and fine brickdust, or lemon skins and sand, rubbed on with an old flannel and polished with a leather.

Tins may be cleaned with soap and whiting and afterwards polished with a leather.

In washing dishes and any other crockery use plenty of hot water and soda; wash glasses, unless greasy, in cold water and polish with a leather.

Keep a small old knife specially for peeling onions. Scald pudding-cloths directly they are used, but do not use soda for them, and let them be perfectly dry before putting away.

After making pastry, put water in the bowl used, scrape the paste-board clean and wash it if necessary, also the rolling-pin, though a neat pastry maker scarcely soils a board. If either a marble slab or a glass rolling pin be used they should be washed each time.

Be careful with the sink in emptying pots and pans. The pipes soon get choked and both expense and trouble are incurred, to say nothing of the injurious smells that may arise if this occurs. Never empty the water from greens down the sink, as it leaves a most unpleasant smell, and always keep it clean and well scrubbed down.

ECONOMY.

A really good cook is never a wasteful one, for the reason that she knows how to turn everything to account. In clever and economical hands a few scraps of cold meat may be minced up, nicely flavoured, and with an egg and a few bread-crumbs, some dainty little rissoles may be the result. Cold vegetables will find their way into salads, as will also scraps of fish flaked; cold potatoes will be mashed and fried, pieces of fat will be tried down, every drop of gravy will be saved, and so on ad infinitum.

Perhaps in no way are servants (and may be mistresses) more extravagant than in the wasting of the bones of joints and birds and pieces of bread. The former should always be broken up and stewed to make stock, and a digester kept supplied with these, and the trimmings will do away with the necessity for making stock in a household of moderate size.

As to the pieces of bread which will sometimes accumulate, they might often be used with advantage for puddings instead of flour; and the dry crust should be put in the oven and afterwards grated for raspings.

FANCY DISHES.

The taste for made dishes has been greatly on the increase of late years, and as far as entrées are concerned they are often the means of using up cold game and poultry and other meats. More difficulty is experienced by an ordinary cook in preparing these than in the usual routine of baking and boiling joints and vegetables. Yet they are well worth a little patience, for they give so much scope for talent, not only in making them savoury and the sauces for them delicate, but in garnishing and ornamentation to render them pretty. Most delicate appetites are stimulated by seeing attractive-looking dishes ; and cooks whose hearts are in their work will find the more they practise decoration in cookery the more interested they will grow in the work. Cold entrées and sweets are specially adapted for ornamentation, in the tasteful blending of colour and the choice of pretty forms, and supper dishes also give scope. Great care, however, must be taken not to let what is used as a garnish interfere, in any way, with the desired flavour of a dish, while the greatest care and nicety is necessary in preparing the sauces for entrées, which, as a rule, form the most important part.

For savoury dishes, aspic jelly is one of the most useful of garnishes, as it is so bright and pretty in itself. Lobster spawn is another good one, as also lobster or Montpélier butter. Truffles and scarlet tongue are also most useful for white sauces or meats, while bright-coloured vegetables and the white and yolk of eggs may play an important part. For the tiny little *appetisans*, now so fashionable, all sorts of pretty decoration should be used, and the main result to be arrived at in them should be good contrasts in both flavour and appearance. A silver plate full of these may be made to look most tempting, if they are varied to suit different tastes ; thus, a few croutons may be spread with caviare, with crossbars and narrow strips of white of egg, which will contrast nicely with others of chopped prawns on croutons spread with Montpélier butter. The basis of these little hors d'œuvres is almost invariably made of small croutons stamped with a cutter from thin slices of bread, and fried a bright golden brown in butter ; and on them may be placed or spread such things as filleted anchovies, stuffed olives, a farce made of sardines, pounded and flavoured and decorated with lobster spawn, etc., bearing in mind that they should be made to look as pretty as possible.

MODES OF COOKING.

As actually different methods of cooking, there are six : namely, baking, boiling, broiling, frying, roasting and stewing; and in these there are sub-divisions : as simmering, toasting and grilling.

The easiest method may be considered stewing, by which process all the inferior parts of meat are cooked better than by any other ; while the most difficult mode, yet the one probably in use the first, it entailing the simplest of utensils, or rather tools, may be reckoned broiling.

We treat separately of all these modes of cooking and of their appropriateness to different kinds of food, and under the head of utensils for cooking we have enumerated those considered best for the different methods.

BAKING.

Baking is one of the most convenient and economical modes of cooking. There is a great prejudice against it, as far as regards meat, by comparing it with roasting; but, though we are ready to acknowledge that there can be no finer or better way of cooking a fine joint or large bird than by roasting it before a good and well-kept-up fire, yet there are many small joints and birds that can be equally well cooked in the oven. Further than this, it is often the fault of the cook if baked meat is not of good flavour. A little fat burnt on the trays of the oven, for example, will give a most unpleasant taste; and again, most cooks are apt to neglect the basting of a joint not always before them as one in the front of the fire would be. It is more trouble to open the door, draw the baking-tin to the edge and baste than to take up the ladle and use it in passing to and fro ; and in this way many a good joint gets spoilt that could have been cooked perfectly well by baking.

Amongst the food most suitable for cooking in this manner we may mention a shoulder or half a shoulder of mutton, pork, either leg or loin, a goose or duck, a pig, a ham covered with a crust of flour and water, and in fact most fat meats. Poor meat, with but little fat, will come away from the bone in baking, and is better cooked in some other way.

Such fish as haddocks, herrings or mackerel are excellent baked, and it is the usual way in which to cook mullet.

The necessity for the oven for all such things as bread, pies and cakes is too obvious to need comment; in fact, in spite of its being held in not very high estimation by many professional cooks, it would be a great deal harder to do without it than with the bottle-jack.

The main thing is, as we have said before, to have the oven perfectly clean and to keep it at a proper heat; also to baste well.

Utensils for baking are now so well constructed that it is much easier to cook in this way than it used to be; but where these new baking tins and dishes are not found, one or two facts are worth knowing, namely, that a jar of water will absorb impurities if placed in the oven while it is being used; and such things as a goose or duck should be reversed and put back upwards while baking to get thoroughly done. To test the heat of the oven, which is a precaution everyone should take, cooks often use a sheet of white writing-paper, which should brown and curl up in an oven ready for pastry, or flour which takes every shade from biscuits to coffee, according to the heat; but special thermometers are made for the purpose. For cooking meat the oven should be about 300° ; for bread at first 560°, but afterwards lowered, and for pastry about the same—very rich pastry requires the hottest oven. Experience will teach one to gauge the heat fairly accurately with the hand. By careful testing, it has been estimated that the average loss per cent. in meat by any form of cooking is from one-fifth to one-third of its whole weight; that in beef roasted the loss is thirty-two per cent., in baking thirty per cent., and in mutton there is a greater proportionate loss. Thus in saying that baking is a more economical mode of cooking than roasting we make no error.

One word of caution we may give the cook and that is not to attempt to cook in the oven at the same time things requiring different degrees of heat, nor to expect that the more delicately flavoured foods will not be affected by the smell of the stronger flavoured ones if placed together to bake.

BOILING.

It is said that this mode of cooking food is the easiest of all; but it demands as much, if not more care and watchfulness than other modes.

The main facts to remember as necessary in boiling are these that unless the water really boils all the time the food is cooking no certain time can be allowed for the preparation of any food in this manner; that in the case of boiling meat the water must be kept clear of scum ; that each thing should be taken from the fire the moment it is sufficiently cooked. This last fact is an important one in some of the most simple things to cook, such as an egg or a potato. In either case if these are allowed to remain boiling a minute or so too much they are spoiled; therefore we assert that boiling needs careful watching and vigilance in the cook.

In the case of boiling, almost everything in the way of food, the slower the process the better, meat especially requiring slow boiling; for if it be done fast it will be hard and tasteless.

When the water in which meat is placed is coming to the boil the scum always rises, and unless it be at once removed the appearance of the joint will be spoilt. After skimming, it is best to put in a little cold water which will cause the rest of the scum to rise.

Some wrap meat in a cloth to preserve its whiteness; but it does not improve its flavour, and there can be no necessity to do this if the water has been properly skimmed.

Meat for boiling should be chosen of even thickness, or one part will be done well and the other too much or too little. The usual rule for time is a quarter of an hour to a pound; but this may be exceeded if the joint boils very slowly; and a much longer time must be allowed for pork than any other meat. This applies only to what is put into *cold* water and brought very gently to the boil, thus a leg of mutton of fair size should take about three-quarters of an hour. If a saucepan containing water be placed over a steady fire the water will grow continually hotter till it reaches boiling point, after which the regular accessions of heat are wholly spent in converting it into steam. The stronger the fire the more quickly does this occur, but once boiling point is reached the ultimatum of heat has been arrived at, and the water will become no hotter however fiercely it boils. In our " Cook's Time Table " the times given for boiling are, in all cases, after the water has reached boiling point; freshly killed meat takes long boiling, old meat longer than young; and the colder the weather the more time should be allowed. Frozen meat must be stewed before it is either boiled or roasted, for it is impossible to cook it tender if this be not done, let it be done ever so slowly and gently. In cold weather it should be brought into a place of which the temperature is not less than 45° Fahrenheit the night before it is wanted to be cooked.

Let there be always room in the saucepan for what is to be boiled, but not too much, as there is then waste of fuel in boiling. Let the covers fit closely, not only to prevent unnecessary evaporation of the water, but to prevent the escape of the nutritive matter.

Salted meat should be well washed clear of the brine before it is put in the water ; and this, as well as all other meat, should be taken off as soon as it is done or it will be sodden and lose its flavour. A good plan is to put a small trivet under a large joint of meat, so that that side should not be too much done. Avoid sticking a fork into what is being boiled, especially beetroot, which loses its colour entirely if this be done.

Never throw away the liquor in which poultry or joints have been boiled, but use it as the basis or stock for soup. If too salt, dilute it with water and use it for pea or lentil soup. With the exception of potatoes, the water in which any vegetable has been boiled is better for broth or gravy than plain water.

Some cooks think it is sufficient to put meat into a saucepan, set it on the fire, and allow a certain time for it to cook, forgetting the facts that we may again briefly enumerate, so important are they : that it should come *slowly* to the boil; that it must be continually *skimmed ;* that after boiling it should only be *simmered.*

It may be that this mode of cooking requires less talent than any other, but we have no hesitation in saying that of all modes it requires the most patience. Some cooks think it better to put meat into boiling water, as by s) doing an impervious crust is formed on the outside, which prevents the juice from escaping. A cut leg of mutton should have a paste of flour and water over it, to prevent the escape of the juice ; and this is one of the parts of meat that is better if plunged into boiling water.

BROILING.

For this mode of cooking a hot fire is required, and the heat need not be lessened afterwards, as in the case of roasting, as the broiling is so quickly done. Like roasting, it is not an economical mode of cooking, as a great deal of fuel is needed for a good broiling fire, the meat loses weight, and only the best kinds can be submitted to this process with satisfactory results.

The great art in broiling is to keep in the juice of what is cooked, and this cannot be done without constant turning, which should be done with tongs, never sticking in a fork and so making holes in the meat. If there are no tongs at hand, put the fork into the fat and not into the lean. Some few things need not be turned in broiling ; a mushroom, for instance, which is cooked stalk upwards; but there is one rule in this manner of cooking that always applies, and that is to use a hot gridiron and have it greased before putting on it what has to be cooked.

The same rules apply to toasting as to broiling, as far as the fire is concerned. If it is wanted to have it brown outside and moist in, it must be held to a quick, hot fire, so that the surface browns before the middle has lost its moisture.

FRYING.

Frying is the quickest mode of cooking, because melted fat or oil can be brought to a high temperature, and in contact with it the food fried is rapidly heated ; but the description used for this mode of cooking very often, that of putting fish, etc , into boiling fat, is erroneous, because, though fat or oil may be made hotter than boiling water, it *does not boil.*

By reason of the expedition of this manner of cooking, it may be easily realised that it is not a mode to apply to very solid or tough foods, that, to have done thoroughly, must be cooked slowly. One thing necessary to know for frying to be successful is when the fat is ready for the food to be put in. Thermometers are constructed specially for this purpose, and may be found in many large kitchens, but one can arrive at the fact with simple materials always at hand. About 350° is a suitable temperature for ordinary frying and the fat can be tested by putting in a few drops of water or a piece of bread. If, when the former is put in, the fat bubbles smartly, it may be taken that it has reached or even exceeded that temperature ; while if a piece of bread be put in and taken out after thirty seconds and found crisp, that will be found an equally safe criterion.

The most usual mode of frying in ordinary kitchens is in an ordinary frying-pan ; this being, in nine cases out of ten, comparatively unsatisfactory, except for what may be termed dry-frying, where no fat or very little is needed to cook the food, such as a rasher of bacon, sprats or any oily matter. Such things as soles, rissoles and potatoes should be immersed in fat to be properly fried, and it is a mistake to imagine this an extravagant mode of cooking, unless it be practised by extravagant people. A panful of oil can be used again and again for the same purpose, if only properly taken care of ; and out of it, when fried, the food will come unburnt, and free from the grease, so difficult to avoid in using a frying pan.

An iron saucepan and not a tin one, should be taken for this kind of frying ; and for all delicate things that should not be handled or touched too much, a frying basket should be used ; failing this, use a slice (not a tin one, as that might melt). And let all cooks, amateur or others, remember that the main point in good frying is to serve the food dry, free from grease and very hot ; and that, to attain this desired result, every atom of grease should be drained away before the fire ere the food be served.

Such fish as whitebait, or such delicate things as rissoles are uneatable when greasy ; and care and practice are needed to send them to table perfectly done ; but a consolation for the trouble taken to do this properly may be found in the fact that greater credit is deemed due for successful frying than for almost any other mode of cooking. Fat for frying should be good and well clarified. Pure olive oil may be considered the best ; but good salt butter, mutton fat or beef dripping answers equally well, the former for sweet, the two latter for savoury foods. Lard is the worst fat for frying, as it so often gives an unpleasant taste to what is cooked. A golden rule in frying is to have the articles as dry as possible. If fish, dry it in a cloth, then thoroughly cover it with egg and bread-crumbs, or dredge with flour. Never put anything damp into the fat, and always have the fat ready for cooking beforehand ; also remember that whereas one may leave a roast or a boil to take care of itself for a time, one should never leave that which is cooked by such an expeditious mode as frying.

Fat meats are better grilled than fried, as the fat is lost by the former mode of cooking and retained by the latter.

ROASTING.

Perhaps for the reason that ours is the country famous for its large joints, this mode of cooking is the favourite one in England; but whereas boiling or stewing may be called the cheapest modes of cooking, roasting is certainly the most extravagant, not only from the loss the meat sustains in the process, but by reason of the cost of so much more fuel required than for other modes.

Roast meat is generally considered more digestible than baked meat, and it is certainly superior in flavour to that cooked in the oven, but small, thin and either sinewy or gelatinous joints of meat are not suitable for roasting. The object in roasting is to harden the surface albumen, and so imprison the juice of the meat; and to do this, that which is to be roasted must first be subjected to a very hot fire and afterwards be drawn away, so that it may be thoroughly cooked, without being burnt. The larger the joint the smaller should be the fire, lest the joint or bird should be blackened outside and raw in, as a bad roaster will serve it; while a perfectly cooked joint should only be a bright brown outside and the inside have only reached the moderate heat that coagulates the albumen and swells and softens the fibrine. Cooked more than this meat is less digestible.

The better the meat the less it will lose in roasting, and the fact of American meat dwindling and shrinking more than our own is one of the reasons why it is considered inferior. But we venture to say the better the cook the smaller will be the waste in this process, for she will not only carefully keep the fire in good order for what is being cooked; but she will not neglect that essential thing in roasting, namely basting. By doing this thoroughly there is no fear of any part of the outside of the food being too dry to eat, and there will certainly be a fair supply of good gravy.

STEWING.

Of all methods of cooking this is the most economical, for by it nothing is wasted, less fire is required than for any other mode, and the cheaper and coarser meats may be used.

Stewing requires a heat much below that of boiling water, 165° being about stewing point. Too often what should be stewed is, through carelessness, boiled, with the result of hard and tasteless dishes. A stew should not necessarily bubble; it should stand by the side of the stove and cook slowly and thoroughly; and the amateur cook must bear in mind that it is a mode of cooking in which haste must be avoided. Where vegetables are to form part of stews, as they so often do, unless they are young and tender, it is best to boil them first and use the liquor in which they were boiled for the stew; but in the case of onions for a brown stew, they should be fried instead; as also a steak for the same purpose.

As little water as possible should be used for stewing, as by such a long process so much of the juices of the food go to add to the gravy. One of the best stews as a savoury one is made by putting a small piece of butter in a pan, and, when it has melted, slicing in some onions ; and again, when these have yielded a fair amount of juice, adding some beef, cut up small, and seasoning ; after which the lid should be put on and not again taken off till there has been time enough allowed to stew the meat in the liquor from the onions ; the pan, however, being occasionally shaken.

Most gravies in stews will bear a good deal of thickening, and all should be well flavoured and salted according to taste, the ess there is to add in the way of pepper, salt or sauce to a stew after it is served the better will be the dish.

VEGETARIAN COOKERY.

One of the greatest boons that vegetarianism has brought us is the teaching of how to use and treat a larger number of vegetables, so as to make a larger number of good dishes from them, and thus bring us more on a level with our Continental neighbours. It has always been urged against English cookery that we do not know how to cook vegetables. Let us hope that vegetarianism, if it does nothing else, will open to us a wider field in the way of foods as nourishing and palatable as those we have been wont to consider our regular daily fare—foods, in many cases, more cheap and digestible than meat ones.

For children and delicate persons an occasional vegetarian meal is an excellent dish if properly prepared, and in the country most celebrated for its cooking the diet on the fast days ordered by its Church is esteemed very highly by most English people.

Recently the secrets of longevity, as stated by a physician who had arrived at a very great age, were, " working hard and eating but little meat." If he were right there are many who would feel inclined to become vegetarians, but, without making any hard and fast rules, or restricting oneself to none but what are not animal foods, for many, less meat would be more healthy diet if only the substitutes for it were well cooked and varied. This is what vegetarianism has done. It has developed a taste, and consequently a demand, for more foods, and in most cases cheaper ones ; and therefore we should be grateful that there are many disciples of it amongst us. It is argued thus, that in cold climates such as ours there is the necessity for the consumption of a great deal of meat, but in this argument many forget that we do not have cold weather throughout the year, and that if we need much meat in winter we cannot do so in summer.

Whether, however, grown people take too much animal food or not, t is certain that in many households children are allowed to do so, and some of the simple vegetarian dishes, for which we give recipes, will be found to find favour with the young folk, and to be more easily digested by them, and, therefore, more nourishing for them than heavier foods taken regularly would be.

HOW TO TRUSS POULTRY AND GAME.

ONE of the most necessary things for those who wish to become cooks to learn is the proper mode of trussing all kinds of poultry and game; and by trussing we mean to include the whole preparation of the bird or animal—the plucking, singeing, etc., required before it will be ready for cooking.

We strongly advise all cooks to learn how to truss even if they live in places where the poultry is generally sent ready for cooking, and it is no bad beginning, after careful examination, to undo and re-truss a bird.

Plucking a bird may be considered a very simple operation, one that anyone could undertake; yet like everything else there is a right way and a wrong of doing it, and more care and nicety is needed to remove all the feathers without injuring the skin than those who had never attempted the task would be apt to imagine. In some cases the skin is very tender (as for example that of grouse) and it is usual to leave the breast feathers on till the bird has been trussed, for nothing so spoils the appearance of either poultry or game as a broken skin.

The right way to begin to pluck a bird is to hold it by the wing in the left hand and begin to pluck from under the wing, then reverse it and pluck from the other side, removing all feathers and only leaving the down, which must then be singed off. To

BIRD BEING SINGED.

do this, hold the bird in the left hand and move a lighted paper quickly over it, being very careful not to scorch the skin. Bearing in mind how the bird is to be trussed afterwards, see that those parts that will then be hidden are perfectly free from down, as they cannot, like the rest of the bird, be singed again afterwards. Having got rid of the feathers, the next thing will be to draw the bird—that is, if it be one that requires drawing.

According to the size of the bird, different ways of doing this are essential;

but safely reckoning that the most common and oftenest found in most households is a chicken or fowl, we will begin with that.

DRAWING OF FOWL.

Lay the bird on its back on a board, cut a slit in the skin of the neck and out of this slit pull out the neck and cut it off at the root; then cut off the skin, leaving just enough for a flap. The next thing is to loosen the inside, which must be done through this opening with the middle finger (this applies to all birds sufficiently large), and if this be done thoroughly there will afterwards be but little trouble to draw the fowl. To do this cut off the vent, and, holding the bird firmly in the left hand, again with the middle finger, take out the entrails. Be most careful in doing this not to break any part, because if the gall bladder be injured it will give the bird a most bitter taste. Should an accident occur, however, the evil may be remedied by washing out the bird and drying it thoroughly. Supposing, however, this is not the case, it will still be necessary to wipe out the inside of the fowl as well as the flap of skin at the neck. After this has been done, the legs of the fowl should be dipped in boiling water, then scraped, the pinions must be cut off, and the bird will then be ready for trussing.

TRUSSING OF FOWL FOR ROASTING.

There are two modes of doing this, one with skewers, the other with a needle. The former is the most simple and usual, so we will take that first. Lay the fowl on its back and run a skewer through the first joint of the pinion on the

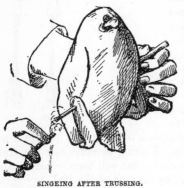

right side (bringing the middle of the leg close to it), then through the fowl to catch the pinion on the left side, even with the other. Next fasten the flap of skin at the neck over the back with a small skewer. To skewer the legs, put one first through the skin of the back on the right side, then through the first joint of the leg. Between the legs catch up a small piece of skin, as shown in the following page, and skewer the left side in the same manner as the right. Next chop off the feet and again singe, being most careful that no down be left on; wash the liver and gizzard and put one in each

SINGEING AFTER TRUSSING.

wing, and the fowl will be ready for roasting.

Trussing with a needle is rather more difficult and is more often done by

SKEWERING OF PINIONS.

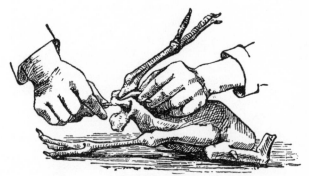

SKEWERING OF LEGS.

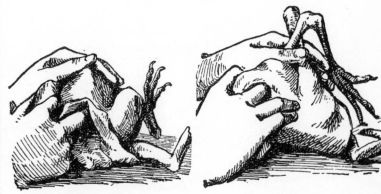

LOOSENING INSIDE.   FOWL BEING DRAWN.

poulterers than ordinary cooks; but it is a very neat way, the needle making much smaller holes than the skewers. The two following illustrations show how

TRUSSING WITH NEEDLE.

FOWL TRUSSED WITH NEEDLE.

this is done, and when this mode of trussing is employed the legs are often put under the fowl and the liver and gizzard omitted.

TRUSSING OF FOWL FOR BOILING.

To truss a fowl neatly for boiling is rather more difficult than to prepare it for roasting, for drawing the skin over the legs without injuring it in any way is not an easy task for the beginner. However, care can do more than skill; and

LOOSENING SKIN OF LEGS.

DRAWING SKIN OVER LEGS.

the first thing to be done is to thoroughly loosen the skin in the manner shown in illustration. Having done this, cut off the legs at the knee-joints and draw gently over the skin. The two following illustrations show the

SKEWERING OF PINIONS.

FOWL TRUSSED FOR BOILING.

skewering of pinions and legs, and it must be borne in mind that a fowl for boiling should be made to look as smooth and round as possible.

TRUSSING OF GOOSE.

This bird will require more careful plucking and singeing than any other; after which the feet and pinions must be cut off at the joints, and the neck close to the back, leaving enough skin to turn over. Next draw it, cutting a slit between the vent and the rump (after having carefully loosened the inside at the throat end), and having washed and wiped the inside, beat the breast bone flat with a wooden rolling-pin. It should now be ready for trussing, and present the appearance shown in page illustration. Put the first skewer through the under part of one wing and bring it through the other then put the second through the first joint of one leg and carry it through to secure the other, see illustrations on following page; next stuff. To do this, cut off the end of the vent and make a hole in the skin large enough for the passage of the rump, so as to keep in the seasoning, and the goose is now ready for cooking, as shown.

TRUSSING OF GROUSE.

Pluck the bird, all except the breast feathers; cut off the head, leaving enough skin to skewer back; then after loosening the inside at the neck, squeeze it out and wipe. To truss it, bring the legs close to the breast between it and the

GROUSE READY FOR TRUSSING.

GROUSE BEING TRUSSED.

side bones, and put a single skewer through the pinions and thick part of the thighs; then carefully remove the breast feathers with the help of a small knife.

TRUSSING OF PIGEON.

Having plucked and drawn the bird, wash it very thoroughly and wipe it quite

PIGEON READY FOR ROASTING.

dry, then cut off head and neck and the toes at the first joint. The legs must next be crossed and fastened by one skewer passed through pinions as well, as shown in following illustration, and the birds will be ready for roasting. Small skewers should be used.

GOOSE READY FOR TRUSSING.

TRUSSING OF GOOSE.

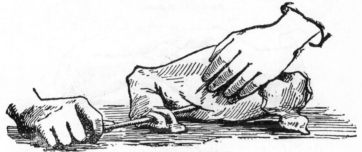

GOOSE READY FOR STUFFING.

GOOSE READY FOR COOKING.

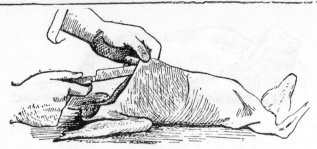

PAUNCHING OF HARE.

SKEWERING OF LEGS.

SKEWERING OF HEAD.

PIGEON BEING SKEWERED.

TRUSSING OF HARE.

The first operation is the skinning, and to do this the belly must be cut open lengthwise and the fore legs off at the first joint, after which the hare should be hung on a hook. Begin by raising the skin of the back and draw it over the hind legs, being careful to leave the tail whole; draw it over the back and when the fore legs are reached they must be slipped out. The head and neck are the most difficult to skin, and here it may be necessary to use a knife to ease the skin; and it must be remembered that it is most important not to damage the ears, as they are always left on with a roast hare.

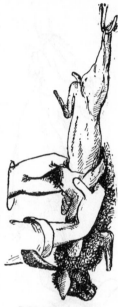

Next cut open and paunch the hare, as in illustration; and, if it be an old one, give it a good wash in vinegar and water. To truss it, cut the sinews of the legs, bring them well forward against the body and skewer with two skewers, one fixing the hind and one the fore legs, as shown. Next put the head well back and skewer it firmly there, then butter two pieces of paper and pin them over the ears.

Great care is needed to preserve the ears of the hare as perfect as possible.

HARE BEING SKINNED.

TRUSSING OF RABBIT.

For roasting, this may be trussed as a hare after it has been emptied,

RABBIT BEING TRUSSED.

washed, and the eyes taken out, the legs being cut off at the fore joints. (See illustration on preceding page.) For boiling, the treatment is so far the same; but, for this mode of cooking, the head, instead of being skewered back is brought round to the side and fixed there.

RABBIT BEING SKEWERED.

This mode of trussing is shown in the illustration of "Boiled Rabbit," in the Dictionary.

TRUSSING OF TURKEY.

Pluck and singe the bird thoroughly, then draw the sinews. To do this break the leg bones close by the feet, and run them on a hook, then pull in the manner shown. Next cut off the legs, as shown in illustration, and the neck close to the back, leaving enough skin to turn over ; take out the crop and loosen the inside at the throat end. To draw the bird cut off the vent, take out the gut, and use a hook to take out the inside (an illustration of this hook will be found on this page). As with a fowl, great care must be taken not to break the gall bladder or the gut joining the gizzard for fear of grit, then wash and thoroughly dry the inside. Next cut the breast-bone through at each side close to the back, and beat it flat with a rolling-pin. Scald the legs and peel off the outer skin, and the bird will be ready for trussing. Three skewers are needed for this purpose, the first put through the pinions, as in illustration on opposite page, the two others at first and second joints of the legs. Next comes the stuffing which should *fill* the bird, when the flaps of skin must be skewered over, and then, if a large turkey, it must be strung as in accompanying illustration.

Pheasants are trussed as grouse, but they can be drawn as a fowl.

Partridges are trussed as grouse.

Plovers, *Quail* and *Woodcock* are trussed as snipe.

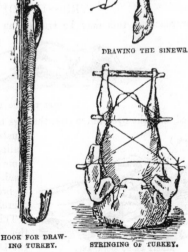

DRAWING THE SINEWS.

TURKEY READY FOR STUFFING.

HOOK FOR DRAW-ING TURKEY.

STRINGING OF TURKEY.

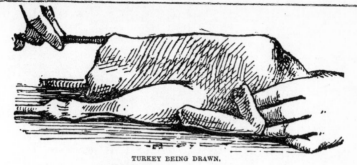

TURKEY BEING DRAWN.

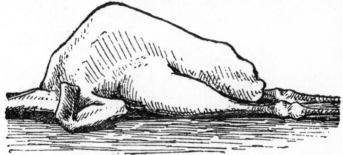

TURKEY READY FOR TRUSSING.

SKEWERING OF PINIONS OF TURKEY.

SKEWERING LEGS OF TURKEY.

TRUSSING OF SNIPE.

These birds are not drawn, and after being plucked, only require wiping on the outside with a damp cloth before being trussed.

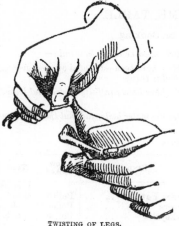

Twist the legs as shown and fasten them close to the body with a small skewer. Skin the neck and head, then bring the beak round under the wing, as in illustration.

TWISTING OF LEGS.

SNIPE TRUSSED.

CARVING OF MEAT, POULTRY AND GAME.

One of the most wasteful ways of treating the above is to carve them badly, and this alone should be reason sufficient for all to learn the art. We say all, for it so often happens that one member of a household alone can carve; and in the absence of that member there is no one who can take the office and make a success.

Compare two joints or birds carved respectively by good and bad carvers when they leave the table. One will present a neat appearance, even if most of it has been disposed of, and just those parts most suitable for eating cold or re-cooking will be left untouched, while the rest will have been cut clean away. The other dish will look ragged and unsightly, scarcely fit to come again to table; and, given the same number of people who have partaken of it as of that properly carved, more will have been consumed. In the hands of a skilful carver food will go much farther because it is divided into proper portions. If a fat piece of beef or mutton be served, the good carver will not cut away nearly all the lean and leave the fat, as cold meat, uneatable. Also he will help in moderate-sized pieces, instead of giving too much to one (in which case some will be wasted) and too little to another; and he will satisfy all by serving them with a hot dish before it has had time to get cold.

In most cases as the meat is carved by master or mistress, so will it be cut in the kitchen. If a joint comes to the servants neatly and properly cut they will endeavour to treat it in the same way, but if it has been hacked about, then will they do the like, just taking what portions they individually like, and thereby wasting much, besides spoiling its good appearance.

THE COOK'S TIME TABLE.

Times to Allow for Cooking.

When consulting these tables the following facts must be borne in mind :—

In every instance the times allowed for Cooking have been estimated by good average fires, properly kept up and suitable for each particular thing.

That during roasting or baking the joints, &c., have been carefully basted and looked after.

That in boiling the times stated have been after the water boils, and that the skimming has not been neglected.

EGGS, TO COOK.

KIND.	How Cooked.	Time.	KIND.	How Cooked.	Time.
		Minutes.			Minutes.
Hens' (New)	Boiled	4 to 6	Guinea Fowls'	Boiled	2 to 3
Ducks'	Boiled	4 to 6	Plovers'	Boiled	30
Geese'	Boiled	6 to 8	Turkeys'	Boiled	6 to 8

Eggs boiled hard for salads, &c., require at least 10 minutes, and should then be put into cold water.

TIMES TO ALLOW FOR COOKING FISH BY VARIOUS MODES.

NAME.	How Cooked.	Size or Quantity.	Time.	NAME.	How Cooked.	Size or Quantity.	Time.
			H. M.				H. M.
Bloaters	Grilled	Medium...	0 5	Plaice	Broiled	Small ...	0 5
Bream	Baked	Medium...	0 30	Plaice (Fillets)	Fried	Large ...	0 5
Brill	Boiled	Large ...	0 20	Salmon (Whole)	Boiled	8 lbs. ...	1 0
Cod (Head) ...	Boiled	Medium...	0 30	Salmon (Head and Shoulders }	Boiled	3 lbs. ...	0 24
Cod (Middle) ...	Boiled	3 lbs. ...	0 30				
Cod (Tail) ...	Boiled	3 lbs. ...	0 25	Salmon (Middle)	Boiled	3 lbs. ...	0 30
Cod Steaks ...	Fried	Thick ...	—	Salmon (Tail)...	Boiled	3 lbs. ...	0 28
John Dory ...	Boiled	Medium...	0 25	Salmon Cutlets	Fried	Thick ...	0 7
Eels	Souché	2 lbs. ...	0 35	Shad...	Boiled	Medium...	0 40
Eels	Stewed	2 lbs. ...	0 45	Skate	Boiled	Medium...	0 30
Flounders ...	Souché	Small ...	0 25	Smelts	Fried	1 doz. ...	0 5
Flounders ...	Fried	Small ...	0 5	Soles	Boiled	Large ...	0 9
Haddocks ...	Baked	Large ...	0 45	Soles	Fried	Medium...	0 7
Haddocks, Dried	Broiled	Medium...	0 5	Soles	Baked	Medium...	0 20
Halibut Steaks	Fried	Thick ...	0 15	Sprats	Fried	Medium...	0 3
Herrings... ...	Baked	Medium...	0 30	Sturgeon	Baked	Small ...	0 50
Lobster	Boiled	Large ...	0 40	Tench	Stewed	1 fish ...	0 35
Lobster	Boiled	Small ...	0 30	Trout	Baked	Medium...	0 30
Mackerel ...	Boiled	Large ...	0 13	Trout	Stewed	Medium...	0 40
Mackerel ...	Broiled	Small ...	0 10	Turbot	Boiled	Large ...	0 30
Mullet (Red) ...	Baked	Medium...	0 25	Turbot (Cut) ...	Boiled	2 lbs. ...	0 15
Mullet (Grey)...	Baked	Medium...	0 30	Turbot (Filleted)	Fried	Medium...	0 10
Mussels ...	Boiled	1 quart ...	0 20	Whitebait ...	Fried	1 quart ...	0 1½
Oysters	Scallop'd	Small tin	0 15	Whiting	Boiled	Large ...	0 6
Plaice	Fried	Medium...	0 5	Whiting	Fried	Small ...	0 6

From these tables it should be found easy to reckon the times to allow for cooking joints of different weights to those given, by adding or deducting in proportion to that stated. Thus, if a joint of ribs of beef weighing 8 lbs. takes 2 hours to roast, and one of 10, 2½ hours, the time allowed will be found 15 minutes to the lb. between those weights, therefore a joint of 9 lbs. should take 2¼ hours if cooked in the same manner.

TIMES TO ALLOW FOR COOKING BEEF BY VARIOUS MODES.

JOINT.	How Cooked.	Weight.	Time.	Weight.	Time.	Weight.	Time.	Weight.	Time.
		lbs.	H. M.	lbs.	H. M.	lbs.	H. M.	lbs.	H. M.
Aitchbone	Boiled	8 ...	2 0	10 ...	2 30	12 ...	2 45	14 ...	3 0
Baron	Roasted	80 ...	7 0	90 ...	7 30	100 ...	8 0	110 ...	8 30
Brisket	Boiled	7 ...	2 0	8 ...	2 15	10 ...	2 30	12 ...	2 50
Clod	Boiled	30 ...	6 0	40 ...	7 0	50 ...	7 45	80 ...	8 30
Leg of Mutton Piece	Baked	14 ...	3 15	16 ...	3 30	18 ...	3 45	20 ...	4 0
Ribs	Baked	8 ...	1 45	10 ...	2 10	12 ...	2 20	16 ...	3 0
Ribs	Roasted	8 ...	2 0	10 ...	2 30	12 ...	2 45	16 ...	3 30
Ribs (Boned)	Baked	7 ...	2 0	9 ...	2 30	11 ...	2 50	13 ...	3 10
Round	Baked	6 ...	1 30	9 ...	2 10	12 ...	2 45	15 ...	3 15
Rumpsteaks	Grilled	1 ...	0 5	2 ...	0 8	3 ...	0 12	4 ...	0 15
Rumpsteaks	Fried	1 ...	0 8	2 ...	0 10	3 ...	0 14	4 ...	0 18
Shin	Stewed	6 ...	3 30	8 ...	4 0	10 ...	4 15	12 ...	4 30
Silverside (Salt) ...	Boiled	7 ...	2 0	10 ...	2 30	14 ...	3 15	20 ...	4 0
Sirloin	Baked	10 ...	2 30	13 ...	3 10	16 ...	3 40	18 ...	4 0
Sirloin	Roasted	10 ...	2 40	13 ...	3 20	16 ...	4 0	18 ...	4 20
Heart	Baked	4 ...	1 45	5 ...	1 30	6 ...	1 45	8 ...	2 0
Tail	Stewed	1½ ...	1 30	2 ...	1 50	2½ ...	2 10	3 ...	2 20
Tongue	Boiled	6 ...	3 15	7 ...	3 30	8 ...	3 45	9 ...	4 0

TIMES TO ALLOW FOR COOKING MUTTON BY VARIOUS MODES.

JOINT.	How Cooked.	Weight.	Time.	Weight.	Time.	Weight.	Time.	Weight.	Time.
		lbs.	H. M.	lbs.	H. M.	lbs.	H. M.	lbs.	H. M.
Breast	Boiled	3 ...	1 30	4 ...	1 45	5 ...	2 0	6 ...	2 10
Breast	Stewed	3 ...	2 0	4 ...	2 15	5 ...	2 30	6 ...	2 40
Haunch	Roasted	10 ...	3 20	12 ...	4 0	16 ...	4 30	20 ...	5 0
Leg	Baked	7 ...	1 50	10 ...	2 20	12 ...	2 50	16 ...	3 20
Leg	Boiled	7 ...	2 0	10 ...	2 30	12 ...	3 0	16 ...	3 30
Leg	Roasted	7 ...	2 0	10 ...	2 30	12 ...	2 45	16 ...	3 0
Loin	Baked	6 ...	1 30	7 ...	1 45	8 ...	2 0	10 ...	2 20
Loin	Roasted	6 ...	1 40	7 ...	1 50	8 ...	2 10	10 ...	2 30
Loin (Boned)	Baked	5 ...	1 20	6 ...	1 30	7 ...	1 40	8 ...	1 50
Neck (Best End) ...	Baked	3 ...	0 50	4 ...	1 5	5 ...	1 20	6 ...	1 30
Neck	Boiled	3 ...	1 20	4 ...	1 30	5 ...	1 40	6 ...	1 50
Neck (Scrag)	Stewed	1 ...	1 45	1½ ...	2 0	2 ...	2 10	2½ ...	2 15
Saddle	Roasted	12 ...	3 0	14 ...	3 15	16 ...	3 35	20 ...	4 0
Saddle	Baked	12 ...	2 50	14 ...	3 5	16 ...	3 30	20 ...	3 50
Shoulder	Baked	6 ...	1 25	8 ...	1 35	9 ...	1 45	10 ...	2 0
Shoulder	Roasted	6 ...	1 30	8 ...	1 45	9 ...	2 0	10 ...	2 10
Head	Boiled	5 ...	1 30	6 ...	1 45	7 ...	2 0	— ...	—
Heart	Baked	0½ ...	0 30	— ...	—	— ...	—	— ...	—
Kidney	Grilled	1 ...	0 6	— ...	—	— ...	—	— ...	—

TIMES TO ALLOW FOR COOKING LAMB BY VARIOUS MODES.

Joint.	How Cooked.	Weight.	Time.	Weight.	Time.	Weight.	Time.	Weight.	Time.
		lbs.	H. M.	lbs.	H. M.	lbs.	H. M.	lbs.	H. M.
Breast	Stewed	1 ...	1 10	2 ...	1 20	3 ...	1 30	4 ...	1 40
Fore-quarter	Baked	6 ...	1 15	7 ...	1 25	8 ...	1 35	10 ...	1 50
Fore-quarter	Roasted	6 ...	1 20	7 ...	1 35	8 ...	1 45	10 ...	2 0
Hind-quarter	Baked	7 ...	1 25	8 ...	1 35	9 ...	1 42	11 ...	2 0
Hind-quarter	Roasted	7 ...	1 35	8 ...	1 45	9 ...	1 50	11 ...	2 5
Leg	Baked	3 ...	1 15	4 ...	1 20	6 ...	1 30	8 ...	1 45
Leg	Roasted	3 ...	1 20	4 ...	1 30	6 ...	1 40	8 ...	2 0
Loin	Baked	3 ...	0 45	4 ...	1 0	5 ...	1 10	6 ...	1 20
Loin	Roasted	3 ...	0 50	4 ...	1 5	5 ...	1 15	6 ...	1 25
Neck (Best End) ...	Baked	2 ...	0 40	3 ...	0 50	4 ...	1 0	— ...	—
Neck	Roasted	2 ...	0 45	3 ...	1 0	4 ...	1 5	— ...	—
Neck (Scrag)	Stewed	1 ...	1 10	2 ...	1 30	— ...	—	— ...	—
Shoulder	Baked	3 ...	0 45	4 ...	1 0	5 ...	1 10	— ...	—
Shoulder	Roasted	3 ...	0 50	4 ...	1 10	5 ...	1 20	— ...	—

TIMES TO ALLOW FOR COOKING PORK BY VARIOUS MODES.

Part.	How Cooked.	Weight.	Time.	Weight.	Time.	Weight.	Time.	Weight.	Time.
		lbs.	H. M.	lbs.	H. M	lbs.	H. M.	lbs.	H. M.
Ham (Smoked)	Baked	8 ...	3 45	10 ...	4 0	12 ...	4 20	16 ...	5 0
Ham	Boiled	8 ...	3 50	10 ...	4 15	12 ...	4 30	16 ...	5 20
Hand	Boiled	3 ...	2 0	4 ...	2 15	5 ...	3 25	6 ...	3 35
Fore-loin	Baked	6 ...	2 10	8 ...	2 30	10 ...	2 50	12 ...	3 0
Fore-loin	Roasted	6 ...	2 15	8 ...	2 40	10 ...	3 0	12 ...	3 15
Hind-loin	Baked	6 ...	2 10	8 ...	2 30	12 ...	2 50	14 ...	3 0
Hind-loin	Roasted	6 ...	2 15	8 ...	2 40	12 ...	3 0	14 ...	3 15
Leg	Baked	6 ...	2 40	8 ...	3 0	10 ...	3 20	12 ...	3 35
Leg	Boiled	6 ...	3 0	8 ...	3 30	10 ...	4 0	12 ...	4 30
Leg	Roasted	6 ...	2 15	8 ...	3 10	10 ...	3 30	12 ...	3 45
Spare Rib	Roasted	3 ...	1 30	4 ...	1 45	5 ...	3 0	6 ...	2 10
Bacon	Boiled	2 ...	1 30	4 ...	2 0	6 ...	2 20	8 ...	2 40
Face (half)	Boiled	2 ...	1 30	3 ...	1 40	4 ...	1 50	5 ...	2 0

TIMES TO ALLOW FOR COOKING VEAL BY VARIOUS MODES.

Joint.	How Cooked.	Weight.	Time.	Weight.	Time.	Weight.	Time.	Weight.	Time.
		lbs.	H. M.	lbs.	H. M.	lbs.	H. M.	lbs.	H. M.
Breast	Stewed	6 ...	2 15	8 ...	2 30	10 ...	3 0	12 ...	3 30
Cutlet	Fried	1 ...	0 12	2 ...	0 15	3 ...	0 18	4 ...	0 20
Fillet	Baked	9 ...	3 30	12 ...	4 10	14 ...	4 20	16 ...	4 30
Fillet	Roasted	9 ...	3 45	12 ...	4 15	14 ...	4 30	16 ...	4 45
Knuckle	Stewed	3 ...	2 30	5 ...	2 45	6 ...	3 0	7 ...	3 15
Loin	Baked	10 ...	2 45	12 ...	3 0	16 ...	3 15	18 ...	3 30
Loin	Roasted	10 ...	2 50	12 ...	3 10	16 ...	3 30	18 ...	3 40
Shoulder	Baked	8 ...	3 15	10 ...	3 30	12 ...	4 0	14 ...	4 20
Shoulder	Stewed	8 ...	3 30	10 ...	3 50	12 ...	4 10	14 ...	5 0
Head	Boiled	12 ...	2 30	13 ...	2 45	14 ...	3 0	16 ...	3 15
Head	Stewed	12 ...	4 40	13 ...	4 50	14 ...	5 0	16 ...	5 20
Heart	Baked	1 ...	0 40	1½ ...	0 50	— ...	—	— ...	—
Sweetbread	Stewed	1 ...	0 25	1½ ...	0 30	— ...	—	— ...	—

TIMES TO ALLOW FOR COOKING POULTRY AND GAME.

Name.	How Cooked.	Size or Quantity.	Time. H. M.	Name.	How Cooked.	Size or Quantity.	Time. H. M.
Chicken	Boiled	Small ...	0 30	Green Goose ...	Baked	Medium...	0 45
Chicken	Roasted	Small ...	0 30	Green Goose ...	Roasted	Medium...	0 50
Ducklings ...	Baked	Medium...	0 30	Guinea Fowl ...	Baked	Medium...	0 50
Ducklings ...	Roasted	Medium...	0 35	Guinea Fowl ...	Roasted	Medium...	1 0
Ducks	Baked	Large ...	0 50	Larks	Grilled	1 doz. ...	0 10
Ducks	Roasted	Large ...	1 0	Larks	Baked	1 doz. ...	0 15
Fowl	Boiled	Large ...	1 0	Pigeon	Grilled	Medium...	0 15
Fowl	Boiled	Medium...	0 45	Pigeon	Stewed	Medium...	0 30
Fowl	Roasted	Medium...	0 50	Rabbit	Baked	Large ...	0 45
Fowl	Baked	Medium...	0 45	Rabbit	Boiled	Medium...	0 40
Goose	Baked	Large ...	1 45	Rabbit	Roasted	Large ...	0 50
Goose	Baked	Small ...	1 20	Turkey	Baked	Large ...	2 30
Goose	Roasted	Large ...	1 50	Turkey	Boiled	Medium...	1 45
Goose	Roasted	Small ...	1 25	Turkey	Roasted	Large ...	2 40
Blackcock ...	Baked	Large ...	0 45	Plover	Baked	Medium...	0 10
Blackcock ...	Roasted	Large ...	0 50	Plover	Roasted	Medium...	0 12
Duck (Wild) ...	Baked	Medium...	0 20	Ptarmigan ...	Baked	Medium...	0 30
Duck	Roasted	Medium...	0 25	Ptarmigan ...	Roasted	Medium...	0 35
Grouse	Baked	Medium...	0 25	Quail	Baked	Medium ...	0 20
Grouse	Roasted	Medium...	0 30	Quail	Roasted	Medium...	0 25
Hare	Baked	Large ...	1 45	Snipe	Baked	Medium...	0 15
Hare	Jugged	Medium...	3 30	Snipe	Roasted	Medium...	0 20
Hare	Roasted	Large ...	1 55	Teal	Baked	Medium...	0 10
Leveret	Baked	Medium...	0 40	Teal	Roasted	Medium...	0 12
Leveret	Roasted	Medium...	0 45	Venison, Haunch	Baked	Large ...	4 0
Partridge ...	Baked	Medium...	0 25	Venison, Haunch	Roasted	Large ...	4 30
Partridge ...	Roasted	Medium...	0 30	Venison, Haunch	Roasted	Small ...	3 0
Pheasant ...	Baked	Large ...	0 45	Woodcock ...	Baked	Medium...	0 20
Pheasant ...	Roasted	Large ...	0 50	Woodcock ...	Roasted	Medium...	0 25

TIMES TO ALLOW FOR COOKING VEGETABLES.

Name.	How Cooked.	Time. H. M.	Name.	How Cooked.	Time. H. M.
Artichokes	Boiled	0 25	Endive	Stewed	0 15
Artichokes (Jerusalem)	Boiled	0 20	Mushrooms	Broiled	0 12
Asparagus	Boiled	0 16	Onions (Spanish)	Baked	2 0
Asparagus	Stewed	0 25	Onions (Spanish)	Stewed	2 0
Beans (French)	Boiled	0 15	Parsnips...	Boiled	1 0
Beans (Broad)	Boiled	0 20	Peas (Green)	Boiled	0 15
Beans (Haricot)	Boiled	2 30	Potatoes...	Baked	1 30
Beetroot	Boiled	2 30	Potatoes...	Boiled	0 20
Broccoli	Boiled	0 20	Potatoes...	Steamed	0 30
Broccoli Sprouts	Boiled	0 12	Potatoes (New)	Boiled	0 20
Brussels Sprouts	Boiled	0 12	Sea-kale	Boiled	0 15
Cabbage	Boiled	0 30	Savoys	Boiled	0 30
Cabbage (Summer) ...	Boiled	0 12	Spinach	Boiled	0 15
Carrots	Boiled	2 0	Tomatoes	Baked	0 20
Carrots (Young)	Boiled	0 30	Turnips	Boiled	1 0
Cauliflower	Boiled	0 20	Vegetable Marrow ...	Boiled	0 20
Celery	Stewed	0 20			

TABLES OF RELATIVE VALUE

OF FISH OF ALL KINDS, BEEF, MUTTON, LAMB, PORK & VEAL, BY DIFFERENT MODES OF COOKING.

To determine the actual relative value of various kinds of fish, they have one and all, in the following list, been *practically* tested. Each fish, or part of fish, has been weighed before and after cooking, to see what it has lost in the process; then all skin, bone and waste has been removed, and the eatable part alone weighed; comparing the price of the fish as bought for what we actually pay for what is eatable, the result is in many cases surprising. It will be seen that some fish yield so little that however cheaply they may be bought, they are extravagant; while some of the dearer kinds, having so little waste, are in reality the most economical.

It must be remembered by those who take the trouble to test the accuracy of the following tables that of necessity different cooks will arrive at slightly different results for the reason that some cook so much more economically than others by boiling and stewing slowly, and basting well all meats either baked or roasted.

Again in trimming meat, boning or filleting fish, &c., the cook may be either extravagant or saving; while upon the quality of the food also much may depend, inferior meat, for example, shrinking and wasting more than that of good quality.

In the practical hints the results of which are here shown, good provisions have been used, joints of ordinary size, moderately fat, &c., and fire and heat suitable for what had to be cooked has been employed.

TABLE OF RELATIVE VALUE OF VARIOUS KINDS OF FISH.

Name of Fish.	How Cooked.	Average Price per lb.		Loss per lb. by Cooking, Bone and Waste.		Average Cost per lb.	
		s.	*d.*	lb.	oz.	*s.*	*d.*
Brill	Boiled	0	10	0	8	1	8
Cod........................	Boiled	0	7	0	6	0	11
Cod (Head and Shoulders)	Boiled	0	7	0	8	1	2
Cod (Steaks)	Broiled	0	9	0	2½	0	11¼
Dory	Boiled	1	0	0	8½	2	2
Eels	Fried	0	10	0	3	1	0¼
Eels	Stewed	0	10	0	2	0	11½
Flounders..................	Fried	0	5	0	8½	0	10¾
Mackerel	Boiled	0	4	0	4	0	5½
Mackerel	Broiled	0	4	0	5	0	5¾
Mullet (Red)	Fried	1	0	0	4	1	4
Mullet (Grey)	Fried	0	9	0	4	1	0
Plaice	Boiled	0	5	0	5½	0	7½
Plaice	Fried	0	5	0	7	0	9
Salmon (Head)	Boiled	1	6	0	8½	3	1
Salmon (Cutlets)	Fried	2	0	0	3	2	5½
Salmon (Tail)	Boiled	1	9	0	4	2	4
Shad	Boiled	1	0	0	5	1	5½
Skate........................	Boiled	0	6	0	4¼	0	8¾
Smelts	Fried	2	0	0	10	5	4
Soles	Boiled	1	3	0	5½	2	0
Soles	Fried	1	3	0	6½	2	4¼
Trout........................	Boiled	1	0	0	3¼	1	4
Turbot	Boiled	1	4	0	6½	2	4
Whiting	Fried	0	8	0	5	0	11¼

TABLE OF RELATIVE VALUE OF DIFFERENT KINDS OF MEAT

As in the case of fish, all the following parts of beef, mutton, lamb, pork and veal have been specially cooked and carefully tested to arrive at correct results. No pains have been spared to make the tables accurate, and it will be interesting to note that some of the most expensive joints and parts are in reality far cheaper, yielding more actual food than what we usually call cheap ones.

VARIOUS PARTS OF BEEF, RELATIVE VALUE.

Joint or Part.	How Cooked.	Average Price per lb.		Loss per lb. by Cooking, Bone and Waste.		Actual Cost per lb.	
		s.	*d.*	lb.	oz.	*s.*	*d.*
Aitchbone	Boiled	0	7½	0	9¾	1	7
Brisket	Boiled	0	8	0	6¼	1	1½
Buttock (in Steaks)	Stewed	0	11	0	0½	0	11¼
Ribs (Fore)	Roasted	0	11	0	7	1	7½
Ribs (Middle)	Roasted	0	11	0	6½	1	6½
Round	Baked	0	10	0	2	0	11¼
Round (Silverside)	Boiled	0	9	0	3	0	11
Rump Steaks	Broiled	1	2	0	0½	1	2¼
Sirloin	Roasted	0	11	0	4½	1	3¼
Heart	Roasted	0	6	0	0½	0	6¼
Tongue	Boiled	0	8	0	4	0	10½

VARIOUS PARTS OF MUTTON, RELATIVE VALUE.

Joint or Part.	How Cooked.	Average Price per lb.		Loss per lb. by Cooking, Bone and Waste.		Actual Cost per lb.	
		s.	*d.*	lb.	oz.	*s.*	*d.*
Breast	Roasted	0	8	0	5	0	11½
Chump Chop	Grilled	1	1	0	5	1	7
Leg	Boiled	0	10	0	4¾	1	2
Leg	Roasted	0	10	0	5¼	1	3
Loin	Roasted	0	10	0	5	1	2½
Loin Chop	Grilled	1	1	0	4	1	5¼
Neck (best end)	Boiled	0	10	0	4	1	1¼
Neck (Scrag)	Stewed	0	7	0	8	1	2
Saddle	Roasted	0	10	0	3¾	1	1
Shoulder	Roasted	0	9	0	7	1	4
Head	Stewed	0	5	0	8	0	10
Heart	Baked	0	9	0	2	0	10¼
Kidneys	Grilled	1	2	0	3	1	5½

VARIOUS PARTS OF LAMB, RELATIVE VALUE.

Joint or Part.	How Cooked.	Average Price per lb.		Loss per lb. by Cooking, Bone and Waste.		Actual Cost per lb.	
		s.	*d.*	lb.	oz.	*s.*	*d.*
Breast	Stewed	0	0	0	5	1	2½
Fore-quarter	Roasted	1	0	0	4¾	1	5
Hind-quarter	Roasted	[illegible]	[illegible]	0	3	1	4¼
Leg	Roasted	1	1	0	6¼	1	9¾
Loin	Roasted	1	0	0	4½	1	4¾
Neck (in Cutlets)	Fried	0	10	0	8	1	8
Neck (Scrag)	Stewed	0	8	0	7	1	2¼
Shoulder	Roasted	1	0	0	6	1	7

Various Parts of Pork, Relative Value.

Joint or Part.	How Cooked.	Average Price per lb.		Loss per lb. by Cooking, Bone and Waste.		Actual Cost per lb.	
		s.	d.	lb.	oz.	s.	d.
Bacon (Back)	Boiled	0	11	None.		0	11
Bacon (Side)	Fried	0	11	0	4	1	2¾
Bacon (Cushion)...........	Boiled	0	9	0	3¼	0	11¾
Ham	Boiled	1	0	0	6	1	7¾
Ham (Rashers)	Fried	0	8	0	5¼	1	6
Ham (Knuckle)	Boiled	0	8	0	4½	1	0
Leg of Pork	Boiled	0	9	0	4¾	1	1
Leg of Pork	Roasted	0	9	0	4¼	1	1
Loin of Pork (Hind)......	Roasted	0	10	0	6½	1	4¾
Loin of Pork (Fore)	Roasted	0	9	0	6¼	1	3
Pickled Pork	Boiled	0	8	0	1	0	8½

Various Parts of Veal, Relative Value.

Joint or Part.	How Cooked.	Average Price per lb.		Loss per lb. by Cooking, Bone and Waste.		Actual Cost per lb.	
		s.	d.	lb.	oz.	s.	d.
Breast	Roasted	0	10	0	5¼	1	3
Fillet...................	Roasted	1	0	0	4½	1	4¾
Knuckle	Boiled	0	6	0	8½	1	1
Leg (in Cutlets)	Fried	1	2	0	2¾	1	5
Loin	Roasted	0	11	0	7¼	1	8
Neck	Roasted	0	9	0	5	1	1
Shoulder	Roasted	0	9	0	5	1	1
Head	Boiled	0	6	0	6	0	9½
Heart....................	Baked	0	8	0	0½	0	8½
Liver	Fried	0	10	0	0½	0	10½
Sweetbread	Fried	1	4	0	1	1	5
Tongue	Boiled	0	8	0	6	0	11

HAUNCH OF MUTTON.

THE DICTIONARY OF COOKERY.

Art of all arts, that aims to " cure the ills
That flesh is heir to," and save doctors' bills.

LMA Pudding.—
INGREDIENTS *for
good-sizedpudding.*
—6 *oz. of butter,* ½
lb. of flour, ½ *lb.
of pounded white
sugar,* ¼ *lb. of sul-
tanas,*4*eggs.* AVER-
AGE COST, 1*s.* 3*d.*

Beat the butter
to a cream and
strew in slowly the sugar ; when these are
well mixed dredge in the flour and add the
currants, with a few drops of vanilla flavouring if liked, and moisten with the eggs,
which should first be well beaten. Butter
a mould that the pudding will exactly fill,
tie down with a cloth, put into boiling
water and boil for 3 hours. Serve with
sifted sugar strewn over the top.

TIME.—3 *hours.*
SEASONABLE *at any time.*

Almond Cake.—INGREDIENTS.—
½ *lb. of sweet almonds,* 1 *oz. of bitter almonds,*
6 *eggs,* 8 *tablespoonfuls of sifted sugar,* 5
*tablespoonfuls of fine flour, the grated rind
of* 1 *lemon,* 3 *oz. of butter.* AVERAGE COST,
1*s.* 9*d.*

Blanch and pound the almonds to a
paste ; separate the whites from the yolks
of the eggs ; beat the latter and add them
to the almonds. Stir in the sugar, flour
and lemon-rind ; add the butter, which
should be beaten to a cream ; and when all
these ingredients are well mixed, put in
the whites of the eggs, which should be
whisked to a stiff froth. Butter a cake-
mould, put in the mixture, and bake in a
good oven from 1¼ to 1¾ hour.

TIME.—1¼ *to* 1¾ *hour.*
SEASONABLE *at any time.*

Almond Cheesecakes.—IN-
GREDIENTS *for* 12 *cheesecakes.*—4 *oz. of
sweet almonds,* 3 *bitter ones,* 3 *eggs,* 2 *oz. of
butter, the rind of* ¼ *lemon,* 1 *tablespoonful
of lemon-juice,* 3 *oz. of sugar.* AVERAGE
COST, 10*d.*

Blanch and pound the almonds smoothly
in a mortar, with a little rosewater ; stir in
the eggs, which should be well beaten, and

Q

the butter, which should be warmed; add the lemon-peel grated fine, and juice, sweeten and stir well until the whole is thoroughly mixed. Line some patty-pans with puff-paste, put in the mixture and bake for 15 to 20 minutes in a quick oven.

TIME.—20 *minutes, or rather less.*

Almond Icing for Cakes.—IN-

GREDIENTS.—1 *lb.* of castor sugar, 1 *lb.* of sweet almonds, *the whites of* 4 *eggs, a little rosewater.* AVERAGE COST *for a large cake,* 1*s.* 7*d.*

Blanch the almonds and pound them to a paste with a little rosewater. Beat the whites of eggs to a stiff froth, mix them with the almonds, add the sugar and beat all together till quite smooth. Spread the mixture over the cake and put it into the oven to dry.

Almond Milk (for Invalids).—

INGREDIENTS.—2 *oz.* of sweet almonds, 4 *bitter seeds,* 1 *pint of milk,* 1 *pint of water, a little orange-flower water, sugar to taste.* AVERAGE COST, 6*d.*

Blanch and pound the almonds and seeds with the orange-flower water to a smooth paste, rub this into the milk and water, strain, and sweeten according to taste.

Almond Paste.—INGREDIENTS.—

1 *lb.* of *sweet almonds,* 4 *bitter ones,* ½ *lb.* of very finely-sifted castor sugar, *the white of an egg.* AVERAGE COST *for this quantity,* 10*d.*

Blanch the almonds and dry them thoroughly; pound them well in a mortar, wetting them gradually with the white of an egg. When well pounded, put them into a small preserving

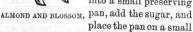

ALMOND AND BLOSSOM. pan, add the sugar, and place the pan on a small but clear fire (a hot plate is better); keep

stirring until the paste is dry, then take it out of the pan, put it between two dishes, and when cold make it into any shape that fancy may dictate, or use it for the tops of cakes.

TIME.—½ *hour.*

Almond Pudding, Baked.—IN-

GREDIENTS. - ¼ *lb.* of almonds, 4 *bitter ones,* 1 *glass of sherry,* 4 *eggs, the rind and juice* of ½ *lemon,* 3 *oz.* of butter, 1 *pint of milk,* 2 *oz.* of bread-crumbs, 2 *tablespoonfuls of sugar.* AVERAGE COST, 1*s.* 6*d.*

Blanch and pound the almonds to a smooth paste with the water; mix these with the butter, which should be melted; beat the eggs, grate the lemon-rind, and strain the juice; add these with the milk, sugar and wine to the other ingredients and stir them well together. When well mixed, put it into a pie-dish lined with puff-paste and bake for ½ hour.

TIME.—½ to ¾ *hour.*

SEASONABLE *at any time.*

Almond Puddings, Small.—IN-

GREDIENTS *for sufficient for 6 persons*—½ *lb.* of *sweet almonds,* 6 *bitter ones,* ¼ *lb.* of *butter,* 3 *eggs,* 2 *tablespoonfuls of sifted sugar,* 2 *tablespoonfuls of cream or milk,* 1 *tablespoonful of brandy.* AVERAGE COST, 1*s.* 10*d.*

Blanch and pound the almonds to a smooth paste with a spoonful of water; warm the butter, mix the almonds with this, and add the other ingredients, leaving out the whites of

SMALL ALMOND PUDDINGS.

2 eggs, and be particular that these are well beaten. Mix well, butter some cups, half fill them, and bake the puddings from 20 minutes to ½ hour. Turn them out on a dish, and serve with sweet sauce, or with sifted sugar only.

TIME.—20 *minutes to* ½ *hour.*

SEASONABLE *at any time.*

Almond Puffs.—INGREDIENTS.—

Equal weights of flour, castor sugar, butter and sweet almonds, allowing 2 bitter almonds to an ounce of the other ingredients. AVERAGE COST, 1d. each.

Blanch and pound the almonds in a mortar to a smooth paste; melt the butter, dredge in the flour, and add the sugar and pounded almonds. Beat the mixture well, and put it into cups or moulds, which should be well buttered, and bake in a moderate oven for about 20 minutes, or longer, should the puffs be large. Turn them out on a dish, the bottom of the puff uppermost, and serve.

TIME.—20 minutes.

SEASONABLE at any time.

Almond Soup.—INGREDIENTS.—

4 lbs. of lean beef, or veal, a few vegetables as for Stock (see STOCK), 6 oz. of vermicelli, 4 blades of mace, 6 cloves, ½ lb. of sweet almonds, the yolks of 6 eggs, 1 gill of thick cream or milk, rather more than 3 quarts of water. AVERAGE COST, 3s. 6d.

Boil the beef or veal, vegetables and spices gently in water that will cover them, till the gravy is very strong, and the meat very tender; then strain off the gravy, and set it on the fire with the specified quantity of vermicelli to 2 quarts. Let it boil till sufficiently cooked. Have ready the almonds, blanched and pounded very fine; the yolks of the eggs boiled hard; mixing the almonds, whilst pounding, with a little of the soup, lest the latter should grow oily. Pound them to a pulp, and keep adding to them, by degrees, a little soup, until they are thoroughly mixed together. Let the soup be cool when mixing, and do it perfectly smooth. Strain it through a sieve, set it on the fire, stir frequently, and serve hot. Just before taking it up, add the cream.

TIME.—From 4 to 5 hours to simmer meat and vegetables; 20 minutes to cook the vermicelli.

SEASONABLE all the year.

Almond Tartlets.—INGREDIENTS

for 1 doz. tartlets.—4 oz. of butter, 4 oz. of pounded sugar, the rind and juice of 2 lemons, 3 eggs, puff paste. AVERAGE COST, 1s. 3d.

ALMOND TARTLETS.

Set the butter in the oven to oil, beat the eggs well, grate the peel of the lemon, and squeeze and strain the juice. Add the sugar to the beaten eggs, then the lemon-peel and juice, lastly the butter, and stir well together. Line some patty-pans with paste, and fill about half full with the mixture, and bake in a quick oven.

TIME.—About 20 minutes to bake the tartlets.

SEASONABLE at any time.

Alpine Eggs.—INGREDIENTS for

sufficient for 6 persons.—6 eggs, ½ lb. of cheese, 3 oz. of butter, chopped parsley, seasoning of pepper and salt. AVERAGE COST, 1s. 2d.

Butter a shallow tin and line it with nearly all the cheese cut in slices, break over this the eggs without breaking the yolks, and season. Grate what remains of the cheese and mix it with the parsley; lay this over the top, and upon it put the remainder of the butter, cut in little pieces. Bake in a quick oven 10 minutes.

TIME.—10 minutes.

SEASONABLE at any time.

Amber Pudding.—INGREDIENTS

to fill a large pie-dish.—6 apples, 1 lemon, 3 eggs, 3 oz, of moist sugar, a litle castor sugar, 2 oz. of butter, a few crystallised cherries, short or puff paste. AVERAGE COST, 1s. 6d.

Peel and core the apples, and stew them with the rind and juice of the lemon and the moist sugar till reduced to a pulp. Grease the bottom of a pie-dish and line it half way down with a strip of paste. Pass the apple marmalade through a sieve, add to it the yolks of the eggs, and after mixing thoroughly, turn into the dish and bake for 15 minutes. Beat the whites of the eggs stiff, adding as much castor sugar as they will take up, put the mixture upon the top of the baked pudding, decorate with the cherries, and place it in a moderate oven to bring to a bright golden colour.

TIME.—½ hour to bake the pudding.
SEASONABLE at any time.

Anchovy Butter.—INGREDIENTS.

—To every ½ lb. of butter allow 6 anchovies, 1 small bunch of parsley. AVERAGE COST, ½ lb., 1s. 2d.

Wash, bone, and pound the anchovies well in a mortar; scald the parsley, chop it, and rub through a sieve; then pound all the ingredients together, mix well, and

THE ANCHOVY.

make the butter into pats immediately. This makes a pretty dish, if fancifully moulded, for breakfast or supper, and should be garnished with parsley.

SEASONABLE at any time.

Anchovy Canapés.—INGREDI-

ENTS.—2 slices of stale bread, 8 anchovies, 2 eggs, butter for frying. AVERAGE COST, 9d.

Cut the bread one third of an inch thick and stamp out with a cutter small rounds about the size of a penny and fry a nice golden brown in the butter. Bone and fillet the anchovies and boil the eggs hard. Curl two fillets on each croûton and fill up the centre with the white of egg chopped fine and the yellow rubbed through a sieve.

SEASONABLE at any time.

Anchovy Sauce (for Fish). — IN-

GREDIENTS.—4 anchovies, 1 oz. of butter, ½ pint of melted butter, cayenne to taste. AVERAGE COST for ½ pint, 6d.

Bone the anchovies, and pound them to a paste, with 1 oz. of butter. Make the melted butter hot, stir in the pounded anchovies and cayenne; simmer for 3 or 4 minutes; and, if liked, add a squeeze of lemon-juice. A more general and expeditious way of making this sauce is to stir in 1½ tablespoonful of anchovy essence to ½ pint of melted butter, and to add seasoning to taste. Boil the whole up for 1 minute, and serve hot.

TIME.—5 minutes.

Anchovy Toast. I.—INGREDIENTS.

—2 or 3 slices of bread, butter for frying, anchovy paste, cayenne.

Toast and butter the bread, or fry it in the butter and cut off the crust. Spread it with the paste and give it a seasoning of cayenne. Serve very hot.

Anchovy Toast. II.—INGREDIENTS

for sufficient for 3 persons.—Stale bread, 6 anchovies, butter for frying, cayenne. AVERAGE COST, 9d.

Cut the bread one third of an inch thick into little squares and fry them a bright brown, bone and fillet the anchovies and lay them on and sprinkle over a few grains of cayenne. Serve very hot.

SEASONABLE at any time.

Anchovies, Fried.—INGREDIENTS.

—1 tablespoonful of oil, ½ a glass of white wine, sufficient flour to thicken, 12 anchovies. AVERAGE COST for this quantity, 9d.

Mix the oil and wine together, with sufficient flour to make them into a thickish paste; cleanse the anchovies, wipe them, dip them in the paste, and fry of a nice brown colour.

TIME.—½ hour.
SEASONABLE all the year.

Anchovies, Potted, or Anchovy Butter.

—INGREDIENTS.—2 *dozen anchovies, ½ lb. of fresh butter, cayenne, pounded mace.* AVERAGE COST, 2s.

Wash the anchovies thoroughly; bone and dry them, and pound them in a mortar to a paste. Mix the butter and seasoning gradually with them, and rub the whole through a sieve. Put it by in small pots for use, and carefully exclude the air with a bladder, as it soon changes the colour of anchovies, besides spoiling them.

Angels on Horseback.

—INGREDIENTS *for dish for 4 persons.*—3 *thin slices of stale bread,* 1 *dozen oysters, a few very thin slices of bacon, some finely chopped parsley, a few drops of lemon juice, Nepaul pepper or cayenne, butter for frying.* AVERAGE COST, 2d. each.

Cut the bacon into little squares each large enough to roll round an oyster, sprinkle over each the chopped herbs, lay on the oysters, season with the pepper and a drop of lemon juice, roll up and run on a skewer and fry in butter till the bacon is cooked. Cut the bread into squares or stamp out small rounds and fry them a bright golden colour and on each lay an oyster. Serve very hot garnished with lemon and parsley.

TIME.—3 *minutes to fry the oysters.*

Apple Cake.

— INGREDIENTS *for large cake.*—8 *apples, sugar to taste, the juice of a lemon and half its rind,* 2 *eggs, half a small cupful of milk,* 3 *oz. of butter,* 2 *oz. of sweet almonds, enough good short crust to line a large plate or tin.* AVERAGE COST, 1s. 8d.

Prepare the apples as for a tart. Put sugar enough to sweeten them into a basin, add the lemon peel grated and the milk. Mix these, then add the eggs whisked and the butter melted, lastly the apples and lemon juice. Line the tin or plate with the paste and put a rim round the edge; put in

the mixture and scatter over the almonds, blanched and chopped. Bake for about ½ hour.

TIME.—½ *an hour.*

Apple Charlotte, A very simple.

—INGREDIENTS *for sufficient for 6 persons.*—*Slices of bread and butter,* 6 *good-sized apples, rind and juice of* 1 *lemon, moist sugar to taste.* AVERAGE COST, 10d.

Butter a pie-dish; place a layer of bread and butter, cutting off the crust, at the bottom; then a layer of apples, pared, cored, and cut into thin slices; sprinkle over these a portion of the lemon peel grated and juice, and sweeten with moist sugar. Place another layer of bread and butter, and then one of apples, proceeding

DISH OF APPLES.

in this manner until the dish is full; then cover it up with the peel of the apples, to preserve the top from browning or burning; bake in a brisk oven for rather more than ¾ hour; turn the charlotte on a dish, sprinkle sifted sugar over, and serve.

TIME.—¾ *hour, or a few minutes longer.*
SEASONABLE *from August to March.*

Apple Cheesecakes.

—INGREDIENTS *for 18 cheesecakes.*—*Sufficient apples to make ½ lb. when cooked, ¼ lb. of sifted sugar, ¼ lb. of butter,* 4 *eggs, the rind and juice of* 1 *lemon, puff paste.* AVERAGE COST, 1s. 8d.

Pare, core, and boil the apples to a pulp; add to these the sugar, the butter, which should be melted, the eggs, leaving out 2 of the whites, and the grated rind and juice of the lemon; stir well; line some patty-pans with puff-paste ; fill them with the mixture, and bake about 20 minutes.

TIME.—*About 20 minutes.*

SEASONABLE *from August to March.*

Apple Custard, Baked.—INGREDIENTS *for large dish.*—8 *large apples, moist sugar to taste,* 3 *tablespoonfuls of cold water, the grated rind of* 1 *lemon,* ¾ *pint of milk,* 3 *eggs,* 3 *oz. of loaf sugar.* AVERAGE COST, 1s. 1d.

Pare and core the apples ; put them into a lined saucepan with the cold water, and, as they heat, beat them to a pulp ; sweeten with the sugar, and add the lemon rind. When cold, put the fruit at the bottom of a pie-dish, and pour over it a custard, made with the above proportion of milk, eggs, and sugar ; place the dish in a moderate oven, and bake from 20 to 30 minutes.

TIME.—*20 to 30 minutes.*

SEASONABLE *from August to March.*

Apple Dumplings, Baked.—INGREDIENTS *for* 8 *dumplings.*—8 *apples, suet crust, sugar to taste.* AVERAGE COST, 1½d. *each.*

Pare and take out the cores of the apples with a scoop, and make a suet crust with 1 lb. of flour to 6 oz. of suet ; fill the cavities of the apples with sugar, then roll them in squares cut from the crust, taking care to join the paste nicely. When they are formed into round balls, put them on a tin and bake them for about ½ hour, or longer, should the apples be very large. When served, sift over them some pounded white sugar. These may be made richer by using puff-paste instead of suet-crust.

TIME.—*From* ½ *to* ¾ *hour, or longer.*

SEASONABLE *from August to March.*

Apple Dumplings, Boiled.—INGREDIENTS *for* 6 *dumplings.*—6 *apples, suet crust, sugar to taste.* AVERAGE COST, 1½d. *each.*

Make the dumplings by the preceding recipe. Put them into floured cloths, tie them securely and place them in boiling

water. Keep them boiling from ¾ to 1 hour ; remove the cloths, and send them hot and quickly to table. Dumplings boiled in knitted cloths have a very pretty

APPLE DUMPLINGS.

appearance when they come to table, or they may be boiled without cloths.

TIME.—1 *hour, or longer should the dumplings be very large.*

SEASONABLE *from August to March.*

Apple Fritters.—INGREDIENTS *for sufficient for* 6 *persons.*—2 *tablespoonfuls of flour,* ½ *oz. of butter,* ⅓ *saltspoonful of salt,* 2 *eggs, milk,* 4 *medium-sized apples, hot lard or clarified beef dripping, sugar, lemon juice.* AVERAGE COST, 1s.

Divide the whites from the yolks of the eggs, and beat them separately. Put the flour into a basin, stir in the butter, which should be melted to a cream ; add the salt, and moisten with sufficient warm milk to make it of a proper consistency, that is to say, a batter that will drop from the spoon. Stir this well, rub down any lumps that may be seen, add the yolks and then the whites of the eggs, which have

APPLE FRITTERS.

been previously well whisked ; beat up the batter for a few minutes, and it is ready for use. Peel and cut the apples into rather thick whole slices, without dividing them, and stamp out the core of each slice with a cutter ; squeeze some lemon juice over a little sifted sugar, dip the slices in this, then throw them into the batter ; have ready a pan of boiling lard or clarified dripping ; take out the pieces of apple one by one, put them into the hot lard, and fry a nice brown, turning them when required.

When done, lay them on a piece of blotting-paper before the fire, to absorb the greasy moisture ; then pile the fritters one above the other ; strew over them some pounded sugar, and serve very hot. The batter is better for being mixed some hours before the fritters are made.

TIME.—*From 7 to 10 minutes to fry the fritters; 5 minutes to drain them.*

SEASONABLE *from August to March.*

Apple Jam.—INGREDIENTS.—
Apples of one sort, preserving sugar, lemons.
AVERAGE COST, 4d. to 6d. *per lb. pot.*

Peel, core and slice the apples, and to every lb. allow ¾ lb. of sugar and the grated rind and juice of half a lemon. Put

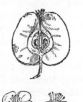

the apples into a jar, stand this in a saucepan of boiling water, and let them stew until quite tender. Next put the apples into a preserving-pan, crush the sugar to small lumps, and add it, with the grated lemon-rind and juice, to the apples. Simmer these over the fire for ½ hour, reckoning from the time the jam begins to simmer properly ; remove the scum as it

APPLE AND BLOSSOM.

rises, and when the jam is done, put it into pots for use. Place a piece of oiled paper over the jam, and, to exclude the air, cover the pots with tissue paper dipped in the white of an egg, and stretched over the top. This jam will keep good for a long time.

TIME.—*From 3 to 4 hours to stew in the jar; ½ hour to boil after the jam begins to simmer.*

SEASONABLE.—*Make this in Autumn, when apples can be had at a reasonable price.*

Apple Jelly. I.—INGREDIENTS.—
Apples, water, loaf sugar, lemon juice.
AVERAGE COST, 6d. *per pot.*

Pare, core and cut the apples into slices, and put them into a jar, with water in the proportion of ½ pint to each lb. Place them in a cool oven, with the jar well covered, and, when the juice is thoroughly drawn and the apples are quite soft, strain them through a jelly-bag. Measure the juice and to every quart allow 2 lbs. of crushed sugar. Put juice and sugar into a preserving pan, boil together for rather more than ½ hour, removing the scum as it rises, then add the lemon-juice just before it is done, and put the jelly into pots for use. This preparation is useful for garnishing sweet dishes, and may be turned out for dessert.

TIME.—*The apples to be put in the oven over-night, and left till morning; rather more than ½ hour to boil the jelly.*

SEASONABLE.—*This should be made in Autumn.*

Apple Jelly. II.—INGREDIENTS.—
6 *lbs. of apples,* 2 *lemons, water ; to every pint of juice allow* ¾ *lb. of loaf sugar.* AVERAGE COST, 6d. *per pot.*

Pare, core, and cut the apples into pieces, and put them in a preserving-pan with sufficient cold water to cover them and the peel of the lemons, which must be taken out when the apples are sufficiently flavoured. Let them boil for an hour ; then drain the syrup from them through a jelly-bag, and measure the juice; to every pint allow ¾ lb. of loaf sugar, and boil these together for ¾ hour, removing every particle of scum as it rises, and keeping the jelly well stirred, that it may not burn ; add the lemon-juice, strained, just before the jelly is done, and store away in small pots.

TIME. — 1 *hour to boil the fruit and water;* ¾ *hour to boil the juice with the sugar.*

SEASONABLE.—*Make this in Autumn.*

Apple Jelly, Clear (for Immediate Eating).

—INGREDIENTS *for* 1½ *pint mould.*— 3 *lbs. of apples, water, loaf sugar, isinglass, lemons.* AVERAGE COST, 1s. 6d.

Pare, core and cut the apples into quarters, and boil them, with the lemon-peel and sufficient water to cover them, until tender; then strain off the apples, and run the juice through a jelly-bag; put the strained juice, with sugar in the proportion of ½ lb. to a pint, and isinglass or gelatine dissolved in boiling water in the proportion of ½ oz. to a pint, into a lined saucepan or preserving-pan; boil all together for about ½ hour, and put the jelly into moulds. When this jelly is clear, and turned out well, it makes a pretty supper dish, with a little custard or whipped cream round it. If required to be kept any length of time, rather a larger proportion of sugar must be used.

TIME.—*About* 1 *hour to boil the apples;* ½ *hour the jelly.*

SEASONABLE *from August to March.*

Apple Jelly, Thick, or Marmalade (for Entremets or Dessert Dishes).

INGREDIENTS.—*Apples, sugar, lemon-peel.*

Peel, core, and boil the apples with only sufficient water to prevent them from burning; beat them to a pulp, and to every lb. of pulp allow ¾ lb. of lump sugar.

APPLE JELLY, STUCK WITH ALMONDS.

Dip the lumps into water; put these into a saucepan and boil till the syrup is thick and can be well skimmed; then add this syrup to the apple pulp, with sufficient grated lemon-peel to flavour the jelly, and stir it over a quick fire for about 20 minutes, or till the apples cease to stick to the bottom of the pan. The jelly is then done, and may be poured into moulds which have been previously dipped in water, when it will turn out nicely. A little custard may be poured round, or it may be stuck with blanched almonds.

TIME.—*From* ½ *to* ¾ *hour to reduce the apples to a pulp;* 20 *minutes to boil after the sugar is added.*

SEASONABLE *from August to March.*

Apple Pudding, Rich Baked.

—INGREDIENTS.—½ lb. *of apple pulp,* ¼ lb. *of loaf sugar,* 4 oz. *of butter, the rind of* 1 *lemon,* 4 *eggs, puff-paste.* AVERAGE COST, 1s. 4d.

Peel, core, and slice the apples, as for sauce, sufficient to make ½ lb. of pulp; put them into a stewpan, with just sufficient water to prevent them from burning, and let them stew until reduced to a pulp. Add the sifted sugar, the grated lemon-rind and the eggs, well beaten. Beat these ingredients well together; then melt the butter, stir it to the other things, put a border of puff-paste round the dish, pour in the mixture, and bake for rather more than ½ hour. The butter should not be added until the pudding is ready for the oven.

TIME.—½ *to* ¾ *hour.*

SEASONABLE *from August to March.*

Apple Pudding, Baked.

—INGREDIENTS *for a large pudding.*—3 *lbs. of apples,* 6 oz. *of moist sugar,* 3 oz. *of butter,* 3 *eggs,* 1 *pint of bread-crumbs, a few cloves.* AVERAGE COST, 1s. 6d.

Pare, core, and cut the apples as for sauce, and boil them until reduced to a pulp with the cloves, which should then be taken out; then add the butter, melted, and the eggs, which should be well whisked. Beat up the pudding for 2 or 3 minutes; butter a pie-dish; put in a layer of bread-crumbs, then the apple, and then another layer of bread-crumbs; flake over these a few tiny pieces of butter, and bake for about ½ hour. A very good economical pudding may be made merely with apples, boiled and sweetened, with the addition of a few strips of lemon-peel. A layer of bread-crumbs should be placed above and below the apples, and the pudding baked for ½ hour.

TIME.—*About ½ hour.*

SEASONABLE *from August to March.*

Apple Batter Pudding, Baked.

—INGREDIENTS *for a pudding large enough for 5 or 6 persons.*—1½ lb. of apples, ¼ lb. of finely-chopped suet, 3 eggs, 3 tablespoonfuls of flour, 1 pint of milk, a little grated nutmeg. AVERAGE COST, 11d.

Mix the flour to a smooth batter with the milk, add the eggs, which should be well whisked, and put the batter into a well-buttered pie-dish. Wipe the apples clean, but do not pare them ; cut them in halves and take out the cores ; lay them in the batter, rind uppermost; shake the suet on the top, over which also grate a little nutmeg; bake in a moderate oven for an hour, and sift over castor sugar when serving. This pudding is also very good with the apples pared, sliced and mixed with the batter.

TIME.—1 *hour.*

Apple Pudding, Boiled.

—INGREDIENTS.—*Suet crust, apples, sugar to taste, a few strips of lemon-peel, a few cloves.* AVERAGE COST, 10d.

Make a good suet crust by either of the given recipes, using for a moderate-sized pudding from ¾ to 1 lb. of flour, with the other ingredients in proportion. Butter a basin ; line it with some paste; pare, core, and cut the apples into slices, and fill the basin with these, putting the sugar in the middle, the flavouring, and cover with crust ; pinch the edges together, flour the cloth, place it over the pudding, tie it securely, and put it into plenty of fast-boiling water; let it boil from 2½ to 3 hours ; then turn it out of the basin and send to table quickly. Apple puddings may also be boiled in a cloth without a basin ; but, when made in this way, must be served without the least delay, as the crust soon becomes heavy. A netted cloth gives them a pretty appearance. This pudding does not spoil by being boiled an extra hour ; care, however, must be taken to keep it well covered with water all the time, and not to allow it to stop boiling.

TIME.— *From 2½ to 3 hours, according to the quality of the apples.*

SEASONABLE *from August to March.*

Apple Sauce (for Geese, Pork, &c.).

—INGREDIENTS *for a goose or pair of ducks.* —1½ lb. of apples, sifted sugar to taste, a piece of butter the size of a walnut; water. AVERAGE COST, 3d.

Peel, core and quarter the apples, and throw them into cold water to preserve their whiteness. Put them in a saucepan, with sufficient water to moisten them, and boil till soft enough to pulp. Beat them up, adding sugar to taste, and the butter.

TIME.—*According to the apples, about ¾ hour.*

Apple Snow. — INGREDIENTS *for moderate sized dish.*—6 large apples, the whites of 6 eggs, the rind of 1 lemon, 6 oz. of castor sugar. AVERAGE COST, 1s.

Peel, core and cut the apples into quarters, and put them into a saucepan with the lemon-peel, and sufficient water to prevent them from burning, about ¼ pint. When they are tender, take out the peel, beat them into a pulp, let them cool, and stir them to the whites of the eggs, which should be previously beaten to a strong froth. Add the sifted sugar, and continue the whisking until the mixture becomes quite stiff, and heap it on a glass dish. The dish may be garnished with preserved barberries or strips of bright-coloured jelly, and if liked a dish of custard may be served with it, or some whipped cream.

TIME.—*From* 30 *to* 40 *minutes to stew the apples.* SEASONABLE *from August to March.*

Apple Snowballs.—INGREDIENTS.

—2 *teacupfuls of rice,* 6 *apples, moist sugar, cloves.* AVERAGE COST, 6*d.*

Boil the rice and milk until three-parts done; then strain it off, and pare and core the apples without dividing them. Put a small quantity of sugar and a clove into each apple, mould the rice round them, and tie each ball separately in a cloth. Boil until the apples are tender; then take them up, remove the cloths, and serve.

TIME.—½ *hour to boil the rice separately;* ½ *to* 1 *hour with the apple.*

SEASONABLE *from August to March.*

Apple Soufflé.—INGREDIENTS *for soufflé for* 6 *persons.*—6 *oz. of rice,* 1 *quart of milk, rind of* ½ *lemon, sugar to taste, the yolks of* 4 *eggs, the whites of* 6, 1½ *oz. of butter,* 4 *tablespoonfuls of apple marmalade.* AVERAGE COST, 1*s.*

Boil the milk with the lemon-peel until the former is well flavoured; then strain it, put in the rice, and let it gradually swell over a slow fire, adding sufficient sugar to sweeten it nicely. Then crush the rice to a smooth pulp with the back of a wooden spoon; line the bottom and sides of a round cake-tin with it, and put it into the oven to set: turn it out of the tin dexterously, and be careful that the border of rice is firm in every part. Mix with the marmalade the beaten yolks of eggs and the butter, and stir these over the fire until the mixture thickens. Take it off the fire; to this add the whites of the eggs, which should be previously beaten to a strong froth; stir all together, and put it into the rice border. Bake in a moderate oven for about ½ hour, or until the soufflé rises very light. It should be watched, and served instantly it rises, or it will immediately fall after it is taken from the oven.

TIME.—½ *hour.*

SEASONABLE *from August to March.*

Apple Tart, Creamed.—INGREDIENTS *for* 1 *tart.*—2 *lbs. of apples,* 3 *oz. of sugar, a few strips of lemon-peel, puff paste.* AVERAGE COST, 1*s.* 3*d.*

Make the tart by the preceding recipe, omitting the icing. When it is baked, cut out the middle of the lid or crust, leaving a border all round the dish. Fill up with a nicely-made boiled custard, grate a little nutmeg over the top, and the pie is ready for table. Whipped cream may be substituted for the custard. This tart is usually eaten cold. It is rather an old-fashioned dish; but, at the same time, extremely nice.

TIME.—½ *to* ¾ *hour.*

SEASONABLE *from August to March.*

Apple Tart or Pie.—INGREDIENTS *for good sized tart.*—2 *lbs. of apples,* ¼ *lb. of moist sugar,* ½ *teaspoonful of finely-minced lemon-peel,* 1 *tablespoonful of lemon-juice.* AVERAGE COST, 10*d.*

Make puff-paste by either of the given recipes, with ½ lb. of flour; place a border of it round the edge of a pie-dish, and fill the dish with apples pared, cored and cut into slices; sweeten with moist sugar, putting it between the apples, add the lemon-peel and juice, and 2 or 3 table-

APPLE TART.

spoonfuls of water; cover with crust, cut it evenly round close to the edge of the pie-dish, and bake in a hot oven from ½ to ¾ hour, or rather longer, should the pie be very large. Whisk the white of an egg to a froth and when three-parts done, brush the pie over with this; then sprinkle upon it some sifted sugar, and then a few drops of water. Put the pie back into the oven, and finish baking, and be particularly careful that it does not catch or burn, *which it is very liable to do after the crust is iced.* If made with a plain crust, the icing may be omitted. The flavouring of an apple pie may be varied by a few spoonfuls of sherry, which very much improve the taste; a few cloves, or a few slices of quince.

TIME.—½ *hour before the crust is iced; 10 to 15 minutes afterwards.*

SEASONABLE *from August to March; but the apples become flavourless after February.*

Apple Trifle.—INGREDIENTS *for moderate-size* trifle.—2 *lbs. of apples, the rind of* ½ *lemon, 6 to 8 oz. of pounded sugar,* ½ *pint of milk,* ½ *pint of cream, 2 eggs.* AVERAGE COST, 1s. 8d.

Peel, core, and cut the apples into thin slices, and put them into a saucepan with 2 tablespoonfuls of water, 6 oz. of sugar, and the grated lemon-rind. Boil all together until quite tender, and pulp through a sieve; put them at the bottom of the dish to form a thick layer. Stir together the milk, half the cream, and the eggs, well beaten, with a little sugar, over the fire, and let the mixture thicken, but do not allow it to reach the boiling-point. When thick, take it off the fire; let it cool a little, then pour it over the apples. Whip the remainder of the cream with sugar, lemon-peel, &c., the same as for other trifles; heap it high over the custard, and garnish with strips of bright apple jelly, preserved cherries, &c.

TIME.—*from 30 to 40 minutes to stew the apples; 10 minutes to stir the custard over the fire.*

SEASONABLE *from August to March.*

Apple Wine.—INGREDIENTS.—10 *lb. of sugar, 4 gallons of cider.* AVERAGE COST, 2s. 6d. *per gallon.*

Put the cider and sugar into a cask that it does not fill within a gallon, and let it stand in a cool place, with the bung out for 2 days, then bung it, leaving a small vent, until the fermentation is over; then bung it securely, and the wine will be ready in a year. The cider used for this wine must be pure and made from ripe, sound fruit, or the wine will not be a success.

TIME.—12 *months in cask.*

SEASONABLE — *make in January or February.*

Apples à la Portugaise.—INGREDIENTS *for* 1 *dish.*—7 *or* 8 *good boiling apples,* ½ *pint of water,* 6 *oz. of sugar, a little apple marmalade, preserved cherries.* AVERAGE COST, 1s.

Peel the apples, and, with a scoop, take out the cores; boil the fruit in the above proportion of sugar and water, without being too much done, and take care the apples do not break. Have ready some apple marmalade; cover the bottom of a glass dish with this, level it, and lay the apples in a sieve to drain; pile then neatly on the marmalade, raising them in the centre, and ornament with the preserved cherries. A plain boiled custard poured over makes a change in this dish.

TIME.—*From 20 to 30 minutes to stew the apples.*

SEASONABLE *from August to March.*

Apples and Rice.—INGREDIENTS *for dish for* 6 *persons.*—8 *good-sized apples,* 3 *oz. of butter, the rind of* ½ *lemon grated,* 6 *oz. of rice,* 1½ *pint of milk, sugar to taste,* ½ *teaspoonful of grated nutmeg, some apricot jam.* AVERAGE COST, 1s.

Peel the apples, halve them, and take out the cores; put them into a stewpan with the butter, strew sufficient sifted sugar over to sweeten them nicely, and add the grated lemon-peel. Stew the apples very gently until tender, taking care they do not break. Boil the rice, with the milk, sugar, and nutmeg, until soft, and, when thoroughly done, dish it, piled high in the centre; arrange the apples on it, warm a little apricot jam, pour it over the whole, and serve hot.

TIME.—*About* 30 *minutes to stew the apples very gently; about* ¾ *hour to cook the rice.*

SEASONABLE *from August to March.*

Apples and Rice, A pretty Dish of.

INGREDIENTS *for dish for 6 persons.*—6 oz. of rice, 1 *quart of milk, the rind of ½ lemon, sugar to taste, ½ saltspoonful of salt, 8 apples, ¼ lb. of sugar, ¼ pint of water, ½ pint of boiled custard.* AVERAGE COST, 1s. 6d.

Flavour the milk with lemon-rind, by boiling them together for a few minutes; then take out the peel, and put in the rice, with sufficient sugar to sweeten it nicely, and boil gently until the rice is quite soft; then let it cool. In the meantime pare, quarter and core the apples, and boil them until tender in water, sweetened according to the kind of the fruit; and, when soft, lift them out on a sieve to drain. Put a middling-sized gallipot in the centre of a dish; lay the rice all round till the top of the gallipot is reached; smooth the rice with the back of a spoon, and stick the apples into it in rows, one row sloping to the right, and the next to the left. Set it in the oven to colour the apples; then, when required for table, remove the gallipot, garnish the rice with preserved fruits, and pour in the middle sufficient custard, made by the recipe for BOILED CUSTARD, to be level with the top of the rice, and serve hot.

TIME.—*From 20 to 30 minutes to stew the apples; ¼ hour to simmer the rice; ¼ hour to bake.*

SEASONABLE *from August to March.*

Apples, Buttered.

INGREDIENTS *for 1 dish.*—*Apple marmalade or a few good boiling apples, ½ pint of water, 6 oz. of sugar, 2 oz. of butter, a little apricot jam.* AVERAGE COST, 1s. 6d.

Pare the apples, and take out the cores with a scoop; boil up the sugar and water for a few minutes; then lay in the apples and simmer them very gently until tender, taking care not to let them break. Have ready sufficient marmalade made by the recipe for APPLE MARMALADE, flavoured with lemon, to cover the bottom of the dish; arrange the apples on this, with a piece of butter placed in each, and in between them a few spoonfuls of apricot jam or marmalade; put the dish in the oven for 10 minutes, then sprinkle over the top sifted sugar, and either brown it before the fire or with a salamander, and serve hot. The syrup that the apples were boiled in should be saved for another time.

TIME.—*From 20 to 30 minutes to stew the apples very gently; 10 minutes in the oven.*

Apples, Compote of (Soyer's Recipe).

INGREDIENTS *for dish for 4 or 5 persons.*—6 *ripe apples, 1 lemon, ½ lb. of lump sugar, ½ pint of water.* AVERAGE COST, 6d. to 9d.

Select the apples of a moderate size, peel them, cut them in halves, remove the cores, and rub each piece over with a little lemon. Put the sugar and water together into a lined saucepan, and let them boil until forming a thickish syrup, then lay in the apples with the rind of the lemon cut thin, and the juice of the same. Let the apples simmer till tender; then take them out very carefully, drain them on a sieve, and reduce the syrup by boiling it quickly for a few

COMPOTE OF APPLES

minutes. When both are cold, arrange the apples neatly on a glass dish, pour over the syrup, flavouring it with a little liqueur if liked, and garnish with strips of green angelica or preserved cherries. Smaller apples may be dressed in the same manner: they should not be divided in half, but peeled, and the cores pushed out with a vegetable-cutter.

TIME.—10 *minutes to boil the sugar and water together; from 20 to 30 minutes to simmer the apples.*

SEASONABLE *from August to March.*

Apples, Flanc of, or Apples

in a raised Crust.—Ingredients.—¾ lb. of short crust, 2 lbs. of moderate-sized apples, the rind and juice of ½ lemon, ½ lb. of white sugar, ¾ pint of water, a few strips of citron or other preserved fruits for garnish. Average Cost, 1s.

Make a plain stiff short crust, roll it out to the thickness of ½ inch, and butter an oval mould; line it with the crust, and press it carefully all round the sides, to obtain the form of the mould, but be particular not to break the paste. Pinch the part that just rises above the mould with the paste-pincers, and fill the case with flour; bake it for about ¾ hour; then take it out of the oven, remove the flour, put the case back in the oven for another ¼ hour, and do not allow it to get scorched. It is now ready for the apples, which should be prepared in the following manner: peel, and take out the cores with a small knife, or a scoop for the purpose, without dividing the apples; put them into a small lined saucepan, just capable of holding them, with sugar, water, lemon-juice and rind, in the above proportion. Simmer them very gently until tender; then take out the apples, let them cool, arrange them in the flanc, or case, and boil down the syrup until reduced to a thick jelly; pour it over the apples, and garnish.

A more simple flanc may be made by rolling out the paste, cutting the bottom of a round or oval shape, and then a narrow strip for the sides: these should be stuck on with the white of an egg to the bottom piece, and the flanc then filled with raw fruit, with sufficient sugar to sweeten it nicely. It will not require so long baking as in a mould; but the crust must be made everywhere of an equal thickness, and so perfectly joined that the juice does not escape. This dish may also be served hot, and should be garnished in the same manner, or a little melted apricot jam may be poured over the apples, which very much improves their flavour.

Time.—Altogether 1 hour to bake the flanc; from 30 to 40 minutes to stew the apples very gently.

Seasonable from August to March.

Apples, Ginger.—Ingredients for

3 dishes—1½ oz. of whole ginger, ¼ pint of whiskey or other spirit, 3 lbs. of apples, 2 lbs. of loaf sugar, the juice of 2 lemons. Average Cost, 2s. 6d.

Bruise the ginger, put it into a small jar, pour over whiskey to cover it, and let it remain for 3 days; then cut the apples into thin slices, after paring and coring them; add the sugar and the lemon juice, which should be strained; and simmer all together very gently until the apples are transparent, but not broken. Serve cold, and garnish the dish with slices of candied lemon-peel or preserved ginger.

Time.—3 days to soak the ginger; about ¾ hour to simmer the apples very gently.

Seasonable from August to March.

(A pretty Supper Dish.)

Apples, Iced, or Apple Hedge-

Hog.—Ingredients for dish for 6 persons. —About 2 dozen good boiling apples, 1 lb. of sugar, ½ pint of water, the rind of ½ lemon, minced very finely, the whites of 2 eggs, 2 tablespoonfuls of pounded sugar, a few sweet almonds. Average Cost, 1s. 9d. to 2s.

Peel and core a dozen of the apples without dividing them, and stew them very gently in a lined saucepan with ½ lb. of the sugar and ½ pint of water, and when tender lift them carefully on to a dish. Have ready the remainder of the apples, pared, cored and cut into thin slices; put them into the same syrup with the other ½ lb. of sugar, the lemon-peel, and boil gently until they are reduced to a marmalade; keeping them stirred, to prevent them from burning. Cover the bottom of the dish with some of the marmalade, and over that a layer of the stewed apples, in the insides of which, and between each, place some of the marmalade; then place another layer of apples, and fill up the cavities with marmalade as before, forming the whole into a raised oval shape. Whip the whites of the eggs to a stiff froth, mix with them the pounded sugar, and cover the apples very smoothly all over with the icing; blanch and cut each almond into 4 or 5 strips; place these strips at equal distances over the icing, sticking up; strew over a little rough pounded sugar, and put the dish in a very slow oven, to colour the almonds, and so allow the apples to get warm through. This dish may also be served cold, and makes a pretty supper one.

TIME.—20 to 30 *minutes to stew the apples.*
SEASONABLE *from August to March.*

Apples in Red Jelly. — INGRE-
DIENTS *for* 1 *dish.*—6 *good-sized apples,* 6 *cloves,* 6 *oz. of pounded sugar,* 1 *lemon,* 2 *teacupfuls of water,* 1 *tablespoonful of gelatine, a few drops of prepared cochineal.*
AVERAGE COST, *with the garnish,* 10d.

Peel and take out the cores of the apples, either with a scoop or a small silver knife, and put into each apple a clove and as much sifted sugar as it will hold. Place them, without touching each other, in a large pie-dish; add more white sugar, the juice of 1 lemon, and 2 teacupfuls of water. Bake in the oven, with a dish over them, until they are done. Look at them frequently, and, as each apple is cooked, place it in a glass dish. They must not be left in the oven after they are done, or they will break, and so would spoil the appearance of the dish. When the apples are neatly arranged in the dish without touching each other, strain the liquor in which they have been stewing into a lined saucepan; add to it the rind of the lemon, and a tablespoonful of gelatine which has been previously dissolved in cold water, and, if not sweet, a little more sugar, and 6 cloves. Boil till quite clear; colour with a few drops of prepared cochineal, and strain the jelly

through a double muslin into a jug; let it cool a *little;* then pour it into the dish round the apples. When quite cold, garnish the tops of the apples with a bright-coloured marmalade, jelly, or the white of an egg beaten to a strong froth, with a little sifted sugar.

TIME.—30 to 50 *minutes to bake the apples.*
SEASONABLE *from August to March.*
(*A pretty Supper Dish.*)

Apples, Stewed, and Custard.
—INGREDIENTS *for large dish.*—8 *good-sized apples, the rind of* ½ *lemon,* ½ *lb. of sugar,* ¾ *pint of water,* ½ *pint of custard.*
AVERAGE COST, 1s.

Pare and take out the cores of the apples without dividing them, and, if possible, leave the stalks on; boil the sugar and water together for 10 minutes; then put in the apples with the lemon-rind, and simmer gently until they are tender, taking care not to let them break. Dish them neatly on a glass dish with the stalks upwards, reduce the syrup by boiling it quickly for a few minutes; let it cool a little, then pour it over the apples. Have ready ½ pint of custard made by the recipe for BOILED CUSTARD; pour it round, but not over, the apples when they are quite cold, and garnish with a little bright-coloured jelly and some blanched almonds.

TIME.—20 to 30 *minutes to stew the apples.*
SEASONABLE *from August to March.*
(*A pretty Dish for a Juvenile Supper.*)

Apples, To Preserve, in
Quarters (in imitation of Ginger). — INGRE-
DIENTS.—6 *lbs. of apples,* 4½ *lbs. of sugar,* 2 *oz. of the best white ginger,* 1 *pint of water.*
AVERAGE COST, *for this quantity,* 2s.

Peel, core and quarter the apples, and put the fruit, sugar and ginger in layers into a wide-mouthed jar, and let them remain for 2 days; then infuse the ginger in 1 pint of boiling water, and cover it closely, and let it remain for 1 day. Put the apples, &c., into a preserving-pan with the water strained from the ginger, and boil till the apples look clear and the syrup is rich, which will be in about an hour. The rind of a lemon may be added just before the apples have finished boiling ; and great care must be taken not to break the pieces of apple in putting them into the jars. Serve on glass dishes for dessert.

TIME.—2 *days for the apples to remain in the jar with sugar, &c.* ; 1 *day to infuse the ginger* ; *about* 1 *hour to boil the apples.*

SEASONABLE, *this should be made in September, October or November.*

Apricot Bouchées.—INGREDIENTS

for 1 *dozen.*—½ *tin of apricots, or* 6 *French ones if in season, some puff paste* (*the cuttings from tarts serve for these*), *loaf sugar,* ¼ *pint of cream.* AVERAGE COST, 1s.

Stamp out small rounds of paste and make a smaller indentation with a round cutter about the size of the fruit, sift over powdered sugar and bake a nice brown in a quick oven.

If fresh fruit is used, cut them in half, take out the stones, and boil in syrup made from loaf sugar and a little water for a few minutes till tender ; the others require no preparation. When the pastry comes out of the oven, press lightly in the centre of each piece to make room for the fruit, and when both are cold lay ½ an apricot hollow upwards in each and fill with the cream whipped to a froth.

SEASONABLE *at any time.*

Apricot Cream.—INGREDIENTS *for*

quart mould.—12 *ripe apricots,* ½ *lb. of sugar,* 1½ *pint of milk, the yolks of* 5 *eggs,* 1 *oz. of gelatine.* AVERAGE COST, 2s. 2d.

Divide the apricots, take out the stones, and boil them in a syrup made with ¼ lb. of sugar and ¼ pint of water, until they form a thin marmalade, which rub through a sieve. Boil the milk with the other ¼ lb. of sugar, let it cool a little, then mix with it the yolks of eggs which have been previously well beaten ; put this mixture into a jug,

place this jug in boiling water, and stir it one way over the fire until it thickens ; but on no account let it boil. Strain through a sieve, add the gelatine, previously boiled with a small quantity of water, and keep stirring it till nearly cold ; then mix the cream with the apricots ; stir well, put it into an oiled mould, and, if convenient, set it on ice ; at any rate, in a very cool place. It should turn out on the dish without any difficulty. In winter-time, when fresh apricots are not obtainable, tinned fruit may be substituted for them.

TIME.—*From* 20 *to* 30 *minutes to boil the apricots.*

SEASONABLE *in August, September, and October.*

Apricot Jam, or Marmalade.

—INGREDIENTS. — *To every lb. of ripe apricots, weighed after being skinned and stoned, allow* ¾ *lb. of sugar.* AVERAGE COST, 6d. *to* 8d. *per pot.*

Pare the apricots, which should be ripe, as thinly as possible, break them in half, and remove the stones. Weigh the fruit, and to every lb. allow the above proportion of loaf sugar. Pound the sugar very finely in a mortar, strew it over the apricots, which should be placed on dishes, and let them remain for 12 hours. Break the stones, blanch the kernels, and put them with the sugar and fruit into a preserving-pan. Let these simmer very gently until clear ; take out the pieces of apricot singly as they become so, and, as fast as the scum rises, carefully remove it. Put the apricots into small jars, pour over them the syrup and kernels, cover the jam with pieces of paper dipped in the purest salad-oil, and stretch over the top of the jars tissue paper, cut about 2 inches larger and brushed over with the white of an egg : when dry, it will be perfectly hard and air-tight.

TIME.—12 *hours, sprinkled with sugar* ; *about* ¾ *hour to boil the jam.*

SEASONABLE.—*Make this in August or September.*

Apricot Pudding, Baked.

INGREDIENTS *for good-sized pudding.*—1 *dozen apricots,* ¾ *pint of bread-crumbs,* 1 *pint of milk,* 3 *oz. of pounded sugar,* 3 *eggs,* 1 *glass of sherry.* AVERAGE COST, *in full season,* 1s. 6d.

Make the milk boiling hot, and pour it on to the bread-crumbs; when half cold, add the sugar, the well-whisked eggs, and the sherry. Divide the apricots in half, scald them until they are soft, and break them up with a spoon, adding a few of the kernels, which should be well pounded in a mortar; then mix the fruit and other ingredients together, put a border of paste round the dish, fill with the mixture, and bake the pudding from ½ to ¾ hour.

TIME.—½ *to* ¾ *hour.*

SEASONABLE *from August to October.*

Apricot Tart.

INGREDIENTS *for* 1 *tart.*—*Sufficient apricots to fill a pie dish, sugar to taste, puff-paste or short crust.* AVERAGE COST, *in season,* 1s. 3d.

Break the apricots in half, take out the stones, and put them into a pie-dish, in the centre of which place a very small cup or jar, bottom uppermost; sweeten with good moist sugar, but add no water. Line the edge of the dish with paste, put on the cover. Bake from ½ to ¾ hour, according to size; and if puff paste is used, glaze it about 10 minutes before the pie is done, and put it into the oven again to set the glaze. Short crust merely requires a little sifted sugar sprinkled over it before being sent to table. Green apricots make very good tarts, but they should be boiled with a little sugar and water before they are covered with the crust.

TIME.—½ *to* ¾ *hour.*

SEASONABLE *in August, September and October; green ones rather earlier.*

Apricots, Compote of.

INGREDIENTS *for compote for* 4 *or* 5 *persons.*—½ *pint of syrup (see* SYRUP*),* 12 *green apricots.* AVERAGE COST, 9d.

Make the syrup by the given recipe, and, when it is ready, put in the apricots whilst the syrup is boiling. Simmer them very gently until tender, taking care not to let them break; take them out carefully, arrange them on a glass dish, let the syrup cool a little, pour it over the apricots, and when cold, serve.

TIME.—*From* 15 *to* 20 *minutes to simmer the apricots.*

SEASONABLE *in June and July, with green apricots.*

Note.—A very nice compote can also be made at a small cost with tinned apricots by putting them in a syrup made from their juice and loaf sugar when made hot, letting them cool in this, then adding a glass or two of liqueur.

Apricots, Flanc of, or
Compote of Apricots in a Raised Crust.

INGREDIENTS *for* 1 *dish.*—¾ *lb. of short crust (see* CRUST*),* 12 *good-sized apricots,* ¾ *pint of water,* ½ *lb. of sugar.* AVERAGE COST, 1s. 6d.

Make a short crust by the given recipe, and line a mould with it. Boil the sugar and water together for 10 minutes; halve the apricots, take out the stones, and simmer them in the syrup until tender; watch them carefully, and take them up, for fear they should break. Arrange them neatly in the flanc or case; boil the syrup until reduced to a jelly; pour it over the fruit, and serve either hot or cold. Greengages, plums of all kinds, peaches, &c., may be done in the same manner, as also currants, raspberries, gooseberries, strawberries, &c.; but with the last-named fruits, a little currant-juice added to them will be found an improvement.

TIME.—*Altogether,*1 *hour to bake the flanc, from* 15 *to* 20 *minutes to simmer the apricots.*

SEASONABLE *in July, August and September.*

Note.—The pretty appearance of this dish depends on the fruit being whole; as each apricot is done, it should be taken out of the syrup immediately.

Apricots and Rice.—Ingredients

for dish for 6 or 8 persons.—*A breakfastcup-ful of rice, a quart of milk, a large cupful of sugar, 4 eggs, 2 dozen ripe apricots, a small piece of butter, 3 tablespoonfuls of apricot marmalade, 2 lemons.* Average Cost, *when the fruit is in full season,* 4s.

Put the rice, milk, butter and 2 table-spoonfuls of sugar in a lined saucepan, together with the rind of 1 lemon, and let all simmer gently until the milk is all absorbed and the rice tender ; then add the eggs, beaten, and boil again, stirring all the time till the eggs are cooked. Take out the lemon-rind, and after putting a galli-pot in the centre of a glass dish, pile the rice round it neatly, smoothing it so as to let it gradually slope towards the edge of

APRICOTS AND RICE.

the dish, leaving the gallipot in until the rice is cold. Take 2 dozen apricots, pare and stone them ; make a syrup of the re-mainder of the sugar with the lemon-juice ; when it is boiling throw in the fruit and boil them quickly, adding a few of the kernels, chopped, for flavouring. Next remove the gallipot from the rice, and put a layer of the apricot marmalade at the bottom of the hollow, with a little of the syrup, and pile the fruit in a pyramid as shown in accompanying illustration. Use the remainder of the kernels for garnishing the rice as a tipsy cake would be.

Time *for boiling the apricots, about 5 minutes.*

Seasonable *in August and September.*

Apricot Iced Eggs. — Ingredi-

ents.—*Apricots or apricot jam, pounded sugar, cream, flavouring of vanilla, saffron.* Average Cost, 3d. *each ice.*

Make some plain white ice as directed in "Ice Cream," and flavour it with vanilla, and make half the quantity with the apricots, colouring it with saffron so as to be the yellow of the yolk of an egg.

Take some small moulds, sold for the purpose, shaped respectively as whole eggs and yolks. Fill the round ones with the yellow apricot ice and freeze, then work the plain ice in the freezing pot, and when ready fill up the whole egg moulds, leav-ing a hollow in the centre, in which

APRICOTS.

place the apricot ices. Close the moulds, and when the ices are frozen, dip the moulds in water and take them out with a fork.

Time.—*25 minutes to freeze.*

Seasonable *in August and September.*

Apricot Wine.—Ingredients.—

12 *lbs. of ripe apricots, 6 oz. of loaf sugar to every quart of liquor.* Average Cost, *when the fruit is in full season,* 1s. *per quart.*

Wipe the apricots, cut them in pieces, and let them boil in two gallons of water. After boiling up let them simmer till the liquor is strongly impregnated with the flavour of the fruit. Strain through a hair-sieve and put 6 oz. of sugar to every quart of liquor. Boil up again, skim very care-fully, and as soon as no more scum appears, put it into an earthen pan. Bottle the following day if the wine is quite clear, and put a lump of sugar into each bottle. It should be a fine wine in 6 months.

Time.—*2 hours to boil the fruit.*

Seasonable.—*Make this in August or September.*

B

April—Dinner for Twelve Persons.

MENU. (*English.*)	Quantity.	Average Cost.	MENU. (*French.*)
		s. d.	
Julienne.	5 pints.	4 6	Julienne.
Stuffed Trout, Fried Whitebait.	3 fish. 2 qts.	7 0 4 0	Truite Farcie et Frite. Blanchaille.
Lobster Cream. Chicken Rissoles.	2 mlds. 2 dishes.	4 0 3 6	Crème de Homard. Croquettes de Volaille.
Quarter of Lamb. Potatoes. Sprouts.	1 joint. 4 lbs. ea.	7 0 1 0	Quartier d'Agneau. Pommes de Terre. Choux.
Ducklings.	3 birds.	9 0	Canetons.
Rhubarb Tart. Vanilla Cream.	2 2 mlds.	2 0 3 6	Tourte à la Rhubarbe. Crème de Vanille.
Cheese Soufflé.	2	2 6	Soufflé de Parmesan.
		£2 8 0	

April—Dinner for Ten Persons.

MENU. (*English.*)	Quantity.	Average Cost.	MENU. (*French.*
		s. d.	
Spring Soup.	5 pints.	3 2	Printanière.
Salmon, Tartar Sauce.	4 lbs. ½ pint.	7 0 0 9	Saumon, Sauce Tartare.
Oyster Patties. Lamb Cutlets.	10 12	4 6 4 0	Petits Pâtes aux Huitres. Côtelettes d'Agneau.
Roast Fillet of Veal. Ham. Potatoes. Spinach.	1 joint. 1 3 lbs. ea.	5 6 6 6 0 9	Rouelle de Veau. Jambon. Pommes de Terre. Epinards.
Ptarmigans.	3 birds.	4 0	Ptarmigans.
Orange Fritters. Gooseberry Tart. Custard.	2 dishes. 1 1½ pint.	1 8 1 4 0 1½	Beignets d'Orange. Tourte aux Groseilles. Crème.
Celery Salad.	2	1 0	Salade de Celeri.
		£2 1 0	

April—Dinner for Eight Persons.

MENU. (*English.*)	Quantity.	Average Cost.	MENU: (*French.*)
		s. d.	
Custard Soup.	2½ pints.	3 0	Consommé à la Royale.
Fried Soles.	3 fish.	4 6	Soles Frits.
Lobster Cutlets. Chicken Cream.	1 dish. 1 dish.	3 0 4 0	Côtelettes de Homard. Crème de Volaille.
Leg of Lamb. Potatoes. Spinach.	1 joint. 3 lbs. ea.	6 0 0 9	Gigot d'Agneau. Pommes de Terre. Epinards.
Rhubarb Tart. Stone Cream.	1 1 mould.	1 6 2 0	Tourte à la Rhubarbe. Crème de Tous-le-Mois.
Cheese Straws.	1 dish.	0 9	Pailles de Parmesan.
		£1 5 6	

April—Dinners for from Six to Twelve Persons.

Clear Soup.

Whiting.

Curried Rabbit.
Beef Rissoles.

Leg of Mutton.
Potatoes.
Sprouts.

Ptarmigan.

Rhubarb Tart.
Custard.
Vanilla Cream.

Gorgonzola
Cheese.

Oysters.
Brown Bread-and-Butter.

Spring Soup.

Turbot, Hollandaise Sauce.

Lamb Cutlets and Spinach.
Chicken Rissoles.

Sirloin, Horseradish Sauce.
Potatoes. Sprouts.

Salad.

Cabinet Pudding
Compôte of
Fruit.

Stilton.
Celery.

Appétisans.

Julienne.

Boiled Salmon.
Cucumber.

Lobster Cream.
Veal Croquettes.

Leg of Lamb.
Potatoes.
Spinach.

Gooseberry Tart.
Whipped Cream.
Orange Jelly.

Cheese Biscuits.

Oxtail Soup.

Filleted Soles.

Stewed Kidneys.

Saddle of Mutton.
Potatoes.
Broccoli.

Asparagus.

Canary Pudding.
Blanc-Mange.
Pastry Sandwiches.

Cheese Straws.

Herrings' Roes, Devilled.

April—Plain Family Dinners for.

No. 1.

Sunday.—Clear soup.—Leg of mutton, vegetables. — Gooseberry tart, cream. — Cheese, celery.—Dessert.

Monday.—Roast ducks. — Cold mutton, vegetables, salad. — Apple Charlotte. — Cheese.

Tuesday.—Fillets of turbot, tartare sauce. —Rissoles made from remains of mutton, broiled steak, vegetables.—Macaroni cheese.

Wednesday.—Vegetable soup. — Hashed duck, boiled beef, vegetables.—Rhubarb tart.—Cheese.

Thursday.—Boiled soles.—Roast chicken, ham, cold beef, vegetables.—Gooseberry fool.

Friday.—Pea soup. — Curried chicken, cold beef, salad, vegetables.—Cabinet pudding.

Saturday.—Salmon cutlets, sharp sauce. —Roast loin of mutton, stuffed, vegetables. —Cheesecakes.

No. 2.

Sunday.—Roast leg or quarter of lamb, brocoli, potatoes.—Rhubarb tart, custard. —Dessert.

Monday.—Skate and caper sauce.—Cold mutton, mashed potatoes, salad.—Lemon pudding.

Tuesday.—Soup.—Hashed mutton, potatoes.—Baked bread and sultana pudding. —Cheese.

Wednesday.—Roast ribs of beef, Yorkshire pudding, greens, potatoes.—Stewed fruit, boiled rice.

Thursday.—Boiled salmon, melted butter.—Cold beef, salad, mashed potatoes.— Cheese biscuits.

Friday.—Mayonnaise of cold salmon.— Hashed beef, fried potatoes.—Baked rice pudding.

Saturday.—Soup from beef bones, with vegetables.—Steak pie, potatoes.—Rhubarb fool.

April—Vegetarian Dinners for.

No. 1.

Vermicelli Soup.

Haricot Beans and Mashed Potatoes.
Plain Fritters.

Savoury Eggs.

Apple Puffs.

No. 2.

Vegetable Soup.

Poached Eggs on Toast,
Potato Salad.

Stewed Rhubarb and Rice.

Pastry Sandwiches.

April—Dinner Table Decorations for.

Those who live in the country will have no trouble in making their tables look pretty if they only go to the fields instead of their gardens, for the flowers for decoration. None can be prettier than these for daylight dinners, that one can scarcely avoid in spring; buttercups, daffodils, and all yellow flowers look better without artificial light, mixed with plenty of tender green foliage or feathery grass. It must be remembered, however, that these wild flowers are not so strong as the cultivated ones, and require plenty of water.

They should be put at once into the vases intended for them, and arranged as lightly and naturally as possible. The cloth should never be strewed with wild flowers, as it may be with hothouse or garden ones; and the former always look well in clear glass where their stems may be seen.

In towns, table decoration in April is not so easy a matter; for, except for those who do not mind an early visit to a market, flowers are scarce and dear. Dessert centres come as aids to eke out a few flowers, and the soft Ponjee silks, or even a cheap art muslin can be made to look very pretty if cleverly puckered and the flowers introduced into their folds.

Fruit, with the exception of grapes, which are now always obtainable, cannot be depended upon to make a dinner-table decoration, there being so few kinds in season during this month.

April, Things in Season.

Fish.—Bream, brill, carp, crabs, dory, flounders, halibut, ling, lobsters, red and grey mullet, mussels, oysters, perch, prawns, salmon (but rather scarce and expensive), shad, shrimps, skate, smelts, soles, tench, turbot, whitings.

Meat.—Beef, lamb, mutton, veal.

Poultry. — Chickens, ducklings, fowls, pigeons, pullets, rabbits.

Game.—Leverets.

Vegetables. — Broccoli, celery, lettuces, young onions, parsnips, radishes, small salad, sea-kale, spinach, sprouts, various herbs.

Fruit. — Apples, nuts, pears, forced cherries, &c.; for tarts, rhubarb.

Arrowroot.—This when unadulterated, is one of the most nutritious and delicate of foods, but it is too often sold mixed with more or less of potato starch. It being so often given to invalids it should be bought of a good firm, such as Crosse and Blackwell, to ensure obtaining the genuine article. When adulterated it soon becomes thin if left after mixing, while the pure arrowroot if mixed to a jelly will remain firm for days.

It is obtained from a plant cultivated in both the East and West Indies, but it is considered that from the latter the best is obtained.

Arrowroot Biscuits, or Drops.

—INGREDIENTS *for 3 or 4 dozen biscuits.*— 6 *oz. of butter*, 4 *eggs*, ½ *lb. of flour*, 6 *oz. of arrowroot*, ½ *lb. of pounded loaf sugar.* AVERAGE COST, 1s. 6d.

Beat the butter to a cream; whisk the eggs to a strong froth, add them to the butter, stir in the flour a little at a time, and beat the mixture well. Break down all the lumps from the arrowroot, and add that with the sugar to the other ingredients. Mix all well together, drop the dough on a buttered tin, in pieces the size of a shilling,

and bake the biscuits about ¼ hour in a slow oven. If the whites of the eggs are separated from the yolks, and both are beaten separately before being added to the other ingredients, the biscuits will be much lighter.

TIME.—¼ *hour.*

SEASONABLE *at any time.*

Arrowroot Blancmange.—INGREDIENTS *for* 1½ *pint mould.*—5 *tablespoonfuls of arrowroot*, 1½ *pint of milk, the rind of* ½ *lemon, sugar to taste.* AVERAGE COST, 6d.

Mix to a smooth batter the arrowroot with ½ pint of the milk; put the other pint on the fire, with the lemon-peel, and let the milk steep until it is well flavoured; then strain the milk, and add it, boiling, to the mixed arrowroot; sweeten it with sifted sugar, and let it boil, stirring it all the time, till it thickens sufficiently to come from the saucepan. Grease a mould with pure salad-oil, pour in the blancmange, and, when quite set, turn it

ARROWROOT.

out on a dish, and pour round it some stewed fruit, or garnish it with red jam. A tablespoonful of brandy, stirred in just before the blancmange is moulded, very much improves the flavour of this sweet dish.

TIME.—*Altogether*, ½ *hour.*

SEASONABLE *at any time.*

Arrowroot Jelly (for Invalids).— INGREDIENTS *for* ½ *pint.*—1 *dessertspoonful of arrowroot*, ½ *pint of water, sugar to taste, nutmeg or other flavouring.* AVERAGE COST, 1½d.

Mix the arrowroot to a smooth paste with a little water and put the rest to boil in a lined saucepan. Pour the arrowroot into the water when it boils, stir it briskly for 5 minutes, then flavour and sweeten to taste. Pour into a wet cup or small mould.

Arrowroot Pudding, Baked or Boiled.

— INGREDIENTS, *for moderate-sized pudding.*—2 *tablespoonfuls of arrow-root*, 1½ *pint of milk*, 1 *oz. of butter, the rind of* ½ *lemon*, 2 *heaped tablespoonfuls of sugar, a little grated nutmeg, puff paste.* AVERAGE COST, 8*d.*

Mix the arrowroot with as much cold milk as will make it into a smooth batter, moderately thick; put the remainder of the milk into a stewpan with the lemon-peel, and let it infuse for about ½ hour; when it boils, strain it gently to the batter, stirring it all the time to keep it smooth; then add the butter; beat this well in until thoroughly mixed, and sweeten with moist sugar. Put the mixture into a pie-dish, round which has been placed a border of paste; grate a little nutmeg over the top, and bake the pudding from 1 to 1¼ hour in a moderate oven, or boil it the same length of time in a well-buttered basin. To enrich this pudding, stir to the other ingredients, just before it is put in the oven, 2 well-whisked eggs, and a tablespoonful of brandy.

TIME.—1 to 1¼ *hour, baked or boiled.*
SEASONABLE *at any time.*

Arrowroot Sauce (for puddings).

—INGREDIENTS, *for sauce for one pudding.* —1 *dessertspoonful of arrowroot*, 4 *dessertspoonfuls of pounded sugar, the juice of* 1 *lemon*, ½ *pint of water.* AVERAGE COST, 3*d.*

Mix the arrowroot smoothly with the water; put this into a stewpan; add the sugar, strained lemon-juice, and grated nutmeg. Stir these ingredients over the fire until they boil, when the sauce is ready for use. A small quantity of wine, or any liqueur, would very much improve the flavour of this sauce: it is usually served

with bread, or any dry pudding that is not very rich.

TIME.—*Altogether*, 15 *minutes.*

Arrowroot, To Make.

—INGREDIENTS.—1 *dessertspoonful of arrowroot*, 3 *tablespoonfuls of cold water*, ½ *pint of boiling water.* AVERAGE COST, 2*d. per pint.*

Mix the arrowroot smoothly in a basin with the cold water, then pour on it the *boiling* water, *stirring* all the time. The water must be *boiling* at the time it is poured on the mixture, or it will not thicken; if mixed with hot water only, it must be put into a clean saucepan, and boiled until it thickens; but this occasions more trouble, and is quite unnecessary, if the water is boiling at first. Put the arrowroot into a tumbler, sweeten it with lump sugar, and flavour it with grated nutmeg or cinnamon, or a piece of lemon-peel, or, when allowed, a little sherry or brandy. As arrowroot is in itself flavourless and insipid, it is almost necessary to add the wine to make it palatable. Arrowroot made with milk instead of water is far nicer, but is not so easily digested. It should be mixed in the same manner, with 3 tablespoonfuls of cold milk, the boiling milk then poured on it, and well stirred. When made in this manner, no wine need be added, but merely sugar, and a little grated nutmeg or lemon-peel.

TIME.—*If obliged to be boiled*, 2 *minutes.*

Artichokes, Boiled.

— INGREDIENTS.—*To each* ½ *gallon of water allow* 1 *heaped tablespoonful of salt, a piece of soda the size of a shilling; artichokes.* AVERAGE COST, 6*d. each.*

Wash the artichokes well in several waters; see that no insects remain about them, and trim away the leaves at the bottom. Cut off the stems and put them into *boiling* water, to which has been added salt and soda in the above proportion. Keep the saucepan uncovered, and let them boil quickly until tender; ascertain when they are done by thrusting a fork in them, or by trying if the leaves can be easily removed. Take them out, let them drain for a minute or two, and serve in a napkin, or with a little white sauce poured over. A tureen of oiled butter should accompany them. This vegetable, unlike

ARTICHOKES.

any other, is considered better for being gathered two or three days before, but they must be well soaked and washed previous to dressing.

TIME.—20 *to* 25 *minutes after water boils.*
SEASONABLE *from July to the beginning of September.*

Artichokes, A French Mode

of Cooking. — INGREDIENTS. — 5 *or* 6 *artichokes; to each ½ gallon of water allow* 1 *heaped tablespoonful of salt,* ½ *teaspoonful of pepper,* 1 *bunch of savoury herbs,* 2 *oz. of butter.* AVERAGE COST, 6*d. each.*

Cut the ends of the leaves, as also the stems; put the artichokes into boiling water, with the above proportion of salt, pepper, herbs and butter; let them boil quickly until tender, keeping the lid of the saucepan off, and when the leaves come out easily, they are cooked enough. To keep them a beautiful green, put a large piece of cinder into a muslin bag, and let it boil with them. Serve with plain oiled butter.

TIME.—20 *to* 25 *minutes.*
SEASONABLE *from July to the beginning of September.*

Artichokes, Fried.—INGREDIENTS.

— 6 *artichokes, salt and water; for the batter—*¼ *lb. of flour, a little salt, the yolk of* 1 *egg, milk, lard for frying.* AVERAGE COST, 6*d. each.*

Trim and boil the artichokes, and rub them over with lemon-juice, to keep them white. When they are quite tender, take them up, remove the chokes, and divide the bottoms; dip each piece into batter, fry them in hot lard or dripping, and garnish the dish with crisped parsley.

TIME.—20 *minutes to boil the artichokes;* 5 *to* 7 *minutes to fry them.*
SEASONABLE *from July to the beginning of September.*

Artichokes à l'Italienne.—IN-

GREDIENTS.—6 *artichokes, salt and butter, about* ½ *pint of good gravy.* AVERAGE COST, 6*d. each.*

Trim and cut the artichokes into quarters, and boil them until tender in water mixed with a little salt and butter. When done, drain them well, and lay them all round the dish, with the leaves outside. Have ready some good gravy, highly flavoured with mushrooms; reduce it until quite thick, and pour it round the artichokes, and serve.

TIME.—20 *to* 25 *minutes to boil the artichokes.*
SEASONABLE *from July to the beginning of September.*

Artichokes, Boiled Jerusalem.

—INGREDIENTS.—*To each* ½ *gallon of water allow* 1 *heaped tablespoonful of salt; artichokes.* AVERAGE COST, 2*d. per lb.*

Wash, peel, and shape the artichokes in a round or oval form, and put them into a saucepan with sufficient *cold* water to cover them, salted in the above proportion. Let them boil gently until tender; take them up, drain them, and serve; send to table with them a tureen of melted butter or cream sauce, a little of which may be poured over the artichokes.

TIME.—*About* 20 *minutes after the water boils.*
SEASONABLE *from September to June.*

Artichokes, Mashed Jerusalem.

INGREDIENTS.—To each ½ gallon of water allow 1 oz. of salt, 15 or 16 artichokes, 1 oz. of butter, pepper and salt to taste. AVERAGE COST, 2d. per lb.

Boil the artichokes as in the preceding recipe until tender; drain and press the water from them, and beat them up with a fork. When thoroughly mashed and free from lumps, put them into a saucepan with the butter and a seasoning of white pepper and salt; keep stirring over the fire until the artichokes are quite hot, and serve. A pretty way of serving Jerusalem artichokes is to shape the artichokes in the form of a pear, and to serve them covered with white sauce, garnished with Brussels sprouts.

TIME.—About 20 minutes.

SEASONABLE from September to June

Artichoke (Jerusalem) Soup.

INGREDIENTS.—3 slices of lean bacon or ham, ½ a head of celery, 1 turnip, 1 onion, 3 oz. of butter, 4 lbs. of artichokes, 1 pint of boiling milk, salt and cayenne to taste, 2 lumps of sugar, 2½ quarts of white stock. AVERAGE COST, per quart, 1s. 2d.

Put the bacon and vegetables, which should be cut into thin slices, into the stewpan with the butter. Braise these for ¼ of an hour, keeping them well stirred. Wash and pare the artichokes, and after cutting them into thin slices, add them, with a pint of stock, to the other ingredients. When these have gently stewed down to a smooth pulp, put in the remainder of the stock. Stir it well, adding the seasoning, and when it has simmered for five minutes, pass it through a strainer. Pour it back into the stewpan, let it again simmer five minutes, taking care to skim it well, and stir it to the boiling milk or cream. Serve with small sippets of bread fried in butter.

TIME.—1 hour.

SEASONABLE from June to October.

Asparagus, Boiled.

INGREDIENTS.—To each ½ gallon of water allow 1 heaped tablespoonful of salt, asparagus. AVERAGE COST, in full season, for 100 heads, 2s. 6d.

Asparagus should be dressed as soon as possible after it is cut, although it may be kept for a day or two by putting the stalks into cold water; yet to be good, like every other vegetable, it cannot be cooked too fresh. Scrape the white part of the stems, beginning from the head, and throw them into cold water; then tie them into bundles of about 20 each, keeping the heads all one way, and cut the stalks evenly that

ASPARAGUS.

they may all be the same length; put them into boiling water, with salt in the above proportion; keep them boiling quickly until tender, with the saucepan uncovered When the asparagus is done, dish it upon toast, which should be dipped in the water it was cooked in, and leave the white ends outward each way, with the points meeting in the middle. Serve with a tureen of oiled butter.

TIME.—15 to 18 minutes after the water boils.

SEASONABLE.—May be had forced from January, but cheapest in May, June and July.

Asparagus Pudding.

INGREDIENTS for 1 pudding.—½ pint of asparagus cut in peas, 4 eggs, 2 tablespoonfuls of flour, 1 tablespoonful of very finely minced ham, 1 oz. of butter, pepper and salt to taste, milk. AVERAGE COST, 2s. 6d.

Cut up the nice green tender parts of asparagus, about the size of peas; put them into a basin with the eggs, which should be well beaten, and the flour, ham, butter, pepper and salt. Mix all these ingredients well together, and moisten with sufficient milk to make the pudding of the consistency of thick batter; put it into a pint buttered mould, tie it down tightly with a floured cloth, place it in *boiling water*, and let it boil for 2 hours; turn it out of the mould on to a hot dish, and pour plain melted or oiled butter *round*, but not over the pudding. Green pea pudding may be made in exactly the same manner, substituting peas for the asparagus.

TIME.—2 *hours*.

SEASONABLE *in May, June, and July*.

Asparagus Sauce.—INGREDIENTS *for sauce for good-sized dish.—A medium-sized bundle of green asparagus, 1 oz. of butter, 3 green onions, a little parsley, a large lump of sugar, 4 tablespoonfuls of Tournée Sauce.* AVERAGE COST, 1s. 4d.

Break the asparagus where it is tender, and after washing it, put it into boiling water with salt in it to make it green.

ASPARAGUS TONGS.

When tender take the asparagus out, put it in cold water and drain on a cloth till all the moisture is absorbed. Put the butter, parsley and onions sliced into a pan, and afterwards lay in the asparagus and fry over a sharp fire for 5 minutes. Add salt to taste, the sugar and the sauce, and simmer for another 5 minutes; then rub through a tammy and, if not of a very good colour, add a little spinach green.

TIME.—¾ *hour to boil the asparagus and make the sauce.*

SEASONABLE *January to July*.

Asparagus Soup.—INGREDIENTS. 100 *heads of asparagus, 2 quarts of medium stock (see* STOCK), *1 pint of water, salt.* AVERAGE COST, 1s. 9d. *per quart.*

Scrape the asparagus, but do not cut off any of the stems, and boil it in a pint of

water salted, *until the heads are nearly done.* Then drain the asparagus, cut off the green heads very neatly, and put them on one side until the soup is ready. If the stock is not made, add the stems of asparagus to the rest of the vegetables; if, however, the stock is ready, boil the stems a little longer in the same water that they were first cooked in. Then strain them off, add the asparagus water to the stock, and when all is boiling drop in the green heads (or peas as they are called), and simmer for 2 or 3 minutes. If the soup boils long after the asparagus is put in, the appearance of the vegetable would be quite spoiled. A small quantity of sherry or other white wine added after the soup is put into the tureen would improve this soup very much. Sometimes a French roll is cut up and served in it.

ASPARAGUS.

TIME.—To nearly cook *the asparagus,* 12 *minutes*.

SEASONABLE *from May to August*.

Asparagus, Stewed.—INGREDIENTS.—100 *heads of asparagus, ¼ lb. of bread-crumbs, 3 oz. of butter, 2 eggs, a little mace, salt.* AVERAGE COST, 3s.

Scrape the asparagus and cut each head twice across into equal parts, lay the heads aside and boil the other parts till half done.

ASPARAGUS.

Put the butter into a stew-pan with the seasoning and the asparagus, heads as well as stems, and simmer gently for 1½ hour.

Shortly before serving add the bread-crumbs and the yolks of the eggs. Serve with the sauce poured over the asparagus.

Time.—1½ hour.

Seasonable *from May to August.*

Aspic Jelly, Moulded with Vegetables.

— Ingredients *for quart mould.*—1 *pint of aspic jelly, any cold boiled vegetables, such as asparagus tops, green peas, carrots, turnips, or beetroot in dice, cucumber (about 1 pint in all), 2 hard-boiled eggs.* Average Cost, 1s.

Coat a wetted mould with the melted jelly, and when cold arrange in it some of the vegetables, with due regard to colour and contrast; then add some more jelly and when cool some more vegetables, with

SALAD IN ASPIC JELLY.

the hard-boiled egg cut in slices, and so on till the mould is full. This if nicely arranged is a pretty dish and a very nice accompaniment to cold meats, and, if the vegetables in season are those in which a bright colour cannot be found, to give the dish effect the jelly may be coloured with cochineal.

Seasonable *in Summer, or at any time according to the vegetables used.*

Aspic Jelly, A Quicker and more Economical way of making.

— Ingredients.—1½ *oz. of gelatine, 2 quarts of any kind of stock, 1 carrot, 1 turnip, 1 shalot, 3 or 4 cloves, the same of pepper-corns, 1 lemon, a tablespoonful of vinegar, a bouquet of herbs, the white of one egg and some shells.* Average Cost *for this quantity,* 1s. 6d.

Put all in a stewpan and whisk over the fire till boiling, let it boil well up, settle for ¼ hour at the side of the stove, then strain.

For a garnish, part of the jelly may be coloured with a little cochineal, and in using it, it is best to cut it first in thin slices and then in diamonds, or it may be simply roughed with a fork.

Time.—½ hour.

Aspic, or Ornamental Savoury Jelly.

—Ingredients.—4 *lbs. of knuckle of veal, 1 cow-heel, 3 or 4 slices of ham, any poultry trimmings, 2 carrots, 1 onion, 1 faggot of savoury herbs, 1 glass of sherry, 3 quarts of water, seasoning to taste of salt and whole white pepper, 3 eggs.* Average Cost, 4s.

Lay the ham on the bottom of a stewpan, cut up the veal and cow-heel into small pieces, and lay them on the ham; add the poultry trimmings, vegetables, herbs, sherry, and water, and let the whole simmer very gently for 4 hours, carefully taking away all scum that may rise to the surface; strain through a fine sieve, and pour into an earthen pan to get cold.

SAVORY JELLY.

Have ready a clean stewpan, put in the jelly, and be particular to leave the sediment behind, or it will not be clear. Add the whites of 3 eggs, with salt and pepper, to clarify; keep stirring over the fire till the whole becomes very white; then draw it to the side, and let it stand till clear. When this is the case, strain it through a cloth or jelly-bag, and use it for moulding poultry, garnishing, &c. Tarragon vinegar may be added to give an additional flavour.

Time.—*Altogether,* 4½ *hours.*

August—Dinner for Twelve Persons.

MENU. (*English.*)	Quantity.	Average Cost.		MENU. (*French.*)
		s.	*d.*	
Appétisans.	2 dishes.	1	6	Appétisans.
Crayfish Soup.	5 pints.	8	9	Potage d'Ecrevisses.
Stewed Trout.	4 fish.	6	6	Truite au Vin Rouge.
Turbot,	1 fish.	10	0	Turbot,
Hollandaise Sauce.	2 turs.	2	0	Sauce Hollandaise.
Salmi of Game.	2 dishes.	6	0	Salmis de Gibier.
Minced Veal with Béchamel Sauce.	2 dishes.	4	0	Emincé de Veau au Béchamel.
Saddle of Mutton.	1 joint.	10	0	Selle de Mouton.
Potatoes. French Beans.	4 lbs. ea.	1	0	Pommes de Terre. Haricots Verts.
Black Game.	3 birds.	4	6	Coqs de Bruyère.
Compôte of Fruit.	2 dishes.	3	6	Compôte de Fruit.
Raspberry Tart.	2	2	3	Tourte aux Framboises.
Vanilla Cream.	2 mlds.	3	0	Crême de Vanille.
Cheese Straws.	2 dishes.	1	6	Pailles de Parmesan.
		£3 5	6	

August—Dinner for Ten Persons.

MENU. (*English.*)	Quantity.	Average Cost.		MENU. (*French.*)
		s.	*d.*	
Lobster Soup.	2 quarts	7	0	Bisque de Homard.
Salmon.	3½ lbs.	6	0	Saumon,
Dutch Sauce.	2 turs.	2	0	Sauce Hollandaise.
Chaudfroid of Chicken.	2 dishes.	5	0	Chaudfroid de Volaille.
Rissoles of Game.	2 dishes.	3	0	Rissolettes de Gibier.
Haunch of Mutton.	1 joint.	11	0	Hanche de Mouton.
Potatoes. Spinach.	3 lbs. ea.	0	9	Pommes de Terre. Epinards.
Grouse.	5 birds.	10	0	Coqs de Bruyère.
Almond Pudding.	2	3	0	Pouding d'Amandes.
Marbled Jelly.	1 mould.	2	9	Gelée Marbrée.
Iced Gooseberry Fool.	2 dishes.	1	6	Crême de Groseilles Glacée.
		£2 12	0	

August—Dinner for Eight Persons.

MENU. (*English.*)	Quantity.	Average Cost.		MENU. (*French.*)
		s.	*d.*	
White Soup.	3 pints.	4	6	Potage Lait d'Amandes.
Salmon Cutlets (Cold).	3 lbs.	5	0	Côtelettes de Saumon.
Horseradish Sauce.	1 tur.	0	6	Sauce Raifort.
Vol-au-vent of Chicken.	1 dish.	4	0	Vol-au-vent de Volaille.
Beef Croquettes.	12	2	0	Croquettes de Bœuf.
Leg of Lamb.	1 joint.	5	0	Gigot d'Agneau.
Potatoes. French Beans.	3 lbs. ea.	0	9	Pommes de Terre. Haricots Verts.
Macaroni and Pine Apple.	1 dish.	1	9	Macaroni aux Ananas.
Noyeau Cream.	1 mould.	2	0	Crême au Noyeau.
		£1 5	6	

August—Dinners for from Six to Twelve Persons.

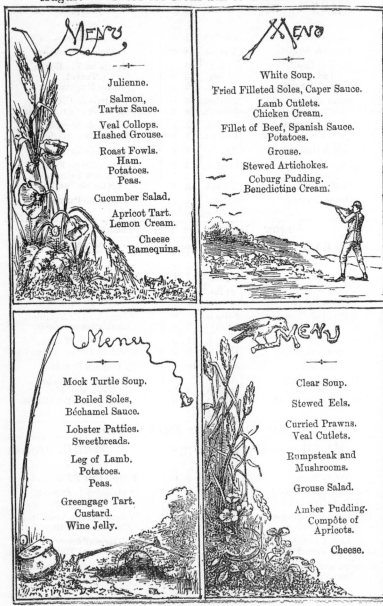

Menu.

Julienne.

Salmon,
Tartar Sauce.

Veal Collops.
Hashed Grouse.

Roast Fowls.
Ham.
Potatoes.
Peas.

Cucumber Salad.

Apricot Tart.
Lemon Cream.

Cheese
Ramequins.

Menu

White Soup.
Fried Filleted Soles, Caper Sauce.
Lamb Cutlets.
Chicken Cream.
Fillet of Beef, Spanish Sauce.
Potatoes.
Grouse.
Stewed Artichokes.
Coburg Pudding.
Benedictine Cream.

Menu

Mock Turtle Soup.

Boiled Soles,
Béchamel Sauce.

Lobster Patties.
Sweetbreads.

Leg of Lamb.
Potatoes.
Peas.

Greengage Tart.
Custard.
Wine Jelly.

Menu

Clear Soup.

Stewed Eels.

Curried Prawns.
Veal Cutlets.

Rumpsteak and
Mushrooms.

Grouse Salad.

Amber Pudding.
Compôte of
Apricots.

Cheese.

August—Plain Family Dinners for.

No. 1.

Sunday.—Roast lamb, peas, potatoes, mint sauce. — Cold apple tart, custard, bread-and-butter pudding.

Monday.— Macaroni soup.—Cold lamb, salad, mashed potatoes.—Lemon pudding. —Cheese.

Tuesday.—Boiled soles, caper sauce.—Rump steak, potatoes, French beans. — Stewed plums and rice.

Wednesday.—Roast sirloin of beef, potatoes, peas, horseradish sauce. — Pastry sandwiches, cornflour blancmange.

Thursday.—Soup.—Mutton cutlets, cold beef, salad, potatoes.—Apple pudding.

Friday.—Beef rissoles.—Roast chicken, bacon, cabbage, potatoes. — Sweet omelette.

Saturday.—Stewed eels.—Veal cutlets, hashed chicken, potatoes.—Cheese salad.

No. 2.

Sunday.—Boiled leg of mutton, caper sauce, potatoes, French beans.—Greengage tart, cream.

Monday.— Soup made from liquor in which mutton was boiled.—Cold mutton, cucumber.—Marmalade pudding.

Tuesday. — Flounders souché. — Hashed mutton, potatoes.—Baked bread pudding.

Wednesday.—Roast round of beef, cabbage, potatoes, Yorkshire pudding.—Macaroni cheese.

Thursday. — Lentil soup. — Cold beef, potatoes, salad.—Stewed plums.

Friday.—Salmon boiled, Tartare sauce, cucumber.— Stew from remnant of beef and vegetables.—Savoury macaroni.

Saturday.—Fish salad from cold fish.—Chops from neck of mutton and fried potatoes.—Apple pudding.

August—Vegetarian Dinners for.

No. 1.

Vermicelli Soup.

Lentil Fritters.
Vegetable Stew.

Fruit Tart and Custard.

Cheese Salad.

No. 2.

Purée of Green Peas.

Haricots and Onion Sauce.
Vegetable Pie.

Stewed Fruit and Cream.

Cheese Straws.

August—Dinner Table Decorations for.

This being so generally a hot month, it is well to have the dinner table decorations as cool-looking and refreshing as possible. A hothouse foliage decoration, without any flowers, is pleasant; and, again, ferns in white china receptacles.

For this purpose the pure white stands of different heights, with cupid or old-world figures, or those commonly called the cactus vases are suitable; but it must be remembered that they require a base of colour, and the white china must not be stood upon a white cloth, or no effect will be produced.

A dessert centre of green plush comes in well for these stands, and if they be furnished with only ferns of different tints, a very pretty result is obtained.

Yellow, again, is not an oppressive-looking colour, and the white stands look well upon it, when they may be furnished with yellow or yellow and white flowers. The latter are usually plentiful in August, but the drawback to the many hot-house one is their strong scent, so objectionable at a dinner table.

A simple, inexpensive, yet pretty decoration can be made for a table of ordinary size by three strawberry punnets filled with moss or sand, in the centre of each of which is a delicate fern, say pteris or maidenhair, surrounded by any foliage at command, while trails of green such as ficus repens or asparagus adorn the white cloth.

Still on the advocation of foliage *versus* flowers for this month's dinner table decoration, it may be noticed that any old prettily-shaped baskets with high handles, or some made so by wires, gilded by amateur hands may be made the prettiest receptacles for greenery; while, should colour be desired, they are always available for the introduction of a bow of ribbon.

August, Things in Season:—

Fish.—Brill, carp, crayfish, crabs, dory, eels, flounders, herrings, lobsters, mullet prawns, salmon, shrimps, skate, soles, sturgeon, trout, turbot.

Meat.—Beef, lamb, mutton, veal, buck venison.

Poultry.—Chickens, ducks, fowls, geese, pigeons, plovers, pullets, rabbits, turkey poults, wheatears, wild ducks.

Game.—Leverets, grouse, blackcock.

Vegetables. — Artichokes, asparagus, beans, carrots, cabbages, cauliflowers, celery, cresses, endive, lettuces, mushrooms, onions, peas, potatoes, radishes, sea-kale, small salading, sprouts, turnips, various kitchen herbs, vegetable marrows.

Fruit.— Currants, figs, filberts, gooseberries, grapes, melons, mulberries, nectarines, peaches, pears, pine-apples, plums, raspberries, walnuts.

Auntie's Cakes.—INGREDIENTS.—

1 lb. of flour, 2 teaspoonfuls of baking-powder, 2 lemons, ½ lb. of pounded sugar, ¼ lb. of butter, 4 eggs, a little salt. AVERAGE COST, for this quantity, 1s. 7d.

Mince the peel of the lemons finely, put it into the dry ingredients, and mix together. Beat the butter to a cream, add it to the eggs well beaten, stir well together, then drop the mixture into small buttered patty-pans, and bake 5 minutes in a quick oven.

TIME.—5 *minutes.*

Aunt Martha's Pudding.—IN-

GREDIENTS *for pudding for 5 or 6 persons.* —6 oz. of bread-crumbs, 3 eggs, 2 oz. of butter, 2 oz. of sugar, 1 lemon, ¼ lb. of raisins or sultanas, a teacupful of milk, a little nutmeg. AVERAGE COST, 10d.

Mix the bread-crumbs and sugar together, and pour the milk, boiling, over ; next add the eggs, beaten, the lemon peel grated

and the juice, then the butter and nutmeg, and beat all together for a quarter of an hour. Butter a mould and stick it all over with the raisins, stoned but not halved, then pour in the mixture and boil for 1¼ hour.

TIME.—1¼ *hour to boil the pudding.*
SEASONABLE *at any time.*

Aunt Polly's Pudding.—INGRE-

DIENTS *for pudding for 4 or 5 persons.*—A teacupful each of golden syrup, raisins, bread-crumbs and flour, 4 sponge cakes, 2 eggs, ½ wineglassful of brandy, a few drops of orange-flower water, a little minced candied peel. AVERAGE COST, 1s.

Mix well, then beat all together and pour into a buttered mould. Steam the pudding for 2½ hours, and serve with wine or sweet sauce.

TIME.—2½ *hours to steam the pudding.*
SEASONABLE *at any time.*

Australian Meat.—The prejudice

against Australian meat as it is imported, tinned, would be banished could it be seen as well as told that only the best meat is used for this purpose. Stall fed beasts in Australia are fattened in the same manner as they are in England and their flesh is equally good as that of meat killed at home, the great drawback to it being the necessary over cooking. However, there is a very great deal of difference in both the quality of the meat and the mode of preparing it for importation, and it may be said that the best is obtained from the Australian Meat Company, Fenchurch Avenue, London. In cooking it, or, rather, heating it, for it is always sufficiently cooked to suit most persons' taste, it is well to remove some of the fat first, this fat serving excellently for frying purposes.

Australian mutton is generally considered better than Australian beef, but both properly treated are good food.

"Beef and strong meats may give the weak more strength,
But bread's the staff of life."

ABA au Rhum.—INGREDIENTS *for good-sized cake.*—1 lb. of flour, 6 oz. of butter, 6 eggs, ½ oz. of German yeast, 2 oz. of sugar, ¼ lb. of raisins or sultanas, ¼ lb. of currants, 2 oz. of candied peel, salt. For sauce, ¼ pint of rum, ½ pot of apricot jam, 4 oz. of sugar, ¼ pint of water. AVERAGE COST, 3s.

Make a sponge of ¼ lb. of flour, the yeast, warm water and a little salt. Mix the rest of the ingredients in a large basin, adding the eggs one by one, and beating the mixture thoroughly with the hand till it is light and full of bubbles. When the sponge is risen, which should be in from 1 to 2 hours, mix the two and beat again. Butter a tin, put in the cake and set to the fire. When it has risen to twice its size, bake it in a good oven and turn it out. To make the sauce, boil the water and sugar to a syrup, add the jam and strain, put in

the rum, let it get quite hot, and serve poured over the baba.

TIME.—*2 hours to rise.*
SEASONABLE *in winter.*

Bachelor's Pudding.—INGREDIENTS *for small pudding.*—4 oz. of grated bread, 4 oz. of currants, 2 apples, 2 oz. of sugar, 3 eggs, a few drops of essence of lemon. AVERAGE COST, 8d.

Pare, core and chop the apples finely, add the currants, bread-crumbs and sugar, beat the eggs and add to them the flavouring; then mix all well together and put in a buttered basin. Tie a cloth over this and boil for 3 hours.

TIME.—*3 hours to boil.*
SEASONABLE *at any time.*

Bacon, Boiled.—INGREDIENTS.—*Bacon, water.* AVERAGE COST, 10d. to 1s. *per lb. for the best parts.*

As bacon is frequently excessively salt, let it be soaked in warm water for an hour or two previous to dressing it; then pare off the rusty parts, and scrape the underside and rind as clean as possible. Put it into a saucepan of cold water; let it come gradually to a boil, and as fast as the scum rises to the surface of the water, remove it. Let it simmer very gently until it is *thoroughly* done ; then take it up, strip off the skin, and sprinkle over the bacon a few bread raspings, and garnish with tufts of cauliflower or Brussels sprouts. When served alone, young and tender broad beans or green peas are the usual accompaniments.

BOILED BACON.

TIME.—1 *lb. of bacon,* ¾ *hour;* 2 *lbs.,* 1½ *hour.*

SEASONABLE *at any time.*

Bacon, Broiled Rashers of.—
AVERAGE COST, 10*d.* to 1*s. per lb. for best parts.*

Before purchasing bacon, ascertain that it is perfectly free from rust, which may easily be detected by its yellow colour ; and for broiling, the streaked part of the thick flank is generally the most esteemed. Cut it into *thin* slices, take off the rind, and broil over a nice clear fire ; turn it two or three times, and serve very hot. Should there be any cold bacon left from the previous day, it answers very well for breakfast, cut into slices, and broiled or fried. Poached or fried eggs are commonly served with the bacon.

TIME.—3 *or* 4 *minutes.*

SEASONABLE *at any time.*

Note.—The slices may be curled round, fastened by small skewers, and toasted before the fire.

Bacon and Hams, Curing of.
—The carcass of the hog, after hanging over-night to cool, is laid on a strong bench or stool, and the head is separated from the body at the neck close behind the ears ; the feet and also the internal fat are removed. The carcass is next divided into two sides in the following manner :—
The ribs are divided about an inch from the spine on each side, and the spine, with the ends of the ribs attached, together with the internal flesh between it and the kidneys, and also the flesh above it, throughout the whole length of the sides are removed. The portion of the carcass thus cut out is in the form of a wedge— the breadth of the interior consisting of the breadth of the spine, and about an inch of the ribs on each side, being diminished to about half an inch at the exterior or skin along the back. The breast-bone and also the first anterior rib are also dissected from the side. Sometimes the whole of the ribs are removed ; but this, for reasons afterwards to be noticed, is a very bad practice. When the hams are cured separately from the sides, which is generally the case, they are cut out so as to include the hock bone, in a similar manner to the London mode of cutting a haunch of mutton. The carcass of the hog thus cut up is ready for being salted, which process, in large curing establishments, is generally as follows :— The skin side of the pork is rubbed over with a mixture of fifty parts by weight of salt, and one part of saltpetre in powder, and the incised parts of the ham or flitch, and the inside of the flitch, covered with the same. The salted bacon, in pairs of flitches with the insides to each other, is piled one pair of flitches above another on benches slightly inclined, and furnished with spouts or troughs to convey the brine to receivers in the floor of the salting-house, to be afterwards used for pickling pork for navy purposes. In this state the bacon remains a fortnight, which is sufficient for flitches cut from hogs of a carcass weight less than 15 stone (14 lbs. to the stone). Flitches of a larger size, at the expiration of that time, are wiped dry and reversed in their place in the pile, having, at the same time, about half the first quantity of fresh, dry common salt sprinkled over the inside and incised parts ; after which they remain on the

benches for another week. Hams, being thicker than flitches, will require, when less than 20 lbs. weight, 3 weeks, and when above that weight, 4 weeks to remain under the above described process. The next and last process in the preparation of bacon and hams, previous to being sent to market, is drying. This is effected by hanging the flitches and hams for 2 or 3 weeks in a room heated by stoves, or in a smoke-house, in which they are exposed for the same length of time to the smoke arising from the slow combustion of the sawdust of oak or other hard wood. The latter mode of completing the curing process has some advantages over the other, as by it the meat is subject to the action of *creosote*, a volatile oil produced by the combustion of the sawdust, which is powerfully antiseptic. The process also furnishing a thin covering of a resinous varnish, excludes the air not only from the muscle, but also from the fat—thus effectually preventing the meat from becoming rusted; and the principal reasons for condemning the practice of removing the ribs from the flitches of pork are, that by so doing the meat becomes unpleasantly hard and pungent in the process of salting, and, by being more exposed to the action of the air, becomes sooner and more extensively rusted. Notwithstanding its superior efficacy in completing the process of curing, the flavour which smoke-drying imparts to meat is disliked by many persons, and it is therefore by no means the most general mode of drying adopted by mercantile curers. A very impure variety of *pyroligneous* acid, or vinegar made from the destructive distillation of wood, is sometimes used, on account of the highly preservative power of the creosote which it contains, and also to impart the smoke-flavour; in which latter object, however, the coarse flavour of tar is given, rather than that derived from the smoke from combustion of wood. A considerable portion of the bacon and hams salted in Ireland is exported from that country packed amongst salt, in bales, immediately from the salting process, without having been in any degree dried In the process of salting above described, pork loses from 8 to 10 per cent. of its weight, according to the size and quality of the meat; and a further diminution of weight to the extent of 5 to 6 per cent. takes place in drying during the first fortnight after being taken out of salt; so that the total loss in weight occasioned by the preparation of bacon and hams in a proper state for market is not less on an average than 15 per cent. on the weight of the fresh pork.

Bacon, To Cure, and Keep it free from Rust (COBBETT's Recipe).—The two sides that remain, and which are called flitches, are to be cured for bacon. They are first rubbed with salt on their insides, or flesh sides, then placed one on the other, the flesh sides uppermost, in a salting-trough which has a gutter round its edges to drain away the brine; for, to have sweet and fine bacon, the flitches must not be sopping in brine, which gives it the sort of vile taste that barrel and sea-pork have. Everyone knows how different is the taste of fresh dry salt from that of salt in a dissolved state; therefore, change the salt often—once in 4 or 5 days; let it melt and sink in, but not lie too long; twice change the flitches, put that at bottom which was first on the top; this mode will cost you a great deal more in salt than the sopping mode; but without it, your bacon will not be so sweet and fine, nor keep so well As for the time required in making your flitches sufficiently salt, it depends on circumstances. It takes a longer time for a thick than a thin flitch; and longer in dry than in damp weather, or in a dry than in a damp place; but for the flitches of a hog of five score, in weather not very dry or damp, about 6 weeks may do, and if yours is to be fat, which receives little

I

injury from over-salting, give time enough, for you to have bacon until Christmas comes again. The place for salting should, like a dairy, always be cool, but well ventilated; confined air, though cool, will taint meat sooner than the midday sun accompanied by a breeze. With regard to smoking the bacon, two precautions are necessary : first, to hang the flitches where no rain comes down upon them; and next, that the smoke must proceed from wood, not peat, turf or coal. As to the time required to smoke a flitch, it depends a good deal upon whether there be a constant fire beneath, and whether the fire be large or small; a month will do, if the fire be pretty constant and rich, as a farm-house fire usually is; but over-smoking, or rather too long hanging in the air, makes the bacon rust; great attention should therefore be paid to this matter. The flitch ought not to be dried up to the hardness of a board, and yet it ought to be perfectly dry. Before you hang it up, lay it on the floor, scatter the flesh side pretty thickly over with bran, or with some fine sawdust, not of deal or fir; rub it on the flesh, or pat it well down upon it; this keeps the smoke from getting into the little openings, and makes a sort of crust to be dried on. To keep the bacon sweet and good, and free from hoppers, sift fine some clean and dry wood ashes. Put some at the bottom of a box or chest long enough to hold a flitch of bacon; lay in one flitch, then put in more ashes, then another flitch, and cover this with six or eight inches of the ashes. The place where the box or chest is kept ought to be dry, and, should the ashes become damp, they should be put in the fireplace to dry, and when cold, put back again. With these precautions, the bacon will be as good at the end of the year as on the first day. For simple general rules, these may be safely taken as a guide; and those who implicitly follow the directions given, will possess at the expiration of from 6 weeks to 2 months well-flavoured and well-cured bacon.

Bacon or Hams, to Cure in the Devonshire Way. — INGREDIENTS. — *To every 14 lbs. of meat allow 2 oz. of saltpetre, 2 oz. of salt prunella, 1 lb. of common salt. For the pickle, 3 gallons of water, 5 lbs. of common salt, 7 lbs. of coarse sugar, 3 lbs. of bay salt.*

Weigh the sides, hams and cheeks, and to every 14 lbs. allow the above proportion of saltpetre, salt prunella, and common salt. Pound and mix these together, and rub well into the meat; lay it on a stone trough or tub, rubbing it thoroughly, and turning it daily for two successive days. At the end of the second day, pour on it a pickle made as follows :—Put the above ingredients into a saucepan, set it on the fire, and stir frequently; remove all the scum, allow it to boil for $\frac{1}{4}$ hour, and pour it hot over the meat. Let the hams, &c., be well rubbed and turned daily; if the meat is small, a fortnight will be sufficient for the sides and shoulders to remain in the pickle, and the hams 3 weeks; if from 30 lbs. and upwards, 3 weeks will be required for the sides, &c., and from 4 to 5 weeks for the hams. On taking the pieces out, let them drain for an hour, cover with dry sawdust, and smoke from a fortnight to 3 weeks. Boil and carefully skim the pickle after using, and it will keep good, closely corked, for 2 years. When boiling it for use, add about 2 lbs. of common salt, and the same of treacle, to allow for waste. Tongues are excellent put into this pickle cold, having first been rubbed well with saltpetre and salt, and allowed to remain 24 hours, not forgetting to make a deep incision under the thick part of the tongue, so as to allow the pickle to penetrate more readily. A fortnight or 3 weeks, according to the size of the tongue, will be sufficient.

TIME.—*Small meat to remain in the pickle a fortnight, hams 3 weeks; to be smoked from a fortnight to 3 weeks.*

Bacon, To Cure in the Wiltshire Way.

INGREDIENTS. — 1½ lb. of coarse sugar, ½ lb. of bay salt, 6 oz. of salt-petre, 1 lb. of common salt.

Sprinkle each flitch with salt, and let the blood drain off for 24 hours; then pound and mix the above ingredients well together and rub it well into the meat, which should be turned every day for a month; hang it to dry, and smoke it for 10 days.

TIME.—*To remain in the pickle from 3 to 4 weeks; to be smoked 10 days, or rather longer.*

Bacon, Constituents of.

One of the most popular articles of food in England, bacon is cured and smoked in many of our counties, and immense quantities are imported here from British Colonies as well as foreign countries; these imports during the last few years having been greatly on the increase.

Of all salted meats bacon is most easily digested. It contains, as will be seen by the following analysis, only one part of flesh-forming properties to twenty of heat givers, reckoned as starch, and this may be taken as a fair average of the quality of the food.

CONSTITUENTS OF 1 LB. OF BACON.

	oz.	grs.
Water	3	250
Nitrogenous Matter	1	132
Fat	10	191
Mineral Matter	0	301
	16	0

Bain Marie, The,

is an open kind of vessel, as shown in the engraving, and is a utensil much used in modern cookery, both in English and French kitchens. It is filled with boiling or nearly boiling water; and into this water should be put all the stewpans containing those ingredients which it is desired to keep hot. The quantity and quality of the contents of these vessels are not at all affected; and if the hour of dinner is uncertain in any establishment, by reason of the nature of the master's business, nothing is so sure a

BAIN MARIE.

means of preserving the flavour of all dishes as the employment of the bain marie.

Banana Cream.

INGREDIENTS *for small mould.* — 6 bananas, ½ pint of cream, 1 lemon, sugar to taste, 1½ oz. of gelatine, a little water, flavouring of Benedictine. AVERAGE COST, 2s. 3d.

Dissolve the gelatine in ½ a teacupful of water, and put it with the bananas, skinned, the lemon rind and juice, and a little loaf sugar, and simmer for about 10 minutes. When cold, beat up with the cream, flavour with the liqueur, and pour in a wet mould. Set the mould in a very cool place, or on ice.

TIME.—*About 10 minutes to simmer.*
SEASONABLE *in autumn and winter.*

Bakewell Pudding.

INGREDIENTS *for small pudding.*—¾ pint of breadcrumbs, 1 pint of milk, 3 eggs, 2 oz. of sugar, 3 oz. of butter, 1 oz. of almonds, pounded, some jam. AVERAGE COST, 1s. 3d.

Butter a pie dish and put in it the breadcrumbs, covering them with a layer of strawberry or any other kind of jam. Mix the milk with the eggs beaten, the almonds pounded, sugar and butter; beat all well together, pour into the dish and bake 1 hour in a moderate oven.

TIME.—1 *hour.*
SEASONABLE *at any time.*

Baking.

Baking, which is one of the subdivisions of roasting, may be considered as one of the most convenient modes of cooking.

Baked meat is not considered so good as that which is roasted, but a great deal of the (sometimes to be detected) disagreeable flavour may be attributed to the want of cleanliness in an oven, the cooking of various dishes at the same time, or the fat which is often allowed to burn on the sides. Not only has a great improvement been made in the construction of modern ovens, but there are now utensils for baking that render the cooked meats of far superior flavour than when baked by the old mode.

TIN BAKING DISH.

If however the meat be put in one of the old-fashioned tins or earthenware pans, a jar of water should go with it into the oven to absorb any disagreeable odour. There are some meats that are as well cooked baked, as roasted, but not many (partly for the reason that in the oven they do not get so well basted as before the fire), as for example, a shoulder of mutton and baked potatoes, a fillet or breast of veal, and a sucking-pig. For meats, the oven should not only be of a good heat but that heat should be kept up. Pastry and bread require a quick oven when first put in, but the heat may be slightly lessened afterwards, because in ordinary ovens where the chief heat is at one side only, they must be turned for fear of burning.

Barberries.—A fruit of such great acidity, that even birds refuse to eat it. In this respect, it nearly approaches the tamarind. When boiled with sugar, it makes a very agreeable preserve, or jelly, according to the different modes of preparing it. Barberries are also used as a dry sweet meat. The berries form a pretty garnish.

Barberries, To Preserve, in Bunches.—INGREDIENTS.—1 pint of syrup, barberries.

Prepare some small pieces of clean white wood, 3 inches long and ¼ inch wide, and tie the fruit on to these in nice bunches. Have ready some clear syrup (see SYRUP), put in the barberries, and simmer them in it for 2 successive days, boiling them for nearly ½ hour each day, and covering them each time with the syrup when cold. When the fruit looks perfectly clear it is sufficiently done, and should be stowed away in pots, with the syrup poured over, or the fruit may be candied.

TIME.—½ hour to simmer each day.
SEASONABLE in Autumn.

Barley.—Barley was originally a native grass of Western Temperate Asia. It is a very hardy plant and may be grown in high Northern Latitudes. The main part of that grown in England is used for malt in making beer. Pot and pearl barley, from which the fibrous parts of the grain are more or less completely removed form useful foods. Pot barley is the coarsest kind and, from the same quantity of grain which produces, for example, 2 lbs. of this, only half that quantity of fine pearl barley is obtained. Barley is not a watery food and is very rich in starch.

CONSTITUENT PARTS OF 1 LB. OF PEARL BARLEY.

					oz.	grs.
Water	...	...	...	...	2	146
Fibrin, etc.	...	...	...	...	0	434
Starch, etc.	...	...	...	...	12	120
Fat	...	...	...	...	0	91
Mineral Matter	...	...	...	...	0	77
					16	0

Barley Gruel (Patent Barley).—INGREDIENTS.—1 tablespoonful of Patent Barley (flour); pinch of salt; a little cold water; ½ pint boiling water (or milk); sugar or port to taste. AVERAGE COST, 2½d. without spirit.

Mix the barley well with cold water, until a smooth paste about the thickness of cream is formed; then add to this ½ pint of boiling water (or milk, which is preferable); put into an enamelled saucepan; add sugar or wine to taste; simmer for 10 minutes, stirring all the time with a silver or wooden spoon.

TIME.—10 *minutes.*

SUFFICIENT to make ½ pint.

Barley Soup.—INGREDIENTS.—2 *lbs* of shin of beef, ¼ lb. of pearl barley, a large bunch of parsley, 4 onions, 6 potatoes, salt and pepper, 4 quarts of water. AVERAGE COST, 4d. per quart.

Put in all the ingredients, and simmer gently for 3 hours.

TIME.—3 *hours.*

SEASONABLE *all the year.*

Barley-Sugar, To Make.—INGREDIENTS *for 6 sticks.*—2 *lbs. of sugar, ½ pint of water, the white of an egg.* AVERAGE COST, 7d.

Put the sugar into a well-tinned saucepan, with the water, and, when the former is dissolved, set it over a moderate fire, adding the egg, well-beaten, before the mixture gets warm, and stir it well together. When it boils, remove the scum as it rises, and keep it boiling until no more appears, and the syrup looks perfectly clear; then strain it through a fine sieve or muslin bag, and put it back into the saucepan. Boil it again like caramel, until it is brittle when a little is dropped in a basin of cold water: it is then sufficiently boiled. Add a little lemon-juice and a few drops of essence of lemon, and let it stand for a minute or two. Have ready a marble slab or large dish, rubbed over with salad-oil: pour on it the sugar, and cut it into strips with a pair of scissors: these strips should then be twisted, and the barley-sugar stored away in a very dry place. It may be formed into lozenges or drops, by dropping the sugar in a very small quantity at a time on the oiled slab or dish.

TIME.—¼ *hour.*

Barley-Water, To Make.—INGREDIENTS *for 1 quart.*—2 *oz. of pearl barley, 2 quarts of boiling water, 1 pint of cold water.*

Wash the barley in cold water; put it into a saucepan with the above proportion of cold water, and when it has boiled for about ¼ hour, strain off the water, and add the 2 quarts of fresh boiling water. Boil it until the liquid is reduced one half; strain it, and it will be ready for use. It may be flavoured with lemon-peel, after being sweetened, or a small piece may be simmered with the barley. When the invalid may take it, a little lemon-juice gives this pleasant drink in illness a very nice flavour. A very nutritious and extremely pleasant drink may be made more quickly and easily prepared by using " Robinson's Patent Barley," following directions given with each packet.

TIME.—*To boil until the liquid is reduced one half.*

Baroness Pudding (Author's Recipe).—INGREDIENTS *for a large pudding.*—¾ *lb. of suet, ¾ lb. of raisins, weighed after being stoned, ¾ lb. of flour, ½ pint of milk, ¼ saltspoonful of salt.* AVERAGE COST, 1s. 2d.

Prepare the suet, by carefully freeing it from skin, and chop it finely; stone the raisins, and cut them in halves, and mix both these ingredients with the salt and flour; moisten the whole with the above proportion of milk, stir the mixture well, and tie the pudding in a floured cloth, which has been previously wrung out in boiling water. Put the pudding into a saucepan of boiling water, and let it boil, without ceasing, 4½ hours. Serve with plain sifted sugar only, a little of which may be sprinkled over the pudding.

TIME.—4½ *hours.*

SEASONABLE *in winter, when fresh fruit is not obtainable.*

Batter Pudding, Baked. — INGREDIENTS *for a good-sized pudding.*—1½

pint of milk, 4 tablespoonfuls of flour, 2 oz. of butter, 3 eggs, a little salt. AVERAGE COST, 8d.

Mix the flour with a small quantity of cold milk; make the remainder hot, and pour it on to the flour, keeping the mixture well stirred; add the butter, eggs and salt; beat the whole well, and put the pudding into a buttered pie-dish; bake for ¾ hour, and serve with sweet sauce, wine sauce, or stewed fruit. Baked in small cups, very pretty little puddings may be made; they should be eaten with the same accompaniments as above.

TIME.—¾ hour.

SEASONABLE at any time.

Batter Pudding, Baked, with Dried or Fresh Fruit.

—INGREDIENTS for a large pudding.—1½ pint of milk, 4 tablespoonfuls of flour, 3 eggs, 2 oz. of finely-shredded suet, ¼ lb. of currants, a pinch of salt. AVERAGE COST, with dried fruit, 10d.

Mix the milk, flour and eggs to a smooth batter; add a little salt, the suet and the currants, which should be well washed, picked and dried; put the mixture into a buttered pie-dish, and bake in a moderate oven for 1¼ hour. When fresh fruits are in season, this pudding is exceedingly nice with damsons, plums, red currants, gooseberries or apples; when made with these, the pudding must be thickly sprinkled over with sifted sugar. Boiled batter pudding, with fruit, is made in the same manner, by putting the fruit into a buttered basin, and filling it up with batter made in the above proportion, but omitting the suet. It must be sent quickly to table and covered plentifully with sifted sugar.

TIME.—Baked batter pudding, with fruit, 1¼ to 1½ hour; boiled ditto, 1½ to 1¾ hour, allowing that both are made in the above proportion of batter. Smaller puddings will be done enough in ¾ or 1 hour.

SEASONABLE at any time, with dried fruits.

Batter Pudding, Boiled.

—INGREDIENTS for good-sized pudding.—3 eggs 1 oz. of butter, 1 pint of milk, 3 tablespoonfuls of flour, a little salt. AVERAGE COST 7d.

Put the flour into a basin, and add sufficient milk to moisten it; carefully rub down all the lumps with a spoon, then pour in the remainder of the milk, and stir in the butter, which should be previously melted; keep beating the mixture, add the eggs and a pinch of salt, and, when the batter is quite smooth, put it into a well-buttered basin, tie it down very tightly, and put it into boiling water; move the basin about for a few minutes after it is put into the water, to prevent the flour settling in any part, and boil for 1¼ hour. This pudding may also be boiled in a floured cloth that has been wetted in hot water: it will then take a few minutes less than when boiled in a basin. Send batter puddings very quickly to table, and serve with sweet sauce, wine sauce, stewed fruit, or jam of any kind, when the latter is used, a little of it may be placed round the dish in small quantities, as a garnish.

TIME—1¼ hour in a basin, 1 hour in a cloth.

SEASONABLE at any time.

Batter Pudding, with Orange Marmalade.

—INGREDIENTS for a pudding large enough for 6 persons.—4 eggs, 1 pint of milk, 1½ oz. of loaf sugar, 3 tablespoonfuls of flour, ½ pot of marmalade. AVERAGE COST, 1s. 2d.

Make the batter with the above ingredients, put it into a well-buttered basin, tie it down with a cloth, and boil for 1 hour. As soon as it is turned out of the basin, put a small jar of orange marmalade all over the top, and send the pudding very quickly to table. It is advisable to warm the marmalade to make it liquid.

TIME.—1 hour.

SEASONABLE at any time; but more suitable for a winter pudding.

Bean Croquettes.—INGREDIENTS.

—*Cold boiled beans, bread-crumbs, onion, egg, or flour and milk, oil or butter for frying.*

SCARLET RUNNER.

Mash the beans, add flavouring of salt, pepper and chopped onion, and enough bread-crumbs to make a paste stiff enough to mould. Form the mixture into balls or cakes, egg-and bread-crumb them, or dip them in milk and then in flour, and fry a nice bright brown in oil or butter. Serve very hot, with sauce or brown gravy. Peas, the ordinary split ones, or German lentils, may be substituted for the beans, and parsley and herbs, with a little lemon-peel, may be used if preferred to the onion.

Beans and Tomatoes.—INGRE-

DIENTS. — *Baked or boiled haricot beans about 1 lb., ½ pint of the liquor in which they were cooked, 1 oz. of flour, 1 oz. of butter, 2 tablespoonfuls of tomato sauce.*

Having strained the beans, thicken the liquor with the flour and butter, put in the sauce and let the mixture boil; then add the beans and serve as soon as they are hot.

Beans, Boiled Broad.—INGRE-

DIENTS.—*To each ½ gallon of water allow 1 heaped tablespoonful of salt; beans.* AVERAGE COST, 6d. per peck.

This is a favourite vegetable with many persons, but, to be nice, should be young and freshly gathered. After shelling the beans, put them into *boiling* water, salted in the above proportion, and let them boil rapidly until tender. Drain them well in a colander; dish, put a small piece of butter on the top, and serve with them, separ-ately, a tureen of parsley and butter. Boiled bacon is very often an accompaniment to this vegetable, but the beans should be cooked separately. It is usually served with the beans laid round, and the parsley and but-ter in a tureen. Beans also make an excellent garnish to a ham, and when used for this pur-pose, if very old, should have their skins removed.

BROAD BEANS.

TIME.—*Very young beans, 15 minutes; when a moderate size, 20 to 25 minutes, or longer.*

SEASONABLE *in July and August.*

Beans, Boiled French.—INGRE-

DIENTS.—*To each ½ gallon of water allow 1 heaped tablespoonful of salt, a very small piece of soda.* AVERAGE COST, 2d. per lb.

This vegetable should always be eaten young, as when allowed to grow too long it

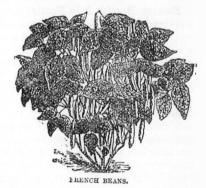

FRENCH BEANS.

tastes stringy and tough when cooked. Cut off the heads and tails, and a thin strip on each side of the beans to remove the strings; then divide each bean into 4 or 6 pieces, according to size, cutting them lengthways in a slanting direction, and as they are cut put them into cold water, with a small quantity of salt dissolved in it. Have ready a saucepan of boiling water, with salt and soda in the above proportion; put in the beans, keep them boiling quickly, with the lid uncovered, and be careful that they do not get smoked. When tender, which may be ascertained by their sinking to the bottom of the saucepan, take them up, pour them into a colander, and when drained, dish, putting small pieces of butter on the top and serve with or without melted butter. When very young, beans are sometimes served whole: thus dressed, their colour and flavour are much better preserved, but the more general way of sending them to table is to cut them into thin strips.

TIME.—*Very young beans,* 10 *to* 12 *minutes; moderate size,* 15 *to* 20 *minutes, after the water boils.*

SEASONABLE *from the middle of July to the end of September, but may be had forced from February to the beginning of June.*

Beans, Broad, à la Poulette.—

INGREDIENTS *for one vegetable dish.* — 2 *pints of broad beans,* ½ *pint of stock or broth, a small bunch of savoury herbs, including parsley, a small lump of sugar, the yolk of* 1 *egg,* ¼ *pint of cream or milk, pepper and salt to taste.* AVERAGE COST, 1s. 4d.

Procure some young and freshly-gathered beans, and shell sufficient to make 2 pints; boil them, as in the preceding recipe, until nearly done; then drain them and put them into a stewpan with the stock, finely-minced herbs and sugar. Stew the beans until perfectly tender, and the liquor has dried away a little; then beat up the yolk of an egg with the cream, add this to the beans, let the whole get thoroughly hot, and when on the point of simmering, serve. Should the beans be very large, the skin should be removed previously to boiling them.

TIME.—10 *minutes to boil the beans,* 1[ ] *minutes to stew them in the stock.*

SEASONABLE *in July and August.*

Beans, Curried. — INGREDIENT[S]

for sufficient for 4 *persons.*—½ *pint of harico[t] beans,* 1 *apple,* 1 *onion,* 1 *dessertspoonful o[f] curry-powder and flour mixed, a littl[e] butter,* ¼ *pint of water,* ½ *lb. of rice.* AVER[-]AGE COST, 7d.

Bake the beans in water in a slow oven till tender, chop the onion and apple fin[e] and fry in butter; next add the flour an[d] curry, and last of all the water. Boil an[d] thicken, then add the beans and serve with a border of boiled rice.

Beans, French Mode of Cook[-]

ing French.—INGREDIENTS *for dish fo[r]* 3 *persons.*—1 *lb. of French beans,* 3 *oz. o[f] fresh butter, pepper and salt to taste, the juic[e] of* ½ *lemon.* AVERAGE COST, 2d. per lb.

Cut and boil the beans by recipe unde[r] "Beans, Boiled French," and when tende[r] put them into a stewpan, and shake ove[r] the fire, to dry away the moisture fro[m] the beans. When quite dry and hot, ad[d] the butter, pepper, salt and lemon-juice keep moving the stewpan, without usin[g] a spoon, as that would break the beans and when the butter is melted, and all i[s] thoroughly hot, serve. If the butter shoul[d] not mix well, add a tablespoonful of gravy and serve very quickly.

TIME.—*About* ¼ *hour to boil the beans* 10 *minutes to shake them over the fire.*

SEASONABLE *from the middle of July t[o] the end of September.*

Beans, Haricots Blancs, o[r]

White Haricot, and Minced Onions.—INGREDIENTS *for dish for* 4 *or* 5 *persons.*—1 *quart of white haricot beans,* 4 *middling sized onions,* ¼ *pint of good brown gravy pepper and salt to taste; a little flour.* AVERAGE COST, 10d.

Peel and mince the onions not too finely and fry them in butter of a light brow[n] colour; dredge over them a little flour, and add the gravy and a seasoning of pepper and salt. Have ready a quart of haricot beans well boiled and drained; put them with the onions and gravy, mix all well together, and serve very hot.

TIME.—*From 2 to 2½ hours to boil the beans; 5 minutes to fry the onions.*

SEASONABLE *in winter.*

Beans, Haricots Blancs, à la Maitre d'Hotel.

— INGREDIENTS *for dish for 4 or 5 persons.* — 1 *quart of white haricot beans, ¼ lb. of fresh butter, 1 tablespoonful of minced parsley, pepper and salt to taste, the juice of ½ lemon.* AVERAGE COST, 9d.

Should the beans be very dry, soak them for an hour or two in cold water, and boil them until perfectly tender, as in the preceding recipe. If the water should boil away, replenish it with a little more cold, which makes the skin of the beans tender. Let them be very thoroughly done; drain them well; then add to them the butter, minced parsley, and

HARICOT BEANS.

a seasoning of pepper and salt. Keep moving the stewpan over the fire, without using a spoon, as this would break the beans; and, when the various ingredients are well mixed with them, squeeze in the lemon-juice and serve very hot.

TIME.—*From 2 to 2½ hours to boil the beans.*

SEASONABLE *in winter.*

Beans, Haricots Blancs, To Boil.

—INGREDIENTS *for dish for 4 or 5 persons.*—1 *quart of white haricot beans, 2 quarts of soft water, 1½ oz. of butter, 1 heaped tablespoonful of salt.* AVERAGE COST, 6d.

Put the beans into cold water, let them soak from 2 to 4 hours, according to their age; then put them into cold water salted in the above proportion, bring them to boil, and let them simmer very slowly until tender; pour the water away from them, and let them stand by the side of the fire, with the lid of the saucepan partially off, to allow the beans to dry; then add 1 oz. of butter and a seasoning of pepper and salt. Shake the beans about for a minute or two, and serve; do not stir them with a spoon, for fear of breaking them to pieces.

TIME.—*After the water boils, from 2 to 2½ hours.*

SEASONABLE *in winter, when other vegetables are scarce.*

Note.—Haricots blancs, when new and fresh, should be put into boiling water, and do not require any soaking previous to dressing.

Béchamel Maigre, or Without Meat.

—INGREDIENTS.—2 *onions, 1 blade of mace, mushroom trimmings, a small bunch of parsley, 1 oz. of butter, flour, ½ pint of water, 1 pint of milk, salt, the juice of ¼ lemon, 2 eggs.*—AVERAGE COST, 9d.

Put in a stewpan the milk and ½ pint of water, with the onions, mace, mushrooms, parsley and salt. Let these simmer gently for 20 minutes. In the meantime, rub on a plate 1 oz. of flour and butter; put it to the liquor and stir it well till it boils up; then place it by the side of the fire, and continue stirring until it is perfectly smooth. Now strain it through a sieve into a basin, after which put it back in the stewpan, and add the lemon-juice. Beat up the yolks of the eggs with about 4 dessertspoonfuls of milk; strain this to the sauce, keep stirring it over the fire, *but do not let it boil, or it will curdle.*

TIME.—*Altogether, ¾ hour.*

Béchamel, or French White Sauce.

—INGREDIENTS.—1 *small bunch of parsley, 2 cloves, ½ bay leaf, 1 small bunch of savoury herbs, salt to taste; 3 or 4 mush-*

rooms, when obtainable; 2 *pints of white stock,* 1 *pint of milk or cream,* 1 *tablespoonful of arrowroot.* AVERAGE COST, 2s.

Put the stock into a stewpan, with the parsley, cloves, bay leaf, herbs and mushrooms; add a seasoning of salt but no pepper, as that would give the sauce a dusty appearance, and should be avoided. When it has boiled long enough to extract the flavour of the herbs, &c., strain it and boil it up quickly again, until it is nearly half reduced. Now mix the arrowroot smoothly with the milk or cream, and let it simmer very gently for 5 minutes over a slow fire; pour to it the stock, and continue to simmer slowly for 10 minutes, if the sauce be thick; if, on the contrary, it be too thin, it must be stirred over a sharp fire till it thickens. Always make it thick, as it can easily be thinned with cream, milk or white stock. This sauce is excellent for pouring over boiled fowls and for made dishes.

TIME.—*Altogether,* 2 *hours.*

Beef.—The manner in which a side of beef is cut up in London and most large towns is here shown.

The meat on those parts of the animal in which the muscles are least called into action is most tender and succulent; as, for instance, along the back, from the rump to the hinder part of the shoulder; whilst the limbs, shoulder and neck are the toughest, driest and least-esteemed.

The names of the several joints in the hind and fore quarters of a side of beef, and the purposes for which they are used, are as follows:—

Hind Quarter:—

1. Sirloin—the two sirloins, cut together in one joint form a baron; this, when roasted, is the famous national dish of Englishmen, at entertainments, on occasion of rejoicing.
2. Rump—the finest part for steaks.
3. Aitchbone—boiling piece.
4. Buttock—prime boiling piece.
5. Mouse-round—boiling or stewing.
6. Hock—stewing.
7. Thick flank, cut with the udder-fat—primest boiling piece.
8. Thin flank—boiling.

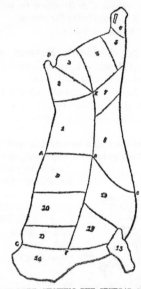

SIDE OF BEEF, SHOWING THE SEVERAL JOINTS.

Fore Quarter:—

9. Five ribs, called the fore-rib—this is considered the primest roasting piece.
10. Four ribs, called the middle rib—greatly esteemed by housekeepers as the most economical joint for roasting.
11. Two ribs, called the chuck rib—used for second quality of steaks.
12. Leg-of-Mutton piece—the muscles of the shoulder dissected from the breast.
13. Brisket or breast—used for boiling, after being salted.
14. Neck, clod and sticking-piece—used for soups, gravies, stocks, pies, and mincing for sausages.
15. Shin—stewing.

The following is a classification of the qualities of meat, according to the several joints of beef, when cut up in the London manner :—

First class—Includes the sirloin, with the kidney suet (1), the rump-steak piece (2), the fore-rib (9).

Second class—The buttock (4), the thick flank (7), the middle-rib (10).

Third class — The aitchbone (3), the mouse-round (5), the thin flank (8), the chuck (11), the leg-of-mutton piece (12), the brisket (13).

Fourth class—The neck, clod and sticking-piece (14).

Fifth class—The hock (6), the shin (15).

Where the demand for the most esteemed and highest-priced joints is great the carcass is so divided as to obtain the greatest amount of meat upon these. In some places, however, where, from a greater equality in the social conditions and habits of the inhabitants, the demand for, and the prices of the different parts of the carcass are more equalised, there is not the same reason for the butcher to cut the best joints so large.

The sirloin, cut where the fillet is thickest, and the middle ribs are generally considered the prime joints for roasting, the silver side of the round (salted) for boiling, and the rump steak for broiling ; but one excellent joint for roasting is often overlooked, that is the aitchbone. This, boned and rolled, and either baked or roasted, is both tender and full of flavour, and in spite of its being a bony joint, when it is reckoned that the bones yield an excellent soup, and that the price charged is little more than half what is demanded for a sirloin, it will be found to be a very economical joint for a large family.

The best beef is considered to be obtained from the shorthorns.

Australian beef, though inferior in flavour and quality to the English, is yet exceedingly good, and can always be obtained at a lower price. At first when imported the best parts only were sent, but now it arrives (frozen) in quarters, and is cut up and sold as English meat, only at a lower rate, thus putting good meat within the reach of all.

Beef should never be hung till it is the least degree high. It will not keep so long as mutton, and in damp weather it soon spoils. It should always be kept in a dry and airy place.

Beef, Aitchbone of, Salted, Boiled.

— INGREDIENTS — *Beef, water.*
AVERAGE COST, 6*d.* or 7*d. per lb.*

After this joint has been in salt 5 or 6 days it will be ready for use, and will not take so long boiling as a round, for it is not so solid. Wash the meat, and if too salt, soak it for a few hours, changing the water once or twice, till the required freshness is obtained. Put into a saucepan or boiling-pot sufficient water to cover the meat; set it over the fire, and when it boils, plunge in the joint, and let it boil up quickly. Now draw the

AITCHBONE OF BEEF.

pot to the side of the fire, and let the process be very gradual, as the water must only simmer, or the meat will be hard and tough. Carefully remove the scum from the surface of the water, and continue doing this for a few minutes after it first boils. Carrots and turnips are served with this dish, and sometimes suet dumplings, which may be boiled with the beef. Garnish with a few of the carrots and turnips, and serve the remainder in a vegetable-dish.

TIME.—*An aitchbone of* 10 *lbs.,* 3 *hours after the water boils;* one of 20 *lbs.,* 4½ *hours.*

SEASONABLE *all the year, but best from September to March.*

Note.—The liquor in which the meat has been boiled may be easily converted into a very excellent pea-soup. It will require very few vegetables, as it will be impregnated with the flavour of those boiled with the meat.

Beef à la Mode.—INGREDIENTS

for dish for 8 *persons.*—6 or 7 *lbs. of the thick flank of beef, a few slices of fat bacon,* 1 *teacupful of vinegar, black pepper, allspice,* 2 *cloves well mixed and finely pounded, making altogether* 1 *heaped teaspoonful; salt to taste,* 1 *bunch of savoury herbs, including parsley, all finely minced and well mixed;* 3 *onions,* 2 *large carrots,* 1 *turnip,* 1 *head of celery,* 1½ *pint of water,* 1 *glass of port wine.* AVERAGE COST, 5s.

Slice and fry the onions of a pale brown, cut up the other vegetables in small pieces, and prepare the beef for stewing in the following manner:—Choose a fine piece of beef, cut the bacon into long slices, about an inch in thickness, dip them into vinegar, and then into a little of the above seasoning of spice, &c., mixed with the same quantity of minced herbs. With a sharp knife make holes deep enough to let in the bacon; then rub the beef over with the remainder of the seasoning and herbs, and bind it up in a nice shape with tape. Have ready a well-tinned stewpan (it should not be much larger than the piece of meat you are cooking), into which put the beef, with the vegetables, vinegar and water. Let it simmer *very gently* for 5 hours, or rather longer, should the meat not be extremely tender, and turn it once or twice. When ready to serve, take out the beef, remove the tape, and put it on a hot dish. Skim off every particle of fat from the gravy, add the port wine, just let it boil, pour it over the beef, and it is ready to serve. Great care must be taken that this does

not boil fast, or the meat will be tough and tasteless—it should only just bubble. When convenient, all kinds of stews, &c., should be cooked on a hot plate, as the process is so much more gradual than on an open fire.

TIME.—5 *hours or rather more.*

SEASONABLE *all the year, but more suitable for a winter dish.*

Beef à la Mode (Economical).—

INGREDIENTS *for dish for* 6 *persons.*—About 3 *lbs. of clod or sticking piece,* 2 *oz. of clarified dripping,* 1 *large onion, flour,* 2 *quarts of water,* 12 *berries of allspice,* 2 *bay-leaves,* ½ *teaspoonful of whole black pepper, salt to taste.* AVERAGE COST, 1s. 8d.

Cut the beef into small pieces and roll them in flour; put the dripping into a stewpan with the onion, which should be sliced thin. Let it get quite hot; lay in the pieces of beef, and stir them well about. When nicely browned all over, add *by degrees* boiling water in the above proportion, and, as the water is added, keep the whole well stirred. Put in the spice, bay-leaves and seasoning, cover the stewpan closely, and set it by the side of the fire to stew very *gently,* till the meat becomes quite tender, which will be in about 3 hours, when it will be ready to serve. Remove the bay-leaves before it is sent to table.

TIME.—3 *hours.*

SEASONABLE *at any time.*

Beef, Baked. I. (Cold Meat

Cookery.) — INGREDIENTS *for large pie.* —about 2 *lbs of cold roast beef,* 2 *small onions,* 1 *large carrot or two small ones,* 1 *turnip, a small bunch of savoury herbs, salt and pepper to taste, quite a pint of gravy,* 3 *tablespoonfuls of ale, dripping crust or mashed potatoes.* AVERAGE COST, *exclusive of the beef,* 8d.

Cut the beef in slices, allowing a small amount of fat to each slice; place a layer of this in the bottom of a pie-dish, with a portion of the onions, carrots and turnips, which must be sliced; mince the herbs, strew them over the meat, and season with pepper and salt. Then put another layer of meat, vegetables and seasoning; and proceed in this manner until all the ingredients are used. Pour in the gravy and ale (water may be substituted for the former, but it is not so nice), cover with a crust or mashed potatoes, and bake for ½ hour, or rather longer.

TIME.—*Rather more than ½ hour.*

SEASONABLE *at any time.*

Note.—It is as well to parboil the carrots and turnips before adding them to the meat, and to use some of the liquor in which they were boiled as a substitute for gravy; that is to say, when there is no gravy at hand. Be particular to cut the onions in very *thin* slices.

Beef, Baked. II. (Cold Meat Cookery.)—INGREDIENTS.— *Slices of cold roast beef, salt and pepper to taste,* 1 *sliced onion,* 1 *teaspoonful of minced savoury herbs,* 12 *tablespoonfuls of gravy or sauce of any kind, mashed potatoes.* AVERAGE COST, *for large pie dish,* 1s. 3d.

Butter the sides of a deep dish, and spread mashed potatoes over the bottom of it; on this place layers of beef in thin slices (this may be minced, if there is not sufficient beef to cut into slices), well seasoned with pepper and salt, and a very little onion and herbs, which should be previously fried of a nice brown; then put another layer of mashed potatoes, and beef, and other ingredients, as before; pour in the gravy or sauce, cover the whole with another layer of potatoes, and bake for ½ hour. This may be served in the dish, or turned out.

TIME.—½ *hour.*

SEASONABLE *at any time.*

Beef, Boiled Round of.—INGRE-DIENTS.—*Beef, water.* AVERAGE COST, 9d. per lb.

As a whole round of beef, generally speaking, is too large for small families,

and very seldom required, we here give the recipe for dressing a portion of the silver side of the round. Take from 12 to 16 lbs., after it has been in salt about 10 days; just wash off the salt, skewer it up in a nice round-looking form, and bind it with tape to keep the skewers in their places. Put it in a saucepan of boiling water, set it upon a good fire, and when it begins to boil, carefully remove all scum from the surface, as, if this is not attended to, it sinks on to the meat, and, when brought to table, presents a very unsightly appearance. After it is well skimmed, draw the pot to the corner of the fire, allow the liquor to cool, then let the beef simmer

BOILED ROUND OF BEEF.

very gently until done. Remove the tape and skewers, which should be replaced by a silver one; pour over a little of the pot-liquor, and garnish with carrots. Carrots, and turnips, and sometimes suet dumplings accompany this dish; and these may all be boiled with the beef. The pot-liquor should be saved, and converted into pea-soup; and the outside slices, which are generally hard, and of an uninviting appearance, may be cut off before being sent to table, and potted. These make an excellent relish for the breakfast or luncheon table.

TIME.—*Part of a round of beef, weighing* 12 *lbs., about* 3 *hours after the water boils.*

SEASONABLE *all the year, but more suitable for winter.*

Soyer's Recipe for Preserving the Gravy in Salt Meat, when it is to be served Cold.—Fill two tubs with cold water, into which throw a few pounds of rough ice ; and when the meat is done, put it into one of the tubs of ice-water ; let it remain 1 minute, when take out, and put it in the other tub. Fill the first tub again with water, and continue this process for about 20 minutes ; then set it upon a dish, and let it remain until quite cold. When cut, the fat will be as white as possible, besides having saved the whole of the gravy. If there is no ice, spring water will answer the same purpose, but will require to be more frequently changed.

Note.—The brisket and rump may be boiled by the above recipe; of course allowing more or less time, according to the size of the joint.

Beef Bones, Broiled. — (Cold Meat Cookery.)—INGREDIENTS.—*The bones of ribs or sirloin ; salt, pepper and cayenne.*

Separate the bones, taking care that the meat on them is not too thick in any part ; sprinkle them well with the above seasoning, and broil over a very clear fire. When nicely browned, they are done ; but do not allow them to blacken.

Beef, Brisket of, à la Flamande.—INGREDIENTS *for dish for 8 or 10 persons.—About 6 or 8 lbs. of the brisket of beef, 4 or 5 slices of bacon, 2 carrots, 1 onion, a bunch of savoury herbs, salt and pepper to taste, 4 cloves, 4 whole allspice, 2 blades of mace.* AVERAGE COST, *4s. 3d.*

Choose that portion of the brisket which contains the gristle, trim it, and put it into a stewpan with the slices of bacon, which should be placed under and over the meat. Add the vegetables, herbs, spices and seasoning, and cover with a little weak stock or water ; shut the stewpan-lid as closely as possible, and simmer very gently for 4 hours. Strain the liquor, reserve a portion of it for sauce, and the remainder boil quickly over a sharp fire until reduced to a glaze, with which glaze the meat. Garnish the dish with scooped carrots and turnips, and, when liked, a little cabbage ;

all of which must be cooked separately. Thicken and flavour the liquor that was saved for sauce, pour it round the meat and serve. The beef may also be garnished with glazed onions, artichoke-bottoms, &c.

TIME.—*4 hours.*

SEASONABLE *at any time.*

Beef, Brisket of, Stewed.—INGREDIENTS *for dish for 10 persons.—7 lbs. of the brisket of beef, vinegar and salt, 6 carrots, 6 turnips, 6 small onions, 1 blade of pounded mace, 2 whole allspice pounded, thickening of butter and flour, 2 tablespoonfuls of ketchup, stock or water.* AVERAGE COST, *4s. 8d.*

About an hour before dressing it, rub the meat over with vinegar and salt ; put it into a stewpan, with sufficient stock to cover it (when this is not at hand, water may be substituted for it), and be particular that the stewpan is not much larger than the meat. Skim well, and when it has simmered very gently for 1 hour, put in the vegetables, and continue simmering till the meat is perfectly tender. Draw out the bones, dish the meat, and garnish either with tufts of cauliflower or braised cabbage cut in quarters. Thicken as much gravy as required, with a little butter and flour ; add spices and ketchup in the above proportion, give one boil, pour some of it over the meat, and the remainder send in a tureen.

TIME.—*Rather more than 3 hours.*

SEASONABLE *at any time.*

Note.—The remainder of the liquor in which the beef was boiled may be served as a soup, or it may be sent to table with the meat in a tureen.

Beef, Broiled, and Mushroom Sauce. (Cold Meat Cookery.)—INGREDIENTS.—*2 or 3 dozen small button mushrooms, 1 oz. of butter, salt and cayenne to taste, 1 tablespoonful of mushroom ketchup, mashed potatoes, slices of cold roast beef.* AVERAGE COST, *exclusive of the meat, 8d.*

Wipe the mushrooms free from grit with a piece of flannel, and salt; put them in a stewpan with the butter, seasoning and ketchup; stir over the fire until the mushrooms are quite done, when pour it in the middle of the mashed potatoes, browned. Then place round the potatoes slices of cold roast beef, nicely broiled over a clear fire. In making the mushroom sauce the ketchup may be dispensed with, if there is sufficient gravy.

TIME.—¼ *hour.*

SEASONABLE *from August to October.*

Beef, Broiled, and Oyster Sauce. (Cold Meat Cookery.)—INGREDIENTS *for small dish.*—1 *dozen oysters,* 3 *cloves,* 1 *blade of mace,* 2 *oz. of butter,* ½ *teaspoonful of flour, cayenne and salt to taste, mashed potatoes, a few slices of cold roast beef.* AVERAGE COST, *exclusive of the meat,* 1s. 6d.

Put the oysters in a stewpan, with their liquor strained; add the cloves, mace, butter, flour and seasoning, and let them simmer gently for 5 minutes. Have ready in the centre of a dish a round wall of mashed potatoes, browned; into the middle pour the oyster sauce quite hot, and round the potatoes place, in layers, slices of the beef, which should be previously broiled over a nice clear fire.

TIME.—5 *minutes.*

SEASONABLE *from September to April.*

Beef Bubble - and - Squeak. (Cold Meat Cookery.)—INGREDIENTS *for small dish.*—A *few thin slices of cold boiled beef; butter, cabbage,* 1 *sliced onion, pepper and salt to taste.* AVERAGE COST, *exclusive of the meat,* 4d.

Fry the slices of beef gently in a little butter, taking care not to dry them up. Lay them on a flat dish, and cover with fried greens. The greens may be prepared from cabbage sprouts or green savoys. They should be boiled till tender, well drained, minced, and placed till quite hot in a frying-pan, with butter, a sliced onion, and seasoning of pepper and salt. When the onion is done it is ready to serve.

TIME.—*Altogether,* ½ *hour.*

SEASONABLE *at any time.*

Beef Cake. (Cold Meat Cookery.)—INGREDIENTS.—*The remains of cold roast beef; to each pound of cold meat allow* ¼ *lb. of bacon or ham; seasoning to taste of pepper and salt,* 1 *small bunch of minced savoury herbs,* 1 *or* 2 *eggs.* AVERAGE COST, *with* 1 *lb. of cold beef,* 5d.

Mince the beef very finely (if underdone it will be better), add to it the bacon, which must also be chopped very small, and mix well together. Season, stir in the herbs, and bind with an egg, or 2 should 1 not be sufficient. Make it into small square cakes, about ½ inch thick, fry them in hot dripping, drain them, and serve in a dish with good gravy poured round.

TIME.—10 *minutes.*

SEASONABLE *at any time.*

Beef Carving:—

Beef, Aitchbone of.—A boiled aitchbone of beef is not a difficult joint to carve, as will be seen on reference to the accompanying engraving. By following with the knife

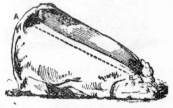

the direction of the line from A to B, nice slices will be easily cut. It may be necessary, as in a round of beef, to cut a thick slice off the outside before commencing to serve. When roasted the bones are usually removed before cooking, and it is then carved like the round.

Beef, Brisket of.—There is but little description necessary to add to show the carving of a boiled brisket of beef, beyond the engraving here inserted. The only point to be observed is that the joint should be cut evenly and firmly quite across the

bones, so that on its reappearance at table it should not have a jagged and untidy look.

Beef, Ribs of.—This dish resembles the sirloin, except that it has no fillet or undercut. As explained in the recipes, the end piece is often cut off, salted and boiled. The mode of carving is similar to that of the sirloin, viz., in the direction of the dotted line from A to B. This joint will be the more easily cut if the plan be pursued which is suggested in carving the sirloin: namely, the inserting of the knife immediately between the bone and the meat, before commencing to cut it into slices.

All joints of roast beef should be cut in even and thin slices. Horseradish, finely scraped, may be served as a garnish, but horseradish sauce is preferable for eating with the beef. Some carve this straight across as the fillet in a sirloin, giving at each helping a slice of the fat end of the meat.

Beef, A Round of.—A round of beef is more easily carved than any other joint of beef, but, to manage it properly, a thin-bladed and very sharp knife is necessary. Off the outside of the joint, at its top, a thick slice should first be cut, so as to leave the surface smooth; then thin and even slices should be cleverly carved in the

direction of the line A to B; and with each slice of the lean a delicate morsel of the fat should be served.

Beef, Sirloin of.—This dish is served differently at various tables, some preferring it to come to table with the fillet, or, as it is usually called, the undercut, uppermost. The reverse way, as shown in the cut, is that most usually adopted. Still the undercut is best eaten when hot; consequently, the carver himself may raise the joint, and cut some slices from the under side, in the direction of from A to B, as the fillet is very much preferred by some eaters.

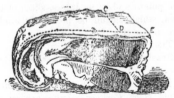

The upper part of the sirloin should be cut in the direction of the line from E to F, or it may be cut in the way named secondly in carving ribs and shown here, C to D, and care should be taken to carve it evenly and in thin slices. It will be found a great assistance, in carving this joint well, if the knife be first inserted just above the bone at the bottom, and run sharply along between the bone and meat, and also to divide

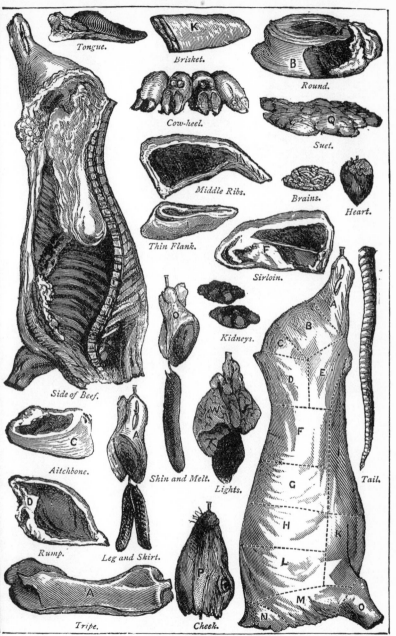

Tongue.

Brisket. **K**

Round. **B**

Cow-heel.

Suet. **Q**

Middle Ribs.

Brains.

Heart.

Thin Flank.

Sirloin. **F**

Side of Beef.

Kidneys. **O**

Aitchbone. **C**

Shin and Melt. **A**

Lights. **W**

Tail.

Rump. **D**

Leg and Skirt.

Tripe. **A**

Cheek. **P**

Various Parts of Beef.

the meat from the bone in the same way at the side of the joint; the slices will then come away more readily. With the sirloin, very finely-scraped horseradish is usually served, and a little given, when liked, to each guest. Horseradish sauce is preferable, however, for serving on the plate, although the scraped horseradish may still be used as a garnish.

Beef Tongue.—Passing the knife down in the direction of from A to B, a not too thin slice should be helped; and the carving of a tongue may be continued in this way until

the best portions of the upper side are served. The fat which lies about the root can be served by turning the tongue, and cutting in the direction of from C to D.

Beef, Collared.—INGREDIENTS.—

7 *lbs. of the thin end of the flank of beef, 2 oz. of coarse sugar, 6 oz. of salt, 1 oz. of saltpetre, 1 large handful of parsley, minced, 1 dessertspoonful of minced sage, a bunch of savoury herbs, ½ teaspoonful of pounded allspice; salt and pepper to taste.* AVERAGE COST, 4*d.*

Choose fine tender beef, but not too fat; lay it in a dish, rub in the sugar, salt and

COLLARED BEEF.

saltpetre, and let it remain in the pickle for a week or ten days, turning and rubbing it every day. Then bone it, remove

all the gristle and the coarse skin of the inside part, and sprinkle it thickly with parsley, herbs, spice and seasoning in the the above proportion, taking care that the former are finely minced, and the latter well pounded. Roll the meat up in a cloth as tightly as possible; bind it firmly with broad tape, and boil it gently for 6 hours. Immediately on taking it out of the pot put it under a good weight, without undoing it, and let it remain until cold. This dish is a very nice addition to the breakfast-table and looks better if glazed.

TIME.—6 *hours.*

SEASONABLE *at any time.*

Note.—During the time the beef is in pickle it should be kept cool, and regularly rubbed and turned every day.

Beef Collops.—INGREDIENTS *for dish for 6 persons.*—2 *lbs. of rumpsteak, 2 oz. of butter, 1 pint of gravy (water may be substituted for this), salt and pepper to taste, 1 shalot, finely minced, a pickled walnut, 1 teaspoonful of capers.* AVERAGE COST, 2*s.* 9*d.*

Have the steak cut thin, and divide it in pieces about 3 inches long; beat these with the blade of a knife, and dredge with flour. Put them in a frying-pan with the butter, and let them fry for about 3 minutes; then lay them in a small stewpan, and pour over them the gravy. Add a piece of butter kneaded with a little flour, put in the seasoning and all the other ingredients, and let the whole simmer, but not boil, for 10 minutes. Serve in a hot covered dish.

TIME.—10 *minutes.*

SEASONABLE *at any time.*

Beef, Curried. (Cold Meat Cookery.)

—INGREDIENTS *for small dish.*—*A few slices of tolerably lean cold roast beef, 2 oz. of butter, 2 onions, 1 wineglassful of beer, a dessertspoonful of curry-powder.* AVERAGE COST, *exclusive of the meat,* 4*d.*

Cut up the beef into pieces about 1 inch square, put the butter into a stewpan with

E

the onions sliced, and fry them of a light brown colour. Add all the other ingredients, and stir gently over a brisk fire for about 10 minutes. Should this be thought too dry, more beer, or a spoonful or two of gravy or water, may be added; but a good curry should not be very thin. Place it in a deep dish, with an edging of dry boiled rice, in the same manner as for other curries.

TIME.—10 *minutes.*

SEASONABLE *in winter.*

Beef, Fricandeau of.—INGREDI-

ENTS *for dish for 6 persons.—About 3 lbs. of the inside fillet of the sirloin (a piece of the rump may be substituted for this), pepper and salt to taste, 3 cloves, 2 blades of mace, 3 whole allspice, 1 pint of stock (see* STOCK), *or water, 1 glass of sherry, 1 bunch of savoury herbs, 2 shalots, bacon.* AVERAGE COST, 4s. 6d.

Cut some bacon into thin strips, and sprinkle over them a seasoning of pepper and salt, mixed with cloves, mace, and allspice, well pounded. Lard the beef with these, put it into a stewpan with the stock or water, sherry, herbs, shalots, 2 cloves, and more pepper and salt. Stew the meat gently until tender, when take it out, cover it closely, skim off all the fat from the gravy, and strain it. Set it on the fire, and boil till it becomes a glaze. Glaze the larded side of the beef with this, and serve on sorrel sauce, which is made as follows:—Wash and pick some sorrel, and put it into a stewpan with only the water that hangs about it. Keep stirring, to prevent its burning, and when done, lay it in a sieve to drain. Chop it, and stew it with a small piece of butter and 4 or 5 tablespoonfuls of good gravy, for an hour, then rub it through a sieve. If too acid, add sugar; a little cabbage-lettuce boiled with the sorrel will be found an improvement.

TIME.—2 *hours to gently stew the meat.*

SEASONABLE *at any time.*

Beef, Fried Salt. (Cold Meat

Cookery.)—INGREDIENTS.—*A few slices of cold salt beef, pepper to taste, 3 oz. of butter, mashed potatoes.* AVERAGE COST, *exclusive of the meat,* 4d.

Cut any part of cold salt beef into thin slices, fry them gently in butter, and season with a little pepper. Have ready some very hot mashed potatoes, lay the slices of beef on them, and garnish with 3 or 4 pickled gherkins. Cold salt beef, warmed in a little liquor from mixed pickle, drained, and served as above, will be found good.

TIME.—*About 5 minutes.*

SEASONABLE *at any time.*

Beef Fritters. (Cold Meat Cookery.)

INGREDIENTS.—*The remains of cold roast beef, pepper and salt to taste, ¾ lb. of flour, ¼ pint of water, 2 oz. of butter, the whites of 2 eggs.* AVERAGE COST, *exclusive of meat,* 6d.

Mix very smoothly, and by degrees, the flour with the above proportion of water; stir in 2 oz. of butter, which must be melted but not oiled, and just before it is to be used, add the whites of two well-whisked eggs. Should the batter be too thick, more water must be added. Pare down the cold beef into thin shreds, season with pepper and salt, and mix it with the batter, or the beef may be cut in thin slices and dipped in the batter. Drop a small quantity at a time into a pan of boiling lard, and fry from 7 to 10 minutes, according to the size. When done on one side, turn and brown them on the other. Let them dry for a minute or two before the fire, and serve on a folded napkin. A small quantity of finely-minced onions, mixed with the batter, is thought by some to be an improvement.

TIME.—*From 7 to 10 minutes.*

SEASONABLE *at any time.*

Beef, Hashed. I. (Cold Meat

Cookery.)—INGREDIENTS *for small dish.—Gravy saved from the meat, 1 teaspoonful of tomato sauce, one teaspoonful of Harvey's sauce, one teaspoonful of good mushroom ketchup, ½ a glass of port wine or strong ale, pepper and salt to taste, a little flour to thicken, 1 onion finely minced, a few slices of cold roast beef.* AVERAGE COST, *exclusive of the meat, 4d.*

Put all the ingredients but the beef into a stewpan with whatever gravy may have been saved from the meat the day it was roasted; simmer these gently for 10 minutes, then take the stewpan off the fire; let the gravy cool and skim off the fat. Cut the beef into thin slices, dredge them with flour, and lay them in the gravy; let the whole simmer gently for 5 minutes, but not boil, or the meat will be tough and hard. Serve very hot, and garnish with sippets of toasted bread.

TIME.—*20 minutes.*

SEASONABLE *at any time.*

Beef, Hashed. II. (Cold Meat Cookery.)—INGREDIENTS *for small dish.— The remains of ribs or sirloin of beef, 2 onions, 1 carrot, 1 bunch of herbs, pepper and salt to taste, ½ blade of pounded mace, thickening of flour, rather more than 1 pint of water.* AVERAGE COST, *exclusive of the meat, 6d.*

Take off all the meat from the bones of ribs or sirloin of beef; remove the outside brown and gristle; place the meat on one side, and well stew the bones and pieces with the above ingredients, for about 2 hours, till it becomes a strong gravy, and is reduced to rather more than ½ pint; strain this, thicken with a teaspoonful of flour, and let the gravy cool; skim off all the fat; lay in the meat, let it get hot through, but do not allow it to boil; and garnish with sippets of toasted bread. The gravy should be flavoured as in the preceding recipe.

TIME.—*Rather more than 2 hours.*

SEASONABLE *at any time.*

Note.—Either of the above recipes may be served in walls of mashed potatoes, browned,

in which case the sippets should be omitted. *Be careful that hashed meat does not boil, or it will become tough.*

Beef, Hunter's.—INGREDIENTS.— *For a round of beef weighing 25 lbs. allow 3 oz. of saltpetre, 3 oz. of coarse sugar, 1 oz. of cloves, 1 grated nutmeg, ½ oz. of allspice, 1 lb. of salt, ½ lb. of bay salt.*

Hang the beef for 2 or 3 days, and remove the bone. Pound spices, salt, &c., in the above proportion, and let them be reduced to the finest powder. Put the beef into a pan, rub all the ingredients well into it, and turn and rub it every day for rather more than a fortnight. When it has been sufficiently long in pickle, wash the meat, bind it up securely with tape, and put it into a pan with ½ pint of water at the bottom; mince some suet, cover the top of the meat with it, and over the pan put a common crust of flour and water; bake for 6 hours, and when cold, remove the paste. Save the gravy that flows from it, as it adds greatly to the flavour of hashes, stews, &c. The beef may be glazed, and garnished with meat jelly.

TIME.—*6 hours.*

SEASONABLE *all the year.*

Note.—In salting or pickling beef or pork for family consumption, it not being generally required to be kept for a great length of time, a less quantity of salt and a larger quantity of other matters more adapted to retain mellowness in meat may be employed, which could not be adopted by the curer of the immense quantities of meat required to be preserved for victualling the shipping of this maritime country. Sugar, which is well known to possess the preserving principle in a very great degree, without the pungency and astringency of salt, may be, and is, very generally used in the preserving of meat for family consumption. Although it acts without corrugating or contracting the fibres of meat, as is the case in the action of salt, and, therefore, does not impair its mellowness, yet its use in sufficient quantities for preservative effect, without the addition of other antiseptics, would impart a flavour not agreeable to the taste of many persons. It may be used, however, together with salt, with the greatest advantage in imparting mildness and mellowness to cured meat, in a proportion of about one part by weight to four of the mixture; and, perhaps, now that sugar is so much lower in price than it was in former years, one of the obstructions to its more frequent use is removed.

Beef Kidney, To Dress.—IN-
GREDIENTS *for dish for 4 persons.*—1 *kidney, clarified butter, pepper and salt to taste, a small quantity of highly-seasoned gravy,* 1 *tablespoonful of lemon-juice,* ¼ *teaspoonful of powdered sugar.* AVERAGE COST, 1s.

Cut the kidney into neat slices, put them into warm water to soak for 2 hours, and change the water 2 or 3 times ; then lay them on a clean cloth to dry the water from them, place them in a frying-pan with some clarified butter, and fry them of a nice brown; season each side with pepper and salt, put them round the dish with the gravy in the middle. Before pouring the gravy in the dish, add the lemon-juice and sugar.

TIME.—*From 5 to 10 minutes.*
SEASONABLE *at any time.*

Beef Kidney, To Dress.—·IN-
GREDIENTS *for small dish.*—1 *kidney,* 1 *dessertspoonful of minced parsley,* 1 *teaspoonful of minced shalot, salt and pepper to taste,* ¼ *pint of gravy (follow one of the gravy recipes) ; if there be no gravy or stock at hand,* 2 *tablespoonfuls of sherry.* AVERAGE COST, 1s. 3d.

Take off a little of the kidney fat, mince it very fine, and put it in a frying-pan ; slice the kidney, sprinkle over it parsley and shalots in the above proportion, add a seasoning of pepper and salt, and fry it of a nice brown. When it is done enough, dredge over a little flour, and pour in the gravy and sherry. Let it just simmer, but not boil any more, or the kidney would harden ; serve very hot, and garnish with croûtons. Where the flavour of the shalot is disliked it may be omitted, and a small quantity of savoury herbs substituted for it.

TIME.—*From 5 to 10 minutes, according to the thickness of the slices.*
SEASONABLE *at any time.*

Beef Kidney, To Dress (A more simple method).—Cut the kidneys into thin slices, flour them, and fry of a nice brown. When done, make a gravy in the pan by pouring away the fat, putting in a small piece of butter, ¼ pint of boiling water, pepper and salt, a dessertspoonful of lemon-juice, and a tablespoonful of mushroom ketchup. Let the gravy just boil up, pour over the kidney, and serve.

Beef, Minced. (Cold Meat Cookery.)
INGREDIENTS.—1 *oz. of butter,* 1 *small onion,* 12 *tablespoonfuls of gravy left from the meat,* 1 *tablespoonful of strong ale,* 1 *teaspoonful of flour, salt and pepper to taste, a few slices of lean roast beef.* AVERAGE COST, *exclusive of the meat,* 3d.

Put into a stewpan the butter with an onion chopped fine ; add the gravy, ale, and a teaspoonful of flour to thicken ; season with pepper and salt, and stir these ingredients over the fire until the onion is a rich brown. Cut (but do not chop) the meat *very fine,* add it to the gravy, stir till quite hot, and serve. Garnish with sippets of toasted bread. Be careful in not allowing the gravy to boil after the meat is added, as it would render it hard and tough.

TIME.—*About* ½ *hour.*
SEASONABLE *at any time.*

Beef, Minced.—INGREDIENTS *for dish for 2 or 3 persons.*—1 *lb. of rump-steak, salt and pepper to taste,* 2 *oz. of butter,* 1 *onion minced,* ¼ *pint of water,* 1 *tablespoonful of Harvey's sauce, or lemon-juice, or mushroom ketchup,* 1 *small bunch of savoury herbs.* AVERAGE COST, 1s. 6d.

Mince the beef and onion very small, and fry the latter in butter until of a pale brown. Put all the ingredients together in a stewpan, and boil gently for about 10 minutes; garnish with sippets of toasted bread, and serve very hot.

TIME.—10 *minutes.*

SEASONABLE *at any time.*

Beef, Miniature Round of.—IN-
GREDIENTS.—*From* 5 *to* 10 *lbs. of ribs of beef, sufficient brine to cover the meat.* AVERAGE COST, 10*d. per lb.*

Choose a fine rib, have the bone removed, rub some salt over the inside, and skewer the meat up into a nice round form, and bind it with tape. Put it into sufficient brine to cover it (*see* BEEF PICKLE), and let it remain for 6 days, turning the meat every day. When required to be dressed, drain from the pickle, and put the meat into very hot water; boil it rapidly for a few minutes, then draw the pot to the side of the fire, and simmer the beef very gently until done. Remove the skewer, and replace it by a plated or silver one. Carrots and turnips should be served with this dish, and may be boiled with the meat.

TIME.—*A small round of 8 lbs., about 2 hours after the water boils; one of 12 lbs. about 3 hours.*

SEASONABLE *at any time.*

(*An excellent Dish for a small Family.*)

Note.—Should the joint be very small, 4 or 5 days will be sufficient time to salt it.

Beef, Miroton of. (Cold Meat Cookery.)—INGREDIENTS *for small dish.—A few slices of cold roast beef. 2 oz. of butter, salt and pepper to taste, 3 onions, ½ pint of gravy.* AVERAGE COST, *exclusive of the meat,* 5*d.*

Slice the onions and put them into the frying-pan with the cold beef and butter; place it over the fire, and keep turning and stirring the ingredients to prevent them burning. When a pale brown, add the gravy and seasoning; let it simmer for a few minutes, and serve very hot. The dish is excellent and economical.

TIME.—5 *minutes.*

SEASONABLE *at any time.*

Beef Olives. INGREDIENTS *for small dish.—*1 *lb. of rump-steak,* 1 *egg,* 1 *table-spoonful of minced savoury herbs, pepper and salt to taste,* 1 *pint of stock,* 2 *or* 3 *slices of bacon,* 2 *tablespoonfuls of any kind of store sauce, a slight thickening of butter and flour.* AVERAGE COST, 2*s.*

Have the steaks cut very thin, beat them to make them level, cut them into 6 or 7 pieces, brush over with egg, and sprinkle with herbs, which should be very finely minced; season with pepper and salt, roll up the pieces tightly, and fasten with a small skewer. Put the stock in a stew-pan that will exactly hold the ingredients, for, by being pressed together they will keep their shape better; lay in the rolls of meat, cover them with the bacon, cut in thin slices, and over that put a piece of paper. Stew them very *gently* for full 2 hours; for the slower they are done the better. Take them out, remove the skewers, thicken the gravy with butter and flour, and flavour with any store sauce that may be preferred. Give one boil, pour over the meat, and serve.

TIME.—2 *hours.*

SEASONABLE *at any time.*

Beef Olives (Economical). (Cold Meat Cookery.)—INGREDIENTS.—*The re-mains of underdone cold roast beef, bread-crumbs,* 1 *shalot finely minced, pepper and salt to taste, gravy made from the beef bones, thickening of butter and flour,* 1 *table-spoonful of mushroom ketchup.*

Cut some slices of underdone roast beef about ¼ of an inch thick; sprinkle over them some bread-crumbs, minced shalot, and a little of the fat and seasoning; roll them, and fasten with a small skewer. Have ready some gravy made from the beef bones; put in the pieces of meat, and stew them till tender, which will be about 1¼ hour, or rather longer. Arrange the meat in a dish, thicken and flavour the gravy, and pour it over the meat, when it is ready to serve.

TIME.—1½ *hour.* SEASONABLE *at any time.*

Beef Palates, To Dress.—INGRE-
DIENTS.—*4 palates, sufficient gravy to cover them, cayenne to taste, 1 tablespoonful of mushroom ketchup, 1 tablespoonful of pickled onion liquor, thickening of butter and flour.*

Wash the palates, and put them into a stewpan, with sufficient water to cover them, and let them boil until perfectly tender, or until the upper skin may be easily peeled off. Have ready sufficient gravy to cover them; add a good seasoning of cayenne, and thicken with a little butter kneaded with flour; let it boil up, and skim. Cut the palates into square pieces, put them in the gravy, and let them simmer gently for ½ hour; add ketchup and onion-liquor, give one boil, and serve.

TIME.—*From 3 to 5 hours to boil the palates.*

SEASONABLE *at any time.*

Note.—Palates may be dressed in various ways, with good onion sauce, tomato sauce, &c. &c., and may also be served in a *vol-au-vent;* but the above will be found a more simple method of dressing them.

Beef Pickle. (This may also be
used for any kind of Meat, Tongues, or Hams.)—INGREDIENTS.—*6 lbs. of salt, 2 lbs. of fine sugar, 3 oz. of powdered saltpetre, 3 gallons of spring water.*

Boil all the ingredients gently together, so long as any scum or impurity arises, which carefully remove; when quite cold, pour it over the meat, every part of which must be covered with the brine. This may be used for pickling any kind of meat, and may be kept for some time, if boiled up occasionally with an addition of the ingredients.

TIME.—*A ham should be kept in pickle for a fortnight; a piece of beef weighing 1½ lbs., 12 or 15 days; a tongue, 10 days or a fortnight.*

Note.—For salting and pickling meat, it is a good plan to rub in only half the quantity of salt directed, and to let it remain for a day or two to disgorge and effectually to get rid of the blood and slime; then rub in the remainder of the salt and other ingredients, and proceed as above. This rule may be applied to all recipes for salting and pickling meat.

Beef, Pickled part of a Round
for Hanging.—INGREDIENTS.—*For 14 lbs. of a round of beef allow 1½ lb. of salt, ½ oz. of powdered saltpetre; or 1 lb. of salt, ½ lb. of sugar, ½ oz. of powdered saltpetre.*

Rub in, and sprinkle either of the above mixtures on 14 lbs. of meat. Keep it in an earthenware pan, or a deep wooden tray, and turn twice a week during 3 weeks; then bind up the beef tightly with coarse linen tape, and hang it in a kitchen in which a fire is constantly kept, for 3 weeks. Pork, hams, and bacon may be cured in a similar way, but will require double the quantity of the salting mixture; and if not smoke-dried, they should be taken down from hanging after 3 or 4 weeks, and afterwards kept in boxes or tubs, amongst dry oat-husks.

TIME.—*2 or 3 weeks to remain in the brine; to be hung 3 weeks.*

SEASONABLE *at any time.*

Note.—The meat may be boiled fresh from this pickle, instead of smoking it.

Beef, Potted. I. (Cold Meat Cookery.)
—INGREDIENTS.—*2 lbs. of lean beef, 1 tablespoonful of water, ¼ lb. of butter, a seasoning to taste, of salt, cayenne, and black pepper, anchovy sauce.* AVERAGE COST, 2s.

Procure a nice piece of lean beef, as free as possible from gristle, skin, &c., and put it into a jar (if at hand, one with a lid) with 1 tablespoonful of water. Cover it *closely,* and put the jar into a saucepan of boiling water, letting the water come within 2 inches of the top of the jar. Boil gently for 3½ hours, then take the beef, chop it very small with a chopping-knife, and pound it thoroughly in a mortar. Mix with it by degrees all, or a portion, of the gravy that will have run from it, and a little clarified butter; add the seasoning put it in small pots for use, and cover with a little butter just warmed and poured over. If much gravy is added to it, it will keep but a short time ; on the contrary, if a large proportion of butter is used, it may be preserved for some time.

TIME.—3½ hours.

SEASONABLE at any time.

Beef, Potted. II. (Cold Meat Cookery.)

—INGREDIENTS.—The remains of cold roast or boiled beef, butter, cayenne to taste, blades of pounded mace.

The outside slices of boiled beef may, with a little trouble, be converted into a very nice addition to the breakfast-table. Cut up the meat into small pieces and pound it well with a little butter, in a mortar ; add a seasoning of cayenne and mace, and be very particular that the latter spice is reduced to the finest powder. When all the ingredients are thoroughly mixed, put them into glass or earthen potting-pots, and pour on the top a coating of clarified butter.

SEASONABLE at any time.

Note.—If cold roast beef is used, remove all pieces of gristle and dry outside pieces, as these do not pound well.

Beef Ragout. (Cold Meat Cookery.)

—INGREDIENTS for large dish.—About 2 lbs. of cold roast beef, 6 onions, pepper, salt, and mixed spices to taste; ½ pint of boiling water, 3 tablespoonfuls of gravy. AVERAGE COST, exclusive of the meat, 6d.

Cut the beef into rather large pieces, and put them into a stewpan with the onions, which must be sliced. Season well with pepper, salt, and mixed spices, and pour over about ½ pint of boiling water, and gravy in the above proportion (gravy saved from the meat answers the purpose); let the whole stew very gently for about 2 hours, and serve with pickled walnuts, gherkins, or capers, just warmed in the gravy.

TIME, 2 hours.

SEASONABLE at any time.

Beef Rissoles. (Cold Meat Cookery.)

—INGREDIENTS.—The remains of cold roast beef; to each pound of meat allow ¾ lb. of bread-crumbs, salt and pepper to taste, a few chopped savoury herbs, ½ a teaspoonful of minced lemon-peel, 1 or 2 eggs. AVERAGE COST, exclusive of 1 lb. of meat, 3d.

Mince the beef, which should be lean, very fine, and mix with this bread-crumbs, herbs, seasoning and lemon-peel, in the above proportion, to each pound of meat. Make all into a thick paste with 1 or 2 eggs ; divide into balls or cones, and fry a

RISSOLES OF BEEF.

rich brown. Garnish the dish with fried parsley, and send to table some good brown gravy in a tureen. Instead of garnishing with fried parsley, gravy may be poured in the dish round the rissoles ; in this case, it will not be necessary to send any in a tureen. These rissoles may be dipped in egg-and-crumbs before frying.

TIME.—From 5 to 10 minutes, according to size.

SEASONABLE at any time.

Beef, Roast Fillet of (Larded).

—INGREDIENTS for dish for 6 persons.— About 3 lbs. of the inside fillet of the sirloin, 1 onion, a small bunch of parsley, salt and pepper to taste, sufficient vinegar to cover the meat, glaze, Spanish sauce (see SAUCE). AVERAGE COST, exclusive of the sauce, 4s.

Lard the beef with bacon, and put it into a pan with sufficient vinegar to cover it, with an onion sliced, parsley, and seasoning, and let it remain in this pickle for 12 hours. Roast it before a nice clear fire for about 1¼ hour, and, when done, glaze it. Pour some Spanish sauce round the beef, and the remainder serve in a tureen. It may be garnished with Spanish onions, boiled and glazed.

TIME.—1¼ hour.

SEASONABLE at any time.

Beef, Roast Ribs of.—INGREDIENTS.—*Beef, a little salt.* AVERAGE COST, 10d. per lb.

The fore-rib is considered the primest roasting piece, but the middle-rib is considered the most economical. Let the meat be well hung (should the weather permit), having previously cut off the ends of the bones, which should be salted for a few days, and then boiled. Put the meat down to a nice clear fire, with some clean dripping in the pan, dredge the joint with a little flour, and keep continually basting it all the time it is cooking. Sprinkle some fine salt over it (this must never be

done until the joint is dished, as it draws the juices from the meat); pour the dripping from the pan, put in a

BEEF PRESSED.

little boiling water, and *strain* the gravy over the meat. Garnish with tufts of scraped horseradish, and send horseradish sauce to table with it. A Yorkshire pudding sometimes accompanies this dish, and, if lightly made and well cooked, will be found a very agreeable addition.

TIME.—10 *lbs. of beef,* 2½ *hours;* 14 *to* 18 *lbs., from* 3½ *to* 4 *hours.*

SEASONABLE at any time.

Beef, Roast Ribs of, Boned and Rolled (a very convenient Joint for a Family).—INGREDIENTS.—1 or 2 *ribs of beef.* AVERAGE COST, 10 per lb.

Choose a fine rib of beef, and have it cut according to the weight you require, either wide or narrow. Bone and roll the meat round, secure it with wooden skewers, and if necessary, bind it round with a

piece of tape. Spit the beef firmly, or, if a bottle-jack is used, put the joint on the hook, and place it *near* a nice clear fire. Let it remain so till the outside of the meat is set, when draw it to a distance, and keep continually basting until the meat is done, which can be ascertained by the steam from it drawing towards the fire. As this joint is solid, rather more than ¼ hour must be allowed for each lb. Remove the skewers, put in a plated or silver one, and send the joint to table, with gravy in the dish, and garnish with tufts of horseradish. Horseradish sauce is a great improvement to roast beef.

TIME.—*For* 10 *lbs. of the rolled ribs,* 3 *hours (as the joint is very solid, we have allowed an extra* ½ *hour); for* 6 *lbs.,* 1½ *hour.*

SEASONABLE all the year.

Note.—When the weight exceeds 10 lbs., we would not advise the above method of boning or rolling; only in the case of 1 or 2 ribs, when the joint cannot stand upright in the dish, and would look awkwardly. The bones should be put on with a few vegetables and herbs, and made into stock or soup.

Beef, Roast Sirloin of.—INGREDIENTS.—*Beef, a little salt.* AVERAGE COST, 10d. per lb.

As a joint cannot be well roasted without a good fire, see that it is well made up about ¾ hour before it is required, so that when the joint is put down, it is clear and

ROAST SIRLOIN OF BEEF.

bright. Choose a nice sirloin, the weight of which should not exceed 16 lbs., as the outside would be too much done, whilst the inside would not be done enough. Spit it or hook it on to the jack firmly, dredge it slightly with flour, and place it near the fire at first. Then draw it to a distance, and keep continually basting until the meat is done. Dish the meat, sprinkle a small quantity of salt over it, empty the dripping pan of all the dripping, pour in some boiling water, stir it about, and strain over the meat. Garnish with tufts of horseradish, and send horseradish sauce and Yorkshire pudding to table with it.

The rump, round, and other pieces of beef are roasted in the same manner, allowing for solid joints rather more than ¼ hour to every lb.

TIME.—*A sirloin of 10 lbs., 2½ hours; 14 to 16 lbs., about 4 or 4½ hours.*

SEASONABLE *at any time.*

Note.—The above is the usual method of roasting meat; but to have it in perfection and the meat should at first be laid quite close to the fire, and when the outside is set and firm, drawn away to a good distance, and then left to roast very slowly. Where economy is studied, this plan would not answer, as the meat requires to be at the fire double the time of the ordinary way of cooking; consequently, double the quantity of fuel would be consumed.

Beef, Rolled, to eat like Hare.

—INGREDIENTS *for dish for 6 persons.*— *About 3 lbs. of the inside of the sirloin, 2 glasses of port wine, 2 glasses of vinegar, a small quantity of forcemeat, 1 teaspoonful of pounded allspice.* AVERAGE COST, 4s.

Take the inside of a large sirloin, soak it in 1 glass of port wine and 1 glass of vinegar, mixed, and let it remain for 2 days. Make a forcemeat (see FORCEMEAT), lay it on the meat, and bind it up securely. Roast it before a nice clear fire, and baste it with 1 glass each of port wine and vinegar, with which mix a teaspoonful of pounded allspice. Serve, with a good gravy in the dish, and send red-currant jelly to table with it.

TIME.—*A piece of 5 lbs. about 1½ hour before a brisk fire.*

SEASONABLE *at any time.*

Beef Rolls. (Cold Meat Cookery.)—

INGREDIENTS.—*The remains of cold roast or boiled beef, seasoning to taste, of salt, pepper, and minced herbs; puff-paste.*

Mince the beef tolerably fine with a small amount of its own fat; add a seasoning of pepper, salt, and chopped herbs; put the whole into a roll of puff-paste, and bake for ½ hour, or rather longer should the roll be very large. Beef patties may be made of cold meat, by mincing and seasoning beef as directed above, and baking in a rich puff-paste in patty-tins.

TIME.—½ *hour.*

SEASONABLE *at any time.*

Beef Sausages.—INGREDIENTS.—

To every lb. of suet allow 2 lbs. of lean beef; seasoning to taste, of salt, pepper, and mixed spices.

Clear the suet from skin, and chop that and the beef as finely as possible; season with pepper, salt, and spices, and mix the whole well together. Make it into flat cakes, or put it in well-cleansed skins, and fry of a nice brown. Many persons pound the meat in a mortar after it is chopped, but this is not necessary when the meat is minced finely.

TIME.—10 *minutes to fry.*

SEASONABLE *at any time.*

Beef, Sliced and Broiled.—

(Cold Meat Cookery.)—INGREDIENTS.—*A few slices of cold roast beef, 4 or 5 potatoes, a thin batter, pepper and salt to taste.*

Pare the potatoes as you would peel an apple; fry the parings in a thin batter seasoned with salt and pepper, until they are of a light brown colour, and place them on a dish over some slices of beef, which should be nicely seasoned and broiled.

TIME.—5 *minutes to broil the meat.*

SEASONABLE *at any time.*

(*A Breakfast dish.*)

Beef, Spiced. (To Serve Cold.)—

INGREDIENTS.—14 *lbs. of the thick flank or*

rump of beef, ½ lb. of coarse sugar, 1 oz. of saltpetre, ¼ lb. of pounded allspice, 1 lb. of common salt. AVERAGE COST, 7d. per lb.

Rub the sugar well into the beef, and let it lie for 12 hours; then rub the saltpetre and allspice, both of which should be pounded, over the meat, and let it remain for another 12 hours; then rub in the salt. Turn daily in the liquor for a fortnight; soak it for a few hours in water, dry with a cloth, cover with a coarse paste, put a little water at the bottom of the pan, and bake in a moderate oven for 4 hours. If it is not covered with a paste be careful to put the beef into a deep vessel, and cover with a plate, or it will be too crisp. During the time the meat is in the oven it should be turned once or twice.

TIME.—4 *hours.*
SEASONABLE *at any time.*

Beef-Steak Pie.—INGREDIENTS *for good-sized pie.*—2 lbs. of buttock steak, ¼ lb. of ox kidney, pepper, salt and a few minced herbs if liked, 6 oz. of dripping or lard, 1 lb. of flour, sauce. AVERAGE COST, 2s. 6d.

Cut the beef in even square pieces, slice the kidney, freeing it from skin and gristle, and lay them in a pie-dish with a plentiful seasoning of salt and pepper till the dish is full. Pour in a little water and a dessert-spoonful of any good sauce; turn a tin over the dish and put it in the oven to partly cook the meat while the crust is made. Rub the dripping or lard into the flour, add a teaspoonful of salt, and mix with sufficient water to

BEEF-STEAK PIE.

make a short crust. Let the dish cool after taking it out of the oven, border it with a narrow strip of the paste, and lay over the crust; ornament it with a paste jagger or fork at the edges and with cut leaves and a flower at the top. Wash over with beaten egg and put in the oven.

TIME.—*About ¾ hour after putting on the crust.*
SEASONABLE *at any time.*

Beef, Stewed.—INGREDIENTS *for dish for 4 or 5 persons.*—A thick beef or rump-steak of about 2 lbs., an onion, some bread-crumbs, pepper and salt, 2 oz. of butter. AVERAGE COST, 2s. 3d.

Mince the onion fine, mix it with the bread, pepper, and salt; make deep incisions in the beef, but do not cut it through; fill the spaces with the bread, &c. Roll up the steak and put it into a stewpan with the butter; let it stew very gently for more than 2 hours; serve it with its own gravy, thickened with a little flour and flavoured as may be required, either with tomato sauce, ketchup, or Harvey's sauce.

TIME.—*About 2 hours, or rather more.*
SEASONABLE *at any time.*
(*A Polish dish.*)

Beef, Stewed Rump of.—INGREDIENTS *for a large dish.*—½ rump of beef, sufficient stock to cover it, 4 tablespoonful of vinegar, 2 tablespoonfuls of ketchup, a bunch of savoury herbs, 2 onions, 12 cloves, pepper and salt to taste, thickening of butter and flour, 1 glass of port wine. AVERAGE COST, 10d. per lb.

Cut out the bone, sprinkle the meat with a little cayenne (this must be sparingly used), and bind and tie it firmly up with tape; put it into a stewpan with sufficient stock to cover it, add vinegar, ketchup, herbs, onions, cloves, and seasonings in the above proportions, and simmer very gently for 4 or 5 hours, or until the meat is perfectly tender, which may be ascertained by piercing it with a thin skewer. When done, remove the tape, lay it in a deep dish, which keep hot; strain and skim the gravy, thicken it with butter and flour, add a glass of port wine and any flavouring to make the gravy rich and palatable; let it boil up, pour over the meat, and serve. This dish may be very much enriched by garnishing with force-meat balls, or filling up the space whence the bone is taken with a good forcemeat; sliced carrots, turnips, and onions boiled with the meat are also a great improvement, and, where expense is not objected to, it may be glazed. This, however, is not necessary where a good gravy is poured round and over the meat.

TIME.—½ *rump stewed gently from 4 to* *hours.*

SEASONABLE *at any time.*

Note.—A stock or gravy in which to boil the meat may be made of the bone and trimmings, by boiling them with water, and adding carrots, onions, turnips, and a bunch of sweet herbs. To make this dish richer and more savoury, half-roast the rump, and afterwards stew it in strong stock and a little Madeira. This is an expensive method, and is not, after all, much better than a plainer-dressed joint.

Beef, Stewed Shin of.—INGRE-DIENTS.—*A shin of beef*, 1 *head of celery*, 1 *onion, a faggot of savoury herbs, ½ tea-spoonful of allspice, ½ teaspoonful of whole black pepper, 4 carrots, 12 button onions, 2 turnips, thickening of butter and flour, 3 tablespoonfuls of mushroom ketchup, 2 tablespoonfuls of port wine; pepper and salt to taste.* AVERAGE COST, 5*d. per lb.*

Have the bone sawn into 4 or 5 pieces, cover with hot water, bring it to a boil, and remove any scum that may rise to the surface. Put in the celery, onion, herbs, spice, and seasoning, and simmer very gently until the meat is tender. Peel the vegetables, cut them into any shape fancy may dictate, and boil them with the onions until tender; lift out the beef, put it on a dish, which keep hot, and thicken with butter and flour as much of the liquor as will be wanted for gravy; keep stirring till it boils, then strain and skim. Put the gravy back in the stewpan, add the season-ing, port wine, and ketchup, give one boil, and pour it over the beef; garnish with the boiled carrots, turnips and onions.

TIME.—*The meat to be stewed about* 4 *hours.*

SEASONABLE *at any time.*

Beef-Tea.—INGREDIENTS *for* 1 *pint.* —1 *lb. of lean gravy-beef, 1½ pint of water,* 1 *saltspoonful of salt.* AVERAGE COST, 8*d.*

Have the meat cut without fat and bone, and choose a nice fleshy piece. Cut it into small pieces about the size of dice, and put it into a clean saucepan. Add the water *cold* to it; put it on the fire, and bring it to the boiling-point; then skim well. Put in the salt when the water boils, and *simmer* the beef-tea *gently* from ½ to ¾ hour, re-moving any more scum should it appear on the surface. Strain the tea through a hair sieve, and set it by in a cool place. When wanted for use, remove every par-ticle of fat from the top; warm up as much as may be required, adding, if necessary, a little more salt. This pre-paration is simple beef-tea, and is to be administered to those invalids to whom flavourings and seasonings are not allowed. When the patient is very weak, use double the quantity of meat to the same propor-tion of water. Should the invalid be able to take the tea prepared in a more palata-ble manner, it is easy to make it so by following the directions in Soyer's recipe, which is an admirable one for making savoury beef-tea. Beef-tea is always better when made the day before it is wanted, and then warmed up. It is a good plan to put the tea into a small cup or basin, and to place this basin in a sauce-pan of boiling water When the tea is hot, it is ready to serve.

TIME.—½ *to* ¾ *hour.*

Beef-Tea, Baked.—INGREDIENTS *for* 1 *pint.*—1 *lb. of fleshy beef,* 1 *pint of water, ½ saltspoonful of salt.* AVERAGE COST, 8*d.*

Cut the beef into small square pieces, after trimming off all the fat, and put it into a baking-jar (these jars are sold expressly for the purpose of making soups, gravies, &c., in the oven, and are arranged with tightly-fitting lids) with the above proportion of water and salt; close the jar well, place it in a warm but not hot oven, and bake for 3 or 4 hours. When the oven is very fierce in the daytime, it is a good plan to put the jar in at night, and let it remain until next morning, when the tea will be done. It should be strained, and put by in a cool place until wanted. It may also be flavoured with an onion, a clove, and a few sweet herbs, &c., when the stomach is sufficiently strong to take these.

TIME.—*3 or 4 hours, or to be left in the oven all night.*

Note.—A good substitute for beef-tea may be made by using Liebig's Extract of Beef.

Beef-Tea Custard.—INGREDIENTS *for large breakfastcupful.—½ pint of beef-tea made by one of the preceding recipes, the yolks of two eggs, the white of one, salt.* AVERAGE COST, 6d.

Beat the eggs and mix them well with the beef-tea, adding salt to taste, butter a basin, put in the mixture, tie a buttered paper over and steam for 20 minutes. The water should bubble after the custard is in.

This can be eaten either hot or cold; or, cut in small pieces, it can be put in hot beef-tea. It is a nice and nourishing food for invalids.

TIME.—*20 minutes to steam the custard.*

Beef-Tea, Quickly Made.—INGREDIENTS *for 1 pint.—1 lb. of lean beef, 1 pint of water.* AVERAGE COST, 8d.

With a sharp knife scrape the beef into fibres; this should be done on a board, Put the scraped meat into a china cup or basin, and add the water lukewarm. Let it stand for 20 minutes, then put the whole into a lined saucepan, and let it cook long enough to colour it, but no more, 5 minutes is quite sufficient.

TIME.—*In all about ½ an hour.*

Beef-Tea, Savoury. (SOYER' Recipe.)—INGREDIENTS *for 1 pint.—1 lb of solid beef, 1 oz. of butter, 1 clove, 2 butto onions or ½ a large one, 1 saltspoonful o salt, 1 quart of water.* AVERAGE COST, 9d

Cut the beef into very small dice; pu it into a stewpan with the butter, clove onion, and salt; stir the meat round ove the fire for a few minutes until it produce a thin gravy, then add the water, and le it simmer gently from ½ to ¾ of an hour

BEEF-TEA TRAY.

skimming off every particle of fat. Whe done, strain it through a sieve, and put i by in a cool place until required. Th same, if wanted quite plain, is done b merely omitting the vegetables, salt, an clove; the butter cannot be objectionable as it is taken out in skimming.

TIME.—*½ to ¾ hour.*

Note.—The meat left from beef-tea may b boiled a little longer, and pounded with spices &c., for potting. It makes a very nice breakfas dish.

Beef-Tea, Substitute for.—

When beef-tea cannot be taken by a invalid, and when it is necessary to ad minister the largest amount of nourish ment in the smallest or most condensec form, Brand's extract of meat will be found invaluable. A spoonful will be bu little trouble to take or administer, yet i contains as much nourishment as ar ordinary cupful of beef-tea. Where the invalid suffers from sickness or nausea this preparation, which can be taken cold and which is not at all strongly flavoured will be found infinitely pleasanter and more refreshing than hot beef-tea.

Beetroot, Boiled.—INGREDIENTS.
—*Beetroot, boiling water.* AVERAGE COST, *2d. each.*

When large, young, and juicy, this vegetable makes a very excellent addition to winter salads, and may easily be converted into an economical and quickly-made pickle. (*See*BEETROOT, PICKLED.) Beetroot is more frequently served cold than hot ; when the latter mode is preferred, melted butter should be sent to table with it. It may also be stewed with button

BEETROOT.

onions, or boiled and served with roasted onions. Wash the beets thoroughly ; but do not prick or break the skin before they are cooked, as they would lose their beautiful colour in boiling. Put them into boiling water, and let them boil until tender, keeping them well covered. If to be served hot, remove the peel quickly, rubbing and not cutting it off, cut the beetroot into thick slices, and send to table with melted butter. For salads, pickle, &c., let the root cool, then peel and cut it into slices.

TIME.—*Small beetroot,* 1½ *to* 2 *hours; large* 2½ *to* 3 *hours.*

SEASONABLE.—*May be had at any time.*

Beetroot, Pickled.—INGREDIENTS.—*Sufficient vinegar to cover the beets,* 2 *oz. of whole pepper,* 2 *oz. of allspice to each gallon of vinegar.* AVERAGE COST, *2d. each.*

Wash the beets free from dirt, and be very careful not to prick the outside skin, or they would lose their beautiful colour. Put them into boiling water, let them simmer gently, and when about three-

parts done, which will be in 1½ hour, take them out and let them cool. Boil the vinegar with pepper and allspice, in the above proportion, for 10 minutes, and when cold, pour it on the beets, which must be peeled and cut into slices about ½ inch thick. Cover with bladder to exclude the air, and in a week they will be fit for use.

TIME.—*One week.*

SEASONABLE, *make this pickle in the Autumn.*

Beignets Soufflés.—INGREDIENTS *for small dish.*—½ *pint of water,* 3 *eggs,* 1 *dessertspoonful of white sugar,* 3 *oz. of butter, flavouring of vanilla, fat for frying.* AVERAGE COST, 8*d.*

Boil the butter in the water and stir in enough flour to make the mixture stiff enough to leave the sides of the saucepan ; then add the yolks of the eggs, and beat the mixture well. When cold, add the whites of the eggs beaten to a stiff froth with the sugar, and flavouring, and fry in spoonfuls in very hot fat. Serve immediately. Grated cheese can be substituted for the flavouring of vanilla, when a little cayenne must take the place of the sugar.

TIME.—5 *minutes to fry.*

SEASONABLE *at any time.*

Benton Sauce (to serve with Hot or Cold Roast Beef.)—INGREDIENTS *for* 1 *tureen.*—1 *tablespoonful of scraped horseradish,* 1 *teaspoonful of made mustard,* 1 *teaspoonful of pounded sugar,* 4 *tablespoonfuls of vinegar.* AVERAGE COST, 2*d.*

Grate or scrape the horseradish very fine, and mix it with the other ingredients, which must be all well blended together ; serve in a tureen. With cold meat this sauce is a very good substitute for pickles.

Beverages. — Beverages may be divided into three classes :—

1. Those of the simplest kind, neither effervescent nor fermented, often infusions

or decoctions of various substances, such as water, toast and water, barley water, whey, milk, lemonade, tea, coffee, &c.

2. Beverages containing a considerable amount of carbolic acid, such as ginger beer, soda water, and various mineral waters, both natural and artificial.

3. Beverages containing alcohol, such as wine and water, spirit and water, bishop, punch, &c. To whichever class, however, the·beverages belong, the basis of them all is water, and no·need is greater than that of obtaining a good supply of sufficiently pure water.

Water *absolutely* pure, *i.e.*, consisting only of two parts of hydrogen to one of oxygen, can only be obtained by distillation, and is very flat and tasteless; but sufficiently pure we can have it, if not by filtering then by boiling. The latter means should not be resorted to unless necessary, because it renders the water dull in appearance and insipid in taste, the dissolved air and gases having been driven off in the process.

There are now, however, some kinds of aërated filters that improve the quality of boiled water, and it is also freshened and brightened by pouring it from one jug to another several times.

Statistics prove that in Great Britain more is spent upon alcoholic drinks than upon anything else; but as they are so much more expensive than other drinks, it does not follow that we consume a greater quantity of them than those non-alcoholic, of which the most popular is, in this country, tea. Previous to the middle of the 17th century it was not much known in England, and in 1666 it was sold at sixty shillings the pound; since when the consumption has increased from 5,000 lbs. to 50,000,000 lbs., while the price, in inverse ratio, has come down from £3 to 2s. per lb., or even less.

Next in order of popularity of non-alcoholic drinks may be mentioned coffee

and cocoa, the former being a stimulating, and the latter a nourishing drink.

In their order will be found the recipes for the making of tea, coffee and cocoa, as well as home-made wines, liqueurs and cups.

Beverages, Recipes for.—Directions for making the following appear under their respective headings :—

Almond Milk.	Lemon Wine.
Apple Wine.	Lemonade.
Barley Water.	Loving Cup.
Bishop.	Malt Wine.
Burgundy Cup.	May Drink.
Champagne Cup.	Mead.
Cherry Brandy.	Mulled Ale.
Chocolate.	Mulled Wine.
Cider Cup.	Nectar.
Claret Cup.	Negus.
Clove Liqueur.	Noyeau.
Cocoa.	Orange Brandy.
Coffee.	Punch (Cold).
Cowslip Wine.	Punch (Hot).
Egg Wine.	Raspberry Vinegar.
Elder Wine.	Shandy Gaff.
Ginger Beer.	Sherry Cobler.
Ginger Wine.	Syllabub.
Gooseberry Vinegar.	Toast and Water.
Gooseberry Wine.	Vanilla Liqueur.
Lemon Syrup.	

Biscuits.—Now that Huntley and Palmers, and Peek, Frean and Co. have brought the manufacture of biscuits to such perfection, there are but few people who consider it worth while making them at home; but for those few who prefer to have their own, as well as for those who have large families of children, we give a few well-tried recipes for simple kinds.

Biscuits for Butter or Cheese

—INGREDIENTS.— *To every lb. of flour allow 2 oz. of butter, about ½ pint of skimmed milk.*

Warm the butter in milk until the former is dissolved, and then mix it with the flour into a very stiff paste; beat it with a rolling-pin until the dough looks perfectly smooth. Roll it out thin; cut it into biscuits,

DESSERT BISCUITS.   SAVOY BISCUITS.

prick them, and bake them from 6 to 10 minutes. The above is the proportion of milk which we think would convert the flour into a stiff paste; but should it be found too much, an extra spoonful or two of flour must be put in. These biscuits are very nice for the cheese course.

TIME.—6 to 10 *minutes*.

SEASONABLE *at any time*.

Biscuits, Plain, for Cheese.

—INGREDIENTS.—1 *lb. of flour, the yolk of* 1 *egg, milk*. AVERAGE COST, 4*d*.

Mix the flour and the yolk of the egg with sufficient milk to make the whole into a very stiff paste ; beat it well, and knead it until it is perfectly smooth. Roll the paste out *very thin*; with a round cutter shape it into small biscuits, and bake them a nice brown in a slow oven from 12 to 18 minutes.

SODA BISCUITS.

TIME.—12 to 18 *minutes*.

SEASONABLE *at any time*.

Biscuits, Recipes for.—Directions

for making the following appear under their respective headings:—

Arrowroot.	For Butter or	Plain.
Cheese.	Cheese.	Raised.
Cocoa Nut.	Ginger.	Savoy.
Dessert.	Lemon.	Seed. | Soda.

Bishop.—INGREDIENTS *for sufficient*

for 6 persons.—1 *bottle of port,* 2 *lemons,* 2 *oz. of loaf sugar,* 1 *tumbler of water, spice to taste*. AVERAGE COST, 4*s*.

Stick one of the lemons with cloves and bake it. Boil the spice in the water, boil the wine, taking off some of the spirit with a lighted paper. Add the water and the baked lemon, and let it stand near the fire while rubbing the sugar on the rind of the other lemon. Warm a bowl, put the lumps of sugar in, squeeze over half the juice of the lemon, then pour the wine into the bowl and serve.

SEASONABLE *in winter*.

Black-cock, Fillets of, à la

Financiere.—INGREDIENTS *for large entrée dish.*—2 *birds,* 1 *pint of weak stock, cayenne and salt to taste, financière sauce*. AVERAGE COST, 5*s. per brace*.

Cut the birds into neat fillets and stew in the stock till tender; put them on an entrée dish, squeeze over a few drops of lemon, and pour over a good financière sauce. The trimmings of the birds may be stewed first to make a gravy, which should be slightly thickened, and is improved by a glass of sherry, to use in place of the sauce.

TIME.—½ *hour*.

SEASONABLE *in autumn*.

Black-cock, To Carve.—Skilful

carving of game undoubtedly adds to the pleasure of the guests at a dinner-table; for game seems pre-eminently to be composed of such delicate limbs and tender flesh that an inapt practitioner appears to more disadvantage when mauling these pretty and favourite dishes, than larger and more robust *pièces de résistance*. This bird is variously served, with or without the head on ; and, although we do not personally object to the appearance of the head as shown in the woodcut, yet it seems to be more in vogue to serve it without. The carving is not difficult, but should be elegantly and deftly done. Slices from the breast, cut in the direction of the dotted line from B to A, should be taken off, the

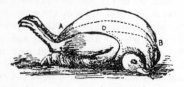

merrythought displaced, and the leg and wing removed by running the knife along from C to D. The thigh is considered a great delicacy.

Black-cock, To Roast.—INGRE-DIENTS.—*Black-cock, butter, toast.* AVER-AGE COST, 5s. *per brace.*

Let these birds hang for a few days, or they will be tough and tasteless, if not well kept. Pluck and draw them, and wipe the insides and outsides with a damp cloth, as washing spoils the flavour. Cut off the heads, and truss them the same as a roast fowl, cutting off the toes, and scalding and peeling the feet. Truss-ing them with the head on, as shown in

LOAST BLACK-COCK.

the engraving, is still practised by many cooks, but the former method is now con-sidered the best. Put them down to a brisk fire, well baste them with butter, and serve with a piece of toast under, and a good gravy and bread sauce. After truss-ing, some cooks cover the breast with vine-leaves and slices of bacon, and then roast them. They should be served in the same manner and with the same accompaniments as with the plainly-roasted birds.

TIME.—45 *to* 50 *minutes.*

SEASONABLE *from the middle of August to the end of December.*

Blancmange. — INGREDIENTS *for quart mould.*—1 *pint of new milk,* 1¼ oz. *of isinglass, the rind of* ½ *lemon,* ¼ *lb. of loaf sugar,* 10 *bitter almonds,* ½ oz. *of sweet almonds,* 1 *pint of cream.* AVERAGE COST, 3s.

Put the milk into a saucepan, with the isinglass, lemon-rind, and sugar, and let these ingredients stand by the side of the fire until the milk is well flavoured; add the almonds, which should be blanched and pounded in a mortar to a paste, and let the milk just boil up; strain it through a fine sieve or muslin into a jug, add the cream, and stir the mixture occasionally until nearly cold. Let it stand for a few minutes, then pour it into the mould, which should be previously oiled with the purest salad-oil, or dipped in cold water. There will be a sediment at the bottom of the jug, which must not be poured into the mould, as, when turned out, it would very much dis-figure the appearance of the blancmange. This blancmange may be made very much richer by using 1½ pint of cream, and melting the isinglass in ½ pint of boiling water. The flavour may also be very much varied by add-ing bay-leaves, laurel-leaves, or essence of vanilla, instead of the lemon-rind and al-monds. Noy-eau, Mara-schino, Curacoa or any favour-

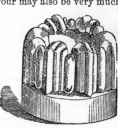

BLANCMANGE MOULD.

ite liqueur, added in small proportions, very much enhances the flavour of this always favourite dish. In turning it out, just loosen the edges of the blancmange from the mould, place a dish on it, and turn it quickly over; it should come out easily, and the blancmange have a smooth glossy appearance when the mould is oiled.

TIME.—*About 1½ hour to steep the lemon-rind and almonds in the milk.*

SEASONABLE *at any time.*

Blancmange, Cheap. — INGRE-DIENTS *for quart mould.*—¼ lb. of sugar, 1 quart of milk, 1½ oz. of gelatine, the rind of lemon, 4 laurel-leaves. AVERAGE COST, 1s.

Put all the ingredients into a lined sauce-pan, and boil gently until the isinglass is dissolved ; taste it occasionally to ascertain when it is sufficiently flavoured with the laurel-leaves ; then take them out, and keep stirring the mixture over the fire for about

BLANCMANGE.

0 minutes. Strain it through a fine sieve into a jug, and, when nearly cold, pour it into a well-oiled mould, omitting the sedi-ment at the bottom. After turning out it may be garnished with bright-coloured jelly, or a little of the blancmange may be coloured with cochineal.

TIME.—½ *hour.*

SEASONABLE *at any time.*

Note.—A nice blancmange, if wanted quickly, can be made by using the powders prepared by Goodall, Backhouse and Co., or Yeatman. A blancmange for children may be made of Brown and Polson's Corn-flour.

Blancmange for Invalids.— INGREDIENTS *for large shape.*—1 quart of new milk, 1½ oz. of Swinborne's isinglass, ½ pint of cream, sugar and flavouring to taste. AVERAGE COST, 1s. 6d.

Soak the isinglass in the milk, then boil it, stirring it until the isinglass is dissolved. Add sugar and any flavouring that may be preferred with the cream. Stir it again till it nearly boils, strain it, keep stirring till nearly cold, then put it in a mould.

TIME.—½ *hour.*

Blonde Sauce (for Fish).—INGRE-DIENTS.—½ pint of melted butter, 3 table-spoonfuls of stock, 1 onion, 2 mushrooms, 1 lemon, 1 glass of sherry, yolks of 3 eggs, parsley. AVERAGE COST, 8d. per pint.

Slice the onion, chop the mushrooms and parsley, and put them into a stewpan with the butter, stock and sherry, and the rind and juice of the lemon. Simmer slowly for ½ hour, then whisk the yolks of the eggs and add to the sauce. Stir for a few minutes over the fire, strain through a sieve, and serve in a tureen.

TIME.—*In all, 36 minutes.*

SEASONABLE *at any time.*

Boiling.—Of all modes of cooking, this is the commonest, if not the easiest. Anything can be boiled. It is upon keeping the water at the right heat that the success of the method depends. It is equally hot whether it boils fast or slowly. Fast boiling is in almost every instance, a mistake. It does not expediate the cooking ; it wastes a great amount of fuel, and it hardens everything in the way of meat or poultry ;

BOILING-POT.

whereas gentle simmering will render the food palatable and tender.

Such things, however, as flour foods (one of the principal ones, rice) should be kept in fast-boiling water, which prevents the grains from falling to the bottom in the saucepan, as it prevents the flour pudding from sticking.

In boiling fish, it should be put in water as hot as the skin will bear, without tearing and wrinkling, and vinegar or white wine should be added to prevent its breaking.

Vegetables may be boiled quickly ; and, in the case of green ones, with the saucepan lid off. The usual time to allow for boiling meat is ¼ hour to the lb. ; but if the boiling be very gentle, a little more is desirable.

Boudin à la Reine. (An Entrée ; M. UDE's Recipe.)—INGREDIENTS *for one entrée dish.—The remains of cold roast fowls, 1 pint of Béchamel, salt and cayenne to taste, egg and bread-crumbs.* AVERAGE COST, *exclusive of the cold fowl, 1s. 3d.*

Take the breasts and nice white meat from the fowls ; cut it into small dice of an equal size, and throw them into some good Béchamel (see BÉCHAMEL) ; season with salt and cayenne, and put the mixture into a dish to cool. When this preparation is quite cold, cut it into two equal parts, which should be made into boudins of a 'ong shape, the size of the dish they are intended to be served on ; roll them in flour, egg-and-bread-crumb them, and be careful that the ends are well covered with the crumbs, otherwise they will break in the frying-pan ; fry them a nice colour, put them before the fire to drain the greasy moisture from them, and serve with the remainder of the Béchamel heated and poured round : this should be thinned with a little stock.

TIME.—10 *minutes to fry the boudins.*

Brandy Cherries.—INGREDIENTS. —*Morella cherries, good French brandy ; to every lb. of cherries allow half the quantity of pounded sugar.*

Have ready some wide-mouthed glass bottles, perfectly clean and dry. Gather the cherries (not too ripe), and cut off half their stalks. Put them in the bottles, strewing the sugar between each layer ; and when the bottles are nearly full, pour in enough brandy to cover them.

A few blanched bitter almonds or peach kernels is thought to be an improvement.

Put corks or bungs in the bottles, tie them over with bladder, and store in a d place. The cherries will be fit to eat in or 3 months, and will keep good for year

SEASONABLE *in August and September*

Brawn, To Make.—INGREDIEN *for large mould or moulds.—To a pig's he weighing 6 lbs., allow 1½ lb. of lean beef, tablespoonfuls of salt, 2 teaspoonfuls pepper, a little cayenne, 6 pounded clove* AVERAGE COST, 3s. 3d.

Cut off the cheeks and salt them, unle the head be small, when all may be use After carefully cleaning the head, put on in sufficient cold water to cover it, wi the beef, and skim it just before it boil A head weighing 6 lbs. will require boili from 2 to 3 hours. When sufficiently boil to come off the bones easily, put it into hot pan, remove the bones, and chop t meat with a sharp knife before the fir together with the beef. *It is necessary do this as quickly as possible to prevent t fat settling in it.* Sprinkle in the seaso ing, which should have been previous mixed. Stir it well and put it quickly in a brawn-tin, if you have one ; if not, cake-tin or mould will answer the purpos if the meat is well pressed with weight which must not be removed for sever hours. When quite cold, dip the tin in boiling water for a minute or two, and t preparation will turn out and be fit f use.

TIME.—*From 2 to 3 hours.*

SEASONABLE *from September to March.*

Note.—The liquor in which the head w boiled will make good pea-soup, and the fa if skimmed off and boiled in water, and afte wards poured into cold water, answers the pu pose of lard. Very nice brawn is also ma from calf's foot used for jelly.

Bread, American.—INGREDIENT —1 *pint of white Indian meal, ½ pint flour, 3 eggs (white and yolks beaten sepa ately), rather more than a pint of milk, large tablespoonful of butter, melted, bu*

ot hot; 1 large tablespoonful of white sugar, 1 teaspoonful of carbonate of soda dissolved in hot water, a teaspoonful of cream of tartar sifted in with the flour and added the last thing, 1 tablespoonful of salt. AVERAGE COST, 7d.

Mix the ingredients well together, then bake in a well-greased mould, steadily, for ½ hour. Turn it out and eat at once.

In cutting corn bread, hold the knife perpendicularly, so as to avoid crushing the spongy interior.

TIME.—¾ hour.

Bread-and-Butter Fritters.—

INGREDIENTS for dish for 4 or 5 persons.—Batter, 8 slices of bread and butter, 3 or 4 tablespoonfuls of jam. AVERAGE COST, 9d.

Make a batter, the same as for apple fritters; cut some slices of bread and butter, not very thick; spread half of them with any jam that may be preferred, and cover with the other slices; slightly press them together, and cut them out in square, long, or round pieces. Dip them in the batter, and fry in boiling lard for about 10 minutes; drain them before the fire on a piece of blotting-paper or cloth. Dish them, sprinkle over sifted sugar, and serve.

TIME.—About 10 minutes.
SEASONABLE at any time.

Bread-and-Butter Pudding,

Baked.—INGREDIENTS for large pudding.—9 thin slices of bread and butter, 1½ pint of milk, 3 eggs, sugar to taste, ¼ lb. of currants, flavouring of vanilla, grated lemon-peel, or nutmeg. AVERAGE COST, 10d.

Cut 9 slices of bread and butter, not very thick, and put them into a pie dish, with currants between each layer, and on the top. Sweeten and flavour the milk, either by infusing a little lemon-peel in it, or by adding a few drops of essence of vanilla; well whisk the eggs, and stir

these to the milk. Strain this over the bread and butter, and bake in a moderate oven for 1 hour or rather longer. This pudding may be very much enriched by adding cream, candied peel, or more eggs than stated above. It should not be turned out, but sent to table in the pie-dish, and is better for being made about two hours before it is baked.

TIME.—1 hour, or rather longer.
SEASONABLE at any time.

Bread, Baking-Powder. — IN-

GREDIENTS.—2 lbs. of flour, 3 teaspoonfuls of Borwick's baking-powder, 1 breakfastcupful of milk, 1 teaspoonful of salt. AVERAGE COST, 6d.

Mix the salt and powder well with the flour, add the milk, and work the whole quickly into a light dough. Divide in loaves, and put in a well-heated oven at once, and bake for an hour. Sour milk, or buttermilk may be used for this bread, when a little carbonate of soda and a little less of baking-powder will be an improvement.

TWIST.

TIME.—1 hour.

Bread-Croutons (for Made

Dishes).—INGREDIENTS.—Slices of bread, butter or clarified dripping for frying.

Cut the bread ¼ inch thick, and stamp it out in small rounds with a cutter. Fry a bright golden brown in butter or clarified dripping.

Bread-Crumbs, Fried.—Cut the

bread into thin slices, place them in a cool oven overnight, and when thoroughly dry and crisp, roll them down into fine crumbs. Put some lard, or clarified dripping, into a frying-pan; bring it to the boiling point, throw in the crumbs and fry them very quickly. Directly they are done, lift them out with a slice, and drain them before the fire from all greasy moisture. When quite crisp, they are ready for use. The fat they are fried in should be clear, and the crumbs should not have the slightest appearance or taste of having been, in the least degree, burnt.

Bread, Fried (for Borders).— Proceed by frying some slices of bread, cut in any fanciful shape, in boiling lard. When quite crisp, dip one side of the sippet into the beaten white of an egg mixed with a little flour, and place it on the edge of the dish. Continue in this manner till the border is completed, arranging the sippets a pale and a dark one alternately.

Bread, Fried Sippets of (for Garnishing many Dishes).—Cut the bread into thin slices, and stamp them out in whatever shape you like—rings, crosses, diamonds, &c. &c. Fry them in the same manner as the bread crumbs, in clear boiling lard or clarified dripping, and drain them until thoroughly crisp before the fire. When variety is desired, fry some of a pale colour and others of a darker hue.

Bread-Making. — Panification, or bread-making, consists of the following processes, in the case of Wheaten Flour. Fifty or sixty per cent. of water is added to the flour, with the addition of some leavening matter, and preferably, of yeast from malt and hops. All kinds of leavening matter have, however, been, and are still used in different parts of the world: in the East Indies, "toddy," which is a liquor that flows from the wounded cocoa-nut tree; and in the West Indies, "dunder," or the refuse of the distillation of rum. The dough then undergoes the well-known process called *kneading*. The yeast produces fermentation, a process which may be thus described:—The dough reacting upon the leavening matter introduced, the starch of the flour is transformed into saccharine matter, the saccharine matter

being afterwards changed into alcohol and carbonic acid. The dough must be well "bound," and yet allow the escape of the little bubbles of carbonic acid which accompany the fermentation, and which, in their passage, cause the numerous little holes which are seen in light bread.

The yeast must be good and fresh, if the bread is to be digestible and nice. Stale yeast produces, instead of vinous fermentation, an acetous fermentation, which flavours the bread and makes it disagreeable. A poor thin yeast produces an imperfect fermentation, the result being a heavy, unwholesome loaf.

When the dough is well kneaded, it is left to stand for some time, and then, as soon as it begins to swell, it is divided into loaves; after which it is again left to stand, when it once more swells up and manifests for the last time the symptoms of fermentation. It is then put into the oven, where the water contained in the dough is partly evaporated, and the loaves swell up again, while a yellow crust begins to form upon the surface. When the bread is sufficiently baked, the bottom crust is hard and resonant struck with the finger, while the crumb is elastic, and rises again after being pressed down with the finger. The bread is, in all probability, baked sufficient, if, on opening the door of the oven, you are met by a cloud of steam, which quickly passes away.

One word as to the unwholesomeness of new bread and hot rolls. When bread is taken out of the oven, it is full of moisture; the starch is held together in masses, and the bread, instead of being crusted, so as to expose each grain of starch to the saliva, actually prevents their digestion by being formed by the teeth into leather poreless masses, which lie on the stomach like so many bullets. Bread should always be least a day old before it is eaten and, if properly made, and kept in a cool dry place, ought to be perfectly soft and alatable at the end of three or four days. Hot rolls, swimming in butter, are most indigestible.

A quickly-made and nice bread can be had by using Yeatman's Yeast Powder instead of ordinary yeast.

Aërated Bread.—Dr. Dauglish, of Malvern, was the inventor of the process for making bread "light," without the use of leaven. The ordinary process of bread-making by fermentation is tedious, and much labour of human hands is requisite in the kneading, in order that the dough may be thoroughly interpenetrated with the leaven. This process impregnates the bread, by the application of machinery, with carbonic acid gas, or fixed air. Different opinions are expressed about the bread; but it is curious to note that, as corn is now reaped by machinery, and dough is baked by machinery, the whole process of bread-making is probably in course of undergoing changes which will emancipate both the housewife and the professional baker from a large amount of labour.

In the production of Aërated Bread, wheaten flour, water, salt, and carbonic acid gas (generated by proper machinery), are the only materials employed. We need not inform our readers that carbonic acid gas is the source of the effervescence, whether in common water coming from a depth, or in lemonade, or any aërated drink. Its action, in the new bread, takes the place of fermentation in the old.

In the patent process, the dough is mixed in a great iron ball, inside which is a system of paddles, perpetually turning, and doing the kneading part of the business. Into this globe the flour is dropped till it is full, and then the common atmospheric air is pumped out, and the pure gas turned on. The gas is followed by the water, which has been aërated for the purpose, and then begins the churning or kneading part of the business.

Of course, it is not long before we have the dough, and very "light" and nice it looks. This is caught in tins, and passed on to the floor of the oven, which is an endless floor, moving slowly through the fire. Done to a turn, the loaves emerge at the other end of the apartment—and the Aërated Bread is made.

It may be added, that it is a good plan to change one's baker from time to time, and so secure a change in the quality of the bread that is eaten.

Mixed Breads.—Rye bread is hard of digestion, and requires longer and slower baking than wheaten bread. It is better when made with leaven of wheaten flour rather than yeast, and turns out lighter. It should not be eaten till two days old. It will keep a long time.

A good bread may be made by mixing rye-flour, wheat-flour, and rice-paste, in equal proportions; also by mixing rye, wheat, and barley. In Norway, it is said that they only bake their barley bread once a year, such is its "keeping" quality.

Indian-corn flour mixed with wheat-flour (half with half) makes a nice bread, but it is not considered very digestible, though it keeps well.

Rice cannot be made into bread, nor can potatoes; but one-third potato-flour to three-fourths wheaten flour makes a tolerably good loaf.

A very good bread, better than the ordinary sort, and of a delicious flavour, is said to be produced by adopting the following recipe:—Take ten parts of wheat-flour, five parts of potato-flour, one part of rice-paste; knead together, add the yeast, and bake as usual. This is, of course, cheaper than wheaten bread.

Flour, when freshly ground, is too glutinous to make good bread, and should therefore not be used immediately, but should be kept dry for a few weeks, and stirred occasionally until it becomes dry, and crumbles easily between the fingers.

Flour should be perfectly dry before being used for bread or cakes; if at all damp, the preparation is sure to be heavy. Before mixing it with the other ingredients, it is a good plan to place it for an hour or two before the fire, until it feels warm and dry.

Yeast from home-brewed beer is generally preferred to any other; it is very bitter, and on that account should be well washed, and put away until the thick mass settles. If it still continues bitter, the process should be repeated; and, before being used, all the water floating at the top must be poured off. German yeast is now very much used, and should be moistened, and thoroughly mixed with the milk or water with which the bread is to ₂e made.

The following observations are extracted from a valuable work on bread making, and will be found very useful to our readers:—

The first thing required for making wholesome bread is the utmost cleanliness; the next is the soundness and sweetness of all the ingredients used for it; and, in addition to these, there must be attention and care through the whole process.

An almost certain way of spoiling dough is to leave it half-made, and to allow it to become cold before it is finished. The other most common causes of failure are using yeast which is no longer sweet, or which has been frozen, or has had hot liquid poured over it.

Too small a proportion of yeast, or insufficient time allowed for the dough to rise, will cause the bread to be heavy.

Heavy bread will also most likely be the result of making the dough very hard, and letting it become quite cold, particularly in winter.

If either the sponge or the dough be permitted to overwork itself, that is to say, if the mixing and kneading be neglected when it has reached the proper point for either, sour bread will probably be the con-

sequence in warm weather, and bad brea₍ in any. The goodness will also be endar₍ gered by placing it so near the fire as t₍ make any part of it hot, instead of mair₍ taining the gentle and equal degree of hea₍ required for its due fermentation.

Milk or Butter.—Milk which is not pe₍ fectly sweet will not only injure the flavou₍ of the bread, but, in sultry weather, wi₍ often cause it to be quite uneatable; y₍ either of them, if *fresh and good*, will mater₍ ally improve its quality.

To keep bread sweet and fresh, as soo₍ as it is cold it should be put into a clea₍ earthen pan, with a cover to it; this pa₍ should be placed at a little distance fro₍ the ground, to allow a current of air ₍ pass underneath. Some persons prefe₍ keeping bread on clean wooden shelve₍ without being covered, that the crust ma₍ not soften. Stale bread may be freshene₍ by warming it through in a gentle ove₍ Stale pastry, cakes, &c., may also be im₍ proved by this method.

The utensils required for making brea₍ on a moderate scale, are a kneading-troug₍ or pan, sufficiently large that the dough ma₍ be kneaded freely without throwing the flo₍ over the edges, and also to allow for i₍ rising; a hair-sieve for straining yeas₍ and one or two strong spoons.

Yeast must always be good of its kin₍ and in a fitting state to produce ready an₍ proper fermentation. Yeast of strong bee₍ or ale produces more effect than that ₍ milder kinds; and the fresher the yea₍ the smaller the quantity will be required ₍ raise the dough.

As a general rule the oven for bakin₍ bread should be rather quick, and the hea₍ so regulated as to penetrate the doug₍ without hardening the outside. The ove₍ door should not be opened after the brea₍ is put in until the dough is set, or has b₍ come firm, as the cool air admitted wi₍ have an unfavourable effect on it.

Brick ovens are generally considered th₍ best adapted for baking bread; the₍

hould be heated with wood faggots, and
hen swept and mopped out to cleanse
hem for the reception of the bread. Iron
ovens are more difficult to manage, being
apt to burn the surface of the bread before
he middle is baked. To remedy this, a
ew clean bricks should be set at the bottom
of the oven, close together, to receive the
ins of bread. In many modern stoves
he ovens are so much improved that they
ake admirably, and they can always be
rought to the required temperature, when
t is higher than is needed, by leaving the
loor open for a time.

Bread, Recipes for.—Directions
or making the following appear under
heir respective headings:—

American.	Fried.
Baking-Powder.	Home-Made.
Croûtons.	,, ,, A Peck of.
Crumbs, Fried.	Rice.

Bread, Rice.—INGREDIENTS *for* 3
medium-sized loaves.—4 *lbs. of wheat flour,*
lb. of rice, 3 *tablespoonfuls of yeast,* ¼ *oz.*
f salt. AVERAGE COST, 10*d.*

Boil the rice till quite tender; pour off
he water, and put the rice warm to the
our; mix well together with the yeast,
alt, and sufficient warm water to make
he whole into a smooth dough; let it rise
y the side of the fire, then make into
oaves, which bake from 1½ to 2 hours,
ccording to the size. An improvement
pon this bread is made by boiling the
ice in milk, in which case it should be
aixed with the flour without straining.

TIME.—1½ to 2 *hours.*

Bread Sauce (to Serve with Roast
urkey, Fowl, Game, &c.).—INGREDIENTS.
r large tureenful.—1 *pint of milk,* ¾ *lb. of*
e crumb of a stale loaf, 1 *onion; pounded*
ace, cayenne, and salt to taste, ¼ *oz. of*
utter. AVERAGE COST, 4*d.*

Peel and quarter the onion, and simmer

it in the milk till perfectly tender. Break
the bread, which should be stale, into
small pieces, carefully picking out any
hard or side pieces; put it in a very clean
saucepan, strain the milk over it, cover it
up, and let it remain for an hour to soak.
Now beat it up with a fork very smoothly,
add a seasoning of pounded mace, cayenne,
and salt, with ½ oz. of butter; give the
whole one boil, and serve. To enrich this
sauce, a small quantity of cream may be
added just before sending it to table.

TIME.—*Altogether* 1¾ *hour.*

Bread Sauce (to Serve with Roast
Turkey, Fowl, Game, &c).—INGREDIENTS.
—*Giblets of poultry,* ¾ *lb. of the crumb of a*
stale loaf, 1 *onion,* 12 *whole peppers,* 1 *blade*
of mace, salt to taste, 2 *tablespoonfuls of*
cream, 1 *pint of water.* AVERAGE COST, 6*d.*

Put the giblets, with the head, neck, legs,
&c, into a stewpan; add the onion, pepper,
mace, salt, and rather more than 1 pint
of water. Let this simmer for an hour,
when strain the liquor over the bread,
which should be previously grated or
broken into small pieces. Cover up the
saucepan, and leave it for an hour by the
side of the fire; then beat the sauce up
with a fork until no lumps remain, and the
whole is nice and smooth. Let it boil for 3
or 4 minutes; keep stirring it until it is
rather thick; when add 2 tablespoonfuls
of cream and serve very hot.

TIME.—2¼ *hours.*

Bread, To Make a Peck of
Good.—INGREDIENTS.—3 *lbs. of potatoes,*
6 *pints of cold water,* ½ *pint of good yeast,*
a peck of flour, 2 *oz. of salt.*

Peel and boil the potatoes; beat them to
a cream while warm; then add 1 pint of
cold water, strain through a colander, and
add to it ½ pint of good yeast, which should
have been put in water overnight to take
off its bitterness. Stir all well together
with a wooden spoon, and pour the mixture
into the centre of the flour; mix it to the

substance of cream, cover it over closely, and let it remain near the fire for an hour; then add the 5 pints of water, milk-warm, with two oz. of salt; pour this in, and mix the whole to a nice light dough. Let it remain for about 2 hours; then make it into 7 loaves, and bake for about 1½ hour in a good oven. When baked, the bread should weigh nearly 20 lbs.

TIME.—*About 1½ hour.*

Bread, To Make Good Home-made. (Miss ACTON'S Recipe.) — INGRE-DIENTS.—1 *quartern of flour, 1 large table-spoonful of solid brewer's yeast, or nearly 1 oz. of fresh German yeast, 1¼ to 1½ pint of warm milk-and-water.*

Put the flour into a large earthenware bowl or deep pan; then, with a strong metal or

HOME-MADE BREAD.

wooden spoon, hollow out the middle; but do not clear it entirely away from the bottom of the pan, as, in that case, the sponge, or leaven (as it was formerly termed) would stick to it, which it ought not to do. Next, take either a large tablespoonful of brewer's yeast which has been rendered solid by mixing it with plenty of cold water, and letting it afterwards stand to settle for a day and night; or, nearly an ounce of German yeast; put it into a large basin, and proceed to mix it, so that it shall be as smooth as cream, with ¾ pint of warm milk-and-water, or with water only; though even a very little milk will much improve the bread. Pour the yeast into the hole made in the flour, and stir into it as much of that which lies round it as will make a thick batter, in which there must be no

lumps. Strew plenty of flour on the top; throw a thick clean cloth over, and set where the air is warm; but do not place upon the kitchen fender, for it will become too much heated there. Look at it from time to time; when it has been laid f

COTTAGE LOAF.

nearly an hour, and when the yeast ha risen and broken through the flour, so tha bubbles appear in it, you will know that is ready to be made up into dough. The place the pan on a strong chair, or dresse or table of convenient height; pour in the sponge the remainder of the warm mil and-water; stir into it as much of the flo as you can with a spoon; then wipe it o clean with your fingers, and lay it asid Next take plenty of the remaining flou throw it on the top of the leaven, and begi with the knuckles of both hands, to knea it well. When the flour is nearly a kneaded in, begin to draw the edges of th dough towards the middle, in order to m the whole thoroughly; and when it is fr

TIN BREAD.

from flour and lumps and crumbs, an does not stick to the hands when touche it will be done, and may be covered wit the cloth, and left to rise a second tim In ¾ hour look at it, and should it hav swollen very much and begin to crack it will be light enough to bake. Tur

Breakfast and Tea China.

4 Breakfast Cups, 2 Bread and Butter Plates, 1 Teapot, 1 Butter Dish, 1 Sardine Box
2 Coffee Cups, Afternoon Tea Set, 1 Milk Jug, 1 Jug, 1 Bread Dish, 1 Bacon Dish
1 Marmalade Jar, 4 Tea Cups.

it then on to a paste-board or very clean dresser, and with a large sharp knife divide it in two; make it up quickly into loaves, and despatch it to the oven: make one or two incisions across the tops of the loaves, as they will rise more easily if this be done. If baked in tins or pans, rub them with a tiny piece of butter laid on a piece of clean paper, to prevent the dough from sticking to them. All bread should be turned upside down, or on its side, as soon as it is drawn from the oven; if this be neglected, the under part of the loaves will become wet and blistered from the steam, which cannot then escape from them. *To make the dough without setting a sponge,* merely mix the yeast with the greater part of the warm milk-and-water, and wet up the whole of the flour at once after a little salt has been stirred in, proceeding exactly, in every other respect, in the directions just given. As the dough will *soften* in the rising, it should be made quite firm at first, or it will be too lithe by the time it is ready for the oven.

FRENCH ROLL.

TIME.—*To be left to rise an hour the first time, ¾ hour the second time; to be baked from 1 hour to 1¼ hour, or baked in one loaf from 1½ to 2 hours.*

Breakfast Cakes.

—INGREDIENTS, 1 *lb. of bread dough,* 2 *oz. of butter,* 2 *oz. of sugar,* 2 *eggs.* AVERAGE COST, 6*d.*

Beat all well together in the same manner as eggs are beaten, using the hand instead of a whisk. Set in a plain mould to rise for ¾ hour, then bake in a gentle oven. When cut it should present a honey-comb appearance. It makes very good toast when stale.

TIME.—1¼ *hour.*

Breakfast Cakes, American.

—INGREDIENTS.—1 *quart of milk,* 1 *large spoonful of sugar,* 1 *teacupful of yeast,* 2 *eggs, salt, flour.* AVERAGE COST, 1*d. each.*

Make the batter as thick as for bread biscuits. Make it overnight, and if sour in the morning, add ½ teaspoonful of soda dissolved in a little milk. Serve hot with butter.

TIME.—½ *hour to bake.*

Breakfasts.

—It will not be necessary to give here a long bill of fare of cold joints, &c., which may be placed on the sideboard, and do duty at the breakfast-table. Suffice it to say, that any cold meat the larder may furnish should be nicely garnished and be placed on the buffet. Collared and potted meats or fish, cold game or poultry, veal-and-ham pies, game-and-rumpsteak pies, are all suitable dishes for the breakfast-table; as also cold ham, tongue, &c. &c.

The following list of hot dishes may perhaps assist our readers in knowing what to provide for the comfortable meal called breakfast. Broiled fish, such as mackerel, whiting, herrings, dried haddocks, &c.; mutton chops and rump-steaks, broiled sheep's kidneys, kidneys à la maître d'hôtel, sausages, plain rashers of bacon, bacon and poached eggs, ham and poached eggs, omelets, plain boiled eggs, œufs-au-plat, poached eggs on toast, muffins, toast, marmalade, butter, &c. &c.

In the summer and when they are obtainable, always have a vase of freshly-gathered flowers on the breakfast-table, and, when convenient, a nicely-arranged dish of fruit; when strawberries are in season, these are particularly refreshing; as also grapes, or even currants, and it is well known that breakfast time is the most wholesome one to partake of fruit.

Bride Cake.

—INGREDIENTS *for large cake.*—5 *lbs. of fine flour,* 3 *lbs. of butter,* 2 *lbs. of currants,* 2 *lbs. of plums or sultanas,* 2 *lbs. of pounded loaf sugar, spice to taste,* 16 *eggs,* 1 *lb. of sweet almonds,* 1 *lb. of* candied peel, ½ pint of white wine, 3 glasses of brandy. AVERAGE COST, 12s. 6d.

Sift the flour, which should be of the best quality and perfectly dry ; wash, pick, and dry the currants, grate the nutmeg and see that the other spice is in the finest powder. The almonds should be pounded in a mortar with a little orange-flower water, the peel cut in neat slices, the plums carefully stoned and cut in half or chopped, and the eggs thoroughly whisked.

Work the butter with the hand till it is like cream, stir in the sugar, beat the whites of the eggs to a solid froth, and add to the butter and sugar. Next beat the yolks of the eggs, add them with the flavouring of spice to the flour, then beat the whole together for half an hour. Mix in the currants, almonds, and candied peel with the wine and brandy, and having lined an opening mould with buttered paper put the mixture in and bake in a fairly quick oven, the top of the cake, to prevent burning, being covered with a buttered paper.

In baking a rich cake of this kind great attention must be paid to the heat of the oven ; it should not be too fierce, but have moderate heat and bake the cake through. To ascertain if it is done, plunge in a clean knife and withdraw it quickly, and if the blade is bright and not sticky the cake is done.

Spread with a thick layer of almond paste and over that put a thick layer of sugar icing. This cake will serve also for a christening one, when the name is generally worked in coloured sugar, and a tiny sugar cradle (these are sold at the confectioners' for the purpose) put on the top.

TIME.—5 to 6 hours.

Brill.—INGREDIENTS.—¼ lb. of salt to each gallon of water; a little vinegar. AVERAGE COST, from 4s. to 6s. each.

Clean the brill, cut off the fins, and rub it over with a little lemon-juice, to preserve its whiteness. Set the fish in sufficient cold water to cover it; throw in salt, in the above proportions, and a little vinegar, and bring it gradually to boil; simmer very gently till the fish is done, which will be in about 10 minutes for a small brill, reckoning from the time the water begins to simmer. It is difficult to give the *exact* number of minutes required for cooking a brill, as the fish varies somewhat in thickness, but the cook can always bear in mind that fish of every description should be *very thoroughly dressed*, and never come to table in the

THE BRILL.

least degree underdone. The time for boiling of course depends entirely on the size of the fish. Serve it on a hot napkin, and garnish with cut lemon, parsley, horseradish and a little lobster coral sprinkled over the fish. Send lobster or shrimp sauce and plain melted butter to table with it.

TIME.—*After the water boils, a small brill, 10 minutes ; a medium-sized brill, 15 to 20 minutes ; a large brill, ½ hour.*

SEASONABLE *from August to April.*

To choose Brill.—The flesh of this fish, like that of turbot, should be of a yellowish tint, and should be chosen on account of its thickness. If the flesh has a bluish tint, it is not good.

A Brill and John Dory are carved in the same manner as a Turbot.

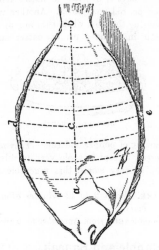

HOW TO CARVE A BRILL.

Note.—The thick parts of the middle of the back are the best slices in a brill or turbot; and the rich gelatinous skin covering the fish, as well as a little of the thick part of the fins, are dainty morsels, and should be placed on each plate.

Brilla Soup.—Ingredients *for sufficient for 10 persons.*—4 lbs. *of shin of beef,* 3 *carrots,* 2 *turnips, a large sprig of thyme,* 2 *onions,* 1 *head of celery, salt and pepper to taste,* 4 *quarts of water.* Average Cost, 3s. 8d.

Take the beef, cut off all the meat from the bone, in nice square pieces, and boil the bone for 4 hours. Strain the liquor, let it cool, and take off the fat; then put the pieces of meat in the cold liquor; cut small the carrots, turnips, and celery; chop the onions, add them with the thyme and seasoning, and simmer till the meat is tender. If not brown enough, colour it with browning.

Time.—6 *hours.*

Brioches.—Ingredients.—1 *lb. of flour,* ¾ *lb. of butter,* ¼ *oz. of German yeast,* 2 *oz. of sugar,* 6 *eggs, salt, water.* Average Cost, 1s. 8d.

Put a little of the flour (about a quarter) on a board, hollow it in the centre and put in the yeast dissolved in a little warm water. Mix and set the sponge to rise in a covered pan near the fire. Put the remainder of the flour on the board, and after making a hole in the centre, put in the salt, butter, sugar and 4 eggs, and break in the other two, one after the other, and work till the paste is smooth. When the sponge has risen to double its original size, mix it with the paste and again set it to rise for 2 hours. Then put the paste on a board, press it out and fold it over two or three times and a third time set it to rise for 2 hours; once more press it out, fold it up and put it on ice till firm. This paste can be used to form small cakes, or for cases for compotes or custards.

Broiling.—Broiling is an excellent mode of cooking tender, juicy meat, from the best joints fish, &c., but it is not suited to any other kinds; neither is it an economical way of cooking, by reason of its taking so much fuel to make a good broiling fire, also the meat losing more weight than in other modes of cooking.

To broil successfully there must be a hot, clear fire, to start with, so that the albumen of the meat, suddenly heated, becomes hardened, and a crust is formed which effectually retains the juice. The gridiron should be hot and well-greased. For broiling, the food should be turned often with tongs or some instrument that will not make holes or cut.

There are a few things that do not require turning, of which one is a mushroom, which should be broiled stalk upwards. Salmon cutlets are usually wrapped in paper. Split fish should have the cut side put to the fire first, afterwards the skin

Browning for Gravies and Sauces.

—The browning for stock answers equally well for sauces and gravies, when it is absolutely necessary to colour them in this manner; but where they can be made to look brown by using ketchup, wine, browned flour, tomatoes, or any coloured sauce, it is far preferable. As, however, in cooking so much depends on appearance, perhaps it would be as well for the inexperienced cook to use the artificial means. When no browning is at hand, and you wish to heighten the colour of your gravy, dissolve a lump of sugar in an iron spoon close to a sharp fire; when it is in a liquid state, drop it into the sauce or gravy quite hot. Care, however, must be taken not to put in too much, as it would impart a very disagreeable flavour to the preparation.

Browning, for Stock.

— INGREDIENTS.—2 oz. of powdered sugar, and ½ a pint of water.

Place the sugar in a stewpan over a slow fire until it begins to melt, keeping it stirred with a wooden spoon until it becomes black, when add the water, and let it dissolve. Cork closely, and use a few drops when required.

Note.—In France, burnt onions are made use of for the purpose of browning. As a general rule, the process of browning is to be discouraged, as apt to impart a slightly unpleasant flavour to the stock, and consequently all soups made from it.

Brussels - Sprouts, Boiled.

— INGREDIENTS.—To each ½ gallon of water allow 1 heaped tablespoonful of salt; a very small piece of soda. AVERAGE COST, 2d. per lb.

Clean the sprouts from insects, nicely wash them, and pick off any dead or discoloured leaves from the outsides; put them into a saucepan of *boiling* water, with salt and soda in the above proportion; keep the pan uncovered, and let them boil quickly over a brisk fire until tender, drain, dish, and serve with a tureen of melted butter, or with a maître d'hôtel sauce poured over them. Another mode of serving them is, when they are dished, to stir in about 1 oz. of butter and a

BRUSSELS SPROUTS.

seasoning of pepper and salt. They must, however, be sent to table very quickly, as, being so very small, this vegetable soon cools.

TIME.—*From 9 to 12 minutes after the water boils.*

SEASONABLE *from November to March.*

Bubble-and-Squeak. (Cold Meat Cookery.)

— INGREDIENTS. — *A few thin slices of cold boiled beef, butter, cabbage, 1 sliced onion, pepper and salt to taste.* AVERAGE COST, *exclusive of the cold beef,* 3d.

Fry the slices of beef gently in a little butter, taking care not to dry them up. Lay them on a flat dish, and cover with fried greens. The greens may be prepared from cabbage sprouts or green savoys. They should be boiled till tender, well drained, minced, and placed till quite hot in a fryingpan, with butter, a sliced onion, and seasoning of pepper and salt. When the onion is done, it is ready serve.

TIME.—*Altogether, ½ hour.*

SEASONABLE *at any time.*

Bullock's Heart, To Dress a.

—INGREDIENTS *for dish for 6 to 8 persons.*— 1 *heart, stuffing of veal forcemeat.* AVERAGE COST, 2s. 6d.

Put the heart into warm water to soak for 2 hours; then wipe it well with a cloth, and, after cutting off the lobes, stuff the inside with a highly-seasoned forcemeat. Fasten it in, by means of a needle and coarse thread; tie the heart up in paper, and set it before a good fire, being very particular to keep it well basted, or it will be dry, there being very little of its own fat. Two or three minutes before dishing, remove the paper, baste well, and serve with good gravy and red-currant jelly or melted butter. If the heart is very large, it will require 2 hours, and, covered with a caul, may be baked as well as roasted.

TIME.—*Large heart, 2 hours.*

SEASONABLE *all the year.*

Note.—This is an excellent family dish, is very savoury, and, though not seen at many good tables, may be recommended for its cheapness and economy.

Buns, Bath.—INGREDIENTS *for* 1 *dozen buns.*—1¼ *lb. of flour,* 4 *eggs,* 1 *oz. of German yeast,* ¼ *lb. of butter,* ¼ *lb. of sugar,* 2 *oz. of candied peel, some caraway comfits.* AVERAGE COST, 1s.

Dissolve the yeast in 4 tablespoonfuls of water and mix it with the yolks of the eggs, 3 of the whites, and ¼ lb. of flour. Beat the mixture in a bowl and set it before the fire to rise. Rub the butter with the flour, add the peel sliced (reserving a few strips for the tops of the buns, and a few comfits). When the sponge has risen sufficiently, mix all together, and set to rise again with a cloth thrown over. Form the buns, brush them over with the remaining white of egg, ornament them with the peel and a few comfits, and bake in a quick oven.

TIME *to bake,* ½ *hour.*

Buns, Hot Cross.— INGREDIENTS *for* 2 *dozen buns.*—2 *lbs. of flour,* ½ *lb. of sugar,* 1 *wineglassful of yeast,* 1 *pint of milk,* ½ *lb. of butter,* 1 *lb. of currants,* ½ *teaspoonful of salt,* 1 *teaspoonful of mixed spice,* AVERAGE COST, 1s. 10d.

Mix the flour and sugar, spice and currants; make a hole in the middle of the flour, and put in a glassful of thick yeast and the milk, warmed; make a batter of the surrounding milk and flour, and set the pan covered before the fire, till the leaven begins to ferment. Put to the mass the butter melted, and enough milk to make a soft paste of all the flour. Form the buns, and lay them a little distance apart on buttered tins to rise for ½ an hour. Cross them with a knife and bake in a quick oven.

TIME.—20 *minutes to bake.*

SEASONABLE *on Good Friday.*

Buns, Light.—INGREDIENTS *for* 1 *dozen buns.*—½ *teaspoonful of tartaric acid,* ½ *teaspoonful of bicarbonate of soda,* 1 *lb. of flour,* 2 *oz. of butter,* 2 *oz. of loaf sugar,* ¼ *lb. of currants or raisins—when liked, a few caraway seeds,* ½ *pint of cold new milk,* 1 *egg.* AVERAGE COST, 9d.

Rub the tartaric acid, soda, and flour all together through a hair sieve; work the butter into the flour; add the sugar, currants, and caraway seeds, when the flavour of the latter is liked. Mix all these ingredients well together; make a hole in the middle of the

BUNS.

flour, and pour in the milk, mixed with the egg, which should be well beaten; mix quickly, and set the dough, with a fork, on baking-tins, and bake the buns for about 20 minutes. This mixture makes a very good cake, and if put into a tin, should be baked 1½ hour. The same quantity of flour, soda, and tartaric acid, with ½ pint of milk and a little salt, will make either bread or tea-cakes, if wanted quickly.

TIME.—20 *minutes for the buns; if made into a cake,* 1½ *hour.*

Buns, Plain.

Buns, Plain.—INGREDIENTS *for* 12 *buns.*—1 *lb. of flour,* 6 *oz. of good butter,* ¼ *lb. of sugar,* 1 *egg, nearly* ¼ *pint of milk,* 2 *small teaspoonfuls of baking-powder, a few drops of essence of lemon.* AVERAGE COST,1*s.*

Warm the butter, without oiling it ; beat it with a wooden spoon ; stir the flour in gradually with the sugar, and mix these ingredients well together. Make the milk lukewarm, beat up with it the yolk of the egg and the essence of lemon, and stir these to the flour, &c. Add the baking-powder, beat the dough well for about 10 minutes, divide it into 12 pieces, put them into buttered tins or cups, and bake in a brisk oven from 20 to 30 minutes.

TIME.—20 *to* 30 *minutes.*

SEASONABLE *at any time.*

Buns, Recipes for.

Buns, Recipes for.—Directions for making the following appear under their respective headings :—

| Bath. | Light. | Victoria. |
| Hot Cross. | Plain. | |

Buns, Victoria.

Buns, Victoria.—INGREDIENTS *for* 6 *buns.*—2 *oz. of pounded loaf sugar,* 1 *egg,* 1½ *oz. of ground rice,* 2 *oz. of butter,* 1½ *oz. of currants, a few thin slices of candied peel, flour.* AVERAGE COST, 6*d.*

Whisk the egg, stir in the sugar, and beat these ingredients both together ; beat the butter to a cream, stir in the ground rice, currants, and candied-peel, and as much flour as will make it of such a consistency that it may be rolled into 6 or 8 balls. Place these on a buttered tin, and bake them from ½ to ¾ hour. They should be put into the oven immediately or they will become heavy, and the oven should be tolerably brisk.

TIME.—½ *to* ¾ *hour.*

SEASONABLE *at any time.*

Butter, Anchovy.

Butter, Anchovy.—INGREDIENTS. —6 *anchovies,* 1 *lb. of butter, a small bunch of parsley.* AVERAGE COST, 1*s.* 8*d.*

Wash, bone, and pound the anchovies, scald the parsley, chop it and rub it through a sieve, then rub all the ingredients together thoroughly. This is very nice served with cold fish.

SEASONABLE *at any time.*

Butter, Browned.

Butter, Browned.—INGREDIENTS. —¼ *lb. of butter,* 1 *tablespoonful of minced parsley,* 3 *tablespoonfuls of vinegar, salt and pepper to taste.*

Put the butter into a frying-pan over a nice clear fire, and when it smokes, throw in the parsley, and add the vinegar and seasoning. Let the whole simmer for a minute or two, when it is ready to serve. This is a very good sauce for skate.

TIME.—¼ *hour.*

Butter, Clarified.

Butter, Clarified.— Put the butter in a basin before the fire, and when it melts, stir it round once or twice and let it settle. Do not strain it unless absolutely necessary, as it causes so much waste. Pour it gently off into a clean dry jar, carefully leaving all sediment behind. Let it cool, and carefully exclude the air by means of a bladder or piece of wash-leather tied over. If the butter is salt, it may be washed before melting, when it is to be used for sweet dishes.

Butter, Constituent Parts of.

Butter, Constituent Parts of. —This article of food so largely used in England and the Continent is now made in very great quantities in factories in the United States and Sweden. A great deal of butter of good quality is imported to England from both Ireland and Holland, and our own best fresh butter comes from Buckinghamshire, Suffolk, Devonshire, Oxfordshire and Yorkshire. In Devonshire the butter is made from the clotted cream for which that county is famous and the process of turning it into butter is but a short one.

In other parts it is reckoned that the butter should come in about 15 minutes

Fresh Butter.

Brittany Butter.

Hens' Eggs.

Turkeys' Eggs.

Gorgonzola Cheese.

Cream Cheese.

Camembert Cheese.

Bondon Cheese.

Ball of Butter.

Ducks' Eggs.

Cheddar Cheese.

Curled Butter.

Pat of Butter.

Cheshire Cheese.

Yorkshire Cheese.

Stilton Cheese.

Butter, Eggs and Cheese.

Butter, Eggs and Cheese.

churning, but it must be remembered that the temperature of the cream must be exact, and the thermometer of the dairy when churning begins should register from 55 to 60.

Butter contains a large amount of heat-giving properties, but the flesh-forming ones in it are very small and, with regard to its dietetic qualities, may be regarded almost in the light of animal oil or vegetable fat.

CONSTITUENT PARTS OF 1 LB. OF BUTTER.

	oz.	grs.
Water	1	262
Albumenoids	0	70
Starch, Sugar, etc....	0	21
Fat	14	14
Mineral Matter	0	70
	16	0

Butter, Curled.—Tie a strong cloth by two of the corners to an iron hook in the wall; make a knot with the other two

ends, so that a stick might pass through. Put the butter into the cloth; twist it tightly over a dish, into which the butter will fall through the

CURLED BUTTER.

knot, so forming small and pretty little strings. The butter may then be garnished with parsley, if to serve with a cheese course; or it may be sent to table plain for breakfast, in an ornamental dish. Squirted butter for garnishing hams, salads, eggs, &c., is made by forming a piece of stiff paper in the shape of a cornet, and squeezing the butter in fine strings from the hole at the bottom. Scooped butter is made by dipping a teaspoon or scooper in warm water, and then scooping the butter quickly and thin. In warm weather, it would not be necessary to heat the spoon.

Butter, Fairy. — INGREDIENTS. — *The yolks of two hard-boiled eggs, 1 table-spoonful of orange-flower water, 2 table-spoonfuls of pounded sugar, ¼ lb. of good fresh butter.* AVERAGE COST, 7d.

Beat the yolks of the eggs smoothly in a mortar, with the orange-flower water and the

sugar, until the whole is reduced to a fine paste; add the butter and force all through an old but clean cloth by wringing the cloth and squeezing the but-

BRITTANY BUTTER.

ter very hard. The butter will then drop on the plate in large and small pieces, according to the holes in the cloth. Plain butter may be done in the same manner, and is very quickly prepared, besides having a very good effect.

Butter, Lobster.—INGREDIENTS.— *Lobster coral, fresh butter, salt and cayenne.*

Rub down in a mortar the coral and add to it the butter, blending well together till a deep red colour is obtained; add cayenne and salt to taste, put it into pots and tie over closely.

SEASONABLE *at any time.*

Butter, Maitre d'Hotel (for putting into Broiled Fish just before it is sent to table).—INGREDIENTS.—*¼ lb. of butter, 2 dessertspoonfuls of minced parsley, salt and pepper to taste, the juice of 1 large lemon.* AVERAGE COST, 6d.

Work the above ingredients well together, and let them be thoroughly mixed with a wooden spoon. If this is used as a sauce, it may be poured either under or over the meat or fish it is intended to be served with.

Note.—4 tablespoonfuls of Béchamel, 2 tablespoonfuls of white stock, with 2 ounces of the above maitre d'hôtel butter stirred into it, and just allowed to simmer for 1 minute, will be found an excellent hot maitre d'hôtel sauce.

Butter, Melted.—INGREDIENTS.— *¼ lb. of butter, a dessertspoonful of flour, 1 wineglassful of water, salt to taste.* AVERAGE COST, 4½d.

Cut the butter up into small pieces, put it into a saucepan, dredge over the flour, and add the water and a seasoning of salt; stir it *one way* constantly till the whole of the ingredients are melted and thoroughly blended. Let it just boil, when it is ready to serve. If the butter is to be melted with cream, use the same quantity as of water, but omit the flour; keep stirring it but do not allow it to boil.

TIME.—1 *minute to simmer.*

Butter, Melted (more economical).

—INGREDIENTS.—2 *oz. of butter,* 1 *dessert-spoonful of flour, salt to taste,* ½ *pint of water.* AVERAGE COST, 2*d.*

Mix the flour and water to a smooth batter, which put into a saucepan. Add the butter and a seasoning of salt, keep stirring *one way* till all the ingredients are melted and perfectly smooth; let the whole boil for a minute or two, and serve.

TIME.—2 *minutes to simmer.*

Butter, Melted. (The French Sauce

Blanche.)—INGREDIENTS.—¼ *lb. of fresh butter,* 1 *tablespoonful of flour, salt to taste,* ½ *gill of water,* ½ *spoonful of white vinegar, a very little grated nutmeg.* AVERAGE COST, 3*d.*

Mix the flour and water to a smooth batter, carefully rubbing down with the back of a spoon any lumps that may appear. Put it in a saucepan with all the other ingredients, and let it thicken on the fire, but do not allow it to boil, lest it should taste of the flour.

TIME.—1 *minute to simmer.*

Butter, Melted, made with

Milk.—INGREDIENTS.—1 *teaspoonful of flour,* 2 *oz. of butter,* ⅓ *pint of milk, a few grains of salt.* AVERAGE COST, 3*d.*

Mix the butter and flour smoothly together on a plate, put it into a lined saucepan, and pour in the milk. Keep stirring it *one way* over a sharp fire; let it boil quickly for a minute or two, and it is ready

to serve. This is a very good foundation for onion, lobster, or oyster sauce; using milk instead of water makes it look much whiter and more delicate.

TIME.—*Altogether,* 10 *minutes.*

Butter, Montpelier. — INGREDI-

ENTS. — *Watercress, fresh butter, pepper or cayenne, salt.*

Pick the leaves from the cress, which must be green and fresh, chop them finely, dry them in a cloth and mince again, then knead up with fresh butter till it is of a bright green, seasoning with pepper or cayenne, and salt.

This is useful for spreading croûtons to make a garnish for savoury dishes, or for appetisans.

SEASONABLE *at any time.*

Butter, Rancid, What to do

with.—When butter has become very rancid, it should be melted several times by a moderate heat, with or without the addition of water, and as soon as it has been we'l kneaded, after the cooling, in order to ex-

DISH OF ROLLED BUTTER.

tract any water it may have retained, it should be put into brown freestone pots, sheltered from the contact of the air. The French often add to it, after it has been melted, a piece of toasted bread, which helps to destroy the tendency of the butter to rancidity.

Butter, to Keep Fresh.—Butter

may be kept fresh for ten or twelve days by a very simple process. Knead it well in cold water till the buttermilk is extracted; then put it in a glazed jar, which invert in another, putting into the latter a sufficient quantity of water to exclude the air. Renew the water every day.

*" Can choice and costly dainties taste more sweet
Than simple ones by honest labour earned?"*

CABBAGE, Boiled.

INGREDIENTS.—To each ½ gallon of water allow 1 heaped tablespoonful of salt; a very small piece of soda. AVERAGE COST, 1d. and 2d. each.

Pick off all the dead outside leaves, cut off as much of the stalk as possible, and cut the cabbages across twice, at the stalk end; if they should be very large, quarter them. Wash them well in cold water, place them in a colander and drain; then put them into *plenty* of *fast-boiling* water, to which have been added salt and soda in the above proportions. Stir them down once or twice in the water, keep the pan uncovered, and let them boil quickly until tender. The instant they are done, take them up into a colander, place a plate over them, let them thoroughly drain, dish, cut across and across into small squares, and serve.

TIME.—*Large cabbages, or Savoys, ½ to ¾ hour, young summer cabbage, 10 to 13 minutes, after the water boils.*

SEASONABLE, *cabbages and sprouts of various kinds, at any time.*

Cabbage, Red, Pickled.—INGREDIENTS.—*Red cabbages, salt, and water; to each quart of vinegar, ½ oz. of ginger well bruised, 1 oz. of whole black pepper, and, when liked, a little cayenne.* AVERAGE COST, 6d. each.

Take off the outside decayed leaves of a nice red cabbage, cut it in quarters, remove the stalks, and cut it across in very thin slices. Lay these on a dish, and strew them plentifully with salt, covering them with another dish. Let them remain for 24 hours; turn to a colander to drain, and, if necessary, wipe lightly with a clean soft cloth. Put them in a jar; boil up the vinegar with spices in the above proportion, and, when cold, pour it over the cabbage. It will be fit for use in a week or two, but if kept for a very long

CABBAGE SEEDLING.

M

time, the cabbage is liable to get soft and to discolour. To be really nice and crisp, and of a good red colour, it should be eaten almost immediately after it is made. A little bruised cochineal boiled with the vinegar adds much to the appearance of this pickle. Tie down with bladder, and keep in a dry place.

SEASONABLE *in July and August, but the pickle will be much more crisp if the frost has just touched the leaves.*

Cabbage, Red, Stewed.—INGRE-
DIENTS.—1 *red cabbage, a small slice of ham, ½ oz. of fresh butter, 1 pint of weak stock or broth, 1 gill of vinegar, salt and pepper to taste, 1 tablespoonful of pounded sugar.* AVERAGE COST, 6d. *each.*

Cut the cabbage into very thin slices, put it into a stewpan, with the ham cut in dice, the butter, ½ pint of stock, and the vinegar ; cover the pan closely, and let it stew for 1 hour. When it is very tender, add the remainder of the stock, a seasoning of salt and pepper, and the pounded sugar ; mix all well together, stir over the fire until nearly all the liquor is dried away, and serve. Fried sausages are usually sent to table with this dish ; they should be laid round and on the cabbage, as a garnish.

TIME.—*Rather more than 1 hour.*

SEASONABLE *from September to January.*

Cabbages.—To these cauliflowers,
broccoli sprouts, savoys and Scotch kale owe their origin. All are wholesome foods, richer, like all fresh vegetable, in heat-givers than flesh-formers in the proportion of 4⅜ parts of the former to 1 of the latter. They contain more water, chiefly in the inner leaves, than potatoes, parsnips, beetroot, or Jerusalem artichokes, but less than onions, vegetable marrows, or turnips, and the same quantity as carrots and tomatoes.

Cabbages should always be boiled in plenty of water, quickly, and with the lid off the saucepan and a tiny piece of soda may be added to keep them green.

The very young white leaves of a white-hearted cabbage chopped fine are a fairly good substitute for lettuce in salad when the latter are scarce.

CONSTITUENT PARTS OF 1 LB. OF
CABBAGE.

					oz.	grs.
Water	...	...	...	...	14	105
Albumenoids	...	...	...	0	105
Starch, etc. ...	...	...	...	1	108
Fat ...	...	...	...	...	0	35
Mineral Matter	...	...	...	0	84
					16	0

Cabbage Soup.—INGREDIENTS *for
soup for 8 persons.*—1 *large cabbage, 3 carrots, 2 onions, 4 or 5 slices of lean bacon, salt and pepper to taste, 2 quarts of medium stock.* AVERAGE COST, 1s. *per quart.*

Scald the cabbage, cut it up and drain it. Line the stewpan with the bacon, put in the cabbage, carrots, and onions ; moisten with skimmings from the stock, and simmer very gently, till the cabbage is tender ; add the stock, stew softly for half an hour, and carefully skim off every particle of fat. Season and serve.

TIME.—1½ *hour.*

SEASONABLE *in winter.*

Cabinet, or Boiled Bread-and-
Butter Pudding, Plain. —INGREDIENTS *for good-sized pudding.*—2 oz. *of raisins, a few thin slices of bread and butter, 3 eggs, 1 pint of milk, sugar to taste, ¼ nutmeg.* AVERAGE COST, 9d.

Butter a pudding-basin, and line the inside with a layer of raisins that have been previously stoned ; then nearly fill the basin with slices of bread and butter with the crust cut off, and, in another basin, beat the eggs ; add to them the milk, sugar and grated nutmeg ; mix all well together, and pour the whole on to the bread and butter ; let it stand ½ hour, then tie a floured cloth over it ; boil for 1 hour, and serve with sweet sauce. Care must be taken that the basin is quite full before the cloth is tied over.

TIME.—1 hour.

SEASONABLE at any time.

Cabinet, or Chancellor's

Pudding.—INGREDIENTS for pudding large enough for 6 persons.—1½ oz. of candied peel, 4 oz. of currants, a handful of sultanas, a few slices of Savoy cake, sponge cake, or French roll, 4 eggs, 1 pint of milk, grated lemon-rind, ¼ nutmeg, 3 tablespoonfuls of sugar. AVERAGE COST, 1s. 3d.

Melt some butter to oil, and with it, well grease the mould or basin in which the pudding is to be boiled, taking care that it is buttered in every part. Cut the peel into thin slices, and place these in a fanciful device at the bottom of the mould, and fill in the spaces between with currants and sultanas; then add a few slices of sponge cake or French roll; drop a few drops of melted butter on these, and between each layer sprinkle a few currants. Proceed in this manner until the mould is nearly full; then flavour the milk with nutmeg and grated lemon-rind; add the sugar, and stir to this the eggs, which should be well beaten. Beat this mixture for a few minutes; then strain it into the mould, which should be quite full; tie a piece of buttered paper over it, and let it stand for 2 hours; then tie it down with a cloth, put it into boiling water, and let it boil slowly for 1 hour. In taking it up, let it stand for a minute or two before the cloth is removed; then quickly turn it out of the mould or basin, and serve with sweet sauce separately. The flavouring of this pudding may be varied by substituting for the lemon-rind essence of vanilla or bitter almonds; and it may be made much richer by using cream; but this is not at all necessary.

TIME.—1 hour.

SEASONABLE at any time.

Café au Lait.—This is merely very

strong coffee added to a large proportion of good hot milk; about 6 tablespoonfuls of strong coffee being quite sufficient for a breakfastcupful of milk. Of the essence, which answers admirably for café au lait, so much would not be required. This preparation is infinitely superior to the weak watery coffee so often served at English tables. A little cream mixed with the milk, if the latter cannot be depended on for richness, improves the taste of the coffee, as also the richness of the beverage.

Café Noir.—This is usually handed

round after dinner, and should be drunk well sweetened, with the addition of a little brandy or liqueurs, which may be added or not at pleasure. The coffee should be made very strong, and served in very small cups, but never mixed with milk or cream. Café noir may be made of the essence of coffee by pouring a tablespoonful into each cup, and filling it up with boiling water. This is a very simple and expeditious manner of preparing coffee for a large party, but the essence for it must be made very good, and kept well corked until required for use.

Cake, Christmas.—INGREDIENTS

for good-sized cake.—5 teacupfuls of flour, 1 teacupful of melted butter, 1 teacupful of cream, 1 teacupful of treacle, 1 teacupful of moist sugar, 2 eggs, ½ oz. of powdered ginger, ½ lb. of raisins, 1 teaspoonful of carbonate of soda, 1 tablespoonful of vinegar. AVERAGE COST, 1s. 6d.

Make the butter sufficiently warm to melt it, but do not allow it to oil; put the flour into a basin, add to it the sugar, ginger, and raisins, which should be stoned and cut into small pieces. When these dry ingredients are thoroughly mixed, stir in the butter, cream, treacle, and well-whisked eggs, and beat the mixture for a few minutes. Dissolve the soda in the vinegar, add it to the dough, and be particular that these latter ingredients are well incorporated with the others; put the cake into a buttered mould or tin, place it in a moderate oven immediately, and bake it from 1¾ to 2¼ hours.

TIME.—1¾ to 2¼ hours.

Cake, Common. (Suitable for sending to Children at School.)—

INGREDIENTS for large cake.—2 lbs. of flour, 4 oz. of butter or clarified dripping, ½ oz. of caraway seeds, ¼ oz. of allspice, ½ lb. of pounded sugar, 1 lb. of currants, 1 pint of milk, 3 tablespoonfuls of fresh yeast. AVERAGE COST, 1s. 7d.

Rub the butter lightly into the flour; add all the dry ingredients, and mix these well together. Make the milk warm, but not hot; stir in the yeast, and with this liquid mix the whole into a light dough; knead it well, and line the cake tins with strips of buttered paper; this paper should be about 6 inches higher than the top of the tin. Put in the dough; stand it in a warm place to rise for more than an hour, then bake the cakes in a well-heated oven. If this quantity be divided into two, they will take from 1½ to 2 hours baking.

TIME.—1½ to 2 hours.

Cake, Economical.—

INGREDIENTS.—1 lb. of flour, ¼ lb. of sugar, ¼ lb. of butter or lard, ½ lb. of currants, 1 teaspoonful of carbonate of soda, the whites of 4 eggs, ½ pint of milk. AVERAGE COST, 1s. 3d.

In making many sweet dishes, the whites of eggs are not required, and if well beaten and added to the above ingredients, make an excellent cake with or without currants. Beat the butter to a cream, well whisk the whites of the eggs, and stir all the ingredients together but the soda, which must not be added until all is well mixed, and the cake is ready to be put into the oven. When the

CAKE-MOULD.

mixture has been well beaten, stir in the soda, put the cake into a buttered mould, and bake it in a moderate oven for 1½ hour.

TIME.—1½ hour.

Cake, Good Holiday.—

INGREDIENTS for large cake.—1½d.-worth of Borwick's baking-powder, 2 lbs. of flour, 6 oz. of butter, ¼ lb. of lard, 1 lb. of currants, ½ lb. of stoned and cut raisins, ¼ lb. of mixed candied peel, ½ lb. of moist sugar, 3 eggs, ¾ pint of cold milk. AVERAGE COST, 2s. 7d.

Mix the baking-powder with the flour; then rub in the butter and lard; have ready the currants, washed, picked, and dried, the raisins stoned and cut into small pieces (not chopped), and the peel cut into neat slices. Add these with the sugar to the flour, &c.,

MADEIRA CAKE.

and mix all the dry ingredients well together. Whisk the eggs, stir to them the milk, and with this liquid moisten the cake; beat it up well, that all may be very thoroughly mixed; line a cake tin with buttered paper, put in the cake, and bake it from 2¼ to 2¾ hours in a good oven. To ascertain when it is done, plunge a clean knife into the middle of it, and if, on withdrawing it, the knife looks clean, and not sticky, the cake is done. To prevent it burning at the top, a piece of clean paper may be put over whilst the cake is soaking, or being thoroughly cooked in the middle. A steamer, such as is used for steaming potatoes, makes a very good cake tin, if it be lined at the bottom and sides with buttered paper.

TIME.—2¼ to 2¾ hours.

SEASONABLE at any time.

Cake, Luncheon.—

INGREDIENTS.—½ lb. of butter, 1 lb. of flour, ½ oz. of caraway seeds, ½ lb. of currants, 6 oz. of moist sugar, 1 oz. of candied peel, 3 eggs, ½ pint of

Twelfth Cake.

Baba.

Tennis Cake.

Gateau.

Madeira Cake.

Margipan.

Wedding Cake.

Rout Cakes.

Shortbread.

Petit Fours.

Sponge Cake.

Christening Cake.

Fancy Cake.

Cakes.

milk, 1 *small teaspoonful of carbonate of soda.* AVERAGE COST, 1s. 6d.

Rub the butter into the flour until it is quite fine; add the caraway seeds, currants which should be nicely washed, picked and dried), sugar, and candied peel cut into thin slices; mix these well together, and

SMALL POUND CAKES.

moisten with the eggs, which should be well whisked. Boil the milk, and add to it, whilst boiling, the carbonate of soda, which must be well stirred into it, and, with the milk, mix the other ingredients. Butter a tin, pour the cake into , and bake it in a moderate oven from 1 o 1½ hour.

TIME.—1 *to* 1½ *hour.*

SEASONABLE *at any time.*

Cake, Nice Plain.—INGREDIENTS.

-1 lb. of flour, 1 teaspoonful of Borwick's aking-powder, ¼ lb. of good dripping, 1 acupful of moist sugar, 3 eggs, 1 breakfast- upful of milk, 1 oz. of caraway seeds, ½ lb. * currants. AVERAGE COST, 1s.

Put the flour and the baking-powder into basin; stir these together; then rub in he dripping, add the sugar, caraway seeds, nd currants; whisk the eggs with the ilk, and beat all together very thoroughly ntil the ingredients are well mixed. utter a tin, put in the cake, and bake it rom 1½ to 2 hours. Let the dripping be uite clean before using; to insure this, it a good plan to clarify it. Beef dripping better than any other for cakes, &c., as utton dripping frequently has a very un- leasant flavour, which would be imparted the preparation.

TIME.—1½ *to* 2 *hours.*

SEASONABLE *at any time.*

Cake, Nice Useful.—INGRE-

IENTS.—¼ lb. of butter, 6 oz. of currants, ¼ . of sugar, 1 lb. of dried flour, 2 teaspoon- ls of baking-powder, 3 eggs, 1 teacupful of

milk, 2 oz. *of sweet almonds,* 1 oz. *of candied peel.* AVERAGE COST, 1s. 4d.

Beat the butter to a cream; wash, pick, and dry the currants; whisk the eggs; blanch and chop the almonds, and cut the peel into neat slices. When all these are ready, mix the dry ingredients together; then add the butter, milk and eggs, and beat the mixture well for a few minutes. Put the cake into a buttered tin or mould, and bake

SPONGE CAKE.

it for rather more than 1½ hour. The currants and candied peel may be omitted, and a litle lemon or almond flavouring sub- stituted for them; made in this manner, the cake will be found very good.

TIME.—*Rather more than* 1½ *hour.*

Cake, Pavini.—INGREDIENTS.—

½ lb. *of flour,* ½ lb. *of ground rice,* ½ lb. *of raisins stoned and cut into small pieces,* ¼ lb. *of currants,* ¼ lb. *of butter,* 2 oz. *of sweet almonds,* ¼ lb. *of sifted loaf sugar, a little nutmeg grated,* 1 pint *of milk,* 1 *tea- spoonful of carbonate of soda.* AVERAGE COST, 1s. 6d.

Stone and cut the raisins into small pieces; wash, pick, and dry the currants; melt the butter to a cream, but without oiling it; blanch and chop the almonds, and grate the nutmeg. When all these in- gredients are thus prepared, mix them well together; make the milk warm, stir in the soda, and with this liquid make the whole into a paste. Butter a mould, rather more than half fill it with the dough, and bake the cake in a moderate oven from 1½ to 2 hours, or less time should it be made into two cakes.

TIME.—1½ *to* 2 *hours.*

SEASONABLE *at any time.*

Cake, Plain, for Children.—

INGREDIENTS.—1 *quartern of dough,* ½ lb. *of moist sugar,* ½ lb. *of butter or good beef drip-*

ping, ¼ pint of warm milk, ½ grated nutmeg or ⅓ oz. of caraway seeds. AVERAGE COST, 1s.

If you are not in the habit of making bread at home, procure the dough from the baker's, and as soon as it comes in put it into a basin near the fire; cover the basin with a thick cloth, and let the dough remain a little while to rise. In the meantime, beat the butter to a cream, and make the milk warm; and when the dough has risen, mix with it thoroughly all the above ingredients, and knead the cake well for a few minutes. Butter some cake tins, half fill them, and stand them in a warm place, to allow the dough to rise again. When the tins are three-parts full, put the cakes into a good oven, and bake them from 1¾ to 2 hours. A few currants might be substituted for the caraway seeds when the flavour of the latter is disliked.

SEED CAKE.

TIME.—*1¼ to 2 hours.*

SEASONABLE *at any time.*

Cakes, Making and Baking of.

—*Eggs* should always be broken into a cup, the whites and yolks separated, and they should always be strained. Breaking the eggs thus, the bad ones may be easily rejected without spoiling the others, and so cause no waste. As eggs are used instead of yeast, they should be very thoroughly whisked; they are generally sufficiently beaten when thick enough to carry the drop that falls from the whisk.

Loaf Sugar should be well pounded, and then sifted through a fine sieve.

Currants should be nicely washed, picked, dried in a cloth, and then carefully examined, that no pieces of grit or stone may be left amongst them. They should then be laid on a dish before the fire, to become thoroughly dry; as, if added damp to the other ingredients, cakes will be liable to be heavy.

Good Butter should always be used for cakes; and if required beaten to a cream,

it saves much time and labour to warm, but not melt, it before beating.

The heat of the oven is of great importance, especially for large cakes. If the heat be not tolerably fierce, the batter will not rise. If the oven is too quick and there is any danger of the cake burning or catching, put a sheet of clean white paper over the top.

To know when a cake is sufficiently baked, plunge a clean knife into the middle of it; draw it quickly out, and if it looks in the least sticky put the cake back and close the oven door until the cake is done. Cakes should be kept in closed tin canisters or jars, and in a dry place. Those made with yeast do not keep so long as those made without it.

Cakes, Recipes for.—Directions

for making the following appear under their respective headings:—

Note.—Very good cakes are now made by the principal biscuit manufacturers, Huntley an

Palmer, and Peek, Frean and Co., these keeping fresh longer than those obtained from a baker or confectioner.

TENNIS CAKE.

Calf.—The manner of cutting up a calf for the English market is to divide the carcass into four quarters, with eleven ribs

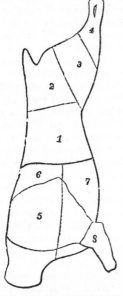

SIDE OF A CALF, SHOWING THE SEVERAL JOINTS.

to each fore quarter; which are again sub-divided into joints, as exemplified on the cut.

Hind Quarter :—

1. The loin.
2. The chump, consisting of the rump and hock-bone.

3. The fillet.
4. The hock, or hind knuckle.

Fore Quarter :—

5. The shoulder.
6. The neck.
7. The breast.
8. The fore knuckle.

The several parts of a moderately-sized well-fed calf, about eight weeks old, are nearly of the following weights :—loin and chump 18 lbs., fillet 12½ lbs., hind knuckle 5½ lbs., shoulder 11 lbs., neck 11 lbs., breast 9 lbs., and fore knuckle 5 lbs.; making a total of 144 lbs. weight. The London mode of cutting the carcass is considered better than that pursued in Edinburgh, as giving three roasting joints and one boiling in each quarter; besides the pieces being more equally divided, as regards flesh, and from the handsomer appearance they make on the table.

Calf's Feet, Baked or Stewed.

—INGREDIENTS *for sufficient for 2 persons.* —1 *calf's foot,* 1 *pint of milk,* 1 *pint of water,* 1 *blade of mace, the rind of* ½ *lemon, pepper and salt to taste.* AVERAGE COST, 1s.

Well clean the foot, and either stew or bake it in the milk-and-water with the other ingredients from 3 to 4 hours. To enhance the flavour, an onion and a small quantity of celery may be added, if approved; ½ a teacupful of cream, stirred in just before serving, is also a great improvement to this dish.

TIME.—3 *to 4 hours.*

SEASONABLE *from March to October.*

Calf's Feet, Boiled, and Parsley and Butter.

—INGREDIENTS *for dish for 4 or 5 persons.*—2 *calf's feet,* 2 *slices of bacon,* 2 *oz. of butter,* 2 *tablespoonfuls of lemon-juice, salt and whole pepper to taste,* 1 *onion, a bunch of savoury herbs,* 4 *cloves,* 1 *blade of mace, water, parsley and butter.* AVERAGE COST, 2s.

Procure 2 white calf's feet; bone them

as far as the first joint, and put them into warm water to soak for 2 hours. Then put the bacon, butter, lemon-juice, onions, herbs, spices and seasoning into a stewpan ; lay in the feet, and pour in just sufficient water to cover the whole. Stew gently for about 3 hours ; take out the feet, dish them and cover with parsley and butter. The liquor they were boiled in should be strained and put by in a clean basin for use : it will be found very good as an addition to gravies, &c.

TIME.—*Rather more than 3 hours.*

SEASONABLE *from March to October.*

Calf's Feet, Fricasseed.—INGRE-

DIENTS.—*A set of calf's feet ; for the batter, allow for each egg 1 tablespoonful of flour, 1 tablespoonful of bread-crumbs, hot lard, or clarified dripping, pepper and salt to taste.* AVERAGE COST, 9d. each.

If the feet are purchased uncleaned, dip them into warm water repeatedly, and scrape off the hair, first one foot and then the other, until the skin looks perfectly clean, a saucepan of water being kept by the fire until they are finished. After washing and soaking in cold water, boil them in just sufficient water to cover them, until the bones come easily away. Then pick them out, and after straining the liquor into a clean vessel, put the meat into a pie-dish until the next day. Now cut it down in slices about ½ inch thick, lay on them a stiff batter made of egg, flour and bread-crumbs in the above proportion ; season with pepper and salt, and plunge them into a pan of boiling lard. Fry the slices a nice brown, dry them before the fire for a minute or two, dish them on a napkin, and garnish with tufts of parsley. This should be eaten with melted butter, mustard and vinegar. Be careful to have the lard boiling to *set* the batter, or the pieces of feet will run about the pan. The liquor they were boiled in should be saved, and will be found useful for enriching gravies, making jellies, &c.

TIME.—*About 3 hours to stew the feet, 10 or 15 minutes to fry them.*

SEASONABLE *from March to October.*

Note.—This dish can be highly recommended to delicate persons.

Calf's Feet Jelly.—INGREDIENTS

for 3 pints.—1 *quart of calf's feet stock, ½ lb. of sugar, ½ pint of sherry, 1 glass of brandy, the shells and whites of 5 eggs, the rind and juice of 2 lemons, ½ oz. of isinglass.*

Prepare the stock as directed in recipe for stock, taking care to leave the sediment, and to remove all the fat from the surface. Put it into a saucepan cold, without clarifying it ; add the remaining ingredients, and stir them well together before the saucepan is placed on the fire. Then simmer the mixture gently for ¼ hour, but *do not stir it after it begins to warm.* Throw in a teacupful of cold water, boil for another 5 minutes, and keep the saucepan covered by the side of the fire for about ½ hour, but do not let it boil again. In simmering, the head or scum may be carefully removed as it rises ; but particular attention must be given to the jelly, that it be not stirred in the slightest degree after it is heated. The isinglass should be added when the jelly begins to boil ; this assists to clear it, and makes it firmer for turning out. Wring out a jelly-bag in hot water ; fasten it on to a stand, or the back of a chair ; place it near the fire with a basin underneath it, and run the jelly through it. Should it not be perfectly clear the first time, repeat the process until the desired brilliancy is obtained. Soak the moulds in water, drain them for half a second, pour in the jelly, and put it in a cool place to set. If ice is at hand, surround the moulds with it, and the jelly will set sooner, and be firmer when turned out. In summer it is necessary to have ice in which to put the moulds, or the cook will be, very likely, disappointed, by her jellies being in too iquid a state to turn out properly, unless a great deal of isinglass is used. When wanted for table, dip the moulds in hot water for a minute, wipe the outside with a cloth, lay a dish on the top of the mould, turn it quickly over, and the jelly should slip out easily. It is sometimes served broken into square lumps, and piled high in glasses. Earthenware moulds are preferable to those of pewter or tin for red jellies, the colour and transparency of the composition being often spoiled by using the latter. To make this jelly more economically, raisin wine may be substituted for the sherry and brandy, and the stock made from cow-heels, instead of calf's feet.

TIME.—20 *minutes to simmer the jelly,* ½ *hour to remain covered.*

SEASONABLE *at any time.*

Note. — As lemon-juice, unless carefully strained, is liable to make the jelly muddy, see that it is clear before it is added to the other ingredients. Omit the brandy when the flavour is objected to.

Calf's Foot Broth.—INGREDIENTS *for* 1½ *pint of broth.*—1 *calf's foot,* 3 *pints of water,* 1 *small lump of sugar, nutmeg to taste, the yolk of* 1 *egg, a piece of butter the size of a nut.* AVERAGE COST, 11*d.*

Stew the foot in the water with the lemon-peel *very gently,* until the liquid is half wasted, removing any scum should it rise to the surface. Set it by in a basin until quite cold, then take off every particle of fat. Warm up about ½ pint of the broth, adding the butter, sugar, and a very small quantity of grated nutmeg ; take it off the fire for a minute or two, then add the beaten yolk of the egg ; keep stirring over the fire until the mixture thickens, but do not allow it to boil again after the egg is added, or it will curdle, and the broth will be spoiled.

TIME.—*To be boiled until the liquid is reduced one half.*

SEASONABLE *from March to October.*

Calf's Head à la Maitre d'Hotel.
(Cold Meat Cookery.)—INGREDIENTS *for small dish.—The remains of a cold calf's head, rather more than* ½ *pint of maitre d'hôtel sauce.* AVERAGE COST, *exclusive of the meat,* 1*s.*

Make the sauce by the given recipe, and have it sufficiently thick that it may nicely cover the meat ; remove the bones from the head, and cut the meat into neat slices. When the sauce is ready, lay in the meat; *gradually* warm it through, and, after it boils up, let it simmer very gently for 5 minutes, and serve.

TIME.—*Rather more than* 1½ *hour.*

SEASONABLE *from March to October.*

Calf's Head, Boiled. (With the Skin on.)—INGREDIENTS *for dish for* 8 *or* 9 *persons.—Calf's head, boiling water, breadcrumbs,* 1 *large bunch of parsley, butter, white pepper and salt to taste,* 4 *tablespoonfuls of melted butter,* 1 *tablespoonful of lemon-juice,* 2 *or* 3 *grains of cayenne.* AVERAGE COST, 4*s.* 6*d.*

Put the head into boiling water, and let it remain by the side of the fire for 3 or 4 minutes ; take it out, hold it by the ear, and with the back of a knife scrape off the hair (should it not come off easily, dip the head again into boiling water). When perfectly clean, take the eyes out, cut off the ears, and remove the brain, which soak for an hour in warm water. Put the head into hot water to soak for a few minutes, to make it look white, and then have ready a stewpan, into which lay the head ; cover it with cold water, and bring it gradually to boil. Remove the scum, and add a little salt, which assists to throw it up. Simmer it very gently from 2½ to 3 hours, and when nearly done, boil the brains for ¼ hour; skin and chop them, not too finely, and add a tablespoonful of minced parsley which has been previously scalded. Season with pepper and salt, and stir the brains, parsley, &c., into about 4 tablespoonfuls of melted butter; add the lemon-juice and cayenne, and keep these hot by the side of the fire. Take up the head, cut out the tongue, skin it, put it on a small dish with the brains round it; sprinkle over the head a few bread-crumbs mixed with a little minced parsley; brown these before the fire, and serve with a tureen of parsley and butter, and either boiled bacon, ham or pickled pork as an accompaniment.

TIME.—2½ to 3 hours.

SEASONABLE from March to October.

Calf's Head, Boiled. (Without the Skin.) — INGREDIENTS for dish for 8 persons. — Calf's head, water, a little salt, 4 tablespoonfuls of melted butter, 1 tablespoonful of minced parsley, pepper and salt to taste, 1 tablespoonful of lemon-juice. AVERAGE COST, 4s. 6d.

After the head has been thoroughly cleaned, and the brains removed, soak it in

CALF'S HEAD.

warm water to blanch it. Lay the brains also into warm water to soak and let them remain for about an hour. Put the head into a stewpan, with sufficient cold water to cover it, and, when it boils, add a little salt; take off every particle of scum as it rises, and boil the head until perfectly

HALF A CALF'S HEAD.

tender. Boil the brains, chop them, and mix with them melted butter, minced parsley, pepper, salt and lemon-juice in the above proportion. Take up the head, skin

the tongue, and put it on a small dish with the brains round it. Have ready some parsley and butter, smother the head with it and the remainder send to table in a tureen Bacon, ham, pickled pork, or a pig's cheek are indispensable with calf's head. The brains are sometimes chopped with hard boiled eggs, and mixed with a little Béchamel or white sauce.

TIME.—From 1½ to 2¼ hours.

SEASONABLE from March to October.

Note.—The liquor in which the head was boiled should be saved: it makes excellent soup, and will be found a nice addition to gravies, &c. Half a calf's head is as frequently served as a whole one, it being a more convenient-sized joint for a small family. It is cooked in the same manner, and served with the same sauces as in the preceding recipe.

Calf's Head, Collared.—INGREDIENTS.—A calf's head, 4 tablespoonfuls of minced parsley, 4 blades of pounded mace, ½ teaspoonful of grated nutmeg, white pepper to taste, a few thick slices of ham, the yolks of 6 eggs boiled hard. AVERAGE COST 5s. 6d.

Scald the head for a few minutes; take it out of the water, and with a blunt knife scrape off all the hair. Clean it nicely divide the head and remove the brains Boil it tender enough to take out the bones which will be in about 2 hours. When the head is boned, flatten it on the table, sprinkle over it a thick layer of parsley, then a layer of ham, and then the yolks of the eggs cut into thin rings and put a seasoning of pounded mace, nutmeg and white pepper between each layer; roll the head up in a cloth, and tie it up as tightly as possible. Boil it for 4 hours, and when it is taken out of the pot, place a heavy weight on the top, the same as for other collared meats. Let it remain till cold; then remove the cloth and binding, and it will be ready to serve.

TIME.—Altogether, 5 hours.

SEASONABLE from March to October.

Calf's Head, Fricasseed.

Cold Meat Cookery.)—INGREDIENTS.—
The remains of a boiled calf's head, 1½ pint
of the liquor in which the head was boiled, 1
blade of pounded mace, 1 onion minced, a
bunch of savoury herbs, salt and white
pepper to taste, thickening of butter and
flour, the yolks of 2 eggs, 1 tablespoonful
of lemon-juice, forcemeat balls. AVERAGE
COST, exclusive of the meat, 6d.

Remove all the bones from the head, and
cut the meat into nice square pieces. Put
½ pint of the liquor it was boiled in into a
saucepan, with mace, onions, herbs and
seasoning in the above proportion; let this
simmer gently for ¾ hour, then strain it and
put in the meat. When quite hot through,
thicken the gravy with a little butter rolled
in flour, and just before dishing the
fricassee, put in the beaten yolks of eggs,
and lemon-juice; but be particular, after
these two latter ingredients are added, that
the sauce does not boil, or it will curdle.
Garnish with forcemeat balls and curled
slices of broiled bacon. To insure the
sauce being smooth, it is a good plan to
dish the meat first, and then to add the
eggs to the gravy: when these are set, the
sauce may be poured over the meat.

TIME.—Altogether, 1¼ hour.

Calf's Head, Hashed. (Cold

Meat Cookery.) — INGREDIENTS.—The remains of a cold boiled calf's head, 1 quart
of the liquor in which it was boiled, a faggot
of savoury herbs, 1 onion, 1 carrot, a strip
of lemon-peel, 2 blades of pounded mace,
salt and white pepper to taste, a very little
cayenne, rather more than 2 tablespoonfuls
of sherry, 1 tablespoonful of lemon-juice, 1
tablespoonful of mushroom ketchup, forcemeat balls. AVERAGE COST, exclusive of
the meat, 9d.

Cut the meat into neat slices, and put
the bones and trimmings into a stewpan
with the above proportion of liquor that
the head was boiled in. Add a bunch of
savoury herbs, 1 onion, 1 carrot, a strip of
lemon-peel, and 2 blades of pounded mace,
and let these boil for 1 hour, or until the
gravy is reduced nearly half. Strain it into
a clean stewpan, thicken it with a little
butter and flour, and add a flavouring of
sherry, lemon-juice and ketchup, in the
above proportion; season with pepper, salt
and a little cayenne; put in the meat, let
it gradually warm through, but not boil
more than two or three minutes. Garnish
the dish with forcemeat balls and pieces of
bacon rolled and toasted, placed alternately,
and send it to table very hot.

TIME.—Altogether, 1½ hour.

SEASONABLE from March to October.

Calf's Head, Moulded. (Cold Meat

Cookery.)—INGREDIENTS.—The remains of
a calf's head, some thin slices of ham or
bacon, 6 eggs boiled hard, 1 dessertspoonful
of salt, pepper, mixed spice, and parsley, ½
pint of good white gravy. AVERAGE COST,
exclusive of the meat, 1s. 4d.

Cut the head into thin slices. Butter a
tin mould, cut the yolks of eggs in half,
and put some of them round the tin;
sprinkle some of the parsley, spice, &c.,
over it; then put in the head and the
bacon in layers, adding occasionally more
eggs and spice till the whole of the head is
used. Pour in the gravy, cover the top
with a thin paste of flour and water, and
bake ¾ of an hour. Take off the paste,
and, when cold, turn it out.

TIME.—From ¾ to 1 hour to bake the preparation.

SEASONABLE from March to October.

Calf's Head, To Carve.—This is

not altogether the most easy-looking dish
to cut when it is put before a carver for the
first time; there is not much real difficulty
in the operation, however, when the head
has been attentively examined, and, after
the manner of a phrenologist, you get to
know its bumps, good and bad. In the
first place, inserting the knife quite down

to the bo... , cut slices in the direction of the line A to B ; with each of these should be helped a piece of what is called the throat sweetbread, cut in the direction of from C to D. The eye, and the flesh round, are favourite morsels with many, and should be given to those at the table who are known to be the greatest connoisseurs.

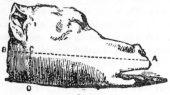

CALF'S HEAD.

The jawbone being removed, there will then be found some nice lean ; and the palate, which is reckoned by some a tit-bit, lies under the head. On a separate dish there is always served the tongue and brains, and each guest should be asked to take some of these.

Calf's Liver and Bacon.—INGREDIENTS for large dish.—2 lbs. of liver, bacon, pepper and salt to taste, a small piece of butter, flour, 2 tablespoonfuls of lemon-juice, ¼ pint of water. AVERAGE COST, 2s. 6d.

Cut the liver in thin slices, and cut as many slices of bacon as there are of liver; fry the bacon first, and put that on a hot dish before the fire. Fry the liver in the fat which comes from the bacon, after seasoning it with pepper and salt and dredging over it a very little flour. Turn the liver occasionally to prevent its burning, and when done lay it round the dish with a piece of bacon between each. Pour away the bacon fat, put in a small piece of butter, dredge in a little flour, add the lemon-juice and water, give one boil, and pour it in the middle of the dish.

TIME.—According to the thickness of the slices, from 5 to 10 minutes.

SEASONABLE from March to October.

Calf's Liver aux Fines Herbe[s] and Sauce Piquante.—INGREDIENTS fo[r] dish for 8 persons.—A calf's liver, flour, bunch of savoury herbs, including parsley when liked, 2 minced shalots ; 1 teaspoonf[ul] of flour, 1 tablespoonful of vinegar, 1 tabl[e] spoonful of lemon-juice, pepper and salt [to] taste, ¼ pint of water. AVERAGE COST, 2s[.]

Procure a calf's liver as white as poss[i] ble, and cut it into slices of a good an[d] equal shape. Dip them in flour, and fr[y] them of a good colour in a little butte[r.] When they are done, put them on a dis[h] which keep hot before the fire. Mince th[e] herbs very fine, put them in the fryin[g] pan with a little more butter ; add the re[] maining ingredients, simmer gently unt[il] the herbs are done, and pour over the live[r.]

TIME.—According to the thickness of th[e] slices, from 5 to 10 minutes.

SEASONABLE from March to October.

Calf's Liver, Larded an[d] Roasted.—INGREDIENTS for dish for 8 per[] sons.—A calf's liver, vinegar, 1 onion, 3 o[r] 4 sprigs of parsley and thyme, salt an[d] pepper to taste, 1 bay leaf, lardoons, brow[n] gravy. AVERAGE COST, 2s. 10d.

Take a fine white liver, and lard it th[e] same as a fricandeau ; put it into vinega[r] with an onion cut in slices, parsley, thyme[,] bay-leaf and seasoning in the above pro[] portion. Let it remain in this pickle fo[r] 24 hours, then roast and baste it frequentl[y] with the vinegar, &c. ; glaze it, serve unde[r] it a good brown gravy, or sauce piquante[,] and send it to table very hot.

TIME.—Rather more than 1 hour.

SEASONABLE from March to October.

Note.—Calf's liver stuffed with forcemeat (se[e] FORCEMEAT), to which has been added a little fa[t] bacon, will be found a very savoury dish. I[t] should be larded or wrapped in buttered paper and roasted before a clear fire. Brown gravy and currant jelly should be served with it.

Camp Vinegar.—INGREDIENTS.— 1 head of garlic, ½ oz. of cayenne, 2 tea[] spoonfuls of soy, 2 ditto walnut ketchup, [1]

t of vinegar, cochineal to colour. AVER-
E COST, 8*d.*

Slice the garlic, and put it, with all the
ove ingredients, into a clean bottle. Let
stand to infuse for a month, when strain
off quite clear, and it will be fit for use.
eep it in small bottles well sealed to ex-
ade the air.

Canapés, Anchovy.— INGREDI-
TS *for 12 canapés.—2 slices of stale bread,*
anchovies, 2 eggs, butter or clarified dr p
ng, for frying. AVERAGE COST, 9*d.*

Cut the bread one-third of an inch thick
d stamp it out in little rounds. Fry
em till of a bright golden brown. Boil the
gs hard, and wash, bone and fillet the
nchovies. Curl two fillets in each round
' bread, and fill the centre with chopped
hite of egg and the yellow rubbed through
sieve.

SEASONABLE *at any time.*

Canapés, Lobster.—INGREDIENTS
r 12 canapés.—12 croûtons, prepared as
preceding recipe, a little lobster butter,
e tail of a small lobster, oil, vinegar and
epper, a few capers. AVERAGE COST, 10*d.*

Cut small slices of the lobster, and
oak them for a few minutes in oil and
inegar. Spread the croûtons with the
utter, lay a slice on each, and two or
hree layers on the top, add a slight season-
g of pepper, and serve on a stamped
aper garnished with parsley or watercress.

SEASONABLE *at any time.*

Canapés, Savoury.— INGREDI-
NTS *for sufficient for 6 persons.—6 oysters,*
 anchovies, 1 sardine, a few shrimps, a
 mall head of celery, 1 small shalot, a little
 ress, mayonnaise sauce, some tarragon, mont-
 elier butter, 1 hard-boiled egg, lobster coral,
 spic jelly. AVERAGE COST, 2*s.*

Pound the shalot, shred the celery, bone
nd scale the fish, and mix, with the cress
nd tarragon, chopped finely. Fill small
rioche cases with the mixture, and run a
ittle butter round the edges, strew some

chopped hard-boiled egg and lobster coral
on the top of each, and garnish with some
aspic jelly, roughed with a fork, and some
fresh parsley.

SEASONABLE *in autumn and winter, as a*
savoury at dinner.

Canary Pudding. (Very good.)—
INGREDIENTS *for pudding, sufficient for*
5 persons.—The weight of 3 eggs in sugar and
butter, the weight of 2 eggs in flour, the rind
of 1 small lemon, 3 eggs. AVERAGE COST, 9*d.*

Melt the butter to a liquid state, but do
not allow it to oil; stir to this the sugar
and finely-minced lemon-peel, and gradually
dredge in the flour, keeping the mixture
well stirred; whisk the eggs; add these to
the pudding; beat all the ingredients until
thoroughly blended, and put them into a
buttered mould or basin; boil for 2 hours,
and serve with sweet sauce.

TIME.—2 *hours.*

SEASONABLE *at any time.*

Candied Chestnuts.—INGREDI-
ENTS. — *Chestnuts, lemon-juice, clarified*
sugar.

Take off the outer skin of the nuts, and
put them into a pan of boiling water for a
minute or so till the second skin comes off
easily; after this throw them into another
pan of boiling water and boil till tender.
Squeeze the juice of a lemon into a basin of
lukewarm water and put the chestnuts in
this when done; when cool dip them in
clarified sugar (*see* RECIPE) and lay on a
slab to dry.

Candied Walnuts.—INGREDIENTS.
—*Walnuts, liqueur, clarified sugar, lemon.*

Proceed in the same manner as in the
preceding recipe for Candied Chestnuts, but
flavour the sugar with a little Benedictine
or other liqueur. A flavouring can also
be given to the chestnuts in the same way.

Cannelons, or Fried Puffs.—
INGREDIENTS *for dish for 6 persons.—½ lb.*
of puff-paste; apricot, or any kind of preserve

that may be preferred; hot lard. AVERAGE COST, 1s.

Cannelons, which are made of puff-paste rolled very thin, with jam inclosed, and cut out in long narrow rolls or puffs, make a very pretty and elegant dish. Make some good puff-paste by the recipe given; roll it out very thin, and cut it into pieces of an equal size, about 2 inches wide and 8 inches long; place upon each piece a spoonful of jam, wet the edges with the white of egg, and fold the paste over *twice;* slightly press the edges together, that the jam may not escape in the frying; and when all are prepared, fry them in boiling lard until of a nice brown, letting them remain by the side of the fire after they are coloured, that the paste may be thoroughly done. Drain them before the fire, dish on a d'oyley, sprinkle over them sifted sugar, and serve. These cannelons are very delicious made with fresh instead of preserved fruit, such as strawberries, raspberries, or currants: it should be laid in the paste, plenty of pounded sugar sprinkled over, and folded and fried in the same manner as stated above.

TIME.—*About* 10 *minutes.*
SEASONABLE, *with jam, at any time.*

Caper Sauce (for Fish).—INGREDIENTS *for* 1 *tureen.*—½ *pint of melted butter,*

THE CAPER.

3 *dessertspoonfuls of capers,* 1 *dessertspoonful of their liquor, a small piece of glaze, if at hand* (*this may be dispensed with*), ¼ *teaspoonful of salt, ditto of pepper,* 1 *tablespoonful of anchovy essence.* AVERAGE COST, 6d.

Cut the capers across once or twice, but do not chop them fine; put them in a saucepan with ½ pint of good melted butter, and add all the other ingredients. Keep

stirring the whole until it just simmer when it is ready to serve.

TIME.—1 *minute to simmer.*

Caper Sauce (for Boiled Mutton).—INGREDIENTS *for sufficient for a joint.*— pint of melted butter,* 3 *tablespoonfuls capers or nasturtiums,* 1 *tablespoonful their liquor.* AVERAGE COST, 5d.

Chop the capers twice or thrice, and ad them, with their liquor, to ½ pint of melte butter, made very smoothly with milk keep stirring well; let the sauce jus simmer, and serve in a tureen. Pickle nasturtium-pods are fine-flavoured, and b many are eaten in preference to caper They make an excellent sauce.

TIME.—2 *minutes to simmer.*

Caper Sauce, A Substitute for —INGREDIENTS *for sufficient for* 1 *joint.*— pint of melted butter,* 2 *tablespoonfuls of cu parsley,* ½ *teaspoonful of salt,* 1 *tablespoon ful of vinegar.* AVERAGE COST, 3d.

Boil the parsley slowly to let it become bad colour; cut, but do not chop it fin Add it to ½ pint of smoothly-made melte butter, with salt and vinegar in the abov proportions. Boil up and serve.

TIME.—2 *minutes to simmer.*

Capsicums, Pickled.—INGREDI ENTS.—*Vinegar,* ¼ *oz. of pounded mace an* ¼ *oz. of grated nutmeg, to each quart; brine.*

THE CAPSICUM.

Gather the pods with the stalks on, before they turn red; slit them down the side with a small-pointed knife, and remove the seeds only; put them in a strong brine for 3 days, changing it every morning; then take them out, lay them on a cloth, with anothe one over them, until they are perfectly fre

om moisture. Boil sufficient vinegar to
ver them, with mace and nutmeg in the
ove proportions; put the pods in a jar,
ur over the vinegar when cold, and ex-
de them from the air by means of a wet
adder tied over.

Carp, Baked. — INGREDIENTS.—1
rp, *forcemeat, bread-crumbs,* 1 *oz. of
tter,* ½ *pint of stock* (see STOCK), ½ *pint of
rt wine,* 6 *anchovies,* 2 *onions sliced,* 1
y-leaf, a faggot of sweet herbs, flour to
icken, the juice of 1 lemon; cayenne and
lt to taste;* ½ *teaspoonful of powdered
gar.*

Stuff the carp with a delicate forcemeat,
ter thoroughly cleansing it, and sew it
, to prevent the stuffing from falling out.
ub it over with an egg, and sprinkle it
th bread-crumbs; lay it in a deep earthen
sh, and drop the butter, oiled, over the
ead-crumbs. Add the stock, onions,
y-leaf, herbs, wine and anchovies, and

THE CARP.

ke for 1 hour. Put 1 oz. of butter into a
ewpan, melt it, and dredge in sufficient
ur to dry it up; put in the strained
uor from the carp, stir frequently, and
en it has boiled, add the lemon-juice and
asoning. Serve the carp on a dish
rnished with parsley and cut lemon, and
e sauce in a boat.

TIME.—1¼ hour.

SEASONABLE *from March to October.*

Carp, Stewed.—INGREDIENTS.—1
rp, salt, stock,* 2 *onions,* 6 *cloves,* 12
ppercorns, 1 *blade of mace,* ¼ *pint of port
ne, the juice of* ½ *lemon, cayenne and salt
taste, a faggot of savoury herbs.*

Scale the fish, clean it nicely, and, if
very large, divide it; lay it in the stewpan,
after having rubbed a little salt on it, and
put in sufficient stock to cover it; add the
herbs, onions and spices, and stew gently
for 1 hour, or rather more should it be
very large. Dish up the fish with great
care, strain the liquor, and add to it the
port wine, lemon-juice and cayenne; give
one boil, pour it over the fish and serve.

TIME.—1¼ hour.

SEASONABLE *from March to October.*

Note.— This fish can be boiled plain and
served with parsley and butter. Chub and
Char may be cooked in the same manner as the
above, as also Dace and Roach.

Carrot Jam (to imitate Apricot Preserve).—INGREDIENTS.—*Carrots; to every
lb. of carrot pulp allow* 1 *lb. of pounded
sugar, the grated rind of* 1 *lemon, the
strained juice of* 2, 6 *chopped bitter almonds,*
2 *tablespoonfuls of brandy.* AVERAGE COST
per lb., 6d.

Select young carrots; wash and scrape
them clean, cut them into round pieces, put
them into a saucepan with sufficient water
to cover them, and let them simmer until
perfectly soft; then beat them through a
sieve. Weigh the pulp, and to every lb.
allow the above ingredients. Put the pulp
into a preserving-pan with the sugar, and
let this boil for 5 minutes, stirring and
skimming all the time. When cold, add
the lemon-rind and juice, almonds and
brandy; mix these well with the jam; then
put it into pots, which must be well
covered and kept in a dry place. The
brandy may be omitted, but the preserve
will then not keep: with the brandy it will
remain good for months.

TIME.—*About* ¾ *hour to boil the carrots;*
5 *minutes to simmer the pulp.*

SEASONABLE *from July to December.*

**Carrot Pudding, Baked or
Boiled.**—INGREDIENTS *for pudding for 5
or 6 persons.*—½ *lb. of bread-crumbs,* 4 *oz.*

of suet, ¼ lb. of stoned raisins, ¾ lb. of carrots, ¼ lb. of currants, 3 oz. of sugar, 2 eggs, milk, a little nutmeg. AVERAGE COST, 1s.

CARROTS.

Boil the carrots until tender enough to mash to a pulp ; add the remaining ingredients, and moisten with sufficient milk to make the pudding of the consistency of thick batter. If to be boiled, put the mixture into a buttered basin, tie it down with a cloth, and boil for 2½ hours ; if to be baked, put it into a pie-dish, and bake for nearly an hour ; turn it out of the dish, strew sifted sugar over it, and serve.

TIME.—2½ hours to boil ; 1 hour to bake.
SEASONABLE from September to March.

Carrot Soup.—INGREDIENTS for 4 quarts.

—4 quarts of liquor in which a leg of mutton or a joint of beef has been boiled, a few beef-bones, 6 large carrots, 2 large onions, 1 turnip ; seasoning of salt and pepper to taste ; cayenne. AVERAGE COST, exclusive of the liquor, 6d.

Put the liquor, bones, onions, turnip, pepper and salt into a stewpan, and simmer for 3 hours. Scrape and cut the carrots thin, strain the soup on them, and stew them till soft enough to pulp through a hair sieve or coarse cloth ; then boil the pulp with the soup, which should be of the consistency of pea-soup. Add cayenne. Pulp only the red part of the carrot, and make this soup the day before it is wanted.

TIME.—4½ hours.
SEASONABLE from October to March.

Carrot Soup.—INGREDIENTS for 2 quarts.

—2 lbs. of carrots, 3 oz. of butter, seasoning to taste of salt and cayenne, 2 quarts of stock or gravy soup. AVERAGE COST, 1s. 8d.

Scrape and cut out all specks from t[he] carrots, wash and wipe them dry, and th[en] reduce them into quarter-inch slices. P[ut] the butter into a large stewpan, and wh[en] it is melted, add 2 lbs. of the sliced carro[t] and let them stew gently for an hour, wit[h]out browning. Add to them the soup, a[nd] allow them to simmer till tender—say f[or] nearly an hour. Press them through [a] strainer with the soup, and add salt a[nd] cayenne if required. Boil the whole gent[ly] for 5 minutes, skim well and serve as h[ot] as possible.

TIME.—1¼ hour.
SEASONABLE from October to March.

Carrots, Boiled.—INGREDIENTS.

To each ½ gallon of water, allow one heap[ed] tablespoonful of salt ; carrots. AVERA[GE] COST, 6d. for large bunch.

Cut off the green tops, wash and scra[pe] the carrots, and should there be any bla[ck] specks, remove them. If very large, c[ut] them in halves, divide them lengthwise i[nto] four pieces, and put them into boiling wat[er] salted in the above proportion ; let th[em] boil until tender, which may be ascertain[ed] by thrusting a fork into them : dish, a[nd] serve very hot. This vegetable is an ind[is]pensable accompaniment to boiled be[ef] When thus served, it is usually boiled w[ith] the beef ; a few carrots are placed round t[he] dish as a garnish, and the remainder se[nt] to table in a vegetable-dish. Young carr[ots] do not require nearly so much boiling, n[or] should they be divided : these make a n[ice] addition to stewed veal, &c.

TIME.—Large carrots, 1¾ to 2¼ hou[rs] young ones, about ½ hour.
SEASONABLE.—Young carrots from A[pril] to July, old ones at any time.

Carrots, Sliced.—INGREDIENTS,

dish for 4 persons.—5 or 6 large carrot[s] large lump of sugar, 1 pint of weak stoc[k] oz. of fresh butter, salt to taste. AVERA[GE] COST, 8d.

Scrape and wash the carrots, cut th[em]

to slices of an equal size, and boil them
, salt and water until half done; drain
.em well, put them into a stewpan with
e sugar and stock, and let them boil
·er a brisk fire. When reduced to a
aze, add the fresh butter and a season-
g of salt; shake the stewpan about
ell, and when the butter is well mixed
ith the carrots, serve. There should
. no sauce in the dish when it comes to
ble, but it should all adhere to the
rrots.

TIME.—*Altogether, ¾ hour.*

SEASONABLE.—*Young carrots from April
July; old ones at any time.*

Carrots, Stewed.—INGREDIENTS
· *dish for 6 persons.—*7 or 8 large carrots,
teacupful of broth, pepper and salt to
ste, ½ teacupful of cream, thickening of
tter and flour. AVERAGE COST, 9d.

Scrape the carrots nicely, half boil, and
·ce them into a stewpan; add the broth,
·pper and salt, and cream; simmer till
·nder, and be careful the carrots are not
·oken. A few minutes before serving,
·x a little flour with about 1 oz. of butter;
·icken the gravy with this, let it just boil
·, and serve.

TIME —*About ¾ hour to boil the carrots,
·ut 20 minutes to cook them after they are
·ced.*

SEASONABLE.—*Young carrots from April
July; old ones at any time.*

Carrots, To Dress (in the German
·y).—INGREDIENTS *for large dish.*—8
·ge carrots, 3 oz. of butter, salt to taste, a
·y little grated nutmeg, 1 tablespoonful of
·ely minced parsley, 1 dessertspoonful of
·nced onion, rather more than 1 pint of
·ak stock or broth, 1 tablespoonful of flour.
·ERAGE COST, 1s.

·Wash and scrape the carrots, and cut
·em into slices of about ¼ inch in thick-
·ss. Put the butter into a stewpan; when
·s melted, lay in the ·arrots, with salt,

nutmeg, parsley and onion in the above
proportions. Toss the stewpan over the
fire for a few minutes, and when the carrots
are well saturated with the butter, pour in
the stock and simmer gently until they
are nearly tender. Then put into another
stewpan a small piece of butter; dredge in
about a tablespoonful of flour, stir this
over the fire, and when of a nice brown
colour, add the liquor that the carrots have
been boiling in; let this just boil up, pour
it over the carrots in the other stewpan,
and let them finish simmering until quite
tender. Serve very hot. This vegetable,
dressed as above, is a favourite accompaniment to roast pork, sausages, &c. &c.

TIME.—*About ¾ hour.*

SEASONABLE.—*Young carrots from April
to July; old ones at any time.*

Cauliflowers à la Sauce
Blanche.—INGREDIENTS *for large dish.*—
3 cauliflowers, ½ pint of sauce blanche, or
French melted butter, 2 oz. of butter, salt
and water. AVERAGE COST, 1s. 2d.

Cleanse the cauliflowers as in the suc-
ceeding recipe, and cut the stalks off flat at
the bottom; boil them until tender in salt

CAULIFLOWER.

and water, to which the above proportion
of butter has been added, and be careful to
take them up the moment they are done,
or they will break and the appearance of
the dish will be spoiled. Drain them well,
and dish them in the shape of a large

N

cauliflower. Have ready ½ pint of sauce made by recipe, pour it over the flowers, and serve hot and quickly.

TIME. — *Small cauliflowers, 12 to 15 minutes; large ones, 20 to 25 minutes, after the water boils.*

SEASONABLE *from the beginning of June to the end of September.*

Cauliflowers or Broccoli,

Boiled — INGREDIENTS.—*To each ½ gallon of water allow 1 heaped tablespoonful of salt.* AVERAGE COST, 3d. to 6d. each, according to size.

Choose cauliflowers that are close and white; trim off the decayed outside leaves, and cut the stalk off flat at the bottom. Open the flower a little in places to remove the insects, which are generally found about the stalk, and let the cauliflowers lie in salt and water for an hour previous to dressing them, with their heads downwards: this will effectually draw out all the vermin. Then put them into fast-boiling water, with the addition of salt in the above proportion and let them boil briskly over a good fire, keeping the saucepan uncovered, and the water well skimmed.

BOILED CAULIFLOWER.

When the cauliflowers are tender, take them up with a slice; let them drain, and, if large enough, place them upright in the dish. Serve with plain melted butter, a little of which may be poured over the flower.

TIME. — *Small cauliflower, 12 to 15 minutes, large one 20 to 25 minutes, after the water boils.*

SEASONABLE *from the beginning of June to the end of September.*

Cauliflowers, with Parmesa Cheese.

— INGREDIENTS *for dish for persons.—2 or 3 cauliflowers, rather mo than ½ pint of white sauce, 2 tablespoonfu of grated Parmesan or other cheese, 2 o of fresh butter, 3 tablespoonfuls of brea crumbs.* AVERAGE COST, 1s. 6d.

Cleanse and boil the cauliflowers by th preceding recipe, drain them, and di them with the flowers standing uprigh Have ready the above proportion of whi sauce; pour sufficient of it over the cau flowers just to cover the top; sprinkle ov this some rasped cheese and bread-crumb

FRIED CAULIFLOWERS.

and drop on these the butter, which shou be melted, but not oiled. Brown with salamander, or before the fire, and po round, but not over, the flowers the mainder of the sauce, with which should mixed a small quantity of grated cheese.

TIME.—*Altogether, ½ hour.*

SEASONABLE *from the beginning of Ju to the end of September.*

Cayenne Cheeses.

— INGREDIEN *for sufficient for 6 persons.—4 oz. of butt ½ lb. of flour, 4 oz. of grated cheese, ½ te spoonful of cayenne, ½ teaspoonful of sal water.* AVERAGE COST, 10d.

Rub the butter in the flour; add t grated cheese, cayenne and salt, and m these ingredients well together. Moist with sufficient water to make the whe into a paste; roll out, and cut into finge about 4 inches in length. Bake them in moderate oven a very light colour, a serve very hot.

TIME.—*15 to 20 minutes.*

SEASONABLE *at any time.*

Cayenne Vinegar, or Essence of Cayenne. — INGREDIENTS.— $\frac{1}{2}$ oz. of cayenne pepper, $\frac{1}{2}$ pint of strong spirit, or 1 pint of vinegar.

Put the vinegar, or spirit, into a bottle, with the above proportion of cayenne, and let it steep for a month, when strain off and bottle for use. This is excellent seasoning for soups or sauces, but must be used very sparingly.

Celery.—With a good heart, and nicely blanched, this vegetable is generally eaten raw, and is usually served with the cheese. Let the roots be washed free from dirt, all the decayed and outside leaves being cut off, preserving as much of the stalk as possible, and all specks or blemishes being carefully removed. Should the celery be large, divide it lengthwise into quarters, and place it, root downwards, in a celery-glass, which should be rather more than half filled with water. The top leaves may be curled, by shredding them in narrow strips with the point of a clean skewer, at a distance of about 4 inches from the top.

SEASONABLE *from October to April.*

Note.—This vegetable is exceedingly useful for flavouring soups, sauces, &c. (the outside leaves alone serve for this purpose), and makes a very nice addition to winter salad.

Celery Salad.—INGREDIENTS *for dish for 4 persons.*—$\frac{1}{2}$ head of celery, $\frac{1}{4}$ lb. of cheese, stilton or cheddar, mayonnaise sauce. AVERAGE COST, 6d.

Cleanse the celery and cut it in small dice, cut the cheese in small squares, and mix these two ingredients with enough mayonnaise sauce just to mask them. Serve garnished with watercress, in a glass dish.

SEASONABLE *at any time.*

Celery Sauce. (For Boiled Turkey, Poultry, &c.)—INGREDIENTS *for sufficient for a turkey.*—4 large heads of celery, 1 pint of white stock, 2 blades of mace, 1 small bunch

of savoury herbs; thickening of butter and flour, or arrowroot, $\frac{1}{2}$ pint of cream or milk, lemon-juice. AVERAGE COST, *with cream,* 2s.

Boil the celery in salt and water until tender, and cut it into pieces 2 inches long. Put the stock into a stewpan with the mace and herbs, and let it simmer for $\frac{1}{2}$ hour to extract their flavour. Then strain the liquor, add the celery, and a thickening of butter kneaded with flour, or, what is still better, with arrowroot; just before serving, put in the cream, boil it up, and squeeze in a little lemon-juice. If necessary, add a seasoning of salt and white pepper.

TIME.—*25 minutes to boil the celery.*

Note.—This sauce may be made brown by using gravy instead of white stock, and flavouring it with mushroom ketchup or Harvey's Sauce.

Celery Sauce. (A more simple Recipe.) — INGREDIENTS *for sufficient for a turkey.*—4 heads of celery, $\frac{1}{2}$ pint of melted butter made with milk, 1 blade of pounded mace; salt and white pepper to taste. AVERAGE COST, 1s.

Wash the celery, boil it in salt and water till tender, and cut it into pieces 2 inches long; make $\frac{1}{2}$ pint of melted butter by recipe; put in the celery, pounded mace, and seasoning; simmer for 3 minutes, when the sauce will be ready to serve.

TIME.—*25 minutes to boil the celery.*

Celery Soup. — INGREDIENTS *for soup for 9 or 10 persons.*—9 heads of celery, 1 teaspoonful of salt, nutmeg to taste, 1 lump of sugar, $\frac{1}{2}$ pint of strong stock, a pint of cream or milk, and 2 quarts of boiling water. AVERAGE COST, *with cream,* 3s. 6d.

Cut the celery into small pieces; throw it into the water, seasoned with the nutmeg, salt and sugar. Boil it till sufficiently tender; pass it through a sieve, add the stock, and simmer it for half an hour. Now put in the cream, bring it to the boiling-point, and serve immediately.

TIME.—1 *hour.*

SEASONABLE *from Septembe to March.*

Note.—This soup can be made brown instead of white, by omitting the cream, and colouring it a little. When celery cannot be procured, half a drachm of the seed, finely pounded, will give a flavour to the soup, if put in a quarter of an hour before it is done. A little of the essence of celery will answer the same purpose.

Celery, Stewed, à la Crême.—

INGREDIENTS *for dish for 6 persons.* — 4 *heads of celery; to each ½ gallon of water allow* 1 *heaped tablespoonful of salt,* 1 *blade of pounded mace, ½ pint of cream.* AVERAGE COST, 1s. 4d.

Wash the celery thoroughly; trim and boil it in salt and water until tender. Put the cream and pounded mace into a stewpan, shake it over the fire until the cream thickens, dish the celery, pour over the sauce and serve.

TIME.—*Large heads of celery, 25 minutes; small ones, 15 to 20 minutes.*

SEASONABLE *from October to April.*

Celery, Stewed, with White

Sauce.—INGREDIENTS *for large dish.* —6 *heads of celery,* 1 *oz. of butter; to each half gallon of water allow* 1 *heaped teaspoonful of salt, ½ pint of white sauce (see* WHITE SAUCE*).* AVERAGE COST, 1s. 4d.

Have ready sufficient boiling water just to cover the celery, with salt and butter in the above proportion. Wash the celery well, cut off the decayed outside leaves, trim away the green tops, and shape the root into a point; put it into the boiling water, let it boil rapidly until tender, then take it out, drain well, place it upon a dish, and pour over it about ½ pint of white sauce, made by recipe. It may also be plainly boiled as above, placed on toast, and melted butter poured over, the same as asparagus is dished.

TIME.—*Large heads of celery, 25 minutes; small ones 15 to 20 minutes, after water boils.*

SEASONABLE *from October to April.*

Celery, Stewed, with White

Sauce.—INGREDIENTS *for sufficient for 6 or 8 persons.*—6 *heads of celery, ½ pint of white stock or weak broth,* 4 *tablespoonfuls of cream, thickening of butter and flour,* 1 *blade of pounded mace, a very little grated nutmeg; pepper and salt to taste.* AVERAGE COST. 1s. 8d.

Wash the celery, strip off the outer leaves, and cut it into lengths of about 4 inches. Put these into a saucepan with the

CELERY.

broth, and stew till tender, which will be in from 20 to 25 minutes; then add the remaining ingredients, simmer altogether for 4 or 5 minutes, pour into a dish, and serve. It may be garnished with sippets of toasted bread.

TIME.—*Altogether, ½ hour.*

SEASONABLE *from October to April.*

Note. — By cutting the celery into smaller pieces, by stewing it a little longer, and, when done, by pressing it through a sieve, the above stew may be converted into a Purée of Celery.

Celery Vinegar. —INGREDIENTS.—

¼ oz. of celery seed, 1 pint of vinegar.

Crush the seed by pounding it in a mortar; boil the vinegar, and when cold, pour it to the seed; let it infuse for a fortnight, when strain and bottle off for use. This is frequently used in salads.

Champagne-Cup.— Ingredients *for cup for 4 persons.* — 1 *quart bottle of champagne,* 2 *bottles of Schweppe's soda-water,* 1 *liqueur-glass of brandy or curaçoa,* 2 *tablespoonfuls of powdered sugar,* 1 *lb. of pounded ice, a sprig of green borage.* Average Cost, 6s.

Put all the ingredients into a silver cup or bowl; stir them together, and serve the same as claret-cup. Should the above proportion of sugar not be found sufficient to suit some tastes, increase the quantity. When borage is not easily obtainable, substitute for it a few slices of cucumber.

Seasonable.—*Suitable for pic-nics, balls, and other festive occasions.*

Charlotte aux Pommes.— Ingredients *for dish for 6 persons.—A few slices of rather stale bread* ½ *inch thick, clarified butter, apple marmalade, with about* 2 *dozen apples,* ½ *glass of sherry.* Average Cost, 1s. 4d.

Cut a slice of bread the same shape as the bottom of a plain round mould, which

CHARLOTTE AUX POMMES.

has been well buttered, and a few strips the height of the mould, and about 1½ inch wide; dip the bread in clarified butter (or spread it with cold butter, if not wanted quite so rich); place the round piece at the bottom of the mould, and set the narrow strips up the sides of it, overlapping each other a little, that no juice from the apples may escape, and that they may hold firmly to the mould. Brush the *interior* over with the white of egg (this will assist to make

the case firmer); fill it with the apple marmalade, with the addition of a little sherry, and cover them with a round piece of bread, also brushed over with egg, the same as the bottom; slightly press the bread down to make it adhere to the other pieces; put a plate on the top, and bake the *charlotte* in a brisk oven, of a light colour. Turn it out on the dish, strew sifted sugar over the top, and pour round it a little melted apricot jam.

Time.—40 *to* 50 *minutes.*

Seasonable *from July to March.*

Charlotte aux Pommes. (An Easy Method of Making.)—Ingredients *for dish for 6 persons.—*½ *lb. of flour,* ¼ *lb. of butter,* ¼ *lb. of powdered sugar,* ½ *teaspoonful of baking-powder,* 1 *egg, milk,* 1 *glass of raisin-wine, apple marmalade,* ¼ *pint of cream,* 2 *dessertspoonfuls of pounded sugar,* 2 *tablespoonfuls of lemon-juice.* Average Cost, 2s.

Make a cake with the flour, butter, sugar and baking-powder; moisten with the egg and sufficient milk to make it the proper consistency, and bake it in a round tin. When cold, scoop out the middle, leaving a good thickness all round the sides, to prevent them breaking; take some of the scooped-out pieces, which should be trimmed into neat slices; lay them in the cake, and pour over sufficient raisin-wine, with the addition of a little brandy, if approved, to soak them well. Have ready some apple marmalade, made by recipe; place a layer of this over the soaked cake, then a layer of cake and a layer of apples; whip the cream to a froth, mixing with it the sugar and lemon-juice; pile it on the top of the *charlotte,* and garnish it with pieces of clear apple jelly. This dish is served cold, but may be eaten hot by omitting the cream, and merely garnishing the top with bright jelly just before it is sent to table.

Time.—1 *hour to bake the cake.*

Seasonable *from July to March.*

Charlotte Russe.—INGREDIENTS *for dish for 6 persons.*—About 18 Savoy *biscuits, ¾ pint of cream, flavouring of vanilla, liqueurs, or wine,* 1 *tablespoonful of pounded sugar,* ½ oz. *of isinglass.* AVERAGE COST, 2s. 2d.

Procure about 18 Savoy biscuits, or ladies'-fingers, as they are sometimes called; brush the edges of them with the white of an egg, and line the bottom of a plain round mould, placing them like a star or rosette. Stand them upright all round the edge, carefully put them so closely together that the white of egg connects them firmly, and place this case in the oven for about 5 minutes, just to dry the egg. Whisk the cream to a stiff froth, with the sugar, flavouring and melted isinglass; fill the charlotte with it, cover with a slice of sponge cake cut in the shape of the mould; place it in ice, where let it remain till ready for table; then turn it on a dish, remove the mould, and serve. 1 tablespoonful of liqueur of any kind, or 4 tablespoonfuls of wine, would nicely flavour the above proportion of cream. For arranging the biscuits in the mould, cut them to the shape required, so that they fit in nicely, and level them with the mould at the top, that, when turned out, there may be something firm to rest upon. Great care and attention is required in the turning out of this dish, that the cream does not burst the case; and the edges of the biscuits must have the smallest quantity of egg brushed over them, or it would stick to the mould, and so prevent the charlotte from coming away properly.

TIME.—5 *minutes in the oven.*
SEASONABLE *at any time.*

Cheese.—Cheese is the curd formed from milk by artificial coagulation, pressed and dried for use. Curd, called also casein and caseous matter, or the basis of cheese, exists in the milk, and not in the cream,

and requires only to be separated by coagulation: the coagulation, however, supposes some alteration of the curd. By means of the substance employed to coagulate it, it is rendered insoluble in water. When the curd is freed from the whey, kneaded and pressed to expel it entirely, it becomes cheese; this assumes a degree of transparency, and possesses many of the properties of coagulated albumen. If it be well dried, it does not change by exposure to the air; but if it contain moisture, it soon putrefies; it therefore requires some salt to preserve it, and this acts likewise as a kind of seasoning. All our cheese is coloured more or less, except that made from skimmed milk.

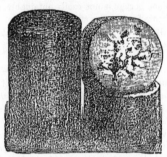

STILTON CHEESE.

The colouring substances employed are arnatto, turmeric, or marigold, all perfectly harmless unless they are adulterated; and it is said that arnatto sometimes contains red lead.

Cheese varies in quality and richness according to the materials of which it is composed. It is made—1. Of entire milk, as in Cheshire; 2. of milk and cream, as at Stilton; 3. of new milk mixed with skimmed milk, as in Gloucestershire; 4. of skimmed milk only, as in Suffolk, Holland, and Italy.

The principal varieties of cheese used in England are the following: *Cheshire cheese* famed all over Europe for its rich quality and fine piquant flavour. It is made of entire new milk, the cream not being taken off. *Gloucester cheese* is much milder in its taste than the Cheshire. There are two kinds of Gloucester cheese, single and double: — *Single Gloucester* is made of skimmed milk, or of the milk deprived of half the cream; *Double Gloucester* is a cheese that pleases almost every palate; it is made of the whole milk and cream.

CHEDDAR CHEESE.

Stilton cheese is made by adding the cream of one day to the entire milk of the next: it was first made at Stilton, in Leicestershire. *Sage cheese* is so called from the practice of colouring some curd with bruised sage, marigold-leaves and parsley, and mixing this with some uncoloured curd. With the Romans, and during the middle ages, this practice was extensively adopted. *Cheddar cheese* much resembles Parmesan. It has a very agreeable taste and flavour, and has a spongy appearance. *Brickbat cheese* has nothing remarkable except its form. It is made by turning with rennet a mixture of cream and new milk; the curd is put into a wooden vessel the shape of a brick, and is then pressed and dried in the usual way. *Dunlop cheese* has a peculiarly mild and rich taste: the best is made entirely from new milk. *New cheese* (as it is called in London) is made chiefly in Lincolnshire, and is either made of all cream, or, like Stilton, by adding the cream of one day's milking to the milk that comes immediately from the cow: they are extremely thin, and are compressed gently two or three times, turned for a few days, and then eaten new, with radishes, salad, &c. *Skimmed milk cheese* is made for sea voyages principally. An excellent, but little known English cheese is called *Wensleydale*, taking its name from the small village in Yorkshire where it is made. Dorsetshire produces a very good cheese called *Blue Veiny*, from its blue veined appearance. Both these cheeses resemble Stilton. *Parmesan cheese* is made in Parma and Piacenza. It is the most celebrated of all cheeses; it is made entirely of skimmed cow's milk; the high flavour which it has is supposed to be owing to the rich herbage of the meadows of the Po, where the cows are pastured. The best Parmesan is kept for three or four years, and none is carried to market till it is at least six months old. *Dutch cheese* derives its peculiar pungent taste from the practice adopted in Holland of coagulating the milk with muriatic acid instead of rennet. *Swiss cheeses*, in their several varieties, are all remarkable for their fine flavour; that from *Gruyère*, a bailiwick in the canton of Fribourg, is best known in England; it is flavoured by the dried herb of *melilotos officinalis* in powder. Cheese from milk and potatoes is manufactured in Thuringia and Saxony. *Camembert* is a very much esteemed cheese coming from Brittany, it is small and flat, with a dark rind. *Roquefort* is a rich cheese made in

GORGONZOLA CHEESE. CREAM CHEESE.

the south of France, from the milk of sheep and goats. *Cream cheese*, although so called, is not properly cheese, but is nothing more than cream dried sufficiently to be cut with a knife.

Cheese.—In families where much cheese is consumed, and it is bought in large quantities, a piece from the whole cheese should be cut, the larger quantity spread with a thickly-buttered sheet of white paper, and the outside occasionally wiped. To keep cheeses moist that are in daily use, when they come from table a damp cloth should be wrapped round them, and the cheese put into a pan with a cover to it, in a cool but not very dry place. To ripen cheeses, and bring them forward, put them into a damp cellar; and to check too large a production of mites, spirits may be poured into the parts affected. Pieces of cheese which are too near the rind, or too dry to put on table, may be made into Welsh rarebits, or grated down and mixed with macaroni. Cheeses may be preserved in a perfect state for years, by covering them with parchment made pliable by soaking in water, or by rubbing them over with a coating of melted fat. The cheeses selected should be free from cracks or bruises of any kind.

Cheese Biscuits.—INGREDIENTS

for small dish.—3 oz. of grated cheese, 3 oz. of flour, 3 oz. of butter, the yolk of an egg, cayenne. AVERAGE COST, 6d.

Season the cheese well with cayenne, and rub it, with the butter, in the flour, moisten with the yolk of an egg. Roll out the paste very thin, and cut into biscuits with a tin cutter. Bake a light brown in a quick oven. These biscuits may be served either hot or cold, and will keep a long time good if put in a tin.

TIME.—10 *minutes to bake.*

Cheese, Constituent Parts of.

—The chief kinds of cheese may be classified under the heads of cream cheeses, whole milk cheeses, and skimmed milk cheeses; but besides these distinct classes there are many graduations from the richest to the poorest quality.

Some of the English cheeses are mixtures of cream and milk, others of whole and skimmed milk, therefore the line of demarcation is but slight.

Stilton, which by most people is esteemed the best of all cheeses, does not contain so much milk fat as some others, yet it is much richer than Cheddar, which may be said to represent the average good quality of a whole milk cheese, and is one of the nicest and most popular of our English ones. After these come Cheshire and Gloucester to show a reduction in their proportion of milk fat, American ones a still greater reduction; while as an example of a cheese of only skimmed milk, a Dutch one may be quoted.

Cheese after, or with, other foods richer in heat-giving properties, is considered more digestible than when taken alone, and the richer and riper kinds are more easily assimilated; but whatever opinions are entertained as to its wholesomeness as an article of diet, it is certain that an enormous amount is made and consumed in this country. A fact to prove this is the great quantity of cheese made in the factories of the United States, and sent from thence to England; it being stated that out of 97,000,000 lbs. manufactured there in one year, the greater part was imported to Great Britain.

CONSTITUENT PARTS OF 1 LB. OF CHEESE OF GOOD QUALITY.

				oz.	grs.
Water	...	...	...	5	214
Albuminoids	...	...	...	4	294
Starch, &c. ...	...	...	...	0	140
Fat ...	...	...	...	4	322
Mineral Matter	...	...	...	0	341
				16	0

Cheese, Mode of Serving.—

The usual mode of serving cheese at good tables is to cut a small quantity of it into neat square pieces, and to put them into a glass cheese-dish, this dish being handed round. Should the cheese crumble much, of course this method is rather wasteful, and it may then be put on the table in the piece, and the host may cut from it. When served thus, the cheese must always be carefully scraped, and laid on a white d'oyley or

apkin, neatly folded. A Stilton cheese
should have a serviette pinned round it, and

CHEESE-GLASS.

be cut with a silver scoop. Cream cheese
is often served in a cheese course, and,
sometimes, grated Parmesan: the latter
should be put into a covered glass dish.
Rusks, cheese-biscuits, pats or slices of
butter, and salad, cucumber, or watercresses, should always form part of a
cheese course.

Cheese, Pounded.—Ingredients.
—To every lb. of cheese allow 3 oz. of fresh
butter.

To pound cheese is an economical way of
using it if it has become dry; it is exceedingly good spread on bread, and is the best
way of eating it for those whose digestion
is weak. Cut up the cheese into small
pieces, and pound it smoothly in a mortar,
adding butter in the above proportion.
Press it down into a jar, covered with clarified butter, and it will keep for several days.
The flavour may be very much increased by
adding mixed mustard (about a teaspoonful
to every pound), or cayenne, or pounded
mace. Curry-powder is also not unfre-
quently mixed with it.

Cheese Sandwiches.— Ingredi-
ents.—Slices of brown bread-and-butter,
thin slices of cheese.

Cut from a nice fat Cheshire, or any good
rich cheese, some slices about ½ inch thick,
and place them between some slices of
brown bread-and-butter, like sandwiches.
Place them on a plate in the oven, and,
when the bread is toasted, serve on a napkin very hot and very quickly.

Time.—10 minutes in a brisk oven.
Seasonable at any time.

Cheese Straws.—Ingredients for
small dish.—2 oz. of butter, 2 oz. of flour, 2
oz. of bread-crumbs, 2 oz. of cheese, a little
salt and cayenne. Average Cost, 4d.

Grate the cheese, and mix the ingredients
into a paste, seasoning with the cayenne
and salt to taste. Roll out very thin, and cut
into strips ¼ inch wide, and 6 inches long;
then twist several times and lay on a but-

CHEESE STRAWS.

tered tin to bake. They may be served
either hot or cold.

Time.—5 minutes to bake.
Seasonable at any time.

Cheese, Toasted, or Scotch
Rare-bit.—Ingredients.—A few slices of
rich cheese, toast, mustard, and pepper.
Average Cost, 1½d. per slice.

Cut some nice rich sound cheese into
rather thin slices; melt it in a cheese-toaster
on a hot plate or over steam, and, when
melted, add a small quantity of mixed
mustard and a seasoning of pepper; stir the
cheese until it is completely dissolved, then
brown it before the fire, or with a salamander. Fill the bottom of the cheese-toaster
with hot water, and serve with dry or buttered toast, whichever may be preferred.
Our engraving illustrates a cheese-toaster
with hot-water reservoir; the cheese is

HOT-WATER CHEESE DISH.

melted in the upper tin, which is placed in
another vessel of boiling water, so keeping
the preparation beautifully hot. A small
quantity of porter or port wine is sometimes mixed with the cheese; and, if it be
not very rich, a few pieces of butter may

be mixed with it to great advantage. Sometimes the melted cheese is spread on the toast, and then laid in the cheese-dish at the top of the hot water. Whichever way it is served, it is highly necessary that the mixture be very hot, and very quickly sent to table, or it will be worthless.

TIME.—*About 5 minutes to melt the cheese.*

SEASONABLE *at any time.*

Cheese, Toasted, or Welsh Rare-bit.—INGREDIENTS.—*Slices of bread, butter, Cheshire or Gloucester cheese, mustard, and pepper.* AVERAGE COST, 1½d. per slice.

Cut the bread into slices about ½ inch in thickness; pare off the crust, toast the bread slightly without hardening or burning it, and spread it with butter. Cut some slices, not quite so large as the bread, from a good rich fat cheese; lay them on the toasted bread in a cheese-toaster; be careful that the cheese does not burn, and let it be equally melted. Spread over the top a little made mustard and a seasoning of pepper, and serve very hot, with very hot plates. To facilitate the melting of the cheese, it may be cut into thin flakes, or toasted on one side before it is laid on the bread. As it is so essential to send this dish hot to table, it is a good plan to melt the cheese in small round silver or metal pans, and to send these pans to table, allowing one for each guest. Slices of dry or buttered toast should always accompany them, with mustard, pepper and salt.

TIME.— *About 5 minutes to melt the cheese.*

SEASONABLE *at any time.*

Note.—Should the cheese be dry, a little butter mixed with it will be an improvement.

Cheesecakes. — INGREDIENTS *for large dish of cheesecakes.*—8 oz. of pressed curds, 2 oz. of ratafias, 6 oz. of sugar, 2 oz. of butter, the yolks of 6 eggs, nutmegs, salt,

rind of 2 oranges or lemons, puff paste. AVERAGE COST, 1s. 9d.

Rub the sugar on the orange or lemon rind, and scrape it off. Press the curd in a napkin, to get rid of moisture; pound it thoroughly in a mortar, with the other ingredients, till the whole becomes a soft paste. Line 2 dozen, or more, tartlet-pans with good puff-paste, garnish these with the cheese-custard, place a strip of candied-peel on the top of each, and bake, in a moderate oven, a light colour; when done, shake a little sifted sugar over them. Currants, dried cherries, sultanas and citron may be used instead of candied-peel.

TIME.—*20 minutes to bake.*

SEASONABLE *at any time.*

Cherokee, or Store Sauce.—INGREDIENTS.—½ oz. of cayenne pepper, 5 cloves of garlic, 2 tablespoonfuls of soy, 1 tablespoonful of walnut ketchup, 1 pint of vinegar.

Boil all the ingredients *gently* for about ½ hour; strain the liquor, and bottle off for use.

TIME.—½ *hour.*

SEASONABLE.—*This sauce can be made at any time.*

Cherries, Dried.—Cherries may be put into a slow oven and thoroughly dried before they begin to change colour; they should then be taken out of the oven, tied in bunches, and stored away in a dry place. In the winter, they may be cooked with sugar for dessert, the same as Normandy pippins. Particular care must be taken that the oven be not too hot. Another

CHERRY.

method of drying cherries is to stone them, and to put them into a preserving-pan, with plenty of loaf sugar strewed amongst them. They should be simmered till the fruit shrivels, when they should be strained from the juice. The cherries should then be placed in an oven cool enough to dry without baking them. About 5 oz. of sugar would be required for 1 lb. of cherries, and the same syrup may be used again to do another quantity of fruit.

Cherries, Morella, To Preserve.

— INGREDIENTS. — *To every lb. of cherries allow* $1\frac{1}{4}$ *lb. of sugar*, 1 *gill of water.* AVERAGE COST, 8d. *per pot.*

Select ripe cherries, pick off the stalks, and reject all that have any blemishes. Boil the sugar and water together for 5 minutes; put in the cherries, and boil them for 10 minutes, removing the scum as it rises. Then turn the fruit, &c., into a pan, and let it remain until the next day, when boil it all again for another 10 minutes, and, if necessary, skim well. Put the cherries into small pots, pour over them the syrup, and, when cold, cover down with oiled papers, and the tops of the jars with tissue-paper, brushed over on both sides with the white of egg, and keep in a dry place.

TIME.—*Altogether*, 25 *minutes to boil.*
SEASONABLE. — *Make this in July or August.*

Cherries, To Preserve, in Syrup

(very delicious). — INGREDIENTS.— 4 *lbs. of cherries*, 3 *lbs. of sugar*, 1 *pint of white-currant juice.* AVERAGE COST, *for this quantity*, 3s. 6d.

Let the cherries be as clear and as transparent as possible, and perfectly ripe; pick off the stalks, and remove the stones, damaging the fruit as little as you can. Make a syrup with the above proportion of sugar, mix the cherries with it, and boil them for about 15 minutes, carefully skimming them; turn them gently into a pan, and let them remain till the next day, then drain the cherries on a sieve, and put the syrup and white-currant juice into the preserving-pan again. Boil these together until the syrup is somewhat reduced and rather thick, then put in the cherries, and let them boil for about five minutes; take them off the fire, skim the syrup, put the cherries into small pots or wide-mouthed bottles; pour the syrup over, and, when quite cold, tie them down carefully, so that the air is quite excluded.

TIME.—15 *minutes to boil the cherries in the syrup;* 10 *minutes to boil the syrup and currant-juice;* 5 *minutes to boil the cherries the second time.*
SEASONABLE. — *Make this in July or August.*

Cherry Brandy.— INGREDIENTS.—

4 *lbs. of Morella cherries picked just ripe*, 3 *bottles of good French brandy*, $3\frac{1}{4}$ *lbs. of white sugar.* AVERAGE COST, 18s.

Have the cherries perfectly dry, and, after pricking them with a needle, drop them in a large stone wine-jar. Pour over them the sugar, pounded, and the brandy, give them an occasional shake, and the liqueur should be fit to drink in 3 months.

TIME.—3 *months.*
SEASONABLE.—*Make this in August.*

Cherry Jam. — INGREDIENTS. — *To every lb. of fruit, weighed before stoning, which should be allowed for each pot of jam, allow* $\frac{1}{2}$ *lb. of sugar; to every* 6 *lbs. of fruit allow* 1 *pint of red-currant juice, and to every pint of juice* 1 *lb. of sugar.* AVERAGE COST, 7d. *per pot.*

Weigh the fruit before stoning, and allow half the weight of sugar; stone the cherries, and boil them in a preserving-pan until nearly all the juice is dried up; then add the sugar, which should be crushed to powder, and the currant-juice, allowing 1 pint to every 6 lbs. of cherries (original weight), and 1 pound of sugar to every pint of juice. Boil all together until it jellies, which will be in from 20 minutes to $\frac{1}{2}$ hour; skim the jam well, keep it well stirred, and a few minutes before it is done, crack some of the stones, and add the kernels: these impart a very delicious flavour to the jam.

TIME.—*According to the quality of the cherries, from ¾ to 1 hour to boil them; 20 minutes to ½ hour with the sugar.*

SEASONABLE. — *Make this in July or August.*

Cherry Sauce (for Sweet Puddings).

(German Recipe).—INGREDIENTS *for sufficient for large pudding.*—1 lb. of cherries, 1 tablespoonful of flour, 1 oz. of butter, ½ pint of water, 1 wineglassful of port wine, a little grated lemon-rind, 4 pounded cloves, 2 tablespoonfuls of lemon-juice, sugar to taste. AVERAGE COST, 1s.

Stone the cherries, and pound the kernels in a mortar to a smooth paste; put the butter and flour into a saucepan, stir them over the fire until of a pale brown, then add the cherries, the pounded kernels, the wine, and the water. Simmer these gently for ¼ hour, or until the cherries are quite cooked, and rub the whole through a hair sieve; add the remaining ingredients, let the sauce boil for another 5 minutes, and serve. This is a delicious sauce to serve with boiled batter pudding, and when thus used, should be sent to table poured over the pudding.

TIME.—*20 minutes to ½ hour.*

SEASONABLE *in June, July and August.*

Cherry Tart. — INGREDIENTS *for medium-sized tart.*—1½ lb. of cherries, 2 small tablespoonfuls of moist sugar, ½ lb. of short crust. AVERAGE COST, 10d.

Pick the stalks from the cherries, put them, with the sugar, into a *deep* pie-dish just capable of holding them, with a small cup placed upside-down in the midst of them. Make a short crust with ½ pound of flour, by either of the recipes for short crust; lay a border round the edge of the dish, put on the cover, and ornament the edges; bake in a brisk oven from ½ hour to 40 minutes; strew finely-sifted sugar over, and serve hot or cold, although the latter is the more usual mode. It is more economical to make two or three tarts at one time, as the trimmings from one tart answer for lining the edges of the dish for another, and so much paste is not required as when they are made singly. Unless for family use, never make fruit pies in very *large* dishes; select them, however, as *deep* as possible.

TIME.—*½ hour to 40 minutes.*

SEASONABLE *in June, July and August.*

Note.—A few currants added to the cherries will be found to impart a nice piquant taste to them.

Chestnut Sauce (for Fowls or Turkey). — INGREDIENTS.—½ lb. of chestnuts, ½ pint of white stock, 2 strips of lemon-peel, cayenne to taste, ¼ pint of cream or milk. AVERAGE COST, 8d.

Peel off the outside skin of the chestnuts, and put them into boiling water for a few minutes; take off the thin inside peel, and put them into a saucepan, with the white stock and lemon-peel, and let them simmer for 1½ hour, or until the chestnuts are

CHESTNUT.

quite tender. Rub the whole through a hair-sieve with a wooden spoon; add seasoning and the cream; let it just simmer, but not boil, and keep stirring all the time. Serve very hot and quickly. If milk is used instead of cream, a very small quantity of thickening may be required; that, of course, the cook will determine.

TIME.—*Altogether, nearly 2 hours.*

SEASONABLE *in winter.*

Chestnut Sauce, Brown.

INGREDIENTS *for* 1 *tureen.*—½ *lb. of chestnuts,* ½ *pint of stock,* 2 *lumps of sugar,* 4 *tablespoonfuls of Spanish sauce* (*see recipe*). AVERAGE COST, 8*d.*

Prepare the chestnuts as in the preceding recipe, by scalding and peeling them; put them in a stewpan with the stock and sugar, and simmer them till tender. When done, add Spanish sauce in the above proportion, and rub the whole through a tammy. Keep this sauce rather liquid, as it is liable to thicken.

TIME.—1½ *hour to simmer the chestnuts.*

Chestnut (Spanish) Soup.

INGREDIENTS *for* 1 *quart.*—¾ *lb. of Spanish chestnuts,* ¼ *pint of cream; seasoning to taste of salt, cayenne and mace;* 1 *quart of stock.* AVERAGE COST, 1*s.* 2*d.*

Take the outer rind from the chestnuts, and put them into a large pan of warm water. As soon as this becomes too hot for the fingers to remain in it, take out the chestnuts, peel them quickly, and immerse them in cold water, and wipe and weigh them. Now cover them with good stock, and stew them gently for rather more than ¾ of an hour, or until they break when touched with a fork; then drain, pound, and rub them through a fine sieve reversed; add sufficient stock, mace, cayenne and salt, and stir it often until it boils, and put in the cream. The stock in which the chestnuts are boiled can be used for the soup, when its sweetness is not objected to, or it may, in part, be added to it; and the rule is that ¾ lb. of chestnuts should be given to each quart of soup.

TIME.—*Rather more than* 1 *hour.*

SEASONABLE *from October to February.*

Chickens, Boiled.

INGREDIENTS.—*A pair of chickens, water.* AVERAGE COST, 5*s. per pair.*

Choosing and Trussing. — In choosing fowls for boiling, it should be borne in mind that those which are not black-legged are generally much whiter when dressed. Pick, draw, singe, wash and truss them in the following manner, without the livers in the wings; and, in drawing, be careful not to break the gall-bladder. Cut off the neck, leaving sufficient skin to skewer back. Cut the feet off to the first joint, tuck the stumps into a slit made on each side of the belly, twist the wings over the back of the fowl, and secure the top of the leg and the bottom of the wing together by running a skewer through them and the body. The other side must be done in the same manner. Should the fowl be very large and old, draw the sinews of the legs before tucking them in. Make a slit in the apron of the fowl, large enough to admit the parson's nose, and tie a string on the tops of the legs to keep them in their proper place.

When they are firmly trussed, put them into a stewpan with plenty of hot water, bring it to boil, and carefully remove all the scum as it rises. *Simmer very gently* until the fowl is tender, and bear in mind that the slower it boils the plumper and whiter will the fowl be. Many cooks wrap them in a floured cloth to preserve the colour, and to prevent the scum from clinging to them; in this case, a few slices of lemon should be placed on the breasts, over these a sheet of buttered paper, and then the cloth; cooking them in this manner renders the flesh very white. Boiled ham, bacon, boiled tongue, or pickled pork, are the usual accompaniments to boiled fowls, and they may be served with Béchamel, white sauce, parsley and butter, oyster, lemon, liver, celery or mushroom sauce. A little should be poured over the fowls after the skewers are removed, and the remainder sent in a tureen to table.

TIME.—*Large fowl,* 1 *hour; moderate-sized one,* ¾ *hour; chicken, from* 20 *minutes to* ½ *hour.*

SEASONABLE *all the year, but scarce in early spring.*

Chicken Broth. — INGREDIENTS
for 1 pint of good broth.—½ *fowl, or the inferior joints of a whole one; 1 quart of water, 1 blade of mace, ½ onion, a small bunch of sweet herbs, salt to taste, 10 peppercorns.* AVERAGE COST, 1s. 6d.

An old fowl not suitable for eating may be converted into very good broth; or, if a young one be used, the inferior joints may be put in the broth, and the best pieces reserved for dressing in some other manner. Put the fowl into a saucepan, stew all the ingredients, and simmer gently for 1½ hour, carefully skimming the broth well. When done, strain and put by in a cool place until wanted; then take all the fat off the top, warm up as much as may be required, and serve. This broth is, of course, only for those invalids whose stomachs are strong enough to digest it with a flavouring of herbs, &c. It may be made in the same manner as beef tea, with water and salt only, but the preparation will be but tasteless and insipid. When the invalid cannot digest this chicken broth with the flavouring, we would recommend plain beef tea in preference to plain chicken tea, which it would be without the addition of herbs, onions, &c.

TIME.—1½ *hour.*

Chicken, Chaudfroid of. —
INGREDIENTS *for dish sufficient for 8 persons.*—2 *roasted fowls, 1 quart of stock, yolks of 2 eggs, ½ gill of white wine, 2 oz. of butter, 1 lemon, 2 oz. of flour, 2 shalots, 3 cloves, sweet herbs.* AVERAGE COST, 7s.

Cut the fowls into neat small joints and lay them aside. Boil the bones and trimmings with the stock, wine, lemon-peel, shalots and herbs (taking out the peel when sufficient of its flavour has been extracted) for 2 to 3 hours. Melt the butter in a stewpan, add the flour and the stock and the yolks of the eggs. The sauce should be thick enough to adhere to the pieces of fowl when they are dipped into it as it begins to cool. Coat each joint thoroughly with the sauce, and arrange them in a ring in a dish with garnish of aspic jelly, red or yellow, truffles, &c. If liked, a border mould of jelly can be used, and the chicken piled in the centre. It is usual to make the sauce white, but it may be made brown, with a garnish of white of egg cut into fancy shapes.

TIME.—2 *hours.*

SEASONABLE, *for an entrée, at any time.*

Chicken, Curried. (Cold Meat Cookery.)—INGREDIENTS.—*The remains of cold roast fowls, 2 large onions, 1 apple, 2 oz. of butter, 1 dessertspoonful of curry-powder, 1 teaspoonful of flour, ½ pint of gravy, 1 tablespoonful of lemon-juice.* AVERAGE COST, *exclusive of the fowl, 7d.*

Slice the onions, peel, core and chop the apple, and cut the fowl into neat joints; fry these in the butter of a nice brown, then add the curry-powder, flour and gravy, and stew for about 20 minutes. Put in the lemon-juice, and serve with boiled rice, either placed in a ridge round the dish or separately. Two or three shalots or a little garlic may be added, if approved.

TIME.—*Altogether, ½ hour.*

SEASONABLE *in winter.*

Chicken Cutlets.—INGREDIENTS
for 1 large entrée.—2 *chickens; seasoning to taste of salt, white pepper and cayenne; 2 blades of pounded mace, egg and bread-crumbs, clarified butter, 1 strip of lemon-rind, 2 carrots, 1 onion, 2 tablespoonfuls of mushroom ketchup, thickening of butter and flour, 1 egg.* AVERAGE COST, 4s. 6d.

Remove the breast and leg-bones of the chickens; cut the meat into neat pieces after having skinned it, and season the cutlets with pepper, salt, pounded mace and cayenne. Put the bones, trimmings, &c., into a stewpan with 1 pint of water, adding carrots, onions and lemon-peel in the above proportion; stew gently for 1½ hour, and strain the gravy. Thicken it with butter and flour, add the ketchup and 1 egg well beaten; stir it over the fire, and bring it to the simmering-point, but do not allow it to boil. In the meantime, egg and bread-crumb the cutlets, and give them a few drops of clarified butter; fry them a delicate brown, occasionally turning them; arrange them pyramidically on the dish, and pour over them the sauce.

TIME.—10 *minutes to fry the cutlets.*

SEASONABLE *from April to July.*

Chicken Cutlets, French.—

(Cold Meat Cookery.)—INGREDIENTS *for an entrée.—The remains of cold roast or boiled fowl, fried bread, clarified butter, the yolk of* 1 *egg, bread-crumbs,* ½ *teaspoonful of finely-minced lemon-peel; salt, cayenne and mace to taste. For sauce—*1 *oz. of butter,* 2 *minced shalots, a few slices of carrot, a small bunch of savoury herbs, including parsley,* 1 *blade of pounded mace,* 5 *peppercorns,* ½ *pint of gravy.* AVERAGE COST, *exclusive of the cold fowl,* 9*d.*

Cut the fowls into as many nice cutlets as possible; take a corresponding number of croutons about the same size, all cut one shape; fry them a pale brown, put them before the fire, then dip the cutlets into clarified butter mixed with the yolk of an egg; cover with bread-crumbs seasoned in the above proportion, with lemon-peel, mace, salt and cayenne; fry them for about 5 minutes, put each piece on one of the croutons, pile them high in the dish, and serve with the following sauce, which should be made ready for the cutlets: put the butter into a stewpan, add the shalots, carrots, herbs, mace and peppercorns; fry for 10 minutes, or rather longer; pour in ½ pint of good gravy, made of the chicken-bones; stew gently for 20 minutes, strain it, and serve.

TIME.—5 *minutes to fry the cutlets;* 35 *minutes to make the gravy.*

SEASONABLE *from April to July.*

Chicken, Fricasséed.—INGREDIENTS *for an entrée for* 8 *persons.—*2 *small fowls, or* 1 *large one,* 3 *oz. of butter, a bunch of parsley and green onions,* 1 *clove,* 2 *blades of mace,* 1 *shalot,* 1 *bay-leaf, salt and white pepper to taste,* ½ *pint of milk, the yolk of* 3 *eggs.* AVERAGE COST, 4*s.* 9*d.*

Choose a couple of fat plump chickens, and after drawing, singeing and washing them, skin and carve them into joints; blanch these in boiling water for 2 or 3 minutes, take them out and immerse them in cold water to render them white. Put the trimmings, with the necks and legs, into a stewpan; add the parsley, onions, clove, mace, shalot, bay-leaf and a seasoning of pepper and salt; pour to these the water that the chickens were blanched in, and simmer gently for rather more than 1 hour. Have ready another stewpan; put in the joints of fowl, with the above proportion of butter; dredge them with flour, let them get hot, but do not brown them much; then moisten the fricassée with the gravy made from the trimmings, &c., and stew very gently for ½ hour. Lift the fowl into another stewpan, skim the sauce, reduce it quickly over the fire by letting it boil fast, and strain it over them. Add the milk, and a seasoning of pounded mace and cayenne; let it boil up, and when ready to serve, stir to it the well-beaten yolks of 3 eggs; these should not be put in till the last moment, and the sauce should by made hot, but must *not boil,* or it will instantly curdle. A few button-mushrooms stewed with the fowl are by many persons considered an improvement.

TIME.—1 *hour to make the gravy;* ½ *hour to simmer the fowl.*

SEASONABLE *at any time.*

Chickens, German Mode of Cooking.—INGREDIENTS.—2 *chickens, lardoons, French rolls,* 3 *oz. of butter, bread-crumbs,* 1 *onion,* 1 *egg, parsley and thyme, grated lemon-peel, a small cup of cream.* AVERAGE COST, 5*s.*

Stuff the chickens with a forcemeat made of French rolls, a little butter, egg, finely chopped onion, parsley, thyme and grated lemon-peel; then lard and bread-crumb them, putting a piece of fat over the breasts that they may not become too brown. Place them in a stewpan with 1 oz. of butter, leave uncovered for a short time, then cover and bake for 1½ hour. Half an hour before serving, add the cream and baste thoroughly over a hotter fire.

TIME.—1½ hour.

SEASONABLE at any time.

Chicken (or Fowl) Patties.

(Cold Meat Cookery.)—INGREDIENTS.—*The remains of cold roast chicken or fowl; to every ¼ lb. of meat allow 2 oz. of ham, 3 tablespoonfuls of cream, 2 tablespoonfuls of veal gravy, ½ teaspoonful of minced lemon-peel; cayenne, salt and pepper to taste; 1 tablespoonful of lemon-juice, 1 oz. of butter rolled in flour, puff paste.*

Mince very small the white meat from a cold roast fowl, after removing all the skin; weigh it, and to every ¼ lb. of meat allow the above proportion of minced ham. Put

(_ICKEN PATTIES.

these into a stewpan with the remaining ingredients, stir over the fire for 10 minutes or ¼ hour, taking care that the mixture does not burn. Roll out some puff paste about ¼ inch in thickness, line the patty-pans with this, put upon each a small piece of bread, and cover with another layer of paste; brush over with the yolk of an egg, and bake in a brisk oven for about ¼ hour. When done, cut a round piece cut of the top, and, with a small spoon, take out the bread (be particular in not breaking the outside border of the crust), and fill the patties with the mixture.

TIME.—¼ hour to prepare the meat; not quite ¼ hour to bake the crust.

SEASONABLE at any time.

Chicken (or Fowl) Pie.—INGRE-

DIENTS for large pie. — *2 small fowls or 1 large one, white pepper and salt to taste, ½ teaspoonful of grated nutmeg, ½ teaspoonful of pounded mace, forcemeat, a few slices of ham, 3 hard-boiled eggs, ½ pint of water, puff crust.* AVERAGE COST, 5s. 6d.

Skin and cut up the fowls into joints, and put the necks, legs and backbones in a stewpan, with a little water, an onion, a bunch of savoury herbs, and a blade of mace; let these stew for about an hour, and, when done, strain off the liquor: this is for gravy. Put a layer of fowl at the bottom of a pie-dish, then a layer of ham, then one of forcemeat and hard-boiled eggs cut in rings; between the layers put a seasoning of pounded mace, nutmeg, pepper and salt. Proceed in this manner until the dish is full, and pour in about ½ pint of water; border the edge of the dish with puff crust, put on the cover, ornament the top, and glaze it by brushing over it the yolk of an egg. Bake from 1¼ to 1½ hour, should the pie be very large, and, when done, pour in at the top the gravy made from the bones. If to be eaten cold, and wished particularly nice, the joints of the fowls should be boned, and placed in the dish with alternate layers of forcemeat; sausage-meat may also be substituted for the forcemeat, and is now very much used. When the chickens are boned, and mixed with sausage-meat, the pie will take about 2 hours to bake. It should be covered with a piece of paper when about half done, to prevent the paste being dried up or scorched.

TIME.—For a pie with unboned meat, 1¼ to 1½ hour; with boned meat and sausage or forcemeat, 1½ to 2 hours.

SEASONABLE at any time.

Chicken, Potted. (A Luncheon or Breakfast Dish.)

INGREDIENTS.—*The remains of cold roast chicken; to every lb. of meat allow* ¼ *lb. of fresh butter, salt and cayenne to taste, 1 teaspoonful of pounded mace,* ½ *small nutmeg.*

Strip the meat from the bones of cold roast fowl; when it is freed from gristle and skin, weigh it, and to every lb. of meat allow the above proportion of butter, seasoning and spices. Cut the meat into small pieces, pound it well with the fresh butter, sprinkle in the spices gradually, and keep pounding until reduced to a perfectly smooth paste. Put it into potting-pots for use, and cover it with clarified butter, about ¼ inch in thickness, and, if to be kept for some time, tie over a bladder. 2 or 3 slices of ham, minced and pounded with the above ingredients, will be found an improvement. It should be kept in a dry place.

SEASONABLE *at any time.*

Chicken (or Fowl) Salad.

INGREDIENTS *for salad for 5 or 6 persons.—The remains of cold roast or boiled chicken, 2 lettuces, a little endive, 1 cucumber, a few slices of boiled beetroot, salad-dressing.* AVERAGE COST, *exclusive of the cold fowl,* 10d.

Trim neatly the remains of the chicken; wash, dry, and slice the lettuces, and place in the middle of a dish; put the pieces of

CHICKEN VOL-AU-VENT.

fowl on the top, and pour the salad-dressing over them. Garnish the edge of the salad with hard-boiled eggs cut in rings, sliced cucumber, and boiled beetroot cut in slices. Instead of cutting the eggs in rings, the yolks may be rubbed through a hair sieve, and the whites chopped very

finely, and arranged on the salad in small bunches, yellow and white alternately. This should not be made long before it is wanted for table.

SEASONABLE *at any time.*

Chili Vinegar.

INGREDIENTS.—50 *fresh red English chilis, 1 pint of vinegar.*

Pound or cut the chilis in halves, and infuse them in the vinegar for a fortnight, when it will be fit for use. This will be found an agreeable relish to fish, as many people cannot eat it without the addition of an acid and cayenne pepper.

China Chilo.

INGREDIENTS *for dish for 4 persons.—*1½ *lb. of leg, loin or neck of mutton, 2 onions, 2 lettuces, 1 pint of green peas, 1 teaspoonful of salt, 1 teaspoonful of pepper,* ¼ *pint of water,* ¼ *lb. of clarified butter, when liked, a little cayenne.* AVERAGE COST, 2s.

Mince the above quantity of undressed leg, loin or neck of mutton, adding a little of the fat, also minced; put it into a stew-pan with the remaining ingredients, previously shredding the lettuce and onion rather fine; closely cover the stewpan, after the ingredients have been well stirred, and simmer gently for rather more than 2 hours. Serve in a dish, with a border of rice round, the same as for curry.

TIME.—*Rather more than 2 hours.*

SEASONABLE *from June to August.*

Chocolate Almonds.

INGREDIENTS.—*Almonds, chocolate.*

Blanch the almonds: putting them in hot water, then rubbing off the skin. Melt some chocolate, take up each almond or a long pin, dip in the chocolate and lay on a buttered slab to cool.

Chocolate Cakes.

INGREDIENTS.—1 *lb. of white sugar pounded and sifted, 1 oz. of chocolate, water.* AVERAGE COST, 4½d.

Scrape the chocolate to a powder and mix it with the sugar. Make into a paste with cold water, then boil up gently and drop with a silver or bone spoon on thick white paper slightly greased. Coffee drops or cakes can be made in the same manner.

Chocolate Cream.

INGREDIENTS *for quart mould.*—3 oz. of grated chocolate, ¼ lb. of sugar, 1 pint of milk, ½ pint of cream, 1½ oz. of clarified isinglass or gelatine, the yolks of 4 eggs. AVERAGE COST, 2s.

Beat the yolks of the eggs well, put them into a basin with the grated chocolate, the sugar, and 1 pint of milk; stir these

CREAM-MOULD.

ingredients well together, pour them into a jug, and set this jug in a saucepan of boiling water; stir it one way until the mixture thickens, but *do not allow it to boil*, or it will curdle. Strain the cream through a sieve into a basin; stir in the isinglass or gelatine and the ½ pint of cream, which should be well whipped; mix all well together, and pour it into a mould which has been previously oiled with the purest salad oil, and, if at hand, set it in ice until wanted for table.

TIME.—*About* 10 *minutes to stir the mixture over the fire.*

SEASONABLE *at any time.*

Chocolate Creams.

INGREDIENTS.—1 lb. of sugar, 3 oz of best arrowroot, rather more than ¾ pint of water, chocolate. AVERAGE COST, 8d.

Mix the arrowroot with the water and put it in a lined saucepan; add the sugar and boil 10 minutes, stirring quickly the

while; then take it off the fire and stir till it begins to cool, when flavour with vanilla or any other essence. Roll the mixture in little balls, melt some chocolate, dip each ball in it and lay on a buttered slab to cool.

Chocolate Ice Cream.

INGREDIENTS *for 8 ices.*—6 oz. of chocolate, ½ pint of new milk, 1 pint of cream, ½ lb. of white sugar. AVERAGE COST, 2s. per quart.

Scrape the chocolate into the milk and blend thoroughly, add the cream and sugar, strain, put it into the freezing machine and stir or shake till it begins to set. If it is required moulded it must be put into the mould before it gets too hard, after which it must be again set on ice.

TIME.—25 *minutes to freeze.*

SEASONABLE *at any time.*

Chocolate Icing.

INGREDIENTS *for medium-sized cake.*—¼ lb. of sugar, 3 oz of chocolate, grated, flavouring of vanilla, a small cupful of water. AVERAGE COST, 6d

Melt over a slow fire, spread the cake, and dry in a cool oven.

Chocolate Soufflé.

INGREDIENTS *for moderate-sized soufflé.*—4 eggs, 3 teaspoonfuls of pounded sugar, 1 teaspoonful of flour, 3 oz. of the best chocolate. AVERAGE COST, 9d.

Break the eggs, separating the whites from the yolks, and put them into different basins; add to the yolks the sugar, flour and chocolate, which should be very finely grated, and stir these ingredients for 5 minutes. Then well whisk the whites of the eggs in the other basin until they are stiff, and, when firm, mix lightly with the yolks till the whole forms a smooth and light substance; butter a round soufflé or cake-tin, put in the mixture, and bake in a moderate oven from 15 to 20 minutes. Pin a white napkin round the tin, strew sifted sugar over the top of the soufflé, and send it immediately to table. The proper appearance of this dish depends entirely on the xpedition with which it is served; and ome cooks, to preserve its lightness, hold salamander over the soufflé until it is laced on the table. If allowed to stand after t comes from the oven it will be entirely poiled, as it falls almost immediately.

TIME.—15 to 20 minutes.

SEASONABLE at any time.

Chocolate, To Make.—INGREDI-

NTS.—Allow ½ oz. of chocolate to ach person; to every oz. allow ½ int of water, ½ pint of milk.

Make the milk-and-water hot; crape the chocolate into it, and tir the mixture constantly and uickly until the chocolate is dis-olved; bring it to the boiling-oint, stir it well, and serve di-ctly with white sugar. Choco-te prepared with a mill, as shown a the engraving, is made by putting a the scraped chocolate, pouring over it ne boiling milk-and-water, and milling it ver the fire until hot and frothy.

MILL.

Cider Cup.— INGREDIENTS for cup

r 4 persons.—1 quart bottle of cider, 1 ttle of Harstin's seltzer, ½ a glass of brandy liqueur, 1 lemon, 2 tablespoonfuls of unded sugar, borage, or a few slices of cu-mber.   AVERAGE COST, 2s.

Put the sugar in a jug with the lemon nd and half the juice, pour over the andy, and set on ice. When the cup is ifficiently flavoured with the lemon peel, ke it out and add the seltzer; then pour t into a glass jug in which have been aced a few sprigs of borage.

SEASONABLE in summer.

Clarified Sugar.—INGREDIENTS.—

lbs. of sugar, 1 pint of water, 1 egg. AVER-E COST, 7d.

Beat the egg (the white only), and put it, th the water and sugar, into a preserv-g-pan. When the sugar has dissolved, put e pan on the fire, and, when it boils, throw in a cup of cold water. Bring it (without stirring) to boiling point again; then place the pan by the side of the fire for the syrup to settle. Remove all the scum, and the sugar will be ready for use.

TIME.—20 minutes for the sugar to dis-solve, 5 minutes to boil.

Claret Cup.—INGREDIENTS for suffi-

cient for 4 persons.—1 bottle of claret, 1 bottle of soda-water, about ½ lb. of pounded ice, 4 tablespoonfuls of pow-dered sugar, 1 liqueur-glass of Maraschino, a sprig of green borage. AVERAGE COST, 3s.

Put all the ingredi-ents into a silver cup, regulating the proportion of ice by the state of the weather; if very warm, a larger quantity would be necessary.

CLARET CUP.

Clove Liqueur.—INGREDIENTS.—¼

lb. of cloves, ¼ lb. of coriander seed, ½ lb. of loaf sugar, 24 fine black cherries, 1 quart of spirit.

Bruise the cloves and coriander seed, and infuse the whole of the ingredients for a month; after which, strain and bottle.

Coburg Puddings.—INGREDIENTS

for puddings sufficient for 7 or 8 persons.—1 pint new milk, 6 oz. of sugar, 6 oz. of flour, 6 oz. of butter, 6 oz. of currants, brandy and other flavouring to taste. AVERAGE COST, 1s. 9d.

Mix the flour and milk to a smooth batter, add the remaining ingredients very gradually, and when well mixed put it into 8 cups, previously buttered, half full and bake for ¾ of an hour. Turn the puddings out on a dish, strew over a little sifted sugar and serve with wine sauce.

TIME.—¾ hour.

SEASONABLE at any time.

Cock-a-Leekie.—INGREDIENTS *for 4 quarts of soup.*—*A capon or large fowl (sometimes an old cock, from which the recipe takes its name, is used), which should be trussed as for boiling,* 2 *or* 3 *bunches of fine leeks,* 5 *quarts of stock (see* STOCK*), pepper and salt to taste.* AVERAGE COST, 5s. 6d.

Wash the leeks well (and, if old, scald them in boiling water for a few minutes), taking off the roots and part of the heads, and cut them into lengths of about an inch. Put the fowl into the stock, with, at first, one half of the leeks, and allow it to simmer gently. In half an hour add the remaining leeks, and then it may simmer for 3 or 4 hours longer. It should be carefully skimmed, and can be seasoned to taste. In serving, take out the fowl and carve it neatly, placing the pieces in a tureen, and pouring over them the soup, which should be very thick of leeks (a *purée* of leeks, the French would call it).

TIME.—4 *hours.*
SEASONABLE *in winter.*

Note.—Without the fowl, the above, which would then be merely called leek soup, is very good, and also economical.

Cocoa-nut Biscuits. — INGREDIENTS.—10 *oz. of sifted sugar,* 3 *eggs,* 6 *oz. of grated cocoa-nut.* AVERAGE COST, 9d.

Whisk the eggs until they are very light, then add the sugar gradually, afterwards the grated cocoa-nut. Roll a tablespoonful at a time of the paste in the form of a pyramid, place them on paper and the paper on tins and bake the biscuits in rather a cool oven till they are just coloured a light brown.

TIME.—*To bake, about* 15 *minutes.*
SEASONABLE *at any time.*

Cocoa-nut Candy.—INGREDIENTS. —1 *lb. of sugar,* ½ *pint of cold water,* 6 *oz. of grated cocoa-nut.* AVERAGE COST, 6d.

Put the sugar and water into a pipkin to

dissolve, boil it 5 minutes, then strain, p in the cocoa-nut, put the pipkin again the fire, and stir till the candy rises ; the spread on sheets of writing-paper that ha

COCOA-NUT PALM.

been warmed before the fire, and before t candy is quite cold, take it off the pap and cut it in small squares. Let it thoroughly dry before it is put away.

Cocoa, To Make.—INGREDIEN —Put into the cup half a teaspoonful Fry's Pure Concentrated Cocoa, and spoonful of fine white sugar; fill up slowly with boiling water, stirring the while. Add milk or cream to suit the palate, and more sugar if required.

COCOA-BEAN.

The extreme solu bility and strength of this choice Cocoa are strikingly apparent on the addition of the milk or crea although the Cocoa may be used witho either.

Cocoa, To Make.—INGREDIEN —Put a large teaspoonful of Fry's Mal Cocoa into a breakfast cup, and make it i smooth paste, with sufficient *cold* milk; ᴨen fill up with water not quite boiling, ᴵdding cream and sugar to taste. If desired, ᴵilk, or milk and water, may be used in ᴵace of the plain water.

Cod.—Cod should be chosen for the ᴵble when it is plump and round near the ᴵil, when the hollow behind the head is ᴵeep, and when the sides are undulated as they were ribbed. The glutinous parts ᵇout the head lose their delicate flavour ᴵter the fish has been twenty-four hours ᴵut of the water. The great point by ᴵhich the cod should be judged is the

THE COD.

ᴵrmness of its flesh; and, although the ᴵd is not firm when it is alive, its quality ᴵay be arrived at by pressing the finger ᴵto the flesh: if this rises immediately, ᴵe flesh is good; if not, it is stale. ᴵnother sign of its goodness is, if the ᴵsh, when it is cut, exhibits a bronze ap-ᴵearance, like the silver side of a round of ᴵeef; when this is the case the flesh will ᴵ firm when cooked. Stiffness in a cod, ᴵ in any other fish, is a sure sign of ᴵeshness, though not always of quality. ᴵometimes codfish, though exhibiting signs ᴵ rough usage, will eat much better than ᴵose with red gills, so strongly recom-ᴵended by many cookery books. This ᴵppearance is generally caused by the fish ᴵaving been knocked about at sea, in the ᴵell-boats, in which they are conveyed ᴵom the fishing-grounds to market.

Cod à la Béchamel. (Cold Meat Cookery.)—INGREDIENTS *for small dish.*—*Any remains of cold cod,* 4 *table-spoonfuls of béchamel* (*see* BÉCHAMEL SAUCE), 2 *oz. of butter: seasoning to taste of pepper and salt; fried bread, and a few bread-crumbs.*

Flake the cod carefully, leaving out all skin and bone; put the béchamel in a stewpan with the butter, and stir it over the fire till the latter is melted; add seasoning, put in the fish, and mix it well with the sauce. Make a border of fried bread round the dish, lay in the fish. sprinkle over with bread-crumbs, and baste with butter. Brown either before the fire or with a salamander, and garnish with toasted bread cut in fanciful shapes.

TIME.—½ *hour.*

Cod à la Crême.—INGREDIENTS *for dish for 3 persons.*—1 *large slice of cod,* 1 *oz. of butter,* 1 *chopped shalot, a little minced parsley,* ¼ *teacupful of white stock,* ¼ *pint of milk or cream, flour to thicken, cayenne and lemon-juice to taste,* ½ *teaspoon-ful of powdered sugar.* AVERAGE COST, *with milk,* 1*s.*

Boil the cod, and while hot, break it into flakes; put the butter, shalot, parsley and stock into a stewpan, and let them boil for five minutes. Stir in sufficient flour to thicken, and pour to it the milk or cream. Simmer for 10 minutes, add the cayenne and sugar, and, when liked, a little lemon-juice. Put the fish in the sauce to warm gradually, but do not let it boil. Serve in a dish garnished with croutons.

TIME.—*Rather more than* ½ *hour.*

SEASONABLE *from November to March.*

Note—The remains of fish from the preceding day answer very well for this dish.

Cod à l'Italienne.—INGREDIENTS *for dish for 4 or 5 persons.*—2 *slices of crimped cod,* 1 *shalot,* 1 *slice of ham minced very fine,* ½ *pint of white stock, when liked,* ½ *teaspoon-ful of cream; salt to taste, a few* **drops** c

garlic vinegar, a little lemon-juice, ½ teaspoonful of powdered sugar. AVERAGE COST, 2s.

Chop the shalots, mince the ham very fine, pour on the stock, and simmer for 15 minutes. If the colour should not be good, add cream in the above proportion, and strain it through a fine sieve; season it, and put in the vinegar, lemon juice and sugar. Now boil the cod, take out the middle bone, and skin it; put it on the dish without breaking, and pour the sauce over it.

TIME.—¾ hour.

SEASONABLE from November to March.

Cod à la Maître d'Hôtel.—INGREDIENTS for dish for 4 or 5 persons.—2 lbs. of cod, ¼ lb. of butter, a little chopped shalot and parsley; pepper to taste; ¼ teaspoonful of grated nutmeg, or rather less when the flavour is not liked; the juice of ¼ lemon. AVERAGE COST, with fresh fish, 1s. 6d.; with remains of cold fish, 6d.

Boil the cod, and either leave it whole, or, what is still better, flake it from the bone, and take off the skin. Put it into a stewpan with the butter, parsley, shalot, pepper and nutmeg. Melt the butter gradually, and be very careful that it does not become like oil. When all is well mixed and thoroughly hot, add the lemon-juice, and serve.

TIME.—½ hour.

SEASONABLE from November to March.

Note.— Cod that has been left will do for this.

Cod, Curried.— INGREDIENTS for dish sufficient for 4 persons.— 2 slices of large cod, or the remains of any cold fish; 3 oz. of butter, 1 onion sliced, a teacupful of white stock, thickening of butter and flour, 1 small teaspoonful of curry-powder, ¼ pint of cream, salt and cayenne to taste. AVERAGE COST, with fresh fish, 2s. 7d.

Flake the fish, and fry it of a nice brown colour with the butter and onions; put

this in a stewpan, add the stock and thickening, and simmer for ten minutes. Stir curry-powder into the cream; put it, with the seasoning, to the other ingredients give one boil, and serve.

TIME.—¾ hour.

SEASONABLE from November to March.

Cod Pie.—INGREDIENTS for pie for persons.—2 slices of cod; pepper and salt taste; ½ a teaspoonful of grated nutmeg, large blade of pounded mace, 2 oz. of butter ½ pint of stock, a paste crust (see PASTRY) For sauce—1 tablespoonful of stock, ¼ pint of cream or milk, thickening of flour or butter, lemon-peel, chopped very fine, to taste 12 oysters. AVERAGE COST, 2s. 9d.

Lay the cod in salt for 4 hours, then wash it and place it in a dish; season, and add the butter and stock; cover with the crust and bake for 1 hour, or rather more. Now make the sauce, by mixing the ingredients named above; give it one boil, and pour into the pie by a hole made at the top of the crust, which can easily be covered by a small piece of pastry cut and baked in a fanciful shape—such as a leaf or otherwise

TIME.—1½ hour.

SEASONABLE from November to March.

Note.—The remains of cold fish may be used for this pie.

Cod Pie (Economical). (Cold Meat Cookery.)—INGREDIENTS.—Any remains of cold cod, 12 oysters, or oyster sauce left from day before, sufficient melted butter to moisten it; mashed potatoes enough to fill up the dish. AVERAGE COST, exclusive the fish, with fresh oysters, 1s. 6d.

Flake the fish from the bone, and carefully take away all the skin. Lay it in a pie-dish, pour over the melted butter and oysters (or oyster sauce, if there is any left and cover with mashed potatoes. Bake for ½ an hour, and send to table of a nice brown colour.

TIME.—½ hour.

SEASONABLE from November to March.

Cod, Salt (commonly called "Salt Fish.")

—INGREDIENTS.—*Sufficient water to cover the fish.* AVERAGE COST, 4d. to 6d. per lb.

Wash the fish, and lay it all night in water, with a ¼ pint of vinegar. When thoroughly soaked, take it out, see that it is perfectly clean, and put it in the fish-kettle, with sufficient cold water to cover it. Heat it gradually, but do not let it boil much, or the fish will be hard. Skim well, and when done, drain the fish, and put it on a napkin garnished with hard-boiled eggs cut in rings.

TIME.—*About 1 hour.*

SEASONABLE *in the spring.*

Note.—Serve with egg sauce and parsnips. This is a usual dish on Ash Wednesdays.

Cod's Head and Shoulders.

—INGREDIENTS.—*Sufficient water to cover the fish; 5 oz. of salt to each gallon of water.* AVERAGE COST, 6d. per lb.

Cleanse the fish thoroughly, and rub a little salt over the thick part and inside of the fish 1 or 2 hours before dressing it, as this very much improves the flavour. Lay it in the fish-kettle, with sufficient cold water to cover it.

Be very particular not to pour the water on the fish, as it is liable to break it, and only keep it just simmering. If the water should boil away, add a little by pouring it in at the side of the kettle, and not on the fish. Add salt in the above proportion, and bring it gradually to a boil. Skim very carefully, draw it to the side of the fire, and let it gently simmer till done. Take it out and drain it; serve on a hot napkin, and garnish with cut lemon and parsley.

TIME.—*According to size, ½ an hour more or less.*

SEASONABLE *from November to March.*

Note. — Oyster or shrimp sauce and plain melted butter should be served with this.

Cod's Head and Shoulders, To Carve.

—First run the knife along the centre of the side of the fish, namely, from *d* to *b*, down to the bone; then carve it in unbroken slices downwards from *d* to *e*, or upwards from *d* to *c*, as shown in the engraving.

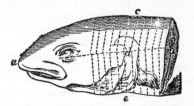

The carver should ask the guests if they would like a portion of the roe and liver.

Note.—Of this fish, the parts about the backbone and shoulders are the firmest and most esteemed by connoisseurs. The sound, which lines the fish beneath the backbone, is considered a delicacy, as are also the gelatinous parts about the head and neck.

Cod Sounds.

—Should be soaked in salt and water, and thoroughly washed before dressing them. They are considered a great delicacy, and may either be broiled, fried, or boiled; if they are boiled, mix a little milk with the water.

Cod Sounds en Poule.

—INGREDIENTS.—*For forcemeat, 12 chopped oysters, 3 chopped anchovies, ¼ lb. of bread crumbs, 1 oz. of butter, 2 eggs, seasoning of salt, pepper, nutmeg and mace to taste; 4 cod sounds.* AVERAGE COST, 3s.

Make the forcemeat by mixing the ingredients well together. Wash the sounds, and boil them in milk and water for ½ an hour; take them out, and let them cool. Cover each with a layer of forcemeat, roll them up in a nice form, and skewer them. Rub over with lard, dredge with flour, and cook them gently before the fire in a Dutch oven.

TIME.—*1 hour.*

Coffee, Essence of. — INGREDI-

ENTS.—*To every ¼ lb. of ground coffee allow 1 small teaspoonful of powdered chicory, 3 small teacupfuls or 1 pint of water.*

Let the coffee be freshly ground, and, if possible, freshly roasted; put it into a percolater, or filter, with the chicory, and pour slowly over it the above proportion of boiling water. When it has all filtered through, warm the coffee sufficiently by bring it to the simmering-point, but do not allow it to boil; then filter it a second time, put it into a clean and dry bottle, cork it well, and it will remain good for several days. Two tablespoonfuls of this essence are quite sufficient for a breakfast-cupful of hot milk. This essence will be found particularly useful to those persons who have to rise extremely early; and having only the milk to make boiling, is very easily and quickly prepared. When the essence is bottled, pour another 3 tea-cupfuls of *boiling* water slowly on the grounds, which, when filtered through, will be a very weak coffee. The next time there is essence to be prepared, make this weak coffee boiling, and pour it on the ground coffee instead of water.

TIME.—*To be filtered once, then brought to the simmering point, and filtered again.*

Note.—Coffee Essence can now be obtained ready for use thus saving time and trouble. That prepared by Messrs. Thos. Symington, containing only sugar in addition to the soluble constituents of fresh coffee, forms an excellent substitute. Very good essence of coffee is also made by Branson and Co., and E. Clark and Co.

Coffee, Nutritious.—INGREDIENTS

for one large cup.—½ oz. of ground coffee, 1 pint of milk.

Let the coffee be freshly ground; put it into a saucepan with the milk, which should be made nearly boiling before the coffee is put in, and boil together for 3 minutes; clear it by pouring some of it into a cup, and then back again, and leave it on the hob for a few minutes to settle

thoroughly. This coffee may be made still more nutritious by the addition of an egg well beaten, and put into the coffee-cup.

TIME.—*5 minutes to boil, 5 minutes to settle.*

Coffee, Simple Method of

Making.—INGREDIENTS.—*Allow ½ oz., or 1 tablespoonful, of coffee to each person; to every oz. allow ½ pint of water.*

Have a small iron ring made to fit the top of the coffee-pot inside, and to this ring sew a small muslin bag (the muslin for the purpose must not be too thin). Fit the bag into the pot, warm the pot with some boiling water; throw this away, and put the ground coffee into the bag; pour over as much boiling water as is required, close the lid, and, when all the water has filtered through, remove the bag, and send the coffee to table. Making it in this manner prevents the necessity of pouring the coffee from one vessel to another, which cools and spoils it. The water should be poured on the coffee gradually, so that the infusion may be stronger; and the bag must be well made, that none of the grounds may escape through the seams, and so make the coffee thick and muddy.

Coffee, To Make.—INGREDIENTS.

—*Allow ½ oz., or 1 tablespoonful, of ground coffee to each person; to every oz. of coffee allow ½ pint of water.*

To make coffee good, *it should never be boiled*, but the boiling water merely poured on it, the same as for tea. The coffee should always be purchased in the berry—if possible, freshly roasted; and it should never be ground long before it is wanted for use. There are very many new kinds of coffee-pots, but the method of making the coffee is nearly always the same, namely, pouring the boiling water on the powder, and allowing it to filter through. Our illustration shows one of Loysel's Hydrostatic Urns, which are admirably adapted for making good and clear coffee, which should be made in the following manner: — Warm the urn with boiling water, remove the lid and movable filter, and place the ground coffee at the bottom of the urn. Put the movable filter over this, and screw the lid, inverted, tightly on the end of the centre pipe. Pour into the inverted lid the above proportion of boiling

LOYSEL'S HYDROSTATIC URN.

water, and when all the water so poured has disappeared from the funnel, and made its way down the centre pipe and up again through the ground coffee by *hydrostatic pressure*, unscrew the lid and cover the urn. Pour back direct into the urn, *not through the funnel*, one, two or three cups, according to the size of the percolater, in order to make the infusion of uniform strength; the contents will then be ready for use, and should run from the tap strong, hot and clear. The coffee made in these urns generally turns out very good, and there is but one objection to them—the coffee runs rather slowly from the tap; this is of no consequence where there is a small party, but tedious where there are many persons to provide for. A remedy for this objection may be suggested, namely, to make the coffee very strong, so that not more than one third of a cup would be required, as the rest would be filled up with milk. Making coffee in filters or percolaters does away with the necessity of using isinglass, white of egg, and various other

preparations, to clear it. Coffee should always be served very hot, and, if possible, in the same vessel in which it is made, as pouring it from one pot to another cools, and consequently spoils it. Many persons may think that the proportion of water we have given for each ounce of coffee is rather small; it is so, and the coffee produced from it will be very strong; one third of a cup will be found quite sufficient, which should be filled with nice hot milk, or milk and cream mixed. This is the *café au lait* for which our neighbours over the Channel are so justly celebrated. Should the ordinary method of making coffee be preferred, use double the quantity of water, and, in pouring it into the cups, put in more coffee and less milk.

Coffee, To Roast. (A French

Recipe.)—It being an acknowledged fact that French coffee is decidedly superior to that made in England, and as the roasting of the berry is of great importance to the flavour of the preparation, it will be useful and interesting to know how they manage these things in France. In Paris there are two houses justly celebrated for the flavour of their coffee—*La Maison Corcellet* and *La Maison Royer de Chartres;* and to obta'n this flavour, before roasting, they add to every 3 lbs. of coffee a piece of butter the

COFFEE CUSTARD.

size of a nut, and a dessertspoonful of powdered sugar; it is then roasted in the usual manner. The addition of the butter and sugar develops the flavour and aroma of the berry; but it must be borne in mind, that the quality of the butter must be of the very best description.

College Puddings.—INGREDIENTS

for 6 puddings.—1 pint of bread-crumbs, 6 oz. of suet finely chopped, ¼ lb. of currants, a little candied peel, 3 oz. of sugar, 3 eggs, 3 tablespoonfuls of brandy, a grate of nutmeg. AVERAGE COST, 1s. 2d.

Put the bread-crumbs into a basin with the sugar, candied peel, currants, suet and nutmeg, and stir these ingredients till well mixed. Beat up the eggs, and moisten the pudding with these and the brandy, beaten well, then form the mixture into round balls, which fry in hot lard or clarified dripping, turning them several times, and letting them stew till thoroughly done. Drain on blotting-paper and serve with wine sauce.

TIME.—15 to 20 minutes.

SEASONABLE at any time.

Collops, Scotch. (Cold Meat

Cookery.)—INGREDIENTS.—The remains of cold roast veal, a little butter, flour, ¼ pint of water, 1 onion, 1 blade of pounded mace, 1 tablespoonful of lemon-juice, ½ teaspoonful of finely-minced lemon-peel, 2 tablespoonfuls of sherry, 1 tablespoonful of mushroom ketchup. AVERAGE COST, exclusive of the cold meat, 6d.

Cut the veal the same thickness as for cutlets, rather larger than a crown piece; flour the meat well, and fry a light brown in butter; dredge again with flour, and add ½ pint of water, pouring it in by degrees; set it on the fire, and when it boils, add the onion and mace, and let it simmer very gently about ¾ hour; flavour the gravy with lemon juice, peel, wine and ketchup, in the above proportion; give one boil, and serve.

TIME.—¾ hour.

SEASONABLE from March to October.

Collops, Scotch, White. (Cold

Meat Cookery.)—INGREDIENTS.—The remains of cold roast veal, 2 blades of pounded mace, cayenne and salt to taste, a little butter, 1 dessertspoonful of flour, ¼ pint of water, 1 teaspoonful of anchovy sauce, 1 tablespoonful of lemon-juice, ¼ teaspoonful of lemon-peel, 1 tablespoonful of mushroom ketchup, 3 tablespoonfuls of cream, 1 tablespoonful of sherry. AVERAGE COST, exclusive of the cold meat, 7d.

Cut the veal into thin slices about 3 inches in width; hack them with a knife and grate on them the nutmeg, mace, cayenne and salt, and fry them in a little butter. Dish them, and make a gravy in the pan by putting in the remaining ingredients. Give one boil, and pour it over the collops; garnish with lemon and slices of toasted bacon, rolled. Forcemeat balls may be added to this dish. If cream is not at hand, substitute the yolk of an egg beaten up well with a little milk.

TIME.—About 5 or 7 minutes.

SEASONABLE from May to October.

Compôte. —By this is generally un-

derstood a confiture made at the moment of need, and with much less sugar than would be ordinarily put to preserves. They are very wholesome things, suitable to most stomachs which cannot accommodate themselves to raw fruit or a large portion of sugar: they are the happy medium, and far better than ordinary stewed fruit. For Fruit Compôtes refer to the recipes relating to the various fruits. A compôte of fruit makes a nice dinner dish if served in a crust of puff-paste after the style of a vol au vent, or in a sponge cake, the centre of which is scooped out to contain the fruit, with a little whipped cream put on the top of the fruit. By many the sponge-cake crust is preferred if soaked with a little sherry as a tipsy cake.

Confectionary.— In speaking of

confectionary, it should be remarked that many preparations come under that head for the various fruits, flowers, herbs, roots and juices which, when boiled with sugar, were formerly employed in pharmacy as well as for sweetmeats, were called con-

ections, from the Latin word *conficere,* "to make up;" but the term confectionary embraces a very large class indeed of sweet foods, many kinds of which should not be attempted in the ordinary cuisine. Apart from these—cakes, biscuits and tarts, &c., the class of sweetmeats, called confections may be thus classified:—1. Liquid confects, or fruits, either whole or in pieces, preserved by being immersed in a fluid transparent syrup; as the liquid confects of apricots, green citrons, and many foreign fruits. 2. Dry confects are those which after having been boiled in the syrup, are taken out and put to dry in an oven, as citron and orange-peel, &c. 3. Marmalade, jams and pastes, a kind of soft compounds made of the pulp of fruits or other vegetable substances, beaten up with sugar or honey; such as oranges, apricots, pears, &c. 4. Jellies are the juices of fruits boiled with sugar to a pretty thick consistency, so as, upon cooling, to form a trembling jelly; as currant, gooseberry, apple jelly, &c. 5. Conserves are a kind of dry confects, made by beating up flowers, fruits, &c., with sugar, not dissolved. 6. Candies are fruits candied over with sugar after having been boiled in the syrup. Scotch confections are generally considered the cleverest, next to the French, and Wotherspoon and Co, of Paisley are a celebrated firm. Sweet, such as toffee, candies, fruit drops, &c., are now so cheap that few people think it worth while to make them for the children, but many of these bought sweets are greatly adulterated, and instead of risking the harm that these cheap sweets might do, it would be well now and then to make a little store of good wholesome home-made ones, such as Everton toffee or barley sugar.

Corn Cake. (Very good for a Breakfast Cake.) — INGREDIENTS *for 4 cakes.*—½ *lb. of corn meal,* 1 *egg,* ½ *lb. of golden syrup,* 2 *teaspoonfuls of baking powder, milk, salt.* AVERAGE COST, 4*d.*

Mix all the ingredients together, using as much milk as is required to make them into a stiff paste. Bake on buttered tin plates in a quick oven and serve hot.

TIME.—20 *minutes.*

SEASONABLE *at any time.*

Cornflour Cake. — INGREDIENTS *for 12 small cakes.*—6 *oz. of cornflour,* 6 *oz. of sifted sugar,* 4 *oz. of butter,* 3 *eggs, flavouring of vanilla.* AVERAGE COST, 1*s.*

Melt the butter, add the other ingredients, and beat for 20 minutes. Butter some small tins (large patty pans will do), put in the mixture, and bake at once in a good oven.

TIME.—¼ *hour.*

SEASONABLE *at any time.*

Cow-Heel, Fried.—INGREDIENTS. —2 *ox-feet, the yolk of* 1 *egg, bread-crumbs, parsley, salt and cayenne to taste, boiling butter.* AVERAGE COST, 1*s.* 3*d.*

Wash, scald and thoroughly clean the feet, and cut them into pieces about 2 inches long; have ready some fine bread-crumbs mixed with a little minced parsley, cayenne and salt; dip the pieces of heel into the yolk of egg, sprinkle them with the bread-crumbs, and fry them until of a nice brown in boiling butter.

TIME.—¼ *hour.*

SEASONABLE *at any time.*

Note.—Ox-feet may be dressed in various ways, stewed in gravy or plainly boiled and served with melted butter. When plainly boiled, the liquor will answer for making sweet or relishing jellies, and also to give richness to soups or gravies.

Cow-heel Stock (for Jellies; more economical than Calf's-Feet).— INGREDIENTS *for 3 pints of stock.*—2 *cow-heels,* 3 *quarts of water.* AVERAGE COST, 1*s.* 3*d.*

Procure 2 heels that have only been scalded, and not boiled; split them in two, and remove the fat between the claws; wash them well in warm water, and put them into a saucepan with the above proportion of cold water; bring it gradually to boil, remove all the scum as it rises, and simmer the heels gently from 7 to 8 hours, or until the liquor is reduced one-half; then strain it into a basin, measuring the quantity, and put it in a cool place. Clarify it in the same manner as calf's-feet stock, using, with the other ingredients, about ½ oz. of isinglass to each quart. This stock should be made the day before it is required for use. Two dozen shank-bones of mutton, boiled for 6 or 7 hours, yield a quart of strong firm stock. They should be put on in 2 quarts of water, which should be reduced one-half. Make this also the day before it is required.

TIME.—7 to 8 hours to boil the cow-heels, 6 to 7 hours to boil the shank-bones.

SEASONABLE at any time.

Cowslip Wine.—INGREDIENTS.—
To every gallon of water allow 3 lbs. of lump sugar, the rind of 2 lemons, the juice of 1, the rind and juice of 1 Seville orange, 1 gallon of cowslip pips. To every 4½ gallons of wine allow 1 bottle of brandy. AVERAGE COST, 2s. 9d. per gallon.

Boil the sugar and water together for ½ hour, carefully removing all the scum as it rises. Pour this boiling liquor on the orange and lemon rinds and the juice, which should be strained; when milk-warm, add the cowslip pips or flowers, picked from the stalks and seeds; and to 9 gallons of wine 3 tablespoonfuls of good fresh brewers' yeast. Let it ferment 3 or 4 days, then put all together in a cask with the brandy, and let it remain for 2 months, when bottle it off for use.

TIME.—To be boiled ½ hour; to ferment 3 or 4 days; to remain in the cask 2 months.

SEASONABLE.—Make this in April or May.

Crab, Hot.—INGREDIENTS for dish
for 3 persons.—1 crab, nutmeg, salt and pepper to taste, 3 oz. of butter, ¼ lb. of bread-

crumbs, 3 tablespoonfuls of vinegar. AVERAGE COST, 1s. 5d.

After having boiled the crab, pick the meat out from the shells, and mix with it the nutmeg and seasoning. Cut up the butter in small pieces and add the bread-crumbs and vinegar. Mix all together, pu[t] the whole in the large shell, and brow[n] before the fire or with a salamander.

THE CRAB.

TIME.—1 hour.

SEASONABLE all the year; but not so goo[d] in May, June and July.

Crab Sauce (for Fish; equal t[o]
Lobster Sauce).—INGREDIENTS for 1 tureen —1 small crab; salt, pounded mace an[d] cayenne to taste; ½ pint of melted butte[r] made with milk. AVERAGE COST, 1s.

Choose a nice fresh crab, pick all th[e] meat away from the shell, and cut it int[o] small square pieces. Make ½ pint o[f] melted butter, put in the fish and sea soning; let it gradually warm through, an[d] simmer for 2 minutes; it should not boil.

Crab, To Choose.—The middle
sized crab is the best; and the crab, lik[e] the lobster, should be judged by its weight for if light, it is watery. The averag[e] price of crabs vary from 4d. to 2s., accord ing to size.

Crab, To Dress.—INGREDIENTS fo[r]
sufficient for 3 persons.—1 medium-size[d] crab, 2 tablespoonfuls of vinegar, 1 ditto o[f] oil; salt, white pepper and cayenne, to taste AVERAGE COST, 1s. 3d.

Empty the shells, and thoroughly mi[x] the meat with the above ingredients, an[d] put it in the large shell. Garnish with slice[s] of cut lemon and parsley. The quantity o[f] oil may be increased when it is much liked.

SEASONABLE all the year; but not so goo[d] in May, June and July.

Cracker Pudding. (American Recipe.)—INGREDIENTS *for medium-sized pudding.*—1 *cupful of cracker-crumbs,* ¼ *lb. of beef suet,* 3 *eggs,* 2 *tablespoonfuls of sugar,* 1 *cups of milk,* ½ *teaspoonful of salt.* AVERAGE COST, 10*d.*

Chop the suet very fine and beat the eggs, and while doing this let the cracker-crumbs be soaking in the milk. Mix the eggs and sugar with the cracker, then the suet and salt, and work to a smooth paste. Bake in a buttered pie-dish for ¾ hour. Serve with fruit sauce or stewed fruit.

TIME.—¾ *hour.*

SEASONABLE *at any time.*

Cranberry Sauce.—INGREDIENTS. —1 *pint of cranberries,* ¼ *pint of water, white sugar to taste.*

Wash and pick over the berries, and put them in a lined saucepan with just sufficient water to cover them. Let them stew slowly, stirring often till they are reduced to a pulp. Take them from the fire, sweeten them, and turn into a deep dish or mould to cool. This sauce is a nice accompaniment to roast poultry and game; and it may be strained and cleared, and served like red currant jelly.

TIME.—1 *hour to stew the fruit.*

SEASONABLE *from October to March.*

Crayfish.—Crayfish should be thrown into boiling water, to which has been added a good seasoning of salt and a little vinegar. When done, which will be in ¼ hour, take them out and drain them. Let them cool, arrange them on a napkin, and garnish with plenty of double parsley.

Note.—This fish is frequently used for garnishing boiled turkey, boiled fowl, calf's head, turbot, and all kinds of boiled fish.

Crayfish, Potted. — INGREDIENTS. 50 *crayfish; pounded mace, pepper and salt to taste;* 4 *oz. butter.* AVERAGE COST, 6*s.* 8*d.*

Boil the fish in salt and water, pick out all the meat, and pound it in a mortar to a paste. Whilst pounding, add the butter gradually, and mix in the spice and seasoning. Put it in small pots, and pour over it clarified butter, carefully excluding the air.

TIME.—15 *minutes to boil the crayfish.*

SEASONABLE *all the year.*

Crayfish Soup. — INGREDIENTS *for soup for* 8 *persons.*— 30 *crayfish,* ¼ *lb. of butter,* 6 *anchovies, the crumb of* 1 *French roll, a little lobster-spawn, seasoning to taste,* 2 *quarts of medium stock, or fish stock.* AVERAGE COST, 7*s.*

Shell the crayfish, and put the fish between two plates until they are wanted; pound the shells in a mortar with the butter and anchovies; when well beaten add a pint of stock, and simmer for ¾ of an

THE CRAYFISH.

hour. Strain it through a hair sieve, put the remainder of the stock to it, with the crumb of the roll; give it one boil, and rub it through a tammy, with the lobster-spawn. Put in the fish, but do not let the soup boil after it has been rubbed through the tammy. If necessary, add seasoning.

TIME.—1½ *hour.*

SEASONABLE *from January to July.*

Cream à la Valois.— INGREDIENTS *for* 1½ *pint mould.*—4 *sponge-cakes, jam,* 1 *pint of milk, sugar to taste, the juice of* ½ *lemon,* ¼ *glass of sherry,* 1½ *oz. of isinglass.* AVERAGE COST, 2*s.*

Cut the sponge-cakes into thin slices, place two together with preserve between them, and pour over them a small quantity of sherry mixed, if liked, with a little brandy. Sweeten and flavour the cream with the lemon-juice and sherry; add the isinglass, which should be dissolved in a little water, and beat up the cream well. Place a little in an oiled mould; arrange the pieces of cake in the cream, then fill the mould with the remainder, let it cool, and turn it out on a dish. By oiling the mould the cream will have a much smoother appearance, and will turn out more easily than when merely dipped in cold water.

SEASONABLE at any time.

Cream Cheese.

Cream Cheese. — Cream cheese should be served on a d'oyley, and garnished either with watercresses or parsley; of the former, a plentiful supply should be given, as they add greatly to the appearance of the dish, besides improving the flavour of the cheese.

Cream, Devonshire.

Cream, Devonshire. — The milk should stand 24 hours in the winter, half that time when the weather is very warm. The milk-pan is then set on a stove, and should there remain until the milk is quite hot; but it must not boil, or there will be a thick skin on the surface. When it is sufficiently done the undulations on the surface look thick, and small rings appear. The time required for scalding cream depends on the size of the pan and the heat of the fire, but the slower it is done the better. The pan should be placed in the dairy when the cream is sufficiently scalded, and skimmed the following day. This cream is so much esteemed that it is sent to the London markets in small square tins, and is exceedingly delicious eaten with fresh fruit. In Devonshire, butter is made from this cream, and is usually very firm.

Cream Eggs.

Cream Eggs.—INGREDIENTS for dish for 6 persons.—7 eggs, ½ pint of milk, ½ pint of cream, ¼ lb. of loaf sugar, 2 lemons, 1 oz. of gelatine, a round stale sponge cake, a few strips of angelica and candied citron, 2 glasses of liqueur, a few pistachio nuts. AVERAGE COST, not including the eggs not

used, which can serve for another dish, 3s. 6d.

Break a small piece off the end of the shell of each egg and take out the contents. Make a lemon cream as directed in recipe for same, and fill the egg-shells with it, putting them upright on the unbroken end to cool. Scoop out the centre of the sponge cake after the fashion of a nest, pour over it the liqueur, and stick it with small pieces of the citron and angelica to look like wings. Chop the nuts finely, and scatter over and inside the nest, and when the eggs are cold shell them and lay them in the nest.

This is a very pretty supper dish, and it may be varied by cutting the cream eggs in half lengthways, scooping out as much as the yolk would occupy from each half and filling the cavity with apricot preserve to look like the yolk.

SEASONABLE at any time.

Cream, Italian.

Cream, Italian.—INGREDIENTS for 1½ pint mould.—½ pint of milk, ½ pint of cream, sugar to taste, 1 oz. of isinglass or gelatine, 1 lemon, the yolks of 4 eggs. AVERAGE COST, 1s. 5d.

Put the cream and milk into a saucepan, with sugar to sweeten, and the lemon-rind. Boil until the milk is well flavoured, then strain it into a basin and add the beaten yolks of eggs. Put this mixture into a jug, place the jug in a saucepan of boiling water over the fire, and stir the contents until they thicken, but do not allow them to boil. Take the cream off the fire, stir in the lemon-juice and isinglass, which should be melted, and whip well; fill a mould, place it in ice if at hand, and, when set, turn it out on a dish, and garnish as taste may dictate. The mixture may be whipped and drained, and then put into small glasses, when this mode of serving is preferred.

TIME.—From 5 to 8 minutes to stir the mixture in the jug.

SEASONABLE at any time.

Cream Sauce (for Fish or White Dishes).

—INGREDIENTS *for* 1 *tureen.*—½ *pint of cream*, 2 *oz. of butter*, 1 *teaspoonful of flour, salt and cayenne to taste; when liked, a small quantity of pounded mace or lemon-juice.* AVERAGE COST, 8d.

Put the butter in a very clean saucepan, dredge in the flour, and keep shaking round till the butter is melted. Add the seasoning and cream, and stir the whole till it boils; let it just simmer for 5 minutes, when add either pounded mace or lemon-juice to taste to give it a flavour.

TIME.—*5 minutes to simmer.*

Note.—This sauce may be flavoured with very finely-shredded shalot.

Creams, Jellies, Blancmanges,

Recipes for.—Directions for making the following appear under their respective headings:—

Apricot Cream.
Banana Cream.
Chocolate Cream.
Chocolate Creams.
Ginger Cream.
Italian Cream.
Lemon Cream.
Lemon Cream, Economical.
Lemon Creams.
Lobster Cream.
Noyeau Cream.
Orange Cream.
Orange Creams.
Stone Cream.
Swiss Cream.
Valois Cream.
Vanilla Cream.
Arrowroot Jelly.
Aspic Jelly.
Aspic Jelly, Another Mode.
Aspic Jelly, Moulded, with Vegetables.

Apple Jelly.
Calf's-foot Jelly.
Invalid's Jelly.
Isinglass Jelly.
Jelly, Marbled.
Jelly, with Fresh Fruit.
Jelly of Two Colours.
Jellies, To Make.
Jellies, Bottled.
Lemon Jelly.
Liqueur Jelly.
Open Jelly.
Orange Jelly.
Restorative Jelly.
Savoury Jelly.
Blancmange.
Blancmange, Cheap.
Blancmange, Arrowroot.
Blancmange for Invalids.
Blancmange, Lemon.
Blancmange, Rice.

Cream, Whipped (for putting on Trifles, serving in Glasses, &c.)

—INGREDIENTS.—To every pint of cream allow 3 oz. of pounded sugar, 1 glass of sherry or any kind of sweet white wine, the rind of ½ lemon, the white of 1 egg.

Rub the sugar on the lemon-rind, and pound it in a mortar until quite fine, and beat up the white of the egg until quite stiff; put the cream into a large bowl, with the sugar, wine, and beaten egg, and whip it to a froth; as fast as the froth rises take it off with a skimmer, and put it on a sieve to drain in a cool place. This should be made the day before it is wanted, as the whip is then so much firmer. The cream should be whipped in a cool place, and in summer over ice, if it is obtainable.

TIME.—*About 1 hour to whip the cream.*
SEASONABLE *at any time.*

Crumpets.

—These are made in the same manner as muffins, only, in making the mixture, let it be more like batter than dough. Let it rise for about ½ hour; pour

CRUMPETS.

it into iron rings, which should be ready on a hot-plate, bake them, and when one side appears done, turn them quickly on the other. *To toast them*, have ready a very *bright clear* fire; put the crumpet on a toasting-fork, and hold it before the fire, *not too close*, until it is nicely brown on one side, but do not allow it to blacken; turn it, and brown the other side; then spread it with good butter, cut it in half, and, when all are done, pile them on a hot dish, and send them quickly to table. Muffins and crumpets should always be served on separate dishes, and both toasted and served as expeditiously as possible.

TIME.—*From* 10 *to* 15 *minutes to bake them.*

Crust, Butter (for Boiled Puddings).

—INGREDIENTS.—*To every lb. of flour allow* 4 *oz. of butter,* ½ *pint of water.* AVERAGE COST, 5*d. per lb.*

With a knife, work the flour to a smooth paste with ½ pint of water; roll the crust out rather thin; place the butter over it in small pieces, dredge lightly over it some flour, and fold the paste over; repeat the rolling once more, and the crust will be ready for use. It may be enriched by adding another 2 oz. of butter; but, for ordinary purposes, the above quantity will be found quite sufficient.

Crust, Common (for Raised Pies).

—INGREDIENTS.—*To every lb. of flour allow* ½ *pint of water,* 1½ *oz. of butter,* 1½ *oz. of lard,* ½ *saltspoonful of salt.* AVERAGE COST, 4*d. per lb.*

Put into a saucepan the water, when it boils add the butter and lard, and when these are melted, make a hole in the middle of the flour; pour in the water gradually, beat it well with a wooden spoon, and be particular in not making the paste too soft. When it is well mixed, knead it with the hands until quite stiff, dredging a little flour over the paste and board to prevent them from sticking. When it is well kneaded, place it before the fire, with a cloth covered over it, for a few minutes; it will then be more easily worked into shape. This paste does not taste so nice as a richer one, but it is worked with greater facility, and answers just as well for raised pies, for the crust is seldom eaten.

Crust, Dripping (for Kitchen Puddings, Pies, &c.).—INGREDIENTS.—*To every lb. of flour allow* 6 *oz. of clarified beef dripping,* ½ *pint of water, a little salt.* AVERAGE COST, 3*d. per lb.*

After having clarified the dripping, weigh it, and to every lb. of flour allow the above proportion of dripping. With a knife,

work the flour into a smooth paste with the water, rolling it out three times, each time placing on the crust 2 oz. of the dripping broken into small pieces. If this paste is lightly made, if good dripping is used, and *not too much of it,* it will be found good; and by the addition of two tablespoonfuls of fine moist sugar, it may be converted into a common short crust for fruit pies.

Crust, Flead.—INGREDIENTS.—*To every lb. of flour allow* ½ *lb. of flead,* ½ *pint of water,* ½ *saltspoonful of salt.* AVERAGE COST, 5*d. per lb.*

Clear the flead from skin, and slice it into thin flakes; rub it into the flour, add the salt, and work the whole into a smooth paste, with the above proportion of water, fold the paste over two or three times, beat it well with the rolling-pin, roll it out, and it will be ready for use. The crust made from this will be found extremely light, and may be made into cakes or tarts; it may also be very much enriched by adding more flead to the same proportion of flour.

Crust, Suet (for Pies or Puddings).

INGREDIENTS.—*To every lb. of flour allow* 5 *or* 6 *oz. of beef suet,* ½ *pint of water.* AVERAGE COST, 4*d. per lb.*

Free the suet from skin and shreds, chop it extremely fine, and rub it well into the flour; work the whole to a smooth paste with the above proportion of water; roll it out, and it is ready for use. This crust is quite rich enough for ordinary purposes, but when a better one is desired, use from ½ to ¾ lb. of suet to every lb. of flour. Some cooks, for rich crusts, pound the suet in a mortar, with a small quantity of butter. It should then be laid on the paste in small pieces, the same as for puff-crust, and will be found exceedingly nice for hot tarts. 5 oz. of suet to every lb. of flour will make a very good crust; and even ¼ lb. will answer very well for children, or where the crust is wanted very plain.

Crust, Common Short. — In-gredients.—To every lb. of flour allow 2 oz. of sifted sugar, 3 oz. of butter, about ½ pint of boiling milk. Average Cost, 5d. per lb.

Crumble the butter into the flour as finely as possible, add the sugar, and work the whole up to a smooth paste with the boiling milk. Roll it out thin, and bake in a moderate oven.

Crust, Very good Short (for Fruit Tarts).—Ingredients.—To every lb. of flour allow ½ or ¾ lb. of butter, 1 table-spoonful of sifted sugar, ⅛ pint of water. Average Cost, 8d. per lb.

Rub the butter into the flour, after having ascertained that the latter is perfectly dry; add the sugar, and mix the whole into a stiff paste with about ⅛ pint of water. Roll it out two or three times, folding the paste over each time, and it will be ready for use.

Crust, Another good Short.—Ingredients.—To every lb. of flour allow 8 oz. of butter, the yolks of 2 eggs, 2 oz. of sifted sugar, about ¼ pint of milk. Average Cost, 8d. per lb.

Rub the butter into the flour, add the sugar, and mix the whole as lightly as possible to a smooth paste, with the yolks of the eggs well beaten, and the milk. The proportion of the latter ingredient must be judged of by the size of the eggs; if these are large so much will not be required, and more if the eggs are smaller.

Cucumber Sandwiches. — Ingredients. — Very thin bread-and-butter, cucumber, oil, vinegar, pepper.

Stamp from the slices of bread with a tin cutter little rounds, the size of the cucumber slices. Lay the latter for a few minutes in a mixture of oil, vinegar and pepper; then put them between the rounds of bread-and-butter.

Seasonable in summer.

Cucumber Sauce.—Ingredients. —3 cucumbers, 2 oz. of butter, 6 tablespoon-fuls of brown gravy. Average Cost, 1s.

Peel the cucumbers, quarter them, and take out the seeds; cut them into small

CUCUMBER.

pieces, put them in a cloth, and rub them well to take out the water that hangs about them. Put the butter in a sauce-pan, add the cucumbers, and shake them over a sharp fire until they are of a good colour; then pour over them the gravy,

TELEGRAPH CUCUMBERS.

mixed with the cucumbers, and simmer gently for 10 minutes, when it will be ready to serve.

Time.—Altogether, ½ hour.

Cucumber Sauce, White.—Ingredients.—3 cucumbers, ½ pint of white stock, cayenne and salt to taste, the yolks of 2 eggs. Average Cost, 1s. 2d.

Cut the cucumbers into small pieces, after peeling them and taking out the

P

seeds. Put them in the stewpan with the white stock and seasoning; simmer gently till the cucumbers are tender, which will be in about ¼ hour. Then add the yolks of the eggs well beaten; stir them to the sauce, but do not allow it to boil, and serve very hot.

TIME.—*Altogether ½ hour.*

Cucumber Soup. (French Recipe.)

INGREDIENTS *for soup for 5 persons.*—1 *large cucumber, a piece of butter the size of a walnut, a little chervil and sorrel cut in large pieces, salt and pepper to taste, the yolks of 2 eggs, 1 gill of cream, 1 quart of medium stock.* AVERAGE COST, 1s. 6d.

Pare the cucumber, quarter it, and take out the seeds; cut it in thin slices, put these on a plate with a little salt, to draw the water from them; drain, and put them in a stewpan, with the butter. When they are warmed through, without being browned, pour the stock on them. Add the sorrel, chervil and seasoning, and boil for 40 minutes. Mix the yolks of the eggs, well-beaten, with the cream, which add at the moment of serving.

TIME.—1 *hour.*

SEASONABLE *from June to September.*

Cucumber Vinegar. (A very nice addition to Salads.)—INGREDIENTS.—10 *large cucumbers, or 12 smaller ones,* 1 *quart of vinegar, 2 onions, 2 shalots, 1 tablespoonful of salt, 2 tablespoonfuls of pepper,* ½ *teaspoonful of cayenne.*

Pare and slice the cucumbers, put them in a stone jar or wide-mouthed bottle with the vinegar; slice the onions and shalots, and add them, with all the other ingredients, to the cucumbers. Let it stand 4 or 5 days, boil it all up, and when cold, strain the liquor through a piece of muslin, and store it away in small bottles well sealed. This vinegar is a very nice addition to gravies, hashes, &c., as well as a great improvement to salads, or to eat with cold meat.

Cucumbers à la Poulette.—INGREDIENTS *for dish for 6 persons.*—2 *cucumbers of moderate size, salt and vinegar, 2 oz of butter, flour, ½ pint of broth, 1 teaspoonful of minced parsley, a lump of sugar, the yolks of 2 eggs, salt and pepper to taste* AVERAGE COST, 4d. *each.*

Pare and cut the cucumbers into slices of an equal thickness, and let them remain in a pickle of salt and vinegar for ½ hour then drain them in a cloth, and put them into a stewpan with the butter. Fry them over a brisk fire, but do not brown them and then dredge over them a little flour

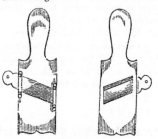

CUCUMBER-SLICES.

add the broth, skim off all the fat, which will rise to the surface, and boil gently until the gravy is somewhat reduced, but the cucumber should not be broken. Stir in the yolks of the eggs, add the parsley, sugar and a seasoning of pepper and salt; bring the whole to the *point of boiling,* and serve.

TIME.—*Altogether,* 1 *hour.*

SEASONABLE *in July, August or September; but may be had, forced, from the beginning of March.*

Cucumbers, Dressed.—INGREDIENTS.—*Cucumber,* 3 *tablespoonfuls of salad-oil,* 4 *tablespoonfuls of vinegar, salt and pepper to taste.* AVERAGE COST, *frame cucumbers,* 4d. *to* 1s.; *field ones,* 1d. *to* 3d. *each.*

Pare the cucumber, cut it equally into *very thin* slices, and *commence* cutting from the *thick end;* if commenced at the stalk, the cucumber will most likely have an exceedingly bitter taste, far from agreeable. For the purpose of slicing cucumbers evenly and very thin, we recommend the slice in preference to an ordinary knife. Put the slices into a dish, sprinkle over a very little salt and some pepper, and pour over oil and vinegar in the above proportion; turn the cucumber about, and it is

CUCUMBER SLICED.

ready to serve. This is a favourite accompaniment to boiled salmon, is a nice addition to all descriptions of salads, and makes a pretty garnish to lobster salad.

SEASONABLE.—*Forced from the beginning of March to the end of June; in full season in July, August and September.*

Cucumbers, Excellent Way of Preserving. - INGREDIENTS. — *Salt and water*, 1 *lb. of lump sugar, the rind of* 1 *lemon*, 1 *oz. of ginger, cucumbers.*

Choose the greenest cucumbers, and those that are most free from seeds; put them in strong salt and water, with a cabbage-leaf to keep them down; tie a paper over them, and put them in a warm place till they are yellow, then wash them and set them over the fire in fresh water with a very little salt, and another cabbage-leaf over them; cover very closely, but take care they do not boil. If they are not a fine green, change the water again, cover them as before, and make them hot. When they are a good colour take them off the fire and let them cool; cut them in quarters, take out the seeds and pulp, and put them into cold water; let them remain for 2 days, changing the water twice each day, to draw out the salt. Put the sugar, with ½ pint of water, in a saucepan over the fire; remove the scum as it rises, and add

the lemon-peel and ginger with the outside scraped off; when the syrup is tolerably thick, take it off the fire, and when *cold*, wipe the cucumbers *dry* and put them in. Boil the syrup once in 2 or 3 days for 3 weeks; strengthen it if required, and let it be quite cold before the cucumbers are put in. Great attention must be paid to the directions in the commencement of this recipe, as, if these are not properly carried out, the result will be far from satisfactory.

SEASONABLE.—*This recipe should be used in June, July or August.*

Cucumbers, Fried.—INGREDIENTS *for dish for* 6 *persons.*—2 *cucumbers, pepper and salt to taste, flour, oil or butter.* AVERAGE COST, 4*d. each.*

Pare the cucumbers, and cut them into slices of an equal thickness, commencing to slice from the thick and not the stalk end of the cucumber. Wipe the slices dry with a cloth, dredge them with flour, and put them into a pan of boiling oil or butter; keep turning them about until brown; lift them out of the pan, let them drain, and serve, piled lightly in a dish. These will be found a great improvement to rump-steak: they should be placed on a dish with the steak on the top.

TIME.—5 *minutes.*

SEASONABLE.—*Forced from the beginning of March to the end of June; in full season in July and August.*

Cucumbers, German Method of Keeping for Winter use.—INGREDIENTS.—*Cucumbers, salt.*

Pare and slice the cucumbers (as for the table), sprinkle well with salt, and let them remain for 24 hours; strain off the liquor, pack in jars, a thick layer of cucumbers and salt alternately; tie down closely, and, when wanted for use, take out the quantity required. Now wash them well in fresh water, and dress as usual with pepper, vinegar and oil.

Cucumbers, Pickled.—INGREDIENTS.—1 oz. of whole pepper, 1 oz. of bruised ginger, sufficient vinegar to cover the cucumbers.

Cut the cucumbers in thick slices, sprinkle salt over them, and let them remain for 24 hours. The next day, drain them well for 6 hours, put them into a jar, pour boiling vinegar over them, and keep them in a warm place. In a short time, boil up the vinegar again, add pepper and ginger in the above proportion, and instantly cover them up. Tie them down with bladder, and in a few days they will be fit for use.

Cucumbers, Stewed.—INGREDIENTS for dish for 8 persons.—3 large cucumbers, flour, butter, rather more than ½ pint of good brown gravy. AVERAGE COST, 1s. 3d.

Cut the cucumbers lengthwise the size of the dish they are intended to be served in; empty them of the seeds, and put them into boiling water with a little salt, and let them simmer for 5 minutes; then take them out, place them in another stewpan, with the gravy, and let them boil over a brisk fire until the cucumbers are tender. Should these be bitter, add a lump of sugar; carefully dish them, skim the sauce, pour over the cucumbers, and serve.

TIME.—Altogether, 20 minutes.

SEASONABLE in June, July and August; but may be had, forced, from the beginning of March.

Cucumbers Stewed with Onions.—INGREDIENTS for dish for 8 persons.—4 cucumbers, 3 moderate-sized onions, not quite 1 pint of white stock, cayenne and salt to taste, the yolks of 2 eggs, a very little grated nutmeg. AVERAGE COST, 1s. 6d.

Pare and slice the cucumbers, take out the seeds, and cut the onions into thin slices; put these both into a stewpan, with the stock, and let them boil for ¼ hour, or longer, should the cucumbers be very large.

Beat up the yolks of 2 eggs; stir these into the sauce; add the cayenne, salt, and grated nutmeg; bring it to the point of boiling, and serve. Do not allow the sauce to boil, or it will curdle. This is a favourite dish with lamb or mutton chops, rumpsteaks, &c.

TIME.—Altogether, 20 minutes.

SEASONABLE in July, August and September; but may be had, forced, from the beginning of March.

Currant and Raspberry Tart, Red.—INGREDIENTS for tart for 6 persons.—1½ pint of picked currants, ½ pint of raspberries, 3 heaped tablespoonfuls of moist sugar, ½ lb. of short crust. AVERAGE COST, 1s.

Strip the currants from the stalks, and put them into a deep pie-dish, with a small cup placed in the midst, bottom upwards; add the raspberries and sugar; place a border of paste round the edge of the dish, cover with crust, ornament the edges, and bake from ½ to ¾ hour; strew some sifted sugar over before being sent to table. This tart is more generally served cold than hot.

TIME.—½ to ¾ hour.

SEASONABLE in June, July and August.

Note.—In tarts of this description carefully avoid washing the fruit.

Currant Dumplings.—INGREDIENTS for dish for 6 persons.—1 lb. of flour, 6 oz. of suet, ½ lb. of currants, rather more than ½ pint of water. AVERAGE COST, 8d.

Chop the suet finely, mix it with the flour, and add the currants, which should be nicely washed, picked and dried; mix the whole to a limp paste with the water (if wanted very nice, use milk); divide it into 7 or 8 dumplings; tie them in cloths, and boil for 1¼ hour. They may be boiled without a cloth: they should then be made into round balls, and dropped into boiling water, and should be moved about at first, to prevent them from sticking to the bottom of the saucepan. Serve with a cut lemon, cold butter and sifted sugar.

TIME.—*In a cloth, 1¼ hour; without, ¾ hour.*

SEASONABLE *at any time.*

Currant Fritters. — INGREDIENTS

for dish for 4 persons.—*½ pint of milk, 2 tablespoonfuls of flour, 4 eggs, 3 tablespoonfuls of boiled rice, 3 tablespoonfuls of currants, sugar to taste, a very little grated nutmeg, hot lard or clarified dripping.* AVERAGE COST, 10*d.*

Put the milk into a basin with the flour, which should previously be rubbed to a smooth batter with a little cold milk; stir these ingredients together; add the eggs, well whisked, the rice, currants, sugar and nutmeg. Beat the mixture for a few minutes, and, if not sufficiently thick, add a little more boiled rice; drop it, in small quantities, into a pan of boiling lard or clarified dripping; fry the fritters a nice brown and, when done, drain them on a piece of blotting-paper, before the fire. Pile them on a white d'oyley, strew over sifted sugar, and serve them very hot. Send a cut lemon to table with them.

CURRANTS.

TIME.—*From 8 to 10 minutes to fry the fritters.*

SEASONABLE *at any time.*

Currant Jam, Black. — INGREDI-

ENTS.—*To every lb. of fruit, weighed before being stripped from the stalks, allow ¾ lb. of loaf sugar, 1 gill of water.* AVERAGE COST, 6*d.* per pot.

Let the fruit be very ripe, and gathered on a dry day. Strip it from the stalks, and put it into a preserving-pan, with a gill of water to each lb. of fruit; boil these to-

gether for 10 minutes; then add the sugar, and boil the jam again for 30 minutes, reckoning from the time when the jam simmers equally all over, or longer, should it not appear to set nicely when a little is poured on to a plate. Keep stirring it to prevent it from burning, carefully remove all the scum, and when done, pour it into pots. Let it cool, cover the top of the jam with oiled paper, and the top of the jars with a piece of tissue paper, brushed over on both sides with the white of an egg; this, when cold, forms a hard stiff cover, and perfectly excludes the air. Great attention must be paid to the stirring of his jam, as it is very liable to burn, on account of the thickness of the juice.

TIME.—10 *minutes to boil the fruit and water; 30 minutes with the sugar, or longer.*

SEASONABLE.—*Make this in July.*

Currant Jam, Red. — INGREDI-

ENTS.—*To every lb. of fruit allow ¾ lb. of loaf sugar.* AVERAGE COST, 6*d.* per lb. pot.

Let the fruit be gathered on a fine day; weigh it, and then strip the currants from the stalks; put them into a preserving-pan with sugar in the above proportion; stir them, and boil them for about ¾ hour. Carefully remove the scum as it rises. Put the jam into pots, and, when cold, cover with oiled papers; over these put a piece of tissue-paper, brushed over on both sides with the white of an egg; press the paper round the top of the pot, and, when dry, the covering will be quite hard and airtight.

TIME.—½ *to ¾ hour, reckoning from the time the jam boils all over.*

SEASONABLE.—*Make this in July.*

Currant Jelly, Black.—INGREDI-

ENTS.—*Black currants; to every pint of juice allow ¼ pint of water, 1 lb. of loaf sugar.* AVERAGE COST, *from 8d. to 10d. per pot.*

Strip the currants from the stalks, which may be done in an expeditious manner by holding the bunch in one hand, and passing a small silver fork down the currants: they will then readily fall from the stalks. Put them into a jar, place this jar in a saucepan of boiling water, and simmer them until their juice is extracted; then strain them, and to every pint of juice allow the above proportion of sugar and water; stir those ingredients together cold until the sugar is dissolved; place the preserving-pan on the fire, and boil the jelly for about ½ hour, reckoning from the time it commences to boil all over, and carefully remove the scum as it rises. If the jelly becomes firm when a little is put on a plate, it is done; it should then be put into *small* pots, and covered the same as the jam in the preceding recipe. If the jelly is wanted very clear, the fruit should not be squeezed dry; but, of course, so much juice will not be obtained. If the fruit is not much squeezed, it may be converted into a jam for immediate eating, by boiling it with a little common sugar: this answers very well for a nursery preserve.

TIME.—*About ¾ hour to extract the juice; ½ hour to boil the jelly.*

SEASONABLE.—*Make this in July.*

Currant Jelly, Red.—INGREDI-

ENTS.—*Red currants; to every pint of juice allow ¾ lb. of loaf sugar.* AVERAGE COST, 8d. to 10d. *per pot.*

Have the fruit gathered in fine weather; pick it from the stalks, put it into a jar, and place this jar in a saucepan of boiling water over the fire, and let it simmer gently until the juice is well drawn from the currants; then strain them through a jelly-bag or fine cloth, and if the jelly is wished very clear, do not squeeze them *too much,* as the skin and pulp from the fruit will be pressed through with the juice, and so make the jelly muddy. Measure the juice, and to each pint allow ¾ lb. of loaf sugar; put these into a preserving-pan, set it over the fire, and keep stirring the jelly

until it is done, carefully removing every particle of scum as it rises, using a wooden or silver spoon for the purpose, as metal or iron ones would spoil the colour of the jelly. When it has boiled from 20 minutes to ½ hour, put a little of the jelly on a plate, and if firm when cool, it is done. Take it off the fire, pour it into small gallipots, cover each of the pots with an oiled paper, and then with a piece of tissue-paper, brushed over on both sides with the white of an egg. Label the pots, adding the year when the jelly was made, and store it away in a dry place. A jam may be made with the currants, if they are not squeezed too dry, by adding a few fresh raspberries, and boiling all together, with sufficient sugar to sweeten it nicely. As this jam is not worth storing away, but is only for immediate eating, a smaller proportion of sugar than usual will be found enough: it answers very well for children's puddings, or for a nursery preserve.

TIME.—*From ¾ to 1 hour to extract the juice; 20 minutes to ½ hour to boil the jelly.*

SEASONABLE.—*Make this in July.*

Note.—Should the above proportion of sugar not be found sufficient for some tastes, add an extra ¼ lb. to every pint of juice, making altogether 1 lb.

Currant Jelly, White.—INGREDI-

ENTS.—*White currants; to every pint of juice allow ¾ lb. of good loaf sugar.* AVERAGE COST, 8d. to 10d. *per pot.*

Pick the currants from the stalks, and put them into a jar; place this jar in a saucepan of boiling water, and simmer until the juice is well drawn from the fruit, which will be in from ¾ to 1 hour. Then strain the currants through a fine cloth or jelly-bag; do not squeeze them too much, or the jelly will not be clear, and put the juice into a very clean preserving-pan, with the sugar. Let this simmer gently over a clear fire until it is firm, and keep stirring and skimming until it is done;

hen pour it into small pots, cover them, and store away in a dry place.

TIME.—¾ *hour to draw the juice;* ½ *hour to boil the jelly.*

SEASONABLE *in July and August.*

Currant Pudding, Boiled.—

Plain and Economical). — INGREDIENTS *for good-sized pudding.*—1 lb. of flour, ½ lb. *of suet,* ½ lb. *of currants, milk.* AVERAGE COST, 10d.

Wash the currants, dry them thoroughly, and pick away any stalks or grit; chop the suet finely; mix all the ingredients together, and moisten with sufficient milk to make the pudding into a stiff batter; tie it up in a floured cloth, put it into boiling water, and boil for 3½ hours; serve with a cut lemon, cold butter, and sifted sugar.

TIME.—3½ *hours.*

SEASONABLE *at any time.*

Currant Pudding, Black or Red.—INGREDIENTS *for pudding for 6 persons.*—1 *quart of red or black currants, measured with the stalks,* ¼ lb. *of moist sugar, suet crust or butter crust.* AVERAGE COST, 10d.

Make, with ¾ lb. of flour, either a suet crust or butter crust (the former is usually made); butter a basin, and line it with part of the crust; add the currants, which should be stripped from the stalks, and sprinkle the sugar over them; put the cover of the pudding on; make the edges very secure, that the juice does not escape; tie it down with a floured cloth, put it into boiling water, and boil from 2½ to 3 hours. Boiled without a basin, allow ½ hour less. We have given rather a large proportion of sugar; but we find fruit puddings are so much more juicy and palatable when *well sweetened* before they are boiled, besides being more economical. A few raspberries added to red-currant pudding are a very nice addition; about ½ pint would be sufficient for the above quantity of fruit. Fruit puddings are very delicious if, when they are turned out of the basin, the crust is browned with a salamander, or put into a very hot oven for a few minutes to colour it; this makes it crisp on the surface.

TIME.—2½ to 3 *hours; without a basin,* 2½ *hours.*

SEASONABLE *in June, July and August.*

Currants, Iced (for Dessert).—INGREDIENTS.—¼ pint of water, the whites of 2 eggs, currants, pounded sugar.

Select very fine bunches of red or white currants, and well beat the whites of the eggs. Mix these with the water; then take the currants, a bunch at a time, and dip them in; let them drain for a minute or two, and roll them in very fine-pounded sugar. Lay them to dry on paper, when the sugar will crystallize round each currant, and have a very pretty effect. All fresh fruit may be prepared in the same manner; and a mixture of various fruits iced in this manner, and arranged on one dish, looks very well for a summer dessert.

TIME.—¼ *day to dry the fruit.*

SEASONABLE *in summer.*

Curry.—INGREDIENTS.— *Veal, mutton, fowl or rabbit: a large onion, butter, brown gravy or stock, a tablespoonful of Stembridge and Co.'s curry-powder.*

Let the meat be half fried. Cut the onion into small pieces, and fry it in butter till quite brown; add the meat, with a small quantity of brown gravy or stock, also the curry-powder, and stew all for about 20 minutes. This is for a dry curry; more gravy and curry-powder can be used if preferred.

TIME.—20 *minutes.*

SEASONABLE *at any time.*

Curry-Powder. (Founded on Dr. KITCHENER'S Recipe.)—INGREDIENTS.—¼ lb. of coriander seed, ¼ lb. of turmeric, 2 oz. of cinnamon seed, ½ oz. of cayenne, 1 oz. of mustard, 1 oz. of ground ginger, ½ oz. of allspice, 2 oz. of fenugreek seed.

Put all the ingredients in a cool oven, where they should remain one night; then pound them in a mortar, rub them through a sieve, and mix thoroughly together; keep the powder in a bottle, from which the air should be completely excluded.

Curry-Powder. (Captain WHITE'S recipe; most excellent.)—INGREDIENTS. —1 lb. of pale turmeric seed, 4 oz. of cumming seed, 8 oz. of coriander seed, 4 oz. of black pepper, 2 oz. of cayenne pepper, 4 oz. of Jamaica ginger, 10 oz. of caraway seed, ¼ oz. of cardamums.

Mix together all these ingredients, well pounded, and then place the mixture in the sun, or before the fire, stirring it frequently.

Note.—This will be found a most excellent curry-powder, if care be taken to purchase the ingredients at a good druggist's.

Curry St. Leonard's.—INGREDIENTS.—*Chicken or any meat; 2 tablespoonfuls of butter, 2 tablespoonfuls of curry-powder, 4 or 5 leaves of mint, a teacup of good gravy, salt, a dessertspoonful of vinegar, 3 tablespoonfuls of cream, 1 dessertspoonful of Stembridge's chutnee.*

Fry together for 10 minutes the butter, curry-powder and mint; then add the meat *cut into small pieces,* also the gravy, salt and vinegar. Let all these simmer for 20 minutes, and then pour over the cream, and serve quite hot.

TIME.—30 *minutes.*
SEASONABLE *at any time.*

Custards, Boiled.—INGREDIENTS *for 8 custards.*—1 *pint of milk, 3 eggs, 3 oz. of loaf sugar, 3 laurel-leaves, or the rind of ½ lemon, or a few drops of essence of vanilla, 1 tablespoonful of brandy.* AVERAGE COST, 9d.

Put the milk into a *lined* saucepan, with the sugar and whichever of the above flavourings may be preferred (the lemon-rind flavours custards most deliciously),

and let the milk steep by the side of the fire until it is well flavoured. Bring it t the point of boiling, then strain it into basin; whisk the eggs well, and, when th milk has cooled a little, stir in the eggs and *strain* this mixture into a jug. Plac this jug in a saucepan of boiling wate over the fire; keep stirring the custard *on way* until it thickens; but on no accoun allow it to reach the boiling point, as i will instantly curdle and be full of lumps Take it off the fire, stir in the brandy, an when this is well mixed with the custard pour it into glasses, which should be rathe more than three-parts full; grate a littl nutmeg over the top, and the dish is read for table. To make custards richer, duck eggs should be used, when obtainable

CUSTARDS IN GLASSES.

they add very much to the flavour an richness, and so many are not required a of the ordinary eggs, 2 ducks' eggs to th pint of milk making a delicious custard When desired extremely rich and good cream should be substituted for the milk and double the quantity of eggs used t those mentioned, omitting the whites.

TIME.—½ *hour to infuse the lemon-rind about* 10 *minutes to stir the custard.*
SEASONABLE *at any time.*

Custard Pudding, Baked.—IN GREDIENTS *for pudding for 4 or 5 persons* —1½ *pint of milk, the rind of ¼ lemon, ¼ lb. of moist sugar, 3 eggs.* AVERAGE COST 7d.

Put the milk into a saucepan with th sugar and lemon-rind, and let this infus for about ½ hour, or until the milk is wel flavoured: whisk the eggs, yolks an whites; pour the milk to them, stirring a the while; then have ready a pie-dish lined at the edge with paste ready baked strain the custard into the dish, grate a little nutmeg over the top, and bake in a very slow oven for about ½ hour or rather longer. The flavour of this pudding may be varied by substituting bitter almonds for the lemon-rind; and it may be very much enriched by using half cream and half milk, and doubling the quantity of eggs.

TIME.—½ to ¾ hour.

SEASONABLE at any time.

Note.—This pudding is usually served cold with fruit tarts.

Custard Pudding, Boiled.—IN-

GREDIENTS *for pudding sufficient for 6 persons.*—1 pint of milk, 1 tablespoonful of flour, 4 eggs, flavouring to taste. AVERAGE COST, 7d.

Flavour the milk by infusing in it a little lemon rind or cinnamon; whisk the eggs, stir the flour gradually to these, and pour over them the milk, and stir the mixture well. Butter a basin that will exactly hold it; put in the custard and tie a floured cloth over; plunge it into boiling water, and turn it about for a few minutes, to prevent the flour from settling in one part. Boil it slowly for ½ hour; turn it out of the basin, and serve. The pudding may be garnished with red-currant jelly, and sweet sauce may be sent to table with it.

TIME.—½ hour.

SEASONABLE at any time.

Note.—Very nice custards and custard puddings may be quickly made by using Goodall, Backhouse and Co.'s or A. Bird and Sons' custard powder.

Custard Sauce (for Sweet Pud-

dings or Tarts).—INGREDIENTS *for sufficient for 1 large pudding.*—½ pint of milk, 4 eggs, 3 oz. of pounded sugar, 1 tablespoonful of brandy. AVERAGE COST, 5d.

Put the milk in a very clean saucepan, and let it boil. Beat the eggs, stir to them the milk and pounded sugar, and put the

mixture into a jug. Place the jug in a saucepan of boiling water; keep stirring well until it thickens, but do not allow it to boil, or it will curdle. Serve the sauce in a tureen, stir in the brandy, and grate a little nutmeg over the top. This sauce may be made very much nicer by using cream instead of milk; but the above recipe will be found quite good enough for ordinary purposes.

Custard Tartlets, or Fan-

chonnettes.—INGREDIENTS *for 12 tartlets* —*For the custard,* 4 eggs, ¾ pint of milk, 2 oz. of butter, 2 oz. of pounded sugar, 3 dessertspoonfuls of flour, flavouring to taste; the whites of 2 eggs, 2 oz. of pounded sugar AVERAGE COST, 1s.

Well beat the eggs, stir to them the milk, the butter, which should be beaten to a cream, the sugar, and flour; mix these ingredients well together, put them into a very clean saucepan, and bring them to the simmering point, but do not allow them to boil. Flavour with essence of vanilla, bitter almonds, lemon, grated chocolate, or any flavouring ingredient that may be preferred. Line some round tartlet-pans with good puff-paste; fill them with the custard, and bake in a moderate oven for about 20 minutes; then take them out of the pans; let them cool, and in the meantime whisk the whites of the eggs to a stiff froth; stir into this the pounded sugar, and spread smoothly over the tartlets a little of this mixture. Put them in the oven again to set the icing, but be particular that they do not scorch; when the icing looks crisp, they are done. Arrange them, piled high in the centre, on a white napkin or paper.

TIME.—20 *minutes to bake the tartlets;* 5 *minutes after being iced.*

SEASONABLE at any time.

Note.—The icing may be omitted on the top of the tartlets, and a spoonful of any kind of preserve put at the bottom of the custard instead: this varies both the flavour and appearance of this dish.

Cutlet, The Invalid's.

INGREDIENTS *for cutlet for 1 person.* — 1 *nice cutlet from a loin or neck of mutton*, 2 *tea-cupfuls of water*, 1 *very small stick of celery, pepper and salt to taste.* AVERAGE COST, 5d.

Have the cutlet cut from a very nice loin or neck of mutton; take off all the fat; put it into a stewpan, with the other ingredients; stew *very gently* indeed for nearly 2 hours, and skim off every particle of fat that may rise to the surface from time to time. The celery should be cut into thin slices before it is added to the meat, and care must be taken not to put in too much of this ingredient, or the dish will not be good. If the water is allowed to boil fast, the cutlet will be hard.

TIME.—2 *hours' very gentle stewing.*
SEASONABLE *at any time.*

Cutlets, Mutton, Italian.

INGREDIENTS *for dish for 6 persons.* — *About* 3 *lbs. of the neck of mutton, clarified butter, the yolk of* 1 *egg,* 4 *tablespoonfuls of bread-crumbs,* 1 *tablespoonful of minced savoury herbs,* 1 *tablespoonful of minced parsley,* 1 *teaspoonful of minced shalot,* 1 *saltspoonful of finely-chopped lemon-peel; pepper, salt, and pounded mace to taste; flour,* ½ *pint of hot broth or water,* 2 *teaspoonfuls of Harvey's sauce,* 1 *teaspoonful of soy,* 2 *teaspoonfuls of tarragon vinegar,* 1 *tablespoonful of port wine.* AVERAGE COST, 2s. 6d.

Cut the mutton into nicely-shaped cutlets, flatten them, and trim off some of the fat, dip them in clarified butter, and then into the beaten yolk of an egg. Mix well together bread-crumbs, herbs, parsley, shalot, lemon-peel, and seasoning in the above proportion, and cover the cutlet with these ingredients. Melt some butter in a frying-pan, lay in the cutlets, and fry them a nice brown; take them out, and keep them hot before the fire. Dredge some flour into the pan, and, if there is no sufficient butter, add a little more; stir till it looks brown, then put in the hot broth or water, and the remaining ingredients give one boil, and pour round the cutlets. If the gravy should not be thick enough add a little more flour. Mushrooms, when obtainable, are a great improvement to this dish, and when not in season mushroom-powder may be substituted for them.

TIME.—10 *minutes; rather longer should the cutlets be very thick.*
SEASONABLE *at any time.*

Cutlets of Cold Mutton. (Cold

Meat Cookery.) — INGREDIENTS.—*The remains of cold loin or neck of mutton,* 1 *egg, bread-crumbs, brown gravy or tomato sauce.* AVERAGE COST, *exclusive of the meat*, 3d.

Cut the remains of cold loin or neck of mutton into cutlets, trim them, and take away a portion of the fat, should there be too much; dip them in beaten egg, and sprinkle with bread-crumbs, and fry them a nice brown in hot dripping. Arrange them on a dish, and pour round them either a good gravy or hot tomato sauce.

TIME.—*About* 7 *minutes.*
SEASONABLE *at any time.*

CUTLETS AND PEAS.

" Dinner we have heard to be the strongest line defining
The difference 'twixt man and beast, the former only dining."

DAMPFNUDELN.

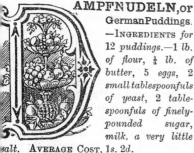

DAMPFNUDELN, or German Puddings. —INGREDIENTS *for 12 puddings.*—1 *lb. of flour,* ¼ *lb. of butter,* 5 *eggs,* 2 *small tablespoonfuls of yeast,* 2 *tablespoonfuls of finely-pounded sugar, milk, a very little salt.* AVERAGE COST, 1s. 2d.

Put the flour into a basin, make a hole in the centre, into which put the yeast, and rather more than ¼ pint of warm milk; make this into a batter with the middle of the flour, and let the sponge rise in a warm temperature. When sufficiently risen, mix the eggs, butter, sugar and salt, with a little more warm milk, and knead the whole well together with the hands, beating the dough until it is perfectly smooth, and it drops from the fingers. Then cover the basin with a cloth, put it in a warm place, and when the dough has nicely risen, knead it into small balls; butter the bottom of a deep sauté-pan, strew over some pounded sugar, and let the dampfnudeln be laid in, but do not let them touch one another;

DAMSON CHEESE.

then pour over sufficient milk to cover them, put on the lid and let them rise to twice their original size by the side of the fire. Now place them in the oven for a few minutes to acquire a nice brown colour, and serve them on a napkin, with custard sauce flavoured with vanilla, or a compôte of any fruit that may be preferred.

TIME.—½ to ¾ *hour for the sponge to rise;* 10 *to* 15 *minutes for the puddings to rise;* 10 *minutes to bake them in a brisk oven.*

SEASONABLE *at any time.*

Damson Cheese.— INGREDIENTS, 1½ *pint of damsons to each pot.*—*Damsons; to every lb. of fruit pulp allow* ½ *lb. of loaf sugar.* AVERAGE COST, 10d. *per small pot.*

Pick the stalks from the damsons, and put them into a preserving-pan; simmer them over the fire until they are soft, occasionally stirring them; then beat them through a coarse sieve, and put the pulp and juice into the preserving-pan, with sugar in the above proportion, having previously carefully weighed them. Stir the sugar well in, and simmer the damsons slowly for 2 hours. Skim well, then boil the preserve quickly for ½ hour, or until it looks firm and hard in the spoon; put it quickly into shallow pots, or very tiny earthenware moulds, and when cold, cover it, with oiled papers, and the jars with tissue-paper brushed over on both sides with the white of an egg. A few of the stones may be cracked, and the kernels boiled with the damsons, which very much improves the flavour of the cheese.

TIME.—*1 hour to boil the damsons without the sugar; 2 hours to simmer them slowly, ½ hour quickly.*

SEASONABLE.—*Make this in September or October.*

Damson Jam.—INGREDIENTS, 1½ pint of damsons to each lb. pot.—Damsons; to every lb. of fruit allow ¾ lb. of loaf sugar. AVERAGE COST, 6d. per pot.

Have the fruit gathered in dry weather, pick it over, and reject any that is at all blemished. Stone the damsons, weigh them, and to every lb. allow ¾ lb. of loaf sugar. Put the fruit and sugar into a preserving-pan; keep stirring them gently until the sugar is dissolved, and carefully

remove the scum as it rises. Boil the jam for about an hour, reckoning from the time it commences to simmer all over alike; it must be well stirred all the time, or it will be liable to burn and stick to the pan, which will cause the jam to have a very disagreeable flavour. When the jam looks firm, and

DAMSONS.

the juice appears to set, it is done; then take it off the fire, put it into pots, cover it down, when quite cold, with oiled and egged papers, and store it away in a dry place.

TIME.—*1 hour after the jam simmers all over.*

SEASONABLE.—*Make this in September or October.*

Damson Pudding.—INGREDIENTS for pudding for 6 persons.—1½ pint of damsons, ¼ lb. of moist sugar, ¾ lb. of suet or butter crust. AVERAGE COST, 10d.

Make a suet crust with ¾ lb. of flour by recipe; line a buttered pudding-basin with a portion of it; fill the basin with the damsons, sweeten them, and put on the lid, pinch the edges of the crust together, that the juice does not escape; tie over a floured cloth, put the pudding into boiling water, and boil from 2½ to 3 hours.

TIME.—*2½ to 3 hours.*

SEASONABLE *in September and October.*

Damson Tart.—INGREDIENTS for small tart.—1½ pint of damsons, ¼ lb. of moist sugar, ½ lb. of short or puff crust. AVERAGE COST, 10d.

Put the damsons, with the sugar between them, into a deep pie-dish, in the midst of which place a small cup or jar turned upside down; pile the fruit high in the middle, line the edges of the dish with short or puff crust, whichever may be preferred; put on the cover, ornament the edges, and bake from ½ to ¾ hour in a good oven. If puff-crust is used, about 10 minutes before the pie is done take it out of the oven, brush it over with the white of an egg beaten to a froth with the blade of a knife; strew some sifted sugar over, and a few drops of water, and put the tart back to finish baking: with short crust, a little plain sifted sugar, sprinkled over, is all that will be required.

TIME.—*½ to ¾ hour.*

SEASONABLE *in September and October.*

Damsons, Baked (for Winter Use) —INGREDIENTS.—*To every lb. of fruit allow 6 oz. of pounded sugar; melted mutton suet.*

Choose sound fruit, not too ripe; pick off the stalks, weigh it, and to every lb. allow the above proportion of pounded sugar. Put the fruit into large dry stone jars, sprinkling the sugar amongst it; cover the jars with saucers, place them in a rather cool oven, and bake the fruit until it is quite tender. When cold, cover the top of the fruit with a piece of white paper cut to the size of the jar; pour over this melted mutton suet about an inch thick, and cover the tops of the jars with thick brown paper well tied down. Keep the jars in a cool dry place, and the fruit will remain good till the following Christmas, but not much longer.

TIME.—*From 5 to 6 hours to bake the damsons in a very cool oven.*

SEASONABLE *in September and October.*

Damsons, Compôte of.— INGRE-
DIENTS *for dish for 4 or 5 persons.*—1 *quart of damsons,* 1 *pint of syrup (see* SYRUP). AVERAGE COST, 9d.

Procure sound ripe damsons, pick the stalks from them, and put them into boiling syrup made by the recipe. Simmer them gently until the fruit is tender, but not sufficiently soft to break; take them up, boil the syrup for 5 minutes, pour it over the damsons, and serve. This should be sent to table in a glass dish.

TIME.—*About ¼ hour to simmer the damsons; 5 minutes to boil the syrup.*

SEASONABLE *in September and October.*

Damsons, Preserved.—INGREDI-
ENTS.—*To every quart of damsons allow ½ lb. of loaf sugar.* AVERAGE COST, 6d. *per quart.*

Put the damsons (which should be picked from the stalks and quite free from blemishes) into a jar, with pounded sugar sprinkled amongst them in the above proportion; tie the jar closely down, set it in a saucepan of cold water; bring it gradually to boil, and simmer gently until the damsons are soft, without being broken. Let them stand till cold; then strain the juice from them, boil it up well, strain it through a jelly-bag, and pour it over the fruit. Let it cool, cover with oiled papers,

and the jars with tissue-paper, brushed over on both sides with the white of an egg, and store away in a dry place.

TIME.—*About ¾ hour to simmer the fruit after the water boils; ¼ hour to boil the juice.*

SEASONABLE.—*Make this in September or October.*

Damsons, or any kind of Plums, To Preserve. (Useful in Winter.)
—INGREDIENTS.—*Damsons or plums; boiling water.* AVERAGE COST, 6d. *per quart.*

Pick the fruit into clean, dry stone jars. taking care to leave out all that are broken or blemished. When full, pour boiling water on the plums, until it stands one inch above the fruit; cut a piece of paper to fit the inside of the jar, over which pour melted mutton-suet; cover down with brown paper, and keep the jars in a dry, cool place. When used, the suet should be removed, the water poured off, and the jelly at the bottom of the jar used and mixed with the fruit.

SEASONABLE *in September and October.*

Darioles à la Vanille. (Sweet Entremets)—INGREDIENTS *for 6 or 7 darioles.*—½ *pint of milk,* ½ *pint of cream,* 2 oz. *of flour,* 3 oz. *of pounded sugar,* 6 *eggs,* 2 oz. *of butter, puff-paste, flavouring of essence of vanilla.* AVERAGE COST, 1s. 8d.

Mix the flour to a smooth batter, with the milk; stir in the cream, sugar, the eggs, which should be well whisked, and the butter, which should be beaten to a cream. Put in some essence of vanilla, drop by drop, until the mixture is well flavoured; line some dariole-moulds with puff-paste, three-parts fill them with the batter, and bake in a good oven from 25 to 35 minutes. Turn them out of the moulds on a dish, without breaking them; strew over sifted

DARIOLE MOULD.

sugar, and serve. The flavouring of the darioles may be varied by substituting lemon, cinnamon, or almonds for the vanilla.

TIME.—25 *to* 35 *minutes.*

SEASONABLE *at any time.*

Darioles of Eggs.

INGREDIENTS *for* 6 *darioles* —5 *eggs*, 4 *oz. of bread-crumbs, a tomato, a little chopped parsley*, 3 *tablespoonfuls of white sauce, seasoning.* AVERAGE COST, 8*d.*

Boil 3 eggs hard, and chop them and mix them with the other ingredients (the tomato skinned and mashed), and the yolks of 2 eggs raw. Put the mixture in buttered moulds, cover with buttered paper and steam for 20 minutes.

TIME.—20 *minutes.*

SEASONABLE *at any time.*

Darioles of Oysters.

INGREDIENTS *for sufficient to fill* 3 *or* 4 *dariole moulds.*—2 *oz. of flour*, 2 *eggs*, 1 *oz. of butter*, ½ *pint of milk*, 1 *dozen oysters, seasoning of nutmeg, cayenne, salt and lemon-juice.* AVERAGE COST, 1*s.* 6*d.*

· Beard the · oysters and scald them in their own liquor, after which strain and

EDIBLE OYSTERS.

cut each oyster in four pieces. Put the flour and butter in a saucepan with the liquor from the oysters and the milk, and stir till boiling point is reached, when add the seasoning (this dish should be well flavoured), and the eggs previously well beaten. Put in the oysters just long enough to heat them thoroughly, then

pour the mixture into well-buttered dariol moulds, and steam gently for about 2 minutes.

TIME.—20 *minutes.*

SEASONABLE *from September to May.*

Dark Sauce (for Game, Fish, Cutlets and other entrées).

INGREDIENTS.— *An onion*, 2 *tablespoonfuls of flour, a ounce of butter*, ½ *pint of stock or gravy, on glass of port or sherry*, 2 *tablespoonfuls o black currant jam or jelly*, 1 *tablespoonfu of vinegar*, 2 *or* 3 *bay-leaves, a few cloves lemon-peel, salt, pepper and a teaspoonfu of chili vinegar, or some cayenne for season ing.* AVERAGE COST, 9*d. per pint.*

Chop the onion, and put it, with the flou and butter, in a saucepan to brown. Ad the stock with a small piece of lemon-pee and the other ingredients, and when we mixed, boil for about 5 minutes and strain Serve hot with poultry, &c.

TIME.—5 *minutes to boil the sauce.*

SEASONABLE *at any time.*

Note.—This is a nice sauce to serve with warmed-up poultry or game, and has th advantage of being easily and quickly mad with ingredients that are generally at hand i an ordinary household.

Date Pudding.

INGREDIENTS *fo pudding for from* 4 *to* 6 *persons.*—¾ *lb. o dates*, ½ *lb. of suet*, ½ *lb. of bread-crumbs, few almonds, treacle, a saltspoonful of sal* AVERAGE COST, 10*d.*

Chop the suet finely, also the dates afte taking out the stones; blanch the almonds and divide in small pieces. Mix the ingre dients together, adding treacle or golde syrup enough to form it into a paste then put it in a plain mould or basin well buttered, tie it down and boil for hours.

TIME.—2 *hours to boil the pudding.*

SEASONABLE *at any time, but useful fo a winter pudding when fresh fruit scarce.*

December—Dinner for Twelve Persons.

MENU. (*English.*)	Quantity.	Average Cost.		MENU. (*French.*)
		s.	d.	
Caviare.	2 dishes.	1	6	Caviare.
Game Soup.	5 pints.	7	6	Consommé de Gibier.
John Dory.	2 fish.	6	0	Doret.
Filleted Soles.	2 pairs.	4	0	Filets de Soles.
Salmi of Wild Duck.	2 dishes.	6	6	Salmis de Canards Sauvages.
Chicken Cream.	2 mlds.	7	0	Crême de Volaille.
Saddle of Mutton.	1 joint.	10	6	Selle de Mouton.
Potatoes. Brussels Sprouts.	4 lbs. ea.	1	0	Pommes de Terre. Choux.
Snipe.	12 birds.	15	0	Bécassines.
Benedictine Soufflé.	2 dishes.	6	0	Soufflé à la Benedictine.
Golden Jelly.	2 mlds.	4	0	Gelée Dorée
		£3 9	0	

December—Dinner for Ten Persons.

MENU. (*English.*)	Quantity.	Average Cost.		MENU. (*French.*)
		s.	d.	
Gravy Soup.	2 quarts	2	0	Bouillon.
Brill,	1 fish.	4	6	Barbue,
Shrimp Sauce.	2 turs.	1	0	Sauce aux Crevettes.
Scalloped Oysters.	10 shells	7	0	Huîtres à la Poulette.
Mutton Cutlets.	2 dishes.	3	0	Côtelettes de Mouton.
Roast Turkey.	1 bird.	9	0	Dindonneau Roti.
Ham.	1	7	0	Jambon.
Potatoes. Stewed Celery.	3 lb. 3 hd.	1	0	Pommes de Terre. Céleri.
Russian Salad.	2	2	6	Salade à la Russe.
Plum Pudding.	1	4	0	Pouding à la Valentia.
Maraschino Jelly.	2 mlds.	3	6	Gelée au Maraschino.
		£2 4	6	

December—Dinner for Eight Persons.

MENU. (*English.*)	Quantity.	Average Cos .		MENU. (*French.*)
		s.	d.	
Mulligatawny Soup.	3½ pints.	3	2	Soupe de l'Inde.
Cod's Head and Shoulders,	4 lbs.	2	0	Cabillaud,
Oyster Sauce.	2 turs.	3	0	Sauce aux Huîtres.
Pâté de Foie Gras in Aspic Jelly.	1 mould.	3	6	Pâté de Foie Gras en Aspic.
Stewed Sweetbreads.	1 dish.	4	0	Ris de Veau.
Sirloin of Beef,	1 joint.	8	6	Aloyau,
Horseradish Sauce.	1 tur.	0	6	Sauce Raifort.
Potatoes. Artichokes.	3 lbs. ea.	0	9	Pommes de Terre. Artichauts.
Black Game.	2 birds.	6	0	Coqs de Bruyère.
Banana Fritters.	1 dish.	2	0	Beignets de Bananas.
Mince Pies.	10	1	8	Mince Pies.
Cheese Straws.	1 dish.	0	6	Pailles de Parmesan.
		£1 15	7	

December—Dinners for from Six to Twelve Persons.

Menu

Mock Turtle Soup.

Brill,
Lobster Sauce.

Stewed Artichokes.
Hashed Game.

Sirloin of Beef.
Potatoes.
Scotch Kale

Exeter Pudding.
Orange Jelly.

Cheese.

Menu

Oxtail Soup.

Soles with Cream Sauce.

Stuffed Tomatoes.
Beef Olives.

Leg of Mutton.
Potatoes.
Broccoli.

Pheasants.

Charlotte Russe.
Puff-paste Rings.
Lemon Cream.

Menu

Julienne.

Brill,
Shrimp Sauce.

Stewed Pigeons.

Saddle of Mutton.
Potatoes.
Stewed Celery.

Salad.

Plum Pudding.
Trifle.

Menu

Oyster Soup.

Turbot,
Tartare Sauce.

Vol-au-Vent of Chicken.

Sirloin of Beef.
Potatoes.
Cabbage.

Partridges.

Amber Pudding.
Mince Pies.

December—Plain Family Dinners for.

No. 1.

Sunday.—Roast ribs of beef, boned and rolled, horseradish sauce, potatoes, Brussels sprouts.—Mince pies, plain apple charlotte.

Monday.—Pea soup.—Cold beef, winter salad, mashed potatoes.—Apple dumplings baked.

Tuesday.—Cod and oyster sauce.—Stewed beef and vegetables.—Fig pudding.

Wednesday. — Soup. — Leg of mutton, Jerusalem artichokes, potatoes.—Lemon pudding.

Thursday. — Cold mutton, beetroot, mashed potatoes.— Pheasants. — Macaroni cheese.

Friday. — Soles souché. — Roast loin of pork, greens, potatoes.—Cabinet pudding.

Saturday.—Soup.—Mutton rissoles, cold pork, salad, baked potatoes.—Remains of cabinet pudding warmed, with arrowroot sauce.

No. 2.

Sunday.—Roast turkey, sausages, Scotch kale, potatoes.—Mince pies, ground rice pudding.

Monday. — Beef olives —Cold turkey, salad, mashed potatoes.—Sponge cake pudding.

Tuesday. —Fried soles.—Boiled mutton, caper sauce, mashed turnips, potatoes.—Stewed prunes, baked rice pudding.

Wednesday.—Soup made from liquor in which mutton was boiled, bones of turkey, etc.—Hashed mutton, fried potatoes. — Apple charlotte.

Thursday.—Steak and kidney pie, potatoes, greens.—Pheasants.—Apple fritters.

Friday.— Cod cutlets fried and Tartare sauce.—Boiled leg of pork, potatoes, cabbage.—Sago pudding.

Saturday.—Soup.—Cold pork, potatoes, winter salad.—Plain plum pudding.

December—Vegetarian Dinners for.

No. 1.

Pea Soup.

Forcemeat Fritters.
Vegetable Pie.

Savoury Rice.
Mince Pies.

Cheese Salad.

No. 2.

Macaroni Soup.

Vegetable Goose.
Fried Potatoes.

Plum Pudding.
Custard.

Cheese.

December—Dinner Table Decorations for.

Those with hot-houses and their supplies of flowers and foliage at their disposal for table decoration will have no trouble with the floral arrangement of their dinner-tables ; there is always (or should be) an abundance of coloured and green foliage, even if flowers be scarce ; but those not possessing these luxuries are often sorely troubled how to decorate. A plush centre of rich colour such as red or old gold renders but little in the way of flowers necessary ; but if this can be fringed with holly and brown ivy, it adds greatly to its effect. Upon these centre pieces of dark tint, white china vases look better than almost any other kind, and in them growing ferns such as maidenhair or pteris may well take the place of flowers, the cloth itself giving the colour. Tiny palms, too, such as cocus weddeliana, are even more delicate and light in appearance than ferns

Still, for those who consider flowers indispensable, there are some that can be procured. Chrysanthemums of many tints should still be had, and the yellow and brown ones have a soft, rich effect when intermingled. To all decorations for whatever season the same rule applies : whatever flowers are used the receptacles for them should be chosen to harmonize with their mode of growth and colour. Low-growing flowers in high stands, and those with long stalks in squat vases or brackets, being unnatural, can never look well.

Q

December, Things in Season:

Fish.—Brill, cod, crabs, crayfish, dory, eels, flounders, haddocks, halibut, herrings, lobsters, mussels, mullet, oysters, prawns, shrimps, skate, smelts, sprats, soles, turbot, whiting.

Meat.—Beef, house lamb, mutton, pork, doe venison.

Poultry.—Capons, chickens, fowls, geese, pigeons, plovers, pullets, quails, rabbits, teal, turkeys, widgeons, wild duck.

Game. — Hares, partridges, pheasants, snipe, woodcock, grouse.

Vegetables. — Jerusalem artichokes, broccoli, cabbages, carrots, celery, leeks, onions, potatoes, parsnips, Scotch kale, turnips, winter spinach.

Fruit. — Apples, chestnuts, filberts, grapes, medlars, oranges, pears, walnuts.

Dessert.—With moderns the dessert is not so profuse, nor does it hold the same relationship to the dinner that it held with the ancients—the Romans more especially. On ivory tables they would spread hundreds of different kinds of raw, cooked, and preserved fruits, tarts and cakes, as substitutes for the more substantial comestibles with which the guests were satiated. However, as late as the reigns of our two last Georges, fabulous sums were often expended upon fanciful desserts. The extravagance in dessert of the present day may be said to be in the flowers and other decorations more than in the fruit, the latter being quite subsidiary to the former. The dessert certainly repays, in its general effect, the expenditure upon it of much pains : and it may be said, that if there be any poetry at all in meals, or the process of feeding, there is poetry in the dessert, the materials for which should be selected with taste, and, of course, must depend, in a great measure, upon the season. Pines, melons, grapes, peaches, nectarines, plums, strawberries, apples, pears, oranges, almonds, raisins,

figs, walnuts, filberts, medlars, cherries &c. &c., all kinds of dried fruits, and choice and delicately-flavoured cakes and biscuits make up the dessert, together with the most costly and *recherché* wines. The shape, pattern and material of the dessert service are subject to changes of fashion ; some persons selecting china chaste in pattern and colour ; others elegantly-shaped glass ones intermingled with gold. The beauty of the dessert services at the tables of the wealthy tend to enhance the splendour of the plate. The garnishing of dessert needs especial attention, as the contrast of the brilliant coloured fruits with nicely-arranged foliage is very charming. Leaves for this purpose should be those of fruit if not of *the* one they decorate. Strawberry, and vine leaves have a pleasing effect ; and for winter desserts, the bay, cuba and laurel are sometimes used. A dessert would not now be considered complete without candied and preserved fruits and confections. The candied fruits may be purchased at a less cost than they can be manufactured at home. They are preserved abroad in most ornamental and elegant forms. And since, from the facilities of travel, we have become so familiar with the tables of the French, chocolate in different forms is indispensable to our desserts. Olives too, should not be omitted ; these should be served in a small, deep glass dish.

Dessert Biscuits (which may be flavoured with ground ginger, cinnamon &c.)—INGREDIENTS *for* 4 *dishes of biscuits.*—1 *lb. of flour,* ½ *lb. of butter,* ½ *lb. of sifted sugar, the yolks of* 6 *eggs, flavouring to taste.* AVERAGE COST, 1*s.* 6*d.*

Put the butter into a basin ; warm it, but do not allow it to oil ; then with the hand beat it to a cream. Add the flour by degrees, then the sugar and flavouring, and moisten the whole with the yolks of the eggs, which should previously be well beaten. When all the ingredients are

thoroughly incorporated, drop the mixture
from a spoon on to a buttered paper, leaving a distance between each cake, for they
spread as soon as they begin to get warm.
Bake in rather a slow oven from 12 to 18
minutes, and do not let the biscuits acquire too much colour. In making the
above quantity, half may be flavoured with
ground ginger and the other half with es-
ence of lemon or currants, to make a
variety. With whatever the preparation
is flavoured, so are the biscuits called, and
an endless variety may be made in this
manner.

Time.—12 to 18 minutes, or rather longer,
in a very slow oven.

Dessert Dishes.—The usual dishes
for fruit are compôtes of various heights,
and the fruit can be arranged and shown to
better advantage on these dishes than on the
short flat ones. The fruit should always
be gathered on the same day that it is
required for table, and should be tastefully
arranged on the dishes, with leaves between
and round it. By purchasing fruits that
are in season, a dessert can be supplied at
very moderate cost. These, with a few
fancy biscuits, crystallised fruit, bon-bons,
&c., are sufficient for an ordinary dessert.
When fresh fruit cannot be obtained, dried
and foreign fruits, compôtes, baked pears,
stewed Normandy pippins, &c. &c., must
supply its place, with the addition of
crystallised biscuits, &c. In decorating a
table, whether for luncheon, dessert, or
supper, a vase or two of flowers should
never be forgotten, as they add so much to
the elegance of the tout ensemble. In
summer and autumn, ladies residing in the
country can always manage to have a few
freshly-gathered flowers on their tables,
and should never be without this inexpensive luxury. On the Continent, vases
or epergnes filled with flowers are invariably placed down the centre of the dinner-
table at regular distances. Ices for dessert

are usually moulded; when this is not the
case, they are handed round in glasses,
with wafers to accompany them. Each
fruit should be served on a separate dish,
and no strong-smelling fruits should be put
upon the table during dinner; many
people have only floral or foliage decoration, and the dessert put on afterwards.
A basin or glass of finely-pounded lump
sugar must never be omitted at a dessert,
as also a glass jug of fresh cold water (iced,
in summer), and two goblets by its side.
Grape scissors, a melon-knife and fork,
and nutcrackers, should always be put on
table, if there are dishes of fruit requiring
them. Finger-glasses are placed at the
right of each person, nearly half filled with
cold spring water, and in winter with tepid
water. After the dishes are placed, and
every one is provided with plates, glasses,
spoons, &c., the wine should be put at
each end of the table, cooled or otherwise,
according to the season. If the party be
small, the wine may be placed only at the
top of the table, near the host. The
following dishes may be introduced at
dessert, according to season:—

Almonds and Raisins. — These are
usually served on glass dishes, the fruit

ALMONDS AND RAISINS.

piled high in the centre, and the almonds
blanched and strewn over. To blanch the
almonds, put them into a small mug or
teacup, pour over them boiling water, let
them remain for 2 or 3 minutes, and the
skins may then be easily removed. Figs,
dates, French plums, &c., are all served
on small glass plates or oval dishes, but
without the almonds.

Seasonable at any time, but more suitable in winter, when fresh fruit is not
obtainable.

Apples.—The apples should be nicely wiped with a dry cloth, and arranged on a dish, piled high in the centre, with evergreen leaves between each layer. The inferior apples should form the bottom layer, with the bright-coloured large ones at the top. The leaves of the laurel, bay,

APPLES.

holly, or any shrub green in winter are suitable for garnishing dessert dishes. Oranges may be arranged in the same manner; they should also be wiped with a dry cloth before being sent to table.

Apricots, Peaches, Plums, Nectarines or Green Figs. — The beautiful colouring of these fruits, which should be

GREEN FIGS.

arranged separately, renders anything more than a few green leaves for garnish superfluous.

SEASONABLE *in autumn.*

Bananas.—These are not a pretty fruit, and require the garnish of some bright-green foliage.

Box of Chocolate.—This is served in an ornamental box, placed on a glass plate or dish.

SEASONABLE.—*May be purchased at any time.*

Box of French Plums. — If the box which contains them is exceedingly orna-

mental, it may be placed on the table; small, on a glass dish; if large, withou

BOX OF CHOCOLATE.

one. French plums may also be arrange on a glass plate, and garnished with bright coloured sweetmeats, which make a ver good effect. All fancy boxes of preserve and crystallised fruit may be put on t

BOX OF FRENCH PLUMS.

table or not, at pleasure. These littl matters of detail must, of course, be le to individual taste.

SEASONABLE.—*May be purchased all t year; but are in greater perfection in t winter.*

Currants, Cherries, Gooseberries **Raspberries.**—These small fruits look we in fruit baskets, the handles twined wi green creeper. White and red curran may be blended with good effect.

SEASONABLE *in summer.*

Dish of Nuts.—These are mere arranged piled high in the centre of t dish, as shown in the engraving, with

DISH OF FILBERTS.

without leaves round the edge. Filbe should always be served with the ou skin or husk on them; and walnuts shou be well wiped with a damp cloth, and th th a dry one, to remove the unpleasant icky feeling the shells frequently have.

SEASONABLE.—*Filberts from September March; walnuts from September to nuary.*

Dish of Strawberries. — Fine strawrries, arranged with the stalks inwards. ok exceedingly well. The inferior ones ould be placed at the bottom of the dish, d the others put in rows pyramidically, th the stalks downwards, so that when e whole is completed, nothing but the red

STRAWBERRY DISH.

rt of the fruit is visible. The fruit should gathered with rather long stalks, as there then something to support it, and it can placed more upright in each layer. A w of the finest should be reserved to crown e top; if to be served with cream, the lks should be removed.

SEASONABLE *in June and July.*

Grapes, White and Black. — These autiful fruits may be blended with excelt effect, and should always be arranged

GRAPES.

th their own leaves, as easily and natury as possible, only touching the stalks for s purpose, and leaving them to show at e top. Where the dishes in which they

are put admit, grapes look well hanging a little over the edge.

SEASONABLE. — *Can be bought all the year; best in autumn.*

Pine and Melon. — A few vine leaves should first be placed upon the dish. Pines should be stood upright, and a slice cut from the bottom if they will not stand with-

PINE.

out. A small melon should be placed stalk upward; a large one laid on its side.

MELON.

Devilled Biscuits.—INGREDIENTS *for dish for 6 persons.*—8 *milk biscuits,* 1½ *oz. of butter, cayenne and salt.* AVERAGE COST, 3*d.*

Butter the biscuits well on both sides, seasoning with cayenne and a little salt, and put them in a tin in the oven to get thoroughly hot.

SEASONABLE *at any time.*

Devilled Lobster.—INGREDIENTS

for dish for 4 or 5 persons.—A large lobster,
some salad dressing, cayenne and finely-
grated bread-crumbs. AVERAGE COST,
2s. 6d.

Cut the meat in small dice. Make a salad
dressing, using butter in the place of oil,
mix it with the lobster, adding cayenne and
3 tablespoonfuls of bread-crumbs. Put the
mixture in the shell, put some bread crumbs
and bits of butter over the top, and bake
for 20 minutes, or a little more if not well
browned in that time.

TIME.—20 *minutes.*
SEASONABLE *at any time.*

Devilled Oysters. — INGREDIENTS

for dish for 4 persons.—2 dozen oysters,
cayenne, salt, 2 oz. of butter. AVERAGE
COST, 3s. 3d.

Open the oysters without spilling the
liquor. Put under each oyster in the shell
a very little salt, and a good seasoning of
cayenne, and on the top of each a little
piece of butter. Put them on a gridiron
over a bright clear fire for about 4 or 5
minutes, and serve with thin brown bread-
and-butter.

TIME.—4 *or 5 minutes.*
SEASONABLE *from September to May.*

Devonshire Junket.—INGREDI-

ENTS *for dish for 6 persons.—1 pint of new*
milk, 2 dessertspoonfuls of brandy, 1 dessert-
spoonful of sugar, and 1½ dessertspoonful
of prepared rennet; thick cream, pounded
cinnamon, or grated nutmeg. AVERAGE
COST, 10d.

Make the milk blood-warm; put it into
a deep dish with the brandy, sugar, and
rennet; stir it all together, and cover it
over until it is set. Then spread some
thick or clotted cream over the top, grate
some nutmeg, and strew some sugar over,
and the dish will be ready to serve.

TIME.—*About 2 hours to set the milk.*
SEASONABLE *at any time.*

Dinner, being the grand solid meal
the day, is a matter of considerable in
portance; and a well-served table is a stri
ing index of human ingenuity and resourc

The elegance with which a dinner
served depends, of course, partly upon th
means, but still more upon the taste of t
master and mistress of the house. It m
be observed, in general, that there shou
always be flowers on the table, and,
they form no item of expense where a ga
den is, there is no reason why they shou
not be employed every day.

The variety of the dishes which furni
forth a modern dinner-table does n
necessarily imply anything unwholeson
or anything capricious. Food that is n
well relished cannot be well digested; a
the appetite of the overworked man
business, or statesman, or of any dwell
in towns, whose occupations are exciti
and exhausting, is jaded, and requir
stimulation. Men and women who are
rude health, and who have plenty of a
and exercise, eat the simplest food wi
relish, and commonly digest it well; b
those conditions are out of the reach
many men. They must suit their mode
dining to their mode of living, if they ca
not choose the latter. It is in serving
food that is at once appetising and who
some that the skill of the modern hous
wife is severely tasked; and she h
scarcely a more important duty to fulf
It is, in fact, her particular vocation,
virtue of which she may be said to ho
the health of the family, and of t
friends of the family, in her hands fro
day to day.

The following aphorisms and sho
directions in relation to dinner-parti
are well deserving of notice:—"Let t
number of your guests never exce
twelve, so that the conversation may
general. Let the temperature of t
dining-room be about 68°. Let the dishe
if few in number, be proportionally goo
To invite a person to your house is

ake charge of his happiness so long as
.e is beneath your roof. The mistress of
he house should always be certain that
he coffee is excellent; whilst the master
should be answerable for the quality of his
vines and liqueurs."

Dinners à la Russe are now so general as
o need no comment here. The dishes are
ut up on a sideboard, and handed round
o the guests, and each dish may be con-
idered a course. They should not be
ttempted if there be not sufficient ser-
ants to wait, or without an experienced
arver amongst them; but even if the
oints and birds are put upon the table,
verything else may be handed. The table
or a dinner à la Russe should be laid with
lowers, plants and foliage, and (if liked)
ome of the dessert dishes. A *menu* or
ill of fare should be placed by the side of
ach guest.

Dormers.

(Cold Meat Cookery.)—
INGREDIENTS *for dish for 2 or 3 persons.—
lb. of cold mutton, 2 oz. of beef suet, pep-
er and salt to taste, 3 oz. of boiled rice, 1
gg, bread-crumbs, made gravy.* AVERAGE
COST, *exclusive of the meat, 4d.*

Chop the meat, suet, and rice finely; mix
vell together, and add a high seasoning of
epper and salt, and roll into sausages;
over them with egg and bread-crumbs,
nd fry in hot dripping of a nice brown.
erve in a dish with made gravy poured
ound them, and a little in a tureen.

TIME.—¼ *hour to fry the sausages.*
SEASONABLE *at any time.*

Draught for Summer.

—INGREDI-
NTS.—*The juice of 1 lemon, a tumblerful
f cold water, pounded sugar to taste, ½
mall teaspoonful of carbonate of soda.*

Squeeze the juice from the lemon; strain,
nd add it to the water, with sufficient
ounded sugar to sweeten the whole nicely.
Vhen well mixed, put in the soda, stir
vell, and drink while the mixture is in an
ffervescing state.

Drink, Pleasant, for Warm Weather.

—INGREDIENTS. — *To every ½
pint of good ale allow 1 bottle of ginger beer.*

For this beverage the ginger beer must
be in an effervescing state, and the beer
not in the least turned or sour. Mix them
together and drink immediately. The
draught is refreshing and wholesome, as
the ginger corrects the action of the beer.
It does not deteriorate by standing a little,
but, of course, is better when taken fresh.

Dripping, To Clarify.

—Good and
fresh dripping answers very well for
basting everything except game and
poultry, and, when well clarified, serves
for frying nearly as well as lard; it should
be kept in a cool place, and will remain
good some time. To clarify it put the
dripping into a basin, pour over it boiling
water, and keep stirring the whole to wash
away the impurities. Let it stand to cool,
when the water and dirty sediment will
settle at the bottom of the basin. Remove
the dripping, and put it away in jars or
basins for use.

Another Way.—Put the dripping into a
clean saucepan, and let it boil for a few
minutes over a slow fire, and be careful to
skim it well. Let it stand to cool a little,
then strain through a piece of muslin into
jars for use. Beef dripping is preferable
to any other for cooking purposes, as, with
mutton dripping, there is liable to be a
tallowy taste and smell.

Drop Cakes.

—INGREDIENTS *for 12
cakes.—2 cupfuls of sugar, pounded, 2 oz.
of flour, 1 oz. of butter, 2 eggs, salt.* AVER-
AGE COST, 1s.

Beat the butter with half the sugar,
whisk the eggs, add them with the remainder of the ingredients, and beat for
15 minutes. Drop the mixture on buttered
tins, and bake for 15 minutes in a moderate
oven.

TIME.—½ *hour.*
SEASONABLE *at any time.*

Duck and Peas, Stewed. (Cold Meat Cookery.)

INGREDIENTS *for dish sufficient for 4 persons.*—*The remains of cold roast duck, 2 oz. of butter, 3 or 4 slices of lean ham or bacon, 1 tablespoonful of flour, 2 pints of thin gravy, 1, or a small bunch of green onions, 3 sprigs of parsley, 3 cloves, 1 pint of young green peas, cayenne and salt to taste, 1 teaspoonful of pounded sugar.* AVERAGE COST, *exclusive of the duck, 1s. 3d.*

Put the butter into a stewpan; cut up the duck into joints, lay them in with the slices of lean ham or bacon; make it brown, then dredge in a tablespoonful of flour, and stir this well in before adding the gravy. Put in the onion, parsley, cloves, and gravy, and when it has simmered for ¼ hour, add a pint of young green peas, and stew gently for about ½ hour. Season with cayenne, salt, and sugar; take out the duck, place it round the dish, and the peas in the middle.

TIME.—¾ *hour.*

SEASONABLE *from June to August.*

Duck and Peas, Stewed. (Cold Meat Cookery.)

INGREDIENTS *for dish sufficient for 4 persons.*—*The remains of cold roast duck, ½ pint of good gravy, cayenne and salt to taste, ½ teaspoonful of minced lemon-peel, 1 teaspoonful of pounded sugar, 2 oz. of butter rolled in flour, 1½ pint of green peas.* AVERAGE COST, *exclusive of duck, 1s.*

Cut up the duck into joints, lay it in the gravy, and add a seasoning of cayenne, salt, and minced lemon-peel; let this gradually warm through, but not boil. Throw the peas into boiling water slightly salted, and boil them rapidly until tender. Drain them, stir in the pounded sugar, and the butter rolled in flour; shake them over the fire for 2 or 3 minutes, and serve in the centre of the dish, with the duck laid round.

TIME.—15 *minutes to boil the peas, when they are full grown.*

SEASONABLE *from June to August.*

Duck, Hashed. (Cold Meat Cookery.)

INGREDIENTS.—*The remains of cold roast duck, rather more than 1 pint of weak stock or water, 1 onion, 1 oz. of butter, thickening of butter and flour, salt and cayenne to taste, ½ teaspoonful of minced lemon-peel, 1 dessertspoonful of lemon-juice, ½ glass of port wine.* AVERAGE COST, *exclusive of cold duck, 4d.*

Cut the duck into nice joints, and put the trimmings into a stewpan; slice and fry the onion in a little butter; add these to the trimmings, pour in the above proportion of weak stock or water, and stew gently for 1 hour. Strain the liquor, thicken it with butter and flour, season with salt and cayenne, and add the remaining ingredients; boil it up and skim well; lay in the pieces of duck, and let them get thoroughly hot through by the side of the fire, but do not allow them to

AYLESBURY DUCKS.

boil; they should soak in the gravy for about ½ hour. Garnish with sippets of toasted bread. The hash may be made richer by using a stronger and more highly flavoured gravy; a little spice or pounded mace may also be added, when their flavour is liked.

TIME.—1½ *hour.*

SEASONABLE *from November to February; ducklings from May to August.*

Ducks, Roast.

INGREDIENTS.—*A couple of ducks; sage-and-onion stuffing, a little flour.* AVERAGE COST, 5s. to 7s. *per pair.*

Choosing and Trussing.—Choose ducks ith plump bellies, and with thick and ellowish feet. They should be trussed ith the feet on, which should be scalded, nd the skin peeled off, and then turned p close to the legs. Run a skewer rough the middle of each leg, after aving drawn them as close as possible to e body, to plump up the breast, passing e same quite through the body. Cut off e heads and necks, and the pinions at the rst joint; bring these close to the sides, vist the feet round, and truss them at the ack of the bird. After the duck is tuffed, both ends should be secured with tring, so as to keep in the seasoning.

To insure ducks being tender, never ress them the same day they are killed; nd, if the weather permits, they should ang a day or two. Make a stuffing of age and onion sufficient for one duck, and eave the other unseasoned, as the flavour not liked by everybody. Put them down a brisk clear fire, and keep them well asted the whole of the time they are ooking. A few minutes before serving, redge them lightly with flour, to make

ROAST DUCK.

hem froth and look plump; and when the team draws towards the fire, send them to able hot and quickly, with a good brown ravy poured *round*, but not *over* the ucks, and a little of the same in a tureen. Vhen in season, green peas should invariably accompany this dish.

TIME.—*Full-grown ducks from ¾ to 1 our; ducklings from 25 to 35 minutes.*

SEASONABLE.—*Ducklings from April to ugust; ducks from November to February.*

Duck, Roast, To Carve.—No ishes require so much knowledge and

skill in their carving as do game and poultry; for it is necessary to be well acquainted with the anatomy of the bird in order to place the knife at exactly the proper point. A tough fowl and an old goose are sad triers of a carver's powers and temper, and, indeed, sometimes of the good humour of those in the neighbourhood of the carver; for a sudden tilt of the dish may eventuate in the placing of a quantity of the gravy in the lap of the right or left-hand supporter of the host. We will endeavour to assist those who are unacquainted with the " gentle art of carving," and also those who are but slightly acquainted with it, by simply describing the rules to follow, and referring to the distinctly-marked illustrations of each dish, which will further help to bring

LEG, WING, AND NECKBONE OF DUCK.

light to the minds of the uninitiated. If the bird be a young duckling, it may be carved like a fowl, *viz.*, by first taking off the leg and the wing on either side; but in cases where the duckling is very small, it will be as well not to separate the leg from the wing, as they will not then form too large a portion for a single serving. After the legs and wings are disposed of, the remainder of the duck will be also carved in the same manner as a fowl; and not much difficulty will be experienced, as ducklings are tender, and the joints are easily broken by a little gentle forcing, or penetrated by the knife. In cases where the duck is a large bird, the better plan to pursue is then to carve it like a goose, that is, by cutting pieces from the breast in the direction indicated by the lines marked from A to B, commencing to carve the slices close to the wing, and then proceeding upwards from that to the breastbone. If more should be wanted than can be obtained from both sides of the breast, then the legs and wings must be attacked, in the same way as is described in connection with carving a fowl. It may be here remarked, that as the legs of a duck are placed far more backward than those of a fowl, their position causing the waddling motion of the bird, the thigh-bones will be found considerably nearer towards the backbone than in a chicken; this is the only difference worth mentioning. The carver should ask each guest if a portion of stuffing would be agreeable, and in order to get at this, a cut should be

ROAST DUCK.

made below the breast, as shown by the line from C to D, at the part called the "apron," and the spoon inserted. (As described in the recipe, it is an excellent plan, when a couple of ducks are served, to have one with, and the other without, stuffing.) As to the prime parts of a duck, it has been said that " the wing of a flier and the leg of a swimmer " are severally the best portions. Some persons are fond of the feet of the duck; and, in trussing, these should never be taken off. The leg, wing, and neckbone are here shown; so that it will be easy to see the shape they should be when cut off.

Note.—Ducklings are trussed and roasted in the same manner, and served with the same sauces and accompaniments. When in season do not omit apple sauce.

Duck, Stewed, with Turnips.

(Cold Meat Cookery.)—INGREDIENTS.—*The remains of cold duck, ½ pint of good gravy, 4 shalots, a few slices of carrot, a small bunch of savoury herbs, 1 blade of pounded mace, 1 lb. of turnips weighed after being peeled, 2 oz. of butter, pepper and salt to taste.* AVERAGE COST, *exclusive of the cold duck, 9d.*

Cut up the duck into joints, fry the shalots, carrots and herbs, and put them with the duck, into the gravy. Cut about 1 lb. of turnips into ½-inch squares, put the butter into a stewpan, and stew them till quite tender, which will be in about ½ hour, or rather more; season with pepper and salt, and serve on the centre of the dish, with the duck, &c., laid round.

TIME.—*Rather more than ½ hour to stew the turnips.*

SEASONABLE *from November to February.*

Duck, To Ragout a Whole.—

INGREDIENTS *for dish sufficient for persons.*—1 *large duck, pepper and salt to taste, good beef gravy, 2 onions sliced, sage-leaves, a few leaves of lemon thyme, thickening of butter and flour.* AVERAGE COST, 3s. 6d.

After having emptied and singed the duck, season it inside with pepper and salt, and truss it. Roast it before a clear fire for about 20 minutes, and let it acquire a nice brown colour. Put it into a stewpan with sufficient well-seasoned beef gravy to cover it; slice and fry the onions, and add these, with the sage-leaves and lemon thyme, both of which should be finely minced, to the stock. Simmer gently until the duck is tender; strain, skim, and thicken the gravy with a little butter and flour; boil it up, pour over the duck and serve. When in season about 1½ pint of young green peas, boiled separately, and put in the ragout, very much improve this dish.

TIME.—20 *minutes to roast the duck; 20 minutes to stew it.*

SEASONABLE *from November to February; ducklings from April to August.*

Duck, Wild, Hashed.—Ingredients

for dish sufficient for 4 persons.—The remains of cold roast wild duck, 1 pint of good brown gravy, 2 tablespoonfuls of bread-crumbs, 1 glass of claret, salt, cayenne, and mixed spices to taste; 1 tablespoonful of lemon or Seville orange-juice. Average Cost, *exclusive of the duck,* 10d.

Cut the remains of the duck into neat joints, put them into a stewpan, with all the above ingredients; let them get gradually hot by the side of the fire, and occasionally stir the contents; when on the point of boiling, serve, and garnish the dish with sippets of toasted bread.

Time.—*About ¼ hour.*

Seasonable *from November to February.*

Duck, Wild, Ragout of.—Ingredients

for dish sufficient for 6 persons.—2 wild ducks, 4 shalots, 1 pint of stock (see Stock*), 1 glass of port wine, 1 oz. of butter, a little flour, the juice of ½ lemon, cayenne and salt to taste.* Average Cost, 5s.

Ducks that have been dressed and left from the preceding day will answer for this dish. Cut them into joints, reserve the legs, wings, and breasts until wanted; put the trimmings into a stewpan with the shalots and stock, and let them simmer for about ½ hour, and strain the gravy. Put the butter into a stewpan; when melted, dredge in a little flour, and pour in the gravy made from the bones; give it one boil, and strain it again; add the wine, lemon-juice, and cayenne; lay in the pieces of duck, and let the whole gradually warm through, but do not allow it to boil, or the duck will be hard. The gravy should not be too thick, and should be very highly seasoned. The squeeze of a Seville orange is a great improvement to this dish.

Time.—*About ½ hour to make the gravy; ¼ hour for the duck gradually to warm through.*

Seasonable *from November to February*

Duck, Wild, Roast.—Ingredients.—*Wild duck, flour, butter.* Average Cost, 4s. to 5s. *a brace.*

Carefully pluck and draw them; cut off the heads close to the necks, leaving sufficient skin to turn over, and do not cut off the feet; some twist each leg at the

WILD DUCK.

knuckle, and rest the claws on each side of the breast; others truss them as shown in our illustration. Roast the birds before a quick fire, and, when they are first put down, let them remain for 5 minutes without basting (this will keep the gravy in); afterwards baste plentifully with butter, and a few minutes before serving, dredge them lightly with flour; baste well, and send them to table nicely frothed, and full of gravy. If overdone, the birds will lose their flavour. Serve with a good gravy in the dish, or orange gravy, and send to table with them a cut lemon. To take off the fishy taste which wild fowl sometimes have, baste them for a few minutes with hot water to which have been added an onion and a little salt; then take away the pan, and baste with butter.

Time.—*When liked underdressed, 20 to 25 minutes; well done, 25 to 35 minutes.*

Seasonable *from November to February.*

Duck, Wild, To Carve.—As game

is almost universally served as a dainty, and not as a dish to stand the assaults of an altogether fresh appetite, these dishes are not usually cut up entirely, but only those parts are served of each which are considered the best-flavoured and the primest. Of wild fowl, the breast alone is considered by epicures worth eating, and slices are cut from this, in the direction indicated by the lines, from A to B; if necessary, the leg and the wing can be taken off by passing the knife from C to D,

WILD DUCK.

and by generally following the directions described for carving boiled fowl.

Dumplings, Sussex, or Hard.

—INGREDIENTS for 6 dumplings.—1 lb. of flour, ½ pint of water, ½ saltspoonful of salt. AVERAGE COST, 2d.

Mix the flour and water together to a smooth paste, previously adding a small quantity of salt. Form this into small round dumplings; drop them into boiling water, and boil from ½ to ¾ hour. They may be served with roast or boiled meat; in the latter case they may be cooked with the meat, but should be dropped into the water when it is quite boiling.

TIME.—½ to ¾ hour.
SEASONABLE at any time.

Dutch Flummery.—INGREDIENTS

for quart mould. — 1½ oz. of isinglass or gelatine, the rind and juice of 1 lemon, 1 pint of water, 4 eggs, 1 pint of sherry, madeira, or raisin wine; sifted sugar to taste. AVERAGE COST, 2s. 6d.

Put the water, isinglass, and lemon-rind into a lined saucepan, and simmer gently until the isinglass is dissolved; strain this into a basin, stir in the eggs, which should be well beaten, the lemon-juice, which should be strained, and the wine; sweeten to taste with pounded sugar, mix all well together, pour it into a jug, set this jug in a saucepan of boiling water over the fire, and keep stirring it one way until it thickens; but take care that it does not boil.

Strain it into a mould that has been oile or laid in water for a short time, and put in a cool place to set. A tablespoonful o brandy, stirred in just before it is poure into the mould, improves the flavour of thi dish: it is better if it is made the day be fore it is required for table.

TIME.—¼ hour to simmer the isinglass about ¼ hour to stir the mixture over the fir

SEASONABLE at any time.

Dutch Sauce. (For Fish.) — IN

GREDIENTS.—½ teaspoonful of flour, 2 oz. o butter, 2 tablespoonfuls of vinegar, 4 tabl spoonfuls of water, the yolks of 2 eggs, th juice of ½ lemon; salt to taste. AVERAG COST, 6d.

Put all the ingredients, except the lemon juice, into a stewpan; set it over the fire and keep continually stirring. When it i sufficiently thick, take it off, as it shoul not boil. If, however, it happens to curdle strain the sauce through a tammy, add th lemon-juice, and serve. Taragon vinega may be used instead of plain, and by man is considered far preferable.

Note.—This sauce may be poured hot ove salad, and left to get quite cold, when it shoul be thick, smooth, and somewhat stiff. Excellen salads may be made of hard eggs, or the remain of salt fish flaked nicely from the bone, by poun ing over a little of the above mixture when ho and allowing it to cool.

Dutch Sauce, Green, or Hol

landaise Verte.—INGREDIENTS.—6 table spoonfuls of Béchamel, seasoning to taste o salt and cayenne, a little parsley-green t colour, the juice of ½ a lemon. AVERAG COST, 4d.

Put the Béchamel into a saucepan with the seasoning, and bring it to a boil. Mak a green colouring by pounding some parsle in a mortar, and squeezing all the juic from it. Let this just simmer, when ad it to the sauce. A moment before serving put in the lemon-juice, but not before; fo otherwise the sauce would turn yellow, an its appearance be thus spoiled.

"*Eat with good appetite nor need
Epicurean sauce.*"—OLD BALLAD.

CLAIRS. — INGRE-DIENTS.— 2 oz. of butter, 1 dessert-spoonful of white sugar, 3 eggs, ½ pint of water, ½ lb. of flour, vanilla flavouring. AVERAGE COST, 6d.

Boil the butter and water to-gether, and stir in enough flour to make the mixture thick enough to leave the sides of the sauce-pan, then add the yolks of the eggs and beat well. When cold, add the whites of the eggs beaten to a stiff froth, with the flavouring. Bake either in strips or round cakes in a moderate oven. When cold, they may be glazed with chocolate or other icing, and a slit may be made to hold some whipped and flavoured cream.

TIME.—*About 15 minutes to bake.*
SEASONABLE *at any time.*

Eel Broth. — INGREDIENTS for 1½ pint of broth.—½ lb. of eel, a small bunch of sweet herbs, including parsley, ¼ onion, 10 peppercorns, 3 pints of water, 2 cloves, salt and pepper to taste. AVERAGE COST, 6d.

After having cleaned and skinned the eel, cut it into small pieces, and put it into a stewpan with the other ingredients; simmer gently until the liquid is reduced to nearly half, carefully removing the scum as it rises. Strain it through a hair sieve: put it by in a cool place, and, when wanted, take off all the fat on the top; warm up as much as is required, and serve with sippets of toasted bread. This is a very nutritious broth, and easy of digestion.

TIME.—*To be simmered until the liquor is reduced to half.*
SEASONABLE *from June to March.*

Eel Pie. — INGREDIENTS *for small pie.*—1 lb. of eels, a little chopped parsley, 1 shalot, pepper and salt to taste, the juice of ½ lemon, a small quantity of forcemeat, ¼ pint of Béchamel; puff paste. AVERAGE COST, 1s. 9d.

Skin and wash the eels, cut them in pieces 2 inches long, and line the bottom of the pie-dish with forcemeat. Put in the eels, and sprinkle them with the parsley, shalots, nutmeg, seasoning and lemon-juice, and cover with puff-paste. Bake for 1 hour, or rather more ; make the Béchamel hot, and pour it into the pie.

TIME.—*Rather more than 1 hour.*

SEASONABLE *from August to March.*

Eel Soup.

INGREDIENTS *for soup for 10 persons.*—3 lbs. of eels, 1 onion, 2 oz. of butter, 3 blades of mace, 1 bunch of sweet herbs, ¼ oz. of peppercorns, salt to taste, 2 tablespoonfuls of flour, ¼ pint of cream, 2 quarts of water. AVERAGE COST. 3s.

Wash the eels, cut them into thin slices, and put them into the stewpan with the butter ; let them simmer for a few minutes th.; pour the water to them, and add the onion, cut in thin slices, the herbs, mace and seasoning. Simmer till the eels are tender, but do not break the fish. Take them out carefully, mix the flour smoothly to a batter with the cream, bring it to a boil, pour over the eels, and serve.

TIME.—*1 hour, or rather more.*

SEASONABLE *from June to March.*

Note.—This soup may be flavoured differently by omitting the cream, and adding a little ketchup or Harvey's sauce.

Eels, Boiled.

INGREDIENTS *for dish sufficient for 4 or 5 persons.*—4 small eels, sufficient water to cover them ; a large bunch of parsley. AVERAGE COST, 10d. per lb.

Choose small eels for boiling ; put them into a stewpan with the parsley, and just sufficient water to cover them ; simmer till tender. Take them out, pour a little parsley and butter over them, and serve some in a tureen.

TIME.—*½ hour.*

SEASONABLE *from June to March.*

Eel, Collared.

INGREDIENTS. —1 large eel ; pepper and salt to taste ; 2 blades of mace, 2 cloves, a little allspice very finely pounded, 6 leaves of sage, and a small bunch

of herbs minced very small. AVERAGE COST, 10d. per lb.

Bone the eel and skin it ; split it, and sprinkle it over with the ingredients, taking care that the spices are very finely pounded, and the herbs chopped very small. Roll it up and bind with a broad

COLLARED EEL.

piece of tape, and boil it in water, mixed with a little salt and vinegar, till tender. It may either be served whole or cut in slices ; and when cold, the eel should be kept in the liquor it was boiled in, but with a little more vinegar put to it.

TIME.—*2 hours.*

SEASONABLE *from August to March.*

Eels, Fried.

INGREDIENTS *for dish sufficient for 2 or 3 persons.* —1 lb. of eels, egg, a few bread-crumbs, hot lard. AVERAGE COST, 1s.

Wash the eels, cut them into pieces 3 inches long, trim and wipe them very dry, dredge with flour, rub them over with egg

FRIED EELS.

and cover with bread-crumbs ; fry a nice brown in hot lard. If the eels are small curl them round, instead of cutting them up. Garnish with fried parsley.

TIME.—*20 minutes, or rather less.*

SEASONABLE *from June to March.*

Eels en Matelote.

INGREDIENTS *for dish for 6 persons.*—2 lbs. of eels, 5 or 6 young onions, a few mushrooms, when obtainable ; salt, pepper and nutmeg to taste ; 1 laurel leaf, ½ pint of port wine, *pint of medium stock, butter and flour to thicken.* AVERAGE COST, 3s.

Rub the stewpan with butter, dredge in a little flour, add the onions cut very small, slightly brown them, and put in all the other ingredients. Wash and cut up the eels into pieces 3 inches long; put them in the stewpan and simmer for ½ hour. Make round the dish a border of croûtons; arrange the eels in a pyramid in the centre, and pour over the sauce. Serve very hot.

TIME.—¾ *hour.*

SEASONABLE *from August to March.*

Eels, Stewed.—INGREDIENTS *for dish sufficient for 6 persons.*—2 *lbs. of eels,* 1 *pint of rich strong stock,* 1 *onion,* 3 *cloves, a piece of lemon-peel,* 1 *glass of port or madeira,* 3 *tablespoonfuls of cream; thickening of flour; cayenne and lemon-juice to taste.* AVERAGE COST, 3s.

Wash and skin the eels, and cut them into pieces about 3 inches long; pepper and salt them, and lay them in a stewpan; pour over the stock, add the onion stuck with cloves, the lemon-peel and the wine. Stew gently for ½ hour, or rather more, and lift them carefully on a dish, which keep hot. Strain the gravy, stir in the cream and sufficient flour to thicken; mix all together, boil for 2 minutes, and add the cayenne and lemon-juice; pour over the eels and serve.

TIME.—¾ *hour.*

SEASONABLE *from June to March.*

Eels, Stewed.—INGREDIENTS *for dish for 6 persons.*—2 *lbs. of middling-sized eels,* 1 *pint of medium stock,* ¼ *pint of port wine; salt, cayenne and mace to taste;* 1 *teaspoonful of anchovy sauce, the juice of* ½ *a lemon.* AVERAGE COST, 2s. 6d.

Skin, wash and clean the eels thoroughly; cut them into pieces 3 inches long, and put them into strong salt-and-water for 1 hour; dry them well with a cloth, and fry them brown. Put the stock on,

with the heads and tails of the eels, and simmer for ½ hour; strain it, and add all the other ingredients. Put in the eels, and stew gently for ½ hour, when serve.

TIME. —2 *hours.*

SEASONABLE *from June to March.*

Eels à la Tartare.—INGREDIENTS *for dish for 6 persons.*—2 *lbs. of eels,* 1 *carrot,* 1 *onion, a little flour,* 1 *glass of sherry; salt, pepper and nutmeg to taste; bread-crumbs,* 1 *egg,* 2 *tablespoonfuls of vinegar.* AVERAGE COST, *exclusive of the sauce,* 2s. 3d.

Rub the butter on the bottom of the stewpan; cut up the carrot and onion, and stir them over the fire for 5 minutes; dredge in a little flour, add the wine and seasoning, and boil for ½ an hour. Skin and wash the eels, cut them into pieces, put them to the other ingredients, and simmer till tender. When they are done, take them o let them get cold, cover them with egg and bread-crumbs, and fry them a nice brown. Put them on a dish, pour sauce piquante over, and serve them hot.

TIME.—1½ *hour.*

SEASONABLE *from August to March.*

Eggs.—There is only one opinion as to the nutritive properties of eggs, although the qualities of those belonging to different birds vary somewhat. Those of the common hen are most esteemed as delicate food, particularly when "new-laid." The quality of eggs depends much upon the food given to the hen. Eggs in general are considered most easily digestible when little subjected to the art of cookery. The lightest way of dressing them is by poaching, which is effected by putting them for a minute or two into brisk boiling water: this coagulates the external white, without doing the inner part too much. Eggs are much better when new-laid than a day or two afterwards. The usual time allotted for boiling hens' eggs in the shell is 3 to 3¼ minutes: less time than that in boiling

water will not be sufficient to solidify the white, and more will make the yolk hard and less digestible; it is very difficult to *guess* accurately as to the time. Great care should be employed in putting them into the water, to prevent cracking the shell, which inevitably causes a portion of

HENS' EGGS. GEESE'S EGGS.

the white to exude, and lets water into the egg. For the purpose of placing eggs in water, always choose a *large* spoon in preference to a small one. Eggs are often beaten up raw in nutritive beverages.

The eggs of the *turkey* are almost as mild as those of the hen; the egg of the *goose* is 'arge, but well tasted. *Ducks' eggs* have a rich flavour; the albumen is slightly transparent, or bluish, when set, or coagulated by boiling, which requires less time than hens' eggs. *Guinea-fowl eggs* are smaller and more delicate than those of the hen. Eggs of *wild fowl* are generally coloured, often spotted; and the taste generally partakes somewhat of the bird

DUCKS' EGGS. TURKEYS' EGGS.

they belong to. Those of land birds that are eaten, as the *plover*, almost invariably boiled a long time and eaten cold, *lapwing, ruff*, &c., are in general much esteemed; but those of *sea-fowl* have, more or less, a strong fishy taste. The eggs of the *turtle* are very numerous: they consist of yolk only, without shell, and are delicious.

When fresh eggs are dropped into a

vessel *full* of boiling water, they crack, because the eggs being well filled, the shells give way to the efforts of the interior fluids, dilated by heat. If the volume of hot water be small, the shells do not crack, because its temperature is reduced by the eggs before the interior dilatation can take place. Stale eggs, again, do not crack, because the air inside is easily compressed.

Egg Balls (for Soups and made Dishes).—INGREDIENTS.—8 *eggs, a little flour; seasoning of salt to taste.*

Boil 6 eggs for 20 minutes, strip off the shells, take the yolks and pound them in a mortar. Beat the yolks of the 2 uncooked eggs; add them, with a little flour and salt, to those pounded; mix all well together, and roll into balls. Boil them before they are put into the soup or other dish they may be intended for.

Egg Sauce (for Salt Fish).—INGREDIENTS *for sauce for 4 lbs. of fish.*—4 *eggs, ½ pint of melted butter, when liked, a very little lemon-juice.* AVERAGE COST, 6d.

Boil the eggs until quite hard, which will be in about 20 minutes, and put them into cold water for ½ hour. Strip off the shells, chop the eggs into small pieces, not, however, too fine. Make the melted butter very smooth, and when boiling, stir in the eggs, and serve very hot. Lemon-juice may be added at pleasure.

TIME.—20 *minutes to boil the eggs.*

Note.—When a thicker sauce is required, use one or two more eggs to the same quantity of melted butter.

Egg Soup.—INGREDIENTS *for soup for 8 persons.*—A *tablespoonful of flour, 4 eggs, 2 small blades of finely-pounded mace, 2 quarts of stock.* AVERAGE COST, 1s. 8d.

Beat up the flour smoothly in a teaspoonful of cold stock, and put in the eggs; throw them into boiling stock, stirring all the time. Simmer for ¼ of an hour. Season

...nd serve with a French roll in the tureen, or fried sippets of bread.

TIME.—½ an hour.

SEASONABLE all the year.

Egg Wine.—INGREDIENTS for glass for 1 person.—1 egg, 1 tablespoonful and ½ glass of cold water, 1 glass of sherry, sugar and grated nutmeg to taste.

Beat the egg, mixing with it a tablespoonful of cold water; make the wine-and-water hot, but not boiling; pour it on the egg, stirring all the time. Add sufficient lump sugar to sweeten the mixture, and a little grated nutmeg; put all into a very clean saucepan, set it on a gentle fire, and stir the contents one way until they thicken, but do not allow them to boil. Serve in a glass with sippets of toasted bread or plain crisp biscuits. When the egg is not warmed, the mixture will be found easier of digestion, but it is not so pleasant a drink.

Eggs, Alpine.—INGREDIENTS for dish for 3 or 4 persons.—4 eggs, 6 oz. of cheese, 2 oz. of butter, a little chopped parsley, pepper and salt. AVERAGE COST, 10d.

Butter a baking-tin thoroughly, and line it with the greater part of the cheese cut in slices; break over this the eggs without breaking the yolks, and season with pepper and salt. Grate the remainder of the cheese and put with it the chopped parsley; lay this over the top, and upon it put small pieces of butter. Bake in a quick oven for 10 minutes.

TIME.—To bake, 10 minutes.

SEASONABLE at any time.

Eggs, To Boil (for Breakfast, Salads, &c.). — Eggs for boiling cannot be too fresh, or boiled too soon after they are laid; but rather a longer time should be allowed for boiling a new-laid egg than for one that is three or four days old. Have ready a saucepan of boiling water; put the eggs into it gently with a spoon,

letting the spoon touch the bottom of the saucepan before it is withdrawn, that the egg may not fall, and consequently crack. For those who like eggs lightly boiled, 3 minutes will be found sufficient; 3¾ to 4 minutes will be ample time to set the white nicely; and if liked hard, 6 to 7 minutes will not be found too long. Should the eggs be unusually large, as those of black Spanish fowls sometimes are, allow an extra ½ minute for them. Eggs for

EGG-STAND FOR THE BREAKFAST-TABLE.

salads should be boiled from 10 minutes to ¼ hour, and should be placed in a basin of cold water for a few minutes; they should then be rolled on the table with the hand, and the shell will peel off easily.

TIME.—To boil eggs lightly, for invalids or children, 3 minutes; to boil eggs to suit the generality of taste, 3¾ to 4 minutes; to boil eggs hard, 6 to 7 minutes; for salads, 10 to 15 minutes.

Eggs, Buttered.—INGREDIENTS for sufficient for 4 persons.—4 new-laid eggs, 2 oz. of butter, 4 slices of hot buttered toast. AVERAGE COST, 8d.

Procure the eggs new-laid if possible; break them into a basin, and beat them well; put the butter into another basin, which place in boiling water, and stir till the butter is melted. Pour that and the eggs into a lined saucepan; hold it over a gentle fire, and, as the mixture begins to warm, pour it two or three times into the basin, and back again, that the two ingre-

R

dients may be well incorporated. Keep stirring the eggs and butter one way until they are hot, *without boiling*, and serve on hot buttered toast. If the mixture is allowed to boil, it will curdle, and so be entirely spoiled.

TIME.—*About 5 minutes to make the eggs hot.*

SEASONABLE *at any time.*

Eggs, Constituent Parts of. —

Eggs are an almost invaluable article of diet, and we have no other food that can take their place in invalid cookery. Extremely nutritive, they contain as great flesh-forming and heat-giving properties as an equal weight of butcher's meat, and, either raw or lightly boiled, are far more easy of digestion than meat. It is calculated that 18 eggs contain enough nutrient properties to sustain a working man during a day.

The most costly and the most esteemed as a delicacy are plovers' eggs, which are usually eaten hard boiled and cold, but the most used are hens' eggs. Enormous quantities of them are imported into Great Britain from all parts, and an instance of this may be found in a recent quotation of no less than 17¼ millions arriving within three months.

CONSTITUENTS OF 1 LB. WEIGHT OF EGGS.

				oz.	grs.
Water	...	...	...	11	206
Albumenoids	...	...	...	2	105
Fat ...	...	...	...	1	332
Mineral Matters...	...	...	0	231
				16	0

Eggs, Curried.—INGREDIENTS *for dish for 4 persons.*—6 eggs, 2 teaspoonfuls of curry-powder, 1½ pint of good gravy, thickening of flour and butter. AVERAGE COST, 1s. 3d.

Mix the curry-powder to a paste with a little of the gravy, and rub it with a spoon, adding the gravy until it is completely amalgamated. Simmer it till it is reduced to a little more than ½ a pint, then thicken

with flour and butter. Boil the eggs hard and cut them in quarters, and warm for minutes in the curry. Serve very hot with boiled rice.

TIME.—*4 hours to simmer slowly.*

SEASONABLE *at any time.*

Eggs, To Choose. — In choosing

eggs, apply the tongue to the large end of the egg, and, if it feels warm, it is new, and may be relied on as a fresh egg. Another mode of ascertaining their freshness is to hold them before a lighted candle or to the light, and if the egg looks clear, it will be tolerably good; if thick, it is stale; and if there is a black spot attached to the shell, it is worthless. No egg should be used for culinary purposes with the slightest taint in it, as it will render perfectly useless those with which it has been mixed. Eggs that are purchased, and that cannot be relied on, should always be broken in a cup, and then put into a basin: by this means stale or bad eggs may be easily rejected, without wasting the others.

Eggs, Ducks'. — Ducks' eggs are

usually so strongly flavoured that, plainly boiled, they are not good for eating; they answer, however, very well for various culinary preparations where eggs are required; such as custards, &c. &c. Being so large and highly-flavoured, 1 duck's egg will go as far as two small hens' eggs, besides making whatever they are mixed with exceedingly rich. They also are admirable when used in puddings.

Eggs, Fried.— INGREDIENTS *for small dish.*—4 eggs, 3 oz. of lard, butter or clarified dripping. AVERAGE COST, 7d.

Place a delicately-clean frying-pan over a gentle fire; put in the fat, and allow it to come to the boiling-point. Break the eggs into cups, slip them into the boiling fat, and let them remain until the whites are delicately set; and, whilst they are frying, ladle a little of the fat over them.

Take them up with a slice, drain them for a minute from their greasy moisture, trim them neatly, and serve on slices of fried bacon or ham; or the eggs may be placed in the middle of the dish, with the bacon put round as a garnish.

TIME.—2 to 3 minutes.

SEASONABLE at any time.

Eggs à la Maître d'Hôtel.—

INGREDIENTS for dish for 4 persons.—¼ lb. of fresh butter, 1 tablespoonful of flour, ½ pint of milk, pepper and salt to taste, 1 tablespoonful of minced parsley, the juice of ½ a lemon, 6 eggs. AVERAGE COST, 1s.

Put the flour and half the butter into a stewpan; stir them over the fire until the mixture thickens; pour in the milk, which should be boiling; add a seasoning of pepper and salt, and simmer the whole for 5 minutes. Put the remainder of the butter into the sauce, and add the minced parsley; then boil the eggs hard, strip off the shell, cut the eggs into quarters, and put them on a dish. Bring the sauce to the boiling-point, add the lemon-juice, pour over the eggs and serve.

TIME.—5 minutes to boil the sauce; the eggs, 10 to 15 minutes.

SEASONABLE at any time.

Eggs, to Pickle.—INGREDIENTS.—

16 eggs, 1 quart of vinegar, ½ oz. of black pepper, ½ oz. of Jamaica pepper, ½ oz. of ginger. AVERAGE COST, 1s. 10d.

Boil the eggs for 12 minutes, then dip them into cold water, and take off the shells. Put the vinegar, with the pepper and ginger into a stewpan, and let it simmer for 10 minutes. Now place the eggs in a jar, pour over them the vinegar, &c., boiling hot, and, when cold, tie them down with bladder to exclude the air. This pickle will be ready for use in a month.

SEASONABLE. — This should be made about Easter, as at this time eggs are plentiful and cheap. A store of pickled eggs will be found very useful.

Eggs au Plat, or au Miroir

(served on the Dish in which they are Cooked).—INGREDIENTS for dish for 2 or 3 persons.—4 eggs, 1 oz. of butter, pepper and salt to taste. AVERAGE COST, 5d.

Butter a dish rather thickly with good fresh butter; melt it, break the eggs into it the same as for poaching, sprinkle them with white pepper and fine salt, and put the remainder of the butter, cut into very small pieces, on the top of them. Put the dish on a hot plate, or in the oven, or before the fire, and let it remain until the whites become set, but not hard, when serve immediately, placing the dish they were cooked in on another. To hasten the cooking of the eggs, a salamander may be held over them for a minute; but great care must be taken that they are not too much done. This is an exceedingly nice dish, and one very easily prepared for breakfast.

TIME.—3 minutes.

SEASONABLE at any time.

Eggs, Plovers'.—Plovers' eggs are

sometimes served boiled hard and cold; they may also be shelled, and served the same as eggs à la tripe, with a good Béchamel sauce or brown gravy poured over them. Their principal use, however, is for salads and other savoury cold dishes, the beautiful colour of the white being generally so much admired.

Eggs, Poached.—INGREDIENTS.—

Eggs, water. To every pint of water allow 1 tablespoonful of vinegar. AVERAGE COST, 1d. to 2d. each.

Eggs for poaching should be perfectly fresh, but not quite new-laid; those that are about 36 hours old are the best for the purpose. If quite new-laid, the white is so milky it is almost impossible to set it; and on the other hand, if the egg be at all stale, it is equally difficult to poach it nicely. Strain some boiling water into a deep clean frying-pan, break the egg into a cup without damaging the yolk, and, when the water boils, remove the pan to the side of the fire, and gently slip the egg into it. Place the pan over a gentle fire, and keep the water simmering until the white looks nicely set, when the egg is ready. Take it up gently with a slice, cut away the ragged edges of the white, and serve either on toasted bread or on slices of ham or bacon, or on spinach, &c. A poached egg should not be overdone, as its appearance and taste will be quite spoiled if the yolk be allowed to harden. When the egg is slipped into the water, the white should be gathered together,

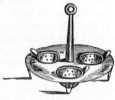

TIN EGG-POACHER.

to keep it a little in form, or the cup should be turned over it for ½ minute. To poach an egg to perfection is rather a difficult operation; so, for inexperienced cooks, a tin egg-poacher may be purchased, which greatly facilitates this manner of dressing eggs. Our illustration clearly shows what it is: it consists of a tin plate with a handle, with a space for three perforated cups. An egg should be broken into each cup, and the machine then placed in a stewpan of boiling water, which has been previously strained. When the whites of the eggs appear set, they are done, and should then be carefully slipped on to the toast or spinach, or with whatever they are served. In poaching eggs in a frying-pan, never do more than four at a time; and, when a little vinegar is liked mixed with the water in which the eggs are done, use the above proportion.

TIME.—2½ to 3½ minutes, according to the size of the eggs.

SEASONABLE at any time, but less plentiful in winter.

Eggs, Poached, with Cream.
—INGREDIENTS for dish for 2 or 3 persons. —1 pint of water, 1 teaspoonful of salt, 4 teaspoonfuls of vinegar, 4 fresh eggs, ½ gill of cream, salt, pepper, 1 oz. of butter. AVERAGE COST, 10d.

Put the water, vinegar and salt into a frying-pan, and break each egg into a separate cup; bring the water, &c., to boil, and slip the eggs gently into it without breaking the yolks. Simmer them from 3 to 4 minutes, but not longer, and with a slice lift them out on to a hot dish, and trim the edges. Empty the pan of its contents, put in the cream, add a seasoning to taste of pepper and salt, bring the whole to the boiling-point; then add the butter, broken into small pieces; toss the pan round and round till the butter is melted, pour it over the eggs, and serve. To insure the eggs not being spoiled whilst the cream, &c., is preparing, it is a good plan to warm the cream with the butter, &c., before the eggs are poached, so that it may be poured over them immediately after they are dished.

TIME.—3 to 4 minutes to poach the eggs, 5 minutes to warm the cream.

SEASONABLE at any time.

Eggs, Savoury.—INGREDIENTS for dish for 4 persons.—4 eggs, ½ oz. of butter, anchovy sauce or paste, cayenne, 8 croûtons, Montpélier butter, aspic jelly. AVERAGE COST, 1s.

Boil the eggs for 10 minutes and put them into cold water; when cold shell them and cut them in half, cut off a small piece at each end, so that they will stand, and take out the yolks. Spread the croûtons with Montpélier butter (plain butter and rounds of toast may be substituted), and stand on each half an egg. Pound the yolks with the anchovy, adding enough to flavour the egg, the cayenne to taste, and the butter, and fill the whites with the mixture. Arrange the croûtons with the eggs in a ring on a plate or dish, and garnish with a little aspic jelly, if at hand, roughed with a fork, and watercress or parsley.

SEASONABLE *at any time.*

Eggs, Scotch.—INGREDIENTS *for dish for 4 persons.*—6 eggs, 6 *tablespoonfuls of forcemeat, made with anchovies or ham for flavouring, hot lard,* ½ *pint of good brown gravy.* AVERAGE COST, 1s. 2d.

Boil the eggs for 10 minutes, strip them from the shells, and cover them with forcemeat. Fry a nice brown in boiling lard, drain them before the fire from their greasy moisture, dish them, and pour round from ¼ to ½ a pint of good brown gravy. To enhance the appearance of the eggs, they may be rolled in beaten egg and sprinkled with bread-crumbs : but this is scarcely necessary if they are carefully fried. The flavour of the ham or the anchovy in the forcemeat must preponderate, as it should be very relishing.

TIME.—10 *minutes to boil the eggs,* 5 *to* 7 *minutes to fry them.*

SEASONABLE *at any time.*

Eggs, Scrambled.—INGREDIENTS *for dish for 4 persons.*—6 eggs, 1 oz. of butter, pepper, salt, 4 slices of buttered toast. AVERAGE COST, 9d.

Put the butter in a saucepan, and break into it the eggs, and season well with pepper and salt. Beat the mixture while cooking with a fork, but do not thoroughly amalgamate the yolks and whites. After about 2 minutes, remove the pan to the side of the fire to finish cooking. The eggs should be set. Have ready some slices of toast hot and buttered, spread on them the egg and serve immediately.

TIME.—5 *minutes.*

SEASONABLE *at any time.*

Eggs, Snow, or Œufs à la Neige (a cheap and pretty Supper Dish).—INGREDIENTS *for medium-sized dish.*— 4

eggs, ¾ *pint of milk, pounded sugar to taste, flavouring of vanilla, lemon-rind, or orange-flower water.* AVERAGE COST, 7d.

Put the milk into a saucepan with sufficient sugar to sweeten it nicely, and the rind of ½ lemon. Let this steep by the side of the fire for ½ hour, when take out the peel ; separate the whites from the yolks of the eggs, and whisk the former to a perfectly stiff froth, or until there is no liquid remaining ; bring the milk to the boiling-point, drop in the snow a tablespoonful at a time, and keep turning the eggs until sufficiently cooked. Then place them on a glass dish, beat up the yolks of the eggs, stir to them the milk, add a little more sugar, and strain this mixture into a jug ; place the jug in a saucepan of boiling water, and stir it one way until the mixture thickens, but do not allow it to boil, or it will curdle. Pour this custard over the eggs, when they should rise to the surface. They make an exceedingly pretty addition to a supper, and should be put in a cold place after being made. When they are flavoured with vanilla or orange-flowered water, it is not necessary to steep the milk. A few drops of the essence of either may be poured into the milk just before the whites are poached. In making the custard a little more flavouring and sugar should always be added.

TIME.—*About* 2 *minutes to poach the whites ;* 8 *minutes to stir the custard.*

SEASONABLE *at any time.*

Eggs, to keep Fresh for several weeks.—Have ready a large saucepan, capable of holding 3 or 4 quarts, full of boiling water. Put the eggs into a cabbage-net, say 20 at a time, and hold them in the water (which must be kept boiling) *for* 20 *seconds.* Proceed in this manner till you have done as many eggs as you wish to preserve, then pack them away in sawdust. We have tried this method of preserving eggs, and can vouch for its excellence. They will be found, at the end of 2 or 3 months, quite good enough for culinary purposes, and although the white may be a little tougher than that of a new-laid egg, the yolk will be nearly the same. Many persons keep eggs for a long time by smearing the shells with butter or sweet oil: they should then be packed in plenty of bran or sawdust, and the eggs not allowed to touch each other. Eggs for storing should be collected in fine weather, and should not be more than 24 hours old when they are packed away, or their flavour, when used, cannot be relied on. Another simple way of preserving eggs is to immerse them in lime-water soon after they have been laid, and then to put the vessel containing the lime-water in a cellar or cool outhouse.

SEASONABLE.—*The best time for preserving eggs is from April to September.*

Eggs à la Tripe.— INGREDIENTS
for dish for 6 persons.—8 eggs, ¾ *pint of Béchamel sauce, dessertspoonful of finely-minced parsley.* AVERAGE COST, 1s.

Boil the eggs hard; put them into cold water, peel them, take out the yolks whole, and shred the whites. Make ¾ pint of Béchamel sauce, add the parsley, and when the sauce is quite hot, put the yolks of the eggs into the middle of the dish, and the shreds of the whites around them; pour over the sauce and garnish with leaves of puff paste or fried croûtons. There is no necessity for putting the eggs into the saucepan with the Béchamel; the sauce, being quite hot, will warm the eggs sufficiently.

TIME.—*10 minutes to boil the eggs.*
SEASONABLE *at any time.*

Elder Wine.— INGREDIENTS. — *To every 3 gallons of water allow* 1 *peck of elderberries; to every gallon of juice allow* 3 *lbs. of sugar,* ½ *oz. of ground ginger,* 6 *cloves,* 1 *lb. of good Turkey raisins;* ¼ *pint of brandy to every gallon of wine. To every* 9 *gallons of wine,* 3 *or* 4 *tablespoonfuls of fresh brewer's yeast.*

Pour the water, quite boiling, on the elderberries, which should be picked from the stalks, and let these stand covered for 24 hours; then strain the whole through a sieve or bag, breaking the fruit to express all the juice from it. Measure the liquor, and to every gallon allow the above proportion of sugar. Boil the juice and sugar with the ginger, cloves and raisins

ELDERBERRIES.

for 1 hour, skimming the liquor the whole time; let it stand until milk-warm, then put it into a clean dry cask, with 3 or 4 tablespoonfuls of good fresh yeast to every 9 gallons of wine. Let it ferment for about a fortnight; then add the brandy, bung up the cask, and let it stand some months before it is bottled, when it will be found excellent. A bunch of hops suspended to a string from the bung, some persons say, will preserve the wine good for several years. Elder wine is usually mulled, and served with sippets of toasted bread and a little grated nutmeg.

TIME.—*To stand covered for 24 hours; to be boiled 1 hour.*
SEASONABLE.—*Make this in September.*

Empress Pudding. — INGREDI-
ENTS *for large pudding.*—¼ *lb. of rice,* 2 *oz. of butter,* 3 *eggs, jam, sufficient milk to soften the rice.* AVERAGE COST, 1s.

Boil the rice in the milk until very soft; then add the butter, boil it for a few minutes after the latter ingredient is put in, and set it by to cool. Well beat the eggs, stir these in, and line a dish with puff paste; put over this a layer of rice, then a thin layer of any kind of jam, then another layer of rice, and proceed in this manner until the dish is full; and bake in a moderate oven for ¾ hour. This pudding may be eaten hot or cold; if the latter, it will be much improved by having a boiled custard poured over it.

TIME.—¾ hour.

SEASONABLE at any time.

Endive.—This vegetable, so beautiful in appearance, makes an excellent addition to winter salad, when lettuces and other salads are not obtainable. It is usually placed cut up in the centre of the dish, and looks pretty with slices of beet and hard-boiled eggs.

Endive à la Française. — INGREDIENTS for dish for 5 or 6 persons.—6 heads of endive, 1 pint of broth, 3 oz. of fresh butter; salt, pepper and grated nutmeg to taste. AVERAGE COST, 1s. 2d.

Wash and boil the endive as in the preceding recipe; chop it rather fine, and put into a stewpan with the broth; boil over a brisk fire until the sauce is all reduced; then in the butter, pepper, salt and grated nutmeg (the latter must be very sparingly used); mix all well together, bring it to the boiling-point, and serve very hot.

TIME.—10 minutes to boil, 5 minutes to simmer in the broth.

SEASONABLE from November to March.

Endive, Stewed. — INGREDIENTS for dish sufficient for 6 persons.—6 heads of endive, salt and water, 1 pint of broth, thickening of butter and flour, 1 tablespoonful of lemon-juice, a small lump of sugar. AVERAGE COST, 1s.

Wash and free the endive thoroughly from insects, remove the green part of the leaves, and put it into boiling water, slightly salted. Let it remain for 10 minutes, then take it out, drain it till there is no water remaining, and chop it very fine. Put it into a stewpan with the broth; add a little salt and a lump of sugar, and boil until the endive is perfectly tender. When done, which may be ascertained by squeezing a piece between the thumb and finger, add a thickening of butter and flour and the lemon-juice; let the sauce boil up, and serve.

TIME.—10 minutes to boil, 5 minutes to simmer in the broth.

SEASONABLE from November to March.

Epicurean Sauce (for Steaks, Chops, Gravies or Fish).—INGREDIENTS.— ¼ pint of walnut ketchup, ¼ pint of mushroom ditto, 2 tablespoonfuls of Indian soy, 2 tablespoonfuls of port wine; ¼ oz. of white pepper, 2 oz. of shalots, ¼ oz. of cayenne, ¼ oz. of cloves, ¾ pint of vinegar. AVERAGE COST, 1s. 9d.

Put the whole of the ingredients into a bottle, and let it remain for a fortnight in a warm place, occasionally shaking up the contents. Strain, and bottle off for use. This sauce will be found an agreeable addition to gravies, hashes, stews, &c.

Exeter Pudding. (Very Rich).—INGREDIENTS for large Pudding.—10 oz. of bread-crumbs, 4 oz. of sago, 7 oz. of finely-chopped suet, 6 oz. of moist sugar, the rind of ½ lemon, ¼ pint of rum, 7 eggs, 4 tablespoonfuls of cream, 4 small sponge-cakes, 2 oz. of ratafias, ½ lb. of jam. AVERAGE COST, 2s. 8d.

Put the bread-crumbs into a basin with the sago, suet, sugar, minced lemon-peel, rum and 4 eggs; stir these ingredients well together, then add 3 more eggs and the cream, and let the mixture be well beaten. Then butter a mould, strew in a few bread-crumbs, and cover the bottom with a layer of ratafias; then put in a layer of the mixture, then a layer of sliced sponge-cake, spread thickly with any kind of jam; then add some ratafias, then some of the mixture and sponge-cake, and so on until the mould is full, taking care that a layer of the mixture is on the top of the pudding. Bake in a good oven from ¾ to 1 hour and serve, with or without wine sauce.

TIME.—From 1 to 1¼ hour.

SEASONABLE at any time.

"*Fill your baskets high
With fennel green and balm, and golden pines.*"—KEATS.

FAIRY BUTTER.

FAIRY BUTTER.—INGREDIENTS *for good-sized dish.* — $\frac{1}{4}$ *lb. of fresh butter, 2 eggs, 2 tablespoonfuls of pounded sugar, 1 tablespoonful of orange-flower water.* AVERAGE COST, 8d.

Boil the eggs hard, and, when cold, take out the yolks, and pound them in a mortar with the sugar and the orange-flower water to a smooth paste, then incorporate with it the butter. Put the paste in an old, clean, coarse cloth, and force it through by wringing the cloth hard and squeezing the butter through it. The butter should then drop on the dish or plate in irregular pieces according to the holes in the cloth, and should have a pretty effect. Plain butter may be done in the same manner.

Fancy Cakes (Petits Fours). — INGREDIENTS.—*Any sweet paste or slices of sponge or pound cake, icing of plain sugar, or of any fancy kind, such as rose or chocolate; small crystalised fruits, strips of*

FARMERS' FRUIT CAKE.

angelica or candied-peel, blanched almonds, pistachio nuts, or any garnish desired.

These pretty little cakes, which cost so much to buy from a pastrycook, can easily be made at home. The simplest mode of doing so is to stamp out small rounds, stars, &c., from slices of stale sponge or pound cake with a fancy cutter; to cover them with icing, and, before it is quite set, to garnish them, according to taste, with the ingredients named above.

Farmers' Fruit Cake.—INGREDIENTS *for good-sized cake.*—*1 lb. of apples, 1 teacupful of golden syrup, 1 of sugar, $\frac{1}{2}$ a cupful of sour milk, $\frac{1}{4}$ lb. of butter, 2 teaspoonfuls of cinnamon, 1 of soda, 1 of cloves, 1 egg, about 1 lb. of flour, or enough to make these ingredients into a smooth paste.* AVERAGE COST, 1s.

Peel, core and chop the apples fine, and let them simmer in the syrup till tender. Work the butter into the flour, next the sugar and spices, mixing well, then add the milk, the egg and the syrup and apples before they are cold. Beat the cake well, and bake it in a buttered tin for $\frac{1}{2}$ to $\frac{3}{4}$ hour in a moderate oven.

TIME.—$\frac{1}{2}$ *to* $\frac{3}{4}$ *hour to bake the cake.*
SEASONABLE *at any time.*

February—Dinner for Twelve Persons.

MENU. (*English*.)	Quantity.	Average Cost.		MENU. (*French.*)
		s.	d.	
Asparagus Soup.	2 quarts	6	0	Potage aux Pointes d'Asperge.
Red Mullet.	12 fish.	8	0	Rougets.
Baked Sweetbreads.	2 dishes.	6	6	Ris de Veau au Gratin.
Curried Chicken.	2 dishes.	4	6	Poulet au Kari.
Saddle of Mutton.	1 joint.	10	0	Selle de Mouton.
Potatoes. Spinach.	4 lbs. ea.	1	0	Pommes de Terre. Epinards.
Larded Guinea Fowl.	3 birds.	10	6	Pintade Lardée.
Compôte of Fruit.	2 dishes.	3	6	Compôte de Fruit.
Lemon Pudding.	1	2	0	Pouding de Citron.
Cheese Biscuits.	2 dishes.	1	0	Biscuits de Fromage.
		£2 13	0	

February—Dinner for Ten Persons.

MENU. (*English*.)	Quantity.	Average Cost.		MENU. (*French.*)
		s.	d.	
Julienne.	3½ pints.	3	6	Julienne.
Cod,	4 lbs.	2	0	Cabillaud,
Italian Sauce.	2 turs.	1	0	Sauce Italienne.
Croquettes of Chicken.	1 dish.	2	6	Croquettes de Volaille.
Mutton Cutlets.	1 dish.	3	0	Cotelettes de Mouton.
Fillet of Veal.	1 joint.	6	0	Rouelle de Veau Rotie.
Ham.	1	7	0	Jambon.
Potatoes. Brussels Sprouts.	4 lbs. ea.	1	0	Pommes de Terre. Choux.
Partridges.	4 birds.	8	0	Perdreaux.
Almond Pudding.	1	2	0	Pouding d'Amandes.
Liqueur Jelly.	1 mould.	2	6	Gelée à la Marasquin.
		£1 18	6	

February—Dinner for Eight Persons.

MENU. (*English*.)	Quantity.	Average Cost.		MENU. (*French.*)
		s.	d.	
Oysters.	2 doz.	4	0	Huitres.
Ox-Tail Soup.	3 pints.	2	0	Potage de Queue de Bœuf.
Croquettes of Turkey.	1 dish.	2	0	Croquettes de Dinde.
Beef Olives.	1 dish.	2	6	Olives de Bœuf.
Capon, Stuffed.	1 bird.	5	6	Chapon Farci.
Ham.	1	6	0	Jambon.
Potatoes. Savoy.	3 lbs. 1	0	6	Pommes de Terre. Choux.
Benedictine Cream.	1 mould.	2	6	Crême à la Benedictine.
Apricot Tartlets.	1 dish.	2	0	Bouchées d'Abricots.
Cheese Straws.	1 dish.	0	9	Pailles de Parmesan.
		£1 7	9	

February—Dinners for from Six to Twelve Persons.

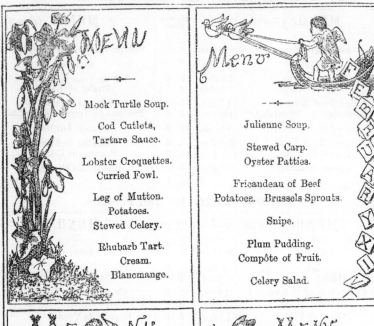

MENU

Mock Turtle Soup.

Cod Cutlets,
Tartare Sauce.

Lobster Croquettes.
Curried Fowl.

Leg of Mutton.
Potatoes.
Stewed Celery.

Rhubarb Tart.
Cream.
Blancmange.

Menu

Julienne Soup.

Stewed Carp.
Oyster Patties.

Fricandeau of Beef
Potatoes. Brussels Sprouts.

Snipe.

Plum Pudding.
Compôte of Fruit.

Celery Salad.

FEBRUARY XIV

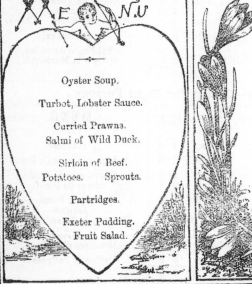

MENU

Oyster Soup.

Turbot, Lobster Sauce.

Curried Prawns.
Salmi of Wild Duck.

Sirloin of Beef.
Potatoes.   Sprouts.

Partridges.

Exeter Pudding.
Fruit Salad.

MENU

Hare Soup.

Brill, Oyster Sauce.

Stewed Pigeons.

Fillet of Beef,
Horseradish Sauce.
Potatoes.   Sea-kale.

Wild Duck.

Coburg Pudding.
Creamed Apple
Tart.

February—Plain Family Dinners for.

No. 1.

Sunday.—Roast sirloin of beef, horse-radish sauce, broccoli, potatoes. — Apple tart, custard pudding.—Cheese —Dessert.

Monday. — Mulligatawny soup. — Cold beef, mashed potatoes, winter salad.—Sultana pudding.

Tuesday.—Fried soles.—Roast shoulder of mutton, potatoes, greens.—Cheese biscuits.

Wednesday.—Rissoles from cold beef.—Cold mutton, salad, potatoes.—Batter pudding with marmalade.

Thursday.—Roast fowls, boiled bacon, potatoes, stewed celery.—Tapioca pudding.

Friday. — Baked haddock, stuffed. — Hashed fowl and celery sauce, potatoes.—Cheese salad.

Saturday.—Stewed steak with vegetables, potatoes.—Baked jam tart.

No. 2.

Sunday.—Boiled beef, carrots, turnips, potatoes.—Mince pies, baked bread-and-butter pudding.

Monday.—Pea soup from beef liquor.—Cold beef, mashed potatoes, salad.—Baked apple dumplings.

Tuesday.—Beef and potato pie, mutton cutlets, vegetables.—Ground rice pudding.

Wednesday.—Roast loin of pork, apple sauce, greens, potatoes.—Stewed prunes and boiled rice.

Thursday.—Brill and shrimp sauce.—Cold pork, salad, potatoes. — Macaroni cheese.

Friday.—Rissoles from cold fish.—Rabbit pie, potatoes.—Orange fritters.

Saturday. — Curried pork, remains of rabbit pie, potatoes. — Gingerbread pudding.

February—Vegetarian Dinners for.

No. 1.

Pea Soup.

Stew of Vegetables.
Curried Eggs.

Welsh Rare-bit.

Dessert.

No. 2.

Wheat Meal and Milk.

Fried Greens and Potatoes.
Haricots.

Mince Pies.   Custard.

Dessert.

February—Dinner Table Decorations for.

Pretty as the earliest "flowers that bloom in the spring" are, they do not lend themselves very well for table decorations, the majority of them being white or of very pale colour. Foliage, too, is scarce, and it is not always an easy matter to find anything wherewith to fill the vases.

Well for those who have dried some golden bracken and some grasses, or who have pressed some ferns during the summer, for they will find them very useful now.

Hot-house flowers, of course, can be had for those who can afford them, but for the many who cannot, we may suggest something less costly. Coloured centres come in well to eke out scanty supplies of flowers, also coloured vases give good effect to white ones. A pretty low decoration can be made with snowdrops and ivy, some of which should be trailed on the cloth.

Golden arbor vitæ, too, is very useful for fringing a cloth, or for trailing with tiny sprays of bright green box. With these, if a few scarlet geraniums can be had, a pretty result can be obtained. There may still be a good supply of chrysanthemums, and they are a host in themselves. They look very pretty in white china vases, such as are now so often used, and which should be put on a coloured ground. Not too many colours in these flowers should be found in one decoration, or yellow and brown, or red and white, are most effective. A quickly arranged dinner table can be furnished with some pretty ferns, in pots tied up with coloured silk; and if some ribbons to correspond are trailed from them, to tie in little bunches to lie on the cloth, it is all that is necessary to make a pretty table.

February, Things in Season:—

Fish.—Brill, carp; cod may be bought, but it is not so good as in January; crabs, crayfish, dory, eels, flounders, haddocks, herrings, ling, lobsters, mussels, mullet, oysters, pike, plaice, prawns, shrimps, skate, smelts, soles, sprats, sturgeon, tench, thornback, turbot, whiting.

Meat.—Beef, house lamb, mutton, pork, veal.

Poultry.— Capons, chickens, ducklings, tame and wild pigeons, pullets with eggs, turkeys, wild-fowl, though now not in full season.

Game.—Grouse, hares, partridges, pheasants, snipe, woodcock.

Vegetables. — Artichokes (Jerusalem), asparagus (forced), beetroot, broccoli (purple and white), Brussels sprouts, cabbages, carrots, celery, chervil, cresses, cucumbers (forced), endive, kidney-beans, lettuces, parsnips, potatoes, savoys, spinach, turnips —various herbs.

Fruit.—Apples (golden and Dutch pippins), grapes, medlars, nuts, oranges, pears (Bon Chrétien), rhubarb (forced and Foreign), walnuts.

Fennel Sauce (for Mackerel).—In-

GREDIENTS *for sauce for 4 mackerel.* —½ *pint*

FENNEL.

of melted butter, rather more than 1 table-spoonful of chopped fennel. AVERAGE COST, 4*d*.

Make the melted butter very smooth, chop the fennel rather small, carefully cleansing it from any grit or dirt, and put it to the butter when this is on the point of boiling. Simmer for a minute or two, and serve in a tureen.

TIME.—*2 minutes.*

Fig Pudding. — INGREDIENTS *for*

large pudding.—1½ *lb. of figs,* ¾ *lb. of suet,* ½ *lb. of flour,* ½ *lb. of bread-crumbs, 2 eggs, milk.* AVERAGE COST, 1*s.* 9*d.*

Cut the figs into small pieces, grate the bread finely, and chop the suet very small; mix these well together, add the flour, the eggs, which should be well beaten, and sufficient milk to form the whole into a stiff paste; butter a mould or basin, press the pudding into it very closely, tie it down with a cloth, and boil for 3 hours, or rather longer; turn it out of the mould, and serve with wine sauce or cream.

TIME.—*3 hours, or longer.*

SEASONABLE. — *Suitable for a winter pudding.*

Fig Pudding. (Staffordshire Recipe).

—INGREDIENTS *for good-sized pudding.*— 1 *lb. of figs, 6 oz. of suet,* ¾ *lb. of flour, milk.* AVERAGE COST, 1*s.*

Chop the suet finely, mix with it the flour, and make these into a smooth paste with milk; roll it out to the thickness of about ½ inch, cut the figs in small pieces, and strew them over the paste; roll it up, make the ends secure, tie the pudding in a cloth, and boil it from 1½ to 2 hours.

TIME.—1½ *to 2 hours.*

SEASONABLE *at any time.*

Figs, Compôte of Green.— IN-

GREDIENTS *for dish for 6 persons.*—1 *pint of syrup,* 1½ *lb. of green figs, the rind of* ½ *lemon.* AVERAGE COST, 1*s.* 9*d.*

Make a syrup as directed, boiling with it the lemon-rind, and carefully removing all the scum as it rises. Put in the figs, and simmer them very slowly until ten

Dressed Crab

Oysters.

Whitebait

Lobster

Brochet of Smelts

Red Mullet in cases

Salmon

Brill

Turbot

Whiting

Eels

Mackerel

Haddock

Cod

Trout

Soles.

FISH

ler ; dish them on a glass dish ; reduce he syrup by boiling it quickly for 5 minutes ; take out the lemon-peel, pour the syrup over the figs, and the compôte,

COMPÔTE OF FIGS.

when cold, will be ready for table. A little port wine or lemon-juice, added ust before the figs are done, will be found an improvement.

TIME.—2 *to* 3 *hours to stew the figs.*
SEASONABLE *in August and September.*

Financière Sauce (for Fish).—IN-GREDIENTS.—½ *pint of Spanish sauce,* ½ *pint sherry or madeira,* ½ *pint of essence of truffles,* ½ *pint essence of mushrooms.*

Boil these ingredients together steadily or 6 minutes, then strain.

TIME.—½ *hour.*
SEASONABLE *at any time.*

Financière Sauce (for Game or Poultry).—INGREDIENTS.—1 *pint Spanish sauce,* ¼ *pint essence of truffles,* ¼ *pint essence of mushrooms.*

Put the ingredients into a stewpan, and reduce over a good fire for 10 minutes, train and put by till wanted.

TIME.—10 *minutes.*
SEASONABLE *at any time.*

Fish.—Fish shortly before they spawn re, in general, best in condition. When he spawning is just over, they are out of eason, and unfit for human food.

When fish is out of season, it has a transparent, bluish tinge, however much may be boiled ; whenever it is in season, s muscles are firm, and boil white and urdy.

As food for invalids, white fish, such s the ling, cod, haddock and whiting, are he best ; flat fish, as soles, skate, turbot nd flounders, are also good.

Salmon, mackerel, herrings and trout

soon spoil or decompose after they are killed ; therefore, to be in perfection, they should be prepared for the table on the day they are caught. With flat fish, this is not of such consequence, as they will keep longer. The turbot, for example, is improved by being kept for a few hours.

Fish, Constituent Parts of.—

The class of fish yields a larger number of species used as food by man than either birds or quadrupeds ; and there are but few fish in the waters of Great Britain that may not be eaten with impunity.

Fish on the whole is not so digestible as meat ; but the whiting, and after that the sole, the plaice and the flounder are light and delicate, and for that reason most in demand for invalids. Those fish which are the most oily and fat, such as salmon and conger eel, are the most difficult of digestion.

All fish in consequence of its highly nitrogenous character, requires the abundant use of starchy foods in combination with it, to supply sufficient heat givers with the flesh forming qualities it contains. Oysters will always be valuable species, not only from their delicacy of flavour, but for the ease with which they can be taken by invalids, and for the nutrient qualities they possess.

Lobsters and crabs are far more difficult of digestion, and mussels, and sometimes other shell fish, are too often found in a semi-decomposed state, when they are very unwholesome, if not poisonous.

We select for analysis two contrasting kinds of fish, the salmon and the sole.

CONSTITUENTS OF 1 LB. OF FISH.

	SALMON.		SOLE.	
	oz.	grs.	oz.	grs.
Water	12	143	13	374
Nitrogenous Matters	2	43	1	350
Fat	0	301	0	14
Mineral Matters ...	0	387	0	136
	16	0	16	0

Fish, General Directions for Dressing.

—In dressing fish of any kind, the first point to be attended to is to see that it is perfectly clean. It is a common error to wash it too much; by doing so the flavour is diminished. If the fish is to be boiled, a little salt and vinegar should be put into the water, to give it firmness, after it is cleaned. Cod-fish, whiting and haddock are none the worse for being a little salted and kept a day; and, if the weather be not very hot, they will be good for two days.

When fish is cheap and plentiful, and a larger quantity is purchased than is immediately wanted, the overplus of such as will bear it should be potted, or pickled, or salted, and hung up; or it may be fried, that it may be served for stewing the next day. Fresh-water fish, having frequently a muddy smell and taste, should be soaked in strong salt and water, after it has been well cleaned. If of a sufficient size, it may be scalded in salt and water, and afterwards dried and dressed.

Fish should be put into cold water and set on the fire to do very gently, or the outside will break before the inner part is done. Unless the fishes are small, they should never be put into warm water; nor should water, either hot or cold, be poured on to the fish, as it is liable to break the skin; if it should be necessary to add a little water whilst the fish is cooking, it ought to be poured in gently at the side of the vessel. The fish-plate may be drawn up, to see if the fish be ready, which may be shown by its easily separating from the bone. It should then be immediately taken out of the water, or it will become woolly. The fish-plate should be set crossways over the kettle, to keep hot for serving, and a cloth laid over the fish, to prevent its losing its colour.

In garnishing fish great attention is required, and plenty of parsley, horse-radish, and lemon should be used. If fried parsley be used, it must be washed, and picked, and thrown into fresh water. When the lard or dripping boils, throw the parsley into it immediately from the water, and instantly it will be green and crisp, and must be taken up with a slice. When well done, and with very good sauce, fish is more appreciated than almost any other dish. The liver and roe, in some instances, should be placed on the dish, in order that they may be distributed in the course of serving; but to each recipe will be appended the proper mode of serving and garnishing.

If fish is to be fried or broiled it must be dried in a nice soft cloth after it is well cleaned and washed. If for frying, brush

FISH KETTLE.

it over with egg, and sprinkle it with some fine crumbs of bread. If done a second time with the egg and bread, the fish will look so much the better. If required to be very nice, a sheet of white blotting-paper must be placed to receive it, that it may be free from all grease; it must also be of a beautiful colour, and all the crumbs appear distinct. Butter gives a bad colour; lard and clarified dripping are most frequently used; but oil is the best, if the expense be no objection. Where much fish is used, oil does not cost more than any other fat for frying, as it can be used more than once. The fish should be put into the lard when boiling, and there should be a sufficiency of this to cover it.

When fish is broiled, it must be seasoned, floured and laid on a very clean gridiron, which, when hot, should be rubbed with a bit of suet, to prevent the fish from stick-

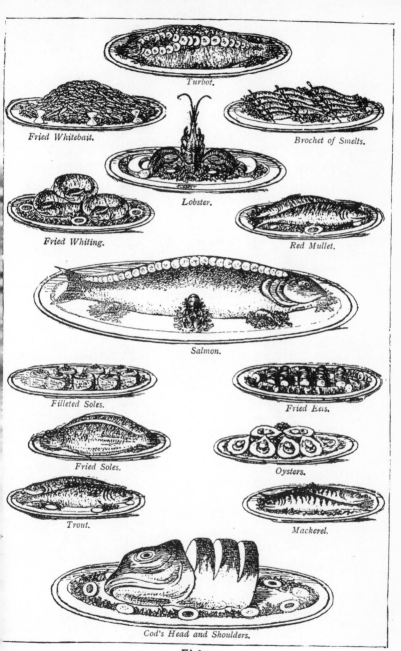

Turbot.

Fried Whitebait.

Brochet of Smelts.

Lobster.

Fried Whiting.

Red Mullet.

Salmon.

Filleted Soles.

Fried Eels.

Fried Soles.

Oysters.

Trout.

Mackerel.

Cod's Head and Shoulders.

Fish.

ing. It must be broiled over a very clear fire, that it may not taste smoky; and not too near, that it may not be scorched.

In choosing fish, it is well to remember that it is possible it may be *fresh*, and yet not *good*. Under the head of each particular fish in this work, are appended rules for its choice, and the months when it is in season. Nothing can be of greater consequence to a cook than to have the fish good; as, if this important course in a dinner does not give satisfaction, it is rarely that the repast goes off well.

Fish, General Directions for Carving.

—In carving fish, care should be taken to help it in perfect flakes, as, if these are broken, the beauty of the fish is lost. The carver should be acquainted, too, with the choicest parts and morsels; and to give each guest an equal share of these *tit-bits* should be his maxim. Steel knives and forks should on no account be used in helping fish, as these are liable to impart to it a very disagreeable flavour. When silver fish-carvers are considered too dear to be bought, good electro-plated ones answer very well, and are inexpensive.

Fish Cake. — Ingredients. — *The remains of any cold fish*, 1 *onion*, 1 *faggot of sweet herbs; salt and pepper to taste*, 1 *pint of water, equal quantities of bread-crumbs and cold potatoes*, ½ *teaspoonful of parsley*, 1 *egg, bread-crumbs*. Average Cost, *exclusive of the cold fish*, 6*d*.

Pick the meat from the bones of the fish, which latter put, with the head and fins, into a stewpan with the water; add pepper and salt, the onion and herbs, and stew slowly for gravy about 2 hours; chop the fish fine, and mix it well with bread-crumbs and cold potatoes, adding the parsley and seasoning; make the whole into a cake with the white of an egg, brush it over with the yolk of the egg, cover with bread-crumbs, fry of a light brown; strain the gravy, pour it over, and stew gently for ¼ of an hour, stirring it carefully once or twice. Serve hot, and garnish with thin slices of lemon and parsley.

Time.—½ *hour after the gravy is made.*
Seasonable *at any time.*

Fish Croquettes.—Ingredients.

—*Remains of cold fish, egg, bread-crumbs, cayenne, salt; fat for frying.*

Flake the fish finely, season it well with cayenne and salt, add an equal quantity of grated bread-crumbs, and make into a paste with beaten eggs. Form into croquettes, dip in egg, then in bread-crumbs, and fry a bright golden brown.

Time.—10 *minutes to fry.*
Seasonable *at any time.*

Fish and Oyster Pie. (Cold Meat Cookery.)—Ingredients. — *Any remains of cold fish, such as cod or haddock; some oysters, either fresh or tinned, pepper and salt to taste, bread-crumbs sufficient for the quantity of fish*, 1 *teaspoonful of finely-chopped parsley, cayenne, salt, seasoning.*

Clear the fish from the bones, and put a layer of it in a pie-dish, which sprinkle with pepper and salt; then a layer of bread-crumbs, oysters and chopped parsley. Repeat this till the dish is quite full. You may form a covering either of bread-crumbs, which should be browned, or puff-paste, which should be cut into long strips, and laid in cross-bars over the fish, with a line of the paste first laid round the edge. Before putting on the top, pour in some made melted butter, or a little thin white sauce, and the oyster-liquor, and bake.

Time.—*If made of cooked fish,* ¼ *hour; if made of fresh fish and puff-paste,* ¾ *hour.*
Seasonable *from September to April.*

Note.—A nice little dish may be made by flaking any cold fish, adding a few oysters, seasoning with pepper and salt, and covering with mashed potatoes; ¼ hour will bake it.

Fish Pie, with Tench and Eels.

—INGREDIENTS *for dish for 4 or 5 persons.*
—2 *tench, 2 eels, 2 onions, a faggot of herbs,*
4 *blades of mace,* 3 *anchovies,* 1 *pint of water,*
pepper and salt to taste, 1 *teaspoonful of*
chopped parsley, the yolks of 4 hard-boiled
eggs, puff-paste. AVERAGE COST, 2s. 2d.

Clean and bone the tench, skin and bone
the eels, and cut them into pieces 2 inches
long, and leave the sides of the tench whole.
Put the bones into a stewpan with the
onions, herbs, mace, anchovies, water and
seasoning, and let them simmer gently for
1 hour. Strain it off, put it to cool, and
skim off all the fat. Lay the tench and
eels in a pie-dish, and between each layer
put seasoning, chopped parsley, and hard-
boiled eggs; pour in part of the strained
liquor, cover in with puff-paste, and bake
for ½ hour or rather more. The oven should
be rather quick, and when done, heat the
remainder of the liquor, which pour into
the pie.

TIME.—½ *hour to bake, or rather more if*
the oven is slow.

Fish Sauce.—INGREDIENTS.—1½ oz.
of cayenne, 2 *tablespoonfuls of walnut ket-*
chup, 2 *tablespoonfuls of soy, a few shreds*
of garlic and shalot, 1 *quart of vinegar.*
AVERAGE COST, 1s.

Put all the ingredients into a large bottle,
and shake well every day for a fortnight.
Keep it in small bottles well sealed, and in
a few days it will be fit for use.

Fish, Scalloped. (Cold Meat Cook-
ery.)—INGREDIENTS *for dish for 3 persons.*
—*Remains of cold fish of any sort,* ¼ *pint of*
cream, ½ *tablespoonful of anchovy sauce,* ½
teaspoonful of made mustard, ditto of wal-
nut ketchup, pepper and salt to taste (the
above quantities are for ½ *lb. of fish when*
picked), bread-crumbs. AVERAGE COST,
exclusive of the cold fish, 7d.

Put all the ingredients into a stewpan,
carefully picking the fish from the bones;
set it on the fire, let it remain till nearly

hot, occasionally stir the contents, but do
not allow it to boil. When done, put the
fish into a deep dish or scallop shell with a
good quantity of bread-crumbs; place
small pieces of butter on the top, set in a
Dutch oven before the fire to brown, or use
a salamander.

TIME.—¼ *hour.*
SEASONABLE *at any time.*

Fish, Scalloped. (Cold Meat Cook-
ery.)—INGREDIENTS.—*Any cold fish,* 1 *egg,*
milk, 1 *large blade of pounded mace,* 1
tablespoonful of flour, 1 *teaspoonful of an-*
chovy sauce, pepper and salt to taste, bread-
crumbs, butter. AVERAGE COST, *exclusive*
of the fish, 4d.

Pick the fish carefully from the bones,
and moisten with milk and the egg; add
the other ingredients, and place in a deep
dish or scallop shells; cover with bread-
crumbs, butter the top, and brown before
the fire; when quite hot, serve.

Fish Souchy. — INGREDIENTS. —
Any fish such as flounders, soles or eels,
water, chopped parsley, carrots and turnips
cut as for Julienne, salt, water.

Put the water on the fire with sufficient
salt to make it taste of it, and the vegetables. When nearly done, add the fish,
stew till tender, and just before serving, add
the chopped parsley.

Fish Stock.—INGREDIENTS. — 2 *lbs.*
of beef or veal (these can be omitted), any
kind of trimmings of white fish which are
to be dressed for table, 2 *onions, the rind*
of half a lemon, a bunch of sweet herbs, 2
carrots, 2 *quarts of water.* AVERAGE COST,
without meat, 3d. *per quart.*

Cut up the fish, and put it, with the other
ingredients, into the water. Simmer for 2
hours; skim the liquor carefully, and strain
it. When a richer stock is wanted fry the
vegetables and fish before adding the water.

TIME.—2 *hours.*

Note.—Do not make fish stock long before it
is wanted, as it soon turns sour.

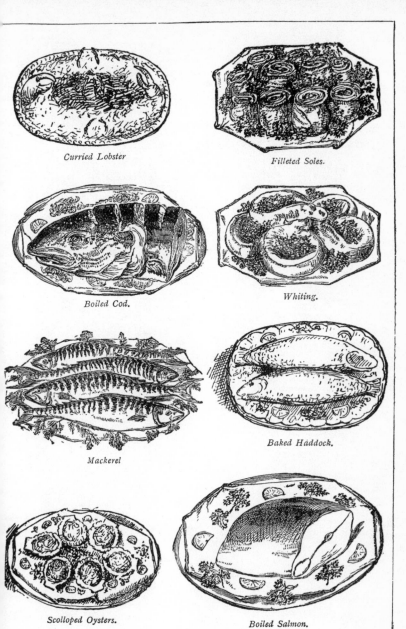

Curried Lobster

Filleted Soles.

Boiled Cod.

Whiting.

Mackerel

Baked Haddock.

Scolloped Oysters.

Boiled Salmon.

Fish.

Flounders, Boiled. — INGREDI-

NTS.—*Sufficient water to cover the floun-ers, salt in the proportion of 6 oz. to each allon, a little vinegar.* AVERAGE COST, *1. to 3d. each.*

Put on a kettle with enough water to over the flounders, lay in the fish, add salt ad vinegar in the above proportions, and hen it boils, simmer very gently for 5 inutes. They must not boil fast, or they ill break. Serve with plain melted butter, arsley and butter, or caper sauce.

TIME.—*After the water boils, 5 minutes.*
SEASONABLE *from August to November.*

Flounders, Fried.—INGREDIENTS.

-*Flounders, egg and bread-crumbs; boiling ard.* AVERAGE COST, *from 1d. to 3d. each.*

Cleanse the fish, and, two hours before aey are wanted, rub them inside and out ith salt, to render them firm; wash and

FLOUNDERS.

ipe them very dry, dip them into egg, ad sprinkle over with bread-crumbs; fry aem in boiling lard, dish on a hot napkin, ad garnish with crisped parsley.

TIME.—*From 5 to 10 minutes, according* * size.*
SEASONABLE *from August to November.*

Flour, Baked or Boiled (for

ifants' or Invalids' Food).—Tie the flour a a cloth as a pudding, put it in boiling ater and boil 3 hours. Scrape the inner art of the ball, and use a tablespoonful * a pint of milk to make gruel. To ake it, put it on a tin in the oven, and ake till it is a light brown colour. Flour eated in either of these ways is more igestible than used in its raw state.

Flowers, Almond.—INGREDIENTS.

—*Puff-paste; to every ¼ lb. of paste allow 3 oz. of almonds, sifted sugar, the white of an egg.*

Roll the paste out to the thickness of ¼ inch, and, with a round fluted cutter, stamp out as many pieces as may be required. Work the paste up again, roll it out, and, with a smaller cutter, stamp out some pieces the size of a shilling. Brush the larger pieces over with the white of an egg, and place one of the smaller pieces on each. Blanch and cut the almonds into strips lengthwise; press them slanting into the paste closely round the rings; and when they are all completed, sift over some pounded sugar, and bake for about ¼ hour or twenty minutes. Garnish between the almonds with strips of apple jelly, and place in centre of the ring a small quantity of gooseberry jam; pile them high on the dish and serve.

TIME.—¼ *hour or 20 minutes.*
SEASONABLE *at any time.*

Flummery.—INGREDIENTS *for quart*

mould.—1 *oz. of gelatine, the rind and juice of 1 lemon, 4 eggs, 1 pint of raisin wine, loaf sugar to taste, 1 pint of water.* AVERAGE COST, *1s. 6d.*

Put the gelatine with the lemon-rind in the water in a lined saucepan, and simmer gently until the gelatine is dissolved; strain into a basin and add the eggs, well beaten, the lemon-juice, strained, and the wine; sweeten to taste with pounded loaf sugar; mix all well together and pour the mixture into a jug. Put this jug, as a custard, in a pan of boiling water, and keep stirring until the mixture thickens, but do not let it *boil.* Strain it into an oiled or wetted mould, and put it in a cool place to set. It is better to make this dish the day before it is required.

TIME.—15 *minutes to simmer the gela-line,* 15 *minutes to stir.*
SEASONABLE *at any time.*

Foie Gras in Aspic. — Ingredients *for* 1½ *pint shape.*—1¼ *pint of aspic
jelly, a few sprays of chervil, a small piece
of truffle, a small pot of foie gras pâté.*
Average Cost, 2*s.* 6*d.*

Melt the jelly, and coat a border mould
with it. In this, arrange small dice of the
truffle and sprays of the chervil, then add
a little more jelly. Cut the foie gras in
thin slices about 1 inch square, and arrange
them with the remainder of the truffle and
chervil, with jelly, between in the mould till
it is full. When cold, turn out and fill the
centre with fresh cut salad.

Seasonable *at any time.*

Fondue.—Ingredients *for dish sufficient for 4 or 5 persons.*—4 *eggs, the weight
of* 2 *in Parmesan or good Cheshire cheese,
the weight of one in butter; pepper and
salt to taste.* Average Cost, 10*d.*

Separate the yolks from the whites of the
eggs; beat the former in a basin, and grate
the cheese, or cut it into *very thin* flakes.
Parmesan or Cheshire cheese may be used,
whichever is the most convenient, although
the former is considered more suitable for
this dish; or an equal quantity of each may
be used. Break the butter into small
pieces, add to it the other ingredients, with
sufficient pepper and salt to season nicely,
and beat the mixture thoroughly. Well
whisk the whites of the eggs, stir them
lightly in, and either bake the fondue in a
soufflé-dish or small round cake-tin. Fill the
dish only half full, as the fondue should
rise very much. Pin a napkin round the
tin or dish, and serve very hot and very
quickly. If allowed to stand after it is
withdrawn from the oven, the beauty and
lightness of this preparation will be entirely
spoiled.

Time.—*From* 15 *to* 20 *minutes.*
Seasonable *at any time.*

Fondue, Brillat Savarin's. (An
excellent Recipe.)— Ingredients. — *Eggs,
cheese, butter, pepper and salt.*

Take the same number of eggs as there
are guests; weigh the eggs in the shell,
allow a third of their weight in Gruyère
cheese, and a piece of butter one-sixth the
weight of the cheese. Break the eggs into
a basin, beat them well; add the cheese
which should be grated, and the butter
which should be broken into small pieces.
Stir these ingredients together with a
wooden spoon; put the mixture into a
lined saucepan, place it over the fire, and
stir it until the substance is thick and soft.
Put in a little salt, according to the age of
the cheese, and a good sprinkling of pepper,
and serve the fondue on a very hot silver
or metal plate. Do not allow the fondue
to remain on the fire after the mixture is
set, as, if it boils, it will be entirely spoiled.
Brillat Savarin recommends that some
choice Burgundy should be handed round
with this dish. We have given this recipe
exactly as he recommends it to be made,
but we have tried it with good Cheshire
cheese, and found it answer remarkably
well.

Time.—*About* 4 *minutes to set the mixture.*

Seasonable *at any time.*

Food for Infants, and its Pre-
paration. — The articles generally employed as food for infants consist of arrowroot, bread, flour, baked flour, prepared
groats, farinaceous food, biscuit-powder,
biscuits, tops-and-bottoms, and semolina, or
manna croup, as it is otherwise called,
which, like tapioca, is the prepared pith of
certain vegetable substances. Of this list
the least efficacious, though, perhaps, the
most believed in, is arrowroot, which only
as a mere agent, for change, and then only
for a very short time, should ever be employed as a means of diet in infancy or
childhood. It is thin, flatulent and innutritious food, and incapable of supporting
infantile life and energy. Bread, though
the universal *régime* with the labouring
poor, where the infant's stomach and diges

ive powers are a reflex, in minature, of the father's, should never be given to an infant under three months, and, even then, however finely beaten up and smoothly made, is a very questionable diet. Flour, when well boiled, though infinitely better than arrowroot, is still only a kind of fermentative paste, that counteracts its own good by after-acidity and flatulence.

Baked flour, when cooked into a pale brown mass, and finely powdered, makes a far superior food to the others, and may be considered as a very useful diet, especially for a change. Prepared groats may be classed with arrowroot and raw flour, as innutritious.

We may observe in this place that an occasional change in the character of the food is highly desirable, both as regards the health and benefit of the child; and, though the interruption should only last for a day, the change will be advantageous.

The packets sold as farinaceous food are unquestionably the best aliment that can be given from the first to a baby, and may be continued, with the exception of an occasional change, without alteration of the material, till the child is able to take its regular meals of animal and vegetable food. Some infants are so constituted as to require a frequent and a total change in their system of living, seeming to thrive for a certain time on any food given to them, but if persevered in too long, declining in bulk and appearance as rapidly as they had previously progressed. In such cases, the food should be immediately changed, and when that which appeared to agree best with the child is resumed, it should be altered in its quality, and perhaps in its consistency.

For the farinaceous food, there are directions with each packet, containing instructions for the making; but whatever the food employed is, enough should be made at once to last the day and night; at first, about a pint basinful, but, as the child advances, a quart will hardly be too much.

In all cases, let the food boil a sufficient time, constantly stirring, and taking every precaution that it does not get burnt, in which case it is on no account to be used.

The food should always be made with water, the whole sweetened at once, and of such a consistency that, when poured out, and it has had time to cool, it will cut with the firmness of a pudding or custard. One or two spoonfuls are to be put into the pap saucepan and stood on the hob till the heat has softened it, when enough milk is to be added, and carefully mixed with the food, till the whole has the consistency of ordinary cream; it is then to be poured into the nursing-bottle, and the food having been drawn through to warm the nipple, it is to be placed in the child's mouth. For the first month or more, half a bottleful will be quite enough to give the infant at one time; but, as the child grows, it will be necessary not only to increase the quantity given at each time, but also gradually to make its food more consistent, and, after the third month, to add an egg to every pint basin of food made. At night, the mother puts the food into the covered pan of her lamp, instead of the saucepan—that is, enough for one supply, and, having lighted the rush, she will find, on the waking of her child, the food sufficiently hot to bear the cooling addition of the milk. But, whether night or day, the same food should never be heated twice, and what the child leaves should be thrown away.

The biscuit powder is used in the same manner as the farinaceous food, and both prepared much after the fashion of making starch. But when tops-and-bottoms, or the whole biscuit, are employed, they require soaking in cold water for some time previously to boiling. The biscuit or biscuits are then to be slowly boiled in as much water as will, when thoroughly soft, allow of their being beaten by a three-pronged fork into a fine, smooth and even pulp, and which, when poured into a basin and become cold, will cut out like a custard. If two large biscuits have been so treated, and the child is six or seven months old, beat up two eggs, sufficient sugar to properly sweeten it, and about a pint of skimmed milk. Pour this on the beaten biscuits in the saucepan, stirring constantly; boil for about 5 minutes, pour into a basin, and use, when cold, in the same manner as the other.

This makes an admirable food, at once nutritious and strengthening. When tops-and-bottoms or rusks are used, the quantity of the egg may be reduced, or altogether omitted.

Semolina, or manna croup, being in little hard grains, like a fine millet-seed, must be boiled for some time, and the milk, sugar and egg added to it on the fire, and boiled for a few minutes longer, and, when cold, used as the other preparations.

Many persons entertain a belief that cow's milk is hurtful to infants, and, consequently, refrain from giving it; but this is a very great mistake, for both sugar and milk should form a large portion of every meal an infant takes. The only objection, moreover, is, that the milk from different cows varies in quality; and for this reason condensed milk is preferred for infant's food.

Forcemeats. — The points which cooks should, in this branch of cookery, more particularly observe, are the thorough chopping of the suet, the complete mincing of the herbs, the careful grating of the bread-crumbs, and the perfect mixing of the whole. These are the three principal ingredients of forcemeats, and they can scarcely be cut too small, as nothing like a lump or fibre should be anywhere perceptible. To conclude, the flavour of no one spice or herb should be permitted to predominate.

Forcemeat Balls (for Fish Soup). — INGREDIENTS *for large tureen of soup.*—1 *middling-sized lobster,* ½ *an anchovy,* 1 *head of boiled celery, the yolk of a hard-boiled egg; salt, cayenne and mace to taste,* 4 *tablespoonfuls of bread-crumbs,* 2 *oz. of butter,* 2 *eggs.* AVERAGE COST 2s. 6d.

Pick the meat from the shell of the lobster, and pound it, with the soft parts, in a mortar; add the celery, the yolk of the hard-boiled egg, seasoning and bread-crumbs. Continue pounding until the whole is nicely amalgamated. Warm the butter till it is in a liquid state; well whisk the eggs, and work these up with the pounded lobster-meat. Make the balls of about an inch in diameter, and fry of a nice pale brown.

SEASONABLE *at any time.*

Forcemeat, French.—It will be well to state, in the beginning of this recipe, that French forcemeat, or quenelles, consist of the blending of three separate processes; namely, panada, udder and whatever meat you intend using.

Panada.—INGREDIENTS.—*The crumb of* 2 *penny rolls,* 4 *tablespoonfuls of white stock,* 1 *oz. of butter,* 1 *slice of ham,* 1 *bay-leaf, a little minced parsley,* 2 *shalots,* 1 *clove,* 2 *blades of mace, a few mushrooms, butter, the yolks of* 2 *eggs.*

Soak the crumb of the rolls in milk for about ½ hour, then take it out, and squeeze so as to press the milk from it; put the soaked bread into a stewpan with the above quantity of white stock, and set it on one side; then put into a separate stewpan 1 oz. of butter, a slice of lean ham cut small, with a bay-leaf, herbs, mushrooms, spices, &c., in the above proportions, and fry them gently over a slow fire. When done, moisten with 2 teacupfuls of white stock, boil for 20 minutes, and strain the whole through a sieve over the panada in the other stewpan. Place it over the fire, keep constantly stirring to prevent it burning, and, when quite dry, put in a small piece of butter, Let this again dry up by stirring over the fire; then add the yolks of 2 eggs, mix well, ut the panada to cool on a clean plate, nd use it when required. Panada should lways be well flavoured, as the forcemeat eceives no taste from any of the other in-redients used in its preparation.

Boiled Calf's Udder for French Force-meat.—Put the udder into a stewpan with ufficient water to cover it; let it stew ently till quite done, when take it out to ool. Trim all the upper parts, cut it into mall pieces, and pound well in a mortar, ill it can be rubbed through a sieve. That ortion which passes through the strainer s one of the three ingredients of which rench forcemeats are generally composed; ut many cooks substitute butter for this, eing a less troublesome and more expedi-ous mode of preparation.

Forcemeat (for Cold Savoury Pies). -Ingredients for 1 large pie.—1 lb. of eal, 1 lb. of fat bacon; salt, cayenne, epper and pounded mace to taste; a very ttle nutmeg, the same of chopped lemon-eel, ½ teaspoonful of chopped parsley, ½ easpoonful of minced savoury herbs, 1 or 2 ggs. Average Cost, 9d.

Chop the veal and bacon together, and ut them into a mortar with the other ngredients mentioned above. Pound well, nd bind with 1 or 2 eggs which have been reviously beaten and strained. Work the hole well together, and the forcemeat ill be ready for use. If the pie is not to e eaten immediately, omit the herbs and arsley, as these will prevent it from eeping. Mushrooms or truffles may be dded.

Forcemeat (for Pike, Carp, Haddock, nd various kinds of Fish).—Ingredients r sufficient for 1 good-sized fish.—1 oz. of esh butter, 1 oz. of suet, 1 oz. of fat bacon, small teaspoonful of minced savoury erbs, including parsley; a little onion, hen liked, shredded very fine; salt, nut-eg and cayenne to taste; 4 oz. of bread-rumbs, 1 egg. Average Cost, 4d.

Mix all the ingredients well together, carefully mincing them very finely; beat up the egg, moisten with it, and work the whole very smoothly together. Oysters or anchovies may be added to this forcemeat, and will be found a great improvement.

Forcemeat (for Baked Pike).—In-gredients sufficient for good-sized fish.—3 oz. of bread-crumbs, 1 teaspoonful of minced savoury herbs, 8 oysters, 2 anchovies (these may be dispensed with), 2 oz. of suet; salt, pepper and pounded mace to taste; 6 tablespoonfuls of cream or milk, the yolks of 2 eggs. Average Cost, 1s. 1d.

Beard and mince the oysters, prepare and mix the other ingredients, and blend the whole thoroughly together. Moisten with the cream and eggs, put all into a stewpan, and stir it over the fire till it thickens, when put it into the fish, which should have previously been cut open, and sew it up.

Time.—4 or 5 minutes to thicken.

Forcemeat, or Quenelles (for Turtle Soup.) (Soyer's Recipe).—Take a pound and a half of lean veal from the fillet, and cut it in long thin slices; scrape with a knife till nothing but the fibre re-mains; put it into a mortar, pound it 10 minutes, or until in a purée; pass it through a wire sieve (use the remainder in stock); then take 1 lb. of good fresh beef suet, which skin, shred and chop very fine; put it into a mortar and pound it; then add 6 oz. of panada (that is, bread soaked in milk and boiled till nearly dry) with the suet; pound them well together, and add the veal; season with a teaspoonful of salt, a quarter one of pepper, half that of nut-meg; work all well together; then add 4 eggs by degrees, continually pounding the contents of the mortar. When well mixed, take a small piece in a spoon, and poach it in some boiling water; and if it is delicate, firm, and of good flavour, it is ready for use.

Forcemeat, Veal, or Veal Quenelles.—INGREDIENTS.—*Equal quantities of veal, panada and calf's udder, 2 eggs, seasoning to taste of pepper, salt and pounded mace or grated nutmeg; a little flour.*

Take the fleshy part of veal, scrape it with a knife, till all the meat is separated from the sinews, and allow about ½ lb. for an entrée. Chop the meat, and pound it in a mortar till reduced to a paste; then roll it into a ball; make another of panada the same size, and another of udder, taking care that these three balls be of the same size. (It is to be remembered, that equality of *size*, and not of weight, is here necessary.) When the three ingredients are properly prepared, pound them all together in a mortar for some time; for the more quenelles are pounded, the more delicate they are. Now moisten with the eggs, whites and yolks, and continue pounding, adding a seasoning of pepper, spices, &c. When the whole is well blended together, mould it into balls, or whatever shape is intended, roll them in flour, and poach in boiling water, to which a little salt should have been added. If the quenelles are not firm enough, add the yolk of another egg, but omit the white, which only makes them hollow and puffy inside. In the preparation of this recipe, it would be well to bear in mind that the ingredients are to be well pounded and seasoned, and must be made hard or soft according to the dishes they are intended for. For brown or white ragoûts they should be firm, and when the quenelles are used very small, extreme delicacy will be necessary in their preparation. Their flavour may be varied by using the flesh of rabbit, fowl, hare, pheasant, grouse, or an extra quantity of mushroom, parsley, &c.

Forcemeat (for Veal, Turkeys, Fowls, Hare, &c.)—INGREDIENTS *for sufficient for a turkey of moderate size.*—2 *oz. of ham or lean bacon, ¼ lb. of suet, the rind of* half a lemon, 1 *teaspoonful of minced parsley*, 1 *teaspoonful of minced lemon thyme salt, cayenne and pounded mace to taste* 6 *oz. of bread-crumbs, 2 eggs.* AVERAGE COST, 7d.

Shred the ham or bacon, chop the suet lemon-peel, and herbs, taking particular care that all be very finely minced; add a seasoning to taste of salt, cayenne and mace, and blend all thoroughly together with the bread-crumbs, before wetting Now beat and strain the eggs; work these up with the other ingredients, and the forcemeat will be ready for use. When it is made into balls, fry of a nice brown, in boiling lard, or put them on a tin and bake for ½ hour in a moderate oven. As we have stated before, no one flavour should predominate greatly, and the forcemeat should be of sufficient body to cut with a knife and yet not dry and heavy. For very delicate forcemeat, it is advisable to pound the ingredients together before binding with the eggs; but for ordinary cooking mincing very finely answers the purpose.

Note.—In the forcemeat for hare, the liver of the animal is sometimes added. Boil for minutes, mince it very small, and mix it with the other ingredients. If it should be in an unsound state, it must be on no account made use of.

Fowl, Trussing of, for Boiling

—It is a more difficult task to truss a fowl for boiling than for roasting, for it is no

LOOSENING SKIN OF LEGS.

easy to draw the skin over the legs without breaking it.

It is best to cut off the legs at the knee joint, then to loosen the skin as shown

en the skin must be drawn over the legs
s in illustration, next skewer the pinions

DRAWING SKIN OVER LEGS.

nd legs as shown, remembering it should
e the aim of all good cooks to make a

SKEWERING OF PINIONS.

oiled fowl look as neat, plump, and com-
act as possible.

FOWL TRUSSED FOR BOILING.

Fowl, Trussing of, for Roast-
g.—Having drawn the fowl, dip the legs
boiling water, and after scraping them,
at off the claws or the whole feet if pre-
rred, and the tips of pinions.

Skewer the pinions as shown in illustra-
on with one skewer passed through the
rst joint of the one on the right side (the
iddle of the leg being brought close to it),
en through the body and the left
inion.

Next draw the skin over the neck, and
skewer it back with a small skewer.

SKEWERING OF PINIONS.

To skewer the legs, take a long skewer,
and having put it through the skin of the
back, run it through the first joint of the

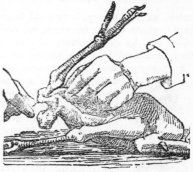

SKEWERING OF LEGS.

leg, taking up a small piece of skin, then
on through the leg on the right side in the
same manner, see illustration.

Fowls, Boiled, à la Béchamel.
—INGREDIENTS.—*A pair of fowls, 1 pint of
Béchamel, a few bunches of boiled broccoli
or cauliflower. AVERAGE COST, 5s. per
pair.*

Truss and boil the fowls; make a pint
of Béchamel sauce; pour some of this over
the fowls, and the remainder send to table
in a tureen. Garnish the dish with bunches
of boiled cauliflowers or broccoli, and serve
very hot. The sauce should be made

sufficiently thick to adhere to the fowls; that for the tureen should be thinned by adding a spoonful or two of stock.

TIME.—*From ½ to 1 hour, according to size.*

SEASONABLE *all the year, but scarce in early spring.*

Fowls, Boiled, To Carve.—

This will not be found a very difficult member of the poultry family to carve,

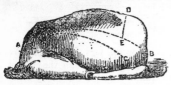

CARVING OF BOILED FOWL.

unless, as may happen, a very old farm-yard occupant, useless for egg-laying purposes, has, by some unlucky mischance, been introduced into the kitchen as a "fine young chicken." Skill, however, and

the application of a small amount of strength, combined with a fine keeping of the temper, will even get over that difficulty. Fixing the fork firmly in the breast, let the knife be firmly passed along the line shown from A to B; then cut downwards from that line to fig. C and the wing, it will be found, can be easily withdrawn. The shape of the wing should

LEG, WING AND NECKBONE OF FOWL.

be like the accompanying engraving. Let the fork be placed inside the leg, which should be gently forced away from the body of the fowl; and the joint, being thus discovered, the carver can readily cut through it, and the leg can be served. When the leg is displaced, it should be of the same shape as that shown in the annexed woodcut. The legs and wings on either side having

been taken off, the carver should draw his knife through the flesh in the direction of the line D to E; by this means the knife can be slipped underneath the merrythought which, being lifted up and pressed backward, will immediately come off. The collar or neck-bones are the next to consider; these lie on each side of the merrythought, close under the upper part of the wings; and, in order to free these from the fowl, they must also be raised by the knife at their broad end, and turned from the body towards the breast-bone until the shorter piece of the bone, as shown in the cut, breaks off. There will now be left only the breast, with the ribs. The breast can be, without difficulty, disengaged from the ribs by cutting through the latter, which will offer little impediment. The side bones are now to be taken off; and to do this, the lower end of the back should be turned from the carver who should press the point of the knife through the top of the backbone, near the centre, bringing it down towards the end of the back completely through the bone. If the knife be now turned in the opposite direction, the joint will be easily separated from the vertebræ. The backbone being now uppermost, the fork should be pressed firmly down on it, whilst at the same time the knife should be employed in raising up the lower small end of the fowl towards the fork, and thus the back will be dislocated about its middle. The wings, breast and merrythought are esteemed the prime part of a fowl, and are usually served to the ladies of the company, to whom legs except as a matter of paramount necessity should not be given. Byron gave it as one reason why he did not like dining with the ladies, that they always had the wings of the fowl, which he himself preferred. We heard a gentleman who, when he might have had a wing, declare his partiality for a leg, saying that he had been obliged to eat legs for so long a time that he had at last come to like them better than the other

nore prized parts. If the fowl is, capon-
like, very large, slices may be carved from
ts breast in the same manner as from a
urkey's.

Fowls, Boiled, with Oysters.

(Excellent).—INGREDIENTS *for dish for 4
ersons.*—1 *young fowl,* 2½ *dozen oysters, the
olks of 2 eggs,* ¼ *pint of cream.* AVERAGE
COST, 5s.

Truss a fowl as for boiling; fill the in-
ide with oysters which have been bearded
nd washed in their own liquor; secure the
nds of the fowl, put it into a jar, and
lunge it into a saucepan of boiling water.
Keep it boiling for 1½ hour, or rather
onger; then take the gravy that has
lowed from the oysters and fowl, of which
here will be a good quantity; stir in the
ream and yolks of eggs, add a few oysters
calded in their liquor; let the sauce get
uite *hot,* but do not allow it to *boil ;*
our some of it over the fowl, and the
emainder send to table in a tureen. A
lade of pounded mace added to the sauce,
vith the cream and eggs, will be found an
mprovement.

TIME —1½ *hour.*
SEASONABLE *from September to April.*

Fowls, Broiled, and Mush-
oom Sauce.—INGREDIENTS *for dish for
persons.*—A *large fowl; seasoning to taste,
f pepper and salt,* 2 *handfuls of button
ushrooms,* 1 *slice of lean ham,* ¾ *pint of
hickened gravy,* 1 *teaspoonful of lemon
uice,* ½ *teaspoonful of pounded sugar.*
AVERAGE COST, 4s. 6d.

Cut the fowl into quarters, roast it until
hree-parts done, and keep it well basted
vhilst at the fire. Take the fowl up, broil
t for a few minutes over a clear fire, and
eason it with pepper and salt. Have ready
ome mushroom sauce made in the fol-
owing manner. Put the mushrooms into
stewpan with a small piece of butter, the
am, a seasoning of pepper and salt, and

the gravy; simmer these gently for ½ hour,
add the lemon-juice and sugar, dish the
fowl, and pour the sauce round them.

BROILED FOWL.

TIME.—*To roast the fowl,* 35 *minutes; to
broil it,* 10 *to* 15 *minutes.*
SEASONABLE.—*In full season from May
to January.*

Fowl, Boiled, and Rice. — IN-
GREDIENTS *for sufficient for 4 persons.*—1
fowl, mutton broth, 2 *onions,* 2 *small blades
of pounded mace, pepper and salt to taste,*
¼ *pint of rice, parsley and butter.* AVERAGE
COST, 2s. 9d.

Truss the fowl as for boiling, and put
it into a stewpan with sufficient clear, well-
skimmed mutton broth to cover it; add the
onion, mace and a seasoning of pepper and
salt; stew very gently for about 1 hour,
should the fowl be large; and about ½ hour
before it is ready, put in the rice, which
should be well washed and soaked. When
the latter is tender, strain it from the
liquor, and put it on a sieve reversed, to
dry before the fire, and, in the meantime,
keep the fowl hot. Dish it, put the rice
round as a border, pour a little parsley and
butter over the fowl, and the remainder
send to table in a tureen.

TIME.—*A large fowl,* 1 *hour.*
SEASONABLE *all the year.*

Fowl, To Bone (for Fricassees,
Curries and Pies).—First carve them entirely into joints, then remove the bones,
beginning with the legs and wings, at the
head of the largest bone; hold this with
the fingers, and work the knife as directed
in the recipe "Fowl, To Stuff and Bone."
The remainder of the bird is too easily
done to require any instructions.

Fowl, Croquettes of. (An Entrée).

—INGREDIENTS.—1 or 2 shalots, or lemon and herb flavouring, 1 oz. of butter, 1 teaspoonful of flour, white sauce; pepper, salt and pounded mace to taste; ½ teaspoonful of pounded sugar, the remains of cold roast fowls, the yolks of 2 eggs, egg and bread-crumbs. AVERAGE COST, exclusive of the cold fowl, 6d.

Mince the fowl, carefully removing all skin and bone, and fry the shalots in the butter; add the minced fowl, dredge in the flour, put in the pepper, salt, mace, pounded sugar and sufficient white sauce to moisten it; stir to it the yolks of 2 well-beaten eggs, and set it by to cool. Then make the mixture up into balls, egg and bread-crumb them and fry a nice brown. They may be served on a border of mashed potatoes, with gravy or sauce in the centre, or dry.

TIME.—10 minutes to fry the balls.

SEASONABLE at any time.

Fowl and Rice, Croquettes of.

(An Entrée).—INGREDIENTS for small dish.—¼ lb. of rice, 1 quart of stock or broth, 3 oz. of butter, minced fowl, egg and bread-crumbs. AVERAGE COST, exclusive of the fowl, 9d.

Put the rice into the above proportion of cold stock or broth, and let it boil very gently for ½ hour; then add the butter, and simmer it till quite dry and soft. When cold, make it into balls, hollow out the inside, and fill with minced fowl made by recipe. The mince should be rather thick. Cover over with rice, dip the balls into egg, sprinkle them with bread-crumbs and fry a nice brown. Dish them, and garnish with fried parsley. Oysters, white sauce, or a little cream, may be stirred into the rice before it cools.

TIME.—½ hour to boil the rice, 10 minutes to fry the croquettes.

SEASONABLE at any time.

Fowl, Curried.

—INGREDIENTS for dish sufficient for 4 persons.—1 fowl, 2 oz. of butter, 3 onions sliced, 1 pint of white veal gravy, 1 teaspoonful of curry-powder, 1 tablespoonful of flour, 1 apple, 4 tablespoonful of cream, 1 tablespoonful of lemon-juice. AVERAGE COST, 3s. 6d.

Put the butter into a stewpan, with the onions sliced, the fowl cut into small joints and the apple peeled, cored and minced. Fry of a pale brown, add the stock, and stew gently for 20 minutes; rub down the curry-powder and flour, with a little of the gravy, quite smoothly, and stir this to the other ingredients; simmer for rather more than ½ hour, and just before serving, add the above proportion of hot cream and lemon-juice. Serve with boiled rice, which may either be heaped lightly on a dish by itself, or put round the curry as a border.

TIME.—50 minutes.

SEASONABLE in the winter.

Note.—This curry may be made of cold fowl but fresh is better.

Fowl, Fricasseed. (Cold Meat Cookery.)—INGREDIENTS.—The remains of cold roast fowl, 1 strip of lemon-peel, 1 blade of pounded mace, 1 bunch of savoury herbs, 1 onion, pepper and salt to taste, 1 pint of water, 1 teaspoonful of flour, ¼ pint of cream the yolks of 2 eggs. AVERAGE COST, exclusive of the cold fowl, 8d.

Carve the fowl into nice joints; make gravy of the trimmings and legs, by stewing with the lemon-peel, mace, herbs, onion, seasoning and water, until reduced to ½ pint; then strain, and put in the fowl. Warm it through, and thicken with a teaspoonful of flour; stir the yolks of the eggs into the cream, add these to the sauce, let it get thoroughly hot, but do not allow it to boil, or it will curdle.

TIME.—1 hour to make the gravy, ½ hour to warm the fowl.

SEASONABLE at any time.

Fowl, Fried. (Cold Meat Cookery.)

—INGREDIENTS.—The remains of cold roast fowl, vinegar, salt and cayenne to taste, 3 or 4 minced shalots. For the batter—½ lb.

f flour, ½ pint of hot water, 2 oz. of butter, he whites of 2 eggs. AVERAGE COST, exlusive of the cold fowl, 8d.

Cut the fowl into nice joints; steep hem for an hour in a little vinegar, with alt, cayenne and minced shalots. Make he batter by mixing the flour and water moothly together; melt in it the butter, nd add the whites of egg beaten to a roth; take out the pieces of fowl, dip hem in the batter, and fry in boiling ard, a nice brown. Pile them high in the lish, and garnish with fried parsley or olled bacon. When approved, a sauce or rravy may be served with them.

TIME.—10 minutes to fry the fowl.
SEASONABLE at any time.

Fowl, Fried. (Cold Meat Cookery.)

—INGREDIENTS.—The remains of cold roast owl, vinegar, salt and cayenne to taste, minced shalots, yolk of egg; to every teacupful of bread-crumbs allow 1 blade of pounded mace, ½ teaspoonful of minced lemon-peel, 1 saltspoonful of salt, a few grains of cayenne. AVERAGE COST, exclusive of the fowl, 4d.

Steep the pieces of fowl as in the preceding recipe, then dip them into the yolk of an egg or clarified butter; sprinkle over bread-crumbs with which have been mixed salt, mace, cayenne and lemon-peel in the above proportion. Fry a light brown, and serve with or without gravy, as preferred.

TIME.—10 minutes to fry the fowl.
SEASONABLE at any time.

Fowl, Fried, and French Beans. (Cold Meat Cookery.)— INGREDIENTS.—The remains of cold roast fowl, the yolk of 1 egg, 2 oz. of butter, 1 blade of pounded mace, ¼ saltspoonful of grated nutmeg, bread-crumbs and chopped parsley. AVERAGE COST, exclusive of cold fowl, 4d.

Cut the fowl into neat joints, brush them over with the yolk of egg, and sprinkle them with bread-crumbs, with which the parsley, nutmeg and mace have been well mixed. Fry the fowl in butter until of a

nice brown, and dish the pieces on French beans, boiled and afterwards simmered for a minute or two in butter. The dish should be garnished with rolled bacon.

TIME.—10 minutes to fry the fowl.
SEASONABLE from July to September.

Fowl au Gratin. (Cold Meat Cookery.)—INGREDIENTS.—The remains of either cold roast or boiled fowl, ½ pint of Béchamel sauce, a dessertspoonful of grated Parmesan cheese, pepper and salt to taste, ¼ saltspoonful of grated nutmeg, ¼ pint of cream, 2 tablespoonfuls of bread-crumbs, fried potatoes.

Mince the fowl, not too finely, and make it hot in the Béchamel sauce, to which the nutmeg, pepper and salt, and cream have been added. When well mixed, put the fowl on a dish, cover it with the bread-crumbs and Parmesan cheese, drop over a little clarified butter, and bake in the oven until of a pale brown. Garnish the dish with fried potatoes.

TIME.—10 minutes to warm the fowl, 10 minutes to bake.

SEASONABLE at any time.

Fowl, Hashed. (Cold Meat Cookery.)

—INGREDIENTS.—The remains of cold roast fowl, 1 pint of water, 1 onion, 1 blade of pounded mace, pepper and salt to taste, 1 small bunch of savoury herbs, thickening of butter and flour, 1½ tablespoonful of mushroom ketchup. AVERAGE COST, exclusive of the fowl, 3d.

Cut off the best joints from the fowl, and the remainder make into gravy, by adding to the bones and trimmings a pint of water, an onion, sliced and fried of a nice brown, the mace, seasoning and herbs. Let these stew gently for 1½ hour, strain the liquor, and thicken with a little flour and butter. Lay in the fowl, thoroughly warm it through, add the ketchup, and garnish with sippets of toasted bread.

TIME.—Altogether 1¾ hour.
SEASONABLE at any time.

Fowl, Hashed. (Indian Fashion.) (Cold Meat Cookery.)—INGREDIENTS.—*The remains of cold roast fowl, 3 or 4 sliced onions, 1 apple, 2 oz. of butter, pounded mace, pepper and salt to taste, 1 tablespoonful of curry powder, 2 tablespoonfuls of vinegar, 1 tablespoonful of flour, 1 teaspoonful of pounded sugar, 1 pint of gravy.* AVERAGE COST, *exclusive of the cold fowl,* 8d.

Cut the onions into slices, mince the apple, and fry these in the butter ; add pounded mace, pepper, salt, curry-powder, vinegar, flour and sugar in the above proportions ; when the onion is brown, put in the gravy, which should be previously made from the bones and trimmings of the fowls, and stew ¾ hour ; add the fowl, cut into nice-sized joints, let it warm through, and when quite tender, serve. The dish should be garnished with an edging of boiled rice.

TIME.—1 *hour.*

SEASONABLE *at any time.*

Fowl, An Indian Dish of. (An Entrée.) (Cold Meat Cookery.)—INGREDIENTS.—*The remains of cold roast fowl, 3 or 4 sliced onions, 1 tablespoonful of curry-powder, salt to taste.* AVERAGE COST, *exclusive of the fowl,* 3d.

Divide the fowl into joints ; slice and fry the onions in a little butter, taking care not to burn them ; sprinkle over the fowl a little curry-powder and salt ; fry these nicely, pile them high in the centre of the dish, cover with the onion, and serve with a cut lemon on a plate. Care must be taken that the onions are not greasy : they should be quite dry, but not burnt.

TIME.—5 *minutes to fry the onions,* 10 *minutes to fry the fowl.*

SEASONABLE *in winter.*

Fowl à la Mayonnaise.—INGREDIENTS *for dish sufficient for 4 persons.*—*A cold roast fowl, Mayonnaise sauce, 4 or 5 young lettuces, 4 hard-boiled eggs, a few watercresses, endive.* AVERAGE COST, 3s. 6d.

Cut the fowl into neat joints, lay them in a deep dish, piling them high in the centre ; mask the fowl with Mayonnaise, and garnish the dish with young lettuces cut up, watercresses, endive and slices of hard boiled eggs. All kinds of cold meat and solid fish may be dressed à la Mayonnaise, and make excellent luncheon or supper dishes. The sauce should not be poured over the fowls until the moment of serving. Should a very large Mayonnaise be required, use 2 fowls instead of one, with an equal proportion of remaining ingredients.

SEASONABLE *from April to September.*

Fowl, Minced. (An Entrée.) (Cold Meat Cookery.)—INGREDIENTS *for moderate-sized dish.*—*The remains of cold roast fowl, 2 hard-boiled eggs, salt, cayenne and pounded mace, 1 onion, 1 faggot of savoury herbs, 6 tablespoonfuls of cream, 1 oz. of butter, 2 teaspoonfuls of flour, ½ teaspoonful of finely-minced lemon-peel, 1 tablespoonful of lemon-juice.* AVERAGE COST, *exclusive of the fowl,* 9d.

Cut out from the fowl all the white meat and mince it finely, without any skin or bone ; put the bones, skin and trimmings into a stewpan, with an onion, a bunch of savoury herbs, a blade of mace and nearly a pint of water ; let this stew for an hour, then strain the liquor. Chop the egg small ; mix them with the fowl ; add salt, cayenne and pounded mace, put in the gravy and remaining ingredients ; let the whole just boil, and serve with sippets of toasted bread.

TIME.—*Rather more than* 1 *hour.*

SEASONABLE *at any time.*

Note.—Another way to make this is to mince the fowl, and warm it in white sauce or Béchamel. When dressed like this, 3 or 4 poached eggs may be placed on the top : oysters, or chopped mushrooms, or balls of oyster forcemeat may be laid round the dish.

Fowl, Minced, à la Béchamel. (Cold Meat Cookery.) — INGREDIENTS *for small dish.—The remains of cold roast fowl* tablespoonfuls of Béchamel sauce, 6 table-poonfuls of white stock, the white of 1 egg, read-crumbs, clarified butter. AVERAGE COST, exclusive of the cold fowl, 8d.

Take the remains of roast fowl, mince he white meat very small, and put it into stewpan with the Béchamel and stock ; tir it well over the fire, and just let it boil up. Pour the mince into a dish, beat up the vhite of egg, spread it over, and strew on t a few grated bread-crumbs ; pour a very ittle clarified butter on the whole, and rown either before the fire or with a sala-mander. This should be served in a silver lish, if not hand.

TIME.—2 or 3 minutes to simmer in the auce.

SEASONABLE at any time.

Fowl, Ragoût of. (Cold Meat Cookery.)—INGREDIENTS for moderate-sized dish.—The remains of cold roast fowl, 3 halots, 2 blades of mace, a faggot of avoury herbs, 2 or 3 slices of lean ham, 1 int of stock or water, pepper and salt to aste, 1 onion, 1 dessertspoonful of flour, 1 ablespoonful of lemon-juice, ½ teaspoonful f pounded sugar, 1 oz. of butter. AVERAGE COST, exclusive of the fowl, 9d.

Cut the fowl up into neat pieces, the same as for a fricassee ; put the trimmings nto a stewpan with the shalots, mace, herbs, ham, onion and stock (water may be ubstituted for this). Boil it slowly for 1 our, strain the liquor, and put a small piece of butter into a stewpan ; when melted, dredge in sufficient flour to dry up the utter, and stir it over the fire. Put in the strained liquor, boil for a few minutes, and strain it again over the pieces of fowl. Squeeze in the lemon-juice, add the sugar and a seasoning of pepper and salt, make t hot, but do not allow it to boil ; lay the fowl neatly on the dish, and garnish with croûtons.

TIME.—Altogether, 1½ hour.

SEASONABLE at any time.

Fowl, Roast.—INGREDIENTS sufficient for 8 persons.—A pair of fowls, a little flour, butter. AVERAGE COST, 5s. to 6s. per pair.

When firmly trussed, singe them all over ; put them down to a bright, clear fire, paper

ROAST FOWL.

the breasts with a sheet of buttered paper, and keep the fowls well basted. Roast them for ¾ hour, more or less, according to the size, and 10 minutes before serving, remove the paper, dredge the fowls with a little fine flour, put a piece of butter into the basting-ladle, and as it melts baste the fowls with it ; when nicely frothed and of a rich colour, serve with good brown gravy (a little of which should be poured over the fowls), and a tureen of well-made bread sauce. Mushroom or oyster sauce are very suitable accompaniments to roast fowl. Chicken is roasted in the same manner.

TIME.—A very large fowl, quite 1 hour, a medium-sized one, ¾ hour ; chicken, ½ hour, or rather longer.

SEASONABLE all the year, but scarce in early spring.

Fowl, Roast, To Carve.—A roast fowl is carved in the same manner as a boiled fowl, viz., by cutting along the line

ROAST FOWL.

from A to B, and then round the leg between it and the wing. The markings and detached pieces, as shown in the engravings under the heading of "Boiled Fowl," supersede the necessity of our lengthily again describing the operation. It may be added that the liver, being considered a delicacy, should be divided, and one half served with each wing. In the case of a fowl being stuffed, it will be proper to give each guest a portion, unless it be not agreeable to some of the party.

Fowl, Roast, Stuffed. — INGREDIENTS *for dish for 4 or 5 persons.—A large fowl, forcemeat, a little flour.* AVERAGE COST, 4s.

Select a large plump fowl, fill the breast with forcemeat, truss it firmly, the same as for a plain roast fowl, dredge it with flour, and put it down to a bright fire. Roast it for nearly or quite an hour, should it be very large ; remove the skewers, and serve with a good brown gravy and a tureen of bread sauce.

TIME.—*Large fowl, nearly or quite* 1 *hour.* SEASONABLE *all the year, but scarce in early spring.*

Note.—Sausage-meat stuffing may be substituted for the forcemeat.

Fowl Sauté, with Peas. (Cold Meat Cookery.)—INGREDIENTS.—*The remains of cold roast fowl,* 2 *oz. of butter, pepper, salt and pounded mace to taste,* 1 *dessertspoonful of flour,* ½ *pint of weak stock,* 1 *pint of green peas,* 1 *teaspoonful of pounded sugar.* AVERAGE COST, *exclusive of the cold fowl,* 9d.

Cut the fowl into nice pieces ; put the butter into a stewpan ; sautez or fry the fowl a nice brown colour, previously sprinkling it with pepper, salt and pounded mace. Dredge in the flour, shake the ingredients well round, then add the stock and peas, and stew till the latter are tender, which will be in about 20 minutes ; put in the pounded sugar and serve, placing the chicken round, and the peas in the middle of the dish. When liked, mushrooms may be substituted for the peas.

TIME.—*Altogether,* 40 *minutes.*
SEASONABLE *from June to August.*

Fowl Scollops. (Cold Meat Cookery.)—INGREDIENTS.—*The remains of cold roast or boiled fowl,* ½ *pint of Béchamel, or white sauce.*

Strip off the skin from the fowl ; cut the meat into thin slices, and warm them in about ½ pint, or rather more of Béchamel or white sauce. When quite hot, serve, and garnish the dish with rolled ham or bacon toasted.

TIME.—1 *minute to simmer the slices of fowl.*
SEASONABLE *at any time.*

Fowl, To Stuff and Bone. (Miss ACTON'S Recipe.) — Cut through the skin down the centre of the back, and raise the flesh carefully on either side with the point of a sharp knife, until the sockets of the wings and thighs are reached. Till a little practice has been gained, it will perhaps be best to bone their joints before proceeding further ; but after they are once detached from it, the whole of the body may be easily separated from the flesh, and taken

FOWL, BONED.

out entire; only the neck, bones and the merrythought will then remain to be removed. The bird thus prepared may either be restored to its original form by filling the legs and wings with forcemeat, and the body with chopped tongue or bacon, sausage meat or forcemeat, such as will give a marbled appearance to the bird when cut, and then be sewed up and trussed as usual ; or the legs and wings may be drawn inside the body, when less stuffing will be required. In any case the fowl when cooked should present a smooth rounded surface easy to carve.

French Cookery.—French cookery ranks deservedly high, and it may be said that in no country is there more interest taken in the art, nor more ambition to excel. We must confess there is, or has been, a certain lack of enterprise amongst those who practice cooking here; and it has been owing to the introduction of French cookery and French cooks that of late, strides have been taken towards arriving at a due appreciation of the importance of good cookery, and mastering its science.

We have now schools within the reach of even the poorest, where English girls can learn, not only how to bake, boil and stew, but what should be treated in these various modes of cooking, and why; also the most economical way of using and cooking food. Advancing higher, we now learn from good cookery books as well as schools how to make the various dainty dishes that used to be out of the reach of English cooks, but " Honour to whom Honour is due ; " it is to the French we owe our inspiration to become perfect in the art of cookery.

Most of the entrées and made dishes which are, by reason of their delicate sauces and flavouring, as well as by the difficulty of their preparation esteemed more highly than simply cooked food, we owe to the cleverness of the French cooks, and it is rare that we ever give them English names; but a still greater advantage in French cookery is how to make the most of and utilize everything in the way of food. In the kitchen of the lower middle class and the poorer of the French people, no matter to what class they belong, there is far less meat—the most costly of our provisions—consumed, than in the same classes here, yet the fare is more varied, more dainty and more appetising than ours.

In one thing we must all agree in reference to French cookery, and that is, that their way of treating vegetables is superior to ours and that in their hands they become not simply accessories, but in themselves one of the pleasantest of foods.

French Terms used in modern Household Cookery, explained.

Appetisans. — Small savouries, such as caviare, stuffed olives, &c., served before or between the courses of a dinner.

Aspic.—A savoury jelly, used as an exterior moulding for cold game, poultry, fish, &c. This, being of a transparent nature, allows the articles which it covers to be seen through it. Also used for decorating or garnishing.

Assiette (plate).—*Assiettes* are the small *entrées* and *hors d'œuvres,* the quantity of which does not exceed what a plate will hold. At dessert, fruits, cheese, chestnuts, biscuits, &c., if served upon a plate, are termed *assiettes.*

Assiette volante is a dish which a servant hands round to the guests, but is not placed upon the table. Small cheese soufflés and different dishes, which ought to be served very hot, are frequently made *assiettes volantes.*

Au-bleu.—Fish dressed in such a manner as to have a *bluish* appearance.

Au-naturel. — Plain simple cookery, generally boiling in water.

Bain-marie.—An open saucepan or kettle of nearly boiling water, in which a smaller vessel can be set for cooking and warming. This is very useful for keeping articles hot, without altering their quantity or quality. If you keep sauce, broth or soup by the fireside, the soup reduces and becomes too strong, and the sauce thickens as well as reduces ; but this is prevented by using the *bain-marie,* in which the water should be very hot, but not boiling.

Batterie de Cuisine.—Set of cooking apparatus.

Béchamel. — French white sauce, now frequently used in English cookery.

Blanchir. — To whiten poultry, vegetables, fruit, &c., by plunging them into boiling water for some time, and afterwards plunging them into cold water, there to remain until they are cold.

Blanquette.—A sort of fricassee.

Bouilli.—Beef or other meat boiled; but, generally speaking, boiled beef is understood by the term.

Bouillie. — A French dish resembling hasty-pudding.

Bouillon.—A thin broth or soup.

Braise.—To stew meat with fat bacon until it is tender, it having previously been blanched.

Braisière.—A saucepan having a lid with ledges, to put fire on the top.

Brider.—To pass a packthread through poultry, game, &c., to keep together their members.

Caramel (burnt sugar).—This is made with a piece of sugar, of the size of a nut, browned in the bottom of a saucepan; upon which a cupful of stock is gradually poured, stirring all the time, and adding the broth little by little. It may be used with the feather of a quill, to colour meats, such as the upper part of fricandeaux; and to impart colour to sauces. Caramel made with water instead of stock may be used to colour *compôtes* and other *entremets.*

Casserole.—A crust of rice, which, after having been moulded into the form of a pie, is baked, and then filled with a fricassee of white meat or a purée of game.

Compôte.—A stew, as of fruit or pigeons.

Consommé.—Rich stock or gravy.

Croquette. — Ball of fried meat, rice, potatoes, &c.

Croûtons.—Fried sippets of bread.

Daubière.—An oval stewpan, in which *daubes* are cooked; *daubes* being meat or fowl stewed in sauce.

Désosser.—To *bone*, or take out the bones from poultry, game or fish. This is an operation requiring considerable experience.

Entrées.—Made dishes served after the fish course.

Entremets.—Small made or sweet dishes.

Escalopes.—Collops; small, round, thin pieces of tender meat, or of fish, beaten

with the handle of a strong knife to make them tender.

Feuilletage.—Puff-paste.

Flamber.—To singe fowl or game after they have been picked.

Foncer.—To put in the bottom of a saucepan slices of ham, veal or thin broad slices of bacon.

Galette.—A broad thin cake.

Gâteau.—A cake, correctly speaking; but used sometimes to denote a pudding and a kind of tart.

Glacer.—To glaze, or spread upon hot meats, or larded fowls, a thick and rich sauce or gravy, called *glaze*. This is laid on with a feather or brush, and in confectionary the term means to ice fruits and pastry with sugar, which glistens on hardening.

Hors-d'œuvres.—Small dishes or *assiettes volantes* of sardines, anchovies and other relishes of this kind, served to the guests during dinner.

Lit.—A bed or layer; articles in thin slices are placed in layers, other articles, or seasoning, being laid between them.

Maigre.— Broth, soup or gravy made without meat.

Matelote.—A rich fish-stew, which is generally composed of carp, eels, trout or barbel. It is made with wine.

Mayonnaise. — Cold sauce or salad dressing.

Menu.—Bill of fare.

Meringue.—A kind of icing made of whites of eggs and sugar, well beaten.

Miroton.—Larger slices of meats than collops, such as slices of beef for a vinaigrette, or ragout or stew of onions.

Mouiller.—To add water, broth or other liquid, during the cooking.

Paner.—To cover with very fine crumbs of bread meats or any other articles to be cooked on the gridiron, in the oven or frying-pan.

Piquer.—To lard with strips of fat bacon, poultry, game, meat, &c. This should always be done according to the vein of the meat, so that in carving you slice the bacon across as well as the meat.

Poêlée.—Stock used instead of water for boiling turkeys, sweetbreads, fowls, and vegetables, to render them less insipid. This is rather an expensive preparation.

Purée.—Vegetables or meat reduced to a very smooth pulp, which is afterwards mixed with enough liquid to make it of the consistency of very thick soup.

Ragoût.—Stew or hash.

Remoulade.—Salad dressing.

Rissoles.—Pastry, made of light puff-paste, and cut into various forms, and fried. They may be filled with fish, meat or poultry.

Roux.—Brown and white ; French thickening.

Salmi. — Ragout of game previously roasted.

Sauce Piquante. — A sharp sauce, in which somewhat of a vinegar flavour predominates.

Sauter.—To dress with a sauce in a saucepan, repeatedly moving it about.

Tamis.—Tammy, a sort of open cloth or sieve through which to strain broth and sauces, so as to rid them of small bones, froth, &c.

Tourte.—Tart. Fruit pie.

Trousser.—To truss a bird; to put together the body and tie the wings and thighs, in order to round it for roasting or boiling, each being tied then with packthread, to keep it in the required form.

Vol-au-vent.—A rich crust of very fine puff-paste, which may be filled with various delicate ragouts or fricassees, of fish, flesh or fowl. Fruit may also be inclosed in a *vol-au-vent*.

Fritters, Plain.—Ingredients *for dish for 4 persons.*—3 oz. of flour, 3 eggs, ½ pint of milk. Average Cost, 4d.

Mix the flour to a smooth batter with a small quantity of the milk ; stir in the eggs, which should be well whisked, and then the remainder of the milk ; beat the whole

to a perfectly smooth batter, and should it be found not quite thin enough, add two or three tablespoonfuls more milk. Have ready a frying-pan, with plenty of boiling lard in it ; drop in rather more than a tablespoonful at a time of the batter, and fry the fritters a nice brown, turning them when

FRITTERS.

sufficiently cooked on one side. Drain them well from the greasy moisture by placing them upon a piece of blotting-paper before the fire ; dish them on a white d'oyley, sprinkle over them sifted sugar, and send to table with them a cut lemon, and plenty of pounded sugar.

TIME.—*From 6 to 8 minutes.*

SEASONABLE *at any time.*

Fritters, Indian. — Ingredients *for dish for 5 or 6 persons.*—3 tablespoonfuls of flour, boiling water, the yolks of 4 eggs, the whites of 2, hot lard or clarified dripping, jam. Average Cost, 9d.

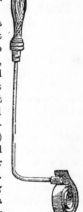

Put the flour into a basin, and pour over it sufficient *boiling* water to make it into a stiff paste, taking care to stir and beat it well, to prevent it getting lumpy. Leave it a little time to cool, and then break into it (*without beating them at first*) the yolks of 4 eggs and the whites of 2, and stir and beat all well together. Have ready some boiling lard or butter; drop a dessertspoonful of batter in at a time, and fry the fritters of a light brown.

FRITTER MOULD.

They should rise so much as to be almost like balls. Serve on a dish, with a spoonful

T

of preserve or marmalade dropped in between each fritter. This is an excellent dish for an hasty addition to dinner, if a guest unexpectedly arrives, it being so easily and quickly made, and it is always a great favourite.

TIME.—*From 5 to 8 minutes to fry the fritters.*

SEASONABLE *at any time.*

Fritters, Omelettes, Pancakes,

Recipes for. — Directions for making the following appear under their respective headings:—

Apple Fritters.	Potato Fritters.
Beef Fritters.	Rice Fritters.
Bread and Butter-	Bachelor's Omelette.
Fritters.	Ham Omelette.
Currant Fritters.	Kidney Omelette.
Indian Fritters.	Plain Omelette.
Orange Fritters.	Plain Sweet Omelette
Pea Fritters.	Sweet Omelette.
Peach Fritters.	French Pancakes.
Pine-apple Fritters.	Indian Pancakes.
Plain Fritters.	Snow Pancakes.

Fruit, to Bottle Fresh. (Very

Useful in Winter.)—INGREDIENTS.—*Fresh fruits, such as currants, raspberries, cherries, gooseberries, plums of all kinds, damsons, &c.; wide-mouthed glass bottles, new corks to fit them tightly.*

Let the fruit be full grown, but not too ripe, and gathered in dry weather. Pick it off the stalks without bruising or breaking the skin, and reject any that is at all blemished; if gathered in the damp, or if the skins are cut at all, the fruit will mould. Have ready some *perfectly dry* glass bottles, and some nice *new* soft corks or bungs; burn a match in each bottle to exhaust the air, and quickly place the fruit in to be preserved; gently cork the bottles, and put them in a very *cool* oven, where let them remain until the fruit has shrunk away a fourth part. Then take the bottles out; *do not open them*, but immediately beat the

corks in tight, cut off the tops, and cover them with melted resin. If kept in a dry place the fruit will remain good for months; and on this principally depends the success of the preparation; for if stored away in a place that is in the least damp, the fruit will soon spoil.

TIME.—*From 5 to 6 hours in a very slow oven.*

Fruit, to Bottle Fresh. —INGRE-

DIENTS.—*Any kind of fresh fruit, such as currants, cherries, gooseberries, all kinds of plums &c.; wide-mouthed glass bottles, new corks to fit them tightly.*

The fruit must be full-grown, not too ripe, and gathered on a very fine day. Let it be carefully picked and put into the bottles, which must be clean and perfectly dry. Tie over the tops of the bottles pieces of bladder; stand the bottles in a large pot, copper or boiler, with cold water to reach to their necks; kindle a fire under, let the water boil, and as the bladders begin to rise and puff, prick them. As soon as the water boils, extinguish the fire, and let the bottles remain where they are, to become cold. The next day remove the bladders, and strew over the fruit a thick layer o f pounded sugar; fit the bottles with cork, and let the cork lie close at hand to its own bottle. Hold for a few moments, in the neck of the bottle, two or three lighted matches, and when they have filled the bottle neck with gas, and before they go out, remove them very quickly; instantly cork the bottles closely, and dip it in bottle-cement.

TIME.—*Altogether about 8 hours.*

Fruit, to Bottle Fresh, with

Sugar. (Very Useful in Winter.)—INGREDIENTS.—*Any kind of fresh fruit; to each quart bottle allow ¼ lb. of pounded sugar.*

Let the fruit be gathered in dry weather. Pick it carefully, and drop it into *clean* and *very dry* quart glass bottles, sprinkling over it the above proportion of pounded sugar to each quart. Put the corks in the bottles, and place them in a copper of cold water up to their necks, with small hay whisps round them, to prevent the bottles from knocking together. Light the fire under, bring the water gradually to boil, and let it simmer gently until the fruit in the bottles is reduced nearly one third. Extinguish the fire, *and let the bottles remain in the water until it is perfectly cold;* then take them out, make the corks secure, and cover them with melted resin or wax.

TIME.—*About ½ hour from the time the water commences to boil.*

Note.—Unless for those possessing very large gardens and a quantity of fruit, it is cheaper and safer to buy it ready bottled. George Whybrow's is one of the best brands.

Fruit Turnovers (suitable for Picnics).— INGREDIENTS.— *Puff-paste, any kind of fruit, sugar to taste.*

Make some puff-paste by recipe; roll it out to the thickness of about ¼ inch, and cut it out in pieces of a circular form; pile the fruit on half of the paste, sprinkle over some sugar, wet the edges and turn the paste over. Press the edges together, ornament them, and brush the turnovers over with the white of an egg; sprinkle over sifted sugar, and bake on tins, in a brisk oven for about 20 minutes. Instead of putting the fruit in raw, it may be boiled down with a little sugar first, and then in-closed in the crust; or jam of any kind, may be substituted for fresh fruit.

TIME.—*20 minutes.*

SEASONABLE *at any time.*

Fruit Turnovers, Apple.—INGREDIENTS *for* 12 *turnovers.*—1 *lb. of paste, short or puff,* 12 *medium-sized or* 16 *small apples, about* ¼ *lb. of sugar, half a lemon.* AVERAGE COST, 1*s.* 6*d.*

Peel, core, and slice the apples, and stew them till tender, but not thoroughly done, with the rind and juice of the lemon, a very little water, and the sugar. Roll out the paste thin, cut it in rounds, and when the fruit is cool, put a little on each, fold over the edges, wetting them to make them stick and bake in a quick oven for 20 minutes.

TIME.—*20 minutes.*

SEASONABLE *from October to March.*

Frying.— Frying is a pleasant and quick mode of cooking, suitable for tender meats of any kind. Melted fat can be brought to a higher temperature than boiling water, although it never *boils;* so it can be understood that frying is not a mode of cooking to be adopted for any tough meat or vegetable food, unless it is only the primary part of their cooking, such as frying vegetables for soups, &c. Such fish as soles, plaice, whitebait, &c., are well cooked by this mode; and the secret of success in frying such things is the use of sufficient fat to *cover* what is being cooked.

APPLE TURNOVER.

" Golden grain, bright fruits,
Sweet herbs which grow for all."—EDWIN ARNOLD.

GAME, HASHED.

GAME PIE.

GAME, Hashed. (Cold Meat Cookery.)—INGREDI-ENTS. — *The remains of cold game, 1 onion stuck with 3 cloves, a few whole peppers, a strip of lemon-peel, salt to taste, thickening of butter and flour, 1 glass of port wine, 1 tablespoonful of lemon-juice, 1 table-spoonful of ketchup, 1 pint of water or weak stock.* AVERAGE COST, exclusive of the cold game, 8d.

Cut the remains of cold game into joints, reserve the best pieces, and the inferior ones and trimmings put into a stewpan with the onion, pepper, lemon-peel, salt and water or weak stock ; stew these for about an hour, and strain the gravy; thicken it with butter and flour ; add the wine, lemon-juice and ketchup ; lay in the pieces of game, and let them gradually warm through by the side of the fire ; do not allow it to boil, or the game will be hard. When on the point of simmering,

serve, and garnish the dish with sippets of toasted bread or fried croutons.

TIME.—*Altogether,* 1¼ *hour.*

SEASONABLE *from August to March.*

Note.—Any kind of game may be hashed by the above recipe, and the flavour may be varied by adding flavoured vinegars, curry powders, &c. ; but we cannot recommend these latter ingredients, as a dish of game should really have a gamey taste ; and if too many sauces, essences, &c., are added to the gravy, they quite overpower and destroy the flavour the dish should possess.

Game Pie.—INGREDIENTS *for large pie.—For the crust 2 lbs. of flour, 1 lb. of butter, 1 pint of water, 4 eggs (yolks only), a teaspoonful of salt. For the pie 1 large pheasant, 2 partridges, a few slices of dressed ham, forcemeat, seasoning of allspice, pepper and salt, gravy.* AVERAGE COST, 9s.

Make a stiff short crust with the ingredients given above, butter a raised pie-mould and line it with the paste. After preparing, cut the birds into small joints, removing as much bone and skin as possible, and having lined the pie with a layer of forcemeat, fill it with the game cut up as described, the ham in very small pieces,

GAME & POULTRY

and the forcemeat in layers, seasoning well. Put on the top of the pie, ornament it, glaze with yolk of egg, and bake in a moderate oven for 4 hours. In the meantime, make a good strong gravy from the bones, reducing it so that it will jelly when

GAME PIE, WITH JELLY.

cold, and pour it with the aid of a funnel through the hole at the top of the pie. A few truffles or mushrooms are a great improvement to this pie, and any other game can be used.

TIME.—4 *hours.*

SEASONABLE *from September to March.*

Game Soup. — INGREDIENTS *for soup for 8 persons.*—2 *partridges or 1 large pheasant, 3 slices of lean ham, 2 oz. of butter, 2 shred onions, 1 head of celery, 1 large carrot, 1 turnip, a small lump of sugar, salt and pepper to taste, 2 quarts of stock.* AVERAGE COST, 2s. 6d. *per quart.*

Cut up the partridges, and braise the pieces in the butter till tender, then take out the best joints and set them aside. Add to the remainder the onions, celery, and 3 pints of the stock. Simmer slowly for 1 hour, strain and take the fat off as clean as possible ; cut the flesh from the parts saved in neat pieces, and add with the sugar and seasoning, give one boil and skim again to have it quite clear. Simmer the carrot and turnip, cut up in the remaining pint of stock, and when quite tender, add to the soup. Bones and trimmings of game, and the inferior parts of birds can be used to make more economical soup.

TIME.—2 *hours.*

SEASONABLE.—*September to February.*

Garlic Vinegar.—INGREDIENTS — 2 *oz. of garlic, 1 quart of wine vinegar.*

Chop the garlic finely, and weigh it, then put it in the above proportion to the vinegar, which must be boiled and allowed to get cold. Infuse for a fortnight, strain and bottle.

TIME.—14 *days.*

Genevese Sauce (for Salmon, Trout, &c.)—INGREDIENTS *sufficient for a salmon.*—1 *small carrot, a small faggot of sweet herbs, including parsley, 1 onion, 5 or 6 mushrooms (when obtainable), 1 bay-leaf, 6 cloves, 1 blade of mace, 2 oz. of butter, 1 glass of sherry, 1½ pint of white stock, thickening of butter and flour, the juice of half a lemon.* AVERAGE COST, 1s. 3d.

Cut up the onion and the carrot into small rings, and put them into a stewpan with the herbs, mushrooms, bay-leaf, cloves and mace ; add the butter, and simmer the whole very gently over a slow fire until the onion is quite tender. Pour in the stock and sherry, and stew slowly for 1 hour, when strain it off into a clean saucepan. Now make a thickening of butter and flour, put it to the sauce, stir it over the fire until perfectly smooth and mellow, add the lemon-juice, give one boil, when it will be ready for table.

TIME.—*Altogether 2 hours.*

SEASONABLE *at any time.*

German Pudding.—INGREDIENTS *for pudding for 4 or 5 persons.*—2 *teaspoonfuls of flour, 1 teaspoonful of arrowroot, 1 pint of milk, 2 oz. of butter, sugar to taste, the rind of ½ lemon, 4 eggs, 3 tablespoonfuls of brandy.* AVERAGE COST, 1s. 3d.

Boil the milk with the lemon-rind until well flavoured ; then strain it, and mix with it the flour, arrowroot, butter and sugar. Boil these ingredients for a few minutes, keeping them well stirred ; then take them off the fire and mix with them the eggs, yolks and whites, beaten separately and added separately. Boil some sugar to candy ; line an oiled mould with this, put in the brandy, then the mixture ; tie down with a cloth, and boil for rather more than 1 hour. When turned out, the brandy and sugar make a nice sauce.

TIME.—*Rather more than* 1 *hour.*

SEASONABLE *at any time.*

German Puffs.—INGREDIENTS *for* 6 *puffs.*—2 *oz. of flour,* 2 *eggs,* ½ *pint of new milk,* 2 *oz. of melted butter, a little salt and nutmeg.* AVERAGE COST, 6*d.*

Let the 2 eggs be well beaten, then mix all the ingredients well together, and beat them up just before they are put into little cups half full for baking. Bake for ¼ hour in a hot oven till the puffs are of a nice brown ; turn out on a flat dish, rub a little butter over each puff, and dust on it powdered sugar.

TIME.—¼ *hour.*

SEASONABLE *at any time.*

German Sauce.—INGREDIENTS.—½ *pint of sauce tournée, the yolks of* 2 *eggs.* AVERAGE COST, 6*d.*

Put the sauce into a stewpan, heat it, and stir to it the beaten yolks of 2 eggs, which have been previously strained. Let it just simmer, but not boil, or the eggs will curdle ; and after they are added to the sauce, it must be stirred without ceasing. This sauce is a general favourite, and is used for many made dishes.

TIME.—1 *minute to simmer.*

SEASONABLE *at any time.*

Gherkins, Pickled. — INGREDIENTS.—*Salt and water,* 1 *oz. of bruised ginger,* ½ *oz. of whole black pepper,* ¼ *oz. of whole black spice,* 4 *cloves,* 2 *blades of mace, a little horseradish.* *This proportion of pepper, spices, &c., for* 1 *quart of vinegar.*

Let the gherkins remain in salt and water for 3 or 4 days, when take them out, wipe perfectly dry, and put them into a stone jar. Boil sufficient vinegar to cover them, with spices and pepper, &c., in the above proportion, for 10 minutes ; pour it, quite boiling, over the gherkins, cover the jar with vine-leaves, and put over them a plate, setting them near the fire, where they must remain all night. Next day drain off the vinegar, boil it up again, and

GHERKINS.

pour it hot over them. Cover up with fresh leaves, and let the whole remain till quite cold. Now tie down closely with bladder to exclude the air, and in a month or two they will be fit for use.

TIME.—4 *days.*

SEASONABLE *from the middle of July to the end of August.*

Giblet Pie.—INGREDIENTS *for moderate-sized pie.*—*A set of duck or goose giblets,* 1 *lb. of rump-steak,* 1 *onion,* ½ *teaspoonful of whole black pepper, a bunch of savoury herbs, plain crust.* AVERAGE COST, *exclusive of the giblets,* 1*s.* 6*d.*

Clean and put the giblets into a stewpan with an onion, whole pepper and a bunch of savoury herbs ; add rather more than a pint of water, and simmer gently for about 1½ hour. Take them out, let them cool, and cut them into pieces ; line the bottom of a pie dish with a few pieces of rump-steak ; add a layer of giblets and a few more pieces of steak ; season with pepper and salt, and pour in the gravy (which should be strained) that the giblets were stewed in ; cover with a plain crust, ornament and glaze it, and bake for rather more than 1½ hour in a brisk oven. Cover a piece of paper over the pie, to prevent the crust taking too much colour.

TIME.—1½ hour to stew the giblets, about 1 hour to bake the pie.

Giblet Soup.—INGREDIENTS for 3 quarts of soup.

—3 sets of goose or duck giblets, 3 lbs. of shin of beef, a few bones, 2 large onions, 2 carrots, 1 large faggot of herbs, salt and pepper to taste, 1 oz. of butter mixed with a dessertspoonful of flour, 3½ quarts of water. AVERAGE COST, 3s. 3d

Scald the giblets, cut the gizzards in 8 pieces, and put them in a stewpan with the beef, bones, onions, herbs, pepper and salt ; add the water, and simmer till the giblets are tender, taking care to skim well. When the giblets are done, take them out, put them in your tureen, strain the soup through a sieve, add the butter, mixed with a dessertspoonful of flour, boil it up for a few minutes, and pour it over the giblets. It can be flavoured with port wine and a little mushroom ketchup if liked. Add salt to taste.

TIME.—3 hours.
SEASONABLE all the year.

Ginger, Apple. (A Dessert Dish.)

—INGREDIENTS sufficient for large dish.— 2 lbs. of any kind of hard apples, 2 lbs. of loaf sugar, 1½ pint of water, 1 oz. of tincture of ginger. AVERAGE COST, 1s. 4d.

Boil the sugar and water until they form a rich syrup, adding the ginger when it boils up. Pare, core and cut the apples into pieces ; dip them in cold water to preserve the colour, and boil them in the syrup until transparent; but be careful not to let them break. Put the pieces of apples into jars, pour over the syrup, and carefully exclude the air, by well covering them. It will remain good some time, if kept in a dry place.

TIME.—5 to 10 minutes to boil the syrup ; about ½ hour to simmer the apples.
SEASONABLE.—Make this in September, October or November.

Ginger-Beer.—INGREDIENTS for 4 dozen bottles.

—2½ lbs. of loaf sugar, 1½ oz. of bruised ginger, 1 oz. of cream of tartar, the rind and juice of 2 lemons, 3 gallons of boiling water, two large tablespoonfuls of thick and fresh brewer's yeast. AVERAGE COST, 1s. 3d.

Peel the lemons, squeeze the juice, strain it, and put the peel and juice into a large earthen pan, with the bruised ginger, cream of tartar and loaf sugar. Put over these ingredients 3 gallons of boiling water ; let it stand until just warm, when add the yeast, which should be thick and perfectly fresh. Stir the contents of the pan well, and let them remain near the fire all night, covering the pan over with a cloth. The next day skim off the yeast, and pour the liquor carefully into another vessel, leaving the sediment ; then bottle immediately, and tie the corks down, and in 3 days the ginger-beer will be fit for use. For some tastes, the above proportion of sugar may be found rather too large, when it may be diminished ; but the beer will not keep so long good.

GINGER.

TIME.—3 days.
SEASONABLE.—This should be made during the summer months.

Note.—A most refreshing summer drink may be easily made with Goodall, Backhouse and Co.'s ginger-beer powder.

Ginger Biscuits. — INGREDIENTS for 4 dozen biscuits.

—1 lb. of flour, 6 oz. of butter, ¼ lb. of pounded loaf sugar, ¾ oz. of *ground ginger,* 2 *eggs.* AVERAGE COST, 1s.

Rub the butter with the flour; add the sugar, ginger and eggs, mix thoroughly, roll out thin, divide into biscuits, stamping them with a cutter, or cutting them with a sharp knife, and bake 5 minutes in a quick oven.

TIME.—5 *minutes.*

SEASONABLE *in winter.*

Ginger Cream.— INGREDIENTS *for good-sized dish.—The yolks of* 4 *eggs,* ½ *pint of cream,* ½ *pint of milk,* 3 *oz. of preserved ginger,* 2 *dessertspoonfuls of syrup, sifted sugar to taste,* 1 *oz. of isinglass or gelatine.* AVERAGE COST, 2s.

Slice the ginger finely : put it into a basin with the syrup, the well-beaten yolks of eggs, and the cream : mix these ingredients well together, and stir them over the fire for about 10 minutes, or until the mixture thickens ; then take it off the fire, whisk till nearly cold, sweeten to taste, add the isinglass, which should be melted and strained, and serve the cream in a glass dish. It may be garnished with slices of preserved ginger or candied citron.

TIME.—*About* 10 *minutes to stir the cream over the fire.*

SEASONABLE *at any time.*

Ginger, Preserved.— Comes from the West Indies. It is made by scalding the roots when they are green and full of sap, then peeling them in cold water and putting them into jars, with a rich syrup ; in which state we receive them. It should

be chosen of a deep yellow colour, with a little transparency. What is dark - coloured, fibrous and stringy is not good.

GINGER.

Ginger roots, fit for preserving and in size equal to West Indian, have been produced in the Royal Agricultural Garden in Edinburgh.

Ginger Pudding. — INGREDIENTS *for good-sized pudding.—* ½ *lb. of flour,* ¼ *lb. of suet,* ¼ *lb. of moist sugar,* 2 *large teaspoonfuls of grated ginger.* AVERAGE COST, 6d.

Shred the suet very fine, mix it with the flour, sugar and ginger ; stir all well together ; butter a basin, and put the mixture in *dry ;* tie a cloth over, and boil 3 hours.

TIME.—3 *hours.*

SEASONABLE *at any time.*

Ginger Wine.— INGREDIENTS *for* 9 *gallons of wine.—To* 9 *gallons of water allow* 27 *lbs. of loaf sugar,* 9 *lemons,* 12 *oz. of bruised ginger,* 3 *tablespoonfuls of yeast,* 2 *lbs. of raisins stoned and chopped,* 1 *pint of brandy.* AVERAGE COST, 12s.

Boil together for 1 hour in a copper (let it previously be well scoured and beautifully clean) the water, sugar, lemon-rinds, and bruised ginger : remove every particle of scum as it rises, and when the liquor is sufficiently boiled, put it into a large tub or pan, as it must not remain in the copper. When nearly cold, add the yeast, which must be thick and very fresh, and, the next day, put all in a dry cask with the strained lemon-juice and chopped raisins. Stir the wine every day for a fortnight ; then add the brandy, stop the cask down by degrees, and in a few weeks it will be fit to bottle.

TIME.—3 *months.*

SEASONABLE.—*The best time for making this wine is either in March or September.*

Note.—Wine made early in March will be fit to bottle in June.

Gingerbread Pudding.— INGREDIENTS *for pudding for* 6 *persons.—* ¾ *lb. of bread-crumbs,* 6 *oz. of suet,* ¾ *lb. of golden syrup,* ½ *oz. of ground ginger,* 2 *eggs, salt,* 1 *teaspoonful of soda.* AVERAGE COST, 10d.

Chop the suet finely and add it to the bread-crumbs, with the salt and the ginger. Mix the soda with a very little milk, and add it to the golden syrup ; then mix all well together with the beaten egg, and pour into a buttered basin. Tie this over with a cloth, and boil for 2 hours or rather more.

Time.—*2 hours.*

Seasonable.—*A nice winter pudding for children.*

Gingerbread, Thick.— Ingredients *for large cake.*—1 lb. of treacle, ¼ lb. of butter, ¼ lb. of coarse brown sugar, 1½ lb. of flour, 1 oz. of ginger, ½ oz. of ground allspice, 1 teaspoonful of carbonate of soda, ¼ pint of warm milk, 3 eggs. Average Cost, 1s. 2d.

Put the flour into a basin, with the sugar, ginger and allspice; mix these together; warm the butter, and add it, with the treacle, to the other ingredients. Stir well;

GINGERBREAD.

make the milk just warm, dissolve the carbonate of soda in it, and mix the whole into a nice smooth dough with the eggs, which should be previously well whisked; pour the mixture into a buttered tin, and bake it from ¾ to 1 hour, or longer, should the gingerbread be very thick. Just before it is done, brush the top over with the yolk of an egg beaten up with a little milk, and put it back in the oven to finish baking.

Time.—*¾ to 1 hour.*

Seasonable *at any time.*

Gingerbread, White.— Ingredients.—1 lb. of flour, ½ lb. of butter, ½ lb. of loaf sugar, the rind of 1 lemon, 1 oz. of ground ginger, 1 nutmeg grated, ½ teaspoonful of carbonate of soda, 1 gill of milk. Average Cost, 1s. 3d.

Rub the butter into the flour; add the sugar, which should be finely pounded and sifted, and the minced lemon-rind, ginger and nutmeg. Mix these well together; make the milk just warm, stir in the soda, and work the whole into a nice smooth paste; roll it out, cut it into cakes, and

bake in a moderate oven from 15 to 20 minutes.

Time.—*15 to 20 minutes.*

Seasonable *at any time.*

Gingerbread-Nuts. (Rich Sweetmeats.)—Ingredients *for about 3 lbs. of nuts.*—1 lb. of treacle, ¼ lb. of clarified butter, 1 lb. of coarse brown sugar, 2 oz. of ground ginger, 1 oz. of candied orange-peel, 1 oz. of candied angelica, ½ oz. of candied lemon-peel, ½ oz. of coriander seeds, ½ oz. of caraway seeds, 1 egg; flour. Average Cost, 1s. 4d.

Put the treacle into a basin, and pour over it the butter, melted so as not to oil, the sugar and ginger. Stir these ingredients well together, and whilst mixing, add the candied peel, which should be cut into very small pieces, but not bruised, and the caraway and coriander seeds, which should be pounded. Having mixed all thoroughly together, break in an egg, and work the whole up with as much fine flour as may be necessary to form a paste. Roll this out and stamp into nuts of any size, and put them on a tin plate, and bake in a slow oven from ¼ to ½ hour.

Time.—*¼ to ½ hour.*

Seasonable *at any time.*

Gingerbread - Nuts, Sunderland. (An Excellent Recipe.)—Ingredients *for 5 lbs. of nuts.*—1¾ lb. of treacle, 1 lb. of moist sugar, 1 lb. of butter, 2¾ lbs. of flour, 1½ oz. of ground ginger, 1½ oz. of allspice, 1½ oz. of coriander seeds. Average Cost, 2s. 6d.

Let the allspice, coriander seeds and ginger be freshly ground; put them into a basin, with the flour and sugar, and mix these ingredients well together; warm the treacle and butter together; then with a spoon work it into the flour, &c., until the whole forms a nice smooth paste. Drop the mixture from the spoon on a piece of buttered paper, and bake in rather a slow oven from 20 minutes to ½ hour. A little candied lemon-peel mixed with the above is an improvement, and a great authority in culinary matters suggests the addition of a little cayenne pepper in gingerbread. Whether it be advisable to use the latter ingredient or not, we leave our readers to decide.

TIME.—20 *minutes to* ½ *hour.*

SEASONABLE *at any time.*

Glaze (for covering Cold Hams, Tongues, &c.) — INGREDIENTS. — *Stock, doubling the quantity of meat in the recipes.*

We may remark at the outset that, unless glaze is wanted in very large quantities, it is seldom made expressly. Either of the stocks, boiled down and reduced very considerably, will be found to produce a very good glaze. Put the stock into a stewpan, over a nice clear fire ; let it boil till it becomes somewhat stiff, when keep stirring, to prevent its burning. The moment it is sufficiently reduced, and come to a glaze, turn it into the glaze-pot before it gets cold. As, however, this is not to be found in every establishment, a white earthenware jar would answer the purpose ; and this may be placed in a vessel of boiling water, to melt the glaze when required. It should never be warmed in a saucepan, except on the principle of the bain marie, lest it should reduce too much, and become black and bitter. If the glaze is wanted of a pale colour, more veal than beef should be used in making the stock ; and it is as well to omit turnips and celery, as these impart a disagreeable bitter flavour. Glaze can be bought ready made, thus saving much time and trouble in small kitchens.

Glaze, To, Cold Joints, &c.— Melt the glaze by placing the vessel which contains it into the bain marie or saucepan of boiling water ; brush it over the meat with a paste-brush, and if in places it is not quite covered, repeat the opera-

tion. The glaze should not be too dark a colour.

Glaze-Kettle.—This is a kettle used for keeping the strong stock boiled down to a jelly, which is known by the name of glaze. It is composed of two tin vessels,

GLAZE-KETTLE.

as shown in the cut, one of which, the upper, containing the glaze, is inserted into one of larger diameter, and containing boiling water.

Golden Pudding. — INGREDIENTS *for pudding large enough for 6 persons.—* ½ *lb. of bread-crumbs,* ¼ *lb. of suet,* ½ *lb. of marmalade,* ¼ *lb. of sugar, 4 eggs.* AVERAGE COST, 1s.

Put the bread-crumbs into a basin ; mix with them the suet, which should be finely minced, the marmalade, and the sugar ; stir all these ingredients well together ; beat the eggs to a froth, moisten the pudding with these, and when well mixed put it into a mould or buttered basin ; tie down with a floured cloth and boil for 2 hours. When turned out, strew a little fine-sifted sugar over the top, and serve.

TIME.—2 *hours.*

SEASONABLE *at any time.*

Note.—The mould may be ornamented with stoned raisins, arranged in any fanciful pattern before the mixture is poured in, which would add very much to the appearance of the pudding. For a plainer pudding for children double the quantity of the bread-crumbs ; and if the eggs do not moisten it sufficiently, use a little milk.

Goose, Green. — INGREDIENTS. —

Goose, 3 oz. of butter, pepper and salt to taste. AVERAGE COST, 4s. to 5s.

Geese are called green till they are about four months old, and should not be stuffed. After it has been singed and trussed, put into the body a seasoning of pepper and salt, and the butter to moisten it inside.

GOOSE READY FOR COOKING.

Roast before a clear fire for about ¾ hour, froth and brown it nicely, and serve with a brown gravy, and, when liked, goose-berry-sauce. This dish should be garnished with watercresses.

TIME.—About ¾ hour.

SEASONABLE in June, July and August.

Goose, Hashed. (Cold Meat Cookery.)—INGREDIENTS.—The remains of cold roast goose, 2 onions, 2 oz. of butter, 1 pint of boiling water, 1 dessertspoonful of flour, pepper and salt to taste, 1 tablespoonful of port wine, 2 tablespoonfuls of mushroom ketchup. AVERAGE COST, exclusive of the cold goose, 6d.

Cut up the goose into pieces of the size required; the inferior joints, trimmings, &c., put into a stewpan to make the gravy; slice and fry the onions in the butter of a very pale brown; add these to the trimmings, and pour over about a pint of boiling water; stew these gently for ¾ hour, then skim and strain the liquor. Thicken it with flour, and flavour with port wine and ketchup in the above proportion; add a seasoning of pepper and salt, and put in the pieces of goose; let these get thoroughly hot through, but do not allow them to boil, and serve with sippets of toasted bread.

TIME—Altogether, rather more than 1 hour.

SEASONABLE from September to March.

Goose, Roast. — INGREDIENTS.—

Goose, 4 large onions, 10 sage-leaves, ¼ lb. of bread-crumbs, 1½ oz. of butter, salt and pepper to taste, 1 egg. AVERAGE COST, for large goose, with stuffing, 7s. 6d.

Select a goose with a clean white skin, plump breast and yellow feet: if these latter are red, the bird is old. Should the weather permit, let it hang for a few days; by so doing the flavour will be very much improved. Pluck, singe, draw and carefully wash and wipe the goose. Make a sage-and-onion stuffing of the above ingredients, put it into the body of the goose, and secure it firmly at both ends by passing the rump through the hole made in the skin, and the other end by tying the skin of the neck to the back: by this means the seasoning will not escape. Put it down to a brisk fire, keep it well basted, and roast from 1½ to 2 hours, according to the size. Remove the skewers, and serve with a tureen of good gravy, and one of well made apple sauce. Should a very highly-flavoured seasoning be preferred, the onions should not be parboiled, but minced raw: of the two methods the mild seasoning is far superior. A ragout, or pie, should be made of the giblets, or they may be stewed down to make gravy. Be careful to serve the goose before the breast falls, or its appearance will be spoiled by coming flattened to table. As this is rather a troublesome bird to carve, a very little gravy should be poured round the goose, but more served in a tureen.

TIME.—A large goose, 1¾ hour; a moderate-sized one, 1¼ to 1½ hour.

SEASONABLE from September to March; in perfection from Michaelmas to Christmas.

Note.—A teaspoonful of made mustard, a saltspoonful of salt, a few grains of cayenne, mixed with a glass of port wine, are sometimes poured into the goose by a slit made in the apron. This sauce is by many considered an improvement.

Goose, Roast, To Carve. — It would not be fair to say that this dish bodes

a great deal of happiness to an inexperienced carver, especially if there is a large party to serve and the slices off the breast should not suffice to satisfy the desires and cravings of many wholesome appetites, produced, may be, by the various sports in vogue at Michaelmas and Christmas. The beginning of the task, however, is not in any way difficult. Evenly-cut slices, not too thick or too thin, should be carved from the breast in the direction of the line

ROAST GOOSE.

from B to C; after the first slice has been cut, a hole should be made with the knife in the part called the apron, passing it round the line as indicated by the figures A, A; here the stuffing is located, and some of this should be served on each plate, unless it is discovered that it is not agreeable to the taste of some one guest. If the carver manages cleverly, he will be able to cut a very large number of fine slices off the breast, and the more so if he commences close down by the wing and carves upwards towards the ridge of the breastbone.

LEG, WING AND NECK-BONE OF GOOSE.

As many slices as can be taken from the breast being carved, the wings should be cut off, and the same process as described in carving boiled fowl is made use of in this instance, only more dexterity and greater force will most probably be required. The shape of the leg, when disengaged from the body of the goose, should be like that shown in the accompanying engraving. It

will be necessary perhaps, in taking off the leg, to turn the goose on its side, and then pressing down the small end of the leg the knife should be passed under it from the top quite down to the joint; the leg being now turned back by the fork, the knife must cut through the joint, loosening the thigh bone from its socket. The merrythought which in a goose is not so large as might be expected, is disengaged in the same way as that of a fowl—by passing the knife under it, and pressing it backwards towards the neck. The neck-bones, of which we give a cut, are freed by the same process as are those of a fowl; and the same may be said of all the other parts of this bird. The breast of a goose is the part most esteemed; all parts, however, are good, and full of juicy flavour.

Goose Stuffing. (SOYER's Recipe.)

—Take 4 apples peeled and cored, 4 onions, 4 leaves of sage, and 4 leaves of lemon-thyme not broken, and boil them in a stew-pan with sufficient water to cover them; when done, pulp them through a sieve, removing the sage and thyme; then add sufficient pulp of mealy potatoes to cause it to be sufficiently dry without sticking to the hand; add pepper and salt, and stuff the bird.

Goose, To Truss a. — Having

plucked and singed the goose, cut off the

GOOSE READY FOR TRUSSING.

feet at the joints, the pinions at the first joint, and the neck close to the back, leaving enough skin to turn over it.

After drawing it, beat the breast-bone flat with a rolling-pin, then put a skewer through the under part of one wing, and bring it through the other as shown in cut above.

Skewer the legs as shown in illustration, with one skewer passed through the first

TRUSSING OF GOOSE.

joint, then through the body to catch the other leg.

Next cut off the end of the vent, and make a hole in the skin large enough for

GOOSE READY FOR STUFFING.

the passage of the rump, to keep in the stuffing.

Fill the goose with plenty of stuffing, then securely fasten down the flap with a small skewer.

It may be necessary to give another singeing to the bird previous to roasting, as it is one from which it is some trouble to get rid of all the down.

The giblets should be put aside when trussing, and afterwards washed and put in water till they are needed.

Goose, Vegetable.—INGREDIENTS for dish for 4 persons.—½ lb. of bread-crumbs, 1 onion, 1 teaspoonful of chopped parsley and herbs, 1 oz. of butter, pepper and salt. AVERAGE COST, 3d.

Soak the bread in cold water, squeeze it nearly dry and mash it, mix with it the herbs and onion minced. Butter a tin, put in the mixture, and put the remainder of the butter cut in small pieces on the top.

Bake in a good oven for 1 hour and serve hot.

TIME.—1 hour.

SEASONABLE at any time.

Gooseberries, Compôte of.— INGREDIENTS for dish sufficient for 6 persons.—Syrup; to 1 pint of syrup allow a quart of gooseberries. AVERAGE COST, 1s.

Top and tail the gooseberries, which should not be very ripe, and pour over them some boiling water; then take them out and plunge them into cold water with which has been mixed a tablespoonful of vinegar, which will assist to keep the fruit a good colour. Make a pint of syrup, and when it boils drain the gooseberries and put them in; simmer them gently until the fruit is nicely pulped and tender, without being broken; then dish the gooseberries on a glass dish, boil the syrup for 2 or 3 minutes, pour over the gooseberries, and serve cold. A glass of liqueur is an improvement to this dish.

TIME.—About 5 minutes to boil the gooseberries in the syrup, 3 minutes to reduce the syrup. SEASONABLE in June.

Gooseberry Chips. (Useful for Dessert.) — INGREDIENTS. — Gooseberries unripe and green, but quite full grown; sifted loaf sugar.

Put the gooseberries when cleaned of tops and tails, into jars, and boil them in a copper till quite soft. To every lb. of pulp put ½ lb. of loaf sugar sifted; the sugar must be stirred in very gently. Then pour out the sweetened pulp on flat dishes, about ⅛ inch thick, which must be set in the sun to dry. When sufficiently dried in the sun, the pulp may be cut into strips, and twisted into any fanciful shapes, bows, &c.

TIME. — For drying, according to the amount of the sun.

SEASONABLE at all times.

Note.—These chips may be kept for years in tin boxes, if packed quite dry, with layers of paper between the rows.

Gooseberry Fool.—Ingredients.

—*Green gooseberries; to every pint of pulp add* 1 *pint of milk, or* ½ *pint of cream and* ½ *pint of milk; sugar to taste.* AVERAGE COST, *with milk,* 6d. *per pint.*

Cut the tops and tails off the gooseberries, put them into a jar with 2 tablespoonfuls of water and a little good moist sugar; set this jar in a saucepan of boiling water, and let it boil until the fruit is soft enough to mash. When done enough, beat it to a pulp, work this pulp through a colander, and stir to every pint the above proportion of milk, or equal quantities of milk and

cream. Ascertain if the mixture is sweet enough, and put in plenty of sugar, or it will not be eatable; and in mixing the milk and gooseberries add the former very gradually to these: serve in a glass dish, or in small glasses. This,

THE GOOSEBERRY.

although a very old-fashioned and homely dish, is, when well made, very delicious, and, if properly sweetened, a very suitable preparation for children. Iced and with a little whipped cream laid over, it is suitable for a dinner party as a sweet.

TIME.—*From* ¾ *to* 1 *hour.*
SEASONABLE *in May and June.*

Gooseberry Jam.— Ingredients,

—*To every lb. of fruit allow* ¾ *lb. of loaf sugar; currant-juice.* AVERAGE COST *per lb. pot,* 6d.

Select red hairy gooseberries; have them gathered in dry weather, when quite ripe, without being too soft. Weigh them; with a pair of scissors cut off the tops and tails, and to every 6 lbs. of fruit have ready ½ pint of red-currant juice, drawn as for jelly. Put the gooseberries and currant-juice into a preserving-pan, let them boil tolerably quickly, keeping them well stirred; when they begin to break, add to them the sugar and keep simmering until the jam becomes firm, carefully skimming and stirring it that it does not burn at the bottom. It should be boiled rather a long time, or it will not keep. Put it into pots (not too large), let it get perfectly cold, then cover the pots down with oiled and egged papers.

TIME.—*About* 1 *hour to boil the goose-berries in the currant-juice, from* ½ *to* ¾ *hour with the sugar.*

SEASONABLE. — *Make this in June or July.*

Gooseberry Jam.— Ingredients

—*To every* 8 *lbs. of red, rough, ripe goose-berries allow* 1 *quart of red-currant juice* 5 *lbs of loaf sugar.* AVERAGE COST *per lb pot,* 6d.

Have the fruit gathered in dry weather and cut off the tops and tails. Prepare

GOOSEBERRIES.

quart of red-currant juice, the same as for red-currant jelly; put it into a preserving pan with the sugar, and keep stirring until the latter is dissolved. Keep it boiling for about 5 minutes; skim well; then put in the gooseberries, and let them boil from to ¾ hour; then turn the whole into an earthen pan, and let it remain for 2 days. Boil the jam up again until it looks clear put it into pots, and when cold, cover with oiled paper, and over the jars put tissue paper brushed over on both sides with the white of an egg, and store away in a dr place. Care must be taken in makin, this, to keep the jam well stirred and wel skimmed, to prevent it burning at th bottom of the pan, and to have it very clear

TIME.—5 *minutes to boil the currant-juice and sugar after the latter is dissolved; from ½ to ¾ hour to simmer the gooseberries the first time, ¼ hour the second time of boiling.*

SEASONABLE. — *Make this in June or July.*

Gooseberry Jam, White or Green.

—INGREDIENTS.—*Equal weight of fruit and sugar, 1½ lb. of fruit is the ordinary allowance for a 1 lb. pot.* AVERAGE COST *per pot, 6d.*

Select the gooseberries not very ripe, either white or green, and top and tail them. Boil the sugar with water (allowing ½ pint to every lb.) for about ¼ hour, carefully removing the scum as it rises; then put in the gooseberries, and simmer gently till clear and firm: try a little of the jam on a plate; if it jellies when cold, it is done, and should then be poured into pots. When cold, cover with oiled paper, and tissue-paper brushed over on both sides with the unbeaten white of an egg, and stow away in a dry place.

TIME.—¼ *hour to boil the sugar and water, ½ hour the jam.*

SEASONABLE.—*Make this in June.*

Gooseberry Jelly.—INGREDIENTS.

Gooseberries; to every pint of juice allow ¾ lb. of loaf sugar.

Put the gooseberries, after cutting off the tops and tails, into a preserving-pan, and stir them over the fire until they are quite soft; then strain them through a sieve, and to every pint of juice allow ¾ lb. of sugar. Boil the juice and sugar together for nearly ¾ hour, stirring and skimming all the time; and if the jelly appears firm when a little of it is poured on to a plate, it is done, and should then be taken up and put into small pots. Cover the pots with oiled and egged papers, the same as for currant jelly, and store away in a dry place.

TIME.—¾ *hour to simmer the gooseberries without the sugar; ¾ hour to boil the juice.*

SEASONABLE.—*Make in July.*

Gooseberry Pudding, Baked.—

INGREDIENTS *for dish sufficient for 4 or 5 persons.—Gooseberries, 3 eggs, 1½ oz. of butter, ½ pint of bread-crumbs, sugar to taste, a little puff-paste.* AVERAGE COST, 1s.

Put the gooseberries into a jar, previously cutting off the tops and tails; place this jar in boiling water, and let it boil until the gooseberries are soft enough to pulp; then beat them through a coarse sieve, and to every pint of pulp add 3 well-whisked eggs, 1½ oz. of butter, ½ pint of bread-crumbs, and sugar to taste; beat the mixture well, put a border of puff-paste round the edge of a pie-dish, put in the pudding, bake for about 40 minutes, strew sifted sugar over and serve.

TIME.—*About 40 minutes.*

SEASONABLE *from May to July.*

Gooseberry Pudding, Boiled.

—INGREDIENTS *for pudding large enough for 6 persons.—¾ lb. of suet crust, 1½ pint of green gooseberries, ¼ lb. of moist sugar.* AVERAGE COST, 1s.

Line a pudding-basin with suet crust rolled out to about ½ inch in thickness, and with a pair of scissors, cut off the tops and tails of the gooseberries; fill the basin with the fruit, put in the sugar, and cover with crust. Pinch the edges of the pudding together, tie over it a floured cloth,

BOILED FRUIT PUDDING.

put it into boiling water, and boil from 2½ to 3 hours; turn it out of the basin, and serve with a jug of cream or milk.

TIME.—2½ *to 3 hours.*

SEASONABLE *from May to July.*

Gooseberry Sauce (for Boiled Mackerel.) — INGREDIENTS *for sufficient sauce for 4 mackerel.—1 pint of green gooseberries, 3 tablespoonfuls of Béchamel (veal gravy may be substituted for this), 2 oz. of fresh butter, seasoning to taste of salt, pepper and grated nutmeg.* AVERAGE COST, 6d.

Boil the gooseberries in water until quite tender; strain them, and rub them through a sieve. Put into a saucepan the Béchamel or gravy, with the butter and seasoning; add the pulp from the gooseberries, mix all well together, and heat gradually through. A little pounded sugar added to this sauce is by many persons considered an improvement, as the saccharine matter takes off the extreme acidity of the unripe fruit.

TIME.— Boil the gooseberries from 20 minutes to ½ hour.

SEASONABLE from May to July.

Gooseberry Tart.—INGREDIENTS for good-sized pie-dish.—1½ pint of gooseberries, ½ lb. of short crust, ¼ lb. of moist sugar. AVERAGE COST, 9d.

With a pair of scissors cut off the tops and tails of the gooseberries; put them into a deep pie-dish, pile the fruit high in the centre, and put in the sugar; line the edge of the dish with short crust, put on the cover, and ornament the edges of the tart; bake in a good oven for about ¾ hour, and before being sent to table, strew over it some fine-sifted sugar. A jug of cream, or a dish of boiled or baked custards, should always accompany this dish.

TIME.—¾ hour.

SEASONABLE from May to July.

Gooseberry Tart. (From Bottled Fruit.)—INGREDIENTS for small tart. — 1 bottle Whybrow's bottled gooseberries, sugar to taste, puff-paste. AVERAGE COST, 1s. 3d.

Empty the bottle into a pie dish, take half the juice and boil it with 2 oz of white sugar till reduced in quantity, then set aside to cool. Put a little sugar with the gooseberries, having first taken away the remainder of the juice, add the syrup, and cover in the usual way with the paste. When the tart is wanted in a hurry, the gooseberries should be put in the dish with half their juice and sugar to taste.

TIME.—15 minutes to bake the tart.

SEASONABLE at any time.

Gooseberry Trifle.—INGREDIENT for one dish.—1 quart of gooseberries, sugar to taste, 1 pint of custard, a plateful whipped cream. AVERAGE COST, 1s. 3d.

Put the gooseberries into a jar, with sufficient moist sugar to sweeten them, and boil them until reduced to a pulp. Put this pulp at the bottom of a trifle-dish, pour over it a pint of custard made by recipe, and, when cold, cover with whipped cream. The cream should be whipped the day before it is wanted for table, as it will then be so much firmer and more solid; but it should not be added to the fruit until a short time before it is required. The dish may be garnished as fancy dictates.

TIME.—About ¾ hour to boil the gooseberries.

SEASONABLE in May, June and July.

Gooseberry Vinegar. (An Excellent Recipe.) — INGREDIENTS for gallons.—2 pecks of crystal gooseberries, gallons of water, 12 lbs. of foot sugar of the coarsest brown quality. AVERAGE COST when the gooseberries have to be purchased 1s. per gallon.

Mash the gooseberries (which should be quite ripe) in a tub with a mallet; put to them the water nearly milk-warm; let this stand 24 hours; then strain it through sieve, and put the sugar to it; mix it well and tun it. These proportions are for 9-gallon cask; and if it be not quite full more water must be added. Let the mixture be stirred from the bottom of the cask two or three times daily for 3 or 4 days, to assist the melting of the sugar; then paste a piece of linen cloth over the bunghole, and set the cask in a warm place, but not in the sun; any corner of a warm kitchen is the best situation for it. The following spring it should be drawn off into stone bottles and the vinegar will be fit for use twelve months after it is made. This will be found a most excellent preparation, greatly superior to much that is sold under the ame of the best white wine vinegar. Many ears' experience has proved that pickle made with this vinegar will keep, when ought vinegar will not preserve the ingredients. The cost per gallon is merely nominal, especially to those who reside in the country and grow their own gooseberries; the coarse sugar is then the only ingredient to be purchased.

TIME.—*To remain in the cask, 9 months.*
SEASONABLE.—*This should be made the end of June or the beginning of July, when gooseberries are ripe and plentiful.*

Gooseberry Wine, Effervescing.—INGREDIENTS.—*To every gallon of water allow 6 lbs. of green gooseberries, 3 lbs. lump sugar.*

This wine should be prepared from unripe gooseberries, in order to avoid the flavour which the fruit would give to the wine when in a mature state. Its briskness depends more upon the time of bottling than upon the unripe state of the fruit, for effervescing wine can be made from fruit that is ripe as well as that which is unripe. The fruit should be selected when it has nearly attained its full growth, and consequently before it shows any tendency to ripen. Any bruised or decayed berries, and those that are very small, should be rejected. The blossom and stalk ends should be removed, and the fruit well bruised in a tub or pan, in such quantities as to insure each berry being broken without crushing the seeds. Pour the water (which should be warm) on the fruit, squeeze and stir it with the hand until all the pulp is removed from the skin and seeds, and cover the whole closely for 24 hours; after which, strain it through a coarse bag, and press it with as much force as can be conveniently applied, to extract the whole of the juice and liquor the fruit may contain. To every 40 or 50 lbs. of fruit one gallon more of hot water may be passed through the *marc*, or husks, in order to obtain any soluble matter that

may remain, and be again pressed. The juice should be put into a tub or pan of sufficient size to contain all of it, and the sugar added to it. Let it be well stirred until the sugar is dissolved, and place the pan in a warm situation; keep it closely covered, and let it ferment for a day or two. It must then be drawn off into clean casks, placed a little on one side for the scum that arises to be thrown out, and the casks kept filled with the remaining "must," that should be reserved for that purpose. When the active fermentation has ceased, the casks should be plugged upright, again filled if necessary, the bungs to be put in loosely, and, after a few days, when the fermentation is a little more languid (which may be known by the hissing noise ceasing), the bungs should be driven in tight, and a spile-hole made to give vent if necessary. About November or December on a clear fine day, the wine should be racked from its lees into clean casks, which may be rinsed with brandy. After a month it should be examined to see if it is sufficiently clear for bottling; if not, it must be fined with isinglass, which may be dissolved in some of the wine: 1 oz. will be sufficient for 9 gallons. In bottling the wine it will be necessary to wire the corks down, or to tie them down with string. Old champagne bottles are the best for this wine. In March or April, or when the gooseberry bushes begin to blossom, the wine must be bottled, in order to insure its being effervescing.

SEASONABLE.—*Make this the end of May or beginning of June, before the berries ripen.*

Gravies, General Stock for.—

By the addition of various store sauces, thickening and flavouring, good stock may be converted into good gravies. It should be borne in mind, however, that the goodness and strength of spices, wines, flavourings, &c., evaporate, and that they lose a great deal of their fragrance if added to the gravy a long time before they are wanted. If this point be attended to, a saving of one half the quantity of these ingredients will be effected, as, with long boiling, the flavour almost entirely passes away. The shank-bones of mutton, previously well soaked, will be found a great assistance in enriching gravies ; a kidney or melt, beef skirt, trimmings of meat, &c. &c., answer very well when only a small quantity is wanted, and a good gravy need not necessarily be so very expensive; for economically prepared dishes are often-times found as savoury and wholesome as dearer ones. The cook should also remember that the fragrance of gravies should not be overpowered by too much spice, or any strong essences,

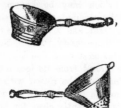

GRAVY STRAINERS.

and that they should always be warmed in a *bain marie*, after they are flavoured, or else in a jar or jug placed in a saucepan full of boiling water. The remains of roast-meat gravy should always be saved ; as when no meat is at hand, a very nice gravy in haste may be made from it, and when added to hashes, regoûts, &c., is a great improvement.

Gravy, A Good Beef (for Poultry, Game, &c.) — INGREDIENTS. — ½ *lb. of lean beef, ½ pint of cold water, 1 shalot or small onion, ½ a teaspoonful of salt, a little pepper,* 1 *tablespoonful of Harvey's sauce or mushroom ketchup, ½ a teaspoonful of arrowroot.* AVERAGE COST, 8d. per pint.

Cut up the beef into small pieces, and put it, with the water, into a stewpan. Add the shalot and seasoning, and simmer gently

for 3 hours, taking care that it does no boil fast. A short time before it is re quired, take the arrowroot, and havin mixed it with a little cold water, pour i into the gravy, which keep stirring, addin the Harvey's sauce, and just letting it boi Strain off the gravy in a tureen, and serv very hot.

TIME.—3 *hours.*

Gravy, Beef, A Quickly Made — INGREDIENTS. — ½ *lb. of shin of bee ½ onion, ¼ carrot, 2 or 3 sprigs of parsle and savoury herbs, a piece of butter abo the size of a walnut; cayenne and ma to taste, ¾ pint of water.* AVERAGE COS 6d.

Cut up the meat into very small piece slice the onion and carrot, and put the into a small saucepan with the butte Keep stirring over a sharp fire until the have taken a little colour, when add th water and the remaining ingredients. Sim mer, for ½ hour, skim well, strain an flavour, when it will be ready for use.

TIME.—½ *hour.*

Gravy, Brown.—INGREDIENTS. 2 *oz. of butter, 2 large onions, 2 lbs. of sh of beef, 2 small slices of lean bacon (if hand), salt and whole pepper to taste,* cloves, 2 *quarts of water. For thickenin* 2 *oz. of butter,* 3 *oz. of flour.* AVERAG COST, 6d. per pint.

Put the butter into a stewpan ; set th on the fire, throw in the onions cut in ring and fry them a light brown ; then add th beef and bacon, which should be cut int small square pieces ; season, and pour in teacupful of water ; let it boil for about t minutes, or until it is of a nice brow colour, occasionally stirring the content Now fill up with water in the above pr portion ; let it boil up, when draw it to th side of the fire to simmer very gently f 1½ hour ; strain, and when cold, take off a the fat. In thickening this gravy, me 3 oz. of butter in a stewpan, add 2 oz.

lour, and stir till of a light-brown colour ; when cold, add to it the strained gravy, and boil it up quickly. This thickening may be kept in larger quantities, and kept in a stone jar for use when wanted.

TIME.—*Altogether 2 hours.*

Gravy, Brown, without Meat.

—INGREDIENTS.—*2 large onions, 1 large carrot, 2 oz. of butter, 3 pints of boiling water, 1 bunch of savoury herbs, a wineglassful of good beer ; salt and pepper to taste.* AVERAGE COST, 4d.

Slice, flour and fry the onions and carrots in the butter until of a nice light-brown colour, then add the boiling water and the remaining ingredients ; let the whole stew gently for about an hour, then strain, and when cold, skim off all the fat. Thicken it, and if thought necessary, add a few drops of colouring.

TIME.—*1 hour.*

Note.—The addition of a small quantity of mushroom ketchup or Harvey's sauce very much improves the flavour of this gravy.

Gravy, Cheap (for Minced Veal.)—

INGREDIENTS. — *Bones and trimmings of old roast or boiled veal, 1½ pint of water, 1 onion, ¼ teaspoonful of minced lemon-peel, teaspoonful of salt, 1 blade of pounded mace, the juice of ¼ lemon ; thickening of butter and flour.* AVERAGE COST, *exclusive of the trimmings,* 2d.

Put all the ingredients into a stewpan, except the thickening and lemon-juice, and let them simmer very gently for rather more than 1 hour, or until the liquor is reduced to a pint, when strain through a hair sieve. Add a thickening of butter and flour, and the lemon-juice ; set it on the fire, and let it just boil up, when it will be ready for use. It may be flavoured with a little tomato sauce, and, where a rather dark-coloured gravy is not objected to, ketchup, or Harvey's sauce, may be added at pleasure.

TIME.—*Rather more than 1 hour.*

Gravy, Cheap (for Hashes, &c.) —

INGREDIENTS.—*Bones and trimmings of the cooked joint intended for hashing, ¼ teaspoonful of salt, ¼ teaspoonful of whole pepper, ¼ teaspoonful of whole allspice, a small faggot of savoury herbs, ½ head of celery, 1 onion, 1 oz. of butter, thickening, sufficient boiling water to cover the bones.* AVERAGE COST, *exclusive of the bones and trimmings,* 4d.

Chop the bones in small pieces, and put them into a stewpan with the trimmings, salt, pepper, spice, herbs and celery. Cover with boiling water, and let the whole simmer gently for 1½ or 2 hours. Slice and fry the onion in the butter till it is of a pale brown, and mix it gradually with the gravy made from the bones ; boil for ¼ hour, and strain into a basin ; now put it back into the stewpan ; flavour with walnut pickle or ketchup, pickled-onion liquor, or any store sauce that may be preferred. Thicken with a little butter and flour, kneaded together on a plate, and the gravy will be ready for use. After the thickening is added, the gravy should just boil to take off the rawness of the flour.

TIME.—*2 hours or rather more.*

Gravy (for Roast Meat.)—INGREDI-

ENTS.—*Gravy, salt.*

Put a common dish with a small quantity of salt in it under the meat, about a quarter of an hour before it is removed from the fire. When the dish is full, take it away, baste the meat, and pour the gravy into the dish on which the joint is to be served.

Gravy (for Venison.)—INGREDIENTS.

—*Trimmings of venison, 3 or 4 mutton shank-bones, salt to taste, 1 pint of water, 2 teaspoonfuls of walnut ketchup.*

Brown the trimmings over a nice clear fire, and put them in a stewpan with the shank-bones and water ; simmer gently for 2 hours, strain and skim, and add the walnut ketchup and a seasoning of salt. Let it just boil, when it is ready to serve.

TIME.—*2 hours.*

Gravy, Jugged. (Excellent.)—

INGREDIENTS.—2 lbs. of shin of beef, ¼ lb. of lean ham, 1 onion or a few shalots, 2 pints of water, salt and whole pepper to taste, 1 blade of mace, a faggot of savoury herbs, ½ a large carrot, ½ a head of celery. AVERAGE COST, 2s. for this quantity.

Cut up the beef and ham into small pieces, and slice the vegetables; take a jar, capable of holding two pints of water, and arrange therein in layers, the ham, meat, vegetables and seasoning, alternately filling up with the above quantity of water; tie down the jar, or put a plate over the top, so that the steam may not escape; place it in the oven, and let it remain there from 6 to 8 hours; should, however, the oven be very hot, less time will be required. When sufficiently cooked, strain the gravy, and when cold remove the fat. It may be flavoured with ketchup, wines, or any other store sauce that may be preferred. It is a good plan to put the jar in a cool oven over-night, to draw the gravy; and then it will not require so long baking the following day.

TIME.—From 6 to 8 hours, according to the oven.

Gravy-Kettle.—

This is an utensil which will not be found in every kitchen; but it is a useful one where it is necessary

GRAVY-KETTLE.

to keep gravies hot for the purpose of pouring over various dishes as they are cooking. It is made of copper, and should consequently be heated over the hot-plate, if there be one, or a charcoal stove.

Gravy made without Meat

(for Fowls.)—INGREDIENTS.—The necks, feet, livers and gizzards of the fowls, 1 slice of toasted bread, ½ onion, 1 faggot of savoury herbs, salt and pepper to taste, ½ pint of water, thickening of butter and flour, 1 dessertspoonful of ketchup. AVERAGE COST 2d.

Wash the feet of the fowls thoroughly clean, and cut them and the neck into small pieces. Put these into a stewpan with the bread, onions, herbs, seasoning, livers and gizzards; pour the water over them and simmer gently for 1 hour. Now take out the liver, pound it, and strain the liquor to it. Add a thickening of butter and flour, and a flavouring of mushroom ketchup; boil it up and serve.

TIME.—1 hour.

Gravy, Rich (for Hashes, Ragoûts &c.)—

INGREDIENTS.—2 lbs. of shin of beef, 1 large onion or a few shalots, a little flour, a bunch of savoury herbs, 2 blades of mace, 2 or 3 cloves, 4 whole allspice, ¼ teaspoonful of whole pepper, 1 slice of lean ham or bacon, ½ a head of celery (when at hand), 2 pints of boiling water, salt and cayenne to taste. AVERAGE COST, 9d. per pint.

Cut the beef into thin slices, as also the onions, dredge them with flour, and fry of a pale brown, but do not allow them to get black; pour in the boiling water, let it boil up and skim. Add the remaining ingredients and simmer the whole very gently for 2 hours, or until all the juices are extracted from the meat; put it by to get cold, when take off all the fat. This gravy may be flavoured with ketchup, store sauces, wine or, in fact, anything that may give additional and suitable relish to the dish it is intended for.

TIME.—Rather more than 2 hours.

Gravy Soup. —

INGREDIENTS for large quantity.—6 lbs. of shin of beef, a knuckle of veal weighing 5 lbs., a few pieces of trimmings, 2 slices of nicely-flavoured lean ham; ¼ lb. of butter, 4 onions, 4 carrots, 1 turnip, nearly a head of celery, 3 *blades of mace*, 6 *cloves, a bunch of savoury herbs, seasoning of salt and pepper to taste, 3 lumps of sugar, 6 quarts of boiling soft water. It can be flavoured with ketchup, Leamington sauce, Harvey's sauce, and a little soy.* AVERAGE COST, *per quart,* 1*s.*

Slightly brown the meat and ham in the butter, but do not' let them burn. When this is done, pour to it the water, and as the scum rises take it off; when no more appears, add all the other ingredients, and let the soup simmer slowly by the fire for 5 hours without stirring it any more from the bottom; take it off and let it settle; skim off all the fat you can, and pass it through a sieve or cloth. When perfectly cold you can remove all the fat, and leave the sediment untouched, which serves very nicely for thick gravies, hashes, &c.

TIME.—7 *hours.*
SEASONABLE *all the year.*

Gravy, Veal (for· White Sauces,

Fricassees, &c.)—INGREDIENTS.—2 *slices of nicely-flavoured lean ham, any poultry trimmings, 2 lbs. of lean veal, a faggot of savoury herbs, including parsley, a few green onions (or one large onion may be substituted for these), a few mushrooms, when obtainable; 1 blade of mace, salt to taste, 3 pints of water.* AVERAGE COST, 1*d. per pint.*

Cut up the ham and veal into small square pieces, put these in a stewpan, moistening them with a small quantity of water; place them over the fire to draw down. When the bottom of the stewpan becomes covered with a white glaze, fill up with water in the above proportion; add the remaining ingredients, stew very slowly for 3 or 4 hours, and do not forget to skim well the moment it boils. Put it by, and when cold take off all the fat. This may be used for Béchamel, sauce tournée, and many other white sauces.

TIME.—3 or 4 *hours.*

Greengage Jam.—INGREDIENTS.—

To every lb. of fruit, weighed before being stoned, allow ¾ *lb. of lump sugar.* AVERAGE COST, 6*d.* to 8*d. per lb. pot.*

Divide the greengages, take out the stones, and put them into a preserving-pan. Bring the fruit to a boil, then add the sugar, and keep stirring it over a gentle fire until it is melted. Remove all

GREENGAGES.

the scum as it rises, and just before the jam is done, boil it rapidly for 5 minutes. To ascertain when it is sufficiently boiled, pour a little on a plate, and if the syrup thickens and appears firm, it is done. Have ready half the kernels blanched; put them into the jam, give them one boil, and pour the preserve into pots. When cold, cover down with oiled papers, and over these, tissue paper brushed over on both sides with the white of an egg.

TIME.—¾ *hour after the sugar is added.*
SEASONABLE.—*Make this in August or September.*

Greengages, Compôte of.—

INGREDIENTS *for dish for 5 or 6 persons.*—1 *pint of syrup, 1 quart of greengages.* AVERAGE COST, 1*s.*

Make a syrup, skim it well, and put in the greengages when the syrup is boiling, having previously removed the stalks and stones from the fruit. Boil gently for ¼ hour, or until the fruit is tender, but take care not to let it break, as the appearance of the dish would be spoiled were the fruit reduced to a pulp. Take the greengages carefully out, place them on a glass dish, boil the syrup for another 5 minutes, let it cool a little, pour over the fruit, and when cold it will be ready for use.

TIME.—¼ *hour to simmer the fruit,* 5 *minutes the syrup.*

SEASONABLE *in July, August and September.*

Greengages, To Preserve and Dry.

INGREDIENTS.—*To every lb. of sugar allow* 1 *lb. of fruit,* ¼ *pint of water.*

For this purpose the fruit must be used before it is quite ripe, and part of the stalk must be left on. Weigh the fruit, rejecting all that is in the least degree blemished, and put it into a lined saucepan with the sugar and water, which should have been previously boiled together to a rich syrup. Boil the fruit in this for 10 minutes, remove it from the fire and drain the greengages. The next day boil up the syrup and put in the fruit again, and let it simmer for 3 minutes, and drain the syrup away. Continue this process for 5 or 6 days, and the last time place the greengages when drained on a hair sieve, and put them in an oven or warm spot to dry; keep them in a box, with paper between each layer, in a place free from damp.

TIME.— 10 *minutes the first time of boiling.*

SEASONABLE.—*Make this in August or September.*

Greengages, Preserved in Syrup.

INGREDIENTS.—*Allow* 1 *lb. of fruit to a* 1 *lb. pot, to every lb. of fruit allow* 1 *lb. of loaf sugar,* ¼ *pint of water.* AVERAGE COST, 6d. *to* 8d. *per lb. pot.*

Boil the sugar and water together for about 10 minutes; divide the greengages, take out the stones, put the fruit into the syrup, and let it simmer gently until nearly tender. Take it off the fire, put it into a large pan, and the next day boil it up again for about 10 minutes with the kernels from the stones, which should be blanched. Put the fruit carefully into jars, pour over it the syrup, and when cold,

cover down, so that the air is quite excluded. Let the syrup be well skimmed both the first and second day of boiling, otherwise it will not be clear.

TIME.—10 *minutes to boil the syrup;* ½ *hour to simmer the fruit the first day,* 10 *minutes the second day.*

SEASONABLE.—*Make this in August or September.*

Greens, Boiled Turnip.

INGREDIENTS.—*To each* ½ *gallon of water allow* 1 *heaped tablespoonful of salt; turnip-greens*

Wash the greens well in two or three waters, and pick off all the decayed and dead leaves; tie them in small bunches, and put them into plenty of boiling water salted in the above proportion. Keep them boiling quickly, with the lid of the saucepan off, and when tender pour them into a colander; let them drain, arrange them in a vegetable-dish, remove the string that the greens were tied with and serve.

TIME.—15 *to* 20 *minutes.*

SEASONABLE *in March, April and May.*

Grouse Pie.

INGREDIENTS *for medium-sized pie.*—2 *birds; cayenne, salt and pepper to taste;* 1 *lb. of rump-steak,* ½ *pint of well-seasoned broth, puff-paste* AVERAGE COST, 6s.

Line the bottom of a pie-dish with the rump-steak cut into neat pieces, and should the grouse be large, cut them into joints; but if small, they may be laid in the pie whole; season highly with salt, cayenne and black pepper; pour in the broth, and cover with a puff-paste; brush the crust over with the yolk of an egg, and bake from ¾ to 1 hour. If the grouse is cut into joints, the backbones and trimmings will make the gravy, by stewing them with an onion, a little sherry, a bunch of herbs, and a blade of mace; this should be poured in after the pie is baked.

TIME.—¾ *to* 1 *hour.*

SEASONABLE *from the* 12th *of August to the beginning of December.*

Grouse, Roast.—INGREDIENTS.—

rouse, butter, a thick slice of toasted bread.
.VERAGE COST, 4s. a brace.

Let the birds hang as long as possible; luck and draw them; wipe, but do not ash them, inside and out, and truss hem. *See* "Grouse, Trussing of." Put hem down to a sharp, clear fire; keep

ROAST GROUSE.

hem well basted the whole of the time they re cooking, and serve them on buttered past, soaked in the dripping-pan, with a ttle melted butter poured over them, or vith bread-sauce and gravy.

TIME.—½ *hour; if liked very thoroughly* one, 35 *minutes.*

SEASONABLE *from the 12th of August to* he beginning of December.

Grouse Salad. (SOYER'S Recipe,

mproved.)—INGREDIENTS.— 4 *eggs, Mont-* elier butter, fresh salad, 2 or 3 grouse; for he sauce, 1 tablespoonful of minced shalot, tablespoonful of pounded sugar, the yolks f 2 eggs, 1 teaspoonful of minced parsley, oz. of salt, 12 tablespoonfuls of oil, 4 table-poonfuls of Chili vinegar, 1 gill of cream, 2 ablespoonfuls of chopped tarragon and hervil.

Boil the eggs hard, shell them, throw hem into cold water, cut a thin slice off he bottom to facilitate the proper placing f them in the dish, cut each one into four, engthwise, and make a very thin, flat bor-ler of the butter, about one inch from the dge of the dish the salad is to be served n; fix the pieces of egg upright close to ach other, the yolk outside, or the yolk nd white alternately; lay in the centre a

fresh salad of whatever is in season, and, having previously roasted the grouse rather underdone, cut it into eight or ten pieces, and prepare the sauce as follows:—Put the shalots into a basin, with the sugar, the yolk of an egg, the parsley and salt, and mix in by degrees the oil and vinegar; when all the ingredients are well mixed, put the sauce on ice or in a cool place. When ready to serve, whip the cream rather thick, which lightly mix with it; then lay the inferior parts of the grouse on the salad, sauce over so as to cover each piece, then lay over the salad and the remainder of the grouse, pour the rest of the sauce over, and serve. The eggs may be ornamented with a little dot of radishes or beetroot on the point. Anchovy and gherkin, cut into small diamonds, may be placed between, or cut gherkins in slices, and a border of them laid round. Tarragon or chervil-leaves are also a pretty addition. The remains of cold black-game, pheasant or partridge may be used in the above manner and will make a very delicate dish.

SEASONABLE *from the 12th of August to the beginning of December.*

Grouse, To Carve.—Grouse may

be carved in the way first described in carving partridge. The backbone of the

GROUSE.

grouse is highly esteemed by many, and this part of many game birds is considered the finest-flavoured.

Grouse, Trussing of.—In plucking

these birds, leave the breast-feathers till after trussing, the skin being delicate and easily broken. Cut off the head, leaving enough skin to skewer back, then loosen the inside at neck and squeeze out the inside. After wiping the inside, bring the legs close to the breast, between it and the

GROUSE READY FOR TRUSSING.

s'de-bones, and put a skewer through the pinions and the thick part of the thighs, Then remove the feathers from the breast with a knife so as to avoid breaking the skin. Partridges and pheasants are trussed

GROUSE READY FOR COOKING.

as grouse, but the latter, being sufficiently large for the passage of the hand, are drawn as fowls.

Gruel, To Make. — INGREDIENTS

for 1 pint of gruel.—1 tablespoonful of Robinson's patent groats, 2 tablespoonfuls of cold water, 1 pint of boiling water.

Mix the prepared groats smoothly with the cold water in a basin; pour over them the boiling water, stirring it all the time. Put it into a very clean saucepan; boil the gruel for 10 minutes, keeping it well stirred; sweeten to taste and serve. It may be flavoured with a small piece of lemon-peel, by boiling it in the gruel, or a little grated nutmeg may be put in; but in these matters the taste of the patient should be consulted. Pour the gruel in a tumbler, and serve. When wine is allowed to the invalid, 2 tablespoonfuls of sherry or port make this preparation very nice. In cases of colds,

the same quantity of spirits is sometime added instead of wine.

TIME.—10 *minutes.*

Gudgeons. — INGREDIENTS. — Eg

and bread-crumbs sufficient for the quantit of fish; hot lard.

Do not scrape off the scales, but take ou the gills and inside, and cleanse thoroughly

THE GUDGEON.

wipe them dry, flour and dip them int egg, and sprinkle over with bread-crumbs Fry of a nice brown.

TIME.—3 or 4 *minutes.*

SEASONABLE *from March to July.*

Guinea Fowl, The.— This bir

takes its name from Guinea, in Africa, wher it is found wild, and in great abundance.

It is gregarious in its habits, associatin in flocks of two or three hundred; delight ing in marshy ground, and at night roostin upon trees or on high situations. In siz it is about the same as a common hen Though domesticated, it retains much o its wild nature and is apt to wander.

Guinea-Fowl, Roast, Larded

—INGREDIENTS.—A guinea-fowl, lardoons flour and salt. AVERAGE COST, 3s. 6d.

When this bird is larded, it should b trussed the same as a pheasant; if plainl roasted, truss it like a turkey. After lard ing and trussing it, put it down to roast a a brisk fire; keep it well basted, and short time before serving, dredge it with little flour, and let it froth nicely. Serv with a little gravy in the dish, and a tureer of the same, and one of well-made bread sauce.

TIME.— Guinea-fowl, larded, 1¼ hour plainly roasted, about 1 hour.

SEASONABLE in winter.

"*Hesperus, thou bringest all good things,*
Home to the weary, to the hungry cheer."—BYRON.

HADDOCK, BAKED.

 **HADDOCK, Baked.—INGREDIENTS.**—*A nice veal forcemeat, butter to taste, egg and bread-crumbs, haddocks.* AVERAGE COST, 6*d.* each.

Scale and clean the fish, without cutting it open much; put in a nice delicate forcemeat, and sew up the slit. Brush it over with egg, sprinkle over bread-crumbs, and baste frequently with butter. Garnish with parsley and cut lemon, and serve with a nice brown gravy. The egg and bread-crumbs can be omitted, and pieces of butter placed over the fish.

TIME.—*Large haddock, ¾ hour; moderate size, ¼ hour.*

SEASONABLE *from August to February.*

Note.—Haddocks may be filleted, rubbed over with egg and bread-crumbs, and fried a nice brown; garnish with crisped parsley.

Haddock, Boiled.—INGREDIENTS.
—*Sufficient water to cover the fish; ¼ lb. of

HADDOCK, BOILED.

salt to each gallon of water.* AVERAGE COST, 6*d.* each.

Scrape the fish, take out the inside, wash it thoroughly, and lay it in a kettle, with enough water to cover it, and salt in the above proportion. Simmer gently from 15 to 20 minutes, or rather more should the

THE HADDOCK.

fish be very large. For small haddocks, fasten the tails in their mouths, and put them into boiling water. 10 to 15 minutes

HADDOCK.

will cook them. Serve with plain melted butter, or anchovy sauce.

TIME.—*Large haddock, ½ hour; small, ¼ hour, or rather less.*

SEASONABLE *from August to February.*

Haddock, Dried.—Dried haddock should be gradually warmed through either before or over a nice clear fire. Rub a little piece of butter over, just before sending it to table.

Haddock, Dried.—INGREDIENTS *for breakfast dish for 4 persons.*—1 *large thick haddock,* 2 *bay-leaves,* 1 *small bunch of savoury herbs, not forgetting parsley, a little butter and pepper; boiling water.* AVERAGE COST, 9*d.*

Cut up the haddock into square pieces, make a basin hot by means of hot water, which pour out. Lay in the fish with the bay-leaves and herbs ; cover with boiling water ; put a plate over to keep in the steam, and let it remain for 10 minutes. Take out the slices, put them in a hot dish, rub over with butter and pepper, and serve.

TIME.—10 *minutes.*

SEASONABLE *at any time but best in winter.*

Haggis.—INGREDIENTS.—*A sheep's pluck and the small fat tripe, a sheep's paunch, a teacupful of oatmeal,* 2 *onions,* 1 *lb. of beef suet, a dessertspoonful of salt, a teaspoonful of pepper,* ¾ *pint of beef gravy.* AVERAGE COST, 3*s.*

Well wash and clean the pluck and the tripe, and boil for ½ hour with the pipe hanging over the edge of the pot, then remove all the pipe, and skin and mince the meat finely. Add the onions, chopped small, the oatmeal, previously dried in the oven, the suet, chopped finely, the seasoning and the gravy, and mix all well together. Have the paunch, which must be whole, thoroughly cleansed, and put the mixture into it, and sew it up loosely, then tie in a cloth as a pudding, leaving room for swelling, and boil slowly, in plenty of water for 3½ hours. Serve hot in a deep dish or tureen.

TIME.—4 *hours.*

SEASONABLE *in winter,*

Half-Pay Pudding.—INGREDIENTS *for pudding sufficient for 6 persons.*—¼ *lb. of suet,* ¼ *lb. of currants,* ¼ *lb. of raisins,* ¼ *lb. of bread-crumbs,* 2 *tablespoonfuls of treacle,* ½ *pint of milk.* AVERAGE COST, 8*d.*

Chop the suet finely ; mix with it the currants, which should be nicely washed and dried, the raisins, which should be stoned, the flour, bread-crumbs and treacle; moisten with the milk, beat up the ingredients until all are thoroughly mixed, put them into a buttered basin, and boil the pudding for 3½ hours.

TIME.—3½ *hours.*

SEASONABLE *at any time.*

Halibut Steaks. (American Recipe.) —INGREDIENTS.—*Some slices of halibut, eggs, crackers or bread-crumbs, hot lard or dripping, salt.*

Wash and wipe the steaks dry, beat the eggs, and roll out the crackers till they are powdered fine (in lieu of these grate bread-crumbs). Dredge the steaks with flour, then dip them in the egg, and cover with cracker or bread-crumbs, and fry on both sides in plenty of hot lard or dripping. They are also very good cut thinner than for frying, and broiled over a clear fire, first being seasoned with pepper and salt. Oyster sauce is a nice accompaniment to this fish, or if a cold one be preferred Tartare.

TIME.—10 *to* 15 *minutes to fry the steaks.*

SEASONABLE *at any time.*

Ham Omelette (A delicious Breakfast Dish.)—INGREDIENTS *for breakfast dish for 4 persons.*—6 *eggs,* 4 *oz. of butter,* ½ *saltspoonful of pepper,* 2 *tablespoonfuls of minced ham.* AVERAGE COST, 1*s.*

Mince the ham very finely, without any fat, and fry it for 2 minutes in a little butter ; then make the batter for the omelette, stir in the ham, and proceed as in the case of a plain omelette. Do not add any salt to the batter, as the ham is usually sufficiently salt to impart a flavour to the omelette. Good lean bacon or tongue, answers equally well for this dish; but they must also be slightly cooked previously to mixing them with the batter. Serve very hot and quickly, without gravy.

TIME.—*From 4 to 6 minutes.*

SEASONABLE *at any time.*

Ham, Fried, and Eggs. (A Breakfast Dish.)—INGREDIENTS. *Ham, eggs; allow 2 eggs and a slice of ham to each person.* AVERAGE COST, 1s. *per lb.*

Cut the ham into slices, and take care that they are of the same thickness in every part. Cut off the rind, and if the ham should be particularly hard and salt, it will be found an improvement to soak it for about 10 minutes in hot water, and then dry it in a cloth. Put it into a cold frying-pan, set it over the fire, and turn the slices 3 or 4 times whilst they are cooking. When done place them on a dish, which should be kept hot in front of the fire during the time the eggs are being poached. Poach the eggs, slip them on to the slices of ham, and serve quickly.

TIME.—*7 or 8 minutes to broil the ham.*

SEASONABLE *at any time.*

Note.—Ham may also be toasted or broiled; but, with the latter method, to insure its being well cooked, the fire must be beautifully clear, or it will have a smoky flavour far from agreeable.

Ham, Potted. (A nice addition to the Breakfast or Luncheon Table.)—INGREDIENTS.—*To 2 lbs. of lean ham allow ½ lb. of fat,* 1 *teaspoonful of pounded mace,* ½ *teaspoonful of pounded allspice,* ½ *nutmeg, pepper to taste, clarified butter.* AVERAGE COST, 2s. 6d.

Cut some slices from the remains of a cold ham, mince them small, and to every 2 lbs. of lean allow the above proportion of fat. Pound the ham in a mortar to a fine paste with the fat, gradually add the seasonings and spices, and be very par-

ticular that all the ingredients are well mixed and the spices well pounded. Press the mixture into potting-pots, pour over clarified butter, and keep it in a cool place.

SEASONABLE *at any time.*

Ham, Potted, that will keep Good for some time.—INGREDIENTS.—*To 4 lbs. of lean ham allow* 1 *lb. of fat,* 2 *teaspoonfuls of pounded mace,* ½ *nutmeg grated, rather more than ½ teaspoonful of cayenne, clarified lard.*

Mince the ham, fat and lean together in the above proportion, and pound it well in a mortar, seasoning it with cayenne pepper, pounded mace and nutmeg; put the mixture into a deep baking-dish, and bake for ½ hour; then press it well into a stone jar, fill up the jar with clarified lard, cover it closely, and paste over it a piece of thick paper. If well seasoned. it will keep a long time in winter, and will be found very convenient for sandwiches, &c.

TIME.—½ *hour.*

SEASONABLE *at any time.*

Ham, To Bake.—INGREDIENTS.—*Ham; a common crust.* AVERAGE COST *of York ham,* 10d. *to* 1s. *per lb.*

As a ham for baking should be well soaked, let it remain in water for at least 12 hours. Wipe it dry, trim away any rusty places underneath, and cover it with a common crust, taking care that this is of sufficient thickness all over to keep the gravy in. Place it in a moderately-heated oven, and bake for nearly 4 hours. Take off the crust and skin, and cover with raspings, the same as for boiled ham, and garnish the knuckle with a paper frill. This method of cooking a ham is, by many persons, considered far superior to boiling it, as it cuts fuller of gravy and has a finer flavour, besides keeping a much longer time good.

TIME.—*A medium-sized ham, 4 hours.*

SEASONABLE *all the year.*

Ham, To Boil.—INGREDIENTS.—

Ham, water, glaze, or raspings. AVERAGE
COST, *for York ham*, 10 *to* 1s. *per lb.*

In choosing a ham, ascertain that it is
perfectly sweet, by running a sharp knife
into it, close to the bone; and if, when the
knife is withdrawn, it has an agreeable
smell, the ham is good; if on the contrary,
the blade has a greasy appearance and
offensive smell, the ham is bad. If it has
been long hung, and is very dry and salt,

BOILED HAM.

let it remain in soak for 24 hours, changing the water frequently. This length of
time is only necessary in the case of its
being very hard; from 8 to 12 hours would
be sufficient for a Yorkshire or a West-
moreland ham. Wash it thoroughly clean,
and trim away from the underside all the
rusty and smoked parts, which would spoil
the appearance. Put it into a boiling-pot,
with sufficient cold water to cover it;
bring it gradually to boil, and as the scum
rises, carefully remove it. Keep it simmering very gently until tender, and be
careful that it does not stop boiling, nor
boil too quickly. When done, take it out of
the pot, strip off the skin, and sprinkle
over it a few fine bread-raspings, put a
frill of cut paper round the knuckle, and
serve. If to be eaten cold, let the ham
remain in the water until nearly cold; by
this method the juices are kept in, and it
will be found infinitely superior to one
taken out of the water hot; it should, however, be borne in mind that the ham must
not remain in the saucepan *all* night.
When the skin is removed, sprinkle over
bread-raspings, or, if wanted particularly
nice, glaze it. Place a paper frill round
the knuckle, and garnish with parsley.

TIME.—*A ham weighing* 10 *lbs.,* 4 *hours*
to simmer gently; 15 *lbs.,* 5 *hours; a ver*
large one, *about* 6 *hours.*

SEASONABLE *all the year.*

Note.—A ham boiled in champagne is though
to have a very superior flavour to one boiled i
water. In large hotels and clubs, what is called
ullage wine is used for this purpose.

Ham, How to Boil to give i
an excellent flavour.—INGREDIENTS.—

Vinegar and water, 2 *heads of celery,*
turnips, 3 *onions, a large bunch of savour*
herbs.

Prepare the ham as in the preceding
recipe, and let it soak for a few hours i
vinegar and water. Put it on in col
water, and when it boils add the vegeta
bles and herbs. Simmer very gently unti
tender, take it out, strip off the skin, cove
with bread-raspings, and put a paper ruch
or frill round the knuckle. This mode o
cooking is for a ham to be eaten hot.

TIME.—*A ham weighing* 10 *lbs.,* 4 *hours*
SEASONABLE *at any time.*

Ham, To Carve.— In cutting
ham, the carver must be guided according
as he desires to practise economy or hav
at once fine slices out of the prime part
Under the first supposition, he will com
mence at the knuckle end, and cut off thi
slices towards the thick part of the ham
To reach the choicer portion, the knife
which must be very sharp and thin, shoul

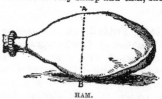

HAM.

be carried quite down to the bone, in th
direction of the line A to B. The slice
should be thin and even, and always cu
down to the bone. There are some wh
like to carve a ham by cutting a hole at th
top, and then slicing pieces off inside th
hole, gradually enlarging the circle; bu

we think this is a plan not to be recommended. A ham, when hot, is usually sent to table with a paper ruffle round the knuckle.

Hams for Curing. (Mons. UDE's Recipe.) — INGREDIENTS. — *For 2 hams weighing about* 16 *or* 18 *lbs. each, allow* 1 *lb. f moist sugar,* 1 *lb. of common salt,* 2 *oz. of saltpetre,* 1 *quart of good vinegar.*

As soon as the pig is cold enough to be ut up, take the 2 hams and rub them well vith common salt, and leave them in a arge pan for 3 days. When the salt has rawn out all the blood, drain the hams, nd throw the brine away. Mix sugar, alt and saltpetre together in the above roportion, rub the hams well with these, nd put them into a vessel large enough to old them, always keeping the salt over hem. Let them remain for 3 days, then our over them a quart of good vinegar. 'urn them in the brine every day for a nonth, then drain them well, and rub them vith bran. Have them smoked over a wood re, and be particular that the hams are ung as high up as possible from the fire ; therwise the fat will melt, and they will ecome dry and hard.

TIME.— *To be pickled* 1 *month ; to be moked* 1 *month.*

SEASONABLE *from October to March.*

Hams, To Cure Sweet in the Westmoreland way. — INGREDIENTS. — . *lbs of common salt,* 3 *lbs. of coarse sugar, lb. of bay-salt,* 3 *quarts of strong beer.*

Before the hams are put into pickle, rub hem the preceding day well with salt, and rain the brine well from them. Put the bove ingredients into a saucepan, and boil or ¼ hour ; pour over the hams ; and let hem remain a month in the pickle. Rub nd turn them every day, but do not take hem out of the pickling-pan, and have hem smoked for a month.

TIME.— *To be pickled* 1 *month ; to be moked* 1 *month.*

SEASONABLE *from October to March.*

Hams, To Pickle. (Suffolk Recipe.) —INGREDIENTS.—*To a ham from* 10 *to* 12 *lbs., allow* 1 *lb. of coarse sugar,* ¾ *lb. of salt,* 1 *oz. of saltpetre,* ½ *a teacupful of vinegar.*

Rub the hams well with common salt, and leave them for a day or two to drain ; then rub well in the above proportion of sugar, salt, saltpetre, and vinegar, and turn them every other day. Keep them in the pickle 1 month, drain them, and send them to be smoked over a wood fire for 3 weeks or a month.

TIME.—*To remain in the pickle* 1 *month ; to be smoked* 3 *weeks or* 1 *month.*

SEASONABLE. — *Hams should be pickled from October to March.*

Hams, To Salt Two, about 12 or 15 lbs. each.—INGREDIENTS.—2 *lbs. of treacle,* ½ *lb. of saltpetre,* 1 *lb. of bay-salt,* 2 *lbs. of common salt.*

Two days before they are put into the pickle, rub the hams well with salt, to draw away all slime and blood. Throw what comes from them away, and then rub them with treacle, saltpetre and salt. Lay them in a deep pan, and let them remain one day ; boil the above proportion of treacle, saltpetre, bay-salt and common salt for ¼ hour, and pour this pickle boiling hot over the hams : there should be sufficient of it to cover them. For a day or two rub them well with it ; afterwards they will only require turning. They ought to remain in this pickle for 3 weeks or a month, and then be sent to be smoked, which will take nearly or quite a month to do. An ox-tongue pickled in this way is most excellent, to be eaten either green or smoked.

TIME.—*To remain in the pickle* 3 *weeks or a month ; to be smoked about a month.*

SEASONABLE *from October to March.*

Hams, To Smoke at Home.— Take an old hogshead, stop up all the crevices, and fix a place to put a cross-stick near the bottom, to hang the articles to be

smoked on. Next, in the side, cut a hole near the top, to introduce an iron pan filled with sawdust and small pieces of green wood. Having turned the tub upside down,

HAM, GARNISHED.

hang the articles upon the cross-stick, introduce the iron pan in the opening, and place a piece of red-hot iron in the pan, cover it with sawdust, and all will be complete. Let a large ham remain 40 hours, and keep up a good smoke. Fish may be smoked in the same manner.

Hare, Broiled. (A Supper or Luncheon Dish.)—INGREDIENTS.—*The legs and shoulders of a roast hare, cayenne and salt to taste, a little butter.*

Cut the legs and shoulders from a roast hare, season them highly with salt and cayenne, and broil them over a very clear fire for 5 minutes. Dish them on a hot dish, rub over them a little cold butter, and send to table very quickly.

TIME.—*5 minutes.*

SEASONABLE *from September to the end of February.*

Hare, Croquettes of.—INGREDIENTS *for small dish sufficient for 4 persons.* —½ *lb. of the remains of cold roast hare,* ½ *lb. of bread, 3 eggs, pepper, salt and cayenne to taste, 1 oz. of butter, 2 tablespoonfuls of stock, bread-crumbs.* AVERAGE COST, *exclusive of the cold hare, 6d.*

Mince the hare as fine as possible, and season it well; soak the bread in the stock, then place it in a stewpan on the fire, add the butter and the yolk of one egg, and beat the mixture to a paste; add the hare and another egg, stir all well together and

set aside to cool. Form the mixture into balls or cones, dip them in beaten egg, then in bread-crumbs, and fry of a nice brown colour. A good brown gravy may be served with these, or some Italian sauce.

TIME.—10 *minutes to fry the croquettes.*

SEASONABLE *from September to the end of February.*

Hare, Hashed. (Cold Meat Cookery.)—INGREDIENTS.—*The remains of cold roast hare, 1 blade of pounded mace, 2 or allspice, pepper and salt to taste, 1 onion, bunch of savoury herbs, 3 tablespoonfuls of port wine, thickening of butter and flour, tablespoonfuls of mushroom ketchup.* AVERAGE COST, 8d.

Cut the cold hare into neat slices, and put the head, bones and trimmings into stewpan, with ¾ pint of water; add the mace, allspice, seasoning, onion and herbs, stew for nearly an hour and strain the gravy; thicken it with butter and flour, add the wine and ketchup, and lay in the pieces of hare, with any stuffing that may be left. Let the whole gradually heat by the side of the fire, and when it has simmered for about 5 minutes, serve and garnish the dish with sippets of toasted bread. Send red-currant jelly to table with it.

TIME—*Rather more than 1 hour.*

SEASONABLE *from September to the end of February.*

Hare, Jugged. (Very good.)—INGREDIENTS *for dish sufficient for 7 or 8 persons.*—1 *hare, 1½ lb. of gravy beef, ½ lb. of butter, 1 onion, 1 lemon, 6 cloves; pepper cayenne and salt to taste;* ¼ *pint of port wine.* AVERAGE COST, 6s. 6d.

Skin, paunch and wash the hare, cut it into pieces, dredge them in flour, and fry in boiling butter. Have ready 1½ pint of gravy made from the above proportion of beef, and thickened with a little flour. Put this into a jar; add the pieces of fried hare, an onion stuck with six cloves, a lemon peeled and cut in half, and a good seasoning of pepper, cayenne and salt; cover the jar down tightly, put it up to the neck into a stewpan of boiling water, and let it stew until the hare is quite tender, taking care to keep the water boiling. When nearly done, pour in the wine, and add a few forcemeat balls; these must be fried or baked in the oven for a few minutes before they are put to the gravy. Serve with red-currant jelly.

TIME.—3½ to 4 hours. If the hare is very old allow 4½ hours.

SEASONABLE from September to the end of February.

Hare, Jugged. (A Quicker and more Economical Way.)—INGREDIENTS for dish sufficient for 8 persons.—1 hare, a bunch of sweet herbs, 2 onions, each stuck with 3 cloves, 6 whole allspice, ½ teaspoonful of black pepper, a strip of lemon-peel, thickening of butter and flour, 2 tablespoonfuls of mushroom ketchup, ¼ pint of port wine. AVERAGE COST, 5s. 6d.

Wash the hare nicely, cut it up into joints (not too large), and flour and brown them as in the preceding recipe; then put them into a stewpan with the herbs, onions, cloves, allspice, pepper and lemon-peel; cover with hot water, and when it boils, carefully remove all the scum, and let it simmer gently till tender, which will be in about 1¾ hour, or longer, should the hare be very old. Take out the pieces of hare, thicken the gravy with flour and butter, add the ketchup and port wine, let it boil for about 10 minutes, strain it through a sieve over the hare and serve. A few fried forcemeat balls should be added at the moment of serving, or instead of frying them, they may be stewed in the gravy about 10 minutes before the hare is wanted for table. Do not omit to serve red-currant jelly with it.

TIME.—Altogether 2 hours.

SEASONABLE from September to the end of February.

Note.—Should there be any left, re-warm it the next day by putting the hare, &c., into a covered jar, and placing this jar in a saucepan of boiling water; this method prevents a great deal of waste.

Hare, Potted. (A Luncheon or Breakfast Dish.)—INGREDIENTS for 6 small pots.—1 hare, a few slices of bacon, a large bunch of savoury herbs, 4 cloves, ½ teaspoonful of whole allspice, 2 carrots, 2 onions, salt and pepper to taste, 1 pint of water, 2 glasses of sherry. AVERAGE COST, 5s. 6d.

Skin, empty and wash the hare; cut it down the middle, and put it into a stewpan with a few slices of bacon under and over it; add the remaining ingredients, and stew very gently until the hare is tender, and the flesh will separate easily from the bones. When done enough take it up, remove the bones, and pound the meat with the bacon, in a mortar, until reduced to a perfectly smooth paste. Should it not be sufficiently seasoned, add a little cayenne, salt and pounded mace, but be careful that these are well mixed with the other ingredients. Press the meat into potting-pots, pour over clarified butter, and keep in a dry place. The liquor that the hare was stewed in should be saved for hashes, soups, &c., &c. Remains of cold hare answer equally well for potting.

TIME.—About 2½ hours to stew the hare.

SEASONABLE from September to the end of February.

Hare, Roast.—INGREDIENTS.—Hare, forcemeat, a little milk, butter.

Choose a young hare; which may be known by its smooth and sharp claws, and by the cleft in the lip not being much spread. To be eaten in perfection, it must hang for some time; and, if properly taken care of, it may be kept for several days. It is better to hang without being paunched; but should it be previously emptied, wipe the inside every day, and sprinkle over it a little pepper and ginger, to prevent the musty taste which long keeping in the damp occasions, and also which affects the stuffing. After it is skinned, wash it well, and soak for an hour in warm water to draw out the blood; if old, let it lie in vinegar for a short time, but wash it well

ROAST HARE.

afterwards in several waters. Make a forcemeat, wipe the hare dry, fill the belly with it, and sew it up. Wrap the ears in a piece of buttered paper. The hare should be kept at a distance from the fire when it is first laid down, or the outside will become dry and hard before the inside is done. Baste it well with milk for a short time, and afterwards with butter; and particular attention must be paid to the basting, so as to preserve the meat on the back juicy and nutritive. When it is almost roasted enough, flour the hare, and baste well with butter. When nicely frothed, dish it, remove the skewers, and send it to table with a little gravy in the dish, and a tureen of the same. Red-currant jelly must also not be forgotten, as this is an indispensable accompaniment to roast hare. For economy, good beef dripping may be substituted for the milk and butter to baste with; but the basting, as we have before stated, must be continued without intermission. If the liver is good, it may be parboiled, minced and mixed with the stuffing; but it should not be used unless quite fresh. Plenty of good gravy should always be served with hare, which otherwise would be rather dry, the

juice of the flesh being extracted in the cooking.

TIME.—*A middling-sized hare, 1¼ hour; a large hare, 1½ to 2 hours.*

SEASONABLE *from September to the end of February.*

Hare, Roast, To Carve.—The

"Grand Carver" of olden times, a functionary of no ordinary dignity, was pleased when he had a hare to manipulate, for his skill and grace had an opportunity of display. *Dinners à la Russe* to a certain extent save modern gentlemen the necessity of learning the art which was in auld lang syne one of the necessary accomplishments of the useful squire; but, until sidetables become universal, or till we see the office of "grand carver" once more instituted, it will be well for all to learn how to assist at the carving of this dish, which, if not the most elegant in appearance, is a very general favourite. The hare, having its head to the left, as shown in the woodcut, should be first served by cutting slices from each side of the backbone, in the direction of the lines from C to D. After these prime parts are disposed of, the leg should next be

ROAST HARE.

disengaged by cutting round the line indicated by the letters E to F. The shoulders will then be taken off by passing the knife round from G to H. The back of the hare should now be divided by cutting quite through its spine, as shown by the line A to B, taking care to feel with the point of the knife for a joint where the back may be readily penetrated. It is the usual plan not to serve any bone in helping hare; and thus the flesh should be sliced from the legs and placed alone on the plate. In large establishments, and where men-cooks are kept, it is often the case that the backbone of the hare, especially in old animals, is taken out, and then the process of carving is, of course considerably facilitated. Stuffing is served with it; and the ears, which should be nicely crisp, and the brains of the hare, are esteemed as delicacies by many connoisseurs.

Hare Soup.—INGREDIENTS *for* 3 *quarts of soup.—A hare fresh-killed*, 1 *lb. of lean gravy beef, a slice of ham*, 1 *carrot*, 2 *onions, a faggot of savoury herbs*, ¼ *oz. of whole black pepper, a little browned flour*, ¼ *pint of port wine, the crumb of two French rolls, salt and cayenne to taste*, 3½ *quarts of water.* AVERAGE COST, 6s.

Skin and paunch the hare, saving the liver and as much blood as possible. Cut it in pieces, and put it in a stewpan with all the ingredients, and simmer gently for 6 hours. This soup should be made the day before it is wanted. Strain through a sieve, put the best parts of the hare in the soup and serve.

TIME.—6 *hours.*
SEASONABLE *from September to March.*

Hare Soup.—Proceed as above; but, instead of putting the joints of the hare in the soup, pick the meat from the bones, pound it in a mortar, and add it, with the crumb of two French rolls, to the soup. Rub all through a sieve; heat slowly, but do not let it boil. Send it to table immediately.

TIME.—8 *hours.*
SEASONABLE *from September to March.*

Hare, Trussing of.—To skin a hare, first cut off the fore feet at the first joint, and the belly open lengthwise. Raise the skin of the back, and draw it over the hind legs, being careful to leave the tail whole; then draw it over the back (see illustration) and slip out the fore legs, easing it, if necessary, with a knife over the neck and head, being careful not to injure the ears, as in a roast hare they should be intact. It is

HARE BEING SKINNED.

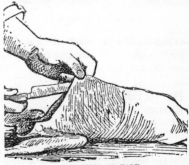

PAUNCHING OF HARE.

better, where a hook is obtainable, to hang the hare upon one, thus leaving both hands free for skinning it.

X

Having cut open the hare, in the way shown in illustration, and paunching it, wash and wipe it inside, then cut the sinews of the legs, and after bringing them

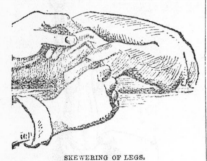

SKEWERING OF LEGS.

well forward against the body, run in two skewers, right through, one fixing the fore, the other the hind legs; next put the head well back, and passing a skewer through

SKEWERING OF HEAD.

the right shoulder (see illustration), skewer it firmly in place. Put the ears in buttered papers before roasting.

Haricot Beans, To Boil. —

INGREDIENTS *for dish for 4 or 5 persons.*—1 *quart of beans, 2 quarts of soft water, 1 oz. of butter, 1 tablespoonful of salt.* AVERAGE COST, 5*d.*

Put the beans in cold water and, according to their age, let them soak from 2 to 4 hours. The older they are the longer time they require. Put them into fresh water (2 quarts of soft) with the salt, bring to the boil, then let them simmer very gently until tender; pour off the water, but leave the pan with the lid partially off by the side of the fire for the beans to dry. Put in the butter and the seasoning of pepper and salt, and shake the pan for a moment or two while the butter melts; then serve very hot.

TIME.—2 *to* 2½ *hours after the water boils.*
SEASONABLE *in winter.*

Haricot Beans and Tomatoes.

—INGREDIENTS *for small dish.*—Baked or *boiled haricot beans, about* 1½ *pint,* ½ *pint of the water in which they were cooked,* 2 *table-spoonfuls of tomato sauce, 1 oz. of flour,* ½ *oz. of butter.* AVERAGE COST, 6*d.*

Having boiled the beans till quite tender, strain off the liquor, and to ¼ pint of it add the thickening of flour and butter, then the sauce, and let it boil. Put in the beans and serve hot. Haricot beans are also good served with fried onions, and when other vegetables are scarce they are useful and very nice when well and thoroughly cooked.

TIME.—2 *to* 2½ *hours to boil the beans.*
SEASONABLE *at any time.*

Herb Powder (for Flavouring when

Fresh Herbs are not obtainable). — INGREDIENTS.—1 *oz. of dried lemon-thyme, 1 oz. of dried winter savoury, 1 oz. of dried sweet marjoram and basil, 2 oz. of dried parsley, 1 oz. of dried lemon-peel.*

Prepare and dry the herbs, pick the leaves from the stalks, pound them and sift them through a hair-sieve; mix in the above proportions, and keep in glass bottles, carefully excluding the air. This we think a far better method of keeping herbs, as the flavour and fragrance do not evaporate so much as when they are merely put in paper bags. Preparing them in this way, you have them ready for use at a moment's notice. Mint, sage, parsley, &c., dried, pounded and each put into separate bottles, will be found very useful in winter.

Herbs, To Dry (for Winter Use.)

—On a very dry day gather the herbs, just before they begin to flower. If this is done when the weather is damp, the herbs will not be so good a colour. (It is very necessary to be particular in little matters like this, for trifles constitute perfection, and herbs nicely dried will be found very acceptable when frost and snow are on the ground. It is hardly necessary, however, to state that the flavour and fragrance of fresh herbs are incomparably finer.) They should be perfectly freed from dirt and dust, and be divided into small bunches, with their roots cut off. Dry them quickly in a very hot oven or before the fire, as by this means most of their flavour will be preserved, and be careful not to burn them; tie them up in paper bags and keep in a dry place. This is a very general way of preserving dried herbs; but we would recommend the plan described in the preceding recipe.

SEASONABLE.—*From the month of July to the end of September is the proper time for storing herbs for winter use.*

Herodotus Pudding.—INGREDIENTS *for medium-sized pudding.*—½ lb. of bread-crumbs, ½ lb. of good figs, 6 oz. of suet, 6 oz. of moist sugar, ⅓ saltspoonful of salt, 2 eggs, nutmeg to taste. AVERAGE COST, 1s.

Mince the suet and figs very finely; add the remaining ingredients, taking care that the eggs are well whisked; beat the mixture for a few minutes, put it into a buttered mould, tie it down with a floured cloth, and boil the pudding for 5 hours. Serve with wine sauce.

TIME.—5 *hours.*

SEASONABLE *at any time.*

Herrings, Fresh White, Baked.

—INGREDIENTS.—*12 herrings, 4 bay-leaves, 12 cloves, 12 allspice, 2 small blades of mace, cayenne pepper and salt to taste, sufficient vinegar to fill up the dish.* AVERAGE COST, 1s. 2d.

Take herrings, cut off the heads, and gut them. Put them in a pie-dish, heads and tails alternately, and between each layer sprinkle over the above ingredients. Cover the fish with the vinegar, and bake for ½ hour, but do not use it till quite cold. The herrings may be cut down the front, the backbone taken out, and closed again. Sprats done in this way are very delicious.

TIME.—½ *an hour.*

To Choose the Herring.—The more scales this fish has, the surer the sign of its freshness. It should also have a bright

THE HERRING.

and silvery look; but if red about the head, it is a sign that it has been dead for some time.

Herrings, Dried; Yarmouth

Bloaters.—The best way to cook these is to make incisions in the skin across the fish, because they do not then require to be so long on the fire, and will be far better than when cut open. The hard roe makes a nice relish by pounding it in a mortar, with a little anchovy, and spreading it on toast. If very dry, soak in warm water 1 hour before dressing. The soft roe, devilled on toast, makes a nice savoury.

Herrings, Red.—May be cooked in the same way as bloaters, but, as they are very salt, they should be soaked some time in cold water first.

Hessian Soup.—INGREDIENTS *for 5 quarts of soup.*—Half an ox's head, 1 pint of split peas, 8 carrots, 6 turnips, 8 potatoes, 6 onions, 1 head of celery, 1 bunch of savoury herbs, pepper and salt to taste, 2 blades of mace, a little allspice, 4 cloves, the

trumb of a French roll, 6 quarts of water.
AVERAGE COST, 2s. 6d.

Clean the head, rub it with salt and water, and soak it for 5 hours in warm water. Simmer it in the water till tender, put it into a pan and let it cool; skim off all the fat, take out the head, and add the vegetables cut up small, and the peas which have been previously soaked; simmer them without the meat, till they are done enough to pulp through a sieve. Put in the seasoning, with the pieces of meat cut up; give one boil and serve.

TIME.—4 *hours.*

SEASONABLE *in winter.*

Note.—An excellent hash or *ragout* can be made by cutting up the nicest parts of the head, thickening and seasoning more highly a little of the soup, and adding a glass of port wine and 2 tablespoonfuls of ketchup.

Hidden Mountain, The. (A pretty Supper Dish.)—INGREDIENTS *for* 1 *dish.*—6 *eggs, a few slices of citron, sugar to taste,* ¼ *pint of cream, a layer of any kind of jam.* AVERAGE COST, 1s. 3d.

Beat the whites and yolks of the eggs separately then mix them and beat well again, adding a few thin slices of citron, the cream, and sufficient pounded sugar to sweeten it nicely. When the mixture is well beaten, put it into a buttered pan, and fry the same as a pancake; but it should be three times the thickness of an ordinary pancake. Cover it with jam, and garnish with slices of citron and preserved cherries if at hand. This dish is served cold.

TIME.—*About* 10 *minutes to fry the mixture.*

SEASONABLE *at any time.*

Hodge - Podge.—INGREDIENTS *for* soup for 12 persons.—2 *lbs. of shin of beef,* 3 *quarts of water,* 1 *pint of table-beer,* 2 *onions,* 2 *carrots,* 2 *turnips,* 1 *head of celery; pepper and salt to taste: thickening of butter and flour.* AVERAGE COST, 2s.

Put the meat, beer and water in a stewpan; simmer for a few minutes, and skim

carefully. Add the vegetables and seasoning; stew gently till the meat is tender Thicken with the butter and flour, and serve with turnips and carrots, or spinach and celery.

TIME.—3 *hours or rather more.*

SEASONABLE *at any time.*

Hodge-Podge. (Cold Meat Cookery.)—INGREDIENTS *for sufficient for* 4 *persons* —*About* 1 *lb. of underdone cold mutton,* 3 *lettuces,* 1 *pint of green peas,* 5 *or* 6 *green onions,* 2 *oz. of butter, pepper and salt to taste,* 1½ *pint of water.* AVERAGE COST *exclusive of the mutton,* 9d.

Mince the mutton, and cut up the lettuces and onions in slices. Put these in a stewpan, with all the ingredients except the peas, and let these simmer very gently for ¾ hour, keeping them well stirred. Boil the peas separately, mix these with the mutton, and serve very hot.

TIME.—¾ *hour.*

SEASONABLE *from the end of May to August.*

Holly-Leaves, To Frost (for Garnishing and Decorating Dessert and Supper Dishes.)— INGREDIENTS.— *Sprigs of holly, oiled butter, coarsely-powder sugar.*

Procure some nice sprigs of holly; pick the leaves from the stalks, and wipe them with a clean cloth free from all moisture; then place them on a dish near the fire, to get thoroughly dry, but not too near to shrivel the leaves; dip them into oiled butter, sprinkle over them some coarsely-powdered sugar, and dry them before the fire. They should be kept in a dry place, as the least damp would spoil their appearance.

TIME.—*About* 10 *minutes to dry before the fire.*

SEASONABLE.—*These may be made at any time; but are more suitable for winter garnishes, when fresh flowers are not easily obtained.*

Honey Cake.

Honey Cake.—INGREDIENTS *for cake sufficient for 4 or 5 persons.*—½ breakfast-cupful of sugar, 1 breakfast-cupful of rich sour cream, 2 breakfast-cupfuls of flour, ½ teaspoonful of carbonate of soda, honey to taste. AVERAGE COST, 8d.

Mix the sugar and cream together; dredge in the flour, with as much honey as will flavour the mixture nicely; stir it well that all the ingredients may be thoroughly mixed; add the carbonate of soda, and beat the cake well for another 5 minutes; put it into a buttered tin, bake it from ½ to ¾ hour, and let it be eaten warm.

TIME.—½ hour to ¾ hour.
SEASONABLE *at any time.*

Honoré Cake.

Honoré Cake.—INGREDIENTS.— *The lower half of a round sponge-cake, a glass of sherry, some meringue paste, sugar, ¼ pint of cream, vanilla flavouring.* AVERAGE COST, 1s. 6d.

Soak the cake in the sherry, colour half the meringue paste pink, and put it in little heaps of alternate colours round the cake to make a wall. Bake in a quick oven till the paste is done. When the cake is cold, whip the cream to a froth with a little sugar and flavouring, and fill up the centre of it. To enrich this cake a layer of apricot jam may be put under the cream.

SEASONABLE *at any time.*

Horseradish.

Horseradish.—AVERAGE COST, 2d. *per stick.*

This root, scraped, is always served with hot roast beef, and is used for garnishing many kinds of boiled fish. Let the horseradish remain in cold water for an hour; wash it well, and with a sharp knife scrape it into very thin shreds, commencing from the thick end of the root. Arrange some of it lightly in a small glass dish, and the remainder use for garnishing the joint; it should be placed in tufts round the border of the dish, with 1 or 2 bunches on the meat.

SEASONABLE *from October to June.*

Horseradish Sauce.

Horseradish Sauce (for Cold Meat, Fish, &c.).—INGREDIENTS *for 1 tureen.*— 1 stick of horseradish, 1 apple, a little vinegar, sugar, ¼ pint of cream. AVERAGE COST, 8d.

Grate the horseradish, bake the apple and let it get cold, take away the skin and core, then mix the two together to a smooth paste with a very little vinegar or lemon-juice, and sugar to taste; lastly add the cream, and mix thoroughly.

This sauce is nice with cold fish, such as salmon or turbot. For meat it can be made more economically by adding another apple and omitting the cream.

SEASONABLE *at any time.*

Horseradish Sauce (to serve with Roast Beef).

Horseradish Sauce (to serve with Roast Beef).—INGREDIENTS *for sufficient for a joint.*—4 tablespoonfuls of grated horseradish, 1 teaspoonful of pounded sugar, 1 teaspoonful of salt, ½ teaspoonful of pepper, 2 teaspoonfuls of made mustard; vinegar. AVERAGE COST, 3d.

Grate the horseradish, and mix it well with the sugar, salt, pepper and mustard; moisten it with sufficient vinegar to give it the consistency of cream, and serve in a tureen; 3 or 4 tablespoonfuls of cream added to the above very much improve the appearance and flavour of this sauce. To heat it to serve with hot roast beef, put in a *bain marie* or a jar, which place in a saucepan of boiling water; make it hot, but do not allow it to boil, or it will curdle.

THE HORSERADISH.

Note.—This sauce is a great improvement on the old-fashioned way of serving cold-scraped horseradish with hot roast beef. The mixing of the cold vinegar with the warm gravy cools and spoils everything on the plate.

Horseradish Vinegar.—INGREDI-
ENTS.—¼ lb. of scraped horseradish, 1 oz. of
minced shalot, 1 drachm of cayenne, 1
quart of vinegar.

Put all the ingredients into a bottle,
which shake well every day for a fortnight.
When it is thoroughly steeped, strain and
bottle, and it will be fit for use immediately. This will be found an agreeable
relish to cold beef, &c.

SEASONABLE.—*This vinegar should be
made either in October or November, as
horseradish is then in its highest perfection.*

Hot Spice. (A Delicious Adjunct to
Chops, Steaks, Gravies, &c.)—INGREDI-
ENTS.—3 drachms each of ginger, black
pepper and cinnamon, 7 cloves, ½ oz. of
mace, ¼ oz. of cayenne, 1 oz. of grated nutmeg, 1½ oz. of white pepper.

Pound the ingredients, and mix them
thoroughly together, taking care that
everything is well blended. Put the spice
in a very dry glass bottle for use. The
quantity of cayenne may be increased,
should the above not be enough to suit the
palate.

Hunter's Pudding.—INGREDIENTS
for pudding sufficient for 10 persons.—1 lb.
of raisins, 1 lb. of currants, 1 lb. of suet,
1 lb. of bread-crumbs, ½ lb. of moist sugar,
6 eggs, 1 tablespoonful of flour, ¼ lb. of mixed
candied peel, 1 glass of brandy, 20 drops of
essence of almonds, 6 cloves. AVERAGE
COST, 3s.

Stone and shred the raisins rather small,
chop the suet finely, and rub the bread unti'
all lumps are well broken ; pound the spice
to powder, cut the candied peel into thin
shreds, and mix all these ingredients well
together, adding the sugar. Beat the
eggs to a strong froth, and as they are
beaten, drop into them the essence of
almonds ; stir these to the dry ingredients
mix well and add the brandy. Tie the
pudding firmly in a cloth, and boil it for 6
hours at the least. 7 or 8 hours would be
still better for it. Serve with boiled custard,
melted red-currant jelly, or brandy sauce.

TIME.—6 to 8 hours.
SEASONABLE *in winter.*

Hunter's Pudding. (A less expensive Recipe.)—INGREDIENTS *for pudding
for 10 persons.*—¾ lb. of raisins, ¾ lb. o
currants, ¾ lb. of suet, ½ lb. of bread-crumbs,
½ lb. of flour, ½ lb. of brown sugar, 3 eggs
½ pint of milk, ¼ lb. of candied peel, flavour
ing of lemon essence. AVERAGE COST
2s. 6d.

Proceed as in preceding recipe, stoning
and chopping the raisins, chopping the
suet, washing and drying the currants
thoroughly and shredding the peel. Put
all the dry ingredients into a basin, adding
a saltspoonful of salt, and mix well
together. Beat the eggs well, add to
them the milk and the essence of lemon,
then add the liquid to the pudding. When
well mixed, tie in a floured cloth, or pour
into a buttered mould, and boil for 6 hours.
Serve with wine or brandy sauce.

TIME.—6 hours to boil the pudding.
SEASONABLE *in winter.*

" I know it well,
Its tinkle tells me that a time is near
Precious to me—it is the dinner bell."—C. S. CALVERLEY.

ICE-CREAMS, Fruit.—INGREDIENTS.—*To every pint of fruit-juice allow 1 pint of cream; sugar to taste.* AVERAGE COST, 1*s. per pint.*

Let the fruit be well ripened; pick it off the stalks, and put it into a large earthen pan. Stir it about with a wooden spoon, breaking it until it is well mashed; then, with the back of the spoon, rub it through a hair sieve. Sweeten it nicely with pounded sugar; whip the cream for a few minutes, add it to the fruit, and whisk the whole again for another 5 minutes. Put the mixture into the freezing-pot, and freeze, taking care to stir the cream, &c., two or three time, and to remove it from the sides of the vessel, that the mixture may be equally frozen and smooth. Ices are usually served in glass plates, but if moulded as they sometimes are for dessert, must have a small quantity of melted isinglass added to them, to enable them to keep their shape. Raspberry, strawberry, currant and all fruit ice-creams are made in the same manner. A little pounded sugar sprinkled over the fruit before it is mashed assists to extract the juice. In winter when fresh fruit is not obtainable, a little jam may be substituted for it; it should be melted and worked through a sieve before being added to the whipped cream; and if the colour should not be good, a little prepared cochineal or beet-root may be put in to improve its appearance.

TIME.—½ *hour to freeze the mixture.*

SEASONABLE, *with fresh fruit, in June, July and August.*

Ice, Lemon-Water. — INGREDIENTS.—*To every pint of syrup allow ½ pint of lemon-juice; the rind of 4 lemons.* AVERAGE COST, 6*d. per pint.*

Rub the sugar on the rinds of the lemons, and with it make the syrup. Strain the lemon-juice, add it to the other ingredients, stir well, and put the mixture into a freezing-pot. Freeze as directed for Ice Pudding, and when the mixture is thoroughly and equally frozen, put it into ice-glasses or plates.

TIME.—1½ hour to freeze the mixture.

SEASONABLE at any time.

Iced Cream, Banana.—INGRE-
DIENTS for 1½ pint mould.—6 bananas, 1½ pint of cream, 1 lemon, sugar to taste, flavouring of Benedictine or other liqueur, water. AVERAGE COST, 2s. 3d.

Skin the fruit and put it in a lined sauce-pan, with the gelatine dissolved in a tea-cupful of water, the lemon-rind and juice, and the loaf sugar, and simmer for about 10 minutes. When cold, beat it up with the cream and flavour with the liqueur. Wet a mould, put in the cream and set to freeze.

TIME.—10 minutes to simmer.

SEASONABLE in autumn and winter.

Note.—A machine for making ice, though a somewhat costly article, is a most useful posses-sion in a large family, particularly in a hot climate or where far from shops. One of the best is called "The Champion."

Iced - Pudding.— INGREDIENTS. —
½ lb. of sweet almonds, 2 oz. of bitter ones, ¾ lb. of sugar, 8 eggs, 1½ pint of milk, a few slices of citron or preserved cherries. AVER-AGE COST, 2s.

Blanch and dry the almonds thoroughly in a cloth, then pound them in a mortar until reduced to a smooth paste; add to these the eggs, well beaten, the sugar and milk; stir these ingredients over the fire until they thicken, but do not allow them to boil; then strain and put the mixture into the freezing-pot; surround it with ice and freeze it. When quite frozen, fill an iced-pudding mould, put on the lid and keep the pudding in ice until required for table; then turn it out on the dish. This pudding may be flavoured with vanilla, curaçoa or maraschino.

TIME.—½ hour to freeze the mixture.

SEASONABLE.—Served all the year round.

Ices.—Ices are composed, it is scarcely necessary to say, of congealed cream or water, combined sometimes with liqueurs or other flavouring ingredients, or more generally with the juices of fruits. At desserts, "At Home" teas in summer, and at dances, ices are scarcely to be dispensed with. The principal utensils required for making ice-creams are ice-tubs, freezing-pots, spaddles and a cellaret. The tub must be large enough to contain about a bushel of ice, pounded small, when brought out of the ice-house, and mixed very care-fully with either salt, nitre or soda. The freezing-pot is best made of pewter. If

ICED-PUDDING MOULD.

it be of tin, as is sometimes the case, the congelation goes on too rapidly in it for the thorough intermingling of its contents, on which the excellence of the ice greatly depends. The spaddle is generally made of copper, kept bright and clean. The cellaret is a tin vessel, in which ices are kept for a short time from dissolving. The method to be pursued in the freezing process must be attended to. When the ice-tub is prepared with fresh pounded ice and salt, the freezing-pot is put into it up to its cover. The articles to be con-gealed are then poured into it and covered over; but to prevent the ingredi-ents from separating and the heaviest of them from falling to the bottom of the mould, it is requisite to turn the freezing-

Benedictine Ice Pudding.

Cream Ice.

Lemon Ice.

Clear Jelly.

Compôte of Oranges.

Nougat.

Gateau.

Compôte of Pears.

Soufflé.

Meringue.

Pine Apple Ice.

Pear Ice.

Orange Ice.

Vanilla Ice.

Chocolate Ice.

Sweet Dishes.

pot round and round by the handle, so as to keep its contents moving until the congelation commences. As soon as this is perceived (the cover of the pot being occasionally taken off for the purpose of noticing when freezing takes place), the cover is immediately closed over it, ice is put upon it, and it is left in this state till it is served. The use of the spaddle is to stir up and remove from the side of the freezing-pot the cream, which in the shaking may have washed against it, and by stirring it in with the rest, to prevent waste of it occurring. Any negligence in stirring the contents of the freezing-pot before congelation takes place will destroy the whole: either the sugar sinks to the bottom and leaves the ice insufficiently sweetened, or lumps are formed, which disfigure and discolour it.

Ices, to make Fruit-Water.—

INGREDIENTS.—*To every pint of fruit-juice allow* 1 *pint of syrup.* AVERAGE COST, 10d. *per pint.*

Select nice ripe fruit; pick off the stalks and put it into a large earthen pan, with a little pounded sugar strewed over; stir it about with a wooden spoon until it is well broken, then rub it through a hair-sieve. Make a syrup, without white of egg; let it cool, add the fruit-juice, mix well together, and put the mixture into the

DISH OF ICES.

freezing pot. Proceed as directed for Ice Puddings, and when the mixture is equally frozen put it into small glasses or in plates. Raspberry, strawberry, currant and other fresh-fruit-water ices are made in the same manner.

TIME.—½ *hour to freeze the mixture.*

SEASONABLE, *with fresh fruit, in June, July and August.*

Ices, Recipes for.—Directions for

making the following appear under their respective headings:—

Banana Ice Cream.	Pine-apple Ice.
Iced Pudding.	Raspberry Ice
Iced Pudding,	Cream.
Nesselrode.	Strawberry Ice
Fruit Ice Cream.	Cream.
Fruit Water Ices.	Vanilla Ice Cream.
Lemon Water Ice.	

Icing, Almond, for Cakes.—

INGREDIENTS.—*To every lb. of finely-pounded loaf sugar, allow* 1 *lb. of sweet almonds, the whites of* 4 *eggs, a little rose-water.*

Blanch the almonds, and pound them (a few at a time) in a mortar to a paste, adding a little rosewater to facilitate the operation. Whisk the whites of the eggs to a strong froth: mix them with the

BENEDICTINE ICE PUDDING.

pounded almonds, stir in the sugar, and beat altogether. When the cake is sufficiently baked, lay on the almond icing, and put it into the oven to dry. Before laying this preparation on the cake, great care must be taken that it is nice and smooth, which is easily accomplished by well beating the mixture.

Icing, Chocolate.—INGREDIENTS

for icing for 1 *large cake.*—½ *lb. of pounded loaf sugar,* 3 *oz. of chocolate, a small tea-cupful of water.* AVERAGE COST, 4d.

Grate the chocolate and put it, with the sugar and water, in a lined saucepan over a slow fire, adding, if there be none in the chocolate, a flavouring of vanilla. When melted smooth, spread on the cake or cakes and dry them in a cool oven.

TIME.—10 *minutes to melt the chocolate.*
SEASONABLE *at any time.*

Icing, Sugar, for Cakes.—INGRE-
DIENTS.—*To every lb. of loaf sugar allow the whites of 4 eggs, 1 oz. of fine starch.*

Beat the eggs to a strong froth, and gradually sift in the sugar, which should be reduced to the finest possible powder, and gradually add the starch, also finely powdered. Beat the mixture well until the sugar is smooth; then with a spoon or broad knife lay the ice equally over the cakes. These should then be placed in a very cool oven, and the icing allowed to dry and harden, but not to colour. The

DECORATION FOR ICED CAKES.

icing may be coloured with strawberry or currant juice, or with prepared cochineal. If it be put on the cakes as soon as they are withdrawn from the oven, it will become firm and hard by the time the cakes are cold. On very rich cakes, such as wedding, christening cakes, &c., a layer of almond icing is usually spread over the top, and over that the white icing as described. All iced cakes should be kept in a very dry place.

Indian Chutney Sauce.—INGRE-
DIENTS.—*8 oz. of sharp, sour apples, pared and cored; 8 oz. of tomatoes, 8 oz. of salt, 8 oz. of brown sugar, 8 oz. of stoned raisins, 4 oz. of cayenne, 4 oz. of powdered ginger.*

2 oz. of garlic, 2 oz. of shalots, 3 quarts of vinegar, 1 quart of lemon-juice.

Chop the apples in small square pieces, and add to them the other ingredients. Mix the whole well together, and put in a well-covered jar. Keep this in a warm place, and stir every day for a month, taking care to put on the lid after this operation; strain, but do not squeeze it dry; store it away in clean jars or bottles for use, and the liquor will serve as an excellent sauce for meat or fish.

SEASONABLE. — *Make this sauce when tomatoes are in full season, that is, from the beginning of September to the end of October.*

Indian Corn, Roasted.—INGRE-
DIENTS.—*Unripe, or green, corn, butter, salt.*

Strip the green ears of their leaves, and roast before a quick fire till the grain is brown. Serve with oiled butter. Indian corn may be used also for soups as peas are.

Indian Maize, Boiled.—INGRE-
DIENTS.—*The ears of young green Indian maize or wheat; to every ½ gallon of water, allow 1 heaped tablespoonful of salt.*

Take off the outside sheath and the fibres, and put the corn into boiling water, when tender, drain, and serve on toast with melted butter.

TIME.—25 *minutes to boil.*
SEASONABLE *in autumn.*

Indian Pudding. — INGREDIENTS
for pudding large enough for 6 persons.—4 large apples, a little grated nutmeg, 1 teaspoonful of minced lemon-peel, 2 large tablespoonfuls of sugar, 6 oz of currants, ¾ lb. of suet crust. AVERAGE COST, 11d.

Pare, core and cut the apples into slices; put them into a saucepan with the nutmeg, lemon-peel and sugar, stew them over the fire till soft; then have ready the above quantity of crust, roll it out thin, spread the apples over the paste, sprinkle over the currants, roll the pudding up, closing the ends properly, tie it in a floured cloth, and boil for 2 hours.

TIME.—*2 hours.*

SEASONABLE *August to March.*

Invalid Cookery.—A few rules to be observed in cooking for invalids :—

Let all the kitchen utensils used in the preparation of invalid cookery be delicately and *scrupulously clean ;* if this be not the case, a disagreeable flavour may be imparted to the preparation, which flavour may disgust, and prevent the patient from taking of the refreshment when brought to him or her.

For invalids, never make a large quantity *of one thing,* as they seldom require much at a time ; and it is desirable that variety be provided for them.

Always have something in readiness ; a little beef tea, nicely made and nicely skimmed, a few spoonfuls of jelly, &c. &c., that it may be administered as soon almost as the invalid wishes for it. If obliged to wait a long time, the patient loses the desire to eat, and often turns against the food when brought to him or her.

In sending dishes or preparations up to invalids, let everything look as tempting as possible. Have a clean tray-cloth laid smoothly over the tray ; let the spoons, tumblers, cups and saucers, &c., be very clean and bright. Gruel served in a tumbler is more appetizing than when served in a basin or cup and saucer.

As milk is an important article of food for the sick, in warm weather let it be kept on ice, to prevent its turning sour. Many other delicacies may also be preserved good in the same manner for some little time.

If the patient be allowed to eat vegetables, never send them up undercooked, or half raw ; and let a small quantity only be temptingly arranged on a dish. This rule will apply to every preparation, as an invalid is much more likely to enjoy his food if small, delicate pieces are served to him.

Never leave food about a sick-room ; if the patient cannot eat it when brought to him, take it away, and bring it to him in an hour or two's time. Miss Nightingale says : " To leave the patient's untasted food by his side from meal to meal, in hopes that he will eat it in the interval, is simply to prevent him taking any food at all." She says, " I have known patients literally incapacitated from taking one article of food after another by this piece of ignorance. Let the food come at the right time, and be taken away, eaten or uneaten, at the right time, but never let a patient have ' something always standing' by him, if you don't wish to disgust him of everything."

Never serve beef tea or broth with the *smallest particle* of fat or grease on the surface. It is better, after making either of these, to allow them to get perfectly cold, when *all the fat* may be easily removed ; then warm up as much as may be required. Two or three pieces of clean whitey-brown paper laid on the broth will absorb any greasy particles that may be floating at the top, as the grease will cling to the paper.

Roast mutton, chickens, rabbits, calves' feet or head, game, fish (simply dressed), and simple puddings are all light food, and easily digested. Of course, these things are only partaken of supposing the patient is in a state of convalescence.

A mutton chop, nicely cut, trimmed and broiled to a turn, is a dish to be recommended for invalids ; but it must not be served *with all the fat* at the end, nor must it be too thickly cut. Let it be cooked over a fire free from smoke, and sent up with the gravy in it, between two very hot plates. Nothing is more disagreeable to an invalid than *smoked* food.

In making toast-and-water, never blacken the bread, but toast it only a nice brown. Never leave toast-and-water to make until the moment it is required, as it cannot then be properly prepared—at least the patient will be obliged to drink it warm, which is anything but agreeable.

In boiling eggs for invalids, let the white be just set; if boiled hard, they will be likely to disagree with the patient.

In Miss Nightingale's admirable "Notes on Nursing," a book that no mother or nurse should be without, she says—"You cannot be too careful as to quality in sick diet. A nurse should never put before a patient milk that is sour, meat or soup that is turned, an egg that is bad, or vegetables underdone." Yet often, she says, she has seen these things brought in to the sick in a state perfectly perceptible to every nose or eye except the nurse's. It is here that the clever nurse appears—she will not bring in the peccant article; but, not to disappoint the patient, she will whip up something else in a few minutes. Remember that sick cookery should half do the work of your poor patient's weak digestion.

She goes on to caution nurses, by saying, "Take care not to spill into your patient's saucer; in other words, take care that the outside bottom rim of his cup shall be quite dry and clean. If, every time he lifts his cup to his lips, he has to carry the saucer with it, or else to drop the liquid upon and to soil his sheet, or bed-gown, or pillow, or, if he is sitting up, his dress, you have no idea what a difference this minute want of care on your part makes to his comfort, and even to his willingness for food."

Invalid's Cutlet.—INGREDIENTS for sufficient for 1 person.—1 nice cutlet from a loin or neck of mutton, 2 teacupfuls of water, 1 very small stick of celery, pepper and salt to taste. AVERAGE COST, 6d.

Have the cutlet cut from a very nice loin or neck of mutton, take off all the fat, put it into a stewpan with the other ingredients; stew very gently indeed for nearly 2

hours, and skim off every particle of fat that may rise to the surface from time to time. The celery should be cut into thin slices before it is added to the meat, and care must be taken not to put in too much of this, or the dish will not be good. If the water is allowed to boil fast, the cutlet will be hard.

TIME.—2 hours very gentle stewing.

SEASONABLE.—Whenever celery may be had.

Invalid's Jelly.—INGREDIENTS for 3 pints of jelly.—6 shanks of mutton, 3 pints of water, a bunch of sweet herbs, pepper and salt to taste, 3 blades of mace, 1 onion, 1 lb. of lean beef, a crust of bread toasted brown. AVERAGE COST, 2s. 6d.

Soak the shanks in plenty of water for some hours, and scrub them well; put them, with the beef and other ingredients, into a saucepan with the water, and let them simmer very gently for 5 hours. Strain the broth, and when cold, take off the fat. It may be eaten either warmed up or cold as a jelly.

TIME.—5 hours.

SEASONABLE at any time.

Invalids, Lemonade for.—INGREDIENTS for 1 pint of lemonade.—½ lemon, lump sugar to taste, 1 pint of boiling water. AVERAGE COST, 1d.

Pare off the rind of the lemon thinly; cut the lemon into 2 or 3 thick slices, and remove as much as possible of the white outside pith and all the pips. Put the slices of lemon, the peel and lump sugar into a jug; pour over the boiling water, cover it closely, and in 2 hours it will be fit to drink. It should either be strained or poured off from the sediment.

TIME.—2 hours.

SEASONABLE at any time.

Italian Cream.—INGREDIENTS for 1½ pint mould.—½ pint of milk, ½ pint of cream, sugar to taste, 1 oz. of isinglass or

gelatine, 1 *lemon, the yolks of* 3 *eggs.*
AVERAGE COST, 1s. 8d.

Put the cream and milk into a saucepan, with sugar to sweeten, and the lemon-rind. Boil until the milk is well flavoured, then strain it into a basin and add the beaten yolks of eggs. Put this mixture into a jug, place the jug in a saucepan of boiling water over the fire and stir the contents until they thicken, but do not allow them to boil. Take the cream off the fire, stir in the lemon-juice and isinglass, which should be melted, and whipped well ; fill a mould, place it in ice if at hand, and, when set, turn it out on a dish, and garnish as taste may dictate. The mixture may be whipped and drained, and then put into small glasses, when this mode of serving is preferred.

TIME.—*From* 5 *to* 8 *minutes to stir the mixture in the jug.*

SEASONABLE *at any time.*

Italian Pudding.— INGREDIENTS *for pudding for* 6 *to* 8 *persons.*—¼ *lb. of any kinds of plain sweet biscuits,* 6 *macaroons or* 2 *dozen ratafias,* 1 *oz. of sultanas,* 2 *oz. of candied peel,* 1 *oz. of pistachio nuts,* ¼ *pint of cream,* ½ *wineglass of rum,* 8 *eggs.* AVERAGE COST, 2s. 3d.

Pound in a mortar the biscuits and ratafias or macaroons to a powder, chop the candied peel, pistachio nuts and sultanas finely and mix with the eggs, beaten, and the rum and cream. Put the mixture in a mould, buttered and lined with paper ; cook in a *bain marie* for 1 hour and serve with Italian punch sauce.

TIME.—1 *hour.*

SEASONABLE *at any time.*

Italian Punch Sauce.—INGREDIENTS *for sauce for* 1 *pudding.*—2 *wineglasses of rum,* ½ *lb. of loaf sugar, the juice of* 1 *orange if in season, if not, that of a lemon, flavouring of vanilla or lemon.* AVERAGE COST, 6d.

Put all, except the fruit juice, in a saucepan and mix thoroughly. A few minutes before the sauce is required set it on the fire, flame the spirit and, after covering the pan for a minute, add the juice and strain.

TIME.—5 *minutes.*

SEASONABLE.—*Can be served with any hot rich pudding.*

Italian Sauce, Brown.—INGREDIENTS *for sauce for small dish.*—A *few chopped mushrooms and shalots,* ½ *pint of stock,* ½ *glass of madeira, the juice of* ½ *lemon,* ½ *teaspoonful of pounded sugar,* 1 *teaspoonful of chopped parsley.* AVERAGE COST, 8d.

Put the stock into a stewpan with the mushrooms, shalots and madeira and stew gently for ¼ hour, then add the remaining ingredients, and let them just boil. When the sauce is done enough, put it in another stewpan and warm it in a *bain marie.* The mushrooms should not be chopped long before they are wanted, as they will then become black.

TIME.—¼ *hour.*

Italian Sauce, White.—INGREDIENTS *for sauce for good-sized dish.*—½ *pint of white stock,* 2 *tablespoonfuls of chopped mushrooms,* 1 *dessertspoonful of chopped shalots,* 1 *slice of ham, minced very fine ;* ¼ *pint of Béchamel ; salt to taste, a few drops of garlic vinegar,* ½ *teaspoonful of pounded sugar, a squeeze of lemon-juice.* AVERAGE COST, 1s.

Put the shalots and mushrooms into a stewpan with the stock and ham and simmer very gently for ½ hour, when add the Béchamel. Let it just boil up and then strain it through a tammy ; season with the above ingredients and serve very hot. If this sauce should not have retained a nice white colour, a little cream may be added.

TIME.—½ *hour.*

"Junkets and jellies and such dainty fare
May all invited freely with me share."—OLD SONG.

JAM Roly-Poly Pudding. — IN-GREDIENTS *for good-sized pudding.*—¾ *lb. of suet-crust,* ¾ *lb. of any kind of jam.* AVERAGE COST, 10*d.*

Make a nice light suet-crust, and roll it out to the thickness of about ½ inch. Spread the jam equally over it, leaving a small margin of paste without any where the pudding joins. Roll it up, fasten the ends securely and tie it in a floured cloth; put the pudding into boiling water and boil for 2 hours. Mincemeat or

JAM PUDDING.

marmalade may be substituted for the jam and makes excellent puddings.

TIME.—2 *hours.*

SEASONABLE.—*Suitable for winter pud-dings, when fresh fruit is not obtainable.*

Jams, Jellies, Marmalades, Recipes for.—Directions for making the following appear under their respective headings:—

Apple Jelly.	Gooseberry Jam,
Apple Jelly	White or Green.
(Another Mode).	Gooseberry Jelly.
Apple Jelly, Clear.	Greengage Jam.
Apricot Jam.	Orange Marmalade.
Carrot Jam.	Orange Marmalade
Cherry Jam.	(Another Mode).
Currant Jam,	Orange Marmalade
Black.	with Honey.
Currant Jam, Red.	Plum Jam.
Currant Jelly,	Quince Marmalade.
Black.	Raspberry Jam.
Currant Jelly, Red.	Raspberry and Cur-
Currant Jelly,	rant Jam.
White.	Raspberry Jelly.
Damson Jam.	Rhubarb Jam.
Gooseberry Jam.	Rhubarb and
Gooseberry Jam	Orange Jam.
(Another Mode.)	Strawberry Jam.

Note.—As in the case of bottled fruits, jam and marmalade are not worth making at home unless there is a large quantity of fruit in the garden. To begin with, there is a great deal of labour and time required to pick and prepare the fruit; and a still more important argumen is that nothing is saved if the fruit has to be bought, although many consider good home-made jam better than any other. The jams prepared by Castell and Brown are excellent in quality and no orange marmalade is superior to Keiller's

January—Dinner for Twelve Persons.

MENU. (*English.*)	Quantity.	Average Cost.		MENU. (*French.*)
		s.	d.	
Mock Turtle Soup.	2 qts.	5	0	Consommé de Tête de Veau.
Turbot.	1 fish.	10	0	Turbot.
Whitebait.	3 pints.	6	0	Blanchailles.
Mutton Cutlets, with	3 lbs.	3	0	Cotelettes de Mouton aux
Spinach.	3 lbs.	0	6	Epinards.
Hashed Game.	2 dishes	3	6	Salmis de Gibier.
Roast Turkey.	1 bird.	12	0	Dindon Roti.
Sausages.	2 lbs.	1	8	Saucisses.
Potatoes. Brussels Sprouts.	3 lbs. ea	0	10	Pommes de Terre. Choux.
Mince Pies.	12	1	0	Mince Pies.
Vanilla Cream.	1 mould.	2	0	Crême de Vanille.
Lemon Jelly.	1 mould.	1	6	Gelée au Citron.
		£2 7	0	

January.—Dinner for Ten Persons.

MENU. (*English.*)	Quantity.	Average Cost.		MENU. (*French.*)
		s.	d.	
Oyster Soup.	3½ pints.	5	0	Potage aux Huitres.
Cod, with Italian Sauce.	4 lbs.	3	6	Cabillaud à l'Italienne.
Chicken Croquets.	2 dishes.	3	0	Croquettes de Volaille.
Stewed Kidneys.	2 dishes.	3	0	Rognons Etuvés.
Sirloin of Beef.	1 joint.	9	0	Aloyau.
Potatoes. Savoys.	3 lbs. 2	0	6	Pommes de Terre. Choux.
Pheasants.	2 birds.	7	0	Faisans.
Exeter Pudding.	1	4	0	Pouding au Rhum.
Cream Eggs.	1 dish.	3	6	Œuffs à la Crême.
Cheese Soufflé.	1	1	6	Soufflé de Parmesan.
		£2 0	0	

January—Dinner for Eight Persons.

MENU. (*English.*)	Quantity.	Average Cost.		MENU. (*French.*)
		s.	d.	
Game Soup.	3 pints.	4	0	Purée de Gibier.
Turbot,	1 fish.	7	0	Turbot,
Lobster Sauce.	1 tur.	2	6	Sauce Homard.
Vol-au-Vent of Oysters.	1	6	0	Vol au-Vent aux Huitres.
Salmi of Black Game.	1 dish.	5	0	Salmis de Coqs de Bruyère.
Saddle of Mutton.	1 joint.	9	6	Selle de Mouton.
Potatoes. Sprouts.	3 lbs. ea.	0	9	Pommes de Terre. Choux.
Compôte of Apples.	1 dish.	2	0	Compôte de Pommes.
Banana Fritters.	1 dish.	1	6	Beignets de Bananes.
Cheese Straws.	1 dish.	0	9	Pailles de Parmesan.
		£1 19	0	

January—Dinners for from Six to Twelve Persons.

Julienne Soup.

Cod,
Italian Sauce.

Sweetbreads.
Rissolettes of Hare.

Turkey.
Ham.
Potatoes.
Sprouts.

Rice Soufflé.
Valois Cream.

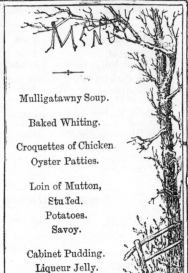

Mulligatawny Soup.

Baked Whiting.

Croquettes of Chicken.
Oyster Patties.

Loin of Mutton,
Stuffed.
Potatoes.
Savoy.

Cabinet Pudding.
Liqueur Jelly.

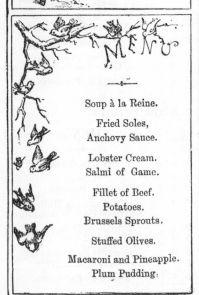

Soup à la Reine.

Fried Soles,
Anchovy Sauce.

Lobster Cream.
Salmi of Game.

Fillet of Beef.
Potatoes.
Brussels Sprouts.

Stuffed Olives.

Macaroni and Pineapple.
Plum Pudding.

Vermicelli Soup.

Cod, with Maître
d Hôtel Butter.

Mutton Cutlets.

Roast Fowls
Sausages.
Potatoes. Sprouts.

Snipe.

Marbled Jelly.
French Rice Pudding.

January—Plain Family Dinners for.

No 1.

Sunday.—Roast sirloin of beef, potatoes, greens, horseradish sauce. — Cold apple tart, custard, blancmange.

Monday.— Soup. — Veal Cutlets. — Cold beef, mashed potatoes, salad.—Cheese.

Tuesday.—Cod fish and oyster sauce.—Curried beef.—Rabbit pie, sprouts, potatoes.—Bread and butter pudding.

Wednesday. — Macaroni soup. — Roast fowls, ham, bread sauce, potatoes.—Jam tart.

Thursday. — Rissoles made from cold chicken.—Leg of mutton, potatoes, mashed turnips.—Plain plum pudding.

Friday.—Fried whiting.—Cold mutton, potatoes, salad.—Gingerbread pudding.

Saturday.—Hashed mutton, potatoes.—Pheasants.—Lemon pudding.

No 2.

Sunday.—Roast turkey, sausages, potatoes, broccoli.—Fruit tart, cream.

Monday.—Pea soup.—Steak and kidney pie, potatoes.—Stewed prunes and rice.—Cheese.

Tuesday.—Hashed turkey, mutton cutlets, potatoes, spinach. — Tapioca pudding.

Wednesday.—Fried soles.—Boiled beef, carrots, potatoes.—Macaroni cheese.

Thursday.—Vegetable soup.—Cold beef, winter salad, mashed potatoes.—Jam pudding.

Friday. — Bubble and squeak. — Roast hare, potatoes.—Batter pudding.

Saturday.—Cod cutlets fried and caper sauce.—Hashed hare, potatoes.—Tinned pine and custard.

January—Vegetarian Dinners for.

No 1.

Pea Soup.

Savoury Omelette.
Lentil Rissoles.

Sea Kale.

Tapioca and Milk.
Stewed Pears.

No. 2.

Savoury Eggs.
Vegetable Stew.

Plum Pudding.

Welsh Rarebit.

Compote of Fruit.

January—Dinner Table Decorations for.

Where coloured leaves and mosses are obtainable, some left from late autumn may still be found, and these in low receptacles of china or glass furnish a dinner table very prettily.

Some natty little receptacles for small pots may be made at this season, of lichen covered twigs, arranged in rustic form and tied with bright coloured ribbons. When not able to procure the lichen or mosses from woods and fields, they can be bought ready prepared.

Fruit in January can be used for decorations, specially grapes and Tangerine oranges, and some prettily coloured candied fruits help to make out a dainty table when both foliage and flowers are scarce.

There are plenty of hot-house flowers to be had, a large proportion of which are white, and these should be arranged in coloured vases, specially crimson ones, and strewed on dark-coloured cloths, in both cases mingled with plenty of foliage, coloured, if it can be had.

A pretty decoration can be made of ferns and foliage only, with or without a coloured cloth. Say a rustic pot in the centre made of the lichen covered twigs of which we have spoken, with a graceful fern or plant in it, and trails of ivy twisted in it to trail upon the cloth. Some smaller rustic stands similarly treated, the number and the placing of which should depend upon the size and shape of the table.

To obtain colour some saques or baskets of satin can be made to hold ferns or flowers, while ribbons can be introduced to tie together little bunches of flowers or foliage laid to each person round the table.

January, Things in Season :—

Fish.—Brill, carp, cod, crabs, crayfish, eels, flounders, haddocks, herrings, lampreys, lobsters, mussels, oysters, perch, pike, plaice, prawns, shrimps, skate, smelts, soles, sprats, sturgeon, turbot, whiting.

Meat.—Beef, house lamb, mutton, pork, veal, venison.

Poultry.—Capons, fowls, tame pigeons, pullets, rabbits, turkeys.

Game.—Grouse, hares, partridges, pheasants, snipe, wild-fowl, woodcock.

Vegetables. — Beetroot, broccoli, cabbages, carrots, celery, chervil, cresses, cucumbers (forced), endive, lettuces, parsnips, potatoes, savoys, spinach, turnips, various herbs.

Fruit.—Apples, grapes, medlars, nuts, oranges, pears, walnuts.

Jaunemange. — INGREDIENTS *for quart moulds.*—1 oz. *of isinglass or gelatine,* 1 *pint of water,* ½ *pint of white wine, the rind and juice of* 1 *large lemon, sugar to taste, the yolks of* 4 *eggs.* AVERAGE COST, 1s. 6d.

Put the isinglass, water and lemon-rind into a saucepan and boil gently until the former is dissolved, then add the strained lemon-juice, the wine and sufficient white sugar to sweeten the whole nicely. Boil for 2 or 3 minutes, straining the mixture into a jug, and add the yolks of the eggs, which should be well beaten ; place the jug in a saucepan of boiling water ; keep stirring the mixture *one way* until it thickens, *but do not allow it to boil;* then take it off the fire and keep stirring until nearly cold. Pour it into a mould, omitting the sediment at the bottom of the jug, and let it remain until quite firm.

TIME.—¼ *hour to boil the isinglass and water; about* 10 *minutes to stir the mixture in the jug.*

SEASONABLE *at any time.*

Jellies of Isinglass and Gelatine.—Isinglass is the purest form of gelatine ; but while chemically there is little difference between the two, practically the difference between the best and inferior varieties of both articles is most strongly marked. In former times Russian isinglass, which should be the dried sounds or swimming bladders of the sturgeon only, was in general use; but its high price introduced cheap imitations. The uncertain strength of the raw products used, chiefly membranes of other fish, simply scraped and washed, rolled and cut up, led to the invention of "Swinborne's Patent Refined Isinglass," which differs from all others, being a cooked article, of uniform strength and purity, tasteless and entirely free from smell. It is largely taken by invalids, is used in infants' food, and is most nutritious in every form of jelly, creams, &c. No article of commerce requires more careful selection of material to insure a wholesome product than gelatine. Held at one time in high estimation as a food, it has latterly been considered of little value because in itself it does not sustain life. Subjected to this test, nearly every useful delicacy would have to be condemned also. Abroad, Liebig pronounced against it, but the gelatine he condemned was chiefly of foreign manufacture and prepared from bones by the use of acids, &c. Our own great chemist, Professor Brande, F.R.S., was careful to draw the distinction between good and bad, and deeming inferior productions unwholesome, he confined his testimony to the merits and nutritious qualities of "Swinborne's Calves' Feet Gelatine," the manufacture of which he thoroughly inspected and approved of.

Jellies, Bottled, How to Mould.—Bottled jellies, of which some of the best we think are sold by the firms of Crosse and Blackwell, and Goodall, Backhouse and Co., are very convenient and

easily prepared sweets. To mould them, uncork the bottle; place it in a saucepan of hot water until the jelly is reduced to a liquid state; taste it, to ascertain whether it is sufficiently flavoured, and if not, add a little wine. Pour the jelly into moulds which have been soaked in water; let it

OPEN MOULD.

set and turn it out by placing the mould in hot water for a minute; then wipe the outside, put a dish on the top and turn it over quickly. The jelly should then slip easily away from the mould and be quite firm. It may be garnished as taste dictates.

Jelly-Bag, How to Make a.—

The very stout flannel called double-mill, used for ironing blankets, is the best material for a jelly-bag, those of home manu-

JELLY-BAG.

facture are the only ones to be relied on for thoroughly clearing the jelly. Care should be taken that the seam of the bag be stitched twice, to secure it against unequal filtration. The most convenient mode of using the bag is to tie it upon a hoop the exact size of the outside of its mouth; and, to do this, strings should be sewn round it at equal distances, it can then be suspended between two chairs. The jelly-bag may, of course, be made any size; but one of twelve or fourteen inches deep and seven or eight inches across the mouth will be sufficient for

ordinary use. The form of a jelly-bag is the fool's-cap.

Jelly, Beef (for Invalids).—INGREDIENTS.—3 lbs. of lean shin of beef, flavouring of lemon-peel, celery, or whatever may be preferred.

Cut the beef into small pieces and put it into a jar with the seasoning and just enough water to cover it. Tie it closely down with brown paper and put it into a cool oven for from 4 to 5 hours. Then strain off the liquor into small moulds or cups, out of which it should turn a firm jelly. It will sometimes, being cold, be retained on the stomach when ordinary beef tea would not, but very little flavouring should be used if it is made for such a patient.

Jelly, Isinglass, or Gelatine. (Substitutes for Calf's Feet.)—INGREDIENTS for 2 quart moulds.—3 oz. of Swinborne's isinglass or gelatine, 2 quarts of water. AVERAGE COST, with flavouring, 2s.

Put the isinglass or gelatine into a saucepan with the above proportion of cold water; bring it quickly to boil, and let it boil very fast, until the liquor is reduced one-half. Remove the scum as it rises, then strain it through a jelly-bag and it will be ready for use. If not required very clear, it may be merely strained through a fine sieve, instead of being run through a bag. Rather more than $\frac{1}{2}$ oz. of isinglass is about the proper quantity to use for a quart of strong calf's-feet stock, and rather more than 2 oz. for the same quantity of fruit juice. As isinglass varies so much in quality and strength, it is difficult to give the exact proportions. The larger the mould, the stiffer should be the jelly; and where there is no ice, more isinglass must be used than if the mixture were frozen. This forms a stock for all kinds of jellies, which may be flavoured in many ways.

TIME.—1½ *hour.*

SEASONABLE *at any time.*

Note.—The above, when boiled, should be perfectly clear, and may be mixed warm with wine, flavourings, fruits, &c., and then run through the bag.

Jelly Moulded with Fresh Fruit, or Macédoine de Fruits.—INGREDIENTS *for quart mould.—Rather more than* 1½ *pint of jelly, a few nice strawberries, or red or white currants, or raspberries, or any fresh fruit that may be in season.* AVERAGE COST, 2s.

Have ready the above proportion of jelly, which must be very clear and rather sweet, the raw fruit requiring an additional quantity of sugar. Select ripe, nice-looking fruit; pick off the stalks unless currants

JELLY MOULDED WITH CHERRIES.

are used, when they are laid in the jelly as they come from the tree. Begin by putting a little jelly at the bottom of the mould, which must harden; then arrange the fruit round the sides of the mould, recollecting that *it will be reversed when turned out;* then pour in some more jelly to make the fruit adhere, and, when that layer is set, put another row of fruit and jelly until the mould is full. If convenient, put it in ice until required for table, then wring a cloth in boiling water, wrap it round the mould for a minute, and turn the jelly carefully out. Peaches, apricots, plums, apples, &c., are better for being boiled in a little clear syrup before they are laid in the jelly; strawberries, raspberries, grapes, cherries, and currants are put in raw. In winter, when fresh fruits are not obtainable, a very pretty jelly may be made with preserved fruits or brandy cherries: these, in a bright and clear jelly, have a very pretty effect;

of course, unless the jelly be *very clear,* the beauty of the dish will be spoiled. It may be garnished with the same fruit as is laid in the jelly; for instance, an open jelly with strawberries might have, piled in the centre, a few of the same fruit prettily arranged, or a little whipped cream might be substituted for the fruit.

TIME.—*One layer of jelly should remain* 2 *hours in a very cool place before another layer is added.*

SEASONABLE, *with fresh fruit, from June to October; with dried, at any time.*

Jelly, Orange, Moulded with slices of Orange.—INGREDIENTS *for quart mould.*—1½ *pint of orange jelly,* 4 *oranges,* ½ *pint of clarified syrup.* AVERAGE COST, 1s. 6d.

Boil ½ lb. of loaf sugar with ½ pint of water until there is no scum left (which must be carefully removed as fast as it rises), and carefully peel the oranges; divide them into thin slices without breaking the thin skin, and put these pieces of orange into the syrup, where let them remain for about 5 minutes; then take them out, and use the syrup for the jelly. When the

JELLY WITH ORANGES.

oranges are well drained, and the jelly is nearly cold, pour a little of the latter into the bottom of the mould; then lay in a few pieces of orange; over these pour a little jelly, and when this is set, place another layer of orange, proceeding in this manner until the mould is full. Put it in ice, or in a cool place, and, before turning it out, wrap a cloth round the mould for a minute

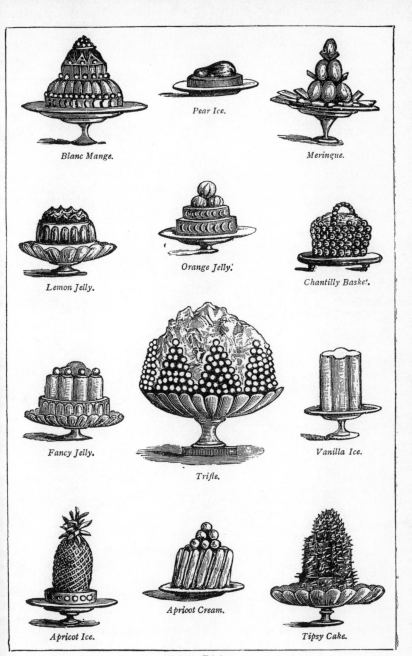

Blanc Mange.

Pear Ice.

Meringue.

Lemon Jelly.

Orange Jelly.

Chantilly Basket.

Fancy Jelly.

Trifle.

Vanilla Ice.

Apricot Ice.

Apricot Cream.

Tipsy Cake.

Sweet Dishes.

or two, which has been wrung out in boiling water.

TIME.—*5 minutes to simmer the oranges.*
SEASONABLE *from November to May.*

Jelly of Two Colours.—INGRE-
DIENTS *for* 1½ *pint mould.*—1½ *pint of calf's feet or gelatine jelly, a few drops of prepared cochineal.* AVERAGE COST, 1s. 3d.

Make 1½ pint of calf's-feet jelly, or, if wished more economical, of clarified syrup and gelatine, flavouring it in any way that may be preferred. Colour one-half of the jelly with a few drops of prepared cochineal, and the other half leave as pale as possible. Have ready a mould well wetted in every part; pour in a small quantity of the red

JELLY OF TWO COLOURS.

jelly, and let this set; when quite firm, pour on it the same quantity of the pale jelly, and let this set; then proceed in this manner until the mould is full, always taking care to let one jelly set before the other is poured in, or the colours would run one into the other. When turned out, the jelly should have a striped appearance. For variety, half the mould may be filled at once with one of the jellies, and, when firm, filled up with the other: this also has a very pretty effect, and is more expeditiously prepared than when the jelly is poured in small quantities into the mould. Blancmange and red jelly, or blancmange and raspberry cream, moulded in the above manner, look very well. The layers of blancmange and jelly should be about an inch in depth, and each layer should be perfectly hardened before another is added. Half a mould of blancmange and half a mould of jelly are frequently served in the same manner. A few pretty dishes may be

made in this way, of jellies or blancmanges left from the preceding day, by melting them separately in a jug placed in a sauce-

OVAL JELLY MOULD.

pan of boiling water, and then moulding them by the foregoing directions.

TIME.—¾ *hour to make the jelly.*

Note.—In making the jelly, use for flavouring a very pale sherry, or the colour will be too dark to contrast nicely with the red jelly.

Jelly, Open, with Whipped
Cream. (A very pretty dish.)—INGREDI-
ENTS *for* 1½ *pint mould.*—1½ *pint of jelly,* ½ *pint of cream,* 1 *glass of sherry, sugar to taste.* AVERAGE COST, 2s. 6d.

Make the above proportion of calf's-feet or isinglass jelly, colouring it and flavouring it in any way that may be preferred; soak a mould, open in the centre, for about ½ hour in cold water; fill it with the jelly,

OPEN JELLY WITH WHIPPED CREAM.

and let it remain in a cool place until perfectly set; then turn it out on a dish; fill the centre with whipped cream, flavoured with sherry and sweetened with pounded sugar; pile this cream high in the centre, and serve. The jelly should be made of rather a dark colour, to contrast nicely with the cream, or the cream may be made pink with colouring and the jelly left pale.

TIME.—¾ hour.

SEASONABLE at any time.

Jelly, Savoury (for Meat Pies).—

INGREDIENTS for a large stock.—3 lbs. of shin of beef, 1 calf's-foot, 3 lbs. of knuckle of veal, poultry trimmings (if for game pies, any game trimmings), 2 onions stuck with cloves, 2 carrots, 4 shalots, a bunch of savoury herbs, 2 bay-leaves, when liked; 2 blades of mace and a little spice; 2 slices of lean ham; rather more than 2 quarts of water. AVERAGE COST, 5s.

Cut up the meat and put it into a stew-pan with all the ingredients except the water; set it over a slow fire to draw down, and, when the gravy ceases to flow from the meat, pour in the water. Let it boil up, then carefully take away all scum from the top. Cover the stewpan closely, and let the stock simmer very gently for 4 hours: if rapidly boiled, the jelly will not be clear. When done, strain it through a fine sieve or flannel bag; and when cold, the jelly should be quite transparent. If this is not the case, clarify it with the white of eggs.

TIME.—4 hours.

Jelly, To make the Stock for,

and to Clarify it.—INGREDIENTS.—2 calf's feet, 6 pints of water. AVERAGE COST, 1s. 6d.

The stock for jellies should always be made the day before it is required for use, as the liquor has time to cool, and the fat can be so much more easily and effectually removed when thoroughly set. Procure 2 nice calf's feet; scald them, to take off the hair; slit them in two, remove the fat from between the claws, and wash the feet well in warm water; put them into a stewpan, with the above proportion of cold water, bring it gradually to boil, then strain it through a sieve into a basin, and put it in

a cool place to set. As the liquor is strained, measure it, to ascertain the proportion for the jelly, allowing something for the sediment and fat at the top. To clarify it, carefully remove all the fat from the top, pour over a little warm water, to wash away any that may remain, and wipe the jelly with a clean cloth; remove the jelly from the sediment, put it into a saucepan, and, supposing the quantity to be a quart, add to it 6 oz. of loaf sugar, the shells and well-whisked whites of 5 eggs, and stir these ingredients together cold; set the saucepan on the fire, but do not stir the jelly after it begins to warm. Let it boil about 10 minutes after it rises to a head, then throw in a teacupful of cold water; let it boil 5 minutes longer, then take the saucepan off, cover it closely and let it remain ½ hour near the fire. Dip the jelly-bag into hot water, wring it out quite dry and fasten it on to a stand or the back of a chair, which must be placed near the fire, to prevent the jelly from setting before it has run through the bag. Place a basin underneath to receive the jelly; then pour it into the bag, and should it not be clear the first time, run it through the bag again. This stock is the foundation of all really good jellies, which may be varied in innumerable ways, by colouring and flavouring with liqueurs, and by moulding it with fresh and preserved fruits. To insure the jelly being firm when turned out, ½ oz. of isinglass clarified might be added to the above proportion of stock. Substitutes for calf's feet are now frequently used in making jellies, which lessen the expense and trouble in preparing this favourite dish; isinglass and gelatine being two of the principal materials employed; but although they may look as nicely as jellies made from good stock, they are never so delicate, and unless the best isinglass or gelatine is used, having very often an unpleasant flavour, somewhat resembling glue, particularly when made with gelatine.

TIME.—*About 6 hours to boil the feet for the stock; to clarify it—¼ hour to boil, ½ hour to stand in the saucepan covered.*

SEASONABLE *from March to October, but may be had all the year.*

John Dory.—INGREDIENTS.—¼ lb. of salt to each gallon of water. AVERAGE COST, 3s. to 5s. each.

This fish, which is esteemed by most people a great delicacy, is dressed in the same way as a turbot, which it resembles in firmness, but not in richness. Cleanse

JOHN DORY.

it thoroughly and cut off the fins; lay it in a fish kettle, cover with cold water and add salt in the above proportion. Bring it gradually to a boil, and simmer gently for ½ hour or rather longer, should the fish be very large. Serve on a hot napkin, and garnish with cut lemon and parsley. Lobster, anchovy or shrimp sauce and plain melted butter should be sent to table with it.

TIME.—*After the water boils, ¼ to ½ hour, according to size.*

SEASONABLE *all the year, but best from September to January.*

Note.—Small John Dory are very good baked, and this is a very nice fish served either boiled or fried in fillets, with a good sauce.

Johnny Cake.—INGREDIENTS *for small cake.*—*A teacupful of yellow Indian meal, a teacupful of flour, a teacupful of water, a teacupful of milk, a large table-spoonful of moist sugar, a dessertspoonful of baking powder, 2 eggs, a little salt, and any flavouring that may be liked, such as a few drops of vanilla or lemon essence.* AVERAGE COST, 5d.

The milk, water and eggs, with the flavouring, should be put in one bowl, and the flour, meal, sugar, baking powder and salt in another. Mix the contents of each bowl separately, then put them together, and again mix well. Butter a tin and pour in the mixture, and put in a hot oven at once or the cake will not be light. Bake for about ½ an hour.

TIME.—*½ hour to bake the cake.*

SEASONABLE *at any time, particularly for a hot cake for breakfast.*

Julienne, Soup à la.—INGREDIENTS *for soup for 8 persons.*—½ lb. of carrots, ½ lb. of turnips, ¼ lb. of onions, 2 or 3 leeks, ½ head of celery, 1 lettuce, a little sorrel and chervil, if liked, 2 oz. of butter, 2 quarts of stock. AVERAGE COST, 2s.

Cut the vegetables into strips of about 1¼ inch long, and be particular they are all the same size, or some will be hard whilst the others will be done to a pulp. Cut the lettuce, sorrel, and chervil into larger pieces; fry the carrots in the butter, and pour the stock boiling to them. When this is done, add all the other vegetables and herbs, and

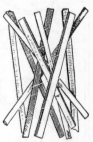

STRIPS OF VEGETABLE.

stew gently for at least an hour. Skim off all the fat, pour the soup over thin slices of bread, cut round about the size of a shilling, and serve.

TIME.—*1½ hour.*

SEASONABLE *all the year.*

Note.—In summer, green peas, asparagus-tops, French beans, &c., can be added. When the vegetables are very strong, instead of frying them in butter at first, they should be blanched, and afterwards simmered in the stock. The vegetables sold ready for Julienne in a condensed form by Chollet and Co., 134, Fenchurch Street, save a great deal of trouble, and are almost equal in flavour to fresh vegetables.

July—Dinners for from Six to Twelve Persons.

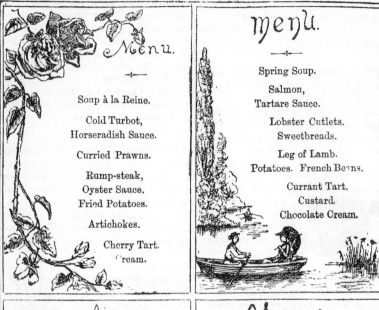

Menu.

Soup à la Reine.

Cold Turbot,
Horseradish Sauce.

Curried Prawns.

Rump-steak,
Oyster Sauce.
Fried Potatoes.

Artichokes.

Cherry Tart.
Cream.

Menu.

Spring Soup.

Salmon,
Tartare Sauce.

Lobster Cutlets.
Sweetbreads.

Leg of Lamb.
Potatoes. French Beans.

Currant Tart.
Custard.
Chocolate Cream.

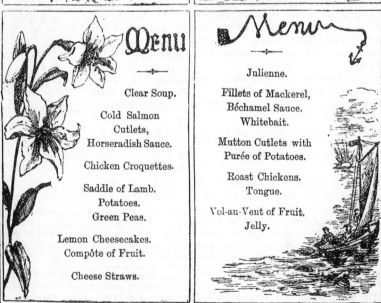

Menu

Clear Soup.

Cold Salmon
Cutlets,
Horseradish Sauce.

Chicken Croquettes.

Saddle of Lamb.
Potatoes.
Green Peas.

Lemon Cheesecakes.
Compôte of Fruit.

Cheese Straws.

Menu

Julienne.

Fillets of Mackerel,
Béchamel Sauce.
Whitebait.

Mutton Cutlets with
Purée of Potatoes.

Roast Chickens.
Tongue.

Vol-au-Vent of Fruit.
Jelly.

July—Dinner for Twelve Persons.

MENU. (*English.*)	Quan ity.	Average Cost.	MENU. (*French.*)
		s. d.	
Clear Soup.	2 quarts	2 6	Consommé à la Royale.
Turbot,	1 fish.	12 0	Turbot,
Dutch Sauce.	2 tur.	1 0	Sauce Hollandaise.
Lobster Cream.	1 mould.	3 6	Crême de Homard.
Chicken Cutlets.	2 dishes.	5 0	Côtelettes de Volaille.
Saddle of Mutton.	1 joint.	10 0	Selle de Mouton.
Potatoes.	4 lbs.	} 1 10 {	Pommes de Terre.
Green Peas.	3 pints.		Petits Pois.
Ducklings.	3 birds.	6 0	Canetons.
Strawberry Cream.	1 mould.	2 6	Crême aux Fraises.
Iced Pudding.	1	5 0	Pouding Glacée.
		£2 9 4	

July—Dinner for Ten Persons.

MENU. (*English.*)	Quantity.	Average Cost.	MENU. (*French.*)
		s. d.	
Crayfish Soup.	3 pints.	6 0	Potage d'Ecrévisses.
Salmon.	3 lbs.	5 6	Saumon.
Whitebait.	2½ pints.	5 0	Blanchaille.
Fricasseed Chicken.	1 dish.	4 6	Fricassée de Volaille.
Quarter of Lamb.	1 joint.	8 6	Quartier d'Agneau.
Potatoes. French Beans.	3 lbs. ea.	1 0	Pommes de Terre. Haricots Verts.
Russian Salad.	1 dish.	1 6	Salade à la Russe.
Vanilla Cream.	1 mould.	2 6	Crême de Vanille.
Macédoine of Fruit.	1	2 6	Macédoine de Fruit.
Ices.	10	2 0	Glaces.
		£1 19 0	

July—Dinner for Eight Persons.

MENU. (*English.*)	Quantity.	Average Cost.	MENU. (*French.*)
		s. d.	
Green Pea Soup.	3 pints.	3 0	Potage aux Petits Pois.
Filleted Soles,	2 fish.	3 0	Filets de Soles,
Sauce à l'Aurore.	1 tur.	0 9	Sauce à l'Aurore.
Turban of Veal.	1 dish.	5 0	Turban de Veau.
Ducks.	1 pair.	7 0	Canetons.
Green Peas.	1 quart.	1 0	Petits Pois.
Potatoes.	3 lbs.	0 3	Pommes de Terre.
Raspberry Cream.	1 mould.	2 6	Crême à la Framboises.
Liqueur Jelly.	1 mould.	2 0	Gelée au Marasquin.
Cheese Soufflé.	1	1 9	Soufflé de Parmesan.
		£1 6 3	

July—Plain Family Dinners for.

No. 1.

Sunday.—Roast quarter of lamb, mint sauce, peas, potatoes.—Cherry tart, custard.

Monday. — Soup. — Cold lamb, salad, potatoes.—Cheese ramakins.

Tuesday.—Boiled mackerel, cucumber.—Stewed steak, vegetables.—Sponge cake pudding.

Wednesday. — Soup. — Boiled chickens, celery sauce, potatoes, beans.—Compôte of fruit.

Thursday. — Croquettes of chicken. — Fillet of beef, vegetables.—Fruit pudding.

Friday.—Boiled salmon, cucumber. — Veal and ham pie, potatoes. — Cheese, celery.

Saturday.—Salmon mayonnaise. — Haricot mutton, potatoes.—Rice pudding.

No. 2.

Sunday.—Roast fillet of veal, bacon, beans, potatoes.—Cold fruit tart, cream.—Cheese.

Monday.—Spring soup.—Cold veal and bacon, salad, potatoes. — Baked batter pudding with fresh fruit.

Tuesday. — Salmon trout, cucumber. — Minced veal, potatoes. — Lemon cheesecakes.

Wednesday.—Roast ducks, peas, potatoes.—College puddings.

Thursday.—Boiled leg of mutton, beans, potatoes.—Half-pay pudding.

Friday.—Broiled salmon, tartar sauce.—Cold mutton, cucumber, potatoes.—Milk pudding.

Saturday. — Soup. — Mutton collops, potatoes.—Jam pudding.

July—Vegetarian Dinners for.

No. 1.

Oatmeal and Milk.

Potato Fritters.
Lentils and Mashed Potatoes.

Raspberry Tart.
Custard.

No. 2.

Vegetable Soup.

Poached Eggs and Spinach.
Haricot Beans.

Compôte of Fruit.
Cream.

July—Dinner Table Decorations for.

—There is not much difficulty in finding table decorations in July, when flowers are so plentiful, and so many kinds are in season ; but it is not the time for gay coloured ones to be used. The cooler, greener and softer the arrangements of the decorations, the pleasanter the effect in hot weather. A glass plateau with a centre piece of iris of pale shades arranged in moss, with a few water lilies laid flat on the plateau forms a pretty decoration, especially if the border be mossed over and fringed with small fern and grass, so as to give the effect of a lake.

Where wild flowers can be obtained they should often be used for the table, as such kinds as marguerites, or cornflowers mingle so well with grasses and look extremely pretty. Grasses are in perfection, both water and field ones, and the latter should be dried for winter use.

July, Things in Season :—

Fish.—Carp, crayfish, dory, flounders, haddocks, herrings, lobsters, mackerel, mullet, pike, plaice, prawns, salmon, shrimps, soles, sturgeon, thornback.

Meat.—Beef, lamb, mutton, veal, buck venison.

Poultry. — Chickens, ducklings, fowls, green geese, leverets, plovers, pullets, rabbits, turkey poults, wheatears, wild ducks (called flappers).

Vegetables. — Artichokes, asparagus, beans, cabbages, carrots, cauliflowers, celery, cresses, endive, lettuces, mushrooms, onions, peas, radishes, small salading, seakale, sprouts, turnips, vegetable marrow, various herbs.

Fruit.—Apricots, cherries, currants, figs, gooseberries, melons, nectarines, pears, pine-apples, plums, raspberries, strawberries, walnuts in high season for pickling.

June—Dinner for Twelve Persons.

MENU. (*English.*)	Quantity.	Average Cost.		MENU. (*French.*)
		s.	*d.*	
Turtle Soup.	2 quarts.	42	0	Tortue.
Salmon,	1 fish.	9	0	Saumon,
Cucumber.	2	1	0	Concombres.
Lobster Cream.	2 mlds.	4	0	Crême de Homard.
Lamb Cutlets and	3 lbs.	} 4	6 {	Côtelettes d'Agnau aux
Peas.	2 pints.			Petits Pois.
Haunch of Venison.	1 joint.	15	0	Hanche de Venaison.
Potatoes. Spinach.	4 lbs. ea.	1	0	Pommes de Terre. Epinards.
Farced Olives.	3 doz.	1	6	Olives Farcies.
Vol-au-vent of Strawberries.	1 dish.	3	6	Vol-au-vent de Fraises.
Maraschino Jelly.	1 mould.	2	6	Gelée au Marasquin.
Iced Pudding.	1	6	0	Pouding Glacée.
		£4 10	0	

June—Dinner for Ten Persons.

MENU. (*English.*)	Quantity.	Average Cost.		MENU. (*French.*)
		s.	*d.*	
Asparagus Soup.	3½ pints.	3	6	Purée d'Asperges.
Salmon,	3½ lbs.	6	0	Saumon,
Lobster Sauce.	1 tur.	2	0	Sauce Homard.
Chaudfroid of Chicken.	1 dish.	4	0	Chaudfroid de Volailles.
Stewed Breast of Lamb.	3 lbs.	3	0	Agnau au Vin Blanc.
Ducks.	3 birds.	9	0	Canetons
Green Peas.	3 pints.	1	6	aux Petits Pois.
Potatoes.	3 lbs.	0	3	Pommes de Terre.
Almond Pudding.	1	2	6	Pouding d'Armandes.
Iced Gooseberry Fool.	1 dish.	1	6	Purée de Groseilles Glacée.
		£1 3	3	

June—Dinner for Eight Persons.

MENU. (*English.*)	Quantity.	Average Cost.		MENU. (*French.*)
		s.	*d.*	
Spring Soup.	3 pints.	2	0	Printanière.
Boiled Filleted Soles	2 fish.	3	0	Soles à la Crême.
Salmon Cutlets.	2½ lbs.	5	0	Côtelettes de Saumon.
Fillet of Beef,	3 lbs.	3	0	Filet du Bœuf
with Spanish Sauce.	1 tur.	1	6	à l'Espagnole.
Gosling.	1 bird.	6	6	Oison.
Potatoes.	3 lbs.	} 1	3 {	Pommes de Terre.
Peas.	1 quart.			Petits Pois.
Foie Gras in Aspic.	1 dish.	2	6	Foie Gras en Aspic.
Gooseberry Tart.	1	1	3	Tourte aux Groseilles.
Vanilla Cream.	1 mould.	2	0	Crême à la Vanille.
		£1 1	0	

June—Dinners for from Six to Twelve Persons.

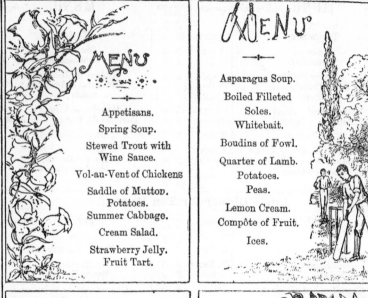

Menu

Appetisans.

Spring Soup.

Stewed Trout with
Wine Sauce.

Vol-au-Vent of Chickens

Saddle of Mutton.
Potatoes.
Summer Cabbage.

Cream Salad.

Strawberry Jelly.
Fruit Tart.

Menu

Asparagus Soup.

Boiled Filleted
Soles.
Whitebait.

Boudins of Fowl.

Quarter of Lamb.
Potatoes.
Peas.

Lemon Cream.
Compôte of Fruit.

Ices.

Menu

Clear Soup.
Broiled Mackerel.

Lobster Cream.
Chicken Rissoles.

Loin of Lamb.
Potatoes.
Greens.

Strawberry Tart.

Casserole of
Rice.
Fruit.

Menu

Appetisans.

Julienne Soup.

Trout,
with Spanish Sauce.

Beef Olives.

Leg of Lamb.
Potatoes.   Peas.

Asparagus.

Cheesecakes.
Fruit Salad

June—Plain Family Dinners for.

No. 1

Sunday.—Spring soup.—Roast chickens, bacon, potatoes, summer cabbage.—Gooseberry tart, cream.

Monday.—Chicken rissoles.—Boiled mutton, caper sauce, vegetables.—Baked batter pudding.

Tuesday. — Salmon, cucumber. — Cold mutton, salad, mashed potatoes.—Stewed fruit.

Wednesday.—Veal and ham pie, hashed mutton, vegetables.—Ground rice pudding.

Thursday. — Boiled mackerel, fennel sauce.—Grilled steak and fried potatoes.—Jam puffs.

Friday.—Roast ribs of beef boned and rolled, peas, potatoes, horseradish sauce.—Corn-flour shape and stewed fruit.

Saturday.—Soup.—Cold beef, salad, potatoes.—Empress pudding.

No. 2

Sunday.—Roast quarter of lamb, mint sauce, green peas, new potatoes.—Fruit tart, custard.

Monday.—Cold lamb, salad, potatoes.—German pudding.

Tuesday.—Boiled salmon, cucumber, tartar sauce.—Hashed lamb, potatoes.—Ratifia pudding.

Wednesday.—Roast sirloin of beef, spinach, potatoes.—Lemon jelly.

Thursday.—Rissoles of cold salmon, cold beef, cucumber, potatoes.—College puddings.

Friday.—Boiled mackerel, melted butter.—Pie made from cold beef, potatoes.—Cheese salad.

Saturday.—Stewed breast of veal with peas, potatoes. — Gooseberry pudding, baked.

June—Vegetarian Dinners for.

No. 1.

Green Pea Soup.

Vegetable Pie.

Compôte of Gooseberries.
Bread and Butter Pudding.

Cheese.

No. 2.

Haricots and Mashed Potatoes.

Russian Salad.

Raspberry and Currant Tart.
Custard.

Cheese and Celery.

June—Dinner Table Decorations for.

—Of all flowers in June roses should take precedence for decorations, for either table or drawing-room, and there is no question but that they look best with only their own foliage. If any other be used it should be maidenhair or other fern. Low receptacles are best for them, either bowls or vases: and for baskets they seem specially intended. The latter should have high handles, if for dinner table decoration, and these may be twined with some climber, and should have a bunch of roses tied on with ribbon, chosen according to the colour of the roses. In small specimen glasses so usually placed before each person on the dinner-table, a single rose, with foliage, looks well. If another flower is required to blend with roses, either white marguerites or stephanotis are the best.

June, Things in Season:—

Fish.—Carp, crayfish, crabs, herrings, lobsters, mackerel, mullet, pike, prawns, salmon, soles, trout, turbot, whitebait, whiting.

Meat.—Beef, lamb, mutton, veal, buck venison.

Poultry.—Chickens, ducklings, fowls, green geese, leverets, plovers, pullets, rabbits, turkey poults, wheatears.

Vegetables. — Artichokes, asparagus, beans, cabbages, carrots, cucumbers, lettuces, onions, parsnips, peas, potatoes, radishes, small salads, sea-kale, spinach—various herbs.

Fruit.—Apricots, cherries, currants, gooseberries, melons, pears, pine-apples, raspberries, rhubarb, strawberries.

" Kickshaws and dainties fit for kings
Upon the table spread."—OLD BALLAD.

KALE BROSE.

KALE BROSE. (A Scotch Recipe.)—INGREDIENTS *for soup for 10 persons.*—Half an ox-head or cow-heel, a teacupful of toasted oatmeal, salt to taste, 2 handfuls of greens, 3 quarts of water. AVERAGE Cost, 8d. per quart.

Make a broth of the ox-head or cow-heel, and boil it till oil floats on the top of the liquor, then boil the greens, shred, in it. Put the oatmeal, with a little salt, into a basin and mix with it quickly a teacupful of the fat broth : it should not run into one doughy mass, but form knots. Stir it into the whole, give one boil and serve very hot.

TIME.—4 *hours.*

SEASONABLE *all the year, but more suitable in winter.*

Kegeree.—INGREDIENTS.—*Any cold fish, 1 teacupful of boiled rice, 1 oz. of butter, 1 teaspoonful of mustard, 2 hard-boiled eggs, salt and cayenne to taste.* AVERAGE COST, 4d.

KIDNEYS, BROILED.

Pick the fish carefully from the bones, flake it, chop the eggs, mix with the other ingredients and serve very hot. The quantities may be varied according to the amount of fish used.

TIME.—¼ *hour after the rice is boiled.*
SEASONABLE *at any time.*

Kidneys, Broiled. (A Breakfast or Supper Dish.)—INGREDIENTS.—*Sheep kidneys, pepper and salt to taste.* AVERAGE COST, 3d. *each.*

Ascertain that the kidneys are fresh and

KIDNEYS.

cut them open, very evenly, longthwise, down to the root, for should one half be thicker than the other, one would be underdone whilst the other would be dried, but do not separate them ; skin them and pass a skewer under the white part of each half to keep them flat and broil over a nice clear fire, placing the inside downwards ; turn them when done enough on one side and cook them on the other. Remove the skewers, place the kidneys on a very hot dish, season with pepper and salt and put a tiny piece of butter in the middle of each; put them on buttered toast, serve very hot and quickly and send very hot plates to table.

TIME.—6 *to 8 minutes.*

SEASONABLE *at any time.*

Kidneys, Fried.—INGREDIENTS.—

Kidneys, butter, pepper and salt to taste. AVERAGE COST, 3*d.* each.

Cut the kidneys open without quite dividing them, remove the skin and put a small piece of butter in the frying-pan. When the butter is melted, lay in the kidneys the flat side downwards and fry them for 7 or 8 minutes, turning them when they are half done. Serve on a piece of dry toast, season with pepper and salt and put a small piece of butter in each kidney; pour the gravy from the pan over them, adding a spoonful of sauce, if liked, and serve very hot.

TIME.—7 *or 8 minutes.*

SEASONABLE *at any time.*

Kidney Omelette. (A favourite French Dish).—INGREDIENTS *for sufficient for 4 or 5 persons.*—6 *eggs,* 1 *saltspoonful of salt,* ½ *saltspoonful of pepper,* 2 *sheep's-kidneys, or* 2 *tablespoonfuls of minced veal kidney,* 3 *oz. of butter.* AVERAGE COST, 1*s.* 3*d.*

Skin the kidneys, cut them into small dice and toss them in a frying pan, in 1 oz. of butter, over the fire for 2 or 3 minutes. Mix the ingredients for the omelette and, when the eggs are well whisked, stir in the pieces of kidney. Make the butter hot in the frying-pan and when it bubbles, pour in the omelette and fry it over a gentle fire from 4 to 6 minutes. When the eggs are set, fold the edges over, so that the omelette assumes an oval form and be careful that it is not too much done; to brown the top, hold the pan before the fire

for a minute or two, or use a salamander until the desired colour is obtained, but never turn an omelette in the pan. Slip it carefully on to a *very hot* dish, or, what is a much safer method, put a dish on the omelette and turn the pan quickly over. It should be served the instant it comes from the fire.

TIME.—4 *to 6 minutes.*

SEASONABLE *at any time.*

Kidney Pudding.—INGREDIENTS.

—3 *sheep's kidneys,* ½ *pint of bread-crumbs,* 3 *oz. of suet, a teacupful of milk,* 1 *egg, seasoning to taste, of minced parsley, herbs, pepper and salt.* AVERAGE COST, 1*s.* 2*d.*

Skin the kidneys and mince them and the suet finely. Put them in a basin with the bread-crumbs and cold seasoning to make the pudding savoury; beat the egg, mix it with the milk, then stir into the other ingredients. Butter a basin, pour in the pudding, cover it with paper and steam for 1 hour. Serve hot with brown sauce or a good gravy.

TIME.—1 *hour to steam.*

SEASONABLE *at any time.*

Kidneys, Stewed.—INGREDIENTS *for dish for 4 to 6 persons.*—*About* 6 *kidneys, a large dessertspoonful of chopped herbs,* 2 *oz. of butter,* 1 *dessertspoonful of flour, a little gravy, juice of* ½ *a lemon, a teaspoonful of Harvey's sauce and mushroom ketchup, cayenne and salt to taste.* AVERAGE COST, 1*s.* 10*d.*

Divide the kidneys in halves and strew the herbs, with cayenne and salt over them; melt the butter in the frying-pan, put in the kidneys and brown them nicely all round; when nearly done, stir in the flour and shake them well; now add the gravy and sauce and stew them for a few minutes, then turn them out into an entrée dish garnished with fried croûtons.

TIME.—10 *or 12 minutes.*

SEASONABLE *at any time.*

Kidney Toast.

INGREDIENTS *for breakfast dish for 2 persons.*—2 *sheep's kidneys, or* ¼ *lb. of bullock's kidney,* 1 *oz. of butter, a squeeze of lemon, cayenne, salt,* 2 *slices of buttered toast.* AVERAGE COST, 8d.

Stew the kidneys in a very little water till quite tender; then skin them, remove the gristle and pound smooth in a mortar with the lemon-juice, butter and seasoning. Spread the mixture on the toast, which should be buttered on both sides and put in the oven to get hot through.

SEASONABLE *at any time.*

Kidneys, with Tomatoes.

INGREDIENTS *for breakfast dish for 4 persons.*—4 *sheep's kidneys,* 4 *tomatoes, a little lemon, bread-crumbs, butter, pepper or cayenne, and salt.* AVERAGE COST, 1s. 6d.

Stew the kidneys till tender, in as little water as possible, and skin the tomatoes. Butter a baking tin, scatter over it some bread-crumbs. Lay first a layer of kidneys, cut in slices, seasoned well with pepper and salt, and a squeeze of lemon, then a layer of the tomatoes, also sliced and seasoned. Moisten with the water in which the kidneys have been stewed, and cover with a layer of bread-crumbs, over which place small pieces of butter. Bake for about 10 minutes.

TIME.—10 *minutes.*

SEASONABLE *in autumn or winter.*

Kouftas.

(Indian Recipe.)—INGREDIENTS.—*The remains of cold chicken, butter, yolk of egg, seasoning of pepper, salt and spice.*

Chop the remains of cold chicken (any scraps will do, or game or meat may be substituted) finely, season it well with pepper, salt and spice, or substitute a little curry-powder for the latter, moisten the mixture with yolk of egg, form it into flat cakes, and fry a nice brown in butter.

TIME.—*About* 10 *minutes to fry the cakes.*

SEASONABLE *at any time.*

Koumiss.

INGREDIENTS.—4 *pints of sweet milk,* 1 *pint of butter milk, a small handful (about* 6 *lumps) of white sugar.*

Mix the two milks together, add the sugar and pour from one jug to another for about 15 minutes, or until the sugar is dissolved. Let it stand in a warm corner of the kitchen for 12 hours, the jug covered with muslin; then bottle in pint bottles, tie down the corks with string and in 4 days it will be ready for use. Let the bottles *lie* on their sides.

TIME.—5 *days.*

SEASONABLE *in warm weather.*

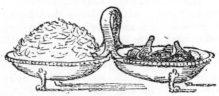

CURRIED KANGAROO TAILS.

" Leverets and larks ! what find we here ?
Let us be merry and enjoy such cheer."—ANON.

A M B. — The most delicious sorts of lamb are those of the South-Down breed, known by their black feet; and of these those which have been exclusively suckled on the milk of the parent ewe, are considered the finest. Next to these in estimation are those fed on the milk of several dams ; and last of all, though the fattest, the grass-fed lamb ; this, however, implies an age much greater than either of the others.

Lamb, in the early part of the season, however reared, is, in London, and indeed generally, sold in quarters, divided with eleven ribs to the forequarter ; but, as the season advances, these are subdivided into two, and the hindquarter in the same manner ; the first consisting of the shoulder, and the neck and breast ; the latter, of the leg and the loin. As lamb, from the juicy nature of its flesh, is especially liable to spoil in unfavourable weather, it should be frequently wiped, so as to remove any moisture that may form on it.

In the purchasing of lamb for the table, there are certain signs by which the experienced judgment is able to form an accurate opinion whether the animal has been lately slaughtered, and whether the joints possess that condition of fibre indicative of good and wholesome meat. The first of these doubts may be solved satisfactorily by the bright and dilated appearance of the eye ; the quality of the forequarter can always be guaranteed by the blue or healthy ruddiness of the jugular, or vein of the neck ; while the rigidity of the knuckle and the firm compact feel of the kidney, will answer in an equally positive manner for the integrity of the hindquarter.

SIDE OF LAMB.

Mode of Cutting up a Side of Lamb in London.—1. Ribs ; 2. Breast ; 3. Shoulder ; 4. Loin ; 5. Leg ; 1, 2, 3. Fore Quarter.

3

Lamb, Breast of, and Green Peas.

INGREDIENTS *for dish for 4 persons.* —1 breast of lamb, a few slices of bacon, ½ pint of stock, 1 lemon, 1 onion, 1 bunch of savoury herbs, green-peas. AVERAGE COST, 10d. per lb.

Remove the skin from a breast of lamb, put it into a saucepan of boiling water, and let it simmer for 5 minutes. Take it out and lay it in cold water. Line the bottom of a stewpan with a few thin slices of bacon; lay the lamb on these; peel the lemon, cut it into slices, and put these on the meat, to keep it white and make it tender; cover with 1 or 2 more slices of bacon; add the stock, onion and herbs, and set it on a slow fire to simmer very gently until tender. Have ready some green peas, put these on a dish and place the lamb on the top of them. The appearance of this dish may be much improved by glazing the lamb, and spinach may be substituted for the peas when variety is desired.

TIME.—1½ hour.

SEASONABLE.—*Grass lamb, from Easter to Michaelmas.*

Lamb, Stewed Breast of.

INGREDIENTS *for dish for 4 persons.* —1 breast of lamb, pepper and salt to taste, sufficient stock to cover it, 1 glass of sherry, thickening of butter and flour. AVERAGE COST, 10d. per lb.

Skin the lamb, cut it into pieces and season them with pepper and salt; lay these in a stewpan, pour in sufficient stock or gravy to cover them, and stew very gently until tender, which will be in about 1½ hour. Just before serving, thicken the sauce with a little butter and flour; add the sherry, give one boil, and pour it over the meat. Green peas or stewed mushrooms may be strewed over the meat, and will be found a very great improvement.

TIME.—1½ hour.

SEASONABLE.—*Grass lamb, from Easter to Michaelmas.*

Lamb, To Carve. — Leg, loin, saddle, shoulder, are carved as mutton.

Lamb Chops.

INGREDIENTS. — Loin of lamb, pepper and salt. AVERAGE COST, 1s. per lb.

Take off the flap from the loin and cut neatly into chops about ¾ inch in thickness. Heat and grease a gridiron and broil the chops a bright pale brown over a clear fire, seasoning them with pepper and salt. They should be served very hot and with very hot plates; and mashed potatoes, spinach or peas form a nice accompaniment to lamb chops.

TIME.—8 to 10 *minutes to broil.*

SEASONABLE *from Easter to Michaelmas.*

Lamb, Fore-quarter of, To Carve.

We always think that a good and practised carver delights in the manipulation of this joint, for there is a little field for his judgment and dexterity which does not always occur in other joints. The separation of the shoulder from the breast is the first point to be attended to; this is done by passing the knife round the dotted line, as shown by the letters A, B, C, D and E, so as to cut through the skin, and then

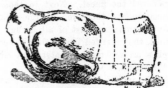

FORE-QUARTER OF LAMB.

by raising with a little force the shoulder, into which the fork should be firmly fixed, it will come away with just a little more exercise of the knife. In dividing the shoulder and breast, the carver should take care not to cut away too much of the meat from the latter, as that would rather spoil its appearance when the shoulder is removed.

The breast and shoulder being separated, it is usual to lay a small piece of butter and sprinkle a little cayenne, lemon-juice and salt between them; and when this is melted and incorporated with the meat and gravy, the shoulder may, as more convenient, be removed into another dish. The next operation is to separate the ribs from the brisket, by cutting through the meat on the line E to F. The joint is then ready to be served to the guests; the ribs being carved in the direction of the lines from I to K, and the brisket from G to H. The carver should ask those at the table what parts they prefer—ribs, brisket, or a piece of the shoulder.

Lamb Cutlets. — INGREDIENTS.—

Loin of lamb, pepper and salt to taste. AVERAGE COST, 1s. per lb.

Trim off the flap from a fine loin of lamb and cut it into cutlets about ¾ inch in thickness. Have ready a bright clear fire; lay the cutlets on a greased gridiron and broil them of a nice brown, turning them when required. Season them with pepper and salt; serve very hot and quickly and garnish with crisped parsley, or place them on mashed potatoes. Asparagus, spinach or peas are the favourite accompaniments to lamb cutlets.

TIME.—*About 8 or 10 minutes.*

SEASONABLE *from Easter to Michaelmas.*

Lamb Cutlets and Spinach.—

INGREDIENTS *for dish for 4 or 5 persons.— 5 cutlets, egg and bread-crumbs, salt and pepper to taste, a little clarified butter.* AVERAGE COST, 1s. per lb.

Cut the cutlets from a neck of lamb and shape them by cutting off the thick part of the chinebone. Trim off most of the fat and all the skin and scrape the top part of the bones quite clean. Brush the cutlets over with egg, sprinkle them with bread-crumbs and season with pepper and salt. Now dip them into clarified butter, sprinkle over a few more bread-crumbs and fry them over a sharp fire, turning them when required. Lay them before the fire to drain and arrange them on a dish with spinach in the centre, which should be previously well boiled, drained, chopped and seasoned.

TIME.—*About 7 or 8 minutes.*

SEASONABLE *from Easter to Michaelmas.*

*Note.—*Peas, asparagus, or French beans may be substituted for the spinach; or lamb cutlets may be served with stewed cucumbers, Soubise sauce, &c. &c.

Lamb, Roast Fore-quarter of.

— INGREDIENTS. — *Lamb, a little salt.* AVERAGE COST, 1s. per lb.

To obtain the flavour of lamb in perfection, it should not be long kept; time to cool is all that it requires; and though the meat may be somewhat thready, the juices and flavour will be infinitely superior to that of lamb that has been killed 2 or 3

FORE-QUARTER OF LAMB.

days. Make up the fire in good time, that it may be clear and brisk when the joint is put down. Place it at a sufficient distance to prevent the fat from burning and baste it constantly till the moment of serving. Lamb should be very *thoroughly* done without being dried up and not the slightest appearance of red gravy should be visible, as in roast mutton; this rule is applicable to all young white meats. Serve with a little gravy made in the dripping-pan, the same as for other roasts and send to table with it a tureen of mint sauce. A cut lemon, a small piece of fresh butter and a little cayenne should also be placed on the table so that when the carver separates the shoulder from the ribs, they may be ready for his use; if, however, he should not be very expert, we would recommend that the cook should divide these joints nicely before coming to table.

TIME.—*Fore-quarter of lamb weighing 10 lbs., 1¾ to 2 hours.*

SEASONABLE —*Grass lamb, from Easter to Michaelmas.*

Lamb's Fry.—INGREDIENTS.—1 *lb. of lamb's fry, 3 pints of water, egg and bread-crumbs, 1 teaspoonful of chopped parsley, salt and pepper to taste.*

Boil the fry for ¼ hour in the above proportion of water, take it out and dry it in a cloth; grate some bread down finely, mix with it a teaspoonful of chopped parsley and a high seasoning of pepper and salt. Brush the fry lightly over with the yolk of an egg, sprinkle over the bread-crumbs and fry for 5 minutes. Serve very hot on a napkin in a dish and garnish with plenty of crisped parsley.

TIME.—¼ *hour to simmer the fry, 5 minutes to fry it.*

SEASONABLE *from Easter to Michaelmas.*

Lamb, Hashed, and Broiled Blade-bone. (Cold Meat Cookery.)—INGREDIENTS. — *The remains of a cold shoulder of lamb, pepper and salt to taste, 2 oz. of butter, about ½ pint of stock or gravy, 1 tablespoonful of shalot vinegar, 3 or 4 pickled gherkins.* AVERAGE COST, *exclusive of the meat, 6d.*

Take the blade-bone from the shoulder, and cut the meat into collops as neatly as possible. Season the bone with pepper and salt, pour a little oiled butter over it and place it in the oven to warm through. Put the stock into a stewpan, add the ketchup and shalot vinegar and lay in the pieces of lamb. Let these heat gradually through, but do not allow them to boil. Take the blade-bone out of the oven and place it on a gridiron over a sharp fire to brown. Slice the gherkins, put them into the hash and dish it with the blade-bone in the

centre. It may be garnished with croûtons or sippets of toasted bread.

TIME.—*Altogether ½ hour.*

SEASONABLE.—*House lamb, from Christmas to March; grass lamb, from Easter to Michaelmas.*

Lamb, Boiled Leg of, à la Béchamel.—INGREDIENTS *for dish for 6 persons.—Leg of lamb, Béchamel sauce.* AVERAGE COST, 1s. *per lb.*

Do not choose a very large joint, but one weighing about 5 lbs. Have ready a saucepan of boiling water, into which plunge the lamb; and when it boils up again, draw it to the side of the fire and let the water cool a little. Then stew very gently for about 1¼ hour, reckoning from the time that the water begins to simmer. Make some Béchamel, dish the lamb, pour the sauce over it and garnish with tufts of boiled cauliflower or carrots. When liked, melted butter may be substituted for the Béchamel; this is a more simple method, but not nearly so nice. Send to table with it some of the sauce in a tureen and boiled cauliflowers or spinach, with whichever vegetable the dish is garnished.

TIME.—1½ *hour after the water simmers.*

SEASONABLE *from Easter to Michaelmas*

Lamb, Roast Leg of.—INGREDIENTS *for dish for 6 persons.—Lamb, a little salt.* AVERAGE COST, 1s. *per lb.*

Place the joint at a good distance from the fire at first and baste well the whole time it is cooking. When nearly done

LEG OF LAMB.

draw it nearer the fire to acquire a nice brown colour. Sprinkle a little fine salt over the meat, empty the dripping-pan of its contents; pour in a little boiling water and strain this over the meat. Serve with mint sauce and for vegetables send peas, spinach or cauliflowers to table with it.

TIME.—*A leg of lamb weighing 5 lbs.,* 1½ *hour.*

SEASONABLE *from Easter to Michaelmas.*

Lamb, Braised Loin of.—INGREDIENTS *for dish for 6 persons.*—A loin of lamb, a few slices of bacon, 1 bunch of green onions, 5 or 6 young carrots, a bunch of savoury herbs, 2 blades of pounded mace, pint of stock, salt to taste. AVERAGE COST, 1s. per lb.

Bone a loin of lamb, and line the bottom

LOIN OF LAMB.

f a stewpan just capable of holding it, with a few thin slices of fat bacon; add the remaining ingredients, cover the meat with a few more slices of bacon, pour in the stock and simmer very *gently* for 2 hours; take it up, dry it, strain and reduce the gravy to a glaze, with which glaze the meat and serve it either on stewed peas, spinach, or stewed cucumbers.

TIME.—*2 hours.*

SEASONABLE *from Easter to Michaelmas.*

Lamb, Roast Saddle of.—INGREDIENTS.—*Lamb; a little salt.* AVERAGE COST, 1s. per lb.

This joint is now very much in vogue, and is generally considered a nice one for a

SADDLE OF LAMB.

small party. Have ready a clear, brisk fire; put down the joint at a little distance, to prevent the fat from scorching and keep it

well basted all the time it is cooking. Serve with mint sauce and send to table with it, either peas, cauliflowers, or spinach.

TIME.—*A small saddle,* 1½ *hour; a large one,* 2 *hours.*

SEASONABLE *from Easter to Michaelmas.*

RIBS OF LAMB.

Note.—Loin and ribs of lamb are roasted in the same manner and served with the same sauces as the above. A loin will take about 1¼ hour; ribs, from 1 to 1¼ hour.

Lamb, Roast Shoulder of.—INGREDIENTS.—*Lamb; a little salt.* AVERAGE COST, 1s. per lb.

Have ready a clear, brisk fire and put down the joint at a sufficient distance from it, that the fat may not burn. Keep constantly basting until done and serve with a little gravy made in the dripping pan and send mint sauce to table with it. Peas, spinach, or cauliflowers are the usual vegetables served with lamb and also a fresh salad.

TIME.—*A shoulder of lamb rather more than* 1 *hour.*

SEASONABLE *from Easter to Michaelmas.*

Lamb, Shoulder of, Stuffed.—INGREDIENTS *for dish for 6 persons.*—Shoulder of lamb, forcemeat, trimmings of veal or beef, 2 onions, ½ head of celery, 1 faggot of savoury herbs, a few slices of fat bacon, 1 quart of stock. AVERAGE COST, 4s. 6d.

Take the blade-bone out of a shoulder of lamb, fill up its place with forcemeat and sew it up with coarse thread. Put it into a stewpan with a few slices of bacon under and over the lamb and add the remaining ingredients. Stew very gently for rather more than 2 hours. Reduce the **gravy**, with which glaze the meat and serve with peas, stewed cucumbers, or sorrel sauce.

TIME.—*Rather more than 2 hours.*

SEASONABLE *from Easter to Michaelmas.*

Lambs' Sweetbreads.

INGREDIENTS *for small entrée.*—2 *sweetbreads*, 1 *egg, bread-crumbs, ½ pint of gravy, 3 table-spoonfuls of sherry.* AVERAGE COST, 3s. 6d.

Soak the sweetbreads in cold water for an hour, then throw them into boiling water to render them firm. Stew them gently for 15 minutes, then take them out and put them in a cloth for all the water to drain off. Brush them over with beaten yolk of egg, cover them with bread-crumbs and brown them before the fire or fry them in hot fat. Make the gravy hot and season it, if necessary, with pepper and salt, add the sherry and pour over the sweetbreads in an entrée dish or one deep enough to hold the gravy.

TIME.—*Rather more than ½ hour.*

SEASONABLE *from Easter to Michaelmas.*

Landrail, or Corn - Crake, Roast.

INGREDIENTS.—3 *or* 4 *birds, butter, fried bread-crumbs.*

Pluck and draw the birds, wipe them inside and out with a damp cloth and truss them in the following manner: Bring the head round under the wing, and the thighs

LANDRAIL.

close to the sides; pass a skewer through them and the body and keep the legs straight. Roast them before a clear fire, keep them well basted and serve on fried bread-crumbs, with a tureen of brown gravy. When liked, bread sauce may also be sent to table with them.

TIME.—12 *to* 20 *minutes.*

SEASONABLE *from August 12th to the middle of September.*

Landrail, To Carve.

—Landrail being trussed like Snipe, with the exception of being drawn, may be carved in the same manner.

Lard, To Melt.

—Melt the inner fat of the pig, by putting it in a stone jar and placing this in a saucepan of boiling water previously stripping off the skin. Let it simmer gently over a bright fire, and as it melts, pour it carefully from the sediment. Put it into small jars or bladders for use and keep it in a cool place. The flead or inside fat of the pig, before it is melted makes exceedingly light crust and is particularly wholesome. It may be preserved a length of time by salting it well and occasionally changing the brine. When wanted for use, wash and wipe it and it will answer for making into paste as well as fresh lard.

AVERAGE COST, 10d. *per lb.*

Lard, To Refine.

—Put the lard into a basin and pour upon it boiling water. When cold, take away the water and repeat the process. Lard so refined, the salt being extracted, is fit for toilet use and, with the addition of a little essence of lemon to scent it, makes a nice cold cream.

Larding.

INGREDIENTS. — *Bacon and larding-needle.*

Bacon for larding should be firm and fat and ought to be cured without any saltpetre, as this reddens white meats. Lay on a table, the hands downwards; trim off any rusty part and cut it into slices of an equal thickness. Place the slices one on the top of another and cut them even into narrow strips, so arranging it that every piece of bacon is of the same size. Bacon for fricandeaux, poultry and game should be about 2 inches in length and rather more than one-eighth of an inch in width. If for larding fillets of beef or loins of veal, the pieces of bacon must be thicker. The following recipe of Soyer is, we think

ery explicit; and any cook, by following
ae directions here given, may be able to
rd, if not well, sufficiently for general
se:—

'Have the fricandeaux trimmed; lay them
ngthwise upon a clean napkin across your
and, forming a kind of bridge with your
umb at the part where you are about to
ommence; then with the point of the lard-
ig-needle make three distinct lines across,
inch apart; run the needle into the third
ne, at the farther side of the fricandeaux,
id bring it out at the first, placing one of
ae lardoons in it; draw the needle through,

BACON FOR LARDING, AND LARDING-NEEDLE.

aving out ¼ inch of the bacon at each
ne; proceed thus to the end of the row;
en make another line ½ inch distant, stick
another row of lardoons, bringing them
at at the second line, leaving the ends of
ae bacon out all the same length; make
ae next row again at the same distance,
inging the ends out between the lardoons
the first row, proceeding in this manner
atil the whole surface is larded in chequered
ws. Everything else is larded in a similar
ay; and, in the case of poultry, hold the
east over a charcoal fire for one minute,
dip it into boiling water, in order to make
e flesh firm."

Lark Pie.

Lark Pie.—INGREDIENTS *for pie for*
persons.—A few thin slices of beef, the
me of bacon, 9 larks, flour; for stuffing,
teacupful of bread-crumbs, ½ teaspoonful
minced lemon-peel, 1 teaspoonful of
inced parsley, 1 egg, salt and pepper to
ste, 1 teaspoonful of chopped shalot, ½
nt of weak stock or water, puff-paste.
VERAGE COST, 3s.

Make a stuffing of bread-crumbs, minced
mon-peel, parsley and the yolk of an egg,

all of which should be well mixed together;
roll the larks in flour and stuff them. Line
the bottom of a pie-dish with a few slices
of beef and bacon; over these place the
larks and season with salt, pepper, minced
parsley and chopped shalot in the above
proportion. Pour in the stock or water,
cover with crust and bake for an hour in a
moderate oven. During the time the pie is
baking, shake it 2 or 3 times to assist in
thickening the gravy, and serve very hot.

TIME.—1 *hour.*

SEASONABLE.—*In full season in Novem-*
ber.

Larks, Roast.

Larks, Roast. — INGREDIENTS. —
Larks, egg and bread-crumbs, fresh butter.
AVERAGE COST, 1s. 6d. *to* 2s. *per dozen.*

These birds are by many persons esteemed a great delicacy and may be either
roasted or broiled. Pick, gut and clean
them; when they are trussed, brush them
over with the yolk of an egg; sprinkle with
bread-crumbs and roast them before a quick
fire; baste them continually with fresh
butter and keep sprinkling with the bread-
crumbs until the birds are well covered.

ROAST LARKS.

Dish them on bread-crumbs fried in clarified butter and garnish the dish with slices
of lemon. Broiled larks are also very
excellent: they should be cooked over a
clear fire, and would take about 10 minutes
or ¼ hour.

TIME.—1 *hour to roast;* 10 *minutes to*
broil.

SEASONABLE.—*In full season in Novem-*
ber.

Note.—Larks may also be plainly roasted, without covering them with egg and bread-crumbs;
they should be dished on fried crumbs.

Larks in Onions.

Larks in Onions. (Italian Recipe.)
—INGREDIENTS *for dish for 5 or 6 persons.*
—8 *larks,* 4 *Spanish onions of equal size,* **3**

thin slices of bacon, ½ pint of stock, a fowl's liver, a bunch of herbs, ¼ lb. of veal forcemeat, pepper and salt. AVERAGE COST, 3s.

Clean and bone the larks, then stuff them with the liver and herbs chopped very fine. Put the bacon at the bottom of a stewpan and upon it the larks; just cover with stock and simmer for about ¼ hour. Peel and blanch the onions, cut them in half and take out enough from each to make room for a lark and a little forcemeat. Put a little in each ½ onion, then a lark, putting on the head (from which the eyes should be removed) with a little forcemeat, then cover with buttered paper and bake long enough to set the stuffing. Lift out with care, and having drained off the fat, glaze and serve with Spanish sauce.

TIME.—½ hour.
SEASONABLE in autumn.

Leamington Sauce. (An excellent Sauce for Flavouring Gravies, Hashes, Soups, &c.) (AUTHOR'S Recipe).—INGREDIENTS. — Walnuts. To each quart of walnut-juice, allow 2 quarts of vinegar, 1 pint of Indian soy, 1 oz. of cayenne, 2 oz. of shalots, ¾ oz. of garlic, ½ pint of port wine.

Be very particular in choosing the walnuts as soon as they appear in the market; for they are more easily bruised before they become hard and shelled. Pound them in a mortar to a pulp, strew some salt over them and let them remain thus for two or three days, occasionally stirring and moving them about. Press out the juice and to each quart of walnut liquor allow the above proportion of vinegar, soy, cayenne, shalots, garlic and port wine. Pound each ingredient separately in a mortar, then mix them well together and store away for use in small bottles. The corks should be well sealed.

SEASONABLE.—This sauce should be made as soon as walnuts are obtainable, from the beginning to the middle of July.

Leek Soup.—INGREDIENTS for sou[ ] for 10 persons.—A sheep's head, 3 quarts water, 12 leeks cut small, pepper and salt [to] taste, oatmeal to thicken. AVERAGE COS[ ] 1s. 3d.

LEEKS.

Prepare the head, either by skinning [or] cleaning the skin very nicely; split it in two; take out the brains and put it into boiling water; add the leeks and seasoning and simmer very gently for 4 hours. Mix smoothly with cold water, as much oatmeal as will make the soup tolerably thick; pour it into the soup; contin[ ] stirring till the whole is blended and we[ ] done, and serve.

TIME.—4½ hours.
SEASONABLE in winter.

Lemon Biscuits.—INGREDIENT[ ] —1¼ lb. of flour, ¾ lb. of loaf sugar, 6 oz. fresh butter, 4 eggs, 1 oz. of lemon-peel, [ ] dessertspoonfuls of lemon-juice. AVERAG[ ] COST, 1s. 4d.

Rub the flour into the butter; stir [in] the pounded sugar and very finely-minc[ed] lemon-peel and, when these ingredients a[re] thoroughly mixed, add the eggs, whi[ch] should be previously well whisked, and t[he] lemon-juice. Beat the mixture well for [a] minute or two, then drop it from a spo[on] on to a buttered tin, about 2 inches apar[t] as the cakes will spread when they g[et] warm; place the tin in the oven and ba[ke] the cakes of a pale brown from 15 to [20] minutes.

TIME.— 15 to 20 minutes.
SEASONABLE at any time.

Lemon Blancmange.—INGRED[I]ENTS for quart mould.—1 quart of mil[k] the yolks of 4 eggs, 3 oz. of ground rice, [ ] oz. of pounded sugar, 1½ oz. of fresh butte[r] the rind of 1 lemon, the juice of 2, ½ oz. [of] gelatine. AVERAGE COST, 1s. 6d.

Make a custard with the yolks of the eggs and ½ pint of the milk and when done ut it into a basin; put half the remainder f the milk into a lined saucepan with the round rice, fresh butter, lemon-rind and oz. of the sugar and let these ingredients

BLANCMANGE MOULD.

boil until the mixture is stiff, stirring them continually; when done, pour it into the bowl where the custard is, mixing both well together. Put the gelatine with the rest of the milk into a saucepan

nd let it stand by the side of the fire ⊕ dissolve; boil for a minute or two, ⣀ir carefully into the basin, adding 3 oz. ▪ore of pounded sugar. When cold, stir ▪ the lemon-juice, which should be care-▪lly strained; and pour the mixture into a ▪ell-oiled mould, leaving out the lemon-▪eel; then set the mould in a pan of ▪ld water until wanted for table. Use ▪gs that have rich-looking yolks; and, ▪ould the weather be very warm, rather ▪ larger proportion of gelatine must be ▪lowed.

TIME.—*Altogether*, ½ *hour*.
SEASONABLE *at any time*.

Lemon Cake. — INGREDIENTS.— 8

▪gs, 3 *tablespoonfuls of orange-flower water*, ▪lb. *of pounded loaf sugar*, 1 *lemon*, ¾ *lb.* ▪ *flour*. AVERAGE COST, 1s. 3d.

Separate the whites from the yolks of ▪e eggs; whisk the former to a stiff froth; ▪d the orange-flower water, the sugar, ▪ated lemon-rind and mix these ingre-▪ents well together. Then beat the yolks ▪ the eggs and add them, with the lemon-▪ice, to the whites, &c.; dredge in the ▪ur gradually; keep beating the mixture ▪ll; put it into a buttered mould and ▪ke the cake about an hour, or rather ▪ger. The addition of a little butter

beaten to a cream, we think, would improve this cake.

TIME.—*About* 1 *hour*.
SEASONABLE *at any time*.

Lemon Cheesecakes. — INGREDIENTS *for* 2 *dozen cheesecakes.*—¼ lb. *of butter*, 1 lb. *of loaf sugar*, 5 *eggs, the rind of* 2 *lemons and the juice of* 3. AVERAGE COST, 1s. 2d.

Put all the ingredients into a stewpan, carefully grating the lemon-rind and straining the juice. Keep stirring the mixture over the fire until the sugar is dissolved, and it begins to thicken; when of the consistency of honey, it is done; then put it into small jars and keep in a dry place. This mixture will remain good 3 or 4 months. When made into cheesecakes, add a few pounded almonds, or candied peel, or grated sweet biscuit; line some patty-pans with good puff-paste, rather more than half fill them with the mixture and bake for about ¼ hour in a good brisk oven.

TIME.—¼ *hour*.
SEASONABLE *at any time*.

Lemon Cheesecakes. (To Keep.) INGREDIENTS *for sufficient to fill* 2 *dozen cheesecakes.*—6 *lemons*, 4 *eggs*, 6 *oz. of butter*, 1 lb. *of loaf sugar*. AVERAGE COST, 1s. 8d.

Grate the rind of the lemons and squeeze the juice of all, add the eggs and the sugar and after mixing thoroughly put in a jug; put the jug in a saucepan of boiling water and stir one way till the mixture is of a smooth paste. When quite cold, cover closely and it will keep good a fortnight or longer in cold weather.

TIME.—20 *minutes*.
SEASONABLE *at any time*.

Lemon Cream. — INGREDIENTS *for* 1½-*pint mould.*—1 *pint of cream, the yolks of* 2 *eggs*, ¼ lb. *of white sugar*, 1 *large lemon*, 1 *oz. of isinglass or gelatine*. AVERAGE COST, 2s. 6d.

Put the cream into a *lined* saucepan with the sugar, lemon-peel and isinglass and simmer these over a gentle fire for about 10 minutes, stirring them all the time. Strain the cream into a jug, add the yolks of eggs, which should be well beaten and put the jug into a saucepan of boiling water; stir the mixture one way until it thickens, *but do not allow it to boil;* take it off the fire and keep stirring it until nearly cold. Strain the lemon-juice into a basin, gradually pour on it the cream and *stir it well* until the juice is well mixed with it. Have ready a well-oiled mould, pour the cream into it and let it remain until perfectly set. When required for table, loosen the edges with a small blunt knife, put a dish on the top of the mould, turn it over quickly and the cream should easily slip away.

TIME.—10 *minutes to boil the cream; about* 10 *minutes to stir it over the fire in the jug.*

SEASONABLE *at any time.*

Lemon Cream, Economical.—

INGREDIENTS *for two* 1½-pint moulds.— 1 *quart of milk,* 8 *bitter almonds,* 2 oz. *of gelatine,* 2 *large lemons,* ¾ lb. *of lump sugar, the yolks of* 6 *eggs.* AVERAGE COST, 2s.

Put the milk into a lined saucepan with the almonds, which should be well pounded

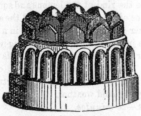

LEMON-CREAM MOULD.

in a mortar, the gelatine, lemon-rind and lump sugar and boil these ingredients for about 5 minutes. Beat up the yolks of the eggs, strain the milk into a jug, add the eggs and pour the mixture backwards and

forwards a few times, until nearly cold; then stir briskly to it the lemon-juice, which should be strained, keep stirring until the cream is almost cold; put it into an oiled mould and let it remain until perfectly set.

LEMON ICE.

The lemon-juice must not be added to the cream when it is warm and should be well stirred after it is put in.

TIME.—5 *minutes to boil the milk.*

SEASONABLE *at any time.*

Lemon Creams, Very Good.—

INGREDIENTS *for* 12 *glasses.*—1 *pint of cream,* 2 *dozen sweet almonds,* 3 *glasses of sherry, the rind and juice of* 2 *lemons, sugar to taste.* AVERAGE COST, 2s. 6d.

Blanch and chop the almonds and put them into a jug with the cream: in another jug put the sherry, lemon-rind, strained juice and sufficient pounded sugar to sweeten the whole nicely. Pour rapidly from one jug to the other till the mixture is well frothed: then pour it into jelly glasses, omitting the lemon-rind. This is a very cool and delicious sweet for summer and may be made less rich by omitting the almonds and substituting orange or raisin wine for the sherry.

TIME.—*Altogether* ½ *hour.*

SEASONABLE *at any time.*

Lemon Creams or Custards.—

INGREDIENTS *for* 12 *glasses.*—5 oz. *of loaf sugar,* 2 *pints of boiling water, the rind of* 1 *lemon and the juice of* 3, 6 *eggs.* AVERAGE COST, 9d.

Make a quart of lemonade in the following manner:—Dissolve the sugar in the boiling water, having previously, with part of the sugar, rubbed off the lemon-rind and add the strained juice. Strain the lemonade into a saucepan and add the eggs, which should be well beaten; stir this *one* *way* over the fire until the mixture thickens, but do not allow it to boil; and serve in custard glasses or on a glass dish. After the boiling water is poured on the sugar and lemon, it should stand covered for about ½ hour before the eggs are added to it, that the flavour of the rind may be extracted.

TIME.—½ *hour to make the lemonade; about 10 minutes to stir the custard over the fire.*

SEASONABLE *at any time.*

Lemon Dumplings.—INGREDIENTS *for 6 dumplings.*—½ lb. of grated bread, ¼ lb. of chopped suet, ¼ lb. of moist sugar, 2 eggs, 1 large lemon. AVERAGE COST, 7d.

Mix the bread, suet and moist sugar well together, adding the lemon-peel, which should be very finely minced. Moisten with the eggs and strained lemon-juice; stir well and put the mixture into small buttered cups. Tie them down and boil for ¾ hour. Turn them out on a dish, strew sifted sugar over them and serve with wine sauce.

TIME.—¾ *hour.*

SEASONABLE *at any time.*

Lemon Jelly.—INGREDIENTS *for 1½-int mould.*—6 *lemons,* ¾ *lb. of lump sugar,* pint of water, 1¼ oz. of isinglass or gelatine, ¼ *pint of sherry.* AVERAGE COST, *with isinglass,* 2s. 6d.

Peel 3 of the lemons, pour ½ pint of boiling water on the rind and let it infuse for hour; put the sugar, isinglass or gelatine and ½ pint of water into a lined saucepan and boil these ingredients for 20 minutes; then put in the strained lemon-juice, the strained infusion of the rind and bring the whole to the point of boiling; skim

well, add the wine and run the jelly through a bag; pour it into a mould that has been wetted or soaked in water; put it in ice, if convenient, where let it remain until required for table. Previously to adding the lemon-juice to the other ingredients, ascertain that it is very nicely strained, as, if this is not properly attended

LEMON JELLY.

to, it is liable to make the jelly thick and muddy. As this jelly is very pale and almost colourless, it answers very well for moulding with a jelly of any bright hue: for instance, half a jelly bright red and the other half made of the above, would have a very good effect. Lemon jelly may also be made with calf's-feet stock, allowing the juice of 3 lemons to every pint of stock.

TIME.—*Altogether* 1 *hour.*

SEASONABLE *at any time.*

Lemon Mincemeat. —INGREDIENTS *for mincemeat for 2 dozen pies.*—2 *large lemons, 6 large apples,* ½ *lb. of suet,* 1 *lb. of currants,* 2 *lb. of sugar,* 2 *oz. of candied lemon-peel,* 1 *oz. of citron, mixed spice to taste.* AVERAGE COST, 1s. 8d.

Pare the lemons, squeeze them and boil the peel until tender enough to mash. Add to the mashed lemon-peel the apples, which should be pared, cored and minced; the chopped suet, currants, sugar, sliced peel and spices. Strain the lemon-juice to these ingredients, stir the mixture well and put it in a jar with a closely-fitting lid. Stir occasionally and in a week or 10 days the mincemeat will be ready for use.

SEASONABLE.—*Make this about the beginning of December.*

Lemon-Peel.—This contains an essential oil of a very high flavour and fragrance and is consequently esteemed both a wholesome and agreeable stomachic. It is used, as will be seen by many recipes in this book, as an ingredient for flavouring a number of various dishes. Under the name of candied lemon-peel, it is cleared of pulp and preserved in sugar, when it becomes an excellent sweetmeat.

Lemon Pudding, Baked.—In-

GREDIENTS *for pudding sufficient for 6 persons.*—4 eggs, 4 oz. of pounded sugar, 1 lemon, 3 oz of butter, puff-paste. AVERAGE COST, 1s.

Beat the eggs to a froth; mix with them the sugar and warm butter; stir these ingredients well together, putting in the grated rind and strained juice of the lemon-peel. Line a shallow dish with puff-paste;

THE LEMON.

put in the mixture and bake in a moderate oven for 40 minutes; turn the pudding out of the dish, strew over it sifted sugar and serve.

TIME.—40 *minutes.*
SEASONABLE *at any time.*

Lemon Pudding, Baked.—In-

GREDIENTS *for pudding for 6 persons.*—10 oz. of bread-crumbs, 2 pints of milk, 2 oz. of butter, 1 lemon, ¼ lb. of pounded sugar, 4 eggs, 1 tablespoonful of brandy. AVERAGE COST, 1s. 4d.

Bring the milk to the boiling point, stir in the butter and pour these hot over the bread-crumbs; add the sugar and very finely-minced lemon-peel; beat the eggs and stir these in with the brandy to the other ingredients; put a paste round the dish and bake for ¾ hour.

TIME.—¾ *hour.*
SEASONABLE *at any time.*

Lemon Pudding, Baked. (Very

Rich.)—INGREDIENTS *for pudding for 6 persons.*—The rind and juice of 2 large lemons, ½ lb. of loaf sugar, ¼ pint of cream the yolks of 8 eggs, 2 oz. of almonds, ½ lb. of butter, melted. AVERAGE COST, 2s. 6d.

Mix the pounded sugar with the cream and add the yolks of eggs and the butter which should be previously warmed. Blanch and pound the almonds and put these, with the grated rind and strained juice of the lemons, to the other ingredients. Stir all well together; line a dish with puff-paste put in the mixture and bake for 1 hour.

TIME.—1 *hour.*
SEASONABLE *at any time.*

Lemon Pudding, Boiled.—In-

GREDIENTS *for large pudding.*—½ lb. of chopped suet, ¾ lb. of bread-crumbs, 2 small lemons, 6 oz. of moist sugar, ¼ lb. of flour, 3 eggs, milk. AVERAGE COST, 1s.

Mix the suet, bread-crumbs, sugar and flour well together, adding the lemon-peel which should be very finely minced, and the juice, which should be strained. When these ingredients are well mixed, moisten with the eggs and sufficient milk to make the pudding of the consistency of thick batter; put it into a well-buttered mould and boil for 3½ hours; turn it out, strew sifted sugar over and serve with wine sauce or not, at pleasure.

TIME.—3½ *hours.*
SEASONABLE *at any time.*

Note.—This pudding may also be baked, and will be found very good. It will take about hours.

Lemon Pudding, Plain.—INGRE-

IENTS *for pudding for 6 persons.*—¾ *lb. of our, 6 oz. of lard or dripping, the juice of 1 arge lemon,* 1 *teacupful of flour, sugar.* AVERAGE COST, 7d.

Make the above proportion of flour and ard into a smooth paste and roll it out to ae thickness of about ½ an inch. Squeeze ae lemon-juice, strain it into a cup, stir ae flour into it and as much moist sugar as ill make it into a stiff and thick paste ; read this mixture over the paste, roll it p, secure the ends and tie the pudding in a oured cloth. Boil for 2 hours.

TIME.—2 *hours.*

SEASONABLE *at any time.*

Lemon Sauce (for Boiled Fowl).—

INGREDIENTS *for sufficient for a pair of wls.*—1 *small lemon,* ¾ *pint of melted utter.* AVERAGE COST, 4d.

Cut the lemon into very thin slices and ese again into very small dice. Have ady ¾ pint of melted butter, put in the mon ; let it just simmer, but not boil and our it over the fowls.

TIME.—1 *minute to simmer.*

Lemon Sauce (for Sweet Puddings).

INGREDIENTS *for sauce for large pud-ng.*—*The rind and juice of* 1 *lemon,* 1 blespoonful *of flour,* 1 *oz. of butter,* 1 *large ineglassful of sherry,* 1 *wineglassful of ater, sugar to taste, the yolks of 4 eggs.* AVERAGE COST, 10d.

Rub the rind of the lemon on to some mps of sugar ; squeeze out the juice and rain it ; put the butter and flour into a ucepan, stir them over the fire and when a pale brown, add the wine, water and rained lemon-juice. Crush the lumps of gar that were rubbed on the lemon ; stir ese into the sauce, which should be very veet. When these ingredients are well ixed and the sugar is melted, put in the aten yolks of 4 eggs ; keep stirring the uce until it thickens, when serve. Do

not, on any account, allow it to boil, or it will curdle and be entirely spoiled.

TIME.—*Altogether,* 15 *minutes.*

Lemon Sauce, White (for Fowls,

Fricassees, &c.).—INGREDIENTS *for suffi-cient for pair of fowls or turkeys.*—¾ *pint of cream, the rind and juice of* 1 *lemon,* ½ *tea-spoonful of whole white pepper,* 1 *sprig of lemon thyme,* 3 *oz. of butter,* 1 *dessertspoon-ful of flour,* 1 *teacupful of white stock ; salt to taste.* AVERAGE COST, 1s. 8d.

Put the cream into a very clean sauce-pan (a lined one is best), with the lemon-peel, pepper and thyme and let these in-fuse for ½ hour, when simmer gently for a few minutes, or until there is a nice flavour of lemon. Strain it and add a thickening of butter and flour in the above propor-tions ; stir this well in and put in the lemon-juice at the moment of serving ; mix the stock with the cream and add a little salt. This sauce should not boil after the cream and stock are mixed together.

TIME.—*Altogether,* ¾ *hour.*

Note.—Where the expense of the cream is objected to, milk may be substituted for it. In this case, an additional dessertspoonful, or rather more, of flour must be added.

Lemon Sponge.—INGREDIENTS *for*

quart mould.—2 *oz. of isinglass or gelatine,* 1¾ *pint of water,* ¾ *lb. of pounded sugar, the juice of* 3 *lemons, the rind of* 1, *the whites of* 3 *eggs.* AVERAGE COST, 2s.

Dissolve the isinglass in the water, strain it into a saucepan and add the sugar, lemon-rind and juice. Boil the whole from 10 to 15 minutes ; strain it again and let it stand till it is cold and begins to stiffen. Beat the whites of the eggs, put them to it and whisk the mixture till it is quite white ; put it into a mould which has been previously wetted and let it remain until perfectly set ; then turn it out and garnish it according to taste.

TIME.—10 *to* 15 *minutes.*

SEASONABLE *at any time.*

Lemon Syrup.—INGREDIENTS.—2 lbs. of loaf sugar, 2 pints of water, 1 oz. of citric acid, ½ drachm of essence of lemon. AVERAGE COST, 9d.

Boil the sugar and water together for ¼ hour and put it into a basin, where let it remain till cold. Beat the citric acid to a powder, mix the essence of lemon with it, then add these two ingredients to the syrup; mix well and bottle for use. Two tablespoonfuls of the syrup are sufficient for a tumbler of cold water and will be found a very refreshing summer drink.

Lemons, To Pickle, with the Peel on. — INGREDIENTS.— 6 lemons, 2 quarts of boiling water; to each quart of vinegar allow ½ oz. of cloves, ½ oz. of white pepper, 1 oz. of bruised ginger, ¼ oz. of mace and chilies, 1 oz. of mustard-seed, ½ stick of sliced horseradish, a few cloves of garlic.

Put the lemons into a brine that will bear an egg; let them remain in it 6 days, stirring them every day; have ready 2 quarts of boiling water, put in the lemons and allow them to boil for ¼ hour; take them out and let them lie in a cloth until perfectly dry and cold. Boil up sufficient vinegar to cover the lemons, with all the above ingredients, allowing the same proportion as stated to each quart of vinegar. Pack the lemons in a jar, pour over the vinegar, &c., boiling hot and tie down with a bladder. They will be fit for use in about 12 months, or rather sooner.

SEASONABLE.—This should be made from November to April.

Lemons, To Pickle without the Peel.—INGREDIENTS.—6 lemons, 1 lb. of fine salt; to each quart of vinegar, the same ingredients as in the last recipe.

Peel the lemons, slit each one down 3 times, so as not to divide them and rub the salt well into the divisions; place them in a pan, where they must remain for a week, turning them every other day; then put

them in a Dutch oven before a clear fir until the salt has become perfectly dry then arrange them in a jar. Pour ove sufficient boiling vinegar to cover them, t which have been added the ingredient mentioned in the foregoing recipe; ti down closely and in about 9 months the will be fit for use.

SEASONABLE.—The best time to mak this is from November to April.

Note.—After this pickle has been made from to 5 months, the liquor may be strained an bottled and will be found an excellent lemo ketchup.

Lemon Wine.—INGREDIENTS.—T 4½ gallons of water allow the pulp of 8 lemons, the rind of 25, 16 lbs. of loaf sugar ½ oz. of isinglass, 1 bottle of brandy.

Peel and slice the lemons, but use onl the rind of 25 of them and put them int the cold water. Let it stand 8 or 9 days squeezing the lemons well every day; the strain the water off and put it into a cas with the sugar. Let it work some time and when it has ceased working, put in th isinglass. Stop the cask down; in abou 6 months put in the brandy and bottle th wine off.

SEASONABLE.—The best time to mak this is in January or February, whe lemons are best and cheapest.

Lemonade. — INGREDIENTS for quart of lemonade.—The rind of 2 lemon the juice of 3 large or 4 small ones, ½ lb. loaf sugar, 1 quart of boiling water. AVE AGE COST, 5d.

Rub some of the sugar, in lumps, on 2 the lemons until they have imbibed all th oil from them and put it with the re mainder of the sugar into a jug; add th lemon-juice (but no pips) and pour over th whole a quart of boiling water. When th sugar is dissolved, strain the lemonad through a fine sieve or piece of muslin an when cool it will be ready for use. Th lemonade will be much improved by havin the white of an egg beaten up in it; a little sherry mixed with it also, makes this beverage much nicer.

Lemonade, Nourishing.—INGREDIENTS *for* 2½ *pints of lemonade.*—1½ *pint of boiling water, the juice of 4 lemons, the rinds of 2, ½ pint of sherry, 4 eggs, 6 oz. of loaf sugar.* AVERAGE COST, 1s. 6d.

Pare off the lemon-rind thinly, put it into a jug with the sugar and pour over the boiling water. Let it cool, then strain it; add the wine, lemon-juice and eggs, previously well beaten and also strained, and the beverage will be ready for use. If thought desirable, the quantity of sherry and water could be lessened and milk substituted for them. To obtain the flavour of the lemon-rind properly a few lumps of the sugar should be rubbed over it, until some of the yellow is absorbed.

TIME.—*Altogether* 1 *hour to make it.*
SEASONABLE *at any time.*

Lentil Porridge.—INGREDIENTS *for sufficient for 2 persons.* — 3 *oz. of lentil flour,* 1 *pint of water, salt,* ½ *oz. of butter.* AVERAGE COST, 2d.

Put the flour and salt in a basin and mix with a little cold water; add the rest of the water boiling, then put on the fire and boil for 10 minutes. Just before serving, stir in the butter. Lentil flour makes a nice porridge mixed with an equal quantity of barley flour.

TIME.—10 *minutes to boil the porridge.*
SEASONABLE *in winter.*

Lentil Rissoles. (Vegetarian Recipe.)—INGREDIENTS *for* 6 *rissoles.*—¼ *lb of lentils, either boiled or baked,* ½ *oz. of butter, pepper, salt and nutmeg, egg and bread-crumbs, a little parsley.* AVERAGE COST, 6d.

Cook the lentils soft enough to mash, drain them, mash them with the butter and add the seasoning. Roll the pastry very thin and stamp it in rounds, into

each of which put some of the lentil mixture; then fold over, wet the edges and stick them together. Dip the rissoles in egg and bread-crumbs and fry in oil or butter.

TIME.—5 *minutes to fry the rissoles.*
SEASONABLE *at any time.*

Lentil Soup.—INGREDIENTS *for soup for 4 persons.*—1 *pint of green German lentils,* 2 *oz. of butter,* 1½ *pint of the liquor in which a joint of pork has been boiled,* 2 *or* 3 *cloves of garlic, pepper and salt.* AVERAGE COST, 8d.

Boil the lentils in a lined saucepan for 15 minutes, then pour off the water, add a small quantity of fresh with the butter and seasoning and simmer till quite soft. Stir in the liquor and add the garlic or some slices of fried onion.

LENTIL.

TIME.—4 *hours.*
SEASONABLE *in winter.*

Lettuces.— These form one of the principal ingredients to summer salads; they should be blanched and be eaten young.

They are seldom served in any other way, but may be stewed and sent to table in a good brown gravy flavoured with lemon-juice. In preparing them for a salad, carefully wash them free from dirt,

LETTUCE.

pick off all the decayed and outer leaves and dry them thoroughly by shaking them in a cloth. Cut off the stalks and either cut or tear the lettuces into small pieces. The manner of cutting them up entirely depends on the salad for which they are intended

In France, the lettuces are sometimes merely wiped with a cloth and not washed, the cooks there declaring that the act of washing them injuriously affects the pleasant crispness of the plant: in this case scrupulous attention must be paid to each leaf, and the grit thoroughly wiped away.

SEASONABLE *from March to the end of August, but may be had all the year.*

Leveret, To Dress a.—INGREDIENTS.—*A leveret, butter, flour.* AVERAGE COST, 4s. each.

Leverets should be trussed in the same manner as a hare, but they do not require stuffing. Roast them before a clear fire and keep them well basted all the time they are cooking. A few minutes before serving, dredge them lightly with flour and froth them nicely. Serve with plain gravy in a dish and send to table red-currant jelly with them.

TIME.—½ to ¾ hour.

SEASONABLE *from May to August, but cheapest in July and August.*

Liaison of Eggs (for Thickening Sauces).—INGREDIENTS.— *The yolks of 3 eggs, 8 tablespoonfuls of milk or cream.* AVERAGE COST, 4d.

Beat up the yolks of the eggs, to which add the milk and strain the whole through a hair-sieve. When the liaison is being added to the sauce it is intended to thicken, care must be exercised to keep stirring it during the whole time, or, otherwise, the eggs will curdle. It should only just simmer, but not boil.

Liqueur Jelly.—INGREDIENTS *for quart mould.—*½ *lb. of lump sugar,* 1½ *oz. of isinglass, or gelatine,* 1½ *pint of water, the juice of 2 lemons,* ¼ *pint of liqueur.* AVERAGE COST, 2s.

Put the sugar, with 1 pint of the water, into a stewpan and boil them gently by the side of the fire until there is no scum re-

maining, which must be carefully removed as fast as it rises. Boil the isinglass with the other ½ pint of water and skim it carefully in the same manner. Strain the lemon-juice and add it, with the clarified isinglass, to the syrup; put in the liqueur and bring the whole to the boiling point. Let the saucepan remain covered by the side of the fire for a few minutes; then pour the jelly through a bag, put it into a mould and set the mould in ice until required for the table. Dip the mould in hot water, wipe the outside, loosen the jelly by passing a knife round the edges and turn it out carefully on a dish. Noyeau, Maraschino, Curaçoa, brandy, or any kind of liqueur answers for this jelly; and, when made with isinglass, liqueur jellies are usually prepared as directed above.

TIME.—10 *minutes to boil the sugar and water.*

SEASONABLE *at any time.*

Liver and Lemon Sauce (for Poultry).— INGREDIENTS *for sauce for a pair of fowls.—The liver of a fowl, 1 lemon, salt to taste,* ½ *pint of melted butter.* AVERAGE COST, 4d.

Wash the liver and let it boil for a few minutes; peel the lemon very thin, remove the white part and pips and cut it into very small dice; mince the liver and a small quantity of the lemon-rind very fine; add these ingredients to ½ pint of smoothly-made melted butter; season with a little salt, put in the cut lemon, heat it gradually, but do not allow it to boil, lest the butter should oil.

TIME.—1 *minute to simmer.*

Liver and Parsley Sauce (for Poultry).—INGREDIENTS *for sauce for pair of chickens.—The liver of a fowl, 1 tablespoonful of minced parsley,* ½ *pint of melted butter.* AVERAGE COST, 4d.

Wash and score the liver, boil it for a few minutes and mince it very fine; blanch or scald a small bunch of parsley, of which there should be sufficient when hopped to fill a tablespoon ; add this with he minced liver to ½ pint of smoothly-made melted butter ; let it just boil ; when serve.

TIME.—1 *minute to simmer.*

Lobsters, To Boil.—INGREDIENTS.

-Lobsters, ¼ lb. of salt to each gallon of water. AVERAGE COST, 1s. to 3s. each.

Buy the lobsters alive and choose those that are heavy and full of motion, which is an indication of their freshness. When the shell is incrusted, it is a sign they are old : medium-sized lobsters are the best. Have ready a stewpan of boiling water, salted in the above proportion ; put in the lobster head downwards and keep it boiling quickly from 20 minutes to ¾ hour, according to its size and do not forget to skim well. If it boils too long, the meat becomes thready and if not done enough, the spawn is not ed : this must be obviated by great atten-ion. Rub the shell over with a little butter or sweet oil, which wipe off again.

TIME.—*Small lobster, 20 minutes to ½ our ; large ditto, ½ to ¾ hour.*

SESAONABLE *all the year, but best from March to October.*

To Choose Boiled Lobsters.—This shell sh, if it has been cooked alive, as ought to have been, will have a stiff-ess in the tail, which, if gently raised, will eturn with a spring. Care, however, must e taken in thus proving it ; for if the tail pulled straight out it will not return ; hen the fish might be pronounced inferior, hich in reality, may not be the case. In rder to be good, lobsters should be weighty r their bulk ; if light, they will be watery ; nd those of the medium size are always e best. Small-sized lobsters are cheapest nd answer very well for sauce.

Lobster Canapés.—INGREDIENTS

r dish for 4 persons.—12 small croûtons ied in butter, a little lobster butter, the ail of a small lobster, oil, capers, pepper nd vinegar. AVERAGE COST, 10d.

Fry the croûtons and when cold spread them with the butter. Cut small slices of the lobster and soak in oil and vinegar for a few minutes. Lay a slice on each croûton and give a seasoning of pepper and cayenne, put 2 or 3 capers on the top and serve on a flat dish, on a stamped paper, garnished with parsley and watercress.

SEASONABLE *at any time.*

Lobster Cream.—INGREDIENTS *for*

quart mould.—1 lobster, 3 eggs, ¼ pint of cream, ½ pint of milk, a cupful of bread crumbs, 2 teaspoonfuls of anchovy sauce, a little cagenne. AVERAGE COST, 2s. 6d.

Boil the milk and pour it over the bread-crumbs, chop the lobster fine and beat the eggs ; and when the crumbs are nearly cold, mix with them ; add the sauce, the season-ing and lastly the cream. Butter a mould, fill it with the mixture, put a buttered paper over the top and steam for an hour. Any good fish sauce may be served with this.

TIME.—1 *hour to steam.*

SEASONABLE *at any time.*

Lobster Curry. (An Entrée.)—IN-

GREDIENTS *for dish for 4 persons.*—1 lobster, 2 onions, 1 oz. of butter, 1 tablespoonful of curry-powder, ½ pint of medium stock, the juice of ½ lemon. AVERAGE COST, 2s. 6d.

Pick the meat from the shell and cut into nice square pieces ; fry the onions of a pale brown in the butter, stir in the curry-powder and stock and simmer till it thickens, when put in the lobster : stew the whole slowly for ½ hour, stirring occasionally ; and just before sending to table, put in the lemon-juice. Serve boiled rice with it, the same as for other curries.

TIME.—*Altogether* ¾ *hour.*

SEASONABLE *at any time.*

Lobster Cutlets. (An Entrée.)—

INGREDIENTS *for dish for 6 persons.*—1 large hen lobster, 1 oz. of fresh butter, ½ salt-spoonful of salt, pounded mace, grated

2 A

nutmeg, cayenne and white pepper to taste, egg and bread-crumbs. AVERAGE COST, 3s. 6d.

Pick the meat from the shell and pound it in a mortar, with the butter and gradu-

THE LOBSTER.

ally add the mace and seasoning, well mixing the ingredients: beat all to a smooth paste and add a little of the spawn; divide the mixture into pieces of an equal size and shape them like cutlets. They should not be very thick. Brush them over with egg and sprinkle with bread-crumbs and stick a short piece of the small claw in the top of each, fry them a nice brown in boiling lard and drain them before the fire on a sieve reversed; arrange them nicely on a dish and pour béchamel in the middle, but not over the cutlets.

TIME.—About 8 minutes after the cutlets are made.

SEASONABLE all the year.

Lobster, Devilled.— INGREDIENTS for dish for 4 persons. —1 medium-sized lobster, some salad dressing, finely-grated bread-crumbs, cayenne. AVERAGE COST, 2s. 6d.

Make a salad dressing, using butter in place of oil, season this well with cayenne and add it to the lobster, chopped fine and a small teacupful of bread-crumbs. Clean the shell and put the mixture in, putting bread-crumbs and a small piece of butter on the top; then bake for about 10 minutes till the crumbs are brown.

TIME.—About 10 minutes.

SEASONABLE at any time.

Lobsters, To Dress.—When the lobster is boiled, rub it over with a little salad oil, which wipe off again; separate the body from the tail, break off the great claws and crack them at the joints, without injuring the meat, split the tail in halves and arrange all neatly in a dish, with the body upright in the middle and garnish with parsley.

Lobster, Hot. — INGREDIENTS for dish for 4 or 5 persons.—1 lobster, 2 oz. of butter, grated nutmeg; salt, pepper and pounded mace to taste; bread-crumbs, 2 eggs. AVERAGE COST, 2s. 6d.

Pound the meat of the lobster to a smooth paste with the butter and seasoning and add a few bread-crumbs. Beat the eggs and make the whole mixture into the form of a lobster; pound the spawn and sprinkle over it. Bake ¼ hour; and just before serving, lay over it the tail and body shell, with the small claws underneath to resemble a lobster.

TIME.—¼ hour.

SEASONABLE at any time.

Lobster Mayonnaise.— INGREDIENTS for dish for 6 persons.—1 large or 2 small lobsters, 1 pint of aspic jelly, 3 hard-boiled eggs, a large lettuce, a few tarragon leaves, capers, truffles (if procurable), stoned olives, pepper and salt, mayonnaise sauce. AVERAGE COST, 3s. 6d.

Put enough melted jelly into a quart border mould as will thinly coat it; and when it begins to set, arrange in it the flesh of the body and claws of the lobster, cut into neat pieces, the tarragon leaves, tiny pieces of the truffle and a few capers; then fill up the mould with jelly. When firmly set, turn out of the mould and fill the centre with the lettuce cut up with the remainder of the lobster. Put a little salad round the mould and mask both that and what is in the centre with a good mayonnaise sauce. Garnish with the truffles sliced the eggs and the small claws of the lobster.

SEASONABLE at any time.

Lobster Patties. — INGREDIENT for 8 patties.—A medium-sized lobster, tablespoonfuls of Béchamel, 6 drops o

anchovy sauce, lemon-juice, cayenne to taste. AVERAGE COST, with the paste, 2s. 9d.

Line the patty-pans with puff-paste and put into each a small piece of bread, cover with paste, brush over with egg and bake of a light colour. Take as much lobster as is required, mince the meat very fine and add the above ingredients; stir it over the fire for 5 minutes; remove the lids of the patty-cases, take out the bread, fill with the mixture and replace the covers.

SEASONABLE at any time.

Lobster, Potted.—INGREDIENTS.—

2 lobsters; seasoning to taste of nutmeg, pounded mace, white pepper and salt; ¼ lb. of butter, 3 or 4 bay-leaves. AVERAGE COST, 4s.

Take out the meat carefully from the shell, but do not cut it up. Put some butter at the bottom of a dish, lay in the lobster as evenly as possible, with the bay-leaves and seasoning between. Cover with butter and bake for ¾ hour in a gentle oven. When done, drain the whole on a sieve and lay the pieces in potting-jars, with the seasoning about them. When cold, pour over it clarified butter; and, if very highly seasoned, it will keep some time.

TIME.—¾ hour.

SEASONABLE at any time.

Note.—Potted lobster may be used cold, or as a fricassee; with cream sauce.

Lobster (à la Mode Française).

—INGREDIENTS for dish for 4 persons.—1 lobster, 4 tablespoonfuls of white stock, 2 tablespoonfuls of cream, pounded mace and cayenne to taste; bread-crumbs. AVERAGE COST, 2s. 6d.

Pick the meat from the shell and cut it up into small square pieces; put the stock, cream and seasoning into a stewpan, add the lobster and let it simmer gently for 6 minutes. Serve it in the shell, which must be nicely cleaned and have a border of puff-paste; cover it with bread-crumbs, place small pieces of butter over and brown before the fire, or with a salamander.

TIME.—½ hour.

SEASONABLE at any time.

Lobster Salad.—INGREDIENTS for

dish for 6 persons.—1 hen lobster, 1 lettuce, endive, small salad (whatever is in season), a little chopped beetroot, 2 hard-boiled eggs, a few slices of cucumber. For dressing, 4 tablespoonfuls of oil, 2 do. of vinegar, 1 teaspoonful of made mustard, the yolks of 2 eggs; cayenne and salt to taste; ¼ teaspoonful of anchovy sauce. These ingredients should be mixed perfectly smooth and form a creamy-looking sauce. AVERAGE COST, 3s.

Wash the salad and thoroughly dry it by shaking it in a cloth. Cut up the lettuces and endive, pour the dressing on them and

LOBSTER SALAD.

lightly throw in the small salad. Mix all well together with the pickings from the body of the lobster; pick the meat from the shell, cut it up into nice square pieces, put half in the salad, the other half reserve for garnishing. Separate the yolks from the whites of 2 hard-boiled eggs; chop the whites very fine and rub the yolks through a sieve and afterwards the coral from the inside. Arrange the salad lightly on a glass dish and garnish, first with a row of sliced cucumber, then with the pieces of lobster, the yolks and whites of eggs, coral and beetroot placed alternately and arranged in small separate bunches, so that the colours contrast nicely.

SEASONABLE from April to October; may be had all the year, but salad is scarce and expensive in winter.

Note.—A few crayfish make a pretty garnish for lobster salad.

Lobster Sauce (to Serve with Turbot, Salmon, Brill, &c.; very Good).—INGREDIENTS *for sauce for a turbot or brill.*—1 *middling-sized hen lobster,* ¾ *pint of melted butter,* 1 *tablespoonful of anchovy sauce,* ½ *oz. of butter, salt and cayenne to taste, a little pounded mace when liked,* 2 *or* 3 *tablespoonfuls of cream.* AVERAGE COST, 2s.

Choose a hen lobster, as this is indispensable, in order to render this sauce as good as it ought to be. Pick the meat from the shells and cut it into small square pieces; put the spawn, which will be found under the tail of the lobster. into a mortar, with ½ oz. of butter and pound it quite smooth; rub it through a hair-sieve and cover up till wanted. Make ¾ pint of melted butter; put in all the ingredients except the lobster-meat and well mix the sauce before the lobster is added to it, as it should retain its square form and not come to table shredded and ragged. Put in the meat, let it get thoroughly hot, but do not allow it to boil, as the colour would immediately be spoiled; for it must be remembered that this sauce should always have a bright red appearance. If it is intended to be served with turbot or brill, a little of the spawn (dried and rubbed through a sieve without butter) should be saved to garnish with; but as the goodness, flavour and appearance of the sauce so much depend on having a proper quantity of spawn, the less used for garnishing the better.

TIME.—1 *minute to simmer.*

SEASONABLE *at any time.*

Note.—Melted butter made with milk will be found to answer very well for lobster sauce, as by employing it a nice white colour will be obtained. Less quantity than the above may be made by using a very small lobster, to which add only ⅓ pint of melted butter and season as above. Where economy is desired, the cream may be dispensed with and the remains of a cold lobster left from table may, with a little care, be converted into a very good sauce.

Lobster Soup.—INGREDIENTS *for soup for* 12 *persons.*—2 *large lobsters or* 6 *small ones; the crumb of a French roll,* 2 *anchovies,* 1 *onion,* 1 *small bunch of sweet herbs,* 1 *strip of lemon-peel,* 2 *oz. of butter, a little nutmeg,* 1 *teaspoonful of flour,* 1 *pint of cream,* 1 *pint of milk; forcemeat balls, mace, salt and pepper to taste, breadcrumbs,* 1 *egg,* 5 *pints of water.* AVERAGE COST, 7s. 6d.

Pick the meat from the lobsters and beat the fins, chine and small claws in a mortar, previously taking away the brown fin and the bag in the head. Put it in a stewpan, with the crumb of the roll, anchovies,

LOBSTER CUT UP.

onions, herbs, lemon-peel and the water; simmer gently till all the goodness is extracted and strain it off. Pound the spawn in a mortar, with the butter, nutmeg and flour and mix with it the cream and milk. Give one boil up, at the same time adding the tails cut in pieces. Make the forcemeat balls with the remainder of the lobster, seasoned with mace, pepper and salt, adding a little flour and a few breadcrumbs; moisten them wih the egg, heat them in the soup and serve.

TIME.—2 *hours or rather more.*

SEASONABLE *from April to October.*

Luncheon. — This is of all meals the most informal. Whether it be one of several courses, a dinner in all but the name, or simply a crust of bread and cheese, depends (or should depend) upon the times chosen for other meals. It should be but a slight repast, unless the dinner hour be very late; but by individual tastes, habits and pursuits, it must be regulated.

Some people consider two meals per diem all that is necessary, and take nothing between a substantial breakfast and a good late dinner; others cannot fast so long, nor would it be healthful for them to do so, but a *very* substantial meal can scarcely be needed by any. In some households the early, or children's dinner, furnishes the staple dish, in all probability a plain joint;

NAUTILUS STAND.

but in high-class houses it is usual to have a good repast, consisting of several savoury dishes and sweets, besides such things as cold game or poultry, or fish. In too many instances, however, cold meat is served, if not daily, yet continually, as giving less trouble than anything else. Where it does not matter how heavy the butcher's bill may be, this may be immaterial, but still cold meat is monotonous and unattractive to many, whereas some small dish that costs but little, except the time of its preparation, would save the joint and please most tastes better. In winter a basin of plain soup forms a nice luncheon, nourishing but still not heavy food, a few rissoles, for which remains of meat or poultry, otherwise unpresentable, might serve, a pie made from cold fish and potatoes, a vegetable stew or pie (excellent ways in which

to re-serve cold vegetables), might make a pleasant change.

SHELL VASE.

We have spoken of the hot joints for the children's dinner, which may also serve for that of servants; but where it is only for the latter, it seems scarcely fair to have it first served and cooled in the dining-room, so that the principal meal in the kitchen comes to its occupants scarcely worth the eating.

Whatever the luncheon be, however, it is an almost invariable rule that less attend-

FINGER GLASS.

ance is exacted than at any other meal; and for that reason it should be carefully impressed upon those who arrange and lay the cloth for the meal, that everything, save hot dishes, should be brought into the room that is likely to be required. Some little decoration should be found for the luncheon-table, such as a pot of fern or a few flowers. On the sideboard should be placed a supply of extra plates, knives, forks and glasses; and cut bread should also be there.

We give four menus for guests' luncheons, two for summer and two for winter, as well as two for picnics that may be useful.

Luncheons for Guests.

Summer.

1.

Mayonnaise of Salmon.

Beef Rissoles.
Cold Lamb.
Mashed Potatoes. Salad.

Cold Fruit Tart.
Custard.
Liqueur Jelly.

Strawberries and Cream.

2.

Fish Salad.

Cold Chicken.
Tongue.
Cucumber.
Veal Cutlets.

Compôte of Fruit.
Tartlets.
Custard Pudding.

Winter.

1.

Julienne.

Scalloped Oysters.

Mutton Cutlets.
Hashed Turkey.
Fried Potatoes.

Amber Pudding.
Stewed Prunes.

Pears. Dried Fruits.

2.

Mock Turtle Soup.

Steak and Mushrooms.
Cold Pheasant.
Potatoes.

Cold Plum Pudding.
Apple Tart.

Apples. Grapes.

Picnic Luncheons.

For Twelve Persons.

Cold Salmon,
Tartar Sauce.
Cucumber.

Quarter of Lamb,
Mint Sauce. Salad.
Pigeon Pie.

Fruit Tarts. Cream.
Jelly.

Cheese Biscuits.

Strawberries.

For Eight Persons.

Lobsters.

Chickens. Tongue.
Small Veal Pie
Salad.

Pastry Sandwiches.
Blancmange.

Cheese. Celery.

Strawberries.
Cream.

Wine, bottled beer, lemonade, soda-water, bread, butter, castor sugar, salt, pepper, mustard, salad dressing, oil, vinegar, plates, knives, forks, spoons, wine-glasses, tumblers, table cloth, serviettes, glass cloths, corkscrews.

> *" Man is a carnivorous production,*
> *And must have meals—at least one meal a day."*—BYRON.

MACARONI (as usually served with the Cheese Course).—I.—INGREDIENTS *for dish for 6 persons.* —½ *lb. of pipe macaroni*, 2 *oz. of butter*, 6 *oz. of Parmesan or Cheshire cheese, pepper and salt to taste, water, bread-crumbs.* AVERAGE COST, 1s.

Put about 3 pints of water into a saucepan with sufficient salt to flavour it; place it on the fire and, when it boils quickly, drop in the macaroni, broken up. Keep the water boiling until it is quite tender; drain the macaroni and put it into a shallow dish. Have ready the grated cheese, either Parmesan or Cheshire; sprinkle it amongst the macaroni and some of the butter cut into small pieces, reserving some of the cheese for the top layer. Season with a little pepper, or cayenne and cover the top layer of cheese with some very fine bread-crumbs. Warm, without oiling, the remainder of the butter and pour it

gently over the bread-crumbs. Place the dish before a bright fire, to brown the crumbs; turn it once or twice, that it may be equally coloured and serve very hot. The top of the macaroni may be browned with a salamander, which is even better than placing it before the fire, as the process is more expeditious; but it should never be browned in the oven, as the butter would oil and so impart a very disagreeable flavour to the dish. In boiling the macaroni let it be perfectly tender, but firm, no part beginning to melt and the form entirely preserved. It may be boiled in plain water, with a little salt, instead of using milk, but should then have a small piece of butter mixed with it.

TIME.—1 *to* 1½ *hour to boil the macaroni*, 5 *minutes to brown it before the fire.*

SEASONABLE *at any time.*

Note.—Riband macaroni may be dressed in the same manner, but does not require boiling so long a time.

Macaroni (as usually served with the Cheese Course). —II. — INGREDIENTS *for dish for 6 persons.*—¼ *lb. of pipe or riband macaroni*, ½ *pint of milk*, ½ *pint of veal or* *beef gravy, the yolks of 2 eggs, 4 tablespoonfuls of cream, 3 oz. of grated Parmesan or Cheshire cheese, 1 oz. of butter.* AVERAGE COST, 1s. 3d.

Wash the macaroni and boil it in the gravy and milk until quite tender, without being broken. Drain it and put it into a rather deep dish. Beat the yolks of the eggs with the cream and 2 tablespoonfuls of the liquor the macaroni was boiled in; make this sufficiently hot to thicken, but do not allow it to boil; pour it over the macaroni, over which sprinkle the grated cheese and the butter, broken into small pieces; brown with a salamander, or before the fire and serve.

TIME.—1 to 1½ hour to boil the macaroni, 5 minutes to thicken the eggs and cream, 5 minutes to brown.

SEASONABLE *at any time.*

Macaroni (as usually served with the Cheese Course).—III.— INGREDIENTS *for dish for 4 persons.—¼ lb. of pipe macaroni, ½ pint of brown gravy, 6 oz. of grated Parmesan cheese.* AVERAGE COST, 9d.

Wash the macaroni and boil it in salt water until quite tender; drain it and put it into a rather deep dish. Have ready a pint of good brown gravy, pour it hot over the macaroni and send it to table with grated Parmesan served on a separate dish. When the flavour is liked, a little pounded mace may be added to the water in which the macaroni is boiled; but this must always be sparingly added, as it will impart a very strong flavour.

TIME.—1 to 1½ hour to boil the macaroni.

SEASONABLE *at any time.*

Macaroni Pudding, Sweet.— INGREDIENTS *for pudding for 6 persons.—2½ oz. of macaroni, 2 pints of milk, the rind of ½ lemon, 3 eggs, sugar and grated nutmeg to taste, 2 tablespoonfuls of brandy.* AVERAGE COST, 1s.

Put the macaroni, with a pint of the milk, into a saucepan, with the lemon-peel and let it simmer gently until the macaroni is tender; then put it into a pie-dish without the peel; mix the other pint of milk with the eggs; stir these well together, adding the sugar and brandy and pour the mixture over the macaroni. Grate a little nutmeg over the top and bake in a moderate oven for ½ hour.

MACARONI.

To make this pudding look nice, a paste should be laid round the edges of the dish and, for variety, a layer of preserve or marmalade may be placed on the macaroni: in this case, omit the brandy.

TIME.—1 hour to simmer the macaroni, ½ hour to bake the pudding.

SEASONABLE *at any time.*

Macaroni Soup. — INGREDIENTS *for soup for 8 persons.—3 oz. of macaroni, a piece of butter the size of a walnut, salt to taste, 2 quarts of clear stock.* AVERAGE COST, 1s. 9d.

Throw the macaroni and butter into boiling water, with a pinch of salt and simmer for ¼ an hour. When it is tender, drain and cut it into thin rings or lengths and drop it into the boiling stock. Stew gently for 15 minutes and serve grated Parmesan cheese with it.

TIME.—¾ to 1 hour.

SEASONABLE *all the year.*

Macaroni, A Sweet Dish of.— INGREDIENTS *for dish for 4 or 5 persons.— ¼ lb. of macaroni, 1½ pint of milk, the rind of ½ lemon, 3 oz. of lump sugar, ¾ pint of custard.* AVERAGE COST, 1s.

Put the milk into a saucepan, with the lemon-peel and sugar; bring it to the boiling point, drop in the macaroni and let it gradually swell over a gentle fire, but do not allow the pipes to break. The form should be entirely preserved and, though tender, should be firm and not soft, with no part beginning to melt. Should the milk dry away before the macaroni is sufficiently swelled, add a little more. Make a custard, place the macaroni on a dish and pour the custard over the hot macaroni; grate over a little nutmeg and, when cold, garnish the dish with slices of candied citron.

TIME.—*From* 40 *to* 50 *minutes to swell the macaroni.*

SEASONABLE *at any time.*

Macaroni and Pine-apple.—

INGREDIENTS *for dish for* 6 *persons.*—1 *pint of any clear jelly,* ½ *tin of preserved pine-apple,* 3 *oz. of loaf sugar,* 6 *oz. of macaroni, milk, cochineal.* AVERAGE COST, 2s.

Boil the macaroni in milk till tender, sweetening it with sugar. Melt the jelly and coat a wetted border mould with it; and in this arrange the pine drained from the syrup and cut in dice. Colour what is left of the jelly with the cochineal and fill up the mould with it; and when the jelly is set, turn it out and fill in the centre with the macaroni, with a good custard poured over.

SEASONABLE *at any time.*

Macaroons.—INGREDIENTS. — ½ *lb.*

of sweet almonds, ½ *lb. of sifted loaf sugar, the whites of* 3 *eggs, wafer paper.* AVERAGE COST, 10d.

Blanch, skin and dry the almonds and pound them well with a little orange-flower or plain water; then add the sifted

MACAROONS.

sugar and the whites of the eggs, which should be beaten to a stiff froth; and mix all the ingredients well together. When the paste looks soft, drop it at equal dis-

tances on to sheets of wafer paper: put a strip of almond on the top of each; strew some syrup over and bake the macaroons in rather a slow oven, of a light brown colour. When hard and set, they are done. They must not be allowed to get very brown, as that would spoil their appearance.

TIME.—*From* 15 *to* 20 *minutes.*

Mackerel.—In choosing this fish,

purchasers should, to a great extent, be regulated by the brightness of its appearance. If it have a transparent, silvery hue, the flesh is good; but if it be red about the head, it is stale.

Mackerel, Baked.—INGREDIENTS

for dish for 8 *persons.*—4 *mackerel, a nice delicate forcemeat,* 3 *oz. of butter; pepper and salt to taste.* AVERAGE COST, 2s.

Clean the fish, take out the roes and fill up with forcemeat and sew up the slit.

MACKEREL.

Flour and put them in a dish, heads and tails alternately, with the roes; and between each layer put some little pieces of butter and pepper and salt. Bake for ½ an hour and either serve with plain melted butter or a maître d'hôtel sauce.

TIME.—½ *hour.*

SEASONABLE *from April to July.*

Note.—Baked mackerel may be dressed in the same way as baked herrings and may also be stewed in wine.

Mackerel, Boiled. — INGREDI-

ENTS.—*Mackerel,* ¼ *lb. of salt to each gallon of water.* AVERAGE COST, 4d. *each.*

Cleanse the inside of the fish thoroughly, and lay it in the kettle, with sufficient water to cover it, with salt as above; bring them gradually to boil, skim well and simmer gently till done ; dish them on a hot napkin, heads and tails alternately, and garnish with fennel. Fennel sauce and plain melted butter are the usual accompaniments to boiled mackerel ; but caper or anchovy sauce is sometimes served with it.

TIME.—*After the water boils*, 10 *minutes ; for large mackerel allow more time.*

SEASONABLE *from April to July.*

Note.—When variety is desired, fillet the mackerel, boil it and pour over parsley and butter ; send some of this to table in a tureen.

Mackerel, Broiled. — INGREDI-ENTS.—*Mackerel, pepper and salt to taste, a small quantity of oil.* AVERAGE COST, 4d. *each.*

Mackerel should never be washed when intended to be broiled, but merely wiped very clean and dry, after taking out the gills and insides. Open the back and put in a little pepper, salt and oil ; broil it over a clear fire, turn it over on both sides and also on the back. When sufficiently cooked, the flesh can be detached from the bone, which will be in about 10 minutes for a small mackerel. Chop a little parsley, work it up in the butter, with pepper and salt to taste and a squeeze of lemon-juice and put it in the back. Serve before the butter is quite melted, with a maître d'hôtel sauce in a tureen.

TIME.—*Small mackerel*, 10 *minutes.*

SEASONABLE *from April to July.*

Mackerel, Fillets of. — INGREDI-ENTS *for dish for 4 or 5 persons.*—2 *large mackerel*, 1 *oz. of butter*, 1 *small bunch of chopped herbs*, 3 *tablespoonfuls of medium stock*, 3 *tablespoonfuls of Béchamel; salt, cayenne and lemon-juice to taste.* AVERAGE COST, 1s. 6d.

Clean the fish and fillet it ; scald the herbs, chop them fine and put them, with the butter and stock, into a stewpan. Lay in the mackerel and simmer very gently for 10 minutes ; take them out and put them

on a hot dish. Dredge in a little flour, add the other ingredients, give one boil and pour it over the mackerel.

TIME.—20 *minutes.*

SEASONABLE *from April to July.*

Note.—Fillets of mackerel may be covered with egg and bread-crumbs and fried of a nice brown. Serve with maître d'hôtel sauce or plain melted butter.

Mackerel, Pickled. — INGREDI-ENTS.—4 *mackerel*, 12 *peppercorns*, 2 *bay-leaves*, ½ *pint of vinegar.* AVERAGE COST 1s. 6d.

Boil the mackerel and lay them in a dish ; take half the liquor they were boiled in add as much vinegar, peppercorns and bay-leaves ; boil for 10 minutes and when cold pour over the fish.

TIME.—½ *hour.*

Mackerel, Potted.—INGREDIENTS —*Mackerel, a blade of mace, cayenne, salt and 2 oz. or more of butter, according to the quantity of mackerel.*

Any remains of cooked mackerel may be potted as follows : pick it well from the bones, break it into very small pieces and put into a stewpan with the butter, pounded mace and other ingredients ; warm it thoroughly, but do not let it boil ; press it into potting pots and pour clarified butter over it.

Madeira Cake.—INGREDIENTS *for large cake.*—¾ lb. *of butter*, 1½ lb. *of flour*, ½ lb. *of castor sugar*, *rind of* 1 *lemon*, 6 *eggs* 2 *oz. of candied peel.* AVERAGE COST 2s. 3d.

Beat the butter to a cream and dredge in the flour, then the sugar and grated lemon rind, lastly the eggs, well whisked. Beat the mixture well and put into a buttered tin ; garnish the top with the peel cut in thin slices and bake in a hot oven from 1½ to 2 hours.

TIME.—1½ *to 2 hours.*

SEASONABLE *at any time.*

Maigre Maitre d'Hôtel Sauce

Hot; made without Meat).—INGREDIENTS.
—½ pint of melted butter, 1 heaped tablespoonful of chopped parsley, salt and pepper
to taste, the juice of ½ large lemon; when
liked, 2 minced shalots. AVERAGE COST,
6d.

Make ½ pint of melted butter, stir in the
above ingredients and let them just boil;
when it is ready to serve.

TIME.—1 minute to simmer.

Maigre Soup (i.e., Soup without

Meat).— INGREDIENTS for soup for 12 persons.—6 oz. of butter, 6 onions, sliced, 4
heads of celery, 2 lettuces, small bunch of
parsley, 2 handfuls of spinach, a few pieces
of bread-crust, 2 blades of mace, salt and
pepper to taste, the yolks of 2 eggs, 3 teaspoonfuls of vinegar, 3 quarts of water.
AVERAGE COST, 1s. 10d.

Melt the butter in a stewpan and put in
the onions to stew gently for 3 or 4 minutes;
then add the celery, spinach, lettuces and
parsley cut small. Stir the ingredients
well for 10 minutes. Now put in the water,
bread, seasoning and mace. Boil gently
for 1½ hour; and at the moment of serving,
beat in the yolks of the eggs and the
vinegar, but do not let it boil, or the eggs
will curdle.

TIME.—2 hours.
SEASONABLE all the year.

Maître d'Hôtel Sauce (Hot;

to serve with Calf's Head, Boiled Eels and
different Fish).—INGREDIENTS for sauce
for dish of medium size.—1 slice of minced
ham, a few poultry trimmings, 2 shalots,
1 clove of garlic, 1 bay-leaf, ¾ pint of water,
2 oz. of butter, 1 dessertspoonful of flour,
1 heaped tablespoonful of chopped parsley;
salt, pepper and cayenne to taste; the juice
of ½ large lemon, ¼ teaspoonful of pounded
sugar. AVERAGE COST, 7d.

Put at the bottom of a stewpan the
minced ham and over it the poultry-trim-

mings (if these are not at hand, veal should
be substituted), with the shalots, garlic
and bay-leaf. Pour in the water and let
the whole simmer gently for 1 hour, or
until the liquor is reduced to a full half
pint.

Then strain this gravy, put it in another
saucepan, make a thickening of butter and
flour in the above proportions and stir it
to the gravy over a nice clear fire, until it
is perfectly smooth and rather thick, care
being taken that the butter does not float
on the surface. Skim well, add the remaining ingredients, let the sauce gradually
heat, but do not allow it to boil. If this
sauce is intended for an entrée, it is necessary to make it of a sufficient thickness, so
that it may adhere to what it is meant to
cover.

Maize Meal or Hominy.—Maize

meal is a preparation, like cornflour, of
starch prepared from maize or Indian
corn, the husk and gluten being separated
by grinding and the action of water. It
is a heat-giver—being nearly all starch—
and not a flesh-former and should therefore, as an article of food, be taken with
milk.

Maize is a native American grass now
grown largely in America, Africa and
Southern States. In the whole ear it is
called a cob and is in America roasted and
eaten as a vegetable, as which it is extremely good; in its grown state it is
known, when boiled, in the United States
as Mush and in Italy as Polenta.

CONSTITUENT PARTS OF 1 LB. OF
MAIZE.

					ozs.	grs.
Water	...	...	...	...	2	140
Fibrine, &c.	...	...	...	...	1	193
Starch, &c.	...	...	...	...	11	51
Fat	...	...	...	...	0	350
Mineral Matter	...	...	...		0	140
					16	0

Maize, Boiled.—Ingredients.—

The ears of young and green Indian wheat; to every ½ gallon of water allow 1 heaped tablespoonful of salt.

MAIZE PLANT.

This vegetable, which makes one of the most delicious dishes brought to table, is unfortunately very rarely seen in Britain; and we wonder that it is not more often cultivated. Our sun, it is true, possesses hardly power sufficient to ripen maize; but, with well-prepared ground and in a favourable position, it might be sufficiently advanced by the beginning of autumn to serve as a vegetable. The outside sheath being taken off and the waving fibres removed, let the ears be placed in boiling water, where they should remain for about 25 minutes (a longer time may be necessary for larger ears than ordinary) ; and, when sufficiently boiled and well drained, they may be sent to table whole and with a piece of toast underneath them. Melted butter should be served with them.

TIME.—25 *to* 35 *minutes.*
SEASONABLE *in autumn.*

Maizena Pudding.—Ingredients

for pudding for 3 persons.—2 *tablespoonfuls of maizena,* 1 *tablespoonful of moist sugar,* 1 *egg,* 1½ *pint of milk.* AVERAGE COST, 4½*d.*

Mix the maizena into a paste with a little cold milk, put the rest of the milk in a saucepan over the fire and when it boils pour it on the paste, stir in the egg and sugar, pour in a deep dish and bake for 15 to 20 minutes.

TIME.—15 *minutes to bake.*
SEASONABLE *at any time.*

Malt Wine.—Ingredients.—5 *gallons of water,* 28 *lbs. of sugar,* 6 *quarts of sweet-wort,* 6 *quarts of tun,* 3 *lbs. of raisins,* ½ *lb. of candy,* 1 *pint of brandy.*

Boil the sugar and water together for 10 minutes; skim it well and put the liquor into a convenient-sized pan or tub. Allow it to cool; then mix it with the sweet-wort and tun. Let it stand for 3 days, then put it into a barrel; here it will work or ferment for another three days or more; then bung up the cask and keep it undisturbed for 2 or 3 months. After this add the raisins (whole), the candy and brandy and, in 6 months' time bottle the wine off. Those who do not brew, may procure the sweet-wort and tun from any brewer. Sweet-wort is the liquor that leaves the mash of malt before it is boiled with the hops; tun is the new beer after the whole of the brewing operation has been completed.

TIME.—*To be boiled* 10 *minutes; to stand* 3 *days after mixing; to ferment* 3 *days; to remain in the cask* 2 *months before the raisins are added; bottle* 6 *month after.*

SEASONABLE.—*Make this in March or October.*

Manchester Pudding (to eat Cold).—Ingredients *for pudding for 6 persons.*—3 *oz. of grated bread,* ½ *pint of milk, a strip of lemon-peel,* 4 *eggs,* 2 *oz. of butter, sugar to taste, puff-paste, jam,* 3 *tablespoonfuls of brandy.* AVERAGE COST, 1*s.* 2*d.*

Flavour the milk with lemon-peel, by infusing it in the milk for ½ hour; then strain it on to the bread-crumbs and boil it for 2 or 3 minutes; add the eggs, leaving out the whites of 2, the butter, sugar and brandy ; stir all these ingredients well together ; border a pie-dish with puff-paste and at the bottom put a thick layer of any kind of jam ; pour the above mixture, cold, on the jam and bake the pudding for an hour. Serve cold, with a little sifted sugar sprinkled over.

TIME.—1 *hour.*

SEASONABLE *at any time.*

Manna Kroup Pudding.— INGREDIENTS *for pudding for 4 or 5 persons.* — 3 *tablespoonfuls of manna kroup,* 12 *bitter almonds,* 1 *pint of milk, sugar to taste,* 3 *eggs.* AVERAGE COST, 8*d.*

Blanch and pound the almonds in a mortar ; mix them with the manna kroup ; pour over these a pint of boiling milk and let them steep for about ¼ hour. When nearly cold, add sugar and the well-beaten eggs ; mix all well together ; put the pudding into a buttered dish and bake for ½ hour.

TIME.—½ *hour.*

SEASONABLE *at any time.*

Mansfield Pudding. —INGREDIENTS *for large pudding.*—The crumb of 2 rolls, 1 *pint of milk, sugar to taste,* 4 *eggs,* 2 *tablespoonfuls of brandy,* 6 *oz. of chopped suet,* 2 *tablespoonfuls of flour,* ½ *lb. of currants,* ½ *teaspoonful of grated nutmeg,* 2 *tablespoonfuls of cream.* AVERAGE COST, 1*s.* 8*d.*

Slice the roll very thin and pour upon it a pint of boiling milk ; let it remain closely covered for ¼ hour, then beat it up with a fork and sweeten with moist sugar ; stir in the chopped suet, flour, currants and nutmeg. Mix these ingredients well together, moisten with the eggs, brandy and cream ; beat the mixture for 2 or 3 minutes, put it into a buttered dish or mould and bake in a moderate oven for 1½ hour. Turn it out, strew sifted sugar over and serve.

TIME.—1¼ *hour.*

SEASONABLE *at any time.*

Marbled Jelly.—INGREDIENTS *for quart shape.*—A quart of any clear sweet jelly, pistachio nuts, cochineal. AVERAGE COST, 2*s.* 6*d.*

Wet a quart mould, coat it with the clear jelly and set a little near the fire, then divide the remainder into 4 basins. Into one put sufficient finely-chopped pistachio nuts to make the jelly green ; colour another red with the cochineal ; leave two plain. When cool, beat one of the plain jellies to a white froth, then with a fork throw lumps of each jelly in turn into the mould, and when full, fill up with the clear melted jelly saved at first. The jelly, when turned out, should have a pretty marbled appearance.

SEASONABLE *at any time.*

Marlborough Pudding. — INGREDIENTS *for pudding of moderate size.*— ¼ lb. of butter, ¼ lb. of powdered lump sugar, 4 *eggs, puff-paste, a layer of any kind of jam.* AVERAGE COST, 1*s.* 2*d.*

Beat the butter to a cream, stir in the powdered sugar, whisk the eggs and add these to the other ingredients. When these are well mixed, line a dish with puff-paste, spread over a layer of any kind of jam that may be preferred, pour in the mixture and bake the pudding for rather more than ½ hour.

TIME.—*Rather more than ½ hour*

SEASONABLE *at any time.*

Marmalade and Vermicelli Pudding.—INGREDIENTS *for pudding for 6 persons.*—1 *breakfastcupful of vermicelli,* 2 *tablespoonfuls of marmalade,* ¼ *lb. of raisins, sugar to taste,* 3 *eggs, milk.* AVERAGE COST, 10*d.*

Pour some boiling milk on the vermicelli and let it remain covered for 10 minutes ; then mix with it the marmalade, stoned raisins, sugar and beaten eggs. Stir all well together, put the mixture into a buttered mould, boil for 1½ hour and serve with custard sauce.

TIME.—1½ *hour.*

SEASONABLE *at any time.*

March—Dinner for Twelve Persons.

MENU. (*English*.)	Quantity.	Average Cost.		MENU. (*French*.)
		s.	*d.*	
Oyster Soup.	2 qts.	6	0	Potage aux Huîtres.
Salmon,	1 fish.	9	0	Saumon,
Tartar Sauce. Cucumber.		1	6	Sauce Tartare. Concombres.
Sweetbreads.	2 dishes.	5	0	Ris de Veau.
Beef Olives.	2 dishes.	3	0	Olives de Bœuf.
Quarter of Lamb.	1 joint.	9	0	Quartier d'Agneau.
Potatoes. Cauliflowers.	2 dishes.	1	4	Pommes de Terre. Choufleur.
Larded Guinea-fowls.	2 birds.	7	0	Pintades Bardées.
Apricot Omelette.	2 dishes.	2	0	Omelette d'Abricots.
Vanilla Cream.	2 mlds.	2	6	Crême de Vanille.
Cheese Biscuits.	2 dishes.	0	8	Biscuits de Fromage.
		£2 7	0	

March—Dinner for Ten Persons.

MENU. (*English*.)	Quantity.	Average Cost.		MENU. (*French*.)
		s.	*d.*	
Julienne Soup.	3½ pints.	2	6	Julienne.
Salmon.	3 lbs.	6	0	Saumon.
Whitebait.	3 pints.	3	6	Blanchailles.
Fried Sweetbreads.	1 dish.	4	0	Ris de Veau Frits.
Chicken Cutlets.	1 dish.	3	6	Côtelettes de Volaille.
Leg of Mutton.	1 joint.	7	0	Gigot de Mouton.
Potatoes. Sea Kale.		2	0	Pommes de Terre. Choux Marins.
Ptarmigan.	2 birds.	3	0	Ptarmigans.
Coburg Pudding.	1	2	6	Pouding à la Coburg.
Swiss Cream.	1 mould.	2	0	Crême.
		£1 16	0	

March—Dinner for Eight Persons.

MENU. (*English*.)	Quantity.	Average Cost.		MENU. (*French*.)
		s.	*d.*	
Spring Soup.	3 pints.	2	0	Printanière.
Fried Whiting.	8 fish.	3	0	Merlans Frits.
Stewed Sweetbread.	1 dish.	4	6	Ris de Veau à la Crême.
Leg of Lamb.	1 joint.	5	6	Gigot d'Agneau.
Potatoes. Savoy.	3 lbs. 1	0	6	Pommes de Terre. Choux.
Ptarmigan.	2 birds.	3	6	Ptarmigans.
Rhubarb Tart.	1	1	3	Tourte à la Rhubarbe.
Cream.	½ pint.	0	9	Crême.
Lemon Jelly.	1 mould.	1	6	Gelée à la Citron.
		£1 2	6	

March—Dinners for from Six to Twelve Persons.

Menu

Ox-Tail Soup.

Soles, with Cream Sauce.
Rissolettes of Hare.

Saddle of Mutton.
Potatoes.
Spinach.

Ducklings.

Maraschino Jelly.
Iced Pudding.

Menu

Vermicelli Soup.

Skate,
Caper Sauce.

Lobster Patties.
Fricasseed Chicken.

Sirloin of Beef,
Horseradish Sauce.
Potatoes.
Cauliflowers.

Casserole of Rice.
Apple Snow.

Menu

Gravy Soup.

Brill,
Lobster Sauce.

Veal Cutlets and
Italian Sauce.

Roast Goose,
Apple Sauce.
Potatoes.

Orange Pudding.
Valois Cream.

Menu

Julienne Soup.

Cod, Oyster Sauce.
Smelts.

Veal Olives.

Sirloin of Beef.
Potatoes.   Sprouts.

Charlotte Russe.
Lemon Sponge.

March—Plain Family Dinners for.

No. 1.

Sunday.—Boiled half calf's head, pickled pork, potatoes, greens.—Plum tart, made with bottled fruit, custard.

Monday.—Mock-turtle soup, made from the liquor in which the head was boiled.—Hashed calf's head, fried potatoes.—Stewed rhubarb.

Tuesday.—Roast boned aitchbone of beef, potatoes, greens, Yorkshire pudding.—Macaroni cheese.

Wednesday.—Fried Whiting.—Cold beef, mashed potatoes, salad. — Baroness pudding.

Thursday.—Soup made from beef bones. Haricot mutton, potatoes.—Russian salad.

Friday.—Stewed eels. — Pie made from cold beef, potatoes.—Cheese, celery.

Saturday. — Half shoulder of mutton, potatoes, Spanish onions.—Lemon pudding.

No. 2.

Sunday.—Roast ribs of beef, baked potatoes, greens.—Fruit tart (bottled fruit), custard.

Monday. — Cold beef, salad, mashed potatoes.—Boiled rhubarb pudding.

Tuesday.—Soup made from beef bones.—Minced beef, potatoes.—Baked ground rice pudding.

Wednesday.—Irish stew, made from neck of mutton. — Apple tart, custard pudding.

Thursday.—Whiting, stuffed and baked. — Beef-steak pie, potatoes. — Bread-and-butter pudding.

Friday.— Loin of mutton, greens, potatoes.—Roly-poly jam pudding.

Saturday.—Pea-soup, fried croûtons.—Cold mutton, mashed potatoes, salad.—Cheese, celery.

March—Vegetarian Dinners for.

No. 1.

Pea Soup.

Vegetable Pie.   Curried Eggs.

Stewed Rhubarb.
Tapioca Pudding.

No. 2.

Vermicelli Soup.

Vegetable Stew.

Hominy Fritters.
Plum Pudding.

March—Dinner Table Decorations for.

Quite the most troublesome of months in which to provide table decorations, it is yet possible to make a pretty arrangement with the flowers and plants usually at our disposal in March.

Growing plants are the most effective and easiest to form a decoration, and pots of snowdrops are perhaps the prettiest. When required for table purposes these, the fairest of Spring blossoms, may be grown in ornamental pots, or the other pots be placed in vases of some fairly bright colour, such as pink or yellow, and they then will need no setting off by coloured tablecloths.

If they are used picked from the plants they should be placed in low receptacles filled with moss, and no hot-house or other fern should be mingled with them.

Daffodils and many other yellow flowers should be had during March, and their colour is a very pretty one for the dinner table. The daffodils look best in rather tall vases, with a very few of their own leaves.

For trailing on the cloth and for blending with flowers, brown ivy comes in well, and the common green ivy need not be despised for decorative purposes when flowers are scarce.

A pretty pot of fern for a centre decoration put in a smart saque of silk or satin with trails of ivy and tiny vases of snowdrops form a simple and quickly-arranged decoration, when hot-house flowers are not to be had ; but a dessert centre of bright colour helps out the flowers, and should be used when colour is needed, the flowers of the season being all of pale tints.

To eke out scanty supplies of flowers, fruit of good colour may be chosen for the table decoration, it being in harmony with the tints of the flowers and foliage.

March, Things in Season:—

Fish.—Bream, brill, carp, crabs, crayfish, dory, eels, flounders, haddocks, herrings, lampreys, lobsters, mussels, oysters, pike, plaice, prawns, salmon, shrimps, skate, smelts, soles, sprats, sturgeon, tench, thornback, turbot, whitebait, whiting.

Meat.—Beef, house lamb, mutton, pork, veal.

Poultry.—Capons, chickens, ducklings, tame and wild pigeons, pullets with eggs, turkeys, wild-fowl, though now not in full season.

Game.—Grouse, hares, partridges, pheasants, snipe, woodcock.

Vegetables. — Asparagus (foreign and forced), beetroot, brocoli (purple and white), Brussels sprouts, cabbages, carrots, celery, chervil, cresses, cucumbers (forced), endive, kidney-beans, lettuces, parsnips, potatoes, savoys, seakale, spinach, turnips, various herbs.

Fruit.—Apples (golden and Dutch pippins), grapes, medlars, nuts, oranges, pears (Bon Chrétien), walnuts.

Marrow-Bones, Boiled. — In-

GREDIENTS.—*Bones, a small piece of common paste, a floured cloth.*

Have the bones neatly sawed into convenient sizes and cover the ends with a small piece of common crust, made with flour and water. Over this tie a floured cloth and place the bones upright in a

MARROW BONES.

saucepan of boiling water, taking care there is sufficient to cover them. Boil them for 2 hours, remove the cloth and paste and serve them upright on a napkin with dry toast. Many persons clear the marrow from the bones after they are cooked, spread it over a slice of toast and add a seasoning of pepper and salt; when served in this manner, it must be very expeditiously sent to table, as it so soon gets cold.

TIME.—*2 hours.*

SEASONABLE *at any time.*

Note.—Marrow-bones may be baked after preparing them as in the preceding recipe; they should be laid in a deep dish and baked for 2 hours.

Marrow Dumplings (to Serve

with Roast Meat, in Soup, with Salad, &c.; German Recipe). — INGREDIENTS *for 6 dumplings.*—1 oz. of beef marrow, 1 oz. of butter, 2 eggs, 2 penny rolls, 1 teaspoonful of minced onion, 1 teaspoonful of minced parsley, salt and grated nutmeg to taste. AVERAGE COST, 6d.

Beat the marrow and butter together to a cream; well whisk the eggs and add these to the other ingredients. When they are well stirred, put in the rolls, which should previously be well soaked in boiling milk, strained and beaten up with a fork. Add the remaining ingredients, omitting the minced onion where the flavour is very much disliked and form the mixture into small round dumplings. Drop these into boiling broth and let them simmer for about 20 minutes or ½ hour. They may be served in soup, with roast meat, or with salad, as in Germany, where they are more frequently sent to table than in this country. They are very good.

TIME.—*20 minutes.*

SEASONABLE *at any time.*

Marrow Pudding, Baked or

Boiled.—INGREDIENTS.—½ pint of bread-crumbs, 1½ pint of milk, 6 oz. of marrow, 4 eggs, ¼ lb. of raisins or currants, or 2 oz. of each; sugar and grated nutmeg to taste.

Make the milk boiling, pour it hot on to the bread-crumbs and let these remain covered for about ½ hour; shred the marrow, beat up the eggs and mix these with the bread-crumbs; add the remaining ingredients, beat the mixture well and either put it into a buttered mould and boil it for

2½ hours, or put it into a pie-dish edged with puff-paste and bake it for rather more than ¾ hour. Before sending it to table, sift a little pounded sugar over, after being turned out of the mould or basin.

TIME.—2½ *hours to boil*, ¾ *hour to bake.*
SEASONABLE *at any time.*

Matelote Sauce.—INGREDIENTS.—
20 *small onions*, 3 *oz. of butter, a lump of sugar, a glass of sherry, a gill of gravy, a dessertspoonful of flour, ½ pint of water, salt, pepper.* AVERAGE COST, 1s. *per pint.*

Peel the onions and put them with the lump of sugar and a little of the butter into a quart saucepan over the fire, shake them in this and add the rest of the butter gradually. When the onions are getting brown, put in the wine and flour and stir gently with a small wooden spoon. When boiling, pour in the gravy and water and simmer till the onions are tender, then season with pepper and salt and a little more sugar if liked and strain. If this sauce be not a rich deep brown, browning should be added.

TIME.—1 *hour.*
SEASONABLE *at any time.*

Mayonnaise (Sauce or Salad Dressing for Cold Chicken, Fish and other Cold Dishes).—INGREDIENTS *for salad for* 6 *persons.—The yolks of* 2 *eggs*, 6 *tablespoonfuls of salad oil*, 3 *tablespoonfuls of vinegar, salt and white pepper to taste*, 1 *tablespoonful of white stock*, 2 *tablespoonfuls of cream.* AVERAGE COST, 7d.

Put the yolks of the eggs into a basin, with a seasoning of pepper and salt and pound them smoothly; have ready the above quantities of oil and vinegar, add them *very gradually* to the eggs, the oil first; continue stirring and rubbing the mixture with a wooden spoon, as herein consists the secret of having a nice smooth sauce. It cannot be stirred too frequently and it should be made in a very cool place, or if ice is at hand, it should be mixed over

it. When the vinegar and oil are well incorporated with the eggs, add the stock and cream, stirring all the time and it will then be ready for use.

For a fish Mayonnaise, this sauce may be coloured with lobster-spawn, pounded; and for poultry or meat, where variety is desired, a little parsley-juice may be used to add to its appearance. Cucumber, tarragon, or any other flavoured vinegar, may be substituted for plain.

Mayonnaise of Salmon.—IN-
GREDIENTS.—*Cold boiled salmon*, 2 *lettuces, a little beetroot and watercress*, 3 *hard-boiled eggs, a very little oil and vinegar, pepper and salt*, ¼ *pint of Mayonnaise sauce.* AVERAGE COST, *exclusive of the cold salmon*, 1s.

Thoroughly wash and dry the lettuces and use the outer leaves, sprinkled with oil and vinegar, to lay on the dish as a foundation for the Mayonnaise. Upon these lay in a circle overlapping one another, small outlets of the salmon well masked in the sauce. In the centre and around these put the remainder of the lettuce shredded finely, and the cress cut up, using first the hearts of the lettuces, then little groups of watercress and decorating these with the best sort and egg, so as to make pretty contrasting colours in the border; then put the remainder of the sauce on the top.

SEASONABLE *in summer.*

May Drink.—INGREDIENTS *for sufficient for* 4 *persons.—A bottle of any light wine, such as hock, half a large lemon*, 6 *black currant leaves*, 6 *oz. of sugar, a little woodruff*, ¼ *pint of water, ice.* AVERAGE COST, 2s.

Steep the leaves and woodruff with the rind of the lemon and the sugar in the water, until it is strongly flavoured. Pour in the wine, stir well, then strain into a glass jug, adding a few fresh leaves of woodruff and some broken ice before serving.

SEASONABLE *in summer.*

May—Dinner for Twelve Persons.

MENU. (*English.*)	Quantity.	Average Cost.		MENU. (*French.*)
		s.	*d.*	
Spring Soup.	2 quarts	2	6	Printanière.
Turbot.	1 fish.	7	6	Turbot.
Whitebait.	3½ pints.	5	6	Blanchailles.
Chicken Patties.	12	3	0	Petits Patés de Volaille.
Sirloin.	1 joint.	7	0	Aloyau.
Potatoes.	4 lbs.	0	4	Pommes de Terre.
Brussels Sprouts.	4 lbs.	1	0	Choux de Bruxelles.
Asparagus.	100	4	0	Asperges.
Noyeau Cream.	2 mlds.	3	0	Crème au Noyeau.
Iced Pudding.	1	5	0	Pouding Glacée.
		£1 18 10		

May—Dinner for Ten Persons.

MENU. (*English.*)	Quantity.	Average Cost.		MENU. (*French.*)
		s.	*d.*	
Almond Soup.	3 pints.	4	0	Potage Lait d'Amandes.
Salmon,	3 lbs.	5	6	Saumon,
Genevese Sauce.	1 tur.	1	0	Sauce Génévèse
Lamb Cutlets.	3 lbs.	3	0	Côtelettes d'Agneau.
Asparagus.	100	3	6	Asperges.
Roast Fowls.	1 pair.	6	0	Volailles.
Ham.	1	7	0	Jambon.
Potatoes.	3 lbs.	0	3	Pommes de Terre.
Peas.	1½ peck.	1	6	Petits Pois.
Vol au Vent of Gooseberries.	1 dish.	2	6	Vol au Vent de Groseilles.
Marbled Jelly.	1 mould.	2	0	Gelée Marbrée.
		£1 16 3		

May—Dinner for Eight Persons.

MENU. (*English.*)	Quantity.	Average Cost.		MENU. (*French.*)
		s.	*d.*	
Spring Soup.	3 pints.	2	0	Printanière.
Fillets of Turbot,	3 lbs.	4	0	Filets de Turbot,
Italian Sauce.	1 tur.	0	9	Sauce Italienne.
Curried Lobster.	1 dish.	4	0	Homard au Kari.
Leg of Lamb.	1 joint.	5	6	Gigot d'Agneau.
Potatoes.	3 lbs.	0	3	Pommes de Terre.
Peas.	1½ peck.	1	6	Petits Pois.
Curaçoa Soufflé.	1	2	6	Soufflé de Curaçoa.
Gooseberry Tart.	1	1	6	Tourte aux Groseilles.
Custard.	1 pint.	0	6	Crème.
		£1 2 6		

May—Dinners for from Six to Twelve Persons.

MENU

Julienne.

Brill, Dutch Sauce.

Lobster Cream.

Turkey Poult.
Ham.
Potatoes. Sprouts.

Salad.

Rhubarb Tart. Custard.
Liqueur Jelly.

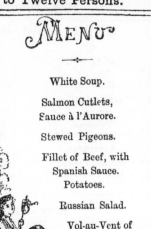

MENU

White Soup.

Salmon Cutlets,
Sauce à l'Aurore.

Stewed Pigeons.

Fillet of Beef, with
Spanish Sauce.
Potatoes.

Russian Salad.

Vol-au-Vent of
Fruit.
Lemon Cream.

Menu

Appetisans.

Spring Soup.

Red Mullet.

Lamb Cutlets.

Ducklings.
Potatoes.   Peas.

Vanilla Soufflé.
Marbled Jelly.

Menu

Clear Soup.

Fried Filleted Soles,
Tartar Sauce.

Leg of Mutton.
Potatoes.
Stewed Celery.

Asparagus.

Lemon Cheesecakes.
Blancmange.

May—Plain Family Dinners for.

No. 1.

Sunday.—Roast fillet of veal, ham, vegetables.—Gooseberry tart, whipped cream or custard.

Monday. — Beef-steak-and-kidney pie, cold veal and ham, salad, mashed potatoes. —Amber pudding.

Tuesday. — Boiled salmon, cucumber, Tartar sauce.—Minced veal, potatoes.—Jam tart.

Wednesday. — Vegetable soup. — Roast chickens, bacon, vegetables. — Macaroni cheese.

Thursday. — Roast leg of lamb, mint sauce, vegetables.—Rhubarb pudding.

Friday. — Croquettes made from cold chicken, cold lamb, salad, mashed potatoes. —Sweet Omelette.

Saturday.—Fried soles, caper sauce.— Stewed steak and vegetables, potatoes.— Cheese biscuits.

No. 2.

Sunday.—Roast lamb, mint sauce, peas, baked potatoes.—Rhubarb tart, custard or cream.

Monday. — Spring soup. — Cold lamb, salad, potatoes.—Arrowroot pudding.

Tuesday.—Stewed breast of veal with vegetables, potatoes. — Sultana pudding baked.

Wednesday. — Roast beef, potatoes, spinach, horseradish sauce. — Stewed rhubarb, plain blancmange.

Thursday.—Soup made from beef bones. —Cold beef, salad, mashed potatoes. — Gooseberry pudding.

Friday.—Fried whiting, melted butter.— Minced beef with poached eggs, potatoes. —Sago pudding.

Saturday.—Haricot mutton, mashed potatoes. — Gooseberry pudding. — Macaroni Cheese.

May—Vegetarian Dinners for.

No. 1.

Fried Potatoes and Greens.
Poached Eggs.

Gooseberry Tart.
Milk Pudding.

Macaroni Cheese.

No. 2.

Lentil Soup.

Haricot Beans and
Mashed Potatoes.

Rhubarb Tart.
Tapioca Pudding.

May—Dinner Table Decorations for.

Wild flowers furnish some of the prettiest of the May decorations, if they can be had fresh and put into water directly they are gathered. They should be plentifully mingled with the grasses that should be growing in profusion in our fields during this month, and the effect will be light and delicate.

As a suggestion for a dinner table decoration, this is a pretty arrangement : A pale green Liberty silk dessert centre of the shade generally called apple green, one of the really Spring tones of colour, on which are placed white china stands filled with moss. In these are white marguerites and buttercups, blended with grasses, every flower and blade put in separately, to gain the light and fairy-like appearance such flowers should present. Here and there in

the puckerings of the soft silk cloth are shrouded and half-hidden, tiny bouquets of flowers ; and to each person, in small specimen tubes, or better still, little fish-globes, a few flowers and grasses.

Water flowers, such as iris and water-lillies, can sometimes be procured as early as May, and than these nothing can be found prettier for table decoration ; but the character of the arrangement should be kept up, and the water flowers should not be intermingled with garden ones, and the foliage and grasses used should be those of water plants.

For a luncheon table, which is of necessity seen by daylight, dark blue corn-flowers are suitable, especially if sapphire glasses are used for claret or light wine.

May, Things in Season:—

Fish.—Carp, chub, crabs, crayfish, dory, herrings, lobsters, mackerel, red and gray mullet, prawns, salmon, shad, smelts, soles, trout, turbot.

Meat.—Beef, lamb, mutton, veal.

Poultry. — Chickens, ducklings, fowls, green geese, leverets, pullets, rabbits.

Vegetables. — Asparagus, beans, early cabbages, carrots, cauliflowers, cresses, cucumbers, lettuces, peas, early potatoes, salads, seakale, various herbs.

Fruit.—Apples, green apricots, cherries, currants for tarts, gooseberries, melons, pears, rhubarb, strawberries.

Mead. — Ingredients. — 1½ lb. of sugar, ½ pint of treacle, 1 oz. of essence of sassafras, 2 oz. of tartaric acid. Average Cost, 6d. per quart.

Pour on to the sugar and treacle 3 pints of boiling water and let it stand till lukewarm; add the tartaric acid and the sassafras, and when cold, bottle. When wanted, put a tablespoonful into a tumbler and fill two thirds full with cold water; stir in a very little soda and drink while foaming.

Seasonable *in hot weather.*

Meat.—In studying several analyses of the same meat there will be seen different results, the reasons for which may be found in the age, the modes of feeding and the peculiarities of various animals. Again there is a great difference in the component parts of different joints of the same meat. There is a very perceptible difference between fat and lean meat; and the more fat the less water does it contain.

If nitrogenous or flesh-forming material is required, lean meat is best, that also containing more saline and mineral matter than is found in fat meat; but where, as in cold countries, heat-givers and force-producers are wanted, then fatter meats are both more economical and useful. Very young meat, particularly that from animals that have been quickly forced to large growth, is very indigestible; and baked meat, even under the new and better system pursued in the construction of ovens, is thought less digestible than that either roasted, boiled, or stewed.

Again, meat twice cooked, or that which has been salted, is not so digestible or nutritive (with the exception however of bacon or ham) as fresh meat.

Constituents of 1 lb. of Various Kinds of Meat.

	BEEF.		MUTTON.	
	oz.	grs.	oz.	grs.
Water ...	8	0	7	16
Albuminoids ...	2	184	2	0
Fat	4	340	6	176
Mineral Matters ...	0	350	0	245
	16	0	16	0

	LAMB.		PORK.		VEAL.	
	oz.	grs.	oz.	grs.	oz.	grs.
Water ...	8	44	6	69	10	0
Albuminoids	1	323	1	263	2	281
Fat	5	263	8	0	2	281
Mineral Matters ...	0	244	0	195	0	512
	16	0	16	0	16	0

Meat Croquettes (from Tinned Meat).—Ingredients *for dish for 4 persons.*—1 *lb. of any kind of tinned meat, ½ the quantity of cold potatoes or breadcrumbs, 3 oz. of dripping or fat from the meat, 1 egg, pepper and salt, hot lard.* Average Cost, 10d.

Chop the meat finely and either mash the potatoes or grate the bread, then mix with the dripping and the seasoning. Make the mixture into small rolls, dip them in beaten egg and bread-crumbs and fry in hot lard a nice bright brown. Serve with or without gravy, as liked, and garnish with fried parsley.

Time. — 4 *or* 5 *minutes to fry the croquettes.*

Seasonable *at any time.*

Loin of Pork

Loin of Mutton boned.

Leg of Lamb

Ribs of Beef boned

Fillet of Veal.

Boiled Beef

Sirloin of Beef.

Breast of Lamb & Peas.

Calf's Head

Sausages.

Heart

Haunch of Venison.

Fore-quarter of Lamb.

Saddle of Mutton.

MEAT

Meat and Macaroni. (Tinned Meat.)

INGREDIENTS *for dish for* 6 *persons.*—*A* 2-*lb. tin of beef,* ¼ *lb. of macaroni, a pinch of powdered cinnamon, pepper, salt,* ½ *pint of stock.* AVERAGE COST, 1s. 6d.

Put the macaroni into sufficient boiling water to cover it and stew till tender. Mince the meat finely and season well, then put it in a stewpan with the stock and let it get hot. Serve on a large round of toast with the macaroni round.

TIME.—*Altogether,* 1½ *hour.*

SEASONABLE *at any time.*

Melons. — AVERAGE COST, *foreign melons,* 1s. *each; English,* 3s. 6d. *to* 7s. 6d. *each.*

This fruit is rarely preserved or cooked in any way, but is sent whole to table on a dish garnished with leaves or flowers, as fancy dictates. A border of any other kind of small fruit, arranged round the melon, has a pretty effect, the colour of the former contrasting nicely with the melon. Plenty of pounded sugar should be served with it; and the fruit should be cut lengthwise, first cutting half through at each end in the other direction, in moderate-sized slices. In America it is frequently eaten with pepper and salt.

SEASONABLE *from July to August or a little later.*

Meringues. — INGREDIENTS *for* 2 *dozen.*—½ *lb. of pounded sugar, the whites of four eggs.* AVERAGE COST, *with cream,* 1s.

Whisk the whites of the eggs to a stiff froth and, with a wooden spoon, stir in quickly the pounded sugar; and have some boards thick enough to put in the oven to prevent the bottom of the meringues from acquiring too much colour. Cut some strips of paper about 2 inches wide; place this paper on the board and drop a tablespoonful at a time of the mixture on the paper, taking care to let all the meringues be the same size. In dropping it from the spoon, give the mixture the form of an egg and keep the meringues about 2 inches apart from each other on the paper. Strew over them some sifted sugar and bake in a moderate oven for ½ hour. As soon as they begin to colour remove them from the oven; take each slip of paper by the two ends and turn it gently on the table and, with a small spoon, take out the soft part of each meringue. Spread some clean paper on the board, turn the meringues upside down and put them into the oven to harden and brown on the other side. When required for table fill them with whipped cream, flavoured with liqueur or vanilla and sweetened with pounded sugar. Join two of the meringues together and

MERINGUES.

pile them high in the dish as shown in the annexed drawing. To vary their appearance finely-chopped almonds may be strewn over them before the sugar is sprinkled over; and they may be garnished with any bright-coloured preserve. Great expedition is necessary in making this sweet dish; as, if the meringues are not put into the oven as soon as the sugar and eggs are mixed, the former melts and the mixture would run on the paper instead of keeping its egg-shape. The sweeter the meringues are made the crisper will they be; but if there is not sufficient sugar mixed with them they will most likely be tough. They are sometimes coloured with cochineal and if kept well covered in a dry place will remain good for a month or six weeks.

TIME.—*Altogether,* ½ *hour.*

SEASONABLE *at any time.*

Military Pudding. — INGREDI-

ENTS *for 6 small puddings.*—½ *lb. of suet,* ½ *lb. of bread-crumbs,* ½ *lb. of moist sugar, the rind and juice of 1 large lemon.* AVERAGE COST, 8*d.*

Chop the suet finely, mix it with the bread-crumbs and sugar and mince the lemon-rind and strain the juice ; stir these into the other ingredients, mix well and put the mixture into small buttered cups and bake for rather more than ¼ hour ; turn them out on the dish and serve with lemon-sauce. The above ingredients may be made into small balls and boiled for about ½ hour ; they should then be served with the same sauce as when baked.

TIME.—*Rather more than* ½ *hour.*

SEASONABLE *at any time.*

Milk.—

Milk, considered to be of all foods in its constituent parts the most perfect, when of good quality is of an opaque white colour; the cream always comes to the top ; the well-known milky odour is strong ; it will boil without alter- ing its appearance in these respects, the little bladders which arise on the surface will renew themselves if broken by the spoon. To boil milk is, in fact, the simplest way of testing its quality. The commonest adulterations of milk are not of a hurtful character. It is a good deal thinned with water and sometimes thickened with a little starch, or coloured with yolk of egg, or even saffron ; but these processes have nothing murderous in them.

Milk, Constituents of.—

As a simple food, milk is the most perfect and the one likely to sustain life longest. Its chief constituents are casein, sugar of milk, milk fat and phosphates ; and these constituents are sufficient to support and keep in good health children and animals without other food.

The quality of cow's milk depends not only upon the breed but the feeding of the animals; where these have a poor and watery diet, the milk being deficient in solids and *vice versa.* In England it is but rarely that any but cow's milk is used but in other countries the inhabitants depend upon the milk of other animals. Thus, in Norway, Sweden and Denmark sheep's milk is used, in Tartary mare's milk, in Switzerland and Spain much of that of goats and in Iceland that of the reindeer. But from whatever animal obtained, the constituents are the same and the proportion of these have but little variation.

CONSTITUENT PARTS OF 1 PINT OF COW'S MILK.

					oz.	grs
Water	...	...	...	...	17	330
Casein	...	...	...	...	0	370
Milk fat	...	...	...	...	0	333
Milk Sugar	...	...	...	...	1	22
Mineral matter	...	...	...	...	0	72

Milk and Cream, To Keep, in

Hot Weather.—When the weather is very warm and it is very difficult to prevent milk from turning sour and spoiling the cream, it should be scalded and it will then remain good for a few hours. It must on no account be allowed to boil, or there will be a skin instead of a cream upon the milk ; and the slower the process the safer will it be. A very good plan to scald milk is to put the pan that contains it into a saucepan or wide kettle of boiling water. When the surface looks thick the milk is sufficiently scalded and it should then be put away in a cool place in the same vessel that it was scalded in. Cream may be kept for 24 hours if scalded without sugar ; and by the addition of the latter ingredient it will remain good double the time if kept in a cool place. All pans, jugs and vessels intended for milk should be kept beautifully clean and well scalded before the milk is put in, as any negligence in this respect may cause large quantities of it to be spoiled ; and milk should never be kept in vessels of zinc or copper. Milk may be preserved good in hot weather for a few hours by placing the jug which contains it in ice, or very cold water; or a pinch of bicarbonate of soda may be introduced into the liquid.

Milk and Cream, Separation

of.—If it be desired that the milk should be freed entirely from cream, it should be poured into a very shallow broad pan or dish, not more than 1½ inch deep, as cream cannot rise through a great depth of milk. In cold and wet weather milk is not so rich as it is in summer and warm weather and the morning's milk is always richer than the evening's. The last-drawn milk of each milking, at all times and seasons, is richer than the first drawn, and on that account should be set apart for cream. Milk should be shaken as little as possible when carried from the cow to the dairy and should be poured into the pans very gently. Persons not keeping cows may always have a little cream, provided the milk they purchase be pure and unadulterated. As soon as it comes in it should be poured into very shallow open pans or pie-dishes, and set by in a very cool place; and in 7 or 8 hours a nice cream should have risen to the surface.

Milk and Cream, Substitute

for, in Tea and Coffee.—INGREDIENTS.— new-laid egg, or 2 yolks, to every large breakfastcupful of tea or coffee.

Beat up the whole of the egg in a basin, put it into a cup and pour over it the tea or coffee quite hot, stirring all the time to prevent the egg from curdling. In point of nourishment, both tea and coffee are much improved by this addition and it is more nourishing if only the yolk be used.

Milk and Suet. (A nourishing

Drink for Invalids.)—INGREDIENTS.—A pint of new milk, ½ oz. of veal suet, 2 lumps of sugar, a pinch of cinnamon or any other flavouring that may be preferred, AVERAGE COST, 3d.

Scrape the suet as fine as possible and boil it slowly in the milk for ½ hour, then add the flavouring and sugar.

TIME.—½ hour.

SEASONABLE at any time.

Milk Soup. (A nice Dish for

Children.)—INGREDIENTS for sufficient soup for 10 children.—2 quarts of milk, 1 salt-spoonful of salt, 1 teaspoonful of powdered cinnamon, 3 teaspoonfuls of pounded sugar, or more if liked, 4 thin slices of bread, the yolks of 4 eggs. AVERAGE COST, 1s. 2d.

Boil the milk with the salt, cinnamon and sugar; lay the bread in a dish, pour over it a little of the milk and keep it hot over a stove, without burning. Beat up the yolks of the eggs, add them to the milk and stir over the fire till it thickens. Do not let it curdle. Pour it upon the bread and serve.

TIME.—¾ hour.

SEASONABLE all the year.

Mince Pies.—INGREDIENTS.—Good

puff-paste, mincemeat.

Make some good puff-paste by recipe; roll half of it out to the thickness of about ¼ inch and line some good-sized pattypans with it; fill them with mincemeat, cover with the paste a little thicker and cut it off all round close to the edge of the tin. Put the pies into a brisk oven, to draw the paste up and bake for 25 minutes, or longer should the pies be very large;

MINCE PIES.

brush them over with the white of an egg, beaten with the blade of a knife to a stiff froth; sprinkle over pounded sugar and put them into the oven for a minute or two, to dry the egg; dish the pies on a white d'oyley and serve hot. They may be merely sprinkled with pounded sugar instead of being glazed, when that mode is preferred. To re-warm them, put the pies on the pattypans and let them remain in the oven for 10 minutes or ¼ hour and they will be almost as good as if freshly made.

TIME.—25 to 30 *minutes* ; 10 *minutes to re-warm them.*

SEASONABLE *at Christmas time.*

Mincemeat.—INGREDIENTS.—2 *lbs. of raisins,* 3 *lbs. of currants,* 1½ *lb. of lean beef,* 3 *lbs. of beef suet,* 2 *lbs. of moist sugar,* 2 *oz. of citron,* 2 *oz. of candied lemon-peel,* 2 *oz. of candied orange-peel,* 1 *large nutmeg,* 2 *lbs. of apples, the rind of* 2 *lemons, the juice of* 1, ½ *pint of brandy.*

Stone and *cut* the raisins once or twice across, but do not chop them ; wash, dry and pick the currants free from stalks and grit and mince the beef and suet, taking care that the latter is chopped very fine; slice the citron and candied peel, grate the nutmeg and pare, core and mince the apples ; mince the lemon-peel, strain the juice and when all the ingredients are thus prepared, mix them well together, adding the brandy when the other things are well blended; press the whole into a jar, carefully exclude the air and the mincemeat will be ready for use in a fortnight. If an additional quantity of spice be preferred, add ½ teaspoonful of pounded mace and the same of pounded allspice. We, however, prefer the mincemeat without the latter ingredients and can vouch for its excellence.

SEASONABLE.—*Make this about the beginning of December.*

Mincemeat, Excellent.—INGREDIENTS.—3 *large lemons,* 3 *large apples,* 1 *lb. of stoned raisins,* 1 *lb. of currants,* 1 *lb. of suet,* 2 *lbs. of moist sugar,* 1 *oz. of sliced candied citron,* 1 *oz. of sliced candied orange-peel and the same quantity of lemon-peel,* 1 *teacupful of brandy,* 2 *tablespoonfuls of orange marmalade.*

Grate the rinds of the lemons ; squeeze

out the juice, strain it and boil the remainder of the lemons until tender enough to pulp or chop very finely. Then add to this pulp the apples, which should be baked and their skins and cores removed ; put in the remaining ingredients one by one and, as they are added, mix everything very thoroughly together. Put the mincemeat into a stone jar with a closely-fitting lid and in a fortnight it will be ready for use.

SEASONABLE.—*This should be made the first or second week in December.*

Mint Vinegar. — INGREDIENTS. — *Vinegar, mint.*

Procure some nice fresh mint, pick the leaves from the stalks and fill a bottle or jar with them. Add vinegar to them until the bottle is full; *cover closely* to exclude the air and let it infuse for a fortnight. Then strain the liquor and put it into small bottles for use, of which the corks should be sealed.

SEASONABLE.—*This should be made in June, July, or August.*

Mint Sauce (to Serve with Roast Lamb). — INGREDIENTS *for* 1 *tureen.* — 4 *dessertspoonfuls of chopped mint,* 2 *dessertspoonfuls of pounded white sugar,* ¼ *pint of vinegar.* AVERAGE COST, 2*d.*

Wash the mint, which should be young and fresh - gathered, free from grit; pick the leaves from the stalks, mince them very fine and put them into a tureen ; add the sugar and vinegar and stir till the former is dissolved. This sauce is better by being made 2 or 3 hours before wanted for table, as the vinegar then becomes impregnated with the flavour of the mint. By many persons, the above proportion of sugar would not be considered sufficient ; but as tastes vary, we have given

MINT.

the quantity which we have found to suit the general palate.

Note.—Where green mint is scarce and not obtainable, mint vinegar may be substituted for it, and will be found very acceptable in early spring.

Mock Turtle Soup. I.—INGRE-DIENTS *for sufficient soup for* 10 *or* 12 *persons.*— ½ *a calf's head,* ¼ *lb. of butter,* ½ *lb. of lean ham,* 2 *tablespoonfuls of minced parsley, a little minced lemon thyme, sweet marjoram, basil,* 2 *onions, a few chopped mushrooms (when obtainable),* 2 *shalots,* 2 *tablespoonfuls of flour,* ¼ *bottle of Madeira or sherry, forcemeat balls, cayenne, salt and mace to taste, the juice of* 1 *lemon and* 1 *Seville orange,* 1 *dessertspoonful of pounded sugar,* 3 *quarts of good stock.* AVERAGE COST, 2s. 6d. *per quart.*

Scald the head with the skin on, remove the brain, tie the head up in a cloth and let it boil for 1 hour. Then take the meat from the bones, cut it into small square pieces and throw them into cold water. Now take the meat, put it into a stewpan and cover with stock; let it boil gently for an hour, or rather more if not quite tender and set it on one side. Melt the butter in another stewpan and add the ham, cut small, with the herbs, parsley, onions, shalots, mushrooms and nearly a pint of stock; let these simmer slowly for 2 hours and then dredge in as much flour as will dry up the butter. Fill up with the remainder of the stock, add the wine, let it stew gently for 10 minutes, rub it through a tammy and put it to the calf's head; season with cayenne and, if required, a little salt; add the juice of the orange and lemon and when liked, ¼ teaspoonful of pounded mace and the sugar. Put in the forcemeat balls, simmer 5 minutes and serve very hot.

TIME.—4½ *hours.*

SEASONABLE *in winter.*

Note.—The bones of the head should be well stewed in the liquor it was first boiled in; and will make good white stock, flavoured with vegetables, &c.

Mock Turtle Soup. II. (More Economical.)—INGREDIENTS *for soup for* 10 *or* 12 *persons.*— *A knuckle of veal weighing* 5 *or* 6 *lbs.,* 2 *cowheels,* 2 *large onions stuck with cloves,* 1 *bunch of sweet herbs,* 3 *blades of mace, salt to taste,* 12 *peppercorns,* 1 *glass of sherry,* 24 *forcemeat balls, a little lemon-juice,* 6 *quarts of water.* AVERAGE COST, 1s. 6d. *per quart.*

Put all the ingredients, except the forcemeat balls and lemon-juice, in an earthen jar and stew for 6 hours. Do not open it till cold. When wanted for use, skim off all the fat and strain carefully; place it on the fire, cut up the meat into inch-and-a-half squares, put it, with the forcemeat balls and lemon-juice, into the soup and serve. It can be flavoured with a tablespoonful of anchovy, or Harvey's sauce.

TIME.—6 *hours.*

SEASONABLE *in winter.*

Monday's Pudding. — INGREDIENTS.—*The remains of cold plum-pudding, brandy, custard made with 4 eggs to every pint of milk.*

Cut the remains of a *good* cold plumpudding into finger-pieces, soak them in a little brandy and lay them cross-barred in a mould until full. Make a custard with the above proportion of milk and eggs, flavouring it with nutmeg or lemon-rind; fill up the mould with it; tie it down with a cloth and boil or steam it for an hour. Serve with a little of the custard poured over, to which has been added a tablespoonful of brandy.

TIME.—1 *hour.*

SEASONABLE *at any time.*

Muffins.— INGREDIENTS. — *To every quart of milk allow* 1½ *oz. of German yeast, a little salt; flour.*

Warm the milk, add to it the yeast and mix these well together; put them into a ɔan and stir in sufficient flour to make the whole into a dough of rather a soft ɔonsistence; cover it over with a cloth and place it in a warm place to rise; and when light and nicely risen, divide the dough into pieces and round them to the shape with the hands; place them in a layer of flour about two inches thick, on wooden trays and let them rise again; when this is effected, they each will exhibit a semi-globular shape. Then place them carefully on a hot-plate or stove and bake them until they are slightly browned, turning them when they are done on one side. Muffins are not easily made, and are more generally purchased than manufactured at home. *To toast them*, divide the edge of the muffin all round, by pulling it open to the depth of about an inch, with the fingers. Put it on a toasting-fork and hold it before a very clear fire until one side is nicely browned, but not burnt; turn and toast it on the other. Do not toast them too quickly, as, if this be done, the middle of the muffin will not be warmed through. When done, divide them by pulling them open; butter them slightly on both sides, put them together again and cut them into halves; when sufficient are toasted and buttered, pile them on a very hot dish and send them very quickly to table.

TIME.—*From* 20 *minutes to* ½ *hour to bake them.*

Mulberries, Preserved.—INGREDIENTS.—*To* 2 *lbs. of fruit and* 1 *pint of juice allow* 2½ *lbs. of loaf sugar.*

Put some of the fruit into a preserving pan, and simmer it gently until the juice is well drawn. Strain it through a bag, measure it, and to every pint allow the above proportion of sugar and fruit. Put the sugar into the preserving-pan, moisten it with the juice, boil it up, skim well and then add the mulberries, which should be ripe, but not soft enough to break to a pulp. Let them stand in the syrup till warm through, then set them on the fire to boil gently; when half done, turn them carefully into an earthen pan, and let them remain till the next day; then boil them as before, and when the syrup is thick and becomes firm when cold, put the preserve into pots.

MULBERRIES.

In making this, care should be taken not to break the mulberries; this may be avoided by gentle stirring, and by simmering the fruit very slowly.

TIME.—¾ *hour to extract the juice;* ¼ *hour to boil the mulberries the first time,* ¼ *hour the second time.*

SEASONABLE *in August and September.*

Mullagatawny Soup.—INGREDIENTS *for soup for* 8 *persons.*—2 *tablespoonfuls of Holbrook's curry-powder,* 6 *onions,* 1 *clove of garlic,* 1 *oz. of pounded almonds, a little lemon-pickle or mango-juice to taste;* 1 *fowl or rabbit;* 4 *slices of lean bacon;* 2 *quarts of medium stock, or, if wanted very good, best stock.* AVERAGE COST, 3*s.* 6*d.*

Slice and fry the onions of a nice colour; line the stewpan with the bacon; cut up the rabbit or fowl into small joints and slightly brown them; put in the fried onions, the garlic and stock, and simmer gently till the meat is tender; skim very carefully and when the meat is done, rub the curry-powder to a smooth batter; add it to the soup with the almonds, which must be first pounded, with a little of the stock. Put in seasoning and lemon-juice or mango-juice to taste, and serve boiled rice with it.

TIME.—2 *hours.*

SEASONABLE *in winter.*

Note.—This soup can also be made with breast of veal or calf's head. Vegetable mullagatawny is made with veal stock, by boiling and pulping chopped vegetable marrow, cucumbers, onions and tomatoes and seasoning with curry.

owder and cayenne. Nice pieces of meat, good urry-powder and strong stock, are necessary to make this soup good.

Mullagatawny Soup. (Made with Tinned Meat.)—INGREDIENTS *for sufficient soup for 6 persons.—A 2-lb. tin of Australian mutton, 2 onions, 2 carrots, 1 turnip, 1 oz. of cooked or uncooked bacon, 2 tablespoonfuls of flour, a bunch of herbs, ½ a teaspoonful of sugar, the juice of a lemon, 1 oz. of curry-powder, a stick of rhubarb or 2 sour apples, 2 quarts of warm water, pepper and salt.* AVERAGE COST, 1s. 8d.

Turn the meat into a basin, take off some of the fat and pour over it the water. Put 2 oz. of the fat with the bacon into a saucepan; and when the fat has melted, add the onions sliced and frizzle for a few minutes; then add the other vegetables and herbs, shaking in with them the flour and curry-powder and fry a few more minutes; then add the water and meat and stir till it boils and thickens thoroughly, when well skim and add the seasoning and lemon-juice. Allow the soup to boil till the vegetables are well cooked, then rub the soup through a hair sieve with a wooden spoon.

TIME.—1 *hour.*

SEASONABLE *in winter.*

Mulled Ale.—INGREDIENTS *for sufficient for 4 persons.—1 quart of good ale, 1 glass of rum, 1 tablespoonful of pounded sugar, a grate of nutmeg, 4 cloves.* AVERAGE COST, 10d.

Put the sugar and cloves in the ale, and make it hot in a mull or saucepan, warm a jug, pour in this and add the rum and grated nutmeg to taste.

SEASONABLE *in winter.*

Mullet, Grey. — INGREDIENTS.—½ *lb. of salt to each gallon of water.* AVERAGE COST, 1s. *each.*

If the fish be very large it should be laid in cold water and gradually brought to a boil; if small put it in boiling water, salted in the above proportion. Serve with anchovy sauce and plain melted butter.

THE GREY MULLET.

TIME. — *According to size, from ¼ to ¾ hour.*

SEASONABLE *from July to October.*

Mullet, Red.—INGREDIENTS.—*Oiled paper, thickening of butter and flour, ½ teaspoonful of anchovy sauce, 1 glass of sherry, cayenne and salt to taste.* AVERAGE COST, *from 1s. to 1s. 6d. each.*

Clean the fish, take out the gills, but leave the inside, fold in oiled paper and bake them gently. When done, take the liquor that flows from the fish, add a thickening of butter kneaded with flour; put in the other ingredients, and let it boil for 2 minutes. Serve the sauce in a tureen, and the fish either with or without the paper cases.

TIME.—*About 25 minutes.*

SEASONABLE *at any time, but more plentiful in summer.*

Note.—Red mullet may be broiled, and should be folded in oiled paper, the same as in the preceding recipe, and seasoned with pepper and salt. They may be served without sauce in their paper cases; but if any is required use melted butter, Italian or anchovy sauce. They should never be plain boiled.

Mushroom Ketchup.—INGREDIENTS.—*To each peck of mushrooms ½ lb. of salt; to each quart of mushroom-liquor ¼ oz. of cayenne, ½ oz. of allspice, ½ oz. of ginger, 2 blades of pounded mace.*

Choose full-grown mushroom flaps, and take care they are perfectly *fresh gathered* when the weather is tolerably dry; for if they are picked during very heavy rain the ketchup from which they are made is liable to get musty, and will not keep long. Put a layer of them in a deep pan, sprinkle salt over them, and then another layer of mushrooms, and so on alternately. Let them remain for a few hours, when break them up with the hand; put them in a nice cool place for 3 days, occasionally stirring and mashing them well, to extract from them as much juice as possible. Now measure the quantity of liquor without straining; and to each quart allow the above proportion of spices, &c. Put all into a stone jar, cover it up very closely, put it in a saucepan of boiling water, set it over the fire and let it boil for 3 hours.

MUSHROOMS.

Have ready a nice clean stewpan, turn into it the contents of the jar, and let the whole simmer very gently for ½ hour; pour it into a jug, where it should stand in a cool place till the next day; then pour it off into another jug, and strain it into very dry clean bottles, and do not squeeze the mushrooms. To each pint of ketchup add a few drops of brandy. Be careful not to shake the contents, but leave all the sediment behind in the jug; cork well, and either seal or resin the cork so as perfectly to exclude the air. When a very clear bright ketchup is wanted, the liquor must be strained through a very fine hair sieve, or flannel bag, *after* it has been very gently poured off; if the operation is not successful it must be repeated until you have quite a clear liquor. It should be

examined occasionally, and, if it is spoiling should be re-boiled with a few peppercorns

SEASONABLE *from the beginning of Sep tember to the middle of October, when thi ketchup should be made.*

Note.—This flavouring ingredient, if genuin and well prepared, is one of the most usefu store sauces to the experienced cook, and n trouble should be spared in its preparation Double ketchup is made by reducing the liquo to half the quantity; for example, 1 quart mus be boiled down to 1 pint. This goes farthe than ordinary ketchup, as so little is required t flavour a good quantity of gravy. The sedimen may also be bottled for immediate use, and wil be found to answer for flavouring *thick* soups o gravies.

Mushroom Powder. (A valuabl addition to Sauces and Gravies, when fresh Mushrooms are not obtainable.)—INGREDI ENTS.—½ *peck of large mushrooms*, 2 *onions 12 cloves*, ¼ *oz. of pounded mace*, 2 *teaspoon fuls of white pepper.*

Peel the mushrooms, wipe them perfectl free from grit and dirt, remove the blac fur, and reject all those that are at a worm-eaten; put them into a stewpan wit the above ingredients, but without water shake them over a clear fire till all th liquor is dried up, and be careful not to le them burn; arrange them on tins and dr them in a slow oven; pound them to a fin powder, which put into small *dry* bottles cork well, seal the corks and keep it in dry place. In using this powder add it t the gravy just before serving, when it wil merely require one boil-up. The flavou imparted by this means to the gravy ough to be exceedingly good.

SEASONABLE.—*This should be made i September or at the beginning of October.*

Note.—If the bottles in which it is store away are not perfectly dry, as also the mush room powder, it will keep good but a very sho time.

Mushroom Pudding. (Vegetaria Recipe.)—INGREDIENTS *for large puddin —1 quart of mushrooms picked and peeled*

pepper and salt, 1¼ lb. of flour, 6 oz. of
butter, 1 teaspoonful of baking-powder, cold
water. AVERAGE COST, 2s.

Make a crust with the flour, baking-
powder and butter (omitting 1 oz.) and line
a greased basin with it. Put in the mushrooms with the rest of the butter and a
good seasoning of pepper and salt and a
little water. Cut a round of paste to cover
the top, wet the edges and pinch together.
Tie in a cloth and boil 1½ hour.

TIME.—1½ hour.

SEASONABLE. — When mushrooms are
plentiful.

Mushroom Sauce, Brown (to
serve with Roast Meat, &c.).—INGREDI-
ENTS for sufficient for small joint or steak.
—½ pint of button-mushrooms, ½ pint of
good beef gravy, 1 tablespoonful of mushroom ketchup (if at hand), thickening of
butter and flour. AVERAGE COST, 6d.

Put the gravy into a saucepan, thicken
it and stir over the fire until it boils. Prepare the mushrooms by cutting off the
stalks and wiping them free from grit and
dirt; the large flap mushrooms cut into
small pieces will answer for a brown sauce,
when the buttons are not obtainable; put
them into the gravy and let them simmer
very gently for about 10 minutes; then
add the ketchup and serve.

TIME.—Rather more than 10 minutes.

SEASONABLE from August to October.

Note.—When fresh mushrooms are not obtainable, the powder may be used as a substitute in
brown sauce.

Mushroom Sauce, Rich and
Good (to serve with Fowls or Rabbits).—
INGREDIENTS for sauce for pair of fowls.—
1 pint of mushroom-buttons, salt to taste, a
little grated nutmeg, 1 blade of pounded
mace, ½ pint of cream, ½ pint of milk, 2 oz.
of butter, flour to thicken. AVERAGE COST,
1s. 9d.

Rub the buttons with a piece of flannel
and salt, to take off the skin; cut off the

stalks and put them in a stewpan with
the above ingredients, previously kneading
together the butter and flour; boil the
whole for about ten minutes, stirring all
the time. Pour some of the sauce over
the fowls and the remainder serve in a
tureen.

TIME.—10 minutes.

SEASONABLE from August to October.

Mushroom Sauce, White (to
serve with Boiled Fowls, Cutlets, &c.).—
INGREDIENTS.—Rather more than ½ pint of
button mushrooms, lemon-juice and water,
1 oz. of butter, ½ pint of Béchamel, ¼ teaspoonful of pounded sugar. AVERAGE
COST, 1s.

Turn the mushrooms white by putting
them into lemon-juice and water, having
previously cut off the stalks and wiped
them perfectly free from grit. Chop them
and put them in a stewpan with the butter.
When the mushrooms are softened, add
the Béchamel and simmer for about 5
minutes; should they, however, not be
done enough, allow rather more time.
They should not boil longer than necessary,
as they would then lose their colour and
flavour. Rub the whole through a tammy
and serve very hot. After this, it should
be warmed in a bain marie.

TIME.—Altogether ¼ hour.

SEASONABLE from August to October.

Mushroom Sauce, White (to
serve with Boiled Fowls, Cutlets, &c.; a
more simple Method).—INGREDIENTS for
sufficient for pair of fowls.—½ pint of melted
butter, made with milk, ½ pint of button
mushrooms, 1 dessertspoonful of mushroom
ketchup, if at hand; cayenne and salt to
taste. AVERAGE COST, 6d.

Make the melted butter with milk and
add to it the mushrooms, which must be
nicely cleaned and free from grit and the
stalks cut off. Let them simmer gently
for about 10 minutes, or until they are

quite tender. Put in the seasoning and ketchup; let it just boil, when serve.

TIME.—*Rather more than* 10 *minutes.*

SEASONABLE *from August to October.*

Mushrooms, Baked. (A Breakfast, Luncheon, or Supper Dish.)—INGREDIENTS *for dish for 4 or 5 persons.*—16 to 20 *mushroom-flaps, butter, pepper to taste.* AVERAGE COST, 1s. 6d.

For this mode of cooking, the mushroom-flaps are better than the buttons and should not be too large. Cut off a portion of the stalk, peel the top and wipe the mushrooms carefully with a piece of flannel and a little fine salt. Put them into a buttered tin baking-dish, with a very small piece of butter placed on each mushroom; sprinkle over a little pepper and let them bake for about 20 minutes, or longer should the mushrooms be very large. Have ready a *very hot* dish, pile the mushrooms high in the centre, pour the gravy round and send them to table quickly, with very *hot* plates.

TIME.—20 *minutes; large mushrooms* ½ *hour.*

SEASONABLE.—*Meadow mushrooms in September and October; cultivated mushrooms may be had at any time.*

Mushrooms, Broiled. (A Breakfast, Luncheon, or Supper Dish)—INGREDIENTS.—*Mushroom-flaps, pepper and salt to taste, butter, lemon-juice.*

Cleanse the mushrooms by wiping them with a piece of flannel and a little salt; cut off a portion of the stalk and peel the tops; broil them over a clear fire, turning them once and arrange them on a very hot dish. Put a small piece of butter on each mushroom, season with pepper and salt, and squeeze over them

BROILED MUSHROOMS.

a few drops of lemon-juice. Place the dish before the fire and when the butter is

melted, serve very hot and quickly. Moderate-sized flaps are better suited to this mode of cooking than the buttons; the latter are better in stews.

TIME.—10 *minutes for medium sized mushrooms.*

SEASONABLE.—*Meadow mushrooms in September and October; cultivated mushrooms may be had at any time.*

Mushrooms, Dried.—Wipe them clean and take away the brown part and peel off the skin; lay them on sheets of paper to dry, in a cool oven, when they will shrivel considerably. Keep them in paper bags, which hang in a dry place. When wanted for use, put them into cold gravy, bring them gradually to simmer and it will be found that they will regain nearly their usual size.

Mushrooms, Pickled.—INGREDIENTS.—*Sufficient vinegar to cover the mushrooms; to each quart of mushrooms, 2 blades of pounded mace, 1 oz. of ground pepper, salt to taste.*

Choose some nice young button mushrooms for pickling and rub off the skin with a piece of flannel and salt and cut off the stalks; if very large, take out the red inside and reject the black ones, as they are too old. Put them into a stewpan, sprinkle salt over them, with pounded mace and pepper in the above proportion; shake them well over a clear fire until the liquor flows and keep them there until they are all dried up again; then add as much vinegar as will cover them; just let it simmer for 1 minute and store it away in stone jars for use. When cold, tie down with bladder and keep in a dry place: they will remain good for a length of time and are generally considered delicious.

SEASONABLE.—*Make this the same time as ketchup, from the beginning of September to the middle of October.*

Mushrooms, To Preserve.—INGREDIENTS.—To each quart of mushrooms, allow 3 oz. of butter, pepper and salt to taste, the juice of 1 lemon, clarified butter.

Peel the mushrooms, put them into cold water, with a little lemon-juice; take them out and dry them very carefully in a cloth. Put the butter into a stewpan capable of holding the mushrooms; when it is melted, add the mushrooms, lemon-juice and a seasoning of pepper and salt; draw them down over a slow fire, and let them remain until their liquor is boiled away and they have become quite dry, but be careful in not allowing them to stick to the bottom of the stewpan. When done, put them into pots and pour over the top clarified butter. If wanted for immediate use, they will keep good a few days without being covered over. To re-warm them, put the mushrooms into a stewpan, strain the butter from them and they will be ready for use.

SEASONABLE.— Meadow mushrooms in September and October; cultivated mushrooms may be had at any time.

Mushrooms, Stewed.—INGREDIENTS for dish for 4 or 5 persons.—1 pint of mushroom buttons, 3 oz. of fresh butter, white pepper and salt to taste, lemon-juice, 1 teaspoonful of flour, cream or milk, ¼ teaspoonful of grated nutmeg. AVERAGE COST, 1s. 3d.

Cut off the ends of the stalks and pare neatly a pint of mushroom-buttons; put them into a basin of water, with a little lemon-juice, as they are done. When all are prepared, take them from the water with the hands, to avoid the sediment; and put them into a stewpan with the fresh butter, white pepper, salt and the juice of ½ lemon; cover the pan closely and let the mushrooms stew gently from 20 to 25 minutes; then thicken the butter with the above proportion of flour, add gradually sufficient cream, or cream and milk, to make the

sauce of a proper consistency and put in the grated nutmeg. If the mushrooms are not perfectly tender, stew them for 5 minutes longer, remove every particle of butter which may be floating on the top and serve.

TIME.—½ hour.

SEASONABLE. — Meadow mushrooms in September and October.

Mushrooms, Stewed in Gravy.

INGREDIENTS for dish for 4 or 5 persons.— 1 pint of mushroom-buttons, 1 pint of brown gravy, ¼ teaspoonful of grated nutmeg, cayenne and salt to taste. AVERAGE COST, 1s.

Make a pint of brown gravy, cut nearly all the stalks away from the mushrooms and peel the tops; put them into a stewpan with the gravy and simmer them gently from 20 minutes to ½ hour. Add the nutmeg and a seasoning of cayenne and salt and serve very hot.

TIME.—20 minutes to ½ hour.

SEASONABLE. — Meadow mushrooms in September and October.

Mustard, How to Mix.—INGREDIENTS.—Mustard, salt and water.

Mustard should be mixed with water that has been boiled and allowed to cool; hot water destroys its essential properties, and raw cold water might cause it to ferment. Put the mustard into a cup with a small pinch of salt, and mix with it very gradually sufficient boiled water to make it drop from the spoon without being watery. Stir and mix well, and  rub the lumps well down with the back of a spoon, as well-mixed mustard should be perfectly free from these. The mustard-pot should not be more than half-full, or rather less if it will not be used for a day

MUSTARD.

2 σ

or two, as it is so much better when it is freshly mixed.

Note.—One of the best brands of mustard is Champion's.

Mustard, Indian. (An excellent Relish to any Cold Meat.) INGREDIENTS. —¼ lb. of Colman's mustard, ¼ lb. of flour, ½ oz. of salt, 4 shalots, 4 tablespoonfuls of vinegar, 4 tablespoonfuls of ketchup, ¼ bottle of anchovy sauce.

Put the mustard, flour and salt into a basin, and make them into a stiff paste with boiling water. Boil the shalots with the vinegar, ketchup and anchovy sauce for 10 minutes, and pour the whole, *boiling*, over the mixture in the basin ; stir well and reduce it to a proper thickness ; put it into a bottle, with a bruised shalot at the bottom and store away for use. This makes an excellent relish and, if properly prepared, will keep for years.

Mustard, Tartar.—INGREDIENTS. —*Horseradish vinegar, cayenne, ½ a tea-cupful of mustard.*

Have ready sufficient horseradish vinegar to mix with the above proportion of mustard ; put the mustard into a cup, with a slight seasoning of cayenne ; mix it perfectly smooth with the vinegar, adding this a little at a time ; rub down with the back of a spoon any lumps that may appear and do not let it be too thin. Mustard may be flavoured in various ways : with tarragon, shalot, celery and many other vinegars, herbs, spices, &c.

Mutton.—Almost every large city has a particular manner of cutting up, or as it is called, dressing the carcase. In London this process is very simple, and as our butchers have found that much skewering back, doubling one part over another, or scoring the inner cuticle or fell tends to spoil the meat and shorten the time it would otherwise keep, they avoid all such treatment easily. The carcase when

flayed (which operation is performed while yet warm), the sheep when hung up and the head removed, presents the profile shown in our cut ; the small numeral indicating the parts or joints into which one-half of the animal is cut. After separating the hind from the fore - quarters, with eleven ribs to the latter, the quarters are usually subdivided in the manner shown in the sketch, in which the several joints are defined by the intervening lines and figures. *Hind quarter :*—No. 1, the leg ; 2, the loin – the two, when cut in one piece, being called the saddle. *Fore quarter :*—No. 3, the shoulder ; 4 and 5 the neck ; No. 5 being called, for distinction, the scrag which is generally afterwards separate from 4, the lower and better joint ; No. 6 the breast. The haunch of mutton, so often served at public dinners and special entertainments, comprises all the leg and so much of the loin, short of the ribs or lap as is indicated on the upper part of the carcase by a dotted line.

SIDE OF MUTTON SHOWING THE SEVERAL JOINTS

Mutton, Baked Minced.—(Cold Meat Cookery.) — INGREDIENTS — *The remains of any joint of cold roast mutton, or 2 onions, 1 bunch of savoury herbs, pepper and salt to taste, 2 blades of pounded mace or nutmeg, 1 teacupful of gravy, mashed potatoes.* AVERAGE COST, *exclusive of the meat,* 4d.

Mince an onion rather fine and fry it light-brown colour, add the herbs and mutton, both of which should be also finely minced and well mixed ; season with pepper and salt and a little pounded mace or nutmeg, and moisten with the above proportion of gravy. Put a layer of potatoes, mashed in the butter, at the bottom of a dish, then the mutton, and then another layer of potatoes, and bake for about ½ hour.

TIME.—½ *hour*.

SEASONABLE *at any time*.

Note.—If there should be a large quantity of meat, use 2 onions instead of 1.

Mutton, Boiled Breast of, and

Caper Sauce.—INGREDIENTS *for dish for 4 or 5 persons.*—*Breast of mutton, breadcrumbs, 2 tablespoonfuls of minced savoury herbs (put a large proportion of parsley), pepper and salt to taste.* AVERAGE COST, 7d. *per lb.*

Cut off the superfluous fat; bone the meat; sprinkle over a layer of breadcrumbs, minced herbs and seasoning; roll and bind it up firmly. Boil *gently* for 2 hours, remove the tape and serve with caper sauce, a little of which should be poured over the meat.

TIME.—2 *hours*.

SEASONABLE *all the year*.

Mutton, An excellent way to

Cook a Breast of.—INGREDIENTS *for dish for 5 persons.*—*Breast of mutton, 2 onions, salt and pepper to taste, flour, a bunch of savoury herbs, green peas.* AVERAGE COST, 7d. *per lb.*

Cut the mutton into pieces about 2 inches square, and let it be tolerably lean; put it into a stewpan with a little fat or butter, and fry it of a nice brown; then dredge in a little flour, slice the onions and put it with the herbs in the stewpan; pour in sufficient water *just* to cover the meat, and simmer the whole gently until the mutton is tender. Take out the meat, strain and skim off all the fat from the gravy, and put both the meat and gravy back into the stewpan; add about a quart of young green peas, and let them boil gently until done. 2 or 3 slices of bacon added and stewed with the mutton give additional flavour; and to insure the peas

being a beautiful green colour they may be boiled in water separately, and added to the stew at the moment of serving.

TIME.—2½ *hours*.

SEASONABLE *from June to August.*

Mutton, Broiled, and Tomato

Sauce. (Cold Meat Cookery.)—INGREDIENTS.—*A few slices of cold mutton, tomato sauce.*

Cut some nice slices from a cold leg or shoulder of mutton; season them with pepper and salt, and broil over a clear fire. Make some tomato sauce, pour it over the mutton and serve. This makes an excellent dish, and must be served very hot.

TIME. — *About* 5 *minutes to broil the mutton.*

SEASONABLE *in September and October, when tomatoes are plentiful and seasonable.*

Mutton Broth, To Make.—IN-

GREDIENTS *for* 1½ *pint of broth.*—1 *lb. of the scrag end of the neck of mutton,* 1 *onion, a bunch of sweet herbs,* ½ *turnip,* 3 *pints of water, pepper and salt to taste.* AVERAGE COST, 7d.

Put the mutton into a stewpan; pour over the water cold and add the other ingredients. When it boils skim it very carefully, cover the pan closely, and let it simmer very gently for an hour; strain it, let it cool, take off all the fat from the surface, and warm up as much as may be required, adding, if the patient be allowed to take it, a teaspoonful of minced parsley which has been previously scalded. Pearl barley or rice are very nice additions to mutton broth, and should be boiled as long as the other ingredients When either of these is added the broth must not be strained, but merely thoroughly skimmed. Plain mutton broth without seasoning is made by merely boiling the mutton, water and salt together, straining it, letting the broth cool, skimming all the fat off, and warming up as much as is required. This preparation would be very tasteless and insipid, but likely to agree with very delicate stomachs, whereas the least addition of other ingredients would have the contrary effect.

TIME.—1 *hour*.

SEASONABLE *at any time.*

Note.—Veal broth may be made in the same manner; the knuckle of a leg or shoulder is the part usually used for this purpose. It is very good with the addition of the inferior joints of a fowl, or a few shank-bones.

Mutton Broth, To Make

Quickly. — INGREDIENTS *for ½ pint of broth.*—1 or 2 *chops from a neck of mutton,* 1 *pint of water, a small bunch of sweet herbs,* ¼ *of an onion, pepper and salt to taste.* AVERAGE COST, 5*d.*

Cut the meat into small pieces; put it into a saucepan with the bones, but no skin or fat; add the other ingredients; cover the saucepan and bring the water quickly to boil. Take the lid off and continue the rapid boiling for 20 minutes, skimming it well during the process; strain the broth into a basin; if there should be any fat left on the surface remove it by laying a piece of thin paper on the top; the greasy particles will adhere to the paper, and so free the preparation from them. To an invalid nothing is more disagreeable than broth served with a quantity of fat floating on the top; to avoid this it is always better to allow it to get thoroughly cool, the fat can then be so easily removed.

TIME.—20 *minutes after the water boils.*

SEASONABLE *at any time.*

Mutton, Haunch of, To Carve.

—A deep cut should, in the first place, be

HAUNCH OF MUTTON.

made quite down to the bone, across the knuckle-end of the joint, along the line A to

B. This will let the gravy escape, and then it should be carved, in not too thick slices, along the whole length of the haunch in the direction of the line from D to C.

Mutton, Leg of, To Carve.—

This homely but capital English joint is almost invariably served at table as shown in the engraving. The carving of it is not

LEG OF MUTTON.

very difficult: the knife should be carried sharply down in the direction of the line from A to B and slices taken from either side, as the guests may desire, some liking the knuckle-end, as well done, and others preferring the more underdone part. The fat should be sought near the line C to D. Some connoisseurs are fond of having this joint dished with the under-side uppermost, so as to get at the finely-grained meat lying under that part of the joint, known as the Pope's eye; but this is an extravagant fashion and one that will hardly find favour in the eyes of many economical British housewives and housekeepers.

Mutton, Loin of, To Carve.—

There is one point in connection with carving a loin of mutton which includes every other; that is, that the joint should be thoroughly well jointed by the butcher before it is cooked. This knack of jointing requires practice and the proper tools; and no one but the butcher is supposed to have these. If the bones be not well jointed, the carving of a loin of mutton is not a gracious business; whereas, if that has been attended to, it is an easy and untroublesome task. The knife should be inserted at letter A, and, after feeling your way between the bones, it should be carried sharply in the direction of the line A to B. As there are some people

LOIN OF MUTTON.

who prefer the outside cut, while others do not like it, the question as to their choice of this should be asked.

Mutton, Saddle of, To Carve.

—Although we have heard, at various intervals, growlings expressed at the inevitable "saddle of mutton" at the dinner-parties of our middle classes, yet we doubt whether any other joint is better liked, when it has been well hung and cooked. There is a diversity of opinion

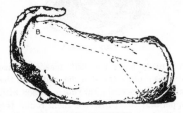

SADDLE OF MUTTON.

respecting the mode of sending this joint to table; but it has only reference to whether or no there shall be any portion of the tail, or, if so, how many joints of the tail. The carving is not difficult: it is usually cut in the direction of the line from B to A, quite down to the bones, in evenly-sliced pieces. A fashion, however, patronised by some, is to carve it obliquely, in the direction of the line from D to C; in which case the joint would be turned round the other way, having the tail end on the right of the carver.

Mutton, Shoulder of, To Carve.

—This is a joint not difficult to carve. The knife should be drawn from the outer edge of the shoulder in the direction of the line from A to B, until the bone of the shoulder is reached. As many slices as can be carved in this manner should be taken and afterwards the meat lying on each side of the blade-bone should be served, by carving in the direction of C to D and C to D. The uppermost side of the shoulder being now finished, the joint should be turned and slices taken

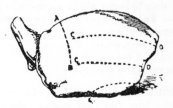

SHOULDER OF MUTTON.

off along its whole length. There are some who prefer this under-side of the shoulder for its juicy flesh, although the grain of the meat is not so fine as that on the other side.

Mutton Chops, Broiled.—IN-
GREDIENTS.—*Loin of mutton, pepper and salt, a small piece of butter.* AVERAGE COST, 1s. per lb.

Cut the chops from a well-hung tender loin of mutton, remove a portion of the fat and trim them into a nice shape; slightly beat and level them; place the gridiron over a bright clear fire, rub the bars with a little fat and lay on the chops. Whilst broiling, frequently turn them and in about 8 minutes they will be done. Season with pepper and salt, dish them on a very hot dish, rub a small piece of butter on each chop, and serve very hot and expeditiously.

TIME.—*About 8 minutes.*
SEASONABLE *at any time.*

Mutton - Collops.

INGREDIENTS *for small dish.—A few slices of a cold leg or loin of mutton, salt and pepper to taste, 1 blade of pounded mace, 1 small bunch of savoury herbs minced very fine, 2 or 3 shalots, 2 or 3 oz. of butter, 1 dessertspoonful of flour, ½ pint of gravy, 1 tablespoonful of lemon-juice.* AVERAGE COST, *exclusive of the meat,* 6d.

Cut some very thin slices from a leg or the chump end of a loin of mutton; sprinkle them with pepper, salt, pounded mace, minced savoury herbs and minced shalot; fry them in butter, stir in a dessertspoonful of flour, add the gravy and lemon-juice, simmer very gently about 5 or 7 minutes, and serve immediately.

TIME.—5 *to* 7 *minutes.*
SEASONABLE *at any time.*

Mutton Croquettes.

INGREDIENTS.—*Lean cold roast mutton, potatoes, flour,* 1 *egg, salt, pepper, hot lard.*

Mince the meat finely, taking away all gristle, and season well with salt and pepper. Boil some potatoes, and mash them with a very little butter and seasoning, then make them into a paste with flour and egg. Roll out this paste and cut into rounds, lay on one half some of the minced meat, then fold over and pinch the edges together as a sausage roll or puff. Fry a nice brown in hot lard.

TIME.—½ *hour.*
SEASONABLE *at any time.*

Mutton, Curried.

(Cold Meat Cookery.)—INGREDIENTS *for small dish.— The remains of any joint of cold mutton,* 2 *onions,* 3 *oz. of butter,* 1 *dessertspoonful of curry-powder,* 1 *dessertspoonful of flour, salt to taste,* ¼ *pint of stock or water.* AVERAGE COST, *exclusive of the meat,* 6d.

Slice the onions in thin rings and put them into a stewpan with the butter, and fry of a light brown; stir in the curry-powder, flour and salt, and mix all together. Cut the meat into nice thin slices (if there is not sufficient to do this it may be minced), and add it to the other ingredients; when well browned, add the stock or gravy and stew gently for about ½ hour. Serve in a dish with a border of boiled rice, or some in a vegetable dish.

TIME.—½ *hour.*
SEASONABLE *in winter.*

Mutton Cutlets, with Mashed Potatoes.

INGREDIENTS *for dish for* 6 *persons.—About* 3 *lbs. of the best end of the neck of mutton, salt and pepper to taste, mashed potatoes.* AVERAGE COST, 2s. 4d.

Procure a well-hung neck of mutton, saw off about 3 inches of the top of the bones, and cut the cutlets of a moderate thickness. Shape them by chopping off the thick part of the chine-bone; beat them flat with a cutlet-chopper, and scrape quite clean a portion of the top of the bone. Broil them over a nice clear fire for about 7 or 8 minutes, and turn them frequently.

MUTTON CUTLETS.

Have ready some smoothly-mashed white potatoes; place these in the middle of the dish; when the cutlets are done, season with pepper and salt; arrange them round the potatoes, with the thick end of the cutlets downwards, and serve very hot and quickly.

TIME.—7 *or* 8 *minutes.*
SEASONABLE *at any time.*

Note.—Cutlets may be served in various ways: with peas, tomatoes, onions, sauce piquant, &c.

Mutton Cutlets, Italian.

INGREDIENTS *for dish for* 6 *persons, as an entrée.—*2 *lbs. of best end of neck of mutton, a tablespoonful of minced parsley,* 4 *oz. of grated bread-crumbs, a teaspoonful of finely-minced onion,* 2 *oz. of butter, a little grated lemon-rind, salt, pepper, mace, flour,* 1 *egg,*

1 *wineglassful of sherry or Madeira, lard for frying.* AVERAGE COST, 2s. 6d.

Cut the meat into even, well-shaped cutlets, paring the bones to flatten them. Mix the bread-crumbs, herbs and seasoning together, melt the butter, dip each cutlet into it, then into beaten egg, and lastly into the bread-crumbs. Put some lard into a frying-pan, and as soon as it boils put in the cutlets and fry them a bright brown, then put them on a hot dish and keep them hot while the gravy is made. To make this, dredge some flour into the pan, and when it is brown, pour in a tea-cupful of boiling water and the wine, and a little sauce or ketchup if liked. Boil up once, then pour round the cutlets, and serve with a garnish of vegetables, such as tufts of cauliflower or green peas.

TIME.—*About* 10 *minutes to fry the cutlets.*

SEASONABLE *at any time.*

Mutton, Braised Fillet of,

with French Beans.—INGREDIENTS *for dish for 4 persons.*—*The chump end of a loin of mutton, buttered paper, French beans, a little glaze,* 1 *pint of gravy.* AVERAGE COST, 10d. *per lb.*

Roll up the mutton in a piece of buttered paper, roast it for 2 hours and do not allow it to acquire the least colour. Have ready some French beans, boiled and drained on a sieve ; remove the paper from the mutton, glaze it ; just heat up the beans in the gravy, and lay them on the dish with the meat over them. The remainder of the gravy may be strained and sent to table in a tureen.

TIME.—2 *hours.*

SEASONABLE *at any time.*

Mutton, Haricot.—INGREDIENTS

for dish for 8 persons.—4 *lbs. of the middle or best end of the neck of mutton,* 3 *carrots,* 3 *turnips,* 3 *onions, pepper and salt to taste,* 1 *tablespoonful of ketchup or Harvey's sauce.* AVERAGE COST, 3s.

Trim off some of the fat, cut the mutton into rather thin chops and put them into a frying-pan with the fat trimmings. Fry of a pale brown, but do not cook them enough for eating. Cut the carrots and turnips into dice and the onions into slices, and slightly fry them in the same fat that the mutton was browned in, but do not allow them to take any colour. Now lay the mutton at the bottom of a stewpan, then the vegetables, and pour over them just sufficient boiling water to cover the whole. Give them a boil, skim well and then set the pan on the side of the fire to simmer gently until the meat is tender. Skim off every particle of fat, add a seasoning of pepper and salt and a little ketchup, and serve. This dish is very much better if made the day before it is wanted for table, as the fat can be so much more easily removed when the gravy is cold. This should be particularly attended to, as it is apt to be rich and greasy if eaten the same day it is made. It should be served in rather a deep dish.

TIME.—2½ *hours to simmer gently.*

SEASONABLE *at any time.*

Mutton, Haricot.—INGREDIENTS

for dish for 4 or 5 persons.—*Breast or scrag of mutton, flour, pepper and salt to taste,* 1 *large onion,* 3 *cloves, a bunch of savoury herbs,* 1 *blade of mace, carrots and turnips, sugar.* AVERAGE COST, 7d. *per lb.*

Cut the mutton into square pieces, and fry them a nice colour ; then dredge over them a little flour and a seasoning of pepper and salt. Put all into a stewpan and moisten with boiling water, adding the onion, stuck with 3 cloves, the mace and herbs. Simmer gently till the meat is done, skim off all the fat and then add the carrots and turnips, which should be previously cut in dice and fried in a little sugar to colour them. Let the whole simmer again for 10 minutes ; take out the onion and bunch of herbs, and serve.

TIME.—*About* 3 *hours to simmer.*

SEASONABLE *at any time.*

Mutton, Haricot. (Cold Meat Cookery.)

INGREDIENTS.— *The remains of cold neck or loin of mutton, 2 oz. of butter, 3 onions, 1 dessertspoonful of flour, ½ pint of good gravy, pepper and salt to taste, 2 tablespoonfuls of port wine, 1 tablespoonful of mushroom ketchup, 2 carrots, 2 turnips, 1 head of celery. AVERAGE COST, exclusive of the meat, 8d.*

Cut the cold mutton into moderate-sized chops and take off the fat; slice the onions and fry them with the chops, in a little butter, of a nice brown colour; stir in the flour, add the gravy, and let it stew gently nearly an hour. In the meantime boil the vegetables until *nearly* tender, slice them, and add them to the mutton about ¼ hour before it is to be served. Season with pepper and salt, add the ketchup and port wine, give one boil, and serve.

TIME.—*1 hour.*
SEASONABLE *at any time.*

Mutton, Hashed.

INGREDIENTS. —*The remains of cold roast shoulder or leg of mutton, 6 whole peppers, 6 whole allspice, a faggot of savoury herbs, ½ head of celery, 1 onion, 2 oz. of butter, flour. AVERAGE COST, exclusive of the meat, 4d.*

Cut the meat in nice even slices from the bones, trimming off all superfluous fat and gristle; chop the bones and fragments of the joints, put them into a stewpan with the pepper, spice, herbs and celery; cover with water and simmer for 1 hour. Slice and fry the onion of a nice pale brown colour, dredge in a little flour to make it thick, and add this to the bones, &c. Stew for ¼ hour, strain the gravy, and let it cool; then skim off every particle of fat, and put it, with the meat, into a stewpan. Flavour with ketchup, Harvey's sauce, tomato sauce, or any flavouring that may be preferred, and let the meat gradually warm through, but not boil, or it will harden. To hash meat properly, it should be laid in cold gravy and only left on the fire just long enough to warm through.

TIME.—*1½ hour to simmer the gravy.*
SEASONABLE *at any time.*

Mutton, Roast Haunch of.

INGREDIENTS.—*Haunch of mutton, a little salt, flour. AVERAGE COST, 10d. per lb.*

Let this joint hang as long as possible without becoming tainted, and while hanging dust flour over it, which keeps off the flies and prevents the air from getting to it. If not well hung, the joint when it comes to table will do credit neither to the butcher nor the cook, as it will not be tender. Wash the outside well, lest it should have a bad flavour from keeping; then flour it and put it down to a nice brisk fire, at some distance so that it may gradually warm through. Keep continually

HAUNCH OF MUTTON.

basting, and about ½ hour before it is served draw it nearer to the fire to get nicely brown. Sprinkle a little fine salt over the meat, pour off the dripping, add a little boiling water slightly salted, and strain this over the joint. Place a paper ruche on the bone, and send red-currant jelly and gravy in a tureen to table with it.

TIME.—*About 4 hours.*
SEASONABLE.—*In best season from September to March.*

Mutton, Boiled Leg of.

INGREDIENTS.—*Mutton, water, salt. AVERAGE COST, 10d. per lb.*

A leg of mutton for boiling should not hang too long, as it will not look a good colour when dressed. Cut off the shankbone, trim the knuckle, and wash and wipe it very clean; plunge it into sufficient boiling water to cover it, let it boil up, then draw the saucepan to the side of the fire, where it should remain till the finger can be borne in the water. Then place it

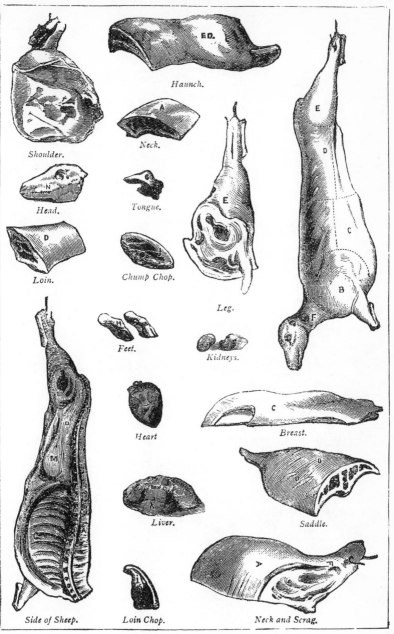

Haunch.

Shoulder.

Neck.

Head.

Tongue.

Loin.

Chump Chop.

Leg.

Feet.

Kidneys.

Heart

Breast.

Liver.

Saddle.

Side of Sheep.

Loin Chop.

Neck and Scrag.

Various Parts of Mutton.

sufficiently near the fire that the water may gently simmer, and be very careful that it does not boil fast, or the meat will be hard. Skim well, add a little salt, and in about 2¼ hours after the water begins to simmer a moderate-sized leg of mutton will be done. Serve with carrots and mashed turnips, which may be boiled with the meat, and send caper sauce to table with it in a tureen.

TIME.—*A moderate-sized leg of mutton of 9 lbs., 2½ hours after the water boils; one of 12 lbs., rather more than 3 hours.*

SEASONABLE *nearly all the year, but not so good in June, July and August.*

Note.—When meat is liked very *thoroughly* cooked, allow more time than stated above. The liquor this joint was boiled in should be converted into soup.

Mutton, Boned Leg of, Stuffed.

—INGREDIENTS.—*A small leg of mutton, weighing 6 or 7 lbs., forcemeat, 2 shalots finely minced.*

Make a forcemeat, to which add 2 finely-minced shalots. Bone the leg of mutton without spoiling the skin, and cut off a great deal of the fat. Fill the hole up whence the bone was taken, with the forcemeat, and sew it up underneath to prevent its falling out. Bind and tie it up compactly, and roast it before a nice clear fire for about 2¼ hours, or rather longer; remove the tape and send it to table with a good gravy. It may be glazed or not as preferred.

TIME.—*2½ hours, or rather longer.*
SEASONABLE *at any time.*

Mutton, Braised Leg of.

—INGREDIENTS *for dish for 8 persons.*—1 *small leg of mutton, 4 carrots, 3 onions, 1 faggot of savoury herbs, a bunch of parsley, seasoning to taste, of pepper and salt, a few slices of bacon, a few veal trimmings, ½ pint of gravy or water.* AVERAGE COST, 5s. 6d.

Line the bottom of a braising-pan with a few slices of bacon, put in the carrots, onions, herbs, parsley and seasoning, and over these place the mutton. Cover the whole with a few more slices of bacon and the veal trimmings, pour in the gravy or water and stew very *gently* for 4 hours. Strain the gravy, reduce it to a glaze over a sharp fire, glaze the mutton with it, and send it to table placed on a dish of white haricot beans boiled tender, or garnished with glazed onions.

TIME.—4 *hours.*
SEASONABLE *at any time.*

Mutton, Roast Leg of.

—INGREDIENTS.—*Leg of mutton, a little salt.* AVERAGE COST, 10d. per lb.

As mutton when freshly killed is never tender, hang it almost as long as it will keep; flour it and put it in a cool airy place for a few days, if the weather will permit. Wash off the flour, wipe it very dry and cut off the shank-bone; put it down to a brisk, clear fire, dredge with flour, and keep continually basting the whole time it is cooking. About 20 minutes before serving, draw it near the

LEG OF MUTTON.

fire to get nicely brown; sprinkle over it a little salt, dish the meat, pour off the dripping, add some boiling water slightly salted, strain it over the joint, and serve.

TIME.—*A leg of mutton weighing 10 lbs., about 2¼ or 2½ hours; one of 7 lbs., about 2 hours, or rather less.*

SEASONABLE *at any time, but not so good in June, July and August.*

Mutton, Roast Loin of.

—INGREDIENTS.—*Loin of mutton, a little salt.* AVERAGE COST, 10d. per lb.

Cut and trim off the superfluous fat, and see that the butcher joints the meat properly, as thereby much annoyance is saved to the carver, when it comes to table. Have ready a nice clear fire (it

LOIN OF MUTTON.

need not be a very wide large one), put down the meat, dredge with flour, and baste well until it is done. Make the gravy as for roast leg of mutton, and serve very hot.

TIME.—*A loin of mutton weighing 6 lbs., 1½ hour or rather longer.*

SEASONABLE *at any time.*

Mutton, Rolled Loin of. (Very Excellent.)—INGREDIENTS *for dish for 8 persons.— About 6 lbs. of a loin of mutton, ½ teaspoonful of pepper, ¼ teaspoonful of pounded allspice, ¼ teaspoonful of mace, ¼ teaspoonful of nutmeg, 6 cloves, forcemeat, 1 glass of port wine, 2 tablespoonfuls of mushroom ketchup.* AVERAGE COST, 5s.

Hang the mutton till tender, bone it and sprinkle over it pepper, mace, cloves, allspice and nutmeg in the above proportion, all of which must be pounded very fine. Let it remain for a day, then make a forcemeat, cover the meat with it and roll and bind it up firmly. Half bake it in a slow oven, let it grow cold, take off the fat and put the gravy into a stewpan ; flour the meat, put it in the gravy and stew it till perfectly tender. Now take out the meat, unbind it, add to the gravy, wine and ketchup as above, give one boil and pour over the meat. Serve with red-currant jelly ; and, if obtainable, a few mushrooms stewed for a few minutes in the gravy will be found a great improvement.

TIME.—*1½ hour to bake the meat, 1½ hour to stew gently.*

SEASONABLE *at any time.*

Note.—This joint will be found very nice if rolled and stuffed, as here directed, and plainly

roasted. It should be well basted and served with a good gravy and currant jelly.

Mutton, Boiled Neck of.—INGREDIENTS *for dish for 6 or 7 persons.— 4 lbs. of the middle or best end of the neck of mutton, a little salt.* AVERAGE COST 9d. per lb.

Trim off a portion of the fat, should there be too much, and if it is to look particularly nice, the chine-bone should be sawn down, the ribs stripped half-way down, and the ends of the bones chopped off ; this is, however, not necessary. Put the meat into sufficient *boiling* water to cover it ; when it boils, add a little salt and remove all the scum. Draw the saucepan to the side of the fire, and let the water get so cool that the finger may be borne in it ; then simmer very *slowly* and gently until the meat is done, which will be in about 1½ hour, or rather more, reckoning from the time that it begins to simmer. Serve with turnips and caper sauce and pour a little of it over the meat. The turnips should be boiled with the mutton ; and when at hand, a few carrots will also be found an improvement. These, however, if very large and thick, must be cut into long thinnish pieces, or they will not be sufficiently done by the time the mutton is ready. Garnish the dish with carrots and turnips, placed alternately round the mutton.

TIME.—*4 lbs. of the neck of mutton, about 1½ hour.*

SEASONABLE *at any time.*

Mutton, Ragout of Cold Neck of. (Cold Meat Cookery.)—INGREDIENTS. —*The remains of a cold neck or loin of mutton, 2 oz. of butter, a little flour, 2 onions sliced, ½ pint of water, 2 small carrots, 2 turnips, pepper and salt to taste.* AVERAGE COST, *exclusive of the meat,* 4d.

Cut the mutton into small chops and trim off the greater portion of the fat ; put the butter into a stewpan, dredge in a little flour, add the sliced onions, and keep stirring till brown; then put in the meat. When this is quite brown, add the water and the carrots and turnips, which should be cut into very thin slices; season with pepper and salt and stew till quite tender, which will be in about ¾ hour. When in season, green peas may be substituted for the carrots and turnips; they should be piled in the centre of the dish and the chops laid round.

TIME.—¾ *hour.*

SEASONABLE, *with peas, from June to August.*

Mutton, Roast Neck of.—INGREDIENTS.—*Neck of mutton; a little salt.* AVERAGE COST, 9*d. per lb.*

For roasting, choose the middle, or the best end of the neck of mutton, and if there is a very large proportion of fat, trim off some of it and save it for making into suet puddings, which will be found exceedingly good. Let the bones be cut short, and see that it is properly jointed before it is laid down to the fire, as they will be more easily separated when they come to table. Place

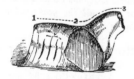

NECK OF MUTTON.

1—2, Best end.   2—3, Scrag.

the joint at a nice brisk fire, dredge it with flour, and keep continually basting until done. A few minutes before serving, draw it nearer the fire to acquire a nice colour, sprinkle over it a little salt, pour off the dripping, add a little boiling water slightly salted; strain this over the meat, and serve. Red-currant jelly may be sent to table with it.

TIME.—4 *lbs. of the neck of mutton, rather more than 1 hour.*

SEASONABLE *at any time.*

Mutton, Stewed Neck of. (Irish Stew.)—INGREDIENTS *for dish for 6 or 8 persons.*—3 *lbs. of the loin or neck of mutton, 4 or 5 large onions, 5 lbs. of potatoes, pepper and salt to taste,* 1¼ *pint of water.* AVERAGE COST, 2s. 9d.

Trim off some of the fat, and cut the meat into chops of moderate thickness. Pare and halve the potatoes, and cut the onions into slices. Put first a layer of potatoes at the bottom of a saucepan, then one of mutton and onions, well seasoned, and so on till the pan is full, the vegetables forming the top layer. Pour in the water and stew very gently for 2½ hours, keeping the saucepan closed the whole time, but shaking it occasionally to prevent burning the stew.

TIME.—2½ *hours.*

SEASONABLE.—*Best in winter.*

Mutton Pie. (Cold Meat Cookery.)—INGREDIENTS.— *The remains of a cold leg, loin, or neck of mutton, pepper and salt to taste, 2 blades of pounded mace, 1 dessertspoonful of chopped parsley, 1 teaspoonful of minced savoury herbs; when liked, a little minced onion or shalot; 3 or 4 potatoes, 1 teacupful of gravy; crust.*

Cold mutton may be made into very good pies, if well seasoned and mixed with a few herbs; if the leg is used, cut it into very thin slices; if the loin or neck, into thin cutlets. Place some at the bottom of the dish; season well with pepper, salt, mace, parsley and herbs; then put a layer of potatoes, sliced, then more mutton, and so on till the dish is full; add the gravy, cover with a crust and bake for 1 hour.

TIME.—1 *hour.*

SEASONABLE *at any time.*

Note.—The remains of an underdone leg of mutton may be converted into a very good family pudding, by cutting the meat into slices and putting them into a basin lined with a suet crust. It should be seasoned well with pepper, salt and minced shalot, covered with a crust, and boiled for about 3 hours.

Mutton Pie.

INGREDIENTS *for dish for 4 or 5 persons.*—2 lbs. *of the neck or loin of mutton, weighed after being boned; 2 kidneys, pepper and salt to taste, 2 teacupfuls of gravy or water, 2 tablespoonfuls of minced parsley ; when liked, a little minced onion or shalot; puff crust.* AVERAGE COST, 2s. 6d.

Bone the mutton and cut the meat into steaks all of the same thickness, and leave but very little fat. Cut up the kidneys, and arrange these with the meat neatly in a pie-dish ; sprinkle over them the minced parsley and a seasoning of pepper and salt ; pour in the gravy, and cover with a tolerably good puff crust. Bake for 1½ hour, or rather longer should the pie be very large, and let the oven be rather brisk. A well-made suet crust may be used instead of puff crust, and will be found exceedingly good.

TIME.—1½ *hour, or rather longer.*

SEASONABLE *at any time.*

Mutton Pudding.

INGREDIENTS *for dish for 6 persons.*—About 2 lbs. *of the chump end of a loin of mutton, weighed after being boned, pepper and salt to taste, suet crust made with milk, in the proportion of 6 oz. of suet to each pound of flour ; a very small quantity of minced onion (this may be omitted when the flavour is not liked).*

Cut the meat into rather thin slices and season them with pepper and salt ; line the pudding-dish with crust ; lay in the meat, and nearly, but do not quite, fill it up with water ; when the flavour is liked, add a small quantity of minced onion ; cover with crust, and proceed in the same manner as directed in recipe for rump-steak-and-kidney pudding.

TIME.—*About 3 hours.*

SEASONABLE *all the year, but more suitable in winter.*

Mutton, Roast Saddle of.

INGREDIENTS.—*Saddle of mutton; a little salt.* AVERAGE COST, 10d. *per lb.*

To insure this joint being tender, let it hang for ten days or a fortnight, if the weather permits. Cut off the tail and flaps and trim away every part that has not indisputable pretensions to be eaten, and have the skin taken off and skewered on again. Put it down to a bright, clear fire, and, when the joint has been cooking for an hour, remove the skin and dredge it

SADDLE OF MUTTON.

with flour. It should not be placed too near the fire, as the fat should not be in the slightest degree burnt, but kept constantly basted, both before and after the skin is removed. Sprinkle some salt over the joint ; make a little gravy in the dripping-pan ; pour it over the meat, which send to table with a tureen of made gravy and red-currant jelly.

TIME.—*A saddle of mutton weighing* 10 lbs., 2½ *hours;* 14 lbs., 3¼ *hours. When liked underdone, allow rather less time.*

SEASONABLE *all the year; not so good when lamb is in full season.*

Mutton, Roast Shoulder of.

INGREDIENTS. — *Shoulder of mutton; a little salt.* AVERAGE COST, 9d. *per lb.*

Put the joint down to a bright, clear fire ; flour it well and keep continually basting.

SHOULDER OF MUTTON.

About ¼ hour before serving, draw it near the fire, that the outside may acquire a nice brown colour, but not sufficiently near to blacken the fat. Sprinkle a little fine salt over the meat, empty the dripping-pan of its contents, pour in a little boiling water slightly salted, and strain this over the joint. Onion sauce, or stewed Spanish onions are usually sent to table with this dish, and sometimes baked potatoes.

TIME.—*A shoulder of mutton weighing 6 or 7 lbs., 1½ hour.*

SEASONABLE *at any time.*

Note.—Shoulder of mutton may be dressed in a variety of ways: boiled, and served with onion sauce ; boned, and stuffed with a good veal forcemeat; or baked, with sliced potatoes in the dripping-pan.

Mutton Soup, Good.— INGREDI-
ENTS *for sufficient for* 12 *persons.—A neck of mutton about* 5 *or* 6 *lbs.*, 3 *carrots,* 3 *turnips,* 2 *onions, a large bunch of sweet herbs, including parsley ; salt and pepper to taste ; a little sherry, if liked;* 3 *quarts of water.* AVERAGE COST, 3*s.* 6*d.*

Lay the ingredients in a covered pan before the fire and let them remain there the whole day, stirring occasionally. The next day put the whole into a stewpan and place it on a brisk fire. When it commences to boil, take the pan off the fire and put it on one side to simmer until the meat is done. When ready for use, take out the meat, dish it up with carrots and turnips, and send it to table ; strain the soup, let it cool, skim off all the fat, season, and thicken it with a tablespoonful, or rather more, of arrowroot ; flavour with a little sherry, simmer for 5 minutes, and serve.

TIME.—15 *hours.*

SEASONABLE *at any time.*

Mutton, with Poached Eggs.
(Cold Meat Cookery.) — INGREDIENTS.— *Cold mutton, underdone if possible, eggs, pepper and salt.*

This dish may be served in two ways. The mutton may be finely minced and seasoned, or slices of it may be cut up the same size and thickness, salted and pep- pered, and grilled till a nice brown over a clear fire. The eggs should be poached while the meat is being cooked, and they should be done evenly in an egg-poacher, or the edges trimmed. When the meat, which may be served plain, or in a wall of mashed potatoes, is ready, the eggs should be laid on the top, and a good gravy, which is improved by a little vinegar or lemon, served with this dish.

TIME.—20 *minutes.*

SEASONABLE *at any time.*

Mutton, with Caper Sauce.
(Tinned Meat.)—INGREDIENTS *for dish for* 6 *persons.—A* 2-*lb. tin of mutton, caper sauce.* AVERAGE COST, 1*s.* 6*d.*

Take off the top of the tin and stand it in a large saucepan filled with boiling water to within a couple of inches of the top. When thoroughly heated, turn out on to a hot dish and serve with caper sauce.

TIME.—½ *hour.*

SEASONABLE *at any time.*

Mutton, with Forcemeat.—IN-
GREDIENTS.—*A leg of mutton, about* 7 *lbs., well hung, lardoons of fat bacon and ham,* 3 *or* 4 *anchovies, parsley, blanched tarragon, garlic, thyme, onions chopped,* 3 *bay-leaves, pepper, salt,* ½ *pint of olive oil,* 2 *tablespoonfuls of vinegar.* AVERAGE COST *of the mutton,* 8½*d.* *to* 9*d.* *per lb.*

Cut off the shank bone of the mutton, lift the skin, partly without injuring it, and lard the leg with the lardoons of bacon and ham, some fillets of anchovies and bits of parsley and blanched tarragon, and (if not objected to) chopped onions, the bay-leaves, pepper and salt. Pour over the oil and vinegar, let the mutton lie in this marinade two to three hours, turning frequently, then take it out, spread over it the herbs, &c., of the marinade, covering with the skin, wrap up in buttered paper, and roast at a brisk fire.

TIME.—2 *hours.*

SEASONABLE *at any time.*

"Now good digestion wait on appetite,
And health on both."- -MACBETH.

NASTURTIUMS, PICKLED.

NASTURTIUMS Pickled. (A very good Substitute for Capers.) IN-GREDIENTS. — *To each pint of vine-gar, 1 oz. of salt, 6 peppercorns, nasturtiums.*

Gather the nasturtium pods on a dry day and wipe them clean with a cloth; put them in a dry glass bottle, with vinegar, salt and

NASTURTIUMS.

pepper, in the above proportion. If there are not enough to fill a bottle, cork up what

NECTARINES, PRESERVED.

there are until there are some more fit; they may be added from day to day. Bung up the bottles and seal or rosin the tops. They will be fit for use in 10 or 12 months; and the best way is to make them one season for the next.

SEASONABLE.—*Look for nasturtium-pods from the end of July to the end of August.*

Nectarines, Preserved.—INGRE-DIENTS.—*To every lb. of sugar allow ¼ pint of water, nectarines.*

Divide the nectarines in two, take out the stones, and make a strong syrup with sugar and water in the above proportion. Put in the nectarines, and boil them until they have thoroughly imbibed the sugar. Keep the fruit as whole as possible, and turn it carefully into a pan. The next day boil it again for a few minutes, take out the nectarines, put them into jars, boil the syrup quickly for 5 minutes, pour it over the fruit, and, when cold, cover the preserve down. The syrup and preserve must be carefully skimmed, or it will not be clear.

TIME.—*10 minutes to boil the sugar and water; 20 minutes to boil the fruit the first*

*time, ten minutes the second time ; 5
minutes to boil the syrup.*

SEASONABLE *in August and September,
but cheapest in September.*

Nectar, Welsh.—INGREDIENTS *for*
2 *gallons.*—1 *lb. of raisins,* 3 *lemons,* 2 *lbs.
of loaf sugar,* 2 *gallons of boiling water.*
AVERAGE COST, 1s. 3d.

Cut the peel of the lemons very thin,
pour upon it the boiling water, and, when
cool, add the strained juice of the lemons,
the sugar and the raisins, stoned and
chopped very fine. Let it stand 4 or 5
days, stirring it every day, then strain it
through a jelly-bag and bottle it for present
use.

TIME.— 4 *or* 5 *days.*

Negus, To Make.—INGREDIENTS.
—*To every pint of port wine allow* 1 *quart
of boiling water,* ¼ *lb. of sugar,* 1 *lemon,
grated nutmeg to taste.* AVERAGE COST,
6d. *per pint.*

As this beverage is more usually drunk
at children's parties than at any other,
the wine need not be very old or expensive
for the purpose, a new fruity wine answering very well for it. Put the wine into a
jug, rub some lumps of sugar (equal to ¼
lb.) on the lemon-rind until all the yellow
part of the skin is absorbed, then squeeze
the juice and strain it. Add the sugar and
lemon-juice to the port wine, with the
grated nutmeg ; pour over it the boiling
water, cover the jug, and, when the
beverage has cooled a little, it will be fit
for use. Negus may also be made of
sherry, or any other sweet white wine, but
is more usually made of port than of any
other beverage.

Nesselrode Pudding. (An Iced
Pudding ; CAREME'S Recipe.)—INGREDI-
ENTS.—40 *chestnuts,* 1 *lb. of sugar, flavouring of vanilla,* 1 *pint of cream, the yolks of*
12 *eggs,* 1 *glass of Maraschino,* 1 *oz. of candied citron,* 2 *oz. of currants,* 2 *oz. of stoned
raisins,* ½ *pint of whipped cream,* 3 *eggs.*
AVERAGE COST, 4s.

Blanch the chestnuts in the boiling water,
remove the husks, and pound them in a
mortar until perfectly smooth, adding a
few spoonfuls of syrup. Then rub them
through a fine sieve and mix them in a
basin with a pint of syrup made from 1
lb. of sugar, clarified and flavoured with
vanilla, 1 pint of cream and the yolks of
12 eggs. Set this mixture over a slow fire,
stirring it *without ceasing*, and, just as it
begins to boil, take it off and pass it
through a tammy. When it is cold, put
it into a freezing-pot, adding the Maraschino, and make the mixture set ; then add
the sliced citron, the currants and stoned
raisins (these two latter should be soaked
the day previously in Maraschino and sugar
pounded with vanilla) ; the whole thus
mingled, add a plateful of whipped cream
mixed with the whites of 3 eggs, beaten to
a froth with a little syrup. When the
pudding is perfectly frozen, put it into a
pine-apple-shaped mould ; close the lid,
place it again in the freezing-pan, covered
over with pounded ice and saltpetre, and
let it remain until required for table ; then
turn the pudding out, and serve.

TIME.—½ *hour to freeze the mixture.*
SEASONABLE *from October to February.*

Nougat. — INGREDIENTS.—*Almonds,
filberts and pistachios, half their weight in
white sugar, liqueur for flavouring, lemon-
juice.*

Blanch, drain, dry and heat the nuts,
which should be cut up small. Melt the
sugar in a stewpan, or copper sugar-boiler,
and put a dessertspoonful of lemon-juice
to each pound ; then add the chopped nuts
and flavouring, and boil for a few minutes,
and pour on an oiled slab to cool.

Nougats à la Crême.—INGREDI-
ENTS *for dish for* 10 *persons.*—1 *lb. of
sweet almonds, a few bitter ones,* 1 *lb. of*

white sugar, 1 *pint of cream, some crystal-lised cherries.* AVERAGE COST, 3*s.*

Blanch, peel and dry the almonds, and cut each almond lengthwise into 4 or 5 slices, then dry them in a slow oven, without allowing them to take colour. Put the sugar in a preserving pan and melt it, stirring it with a wooden spoon to prevent it catching. When a good yellow colour, throw in the almonds, hot from the oven, stirring all the while, then take the pan off the fire and complete the mixing. Have ready a tin plate and some small patty-pans well oiled, then, taking a spoonful of the mixture at a time, flatten it with a lemon on the tin plate as thin as possible, and line the patty-pans, squeezing the nougat close to the sides with the lemon

NOUGATS À LA CRÈME.

Do this as quickly as possible, as the nougat so soon cools. When cold, turn out the moulds out of the pans, fill them with the cream, whipped and flavoured, and place a preserved cherry on the top of each.

TIME.—*About ½ hour to stir the nougat.*
SEASONABLE *at any time.*

November, Things in Season:

Fish.—Brill, cod, crabs, eels, haddocks, oysters, pike, soles, turbot, whiting.

Meat.—Beef, mutton, veal, doe venison.

Poultry.—Chickens, fowls, geese, larks, pigeons, pullets, rabbits, teal, turkeys, widgeon, wild-duck.

Game.—Hares, partridges, pheasants, snipe, woodcock.

Vegetables.—Beetroot, cabbages, carrots, celery, lettuces, late cucumbers, onions, potatoes, salading, spinach, sprouts — various herbs.

Fruit.—Apples, bullaces, chestnuts, filberts, grapes, pears, walnuts.

November, Game Dinners for:

1.

Game Soup.

Fillets of Wild Duck.
Curried Game.

Roast Venison.
Hares.
Ptarmigans.

Quails—Woodcock.
Russian Salad.

Iced Pudding.
Compôte of Pine-apple.

Dessert.

2.

Pheasant Soup.

Salmi of Game.
Croquettes of Hare.

Roast Hare.
Vegetables.

Snipe.

Compôte of Peaches.
Marbled Jelly.

Cheese Salad.

Dessert.

3.

Partridge Soup.

Game Rissoles.
Hashed Wild Duck.

Roast Pheasants.
Fried Potatoes.
Stewed Celery.

Woodcock.

Macaroni and Pine-apple.
Vanilla Cream.

Cheese Soufflé.

Dessert.

November—Dinner for Twelve Persons.

MENU. (English.)	Quantity.	Average Cost.		MENU. (French.)
		s.	d.	
Oysters.	4 doz.	6	0	Huîtres.
Clear Mock Turtle.	5 pints.	4	6	Consommé de Tête de Veau.
Turbot,	4 lbs.	4	0	Turbot,
Horseradish Sauce.	2 turs.	1	0	Sauce Raifort.
Smelts.	3 doz.	4	6	Eperlans.
Lark Pie.	1	6	0	Paté aux Alouettes.
Croquette of Chicken.	2 dishes.	3	0	Croquettes de Volaille.
Saddle of Mutton.	1 joint.	10	6	Selle de Mouton.
Potatoes. Brussels Sprouts.	4 lbs. ea.	1	4	Pommes de Terre. Choux.
Pheasants.	2 birds.	7	0	Faisans.
Curaçoa Soufflé.	1	4	0	Soufflé de Curaçoa.
Marbled Jelly.	2 mlds.	3	6	Gelée Marbrée.
		£2 15	4	

November—Dinner for Ten Persons.

MENU. (English.)	Quantity.	Average Cost.		MENU. (French.)
		s.	d.	
Hare Soup.	2 qts.	3	6	Potage de Levraut.
Brill,	1 fish.	4	0	Barbue,
Lobster Sauce.	2 turs.	2	6	Sauce Homard.
Salmi of Game.	2 dishes.	6	0	Salmi de Gibier.
Leg of Mutton.	1 joint.	7	6	Gigot de Mouton.
Potatoes.	3 lbs.	0	3	Pommes de Terre.
Sea Kale.	2 dishes.	1	3	Choux Marins.
Woodcock.	5 birds.	10	0	Bécasses.
Russian Salad.	1 dish.	1	6	Salade à la Russe.
Almond Pudding.	1	2	6	Pouding d'Amandes.
Vanilla Cream.	1 mould.	2	0	Crême de Vanille.
		£2 1	0	

November—Dinner for Eight Persons.

MENU. (English.)	Quantity.	Average Cost.		MENU. (French.)
		s.	d.	
Ox-Tail Soup.	3 pints.	3	0	Potage de Queue de Bœuf.
Cod's Head and Shoulders,	3 lbs.	2	0	Cabillaud,
Oyster Sauce.	1 tur.	3	6	Sauce aux Huîtres.
Chicken Patties.	10	2	6	Petits Patés de Volailles.
Saddle of Mutton.	1 joint.	10	0	Selle de Mouton.
Potatoes. Spinach.	3 lbs. ea.	1	0	Pommes de Terre. Epinards.
Woodcock.	4 birds.	8	0	Bécasses.
Compôte of Fruit.	1 dish.	3	0	Compôte de Fruit.
Liqueur Jelly.	1 mould.	2	0	Gelée au Marasquin.
		£1 15	0	

November—Dinners for from Six to Twelve Persons.

Menu

Clear Soup.

Turbot, Tartar Sauce

Lobster Cream.
Hashed Game.

Sirloin of Beef.
Potatoes. Sprouts.

Partridges.

Pine-apple Fritters.
Noyeau Cream.

MENU.

Caviare.

Game Soup.

Filleted Soles,
Financière Sauce.

Curried Prawns.
Rump-steak
and Oyster Sauce.

Fried Potatoes.

Pheasants.

Vanilla Soufflé.

Ratafia Pudding.

Menu

Oyster Soup.

Fried Soles,
Sharp Sauce.

Chicken Croquettes.

Leg of Mutton.
Potatoes.
Stewed Celery.

Snipe.

Salad.

Sweet Omelette.
Lemon Cream.

Menu

Appétisans.

Crayfish Soup.

Fillets of Turbot, Cream Sauce.

Rissolettes of Hare.

Truffled Capon.
Mashed Potatoes.

Foie-gras Salad.

Iced Pudding.

Cheese Straws.

November—Plain Family Dinners for.

No 1.

Sunday. — Mulligatawny soup.—Boiled leg of mutton, mashed turnips, potatoes, caper sauce.—Damson tart, custard.

Monday.—Roast fowls, boiled bacon, cold mutton, potatoes, salad.—Gooseberry tart made from bottled fruit, custard.

Tuesday.—Brill, lobster sauce (tinned lobster).—Rissoles of mutton, steak-and-kidney pie, potatoes.—Rice pudding.

Wednesday. — Soup. — Curried chicken, haricot mutton, potatoes.—Cheese.

Thursday.—Flounders souchée.—Boiled silver side of beef, potatoes, cabbage.—stewed prunes.

Friday.—Pea soup.—Cold beef, salad, mashed potatoes.—Apple dumplings.

Saturday.—Curried beef.—Pork chops, potatoes.—Charlotte russe.

No 2.

Sunday.—Roast sirloin of beef, horse-radish sauce, potatoes, sprouts.—Apple tart, whipped cream.

Monday.—Soup.—Cold beef, fried pota-toes, beetroot.—Baked ground rice pud-ding.

Tuesday.—Cod steaks, tartar sauce.—Hashed beef, mashed potatoes.—Macaroni cheese.

Wednesday.—Roast loin of pork, apple sauce, baked potatoes, cabbage.—Bread-and-butter pudding.

Thursday.—Macaroni soup.—Cold pork, beetroot, fried potatoes.—Sweet omelet.

Friday.—Boiled beef, carrots, potatoes.—Baked apple pudding.

Saturday.—Pea soup.—Cold beef, salad, mashed potatoes.—Cheese ramekins.

November—Vegetarian Dinners for.

No 1.

Maize Meal and Milk.

Lentil Rissoles.
Carrot Pudding.

Jam Tart.

Macaroni and Cheese.
Dessert.

No. 2.

Lentil Soup.

Forcemeat Fritters.
Potato Pie.
Fried Vegetables.

Apple Turnovers.

Cheese Straws.

November—Dinner Table Decorations for.

In this, generally the most gloomy month of the year, we want something bright for our tables in the way of flowers and foliage. If hot-house flowers are obtainable, it is an easy task to make a suitable decoration: but the out-door flowers of November are of rather quiet and dark tints.

Chrysanthemums are the most to be de-pended on of all; and with them very pretty arrangements may be made if the colours be well chosen. Like roses, they look very well in fancy baskets, with high handles, ornamented with flowers and rib-bons, which lend additional colour.

Foliage for Chrysanthemums may be either their own or ferns, and if coloured autumnal leaves are still obtainable, they should always be used. An old-gold centre of silk puckered in folds, or a plain plush one looks well with the soft tints of the brown and gold flowers, and one of chestnut colour goes well with the white ones.

Silver stands for flowers come in very well for this season, as they form ornaments by themselves, and so eke out scanty sup-plies.

The drawback, however, to the old-fashioned ones is that they are generally too high, and so impede the view, and it must be borne in mind that in table decor-ation, this should never occur. The host and hostess should be visible to all their guests, as well as to one another.

Some delicate palms and ferns may find a place on dinner tables now, and their fronds, though they are higher than the faces of those seated at table, are too light to obstruct the view.

Noyeau Cream.

—INGREDIENTS *for quart mould.*—1½ oz. of isinglass or gelatine, the juice of 2 lemons, noyeau and pounded sugar to taste, 1 pint of milk, ½ pint of cream. AVERAGE COST, 2s. 6d.

Dissolve the isinglass or gelatine in a little boiling water, add the lemon-juice and strain this to the cream, putting in sufficient noyeau and sugar to flavour, and sweeten the mixture nicely; whip the cream well, put it into an oiled mould, and set the mould in ice or in a cool place; turn it out and garnish the dish to taste.

TIME.—*Altogether* ½ *hour.*
SEASONABLE *at any time.*

Noyeau, Home-made.

— INGREDIENTS.—2 oz. of bitter almonds, 1 oz. of sweet ditto, 1 lb. of loaf sugar, the rinds of 3 lemons, 1 quart of Irish whiskey or gin, 1 tablespoonful of clarified honey, ½ pint of milk.

Blanch and pound the almonds, and mix

with them the sugar, which should also be pounded. Boil the milk, let it stand till quite cold; then mix all the ingredients together, and let them remain for 10 days, shaking them every day. Filter the mixture through blotting-paper, bottle off for use in small bottles, and seal the corks down. This will be found useful for flavouring many sweet dishes. A

NOYEAU.

tablespoonful of the above noyeau added to a pint of boiled custard instead of brandy, as given in our recipe for custard, makes an exceedingly agreeable and delicate flavour.

SEASONABLE. — *May be made at any time.*

Nudeln.

(German Recipe.)—INGREDIENTS *for sufficient for dish for* 8 *to* 10 *persons.*—4 eggs, 2.oz. of butter, grated rusk, flour, milk. AVERAGE COST, 1s.

Make a paste with the eggs, 4 dessert-spoonfuls of milk and flour, and knead it on a paste-board with more flour till it is worked into a stiff dough. Cut into 4 pieces, roll it as thin as possible, and throw over a

NUDELN.

pole to dry. In half-an-hour's time, cut each piece again in 4, lay the pieces upon each other and cut in the narrowest of strips; then shake them apart. The macaroni (for such it is) is then ready for use. When required, boil till tender in plenty of boiling water with salt, turn into a strainer and pour more boiling water over. Serve with grated rusk strewn over the nudeln and a sauce of melted or brown butter.

TIME.—*To be stewed till tender.*
SEASONABLE *at any time.*

Nuts.

—Nuts of all kinds are rather uncompromising things in a dessert to make look at all well.

The best decoration for these may be found in dark green grasses and bright-coloured berries. The brilliant red of barberries, and the intermingling of their pretty foliage with the dark brown of the nuts, give a good effect. Chestnuts, the brightest and prettiest of all nuts, are invariably served, after boiling or roasting in a napkin, with one corner folded back to show its contents. Walnuts should be washed and well dried, as they are so often sticky and dirty to touch when freshly picked.

OATMEAL.

ATMEAL. — One of our most valuable of meals, this is rich in flesh-forming qualities, heat givers and nourishing properties, yet is a cheap food most easily prepared. Scotch oatmeal is of all the best, and all kinds vary in quality according to their freshness. Before exposure to the air it is infinitely superior to what it will become afterwards. As a food it is best to take with milk, which supplies the constituent parts lacking in the meal.

CONSTITUENT PARTS IN 1 LB. OF OATMEAL.

				oz.	grs.
Water	...	...	...	0	350
Albumenoids	...	...	...	2	253
Starch, Sugar, &c.		...	...	10	291
Fat	...	...	...	1	270
Mineral Matter	...	...,	...	0	147
				16	0

Note.—Excellent Scotch oatmeal is sold by Keen, Robinson and Bellville.

OATMEAL SCONES.

Oatmeal Porridge. — INGREDIENTS.—*To each ounce of oatmeal allow 1 pint of water.* AVERAGE COST, 4d. per quart.

Oatmeal porridge is made in several ways. The most usual plan is to boil the water with a little salt in it, and scatter in the meal with one hand while stirring with the other ; then, when thick enough, to set it aside to simmer for from 20 minutes to ½ an hour. An easier way to make it is to put the meal in a basin and pour cold water upon it, to stir it smooth, and then boil it until of the desired consistence. Cold milk and either salt or sugar are generally served with porridge.

TIME.—*20 minutes to ½ hour to simmer.*
SEASONABLE *in winter.*

Oatmeal Scones.—INGREDIENTS. —*Cold porridge, flour.*

A good way of using up cold porridge is to make it into scones. Knead as much flour into it as will make a paste. Roll this out about ¾ inch thick, cut it into three-cornered pieces and bake on a greased griddle or in the oven. Serve hot, split open and buttered ; or they may be spread with treacle for children.

October—Dinner for Twelve Persons.

MENU. (*English.*)	Quantity.	Average Cost.		MENU. (*French.*
		s.	d.	
Oyster Soup.	5 pints.	6	6	Potage aux Huîtres.
Fried Soles.	3 fish.	3	6	Soles Frites.
Red Mullet in Cases.	12 small.	9	0	Rougets en Caisses.
Salmi of Game.	2 dishes.	5	0	Salmis de Gibier.
Saddle of Mutton.	1 joint.	10	0	Selle de Mouton.
Potatoes.	4 lbs.	0	4	Pommes de Terre.
Stewed Celery.	4 heads.	1	0	Céleri.
Vanilla Soufflé.	1	3	0	Soufflé de Vanille.
Apples in Red Jelly.	2 mlds.	4	0	Gelée aux Pommes.
Anchovy Toast.	2 dishes.	1	6	Anchois au Gratin.
		£2 3	10	

October—Dinner for Ten Persons.

MENU. (*English.*)	Quantity.	Average Cost.		MENU. (*French.*)
		s.	d.	
Mock Turtle.	2 quarts.	3	6	Potage de Tête de Veau.
Fried Cod Steaks.	4 lbs.	2	8	Cotelettes de Cabillaud.
Mutton Cutlets and Spinach.	2 dishes.	4	0	Cotelettes de Mouton aux Epinards
Rissolettes of Hare.	1 dish.	2	6	Rissolettes de Levraut.
Sirloin,	1 joint.	7	6	Aloyau
Horseradish Sauce.	1 tur.	0	9	Sauce Raifort.
Potatoes. Savoy.	3 lbs. 2	0	7	Pommes de Terre. Choux.
Wild Duck.	3 birds.	6	0	Canards Sauvages.
Creamed Apple Tart.	1	2	0	Tourte aux Pommes.
Wine Jelly.	1 mould.	2	0	Gelée au Vin.
Stilton.	½ lb.	0	6	Stilton.
		£1 12	0	

October—Dinner for Eight Persons.

MENU. (*English.*)	Quantity.	Average Cost.		MENU. (*French.*)
		s.	d.	
Game Soup.	3½ pints.	5	0	Purée de Gibier.
Fillets of Turbot,	3 lbs.	3	0	Filets de Turbot,
Italian Sauce.	1 tur.	0	9	Sauce Italienne.
Oyster Patties.	10	2	6	Petits Patés aux Huîtres.
Stewed Mushrooms.	1 dish.	2	0	Champignons.
Farced Olives.	1 dish.	1	6	Olives Farcies.
Leg of Mutton.	1 joint	7	0	Gigot de Mouton.
Potatoes. Sprouts.	3 lbs. ea.	1	0	Pommes de Terre. Choux.
Partridges.	3 birds.	6	0	Perdreaux.
Tomato Salad.	1	1	0	Salade aux Tomates.
Charlotte Russe.	1	3	0	Charlotte Russe.
Valois Cream.	1 mould.	2	0	Crême à la Valois.
		£1 14	9	

October—Dinners for from Six to Twelve Persons.

Menu

Ox-tail Soup.

Turbot,
Ravigote Sauce,

Mutton Cutlets and
Spinach.

Roast Goose,
Apple Sauce.
Potatoes.   Savoys.

Salad.

Cabinet Pudding.
Lemon Jelly

Menu

Clear Soup.

Cod Steaks,
Tartar Sauce.

Rissolettes of Game.

Sirloin of Beef,
Horseradish Sauce.
Potatoes. Sprouts.

Wild Duck.

Olives.

Apple Tart and
Cream.
Stone Cream.

Menu

Mock Turtle Soup.

Brill,
Oyster Sauce.

Beef Olives,
Stuffed Tomatoes

Roast Leg of Mutton.
Potatoes.
Mashed Turnips.

Black Game.

Charlotte Russe.
Compôte of Peaches.

Menu

Oyster Soup.

Red Mullet.

Hashed Game.

Stewed Fillet of Beef,
Piquante Sauce.
Mashed Potatoes.

Snipe.

Chocolate Soufflé.
Marbled Jelly.

Cheese Straws.

October—Plain Family Dinners for.

No. 1.	No. 2.
Sunday.—Soup. — Roast goose, apple sauce, potatoes, cabbage.—Damson tart, custard.—Cheese biscuits.	**Sunday.**—Boned and roast aitchbone of beef, Yorkshire pudding, vegetable marrow, potatoes.—Plum tart, custard.
Monday. — Giblet soup. — Steak and tomatoes, potatoes.—Apple pudding.	**Monday.**—Cold beef, mashed potatoes beetroot.—Pancakes.
Tuesday. — Brill and lobster sauce. — Hashed goose, potatoes. — Plain cabinet pudding,	**Tuesday.**—Soup made from bones of beef —Broiled beef and oyster sauce (tinned oysters), fried potatoes. — Savoury rice. — Cheese.
Wednesday.—Fish pie made from cold fish and potatoes. — Boiled aitchbone of beef, carrots, potatoes, suet dumplings.—Cheese biscuits.	**Wednesday.**—Boiled rabbit and pork potatoes, cabbage, onion sauce. — Apple dumplings baked.
Thursday.—Pea soup made from liquor from the beef.—Cold beef, salad, mashed potatoes.—Baked rice pudding.	**Thursday.** — Stewed steak with vegetables, potatoes.—Gingerbread pudding.
Friday. — Baked stuffed haddocks. — Rabbit pie, potatoes.—Celery salad.	**Friday.**—Boiled cod, shrimp sauce.— Pork chops, potatoes.—Macaroni cheese.
Saturday.—Boiled mutton, caper sauce, mashed turnips, potatoes.—Plain apple Charlotte.	**Saturday.**—Fish pie made from cold fish and potatoes.—Fillet of beef (from joint for following day), stewed potatoes.—Celery salad.

October—Vegetarian Dinners for.

No. 1.	No. 2.
Hotch Potch.	Potato Soup.
Potato Rolls. Stewed Tomatoes.	Vegetable Pie. Bread Cutlets.
Savoury Rice. Charlotte Russe.	Plum Tart. Custard.
Welsh Rarebit.	Polenta and Cheese.

October—Dinner Table Decorations for.

Coloured autumn foliage should now be abundant, and blended with green and golden bracken; from it, it is easy to form a beautiful decoration, that is, if we live in the country and can search for it ourselves.

That which stands the journey well, however, we can find in London, and wonderfully good effects can be produced with burberis of different shades of colour, brown ivy and dark green evergreen leaves. Berries. too, come in usefully, and a table if tastefully arranged with barberries and autumn leaves looks lovely. Mountain ash again gives us some beautiful berries, whose rich colour goes well with the autumn leaves.

Here is a suggestion for a decoration for a table of medium size in October :—

In the centre, a tall, graceful, grass-like plant set in the midst of coloured autumn foliage, which varies from white or the palest yellow to dark red, to form a base.

Four or six smaller and similar arrangements at the corners or sides of the table according to its size and shape, and the table strewed with graceful flowing lines of such leaves as burberis, red and green myrtle and brown ivy, mingled with ivy berries and those of the mountain ash.

Virginia creeper alone when of bright colour, mixed with green, forms a beautiful decoration.

October, Things in Season:—

Fish.—Brill, cod, crabs, eels, flounders, haddocks, lobsters, mullet, oysters, plaice, prawns, skate, soles, turbot, whiting.

Meat. — Beef, mutton, pork, veal, venison.

Poultry.—Chickens, fowls, geese, larks, pigeons, pullets, rabbits, teal, turkeys, widgeons, wild ducks.

Game.—Blackcock, grouse, hares, partridges, pheasants, snipes, woodcocks, doe venison.

Vegetables.—Artichokes, beets, cabbages, cauliflowers, carrots, celery, lettuces, mushrooms, onions, potatoes, sprouts, tomatoes, turnips, vegetable marrows, — various herbs.

Fruit.—Apples, black and white bullaces, damsons, figs, filberts, grapes, pears, quinces, walnuts.

Olives, Stuffed.—Ingredients *for savoury for 4 persons.*—1 doz. Spanish olives, forcemeat made from tinned tunny, sardines or anchovies, a little lobster butter, plain butter, cayenne, capers, lemon-juice, 12 croûtons.* Average Cost, 9d.

Free the fish from skin and bone and pound it in a mortar with a little butter,

OLIVES.

a squeeze of lemon-juice and cayenne to taste. Stone the olives, fill them with the forcemeat, fry the croûtons and spread them, when cold, with lobster butter. On each place an olive and put a caper on the top.

Seasonable *at any time.*

Omelette, Bachelor's.—Ingredients *for dish for 2 persons.*—2 or 3 eggs, 2 oz. of butter, 1 teaspoonful of flour, ½ teacupful of milk.* Average Cost, 5d.

Make a thin cream of the flour and milk; then beat up the eggs, mix all together, and add a pinch of salt and a few grains of cayenne. Melt the butter in a small frying-pan, and when very hot pour in the

batter. Let the pan remain for a few minutes over a clear fire; then sprinkle upon the omelette some chopped herbs and a few shreds of onion; double the omelette dexterously, and shake it out of the pan on to a hot dish. A simple sweet omelette can be made by the same process, substituting sugar or preserve for the chopped herbs.

Time.—2 *minutes.*

Seasonable *at any time.*

Omelette, Plain. — Ingredients *for dish for 4 or 5 persons.*—6 eggs, 1 saltspoonful of salt, ½ saltspoonful of pepper, 3 oz. of butter.* Average Cost, 9d.

Break the eggs into a basin, omitting the whites of 3, and beat them up with the salt and pepper until extremely light; then add 1 oz. of the butter broken into small pieces and stir this into the mixture. Put the other 2 oz. of butter into a frying-pan, make it quite hot, and, as soon as it begins to bubble, whisk the eggs, &c., very briskly for a minute or two and pour them into the pan; stir the omelette with a spoon one way until the mixture thickens and becomes firm and, when the whole is set, fold the edges over, so that the omelette assumes an oval form; and when it is nicely brown on one side and quite firm, it is done. To take off the rawness on the upper side, hold the pan before the fire for a minute or two and brown it with a salamander or hot shovel. Serve very expeditiously on a very hot dish and never cook until it is just wanted. The flavour of this omelette may be very much enhanced by adding minced parsley, minced onion or eschalot, or grated cheese, allowing 1 tablespoonful of the former and half the quantity of the latter, to the ab ve proportion of eggs. Shrimps or oysters may also be added : the latter should be scalded in their liquor and then bearded and cut into small pieces. In making an omelette, be particularly careful that it is not too thin; and, to avoid this, do not make it in too large a frying-pan, as the mixture would then spread too much and taste of the outside. It should also not be greasy, burnt or too much done, and should be cooked over a gentle fire, that the whole of the substance may be heated without drying up the outside. Omelettes are sometimes served with gravy; but *this should never be poured over them*, but served in a tureen, as the liquid causes the omelette to become heavy and flat, instead of eating light and soft. In making the gravy, the flavour should not overpower that of the omelette and should be thickened with arrowroot or rice flour.

TIME.—*With* 6 *eggs, in a frying-pan* 18 *or* 20 *inches round,* 4 *to* 6 *minutes.*

SEASONABLE *at any time.*

Omelette, Plain Sweet.—INGRE-
DIENTS *for dish for* 4 *or* 5 *persons.*—6 *eggs,* 3 *oz. of butter,* 2 *oz. of sifted sugar.* AVERAGE COST, 10*d.*

Break the eggs into a basin, omitting the whites of 3; whisk them well, adding the sugar and 1 oz. of butter, which should be broken into small pieces, and stir all these ingredients well together. Make the remainder of the butter quite hot in a small frying-pan, and when it commences to bubble pour in the eggs, &c. Keep stirring them until they begin to set; then turn the edges of the omelette over, to make it an oval shape, and finish cooking it. To brown the top, hold the pan before the fire or use a salamander, and turn it carefully on to a *very hot* dish; sprinkle sifted sugar over, and serve.

TIME.—*From* 4 *to* 6 *minutes.*

SEASONABLE *at any time.*

Omelette, The Cure's, or Ome-
lette au Thon. — INGREDIENTS. — *Take for* 6 *persons the roes of* 2 *carp**; *bleach*

* An American writer says he has followed this recipe, substituting pike, shad, &c., in the place of carp, and can recommend all these also, with a quiet conscience. Any fish, indeed, may be used with success.

them by putting them for 5 *minutes in boiling water slightly salted, a piece of fresh tunny the size of a hen's egg, to which add a small shalot already chopped.*

Mash up together the roe and the tunny, so as to mix them well, and throw the whole into a saucepan with a sufficient quantity of very good butter; whip it up until the butter is melted. This constitutes the specialty of the omelette. Take a second piece of butter, *à discrétion*, mix it with parsley and herbs, place it in a long-shaped dish destined to receive the omelette; squeeze the juice of a lemon over it, and place it on hot embers. Beat up 12 eggs (the fresher the better); throw up the sauté of roe and tunny, stirring it so as to mix all well together; then make your omelette in the usual manner, endeavouring to turn it out long, thick and soft. Spread it carefully on the dish prepared for it, and serve at once. This dish ought to be reserved for recherché déjeûners, or for assemblies where amateurs meet who know how to eat well; washed down with a good old wine, it will work wonders.

Note.—The roe and the tunny must be beaten up (sauté) without allowing them to boil, to prevent their hardening, which would prevent them mixing well with the eggs. Your dish should be hollowed towards the centre to allow the gravy to concentrate, that it may be helped with a spoon. The dish ought to be slightly heated, otherwise the cold china will extract all the heat from the omelette.

Omelette aux Confitures, or
Jam Omelette.—INGREDIENTS *for dish for* 4 *or* 5 *persons.*—6 *eggs,* 3 *oz. of butter,* 3 *tablespoonfuls of apricot, strawberry, or any jam that may be preferred.* AVERAGE COST, 1*s.*

Make an omelette, only, instead of doubling it over, leave it flat in the pan. When quite firm and nicely brown on one side, turn it carefully on to a hot dish, spread over the middle of it the jam, and fold the omelette over on each side; sprinkle ifted sugar over, and serve very quickly. A pretty dish of small omelettes may be made by dividing the batter into 3 or 4 portions, and frying them separately; they should then be spread each one with a different kind of preserve, and the omelettes rolled over. Always sprinkle sweet omelettes with sifted sugar before being sent to table.

TIME.—*4 to 6 minutes.*

SEASONABLE *at any time.*

Omelette Soufflé.—INGREDIENTS

or omelette for 4 persons.—6 *eggs,* 5 *oz. of pounded sugar, flavouring of vanilla, orange-flower water, or lemon-rind,* 3 *oz. of butter,* 1 *dessertspoonful of rice-flour.* AVERAGE COST, 1s.

Separate the yolks from the whites of the eggs, add to the former the sugar, the rice-flour, and either of the above flavourings that may be preferred, and stir these ingredients well together. Whip the whites of the eggs, mix them lightly with the batter and put the butter into a small frying-pan. As soon as it begins to bubble pour the batter into it, and set the pan over a bright but gentle fire; and when the omelette is set, turn the edges over, to make it an oval shape, and slip it on to a silver dish, which has been previously well buttered. Put it in the oven, and bake from 12 to 15 minutes; sprinkle finely-powdered sugar over the soufflé, and *serve it immediately.*

TIME.—*About 4 minutes in the pan; to bake, from 12 to 15 minutes.*

SEASONABLE *at any time.*

Onion Sauce, French, or Sou-

ise.—INGREDIENTS.—½ *pint of Béchamel, bay-leaf, seasoning to taste of pounded mace and cayenne,* 6 *onions, a small piece of ham.* AVERAGE COST, 7*d.*

Peel the onions and cut them in halves; put them into a stewpan with just sufficient water to cover them, and add the bay-leaf, ham, cayenne and mace; be careful to keep the lid closely shut, and simmer them until tender. Take them out and drain thoroughly; rub them through a tammy or sieve (an old one does for the purpose) with a wooden spoon, and put them to ½ pint of Béchamel; keep stirring over the fire until it boils, when serve. If it should require any more seasoning, add it to taste.

TIME.—¾ *hour to boil the onions.*

Onion Sauce, Brown —INGRE-

DIENTS *for large tureen.*—6 *large onions, rather more than ½ pint of good gravy,* 2*oz. of butter, salt and pepper to taste.* AVERAGE COST, 6*d.*

ONION.

Slice and fry the onions of a pale brown in a stewpan, with the above quantity of butter, keeping them well stirred, that they do not get black. When a nice colour, pour over the gravy and let them simmer gently until tender. Now skim off every particle of fat, add the seasoning, and rub the whole through a tammy or sieve; put it back into the saucepan to warm, and, when it boils, serve.

TIME.—*Altogether,* 1 *hour.*

SEASONABLE *from August to March.*

Note.—Where a high flavouring is liked, add 1 tablespoonful of mushroom ketchup, or a small quantity of port wine.

Onion Sauce, White (for Boiled

Rabbits, Roast Shoulder of Mutton, &c.).— INGREDIENTS *for sufficient for a joint.*—5 *large onions, or* 8 *middling-sized ones,* ½ *pint of melted butter made with milk,* ½ *teaspoonful of salt.* AVERAGE COST, 6*d.*

Peel the onions and put them into water to which a little salt has been added, to preserve their whiteness, and let them remain for ¼ hour. Then put them into a stewpan, cover them with water and let them boil until tender, and, if the onions should be very strong, change the water after they have been boiling for ¼ hour. Drain them thoroughly, chop them and rub them through a tammy or sieve. Make ½ pint of melted butter with milk, and when that boils put in the onions, with a seasoning of salt; stir it till it simmers, when it will be ready to serve. If these directions are carefully attended to, this onion sauce will be delicious.

TIME. — *From* ¾ *to* 1 *hour to boil the onions.*

SEASONABLE *from August to March.*

Note.—To make this sauce very mild and delicate, use Spanish onions, which can be procured from the beginning of September to Christmas. 2 or 3 tablespoonfuls of cream, added just before serving, will be found to improve its appearance very much. Small onions, when very young, may be cooked whole and served in melted butter. A sieve or tammy should be kept expressly for onions; on old one answers the purpose, as it is liable to retain the flavour and smell, which of course would be excessively disagreeable in delicate preparations.

Onion Soup. — INGREDIENTS *for soup for 6 persons.*—6 *large onions,* 2 *oz. of butter, salt and pepper to taste,* ½ *pint of cream,* 1 *quart of stock.* AVERAGE COST, 1s. 6d.

Chop the onions, put them in the butter, stir them occasionally, but do not let them brown. When tender, put the stock to them and season; strain the soup and add the boiling cream.

TIME.—½ *hour.*

SEASONABLE *in cold weather.*

Onion Soup, Cheap.—INGREDIENTS *for soup for 8 persons.*—8 *middling-sized onions,* 3 *oz. of butter, a tablespoonful of rice-flour, salt and pepper to taste,* 1 *teaspoonful of powdered sugar, thickening of butter and flour,* 2 *quarts of water.* AVERAGE COST, 8d.

Cut the onions small, put them into the stewpan with the butter and fry them well; mix the rice-flour smoothly with the water, add the onions, seasoning and sugar, and

simmer till tender. Thicken with butter and flour, and serve.

TIME.—2 *hours.*

SEASONABLE *in winter.*

Onions, Burnt (for Gravies).—INGREDIENTS.—½ lb. *of onions,* ½ *pint of water* ½ lb. *of moist sugar,* ½ *pint of vinegar.* AVERAGE COST, 4d.

Peel and chop the onions fine, and put them into a stewpan (not tinned), with the water; let them boil for 5 minutes, then add the sugar, and simmer gently until the mixture becomes nearly black and throws out bubbles of smoke. Have ready the above proportion of boiling vinegar, strain the liquor gradually to it, and keep stirring with a wooden spoon until it is well incorporated. When cold, bottle for use.

TIME—*Altogether,* 1 *hour.*

Onions, Pickled. (A very Simple and exceedingly Good Method.)—INGREDIENTS.—*Pickling onions; to each quart of vinegar,* 2 *teaspoonfuls of allspice,* 2 *tea spoonfuls of whole black pepper.*

Have the onions gathered when quite dry and ripe and, with the fingers, take off the thin outside skin; then, with a silver knife (steel should not be used, as it spoils the colour of the onions), remove one more skin, when the onion will look quite clear. Have ready some very dry bottles or jars and, as fast as they are peeled, put them in. Pour over sufficient cold vinegar to cover them, with pepper and allspice in the above proportions, taking care that each jar has its share of the latter ingredients. Tie down with bladder and put them in a dry place, and in a fortnight they will be fit for use. This is a most simple recipe and very delicious, the onions being nice and crisp. They should be eaten within 6 or 8 months after being done, as the onions are liable to become soft.

SEASONABLE *from the middle of July to the end of August.*

Onions, Pickled.—INGREDIENTS.

—1 *gallon of pickling onions, salt and water, milk; to each ½ gallon of vinegar,* 1 *oz. of bruised ginger,* ¼ *tablespoonful of cayenne,* 1 *oz. of allspice,* 1 *oz. of whole black pepper,* ¼ *oz. of whole nutmeg bruised,* 8 *cloves,* ¼ *oz. of mace.*

Gather the onions, which should not be too small, when they are quite dry and ripe ; wipe off the dirt, but do not pare them ; make a strong solution of salt and water, into which put the onions, and change this morning and night, for 3 days, and save the *last* brine they were put in. Then take the outside skin off and put them into a tin saucepan capable of holding them all, as they are always better done together. Now take equal quantities of milk and the last salt and water the onions were in, and pour this to them ; to this add 2 large spoonfuls of salt, put them over the fire and watch them very attentively. Keep constantly turning the onions about with a wooden skimmer, those at the bottom to the top and *vice versâ,* and let the milk and water run through the holes of the skimmer. Remember, the onions must never boil, or, if they do, they will be good for nothing ; and they should be quite transparent. Keep the onions stirred for a few minutes and, in stirring them, be particular not to break them. Then have ready a pan with a colander, into which turn the onions to drain, covering them with a cloth to keep in the steam. Place on a table an old cloth, 2 or 3 times double ; put the onions on it when quite hot and over them an old piece of blanket ; cover this closely over them, to keep in the steam. Let them remain till the next day, when they will be quite cold and look yellow and shrivelled ; take off the shrivelled skins, when they should be as white as snow. Put them into a pan, make a pickle of vinegar and the remaining ingredients ; boil all these up, and pour hot over the onions in the pan. Cover very closely to keep in all the steam and let them

stand till the following day, when they will be quite cold. Put them into jars or bottles well bunged, and a tablespoonful of the best olive-oil on the top of each jar or bottle. Tie them down with bladder, and let them stand in a cool place for a month or six weeks, when they will be fit for use. They should be beautifully white and eat crisp, without the least softness, and will keep good many months.

SEASONABLE *from the middle of July to the end of August.*

Onions, Spanish, Baked.—IN-

GREDIENTS *for dish for 8 persons.*—4 *or 5 Spanish onions, salt and water.* AVERAGE COST, 8*d.*

Put the onions, with their skins on, into a saucepan of boiling water slightly salted, and let them boil quickly for an hour. Then take them out, wipe them thoroughly, wrap each one in a piece of paper separately, and bake them in a moderate oven for 2 hours,

SPANISH ONIONS.

or longer, should the onions be very large, They may be served in their skins and eaten with a piece of cold butter and a seasoning of pepper and salt ; or they may be peeled and a good brown gravy poured over them.

TIME.—1 *hour to boil,* 2 *hours to bake.*

SEASONABLE *from September to January.*

Onions, Spanish, Pickled.—IN-

GREDIENTS. — *Onions, vinegar ; salt and cayenne to taste.*

Cut the onions in thin slices ; put a layer of them in the bottom of a jar ; sprinkle with salt and cayenne ; then add another layer of onions and season as before. Proceeding in this manner till the jar is full, pour in sufficient vinegar to cover the whole and the pickle will be ready for use in a month.

SEASONABLE.—*May be had in England from September to February.*

Onions, Spanish, Stewed.—

INGREDIENTS *for dish for 8 persons.*—5 or 6 *Spanish onions, 1 pint of good broth or gravy.* AVERAGE COST, 1s.

Peel the onions, taking care not to cut away too much of the tops or tails, or they would then fall to pieces ; put them into a stewpan capable of holding them at the bottom without piling them one on the top of another ; add the broth or gravy and simmer *very gently* until the onions are perfectly tender. Dish them, pour the gravy round, and serve. Instead of using broth, Spanish onions may be stewed with a large piece of butter : they must be done very gradually over a slow fire or hot-plate, and will produce plenty of gravy.

TIME. — *To stew in gravy, 2 hours, or longer if very large.*

SEASONABLE *from September to January.*

Note.—Stewed Spanish onions are a favourite accompaniment to roast shoulder of mutton.

Orange Brandy. (Excellent.)—IN-

GREDIENTS.—*To every ½ gallon of brandy allow ¾ pint of Seville orange-juice, 1¼ lb. of loaf sugar.*

To bring out the full flavour of the orange-peel, rub a few lumps of the sugar on 2 or 3 unpared oranges and put these lumps to the rest. Mix the brandy with the orange-juice, strained, the rinds of 6 of the oranges, pared very thin, and the sugar. Let all stand in a closely-covered jar for about 3 days, stirring it 3 or 4 times a-day. When clear, it should be bottled and closely corked for a year ; it will then be ready for use, but will keep any length of time. This is a most excellent stomachic when taken pure in small quantities ; or, as the strength of the brandy is very little deteriorated by

the other ingredients, it may be diluted with water.

TIME.—*To be stirred every day for 3 days.*

SEASONABLE.—*Make this in March.*

Orange Cream.—INGREDIENTS *for

a quart mould.*—1 oz. *of isinglass, 6 large oranges, 1 lemon, sugar to taste, water, ½ pint of good cream.* AVERAGE COST, 2s. 6d.

Squeeze the juice from the oranges and lemon ; strain it and put it into a saucepan

ORANGE BASKET.

with the isinglass and sufficient water to make it in all 1½ pint. Rub the sugar on the orange and lemon-rind, add it to the other ingredients, and boil all together for about 10 minutes. Strain through a muslin bag and, when cold, beat up with it ½ pint of thick cream. Wet a mould, or soak it in cold water ; pour in the cream and put it

OPEN MOULD.

in a cool place to set. If the weather is very cold, 1 oz. of isinglass will be found sufficient for the above proportion of ingredients.

TIME.—10 *minutes to boil the juice and water.*

SEASONABLE *from November to May.*

Orange Creams. — INGREDIENTS

for 8 creams.—1 *Seville orange, 1 table-spoonful of brandy, ¼ lb. of loaf sugar, the* yolks of 4 eggs, 1 pint of cream. AVERAGE COST, 2s.

Boil the rind of the Seville orange until tender, and beat it in a mortar to a pulp; add to it the brandy, the strained juice of the orange, and the sugar, and beat all together for about 10 minutes, adding the well-beaten yolks of eggs. Bring the cream to the boiling point and pour it very gradually to the other ingredients, and beat the mixture till nearly cold; put it into custard-cups, place the cups in a deep dish of boiling water, where let them remain till quite cold. Take the cups out of the water, wipe them, and garnish the tops of the creams with candied orange-peel or preserved chips.

TIME.—Altogether, ¾ hour.

SEASONABLE from November to May.

Note.—To render this dish more economical, substitute milk for the cream, but add a small pinch of isinglass or gelatine to make the creams firm.

Orange Fritters.

INGREDIENTS for dish for 6 persons.—For the batter, ½ lb. of flour, ½ oz. of butter, ½ saltspoonful of salt, 2 eggs, milk, oranges, hot lard or clarified dripping. AVERAGE COST, 8d.

Make a nice light batter with the above proportion of flour, butter, salt, eggs and sufficient milk to make it the proper consistency; peel the oranges, remove as much of the white skin as possible, and divide each orange into eight pieces without breaking the thin skin, unless it be to remove the pips; dip each piece of orange in the batter. Have ready a pan of boiling lard or clarified dripping; drop in the oranges and fry them a delicate brown from 8 to 10 minutes. When done, lay them on a piece of blotting-paper before the fire, to drain away the greasy moisture, and dish them on a white d'oyley; sprinkle over them plenty of pounded sugar, and serve quickly.

TIME.—8 to 10 minutes to fry the fritters; 5 minutes to drain them.

SEASONABLE from November to May.

Orange Gravy

(for Wildfowl Widgeon, Teal, &c.).—INGREDIENTS for sufficient for 2 or 3 birds.—½ pint of white stock, 1 small onion, 3 or 4 strips of lemon or orange peel, a few leaves of basil, if at hand, the juice of a Seville orange, or lemon, salt and pepper to taste, 1 glass of port wine. AVERAGE COST, 9d.

Put the onion, cut in slices, into a stew-pan with the stock, orange-peel and basil and let them simmer very gently for ¼ hour, or rather longer should the gravy not taste sufficiently of the peel. Strain it off and add to the gravy the remaining ingredients; let the whole heat through, and, when on the point of boiling, serve very hot in a tureen which should have a cover to it.

TIME.—Altogether, ½ hour.

Orange Jelly.

INGREDIENTS for a quart mould.—1 pint of water, 1½ to 2 oz. of isinglass or gelatine, ½ lb. of loaf sugar, 1 Seville orange, 1 lemon, about 9 China oranges. AVERAGE COST, with gelatine, 1s. 8d.

Put the water into a saucepan, with the isinglass or gelatine, sugar and the rind of 1 orange and the same of ½ lemon and stir these over the fire until the isinglass or gelatine is dissolved and remove the scum;

OPEN MOULD.

then add to this the juice of the Seville orange, the juice of the lemon and sufficient juice of China oranges to make in all 1 pint: from 8 to 10 oranges will yield the desired quantity. Stir all together over the fire until it is just on the point of boiling: skim well; then strain the jelly through a very fine sieve or jelly-bag, and, when nearly cold, put it into a mould previously wetted; and, when quite cold, turn it out on a dish and garnish to taste. To insure this jelly being clear, the orange and lemon-juice should be well-strained and the isinglass or gelatine clarified, before they are added to the other ingredients, and, to heighten the colour, a few drops of prepared cochineal may be added.

TIME.—5 *minutes to boil without the juice;* 1 *minute after it is added.*

SEASONABLE *from November to May.*

Orange Marmalade. I.—INGREDIENTS.—*Equal weight of fine loaf sugar and Seville oranges; to* 12 *oranges allow* 1 *pint of water.* AVERAGE COST, 6d. *per lb.*

Let there be an equal weight of loaf sugar and Seville oranges and allow the above proportion of water to every dozen oranges. Peel them carefully, remove a little of the white pith and boil the rinds in water 2 hours, changing the water three times to take off a little of the bitter taste. Break the pulp into small pieces, take out all the pips and cut the boiled rind into chips. Make a syrup with the sugar and water; boil this well, skim it, and, when clear, put in the pulp and chips. Boil all together from 20 minutes to ½ hour; pour it into pots, and, when cold, cover down with bladders, or tissue-paper brushed over on both sides with the white of an egg. The juice and grated rind of 2 lemons to every dozen of oranges, added with the pulp and chips to the syrup, are a very great improvement to this marmalade.

TIME.—2 *hours to boil the orange-rinds;* 10 *minutes to boil the syrup;* 20 *minutes to* ½ *hour to boil the marmalade.*

SEASONABLE.—*This should be made in March or April, as Seville oranges are then in perfection.*

Note.—The best marmalade is made by Keiller, and many are of opinion that when it can be bought so cheaply and good it is scarcely worth making at home.

Orange Marmalade. II.—INGREDIENTS.—*Equal weight of Seville oranges and sugar; to every lb. of sugar allow* ½ *pint of water.* AVERAGE COST, 6d. *per lb. pot.*

Weigh the sugar and oranges, score the skin across and take it off in quarters. Boil these quarters in a muslin bag in water until they are quite soft and they can be pierced easily with the head of a pin; then cut them into chips about 1 inch long and as thin as possible. Should there be a great deal of white stringy pulp, remove it before cutting the rind into chips. Split open the oranges, scrape out the best part of the pulp, with the juice, rejecting the white pith and pips. Make a syrup with the sugar and water; boil it until clear; then put in the chips, pulp and juice and boil the marmalade from 20 minutes to ½ hour, removing all the scum as it rises. In boiling the syrup, clear it carefully from scum before the oranges are added to it.

TIME.—2 *hours to boil the rinds,* 10 *minutes the syrup,* 20 *minutes to* ½ *hour the marmalade.*

SEASONABLE.—*Make this in March or April, when Seville oranges are in perfection.*

Orange Marmalade, An Easy Way of Making. — INGREDIENTS. — *To every lb. of pulp allow* 1½ *lb. of loaf sugar.* AVERAGE COST, 5d. *to* 6d. *per lb.*

Choose some fine Seville oranges or put equal quantities of sweet and bitter oranges; put them whole into a stewpan with sufficient water to cover them and stew them until they become perfectly tender, changing the water 2 or 3 times; drain them, take off the rind, remove the pips from the pulp, weigh it and to every lb. allow 1½ of loaf sugar and ½ pint of the water the oranges were last boiled in. Boil the sugar and water together for 10 minutes; put in the pulp, boil for another 10 minutes; then add the peel cut into

trips and boil the marmalade for another
0 minutes, which completes the process.
'our it into jars; let it cool; then cover
own with bladders, or tissue-paper brushed
ver on both sides with the white of an egg.

TIME.—*2 hours to boil the oranges;
ltogether ½ hour to boil the marmalade.*

SEASONABLE.—*Make this in March or
April.*

Orange Marmalade made with Honey.

INGREDIENTS.—*To* 1 *quart of the
juice and pulp of Seville oranges allow* 1
b. *of the rind,* 2 *lbs. of honey.* AVERAGE
COST, 7d. *or* 8d. *per lb. pot.*

Peel the oranges and boil the rind in
water until tender and cut it into strips.
Take away the pips from the juice and
pulp and put it with the honey and chips
into a preserving-pan: boil all together
for about ½ hour, or until the marmalade
is of the proper consistency; put it into
pots, and, when cold, cover down with
bladders.

TIME.—*2 hours to boil the rind,* ½ *hour
the marmalade.*

SEASONABLE.—*Make this in March or
April.*

Orange Marmalade, Pounded.

INGREDIENTS.—*Weight and* ½ *in sugar
to every lb. of oranges.*

Cut some clear Seville oranges in 4 pieces,
out all the juice and pulp into a basin
and take out the seeds and skins; boil the
rinds in hard water till tender, changing
the water 2 or 3 times while boiling;
drain them well and pound them in a
mortar: then put them into a preserving-
pan with the juice and pulp and their
weight and ½ of sugar; boil rather more
than ½ an hour.

TIME.—*About 2 hours to boil the rinds,
½ an hour the marmalade.*

Orange Pudding, Baked.

INGREDIENTS *for pudding for 4 persons.*—6 oz.
of stale sponge-cake or bruised ratafias, 6

oranges, 1 *pint of milk,* 5 *eggs,* ½ *lb. of sugar.*
AVERAGE COST, 1s. 6d.

Bruise the sponge-cake or ratafias into
fine crumbs and pour upon them the milk,
which should be boiling. Rub the rinds of
2 of the oranges on sugar, and add this, with
the juice of the remainder, to the other
ingredients. Beat up the eggs, stir them
in, sweeten to taste, and put the mixture
into a pie-dish previously lined with puff-
paste. Bake for rather more than ½ hour;
turn it out of the dish, strew sifted sugar
over, and serve.

TIME.—*Rather more than* ½ *hour.*

SEASONABLE *from November to May.*

Orange Pudding, Seville.

INGREDIENTS *for large pudding.*—4 *Seville
oranges,* 4 oz. *of fresh butter,* 12 *almonds,* ½
lb. *of sifted sugar, the juice of* 1 *lemon,* 6
eggs. AVERAGE COST, 1s. 9d.

Boil the oranges and chop them finely,
taking out all the pips. Put the butter,
the almonds, blanched and chopped, and the
sugar, into a saucepan, to which add the
orange-pulp and the lemon-juice. Put it on
a hot-plate to warm, mixing all together
until the butter is thoroughly melted. Turn
the mixture out, let it get cold, then add
the eggs, which should be well whipped.
Put all into a baking-dish, bordered with
puff-paste, and bake from ½ hour to 40
minutes, according to the heat of the oven.

TIME.—½ *hour to 40 minutes.*

SEASONABLE *from November to May.*

Orange Salad.

INGREDIENTS *for
dish for 6 persons.*—6 *oranges,* ¼ *lb. of mus-
catel raisins,* 2 oz. *of pounded sugar,* 4 *tablespoonfuls of brandy.* AVERAGE COST, 1s. 3d.

Peel 5 of the oranges; divide them into
slices without breaking the pulp, and arrange
them on a glass dish. Stone the raisins,
mix them with the sugar and brandy, and
mingle them with the oranges. Squeeze
the juice of the other orange over the whole,
and the dish is ready for table. A little

pounded spice may be put in when the flavour is liked; but this ingredient must be added very sparinlgy.

SEASONABLE *from November to May.*

Orange Wine. (A very Simple and Easy Method of Making a very Superior.)

—INGREDIENTS *for 9 gallons.*—90 *Seville oranges,* 32 *lbs. of lump sugar, water.* AVERAGE COST, 2*s. per gallon.*

Break up the sugar into small pieces and put it into a dry, sweet, 9-gallon cask, placed in a cellar or other storehouse, where it is intended to be kept. Have ready close to the cask two large pans or wooden keelers, into one of which put the peel of the oranges pared quite thin, and into the other the pulp after the juice has been squeezed from it. Strain the juice through a piece of double muslin, and put into the cask with the sugar. Then pour about 1½ gallon of cold spring water on both the peels and the pulp; let it stand for 24 hours, and then strain it into the cask; add more water to the peels and pulp when this is done, and repeat the same process every day for a week: it should take about a week to fill up the cask. Be careful to apportion the quantity as nearly as possible to the seven days, and to stir the contents of the cask each day. On the *third* day after the cask is full—that is, the *tenth* day after the commencement of making—the cask may be securely bunged down. This is a very simple and easy method, and the wine made according to it will be pronounced to be most excellent. There is no troublesome boiling, and all fermentation takes place in the cask. When the above directions are attended to, the wine cannot fail to be good. *It* should be bottled in 8 or 9 months, and will be fit for use in a twelvemonth after the time of making. Ginger wine may be made in precisely the same manner, only, with the 9-gallon cask for ginger wine, 2 lbs. of the best whole ginger, *bruised,* must be put with the sugar.

It will be found convenient to tie the ginger loosely in a muslin bag.

TIME.—*Altogether,* 10 *days to make it.*

SEASONABLE.—*Make this in March, and bottle it in the following January.*

Oranges, Compote of.—INGREDIENTS *for dish for 6 persons.*—1 *pint syrup,* 6 *oranges.* AVERAGE COST, 9*d.*

Peel the oranges, remove as much of the white pith as possible, and divide them into small pieces without breaking the thin skin with which they are surrounded. Make the syrup by recipe, adding the rind of the orange cut into thin narrow strips. When the syrup has been well skimmed and is quite clear, put in the pieces of orange and simmer them for 5 minutes. Take them out carefully with a spoon, without breaking them. and arrange them

COMPOTE OF ORANGES.

on a glass dish. Reduce the syrup by boiling it quickly until thick; let it cool little, pour it over the oranges, and, when cold, they will be ready for table.

TIME.—10 *minutes to boil the syrup; minutes to simmer the oranges;* 5 *minutes to reduce the syrup.*

SEASONABLE *from November to May.*

Oranges, A Pretty Dish of.—

INGREDIENTS *for quart mould.*—6 *large oranges,* ½ *lb. of loaf sugar,* ¼ *pint of water,* ½ *pint of cream,* 2 *tablespoonfuls of any kind of liqueur, sugar to taste.* AVERAGE COST, 1*s.* 9*d.*

Put the sugar and water into a saucepan and boil them until the sugar becomes brittle, which may be ascertained by taking up a small quantity in a spoon, and dipping it in cold water; if the sugar is sufficiently boiled, it will easily snap. Peel the oranges, remove as much of the white pith as possible, and divide them into nice-size lices, without breaking the thin white kin which surrounds the juicy pulp. Place he pieces of orange on small skewers, dip hem into the hot sugar, and arrange them n layers round a plain mould, which hould be well oiled with the purest salad-il. The sides of the mould only should be ined with the oranges, and the centre left pen for the cream. Let the sugar become rm by cooling; turn the oranges carefully ut on a dish, and fill the centre with vhipped cream, flavoured with any kind of iqueur, and sweetened with pounded ugar. This is an exceedingly ornamental nd nice dish for the supper-table.

TIME.—10 *minutes to boil the sugar.*

SEASONABLE *from November to May.*

Oranges, Iced.—INGREDIENTS.—

Oranges; to every lb. of pounded loaf ugar allow the whites of 2 eggs.

Whisk the whites of the eggs well, stir n the sugar, and beat this mixture for ¼ our. Skin the oranges, remove as much of the white pith as possible without njuring the pulp of the fruit; pass a hread through the centre of each orange, lip them into the sugar, and tie them to a stick. Place this stick across the oven, nd let the oranges remain until dry, when they will have the appearance of balls of ice. They make a pretty dessert or supper dish. Care must be taken not to have the oven too fierce, or the oranges would scorch and acquire a brown colour, which would entirely spoil their appearance.

TIME.—*From ½ to 1 hour to dry in a moderate oven.*

SEASONABLE *from November to May.*

Oranges, Preserved.—INGREDI-

ENTS.—*Oranges; to every lb. of juice and pulp allow 2 lbs. of loaf sugar; to every pint of water ½ lb. of loaf sugar.*

Wholly grate or peel the oranges, taking off only the thin outside portion of the rind. Make a small incision where the stalk is taken out, squeeze out as much of the juice as can be obtained, and preserve it in a basin with the pulp that accompanies it. Put the oranges into cold water; let them stand for 3 days, changing the water twice; then boil them in fresh water until they are tender, and put them to drain. Make a syrup with the above proportion of sugar and water, sufficient to cover the oranges; let them stand in it for 2 or 3 days, then drain them well. Weigh the juice and pulp, allow double their weight of sugar, and boil them together until the scum ceases to rise, which must all be carefully removed; put in the oranges, boil them for 10 minutes, place them in jars, pour over them the syrup, and, when cold, cover down. They will be fit for use in a week.

TIME.—3 *days for the oranges to remain in water,* 3 *days in the syrup;* ½ *hour to boil the pulp,* 10 *minutes the oranges.*

SEASONABLE.—*This preserve should be made in February or March, when oranges are plentiful.*

Ortolans, Roast. — INGREDIENTS

for dish for 4 persons.— 4 birds, 4 vine-leaves, 2 rounds of toast, ¼ lb. of butter. AVERAGE COST, 6s.

Keep the birds till tender, then pluck, truss and wipe carefully, but do not draw them. Wrap each bird in a freshly-gathered vine-leaf, tie them on a bird-spit and roast them for 25 minutes, or rather less if they are small. Place the slices of toast in the pan to catch the trail, melt the butter in the pan and baste incessantly. To have ortolans cooked to perfection, it is absolutely necessary that the basting should be kept up. Dish them on the toast, and send some good gravy to table with them.

TIME.—25 *minutes to roast.*

SEASONABLE *from October to February.*

Ox-Cheek Soup. — INGREDIENTS

for soup for 10 persons.—An ox-cheek, 2 oz. of butter, 3 or 4 slices of lean ham or bacon, 1 parsnip, 3 carrots, 2 onions, 2 heads of celery, 3 blades of mace, 4 cloves, a faggot of savoury herbs, 1 bay-leaf, a teaspoonful of salt, half that of pepper, browning, the crust of a French roll, 5 quarts of water. AVERAGE COST, *9d. per quart.*

Lay the ham in the bottom of the stewpan, with the butter; break the bones of the cheek, wash it clean, and put it on the ham. Cut the vegetables small, omitting 1 head of celery; add them to the other ingredients, and set the whole over a slow fire for ¼ of an hour. Now put in the water, and simmer gently till it is reduced to 4 quarts; take out the fleshy part of the cheek, and strain the soup into a clean stewpan; thicken with flour, put in a head of sliced celery, and simmer till the celery is tender. If not a good colour, use a little browning. Cut the meat into small square pieces, pour the soup over, and serve with the crust of a French roll in the tureen. A glass of sherry much improves this soup.

TIME.—*3 to 4 hours.*

SEASONABLE *in winter.*

Ox-Cheek, Stewed. — INGREDIENTS *for dish for 6 persons.—1 cheek, salt and water, 4 or 5 onions, butter and flour, 6 cloves, 3 turnips, 2 carrots, 1 bay-leaf, 1 head of celery, 1 bunch of savoury herbs, cayenne, black pepper and salt to taste, 1 oz. of butter, 2 dessertspoonfuls of flour, 2 tablespoonfuls of Chili vinegar, 2 tablespoonfuls of mushroom ketchup, 2 tablespoonfuls of port wine, 2 tablespoonfuls of Harvey's sauce.* AVERAGE COST, *3s.*

Have the cheek boned, and prepare it the day before it is to be eaten, by cleaning and putting it to soak all night in salt and water. The next day, wipe it dry and clean, and put it into a stewpan. Just cover it with water, skim well when it boils, and let it gently simmer till the meat is quite tender. Slice and fry 3 onions in a little butter and flour, and put them into the gravy; add 2 whole onions, each stuck

with 3 cloves, 3 turnips quartered, 2 carrots sliced, a bay-leaf, 1 head of celery, a bunch of herbs, and seasoning to taste, of cayenne, black pepper and salt. Let these stew till perfectly tender; then take out the cheek, divide into pieces fit to help at table, skim and strain the gravy, and thicken 1½ pint of it with butter and flour in the above proportions. Add the vinegar, ketchup and port wine; put in the pieces of the cheek, let the whole boil up, and serve quite hot. Send it to table in an entrée dish. If the colour of the gravy should not be very good, add a teaspoonful of the browning.

TIME.—*4 hours.*

SEASONABLE *in winter.*

Ox-Tail, Broiled. (An Entrée.) INGREDIENTS *for dish for 8 persons.—2 tails, 1½ pint of stock, salt and cayenne to taste, bread-crumbs, 1 egg.* AVERAGE COST, 5s. 6d.

Joint and cut up the tails into convenient sized pieces, and put them into a stewpan, with the stock, cayenne and salt, and, if liked very savoury, a bunch of sweet herbs. Let them simmer gently for about 2½ hours; then take them out, drain them, and let them cool. Beat an egg upon a plate; dip in each piece of tail, and, afterwards, sprinkle them well with fine bread-crumbs; broil them over a clear fire until for a brownish colour on both sides, and serve with a good gravy, or any sauce that may be preferred.

TIME.—*About 2½ hours.*

SEASONABLE *at any time.*

Note.—These may be more easily prepared by putting the tails in a brisk oven, after they have been dipped in egg and bread-crumb; and, when brown, they are done. They must be boiled the same time as for broiling.

Ox-Tail Soup.—INGREDIENTS *for soup for 10 or 12 persons.—2 ox-tails, 2 slices of ham, 1 oz. of butter, 2 carrots, 2 turnips, 3 onions, 1 leek, 1 head of celery, 1 bunch of savoury herbs, 1 bay-leaf, 12 whole*

peppercorns, 4 cloves, a tablespoonful of salt, 2 tablespoonfuls of ketchup, ½ glass of port wine, 3 quarts of water. AVERAGE COST, 2s. 6d.

Cut up the tails, separating them at the joints; wash them, and put them in a stewpan with the butter. Cut the vegetables into slices and add them, with the peppercorns and herbs. Put in ½ pint of water, and stir it over a sharp fire till the juices are drawn. Fill up the stewpan with the water, and, when boiling, add the salt. Skim well, and simmer very gently for 4 hours, or until the tails are tender. Take them out, skim and strain the soup, thicken with flour, and flavour with the ketchup and port wine. Put back the tails, simmer for 5 minutes, and serve.

TIME.—4½ hours.

SEASONABLE in winter.

Ox-Tails, Stewed.—INGREDIENTS

for dish for 8 persons.—2 ox-tails, 1 onion, 3 cloves, 1 blade of mace, ¼ teaspoonful of whole black pepper, ¼ teaspoonful of allspice, ½ teaspoonful of salt, a small bunch of savoury herbs, thickening of butter and flour, 1 tablespoonful of lemon-juice, 1 tablespoonful of mushroom ketchup. AVERAGE COST, 4s. 6d.

Divide the tails at the joints, wash and put them into a stewpan with sufficient water to cover them, and set them on the fire; when the water boils, remove the scum, and add the onion cut into rings, the spice, seasoning and herbs. Cover the stewpan closely, and let the tails simmer very gently until tender, which will be in about 2½ hours. Take them out, make a thickening of butter and flour, add it to the gravy, and let it boil for ¼ hour. Strain it through a sieve into a saucepan, put back the tails, add the lemon-juice and ketchup; let the whole just boil up, and serve. Garnish with croûtons or sippets of toasted bread.

TIME.—2½ hours to stew the tails.

SEASONABLE all the year.

Oyster Forcemeat (for Roast or Boiled Turkey).—INGREDIENTS for sufficient for a turkey.—½ pint of bread-crumbs, 1½ oz. of chopped suet or some butter, 1 faggot of savoury herbs, ¼ saltspoonful of grated nutmeg, salt and pepper to taste, 2 eggs, 18 oysters. AVERAGE COST, 1s. 10d.

Grate the bread very fine, and be careful that no large lumps remain; put it into a basin with the suet, which must be very finely minced, or when butter is used, that must be cut up into small pieces. Add the herbs, also chopped as small as possible, and seasoning; mix all these well together, until the ingredients are thoroughly mingled. Open and beard the oysters, chop them, but not too small, and add them to the other ingredients. Beat up the eggs, and, with the hand, work all together, until it is smoothly mixed. The

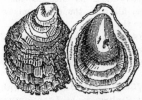

THE EDIBLE OYSTER.

turkey should not be stuffed too full; if there should be too much forcemeat, roll it into balls, fry them, and use them as a garnish.

SEASONABLE from September to April.

Oyster Ketchup.—INGREDIENTS.

—Sufficient oysters to fill a pint measure, 1 pint of sherry, 3 oz. of salt, 1 drachm of cayenne, 2 drachms of pounded mace.

Procure the oysters very fresh, and open sufficient to fill a pint measure; save the liquor and scald the oysters in it, with the sherry; strain the oysters and put them in a mortar, with the salt, cayenne and mace; pound the whole until reduced to a pulp, then add it to the liquor in which they were scalded; boil it again 5 minutes and skim well ; rub the whole through a sieve, and, when cold, bottle and cork closely. The corks should be sealed.

SEASONABLE *from September to April.*

Note.—Cider may be substituted for the sherry.

Oyster Patties.—INGREDIENTS *for*
10 or 12 *patties.*—2 *dozen oysters, 2 oz. of butter, 3 tablespoonfuls of cream, a little lemon-juice, 1 blade of pounded mace; cayenne to taste, puff-paste.* AVERAGE COST, 3s.

Scald the oysters in their own liquor, beard them and cut each one into 3 pieces. Put the butter into a stewpan, dredge in sufficient flour to dry it up; add the strained oyster-liquor, with the other ingredients; put in the oysters and let them heat gradually, but not boil fast. Make the patty-cases as directed for lobster patties, fill with the oyster mixture, and replace the covers.

TIME.—2 *minutes for the oysters to simmer in the mixture.*

SEASONABLE *from September to April.*

Oyster Sauce (to serve with Fish,
Boiled Poultry, &c.).—INGREDIENTS *sufficient for sauce for 6 persons.*—3 *dozen oysters, ½ pint of melted butter, made with milk.* AVERAGE COST, 3s. 3d.

Open the oysters carefully and save their liquor; strain it into a clean saucepan (a lined one is best), put in the oysters and let them just come to the boiling-point, when they should look plump. Take them off the fire immediately and put the whole into a basin. Strain the liquor from them, mix with it sufficient melted butter made with milk to make ½ pint altogether. When this is ready and very smooth, put in the oysters, which should be previously bearded, if you wish the sauce to be really nice. Set it by the side of the fire to get thoroughly hot, *but do not allow it to boil,* or the oysters will immediately harden. Using cream instead of milk

makes this sauce extremely delicious When liked, add a seasoning of cayenn or anchovy sauce ; but, as we have befor stated, a plain sauce *should* be plain an not be overpowered by highly-flavoure essences ; therefore we recommend tha the above directions be implicitly followed and no seasoning added. Never allov fewer than 6 oysters to 1 person, unless th party is very large.

, SEASONABLE *from September to April.*

Note.—A more economical sauce may b made by using a smaller quantity of oysters an not bearding them before they are added to th sauce: this may answer the purpose, but w cannot undertake to recommend it as a mod for making this delicious adjunct to fish, &c.

Oyster Soup.—INGREDIENTS *fo*
soup for 12 persons.—6 *dozen oysters,* ! *quarts of white stock, ½ pint of cream, 2 oz of butter, 1½ oz. of flour; salt, cayenne an mace to taste.* AVERAGE COST, 8s. 6d.

Scald the oysters in their own liquor take them out, beard them and put then in a tureen. Take a pint of the stock put in the beards and the liquor, which must be carefully strained, and simmer fo ½ an hour. Take it off the fire, strain i again, and add the remainder of the stock with the seasoning and mace. Bring it t a boil, add the thickening of butter an flour, simmer for 5 minutes, stir in th boiling cream, pour it over the oysters, an serve.

TIME.—1 *hour.*

SEASONABLE *from September to April.*

Note.—This soup can be made less rich b using milk instead of cream, and thickening wit] arrowroot instead of butter and flour.

Oyster Soup.—INGREDIENTS *fo*
soup for 12 persons.—3 *quarts of good mut ton broth, 6 dozen oysters, 2 oz. of butter 1 oz. of flour.* AVERAGE COST, 7s.

Beard the oysters and scald them i their own liquor; then add it, wel strained, to the broth; thicken with th butter and flour, and simmer for ¼ of a

...our. Put in the oysters, stir well, but do not let it boil, and serve very hot.

TIME.—¾ _hour_.

SEASONABLE _from September to April_.

Oysters, Darioles of.—INGREDI-
ENTS _for dish for 2 persons.—A dozen oysters, 1 oz. of flour, 1 oz. of butter, 2 eggs, pint of milk, seasoning of lemon-juice, salt, cayenne and nutmeg_. AVERAGE COST, s. 6d.

Beard the oysters and scald them in their liquor, strain them and cut each into pieces. Put the butter and flour in a saucepan, with the liquor from the oysters and the milk, and stir till boiling; then add the seasoning and the eggs well beaten, and lastly the oysters. Butter some dariole moulds, well fill them with the mixture, and steam gently for 20 minutes.

TIME.—20 _minutes to steam the darioles_.

SEASONABLE _from September to April_.

Oysters, Fried.—INGREDIENTS _for dish for 4 persons.—3 dozen oysters, 2 oz. of butter, 1 tablespoonful of ketchup, a little chopped lemon-peel, ½ teaspoonful of chopped parsley_. AVERAGE COST, 3s. 3d.

Boil the oysters for 1 minute in their own liquor and drain them; fry them with the butter, ketchup, lemon-peel and parsley; lay them on a dish and garnish with toasted sippets and parsley. This is a delicious delicacy, and is a favourite Italian dish.

TIME.—5 _minutes_.

SEASONABLE _from September to April_.

Oysters Fried in Batter.—IN-
GREDIENTS _for dish for 4 persons. — 3 dozen oysters, 2 eggs, ½ pint of milk, sufficient flour to make the batter; pepper and salt to taste; when liked, a little nutmeg; not lard_. AVERAGE COST, 3s. 6d.

Scald the oysters in their own liquor, beard them, and lay them on a cloth to drain thoroughly. Break the eggs into a basin, mix the flour with them, add the milk gradually, with nutmeg and season-

ing, and put the oysters in the batter. Make some lard hot in a deep frying-pan, put in the oysters, one at a time · when done, take them up with a sharp-pointed skewer and dish them on a napkin. Fried oysters are frequently used for garnishing boiled fish, and then a few bread-crumbs should be added to the flour.

TIME.—5 _or_ 6 _minutes_.

SEASONABLE _from September to April_.

Oysters, To Keep.—Put them in a tub and cover them with salt and water. Let them remain for 12 hours, when they are to be taken out and allowed to stand for another 12 hours without water. If left without water every alternate 12 hours, they will be much better than if constantly kept in it. Never put the same water twice to them.

Oysters, Pickled.—INGREDIENTS.
—100 _oysters; to each_ ½ _pint of vinegar_, 1 _blade of pounded mace_, 1 _strip of lemon-peel_, 12 _black peppercorns_.

Get the oysters in good condition, open them, place them in a saucepan, and let them simmer in their own liquor for about 10 minutes very gently; then take them out one by one, and place them in a jar, and cover them, when cold, with a pickle made as follows:—Measure the oyster-liquor; add to it the same quantity of vinegar, with mace, lemon-peel and pepper in the above proportion, and boil it for 5 minutes; when cold, pour over the oysters and tie them down very closely, as contact with the air spoils them.

SEASONABLE _from September to April_.

Note.— Put this pickle away in small jars: because, directly one is opened, its contents should immediately be eaten, as they soon spoil. The pickle should not be kept more than 2 or 3 months.

Oysters, Sausages of.—INGREDI-
ENTS _for sausages for 6 persons.—2 dozen oysters, 1 lb. of veal, ¼ lb. of suet, 1 egg, 1 slice of bread, some butter, seasoning_. AVERAGE COST, 3s.

Open the oysters, saving the liquor and taking off the beards. Mince the veal and suet finely, then pound them with the oysters to a paste. Soak the bread in the liquor from the oysters, and add that to the paste, pounding it in and adding a seasoning of pepper and salt. Bind the mixture with the egg beaten, and form into small rolls the size of sausages. Fry in butter a bright golden brown, and serve hot with brown bread-and-butter, and a cut lemon.

TIME.—*10 minutes to fry the sausages.*
SEASONABLE *from September to April.*

Oysters, Scalloped.—INGREDI-ENTS *for dish for 4 or 5 persons.*—3 *dozen oysters,* 1 *oz. of butter, flour,* 2 *tablespoonfuls of white stock,* 2 *tablespoonfuls of cream; pepper and salt to taste; bread-crumbs, oiled butter.* AVERAGE COST, 3s. 6d.

Scald the oysters in their own liquor, take them out, beard them, and strain the liquor free from grit. Put 1 oz. of butter into a stewpan; when melted, dredge in

SCALLOPED OYSTERS.

sufficient flour to dry it up; add the stock, cream and strained liquor, and give one boil. Put in the oysters and seasoning; let them gradually heat through, but not boil. Have ready the scallop-shells buttered; lay in the oysters, and as much of the liquid as they will hold; cover them over with bread-crumbs, over which drop a little oiled butter. Brown them in the oven, or before the fire, and serve quickly, and very hot.

TIME.—*Altogether,* ¼ *hour.*

Oysters, Scalloped.—Prepare the oysters as in the preceding recipe, and put them in a scallop-shell or saucer, and be-tween each layer sprinkle over a few

bread-crumbs, pepper, salt and grated nutmeg; place small pieces of butter over and bake before the fire in a Dutch oven. Put sufficient bread-crumbs on the top to make a smooth surface, as the oysters should not be seen.

TIME.—*About* ¼ *hour.*
SEASONABLE *from September to April.*

Oysters (Tinned), Scalloped.—INGREDIENTS *for dish for 2 persons.*—1 *tin of oysters,* 1 *oz. of butter,* ¼ *lb. of bread crumbs, cayenne, salt.* AVERAGE COST, 8d.

Butter a shallow tin, and strew it with bread-crumbs, which very lightly sprinkle with salt. Over the bread-crumbs lay the oysters, seasoning them with cayenne and 3 dessertspoonfuls of their liquor. Cover them with bread-crumbs, and put the remainder of the butter over them in small pieces. Bake them in a Dutch oven or in an ordinary one, afterwards browning them before the fire.

TIME.—*From 10 to 15 minutes to bake.*
SEASONABLE *at any time.*

Oysters, Stewed.—INGREDIENTS *for dish for 4 or 5 persons.*—3 *dozen oysters,* 1 *oz. of butter, flour,* ½ *pint of cream; cayenne and salt to taste;* 1 *blade of pounded mace.*

Scald the oysters in their own liquor, take them out, beard them, and strain the liquor; put the butter into a stewpan, dredge in sufficient flour to dry it up, add the oyster-liquor and mace, and stir it over a sharp fire with a wooden spoon; when it comes to a boil, add the cream, oysters and seasoning. Let all simmer for 1 or 2 minutes, but not longer, or the oysters would harden. Serve on a hot dish, and garnish with croûtons, or toasted sippets of bread. A small piece of lemon-peel boiled with the oyster-liquor, and taken out before the cream is added, will be found an improvement.

TIME.—*Altogether 15 minutes.*
SEASONABLE *from September to April.*

" Pig, pudding and soup, the electrified group,
With the flagon, pop under the sofa in haste."—INGOLDSBY.

PANADA.

ANADA.—INGRE-
DIENTS.—*1 pint of
white stock, 1 slice
of lean ham, 1½ lb. of
butter, 2 penny rolls,
a little minced pars-
ley, 2 shalots, 2 or 3
cloves, 2 blades of
mace, a few mush-
rooms, 2 eggs, salt,
pepper, a little milk.*

AVERAGE COST, 1s. 6d.

Take the crumb from the rolls, and soak
it in milk for ½ an hour, then take it out
and squeeze out the moisture. Put the
soaked bread into a stewpan with one-third
of the stock, and set on one side. Put
into a separate stewpan 1 oz. of butter,
the ham cut small, and the mushrooms and
other seasonings, and fry all gently over a
slow fire. Next moisten them with the remainder of the stock, boil for 20 minutes,
and strain into the other stewpan over the
soaked bread. Place the pan over the fire
and keep constantly stirring, to prevent
burning, and, when the mixture dries, put
in the ½ oz. of butter and let this also dry

PANCAKE, INDIAN.

up ; then add the yolks of the eggs and
mix well. Put the panada on a plate to
cool, and use it with the udder and the veal
or other meat used for quenelles or French
forcemeat.

Pancake, Indian.—INGREDIENTS
for dish sufficient for 3 persons.—*1 pint of
milk, 3 eggs, ¼ lb. of sugar, ½ a teacupful of
rice, flavouring of cinnamon, preserved ginger and cherries, butter for frying.* AVER-
AGE COST, 10d.

Boil the rice in the milk till quite soft,
then beat it to a pulp and add the eggs,
well beaten, the sugar and the flavouring.

INDIAN PANCAKE.

Form into an oval flat cake, and fry on
one side in butter ; then put it carefully on
a hot dish, and garnish with the preserved
fruit.

TIME.—*To fry, 7 or 8 minutes.*
SEASONABLE *at any time.*

Pancakes. — INGREDIENTS *for dish for 4 or 5 persons.*—6 *eggs*, 6 *oz. of flour*, 1½ *pint of milk*, *butter or lard.* AVERAGE COST, 1*s.*

Ascertain that the eggs are fresh, break each one separately in a cup, whisk them well, put them into a basin, with the flour, salt and a few drops of milk, and beat the whole to a perfectly *smooth* batter; then add by degrees the remainder of the milk. The proportion of this latter ingredient must be regulated by the size of the eggs, &c. &c. ; but the batter, when ready for frying, should be of the consistency of thick cream. Place a small frying-pan on the fire to get hot; let it be delicately clean, or the pancakes will stick, and, when quite hot, put into it a small piece of butter or lard, allowing about ⅓ oz. to each pancake. When it is melted, pour in the batter,

PANCAKES.

about ½ teacupful to a pan 5 inches in diameter, and fry it for about 4 minutes, or until it is nicely brown on one side. By only pouring in a small quantity of batter, and so making the pancakes thin, the necessity of turning them (an operation rather difficult to unskilful cooks) is obviated. When the pancake is done, sprinkle over it some pounded sugar, roll it up in the pan, and take it out with a large slice, and place it on a dish before the fire. Proceed in this manner until sufficient are cooked for a dish: then send them quickly to table, and continue to send in a further quantity, as pancakes are never good unless eaten almost immediately they come from the frying-pan. The batter may be flavoured with a little grated lemon-rind, or the pancakes may have preserve rolled in them instead of sugar. Send sifted sugar and a cut lemon to table with them. To render the pancakes

very light, the yolks and whites of the eggs should be beaten separately, and the whites added the last thing to the batter before frying.

TIME.—*From 4 to 5 minutes for a pancake that does not require turning; from 6 to 8 minutes for a thicker one.*

SEASONABLE *at any time, but specially served on Shrove Tuesday.*

Pancakes, Richer.—INGREDIENTS *for 8 pancakes.*—6 *eggs*, ½ *pint of cream*, ¼ *pint of milk*, ¼ *lb. of loaf sugar*, 1 *glass of sherry*, ½ *teaspoonful of grated nutmeg*, *flour.* AVERAGE COST, 2*s.*

Ascertain that the eggs are extremely fresh, beat them well, strain and mix with them the cream, milk, pounded sugar, wine, nutmeg, and as much flour as will make the batter nearly as thick as that for ordinary pancakes. Make the frying-pan hot, wipe it with a clean cloth, put in a small piece of butter or lard, pour in sufficient batter to make a thin pancake, and fry it for about 5 minutes. Dish the pancakes, piled one above the other, strewing sifted sugar between them, and serve.

TIME.—*About 5 minutes.*

SEASONABLE *at any time, but specially served on Shrove Tuesday.*

Pancakes, French.—INGREDIENTS *for dish for 3 persons.*— 2 *eggs*, 2 *oz. of butter*, 2 *oz. of sifted sugar*, 2 *oz. of flour*, ½ *pint of new milk.* AVERAGE COST, 6*d.*

Beat the eggs thoroughly, and put them into a basin with the butter, which should be beaten to a cream; stir in the sugar and flour, and when these ingredients are well mixed, add the milk; keep stirring and beating the mixture for a few minutes; put it on buttered plates, and bake in a quick oven for 20 minutes. Serve with a cut lemon and sifted sugar, or pile the pancakes high on a dish, with a layer of preserve or marmalade between them.

TIME.—20 *minutes.*

SEASONABLE *at any time.*

Pancakes, Snow.— INGREDIENTS

for 8 small pancakes.—3 *tablespoonfuls of flour*, 1 *egg*, 3 *tablespoonfuls of snow, about* ½ *pint of new milk, lard for frying.* AVERAGE COST, 5d.

Mix the flour with the milk by degrees, add the egg, well beaten, and, just before frying, the snow; it should then be all beaten up together quickly, and put into the frying-pan immediately.

SEASONABLE *in winter.*

Pancakes, Fritters and Omelettes, Recipes for.— Directions for

making the following appear under their respective headings :—

Pancake, Indian.	Fritters, Pea.
Pancakes.	,, Peach.
,, Richer.	,, Pine-apple.
,, Plain.	,, Plain.
,, Snow.	,, Potato.
Fritters, Apple.	,, Rice.
,, Beef.	Omelette, Bachelor's.
,, Bread & Butter.	,, Ham.
,, Currant.	,, Kidney.
,, Indian.	,, Plain.
,, Orange.	,, ,, Sweet.

Pan Kail.—INGREDIENTS *for soup for*

8 *persons.*—2 *lbs. of cabbage or Savoy greens;* ¼ *lb. of dripping, salt and pepper to taste, oatmeal for thickening,* 2 *quarts of water.* AVERAGE COST, 4d.

Chop the cabbage very fine, thicken the water with oatmeal, put in the cabbage and dripping; season and simmer for 1½ hour. It can be made sooner by blanching and mashing the greens, adding any good liquor that a joint has been boiled in, and then further thickened with bread or pounded biscuit.

TIME.—1½ *hour.*

SEASONABLE *all the year, but more suitable in winter.*

Paradise Pudding. — INGREDI-

ENTS *for pudding for* 4 *persons.*—3 *eggs*, 3 *apples*, ¼ *lb. of bread-crumbs*, 3 *oz. of sugar,* 3 *oz. of currants, salt and grated nutmeg to taste, the rind of* ½ *lemon*, ½ *wineglassful of brandy.* AVERAGE COST, 10d.

Pare, core and mince the apples into small pieces, and mix them with the other ingredients; beat up the eggs, moisten the mixture with these, and beat it well; stir in the brandy, and put the pudding into a buttered mould; tie it down with a cloth, boil for 1½ hour, and serve with sweet sauce.

TIME.—1½ *hour.*

Parsley and Butter (to serve with

Calf's Head, Boiled Fowls, &c.). — INGREDIENTS *for sauce for large fowl.*—2 *tablespoonfuls of minced parsley*, ½ *pint of melted butter.* AVERAGE COST, 4d.

Put into a saucepan a small quantity of water, slightly salted, and, when it boils, throw in a good bunch of parsley which has been previously washed and tied together in a bunch; let it boil for 5 minutes, drain it, mince the leaves *very fine*, and put the above quantity in a tureen; pour over it ½ pint of smoothly-made melted butter; stir once, that the ingredients may be thoroughly mixed, and serve.

TIME.—5 *minutes to boil the parsley.*

SEASONABLE *at any time.*

Parsley, Fried (for Garnishing).—

INGREDIENTS.—*Parsley, hot lard or clarified dripping.*

Gather some young parsley; wash, pick and dry it thoroughly in a cloth; put it into the wire basket of which we have given an engraving, and hold it in boiling lard or dripping for a minute or two. Directly it is done, lift out the basket, and let it stand before the fire, that the parsley may become thoroughly crisp; and the quicker it is fried the better. Should the kitchen not be furnished with the above article, throw the parsley into the frying-pan, and, when crisp, lift it out with a slice, dry it before the fire, and when thoroughly crisp it will be ready for use.

Wire Basket.—For this recipe a wire basket, as shown in the annexed engraving, will be found very useful. It is very

light and handy, and may be used for other similar purposes besides that just described.

Parsley Juice for Colouring various Dishes).—Procure some nice young parsley; wash it and dry it thoroughly in a cloth; pound the leaves in a mortar till all the juice is extracted, and put the juice in a teacup or small jar; place this in a saucepan of boiling water, and warm it on the *bain-marie* principle just long enough to

PARSLEY.

take off its rawness; let it drain, and it will be ready for colouring.

Substitute for.—Sometimes in the middle of winter, parsley-leaves are not to be had, when the following will be found an excellent substitute :—Tie up a little parsley-seed in a small piece of muslin, and boil it for 10 minutes in a small quantity of water; use this water to make the melted butter with, and throw into it a little boiled spinach, minced rather fine, which will

have an appearance similar to that of parsley.

Parsley, To Preserve, through the Winter.—Use freshly-gathered parsley for keeping, and wash it perfectly free from grit and dirt; put it into boiling water which has been slightly salted and well skimmed, and then let it boil for 2 or 3 minutes; take it out, let it drain, and lay it on a sieve in front of the fire, when it should be dried as expeditiously as possible. Store it away in a very dry place in bottles, and, when wanted for use pour over it a little warm water and let it stand for about 5 minutes.

SEASONABLE.—*This may be done at any time between June and October.*

Parsnips, Boiled.—INGREDIENTS. —*Parsnips; to each ½ gallon of water allow 1 heaped tablespoonful of salt.* AVERAGE COST, 1d. *each.*

Wash the parsnips, scrape them thoroughly, and with the point of the knife remove any black specks about them, and, should they be very large, cut the thick part into quarters. Put them into a saucepan of boiling water salted in the above proportion; boil them rapidly until tender, which may be ascertained by thrusting

THE PARSNIP.

a fork in them; take them up, drain them, and serve in a vegetable-dish. This vegetable is usually served with salt fish, boiled pork, or boiled beef; when sent to table with the latter, a few should be placed alternately with carrots round the dish as a garnish.

TIME.—*Large parsnips, 1 to 1½ hour; small ones, ½ to 1 hour.*

SEASONABLE *from October to May.*

Parsnip Soup.— INGREDIENTS *for soup for 4 or 5 persons.*—1 *lb. of sliced parsnips,* 2 *oz. of butter, salt and cayenne to taste,* 1 *quart of stock.* AVERAGE COST, 6*d.*

Put the parsnips into the stewpan with the butter, which has been previously melted, and simmer them till quite tender. Then add nearly a pint of stock, and boil together for ½ an hour. Pass all through a fine strainer, and put to it the remainder of the stock. Season, boil, and serve immediately.

TIME.—2 *hours.*

SEASONABLE *from October to April.*

Partridge, Broiled. (A Luncheon, Breakfast, or Supper Dish.)—INGREDIENTS *for dish for 6 persons.*—3 *partridges, salt and cayenne to taste, a small piece of butter, brown gravy or mushroom sauce.* AVERAGE COST, 5*s.*

Pluck, draw and cut the partridges in half, and wipe the inside thoroughly with a damp cloth. Season them with salt and cayenne, broil them over a very clear fire, and dish them on a hot dish; rub a small piece of butter over each half, and send them to table with brown gravy or mushroom sauce.

TIME.—*About* ¼ *hour.*

SEASONABLE *from the 1st of September to the beginning of February.*

Partridge Pie.— INGREDIENTS *for pie for 7 or 8 persons.*— 3 *partridges, pepper and salt to taste,* 1 *teaspoonful of minced parsley (when obtainable, a few mushrooms),* ¾ *lb. of veal cutlet, a slice of ham,* ½ *pint of stock, puff-paste.* AVERAGE COST, 7*s.*

Line a pie-dish with a veal cutlet; over that place a slice of ham and a seasoning of pepper and salt. Pluck, draw and wipe the partridges; cut them in half, and cut off the legs at the first joint, and season them inside with pepper, salt, minced parsley and a small piece of butter; place

them in the dish, and pour over the stock; line the edges of the dish with puff-paste, cover with the same, decorate, and brush it over with the yolk of an egg, and bake for ¾ to 1 hour.

TIME.—¾ *to* 1 *hour.*

SEASONABLE *from the 1st of September to the beginning of February.*

Partridge, Potted.—INGREDIENTS. —*Partridges; seasoning to taste, of mace, allspice, white pepper and salt; butter, coarse paste.*

Pluck and draw the birds, and wipe them inside with a damp cloth. Pound well some mace, allspice, white pepper and salt; mix together, and rub every part of the partridges with this. Pack the birds as close as possible in a baking-pan, with plenty of butter over them, and cover with a coarse flour-and-water crust. Tie a paper over this, and bake for rather more than 1½ hour; let the birds get cold, then cut them into pieces for keeping, pack them closely into a large potting-pot, and cover with clarified butter. This should be kept in a cool dry place. The butter used for potted things will answer for basting, or for paste for meat pies.

TIME.—1½ *hour.*

SEASONABLE *from the 1st of September to the beginning of February.*

Partridge, Roast.—INGREDIENTS. —*Partridges; butter.*

Choose young birds, with dark-coloured bills and yellowish legs, and let them hang a few days, or there will be no flavour to the flesh, nor will it be tender. The time they should be kept entirely depends on the taste of those for whom they are intended, as what some persons would consider delicious would be to others disgusting and offensive. Pluck, draw and wipe the partridge inside and out, cut off the head, leaving enough skin to skewer back; bring the legs close to the breast, between it and the side bones, and pass a skewer through the pinions and the thick part of the thighs. When the bird is firmly and plumply trussed, roast it before a nice bright fire; keep it well basted, and. a few minutes before serving, flour and froth it well. Dish it, and serve with gravy and

ROAST PARTRIDGE.

bread sauce, and send to table hot and quickly. A little of the gravy should be poured over the bird.

TIME.—25 to 35 minutes.

SEASONABLE from the 1st of September to the beginning of February.

Partridge Soup.

INGREDIENTS for soup for 8 persons.—2 partridges, 3 slices of lean ham, 2 shred onions, 1 head of celery, 1 large carrot and 1 turnip sliced, then stamped out in rounds with a cutter, 1 small lump of sugar, 2 oz. of butter, salt and pepper to taste, 2 quarts of medium stock. AVERAGE COST, 5s.

Cut the partridges into pieces, and braise them in the butter and ham until quite tender; then take out the legs, wings and breast, and set them by. Keep the backs and other trimmings in the braise, and add the onions and celery; any remains of cold game can be put in, and 3 pints of stock. Simmer slowly for 1 hour, strain it, and skim the fat off as clean as possible; put in the pieces that were taken out, give it one boil, and skim again to have it quite clear, and add the sugar and seasoning. Now simmer the cut carrot and turnip in 1 pint of stock; when quite tender, put them to the partridges, and serve.

TIME.—2 hours.

SEASONABLE from September to February.

Note.—The meat of the partridges may be pounded with the crumb of a French roll, and worked with the soup through a sieve.

Partridges, To Carve.

There are several ways of carving this most familiar game bird. The more usual and summary mode is to carry the knife sharply along the top of the breast-bone of the bird, and cut it quite through, thus dividing it into two precisely equal and similar parts, in the same manner as carving a pigeon. Another plan is to cut it into three pieces: viz., by severing

ROAST PARTRIDGES.

a small wing and leg on either side from the body, by following the line 1 to 2 in the upper woodcut; thus making 2 helpings, when the breast will remain for a third plate. The most elegant manner is that of thrusting back the body from the legs, and then cutting through the breast in the direction shown by the line 1 to 2: this plan will give 4 or more small helpings. A little bread-sauce should be served to each guest.

Partridges, Hashed, or Salmi de Perdreaux.

INGREDIENTS for dish for 6 persons.—3 young partridges, 3 shalots, a slice of lean ham, 1 carrot, 3 or 4 mushrooms, a bunch of savoury herbs, 2 cloves, 6 whole peppers, ¾ pint of stock, 1 glass of sherry or Madeira, a small lump of sugar. AVERAGE COST, 6s.

After the partridges are plucked and drawn, roast them rather underdone, and cover them with paper, as they should not be browned; cut them into joints, take off the skin from the wings, legs and breasts; put these into a stewpan, cover them up, and set by until the gravy is ready. Cut a slice of ham into small pieces, and put them, with the carrots sliced, the shalots, mushrooms, herbs, cloves and pepper, into a stewpan; fry them lightly in a little butter, pour in the stock, add the bones and trimming from the partridges, and simmer for ¼ hour. Strain the gravy, let it cool, and skim off every particle of fat; put it to the legs, wings and breasts, add a glass of sherry or Madeira and a small lump of sugar, let all gradually warm through by the side of the fire, and, when on the point of boiling, serve, and garnish the dish with croûtons. The remains of roast partridge answer very well dressed in this way, although not so good as when the birds are in the first instance only half-roasted. This recipe is equally suitable for pheasants, moor game, &c.; but care must be taken always to skin the joints.

TIME.—*Altogether*, 1 *hour.*

SEASONABLE *from the first of September to the beginning of February.*

Partridges, Stewed.—INGREDI-

ENTS *for dish for* 4 *persons.*—2 *partridges,* 1 *lemon, a little fat bacon,* 2 *onions,* 2 *carrots, sliced,* 1 *onion stuck with* 2 *or* 3 *cloves, a little thyme, parsley,* 2 *bay-leaves, a glass of white wine,* ½ *pint of stock, butter, salt and pepper.* AVERAGE COST, 4s.

Truss the birds with a small lump of butter inside, skewering the skin of the neck over it; place two slices of lemon on

STEWED PARTRIDGES.

the breast of each, and cover with slices of bacon. Put the birds into a stewpan with the other ingredients, and simmer for an hour, then drain, and take off the fat and the lemon just before serving. Strain the gravy, take off all the fat, and thicken with a little butter and flour; pour this sauce in an entrée dish, lay in the birds and garnish with some stewed mushrooms or a purée of green peas.

TIME.—1 *hour to stew the birds.*

SEASONABLE *from September to March.*

Paste, Common, for Family

Pies.—INGREDIENTS *for paste for* 2 *pies of moderate size.* —1¼ *lb. of flour,* ½ *lb. of butter or lard, rather more than* ½ *pint of water.* AVERAGE COST, *with lard,* 6d., *with butter,* 9d.

Rub the butter lightly into the flour, and mix it to a smooth paste with the water; roll it out 2 or 3 times, and it will be ready for use. This paste may be converted into an excellent short crust for sweet tart by adding to the flour, after the butter is rubbed in, 2 tablespoonfuls of fine sifted sugar.

Paste, Puff, French; or, Feuille-

tage. (Founded on M. UDE'S Recipe).— INGREDIENTS.— *Equal quantities of flour and butter—say* 1 *lb. of each;* ½ *saltspoonful of salt, the yolks of* 2 *eggs, rather more than* ¼ *pint of water.* AVERAGE COST, 9d. *per lb.*

Weigh the flour; ascertain that it is perfectly *dry*, and sift it; squeeze all the water from the butter, and wring it in a clean cloth till there is no moisture remaining. Put the flour on the paste-board, work lightly into it 2 oz. of the butter, and then make a hole in the centre; into this well put the yolks of 2 eggs, the salt and about ¼ pint of water (the quantity of this latter ingredient must be regulated by the cook, as it is impossible to give the exact proportion of it); knead up the paste quickly and lightly, and, when quite smooth, roll it out square to the thickness of about ½ an inch. Take care that the butter is perfectly free from moisture, and *as cool* as possible, roll it into a ball, and p'ace this ball of butter on the paste; fold the paste over the butter all round, and secure it by wrapping it well all over. Flatten the paste by rolling it lightly with the rolling-pin until it is quite thin, but not thin enough to allow the butter to break through, and keep the board and paste dredged lightly with flour during the process of making it. This rolling gives it the *first* turn. Now fold the paste in three, and roll out again, and, should the weather be very warm, put it in a cold place on the ground to cool between the several turns; for, unless this is particularly attended to, the paste will be spoiled. Roll out the paste again *twice*, put it by to cool, then roll it out *twice* more, which will make six *turnings* in all. Now fold the paste in two, and it will be ready for use. If properly baked and well made, this crust will be delicious, and should rise in the oven about 4 or 5 inches. The paste should be made rather firm in the first instance, as the ball of butter is liable to break through. Great attention must also be paid to keeping the butter very cool, as, if this is in a liquid or soft state, the paste will not answer at all. Should the cook be dexterous enough to succeed in making this, the paste will have a much better appearance than that made by the process of dividing the butter into 4 parts, and placing it over the rolled-out paste; but, until experience has been acquired, we recommend puff-paste made by recipe. The above paste is used for vols-au-vent, small articles of pastry, and, in fact, everything that requires very light crust.

Paste, Puff, very Good.—INGRE-
DIENTS.—*To every lb. of flour allow* 1 *lb. of butter, and not quite* ½ *pint of water.* AVER-AGE COST, 9d. *per lb.*

Carefully weigh the flour and butter, and have the exact proportion; squeeze the butter well, to extract the water from it, and afterwards wring it in a clean cloth, that no moisture may remain. Sift the flour; see that it is perfectly dry, and proceed in the following manner to make the paste, using a very *clean* paste-board and rolling-pin :—Supposing the quantity to be 1 lb of flour, work the whole into a smooth paste with not quite ½ pint of water, using a knife to mix it with: the proportion of this latter ingredient must be regulated by the discretion of the cook; if too much be

added, the paste, when baked, will be tough. Roll it out until it is of an equal thickness of about an inch; break 4 oz. of butter into small pieces; place these on the paste, sift over it a little flour, fold it over, roll out again and put another 4 oz. of butter. Repeat the rolling and buttering until the paste has been rolled out 4 times, or equal quantities of flour and butter have been used. Do not omit, every time the paste is rolled out, to dredge a little flour over that and the rolling-pin, to prevent both from sticking. Handle the paste as lightly as possible, and do not press heavily upon it with the rolling-pin. The next thing to be considered is the oven, as the baking of pastry requires particular attention. Do not put it into the oven until it is sufficiently hot to raise the paste; for the best-prepared paste, if not properly baked, will be good for nothing. Brushing the paste as often as rolled out, and the pieces of butter placed thereon, with the white of an egg, assists it to rise in *leaves* or *flakes.* As this is the great beauty of puff-paste, it is as well to try this method.

Paste, Puff, Medium.—INGREDI-
ENTS.—*To every* lb. *of flour allow* ½ lb. *of butter,* 3 oz. *of lard, not quite* ½ *pint of water.* AVERAGE COST, 7d.

This paste may be made by the directions in the preceding recipe, only using less butter, and substituting lard for a portion of it. Mix the flour to a smooth paste with not quite ½ pint of water; then roll it out 3 times, the first time covering the paste with butter, the second with lard, and the third with butter. Keep the rolling-pin and paste slightly dredged with flour, to prevent them from sticking, and it will be ready for use.

Paste, Puff. (SOYER'S Recipe.)—IN-
GREDIENTS.—*To every* lb. *of flour allow the yolk of* 1 *egg, the juice of* 1 *lemon,* ½ *salt-spoonful of salt, cold water,* 1 lb. *of fresh butter.* AVERAGE COST, 10d. *per lb.*

Put the flour on to the paste-board; make a hole in the centre, into which put the yolk of the egg, the lemon-juice and salt; mix the whole with cold water (this should be iced in summer, if convenient) into a soft flexible paste, with the right hand, and handle it as little as possible; then squeeze all the buttermilk from the butter, wring it in a cloth, and roll out the paste; place the butter on this, and fold the edges of the paste over, so as to hide it; roll it out again to the thickness of ¼ inch; fold over one-third, over which again pass the rolling-pin; then fold over the other third, thus forming a square; place it with the ends, top and bottom before you, shaking a little flour both under and over, and repeat the rolls and turns twice again, as before. Flour a baking-sheet, put the paste on this, and let it remain on ice or in some cool place for ½ hour; then roll twice more, turning it as before; place it again upon the ice for ¼ hour, give it 2 more rolls, making 7 in all, and it is ready for use when required.

Pastry and Puddings, Directions in connection with the making of.
— A few general remarks respecting the various ingredients of which puddings and pastry are composed may be acceptable in addition to the recipes given in this book.

Flour should be of the best quality and perfectly dry, and sifted before being used; if in the least damp, the paste made from it will certainly be heavy.

Butter, unless fresh is used, should be washed from the salt and well squeezed and wrung in a cloth, to get out all the water and buttermilk, which, if left in, assists to make the paste heavy.

Lard should be perfectly sweet, which may be ascertained by cutting the bladder through; and, if the knife smells sweet, the lard is good.

Suet should be finely chopped, perfectly free from skin and quite sweet; during the process of chopping, it should be

lightly dredged with flour, which prevents the pieces from sticking together. Beef suet is considered the best; but veal suet, or the outside fat of a loin or neck of

PASTE-BOARD AND ROLLING-PIN.

mutton, makes good crusts; as also the skimmings in which a joint of mutton has been boiled, but *without* vegetables.

Clarified Beef Dripping answers very well for kitchen pies, puddings, cakes or for family use. A very good short crust may be made by mixing with it a small quantity of moist sugar; but care must be taken to use the dripping sparingly, or a very disagreeable flavour will be imparted to the paste.

Strict cleanliness must be observed in pastry-making; all the utensils used

PASTE-PINCERS AND JAGGER, FOR ORNAMENTING THE EDGES OF PIE-CRUSTS.

should be perfectly free from dust and dirt, and the things required for pastry kept entirely for that purpose.

In mixing paste, add the water very gradually, work the whole together with the knife-blade, and knead it until perfectly smooth. Those who are inexperienced in pastry-making should work the butter in by breaking it in small pieces, and covering the paste rolled out. It should then be dredged with flour, and the ends folded over and rolled out very

PASTE-CUTTER AND CORNER CUTTER.

thin again; this process must be repeated until all the butter is used.

The art of making paste requires much practice, dexterity and skill: it should be touched as lightly as possible, made with cool hands and in a cool place (a marble slab is better than a board for the purpose), and the coolest part of the

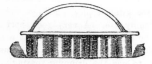

ORNAMENTAL-PASTE CUTTER.

house should be selected for the process during warm weather.

To insure rich paste being light, great expedition must be used in the making and baking; for if it stand long before it is put in the oven, it becomes flat and heavy.

Puff-paste requires a brisk oven, but not too hot, or it would blacken the crust;

PATTY-PANS, PLAIN AND FLUTED.

on the other hand, if the oven be too slack, the paste will be sodden and will not rise, nor will it have any colour.

Paste and all cakes made with baking-powder should be put in the oven directly they are made.

Tart-tins, cake-moulds, dishes for baked puddings, patty-pans, &c., should all be buttered before the article intended to be baked is put in them. Things to be baked on sheets should be placed on

PIE DISH.

buttered paper. Raised-pie paste should have a soaking heat, and paste glazed must have rather a slack oven, that the icing be not scorched. It is better to ice tarts, &c., when they are three-parts baked.

To ascertain when the oven is heated to the proper degree for puff-paste, put a

RAISED-PIE MOULD.

small piece of the paste in previous to baking the whole, and then the heat can thus be judged of.

The freshness of all pudding ingredients is of much importance, as one bad article will taint the whole mixture.

When the *freshness* of eggs is *doubtful*, break each one separately in a cup, before

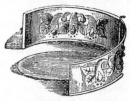

RAISED-PIE MOULD, OPEN.

mixing them all together. Should there be a bad one amongst them it can be thrown away; whereas, if mixed with the good ones, the entire quantity would be spoiled. The yolks and whites beaten separately make the articles they are put into much lighter.

Raisins and dried fruits for puddings should be carefully picked, and in many cases stoned. Currants should be well washed, pressed in a cloth, and placed on a dish before the fire to get thoroughly dry; they should then be picked carefully over, and *every piece of grit or stone* removed from amongst them. To plump them, some cooks pour boiling water over them, and then dry them before the fire.

Batter pudding should be smoothly mixed and free from lumps. To insure this, first mix the flour with a very small proportion of milk, and add the remainder by degrees. Should the pudding be very lumpy, it may be strained through a hair sieve.

All boiled puddings should be put on in *boiling water*, which must not be allowed

BOILED-PUDDING MOULD.

to stop simmering, and the pudding m u s t always be covered with the water; if requisite, the saucepan should be kept filled up.

To prevent a pudding boiled in a cloth from sticking to the bottom of the saucepan, place a small plate or saucer underneath it, and set the pan *on a trivet* over the fire. If a mould is used, this precaution is not necessary; but care must be taken to keep the pudding well-covered with water.

For dishing a boiled pudding, as soon as it comes out of the pot dip it into a basin of cold water, and the cloth will then not adhere to it. Great expedition is necessary in sending puddings to table, as by standing they quickly become heavy, batter puddings particularly.

For baked or boiled puddings, the moulds, cups, or basins should be always buttered before the mixture is put in

them, and they should be put into the saucepan directly they are filled.

Scrupulous attention should be paid to the cleanliness of pudding-cloths, as from neglect in this particular the outsides of boiled puddings frequently taste very disagreeably. As soon as possible after it is taken off the pudding, it should be soaked in water, and then well washed,

BOILED-PUDDING MOULD.

without soap, unless it be very greasy. It should be dried out-of-doors, then folded up and kept in a dry place. When wanted for use, dip it in boiling water and dredge it slightly with flour.

The dry ingredients for puddings are better for being mixed some time before they are wanted; the liquid portion should only be added just before the pudding is put into the saucepan.

A pinch of salt is an improvement to the generality of puddings; but this ingredient should be added very sparingly, as the flavour should not be detected.

When baked puddings are sufficiently solid, turn them out of the dish they

PUDDING BASIN.

were baked in, bottom uppermost, and strew over them fine-sifted sugar.

When pastry or baked puddings are not done through, and yet the outside is sufficiently brown, cover them over with a piece of white paper until thoroughly cooked: this prevents them from getting burnt.

Pastry, To Ice or Glaze.

To glaze pastry, which is the usual method adopted for meat or raised pies, break an egg, separate the yolk from the white, and beat the former for a short time. Then when the pastry is nearly baked, take it out of the oven, brush it over with this beaten yolk of an egg, and put it back in the oven to set the glaze.

To ice pastry, which is the usual method adopted for fruit tarts and sweet dishes of pastry, put the white of an egg on a plate, and with the blade of a knife beat it to a stiff froth. When the pastry is nearly baked, brush it over with this, and sift over some pounded sugar; put it back into the oven to set the glaze, and, in a few minutes, it will be done. Great care should be taken that the paste does not catch or burn in the oven, which it is very liable to do after the icing is laid on. Allow 1 egg and 1½ oz. of sugar to glaze 3 tarts.

Pastry Sandwiches.

INGREDIENTS.—*Puff-paste, jam of any kind, the white of an egg, sifted sugar.* AVERAGE COST, *with ½ lb. of paste, 8d.*

Roll the paste out thin; put half of it on a baking-sheet or tin, and spread equally over it apricot, greengage, or any preserve that may be preferred. Lay over this preserve another thin paste; press the edges together all round, and mark the paste in lines with a knife on the surface, to show where to cut it when baked. Bake from 20 minutes to ½ hour; and, a short time before being done, take the pastry out of the oven, brush it over with the white of an egg, sift over pounded sugar, and put it back in the oven to colour. When cold, cut it into strips; pile these on a dish pyramidically, and serve.

TIME.—*20 minutes to ½ hour.*

SEASONABLE *at any time.*

Pâte Brisée, Crust, French (for Raised Pies).

INGREDIENTS.—*To every lb.* of flour allow ½ saltspoonful of salt, 2 eggs, ½ pint of water, 6 oz. of butter. AVERAGE COST, 1s. per lb.

Spread the flour, which should be sifted and thoroughly dry, on the paste-board; make a hole in the centre, into which put the butter; work it lightly into the flour, and, when quite fine, add the salt; work the whole into a smooth paste with the eggs (yolks and whites) and water, and make it very firm. Knead the paste well, and let it be rather stiff, that the sides of the pie may be easily raised, and that they do not afterwards tumble or shrink.

Note.—This paste may be very much enriched by making it with equal quantities of flour and butter; but then it is not so easily raised as when made plainer.

Paté de Foie Gras Sandwiches.

INGREDIENTS *for sandwiches for 6 persons.—A small tin of foie gras, a little cress, ¼ lb. of butter, brown bread.* AVERAGE COST, 1s.

Cut bread-and-butter from a tin loaf very thin, sprinkle half the slices with the cress freed from half the white stalks, spread the other half with the pâté, and put them together, trimming off the crusts. Arrange them on a dish in a circle as cutlets, overlapping one another, and garnish with parsley or watercress; in using the latter, put a pile in the centre.

SEASONABLE.—*Suitable for afternoon tea, or a savoury at luncheon.*

Patties, Cheese.

INGREDIENTS *for 8 patties.—¼ lb. of cheddar cheese, 1 oz. of butter, 1 oz. of flour, ¾ pint of milk, 4 eggs, salt and cayenne, some scraps of puff-paste.* AVERAGE COST, *exclusive of the paste, 10d.*

Rub the butter and flour together, put them with the milk in a pan over the fire, and stir till boiling. Move the pan aside and stir in the yolks of the eggs one by one, then the cheese grated, and lastly the whites of the eggs, well beaten, and the seasoning. Line some patty-pans with the pastry, pour in the mixture, and bake in a quick oven.

TIME.—15 *minutes to bake the patties.*
SEASONABLE *at any time.*

Patties, Fried. (Cold Meat Cookery.)
—INGREDIENTS.—*Cold roast veal, a few slices of cold ham,* 1 *egg, boiled hard, pounded mace, pepper and salt to taste, gravy, cream,* 1 *teaspoonful of minced lemon-peel, good puff-paste.*

Mince a little cold veal and ham, allowing one-third ham to two-thirds veal; add an egg, boiled hard and chopped, and a seasoning of pounded mace, salt, pepper and lemon-peel; moisten with a little gravy and cream. Make a good puff-paste; roll rather thin, and cut it into round or square pieces; put the mince between two of them, pinch the edges to keep in the gravy, and fry a light brown. They may also be baked in patty-pans; in that case they should be brushed over with the yolk of an egg before they are put in the oven. To make a variety, oysters may be substituted for the ham.

TIME.—15 *minutes to fry the patties.*
SEASONABLE *from March to October.*

Patties, etc., Recipes for.—
Directions for making the following appear under their respective headings:—

Almond Cheese-cakes.	German Puffs.
	Lemon Cheesecakes.
Almond Puffs.	,, ,, To Keep.
Almond Tartlets.	Lobster Patties.
Apple Cheesecakes.	Oyster Patties.
Cheese Patties.	Potato Patties.
Cheesecakes.	Tartlets.
Custard Tartlets.	,, Cream.
Fried Patties.	,, Polish.

Pea Fritters. (Vegetarian Recipe.)
—INGREDIENTS. — *Cold brose, or lentil porridge, bread-crumbs, onion, seasoning, flour, oil or butter for frying.*

Mix with the cold porridge an equal quantity of bread-crumbs, adding some minced onion and seasoning to taste. Shape into flat cakes, flour them, and fry a nice brown in oil or butter.

SEASONABLE. — *A nice little breakfast savoury.*

Pea Soup. (Inexpensive.)—INGRE-DIENTS *for soup for* 12 *persons.*—3 *onions,* 3 *carrots,* 1 *stick of celery,* ¾ *lb. of split peas, a little mint, shred fine;* 1 *tablespoonful of coarse brown sugar, salt and pepper to taste,* 4 *quarts of water, or liquor in which a joint of meat has been boiled.* AVERAGE COST, 7d.

Fry the vegetables for 10 minutes in a little butter or dripping, previously cutting them up into small pieces; pour the water on them, and when boiling add the peas. Let them simmer for nearly 3 hours, or until the peas are thoroughly done. Add the sugar, seasoning and mint; boil for ¼ of an hour, and serve.

TIME.—3½ *hours.*
SEASONABLE *in winter.*

Pea Soup. (Green.)—INGREDIENTS *for soup for* 8 *persons.*—3 *pints of green peas,* ¼ *lb. of butter,* 2 *or* 3 *thin slices of ham,* 3 *onions, sliced,* 2 *shredded lettuces, the crumb of* 2 *French rolls,* 2 *handfuls of spinach,* 1 *lump of sugar,* 2 *quarts of medium stock.* AVERAGE COST, 3s. 6d.

Put the butter, ham, 1 quart of peas, onions and lettuces to a pint of stock, and simmer for an hour; then add the remainder of the stock, with the crumb of the French rolls, and boil for another hour. Now boil the spinach, and squeeze it very dry. Rub the soup through a sieve, and the spinach with it, to colour it. Have ready a pint of *young* peas, boiled; add them to the soup, put in the sugar, give one boil and serve. If necessary, add salt.

TIME.—2½ *hours.*
SEASONABLE *from June to the end of August.*

Note.—It will be well to add, if the peas are not quite young, a little more sugar. Where economy is essential, water may be used instead of stock for this soup, boiling in it likewise the pea-shells; but using a double quantity of vegetables.

Pea Soup, Winter. (Yellow.) —

INGREDIENTS *for soup for* 12 *or* 1½ *persons.* —1 *quart of split peas,* 2 *lbs. of shin of beef, trimmings of meat or poultry, a slice of bacon,* 2 *large carrots,* 2 *turnips,* 5 *large onions,* 1 *head of celery, seasoning to taste,* 2 *quarts of soft water, any bones left from roast meat,* 2 *quarts of common stock, or liquor in which a joint of meat has been boiled.* AVERAGE COST, 6*d. per quart.*

Put the peas to soak over-night in soft water and float off such as rise to the top. Boil them in the water till tender enough to pulp; then add the ingredients mentioned above, and simmer for 2 hours, stirring it occasionally. Pass the whole through a sieve, skim well, season and serve with toasted bread, cut in dice.

TIME.—4 *hours.*

SEASONABLE *all the year round, but more suitable for cold weather.*

Note.—A very nice soup can be made with Symington's pea-soup powder, using it according to instructions, in place of the split peas.

Peach Fritters.—INGREDIENTS *for dish for* 4 *persons.*—For the batter, ½ *lb. of flour,* ½ *oz. of butter,* ½ *saltspoonful of salt,* 2 *eggs, milk. Peaches, about* 6, *hot lard or clarified dripping.* AVERAGE COST, 1*s.*

Make a nice smooth batter; skin, halve and stone the peaches, which should be quite ripe; dip them in the batter, and fry the pieces in hot lard or clarified dripping, which should be boiling before the peaches are put in. From 8 to 10 minutes will be required to fry them; when done, drain them before the fire. Dish them on a white d'oyley. Strew over plenty of pounded sugar, and serve.

TIME.—*From* 8 *to* 10 *minutes to fry the fritters,* 5 *minutes to drain them.*

SEASONABLE *in July, August and September.*

Peaches, Compote of. —INGRE-

DIENTS *for dish for* 6 *persons.*—1 *pint of syrup, about* 15 *small peaches.* AVERAGE COST, 1*s.* 3*d.*

Peaches that are not very large, and that would not look well for dessert, answer very nicely for a compote. Divide the peaches, take out the stones, and pare the

PEACH.

fruit; make a syrup by recipe, put in the peaches, and stew them gently for about 10 minutes. Take them out without breaking, arrange them on a glass dish, boil the syrup for 2 or 3 minutes, let it cool, pour it over the fruit, and, when cold, it will be ready for table.

TIME.—10 *minutes.*

SEASONABLE *in August and September.*

Peaches Preserved in Brandy.

—INGREDIENTS. — *To every lb. of fruit, weighed before being stoned, allow* ¼ *lb. of finely-pounded loaf sugar, brandy.*

Let the fruit be gathered in dry weather; wipe and weigh it, and remove the stones as carefully as possible, without injuring the peaches much. Put them into a jar, sprinkle amongst them pounded loaf sugar in the above proportion, and pour brandy over the fruit. Cover the jar down closely, place it in a saucepan of boiling water over the fire, and bring the brandy to the simmering point, but do not allow it to boil. Take the fruit out carefully, without breaking it; put it into small jars, pour over it the brandy, and, when cold, exclude the air by covering the jars with bladders, or tissue-paper, brushed over on both sides with the white of an egg. Apricots may be done in the same manner, and, if properly prepared, will be found delicious.

TIME.—*From 10 to 20 minutes to bring the brandy to the simmering point.*

SEASONABLE *in August and September.*

Pears à l'Allemande.—INGREDI-
ENTS *for dish for 5 or 6 persons.*—6 *to 8 pears, water, sugar, 2 oz. of butter, the yolk of an egg, ½ oz. of gelatine.* AVERAGE COST, 1s. 2d.

Peel and cut the pears into any form that may be preferred, and steep them in cold water to prevent them turning black ; put them into a saucepan with sufficient cold water to cover them, and boil them with the butter and enough sugar to sweeten them nicely, until tender; then brush the pears over ·with the yolk of an egg, sprinkle them with sifted sugar, and arrange them on a dish. Add the gelatine to the syrup, boil it up quickly for about 5 minutes, strain it over the pears, and let it remain until set. The syrup may be coloured with a little prepared cochineal, which would very much improve the appearance of the dish.

TIME.—*From 20 minutes to ½ hour to stew the pears ; 5 minutes to boil the syrup.*

SEASONABLE *from August to February.*

Pears, Baked.—INGREDIENTS *for dish for 10 persons.*—12 *pears, the rind of 1 lemon, 6 cloves, 10 whole allspice ; to every pint of water allow ½ lb. of loaf sugar.* AVERAGE COST, 1s. 6d.

Pare and cut the pears into halves, and, should they be very large, into quarters ; leave the stalks on, and carefully remove the cores. Place them in a clean baking-jar, with a closely-fitting lid ; add to them the lemon-rind cut in strips, the juice of ½ lemon, the cloves, the pounded allspice, and

sufficient water just to cover the whole, with sugar in the above proportion. Cover the jar down closely, put it into a very cool oven, and bake the pears from 5 to 6 hours, but be very careful that the oven is not too hot. To improve the colour of the fruit, a few drops of prepared cochineal may be added ; but this will not be found necessary, if the pears are very gently baked.

TIME.—*Large pears, 5 to 6 hours, in a very slow oven.*

SEASONABLE *from September to January.*

Pears, Moulded.— INGREDIENTS *for quart mould.*—4 *large pears or 6 small ones, 8 cloves, sugar to taste, water, a small piece of cinnamon, ¼ pint of raisin wine, a strip of lemon-peel, the juice of ½ lemon, ½ oz. of gelatine.* AVERAGE COST, 1s.

Peel and cut the pears into quarters ; put them into a jar with ¾ pint of water, cloves, cinnamon and sufficient sugar to sweeten the whole nicely ; cover down the top of the jar, and bake the pears in a gentle oven until perfectly tender, but do not allow them to break. When done, lay the pears in a plain mould, which should be well wetted, and boil ½ pint of the liquor the pears were baked in with the wine, lemon-peel, strained juice and gelatine. Let these ingredients boil quickly for 5 minutes, then strain the liquid warm over the pears ; put the mould in a cool place, and when the jelly is firm, turn it out on a glass dish.

TIME.—*2 hours to bake the pears in a cool oven.*

SEASONABLE *from August to February.*

Pears, Preserved.—INGREDIENTS.
—*Jargonelle pears ; to every lb. of sugar allow ½ pint of water.*

Procure some Jargonelle pears, not too ripe ; put them into a stewpan with sufficient water to cover them, and simmer them till rather tender, but do not allow them to break ; then put them into cold water. Boil the sugar and water together for 5 minutes, skim well, put in the pears, and simmer them gently for 5 minutes. Repeat the simmering for 3 successive days, taking care not to let the fruit break. The last time of boiling, the syrup should be made rather richer and the fruit boiled for 10 minutes. When the pears are done, drain them from the syrup and dry them in the sun, or in a cool oven; or they may be kept in the syrup, and dried as they are wanted.

TIME.—½ hour to simmer the pears in water, 20 minutes in the syrup.

SEASONABLE.—Most plentiful in September and October.

Pears, Stewed.

Pears, Stewed.—INGREDIENTS for dish for 6 persons.—8 large pears, 5 oz. of loaf sugar, 6 cloves, 6 whole allspice, ½ pint of water, ½ pint of port wine, a few drops of prepared cochineal or carmine. AVERAGE COST, 1s. 8d.

Pare the pears, quarter them, remove the cores, and leave the stalks on; put them into a lined saucepan with the above ingredients, and let them simmer very gently until tender, which will be in from 3 to 4 hours, according to the quality of the pears. They should be watched, and,

STEWED PEARS.

when done, carefully lifted out on to a glass dish without breaking them. Boil up the syrup quickly for 2 or 3 minutes; allow it to cool a little, pour it over the pears, and let them get perfectly cold. To improve the colour of the fruit, a few drops of prepared cochineal may be added, which rather enhances the beauty of this dish. The fruit must not be boiled fast, but only simmered, and watched that it be not too much done.

TIME.—3 to 4 hours.

SEASONABLE from September to January.

Peas. — Peas are one of the most valuable vegetables largely grown in England. Both in their fresh and dry state they are nutritious and pleasant in flavour, but the latter require long and slow boiling.

One pound of peas contains flesh formers equal to 3½ oz. of the dry nitrogenous matter of muscle or flesh, and for one part of flesh formers there are only 2½ parts of heat givers.

The unripe, or green pea, contains a great deal of sugar, and the albumenoid matter in these is more easily digested than in the vegetable in its dry state.

Haricot beans possess the same qualities as peas, and are as good, and, if properly cooked, a pleasant food, not fully appreciated in England.

CONSTITUENTS OF 1 LB. OF PEAS.

	oz.	grs.
Water	2	126
Albumenoids	3	255
Starch, Sugar, &c.	9	108
Fat	0	175
Mineral Matters	0	210
	16	0

Peas, Boiled Green.

Peas, Boiled Green.—INGREDIENTS.—Green peas; to each ½ gallon of water allow 1 small teaspoonful of moist sugar, 1 heaped tablespoonful of salt. AVERAGE COST, from 8d. to 1s. per peck.

This delicious vegetable, to be eaten in perfection, should be young, and not gathered or shelled long before it is dressed. Shell the peas, wash them well in cold water and drain them; then put them into a saucepan with plenty of fast-boiling water, to which salt and moist sugar have been added in the above proportion; let them boil quickly over a brisk fire, with the lid of the saucepan removed, and be careful that the smoke does not draw in. When tender, pour them into a colander; put them into a hot vegetable-dish, and quite in the centre of the peas place a piece of butter the size of a walnut. Many cooks boil a small bunch of mint *with* the peas, or garnish them with it, by boiling a few sprigs in a saucepan by themselves. Should the peas be very old, and difficult to boil a good colour, a very tiny piece of soda may be thrown in the water previous to putting them in ; but this must be very sparingly used, as it causes the peas, when boiled, to have a smashed and broken appearance. With young peas there is not the slightest occasion to use it.

TIME.—*Young peas,* 10 *to* 15 *minutes ; the large sorts, such as marrowfats, &c.,* 18 *to* 24 *minutes ; old peas,* ½ *hour.*

SEASONABLE *from June to the end of August.*

Peas, Green, à la Française.—

INGREDIENTS *for dish for 4 or 5 persons.—* 1 *peck of green peas,* 3 *oz. of fresh butter, a bunch of parsley,* 6 *green onions, flour, a small lump of sugar,* ½ *teaspoonful of salt,* 1 *teaspoonful of flour.* AVERAGE COST, 1s.

Shell sufficient fresh-gathered peas to fill 2 quarts ; put them into cold water with the above proportion of butter, and stir them about until they are well covered with the butter ; drain them in a colander, and put them in a stewpan with the parsley and onions ; dredge over them a little flour, stir the peas well, and moisten them with boiling water ; boil them quickly over a large fire for 20 minutes, or until there is no liquor remaining. Dip a small lump of sugar into some water, that it may soon melt ; put it with the peas, to which add ½ teaspoonful of salt. Take a piece of butter the size of a walnut, work it together with a teaspoonful of flour, and add this to the peas, which should be boiling when it is put in. Keep shaking the stewpan, and, when the peas are nicely thickened, dress them high in the dish, and serve.

TIME.—*Altogether,* ¾ *hour.*

SEASONABLE *from June to the end of August.*

Peas, Stewed Green.—INGREDI-

ENTS *for dish for 4 or 5 persons.—* 1 *peck of peas,* 1 *lettuce,* 1 *onion,* 2 *oz. of butter, pepper and salt to taste,* 1 *egg,* ½ *teaspoonful of powdered sugar.*

Shell the peas, and cut the onion and lettuce into slices ; put these into a stewpan with the butter, pepper and salt, but with no more water than that which hangs around the lettuce from washing. Stew the whole very gently for rather more than 1 hour ; then stir in a well-beaten egg, and about ½ teaspoonful of powdered sugar. When the peas, &c., are nicely thickened, serve ; but, after the egg is added, do not allow them to boil.

TIME.—1¼ *hour.*

SEASONABLE *from June to the end of August.*

Note.—A good substitute for green peas may be found in those prepared by Hall and Co., which, if well soaked and properly cooked, form an excellent vegetable.

Pease Pudding.—INGREDIENTS *for*

pudding for 7 or 8 persons.— 1½ *pint of split peas,* 2 *oz. of butter, pepper and salt to taste.* AVERAGE COST, 5d.

Put the peas to soak over-night, in rain-water, and float off any that are worm-eaten or discoloured. Tie them loosely in a clean cloth, leaving a little room for them to swell, and put them on to boil in cold rain-water, allowing 2½ hours after the water has simmered up. When the peas are tender, take them up and drain ; rub them through a colander with a wooden spoon, add the butter, eggs, pepper and salt ; beat all well together for a few minutes, until the ingredients are well incorporated, then tie them tightly in a floured cloth ; boil the pudding for another hour, turn it on to the dish, and serve very hot. This pudding should always be sent to table with boiled leg of pork, and is an exceedingly nice accompaniment to boiled beef. This pudding is improved by the addition of a couple of eggs, added when the pudding is first taken up.

TIME.—2½ *hours to boil the peas, tied loosely in the cloth; 1 hour for the pudding.*

SEASONABLE *from September to March.*

Perch, Boiled.—INGREDIENTS.—

¼ *lb. of salt to each gallon of water.*

Scale the fish, take out the gills and clean it thoroughly; lay it in boiling water, salted as above, and simmer gently for 10 minutes. If the fish is very large, longer time must be allowed. Garnish with

THE PERCH.

parsley, and serve with plain melted butter, or Dutch sauce. Perch do not preserve so good a flavour when stewed as when dressed in any other way.

TIME.—*Middling-sized perch, ¼ hour.*

SEASONABLE *from September to November.*

Note.—Tench may be boiled the same way, and served with the same sauces.

Perch, Fried.—INGREDIENTS.—*Egg and bread-crumbs, hot lard.*

Scale and clean the fish, brush it over with egg, and cover with bread-crumbs. Have ready some boiling lard; put the fish in, and fry a nice brown. Serve with plain melted butter or anchovy sauce.

TIME.—10 *minutes.*

SEASONABLE *from September to November.*

Note.—Fry tench in the same way.

Perch, Stewed with Wine.—

INGREDIENTS.—*Equal quantities of stock and sherry,* 1 *bay-leaf,* 1 *clove of garlic, a small bunch of parsley,* 2 *cloves, salt to taste; thickening of butter and flour, pepper,* *grated nutmeg, ½ teaspoonful of anchovy sauce.*

Scale the fish and take out the gills, and clean them thoroughly; lay them in a stewpan with sufficient stock and sherry just to cover them. Put in the bay-leaf, garlic, parsley, cloves and salt, and simmer till tender. When done, take out the fish, strain the liquor, add a thickening of butter and flour, the pepper, nutmeg and the anchovy sauce, and stir it over the fire until somewhat reduced, when pour over the fish, and serve.

TIME.—*About* 20 *minutes.*

SEASONABLE *from September to November.*

Petites Bouchées.—INGREDIENTS

for moderate-sized dish. — 6 *oz. of sweet almonds,* ¼ *lb. of sifted sugar, the rind of ½ lemon, the white of* 1 *egg, puff-paste.* AVERAGE COST, 1*s.*

Blanch the almonds and chop them fine; rub the sugar on the lemon-rind and pound it in a mortar; mix this with the almonds and the white of the egg. Roll some puff-paste out; cut it in any shape that may be preferred, such as diamonds, rings, ovals, &c., and spread the above mixture over the paste. Bake the bouchées in an oven, not too hot, and serve cold.

TIME.—¼ *hour, or rather more.*

SEASONABLE *at any time.*

Petits Fours. — INGREDIENTS. —

Sponge or pound cake, icing of any kind, crystallized fruit, pistachio nuts, candied peel.

These pretty little cakes, so dear to buy, and so useful for supper or dessert dishes, may easily be made at home. The simplest way to make them is to cut stale pound or sponge cake in even slices, then to cut it in fancy shapes, to cover them with icing, and to ornament them as taste may direct with the garnishes named above; or with sweetmeats, blanched almonds, or angelica, the latter looking well set as leaves to small bright-coloured fruit, such as a cherry on white icing; or pink blanched almonds and chopped pistachio nuts look pretty.

Pheasant.—If this bird be eaten three days after it has been killed, it then has no peculiarity of flavour; a pullet would be more relished, and a quail would surpass it in aroma. Kept, however, a proper length of time—and this can be ascertained by a slight smell and change of colour—then it becomes a highly-flavoured dish, occupying, so to speak, the middle distance between chicken and

THE PHEASANT.

venison. It is difficult to define any exact time to "hang" a pheasant; but any one possessed of the instincts of gastronomical science can at once detect the right moment when a pheasant should be taken down, in the same way as a good cook knows whether a bird should be removed from the spit, or have a turn or two more.

Pheasant alla Neapolitana. (An Italian Recipe.)—INGREDIENTS *for dish for persons.—A pheasant, lardoons, 2 oz. of utter, ½ lb. of macaroni, ½ pint of beef or eal gravy, 2 tomatoes or some tomato sauce, oz. of Parmesan cheese.* AVERAGE COST, s. 6d.

Having larded the pheasant, roast it before a brisk fire, basting often till done. Cut up the bird very carefully; then put it together again, and serve it on a bed formed of the macaroni, the cheese, tomatoes and gravy stewed together till the former is

perfectly tender. Some good sauce or gravy should be sent to table with this dish.

TIME.—*For the pheasant, ¾ to 1 hour, for the macaroni, 1½ to 1¾ hour.*

SEASONABLE *from October to February.*

Pheasant, Broiled. (A Breakfast or Luncheon Dish.)—INGREDIENTS.—*1 pheasant, a little lard, egg and bread-crumbs, salt and cayenne to taste.*

Cut the legs off at the first joint, and the remainder of the bird into neat pieces; put them into a frying pan with a little lard, and, when browned on both sides and about half-done, take them out and drain them; brush the pieces over with egg, and sprinkle with bread-crumbs, with which has been mixed a good seasoning of cayenne and salt. Broil them over a moderate fire for about 10 minutes, or rather longer, and serve with mushroom-sauce, sauce piquante, or brown gravy in which a few game bones and trimmings have been stewed.

TIME.—*Altogether, ½ hour.*

SEASONABLE *from the 1st of October to the beginning of February.*

Pheasant, To Carve.—Fixing the fork in the breast, let the carver cut slices from it in the direction of the lines from B to A; these are the prime pieces. If there be more guests to satisfy than these slices

ROAST PHEASANT.

will serve, then let the legs and wings be disengaged in the same manner as described in carving boiled fowl, the point where the wing joins the neckbone being carefully found. The merrythought will come out in the same way as that of a fowl. The most valued parts are the same as those which are most considered in a fowl.

Pheasant Cutlets.—INGREDIENTS *for dish for 6 persons.*—2 *pheasants, egg and bread-crumbs, cayenne and salt to taste, brown gravy.* AVERAGE COST, 6s.

Procure 2 young pheasants that have been hung a few days; pluck, draw and wipe them inside; cut them into joints; remove the bones from the best of these; and the backbones, trimmings, &c., put into a stewpan, with a little stock, herbs, vegetables, seasoning, &c., to make the gravy. Flatten and trim the cutlets of a good shape, egg-and-bread-crumb them, broil them over a clear fire, pile them high in the dish, and pour under them the gravy made from the bones, which should be strained, flavoured and thickened. One of the small bones should be stuck on the point of each cutlet.

TIME.—10 *minutes or rather more to broil the cutlets.*

SEASONABLE *from the 1st of October to the beginning of February.*

Pheasant, Roast.—INGREDIENTS. —*Pheasant, flour, butter.* AVERAGE COST, 3s.

Old pheasants may be known by the length and sharpness of their spurs; in young ones they are short and blunt. The cock bird is generally reckoned the best, except when the hen is with egg. They should hang some time before they are dressed, as, if they are cooked fresh, the flesh will be exceedingly dry and tasteless. After the bird is plucked and drawn, wipe the inside with a damp cloth, and truss it in the same manner as partridge. Roast it before a brisk fire, keep it well basted, and flour and froth it nicely. Serve with brown gravy, a little of which should be poured round the bird, and a tureen of bread sauce. 2 or 3 of the pheasant's best tail-feathers are usually stuck in the tail as an ornament.

TIME —½ *to 1 hour, according to the size.*

SEASONABLE *from the 1st of October to the beginning of February.*

Pheasant, Roast, à la Sainte Alliance. (BRILLAT SAVARIN'S Recipe.) —When the pheasant is in good condition to be cooked, it should be plucked, and not before. The bird should then be stuffed in the following manner:—Take two snipes and draw them, putting the bodies on one plate, and the livers, &c., on another. Take off the flesh, and mince it finely with a little beef lard, a few truffles, pepper and salt to taste, and stuff the pheasant carefully with this. Cut a slice of bread, larger

ROAST PHEASANT.

considerably than the bird, and cover it with the liver, &c., and a few truffles; an anchovy and a little fresh butter added to these will do no harm. Put the bread, &c. into the dripping-pan, and, when the bird is roasted, place it on the preparation, and surround it with Florida oranges.

Do not be uneasy, Savarin adds, about your dinner; for a pheasant served in this way is fit for beings better than men. The pheasant itself is a very good bird; and imbibing the dressing and the flavour of the truffle and snipe, it becomes thrice better.

Pheasant Soup.—INGREDIENTS *for soup for 10 or 12 persons.*—2 *pheasants, ½ lb. of butter, 2 slices of ham, 2 large onions sliced, ½ head of celery, the crumb of 2 French rolls, the yolks of 2 eggs, boiled hard, salt and cayenne to taste, a little pounded mace, if liked; 3 quarts of stock.* AVERAGE COST, 7s. 6d.

Cut up the pheasants, flour and braise them in the butter and ham till they are of a nice brown, but not burnt. Put them in a stewpan, with the onions, celery, stock and seasoning, and simmer for 2 hours. Strain the soup ; pound the breasts with the crumb of the roll, previously soaked, and the yolks of the eggs ; put it to the soup, give one boil, and serve.

TIME.—2½ hours.

SEASONABLE *from October to February.*

Note.—Fragments, pieces and bones of cold game may be used to great advantage in this soup, and then 1 pheasant will suffice.

Pickle, An Excellent.—INGREDI-
ENTS.—*Equal quantities of medium-sized onions, cucumbers and sauce-apples;* 1½ *teaspoonful of salt,* ¾ *teaspoonful of cayenne,* 1 *wineglassful of soy,* 1 *wineglassful of sherry ; vinegar.*

Slice sufficient cucumbers, onions and apples to fill a pint stone jar, taking care to cut the slices very thin ; arrange them in alternate layers, adding at the same time salt and cayenne in the above proportion ; pour in the soy and wine, and fill up with vinegar. It will be fit for use the day it is made.

SEASONABLE *in August and September.*

Pickle, Indian. (Very Superior.)
—INGREDIENTS.—*To each gallon of vinegar allow* 6 *cloves of garlic,* 12 *shalots,* 2 *sticks of sliced horseradish,* ¼ *lb. of bruised ginger,* 2 *oz. of whole black pepper,* 1 *oz. of long pepper,* 1 *oz. of allspice,* 12 *cloves,* ¼ *oz. of cayenne,* 2 *oz. of mustard seed,* ¼ *lb. of mustard,* 1 *oz. of turmeric; a white cabbage, cauliflowers, radish-pods, French beans, gherkins, small round pickling-onions, nasturtiums, capsicums, chilies, &c.*

Cut the cabbage, which must be hard and white, into slices, and the cauliflowers into small branches ; sprinkle salt over them in a large dish, and let them remain two days ; then dry them, and put them

into a very large jar, with garlic, shalots, horseradish, ginger, pepper, allspice and cloves, in the above proportions. Boil sufficient vinegar to cover them, which pour over, and, when cold, cover up to keep them free from dust. As the other things for the pickle ripen at different times, they may be added as they are ready ; these will be radish-pods, French beans, gherkins, small onions, nasturtiums, capsicums, chilies, &c. &c. As these are procured, they must, first of all, be washed in a little cold vinegar, wiped, and then simply added to the other ingredients in the large jar, only taking care that they are *covered* by the vinegar. If more vinegar should be wanted to add to the pickle, do not omit first to boil it before adding it to the rest. When you have collected all the things you require, turn all out in a large pan, and thoroughly mix them. Now put the mixed vegetables into smaller jars, without any of the vinegar ; then boil the vinegar again, adding as much more as will be required to fill the different jars, and also cayenne, mustard-seed, turmeric and mustard, which must be well mixed with a little cold vinegar, allowing the quantities named above to each gallon of vinegar. Pour the vinegar, boiling hot, over the pickle, and when cold, tie down with a bladder. If the pickle is wanted for immediate use, the vinegar should be boiled twice more, but the better way is to make it during one season for use during the next. It will keep for years, if care is taken that the vegetables are quite covered by the vinegar.

This recipe was taken from the directions of a lady whose pickle was always pronounced excellent by all who tasted it, and who has, for many years, exactly followed the recipe given above.

Note.—For small families, perhaps the above quantity of pickle will be considered too large ; but this may be decreased at pleasure, taking care to properly proportion the various ingredients.

Pickle, Mixed.

Pickle, Mixed. (Very good.)—IN-GREDIENTS. — *To each gallon of vinegar allow ¼ lb. of bruised ginger, ¼ lb. of mustard, ¼ lb. of salt, 2 oz. of mustard seed, 1½ oz. of turmeric, 1 oz. of ground black pepper, ¼ oz. of cayenne, cauliflowers, onions, celery, sliced cucumbers, gherkins, French beans, nasturtiums, capsicums.*

Have a large jar, with a tightly-fitting lid, in which put as much vinegar as is required, reserving a little to mix the various powders to a smooth paste. Put into a basin the mustard, turmeric, pepper and cayenne; mix them with vinegar, and stir well until no lumps remain; add all the ingredients to the vinegar, and mix well. Keep this liquor in a warm place, and thoroughly stir every morning for a month with a wooden spoon, when it will be ready for the different vegetables to be added to it. As these come into season, have them gathered on a dry day, and, after merely wiping them with a cloth, to free them from moisture, put them into the pickle. The cauliflowers, it may be said, must be divided into small bunches. Put all these into the pickle raw, and at the end of the season, when there have been added as many of the vegetables as could be procured, store it away in jars, and tie over with bladder. As none of the ingredients are boiled, this pickle will not be fit to eat till 12 months have elapsed. Whilst the pickle is being made, keep a wooden spoon tied to the jar; and its contents, it may be repeated, must be stirred every morning.

SEASONABLE.—*Make the pickle-liquor in May or June; as the season arrives for the various vegetables to be picked.*

Pickle for Tongues or Beef.

(Newmarket Recipe.) — INGREDIENTS. — 1 *gallon of soft water, 3 lbs. of coarse salt, 6 oz. of coarse brown sugar, ½ oz. of saltpetre.*

Put all the ingredients into a saucepan, and let them boil for ½ an hour; clear off the scum as it rises, and when done pour the pickle into a pickling-pan. Let it get cold, then put in the meat, and allow it to remain in pickle from 8 to 14 days, according to the size. It will keep good for 6 months if well boiled once a fortnight. Tongues will take 1 month or 6 weeks to be properly cured; and, in salting meat, beef and tongues should always be put in separate vessels.

TIME.—*A moderate-sized tongue should remain in the pickle about a month, and be turned every day.*

Pickle, Universal.

Pickle, Universal.—INGREDIENTS. —*To 6 quarts of vinegar allow 1 lb. of salt, ¼ lb. of ginger, 1 oz. of mace, ½ lb. of shalots, 1 tablespoonful of cayenne, 2 oz. of mustard-seed, 1½ oz. of turmeric.*

Boil all the ingredients together for about 20 minutes; when cold, put them into a jar with whatever vegetables you choose, such as radish-pods, French beans, cauliflowers, gherkins, &c. &c., as these come into season; put them in fresh as you gather them, having previously wiped them perfectly free from moisture and grit. This pickle will be fit for use in about 8 or 9 months.

TIME.—*20 minutes.*

SEASONABLE.—*Make the pickle in May or June, to be ready for the various vegetables.*

Note.—As this pickle takes 2 or 3 months to make—that is to say, nearly that time will elapse before all the different vegetables are added—care must be taken to keep the jar which contains the pickle well covered, either with a closely-fitting lid, or a piece of bladder securely tied over, so as perfectly to exclude the air.

Pickled Herrings.

Pickled Herrings.—INGREDIENTS. —*12 salt herrings, 1 oz. of white pepper, 12 peppercorns, 8 shalots, 1 nutmeg, a few small onions, 1 pint of vinegar, some thyme and bay-leaves.* AVERAGE COST, 2s.

Scale the herrings, take out the roes without cutting the fish more than absolutely necessary, then wash them thoroughly and lay them in milk for 2 days to draw out the salt. Bruise the seasoning, shalots and onions, well together, and stuff the fish with

PICKLED HERRINGS.

part of the mixture ; then place them in layers in an earthen jar, covering them with a layer of small onions, thyme and bay-leaves. Boil the vinegar, and stir the roes smooth in it, then pour over the fish.

SEASONABLE *from August to March.*

Pickles.

— Although pickles may be purchased at shops at as low a rate as they can usually be made for at home, or perhaps even for less, yet we would advise all housewives, who have sufficient time and convenience, to prepare their own. The only general rules, perhaps, worth stating here—as in the recipes all necessary details are explained—are, that the vegetables and fruits used should be sound, and not over-ripe, that they should be perfectly dry, and that the very best vinegar should be used.

In towns where it is often impossible to procure vegetables fit for pickling, it is best to procure them of thoroughly good brands, where one may rely upon the vinegar used being of good quality. Inferior pickles are not only unpleasant condiments ; they are positively injurious to health.

From experience we find that the following firms supply pickles both of good flavour and excellent quality :—

Crosse & Blackwell. | Lazenby and Co.
Holbrook and Co. | Whybrow, George.

Pickles, Recipes for.

—Directions for making the following appear under their respective headings :—

Cabbage, Red.	Mackerel.
Capsicums.	Mushrooms.
Cucumbers.	Nasturtiums.
Eggs.	Onions.
Excellent.	„ A Simple Mode.
Gherkins.	„ Spanish.
Herrings.	Oysters.
Indian.	Mixed.
Lemons, with Peel.	Salmon.
Lemons, without Peel.	Tomatoes & Onions.
	Universal.

Picnics.

—To the young, at any rate, there is no form of entertainment more thoroughly enjoyable than a picnic, provided it be well arranged, with due regard in the choice of those who will for some hours be thrown together without formality, and with but little chaperonage. Little mistakes will invariably occur at all picnics that are not ceremonious ones ; things will be forgotten ; some viands possibly spoilt by bad packing, and such like small troubles ; but these are nothing compared to the mistakes of bringing the wrong people together, of placing them without regard for individual tastes in the vehicles used, or having too many of one sex in the party. At a picnic there is no get-away for anyone, as there is at an evening party or an " at home." However dull or bored one may feel, one must stay to the bitter end of these al fresco entertainments ; ergo, it is necessary, to make them successful, that the guests be well chosen. Picnic parties for children are quite the pleasantest form of amusement for the young folk in summer time ; and there are few of us who cannot look back upon the unalloyed enjoyment of one of them in our youth.

Older grown, we still may enjoy them ; but when we arrive at the age and dignity of chaperonage, it is necessary for our comfort that there should be no hitch in the day's arrangements, and that not too many things be forgotten. We add to the following menus a list of crockery, &c., required, as well as a few articles that are sometimes omitted with disastrous results ; and we may remark that the easiest way to provide a good luncheon is, first to make a menu out, and if the luncheon, as it so often is, be provided by the ladies of the party, for the most experienced to allot to herself and the others the various dishes to bring.

Picnic Luncheons, Menus for :—

1.

Cold Salmon and Tartar Sauce.
Cucumber.

Cold Lamb and Mint Sauce.
Pigeon Pie.
Cold Boiled Beef.
Salad.

Fruit Turnovers.
Pastry Sandwiches.
Jellies. Creams.

Cheese, Butter and Biscuits.
Strawberries and Cream.

2.

Lobster Patties.

Cold Boiled Chicken.
Ham.
Cold Roast Beef.
Veal and Ham Pie.
Cucumber. Salad.

Cheesecakes.
Stewed Fruit and Custard.
Lemon Sponge.

Cheese, Biscuits, Butter.
Fruit of any kind.

Wines, bottled beer, soda - water, lemonade, bread, salad dressing, oil, vinegar, pepper, salt, mustard, plates, knives, forks, spoons, glasses, tumblers, table-cloth, serviettes, glass and other cloths for wiping, corkscrews and champagne opener.

Picnic Menus for Children :—

1.

Ham and Beef Sandwiches.
Rolls containing Minced and Seasoned
Cold Meat.

Fruit and Jam Puffs.
Cakes of several kinds.

Plenty of Fresh Fruit.

2.

Meat Patties.
Egg Sandwiches.

Pastry Sandwiches.
Fruit Turnovers.
Cake.

Fruit of any kind.

Home-made lemonade in bottles that can be thrown away, lime-juice cordials and water.

These it will be seen are for ordinary children's picnics, where it is not convenient to carry plates, dishes, &c. ; but where these can be managed, such a joint as a cold leg of lamb, or some chickens and ham, and plenty of vegetable salad might take the place of the sandwiches and meat patties.

Drinking cups will be needed, and also cups for tea if that be given, in which case there should be provided plenty of cake and cut bread-and-butter, milk, sugar and the tea itself. We may warn those who have not had much experience in providing for children's meals out-of-doors, that they will in all probability eat and drink a great deal more than they would at home ; and that, however good a dinner they may make, after the afternoon romps or rambles, they will yet come with healthy appetites to tea.

For this meal a kettle and teapot must be taken, if they cannot be borrowed ; nor should a box of matches, a little dry wood, and a cloth for wiping cups be forgotten.

Pies and Tarts, Recipes for.—

Directions for making the following appear under their respective headings :—

Pig, Sucking, To Carve. — A

sucking-pig seems, at first sight, rather an elaborate dish, or rather animal, to carve ; but by carefully mastering the details of the business, every difficulty will vanish ; and if a partial failure be at first made, yet all embarrassment will quickly disappear on a second trial. A sucking-pig is usually sent to table in the manner shown in the engraving, being cut straight through, and the head thus divided cut off, and the first point to be attended to is to separate the shoulder from the carcase, by carrying the knife quickly and neatly round the circular line, as shown by the letters A, B, C ; the shoulder will then easily come away. The next step is to take off the leg ; and this is done in the same way, by cutting round this joint in the direction shown by the letters A, B, C, in the same way as the shoulder. The ribs then stand fairly open to the knife, which should be carried down in the direction of the line D to E ; and

three or four helpings will dispose of these. The other half of the pig is served, of course, in the same manner. Different parts of the pig are variously esteemed ; some preferring the flesh of the neck ;

SUCKING PIG.

others the ribs ; and others, again, the shoulders. The truth is, the whole of a sucking-pig is delicious, delicate eating ; but, in carving it. the host should consult the various tastes and fancies of his guests, keeping the larger joints, generally, for the gentlemen of the party.

Pig, Sucking, Roast. — INGRE-

DIENTS for dish for 12 persons.—Pig, 6 oz. of bread-crumbs, 16 sage-leaves, pepper and salt to taste, a piece of butter the size of an egg, salad oil or butter to baste with, about ½ pint of gravy, 1 tablespoonful of lemon-juice. AVERAGE COST, 6s.

A sucking-pig, to be eaten in perfection, should not be more than three weeks old, and should be dressed the same day that it is killed. After preparing the pig for cooking, as in the following recipe, stuff it with finely-grated bread-crumbs, minced sage, pepper, salt and a piece of butter the size of an egg, all of which should be well mixed together, and put into the body of the pig. Sew up the slit neatly, and truss the legs back, to allow the inside to be roasted, and the under part to be crisp. Put the pig down to a bright clear fire, not too near, and let it lay till thoroughly dry ; then have ready some butter tied up in a piece of thin cloth, and rub the pig with this in every part. Keep it well rubbed with the butter the whole of the time it is roasting, and do not allow the crackling to become blistered or burnt. When half-done, hang a pig-iron before the middle part (if this is not obtainable, use a flat-iron), to prevent its being scorched and dried up before the ends are done. Before it is taken from the fire, cut off the head, and part that and the body down the middle. Chop the brains and mix them with the stuffing; add ½ pint of good gravy, a tablespoonful of lemon-juice, and the gravy that flowed from the pig; put a little of this on the dish with the pig, and the remainder send to table in a tureen. Place the halves of the pig back to back in the dish, with one half of the head on each side, and one of the ears at each end, and

ROAST SUCKING-PIG.

send it to table as hot as possible. Instead of butter, many cooks take salad oil for basting, which makes the crackling *crisp ;* and as this is one of the principal things to be considered, perhaps it is desirable to use it; but be particular that it is very pure, or it will impart an unpleasant flavour to the meat. The brains and stuffing may be stirred into a tureen of melted butter instead of gravy, when the latter is not liked. Apple sauce and the old-fashioned currant sauce are not yet quite obsolete as an accompaniment to roast pig.

TIME.—1½ to 2 hours for a small pig.

SEASONABLE *from September to February.*

Pig, Sucking, To Scald a.—

Put the pig into cold water directly it is killed; let it remain for a few minutes, then immerse it in a large pan of boiling water for 2 minutes. Take it out, lay it on a table, and pull off the hair as quickly as possible. When the skin looks clean, make a slit down the belly, take out the entrails, well clean the nostrils and ears, wash the pig in cold water, and wipe it thoroughly dry. Take off the feet at the first joint, and loosen and leave sufficient skin to turn neatly over. If not to be dressed immediately, fold it in a wet cloth to keep it from the air.

Pigs' Cheeks, To Dry.—INGRE-

DIENTS.—*Salt,* ½ *oz. of saltpetre,* 2 *oz. of bay-salt,* 4 *oz. of coarse sugar.*

Cut out the snout, remove the brains, and split the head, taking off the upper bone to make the jowl a good shape; rub it well with salt; next day take away the brine, and salt it again the following day; cover the head with saltpetre, bay salt and coarse sugar, in the above proportion, adding a little common salt. Let the head be often turned, and when it has been in the pickle for 10 days, smoke it for a week or rather longer.

TIME.—*To remain in the pickle* 10 *days; to be smoked,* 1 *week.*

SEASONABLE. — *Should be made from September to March.*

Note.—A pig's cheek, or Bath chap, will require two hours' cooking after the water boils

Pig's Face, Collared. (A Break-

fast or Luncheon Dish.)—INGREDIENTS.— 1 *pig's face; salt. For brine,* 1 *gallon of spring water,* 1 *lb. of common salt,* ½ *handful of chopped juniper-berries,* 6 *bruised cloves,* 2 *bay-leaves, a few sprigs of thyme, basil, sage,* ¼ *oz. of saltpetre. For forcemeat,* ½ *lb. of ham,* ⅓ *lb. of bacon,* 1 *teaspoonful of mixed spices, pepper to taste,* ¼ *lb. of lard,* 1 *tablespoonful of minced parsley,* 6 *young onions.* AVERAGE COST, 2s. 6d.

Singe the head carefully, bone it without

breaking the skin, and rub it well with salt. Make the brine by boiling the above ingredients for ¼ hour, and letting it stand to cool. When cold, pour it over the head, and let it steep in this for 10 days, turning and rubbing it often. Then wipe, drain and dry it. For the forcemeat, pound the ham and bacon very finely, and mix with

PIG'S FACE.

these the remaining ingredients, taking care that the whole is thoroughly incorporated. Spread this equally over the head, roll it tightly in a cloth, and bind it securely with broad tape. Put it into a saucepan with a few meat trimmings, and cover it with stock; let it simmer gently for 4 hours, and be particular that it does not stop boiling the whole time. When quite tender, take it up, put it between 2 dishes with a heavy weight on the top, and when cold, remove the cloth and tape. It should be sent to table on a napkin, or garnished with a piece of white paper with a ruche at the top.

TIME.—4 *hours.*

SEASONABLE *from October to March.*

Pig's Fry, To Dress.—INGREDIENTS *for dish for* 4 *persons.*—1½ *lb. of pig's fry,* 2 *onions, a few sage-leaves,* 3 *lbs. of potatoes, pepper and salt to taste.* AVERAGE COST, 1*s.*

Put the lean fry at the bottom of a piedish, sprinkle over it some minced sage and onion, and a seasoning of pepper and salt; slice the potatoes, put a layer of these on the seasoning, then the fat-fry, then more seasoning, and a layer of potatoes at the top. Fill the dish with boiling water, and bake for 2 hours, or rather longer.

TIME.—*Rather more than* 2 *hours.*

SEASONABLE *from September to March.*

Pig's Liver. (A Savoury and Economical Dish.)—INGREDIENTS *for dish for from* 6 *to* 8 *persons.--The liver and lights of a pig,* 6 *or* 7 *slices of bacon, potatoes,* 1 *large bunch of parsley,* 2 *onions,* 2 *sage-leaves, pepper and salt to taste, a little broth or water.* AVERAGE COST, 1*s.* 6*d.*

Slice the liver and lights, and wash these perfectly clean, and parboil the potatoes; mince the parsley and sage, and chop the onions rather small. Put the meat, potatoes and bacon into a deep tin dish, in alternate layers, with a sprinkling of the herbs, and a seasoning of pepper and salt between them; pour on a little water or broth, and bake in a moderately-heated oven for 2 hours.

TIME.—2 *hours.*

SEASONABLE *from September to March.*

Pig's Pettitoes.—INGREDIENTS.— 2 *pettitoes, a thin slice of bacon,* 1 *onion,* 1 *blade of mace,* 6 *peppercorns,* 3 *or* 4 *sprigs of thyme,* 1 *pint of gravy, pepper and salt to taste, thickening of butter and flour.*

Put the liver, heart and pettitoes into a stewpan with the bacon, mace, peppercorns, thyme, onion and gravy, and simmer these gently for ¼ hour; then take out the heart and liver, and mince them very fine. Keep stewing the feet until quite tender, which will be in from 20 minutes to ½ hour, reckoning from the time that they boiled up first; then put back the minced liver, thicken the gravy with a little butter and flour, season with pepper and salt, and simmer over a gentle fire for 5 minutes, occasionally stirring the contents. Dish the mince, split the feet, and arrange them round alternately with sippets of toasted bread, and pour the gravy in the middle.

TIME.—*Altogether,* 40 *minutes.*

SEASONABLE *from September to March.*

Pigeon, To Carve. — A very straightforward plan is adopted in carving a pigeon; the knife is carried sharply in the direction of the line as shown from A to B, entirely through the bird, cutting it into two precisely equal and similar parts.

PIGEON.

If it is necessary to make three pieces of it, a small wing should be cut off with the leg on either side, thus serving two persons; and, by this means, there will be sufficient meat left on the breast to send to a third person.

Pigeon Pie. (Epsom Grand-Stand Recipe.)—INGREDIENTS.—1½ lb. of rumpsteak, 2 or 3 pigeons, 3 slices of ham, pepper and salt to taste, 2 oz. of butter, 4 eggs, puffcrust. AVERAGE COST, 5s.

Cut the steak into pieces about 2 inches square, and with it line the bottom of a pie-dish, seasoning it well with pepper and salt. Clean the pigeons, cut them in half, rub them with pepper and salt inside and out, and put into each half ½ oz. of butter; lay them on the steak, and a piece of ham on each pigeon. Add the yolks of 4 eggs, and half fill the dish with stock; place a border of puff-paste round the edge of the dish, put on the cover, and ornament it in any way that may be preferred. Clean three of the feet, and place them in a hole made in the crust at the top: this shows what kind of pie it is. Glaze the crust— that is to say, brush it over with the yolk of an egg, and bake it in a well-heated oven for about 1¼ hour. When liked, a seasoning of pounded mace may be added.

TIME.—1¼ hour, or rather less.

SEASONABLE at any time.

Pigeons, Broiled.—INGREDIENTS. —2 pigeons, 2 oz. of butter, pepper and salt to taste. AVERAGE COST, 1s. 8d.

Take care that the pigeons are quite fresh, and carefully pluck, draw and wash them; split the backs, rub the birds over with butter, season them with pepper and salt, and broil them over a moderate fire for ¼ hour or 20 minutes. Serve very hot, with either mushroom sauce or a good gravy. Pigeons may also be plainly boiled, and served with parsley and butter; they should be trussed like boiled fowls and take from ¼ hour to 20 minutes to boil.

TIME.—To broil a pigeon, from ¼ hour to 20 minutes; to boil one, the same time.

SEASONABLE from April to September, but in the greatest perfection from Midsummer to Michaelmas.

Pigeons, Roast.—INGREDIENTS.— 2 pigeons, 3 oz. of butter, pepper and salt to taste.

Trussing.—Pigeons, to be good, should be eaten fresh (if kept a little, the flavour goes off), and they should be drawn as soon as killed. Previous to trussing, they should be carefully cleaned, as no bird requires so much washing. Wipe the birds very dry, season them inside with pepper and salt, and put about ¾ oz. of butter into the body of each; this makes them moist.

ROAST PIGEON.

Place them at a bright fire, and baste them well the whole of the time they are cooking (they will be done enough in from 20 to 30 minutes); garnish with fried parsley, and serve with a tureen of parsley and butter. Bread sauce and gravy, the same as for roast fowl, are exceedingly nice accompaniments to roast pigeons, as also egg-sauce.

TIME.—From 20 minutes to ½ hour.

SEASONABLE from April to September; but in the greatest perfection from Midsummer to Michaelmas.

Pigeons, Stewed.

Pigeons, Stewed.—INGREDIENTS *for dish for 6 persons.*—6 *pigeons, a few slices of bacon,* 3 *oz. of butter,* 2 *tablespoonfuls of minced parsley, sufficient stock to cover the pigeons, thickening of butter and flour,* 1 *tablespoonful of mushroom ketchup,* 1 *tablespoonful of port wine.* AVERAGE COST, 5s. 6d.

Empty and clean the pigeons thoroughly, mince the livers, add to these the parsley and butter, and put it into the insides of the birds. Truss them with the legs inward, and put them into a stewpan with a few slices of bacon placed under and over them; add the stock, and stew gently for rather more than ½ hour. Dish the pigeons, strain the gravy, thicken it with butter and flour, add the ketchup and port wine, give one boil, pour over the pigeons, and serve.

TIME.—*Rather more than ½ hour.*

SEASONABLE *from April to September.*

Pigeons, Trussing of.

Pigeons, Trussing of. — Having plucked and drawn the birds, wash them

PIGEON READY FOR TRUSSING.

thoroughly and wipe them perfectly dry. Cut off the neck and head, and the toes at

PIGEON BEING SKEWERED.

the first joint. Then, for roasting, twist the legs and run a skewer through both pinions and legs as shown. .

PIGEON READY FOR COOKING.

Pike, Baked.

Pike, Baked.—INGREDIENTS.—1 or 2 *pike, a nice delicate stuffing (see* FORCE-MEATS), 1 *egg, bread-crumbs,* ¼ *lb. of butter.*

Scale the fish, take out the gills, wash and wipe it thoroughly dry; stuff it with forcemeat, sew it up, and fasten the tail in the mouth by means of a skewer; brush it over with egg, sprinkle with bread-crumbs and baste with butter before putting it in the oven, which must be well heated. When the pike is of a nice brown colour, cover it with buttered paper, as the outside would become too dry. If 2 are dressed, a little variety may be made by making one of them green with a little chopped parsley mixed with the bread-crumbs. Serve anchovy or Dutch sauce and plain melted butter with it.

TIME.—*According to size,* 1 *hour, more or less.*

SEASONABLE *from September to March.*

Note.—Pike *à la génévèse* may be stewed in the same manner as salmon *à la génévèse.*

Pike, Boiled.

Pike, Boiled.— INGREDIENTS.—¼ *lb. of salt to each gallon of water; a little vinegar.*

Scale and clean the pike, and fasten the tail in its mouth by means of a skewer. Lay it in cold water, and when it boils, throw in the salt and vinegar. The time for boiling depends, of course, on the size of the fish; but a middling-sized pike will take about ½ an hour. Serve with Dutch or anchovy sauce and plain melted butter.

TIME.—*According to size,* ½ *to* 1 *hour*

SEASONABLE *from September to March.*

Pilau. — INGREDIENTS *for dish for* 4 *persons.*—*A chicken or a few cutlets from the neck of mutton, 6 onions, 2 mangoes, if procurable, rice, 6 oz. of butter, seasoning.* AVERAGE COST, 2s. 3d.

Slice the mangoes and peel and mince the onions, and put them in a stewpan with ¾ lb. of butter and a good seasoning of pepper and salt. Cut the chicken into joints, or shape the cutlets neatly and fry

PILAU.

in the rest of the butter; then add to the onions and mangoes in the stewpan and stew for an hour. Boil some rice (about ½ lb.) as for curry, spread it on a hot water dish, on this place the joints of fowl, or the cutlets, and pour over them the sauce.

TIME.—1 *hour to stew.*

SEASONABLE *at any time.*

Pilau (Fowl). (Based on M. SOYER'S Recipe; an Indian Dish.)—INGREDIENTS *for dish for* 5 *or* 6 *persons.*—1 *lb. of rice, 2 oz. of butter, a fowl, 2 quarts of stock or good broth, 40 cardamom-seeds, ½ oz. of coriander-seed, ¼ oz. of cloves, ¼ oz. of allspice, ¼ oz. of mace, ¼ oz. of cinnamon, ½ oz. of peppercorns, 4 onions, 6 thin slices of bacon, 2 hard-boiled eggs.* AVERAGE COST, 5s.

Well wash 1 lb. of the best Patna rice, put it into a frying-pan, with the butter, which keep moving over a slow fire until the rice is lightly browned. Truss the fowl as for boiling, put it into a stewpan with the stock or broth; pound the spices and seeds thoroughly in a mortar, tie them in a piece of muslin and put them in with the fowl. Let it boil slowly until it is nearly done; then add the rice, which should stew until quite tender and almost dry; cut the onions into slices, sprinkle them with flour, and fry, without breaking them, of a nice brown colour. Have ready the slices of bacon curled and grilled, and the eggs, boiled hard. Lay the fowl in the form of a pyramid upon a dish, smother with the rice, garnish with the bacon, fried onions and the hard-boiled eggs cut into quarters, and serve very hot. Before taking the rice out, remove the spices.

TIME.—½ *hour to stew the fowl without the rice;* ½ *hour with it.*

SEASONABLE *at any time.*

Pine-apple Chips. — INGREDIENTS.—*Pine-apples; sugar to taste.*

Pare and slice the fruit thinly, put it on dishes and strew over it plenty of pounded sugar. Keep it in a hot closet, or very slow oven, 8 or 10 days, and turn the fruit every day until dry; then put the pieces of pine on tins and place them in a quick oven for 10 minutes. Let them cool, and store them away in dry boxes, with paper between the layers.

TIME.—8 *to* 10 *days.*

SEASONABLE.—*Foreign pines, in July and August.*

Pine-apple Fritters. (An Elegant Dish.) —INGREDIENTS *for dish for* 4 *or* 5 *persons.*—*A small pine-apple, or a tinned one, a small wineglassful of brandy or liqueur, 2 oz. of sifted sugar; batter as for apple fritters (which see).* AVERAGE COST, 2s.

This elegant dish, although it may appear extravagant, is really not so if made when pine-apples are plentiful. We receive them now in such large quantities from the West Indies, that at times they may be purchased at an exceedingly low rate; it would not, of course, be economical to use the pines which are grown in our English pineries for the purposes of fritters, but tinned pines, which preserve their flavour better than any other fruit, answer well for fritters. Pare the pine with as little waste as possible, cut it into rather thin slices, and soak these slices in the above proportion of brandy or liqueur and pounded sugar for 4 hours; then make a batter the same as for apple fritters, substituting cream for the milk, and using a smaller quantity of flour; when this is ready, dip in the pieces of pine and fry them in boiling lard from 5 to 8 minutes; turn them, when sufficiently brown, on one side, and, when done, drain them from the lard before the fire, dish them on a white d'oyley or paper, strew over them sifted sugar and serve quickly.

TIME.—5 *to* 8 *minutes.*

SEASONABLE *in July and August.*

Pine-apple Ice Cream.

INGREDIENTS *for ices for 8 persons.*—$\frac{1}{4}$ *lb. of tinned pine, the juice of a small lemon,* 1 *pint of cream,* $\frac{1}{2}$ *pint of milk,* $\frac{1}{4}$ *lb. of white sugar.* AVERAGE COST, 2s.

Cut the pine into dice, bruise it in a mortar, then add the lemon-juice, sugar,

PINE-APPLE ICE.

cream and milk. Mix them thoroughly, press through a hair-sieve, and freeze.

TIME.—25 *minutes to freeze the ice.*

SEASONABLE *at any time.*

Pine-apple, Preserved.

INGREDIENTS.—To every lb. *of fruit, weighed after being pared, allow* 1 *lb. of loaf sugar;* $\frac{1}{4}$ *pint of water.* AVERAGE COST, 10d. *per pot.*

The pines for making this preserve should be perfectly sound but ripe. Cut them into rather thick slices, as the fruit shrinks very much in the boiling. Pare off the rind carefully, that none of the pine be wasted; and, in doing so, notch it in and out, as the edge cannot be smoothly cut without great

waste. Dissolve a portion of the sugar in a preserving-pan, with $\frac{1}{4}$ pint of water; when this is melted, gradually add the remainder of the sugar, and boil it until it forms a clear syrup, skimming well. As soon as this is the case, put in the pieces of pine, and boil well for at least $\frac{1}{2}$ hour, or until it looks nearly transparent. Put it into pots, cover down when cold, and store away in a dry place.

TIME.—$\frac{1}{2}$ *hour to boil the fruit.*

SEASONABLE.—*Foreign pines, in July and August.*

Pine-apple, Preserved. (For present use).

INGREDIENTS — *Pine-apple, sugar, water.* AVERAGE COST, 10d. *per lb.*

Cut the pine into slices $\frac{1}{4}$ inch in thickness; peel them, and remove the hard part from the middle. Put the parings and hard pieces into a stewpan, with sufficient water to cover them, and boil for $\frac{1}{4}$ hour. Strain the liquor, and put in the slices of pine. Stew them for 10 minutes, add sufficient sugar to sweeten the whole nicely, and boil again for another $\frac{1}{4}$ hour; skim well, and the preserve will be ready for use. It must be eaten soon, as it will keep but a very short time.

TIME.—$\frac{1}{4}$ *hour to boil the parings in water;* 10 *minutes to boil the pine without sugar,* $\frac{1}{4}$ *hour with sugar.*

SEASONABLE. — *Foreign, in July and August; English, all the year.*

Pine-apple Water Ice.

INGREDIENTS *for sufficient ice for 8 persons.*—$\frac{1}{2}$ *lb. of tinned pine, the juice of a small lemon* 1 *pint of clarified sugar,* $\frac{1}{2}$ *pint of water.* AVERAGE COST, 1s.

Chop the pine thin, bruise it in a mortar, mix it well with the other ingredients, pass it through a sieve, and freeze.

TIME.—25 *minutes to freeze.*

SEASONABLE *at any time.*

Pippins, Normandy, Stewed.

—INGREDIENTS—1 *lb. of Normandy pip-*

pins, 1 *quart of water*, ½ *teaspoonful of powdered cinnamon*, ½ *teaspoonful of ground ginger*, 1 *lb. of moist sugar*, 1 *lemon.* AVERAGE COST, 1s.

Well wash the pippins, and put them into 1 quart of water with the above proportion of cinnamon and ginger, and let them stand 12 hours ; then put these altogether into a stewpan, with the lemon, sliced thinly, and half the moist sugar. Let them boil slowly until the pippins are half done ; then add the remainder of the sugar, and simmer until they are quite tender. Serve on glass dishes for dessert.

TIME.—2 *to* 3 *hours*.
SEASONABLE.—*Suitable for a winter dish*.

Plaice, Fried. — INGREDIENTS. —
Plaice, hot lard, or clarified dripping ; egg and bread-crumbs. AVERAGE COST, 6d. *per lb*.

This fish is fried in the same manner as soles. Wash and wipe them thoroughly dry, and let them remain in a cloth until it

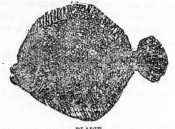

PLAICE.

is time to dress them. Brush them over with egg, and cover with bread-crumbs, mixed with a little flour. Fry of a nice brown in hot dripping or lard, and garnish with fried parsley and cut lemon. Send them to table with shrimp sauce and plain melted butter.

TIME.—*About* 5 *minutes*.
SEASONABLE *from May to November*.

Note.—Plaice may be boiled plain, and served with melted butter. Garnish with parsley and cut lemon.

Plaice, Stewed.—INGREDIENTS *for dish for* 8 *or* 10 *persons.*—4 *or* 5 *plaice*, 2 *onions*, ½ *oz. of ground ginger*, ½ *pint of lemon-juice*, ¼ *pint of water*, 4 *eggs ; cayenne to taste.* AVERAGE COST, 2s.

Cut the fish into pieces about 2 inches wide, salt them, and let them remain for a quarter of an hour. Slice and fry the onions a light brown ; put them in a stewpan, on the top of which put the fish without washing, and add the ginger, lemon-juice and water. Cook slowly for ½ hour, and do not let the fish boil, or it will break. Take it out, and when the liquor is cool, add 4 well-beaten eggs ; simmer till it thickens, when pour over the fish, and serve.

TIME.—¾ *hour*.
SEASONABLE *from May to November*.

Plovers, To Carve.—Plovers may be carved like quails or woodcock, being trussed and served in the same way as those birds.

Plovers, To Dress.—INGREDIENTS *for dish for* 3 *persons.*—3 *plovers, butter, flour, toasted bread.* AVERAGE COST, 3s.

Choosing and Trussing.—Choose those that feel hard at the vent, as that shows their fatness. There are three sorts—the grey, green and bastard plover, or lapwing. They will keep good for some time, but if very stale, the feet will be very dry. Plovers are scarcely fit for anything but roasting ; they are, however, sometimes stewed, and made into a ragoût, but this mode of cooking is not to be recommended.

Pluck off the feathers, wipe the outside of the birds with a damp cloth, and do not draw them ; truss with the head under the wing, put them down to a clear fire, and lay slices of moistened toast in the dripping-pan to catch the trail. Keep them *well* basted, dredge them lightly with flour for a few minutes before they are done, and let them be nicely frothed. Dish them on the toasts, over which the *trail* should be equally spread. Pour round the toast a little good gravy, and send some to table in a tureen.

TIME.—*10 minutes to ¼ hour.*

SEASONABLE.—*In perfection from the beginning of September to the end of January.*

Plucking, Singeing and Dressing of Poultry and Game.

— Under the heading of fowl, goose, &c., will be found detailed the way to truss each particular bird, as well as a hare and a rabbit ; but as all birds are plucked in the same way, it is only necessary to describe the process once.

FOWL BEING PLUCKED.

The bird should be held in the manner shown in illustration, and the feathers first removed from under the wing, and every feather must be taken out, leaving only the down. In plucking grouse, leave the breast feathers in till after trussing, as the skin is tender and apt to break.

When poultry has been plucked it is necessary to singe it, and, to do this, hold it as shown in "Fowl being Singed," and take off all the down left with a lighted paper, which must be moved quickly to avoid scorching the skin. In this singeing, be particularly careful of those parts which will be hidden in the trussing, as the others can be singed again after the bird has been trussed.

In drawing birds, care and knowledge is

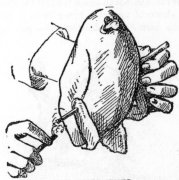

FOWL BEING SINGED.

needed ; and we describe and illustrate the drawing of a fowl, as the mode is the same for all birds of sufficiently large size.

Lay the fowl back downwards upon a table. Cut a slit in the skin of the neck ; then draw it out and cut it off at the root. After this, cut through the skin, leaving

LOOSENING INSIDE OF FOWL.

enough to form a flap ; then through this opening put the middle finger, as shown in illustration, and loosen the inside as carefully and thoroughly as possible, as by this means less trouble is found in afterwards drawing the fowl. Next cut off the head and draw the bird as shown in illustration, being most careful to take out all the entrails, and not to break the gall bladder, which would impart a bitter taste to the whole bird. After drawing, wipe out the

FOWL BEING DRAWN.

bird inside, also the flap of the neck; then dip the legs in boiling water, scrape them and cut off the claws, also the tips of the pinions.

Some few birds are not drawn at all, others are not large enough for the passage of the hand, and these will be found treated under their several headings.

Plum Cake, Common. — INGRE-

DIENTS *for large cake.*—3 *lbs. of flour,* 6 *oz. of butter or good dripping,* 6 *oz. of moist sugar,* 6 *oz. of currants,* ½ *oz. of pounded allspice,* 2 *tablespoonfuls of fresh yeast,* 1 *pint of new milk.* AVERAGE COST, 1s. 6d.

Rub the butter into the flour; add the sugar, currants and allspice; warm the milk, stir to it the yeast, and mix the whole into a dough; knead it well, and put it into 6 buttered tins; place them near the fire for nearly an hour for the dough to rise, then bake the cakes in a good oven from 1 to 1¼ hour. To ascertain when they are done, plunge a clean knife into the middle, and if on withdrawal it comes out clean, the cakes are done.

TIME.—1 *to* 1¼ *hour.*

Plum Cake, A Nice.—INGREDI-

ENTS.—1 *lb. of flour,* ¼ *lb. of butter,* ½ *lb. of sugar,* ½ *lb. of currants,* 2 *oz. of candied lemon-peel,* ½ *pint of milk,* 1 *teaspoonful of ammonia or carbonate of soda.* AVERAGE COST, 1s.

Put the flour into a basin, with the sugar, currants and sliced candied-peel; beat the butter to a cream, and mix all these ingredients together with the milk. Stir the ammonia into 2 tablespoonfuls of milk; add it to the dough, and beat the whole well, until everything is thoroughly mixed, Put the dough into a buttered tin, and bake the cake from 1½ to 2 hours.

TIME.—1½ *to* 2 *hours.*

SEASONABLE *at any time.*

Plum Jam. — INGREDIENTS. — *To every lb. of plums, weighed before being stoned, allow* ¾ *lb. of loaf sugar.*

In making plum jam, the quantity of sugar to each lb. of fruit must be regulated by the quality and size of the fruit, some plums requiring much more sugar than others. Divide the plums, take out the stones; and put them on to large dishes, with roughly-pounded sugar sprinkled over them in the above proportion, and let them remain for one day; then put them into a preserving-pan, stand them by the side of the fire to simmer gently for about ½ hour, and then boil them rapidly for another 15 minutes. The scum must be carefully removed as it rises, and the jam must be well stirred all the time, or it will burn at the bottom of the pan, and so spoil the colour and flavour of the preserve. Some of the stones should be cracked, and a few kernels added to the jam just before it is done; these impart a very delicious flavour to the plums. The above proportion of sugar would answer for Orleans plums; the Impératrice, Magnum bonum and Winesour would not require quite so much.

TIME.—½ *hour to simmer gently;* ¼ *hour to boil rapidly.*

SEASONABLE.—*From the end of July to the beginning of October.*

Best plums for preserving.—Violets, Mussels, Orleans, Impératrice, Magnum-bonum and Winesour.

Plum Pudding, Baked.—INGRE-DIENTS *for pudding for 10 or 12 persons.*—2 *lbs. of flour,* 1 *lb. of currants,* 1 *lb. of raisins,* 1 *lb. of suet,* 2 *eggs,* 1 *pint of milk, a few slices of candied peel.* AVERAGE COST, 2*s.* 3*d.*

Chop the suet finely; mix it with the flour, currants, stoned raisins and candied peel; moisten with the well-beaten eggs, and add sufficient milk to make the pudding of the consistency of very thick batter. Put it into a buttered dish, and bake in a good oven from 2¼ to 2½ hours; turn it out, strew sifted sugar over, and serve. For a very plain pudding, use only half the quantity of fruit, omit the eggs, and substitute milk or water for them. The above ingredients make a large family pudding: for a small one, half the quantity will be found ample; but it must be baked quite 1½ hour.

TIME.—*Large pudding,* 2¼ *to* 2½ *hours; half the size,* 1½ *hour.*

SEASONABLE *in winter.*

Plum Pudding, Excellent, made without Eggs.—INGREDIENTS *for pudding for 6 persons.*—½ *lb. of flour,* 6 *oz. of raisins,* 6 *oz. of currants,* ¼ *lb. of chopped suet,* ¼ *lb. of brown sugar,* ¼ *lb. of mashed carrot,* ¼ *lb. of mashed potatoes,* 1 *tablespoonful of treacle,* 1 *oz. of candied lemon-peel,* 1 *oz. of candied citron.* AVERAGE COST, 1*s.*

Mix the flour, currants, suet and sugar well together; have ready the above proportions of mashed carrot and potato, which stir into the other ingredients; add the treacle and lemon-peel; but put no liquid in the mixture, or it will be spoiled. Tie it loosely in a cloth, or, if put in a basin, do not quite fill it, as the pudding should have room to swell, and boil it for 4 hours. Serve with brandy-sauce. This pudding is better for being mixed overnight.

TIME.—4 *hours.*

SEASONABLE *in winter.*

Plum Pudding, Unrivalled.—INGREDIENTS *for 3 moderate-sized puddings.*—1½ *lb. of muscatel raisins,* 1¾ *lb. of currants,* 1 *lb. of sultana raisins,* 2 *lbs. of the finest moist sugar,* 2 *lbs. of bread-crumbs,* 16 *eggs,* 2 *lbs. of finely-chopped suet,* 6 *oz. of mixed candied peel, the rind of 2 lemons,* 1 *oz. of ground nutmeg,* 1 *oz. of ground cinnamon,* ½ *oz. of pounded bitter almonds,* ½ *pint of brandy.* AVERAGE COST, 7*s.* 6*d.*

Stone and cut up the raisins, but do not chop them; wash and dry the currants, and cut the candied peel into thin slices. Mix all the dry ingredients well together, and moisten with the eggs, which should be well beaten and strained, to the pudding; stir in the brandy, and, when all is thoroughly mixed, well butter and flour a stout new pudding-cloth; put in the pudding, tie it down very tightly and closely, boil from 6 to 8 hours, and serve with brandy-sauce. A few sweet almonds, blanched and cut in strips, and stuck on the pudding, ornament it prettily. This quantity may be divided and boiled in buttered moulds. For small families this is the most desirable way, as the above will be found to make a pudding of rather large dimensions.

TIME.—6 *to* 8 *hours.*

SEASONABLE *in winter.*

Plum Pudding for Children.—INGREDIENTS.—1 *lb. of flour,* 1 *lb. of bread-crumbs,* ¾ *lb. of raisins,* ¾ *lb. of currants,* ¾ *lb. of suet,* 3 *eggs,* ½ *lb. of sugar, milk,* 2 *oz. of candied peel,* 1 *teaspoonful of powdered allspice,* ½ *saltspoonful of salt.* AVERAGE COST, 2*s.*

Let the suet be finely chopped, the raisins stoned, and the currants well washed, picked and dried. Mix these with the other dry ingredients, and stir all well together; beat and strain the eggs to the pudding, stir these in, and add just sufficient milk to make it mix properly. Tie it up in a well-floured cloth, put it into boiling water, and boil for at least 5 hours. Serve with a sprig of holly placed in the middle of the pudding, and a little pounded sugar sprinkled over it.

TIME.—5 *hours.*

SEASONABLE *at Christmas.*

Plum Pudding, Christmas.

(Very Good.)— INGREDIENTS.— 1½ *lb. of raisins,* ½ *lb. of currants,* ½ *lb. of mixed peel,* ¾ *lb. of bread-crumbs,* ¾ *lb. of suet,* 8 *eggs,* 1 *wineglassful of brandy,* 1 *lb. of sugar.* AVERAGE COST, 3s. 6d.

Stone and cut the raisins in halves, but do not chop them; wash, pick and dry the currants, and mince the suet finely; cut the candied peel into thin slices, and grate down the bread into fine crumbs. When all these dry ingredients are prepared, mix

CHRISTMAS PLUM PUDDING IN MOULD.

them well together with the sugar; then moisten the mixture with the eggs, which should be well beaten, and the brandy; stir well, that everything may be very thoroughly blended, and *press* the pudding into a buttered mould; tie it down tightly with a floured cloth, and boil for 5 or 6 hours. It may be boiled in a cloth without a mould, and will require the same time allowed for cooking. As Christmas puddings are usually made a few days before they are required for table, when the pud-

ding is taken out of the pot, hang it up immediately, and put a plate or saucer underneath to catch the water that may drain from it. The day it is to be eaten, plunge it into boiling water, and keep it boiling for at least 2 hours; then turn it out of the mould, and serve with brandy-sauce. On Christmas-day a sprig of holly is usually placed in the middle of the pudding, and about a wineglassful of brandy poured round it, which, at the moment of serving, is lighted, and the pudding thus brought to table encircled in flame.

TIME.—5 *or* 6 *hours the first time of boiling;* 2 *hours the day it is to be served.*

SEASONABLE *on the* 25th *of December, and on various festive occasions till March.*

Note.—Five or six of these puddings should be made at one time, as they will keep good for many weeks, and in cases where unexpected guests arrive, will be found an acceptable and, as it only requires warming through, a quickly-prepared dish. Moulds of every shape and size are manufactured for these puddings, and may be purchased of Messrs. R. & J. Slack, 336, Strand.

Plum Pudding, A Pound.—IN-

GREDIENTS *for pudding for* 12 *persons.*—1 *lb. of suet,* 1 *lb. of currants,* 1 *lb. of stoned raisins,* 8 *eggs,* 1 *grated nutmeg,* 2 *oz. of sliced candied peel,* 1 *teaspoonful of ground ginger,* ½ *lb. of bread-crumbs,* ½ *lb. of flour,* ½ *pint of milk.* AVERAGE COST, 2s.

Chop the suet finely; mix with it the dry ingredients; stir these well together, and add the well-beaten eggs and milk to moisten with. Beat up the mixture well, and should the above proportion of milk not be found sufficient to make it of the proper consistency, a little more should be added. Press the pudding into a mould, tie it in a floured cloth, and boil for 5 hours, or rather longer, and serve with brandy sauce.

TIME.—5 *hours, or longer.*

SEASONABLE *in winter.*

Note.—The above pudding may be baked instead of boiled; it should be put into a buttered mould or tin, and baked for about 2 hours; a smaller one would take about 1¼ hour.

Plum Pudding. (Fresh Fruit.)—

INGREDIENTS *for pudding for 6 or 8 persons.* — ¾ lb. of suet crust, 1½ pint of Orleans or any other kind of plum, ¼ lb. of moist sugar. AVERAGE COST, 10d.

Line a pudding-basin with suet crust rolled out to the thickness of about ½ inch; fill the basin with the fruit, put in the sugar and cover with crust. Fold the edges over, and pinch them together to prevent the

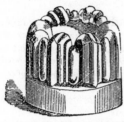

BAKED PUDDING OR CAKE MOULD.

juice escaping. Tie over a floured cloth, put the pudding into boiling water, and boil from 2 to 2½ hours. Turn it out of the basin, and serve quickly.

TIME.—2 to 2½ hours.

SEASONABLE, *with various kinds of plums, from the beginning of August to the beginning of October.*

Plum Pudding. (Vegetarian Recipe.)

—INGREDIENTS *for pudding for 6 persons.* —1 lb. of flour, ½ lb. of sultanas, ½ lb. of currants, ¼ lb. of butter, rind of 1 lemon, 3 eggs, a teaspoonful of baking-powder. AVERAGE COST, 1s. 4d.

Mix the powder with the flour, rub in the butter, add to them the currants, washed and dried, the sultanas, picked over, and a little nutmeg, if liked. Mix with the eggs, well beaten, and a little milk, if necessary. Put the pudding in a buttered basin, and steam for 4 hours. Serve with wine sauce.

TIME.—4 hours.

SEASONABLE *in winter.*

Plum Tart. — INGREDIENTS *for tart*

for 6 persons.—½ lb. of good short crust, 1½ pint of plums, ¼ lb. of moist sugar. AVERAGE COST, 1s.

Line the edges of a deep tart-dish with crust; fill the dish with plums, and place a

PLUM TART.

small cup or jar, upside down, in the midst of them. Put in the sugar, cover the pie with crust, ornament the edges, and bake in a good oven from ½ to ¾ hour. When puff-crust is preferred to short crust, use that made by the given recipe, and glaze the top by brushing it over with the white of an egg, beaten to a stiff froth with a knife; sprinkle over a little sifted sugar, and put the pie in the oven to set the glaze.

TIME.—½ to ¾ hour.

SEASONABLE, *with various kinds of plums, from the beginning of August to the beginning of October.*

Plums, French, Stewed. (A Dessert dish.)—INGREDIENTS—1½ lb. of French plums, ¾ pint of syrup, 1 glass of port wine, the rind and juice of 1 lemon. AVERAGE COST. 1s. 8d.

Stew the plums gently in water for 1 hour; strain the water, and with it make the syrup. When it is clear, put in the plums with the port wine. lemon-juice and rind, and simmer very gently for 1½ hour. Arrange the plums on a glass dish, take out the lemon-rind, pour the syrup over the plums and, when cold, they will be ready for table. A little allspice stewed with the fruit is by many persons considered an improvement.

TIME.—1 hour to stew the plums in water, 1½ hour in the syrup.

SEASONABLE *in winter.*

Plums, To Preserve Dry.—IN-GREDIENTS.—To every lb. of sugar allow ¼ pint of water.

Gather the plums when they are full grown and just turning colour; prick them, put them into a saucepan of cold water and set them on the fire until the water is

on the point of boiling. Then take them out, drain them, and boil them gently in syrup made with the above proportion of sugar and water; and if the plums shrink and will not take the sugar, prick them as they lie in the pan; give them another boil, skim and set them by. The next

FLUMS.

day add some more sugar, boiled almost to candy, to the fruit and syrup; put all together into a wide-mouthed jar and place them in a cool oven for 2 nights; then drain the plums from the syrup, sprinkle a little powdered sugar over and dry them in a cool oven.

TIME.—15 to 20 *minutes to boil the plums in the syrup.*

SEASONABLE *from August to October.*

Plums, Preserved. — INGREDI-

ENTS.—*To every lb. of fruit allow ¾ lb. of loaf sugar; for the thin syrup, ¼ lb. of sugar to each pint of water.*

Select large ripe plums; slightly prick them, to prevent them from bursting, and simmer them very gently in a syrup made with the above proportion of sugar and water. Put them carefully into a pan, let the syrup cool, pour it over the plums and allow them to remain for two days. Having previously weighed the other sugar, dip the lumps quickly into water and put them into a preserving-pan with no more water than hangs about them; and boil the sugar to a syrup, carefully skimming it. Drain the plums from the first syrup; put them into the fresh syrup and simmer them very gently until they are clear: lift them out

singly into pots, pour the syrup over and, when cold, cover down to exclude the air. This preserve will remain good some time if kept in a dry place, and makes a very nice addition to a dessert. The magnum-bonum plums answer for this preserve better than any other kind of plum. Greengages are also very delicious done in this manner.

TIME.—¼ *hour to 20 minutes to simmer the plums in the first syrup; 20 minutes to ½ hour very gentle simmering in the second.*

SEASONABLE *from August to October.*

Poivrade Sauce. — INGREDIENTS

for one dish of ordinary size.—6 oz. of ham, 1 oz. of butter, a clove of garlic, a bay-leaf, a sprig each of sweet thyme and basil, 2 or 3 cloves, 4 young onions, ½ stick of celery, a few sprigs of parsley, ¼ pint of stock, a wineglassful of tarragon vinegar. AVERAGE COST, 1s.

Mince the ham, and fry it in the butter with the onions and herbs and the cloves, over a quick fire, then add the celery, sliced, the vinegar, stock and pepper, and let all simmer for ½ an hour, when strain through a tammy.

TIME.—½ *hour to simmer.*

SEASONABLE *at any time.*

Polenta and Cheese. — INGREDI-

ENTS.—*Cold maize meal porridge, grated cheese, butter or oil, salt and cayenne.*

Cut the polenta into squares about ½ to ¾ inch in thickness, and arrange them in a pie-dish, with grated cheese between and over the top. Put over a few small pieces of butter, or a little oil, and bake in a quick oven till brown. Serve very hot, with freshly-made toast.

Pomeranian Soup. — INGREDI-

ENTS *for soup for 6 or 8 persons.—1 quart of haricot beans, 1 quart of medium stock, a head of celery, sweet herbs, parsley, salt and pepper.* AVERAGE COST, 1s. 6d.

Put the beans in plenty of water, and boil them until perfectly tender, then take half of them and mash them with a little stock, rub them through a sieve, and return them to the saucepan with the rest of the stock, the celery cut in dice (setting aside the unmashed beans), and boil till a smooth soup is obtained. Next add the rest of the beans, the parsley chopped fine, and a seasoning of sweet herbs, salt and pepper, and boil for 15 minutes.

Time.—3½ hours.

Seasonable in winter.

Pooloot. (Indian Recipe.)—Ingre-

dients for dish for 6 persons.—A fowl, 1 lb. of rice, 1 quart of stock, a few thinly-cut rashers of bacon, 6 hard-boiled eggs, a table-spoonful of ground ginger, 6 onions, 1 lemon, peppercorns, cardamums, butter for frying. Average Cost, 4s. 3d.

Truss the fowl as for boiling, boil the rice for 5 minutes, drain it, and put it with the fowl and the stock in a stewpan over a slow fire. Pound 4 of the onions, and squeeze out the juice, which add with that of the lemon, and the ginger tied in a bag. When the fowl is sufficiently done, take it out and keep it hot while the rice

POOLOOT.

dries before the fire, during which time slice and fry the other two onions. Afterwards cut up the fowl and fry it in the same butter as the onions. Pile the rice on a dish, lay over it the joints of fowl, and over these the onions; strew over some peppercorns and cardamums, and garnish with the hard-boiled eggs and the bacon rolled and fried.

Time.—To boil the fowl, ¾ to 1 hour.

Seasonable in winter.

Pop-overs. (American Recipe.)—

Ingredients for small dish.—A teacupful of milk, and the same of flour, 1 egg, a pinch of salt. Average Cost, 2d.

Make a batter of the above ingredients, and pour into a pop-over tin (these are similar to our sheets of tin for tartlets, but the hollows are deeper), and bake in a quick oven.

Time.—About 10 minutes to bake.

Seasonable at any time.

Pork.—In the country, where, for

ordinary consumption, the pork killed for sale is usually both larger and fatter than that supplied to the London consumer, it is customary to remove the skin and fat down to the lean, and, salting that, roast what remains of the joint.

In fresh pork, the leg is the most economical family joint, and the loin the richest. The most economical way of cooking fresh pork is to boil it, but it requires a very long time to get thoroughly done, as the texture of the meat is close.

Pork, to be preserved, is cured in several ways—either by covering it with salt, or immersing it in ready-made brine, where it is kept till required ; or it is only partially salted and then hung up to dry, when the meat is called white bacon; or, after salting, it is hung in wood smoke till the flesh is impregnated with the aroma from the wood. The Wiltshire bacon, which is regarded as the finest in the kingdom, is prepared by laying the sides of a hog in large wooden troughs, and then rubbing into the flesh quantities of powdered bay-salt, made hot in a frying-pan. This process is repeated for four days ; they are then left for three weeks, merely turning the flitches every other day. After that time they are hung up to dry. The hogs usually killed for purposes of bacon in England average from 18 to 20 stone ; on the other hand, the hogs killed in the country for farm-house purposes seldom weigh less than 26 stone. The legs of boars, hogs and, in Germany, those of bears, are prepared differently and called hams.

The practice in vogue formerly in this country was, to cut out the hams and cure them separately; then to remove the ribs, which were roasted as "spare-ribs," and, curing the remainder of the side, call it a "gammon of bacon."

Small pork, to cut for table in joints, is cut up, in most places throughout the kingdom, as represented in the engraving. The side is divided with nine ribs to the fore quarter; and the following is an enumeration of the joints in the two respective quarters:—

SIDE OF A PIG, SHOWING THE SEVERAL JOINTS.

Hind Quarter
1. The leg.
2. The loin.
3. The spring, or belly.

Fore Quarter
4. The hand.
5. The fore-loin.
6. The cheek.

The weight of the several joints of a good pork pig of four stone may be as follows:—

The leg . . . . . . 8 lbs.
The loin and spring . 7 ,,
The hand . . . . . 6 ,,
The chine . . . . . 7 ,,
The cheek . . from 2 to 3 ,,

Of a bacon pig, the legs are reserved for curing, and when cured are called hams; when the meat is separated from the shoulder-blade and bones and cured, it is called bacon. The bones, with part of the meat left on them, are divided into spare-ribs, griskins and chines.

Pork Cheese. (An Excellent Breakfast Dish.)—INGREDIENTS *for dish for 6 persons.*—2 *lbs. of cold roast pork, pepper and salt to taste,* 1 *dessertspoonful of minced parsley,* 4 *leaves of sage, a very small bunch of savoury herbs,* 2 *blades of pounded mace, a little nutmeg,* ½ *teaspoonful of minced lemon-peel; good strong gravy, sufficient to fill the mould.* AVERAGE COST, 2s.

Cut, but do not chop, the pork into fine pieces, and allow ¼ lb. of fat to each pound of lean. Season with pepper and salt; pound well the spices, and chop finely the parsley, sage, herbs and lemon-peel, and mix the whole nicely together. Put it into a mould, fill up with good strong well-flavoured gravy, and bake rather more than one hour. When cold, turn it out of the mould.

TIME.—*Rather more than* 1 *hour.*
SEASONABLE *from October to March.*

Note.—The remains of a pig's head, after the chops are taken off, make most excellent pork cheese.

Pork Cutlets, or Chops.—INGREDIENTS.—*Loin of pork, pepper and salt to taste.* AVERAGE COST, 10d. per lb.

Cut the cutlets from a delicate loin of pork, bone and trim them neatly, and cut away a greater portion of the fat. Season them with pepper; place the gridiron on the fire; when quite hot, lay on the chops, and broil for about ¼ hour, turning them 3 or 4 times; and be particular that they are *thoroughly* done, but not dry. Dish them, sprinkle over a little fine salt, and serve plain, or with tomato sauce, sauce piquante, or pickled gherkins, a few of which should be laid round the dish as a garnish.

TIME.—*About* ¼ *hour.*
SEASONABLE *from October to March.*

Pork Cutlets, or Chops.—INGREDIENTS.—*Loin, or fore-loin of pork, egg and bread-crumbs, salt and pepper to taste; to every tablespoonful of bread-crumbs allow* ½

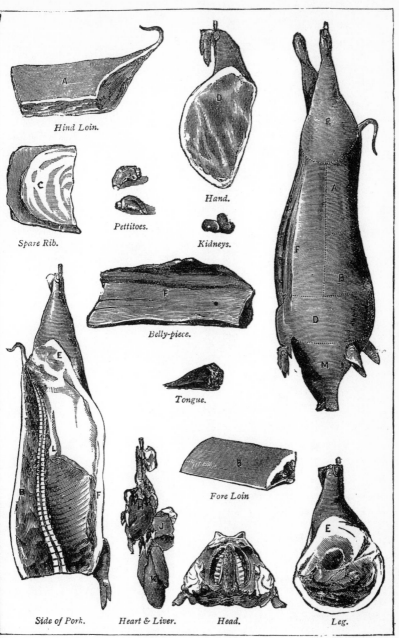

Hind Loin.

Hand.

Spare Rib.

Pettitoes.

Kidneys.

Belly-piece.

Tongue.

Side of Pork.

Heart & Liver.

Head.

Fore Loin

Leg.

Various Parts of Pork.

Various Parts of Pork

teaspoonful of minced sage ; clarified butter.
AVERAGE COST, 10d. per lb.

Cut the cutlets from a loin, or fore-loin of pork ; trim them the same as mutton cutlets, and scrape the top part of the bone. Brush them over with egg, sprinkle with bread-crumbs, with which have been mixed minced sage and a seasoning of pepper and salt; drop a little clarified butter on them, and press the crumbs well down. Put the frying-pan on the fire, put in some lard ; when this is hot, lay in the cutlets, and fry them a light brown on both sides. Take them out, put them before the fire to dry the greasy moisture from them, and dish them on mashed potatoes. Serve with them any sauce that may be preferred ; such as tomato sauce, sauce piquante, sauce Robert, or pickled gherkins.

TIME.—From 15 to 20 minutes.

SEASONABLE from October to March.

Note.—The remains of roast loin of pork may be dressed in the same manner.

Pork Cutlets. (Cold Meat Cookery.)

—INGREDIENTS.—*The remains of cold roast loin of pork,* 1 oz. *of butter,* 2 *onions,* 1 *dessertspoonful of flour,* ½ *pint of gravy, pepper and salt to taste ,* 1 *teaspoonful of vinegar and mustard.* AVERAGE COST, *exclusive of the cold pork,* 4d.

Cut the pork into nice-sized cutlets, trim off most of the fat, and chop the onions. Put the butter into a stewpan, lay in the cutlets and chopped onions, and fry a light brown ; then add the remaining ingredients, simmer gently for 5 or 7 minutes, and serve.

TIME.—5 to 7 minutes.

SEASONABLE from October to March.

Pork, Roast Griskin of.—INGRE-

DIENTS. — *Pork ; a little powdered sage.* AVERAGE COST, 8d. per lb.

As this joint frequently comes to table hard and dry, particular care should be taken that it is well basted. Put it down to a bright fire, and flour it. About 10

minutes before taking it up, sprinkle over some powdered sage ; make a little gravy in the dripping-pan, strain it over the meat and serve with a tureen of apple sauce.

GRISKIN OF PORK.

This joint will be done in far less time than when the skin is left on, consequently, should have the greatest attention that it be not dried up.

TIME.—*Griskin of pork weighing* 6 *lbs.,* 1½ *hour.*

SEASONABLE *from September to March.*

SPARE-RIB OF PORK.

Note.—A spare-rib of pork is roasted in the same manner as above, and would take 1½ hour for one weighing about 6 lbs.

Pork, Hashed.—INGREDIENTS.—*The remains of cold roast pork,* 2 *onions,* 1 *teaspoonful of flour,* 2 *blades of pounded mace,* 2 *cloves,* 1 *tablespoonful of vinegar,* ½ *pint of gravy, pepper and salt to taste.* AVERAGE COST, *exclusive of the meat,* 3d.

Chop the onions and fry them of a nice brown ; cut the pork into thin slices, season them with pepper and salt, and add these to the remaining ingredients. Stew gently for about ½ hour, and serve garnished with sippets of toasted bread.

TIME.—½ hour.

SEASONABLE from October to March.

Pork, Boiled Leg of. — INGREDI-

ENTS.—*Leg of pork ; salt.* AVERAGE COST, 8d. per lb.

For boiling, choose a small, compact

2 M

well-filled leg, and rub it well with salt; let it remain in pickle for a week or ten days, turning and rubbing it every day. An hour before dressing it, put it into cold water for an hour, which improves the colour. If the pork is purchased ready salted, ascertain how long the meat has been in pickle, and soak it accordingly. Put it into a boiling-pot, with sufficient cold water to cover it; let it gradually come to a boil, and remove the scum as it rises. Simmer it very gently until tender, and do not allow it to boil fast, or the knuckle will fall to pieces before the middle of the leg is done. Carrots, turnips or parsnips may be boiled with the pork, some of which should be laid round the dish as a garnish. A well-made pease-pudding is an indispensable accompaniment.

TIME.—*A leg of pork weighing 8 lbs., 3 hours after the water boils, and to be simmered very gently.*

SEASONABLE *from September to March.*

Note.—The liquor in which a leg of pork has been boiled makes excellent pea-soup.

Pork, Roast Leg of.—INGREDI-
ENTS.—*Leg of pork, a little oil, sage-and-onion stuffing.* AVERAGE COST, 8d. per lb.

Choose a small leg of pork, and score the skin across in narrow strips, about $\frac{1}{4}$ inch apart. Cut a slit in the knuckle,

ROAST LEG OF PORK.

loosen the skin, and fill it with sage-and-onion stuffing. Brush the joint over with a little salad-oil (this makes the crackling crisper, and a better colour), and put it down to a bright, clear fire, not too near, as that would cause the skin to blister. Baste it well, and serve with a little gravy made in the dripping-pan, and do not omit

to send to table with it a tureen of well-made apple-sauce.

TIME.—*A leg of pork weighing 8 lbs., about 3 hours.*

SEASONABLE *from September to March.*

Pork, Leg of, To Carve.—This
joint, which is such a favourite one with many people, is easy to carve. The knife should be carried sharply down to the bone, clean through the crackling, in the direction of the line A to B. Sage-and-onion and apple-sauce are usually sent to table with this dish—sometimes the leg of pork is stuffed—and the guests should be

LEG OF PORK.

asked if they will have either or both. A frequent plan, and we think a good one, is now pursued, of sending sage-and-onion to table separately from the joint, as it is not everybody to whom the flavour of this stuffing is agreeable.

Pork, Roast Loin of.—INGREDI-
ENTS.—*Pork; a little salt.* AVERAGE COST, 9d. per lb.

Score the skin in strips rather more than $\frac{1}{4}$ inch apart, and place the joint at a good distance from the fire, on account of the crackling, which would harden before the meat would be heated through, were it placed too near. If very lean, it should be rubbed over with a little salad oil, and kept well basted all the time it is at the fire. Pork should be very thoroughly cooked, but not dry; and be careful never to send it to table the least underdone, as nothing is more unwholesome and disagreeable than underdressed white meats. Serve with apple sauce and a little gravy made in the dripping-pan. A stuffing of sage-and-onion may be made separately, and baked in a flat dish: this method is better than putting it in the meat, as many persons have so great an objection to the flavour.

TIME.—*A loin of pork weighing 5 lbs , about 2 hours; allow more time should it be very fat.*

SEASONABLE *from September to March.*

Pork, Loin of, To Carve.

As with a loin of mutton, it is essential that this be well jointed before cooking, also that the crackling be scored, then there

LOIN OF PORK.

is no difficulty in carving it. The knife is inserted at A and carried to B, and the chops should be divided neatly and evenly.

Pork, To Pickle.

INGREDIENTS.— ¼ lb. of saltpetre, salt. AVERAGE COST, 9d. per lb.

Cut suitable pieces for pickling directly the pig is cold, rub these with salt, and put them in a pan with a sprinkling of that and the saltpetre between the pieces; as it melts on the top, strew on more. Lay a coarse cloth over the pan, a board over that, and a weight on the board, to keep the pork down in the brine. If excluded from the air, it will continue good for nearly 2 years.

SEASONABLE.—*The best time for pickling meat is late in the autumn.*

Pork, Pickled, To Boil.

INGREDIENTS.—*Pork; water.* AVERAGE COST, 9d. per lb.

Should the pork be very salt, let it remain in water about 2 hours before it is dressed; put it into a saucepan with sufficient cold water to cover it, let it gradually come to a boil, then gently simmer until quite tender. Allow ample time for it to cook, as nothing is more disagreeable than underdone pork, and when boiled fast the meat becomes hard. This is sometimes served with boiled poultry and roast veal, instead of bacon: when tender, and not over salt, it will be found equally good.

TIME.—*A piece of pickled pork weighing 2 lbs., 1¼ hour; 4 lbs., rather more than 2 hours.*

SEASONABLE *at any time.*

Pork Pies. (Warwickshire Recipe.)

INGREDIENTS.—*For the crust, 2½ lbs. of lard to 7 lbs. of flour; milk and water. For filling the pies, to every 3 lbs. of meat allow 1 oz. of salt, 2¼ oz. of pepper, a small quantity of cayenne, 1 pint of water.*

Rub into the flour a portion of the lard; the remainder put with sufficient milk and water to mix the crust, and boil this gently for ¼ hour. Pour it boiling on the flour, and knead and beat it till perfectly smooth. Now raise the crust in either a round or oval form, cut up the pork into pieces the size of a nut, season it in the above proportion, and press it compactly into the pie, in alternate layers of fat and lean, and pour in a small quantity of water; lay on the lid, cut the edges smoothly round, and pinch them together. Bake in a brick oven, which should be slow, as the meat is very solid. Very frequently an inexperienced cook finds much difficulty in raising the crust. She should bear in mind that it must not be allowed to get cold, or it will fall immediately: to prevent this, the operation should be performed as near the fire as possible. As considerable dexterity and expertness are necessary to raise the crust with the hand only, a jar of convenient size may be placed in the middle of the paste, and the crust moulded on this;

but be particular that it is kept warm the whole time.

SEASONABLE *from September to March.*

Pork Pies, Little Raised.

INGREDIENTS.—2 *lbs. of flour,* ½ *lb. of butter,* ¼ *lb. of mutton suet, salt and white pepper to taste,* 4 *lbs. of the neck of pork,* 1 *dessertspoonful of powdered sage.* AVERAGE COST, 3s. 6d.

Well dry the flour, mince the suet, and put these with the butter into a saucepan, to be made hot, and add a little salt. When melted, mix it up into a stiff paste, and put it before the fire with a cloth over it until ready to make up ; chop the pork into small pieces, season it with white pepper, salt and powdered sage ; divide the paste into rather small pieces, raise it in a round or oval form, fill with the meat, and bake in a brick oven. These pies will require a fiercer oven than those in the preceding recipe, as they are made so much smaller, and consequently do not require so soaking a heat.

TIME.—*If made small, about* 1½ *hour.*
SEASONABLE *from September to March.*

Pork Steaks and Apples.

(American Recipe.)—INGREDIENTS *for dish for* 4 *persons.*—2 *lbs. of pork, cut in steaks from the loin or neck,* 2 *lbs. of apples, hot lard for frying, pepper and salt.* AVERAGE COST, 2s. 3d.

Trim the steaks neatly, cutting off most of the fat, season them with pepper, heat a gridiron, grease it and put on the steaks and broil them till they are thoroughly done and dry, turning them several times. Peel the apples, take out the cores, and slice them ; then fry in hot lard, and, when drained, put them round the steaks on a hot dish.

TIME.—*About* 15 *minutes to fry.*
SEASONABLE *from October to March.*

Porridge, Hominy.

INGREDIENTS.—*Hominy, water, butter.*

The night before the porridge is required, pour boiling water on a sufficient quantity of hominy, and let it stand till morning. Should it have absorbed the water, add a little more and boil for half an hour, or rather more. Just before serving, stir in a little butter, about a teaspoonful to each person.

SEASONABLE.—*A good breakfast dish in winter.*

Portable Soup.

By reducing very strong stock almost to a glaze, and forming it into little cakes, which should be perfectly dry, and stowed in tin canisters, portable soup can be made at home ; but the many good preparations sold for the purpose save a great deal of trouble and answer excellently well. Johnston's fluid beef is one of the pleasantest, either simply made with water, or better still with some simple vegetable stock.

Note.—The desiccated soup made by F. King and Co., also answers the same purpose as this, as a very small packet will make a good quantity of nice soup.

Potage à la bonne femme.

INGREDIENTS *for soup for* 4 *or* 5 *persons.*—1½ *pint of white stock,* 1 *gill of new milk,* 1 *oz. of butter, a lettuce, an onion, a very small cucumber, the yolks of* 2 *eggs, a pinch of sugar, a handful of sorrel, a little chervil and tarragon, a French roll, salt, nutmeg.* AVERAGE COST, 1s. 9d.

Shred the vegetables, and put the onion in a saucepan with the butter, but do not brown it ; add the vegetables to the onion, and stir them over a slow fire for 10 minutes. Put in the seasoning and stock boiling, and boil for another 10 minutes ; then, when cool, add the yolks of the eggs and the milk. Cut the roll in thin slices, dry them in the oven, then put them in a tureen and pour the soup over.

TIME.—½ *an hour.*
SEASONABLE *in spring or early summer.*

Potato Balls. — Ingredients.—

Mashed potatoes, egg, bread-crumbs, a little parsley, pepper and salt, dripping or lard.

Boil and mash the potatoes, adding a seasoning of pepper and salt, and a little finely-minced parsley. Form the potato

POTATO CROQUETTES.

into balls, dip them in egg and bread-crumbs, and fry in hot lard or dripping till a bright brown. Drain them before the fire, and dish them upon a napkin.

Time.—*10 minutes to fry.*
Seasonable *at any time.*

Potato Cake. — Ingredients *for good-sized cake.*—1 *lb. of potato flour*, 6 *oz. of butter*, ¼ *lb. of castor sugar*, 2 *eggs, flavouring of essence of lemon.* Average Cost, 10*d.*

Beat the butter to a cream, add the flour and next the other ingredients, then beat well together for 10 minutes. Pour into a buttered cake-tin, and bake for 15 to 20 minutes in a quick oven.

Time.—*15 to 20 minutes to bake.*
Seasonable *at any time.*

Potato Fritters.—Ingredients *for dish for 3 or 4 persons.*—2 *large potatoes*, 3 *eggs*, 2 *tablespoonfuls of cream*, 2 *ditto of raisin or sweet wine*, 1 *dessertspoonful of lemon-juice*, ½ *teaspoonful of grated nutmeg, hot lard.* Average Cost, 9*d.*

Boil the potatoes, and beat them up lightly with a fork, but do not use a spoon, as that would make them heavy. Beat the eggs well, leaving out one of the whites; add the other ingredients, and beat all together for at least 20 minutes, or until the batter is extremely light. Put plenty of good lard into a frying-pan, and drop a tablespoonful of the batter at a time into it, and fry the fritters a nice brown. Serve

them with the following sauce:—A glass of sherry mixed with the strained juice of a lemon, and sufficient white sugar to sweeten the whole nicely. Warm these ingredients, and serve the sauce separately in a tureen. The fritters should be neatly dished on a white d'oyley or an ornamented paper, and pounded sugar sprinkled over them. They should be well drained on a piece of blotting-paper before the fire previously to being dished.

Time.—*From 6 to 8 minutes.*
Seasonable *at any time.*

Potato Pasty.—Ingredients *for dish for 4 persons.*—1½ *lb. of rump-steak or mutton cutlets, pepper and salt to taste*, ½ *pint of weak broth or gravy*, 1 *oz. of butter, mashed potatoes.* Average Cost, 1*s.* 10*d.*

Place the meat, cut in small pieces, at the bottom of the pan; season it with pepper and salt, and add the gravy and butter broken into small pieces. Put on

POTATO PASTY PAN.

the perforated plate, with its valve-pipe screwed on, and fill up the whole space to the top of the tube with nicely-mashed potatoes mixed with a little milk, and finish the surface of them in any ornamental manner. If carefully baked, the potatoes will be covered with a delicate brown crust, retaining all the savoury steam rising from the meat. Send it to table as it comes from the oven, with a napkin folded round it.

Time.—*40 to 60 minutes.*
Seasonable *at any time.*

Potato Patties.—Ingredients *for dish for 6 persons.*—¾ *lb. of mealy potatoes*, 2 *oz. of butter*, ½ *pint of milk*, 4 *eggs, bread-crumbs.* Average Cost, 8*d.*

Boil the potatoes, run them through a sieve, adding a little milk and the butter, melted and beaten to a cream. Boil the rest of the milk and pour it boiling over the potatoes, add seasoning of pepper and salt to taste, then stir over the fire into a smooth firm paste. Next add to it 2 well-beaten eggs, and, when the mixture becomes cold, beat up with the yolks of the other 2 eggs, adding the whites of the eggs well-beaten. Butter small patty-pans, sprinkle them with crumbs, fill them with the mixture, and bake a nice bright brown in a hot oven.

TIME.—*Altogether, ½ hour.*
SEASONABLE *at any time.*

Potato Pie.—INGREDIENTS *for dish for 3 persons.*—1 *lb. tin of roast mutton, 2 lbs. of potatoes, 2 oz. of butter, 2 onions, a little sauce, milk, seasoning, bread-crumbs.* AVERAGE COST, 1s. 3d.

Turn out the meat from the tin, taking off most of the fat, then boil and mash the potatoes with a little milk and butter;

SWEET POTATO.

then slice the onions, and fry them in the mutton fat. Butter a pie-dish, line it with the potatoes, next a layer of mutton, cut in small pieces and well seasoned, then a few onions, and so on till the dish is full, scattering a few bread-crumbs and small pieces over the top, and bake.

TIME.—20 *minutes to bake.*
SEASONABLE *at any time.*

Potato Pie. (Vegetarian Recipe.)—INGREDIENTS *for pie for 2 or 3 persons.*— ½ *lb. of potatoes, a small stick of celery, 1*

onion, 1 oz. of sago, 1 oz. of butter, paste to cover the pie, a little milk. AVERAGE COST, 7d.

Fry the onion in a little butter, and fill a pie-dish with it and the celery, and potatoes sliced, strewing in between the layers the sago and seasoning of pepper and salt. Fill up the dish with milk, and cover with a paste; then bake in a good oven for an hour.

TIME.—1 *hour to bake.*
SEASONABLE *at any time.*

Potato Pudding. — INGREDIENTS *for pudding for 5 or 6 persons.*— ½ *lb. of mashed potatoes, 2 oz. of butter, 2 eggs, ¼ pint of milk, 3 tablespoonfuls of sherry, ½ saltspoonful of salt, the juice and rind of 1 small lemon, 2 oz. of sugar.* AVERAGE COST, 8d.

Boil sufficient potatoes to make ½ lb. when mashed; add to these the butter, eggs, milk, sherry, lemon-juice and sugar; mince the lemon-peel very finely, and beat all the ingredients well together. Put the pudding into a buttered pie-dish, and bake for rather more than ½ hour. To enrich it, add a few pounded almonds, and increase the quantity of eggs and butter.

TIME.—½ *hour, or rather longer.*
SEASONABLE *at any time.*

Potato Rissoles.—INGREDIENTS.— *Mashed potatoes, salt and pepper to taste when liked, a very little minced parsley egg and bread-crumbs.*

Boil and mash the potatoes; add a seasoning of pepper and salt, and, when liked, a little minced parsley. Roll the potatoes into small balls, cover them with egg and bread-crumbs, and fry in hot lard for about 10 minutes; let them drain before the fire; dish them on a napkin, and serve.

TIME.—10 *minutes to fry the rissoles.*
SEASONABLE *at any time.*

Note.—The flavour of these rissoles may be very much increased by adding finely-minced tongue or ham, or even chopped onions when these are liked.

Potato Salad. — INGREDIENTS *for salad for 8 persons.*—10 or 12 cold boiled potatoes, 4 tablespoonfuls of tarragon or plain vinegar, 6 tablespoonfuls of salad-oil, pepper and salt to taste, 1 teaspoonful of minced parsley. AVERAGE COST, 4d.

Cut the potatoes into slices about ½ inch in thickness; put these into a salad-bowl with oil and vinegar in the above proportion; season with pepper, salt and a teaspoonful of minced parsley; stir the salad well, that all the ingredients may be thoroughly incorporated, and it is ready to serve. This should be made two or three hours before it is wanted for table. Anchovies, olives or pickles may be added to this salad, as also slices of cold beef, fowl or turkey.

SEASONABLE *at any time.*

Potato Sanders. (Vegetarian Recipe.) — INGREDIENTS. — *Cold boiled potatoes, flour, bread-crumbs, soaked in water, minced parsley or herbs, seasoning, a little minced onion.*

Mix with the mashed potatoes sufficient flour to make a paste, roll this out and cut in small squares. Squeeze the bread dry, add the other ingredients, put a little in each square of paste and close, and bake as a sausage roll.

SEASONABLE *at any time.*

Potato Snow. — INGREDIENTS. — *Potatoes, salt and water.*

Choose large white potatoes, as free from spots as possible; boil them in their skins in salt and water until perfectly tender; drain and *dry them thoroughly* by the side of the fire, and peel them. Put a hot dish before the fire, rub the potatoes through a coarse sieve on to this dish; do not touch them afterwards, or the flakes will fall, and serve as hot as possible.

TIME.—*From ½ to ¾ hour to boil the potatoes.*

SEASONABLE *at any time.*

Potato Soup. — INGREDIENTS *for soup for 8 persons.*—4 lbs. of mealy potatoes, boiled or steamed very dry, pepper and salt to taste, 2 quarts of stock. AVERAGE COST, 1s. 6d.

Mash the boiled potatoes smoothly, that no lumps remain, and gradually put them to the boiling stock; pass it through a sieve, season and simmer for 5 minutes. Skim well, and serve with fried bread.

TIME.—½ hour.

SEASONABLE *from September to March.*

Potato Soup. — INGREDIENTS *for soup for 9 or 10 persons.*—1 lb. of shin of beef, 1 lb. of potatoes, 1 onion, ½ a pint of peas, 2 oz. of rice, 2 heads of celery, pepper and salt to taste; 3 quarts of water.

Cut the beef into thin slices, chop the potatoes and onion, and put them into a stewpan, with the water, peas and rice. Stew gently till the gravy is drawn from the meat; strain it off, take out the beef, and pulp the other ingredients through a coarse sieve. Put the pulp back into the soup, cut up the celery in it, and simmer till this is tender. Season, and serve with fried bread cut into it.

TIME.—3 hours.

SEASONABLE *from September to March.*

Potato Soup. (Very Economical.)— INGREDIENTS *for soup for 4 persons.*—4 middle-sized potatoes, well pared, a thick slice of bread, 6 leeks, peeled and cut into thin slices as far as the white extends upwards from the roots, a teacupful of rice, a teaspoonful of salt, and half that of pepper, and 2 quarts of water. AVERAGE COST, 3½d.

The water must be completely boiling before anything is put into it; then add the whole of the ingredients at once, with the exception of the rice, the salt and the pepper. Cover, and let these come to a brisk boil; put in the others, and let the whole boil slowly for an hour, or till all the ingredients are thoroughly done, and their several juices extracted and mixed.

TIME.—2½ hours.

SEASONABLE *at any time.*

Potatoes.—To Sir Walter Raleigh has generally been attributed the introduction of these valuable vegetables into England, but as a matter of fact, Sir Francis Drake brought them into this country a year before, in 1585, just 20 years after they had been taken to Ireland by Sir John Hawkins.

Besides being in themselves a most useful, in fact, now an almost indispensable food, from potatoes other foods are obtained. The best substitute for arrowroot is made from the starch in potatoes, and, where flour is scarce, they are largely used in bread. Spirit is also made from potatoes by boiling the starch with weak sulphuric acid, which changes it into what is called grape water, this, being fermented, yielding alcohol. Potatoes are deficient in flesh-formers, but rich in heat-giving properties.

CONSTITUENT PARTS OF 1 LB. OF POTATOES.

				oz.	grs.
Water	...	...	...	12	0
Albumenoids	...	...	...	0	161
Starch, sugar, etc.	...	...	...	3	185
Fat ...	...	...	...	0	21
Mineral Matter	...	...	...	0	70
				16	0

Potatoes, Baked.—INGREDIENTS. —*Potatoes.*

Choose large potatoes, as much of a size as possible ; wash them in lukewarm water, and scrub them well, for the browned skin of a baked potato is by many persons considered the better part of it. Put them into a moderate oven and bake them for about two hours, turning them three or four times whilst they are cooking. Serve them in a napkin immediately they are done, as, if kept a long time in the oven, they have a

shrivelled appearance. Potatoes may also be roasted before the fire in an American oven ; but when thus cooked they must be

BAKED POTATOES.

done very slowly. Do not forget to send to table with them some butter.

TIME.—*Large potatoes, in a hot oven,* 1½ *to* 2 *hours ; in a cool oven,* 2 *to* 2½ *hours.*

SEASONABLE *all the year, but not good just before and whilst new potatoes are in season.*

Potatoes, To Boil.—INGREDIENTS *for dish for* 5 *persons.*—10 *or* 12 *potatoes ; to each* ½ *gallon of water allow* 1 *heaped tablespoonful of salt.* AVERAGE COST, 3*d.*

Choose potatoes of an equal size, pare them, take out all the eyes and specks, and as they are peeled, throw them into cold water. Put them into a saucepan with sufficient *cold* water to cover them, with salt in the above proportion, and let them *boil gently* until tender. Ascertain when they are done by thrusting a fork in them,

BOILED POTATOES.

and take them up the moment they feel soft through ; for if they are left in the water afterwards, they become waxy or watery. Drain away the water, put the saucepan by the side of the fire, with the lid partially removed, to allow the steam to escape, and let the potatoes get thoroughly dry, and do not allow them to get burnt. Their superfluous moisture will evaporate, and the potatoes, if a good sort, should be perfectly mealy and dry. Potatoes vary so much in quality and size that it is difficult to give the exact time for boiling; they should be attentively watched, and probed with a fork to ascertain when they are cooked. Send them to table quickly, and very hot, and with an opening in the cover of the dish, that a portion of the steam may evaporate, and not fall back on the potatoes.

TIME.—*Moderate-sized old potatoes*, 15 *to* 20 *minutes after the water boils; large ones*, ½ *hour to* 35 *minutes.*

SEASONABLE *all the year, but not good just before and whilst new potatoes are in season.*

Note.—To keep potatoes hot, after draining the water from them, put a folded cloth or flannel (kept for the purpose) on the top of them, keeping the saucepan-lid partially removed. This will absorb the moisture, and keep them hot some time without spoiling.

Potatoes, To Boil, in their Jackets.—INGREDIENTS *for dish for* 5 *or* 6 *persons.*—10 *or* 12 *potatoes; to each* ½ *gallon of water allow* 1 *heaped tablespoonful of salt.* AVERAGE COST, 3*d.*

To obtain this wholesome and delicious vegetable cooked in perfection it should be boiled and sent to table with the skin on. In Ireland, where, perhaps, the cooking of potatoes is better understood than in any country, they are always served so. Wash the potatoes well, and if necessary, use a clean scrubbing-brush to remove the dirt from them; and, if possible, choose the potatoes so that they may all be as nearly the same size as possible. When thoroughly cleansed, fill the saucepan half full with them, and just cover the potatoes with cold water, salted in the above proportion; they are more quickly boiled with a small quantity of water, and, besides, are more savoury than when drowned in it. Bring them to boil, then draw the pan to the side of the fire, and let them simmer gently until tender. Ascertain when they are done by probing them with a fork;

then pour off the water, uncover the saucepan, and let the potatoes dry by the side of the fire, taking care not to let them burn. Peel them quickly, put them in a very hot vegetable-dish, either with or without a napkin, and serve very quickly. After potatoes are cooked they should never be entirely covered up, as the steam, instead of escaping, falls down on them, and makes them watery and insipid. In Ireland, they are usually served up with the skins on, and a small plate is placed by the side of each guest.

TIME.—*Moderate-sized potatoes, with their skins on*, 20 *to* 25 *minutes after the water boils; large potatoes*, 25 *minutes to* ¾ *hour, or longer;* 5 *minutes to dry them.*

SEASONABLE *all the year, but not good just before and whilst new potatoes are in season.*

Potatoes, New, To Boil.—INGREDIENTS.—*Potatoes; to each* ½ *gallon of water allow* 1 *heaped tablespoonful of salt.* AVERAGE COST, 2*d. per lb.*

Do not have the potatoes dug long before they are dressed, as they are never good when they have been out of the ground some time. Well wash them, rub off the skins with a coarse cloth, and put them into *boiling* water, salted in the above proportion. Let them boil until tender; try them with a fork, and when done, pour the water away from them; let them stand by the side of the fire with the lid of the saucepan partially removed, and when the potatoes are thoroughly dry, put them into a hot vegetable-dish, with a piece of butter the size of a walnut; pile the potatoes over this, and serve. If the potatoes are too old to have the skin rubbed off, boil them in their jackets; drain, peel and serve them as above, with a piece of butter placed in the midst of them.

TIME.—¼ *to* ½ *hour, according to the size.*

SEASONABLE *in May and June, but may be had, forced, in March.*

Potatoes, Fried. (French Fashion.)

—INGREDIENTS. — *Potatoes, hot butter or clarified dripping, salt.*

Peel and cut the potatoes into thin slices, as nearly the same size as possible, or in ribbons with a cutter; make some butter or dripping *hot* in a frying-pan; put in the potatoes, and fry them on both sides until *nearly* cooked. Now take the potatoes out of the fat, make the fat *quite boiling*, then throw in the potatoes for a minute or two until sufficiently done. The immersion of the vegetable in the grease a second time, after it is partially cooked, causes it to puff or "gonfler," as the French say, which is the desired appearance for properly-dressed fried potatoes to possess. When they are crisp and done, take them up, place them on a cloth before the fire to drain the grease from them, and serve very hot, after sprinkling them with salt. These are generally served with pheasants and other game-birds as a garnish, they are also delicious with rump-steak, and, in France, are frequently served thus as a breakfast dish. The remains of cold potatoes may also be sliced and fried by the above recipe, but the slices must be cut a little thicker.

TIME.—*Sliced raw potatoes, 5 minutes; cooked potatoes, 5 minutes.*

SEASONABLE *at any time.*

Potatoes, A German Method

of Cooking.—INGREDIENTS.—8 *to* 10 *middling-sized potatoes,* 3 *oz. of butter,* 2 *table-spoonfuls of flour,* ½ *pint of broth,* 2 *table-spoonfuls of vinegar.* AVERAGE COST, 9*d.*

Put the butter and flour into a stewpan; stir over the fire until the butter is of a nice brown colour, and add the broth and vinegar; peel and cut the potatoes into long thin slices, lay them in the gravy, and let them simmer gently until tender, which will be in from 10 to 15 minutes, and serve very hot. A laurel-leaf simmered with the potatoes is an improvement.

TIME.—10 to 15 *minutes.*

SEASONABLE *at any time.*

Potatoes à la Maître d'Hôtel

INGREDIENTS.—*Potatoes, salt and water, to every* 6 *potatoes allow* 1 *tablespoonful of minced parsley,* 2 *oz. of butter, pepper and salt to taste,* 4 *tablespoonfuls of gravy,* 2 *tablespoonfuls of lemon-juice.*

Wash the potatoes clean, and boil them in salt and water; when they are done drain them, let them cool; then peel and cut the potatoes into thick slices: if these are too thin, they will break in the sauce. Put the butter into a stewpan with the pepper, salt, gravy and parsley; mix these ingredients well together, put in the potatoes, shake them two or three times, that they may be well covered with the sauce, and, when quite hot through, squeeze in the lemon-juice, and serve.

TIME.—½ to ¾ *hour to boil the potatoes,* 10 *minutes for them to heat in the sauce.*

SEASONABLE *all the year.*

Potatoes, Mashed. — INGREDI-

ENTS *for dish for* 6 *persons.*—3 *lbs. of potatoes,* 2 *oz. of butter,* 3 *tablespoonfuls of milk, salt to taste.* AVERAGE COST, 6*d.*

Boil the potatoes in their skins; when done, drain them, and let them get thoroughly dry by the side of the fire; then peel them and, as they are peeled, put them into a clean saucepan, and with a *large fork* beat them to a light paste; add butter, milk and salt in the above proportion, and stir all the ingredients well over the fire. When thoroughly hot, dish them lightly, and draw the fork backwards over the potatoes to make the surface rough, and serve. When dressed in this manner, they may be browned at the top with a salamander, or before the fire. Some cooks press the potatoes into moulds, then turn them out, and brown them in the oven: this is a pretty mode of serving, but it makes them heavy. In whatever way they are sent to table, care must be taken to have them quite free from lumps.

TIME.—½ to ¾ *hour to boil the potatoes.*

SEASONABLE *at any time.*

Potatoes, Very Thin-mashed,
or Purée de Pommes de Terre.— INGRE-
DIENTS.—*To every lb. of mashed potatoes
allow ¼ pint of good broth or stock, 2 oz. of
butter.*

Boil the potatoes, well drain them, and
pound them smoothly in a mortar, or beat
them up with a fork; add the stock or
broth, and rub the potatoes through a sieve.
Put the purée into a very clean saucepan
with the butter; stir it well over the fire
until thoroughly hot, and it will then be
ready to serve. A purée should be rather
thinner than mashed potatoes, and is a
delicious accompaniment to delicately-
broiled mutton cutlets. Cream or milk
may be substituted for the broth when the
latter is not at hand. A casserole of potatoes, which is often used for ragoûts instead
of rice, is made by mashing potatoes rather
thickly, placing them on a dish, and making
an opening in the centre. After having
browned the potatoes in the oven, the dish
should be wiped clean, and the ragoût or
fricassée poured in.

TIME.—*About ½ hour to boil the potatoes;
6 or 7 minutes to warm the purée.*

SEASONABLE *at any time.*

Potatoes, How to use Cold.—
INGREDIENTS.—*The remains of cold potatoes; to every lb. allow 2 tablespoonfuls of
flour, 2 ditto of minced onions, 1 oz. of buttermilk.*

Mash the potatoes with a fork until perfectly free from lumps; stir in the other
ingredients, and add sufficient milk to
moisten them well; press the potatoes into
a mould, and bake in a moderate oven until
nicely brown, which will be in from 20
minutes to ½ hour. Turn them out of the
mould, and serve.

TIME.—*20 minutes to ½ hour.*

SEASONABLE *at any time.*

Potatoes, To Steam.—INGREDI-
ENTS.—*Potatoes; boiling water.*

This mode of cooking potatoes is now
much in vogue, particularly where they are
wanted on a large scale, it being so very
convenient. Pare the potatoes, throw them
into cold water as they are peeled, then put
them into a steamer. Place the steamer
over a saucepan of boiling water, and steam
the potatoes from 20 to 40 minutes, according to the size and sort. When a fork goes
easily through them, they are done; then
take them up, dish, and serve very quickly.

TIME.—*20 to 40 minutes.*

SEASONABLE *all the year, but not so good
whilst new potatoes are in season.*

Pot au Feu.—INGREDIENTS *for soup
for 6 persons.*—*1½ lb. of lean beef, ¼ lb. of
bones, 3 quarts of water, 1 oz. of salt, 2
carrots, 2 turnips, 2 leeks, 1 head of celery,
2 or 3 cloves.* AVERAGE COST, 1s. 6d.

Bone the meat and tie it up with string,
chop the bones and put them at the bottom
of the saucepan, and over them the meat.
Pour in the water and add the salt, and let
boil with the lid of the saucepan leaving an
inch wide opening. As soon as the scum
rises add ½ pint of cold water, and take off
the scum with a skimmer. Repeat this,
boiling and skimming twice after the first
time, and after this the broth should be
perfectly clear. Wipe the edges of the
stewpan carefully and add the vegetables,
which will stop the boiling. As soon as it
boils up again, draw the pan aside, so that
only part of it is over the fire. Place cinders on the fire to subdue the heat, which
should be regular and gentle for 3 hours,
during which the broth should simmer.
Take out the meat and bones, take off all
fat, and pour into the tureen, when, if more
salt be necessary, it should be added.

TIME.—*3 hours to simmer.*

SEASONABLE *at any time.*

Poulet aux Cressons.—INGREDI-
ENTS *for dish for 4 or 5 persons.*—*1 fowl, 1
large bunch of watercresses, 3 tablespoonfuls of vinegar, ¼ pint of gravy.* AVERAGE
COST, 3s.

Truss and roast a fowl by recipe, taking care that it is nicely frothed and brown. Wash and dry the watercresses, pick them nicely and arrange them in a flat layer on a dish. Sprinkle over a little salt and the above proportion of vinegar; place over these the fowl, and pour over it the gravy. A little gravy should be served in a tureen. When not liked, the vinegar may be omitted.

TIME.—*From ½ to 1 hour, according to size.*

SEASONABLE *at any time.*

Poulet à la Marengo.—INGREDIENTS *for dish for 5 persons.*—1 *large fowl,* 4 *tablespoonfuls of salad oil,* 1 *tablespoonful of flour,* 1 *pint of stock or water, about* 28 *mushroom-buttons, salt and pepper to the taste,* 1 *teaspoonful of powdered sugar, a very small piece of garlic.* AVERAGE COST, 3s. 6d.

Cut the fowl into 8 or 10 pieces, put them with the oil into a stewpan, and brown them over a moderate fire; dredge in the above proportion of flour; when that is brown, pour in the stock or water, let it simmer very slowly for rather more than ½ an hour, and skim off the fat as it rises to the top; add the mushrooms, season with pepper, salt, garlic and sugar; take out the fowl, which arrange pyramidically on a dish, with the inferior joints at the bottom. Reduce the sauce by boiling it quickly over the fire, keeping it stirred until sufficiently thick to adhere to the back of the spoon; pour over the fowl, and serve.

TIME.—*Altogether, 50 minutes.*

SEASONABLE *at any time.*

Poultry and Game.—There are about thirty different kinds of birds used as food in Great Britain, but only three animals that come under this class, namely the hare, the rabbit and the deer. The flesh of both hare and rabbit approaches very nearly to the texture and constituents of poultry, but venison is more like that of well-seasoned mutton.

The chief characteristic of the flesh of fowls is the almost total absence of fat, and when it does exist, it renders digestion more difficult. The flesh of game appears to be the only kind of animal food that can be eaten with impunity when decomposed, or, as it is usually termed, "high."

As it would not be possible to give an analysis of the constituent parts of the many kinds of poultry and game, we confine ourselves to that of the one more in request than any other.

CONSTITUENT PARTS OF 1 LB. OF FOWL.

	oz.	grs.
Water	12	107
Albumenoids	3	156
Fat...		Traces
Mineral Matter	0	174
	16	0

Pound Cake.—INGREDIENTS *for large cake.*—1 *lb. of butter,* 1¼ *lb. of flour,* 1 *lb. of pounded loaf sugar,* 1 *lb. of currants,* 9 *eggs,* 2 *oz. of candied peel,* ½ *oz. of citron,* ½ *oz. of sweet almonds; when liked, a little pounded mace.* AVERAGE COST, 3s. 6d.

Work the butter to a cream; dredge in the flour; add the sugar, currants, candied

POUND CAKE.

peel, which should be cut into neat slices, and the almonds, which should be blanched and chopped, and mix all these well together; whisk the eggs, and let them be thoroughly blended with the dry ingredients. Beat the cake well for 20 minutes, and put it into a round tin, lined at the bottom and sides with a strip of white buttered paper. Bake it from 1½ to 2 hours and let the oven be well heated when the cake is first put in, as, if this is not the case, the currants will all sink to the bottom of it. To make this preparation light, the yolks and whites of the eggs should be beaten separately, and added separately to the other ingredients. A glass of wine is sometimes added to the mixture ; but this is scarcely necessary, as the cake will be found quite rich enough without it.

TIME.—1½ to 2 *hours.*

SEASONABLE *at any time.*

Pralines, Lemon.—INGREDIENTS. —*Lemons and sugar.*

Pare some lemons, and cut the rinds into pieces an inch long and very narrow. Boil some sugar nearly to a caramel, put in the lemon shreds, stirring them about well with a large wooden spoon till cold ; then set them on a sieve to shake off the loose sugar, and store in tin boxes.

Pralines, Pistachio. — INGREDIENTS.—*Equal quantities of loaf sugar and pistachio nuts, rose-water for flavouring.*

Dissolve the sugar in water till it can be made into a ball, add to it the nuts, blanched and chopped ; take the pan from the fire, stirring them till they have taken all the sugar, then put the pan on again, and boil to a caramel. Put the pralines next on a sieve, and scatter over sufficient rose-water to flavour them.

Prawn Soup. — INGREDIENTS *for soup for 8 persons.* — *Two quarts of fish stock, two pints of prawns, the crumb of a French roll, anchovy sauce or mushroom ketchup to taste, one blade of mace, ¼ pint of vinegar, a little lemon-juice.* AVERAGE COST, 5s.

Pick out the tails of the prawns, put the bodies in a stewpan with 1 blade of mace, ¼ pint of vinegar and the same quantity of water ; stew them for ¼ hour, and strain off the liquor. Put the fish stock into a stewpan ; add the strained liquor, pound the prawns with the crumb of a roll moist-

ened with a little of the soup, rub them through a tammy and mix them by degrees with the soup ; add ketchup or anchovy sauce to taste, with a little lemon-juice. When it is well cooked, put in a few picked prawns ; let them get thoroughly hot, and serve. If not thick enough, put in a little butter and flour.

TIME.—1 *hour.*

SEASONABLE *at any time.*

Note.—This can be thickened with tomatoes, and vermicelli served in it, which makes it a very tasteful soup.

Prawns, Curried.—INGREDIENTS *for entrée for 3 persons.*—2 *dozen prawns,* 2 *oz. of butter,* 2 *tablespoonfuls of curry-powder, a sour apple, an onion, a small cocoanut, the juice of ½ lemon, ½ pint of stock.* AVERAGE COST, 2s. 6d.

Melt the butter in a stewpan, and fry in it the onion, cut in very thin slices ; stir in the curry-powder, and see that the mixture is smooth before adding the stock, which should first be made hot. Next add the apple, chopped, and a large tablespoonful of grated cocoanut, and salt to taste, and simmer for about ¼ hour. Then put in the

PRAWNS.

prawns, picked, a wineglassful of the cocoanut-milk and the lemon-juice, and let the fish get quite hot. Serve with boiled rice, as other curries.

Tinned prawns can also be used for curry, and cost far less than the fresh ones.

TIME.—15 *minutes to simmer.*

SEASONABLE *at any time.*

Prawns, To Dress.—Cover a dish with a large cup reversed, and over that lay a small white napkin. Arrange the prawns on it in the form of a pyramid, and garnish with plenty of parsley. Sometimes prawns are stuck into a lemon cut in

half the long way, and garnished with parsley.

Preserves. — From the nature of vegetable substances, and chiefly from their not passing so rapidly into the putrescent state as animal bodies, the mode of preserving them is somewhat different, although the general principles are the same. All the means of preservation are put in practice occasionally for fruits and the various parts of vegetables, according to the nature of the species, the climate, the uses to which they are applied, &c. Some are dried, as nuts, raisins, sweet herbs, &c.; others are preserved by means of sugar, such as many fruits whose delicate juices would be lost by drying; some are preserved by means of vinegar, and chiefly used as condiments or pickles; a few also by salting, as French beans; while others are preserved in spirits. We have, however, in this place to treat of the best methods of preserving fruits. Fruit is a most important item in the economy of health; the epicurean can scarcely be said to have any luxuries without it; therefore, as it is so invaluable, when we cannot have it fresh, we must have it preserved. It has long been a desideratum to preserve fruits by some cheap method, yet by such as would keep them fit for the various culinary purposes, as making tarts and other similar dishes. The expense of preserving them with sugar is a serious objection; for, except the sugar be used in considerable quantities, the success is very uncertain. Sugar also overpowers and destroys the sub-acid taste so desirable in many fruits; those which are preserved in this manner are chiefly intended for the dessert. Fruits intended for preservation should be gathered in the morning, in dry weather, with the morning sun upon them, if possible; they will then have their fullest flavour, and keep in good condition longer than when gathered at any other time. Until fruit can be used, it should be

placed in the dairy, an ice-house, or a refrigerator. In an ice house it will remain fresh and plump for several days. Fruit gathered in wet or foggy weather will soon be mildewed, and be of no service for preserves.

Having secured the first and most important contribution to the manufacture of preserves—the fruit, the next consideration is the preparation of the syrup in which the fruit is to be suspended; and this requires much care. In the confectioner's art there is a great nicety in proportioning the degree of concentration of the syrup very exactly to each particular case; and he knows this by signs, and expresses it by certain technical terms. But to distinguish these properly requires very great attention and considerable experience. The principal thing to be acquainted with is the fact that, in proportion as the syrup is longer boiled, its water will become evaporated, and its consistency will be thicker. Great care must be taken in the management of the fire, that the syrup does not boil over, and that the boiling is not carried to such an extent as to burn the sugar.

The first degree or consistency is called *the thread*, which is subdivided into the little and great thread. If you dip the finger into the syrup and apply it to the thumb, the tenacity of the syrup will, on separating the finger and thumb, afford a thread, which shortly breaks: this is the little thread. If the thread, from the greater tenacity, and consequently, greater strength of the syrup, admits of a greater extension of the finger and thumb, it is called the great thread. There are half-a-dozen other terms and experiments for testing the varying thickness of the boiling sugar towards the consistency called *caramel*; but that degree of sugar-boiling belongs to the confectioner. A solution of sugar prepared by dissolving two parts of double-refined sugar (the best sugar is the most economical for preserves) in one of water, and boiling this a little, affords a syrup of the right degree of strength, and which neither ferments nor crystallizes. This appears to be the degree called *smooth* by the confectioners, and is proper to be used for the purposes of preserves. The syrup employed should sometimes be clarified, which is done in the following manner:—Dissolve 2 lbs. of loaf sugar in a pint of water; add to this solution the white of an egg and beat it well. Put the preserving-pan upon the fire with the solution; stir it with a wooden spatula, and when it begins to swell and boil up, throw in some cold water or a little oil to damp the boiling; for, as it rises suddenly, if it should boil over, it would take fire, being of a very inflammable nature. Let it boil up again; then take it off, and remove carefully the scum that has risen. Boil the solution again, throw in a little more cold water, remove the scum, and so on for three or four times successively; then strain it. It is considered to be sufficiently boiled when some taken up in a spoon pours out like oil.

Although sugar passes so easily into the state of fermentation, and is, in fact, the only substance capable of undergoing the vinous stage of that process, yet it will not ferment at all if the quantity be sufficient to constitute a very strong syrup: hence, syrups are used to preserve fruits and other vegetable substances from the changes they would undergo if left to themselves. Before sugar was in use, honey was employed to preserve many vegetable productions, though this substance has now given way to the juice of the sugar-cane.

The fruits that are the most fit for preservation in syrup are apricots, peaches, nectarines, apples, greengages, plums of all kinds and pears. As an example, take some apricots not too ripe, make a small slit at the stem end, and push out the stone; simmer them in water till they are softened and about half done, and afterwards throw them into cold water. When they have cooled, take them out and drain them. Put

the apricots into the preserving-pan with sufficient syrup to cover them; let them boil up three or four times, and then skim them; remove them from the fire, pour them into an earthen pan, and let them cool till next day. Boil them up three days successively, skimming each time, and they will then be finished and in a fit state to be put into pots for use. After each boiling, it is proper to examine into the state of the syrup when cold: if too thin, it will bear additional boiling; if too thick, it may be lowered with more syrup of the usual standard. The reason why the fruit is emptied out of the preserving-pan into an earthen pan is, that the acid of the fruit acts upon the copper, of which the preserving-pans are usually made. From this example the process of preserving fruits by syrup will be easily comprehended. The first object is to soften the fruit by blanching or boiling it in water, in order that the syrup by which it is preserved may penetrate through its substance.

Many fruits, when preserved by boiling, lose much of their peculiar and delicate flavour, as, for instance, pine-apples; and this inconvenience may, in some instances, be remedied by preserving them without heat. Cut the fruit in slices about one-fifth of an inch thick, strew powdered loaf sugar an eighth of an inch thick on the bottom of a jar, and put the slices on it. Put more sugar on this, and then another layer of the slices, and so on till the jar is full. Place the jar with the fruit up to the neck in boiling water, and keep it there till the sugar is completely dissolved, which may take half-an-hour, removing the scum as it rises. Lastly, tie a wet bladder over the mouth of the jar, or cork and wax it.

Any of the fruits that have been preserved in syrup may be converted into dry preserves, by first draining them from the syrup and then drying them in a stove or very moderate oven, adding to them a quantity of powdered loaf-sugar, which will gradually penetrate the fruit, while the liquid parts of the fruit gently evaporate. They should be dried in the stove or oven on a sieve, and turned every six or eight hours, fresh powdered sugar being sifted over them every time they are turned. Afterwards, they are to be kept in a dry situation, in drawers or boxes. Currants and cherries preserved whole in this manner, in bunches, are extremely elegant, and have a fine flavour. In this way it is, also, that orange and lemon chips are preserved.

Marmalades, jams and fruit pastes are of the same nature, and are now in very general request. They are prepared without difficulty, by attending to a very few directions; they are somewhat expensive, but may be kept without spoiling for a considerable time. Marmalades and jams differ little from each other: they are preserves of a half-liquid consistency, made by boiling the pulp of fruits, and sometimes part of the rinds, with sugar. The appellation of marmalade is applied to those confitures which are composed of the firmer fruits, as pine-apples or the rinds of oranges; whereas jams are made of the more juicy berries, such as strawberries, raspberries, currants, mulberries, &c. Fruit pastes are a kind of marmalades, consisting of the pulp of fruits, first evaporated to a proper consistency, and afterwards boiled with sugar. The mixture is then poured into a mould, or spread on sheets of tin, and subsequently dried in the oven or stove till it has acquired the state of a paste. From a sheet of this paste, strips may be cut and formed into any shape that may be desired, as knots, rings, &c. Jams require the same care and attention in the boiling as marmalade: the slightest degree of burning communicates a disagreeable empyreumatic taste; and if they are not boiled sufficiently, they will not keep. That they may keep, it is necessary not to be sparing of sugar.

In all the operations for preserve-making,

when the preserving-pan is used, it should not be placed on the fire, but on a trivet, unless the jam be made on a hot plate, when this is not necessary. If the pan be placed close on to the fire, the preserve is very liable to burn, and the colour and flavour be consequently spoiled.

Fruit jellies are compounds of the juices of fruits combined with sugar, concentrated, by boiling, to such a consistency that the liquid, upon cooling, assumes the form of a tremulous jelly.

Before fruits are candied, they must first be boiled in syrup, after which they are taken out and dried on a stove, or before the fire; the syrup is then to be concentrated, or boiled to a candy heat, and the fruit dipped in it, and again laid on the stove to dry and candy; they are then to be put into boxes, and kept dry.

Conserves consist of fresh vegetable matters beaten into a uniform mass with refined sugar; and they are intended to preserve the virtues and properties of recent flowers, leaves, roots, peels or fruits unaltered, and as near as possible to what they were when freshly gathered, and to give them an agreeable taste.

The last to be mentioned, but not the least important preparation of fruit, is the compote, which can be made at the moment of need, and with much less sugar than would be ordinarily put to preserves. Compotes are very wholesome things, suitable to most stomachs which cannot accommodate themselves to raw fruit or a large portion of sugar. They are the happy medium—far better than ordinary stewed fruit.

Prince of Wales's Soup.—INGREDIENTS *for soup for* 8 *persons.*—12 *turnips, 1 lump of sugar, 2 spoonfuls of strong veal stock, salt and white pepper to taste, 2 quarts of very bright stock.* AVERAGE COST, 2*s.*

Peel the turnips, and, with a cutter, cut

them into balls as round as possible, but very small. Put them in the stock, which must be very bright, and simmer till tender. Add the veal stock and seasoning. Have little pieces of bread cut round, about the size of a shilling ; moisten them with stock; put them into a tureen, and pour the soup over without shaking, for fear of crumbling the bread, which would spoil the appearance of the soup and make it look thick.

TIME.—2 *hours.*

SEASONABLE *in the winter.*

Prunes, Stewed. —INGREDIENTS
for dish for 4 or 5 persons.—1 *lb. of prunes,* ½ *lb. of sugar,* 1 *pint of water.* AVERAGE COST, 10*d.*

Boil the sugar and water together a few minutes, then wash the fruit and put it in and let it boil gently for 2 hours, till it is perfectly tender. Take out the prunes and boil the syrup till it is very thick, then put back the fruit and let it stand till the next day.

TIME.—2½ *hours.*

SEASONABLE *when fresh fruit is scarce.*

Ptarmigan, The, or White
Grouse.—This bird is nearly the same size as red grouse, and is fond of lofty situations, where it braves the severest weather, and is found in most parts of Europe as

THE PTARMIGAN.

well as in Greenland. At Hudson's Bay they appear in such multitudes that so many as sixty or seventy are frequently taken at once in a net. As they are as tame as chickens, this is done without difficulty.

Buffon says that the ptarmigan avoids the solar heat, and prefers the frosts of the summits of the mountains ; for, as the snow melts on the sides of the mountains, it ascends till it gains the top, where it makes a hole and burrows in the snow. In winter, it flies in flocks, and feeds on the wild vegetation of the hills, which imparts to its flesh a bitter, but not altogether unpalatable taste. It is dark-coloured, has something of the flavour of the hare, and is greatly relished and much sought after by some sportsmen.

Ptarmigan, To Carve.—Ptarmigan, being much of the same size, and trussed in the same manner as the red bird, may be carved in the manner described in Partridge and Grouse carving.

Ptarmigan, To Dress the. —
INGREDIENTS.—2 *or 3 birds; butter, flour, fried bread-crumbs.* AVERAGE COST, 2*s.* 6*d. per brace.*

The ptarmigan, or white grouse, when young and tender, are exceedingly fine eating, and should be kept as long as possible, to be good. Pluck, draw and truss them in the same manner as grouse, and roast them

PTARMIGANS.

before a brisk fire. Flour and froth them nicely, and serve on buttered toast, with a tureen of brown gravy. Bread sauce, when liked, may be sent to table with them, and fried bread-crumbs substituted for the toasted bread.

TIME.—*About* ½ *hour.*

SEASONABLE *from the beginning of February to the end of April.*

2 x

Pudding, Aunt Nelly's.—Ingredients *for pudding for 6 persons.*—½ *lb. of
flour,* ½ *lb. of treacle,* ½ *lb. of suet, the rind
and juice of* 1 *lemon, a few strips of candied
lemon-peel,* 3 *tablespoonfuls of cream,* 2 *eggs.*
Average Cost, 1s.

Chop the suet finely; mix it with the
flour, treacle, lemon-peel, minced, and candied lemon-peel; add the cream, lemon-juice
and 2 well-beaten eggs; beat the pudding

SULTANA PUDDING.

well, put it into a buttered basin, tie it
down with a cloth, and boil from 3½ to 4
hours.

Time.—3½ *to* 4 *hours.*

Seasonable *at any time, but more suitable for a winter pudding.*

Pudding, Cold.—Ingredients *for
pudding for 6 persons.*—4 *eggs,* 1 *pint of
milk, sugar to taste, a little grated lemon-
rind,* 2 *oz. of raisins,* 4 *tablespoonfuls of
marmalade, a few slices of sponge-cake.*
Average Cost, 1s.

Sweeten the milk with lump sugar, add a
little grated lemon-rind, and stir to this the

MOULDED PUDDING.

eggs, which should be well-whisked; line a
buttered mould with the raisins, stoned and
cut in half; spread the slices of cake with
the marmalade, and place them in the
mould; then pour in the custard, tie the

pudding down with paper and a cloth, and
boil gently for 1 hour; when cold, turn it
out, and serve.

Time.—1 *hour.*

Seasonable *at any time.*

Pudding - Pies, Folkestone. —
Ingredients *for* 12 *puddings.*—1 *pint of
milk,* 3 *oz. of ground rice,* 3 *oz. of butter,*
¼ *lb. of sugar, flavouring of lemon-peel or
bay-leaf,* 4 *eggs, puff-paste, currants.* Average Cost, 1s. 2d.

Infuse 2 laurel or bay-leaves, or the rind
of ½ lemon in the milk, and when it is well
flavoured, strain it and add the rice; boil
these for ¼ hour, stirring all the time; then
take them off the fire, pour in the butter,
sugar and eggs, and let these latter be well
beaten before they are added to the other
ingredients; when nearly cold, line some
patty-pans with puff-paste, fill with the
custard, strew over each a few currants, and
bake from 20 to 25 minutes in a moderate
oven.

Time.—20 *to* 25 *minutes.*

Seasonable *at any time.*

Puddings, Recipes for.—Directions for making the following appear under
their respective headings:—

Marbled Jelly

Trifle.

Blanc Mange.

Almond Puddings.

Rout Cakes.

Jam Pudding

Tartlets.

Mince Pies

Vanilla Cream.

Apple Marmalade Tart

Cherry Tart.

Pear & Apple Dumplings

Dessert Biscuits.

Charlotte Russe.

Gingerbread Pudding.

Fruit Tart.

Milk Pudding

Christmas Plum Pudding.

Apples & Rice

Pancakes

SWEETS

Puff-paste Rings, or Puits
d'Amour.—INGREDIENTS.—*Puff-paste* (*see*
PASTE), *the white of an egg, sifted loaf
sugar.*

Make some good puff-paste by recipe;
roll it out to the thickness of about ¼ inch,
and, with a round fluted paste-cutter,
stamp out as many pieces as may be
required; then work the paste up again,
and roll it out to the same thickness, and
with a *smaller* cutter, stamp out sufficient
pieces to correspond with the larger ones.
Again stamp out the centre of these
smaller rings; brush over the others with
the white of an egg, place a small ring on
the top of every large circular piece of
paste, egg over the tops, and bake from 15
to 20 minutes. Sift over sugar, put them
back in the oven to colour them; then fill
the rings with preserve of any bright
colour. Dish them high on a napkin, and
serve. So many pretty dishes of pastry
may be made by stamping puff-paste out
with fancy cutters, and filling the pieces,
when baked, with jelly or preserve, that
our space will not allow us to give a
separate recipe for each of them; but as
they are all made from one paste, and only
the shape and garnishing varied, perhaps
it is not necessary, and by exercising a
little ingenuity, variety may always be
obtained. Half-moons, leaves, diamonds,
stars, shamrocks, rings, &c., are the most
appropriate shapes for fancy pastry.

TIME.—15 *to* 25 *minutes.*

SEASONABLE *at any time.*

Pumpkin Pie. (American Recipe.)
—INGREDIENTS *for large pie.*—*Pumpkin,
6 eggs, 3 pints of milk, ½ lb. of loaf sugar,
flavouring of mace and nutmeg.* AVERAGE
COST, 1*s.* 6*d.*

Pare the pumpkin, take out the seeds,
and stew till soft, press it through a sieve,
and to a quart of the pulp allow the ingredients named. Mix first with it the sugar,
then the milk, then the yolks and whites of
the eggs, beaten separately, and beat all

together. Line a pie-dish with puff-paste, pour in the mixture, and bake in a quick oven.

TIME.—¾ *hour to bake the pie.*

SEASONABLE *in summer.*

Pumpkin Pies.—INGREDIENTS.—*To every quart of pumpkin, strained, allow 6 eggs, ¼ lb. of butter, ½ pint of sweet milk, ¾ lb. of white sugar, 1 tablespoonful of French brandy, 1 gill of madeira or sherry.* AVERAGE COST, 2s. *per quart.*

Cut the pumpkin into large pieces; peel these, and put them into cold water over a very slow fire; simmer, without boiling, until every piece is tender; then strain through a colander, and afterwards through coarse muslin, squeezing out every drop of water. To every quart of the pumpkin add the ingredients given above, beating the eggs till thick and light, and stirring the butter and sugar to a cream. When well mixed, bake in a puff-paste.

TIME.—1½ *hour.*

SEASONABLE *in September and October.*

Pumpkin, Preserved.—INGREDIENTS.—*To each lb. of pumpkin allow 1 lb. of roughly-pounded loaf sugar, 1 gill of lemon-juice.*

Obtain a good sweet pumpkin; halve it, take out the seeds and pare off the rind; cut it into neat slices, or into pieces about the size of a five-shilling piece. Weigh the pumpkin, put the slices in a pan or deep dish in layers, with the sugar sprinkled between them; pour the lemon-juice over the top, and let the whole remain for 2 or 3 days. Boil altogether, adding ½ pint of water to every 3 lbs. of sugar used, until the pumpkin becomes tender; then turn the whole into a pan, where let it remain for a week; then drain off the syrup, boil it until it is quite thick: skim, and pour it, boiling, over the pumpkin. A little bruised ginger and lemon-rind, thinly pared, may be boiled in the syrup to flavour the pumpkin.

TIME.—*From ½ to ¾ hour to boil the pumpkin tender.*

SEASONABLE *in September and October, but better when made in the latter month, as the pumpkin is then quite ripe.*

Note.—Vegetable marrows are very good prepared in the same manner, but are not quite so rich.

Punch, Cold. — INGREDIENTS *for bowl for 12 persons.*—1 *bottle of rum, 2 glasses of curaçoa, 1 bottle of champagne, ¼ lb. of pounded sugar, 1 large lemon, ½ pint of water, ice.* AVERAGE COST, 8s.

Put the sugar and lemon-rind into a bowl, with the water, made boiling, poured over them. When the water is cold, and the sugar thoroughly dissolved, add the spirits and champagne and the juice of the lemon, and just before serving, break some ice into the bowl, and take out the lemon-rind. Some thin slices of quartered lemon may be floated on the top of the punch.

SEASONABLE *in Summer.*

Punch, To Make Hot.—INGREDIENTS.—½ *pint of rum, ½ pint of brandy, ¼ lb. of sugar, 1 large lemon, ½ teaspoonful of nutmeg, 1 pint of boiling water.*

Rub the sugar over the lemon until it has absorbed all the yellow part of the skin, then put the sugar into a punch-bowl; add the lemon-juice (free from pips),

PUNCH-BOWL AND LADLE.

and mix these two ingredients well together. Pour over them the boiling water, stir well together, add the rum, brandy, and nutmeg; mix thoroughly, and the punch will be ready to serve. It is very important in making good punch that all the ingredients are thoroughly incorporated; and to insure success, the processes of mixing must be diligently attended to.

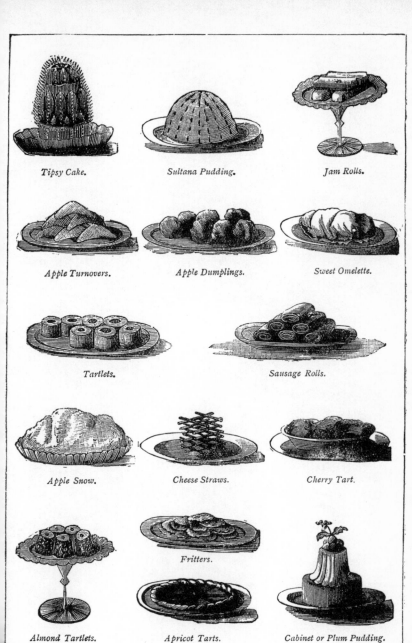

Tipsy Cake.

Sultana Pudding.

Jam Rolls.

Apple Turnovers.

Apple Dumplings.

Sweet Omelette.

Tartlets.

Sausage Rolls.

Apple Snow.

Cheese Straws.

Cherry Tart.

Almond Tartlets.

Fritters.

Apricot Tarts.

Cabinet or Plum Pudding.

Puddings, Tarts, &c.

" Quickly prepare the feast," quoth he,
" And let there be salad and quail."—ANON.

QUAILS, TO DRESS.

UAILS, To Dress.—INGREDIENTS.— *Quails, butter, toast.* AVERAGE COST, 1s. *to* 2s. *each.*

These birds keep good several days, and should be roasted without drawing. Truss them in the same manner as woodcock; roast them before a clear fire, keep them well basted, and serve on toast.

THE QUAIL.

TIME.—*About 20 minutes.*
SEASONABLE *from October to December.*

QUEEN CAKES.

Quails, Carving of.—Quails, being trussed and served like woodcock, may be similarly carved.

Quaking Pudding.—INGREDIENTS *for pudding for 6 persons.*—1 *pint of milk,* 1 *pint of cream,* 2 *tablespoonfuls of flour,* 4 *eggs, sugar and flavouring to taste.* AVERAGE COST, 2s.

Scald the cream and milk, and, when nearly cold, add the other ingredients; then pour in a buttered basin, tie a cloth over and boil for ½ hour. Carefully turn out the pudding, and send fruit or wine sauce to table with it.

TIME.—½ *hour.*
SEASONABLE *at any time.*

Queen Cakes.—INGREDIENTS *for* 18 *cakes.*—1 *lb. of flour,* ½ *lb. of butter,* ½ *lb. of pounded loaf sugar,* 3 *eggs,* 1 *teacupful of cream,* ½ *lb. of currants,* 1 *teaspoonful of carbonate of soda, essence of lemon or almonds to taste.* AVERAGE COST, 1s. 8d.

Work the butter to a cream; dredge in the flour, add the sugar and currants, and mix the ingredients well together. Whisk the eggs, mix them with the cream and flavouring and stir these to the flour; add the carbonate of soda, beat the paste well for 10 minutes, put it into small buttered pans and bake the cakes from ¼ to ½ hour. Grated lemon-rind may be substituted for the lemon or almond flavouring, which will make the cakes equally nice.

TIME.—¼ to ½ hour.
SEASONABLE at any time.

Queen Mab Pudding.

INGREDIENTS for pudding for 6 persons.—1 pint of milk, flavouring of almonds or vanilla, the rind of a lemon, 1 oz. of gelatine, ¼ lb. of loaf sugar, ½ pint of cream, 4 eggs, 2 oz. of dried citron, 2 oz. of crystallized cherries. AVERAGE COST, 2s.

Put into the milk the rind of the lemon, and heat it slowly by the side of the fire till it is well flavoured, then add some vanilla essence or any other that is liked; then add a pinch of salt and the gelatine. When dissolved, strain the milk through a muslin into a clean saucepan, with the sugar and cream, and by degrees the well beaten yolks of the eggs. Next thicken the mixture as a custard over the fire, which should be a gentle one, but do not risk it curdling. When of a good consistence, pour it out and continue stirring until half cold, then add the citron cut in small pieces and the cherries cut in halves. Well oil a mould, pour in the mixture and let it set. Serve cold. This pudding is very nice made with tinned pine-apple cut in dice in the place of the citron and cherries.

TIME.—1½ hour.
SEASONABLE at any time.

Queer Times Pudding.

INGREDIENTS for pudding for 3 or 4 persons.—½ pint of golden syrup, ½ pint of water, 2 teaspoonfuls of carbonate of soda, a teaspoonful of salt, flour. AVERAGE COST, 3d.

Mix the syrup, water, salt and soda together, and add enough flour to make a rather stiff batter. Tie the pudding in a cloth loosely, that it may have room to swell, and boil for 3 hours.

TIME.—3 hours.
SEASONABLE at any time.

Quenelles.

(For Turtle and other Soups.)—INGREDIENTS for sufficient for 6 quarts of soup.—1½ lb. of lean fillet of veal, 1 lb. of beef suet, 6 oz. of panada, 1 teaspoonful of salt, seasoning of pepper and nutmeg, 4 eggs. AVERAGE COST, 2s. 10d.

Cut the veal in long, thin slices, and scrape them with a knife till nothing but the fibre remains, then put it in a mortar, pound it to a paste, which pass through a wire sieve (what remains will do for stock); skin, shred and chop the suet fine, then pound it, adding the panada and pounding them well together. Add the veal and the seasoning, and work all well together, then the eggs slowly, continuing the pounding. When well mixed, take a small piece in a spoon and poach it, and if it is delicate, firm and of a good flavour, it is ready for use.

Quickly Made Pudding.

INGREDIENTS for 6 puddings.—¼ lb. of butter, ½ lb. of sifted sugar, ¼ lb. of flour, 1 pint of milk, 4 eggs, a little grated lemon-rind. AVERAGE COST, 1s.

Make the milk hot; stir in the butter, and let it cool before the other ingredients are added to it; then stir in the sugar, flour and eggs, which should be well whisked; flavour with a little grated lemon-rind, and beat the mixture well. Butter some small cups, rather more than half fill them; bake them 20 minutes to ½ hour, according to the size of the puddings, and serve with fruit, custard or wine-sauce, a little of which may be poured over them.

TIME.—20 minutes to ½ hour.
SEASONABLE at any time.

Quince Jelly.

INGREDIENTS.—To every pint of juice allow 1 lb. of loaf sugar. AVERAGE COST, 10d. per lb. pot.

Pare and slice the quinces, and put them into a preserving-pan with sufficient water to float them. Boil them until tender, and the fruit is reduced to a pulp; strain off the clear juice, and to each pint allow the above proportion of loaf sugar. Boil the juice and sugar together for about ¾ hour;

THE QUINCE.

remove all the scum as it rises, and if the jelly appears firm when a little is poured on a plate, it is done. The residue left on the sieve will answer to make a common marmalade for immediate use, by boiling it with ½ lb. of common sugar to every lb. of pulp.

TIME.—3 *hours to boil the quinces in water; ¾ hour to boil the jelly.*

SEASONABLE *from August to October.*

Quince Marmalade.—INGREDI-
ENTS.—*To every lb. of quince pulp allow ¾ lb. of loaf sugar.* AVERAGE COST, 9d. *per lb. pot.*

Slice the quinces into a preserving-pan, adding sufficient water for them to float: place them on the fire to stew, until reduced to a pulp, keeping them stirred occasionally from the bottom, to prevent their burning; then pass the pulp through a hair sieve, to keep back the skin and seeds. Weigh the pulp, and to each lb. add lump sugar in the above proportion, broken very small. Place the whole on the fire, and keep it well stirred from the bottom of the pan with a wooden spoon, until reduced to a marmalade, which may

be known by dropping a little on a cold plate, when, if it jellies, it is done. Put it into jars whilst hot; let it cool, and cover with pieces of oiled paper cut to the size of the mouths of the jars. The tops of them may be afterwards covered with pieces of bladder, or tissue paper brushed over on both sides with the white of an egg.

TIME.—3 *hours to boil the quinces without the sugar; ¾ hour to boil the pulp with the sugar.*

SEASONABLE *in August, September and October.*

Quinces, Preserved.—INGREDI-
ENTS.—*Quinces, sugar, water.*

Pare and quarter the fruit, then boil in enough water to keep the pieces whole. When they are tender take them out, and to every pound of quince add the same of white sugar. Let them stand with the sugar on until the next day, when the syrup should be as clear as amber; then put them in the pan and boil for 20 minutes more. They may be coloured with a little cochineal. The water in which they were boiled may be made into a jelly with the parings, adding a pound of sugar to each pint of juice, and boiling for ½ an hour.

TIME.—3 *hours.*

SEASONABLE *in August, September and October.*

Quin's Sauce. (An Excellent Fish Sauce.)—INGREDIENTS.—½ *pint of walnut pickle,* ½ *pint of port wine,* 1 *pint of mushroom ketchup,* 1 *dozen anchovies,* 1 *dozen shalots,* ¼ *pint of soy,* ½ *teaspoonful of cayenne.*

Put all the ingredients into a saucepan, having previously chopped the shalots and anchovies very small; simmer for 15 minutes, strain, and, when cold, bottle off for use; the corks should be well sealed to exclude the air.

TIME.—¼ *hour.*

SEASONABLE *at any time.*

" Right royal fare
Lay ready there,
Old England's prime roast beef."—
THE KNIGHT'S GUEST.

ABBIT, Boiled.—IN-GREDIENTS *for dish for 4 persons.—Rabbit; water.* AVERAGE COST, 1s. to 1s. 6d. each.

For boiling, choose rabbits with smooth and sharp claws, as that denotes they are young: should these be blunt and rugged, the ears dry and tough, the animal is old. After emptying and skinning it, wash it well in cold water, and let it soak for about ¼ hour in warm water, to draw out the blood. Bring the head round to the side, and fasten it there by means of a skewer run through that and the body. Put the rabbit into sufficient hot water to cover it, let it boil very gently until tender, which will be in from ½ to ¾ hour, according to its size and age. Dish it, and smother it either with onion, mushroom, or liver-sauce, or parsley-and-butter; the former is, however, generally preferred to any

of the last-named sauces. When liver-sauce is preferred, the liver should be boiled for a few minutes, and minced very finely or

BOILED RABBIT, WITH ONIONS.

rubbed through a sieve, before it is added to the sauce. Boiled salted pork is another usual accompaniment.

TIME.—*A very young rabbit, ½ hour; a large one, ¾ hour; an old one, 1 hour or longer.*

SEASONABLE *from September to February.*

Rabbit, Curried. — INGREDIENTS *for dish for 4 or 5 persons.*—1 *rabbit,* 2 *oz. of butter,* 3 *onions,* 1 *pint of stock,* 1 *tablespoonful of curry-powder,* 1 *tablespoonful of flour,* 1 *tablespoonful of mushroom-powder, the juice of ½ lemon, ½ lb. of rice.* AVERAGE COST, 2s.

Empty, skin and wash the rabbit thoroughly, and cut it neatly into joints. Put it into a stewpan with the butter and sliced onions, and let them acquire a nice brown colour, but do not allow them to blacken. Pour in the stock, which should be boiling; mix the curry-powder and flour smoothly with a little water, add it to the stock, with the mushroom-powder, and simmer gently for rather more than ½ hour; squeeze in the lemon-juice and serve in the centre of a dish, with an edging of boiled rice all round. Where economy is studied, water may be substituted for the stock; in this case, the meat and onions must be very nicely browned. A little sour apple and rasped cocoa-nut stewed with the curry will be found a great improvement, as in other curries.

TIME.—*Altogether,* ¾ *hour.*
SEASONABLE *in winter.*

Rabbit, Fried. — INGREDIENTS *for dish for 4 or 5 persons.*—1 *rabbit, flour, dripping,* 1 *oz. of butter,* 1 *teaspoonful of minced shalot,* 2 *tablespoonfuls of mushroom-ketchup.* AVERAGE COST, 1s. 8d.

Cut the rabbit into neat joints, and flour them well; make the dripping boil in a frying-pan, put in the rabbit, and fry it a nice brown. Have ready a very hot dish, put in the butter, shalot and ketchup; arrange the rabbit pyramidically on this, and serve as quickly as possible.

TIME.—10 *minutes.*
SEASONABLE *from September to February.*

Note.—The rabbit may be brushed over with egg, and sprinkled with bread-crumbs, and fried as above. When cooked in this manner, make a gravy in the pan, and pour it round, but not over, the pieces of rabbit.

Rabbit à la Minute.—INGREDIENTS *for dish for 4 or 5 persons.* —1 *rabbit,* ¼ *lb. of butter, salt and pepper to taste,* 2 *blades of pounded mace,* 3 *dried mushrooms,* 2 *tablespoonfuls of minced parsley,* 2 *teaspoonfuls of flour,* 2 *glasses of sherry,* 1 *pint of water.* AVERAGE COST, 2s. 3d.

Empty, skin and wash the rabbit tho-

roughly, and cut it into joints. Put the butter into a stewpan with the pieces of rabbit; add salt, pepper and pounded mace, and let it cook until three parts done; then put in the remaining ingredients, and boil for about 10 minutes; it will then be ready to serve. Fowls or hare may be dressed in the same manner.

TIME.—*Altogether,* 35 *minutes.*
SEASONABLE *from September to February.*

Rabbit Pie.—INGREDIENTS *for medium-sized pie.*—1 *rabbit, a few slices of ham or bacon, salt and white pepper to taste,* 2 *blades of pounded mace,* ½ *teaspoonful of grated nutmeg, a few forcemeat balls,* 2 *hard-boiled eggs,* ½ *pint of gravy, puff-crust.* AVERAGE COST, 2s. 6d.

Cut up the rabbit (which should be young), remove the breast-bone and bone the legs. Put the rabbit, slices of ham, forcemeat balls and hard-boiled eggs, by turns, in layers, and season each layer with pepper, salt, pounded mace and grated nut-

RABBIT PIE.

meg. Pour in about ½ pint of water, cover with crust, and bake in a well-heated oven for about 1½ hour. Should the crust acquire too much colour, place a piece of paper over it to prevent it from burning. When done, pour in at the top, by means of the hole in the middle of the crust, a little good gravy, which may be made of the breast and leg bones of the rabbit and 2 or 3 shank-bones, flavoured with onion, herbs and spices.

TIME.—1½ *hour.*
SEASONABLE *from September to February.*

Note.—The liver of the rabbit may be boiled, minced and mixed with the forcemeat balls, when the flavour is liked.

Rabbit or Hare, Ragoût of.—

INGREDIENTS *for dish for 5 persons.*—1 *rabbit, 3 teaspoonfuls of flour, 3 sliced onions, 2 oz. of butter, a few thin slices of bacon, pepper and salt to taste, 2 slices of lemon, 1 bay-leaf, 1 glass of port wine.* AVERAGE COST, 2s.

Slice the onions, and put them into a stewpan with the flour and butter; place the pan near the fire, stir well as the butter melts, till the onions become a rich brown colour, and add, by degrees, a little water or gravy till the mixture is of the consistency of cream. Cut some thin slices of bacon; lay in these, with the rabbit, cut into neat joints; add a seasoning of pepper and salt, the lemon and bay-leaf, and let the whole simmer until tender. Pour in the port wine, give one boil, and serve.

TIME.— *About ½ hour to simmer the rabbit.*

SEASONABLE *from September to February.*

Rabbit, Roast or Baked.—

INGREDIENTS *for dish for 4 or 5 persons.*—1 *rabbit, forcemeat, buttered paper, sausage-meat.* AVERAGE COST, 1s. 9d.

Empty, skin and thoroughly wash the rabbit; wipe it dry, line the inside with sausage-meat and forcemeat, to which has been added the minced liver. Sew the stuffing inside, skewer back the head

ROAST RABBIT.

between the shoulders, cut off the fore-joints of the shoulders and legs, bring them close to the body, and secure them by means of a skewer. Wrap the rabbit in buttered paper, and put it down to a bright, clear fire; keep it well basted, and, a few minutes before it is done, remove the paper, flour and froth it, and let it acquire a nice brown colour. Take out the skewers,

and serve with brown gravy and red-currant jelly. To bake the rabbit, proceed in the same manner as above; in a good oven, it will take about the same time as roasting.

TIME.—*A young rabbit, 35 minutes; a large one, about ¾ hour.*

SEASONABLE *from September to February.*

Rabbit Soup.—

INGREDIENTS *for soup for 10 or 12 persons.*—2 *large rabbits, or 3 small ones; a faggot of savoury herbs, ½ head of celery, 2 carrots, 1 onion, 1 blade of mace, salt and white pepper to taste, a little pounded mace, ½ pint of cream, the yolks of 2 eggs, boiled hard, the crumb of a French roll, 3 quarts of water.* AVERAGE COST, 4s.

Make the soup with the legs and shoulders of the rabbits, and keep the nice pieces for a dish or *entrée.* Put them into warm water to draw the blood; when quite clean, put them into a stewpan, with a faggot of herbs, and a teacupful, or rather more, of veal stock or water. Simmer slowly till done through, add the three quarts of water, and boil for an hour. Take out the rabbits, pick the meat from the bones, covering it up to keep it white; put the bones back in the liquor, add the vegetables, and simmer for two hours; skim and strain, and let it cool. Now pound the meat in a mortar, with the yolks of the eggs, and the crumb of the roll previously soaked; rub it through a tammy and gradually add it to the strained liquor, and simmer for 15 minutes. Mix arrow-root or rice-flour with the cream (say 2 dessertspoonfuls), and stir in the soup; bring it to a boil, and serve. This soup must be very white, and instead of thickening it with arrowroot or rice-flour, vermicelli or pearl barley can be boiled in a little stock, and put in five minutes before serving.

TIME.—*Nearly 4 hours.*

SEASONABLE *from September to March.*

Rabbit, Stewed.—INGREDIENTS *for dish for 4 or 5 persons.*—1 *rabbit*, 2 *large onions*, 6 *cloves*, 1 *small teaspoonful of chopped lemon-peel*, *a few forcemeat balls*, *thickening of butter and flour*, 1 *large tablespoonful of mushroom ketchup.* AVERAGE COST, 1s. 9d.

Cut the rabbit into small joints; put them into a stewpan, add the onions, sliced, the cloves and minced lemon-peel. Pour in sufficient water to cover the meat, and, when the rabbit is nearly done, drop in a few forcemeat balls, to which has been added the liver, finely chopped. Thicken the gravy with flour and butter, put in the ketchup, give one boil, and serve.

TIME.—*Rather more than ½ hour.*

SEASONABLE *from September to February.*

Rabbit, Stewed, Larded. — INGREDIENTS *for dish for 4 or 5 persons.*— 1 *rabbit*, *a few strips of bacon*, *rather more than* 1 *pint of good broth or stock*, *a bunch of savoury herbs*, *salt and pepper to taste*, *thickening of butter and flour*, 1 *glass of sherry.* AVERAGE COST, 2s.

Well wash the rabbit, cut it into quarters, lard them with slips of bacon, and fry them; then put them into a stewpan with the broth, herbs and a seasoning of pepper and salt; simmer gently until the rabbit is tender, then strain the gravy, thicken it with butter and flour, add the sherry, let it boil, pour it over the rabbit, and serve. Garnish with slices of cut lemon.

TIME.—*Rather more than ½ hour.*

SEASONABLE *from September to February.*

Rabbits, Stewed in Milk.— INGREDIENTS *for dish for 6 or 7 persons.*—2 *very young rabbits*, *not nearly half grown;* 1½ *pint of milk*, 1 *blade of mace*, 1 *dessertspoonful of flour*, *a little salt and cayenne.* AVERAGE COST, 2s.

Mix the flour very smoothly with 4 tablespoonfuls of the milk, and, when this is well mixed, add the remainder. Cut up the rabbits into joints, put them into a stewpan, with the milk and other ingredients, and simmer them *very gently* until quite tender. Stir the contents from time to time, to keep the milk smooth and prevent it from burning. ½ hour will be sufficient for the cooking of this dish.

TIME.—½ *hour.*

SEASONABLE *from September to February.*

Rabbits, To Carve.—In carving a boiled rabbit, let the knife be drawn on each side of the backbone, the whole length of the rabbit, as shown by the dotted line B to A; thus the rabbit will be in three parts. Now let the back be divided into two equal parts, in the direction of the line from C to D; then let the leg be taken off, as shown by the line E to F, and the

BOILED RABBIT.

shoulder, as shown by the line G to H. This, in our opinion, is the best plan to carve a rabbit, although there are other modes which are preferred by some.

A roast rabbit is rather differently trussed from one that is meant to be boiled; but the carving is nearly similar, as will be seen by the cut. The back should be

ROAST RABBIT.

divided into as many pieces as it will give, and the legs and shoulders can then be disengaged in the same manner as those of the boiled animal.

Rabbit, Trussing of.

Rabbit, Trussing of. — Having skinned, paunched and washed the rabbit, and taken out the eyes, cut off the fore-joints of shoulders and legs, draw the

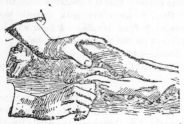

RABBIT BEING SKEWERED.

legs forward close to the body, bring the head round to the side, and skewer through all.

Raised Biscuits.

Raised Biscuits. (American Recipe.)—INGREDIENTS *for large breakfast dish.*—1 *quart of milk*, ¾ *cup of lard*, ¾ *cup of yeast*, 2 *tablespoonfuls of white sugar*, 1 *teaspoonful of salt, flour to make a soft dough.* AVERAGE COST, 10d.

Mix the ingredients over night, melting the lard and slightly warming the milk. In the morning, roll out the dough thick, and form into cakes. Put these into a baking-pan, and when they have risen for 20 minutes, bake them for another 20 minutes or ½ hour.

TIME.—40 *minutes.*

SEASONABLE *at any time.*

Raised Pie of Poultry or Game.

Raised Pie of Poultry or Game.—INGREDIENTS *for large pie.*—To every lb. of flour allow ½ lb. of butter, ½ pint of water, the yolks of 2 eggs, ½ teaspoonful of salt (these are for the crust); 1 large fowl or pheasant, a few slices of veal cutlet, a few slices of dressed ham, forcemeat, seasoning of nutmeg, allspice, pepper and salt, gravy.* AVERAGE COST, 6s.

Make a stiff short crust with the above proportion of butter, flour, water, and eggs, and work it up very smoothly; butter a raised-pie mould, and line it with paste. Previously to making the crust, bone the fowl, or whatever bird is intended to be used, lay it, breast downwards, upon a cloth, and season the inside well with pounded mace, allspice, pepper and salt; then spread over it a layer of forcemeat, then a layer of seasoned veal, and then one of ham, and then another layer of forcemeat, and roll the fowl over, making the skin meet at the back. Line the pie with forcemeat, put in the fowl, and fill up the cavities with slices of seasoned veal, and ham and forcemeat; wet the edges of the pie, put on the cover, pinch the edges together with the paste-pincers, and decorate it with leaves; brush it over with beaten yolk of egg, and bake in a moderate oven for 4 hours. In the mean time, make a good strong gravy from the bones, pour it through a funnel into the hole at the top; cover this hole with a small leaf, and the pie, when cold, will be ready for use. Let it be remembered that the gravy must be considerably reduced before it is poured into the pie, as, when cold, it should form a firm jelly, and not be the least degree in a liquid state. This recipe is suitable for all kinds of poultry or game, using one or more birds, according to the size of the pie intended to be made, but the birds must always be boned. Truffles, mushrooms, &c., added to this pie, make it much nicer; and, to enrich it, lard the fleshy parts of the poultry or game with thin strips of bacon. This method of forming raised pies in a mould is generally called a *timbale*, and has the advantage of being more easily made than one where the paste is raised by the hands; the crust, besides, being eatable. The birds may be cut up if preferred, and are then easier to bone.

TIME.—*Large pie*, 4 *hours.*

SEASONABLE *with poultry, all the year; with game, from September to March.*

Raised Pie of Veal and Ham.

Raised Pie of Veal and Ham.—INGREDIENTS *for very large pie.*—3 or 4 lbs. of veal cutlets, a few slices of bacon or ham, *seasoning of pepper, salt, nutmeg and allspice, forcemeat,* 2 lbs. *of hot-water paste,* ½ pint *of good strong gravy.* AVERAGE COST, 6s.

To raise the crust for a pie with the hands is a very difficult task, and can only be accomplished by skilled and experienced cooks. The process should be seen to be satisfactorily learnt, and plenty of practice given to the making of raised pies, as by that means only will success be insured.

RAISED PIE.

Make a hot-water paste by recipe, and from the mass raise the pie with the hands; if this cannot be accomplished, cut out pieces for the top and bottom, and a long piece for the sides; fasten the bottom and side-piece together by means of egg, and pinch the edges well together; then line the pie with forcemeat, put in a layer of veal, and a plentiful seasoning of salt, pepper, nutmeg and allspice; for, let it be remembered, these pies taste very insipid unless highly seasoned. Over the seasoning place a layer of sliced bacon or cooked ham, and then a layer of forcemeat, veal, seasoning and bacon, and so on until the meat rises to about an inch above the paste; taking care to finish with a layer of forcemeat, to fill all the cavities of the pie, and to lay in the meat firmly and compactly. Brush the top edge of the pie with beaten egg, put on the cover, press the edges, and pinch them round with paste-pincers. Make a hole in the middle of the lid, and ornament the pie with leaves, which should be stuck on with the white of an egg; then brush it all over with the beaten yolk of an egg, and bake the pie in an oven

with a soaking heat from 3 to 4 hours. To ascertain when it is done, run a sharp-pointed knife or skewer through the hole at the top into the middle of the pie, and if the meat feels tender, it is sufficiently baked. Have ready about ½ pint of very strong gravy, pour it through a funnel into the hole at the top, stop up the hole with a small leaf of baked paste, and put the pie away until wanted for use. Should it acquire too much colour in the baking, cover it with white paper, as the crust should not in the least degree be burnt. Mushrooms, truffles and many other ingredients may be added to enrich the flavour of these pies, and the very fleshy parts of the meat may be larded. These pies are more frequently served cold than hot, and form excellent dishes for cold suppers or breakfasts. The cover of the pie is sometimes carefully removed, leaving the perfect edges, and the top decorated with square pieces of very bright aspic jelly; this has an exceedingly pretty effect.

TIME.—*About* 4 *hours.*

SEASONABLE *from March to October.*

Raisin Cheese.—INGREDIENTS.—
To every lb. *of raisins allow* ½ lb. *of loaf sugar; pounded cinnamon and cloves to taste.*

Stone the raisins; put them into a stew-pan with the sugar, cinnamon and cloves, and let them boil for 1½ hour, stirring all the time. Let the preparation cool a little, pour it into a glass dish, and garnish with strips of candied lemon-peel and citron. This will remain good some time, if kept in a dry place.

TIME.—1½ *hour.*

SEASONABLE *at any time.*

Raisin Pudding, Baked. (Plain and Economical.)—INGREDIENTS *for large pudding.*—1 lb. *of flour,* ¾ lb. *of stoned raisins,* ½ lb. *of suet, a pinch of salt,* 1 oz. *of sugar, a little grated nutmeg, milk.* AVERAGE COST, 1s.

Chop the suet finely; stone the raisins and cut them in halves; mix these with the suet, add the salt, sugar and grated nutmeg, and moisten the whole with sufficient milk to make it of the consistency of thick batter. Put the pudding into a pie-dish, and bake for 1½ hour, or rather longer. Turn it out of the dish, strew sifted sugar over, and serve. This is a very plain recipe, and suitable where there is a family of children. It, of course, can be much improved by the addition of candied peel, currants and rather a larger proportion of suet; a few eggs would also make the pudding richer.

TIME.—1½ hour.

SEASONABLE in the winter.

Raisin Pudding, Boiled. (Plain and Economical.)—INGREDIENTS for large pudding.—1 lb. of flour, ½ lb. of stoned raisins, ¼ lb. of chopped suet, ½ saltspoonful of salt, milk. AVERAGE COST, 10d.

After having stoned the raisins, and chopped the suet finely, mix them with the flour, add the salt, and when these dry ingredients are thoroughly mixed, moisten the pudding with sufficient milk to make it into a rather stiff paste. Tie it up in a floured cloth, put it into boiling water, and boil for 4 hours; serve with sifted sugar. This pudding may also be made in a long shape, the same as a rolled jam-pudding, and will not require quite so long boiling—2½ hours would then be quite sufficient.

RAISIN-GRAPE.

TIME.—Made round, 4 hours; in a long shape, 2½ hours.

SEASONABLE in the winter.

Raisin Wine.—INGREDIENTS.—10 lbs. of raisins, 1 lb. of sugar, water. AVERAGE COST, 3s. 6d. per gallon.

Pick some sound large raisins, and chop them very finely. Pour a gallon of hot water upon them, and press the liquor through a bag. Let it stand 12 hours, then put in the sugar, and leave it to ferment. When this has ceased, cask it, bung it, and leave it for 3 months, when draw it off into another cask, which it must quite fill. Bung very closely and bottle 10 months later. A year afterwards it will be ready.

TIME.—About 2 years.

SEASONABLE.—Make this in autumn.

Ramekins (to serve with the Cheese Course).—INGREDIENTS for 9 or 10 tins.— ¼ lb. of Cheshire cheese, ¼ lb. of Parmesan cheese, ¼ lb. of fresh butter, 4 eggs, the crumb of a small roll; pepper, salt and pounded mace to taste. AVERAGE COST, 1s. 4d.

Boil the crumb of the roll in milk for 5 minutes; strain and put it into a mortar; add the cheese, which should be finely scraped, the butter, the yolks of the eggs and seasoning, and pound these ingredients well together. Whisk the whites of the eggs, mix them with the paste, and put it into small tins or cases, which should not be more than half filled. Bake them from 10 to 12 minutes, and serve them very hot and very quickly. This batter answers equally well for macaroni after it is boiled tender.

TIME.—10 or 12 minutes.

SEASONABLE at any time.

Ramekins, Pastry (to serve with the Cheese Course).—INGREDIENTS.—Any pieces of very good light puff-paste, Cheshire, Parmesan or Stilton cheese.

The remains or odd pieces of paste left from large tarts, &c., answer for making these little dishes. Gather up the pieces of paste, roll it out evenly, and sprinkle it with grated cheese of a nice flavour. Fold the paste in three, roll it out again, and sprinkle more cheese over; fold the paste, roll it out, and with a paste-cutter shape it in any way that may be desired. Bake the ramekins in a brisk oven from 10 to 15 minutes, dish them on a hot napkin, and serve quickly. The appearance of this dish may be very much improved by brushing the ramekins over with the yolk of egg before they are placed in the oven.

TIME.—10 to 15 minutes.

SEASONABLE at any time.

Raspberry Cream.
INGREDIENTS for quart mould.—¾ pint of milk, ¾ pint of cream, 1½ oz. of gelatine, raspberry jelly, sugar to taste, 2 tablespoonfuls of brandy. AVERAGE COST, 2s. 3d.

Boil the milk, cream and gelatine together for ¼ hour, or until the latter is melted, and strain it through a hair-sieve into a basin. Let it cool a little; then add to it sufficient raspberry jelly, which, when melted, would make ⅓ pint, and stir well until the ingredients are thoroughly mixed. If not sufficiently sweet, add a little pounded sugar with the brandy; whisk the mixture well until nearly cold, put it into a well-oiled mould, and set it in a cool

RASPBERRY-CREAM MOULD.

place till perfectly set. Raspberry jam may be substituted for the jelly; but must be melted, and rubbed through a sieve, to free it from seeds: in summer, the juice of the fresh fruit may be used, by slightly mashing it with a wooden spoon, and sprinkling sugar over it; the juice that flows from the fruit should then be used for mixing with the cream. If the colour

should not be very good, a few drops of prepared cochineal, or carmine, may be added to improve its appearance.

TIME. — ¼ hour to boil the cream and gelatine.

SEASONABLE, with jelly, at any time.

Note.—Strawberry cream may be made in precisely the same manner, substituting strawberry jam or jelly for the raspberry.

Raspberry and Currant Jam.
INGREDIENTS for 24 pots of jam.—9 lbs. of red currants, 6 lbs. of raspberries, 12 lbs. of loaf sugar. AVERAGE COST, 7s. 6d. to 8s. 6d.

Pick over the currants and stem the raspberries, and put both, with the sugar, in a preserving-pan; and after coming to the boil, boil for ¾ hour. Remove all scum as it rises, and put into pots, covering the jam with oiled paper; and then the pots with tissue-paper, brushed over with white of egg.

TIME.—¾ hour.

SEASONABLE.—Make in July.

Raspberry Ice Cream.
INGREDIENTS for 1 quart.—1 lemon, 1 lb. pot of jam, ¾ pint of cream, ¾ pint of milk, a few drops of cochineal. AVERAGE COST, 1s. 10d.

Strain the lemon-juice over the jam, colour with the cochineal, add the milk and cream, and freeze as other ices.

TIME.—25 minutes to freeze.

SEASONABLE at any time.

Raspberry Jam.
INGREDIENTS.—To every lb. of raspberries allow 1 lb. of sugar, ¼ pint of red-currant juice. AVERAGE COST, 6d. per pot.

Let the fruit for this preserve be gathered in fine weather, and used as soon after it is picked as possible. Take off the stalks, put the raspberries into a preserving-pan, break them well with a wooden spoon, and let them boil for ¼ hour, keeping them well stirred. Then add the currant-juice and sugar, and boil again for ½ hour. Skim the jam well after the sugar is added, or the preserve will not be clear. The addition of the currant-juice is a very great improvement to this preserve, as it gives it a piquant acidity, which the flavour of the raspberries seems to require.

TIME.—¼ hour to simmer the fruit without the sugar; ½ hour after it is added.

SEASONABLE. — Make in July and August.

Raspberry Jelly.—INGREDIENTS.
—To each pint of juice allow ¾ lb. of loaf sugar. AVERAGE COST, 9d. per pot.

Let the raspberries be freshly gathered, quite ripe, and picked from the stalks ; put them into a large jar, after breaking the

fruit a little with a wooden spoon, and place this jar, covered, in a saucepan of boiling water. When the juice is well drawn, which will be in from ¾ to 1 hour, strain the fruit through a fine hair-sieve or cloth ; measure the juice, and to every pint allow the above proportion of loaf sugar. Put the juice and sugar into a

RASPBERRY.

preserving-pan, place it over the fire, and boil gently until the jelly thickens when a little is poured on a plate; carefully remove all the scum as it rises, pour the jelly into small pots, cover down, and keep in a dry place. This jelly answers for making raspberry cream, and for flavouring various sweet dishes, when, in winter, the fresh fruit is not obtainable.

TIME.—¾ to 1 hour to draw the juice.

SEASONABLE.—This should be made in July or August.

Raspberry Liqueur. — INGREDI-
ENTS for 2 quarts.—1 quart of gin, 1 pint of raspberries, 1 lb. of loaf sugar, 1½ pint of water. AVERAGE COST, 3s. 3d.

Put the gin with the fruit in a bottle, which cork closely. Let it stand a fortnight, then boil the sugar and water, and when cold, filter and pour to the gin and fruit. Filter through blotting-paper, and put up in small well-corked bottles.

SEASONABLE.—Make in July.

Raspberry Vinegar. — INGREDI-
ENTS.—3 pints of the best vinegar, 4½ pints of freshly-gathered raspberries; to each pint of liquor allow 1 lb. of pounded loaf sugar and 1 wineglassful of brandy. AVERAGE COST, 1s. per pint.

Let the raspberries be freshly gathered, pick them from the stalks, and put 1½ pint of them into a stone jar; pour 3 pints of the best vinegar over them, and let them remain for 24 hours ; then strain the liquor over another 1½ pint of fresh raspberries. Let them remain another 24 hours, and the following day repeat the process for the third time ; then drain off the liquor without pressing, and pass it through a jelly-bag (previously wetted with plain vinegar) into a stone jar. Add to every pint of the liquor 1 lb. of pounded loaf sugar ; stir them together, and, when the sugar is dissolved, cover the jar, set it upon the fire in a saucepan of boiling water and let it boil for an hour, removing the scum as fast as it rises ; add to each pint a glass of brandy, bottle it and seal the corks. This is an excellent drink in cases of fevers and colds : it should be diluted with cold water, according to the taste or requirement of the patient.

TIME.—To be boiled 1 hour.

SEASONABLE. — Make this in July or August, when raspberries are most plentiful.

Ratafia Pudding.—INGREDIENTS
for larg pudding.—1 quart of milk, 4 eggs, ¼ lb. of ratafias, loaf sugar and flavouring of almonds to taste. AVERAGE COST, 1s.

Well beat the eggs, and add them to the milk, with sugar and almond flavouring to taste. Pour into a pie-dish, and on the top drop the ratafias, right side upwards, till the top is covered. Bake in a good oven for ½ hour.

TIME.—½ *hour.*

SEASONABLE *at any time.*

Ratafias. — INGREDIENTS.—½ *lb. of sweet almonds,* ¼ *lb. of bitter ones,* ¾ *lb. of sifted loaf sugar, the white of* 4 *eggs.* AVERAGE COST, 1s. 2d.

Blanch, skin and dry the almonds, and pound them in a mortar with the white of an egg; stir in the sugar, and gradually add the remaining whites of eggs, taking care that they are very thoroughly whisked. Drop the mixture through a small biscuit syringe, on to cartridge-paper, and bake the cakes from 10 to 12 minutes in rather a quick oven. A very small quantity should be dropped on the paper to form one cake, as the mixture spreads; when baked, the ratafias should be about the size of a large button.

TIME.—10 *to* 12 *minutes.*

Ravigote. (A French Salad Sauce; Mons. UDE'S Recipe.)—INGREDIENTS *for moderate-sized dish.* — 1 *teaspoonful of mushroom ketchup,* 1 *teaspoonful of cavice,* 1 *teaspoonful of chili vinegar,* 1 *teaspoonful of Reading sauce, a piece of butter the size of an egg,* 3 *tablespoonfuls of thick Béchamel,* 1 *tablespoonful of minced parsley,* 3 *tablespoonfuls of cream, salt and pepper to taste.* AVERAGE COST, 9d.

Scald the parsley, mince the leaves very fine and add to it all the other ingredients; after mixing the whole together thoroughly, the sauce will be ready for use.

SEASONABLE *at any time.*

Reading Sauce.—INGREDIENTS.— 2½ *pints of walnut pickle,* 1½ *oz. of shalots,* 1 *quart of spring water,* ¾ *pint of Indian soy,* ½ *oz. of bruised ginger,* ½ *oz. of long pepper,* 1 *oz. of mustard-seed,* 1 *anchovy,* ½ *oz. of cayenne,* ¼ *oz. of dried sweet bay-leaves.*

Bruise the shalots in a mortar, and put them in a stone jar with the walnut-liquor; place it before the fire, and let it boil until reduced to 2 pints. Then, into another jar, put all the ingredients except the bay-leaves, taking care that they are well bruised, so that the flavour may be thoroughly extracted; put this also before the fire, and let it boil for 1 hour or rather more. When the contents of both jars are sufficiently cooked, mix them together, stirring them well as you mix them, and submit them to a slow boiling for ½ hour; cover closely, and let them stand 24 hours in a cool place; then open the jar and add the bay-leaves; let it stand a week longer closed down, when strain through a flannel bag, and it will be ready for use. The above quantities will make ½ gallon.

TIME.—*Altogether,* 3 *hours.*

SEASONABLE.—*This sauce may be made at any time.*

Regency Soup.—INGREDIENTS *for soup for 8 persons.*—*The bones and remains of any cold game, such as of pheasants, partridges, &c.;* 2 *carrots,* 2 *small onions,* 1 *head of celery,* 1 *turnip,* ¼ *lb. of pearl barley, the yolks of* 3 *eggs, boiled hard,* ¼ *pint of cream, salt to taste,* 2 *quarts of medium or common stock.* AVERAGE COST, *exclusive of the cold game,* 2s. 6d.

Place the bones or remains of game in the stewpan, with the vegetables sliced; pour over the stock, and simmer for 2 hours; skim off all the fat, and strain it. Wash the barley and boil it in 2 or 3 waters before putting it to the soup; finish simmering in the soup, and when the barley is done, take out half, and pound the other half with the yolks of the eggs. When you have finished pounding, rub it through a clean tammy, add the cream, and salt if necessary; give one boil, and serve very hot, putting in the barley that was taken out first.

TIME.—2½ *hours.*

SEASONABLE *from September to March.*

Remoulade, or French Salad-

Dressing.—INGREDIENTS *for dressing for salad for 6 persons.*—4 *eggs,* ½ *tablespoonful of made mustard, salt and cayenne to taste.* 3 *tablespoonfuls of olive oil,* 1 *tablespoonful of tarragon or plain vinegar.* AVERAGE COST, 7*d.*

Boil 3 eggs quite hard for about ¼ hour, put them into cold water, and let them remain in it for a few minutes; strip off the shells, put the yolks in a mortar and pound them very smoothly; add to them, very gradually the mustard, seasoning and vinegar, keeping all well stirred and rubbed down with the back of a wooden spoon. Put in the oil very slowly, and when this is thoroughly mixed with the other ingredients, add the yolk of a raw egg and stir well, when it will be ready for use. This sauce should not be curdled; and to prevent this, the only way is to mix a little of everything at a time, and not to cease stirring. The quantities of oil and vinegar may be increased or diminished, according to taste, as many persons would prefer a smaller proportion of the former ingredient.

Green Remoulade is made by using tarragon vinegar instead of plain, and colouring with a little parsley-juice. Harvey's sauce or chili vinegar may be added at pleasure.

TIME.—¼ *hour to boil the eggs.*

Restorative Jelly.

(Invalid's Cookery.)—INGREDIENTS *for a quart.*—1 *bottle of sherry,* 2 *oz. of sugar candy,* 3 *oz. of isinglass,* 2 *oz. of gum arabic.* AVERAGE COST, 5*s.*

Put all in a jar, which cover closely, and let it stand all night; then set it in a sauce pan of water, and let it simmer till the isinglass and candy are dissolved.

SEASONABLE *at any time.*

Rhubarb Jam.

—INGREDIENTS.—*To every lb. of rhubarb allow* 1 *lb. of loaf sugar, the rind of* ½ *lemon.* AVERAGE COST, 4*d. per lb. pot.*

Wipe the rhubarb perfectly dry, take off the string or peel, and weigh it; put it into a preserving-pan, with sugar in the above proportion; mince the lemon-rind very finely, add it to the other ingredients, and place the preserving-pan by the side of the fire; keep stirring to prevent the rhubarb from burning, and when the sugar is welldissolved, put the pan more over the fire, and let the jam boil until it is done, taking care to keep it well skimmed and stirred with a wooden or silver spoon. Pour it into pots, and cover down with oiled and egged papers.

RHUBARB.

TIME.—*If the rhubarb is young and tender,* ¾ *hour, reckoning from the time it simmers equally;* old *rhubarb,* 1¼ *to* 1½ *hour.*

SEASONABLE *from February to May.*

Rhubarb and Orange Jam

(to resemble Scotch Marmalade). — INGREDIENTS.—1 *quart of finely-cut rhubarb,* 6 *oranges,* 1½ *lb. of loaf sugar.* AVERAGE COST, 6*d. per pot.*

Peel the oranges; remove as much of the white pith as possible, divide them and take out the pips; slice the pulp into a preserving-pan, add the rind of half the oranges cut into thin strips, and the loaf sugar, which should be broken small. Peel the rhubarb, cut it into thin pieces, put it to the oranges and stir all together over a gentle fire until the jam is done. Remove all the scum as it rises, put the preserve into pots, and, when cold, cover down. Should the rhubarb be very old, stew it alone for ¼ hour before the other ingredients are added.

TIME.—¾ *to* 1 *hour.*

SEASONABLE *from February to May.*

Rhubarb Pudding, Boiled.—IN-GREDIENTS *for pudding for 6 persons.*—4 *or* 5 *sticks of fine rhubarb,* ¼ *lb. of moist sugar,* ¾ *lb. of suet-crust.* AVERAGE COST, 8*d.*

Make a suet-crust with ¾ lb. of flour, and line a buttered basin with it. Wash and wipe the rhubarb, and, if old, string it—that is to say, pare off the outside skin. Cut it into inch lengths, fill the basin with it, put in the sugar and cover with crust. Pinch the edges of the pudding together, tie over it a floured cloth, put it into boiling water, and boil from 2 to 2½ hours. Turn it out of the basin, and serve with sifted sugar.

TIME.—2 *to* 2½ *hours.*

SEASONABLE *from February to May.*

Rhubarb Tart.—INGREDIENTS *for tart of medium size.*—½ *lb. of puff-paste, about* 5 *sticks of large rhubarb,* ¼ *lb. of moist sugar.* AVERAGE COST, 10*d.*

Make a puff-crust; line the edges of a deep pie-dish with it, and wash, wipe and cut the rhubarb into pieces about 1 inch long. Should it be old and tough, string it—that is to say, pare off the outside skin. Pile the fruit high in the dish, as it shrinks very much in the cooking; put in the sugar, cover with crust, ornament the edges and bake the tart in a well-heated oven from ½ to ¾ hour. If wanted very nice, brush it over with the white of an egg beaten to a stiff froth, then sprinkle on it some sifted sugar, and put it in the oven just to set the glaze: this should be done when the tart is nearly baked. A small quantity of lemon-juice and a little of the peel, minced, are by many persons considered an improvement to the flavour of rhubarb tart.

TIME.—½ *to* ¾ *hour.*

SEASONABLE *from February to May.*

Rhubarb Wine.—INGREDIENTS.—*To every* 5 *lbs. of rhubarb pulp allow* 1 *gallon of cold spring water; to every gallon of liquor allow* 3 *lbs. of loaf sugar,* ½ *oz. of isinglass, the rind of* 1 *lemon.*

Gather the rhubarb about the middle of May; wipe it with a wet cloth, and, with a mallet, bruise it in a large wooden tub, or other convenient means. When reduced to a pulp, weigh it, and to every 5 lbs. add 1 gallon of cold spring water; let these remain for 3 days, stirring 3 or 4 times a day; and on the fourth day, press the pulp through a hair sieve; put the liquor into a tub, and to every gallon put 3 lbs. of loaf sugar, stir in the sugar until it is quite dissolved, and add the lemon-rind; let the liquor remain, and, in 4, 5, or 6 days, the fermentation will begin to subside, and a crust or head will be formed, which should be skimmed off, or the liquor drawn from it when the crust begins to crack or separate. Put the wine into a cask, and if, after that, it ferments, rack it off into another cask, and in a fortnight stop it down. If the wine should have lost any of its original sweetness, add a little more loaf sugar, taking care that the cask is full. Bottle it off in February or March, and in the summer it should be fit to drink. It will improve greatly by keeping; and, should a very brilliant colour be desired, add a little currant-juice.

SEASONABLE. — *Make this about the middle of May.*

Rice.—This grass is chiefly grown in the East, but it is also cultivated in the Southern parts of Europe. It is said to be the chief food of one third of the human race, and it is a fact that more of it is grown and consumed than any other cereal. There is a great deal of starch in rice, but it is lacking, as will be seen by the following analysis of one pound, in flesh-forming qualities. It is useful as a food when employed with others possessing the latter quality, such as meat or eggs.

In cooking rice the best method is steaming, as by boiling it in the water a great part of the constituents in which it is deficient is lost. The husk of rice is largely used in the adulteration of many foods.

CONSTITUENT PARTS OF 1 LB. OF RICE.

					oz.	grs.
Water	...	...	...	...	2	147
Albumenoids	...	...	...	1	87
Starch, &c	...	...	...	...	12	133
Fat	...	...	...	...	...	0	35
Mineral matter	...	...	...	0	35
					16	0

Rice Biscuits or Cakes.—INGRE-DIENTS *for 18 cakes.*—½ *lb. of rice-flour,* ¼ *lb. of pounded lump sugar,* ¼ *lb. of butter,* 2 *eggs.* AVERAGE COST, 8*d.*

Beat the butter to a cream, stir in the rice-flour and pounded sugar, and moisten the whole with the eggs, which should be previously well beaten. Roll out the paste, shape it with a round paste-cutter into small cakes, and bake them from 12 to 18 minutes in a very slow oven.

TIME.—12 *to* 18 *minutes.*

SEASONABLE *at any time.*

Rice Blancmange.—INGREDIENTS *for quart mould.*—¼ *lb. of ground rice,* 3 *oz. of loaf sugar,* 1 *oz. of fresh butter,* 1 *quart of milk, flavouring of lemon-peel, essence of almonds or vanilla, or laurel-leaves.* AVER-AGE COST, 8*d.*

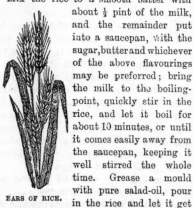

Mix the rice to a smooth batter with about ¼ pint of the milk, and the remainder put into a saucepan, with the sugar, butter and whichever of the above flavourings may be preferred; bring the milk to the boiling-point, quickly stir in the rice, and let it boil for about 10 minutes, or until it comes easily away from the saucepan, keeping it well stirred the whole time. Grease a mould with pure salad-oil, pour in the rice and let it get perfectly set, when it should turn out

EARS OF RICE.

quite easily; garnish it with jam, or pour round a compote of any kind of fruit, just before it is sent to table. This blanc-mange is better for being made the day before it is wanted, as it then has time to become firm. If laurel-leaves are used for flavouring, steep 3 of them in the milk, and take them out before the rice is added; about 8 drops of essence of almonds, or from 12 to 16 drops of essence of vanilla, would be required to flavour the above pro-portion of milk.

TIME.—*From* 10 *to* 15 *minutes to boil the rice.*

SEASONABLE *at any time.*

Rice Bread. — INGREDIENTS.— *To every lb. of rice allow* 4 *lbs. of wheat flour, nearly* 3 *tablespoonfuls of yeast,* ¼ *oz. of salt.*

Boil the rice in water until it is quite tender; pour off the water, and put the rice, before it is cold, to the flour. Mix these well together with the yeast, salt, and sufficient warm water to make the whole into a smooth dough; let it rise by the side of the fire, then form it into loaves, and bake them from 1½ to 2 hours, according to their size. If the rice is boiled in milk instead of water, it makes very delicious bread or cakes. When boiled in this manner, it may be mixed with the flour without straining the liquid from it.

TIME.—1½ *to* 2 *hours.*

Rice, Buttered.—INGREDIENTS.— ¼ *lb. of rice,* 1½ *pint of milk,* 2 *oz. of butter, sugar to taste, grated nutmeg or pounded cinnamon.*

Wash and pick the rice, drain and put it into a saucepan with the milk; let it swell gradually, and, when tender, pour off the milk; stir in the butter, sugar and nutmeg or cinnamon, and, when the butter is thoroughly melted and the whole is quite hot, serve. After the milk is poured off, be particular that the rice does not burn ; to prevent this, do not cease stirring it.

TIME.—*About ¾ hour to swell the rice.*
SEASONABLE *at any time.*

Rice Cake.—INGREDIENTS *for good-sized cake.*—½ *lb. of ground rice,* ½ *lb. of flour,* ½ *lb. of loaf sugar,* 9 *eggs,* 20 *drops of essence of lemon, or the rind of* 1 *lemon,* ¼ *lb. of butter.* AVERAGE COST, 1s. 6d.

Separate the whites from the yolks of the eggs ; whisk them both well, and add to the latter the butter beaten to a cream. Stir in the flour, rice and lemon (if the rind is used it must be very finely minced), and beat the mixture well ; then add the whites of the eggs, beat the cake again

CAKE-MOULD.

for some time, put it into a buttered mould or tin, and bake it for nearly 1½ hour. It may be flavoured with essence of almonds, when this is preferred.

TIME.—*Nearly* 1½ *hour.*
SEASONABLE *at any time.*

Rice, Savoury Casserole of ;
or Rice Border (for Ragoûts, Fricassées and Entrées).—INGREDIENTS *for* 2 *casse-roles.*—1½ *lb. of rice,* 3 *pints of weak stock or broth,* 2 *slices of fat ham,* 1 *teaspoonful of salt.* AVERAGE COST, 1s. 3d.

A casserole of rice, when made in a mould, is not such a difficult operation as when it is moulded by the hand. It forms the basis of an elegant and inexpensive entrée, as the remains of cold fish, flesh, or fowl may be served as ragoûts, fricassées, &c., inclosed in the casserole. It re-

CASSEROLE OF RICE.

quires great nicety in its preparation, the principal thing to attend to being the boil-ing of the rice, as, if this is not sufficiently cooked, the casserole, when moulded, will have a rough appearance, which would en-tirely spoil it. After having washed the rice in two or three waters, drain it well and put it into a stewpan, with the stock, ham and salt ; cover the pan closely, and let the rice gradually swell over a slow fire, occasionally stirring, to prevents its stick-ing. When it is quite soft, strain it, pick out the pieces of ham, and, with the back of a large wooden spoon, mash the rice to a perfectly smooth paste. Then well grease a mould (moulds are made purposely for rice borders), and turn it upside down for a minute or two, to drain away the fat, should there be too much ; put some rice all round the bottom and sides of it ; place a piece of soft bread in the middle, and cover it with rice : press it equally with the spoon, and let it cool. Then dip the mould into hot water, turn the casserole carefully on to a dish, mark where the lid is to be formed on the top, by making an incision with the point of a knife about an inch from tne edge all round, and put it into a *very hot* oven. Brush it over with a little clarified butter, and bake about ½ hour, or rather longer ; then carefully remove the lid, which will be formed by the incision having been made all round, and remove the bread in small pieces, with the point of a penknife, being careful not to injure the casserole. Fill the centre with the ragoût or fricassée, which should be made thick ; put on the cover, glaze it, place it in the oven to set the glaze, and serve as hot as possible. The casserole should not be emptied too much, as it is liable to crack from the weight of whatever is put in ; and, in baking it, let the oven be very hot, or the casserole will probably break.

TIME.—*About ¾ hour to swell the rice.*
SEASONABLE *at any time.*

Rice, Sweet Casserole of.— IN-GREDIENTS *for* 2 *casseroles.*—1½ *lb. of rice,* 3 *pints of milk, sugar to taste, flavouring of* *bitter almonds*, 3 *oz. of butter, the yolks of* 3 *eggs.* AVERAGE COST, 1*s.* 6*d.*

This is made in precisely the same manner as a savoury casserole, only substituting the milk and sugar for the stock and salt. Put the milk into a stewpan, with sufficient essence of bitter almonds to flavour it well ; then add the rice, which should be washed, picked and drained, and let it swell gradually in the milk over a slow fire. When it is tender, stir in the sugar, butter and yolks of eggs ; butter a mould, press in the rice, and proceed in exactly the same manner as in preceding recipe. When the casserole is ready, fill it with a compote of any fruit that may be preferred, or with melted apricot-jam, and serve.

TIME.—*From* ¾ *to* 1 *hour to swell the rice,* ½ *to* ¾ *hour to bake the casserole.*

SEASONABLE *at any time.*

Rice Croquettes.— INGREDIENTS

for 8 *croquettes.*—½ *lb. of rice,* 1 *quart of milk,* 6 *oz. of pounded sugar, flavouring of vanilla, lemon-peel or bitter almonds, egg and bread-crumbs, hot lard.* AVERAGE COST, 10*d.*

Put the rice, milk and sugar into a saucepan, and let the former gradually swell over a gentle fire until all the milk is dried up ; and just before the rice is done, stir in a few drops of essence of any of the above flavourings. Let the rice get cold ; then form it into small round balls, dip them into yolk of egg, sprinkle them with bread-crumbs, and fry them in boiling lard for about 10 minutes, turning them about that they may get equally browned. Drain the greasy moisture from them, by placing them on a cloth in front of the fire for a minute or two ; pile them on a white d'oyley, and send them quickly to table. A small piece of jam is sometimes introduced into the middle of each croquette, which adds very much to the flavour of this dish.

TIME.—*From* ¾ *to* 1 *hour to swell the rice ; about* 10 *minutes to fry the croquettes.*

SEASONABLE *at any time.*

Rice Fritters. — INGREDIENTS *for*

fritters for 5 *or* 6 *persons.*—6 *oz. of rice,* 1 *quart of milk,* 3 *oz. of sugar,* 1 *oz. of fresh butter,* 6 *oz. of orange marmalade,* 4 *eggs.* AVERAGE COST, 1*s.* 3*d.*

Swell the rice in the milk, with the sugar and butter, over a slow fire until it is perfectly tender, which will be in about ¾ hour. When the rice is done, strain away the milk, should there be any left, and mix with it the marmalade and well-beaten eggs ; stir the whole over the fire until the eggs are set ; then spread the mixture on a dish to the thickness of about ½ inch, or rather thicker. When it is perfectly cold, cut it into long strips, dip them in a batter the same as for apple fritters, and fry them a nice brown. Dish them on a white d'oyley, strew sifted sugar over, and serve quickly.

TIME.—*About* ¾ *hour to swell the rice ; from* 7 *to* 10 *minutes to fry the fritters.*

SEASONABLE *at any time.*

Rice Milk. — INGREDIENTS *for dish*

for 4 *children.*—3 *tablespoonfuls of rice,* 1 *quart of milk, sugar to taste ; when liked, a little grated nutmeg.* AVERAGE COST, 5*d.*

Well wash the rice, put it into a saucepan with the milk, and simmer gently until the rice is tender, stirring it from time to time to prevent the milk from burning ; sweeten it, add a little grated nutmeg, and serve. This dish is also very suitable and wholesome for children ; it may be flavoured with a little lemon-peel, and a little finely-minced suet may be boiled with it, which renders it more strengthening and more wholesome. Tapioca, semolina, vermicelli and macaroni may all be dressed in the same manner.

TIME.—*From* ¾ *to* 1 *hour.*

SEASONABLE *at any time.*

Rice Pudding, Rich, Baked.—

INGREDIENTS *for pudding for* 6 *persons.*—1 *small teacupful of rice,* 4 *eggs,* 1 *pint of milk,* 2 *oz. of fresh butter,* 2 *oz. of beef marrow,* ¼ *lb. of currants,* 2 *tablespoonfuls of brandy, nutmeg,* ¼ *lb. of sugar, the rind of* ½ *lemon.* AVERAGE COST, 1s. 4d.

Put the lemon-rind and milk into a stewpan, and let it infuse until the milk is well flavoured with the lemon; in the meantime, boil the rice until tender in water, with a very small quantity of salt, and, when done, let it be thoroughly drained. Beat the eggs, stir to them the milk, which should be strained, the butter, marrow, currants and remaining ingredients; add the rice, and mix all well together. Line the edges of the dish with puff-paste, put in the pudding, and bake for about ¾ hour in a slow oven. Slices of candied-peel may be added at pleasure, or Sultana raisins may be substituted for the currants.

TIME.—¾ *hour.*

SEASONABLE *for a winter pudding, when fresh fruits are not obtainable.*

Rice Pudding, Baked. (Plain and Economical; a nice Pudding for Children.)
—INGREDIENTS *for pudding for* 6 *children.* —1 *teacupful of rice,* 2 *tablespoonfuls of moist sugar,* 1 *quart of milk,* ½ *oz. of butter or* 2 *small tablespoonfuls of chopped suet,* ½ *teaspoonful of grated nutmeg.* AVERAGE COST, 6d.

Wash the rice, put it into a pie-dish with the sugar, pour in the milk, and stir these ingredients well together; then add the butter cut up into very small pieces, or, instead of this, the above proportion of finely-minced suet; grate a little nutmeg over the top, and bake the pudding in a moderate oven, from 1½ to 2 hours. As the rice is not previously cooked, care must be taken that the pudding be very slowly baked, to give plenty of time for the rice to swell, and for it to be very thoroughly done.

TIME.—1½ *to* 2 *hours.*

SEASONABLE *at any time.*

Rice, Plain Boiled.—INGREDIENTS
for pudding for 4 *children.*—½ *lb. of rice.* AVERAGE COST, 2d.

Wash the rice, tie it in a pudding-cloth, allowing room for the rice to swell, and put it into a saucepan of cold water; boil it gently for 2 hours and if, after a time, the cloth seems tied too loosely, take the rice up and tighten the cloth. Serve with sweet melted butter, or cold butter and sugar, or stewed fruit, jam or marmalade, any of which accompaniments are suitable for plain boiled rice.

TIME.—2 *hours after the water boils.*

SEASONABLE *at any time.*

Rice Pudding, Boiled. — INGRE-
DIENTS *for pudding for* 6 *persons.*—¼ *lb. of rice,* 1½ *pint of new milk,* 2 *oz. of butter,* 4 *eggs,* ½ *saltspoonful of salt,* 4 *large tablespoonfuls of moist sugar, flavouring to taste.* AVERAGE COST, 11d.

Stew the rice very gently in the above proportion of new milk, and, when it is tender, pour it into a basin; stir in the butter and let it stand to cool; then beat the eggs, add these to the rice with the sugar, salt and any flavouring that may be approved, such as nutmeg, powdered cinnamon, grated lemon-peel, essence of bitter almonds, or vanilla. When all is well stirred, put the pudding into a buttered basin, tie it down with a cloth, plunge it into boiling water, and boil for 1¼ hour.

TIME.—1¼ *hour.*

SEASONABLE *at any time.*

Rice Pudding, Boiled (with Dried or Fresh Fruit; a nice Dish for the Nursery).—INGREDIENTS *for pudding for* 6 *children.*—½ *lb. of rice,* 1 *pint of any kind of fresh fruit that may be preferred, or* ½ *lb. of raisins or currants.* AVERAGE COST, 6d.

Wash the rice, tie it in a cloth, allowing room for it to swell, and put it into a saucepan of cold water; let it boil for an hour, then take it up, untie the cloth, stir in the fruit, and tie it up again tolerably tight, and put it into the water for the remainder of the time. Boil for another hour, or rather longer and serve with sweet sauce if made with dried fruit, and with plain sifted sugar if made with fresh fruit.

TIME.—1 *hour to boil the rice without the fruit;* 1 *hour, or longer, afterwards.*

SEASONABLE *at any time.*

Note.—This pudding is very good made with apples; they should be pared, cored and cut into thin slices.

Rice Pudding, French; or, Gateau de Riz.

—INGREDIENTS *for pudding for 6 persons.*—¼ *lb. of rice,* 1 *quart of milk, the rind of* 1 *lemon,* ½ *teaspoonful of salt, sugar to taste,* 4 *oz. of butter,* 6 *eggs, bread-crumbs.* AVERAGE COST, 1s. 6d.

Put the milk into a stewpan with the lemon-rind, and let it infuse for ½ hour, or until the former is well flavoured; then take out the peel, have ready the rice, washed, picked and drained; put it into the milk, and let it gradually swell over a very slow fire. Stir in the butter, salt and sugar, and, when properly sweetened, add the yolks of the eggs, and then the whites, both of which should be well beaten and added separately to the rice. Butter a mould, strew in some fine bread-crumbs, and let them be spread equally over it; then carefully pour in the rice, and bake the pudding in a *slow* oven for 1 hour. Turn it out of the mould, and garnish the dish with preserved cherries, or any bright-coloured jelly or jam. This pudding is exceedingly nice flavoured with essence of vanilla.

TIME.—¾ to 1 *hour for the rice to swell; to be baked* 1 *hour in a slow oven.*

SEASONABLE *at any time.*

Rice Pudding, Baked or Boiled Ground.

—INGREDIENTS *for pudding for 6 persons.*—2 *pints of milk,* 6 *tablespoonfuls of ground rice, sugar to taste,* 4 *eggs, flavouring of lemon-rind, nutmeg, bitter-almonds, or bay-leaf.* AVERAGE COST, 11d.

Put 1½ pint of the milk into a stewpan with any of the above flavourings, and bring it to the boiling point, and, with the other ½ pint of milk, mix the ground rice to a smooth batter; strain the boiling milk to this, and stir over the fire until the mixture is tolerably thick; then pour it into a basin, leave it uncovered, and when nearly or quite cold sweeten it to taste, and add the eggs, which should be previously well beaten, with a little salt. Put the pudding into a well-buttered basin, tie it down with a cloth, plunge it into boiling water, and boil for 1½ hour. For a baked pudding, proceed in precisely the same manner, only using half the above proportion of ground rice, with the same quantity of all the other ingredients; an hour will bake the pudding in a moderate oven. Stewed fruit, or preserves, or marmalade, may be served with either the boiled or baked pudding, and will be found an improvement. Ground rice pudding can also be made very nice without eggs.

TIME.—1½ *hour to boil,* 1 *hour to bake.*

SEASONABLE *at any time.*

Rice Pudding, Iced.

—INGREDIENTS *for pudding for 6 persons.*—6 *oz. of rice,* 1 *quart of milk,* ½ *lb. of sugar, the yolks of* 6 *eggs,* 1 *small teaspoonful of essence of vanilla.* AVERAGE COST, 1s. 2d.

Put the rice into a stewpan, with the milk and sugar, and let these simmer over a gentle fire until the rice is sufficiently soft to break up into a smooth mass, and should the milk dry away too much, a little more may be added. Stir the rice occasionally, to prevent its burning, then beat it to a smooth mixture; add the yolks of the eggs, which should be well whisked, and the vanilla (should this flavouring not be liked, essence of bitter almonds may be substituted for it); put this rice custard into the freezing-pot, and proceed as directed in the recipe for Iced Pudding. When wanted for table, turn the pudding out of the mould, and pour over the top and round it a compote of oranges, or any other fruit that may be preferred, taking care that the flavouring in the pudding harmonizes well with the fruit that is served with it.

TIME.—½ hour to freeze the mixture.

SEASONABLE all the year.

Rice Puddings, Miniature.—
INGREDIENTS for 6 small puddings.—¼ lb. of rice, 1½ pint of milk, 2 oz. of fresh butter, 4 eggs, sugar to taste, flavouring of lemon-peel, bitter almonds or vanilla; a few strips of candied peel. AVERAGE COST, 1s.

Let the rice swell in 1 pint of milk over a slow fire, putting with it a strip of lemon-peel; stir to it the butter and the other ½ pint of milk, and let the mixture cool. Then add the well-beaten eggs, and a few drops of essence of almonds or essence of vanilla, whichever may be preferred. Butter well some small cups or moulds, line them with a few pieces of candied peel sliced very thin, fill them three-parts full, and bake for about 40 minutes; turn them out of the cups on to a white d'oyley, or dessert paper, and serve with sweet sauce. The flavouring and candied peel might be omitted, and stewed fruit or preserve served instead, with these puddings.

TIME.—40 minutes.

SEASONABLE at any time.

Rice Snowballs. (A Pretty Dish for Juvenile Suppers.)—INGREDIENTS for dish for 6 children.—6 oz. of rice, 1 quart of milk, flavouring of essence of almonds, sugar to taste, 1 pint of custard. AVERAGE COST, 1s.

Boil the rice in the milk, with sugar and a flavouring of essence of almonds, until the former is tender, adding, if necessary, a little more milk, should it dry away too much. When the rice is quite soft, put it into teacups, or small round jars, and let it remain until cold; then turn the rice out on a deep glass dish, pour over a custard, and on the top of each ball place a small bright-coloured preserve or jelly. Lemon-peel or vanilla may be boiled with the rice instead of the essence of almonds, when

either of these is preferred; but the flavouring of the custard must correspond with that of the rice.

TIME.—About ¾ hour to swell the rice in the milk.

SEASONABLE at any time.

Rice Soufflé.—INGREDIENTS for dish for 4 persons.—3 tablespoonfuls of ground rice, 1 pint of milk, 5 eggs, pounded sugar to taste, flavouring of lemon-rind, vanilla, coffee, chocolate, or anything that may be preferred, a piece of butter the size of a walnut. AVERAGE COST, 10d.

Mix the ground rice with 6 tablespoonfuls of the milk quite smoothly, and put it into a saucepan with the remainder of the milk and butter, and keep stirring it over the fire for about ¼ hour, or until the mixture thickens. Separate the yolks from the whites of the eggs, beat the former in a basin, and stir to them the rice and sufficient pounded sugar to sweeten the soufflé; but add this latter ingredient as sparingly as possible, as, the less sugar there is used the lighter will be the soufflé. Now whisk the whites of the eggs to a stiff froth or snow; mix them with the other preparation, and pour the whole into a soufflé-dish, and put it instantly into the oven; bake it about ½ hour in a moderate oven, take it out, hold a salamander or hot shovel over the top, sprinkle sifted sugar over it, and send to table in the dish it was baked in, either with a napkin pinned round or inclosed in a more ornamental dish. The excellence of this dish entirely depends on the proper whisking of the whites of the eggs, the manner of baking and the expedition with which it is sent to table. Soufflés should be served instantly from the oven, or they will sink and be nothing more than an ordinary pudding.

TIME.—About ½ hour.

SEASONABLE at any time.

Rice Soup.—INGREDIENTS for soup for 8 or 10 persons.—4 oz. of Patna rice, salt

cayenne and mace, 2 *quarts of white stock.* AVERAGE COST, 1s. 9d.

Throw the rice into boiling water, and let it boil until tender ; then pour it into a sieve, and allow it to drain well. Now add it to the stock boiling, and allow it to simmer a few minutes ; season to taste. Serve quickly.

TIME.—1½ *hour.*

SEASONABLE *all the year.*

Rice Soup.—INGREDIENTS *for soup for* 8 *or* 10 *persons.*—6 *oz. of rice, the yolks of* 4 *eggs,* ½ *pint of cream, rather more than* 2 *quarts of stock.* AVERAGE COST, 2s.

Boil the rice in the stock, and rub half of it through a tammy ; put the stock in a stewpan, add all the rice and simmer gently for 5 minutes. Beat the yolks of the eggs, mix them with the cream (previously boiled), and strain through a hair sieve ; take the soup off the fire, add the eggs and cream, stirring frequently. Heat it gradually, stirring all the time ; but do not let it boil, or the eggs will curdle.

TIME.—2 *hours.*

SEASONABLE *all the year.*

Rice, To Boil (for Curries, &c.).— INGREDIENTS *for rice for large curry.*—¾ *lb. of rice, water, salt.* AVERAGE COST, 3d.

Pick, wash and soak the rice in plenty of cold water ; then have ready a saucepan of boiling water, drop the rice into it, and keep it boiling quickly, with the lid removed, until it is tender, but not soft. Take it up, drain it, and put it on a dish before the fire to dry ; do not handle it much with a spoon, but shake it about a little with two forks, that it may all be equally dried, and strew over it a little salt. It is now ready to serve, and may be heaped lightly on a dish by itself, or be laid round the dish as a border, with a curry or fricassée in the centre. The rice, to be well boiled, should be white, dry and with every grain distinct. During the process of boiling, the rice should be

attentively watched, that it be not overdone, as, if this is the case, it will have a mashed and soft appearance.

TIME.—15 *to* 25 *minutes, according to the quality of the rice.*

SEASONABLE *at any time.*

Rice, To Boil (for Curries, &c. ; SOYER'S Recipe).—INGREDIENTS *for rice for large curry.*—1 *lb. of the best Carolina rice,* 2 *quarts of water,* 1½ *oz. of butter, a little salt.* AVERAGE COST, 6d.

Wash the rice well in two waters ; make 2 quarts of water boiling, and throw the rice into it ; boil it until three-parts done, then drain it on a sieve. Butter the bottom and sides of a stewpan, put in the rice, place the lid on tightly, and set it by the side of the fire until the rice is perfectly tender, occasionally shaking the pan to prevent its sticking. Prepared thus, every grain should be separate and white. Either dish it separately, or place it round the curry as a border.

TIME.—15 *to* 25 *minutes.*

SEASONABLE *at any time.*

Roasting, Memoranda in.—The management of the fire is a point of primary importance in roasting. A radiant fire throughout the operation is absolutely necessary to insure a good result. When the article to be dressed is thin and delicate, the fire may be small ; but when the joint is large, the fire must fill the grate. Meat must never be put down before a hollow or exhausted fire, which may soon want recruiting ; on the other hand, if the heat of the fire become too fierce, the meat must be removed to a considerable distance till it has somewhat abated. Some cooks always fail in roasting, though they succeed in nearly everything else. A French writer on the culinary art says that anybody can learn how to cook, but one must be born a roaster. According to Liebig, beef or mutton cannot be said to be sufficiently roasted, until it has acquired throughout

the whole mass a temperature of 158°. But poultry may be well cooked when the inner parts have attained a temperature of 130° to 140°. This depends on the greater amount of blood which beef and mutton contain, the colouring matter of blood not being coagulable under 158°.

Robert Sauce (for Steaks, &c.).—

INGREDIENTS *for sauce for dish for 5 or 6 persons.*—2 *oz. of butter,* 3 *onions,* 1 *teaspoonful of flour,* 4 *tablespoonfuls of gravy or stock, salt and pepper to taste,* 1 *teaspoonful of made mustard,* 1 *teaspoonful of vinegar, the juice of ½ lemon.* AVERAGE COST, 6d.

Put the butter into a stewpan, set it on the fire, and, when browning, throw in the onions, which must be cut into small slices. Fry them brown, but do not burn them; add the flour, shake the onions in it, and give the whole another fry. Put in the gravy and seasoning, and boil it gently for 10 minutes; skim off the fat, add the mustard, vinegar and lemon-juice, give it one boil, and pour round the steaks, or whatever dish the sauce has been prepared for.

TIME.—*Altogether,* ½ *hour.*

SEASONABLE *at any time.*

Note.—This sauce will be found an excellent accompaniment to roast goose, pork, mutton cutlets, and various other dishes.

Rolls, Excellent. — INGREDIENTS

for 6 good-sized rolls.—1 *lb. of flour,* 1 *oz. of butter,* ¼ *pint of milk, a large teaspoonful of yeast, a little salt.* AVERAGE COST, 5d.

Warm the butter in the milk, add to it the yeast and salt, and mix these ingredients well together. Put the flour into a pan, stir in the above ingredients and let the dough rise, covered in a warm place. Knead it well, make it into rolls, let them rise again for a few minutes, and bake in a quick oven. Richer rolls may be made by adding 1 or 2 eggs and a larger proportion of butter, and their appearance improved

by brushing the tops over with yolk of egg or a little milk.

TIME.—*This quantity, divided into 6 rolls, from 15 to 20 minutes.*

Rolls, Hot. — This dish, although

very unwholesome and indigestible, is nevertheless a great favourite, and eaten by many persons. As soon as the rolls

ROLLS.

come from the baker's they should be put into the oven, which, in the early part of the morning, is sure not to be very hot; and the rolls must not be buttered until wanted. When they are quite hot, divide them longthwise into three; put some thin flakes of good butter between the slices, press the rolls together, and put them in the oven for a minute or two, but not longer, or the butter would oil; take them out of the oven, spread the butter equally over, divide the rolls in half, and put them on to a very hot dish, and send them instantly to table.

Rolls, Fluted. — INGREDIENTS. —

Puff-paste, the white of an egg, sifted sugar, jelly or preserve.

Make some good puff-paste (trimmings answer very well for little dishes of this sort); roll it out to the thickness of ¼ inch, and with a round fluted paste-cutter stamp

FRENCH ROLL.

out as many round pieces as may be required; brush over the upper side with the white of an egg; roll up the pieces, pressing the paste lightly together where it joins; place the rolls on a baking-sheet, and bake for about ¼ hour. A few minutes before they are done, brush them over with the white of an egg, strew over sifted sugar, put them back in the oven, and when the icing is firm and of a pale brown colour, they are done. Place a strip of jelly or preserve across each roll, dish them high on a napkin, and serve cold.

TIME.—¼ *hour before being iced; 5 to* 10 *minutes after.*

SEASONABLE *at any time.*

Roux, Brown. (A French Thickening for Gravies and Sauces.)—INGREDIENTS.—6 *oz. of butter,* 9 *oz. of flour.* AVERAGE COST, 7*d.*

Melt the butter in a stewpan over a slow fire, and dredge in, very gradually, the flour; stir it till of a light-brown colour—to obtain this do it very slowly, otherwise the flour will burn and impart a bitter taste to the sauce it is mixed with. Pour it in a jar, and keep it for use; it will remain good some time.

TIME.—*About ½ hour.*

Roux, White (for thickening White Sauces).—Allow the same proportions of butter and flour as in the preceding recipe, and proceed in the same manner as for brown roux; but do not keep it on the fire too long, and take care not to let it colour. This is used for thickening white sauce. Pour it into a jar to use when wanted.

A dessertspoonful will thicken a pint of gravy.

TIME.—¼ *hour.*

Note. — Besides the above, sauces may be thickened with potato flour, ground rice, baked flour, arrowroot, &c.: the latter will be found far preferable to the ordinary flour for white sauces. A slice of bread, toasted and added to gravies, answers the two purposes of thickening and colouring them.

Rump-steak, Fried. — INGREDIENTS.—*Steaks, butter or clarified dripping.* AVERAGE COST, 1*s.* 2*d. per lb.*

Although broiling is a far superior method of cooking steaks to frying them, yet, when the cook is not very expert, the latter mode may be adopted; and, when properly done, the dish may really look very inviting, and the flavour be good. The steaks should be cut rather thinner than for broiling, and with a small quantity of fat to each. Put some butter or clarified dripping into a frying-pan; let it get quite hot, then lay in the steaks. Turn them frequently until done, which will be in about 8 minutes, or rather more should the steaks be very thick. Serve on a very hot dish, in which put a small piece of butter and a tablespoonful of ketchup and season with pepper and salt. They should be sent to table quickly, as when cold the steaks are entirely spoiled.

TIME.—8 *minutes for a medium-sized steak, rather longer for a very thick one.*

SEASONABLE *all the year, but not good in summer, as the meat cannot hang to get tender.*

Note.—Where much gravy is liked, make it in the following manner:—As soon as the steaks are done, dish them, pour a little boiling water into the frying-pan, add a seasoning of pepper and salt, a small piece of butter and a tablespoonful of Harvey's sauce or mushroom ketchup. Hold the pan over the fire for a minute or two, just let the gravy simmer, then pour on the steak, and serve

Rump-steak and Kidney Pudding.—INGREDIENTS *for pudding for 6 persons.* — 2 *lbs. of rump-steak,* 2 *kidneys, seasoning to tas'e, of salt and black pepper, suet-crust made with milk (see* Pastry), *in the proportion of 6 oz. of suet to each 1 lb. of flour.* AVERAGE COST, 3*s.* 4*d.*

Procure some tender rump-steak (that which has been hung a little time), and divide it into pieces about an inch square, and cut each kidney into 8 pieces. Line the basin with crust made with suet and flour in the above proportion, leaving a small piece of crust to overlap the edge. Then cover the bottom with a portion of the steak and a few pieces of kidney ; season with salt and pepper (some add a little flour to thicken the gravy, but it is not necessary), and then add another layer of steak, kidney and seasoning. Proceed in this manner till the basin is full, when pour in sufficient water to come within 2 inches of the top of the basin. Moisten the edges of the crust, cover the pudding over, press the two crusts together, that the gravy may not escape, and turn up the overhanging paste. Wring out a cloth in hot water, flour it and tie up the pudding ; put it into boiling water and let it boil for at least 4 hours. If the water diminishes, always replenish with some hot in a jug, as the

SUSSEX PUDDING DISH.

pudding should be kept covered all the time, and not allowed to stop boiling. When the cloth is removed, cut out a round piece in the top of the crust, to prevent the pudding bursting, and send it to table in the basin, either in an ornamental dish or with a napkin pinned round it. Serve quickly.

TIME.—*For a pudding with 2 lbs. of steak and 2 kidneys allow 4 hours.*

SEASONABLE *all the year, but more suitable in winter.*

Note.—Rump-steak pudding may be very much enriched by adding a few oysters or mushrooms. In Sussex, the inhabitants are noted for their savoury puddings, which are usually made in the manner just described. It differs from the general way of making them, as the meat is cut up into very small pieces and the basin is differently shaped, resembling a very large saucer : on trial, this pudding will be found far nicer, and more full of gravy, than when laid in large pieces in the basin. Where time does not allow for the proper boiling of a meat pudding, it may be made of McCall's tinned meat, with a little fresh kidney cut up small in it.

Rump-steak and Oyster Sauce.

—INGREDIENTS *for dish for 6 persons.*—3 *dozen oysters, ingredients for oyster sauce,* 2 *lb. of rump-steak, seasoning to taste, of pepper and salt.* AVERAGE COST, 5s. 6d.

Make the oyster sauce, and when that is ready, put it by the side of the fire, but do not let it keep boiling. Have the steaks cut of an equal thickness, broil them over a very clear fire, turning them often that the gravy may not escape. In about 8 minutes they will be done, when put them on a very hot dish ; smother with the oyster sauce, and the remainder send to table in a tureen. Serve quickly.

TIME.—*About 8 to 10 minutes, according to the thickness of the steak. Instead of fresh oysters, tinned ones may be used for the sauce.*

SEASONABLE *from September to April.*

Rump-steak or Beef-steak, Broiled.

—INGREDIENTS.—*Steaks, a piece of butter the size of a walnut, salt to taste,* 1 *tablespoonful of good mushroom ketchup or Harvey's sauce.* AVERAGE COST, 1s. 2d. *per lb.*

As the success of a good broil so much depends on the state of the fire, see that it is bright and clear, and perfectly free from smoke, and do not add any fresh fuel just before you require to use the gridiron. Sprinkle a little salt over the fire, put on the gridiron for a few minutes, to get thoroughly hot through ; rub it with a piece of fresh suet, to prevent the meat from sticking, and lay on the steaks, which should be cut of an equal thickness, about ¾ of an inch, or rather thinner, and levelled by beating as *little* as possible with a rolling-pin. Turn them frequently with steak-tongs (if these are not at hand, stick a fork in the edge of the fat, that no gravy escapes), and in from 8 to 10 minutes they will be done. Have ready a very hot dish, into which put the ketchup, and, when liked, a little minced shalot ; dish up the steaks, rub them over with butter and season with pepper and salt. The exact time for broiling steaks must be determined by taste, whether they are liked underdone or well done ; more than from 8 to 10 minutes for a steak ¾ inch in thickness, we think, would spoil and dry up the juices of the meat. Great expedition is necessary in sending broiled steaks to table ; and, to have them in perfection, they should not be cooked till everything else prepared for dinner has been dished up, as their excellence entirely depends on their being served very hot. Garnish with scraped horseradish. Oyster, tomato, onion and many other sauces, are frequent accompaniments to rump-steak, but true lovers of this English dish generally reject all additions but pepper and salt.

TIME.—8 to 10 minutes.

SEASONABLE all the year, but not good in the height of summer, as the meat cannot hang long enough to be tender.

Rump-steak Pie.—INGREDIENTS

for pie for 6 to 8 persons.—2½ lbs. of rump-steak, 2 kidneys, seasoning to taste, of salt, cayenne and black pepper, crust, water, the yolk of an egg. AVERAGE COST, 4s.

Have the steaks cut from a rump that has hung a few days, that they may be tender, and be particular that every portion is perfectly sweet. Cut the steaks into pieces about 2 inches long and 1 wide, allowing a small piece of fat to each piece of lean. Cut the kidneys in 7 or 8 pieces, and arrange the meat in layers in a pie-dish. Between each layer sprinkle a seasoning of salt, pepper, and, when liked, a few grains of cayenne. Fill the dish sufficiently with meat to support the crust, and to give it a nice raised appearance when baked, and not to look flat and hollow. Pour in sufficient water to half fill the dish, and border it with paste (see Pastry) ; brush it over with a little water, and put on the cover ; slightly press down the edges with the thumb, and trim off close to the dish. Ornament the pie with leaves, or pieces of paste cut in any shape that fancy may

direct, brush it over with the beaten yolk of an egg ; make a hole in the top of the crust, and bake in a hot oven for about 1½ hour.

TIME.—In a hot oven, 1½ hour.

SEASONABLE at any time.

Rump-steak Pudding, Baked.

INGREDIENTS for pudding for 5 or 6 persons.—6 oz. of flour, 2 eggs, not quite 1 pint of milk, salt to taste, 1½ lb. of rump-steaks, 1 kidney, pepper and salt. AVERAGE COST, 2s. 6d.

Cut the steaks into nice square pieces, with a small quantity of fat, and the kidney divide into small pieces. Make a batter of flour, eggs and milk in the above proportion ; lay a little of it at the bottom of a pie-dish ; then put in the steaks and kidney, which should be well seasoned with pepper and salt, and pour over the remainder of the batter, and bake for 1½ hour in a brisk but not fierce oven.

TIME.—1½ hour.

SEASONABLE at any time.

Rump-steak, Rolled, Roasted

and Stuffed.—INGREDIENTS for dish for 5 or 6 persons.—2 lbs. of rump-steak, forcemeat, pepper and salt to taste, clarified butter. AVERAGE COST, 2s. 8d.

Have the steaks cut rather thick from a well-hung rump of beef, and sprinkle over them a seasoning of pepper and salt. Make a forcemeat ; spread it over half of the steak ; roll it up, bind and skewer it firmly, that the forcemeat may not escape, and roast it before a nice clear fire for about 1½ hour, or rather longer, should the roll be very large and thick. Keep it constantly basted with butter, and serve with brown gravy, some of which must be poured round the steak, and the remainder sent to table in a tureen.

TIME.—1½ hour.

SEASONABLE all the year, but best in winter.

Rump-steak with Fried Potatoes; or Biftek aux Pommes-de-Terre (à la Mode Française).

—INGREDIENTS *for dish for 6 persons.*—2 *lbs. of steak, 8 potatoes, ¼ lb. of butter, salt and pepper to taste. 1 teaspoonful of minced herbs.* AVERAGE COST, 2*s.* 10*d.*

Put the butter into a frying or *sauté* pan, set it over the fire, and let it get very hot; peel and cut the potatoes into long thin slices; put them into the hot butter, and fry them till of a nice brown colour. Now broil the steaks over a bright clear fire, turning them frequently, that every part may be equally done; as they should not be thick, 5 minutes will broil them. Put the herbs and seasoning in the butter the potatoes were fried in, pour it under the steak, and place the fried potatoes round as a garnish. To have this dish in perfection, a portion of the fillet of the sirloin should be used, as the meat is generally so much more tender than that of the rump, and the steaks should be cut about ½ of an inch in thickness.

TIME.—5 *minutes to broil the steaks, and about the same time to fry the potatoes.*

SEASONABLE *all the year; but not so good in warm weather, as the meat cannot hang to get tender.*

Rump- or Beef-steak, Stewed.

—INGREDIENTS *for dish for 4 or 5 persons* —About 2 *lbs. of beef- or rump-steak, 3 onions, 2 turnips, 3 carrots, 2 or 3 oz. of butter, ½ pint of water, 1 teaspoonful of salt, ½ do. of pepper, 1 tablespoonful of ketchup, 1 tablespoonful of flour.* AVERAGE COST, 2*s.* 10*d.*

Have the steaks cut tolerably thick and rather lean; divide them into convenient-sized pieces, and fry them in the butter a nice brown on both sides. Cleanse and pare the vegetables, cut the onions and carrots into thin slices, and the turnips into dice, and fry these in the same fat that the steaks were done in. Put all into a saucepan, add ½ pint of water, or rather more should it be necessary, and simmer very gently for 2½ or 3 hours; when nearly done, skim well, add salt, pepper and ketchup in the above proportions, and thicken with a tablespoonful of flour, mixed with 2 of cold water. Let it boil up for a minute or two after the thickening is added, and serve. When a vegetable scoop is at hand, use it to cut the vegetables in fanciful shapes; and tomato, Harvey's sauce, or walnut-liquor may be used to flavour the gravy. It is less rich if stewed the previous day, so that the fat may be taken off when cold; when wanted for table it will merely require warming through.

TIME.—3 *hours.*

SEASONABLE *at any time.*

Rusks, To Make. (Suffolk Recipe.)

—INGREDIENTS *for 2 dozen rusks.*—1 *lb. of flour, 2 oz. of butter, ¼ pint of milk, 2 oz. of loaf sugar, 3 eggs, 1 tablespoonful of yeast.* AVERAGE COST, 9*d.*

Put the milk and butter into a saucepan, and keep shaking it round until the latter is melted. Put the flour into a basin, with the sugar, mix these well together, and beat the eggs. Stir them with the yeast to the milk and butter, and, with this liquid, work the flour into a smooth dough. Cover a cloth over the basin, and leave the dough to rise by the side of the fire; then knead it, and divide it into 12 pieces; place them in a brisk oven and bake for about 20 minutes. Take the rusks out, break them in half, and then set them in the oven to get crisp on the other side. When cold, they should be put into tin canisters, to keep them dry; and if intended for the cheese course, the sifted sugar should be omitted.

TIME.—20 *minutes to bake the rusks; 5 minutes to render them crisp after being divided.*

SEASONABLE *at any time.*

Rusks, Another Way of Making.

INGREDIENTS.—¼ *lb. of butter,* 2 *oz. of sugar,* 2 *lbs. of flour,* 4 *eggs,* 1 *quart of milk,* 1 *tablespoonful of yeast, a little salt.* AVERAGE COST, 1s. 6d.

Mix the yeast with the sugar and a small cupful of warm milk, and, after putting the flour in a deep basin, pour it in the centre, and stand to rise in a warm place for an hour. Mix in the flour, the rest of the milk, the eggs and salt, and beat all well with a wooden spoon. Set again to rise in a buttered tin for an hour, and then bake in a moderate oven. When cold, cut into thin slices, and dry in a quick oven, with powdered sugar sprinkled over.

TIME.—*About* 3 *hours.*

SEASONABLE *at any time.*

Rusks, Italian.

A stale Savoy or lemon cake may be converted into very good rusks in the following manner. Cut the cake into slices, divide each slice in two; put them on a baking-sheet, in a slow oven, and when they are of a nice brown and quite hard, they are done. They should be kept in a close tin canister in a dry place, to preserve their crispness.

Russian Salad.

INGREDIENTS.—*Any cold cooked vegetables, such as peas, asparagus, potatoes, carrots, lettuces and cucumbers, some anchovies, fileted and boned; some stoned olives, any cold fish, flaked, mayonnaise sauce, aspic jelly.*

The vegetables should all be cut up small, the lettuce shred finely, and they should then be thoroughly mixed with the flaked fish and the sauce; then the salad should be turned into the dish in which it is to be served, and garnished with the olives, the anchovies and some bright-coloured aspic jelly. A pretty way of serving a Russian salad is shown in our illustration. The aspic, in which is put the fish, is set in a border mould, and, when turned out, the salad is piled in the centre, and a few bright leaves of lettuce cut up finely, with a garnish of slices of beetroot, put round.

SEASONABLE *in summer.*

Note.—Two sweet vegetables, such as beet and carrot, should not be used in the same salad, and both of these should be used sparingly; lettuce and cress should be used in a larger proportion than anything else.

RUSSIAN SALAD.

"*Squares of coloured ice,*
Sweetened with syrup, tinctured with spice."
THOMAS BAILY ALDRICH.

SAGE-AND-ONION STUFFING.

AGE - & - ONION Stuffing (for Geese, Ducks and Pork). —INGREDIENTS.—*4 large onions, 10 sage-leaves, ¼ lb. of bread-crumbs, 1½ oz. of butter, salt and pepper to taste, 1 egg.* AVERAGE COST, *5d.*

Peel the onions, put them into boiling water, let them simmer for 5 minutes or rather longer, and just before they are taken out, put in the sage-leaves for a minute or two to take off their rawness. Chop both these very fine, add the bread, seasoning and butter, and work the whole together with the yolk of an egg, when the stuffing will be ready for use. It should be rather highly seasoned, and the sage-leaves should be very finely chopped. Many cooks do not parboil the onions in the manner just stated, but merely use them raw. The stuffing then, however, is not nearly so mild, and, to

SAGO PUDDING.

many tastes, its strong flavour would be very objectionable. When made for goose, a portion of the liver of the bird, simmered for a few minutes and very finely minced, is frequently added to this stuffing ; and where economy is studied, the egg and butter may be dispensed with.

TIME.—*Rather more than 5 minutes to simmer the onions.*

Sago Pudding.—INGREDIENTS *for pudding for 6 persons.*—*1½ pint of milk, 3 tablespoonfuls of sago, the rind of ½ lemon, 3 oz. of sugar, 3 eggs, 1 oz. of butter, grated nutmeg.* AVERAGE COST, *9d.*

Put the milk and lemon-rind into a stew-pan, place it by the side of the fire, and let it remain until the milk is well flavoured with the lemon ; then strain it, mix with it the sago and sugar, and simmer gently for about 15 minutes. Let the mixture cool a little, and stir to it the eggs, which should be well beaten, and the butter. Pour the pudding into a buttered pie-dish, grate a little nutmeg over the top, and bake from ¾ to 1 hour.

TIME.—¾ to 1 hour, or *longer if the oven is very slow.*

SEASONABLE *at any time.*

Note.—The above pudding may be boiled instead of baked; but then allow 2 extra tablespoonfuls of sago, and boil the pudding in a buttered basin from 1¼ to 1¾ hour.

Sago Sauce for Sweet Puddings.

—INGREDIENTS *for sauce for large pudding.*—1 tablespoonful of sago, ½ pint of water, ¼ pint of port or sherry, the rind and juice of 1 small lemon, sugar to taste; when the flavour is liked, a little pounded cinnamon. AVERAGE COST, 8d.

Wash the sago in two or three waters; then put it into a saucepan with the water and lemon-peel; let it simmer gently by the side of the fire for 10 minutes, then

SAGO PALM.

take out the lemon-peel, add the remaining ingredients, give one boil, and serve. Be particular to strain the lemon-juice before adding it to the sauce. This, on trial, will be found a delicious accompaniment to various boiled puddings, such as those made of bread, raisins, rice, &c.

TIME.—10 *minutes.*

Sago Soup.

—INGREDIENTS *for soup for 8 or 10 persons.*—5 oz. of sago, 2 quarts of medium or cheap stock. AVERAGE COST, 1s. 3d.

Wash the sago in boiling water, add it, by degrees, to the boiling stock, and simmer till the sago is entirely dissolved and forms a sort of jelly.

TIME.—*Nearly an hour.*

SEASONABLE *all the year.*

Note.—The yolks of 2 eggs, beaten up with a little cream, previously boiled, and added at the moment of serving, much improves this soup.

Salad, Boiled.

—INGREDIENTS *for dish for 6 persons.*—2 heads of celery, 1 pint of French beans, lettuce and endive. AVERAGE COST, 8d.

Boil the celery and beans separately until tender, and cut the celery into pieces about 2 inches long. Put these into a salad-bowl or dish; pour over either of the salad dressings, and garnish the dish with a little lettuce finely chopped, blanched endive, or a few tufts of boiled cauliflower. This composition, if less agreeable than vegetables in their raw state, is more wholesome; for salads, however they may be compounded, when eaten uncooked, prove to some people indigestible. Tarragon, chervil, burnet, and boiled onion may be added to the above salad with advantage, as also slices of cold meat, poultry or fish.

SEASONABLE *from July to October.*

Salad Dressing. (Excellent.)

—INGREDIENTS *for dressing for small salad.*—1 teaspoonful of mixed mustard, 1 teaspoonful of pounded sugar, 2 tablespoonfuls of salad oil, 4 tablespoonfuls of milk, 2 tablespoonfuls of Champion's vinegar, cayenne and salt to taste. AVERAGE COST, 3d.

Put the mixed mustard into a salad-bowl with the sugar, and add the oil drop by drop, carefully stirring and mixing all these ingredients well together. Proceed in this manner with the milk and vinegar, which must be added very *gradually*, or the sauce will curdle. Put in the seasoning, when the mixture will be ready for use. If this dressing is properly made, it will have a soft, creamy appearance, and will be found very delicious with crab or cold fried fish (the latter cut into dice), as well as with salads. In mixing salad dressings, the ingredients cannot be added *too gradually*, or *stirred too much*.

This recipe can be confidently recommended by the editress, to whom it was given by an intimate friend noted for her salads.

Salad Dressing. (Excellent.) —

INGREDIENTS *for dressing for large salad.* —4 *eggs*, 1 *teaspoonful of mixed mustard,* ¼ *teaspoonful of white pepper, half that quantity of cayenne, salt to taste, 4 table-spoonfuls of cream, vinegar.* AVERAGE COST, 8*d.*

Boil the eggs until hard, which will be in about ¼ hour or 20 minutes; put them

SALAD IN JELLY.

into cold water, take off the shells, and pound the yolks in a mortar to a smooth paste. Then add all the other ingredients, except the vinegar, and stir them well until the whole are thoroughly incorporated one with the other. Pour in sufficient vinegar to make it of the consistency of cream, taking care to add but little at a time. The mixture will then be ready for use. Oil may be substituted for the cream.

Note.— The whites of the eggs, cut into rings, will serve very well as a garnish to the salad.

Salad Dressing. (Excellent.)—IN-

GREDIENTS *for dressing for 1 salad.—*1 *egg,* 1 *teaspoonful of salad oil,* 1 *teaspoonful of mixed mustard,* ¼ *teaspoonful of salt,* ½ *teaspoonful of pounded sugar,* 2 *tablespoonfuls of vinegar,* 6 *tablespoonfuls of cream.* AVERAGE COST, 6*d.*

Prepare and mix the ingredients by the preceding recipe, and be very particular that the whole is well stirred.

*Note.—*In making salads, the vegetables, &c., should never be added to the sauce very long before they are wanted for table; the dressing, however, may always be prepared some hours before required. Where salads are much in request, it is a good plan to bottle off sufficient dressing for a few days' consumption, as thereby, much time and trouble are saved. If kept in a cool place, it will remain good for 4 or 5 days.

Poetic Recipe for Salad.—The Rev. Sydney Smith's recipe.

" Two large potatoes, pass'd through kitchen sieve,
Smoothness and softness to the salad give:
Of mordant mustard add a single spoon,
Distrust the condiment that bites too soon;
But deem it not, thou man of herbs, a fault,
To add a double quantity of salt;
Four times the spoon with oil of Lucca crown,
And twice with vinegar procured from 'town;'
True flavour needs it, and your poet begs,
The pounded yellow of two well-boil'd eggs.
Let onion's atoms lurk within the bowl,
And, scarce suspected, animate the whole
And, lastly, in the flavour'd compound toss
A magic spoonful of anchovy sauce.
Oh! great and glorious and herbaceous treat,
'Twould tempt the dying anchorite to eat.
Back to the world he'd turn his weary soul,
And plunge his fingers in the salad-bowl."

Salad, French. — INGREDIENTS.—

Lettuces; a little chopped burnet. To every 4 tablespoonfuls of oil allow 1½ *of either tarragon or plain French vinegar;* 1 *salt-spoonful of salt,* ½ *saltspoonful of pepper.*

Wash the lettuces, shake them in a cloth, and cut them into inch lengths. Put the lettuce into a salad-bowl, sprinkle over the chopped burnet, and mix these well together. Put the salt and pepper into the salad-spoon, moisten with the vinegar, disperse this amongst the salad, pour the oil over, and mix the whole well together for at least 5 minutes, when the preparation will be ready for table. This is the very simple and expeditious mode of preparing a salad generally adopted by our French neighbours, who are so noted for the delicious manner in which they dress their bowl. Success will not be obtained if the right vinegar is not procured, therefore we advise our friends who wish to excel in making a French salad to procure a bottle of the best French vinegar, flavoured with tarragon or not, as taste may dictate. Those persons living in or near London, can purchase the vinegar of Messrs. Crosse and Blackwell, Soho Square, at whose establishment the quality of this important ingredient in a salad can be relied on.

TIME.—*To be stirred at least 5 minutes, after all the ingredients are put in.*

SEASONABLE.—*Plentiful in summer, but scarce and dear during the winter season.*

Salad, Fresh Fruit. (A Dessert Dish.)

—Fruit salads are made by stripping the fruit from the stalks, piling it on a dish, and sprinkling over it finely-pounded sugar. They may be made of strawberries, currants, or any of these fruits mixed; peaches also make a very good salad. After the sugar is sprinkled over, about 6 large tablespoonfuls of wine or brandy, or 3 tablespoonfuls of liqueur, should be poured in the middle of the fruit; and, when the flavour is liked, a little pounded cinnamon may be added. In helping the fruit, it should be lightly stirred, that the wine and sugar may be equally distributed.

SEASONABLE *in summer.*

Salad, Red Cabbage. — INGREDIENTS *for large salad.*

—*A small red cabbage, 2 teaspoonfuls of salt, ½ pint of vinegar, 3 teaspoonfuls of oil, a small quantity of cayenne-pepper.* AVERAGE COST, 8*d.*

Take off the outside leaves of a fresh red cabbage, and cut the remainder very finely into small thin slices. Mix with the cabbage the above salad ingredients, and let it remain for two days, when it will be fit for use. This salad will keep very well for a few days. The quantity of the ingredients may, of course, be a little varied, according to taste.

TIME.—2 *days.*

SEASONABLE *in July and August.*

Salad, Summer. — INGREDIENTS *for salad for 8 persons.*

—3 *lettuces, 2 handfuls of mustard-and-cress, 10 young radishes, a few slices of cucumber.* AVERAGE COST, *with dressing,* 10*d.*

Let the herbs be as fresh as possible for a salad, and, if at all stale or dead-looking, let them lie in water for an hour or two, which will very much refresh them. Wash and carefully pick them over, remove decayed or worm-eaten leaves, and drain them thoroughly by swinging them gently in a clean cloth.

SALAD IN BOWL.

With a silver knife, cut the lettuces into small pieces, and the radishes and cucumbers into thin slices; arrange all these ingredients lightly on a dish, with the mustard-and-cress, and pour under, but not over, the salad either of the salad-dressings, and do not stir it up until it is to be eaten. It may be garnished with hard-boiled eggs, cut in slices, sliced cucumbers, nasturtiums, beetroot, and many other things that taste will always suggest to make a pretty and elegant dish. In making a good salad, care must be taken to have the herbs freshly gathered, and *thoroughly drained* before the sauce is added to them, or it will be watery and thin. Young spring onions, cut small, are by many persons considered an improvement to salads; but, before these are added, the cook should always consult the taste of her employer. Slices of cold meat or poultry added to a salad make a convenient and quickly-made summer luncheon-dish; or cold fish, flaked, will also be found exceedingly nice, mixed with it.

SEASONABLE *from May to September.*

Salad, Winter.—Ingredients for salad for 6 persons.—Endive, mustard-and-cress, boiled beetroot, 3 or 4 hard-boiled eggs, celery. Average Cost, 8d.

The above ingredients form the principal constituents of a winter salad, and may be converted into a very pretty dish, by nicely contrasting the various colours and by tastefully garnishing it. Shred the celery into thin pieces, after having carefully washed and cut away all worm-eaten pieces; cleanse the endive and mustard-and-cress free from grit, and arrange these high in the centre of a salad-bowl or dish; garnish with the hard-boiled eggs and beetroot, both of which should be cut in slices; and pour into the dish, but not over the salad, either of the salad dressings. Never dress a salad long before it is required for table, as, by standing, it loses its freshness and pretty crisp and light appearance; the sauce, however, may always be prepared a few hours beforehand, and when required to use, the herbs laid lightly over it.

Seasonable from the end of September to March.

Salads, Recipes for.—Directions for making the following, appear under their respective headings:—

Boiled.	Orange.
Celery.	Potato.
Chicken.	Red Cabbage.
French.	Russian.
Fresh Fruit.	Salmon Mayonnaise
Grouse.	Summer.
Lobster.	Winter.
,, Mayonnaise.	

Salmon à la Genevese.—Ingredients for dish for 6 persons.—2 slices of salmon, 2 chopped shalots, a little parsley, small bunch of herbs, 2 bay-leaves, 2 carrots, pounded mace, cayenne and salt to taste, 4 tablespoonfuls of Madeira, ½ pint of white stock, thickening of butter and flour, 1 teaspoonful of essence of anchovies, the juice of

1 large lemon, or of 2 small ones. Average Cost, 4s.

Rub the bottom of a stewpan over with butter, and put in the shalots, herbs, bay-leaves, carrots, mace and seasoning; stir them for 10 minutes over a clear fire, and add the Madeira or sherry; simmer gently for ½ hour, and strain through a sieve over the fish, which stew in this gravy while on, as the fish is sufficiently cooked; take away all the liquor, except enough to keep the salmon moist, and put into another stewpan; add the stock, thicken with butter and flour, and put in the anchovies, lemon-juice, cayenne and salt; lay the salmon on a hot dish, pour over it part of the sauce, and serve the remainder in a tureen.

Time.—1¼ hour.

Seasonable in spring and summer.

Salmon, Boiled.—Ingredients.—6 oz. of salt to each gallon of water; sufficient water to cover the fish. Average Cost, in full season, 1s. 4d. per lb.

Scale and clean the fish, and be particular that no blood is left inside; lay it in the fish-kettle with sufficient cold water to cover it, adding salt in the above proportion. Bring it quickly to a boil, take off all the scum, and let it simmer gently till the fish is done, which will be when the meat separates easily from the bone. Experience alone can teach the cook to fix the time for boiling fish; but it is especially to be remembered, that it should never be under-dressed, as then nothing is more unwholesome. Neither let it remain in the kettle after it is sufficiently cooked, as that would render it insipid, watery and colourless. Drain it, and if not wanted for a few minutes, keep it warm by means of warm cloths laid over it. Serve on a hot napkin, garnish with cut-lemon and parsley, and send lobster or any other sauce liked, and a dish of dressed cucumber, to table with it.

Time.—8 minutes to each lb. for large thick salmon; 6 minutes for thin fish.

SEASONABLE *from April to August.*

Note.—Cut-lemon should be put on the table with this fish; and a little of the juice squeezed over it is regarded by many persons as a most agreeable addition. Boiled peas are also, by some connoisseurs, considered especially adapted to be served with salmon.

To Choose Salmon.—To be good, the belly should be firm and thick, which may readily be ascertained by feeling it with the thumb and finger. The circumstance of this fish having red gills, though given as a standing rule in most cookery-books, as a sign of its goodness, is not at all to be relied on, as this quality can be easily given them by art.

Salmon and Caper Sauce.—

INGREDIENTS *for dish for 6 persons.*—2 *slices of salmon, 3 oz. of butter, ½ teaspoonful of chopped parsley, 1 shalot; salt, pepper and grated nutmeg to taste; caper sauce.* AVERAGE COST, 3s. 6d.

Lay the salmon in a baking-dish, place pieces of butter over it, and add the other ingredients, rubbing a little of the seasoning into the fish; baste it frequently; when done, take it out and drain for a minute or two; lay it in a dish, pour caper sauce over it, and serve. Salmon dressed in this way, with tomato sauce, is very delicious.

TIME.—*About ¾ hour.*

SEASONABLE *from April to August.*

Salmon, Collared.—INGREDIENTS.

—*A· piece of salmon, say 3 lb., a high seasoning of salt, pounded mace and pepper; water and vinegar, 3 bay-leaves.* AVERAGE COST, 4s.

Split the fish; scale, bone and wash it thoroughly clean; wipe it and rub in the seasoning inside and out; roll it up and bind firmly; lay it in a kettle, cover it with vinegar and water (½ vinegar, in proportion to the water); add the bay-leaves and a good seasoning of salt and whole pepper, and simmer till done. Do not remove the lid. Serve with melted butter or anchovy sauce. For preserving the collared fish,

boil up the liquor in which it was cooked, and add a little more vinegar. Pour over when cold.

TIME.—*¾ hour, or rather more.*

Salmon, Crimped. — Salmon is

frequently dressed in this way, but must be very fresh, and cut into slices 2 or 3 inches thick. Lay these in cold salt and water for 1 hour; have ready some boiling water, salted and well skimmed; put in the fish, and simmer gently for ¼ hour, or rather more should it be very thick; garnish the same as boiled salmon, and serve with the same sauces.

TIME.—*About ¼ hour, according to size.*

Note.—Never use vinegar with salmon, as it spoils the taste and colour of the fish.

Salmon, Curried.—INGREDIENTS.

—*Any remains of boiled salmon, ¾ pint of strong or medium stock, 1 onion, 1 tablespoonful of curry-powder, 1 teaspoonful of Harvey's sauce, 1 teaspoonful of anchovy sauce, 1 oz. of butter, the juice of ½ lemon, cayenne and salt to taste.* AVERAGE COST, *exclusive of the fish, 9d.*

Cut up the onions into small pieces, and fry them of a pale brown in the butter; add all the ingredients but the salmon, and simmer gently till the onion is tender, occasionally stirring the contents; cut the salmon into small square pieces, carefully take away all skin and bone, lay it in the stewpan, and let it gradually heat through; but do not allow it to boil long.

TIME.—*¾ hour.*

Salmon Cutlets. —INGREDIENTS

for dish for 6 persons.— 2 *lbs. of salmon, butter, pepper and salt, some good well-flavoured sauce.* AVERAGE COST, 3s. 6d.

Cut the slices 1 inch thick, and season them with pepper and salt; butter a sheet of white paper, lay each slice on a separate piece, with their ends twisted; broil gently over a clear fire, and serve with anchovy, caper, or any other sauce. When higher seasoning is required, add a few chopped herbs and a little spice.

TIME.—5 *to* 10 *minutes.*

Salmon, Fricandeau of.—INGRE-

DIENTS *for dish for* 6 or 8 *persons.* —3 *lbs. of middle of salmon, lardoons cut fine,* 2 *onions,* 2 *carrots,* 2 *bay-leaves, some thyme, whole pepper, grated nutmeg and salt, a pint of stock.* AVERAGE COST, 5s.

Having scaled, washed and dried the fish, lard it finely, and put it into a stew-pan with the vegetables cut fine, and the rest of the ingredients, and allow it to simmer very gently for 2 hours. Strain the sauce, skim off the fat, reduce it to a glaze, and with it glaze the fricandeau.

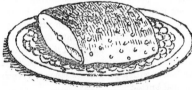

FRICANDEAU OF SALMON.

Serve with the glaze made again into sauce with a little stock, or what is better, with a purée of green peas.

TIME.—2¼ *hours.*

SEASONABLE *from April to August.*

Salmon, Fried. (Jewish Recipe.)—

INGREDIENTS *for dish for* 4 *or* 5 *persons.*— 2 *lbs. of salmon, a small flask of olive oil.* AVERAGE COST, 3s. 6d.

Pour the oil into a small deep pan over a clear fire, and when it ceases to bubble, put in the salmon well cleaned, and cut in two cutlets if too thick, and fry till thoroughly cooked through. It should only be a pale brown, and when it becomes so, raise the pan a little from the fire. When thoroughly done, drain and leave it to get cold, when serve on a fancy paper, garnished with parsley and cut lemon.

TIME.—*About ½ hour to fry the fish.*

SEASONABLE *from April to August.*

Salmon Jelly.—INGREDIENTS *for*

large mould.—1½ *pint of any savoury jelly, stiff enough to turn out, a tin of salmon or the remains of the cold boiled fish,* 2 *hard-boiled eggs, a few slices of beetroot, some very small sprigs of parsley.* AVERAGE COST, 1s. 6d.

Dip a jelly mould in water, then coat it with the jelly. Arrange in it as nicely as possible, some of the salmon cut in neat pieces, the beet stamped with a cutter, the eggs cut in rounds and the parsley in tiny sprigs, and let the jelly cool. Next drain (if tinned salmon be used), put the rest of the fish, with a little seasoning of cayenne and salt, in the centre, and fill up with the jelly.

SEASONABLE *at any time.*

Salmon Mayonnaise.—INGREDI-

ENTS *for mayonnaise for* 8 *persons.*—2 *lbs. of cold boiled salmon,* 2 *large lettuces, some small salad, a little beetroot, a very little oil and vinegar, pepper and salt, rather less than* ½ *pint of mayonnaise sauce.* AVERAGE COST, 4s.

Having cleansed and dried the lettuces, take the outer leaves dipped in a little oil and vinegar, to form a foundation, and upon this lay, as other cutlets, overlapping one another, in a ring, some cut from the salmon, and well mashed with the sauce, in the centre, and round these put the salad cut up, arranging it as prettily and effectively as possible with regard to colour; then pour over the remainder of the sauce and decorate with slices of beet, eggs cut up, or any savoury garnish taste may dictate.

SEASONABLE *in spring and summer.*

Salmon, Pickled. —INGREDIENTS.

—*Salmon,* ½ *oz. of whole pepper,* ½ *oz. of whole allspice,* 1 *teaspoonful of salt,* 2 *bay-leaves, equal quantities of vinegar and the liquor in which the fish was boiled.* AVERAGE COST, *in full season,* 1s. 4d. *per lb.*

After the fish comes from table, lay it in

a nice dish with a cover to it, as it should be excluded from the air, and take away the bone ; boil the liquor and vinegar with the other ingredients for 10 minutes, and let it stand to get cold ; pour it over the salmon, and in 12 hours this will be fit for the table.

TIME.—10 *minutes.*

Salmon, Potted.—INGREDIENTS.—

Salmon, pounded mace, cloves and pepper to taste ; bay-leaves, butter.

Skin the salmon, and clean it thoroughly by wiping with a cloth (water would spoil it) ; cut it into square pieces, which rub with salt ; let them remain till thoroughly drained, then lay them in a dish with the other ingredients, and bake. When quite done, drain them from the gravy, press into pots for use, and, when cold, pour over it clarified butter.

TIME.—$\frac{1}{2}$ *hour.*

Salmon, To Carve.—First run the

knife quite down to the bone, along the side of the fish, from A to B, and also from C to D. Then help the thick part lengthwise, that is, in the direction of the lines from A to B ; and the thin part breadthwise,

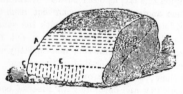

BOILED SALMON.

that is, in the direction of the lines from E to F, as shown in the engraving. A slice of the thick part should always be accompanied by a smaller piece of the thin from the belly, where lies the fat of the fish.

Note.—Many persons, in carving salmon, make the mistake of slicing the thick part of this fish in the opposite direction to that we have stated ; and thus, by the breaking of the flakes, the beauty of its appearance is destroyed.

Salmon, To Cure.—This process

consists in splitting the fish, rubbing it with salt, and then putting it into pickle in tubs provided for the purpose. Here it is kept for about 6 weeks, when it is taken out, pressed and packed in casks, with layers of salt.

Salsify, To Dress.—INGREDIENTS.

Salsify ; to each $\frac{1}{2}$ gallon of water allow 1 heaped tablespoonful of salt, 1 oz. of butter, 2 tablespoonfuls of lemon-juice.

Scrape the roots gently, so as to strip them only of their outside peel ; cut them into pieces about 4 inches long, and, as they are peeled, throw them into water with which has been mixed a little lemon-juice, to prevent their discolouring. Put them into boiling water, with salt, butter and lemon-juice in the above proportion, and let them boil rapidly until tender ; try them with a fork, and, when it penetrates easily, they are done. Drain the salsify, and serve with a good white sauce or French melted butter.

TIME.—30 *to* 50 *minutes.*

SEASONABLE *in winter.*

Note. — This vegetable may be also boiled, sliced and fried in batter of a nice brown. When crisp and a good colour, they should be served with fried parsley in the centre of the dish, and a little fine salt sprinkled over the salsify.

Salt.— Too little attention is often paid

to this most necessary adjunct to the table. There is nothing more disagreeable than wet salt ; equally so, that which is so hard that one spills it in trying to break it up. The best table salt is Bumstead's, and if this is kept in a dry place it keeps in good condition ; but salt-cellars want attending to every time they are used, and, therefore, a jar full of well-dried table salt should always be kept ready to fill them. Another little thing (too often forgotten by servants) to be remembered, should be the removal of the spoons when the cellars are taken from the table.

Sandwich Savouries. — INGRE-
DIENTS *for savoury for 6 persons.*—6 *anchovies,* 2 *rounds of stale bread,* 2 *eggs, butter
for frying.* AVERAGE COST, 9d.

The bread should be cut about one-third
of an inch in thickness, and stamped out
with a cutter in rounds of the size of a 5s.-
piece. These fry in butter till of a bright
golden brown, and set aside. Bone, wash
and fillet the anchovies, and, when the
croûtons are cold, curl two fillets upon each
and fill in the centre with finely-chopped
white of egg and the yolk rubbed through
a sieve.

SEASONABLE *at any time.*

Sandwiches, Anchovy.—INGRE-
DIENTS *for savoury for 6 persons.*—6 *slices
of very thin bread-and-butter,* 6 *anchovies
or some anchovy-paste, mustard-and-cress,
cayenne.* AVERAGE COST, 6d.

Spread half the slices of bread-and-butter
with the anchovies boned and filleted, or
the paste, and the others sprinkle over
with the mustard - and - cress freed from
stalks. Season with a little cayenne, then
put the slices together and cut into neat
sandwiches.

SEASONABLE *at any time.*

Sandwiches, Caviare.—INGRE-
DIENTS *for dish for 6 persons.*—6 *rounds of
very thin brown bread-and-butter, lemon-
juice, caviare, Nepaul pepper.* AVERAGE
COST, 1s.

Spread some caviare on three of the
rounds, squeeze over a very little lemon-
juice, and season with the pepper; then
put over the other slices, and, after cutting
off the crust, cut into fingers. Put a
stamped paper upon the dish, arrange the
fingers in layers, grotto form, and put in
the centre and round a garnish of watercress.

SEASONABLE *at any time.*

Sandwiches, Cucumber. — IN-
GREDIENTS *for small dish.*—*The centre or*

*thickest part of a moderate-sized cucumber,
4 rounds of thin white bread-and-butter,
oil, vinegar and pepper.* AVERAGE COST,
4d.

Peel the cucumber and cut into slices
rather thicker than for a salad, and steep
these rounds for a short time in oil and
vinegar. Stamp out rounds of bread-and-
butter of corresponding size, and make
sandwiches of the cucumber sprinkled
with a litttle pepper. These sandwiches
look best arranged in rings as cutlets, with
garnish of cress or parsley.

SEASONABLE *in summer for afternoon tea.*

Sandwiches, Foie Gras.—IN-
GREDIENTS. — *Bread - and - butter, either
white or brown, foie gras, cayenne.*

Make these sandwiches in the same way
as anchovy ones, with cayenne to taste, if
liked.

Sandwiches, Oyster.—INGREDI-
ENTS *for savoury for 6 persons.*—6 *large
oysters, thin brown bread - and - butter,
cayenne, lemon-juice.* AVERAGE COST,
10d. to 1s.

Having opened the oysters, put them in
a mortar, and pound them with lemon-
juice and cayenne sufficient for flavouring.
Spread the oysters upon half the bread-and-
butter, lay over the other slices, and, after
cutting away the crust, cut into neat
sandwiches, which arrange upon a silver
dish or plate.

SEASONABLE *from September to March.*

Note.—These are useful for hors d'œuvres,
and should be served at the commencement of
dinner, before the soup.

Sandwiches, Victoria.—INGRE-
DIENTS *for dish for 6 persons.*—4 *eggs; their
weight in pounded sugar, butter and flour;*
¼ *saltspoonful of salt, a layer of any kind
of jam or marmalade.* AVERAGE COST,
1s. 3d.

Beat the butter to a cream; dredge in
the flour and pounded sugar; stir these

ingredients well together and add the eggs, which should be previously thoroughly whisked. When the mixture has been well-beaten for about 10 minutes, butter a Yorkshire-pudding tin, pour in the batter, and bake it in a moderate oven for 20 minutes. Let it cool, spread one half of the cake with a layer of nice preserve, place over it the other half of the cake, press the pieces slightly together, and then cut it into long finger-pieces ; pile them in crossbars on a glass dish, and serve.

Time.—20 *minutes.*

Seasonable *at any time.*

Sandwiches, Recipes for.—

Directions for making the following, appear under their respective headings :—

Anchovy.	Cucumber.
Anchovy with An-	Foie Gras.
chovy Paste.	Oyster.
Caviare.	Toast.
Cheese.	Victoria.

Sardine Sauce.—Ingredients *for sauce for moderate-sized dish of fish.*—6 *sardines,* 1 *oz. of butter, the rind of* 1 *lemon,* 1 *shalot,* 1 *pint of gravy or stock, a bay-leaf, salt, pepper, a grate of nutmeg, flour.*

Average Cost, 10*d.*

Bone and chop up the sardines, put the bones into a saucepan with the other ingredients, with the butter worked into a ball with flour, and boil for 15 minutes ; then strain over the chopped fish.

Time.—15 *minutes.*

Seasonable *at any time.*

Sardine Savouries.—Ingredients *for dish for* 6 *persons.*—8 *sardines,* 2 *slices of stale bread, a dessertspoonful each of anchovy and Worcester sauce,* 2 *oz. of butter, a dessertspoonful of flour, cayenne, water and lemon-juice; butter for frying.*

Average Cost, 1*s.*

Having fried the croûtons, scale and bone the sardines, and pound them in a

mortar with the butter, and spread upon the croûtons. Make a mixture of the other ingredients with rather less than ½ pint of water, and simmer till the flour is well cooked, keeping the croûtons hot meanwhile ; then pour the sauce over the croûtons, and serve as hot as possible.

Sauces, General Remarks upon.—

The preparation and appearance of sauces and gravies are of the highest consequence, and in nothing does the talent and taste of the cook more display itself. Their special adaptability to the various viands they are to accompany cannot be too much studied, in order that they may harmonize and blend with them as perfectly, so to speak, as does a pianoforte accompaniment with the voice of the singer.   .

The general basis of most gravies and some sauces is the same stock as that used for soups; and, by the employment of these with, perhaps, an additional slice of ham, a little spice, a few herbs and a slight flavouring from some cold sauce or ketchup, very nice gravies may be made for a very small expenditure. A milt (either of a bullock or sheep), the shank-end of mutton that has already been dressed, and the necks and feet of poultry may all be advantageously used for gravy, where much is not required. It may, then, be established as a rule, that there exists no necessity for good gravies to be expensive, and that there is no occasion, as many would have the world believe, to buy ever so many pounds of fresh meat, in order to furnish an ever so little quantity of gravy.

Brown sauces, generally speaking, should scarcely be so thick as white sauces ; and it is well to bear in mind, that all those which are intended to mask the various dishes of poultry or meat, should be of a sufficient consistency to slightly adhere to the fowls or joints over which they are poured. For browning and thickening sauces, &c., browned flour may be properly employed.

Sauces should possess a decided character; and, whether sharp or sweet, savoury or plain, they should carry out their names in a distinct manner; although, of course, not so much flavoured as to make them too piquant on the one hand, or too mawkish on the other.

Gravies and sauces should be sent to table very hot; and there is all the more necessity for the cook to see to this point, as, from their being usually served in small quantities, they are more liable to cool quickly than if they were in a larger body. Those sauces, of which cream or eggs form a component part, should be well stirred as soon as these ingredients are added to them, and must never be allowed to boil; as, in that case, they would instantly curdle.

Sauce à l'Aurore (for Trout, Soles, &c.).

—INGREDIENTS *for sauce for 2 or 3 soles.*—*The spawn of* 1 *lobster,* 1 *oz. of butter,* ½ *pint of Béchamel, the juice of* ½ *lemon, a high seasoning of salt and cayenne.* AVERAGE COST, 9*d.*

Take the spawn and pound it in a mortar with the butter until quite smooth, and work it through a hair sieve. Put the Béchamel into a stewpan, add the pounded spawn, the lemon-juice, which must be strained, and a plentiful seasoning of cayenne and salt; let it just simmer, but do not allow it to boil, or the beautiful red colour of the sauce will be spoiled. A small spoonful of anchovy essence may be added at pleasure.

TIME.—1 *minute to simmer.*
SEASONABLE *at any time.*

Sauce à la Matelote (for Fish).

—INGREDIENTS *for sauce for good-sized dish of fish.*—½ *pint of Espagnole,* 3 *onions,* 2 *tablespoonfuls of mushroom ketchup,* ½ *glass of port wine, a bunch of sweet herbs,* ½ *bay-leaf, salt and pepper to taste,* 1 *clove,* 2

berries of allspice, a little liquor in which the fish has been boiled, lemon-juice and anchovy sauce. AVERAGE COST, 1*s.* 8*d.*

Slice and fry the onions of a nice brown colour, and put them into a stewpan with the Espagnole, ketchup, wine and a little liquor in which the fish has been boiled. Add the seasoning, herbs and spices, and simmer gently for 10 minutes, stirring well the whole time; strain it through a fine hair sieve, put in the lemon-juice and anchovy sauce, and pour it over the fish.

WICKER SAUCE STAND.

This sauce may be very much enriched by putting in a few small quenelles, or forcemeat balls made of fish, and also glazed onions or mushrooms. These, however, should not be added to the matelote till it is dished.

TIME.—10 *minutes.*
SEASONABLE *at any time.*

Note.—This sauce originally took its name as being similar to that which the French sailor (*matelot*) employed as a relish to the fish he caught and ate. In some cases cider and perry were substituted for the wine. The Norman *matelotes* were very celebrated.

Sauce Aristocratique. (A Store Sauce.)

—INGREDIENTS. — *Green walnuts. To every pint of juice,* 1 *lb. of anchovies,* 1 *drachm of cloves,* 1 *drachm of mace,* 1 *drachm of Jamaica ginger, bruised,* 8 *shalots. To every pint of the boiled liquor,* ½ *pint of vinegar,* ¼ *pint of port wine,* 2 *tablespoonfuls of soy.* AVERAGE COST, 3s. 6d. *per quart.*

Pound the walnuts in a mortar, squeeze out the juice through a strainer, and let it stand to settle. Pour off the clear juice, and to every pint of it add anchovies, spices and cloves in the above proportion. Boil all these together till the anchovies are dissolved, then strain the juice again, put in the shalots (8 to every pint) and boil again. To every pint of the boiled liquor add vinegar, wine and soy in the above quantities, and bottle off for use. Cork well and seal the corks.

SEASONABLE.—*Make this sauce from the beginning to the middle of July, when walnuts are in perfection for sauces and pickling.*

Sauce, Mango Chetney,

Bengal Recipe for Making.—INGREDIENTS.—1½ lb. *of moist sugar,* ¾ lb. *of salt,* ¼ lb. *of garlic,* ¼ lb. *of onions,* ¾ lb. *of powdered ginger,* ¼ lb. *of dried chilies,* ¾ lb. *of mustard seed,* ¾ lb. *of stoned raisins* 2 *bottles of best vinegar,* 30 *large unripe sour apples.* AVERAGE COST, 5s.

The sugar must be made into syrup ; the garlic, onions and ginger be finely pounded in a mortar ; the mustard-seed be washed in cold vinegar, and dried in the sun ; the apples be peeled, cored and sliced, and boiled in a bottle and a half of the vinegar. When all this is done, and the apples are quite cold, put them into a large pan, and gradually mix the whole of the rest of the ingredients, including the remaining half-bottle of vinegar. It must be well stirred until the whole is thoroughly blended, and then put into bottles for use. Tie a piece of wet bladder over the mouths of the bottles, after they are well corked. This chetney is very superior to any which can be bought, and one trial will prove it to be delicious.

Note.—This recipe was given by a native to an English lady, who had long been a resident in India, and who, since her return to her native country, has become quite celebrated among her friends for the excellence of this Eastern relish.

Sauce, Christopher North's

(for Meat or Game).—INGREDIENTS *for sauce for small dish.*—1 *glass of port wine,* 2 *tablespoonfuls of Harvey's sauce,* 1 *dessertspoonful of mushroom ketchup, ditto of pounded white sugar,* 1 *tablespoonful of lemon-juice,* ½ *teaspoonful of cayenne pepper, ditto of salt.* AVERAGE COST, 6d.

Mix all the ingredients thoroughly together, and heat the sauce gradually by placing the vessel in which it is made in a saucepan of boiling water. Do not allow it to boil, and serve directly it is ready. This sauce, if bottled immediately, will keep good for a fortnight, and will be found excellent.

Sauce, Green (for Green Geese or

Ducklings). — INGREDIENTS. — ¼ *pint of sorrel-juice,* 1 *glass of sherry,* ½ *pint of green gooseberries,* 1 *teaspoonful of pounded sugar,* 2 *oz. of fresh butter.*

Boil the gooseberries in water until they are quite tender ; mash them and press them through a sieve ; put the pulp into a saucepan with the above ingredients ; simmer for 3 or 4 minutes, and serve very hot.

TIME.—3 *or* 4 *minutes.*

Sauce Piquante (for Cutlets, Roast

Meat, &c.).—INGREDIENTS *for sauce for dish for* 4 *or* 5 *persons.*—2 *oz. of butter,* 1 *small carrot,* 6 *shalots,* 1 *small bunch of savoury herbs, including parsley,* ½ *bayleaf,* 2 *slices of lean ham,* 2 *cloves,* 6 *peppercorns,* 1 *blade of mace,* 3 *whole allspice,* 4 *tablespoonfuls of vinegar,* ½ *pint of stock,* 1 *small lump of sugar,* ¼ *saltspoonful of cayenne, salt to taste.* AVERAGE COST, 1s.

Put into a stewpan the butter, with the carrots and shalots, both of which must be cut into small slices ; add the herbs, bay-leaf, spices and ham (which must be minced rather finely), and let these ingredients simmer over a slow fire until the bottom of the stewpan is covered with a brown glaze. Keep stirring with a wooden spoon, and put in the remaining ingredients. Simmer very gently for ¼ hour, skim off every particle of fat, strain the sauce through a sieve, and serve very hot. Care must be taken that this sauce be not made too acid, although it should possess a sharpness indicated by its name. Of course the above quantity of vinegar may be increased or diminished at pleasure, according to taste.

TIME.—*Altogether, ½ hour.*
SEASONABLE *at any time.*

Sauce, A Good (for Various Boiled Puddings).

— INGREDIENTS *for sauce for large pudding.*— ¼ lb. *of butter,* ¼ lb. *of pounded sugar, a wineglassful of brandy or rum.* AVERAGE COST, 8d.

Beat the butter to a cream, until no lumps remain; add the pounded sugar and brandy or rum; stir once or twice until the whole is thoroughly mixed, and serve. This sauce may either be poured round the pudding or served in a tureen, according to taste or fancy.

Sauce, Soyer's (for Plum Pudding).

—INGREDIENTS *for sauce for good-sized pudding.*—*The yolks of 3 eggs, 1 tablespoonful of powdered sugar, 1 gill of milk, a very little grated lemon-rind, 2 small wineglassfuls of brandy.* AVERAGE COST, 1s.

Separate the yolks from the whites of 3 eggs, and put the former into a stewpan; add the sugar, milk and grated lemon-rind, and stir over the fire until the mixture thickens; but do *not* allow it to *boil*. Put in the brandy; let the sauce stand by the side of the fire to get quite hot; keep stirring it, and serve in a boat or tureen separately, or pour it over the pudding.

TIME.—*Altogether, 10 minutes.*

Sauce, A Good (for Steaks).

—INGREDIENTS.—1 oz. *of whole black pepper,* ½ oz. *of allspice,* 1 oz. *of salt,* ½ oz. *of grated horseradish,* ½ oz. *of pickled shalots,* 1 pint *of mushroom ketchup or walnut pickle.* AVERAGE COST, 9d.

Pound the ingredients finely in a mortar, and put them into the ketchup or walnut-liquor. Let them stand for a fortnight, when strain off the liquor and bottle for use. Either pour a little of the sauce over the steaks, or mix it in the gravy.

SEASONABLE.—*This can be made at any time.*

Note.—In using a jar of pickled walnuts, there is frequently left a large quantity of liquor. This should be converted into a sauce like the above, and will be found a very useful relish.

Sauce, Sweet (for Pudding).

—INGREDIENTS *for sauce for good-sized pudding.* —½ pint *of melted butter made with milk, 3 teaspoonfuls of pounded sugar, flavouring of grated lemon-rind or cinnamon.* AVERAGE COST, 4d.

Make ½ pint of melted butter, omitting any salt; stir in the sugar, add a little grated lemon-rind, nutmeg or powdered cinnamon, and serve. Previously to making the melted butter, the milk can be flavoured with bitter almonds, by infusing about half a dozen of them in it for about ½ hour; the milk should then be strained before it is added to the other ingredients. This simple sauce may be served for children, with batter, plum, or bread pudding.

TIME.—*Altogether, 15 minutes.*

Sauce, Sweet (for Venison).

—INGREDIENTS *for sauce for small joint.*—*A small jar of red-currant jelly, 1 glass of port wine.* AVERAGE COST, 10d.

Put the above ingredients into a stewpan, set them over the fire, and, when melted, pour in a tureen, and serve. It should not be allowed to boil.

TIME.—5 *minutes to melt the jelly.*

Sauce, Tournée.

— INGREDIENTS *for sauce for 1 entrée.*—1 pint *of white stock, thickening of flour and butter, or white roux, a faggot of savoury herbs, including parsley, 6 chopped mushrooms, 6 green onions.* AVERAGE COST, 6d.

Put the stock into a stewpan with the herbs, onions and mushrooms, and let it simmer very gently for about ½ hour; stir in sufficient thickening to make it of a proper consistency; let it boil for a few minutes, then skim off all the fat, strain and serve. This sauce, with the addition of a little cream, is frequently called velouté.

TIME.—½ *hour.*

Note.—If poultry trimmings are at hand, the stock should be made of these. The above sauce should not be made too thick, as it does not then admit of the fat being nicely removed.

Sauce for Wild Fowl.—INGRE-
DIENTS *for sauce for 2 birds.*—1 *glass of port wine,* 1 *tablespoonful of Leamington sauce,* 1 *tablespoonful of mushroom ketchup,* 1 *tablespoonful of lemon-juice,* 1 *slice of lemon-peel,* 1 *large shalot cut in slices,* 1 *blade of mace, cayenne to taste.* AVERAGE COST, 8d.

Put all the ingredients into a stewpan, set it over the fire, and let it simmer for about 5 minutes; then strain, and serve the sauce in a tureen.

TIME.—5 *minutes.*

Sauces, Recipes for.—Directions for making the following, appear under their respective headings:—

A l'Aurore.	Bread, Another
A la Matelote.	Mode.
Anchovy.	Butter, Melted.
Apple.	,, Another Mode.
Aristocratique.	,, with Milk.
Arrowroot.	Caper, for Fish.
Asparagus.	,, for Mutton.
Béchamel.	,, Substitute for.
,, Maigre.	Celery.
Benton.	,, More Simple.
Blanche.	Cherry.
Blonde.	Chestnut.
Bread.	,, Brown.

Cherokee.	Mango Chutney.
Christopher North's	Mint.
Crab.	Mushroom, Rich.
Cranberry.	,, Brown.
Cucumber.	,, White.
,, White.	,, Another Mode.
Custard.	Onion, Brown.
Dutch.	Onion, French.
Dutch Green.	,, White.
Egg.	Oyster.
Epicurean.	Parsley and Butter.
Fennel.	Piquante.
Financière.	Poivrade.
,, for Poultry and	Quin's.
Game.	Ravigote.
For Wild Fowl.	Reading.
Genevese.	Remoulade.
German.	Robert.
Good, for Puddings.	Sago.
,, for Steaks.	Sardine.
Gooseberry.	Sharp.
Green.	Shrimp.
Horseradish.	Soyer's.
Horseradish, Cold.	Spanish.
Hot Spice.	Sweet, for Puddings.
Indian Chutney.	,, for Venison.
Italian, Brown.	Tamarind.
,, White.	Tartar.
Leamington.	Tomato, for Keep-
Lemon.	ing.
,, White.	,, Another Mode.
,, for Puddings.	,, Hot.
Lobster.	Tournée.
Maître d' Hôtel.	Vanilla Custard.
,, without Meat.	White.

Sauces, Good Store, and for Cooking :—

Brand & Co., South Lambeth.	Ketchup, Walnut.
C. Cocks, Reading.	Vinegar, Camp.
Goodall, Back-house & Co., Leeds.	,, Celery.
	,, Chili.
	,, Cucumber.
Holbrook & Co., Birmingham.	,, Garlic.
	,, Gooseberry.
Ketchup, Oyster.	,, Horseradish.
	,, Raspberry.

Saucer Cake (for Tea).

INGREDIENTS.—¼ lb. of flour, ¼ lb. of fine oatmeal, ¼ lb. of pounded white sugar, ¼ lb. of butter, 2 eggs, 1 oz. of candied orange or lemon-peel. AVERAGE COST, 10d.

Mix the flour and oatmeal together; add the sugar, the candied peel cut into thin slices, the butter beaten to a cream, and the eggs well whisked. Beat the mixture for 10 minutes, put it into a buttered cake-tin or mould, or, if this is not obtainable, a soup-plate answers the purpose, lined with a piece of buttered paper. Bake the cake in a moderate oven from 1 to 1¼ hour, and when cold, put it away in a covered canister. It will remain good some weeks, even if it be cut into slices.

TIME.—1 to 1¼ hour.

SEASONABLE at any time.

Note.—Tous-les-mois is a superior kind of oatmeal

Sauerbraten. (German Recipe.)

INGREDIENTS for dish for 12 persons.—5 lbs. of fillet or rump of beef, 1 quart of mild vinegar, 4 bay-leaves, 2 small nutmegs, 2 oz. each of suet and butter, a dessertspoonful of flour, 2 small carrots, 4 onions, a crust of brown bread, a small cupful of cream, ground cloves, pepper and salt. AVERAGE COST, 6s.

Boil the vinegar with the nutmegs grated and the bay-leaves, and, having washed the

SAUERBRATEN.

meat, lay it in this, and keeping it in a cool place for 3 days in summer or 8 to 10 days in winter, turn it frequently with a wooden fork. When ready for cooking, lard the meat with lardoons, dipped in a mixture of ground cloves, pepper and salt; then having scattered a little salt over the meat, brown it a nice golden colour in a stewpan, with the butter and flour. Next pour in sideways enough water to cover the meat, put on the lid, and, after a few minutes, add the vegetables and the bread, and, weighting the lid down, let all simmer for 2½ hours, adding the cream ½ hour before serving. Take out the meat and put it on a hot plate in the oven. Thicken the gravy with flour, pass through a sieve, bring it to a boil, pour a little over the meat, and send the rest to table in a tureen.

TIME.—About 2½ hours.

SEASONABLE at any time.

Sauerkraut.

INGREDIENTS for dish for 6 persons.—2 lbs. of sauerkraut, 2 oz. each of lard, suet and butter, potato, grated, juniper berries, caraway seeds, salt.

Melt the lard, suet and butter in a stewpan, with a little water and a very little

SAUERKRAUT.

salt, and a few juniper berries and caraway seeds tied in a bag; then add the sauerkraut, cover closely and boil for 1½ hour. Before serving, thicken with either grated potato or peas.

TIME.—1½ hour.

SEASONABLE in autumn and winter.

Note.—Sauerkraut can be bought ready for use in England in small barrels. It is cabbage cut fine, pressed into clean barrels with salt, and allowed to ferment, with a cloth dipped in a solution of spices tied over the top of the barrel.

Sausage-Meat, Fried.

INGREDIENTS.—To every 1 lb. of lean pork, add ¾ lb. of fat bacon, ½ oz. of salt, 1 saltspoonful of pepper, ¼ teaspoonful of grated nutmeg, 1 teaspoonful of minced parsley. AVERAGE COST, 9d. per lb.

Remove from the pork all skin, gristle and bone, and chop it finely with the bacon; add the remaining ingredients and carefully mix all together. Pound it well in a mortar, make it into convenienent-sized cakes, flour these and fry them a nice brown for about 10 minutes. This is a very simple method of making sausage-meat, and on trial will prove very good, its great recommendation being that it is so easily made.

TIME.—10 *minutes.*

SEASONABLE *from September to March.*

Sausage-Meat Stuffing (for Turkeys).

—INGREDIENTS *for stuffing for small turkey.*—6 *oz. of lean pork,* 6 *oz. of fat pork, both weighed after being chopped (beef-suet may be substituted for the latter),* 2 *oz. of bread-crumbs,* 1 *small tablespoonful of minced sage,* 1 *blade of pounded mace, salt and pepper to taste,* 1 *egg.* AVERAGE COST, 9*d.*

Chop the meat and fat very finely, mix with them the other ingredients, taking care that the whole is thoroughly incorporated. Moisten with the egg, and the stuffing will be ready for use. Equal quantities of this stuffing and forcemeat will be found to answer very well, as the herbs, lemon-peel, &c., in the latter, impart a very delicious flavour to the sausage-meat.

Sausage or Meat Rolls.

—INGREDIENTS *for* 12 *rolls.*—1 *lb. of puff-paste, sausage-meat, the yolk of* 1 *egg.* AVERAGE COST, 1*s.* 6*d.*

Make 1 lb. of puff-paste; roll it out to the thickness of about ½ inch, or rather less, and divide it into 8, 10 or 12 squares, according to the size the rolls are intended to be. Place some sausage-meat on one-half of each square, wet the edges of the paste, and fold it over the meat; slightly press the edges together, and trim them neatly with a knife. Brush the rolls over with the yolk of an egg, and bake them in a well-heated oven for about ½ hour, or longer should they be very large. The remains of cold chicken and ham, minced and seasoned, as also cold veal or beef, make very good rolls.

TIME.—½ *hour, or longer if the rolls are large.*

SEASONABLE, *with sausage-meat, from September to March or April.*

Sausages, Beef.

—INGREDIENTS *for* 3 *lbs. of sausages.*—1 *lb. of suet,* 2 *lbs. of lean beef, seasoning to taste, of salt, pepper and mixed spices.* AVERAGE COST, 2*s.*

Clear the suet from skin, and mince that and the beef as finely as possible; season with pepper, salt and spices, and mix the whole well together. Make it into flat cakes, and fry of a nice brown. Many persons pound the meat in a mortar after it is chopped; but this is not necessary when the meat is minced finely.

TIME.—10 *minutes.*

SEASONABLE *at any time.*

Sausages, Fried.

—INGREDIENTS. —*Sausages; a small piece of butter.* AVERAGE COST, *if bought ready made,* 10*d. per lb.*

Prick the sausages with a fork (this prevents them from bursting), and put them into a frying-pan with a small piece of butter. Keep moving the pan about, and turn the sausages 3 or 4 times. In from 10 to 12 minutes they will be sufficiently cooked, unless they are *very large,*

FRIED SAUSAGES.

when a little more time should be allowed for them. Dish them with or without a piece of toast under them, and serve very hot. In some counties, sausages are boiled and served on toast. They should be plunged into boiling water, and simmered for about 10 or 12 minutes.

TIME.—10 *to* 12 *minutes.*

Note.—Sometimes, in close, warm weather, sausages very soon turn sour; to prevent this, put them in the oven for a few minutes with a small piece of butter to keep them moist. When wanted for table, they will not require so long frying as uncooked sausages.

Sausages, Pork. (Author's Oxford Recipe.)

INGREDIENTS *for 2 dozen sausages.*—1 lb. *of pork, fat and lean, without skin or gristle;* 1 lb. *of lean veal,* 1 lb. *of beef suet,* ½ lb. *of bread-crumbs, the rind of* ½ *lemon,* 1 *small nutmeg,* 6 *sage-leaves,* 1 *teaspoonful of pepper,* 2 *teaspoonfuls of salt,* ½ *teaspoonful of savory,* ½ *teaspoonful of marjoram.* AVERAGE COST, 2s. 6d.

Chop the pork, veal and suet finely together, add the bread-crumbs, lemon-peel (which should be well minced), and a small nutmeg grated. Wash and chop the sage-leaves very finely;

SAUSAGES.

add these, with the remaining ingredients, to the sausage-meat, and when thoroughly mixed, either put the meat into skins, or, when wanted for table, form it into little cakes, which should be floured and fried.

SEASONABLE *from October to March.*

Sausages, Veal.

INGREDIENTS.—*Equal quantities of fat bacon and lean veal; to every lb. of meat, allow* 1 *teaspoonful of minced sage, salt and pepper to taste.*

Chop the meat and bacon finely, and to every pound allow the above proportion of very finely-minced sage; add a seasoning of pepper and salt, mix the whole well together, make it into flat cakes, and fry a nice brown.

SEASONABLE *from March to October.*

Savoy Biscuits.

INGREDIENTS *for* 2 *dozen cakes.*—6 oz. *of flour,* 6 oz. *of sugar,* 4 *eggs, the rind of* 1 *lemon.* AVERAGE COST, 7d.

Separate the yolks from the whites of the eggs; beat the former well, add to them the sugar and grated lemon-rind, and beat for 15 minutes; then slowly dredge in the flour, and, after the whites have been whisked to a solid froth, add them, and beat for another 5 minutes. It is better for one person to beat the whites while another is blending the other ingredients. When ready, draw the cake in strips the length of a Savoy biscuit upon thick cartridge paper, and bake in a rather hot oven. They must be carefully watched, as they soon scorch, when their appearance is spoilt for using for Charlotte russe or other sweet fancy dishes.

TIME.—*5 to 8 minutes in a quick oven.*
SEASONABLE *at any time.*

Savoy Cake.

INGREDIENTS —*7 eggs, the weight of 4 in pounded loaf sugar, the weight of all in flour, a little grated lemon-rind, essence of almonds, or orange-flower water.* AVERAGE COST, 10d.

Break the eggs, putting the yolks into one basin and the whites into another. Whisk the former, and mix with them the sugar, the grated lemon-rind, or any other flavouring to taste; beat them well together and add the whites of the eggs, whisked to a froth. Put in the flour by degrees, continuing to beat the mixture for ¼ hour,

SAVOY CAKE WITH PISTACHIOS.

butter a mould, pour in the cake, and bake it from 1¼ to 1½ hour. This is a very nice cake, and it may be iced for a supper table, or cut into slices and spread with jam, which converts it into sandwiches.

TIME.—*1¼ to 1½ hour.*
SEASONABLE *at any time.*

Scotch Cakes.

INGREDIENTS *for a dozen cakes.*—1½ lb. *of flour,* ¾ lb. *of butter,* ¾ lb. *of sugar,* 2 *tablespoonfuls of ground caraway-seed,* ½ *that quantity of cinnamon a little citron or other candied-peel, cut in small slices.* AVERAGE COST, 1s. 6d.

Cream the butter, add the sugar, then slowly the flour; then the flavouring and the citron. Butter some patty-pans and put in the mixture, and bake for 15 minutes.

TIME.—15 *minutes to bake.*

SEASONABLE *at any time.*

Scotch Oat Cake.—INGREDIENTS *for 4 cakes.*—2 *lbs. of meal,* 2 *oz. of butter,* 1 *teaspoonful of carbonate of soda.* AVERAGE COST, 5d.

Put a quarter of the meal into a basin, and a quarter of the butter and soda into a tea-cup, filling this half full with hot water. When the butter and soda are melted, mix quickly with the meal in the basin with a knife, and, after stirring well, turn the mixture out on to a paste-board, and mould it flat and round with the knuckles, spreading it gradually so that it does not crack at the edges. Strew over the cake plenty of dry meal and roll it out thin, then cut from the centre into 3 cakes, and put them on a hot griddle, moving them as they get done from a cool spot to a hotter. By pressing the nail on the surface, it may be known when they are done. Next move them from the fire to the toaster in front of it, and let them dry gradually. Mix the other 3 cakes in the same way, having one ready as another comes off the fire.

TIME.—10 *minutes to bake.*

SEASONABLE *at any time.*

Scrap Cakes. — INGREDIENTS *for 4 dozen cakes.*—2 *lbs. of leaf, or the inside fat of a pig;* 1½ *lb. of flour,* ¼ *lb. of moist sugar,* ½ *lb. of currants,* 1 *oz. of candied lemon-peel, ground allspice to taste.* AVERAGE COST, 2s.

Cut the leaf, or flead, as it is sometimes called, into small pieces; put it into a large dish, which place in a quick oven; be

careful that it does not burn, and in a short time it will be reduced to oil, with the small pieces of leaf floating on the surface; and it is of these that the cakes should be made. Gather all the scraps together, put them into a basin with the flour, and rub them well together. Add the currants, sugar, candied peel, cut into thin slices, and the ground allspice. When all these ingredients are well mixed, moisten with sufficient cold water to make the whole into a nice paste; roll it out thin, cut it into shapes, and bake the cakes in a quick oven from 15 to 20 minutes. These are very economical and wholesome cakes for children, and the lard, melted at home, produced from the flead, is generally better than that you purchase. To prevent the lard from burning, and to insure its being a good colour, it is better to melt it in a jar placed in a saucepan of boiling water; by doing it in this manner, there will be no chance of its discolouring.

TIME.—15 *to* 20 *minutes.*

SEASONABLE *from September to March.*

Sea-Bream, Baked. — INGREDIENTS.—1 *bream; seasoning to taste, of salt, pepper and cayenne;* ¼ *lb. of butter.*

Well wash the bream, but do not remove the scales, and wipe away all moisture with

THE SEA BREAM.

a nice dry cloth. Season it inside and out with salt, pepper and cayenne, and lay it in a baking-dish. Place the butter in small pieces upon the fish, and bake for rather more than ½ an hour. To stuff this fish before baking, will be found a great improvement.

TIME.—*Rather more than ½ hour.*

SEASONABLE *in summer.*

Note.—This fish may be broiled over a nice clear fire, and served with a good brown gravy or white sauce, or it may be stewed in wine.

Sea-Kale, Boiled.—INGREDIENTS.

To each ½ gallon of water allow 1 *heaped tablespoonful of salt.* AVERAGE COST, 9d, *per basket.*

Well wash the kale, cut away any worm-eaten pieces, and tie it into small bunches; put it into *boiling* water, salted in the above proportion, and let it boil quickly until tender. Take it out, drain, untie the bunches, and serve with plain melted

SEA-KALE.

butter or white sauce, a little of which may be poured over the kale. Sea-kale may also be parboiled and stewed in good brown gravy; it will then take about ½ hour altogether.

TIME.—15 *minutes; when liked very thoroughly done, allow an extra* 5 *minutes.*

SEASONABLE *from February to June.*

Sea Pie.—INGREDIENTS *for pie for* 5 *or* 6 *persons.*—1 *lb. of gravy beef,* 3 *lbs. of potatoes, an onion, pepper and salt,* 1 *lb. of suet or dripping crust.* AVERAGE COST, 1s. 5d.

Having washed and peeled the potatoes, put them in cold water till wanted. Line a dish with the crust, then cut up the meat in small pieces and lay in, over it putting the onion sliced, with plenty of seasoning, and a dredge of flour. Fill up with quartered potatoes, and pour in ½ pint of water. Tie the dish in a cloth, plunge it into a saucepan of boiling water, and boil gently for 2 hours.

TIME.—2 *hours.*

SEASONABLE *as a winter dish for children.*

Seed Biscuits.—INGREDIENTS *for* 3 *dozen biscuits.*—1 *lb. of flour,* ¼ *lb. of sifted sugar,* ¼ *lb. of butter,* ½ *oz. of caraway seeds,* 3 *eggs.* AVERAGE COST, 10d.

Beat the butter to a cream; stir in the flour, sugar and caraway seeds; and when these ingredients are well mixed, add the eggs, which should be well whisked. Roll out the paste; with a round cutter shape out the biscuits, and bake them in a moderate oven from 10 to 15 minutes. The tops of the biscuits may be brushed over with a little milk or the white of an egg, and then a little sugar strewn over.

TIME.—10 *or* 15 *minutes.*

SEASONABLE *at any time.*

Seed-Cake, Common.—INGREDIENTS *for good-sized cake.*—½ *quartern of dough,* ¼ *lb. of good dripping,* 6 *oz. of moist sugar,* ½ *oz. of caraway seeds,* 1 *egg.* AVERAGE COST, 8d.

If the dough is sent in from the baker's, put it in a basin covered with a cloth, and

SEED CAKE.

set it in a warm place to rise. Then with a wooden spoon beat the dripping to a liquid; add it, with the other ingredients, to the dough, and beat it until everything is very thoroughly mixed. Put it into a buttered tin, and bake the cake for rather more than 2 hours.

TIME.—*Rather more than 2 hours.*

SEASONABLE *at any time.*

Seed-Cake, A Very Good.—IN-GREDIENTS *for good-sized cake.*—¾ lb. of *butter*, 4 *eggs*, ¾ *lb. of sifted sugar, pounded mace and grated nutmeg to taste*, 1 *lb. of flour*, ¾ *oz. of caraway seeds*, 1 *wineglassful of brandy.* AVERAGE COST, 2s.

Beat the butter to a cream; dredge in the flour; add the sugar, mace, nutmeg and caraway seeds, and mix these ingredients well together. Whisk the eggs, stir to them the brandy, and beat the cake again for 10 minutes. Put it into a tin lined with buttered paper, and bake it from 1½ to 2 hours. This cake would be equally nice made with currants, and omitting the caraway seeds.

TIME.—*1½ to 2 hours.*

SEASONABLE *at any time.*

Seed Cakes.—INGREDIENTS *for 2 dozen cakes.*—½ *lb. of butter*, ½ *lb. of sugar*, 1 *teacupful of milk*, 1 *tablespoonful of caraway seeds*, ¼ *teaspoonful of carbonate of soda*, 4 *eggs, a little salt, flour.* AVERAGE COST, 1s. 3d.

Beat the eggs well, add to them the sugar, the soda, dissolved in a little milk, then the remainder of the milk and the caraway-seeds; add gradually the flour till the paste is sufficiently stiff to roll out and cut into cakes. Stamp them out, or put spoonfuls of this mixture into buttered patty-pans, and bake in a quick oven.

TIME.—*To bake the cakes, from 10 to 15 minutes.*

SEASONABLE *at any time.*

Semolina Pudding, Baked.—INGREDIENTS *for pudding for 6 persons.*—3 *oz. of semolina*, 1½ *pint of milk*, ¼ *lb. of sugar*, 12 *bitter almonds*, 3 *oz. of butter*, 4 *eggs.* AVERAGE COST, 1s. 2d.

Flavour the milk with the bitter almonds,

by infusing them in it by the side of the fire for about ½ hour; then strain it, and mix with it the semolina, sugar and butter. Stir these ingredients over the fire for a few minutes; then take them off, and gradually mix in the eggs, which should be well beaten. Butter a pie-dish, line the edges with puff-paste, put in the pudding, and bake in rather a slow oven from 40 to 50 minutes. Serve with custard sauce or stewed fruit, a little of which may be poured over the pudding.

TIME.—*40 to 50 minutes.*

SEASONABLE *at any time.*

Semolina Pudding. (More Economical.)—INGREDIENTS *for large pudding.* —¼ *lb. of semolina*, 1 *quart of milk*, ¼ *lb. of sugar*, 2 *oz. of butter*, 3 *eggs, the rind of a small lemon.* AVERAGE COST, 1s.

Butter a pie-dish, and put in it the semolina, milk, sugar and lemon rind. Set the dish on the top of the stove long enough for the semolina to soak and the lemon-rind to flavour the pudding; then take out the rind. Beat the eggs well and mix with the pudding, put some small pieces of butter on the top, and bake in a rather slow oven for an hour.

Should any trimmings of puff paste be at hand, they may well be used for edging the dish. Any other flavouring may be substituted for the lemon-rind.

TIME.—*1 hour.*

SEASONABLE *at any time.*

Semolina Soup.—INGREDIENTS.—5 *oz. of semolina*, 2 *quarts of boiling stock* (cheap or medium quality). AVERAGE COST, 10d. per quart.

Drop the semolina into the boiling stock and keep stirring for a short time, to prevent its burning. Simmer gently for ½ hour, and serve.

TIME.—*½ hour.*

SEASONABLE *all the year.*

Note.—Semolina is a good thickening for any soup for family use.

September—Dinner for Twelve Persons.

MENU. (English.)	Quantity.	Average Cost.		MENU. (French.)
		s.	d.	
Oysters.	4 doz.	6	0	Huîtres.
Clear Soup.	2 quarts.	3	6	Consommé.
Boiled Soles,	2 pairs.	6	0	Soles,
Lobster Sauce.	2 tur.	2	6	Sauce Homard.
Red Mullet.	12 fish.	8	0	Rougets.
Grilled Mushrooms.	3 baskts.	4	6	Champignons Grillés.
Hashed Game.	2 dishes	6	0	Salmis de Gibier.
Sirloin.	1 joint.	9	6	Aloyau.
Potatoes. French Beans.	4 lbs. ea.	1	0	Pommes de Terre. Haricots Verts.
Partridges.	6 birds.	12	0	Perdreaux.
Greengage Tart.	2 dishes.	4	0	Tourte aux Prunes Verts.
Custard.	2 dishes	1	6	Crême.
Compôte of Fruit.	2 dishes.	4	6	Compôte de Fruits.
		£3 9	0	

September—Dinner for Ten Persons.

MENU. (English.)	Quantity.	Average Cost.		MENU. (French.)
		s.	d.	
Appetisans.	3 dishes.	2	0	Appétisans.
Soup à la Reine.	2 quarts.	5	6	Soupe à la Reine.
Turbot,	1 fish.	10	0	Turbot,
Green Dutch Sauce.	2 tur.	2	6	Hollandaise Verte.
Salmi of Wild Duck.	1 dish.	5	6	Salmi de Canards Sauvages.
Mutton Cutlets.	1 dish.	4	0	Côtelettes de Mouton.
Goose,	1 bird.	9	6	Oiseau,
Apple Sauce.	2 tur.	0	9	Sauce aux Pommes.
Potatoes. Sprouts.	3 lbs. ea.	0	9	Pommes de Terre. Choux.
Olives, Stuffed.	2½ doz.	2	0	Olives Farcies.
Cream Eggs.	1 dish.	3	0	Œufs à la Crême.
Iced Pudding.	1	5	0	Poud ng Glacé.
		£2 10	6	

September—Dinner for Eight Persons.

MENU. (English.)	Quantity.	Average Cos .		MENU. (French.)
		s.	d.	
Flemish Soup.	3 pints.	2	6	Soupe à la Flamande.
Cold Salmon Cutlets,	1 dish.	4	6	Côtelettes de Saumon,
Horseradish Sauce.	1 tur.	1	0	Sauce Raifort.
Game Croquettes.	1 dish.	3	0	Croquettes de Gibier.
Veal Collops.	1 dish.	3	6	Escalopes de Veau.
Saddle of Mutton.	1 joint	10	6	Selle de Mouton.
Potatoes. French Beans.	3 lbs. ea.	0	9	Pommes de Terre. Haricots Verts.
Sweet Omelette.	1	1	3	Omelette aux Confitures.
Compôte of Peaches.	1	3	0	Compôte de Pêches.
		£1 10	0	

September—Dinners for from Six to Twelve Persons.

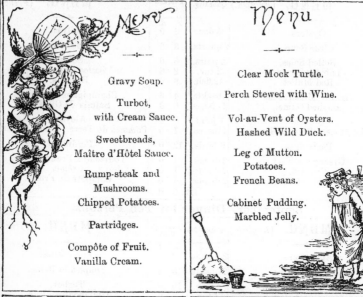

Menu

Gravy Soup.

Turbot,
with Cream Sauce.

Sweetbreads,
Maître d'Hôtel Sauce.

Rump-steak and
Mushrooms.
Chipped Potatoes.

Partridges.

Compôte of Fruit.
Vanilla Cream.

Menu

Clear Mock Turtle.

Perch Stewed with Wine.

Vol-au-Vent of Oysters.
Hashed Wild Duck.

Leg of Mutton.
Potatoes.
French Beans.

Cabinet Pudding.
Marbled Jelly.

Menu

Celery Soup.

Fried Soles, Piquante Sauce.

Oyster Patties.

Sirloin of Beef,
Horseradish Sauce.
Potatoes.   Sprouts.

Olives.

Damson Tart.   Custard.
Stone Cream.

Menu

Julienne.

Turbot,
Shrimp Sauce.

Chicken Croquettes.

Saddle of Mutton.
Potatoes.
Sprouts.

Grouse.

Russian Salad.

Marasquino Jelly.

Ices.

September—Plain Family Dinners for.

No. 1.

Sunday.—Saddle of mutton, potatoes, French beans.—Greengage tart, custard, rice blancmange.—Cheese biscuits, butter. —Dessert of pears, plums and walnuts.

Monday. — Mock turtle soup. — Cold mutton, mashed potatoes, salad.—Cheese ramekins.

Tuesday.—Brill, shrimp sauce.—Hashed mutton, potatoes, vegetable marrow.— Baked milk pudding.

Wednesday.—Rissoles from cold fish.— Steak-and-kidney pie, potatoes, baked Spanish onions.—Apple dumplings.

Thursday.—Roast sirloin of beef, potatoes, French beans, Yorkshire pudding.— Stewed fruit and boiled tapioca.

Friday.—Cold beef, mashed potatoes, tomato salad.—Grouse.—Sweet omelette.— Cheese.

Saturday.—Soup.—Haricot beef with vegetables.—Jam tart, rice pudding.

No. 2.

Sunday.—Roast turkey, sausages, sea-kale, potatoes. — Damson tart, custard pudding.—Cheese, &c.—Dessert of peaches, pears and walnuts.

Monday. — Soup. — Steak-and-kidney pudding, potatoes.—Baked apple custard. —Cheese.

Tuesday.—Rissoles of cold turkey.— Roast loin of mutton, onion sauce, potatoes, sprouts.—Ground rice pudding.

Wednesday.—Cod and oyster sauce.— Haricot mutton, with vegetables, potatoes. —Apple tart and custard.

Thursday.—Fish pie made from cold fish —Boiled round of beef, carrots, potatoes.— Macaroni cheese.

Friday. — Cold beef, roast chickens, cushion of bacon, French beans, potatoes. —Plain plum pudding.

Saturday. — Pea soup. — Minced beef, curried chicken, potatoes.

September—Vegetarian Dinners for.

No. 1.

Brown Vegetable Soup.

Potato Pie.

Croquettes of Hominy.
Stuffed Tomatoes.

Stewed Fruit.
Ground Rice Pudding.

No. 2.

White Soup.

Bean Croquettes.
Macaroni and Tomatoes.

Apple Tart.
Custard.

Celery Salad.

September—Dinner Table Decorations for.

In the country, one has not far to seek for pretty decorations for the table this month. Should the autumn come in early, and coloured leaves, mosses and berries abound, many of these may be used; but October is the best month for the beautiful tints of autumn in natural foliage. Sheaves of corn are appropriate decorations for this month, and if these be set up round tins which contain water, in which poppies and other corn flowers are placed, so that they blend with the corn, the effect is very pretty. Barley is almost prettier than anything else for this purpose, and the little sheaves should be tied with ribbon of the same colour as the flowers used; thus, scarlet for the poppies, and dark blue for the corn flowers. Alpine poppies of various colours are very useful for table decoration, and look best with very little foliage or only grasses.

Towards the end of this month, golden bracken should be gathered and pressed, to serve for winter decoration.

September, Things in Season.

Fish. — Bream, brill, carp, cod, crab, dory, eels, flounders, haddocks, lobsters, mullet, oysters, plaice, prawns, skate, soles, turbot, whiting, whitebait.

Meat.—Beef, lamb, mutton, pork, veal.

Poultry.—Chickens, ducks, fowls, geese, larks, pigeons, pullets, rabbits, teal, turkeys.

Game.—Blackcock, buck venison, grouse, hares, partridges.

Vegetables. — Artichokes, asparagus, beans, cabbage sprouts, carrots, celery, lettuces, mushrooms, onions, peas, potatoes, salads, sea-kale, sprouts, tomatoes, turnips, vegetable marrows, various herbs.

Fruit.—Bullaces, damsons, figs, filberts, grapes, melons, morella cherries, mulberries, nectarines, peaches, pears, plums, quinces, walnuts.

Shad, Baked. — INGREDIENTS *for dish for 6 persons.—A medium-sized shad, ¼ lb. of salt pork, 1 oz. of butter, 2 oz. of bread-crumbs, a glass of port wine, flour, pepper and salt.* AVERAGE COST, 2s. 3d.

Cut the fish open at the gills and wash and scrape it clean, then wipe it with a dry cloth. Make a stuffing with half the pork, the bread-crumbs, chopped parsley and a seasoning of pepper and salt. Fill the fish with this, sew it up, and dredge it with flour, and lay the rest of the pork, cut very thin, over it. Bake 40 minutes in a tin, then lay in a hot dish. Put butter, seasoning, hot water and the wine into the tin to make some gravy, and when it boils, pour it over the fish.

TIME.—40 *minutes to bake the fish.*
SEASONABLE *from April to June.*

Shad, To Dress.—INGREDIENTS.— 1 *shad, oil, pepper and salt.*

Scale, empty and wash the fish carefully, and make two or three incisions across the back. Season it with pepper and salt, and let it remain in oil for ½ hour. Broil it on both sides over a clear fire, and serve with caper sauce. This fish is much esteemed by the French, and by them is considered excellent.

TIME.—*Nearly* 1 *hour.*
SEASONABLE *from April to June.*

Shandy Gaff. — INGREDIENTS *for pint mug, ½ pint of good bitter ale, ½ pint or a bottle of ginger beer; if liked, a dash of liqueur ice.* AVERAGE COST, *without the liqueur, 3d.*

Put some lumps of ice in a tankard, and pour the ale and ginger beer over, adding a little liqueur, if liked.

SEASONABLE *in summer.*

Sharp Sauce. — INGREDIENTS *for good-sized dish of cutlets.—2 oz. of butter, 6 shalots, a small carrot, a small bunch of savoury herbs including parsley, a small bay-leaf, 2 slices of lean ham, 6 peppercorns, 1 blade of mace, 4 tablespoonfuls of vinegar, ½ pint of stock, 3 allspice, a small lump of sugar, salt and cayenne to taste.* AVERAGE COST, 10d.

Slice the carrots and shalots, and put them in a stewpan, with the butter. Add the ham, finely-minced, the spices and the herbs, and let all simmer over a slow fire till the bottom of the stewpan is covered with a brown glaze. Keep stirring with a wooden spoon, and add the remaining ingredients; then simmer very gently for 15 minutes; skim off every atom of fat, strain the sauce, and serve very hot.

TIME.—½ *hour.*
SEASONABLE *at any time.*

Sheep's Brains, en Matelote.—

INGREDIENTS *for dish for 6 persons.—6 sheep's brains, vinegar, salt, a few slices of bacon, 1 small onion, 2 cloves, a small bunch of parsley, sufficient stock or weak broth to cover the brains, 1 tablespoonful of lemon-juice, matelote sauce.* AVERAGE COST, 1s. 6d.

Detach the brains from the head, without breaking them, and put them into a pan of warm water ; remove the skin, and let them remain for 2 hours. Have ready a saucepan of boiling water, add a little vinegar and salt, and put in the brains. When they are quite firm, take them out and put them into very cold water. Place 2 or 3 slices of bacon in a stewpan, put in the brains, the onion, stuck with 2 cloves, the parsley, and a good seasoning of pepper and salt; cover with stock or weak broth, and boil them gently for about 25 minutes. Have ready some croûtons ; arrange these in the dish alternately with the brains, and cover with a matelote sauce, to which has been added the above proportion of lemon-juice.

TIME.—25 *minutes.*

SEASONABLE *at any time.*

Sheep's Feet or Trotters.

(SOYER'S Recipe.)—INGREDIENTS *for dish for 6 or 8 persons.*—12 *feet,* ¼ *lb. of beef or mutton suet,* 2 *onions,* 1 *carrot,* 2 *bay-leaves,* 2 *sprigs of thyme,* 1 *oz. of salt,* ¼ *oz. of pepper,* 2 *tablespoonfuls of flour,* 2½ *quarts of water,* ¼ *lb. of fresh butter,* 1 *teaspoonful of salt,* 1 *teaspoonful of flour,* ¼ *teaspoonful of pepper, a little grated nutmeg, the juice of* 1 *lemon,* 1 *gill of milk, the yolks of* 2 *eggs.* AVERAGE COST, 3s.

Have the feet cleaned, and the long bone extracted from them. Put the suet into a stewpan, with the onions and carrot, sliced, the bay-leaves, thyme, salt and pepper, and let these simmer for 5 minutes. Add two tablespoonfuls of flour and the water, and keep stirring till it boils; then put in the feet. ; Let these simmer for 3 hours, or until perfectly tender, and take them and lay them on a sieve. Mix together on a plate, with the back of a spoon, butter, salt, flour (1 teaspoonful), pepper, nutmeg and lemon-juice, as above, and put the feet, with a gill of milk, into a stewpan. When very hot, add the butter, &c., and stir continually till melted. Now mix the yolks of 2 eggs with 5 tablespoon-fuls of milk ; stir this to the other ingre-

dients, keep moving the pan over the fire continually for a minute or two, but do not allow it to boil after the eggs are added. Serve in a very hot dish, and garnish with croûtons or sippets of toasted bread.

TIME.—3 *hours.*

SEASONABLE *at any time.*

Sheep's Head.

—INGREDIENTS.— 1 *sheep's head, sufficient water to cover it,* 3 *carrots,* 3 *turnips,* 2 *or* 3 *parsnips,* 3 *onions, a small bunch of parsley,* 1 *teaspoonful of pepper,* 3 *teaspoonfuls of salt,* ¼ *lb. of Scotch oatmeal.* AVERAGE COST, 1s. 4d.

Clean the head well, and let it soak in warm water for 2 hours, to get rid of the blood ; put it into a saucepan, with sufficient cold water to cover it, and when it boils, add the vegetables, peeled and sliced, and the remaining ingredients ; before adding the oatmeal, mix it to a smooth batter with a little of the liquor. Keep stirring till it boils up; then shut the saucepan closely, and let it stew gently for 1½ or 2 hours. It may be thickened with rice or barley, but oatmeal is preferable.

TIME.—1½ *to* 2 *hours.*

SEASONABLE *at any time.*

Sheep's Head Soup.

—INGREDIENTS *for soup for 6 persons.*—1 *sheep's head,* 1 *onion,* 1 *leek,* 1 *bunch of sweet herbs, pepper, salt and water.* AVERAGE COST, 1s. 2d.

Wash and clean the head, and soak it for 2 hours, then put it in a deep saucepan, with just enough water to cover it. When the head is thoroughly heated, add 2 quarts of water and boil for 2 hours, after which take out the head and remove the meat from the bones. Put back the bones into the saucepan with the herbs, the onion and leek, cut in small pieces, and seasoning, and simmer another hour. Chop the meat into small pieces, and add it to the soup 10 minutes before serving.

TIME.—3 *hours.*

SEASONABLE *in winter.*

Sherry Cobbler.

INGREDIENTS *for sufficient for 3 persons.—4 glasses of sherry, 1 bottle of soda or seltzer, 1 tablespoonful of pounded sugar, 1 glass of liqueur, ice.* AVERAGE COST, 1s. 6d.

Put into 3 tumblers a lump of ice, a third of the sherry, and a little dash of

TANKARD.

liqueur. Next divide the soda into the 3 glasses, and serve with straws.

SEASONABLE *in summer.*

Shortbread, Scotch.

INGREDIENTS *for 6 good-sized cakes.—2 lbs. of flour, 1 lb. of butter, ¼ lb. of pounded loaf sugar, ½ oz. of caraway seeds, 1 oz. of sweet almonds, a few strips of candied orange-peel.* AVERAGE COST, 1s. 10d.

Beat the butter to a cream, gradually dredge in the flour, and add the sugar, caraway seeds and sweet almonds, which should be blanched and cut into small pieces. Work the paste until it is quite smooth, and divide it into six pieces. Put

SHORTBREAD.

each cake on a separate piece of paper, roll the paste out square to the thickness of about an inch, and pinch it upon all sides. Prick it well, and ornament with one or two strips of candied orange-peel. Put the cakes into a good oven and bake them from 25 to 30 minutes.

TIME.—25 to 30 *minutes.*

SEASONABLE *at any time.*

Note.—Where the flavour of the caraway seeds is disliked, omit them, and add rather a larger proportion of candied peel.

Shrimp Sauce

(for Various Kinds of Fish).—INGREDIENTS *for sauce for small dish of fish.—½ pint of melted butter, ¼ pint of picked shrimps, cayenne to taste.* AVERAGE COST, 6d.

Make the melted butter very smoothly, shell the shrimps (sufficient to make ¼ pint when picked), and put them into the butter; season with cayenne and let the sauce just simmer, but do not allow it to boil. When liked, a teaspoonful of anchovy sauce may be added.

TIME.—1 *minute to simmer.*

Shrimps or Prawns, To Boil.

INGREDIENTS.—¼ *lb. of salt to each gallon of water.* AVERAGE COST, *prawns,* 1s. *per dozen; shrimps,* 4d. *per pint.*

Prawns should be very red, and have no spawn under the tail; much depends on

THE SHRIMP.

their freshness and the way in which they are cooked. Throw them into boiling water, salted as above, and keep them boiling for about 7 or 8 minutes. Shrimps should be done in the same way: but less time should be allowed. It may easily be known when they are done by their changing colour. Care should be taken that they are not over boiled, as they then become tasteless and indigestible.

TIME. — *Prawns, about* 8 *minutes; shrimps, about* 5 *minutes.*

SEASONABLE *all the year.*

Shrimps or Prawns, Buttered.

—INGREDIENTS.—1 *pint of picked prawns or shrimps,* ¾ *pint of stock, thickening of* butter and flour; salt, cayenne and nutmeg to taste. AVERAGE COST, with prawns, 5s.; with shrimps, 1s. 3d.

Pick the prawns or shrimps, and put them in a stewpan with the stock; add a thickening of butter and flour: season and simmer gently for 3 minutes. Serve on a dish garnished with fried bread or toasted sippets. Cream sauce may be substituted for the gravy.

TIME.—3 minutes.

Shrimps, Potted.—INGREDIENTS.

—1 pint of shelled shrimps, ¼ lb. of fresh butter, 1 blade of pounded mace, cayenne to taste; when liked, a little nutmeg. AVERAGE COST, 1s. 3d.

Have ready a pint of picked shrimps, and put them, with the other ingredients, into a stewpan; let them heat gradually in the butter, but do not let it boil. Pour into small pots, and when cold, cover with melted butter, and carefully exclude the air.

TIME.—¼ hour to soak in the butter.

Skate, To Choose.—This fish

should be chosen for its firmness, breadth and thickness, and should have a creamy

THORNBACK SKATE.

appearance. When crimped, it should not be kept longer than a day or two, as all kinds of crimped fish soon become sour. Thornback is often substituted for skate, but is very inferior in quality to the true skate.

Skate, Boiled.—INGREDIENTS.—¼

lb. of salt to each gallon of water. AVERAGE COST, 4d. to 6d. per lb.

Cleanse and skin the skate, lay it in a fish-kettle, with sufficient water to cover it, salted in the above proportion. Let it simmer very gently till done, then dish it on a hot napkin, and serve with shrimp, lobster, or caper sauce.

TIME.—According to size, from ½ to 1 hour.

SEASONABLE from August to April.

Skate, Crimped.—INGREDIENTS.

—½ lb. of salt to each gallon of water. AVERAGE COST, 4d. to 6d. per lb.

Cleanse, skin and cut the fish into slices, which roll and tie round with string. Have ready some water highly salted, put in the fish, and boil till it is done. Drain well, remove the string, dish on a hot napkin, and serve with the same sauces as above. Skate should never be eaten out of season, as it is liable to produce diarrhœa and other diseases. It may be dished without a napkin, and the sauce poured over.

TIME.—About 20 minutes.

SEASONABLE from August to April.

Skate, with Caper Sauce, à la

Française.—INGREDIENTS —2 or 3 slices of skate, ½ pint of vinegar, 2 oz. of salt, ½ teaspoonful of pepper, 1 sliced onion, a small bunch of parsley, 2 bay-leaves, 2 or 3 sprigs of thyme, sufficient water to cover the fish. AVERAGE COST, 4d. to 6d. per lb.

Put in a fish-kettle all the above ingredients and simmer the skate in them till tender. When it is done, skin it neatly, and pour over it some of the liquor in which it has been boiling. Drain it, put it on a hot dish, pour over it caper sauce, and send some of the latter to table in a tureen.

TIME.—½ hour.

SEASONABLE from August to April.

Note.—Skate may also be served with onion sauce, or parsley and butter.

Skate, Small, Fried.—INGREDI-

ENTS. — Skate, sufficient vinegar to cover them, salt and pepper to taste, 1 sliced

onion, a small bunch of parsley, the juice of
½ *lemon, hot dripping.*   AVERAGE COST,
4*d. to* 6*d. per lb.*

Cleanse the skate, lay them in a dish,
with sufficient vinegar to cover them ; add
the salt, pepper, onion, parsley and lemon-
uice, and let the fish remain in this pickle
for ½ hour. Then drain them well, flour
them, and fry of a nice brown in hot dripping. They may be served either with or
without sauce. Skate is not good if dressed
too fresh, unless it is crimped ; it should,
therefore, be kept for a day, but not long
enough to produce a disagreeable smell.

TIME.—10 *minutes.*

SEASONABLE *from August to April.*

Smelts, To Choose.—When good,
this fish is of a fine silvery appearance, and
when alive, their backs are of a dark brown
shade, which, after death, fades to a light
fawn. They ought to have a refreshing
fragrance, resembling that of a cucumber.

Smelts, Baked. —INGREDIENTS.—
12 *smelts, bread-crumbs,* ¼ *lb. of fresh butter,*
2 *blades of pounded mace ; salt and cayenne*
to taste.   AVERAGE COST, 1*s.* 6*d. to* 2*s. per*
dozen.

Wash, and dry the fish thoroughly in a
cloth, and arrange them nicely in a flat
baking-dish. Cover them with fine bread-
crumbs, and place little pieces of butter all
over them. Season, and bake for 15 minutes.
Just before serving, add a squeeze of lemon-
juice, and garnish with fried parsley and
cut lemon.

SEASONABLE *from October to May.*
Sufficient for 6 persons.

Smelts, Fried. — INGREDIENTS. —
Smelts, egg and bread-crumbs, a little flour ;
boiling lard.   AVERAGE COST, 1*s.* 6*d. to* 2*s.*
per dozen.

Smelts should be very fresh, and not
washed more than is necessary to clean
them. Dry them in a cloth, lightly flour,
dip them in egg and sprinkle over with very

fine bread-crumbs, and put them into boiling lard. Fry of a nice pale brown, and be
careful not to take off the light roughness
of the crumbs, or their beauty will be

BROCHET OF SMELTS.

spoiled. Dry them before the fire on a
drainer, and serve with plain melted butter.
This fish is often used as a garnishing.

TIME.—5 *minutes.*

SEASONABLE *from October to May.*

Snipes, To Carve.—One of these
small but delicious birds may be given,
whole, to a gentleman ; but, in helping a
lady, it will be better to cut them quite

SNIPE.

through the centre, from A to B, completely
dividing them into equal and like portions,
and put only one half on the plate.

Snipes, To Dress.—INGREDIENTS.
Snipes, butter, flour, toast. AVERAGE COST,
1*s.* 6*d. to* 2*s. a brace.*

These, like woodcocks, should be dressed
without being drawn. Pluck, and wipe
them outside and truss them. (*See* Trussing).

ROAST SNIPE.

Place four on a skewer, tie them on to the
jack or spit, and roast before a clear fire for
about ¼ hour. Put some pieces of buttered-
toast into the dripping-pan to catch the
trails ; flour and froth the birds nicely, dish

the pieces of toast with the snipes on them; and pour round, but not over them, a little good brown gravy. They should be sent to table very hot and expeditiously, or they will not be worth eating.

TIME.—*About ¼ hour.*

SEASONABLE *from November to February.*

Note.—Ortolans are trussed and dressed in the same manner.

Snow Cake.—INGREDIENTS *for good-sized cake.*—½ *lb. of tous-les-mois, ¼ lb. of white pounded sugar, ¼ lb. of fresh or washed salt butter,* 1 *egg, the juice of* 1 *lemon.* AVERAGE COST, 1s.

Beat the butter to a cream; then add the egg, previously well beaten, and then the other ingredients: if the mixture is not light, add another egg, and beat for ¼ hour, until it turns white and light. Line a flat tin with raised edges, with a sheet of buttered paper; pour in the cake and put it into the oven. It must be rather slow, and the cake not allowed to brown at all. If the oven is properly heated, 1 to 1¼ hour will be long enough to bake it. Let it cool a few minutes, then with a clean, sharp knife cut it into small square pieces, which should be gently removed to a large flat dish to cool before putting away. This will keep for several weeks.

TIME.—1 *to* 1¼ *hour.*

SEASONABLE *at any time.*

Snow Cake. (A genuine Scotch Recipe.)—INGREDIENTS *for a cake of moderate size.*—1 *lb. of arrowroot, ½ lb. of pounded white sugar, ½ lb. of butter, the whites of* 6 *eggs; flavouring to taste of essence of almonds, or vanilla or lemon.* AVERAGE COST, 2s. 3d.

Beat the butter to a cream; stir in the sugar and arrowroot gradually, at the same time beating the mixture. Whisk the whites of the eggs to a stiff froth, add them to the other ingredients, and beat well for 20 minutes. Put in whichever of the above flavourings may be preferred; pour the cake into a buttered mould or tin, and bake it in a moderate oven from 1 to 1½ hour.

TIME.—1 *to* 1½ *hour.*

SEASONABLE *at any time.*

Soda Biscuits.—INGREDIENTS *for* 3 *dozen biscuits.*—1 *lb. of flour, ½ lb. of pounded loaf sugar, ¼ lb. of fresh butter,* 2 *eggs,* 1 *small teaspoonful of carbonate of soda.* AVERAGE COST, 10d.

Put the flour (which should be perfectly dry) into a basin, rub in the butter, add the sugar, and mix these ingredients well together. Whisk the eggs, stir them into the mixture, and beat it well until everything is well incorporated. Quickly stir in the soda, roll the paste out until it is about ½ inch thick, cut it into small round cakes with a tin cutter, and bake them from 12 to 18 minutes in rather a brisk oven. After the soda is added, great expedition is necessary in rolling and cutting out the paste and in putting the biscuits *immediately* into the oven, or they will be heavy.

TIME.—12 *to* 18 *minutes.*

SEASONABLE *at any time.*

Soda Bread.— INGREDIENTS. — *To every* 2 *lbs. of flour allow* 1 *teaspoonful of tartaric acid,* 1 *teaspoonful of salt,* 1 *teaspoonful of carbonate of soda,* 2 *breakfast-cupfuls of cold milk.*

Let the tartaric acid and salt be reduced to the finest possible powder; then mix them well with the flour. Dissolve the soda in the milk, and pour it several times from one basin to another, before adding it to the flour. Work the whole quickly into a light dough, divide it into 2 loaves, and put them into a well-heated oven immediately, and bake for an hour. Sour milk or buttermilk may be used, but then a little less acid will be needed.

TIME.—1 *hour.*

Soda Cake. — INGREDIENTS *for moderate-sized cake.*—¾ *lb. of butter,* 1 *lb. of flour, ½ lb. of currants, ½ lb. of moist*

sugar, 1 *teacupful of milk*, 3 *eggs*, 1 *tea-spoonful of carbonate of soda.* AVERAGE COST, 1*s.* 2*d.*

Rub the butter into the flour, add the currants and sugar, and mix these ingredients well together. Whisk the eggs well, stir them to the flour, &c., with the milk, in which the soda should be previously dissolved, and beat the whole up together with a wooden spoon or beater. Divide the dough into two pieces, put them into buttered moulds or cake-tins, and bake in a moderate oven for nearly an hour. The mixture must be extremely well beaten up, and not allowed to stand after the soda is added to it, but must be placed in the oven immediately. Great care must also be taken that the cakes are quite done through, which may be ascertained by thrusting a knife into the middle of them : if the blade looks bright when withdrawn they are done. If the tops acquire too much colour before the inside is sufficiently baked, cover them over with a piece of clean white paper, to prevent them from burning.

TIME.—1 *hour.*

SEASONABLE *at any time.*

Sole or Cod Pie.—INGREDIENTS

for pie for 4 persons.—1 *lb. of cold boiled sole or cod, seasoning to taste, of pepper, salt and pounded mace,* 1 *dozen oysters,* 3 *table-spoonfuls of white stock,* 1 *teacupful of cream thickened with flour, puff-paste.* AVERAGE COST, *exclusive of the cold fish,* 1*s.* 6*d.*

Clear the fish from the bones, lay it in a pie-dish, and between the layers put a few oysters and a little seasoning ; add the stock, and, when liked, a small quantity of butter; cover with puff-paste and bake for ½ hour. Boil the cream with sufficient flour to thicken it ; pour in the pie, and serve.

TIME.—½ *hour.*

SEASONABLE *at any time.*

Soles, To Choose. — This fish

should be both thick and firm. If the skin is difficult to be taken off, and the flesh looks grey, it is good.

Soles, Baked.—INGREDIENTS *for*

dish for 4 or 5 persons.—2 *soles,* ¼ *lb. of butter, egg and bread-crumbs, minced parsley,* 1 *glass of sherry, lemon-juice; cayenne and salt to taste.* AVERAGE COST, 2*s.* 3*d.*

Clean, skin and well wash the fish, and dry them thoroughly in a cloth. Brush them over with egg, sprinkle with bread-crumbs mixed with a little minced parsley,

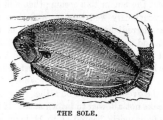

THE SOLE.

lay them in a large flat baking-dish, white side uppermost ; or if it will not hold the two soles, they may each be laid on a dish by itself ; but they must not be put one on the top of the other. Melt the butter, and pour it over the whole, and bake for 20 minutes. Take a portion of the gravy that flows from the fish, add the wine, lemon-juice and seasoning, give it one boil, skim, pour it *under* the fish, and serve.

TIME.—20 *minutes.*

SEASONABLE *at any time.*

Soles, Boiled.—INGREDIENTS.—¼

lb. of salt to each gallon of water. AVERAGE COST, 1*s.* 3*d. per lb.*

Cleanse and wash the fish carefully, cut off the fins, but do not skin it. Lay it in a fish-kettle, with sufficient cold water to cover it, salted in the above proportion. Let it gradually come to a boil, and keep it simmering for a few minutes, according to the size of the fish. Dish it on a hot napkin after well draining it, and garnish with parsley and cut lemon. Shrimp or lobster sauce, and plain melted butter are usually sent to table with this dish.

TIME.—*After the water boils,* 7 *minutes for a middling-sized sole.*

SEASONABLE *at any time.*

Soles, Boiled or Fried, To Carve.

—The usual way of helping this fish is to cut it right through, bone and all, distributing it in nice and not too large pieces. A moderately-sized sole will be sufficient for three slices; namely, the

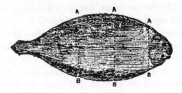

THE SOLE.

head, middle and tail. The guests should be asked which of these they prefer. A small one will only give two slices. If the sole is very large, the upper side may be raised from the bone, and then divided into pieces; and the under side served in the same way.

In helping filleted soles, one fillet is given to each person.

Soles, Filleted, à l'Italienne.

—INGREDIENTS *for dish for 4 or 5 persons. —2 soles; salt, pepper and grated nutmeg to taste; egg and bread-crumbs, butter, the juice of* 1 *lemon.* AVERAGE COST, 1*s.* 3*d. per lb.*

Skin and carefully wash the soles, separate the meat from the bone, and divide each fillet in two pieces. Brush them over with white of egg, sprinkle with bread-crumbs and seasoning, and put them in a baking-dish. Place small pieces of butter over the whole, and bake for ½ hour. When they are nearly done, squeeze the juice of a lemon over them, and serve on a

dish, with Italian sauce (*see* Sauces) poured over them.

TIME.—½ *hour.*

SEASONABLE *at any time.*

Note.—Whiting may be dressed in the same manner, and will be found very delicious.

Soles, Fricasseed.

—INGREDIENTS *for dish for* 6 *persons. —2 middling-sized soles,* 1 *small one,* ½ *teaspoonful of chopped lemon-peel,* 1 *teaspoonful of chopped parsley, a little grated bread; salt, pepper and nutmeg to taste;* 1 *egg,* 2 *oz. of butter,* ½ *pint of good gravy,* 2 *tablespoonfuls of port wine, cayenne and lemon-juice to taste.* AVERAGE COST, 3*s.* 6*d.*

Fry the soles of a nice brown, and drain them well from fat. Take all the meat from the small sole, chop it fine, and mix with it the lemon-peel, parsley, bread and seasoning; work all together with the yolk of an egg and the butter; make this into small balls, and fry them. Thicken the gravy with a dessertspoonful of flour, add the port wine, cayenne and lemon-juice; lay in the 2 soles and balls; let them simmer gently for 5 minutes; serve hot, and garnish with cut lemon.

TIME.—10 *minutes to fry the soles.*

SEASONABLE *at any time.*

Soles, Fried.

— INGREDIENTS *for dish for* 4 *or* 5 *persons. —2 middling-sized soles, hot lard or clarified dripping, egg and bread-crumbs.* AVERAGE COST, 3*s.*

Skin and carefully wash the soles, and cut off the fins, wipe them very dry, and let them remain in the cloth until it is time to dress them. Have ready some fine bread-crumbs and beaten egg; dredge the soles with a little flour, brush them over with egg, and cover with bread-crumbs. Put them in a deep pan, with plenty of clarified dripping or lard (when the expense is not objected to, oil is still better), heated so that it may neither scorch the fish nor make them sodden. When they are sufficiently cooked on one side, turn them carefully and brown them on the other; they may be considered ready when a thick smoke rises. Lift them out carefully, and lay them before the fire on a reversed sieve and soft paper, to absorb the fat. Particular attention should be paid to this, as nothing is more disagreeable than greasy fish; this may be always avoided by dressing them in good time, and allowing a few minutes for them to get thoroughly crisp and free from greasy moisture. Dish them on a hot napkin, garnish with cut lemon and fried parsley, and send them to table with shrimp sauce and plain melted butter.

TIME.—10 *minutes for large soles; less time for small ones.*

SEASONABLE *at any time.*

Soles, Fried, Filleted.—Soles for

filleting should be large, as the flesh can be more easily separated from the bones, and there is less waste. Skin and wash the fish, and raise the meat carefully from the bones, and divide it into nice handsome pieces. The more usual way is to roll the fillets, after dividing each one in two pieces, and either bind them round with twine, or run a small skewer through them. Brush over with egg, and cover with breadcrumbs; fry them a nice bright brown, and garnish with fried parsley and cut lemon. When a pretty dish is desired, this is by far the most elegant mode of dressing soles, as they look much better than when fried whole. Instead of rolling the fillets, they may be cut into square pieces, and arranged in the shape of a pyramid on the dish.

TIME.—*About* 10 *minutes.*

SEASONABLE *at any time.*

Soles or Plaice, Fried. (Jewish

Recipe.) — INGREDIENTS *for dish for* 4 *persons.—A pair of soles, or a large plaice, a small flask of salad oil.* AVERAGE COST, *reckoning half the price of the oil, which may be used again,* 2s.

Pour the oil into a deep pan, and lay in the fish cut in neat fillets, and when the oil ceases to bubble, fry the fish a pale golden brown. Drain very thoroughly, and serve cold with cut lemon and bread-and-butter.

TIME.—5 *to* 10 *minutes to fry the fish.*

SEASONABLE *at any time.*

Soles, with Mushrooms.—IN-

GREDIENTS *for dish for* 4 *or* 5 *persons.*—1 *pint of milk,* 1 *pint of water,* 1 *oz. of butter,* 1 *oz. of salt, a little lemon-juice,* 2 *middling-sized soles.* AVERAGE COST, 2s. 3d.

Cleanse the soles, but do not skin them, and lay them in a fish-kettle with the milk, water, butter, salt and lemon-juice. Bring them gradually to boil, and let them simmer very gently till done, which will be in about 7 minutes. Take them up, drain them well on a cloth, put them on a hot dish, and pour over them a good mushroom sauce. (*See* Sauces.)

TIME.—*After the water boils,* 7 *minutes.*

SEASONABLE *at any time.*

Soles, with Cream Sauce.—

INGREDIENTS *for dish for* 4 *or* 5 *persons.*— 2 *soles : salt, cayenne and pounded mace to taste; the juice of* ½ *lemon, salt and water,* ½ *pint of cream.* AVERAGE COST, 2s. 6d.

Skin, wash and fillet the soles, and divide each fillet in 2 pieces; lay them in cold salt and water, which bring gradually to a boil. When the water boils, take out the fish, lay it in a delicately clean stewpan, and cover with the cream. Add the seasoning, simmer very gently for 10 minutes, and, just before serving, put in the lemon-juice. The fillets may be rolled, and secured by means of a skewer; but this is not so economical a way of dressing them, as double the quantity of cream is required.

TIME.—10 *minutes in the cream.*

SEASONABLE *at any time.*

Note.—This will be found a most delicate and delicious dish.

Soufflé, To Make.—INGREDIENTS
for dish for 4 persons.—3 *heaped tablespoonfuls of potato-flour, rice-flour, arrowroot, or tapioca,* 1 *pint of milk,* 5 *eggs, a piece of butter the size of a walnut, sifted sugar to taste,* ¼ *saltspoonful of salt, flavouring.* AVERAGE COST, 10*d.*

Mix the potato-flour, or whichever one of the above ingredients is used, with a little of the milk; put it into a saucepan, with the remainder of the milk, the butter, salt and sufficient pounded sugar to sweeten the whole nicely. Stir these ingredients over the fire until the mixture thickens; then take it off the fire, and let it cool a little. Separate the whites from the yolks of the eggs, beat the latter, and stir them into the soufflé batter. Now whisk the whites of the eggs to the firmest possible froth, for on this depends the excellence of the dish; stir them to the other ingredients, and add a few drops of essence of any flavouring that may be preferred, such as vanilla, lemon, orange, ginger, &c. &c. Pour the batter into a soufflé-dish, put it immediately into the oven, and bake for about ½ hour; then take it out, put the dish into another more ornamental one, such as is made for the purpose; hold a salamander or hot shovel over the soufflé, strew it with sugar, and send it instantly to table. The secret of making a soufflé well is to have the eggs well whisked, but particularly the whites, the oven not too hot, and to send it to table the moment it comes from the oven.

SOUFFLÉ PAN.

If the soufflé be ever so well made, and it is allowed to stand before being sent to table, its appearance and goodness will be entirely spoiled. Soufflés may be flavoured in various ways, but must be named accordingly. Vanilla is one of the most delicate and the nicest flavourings that can be used for this dish.

TIME.—*About* ½ *hour in the oven; 2 or 3 minutes to hold the salamander over.*

SEASONABLE *at any time.*

Soups, General Directions for
Making.—Lean, juicy beef, mutton and veal form the basis of all good soups; therefore it is advisable to procure those pieces which afford the richest succulence, and such as are fresh-killed. Stale meat renders soups bad, and fat is not well adapted for making them. The principal art in composing good rich soup is so to proportion the several ingredients that the flavour of one shall not predominate over another, and that all the articles of which it is composed shall form an agreeable whole. Care must be taken that the roots and herbs are perfectly well cleaned, and that the water is proportioned to the quantity of meat and other ingredients, allowing a quart of water to a pound of meat for soups, and half that quantity for gravies. In making soups or gravies, gentle stewing or simmering is absolutely necessary. It may be remarked, moreover, that a really good soup can never be made but in a well-closed vessel, although, perhaps, greater wholesomeness is obtained by an occasional exposure to the air. Soups will, in general, take from four to six hours doing, and *are much better prepared the day before they are wanted.* When the soup is cold, the fat may be easily and completely removed; and in pouring it off, care must be taken not to disturb the settlings at the bottom of the vessel, which are so fine that they will escape through a sieve. A very fine hair-sieve or cloth is the best strainer; and if the soup is strained while it is hot, let the tamis or cloth be previously soaked in cold water. Clear soups must be perfectly transparent and thickened soups about the consistency of cream. To obtain a really clear and transparent soup, it is requisite to continue skimming the liquor until there is not a particle of scum remaining, this being

commenced immediately after the water is added to the meat. To thicken and give body to soups and gravies, potato-mucilage, arrowroot, bread-raspings, isinglass, flour and butter, barley, rice, or oatmeal are used. A piece of boiled beef pounded to a pulp, with a bit of butter and flour, and rubbed through a sieve, and gradually incorporated with the soup, will be found

MARJORAM.

an excellent addition. When soups and gravies are kept from day to day in hot weather, they should be warmed up every day, put into fresh - scalded pans or tureens, and placed in a cool larder. In temperate weather, every other day may be sufficient. Stock made only from meat keeps good longer than that boiled with vegetables, the latter being liable to turn the mixture sour, particularly in very warm weather.

Various herbs and vegetables are required for the purpose of making soups and gravies. Of these the principal are— Scotch barley, pearl barley, wheat flour, oatmeal, bread-raspings, peas, beans, rice, vermicelli, macaroni, isinglass, potato-mucilage, mushroom or mushroom-ketchup, parsnips, carrots, beetroot, turnips, garlic, shalots and onions. Sliced onions, fried with butter and flour till they are browned, and then rubbed through a sieve, are excellent to heighten the colour and flavour of brown soups and sauces, and form the basis of many of the fine relishes furnished by the cook. The older and drier the onion, the stronger will be its flavour. Leeks, cucumber, or burnet vinegar; celery or celery seed pounded. The latter, though equally strong, does not impart the delicate sweetness of the fresh vegetable ; and when used as a substitute, its flavour

should be corrected by the addition of a bit of sugar. Cress-seed, parsley, common thyme, lemon thyme, orange thyme, knotted marjoram, sage, mint, winter savory, and basil. As fresh green basil is seldom to be procured, and its fine flavour is soon lost, the best way of preserving the extract is by pouring wine on the fresh leaves.

For the Seasoning of Soups, bay-leaves, tomato, tarragon, chervil, burnet, allspice, cinnamon, ginger, nutmeg, clove, mace, black and white pepper, essence of anchovy, lemon-peel and juice, and Seville orange juice are all taken. The latter imparts a finer flavour than the lemon, and the acid is much milder. These materials, with wine, mushroom ketchup, Harvey's sauce, tomato sauce, combined in various proportions, are, with other ingredients, manipulated into an almost endless variety of excellent soups and gravies. Soups, which are intended to constitute the principal part of a meal, certainly ought not to be flavoured like sauces, which are only designed to give a relish to some particular dish.

Soup-Making, The Chemistry and Economy of.

—Stock being the basis of all meat soups, and, also, of all the principal sauces, it is essential to the success of these culinary operations, to know the most complete and economical method of extracting from a certain quantity of meat the best possible stock or broth. The theory and philosophy of this process we will, therefore, explain, and then proceed to show the practical course to be adopted.

As all meat is principally composed of fibres, fat, gelatine, osmazome and albumen, it is requisite to know that the fibres are inseparable, constituting almost all that remains of the meat after it has undergone a long boiling.

Fat is dissolved by boiling; but as it is contained in cells covered by a very fine membrane, which never dissolves, a portion of it always adheres to the fibres. The other portion rises to the surface of the stock, and is that which has escaped from the cells which were not whole, or which have burst by boiling.

Gelatine is soluble; it is the basis and the nutritious portion of the stock. When there is an abundance of it, it causes the stock, when cold, to become a jelly.

Osmazome is soluble even in cold water, and is that part of the meat which gives flavour and perfume to the stock. The flesh of old animals contains more *osmazome* than that of young ones. Brown meats contain more than white, and the former make the stock more fragrant. By roasting meat, the osmazome appears to acquire higher properties; so, by putting the remains of roast meats into your stock-pot, you obtain a better flavour.

Albumen is of the nature of the white of eggs; it can be dissolved in cold or tepid water, but coagulates when it is put into water not quite at the boiling point. From this property in albumen, it is evident that if the meat is put into the stock-pot when the water boils, or after this is made to boil up quickly, the albumen in both cases, hardens. In the first it rises to the surface, in the second it remains in the meat, but in both it prevents the gelatine and osmazome from dissolving; and hence a thin and tasteless stock will be obtained. It ought to be known too that the coagulation of the albumen in the meat always takes place, more or less, according to the size of the piece, as the parts farthest from the surface always acquire *that degree* of heat which congeals it before entirely dissolving it.

CHERVIL.

Bones ought always to form a component part of the stock-pot. They are composed of an earthy substance—to which they owe

their solidity—of gelatine and a fatty fluid, something like marrow. *Two ounces* of them contain as much gelatine as *one pound* of meat; but in them, this is so incased in the earthy substance, that boiling water can dissolve only the surface of whole bones. By breaking them, however, you can dissolve more, because you multiply their surfaces; and by reducing them to powder or paste, you can dissolve them entirely; but you must not grind them dry. We have said that gelatine forms the basis of stock; but this, though very nourishing, is entirely without taste; and to make the stock savoury, it must contain *osmazome.* Of this, bones do not contain a particle; and that is the reason why stock made entirely of them is not liked; but when you add meat to the broken or pulverised bones, the osmazome contained in it makes the stock sufficiently savoury.

In concluding this part of our subject, the following condensed hints and directions should be attended to in the economy of soup-making:—

Beef makes the best stock; veal stock has less colour and taste; whilst mutton sometimes gives it a tallowy smell, far from agreeable, unless the meat has been previously roasted or broiled. Fowls add very little to the flavour of stock, unless they be old and fat. Pigeons, when they are old, add the most flavour to it; and a rabbit or partridge is also a great improvement. From the freshest meat the best stock is obtained.

If the meat be boiled solely to make stock, it must be cut up into the smallest possible pieces; but, generally speaking, if it is desired to have good stock and a piece of savoury meat as well, it is necessary to put a rather large piece into the stock-pot, say sufficient for two or three days, during which time the stock will keep well in all weathers. Choose the freshest meat, and have it cut as thick as possible; for if it is a thin, flat piece, it will not look well, and will be very soon spoiled by the boiling.

Never wash meat, as it deprives its surface of all its juices; separate it from the bones, and tie it round with tape so that its shape may be preserved, then put it into the stock-pot, and for each pound of meat let there be one pint of water; press it down with the hand, to allow the air which it contains, to escape, and which often raises it to the top of the water.

Put the stock-pot on a gentle fire, so that it may heat gradually. The albumen will first dissolve, afterwards coagulate; and as it is in this state lighter than the liquid, it will rise to the surface, bringing with it all its impurities. It is this which makes *the scum*. The rising of the hardened albumen has the same effect in clarifying stock as the white of eggs and, as a rule it may be said that the more scum there is, the clearer will be the stock. Always take care that the fire is very regular.

STOCK POT.

Remove the scum when it rises thickly, and do not let the stock boil, because then one portion of the scum will be dissolved, and the other go to the bottom of the pot; thus rendering it very difficult to obtain a clear broth. If the fire is regular, it will not be necessary to add cold water in order to make the scum rise; but if the fire is too large at first, it will then be necessary to do so.

When the stock is well skimmed, and begins to boil, put in salt and vegetables, which to every 3 lbs. of meat should consist of three carrots, two turnips, one parsnip, a few leeks and a little celery. You can add, according to taste, a piece of cabbage, two or three cloves stuck in an onion, and a tomato. The latter gives a very agreeable flavour to the stock. If burnt onion be added, it ought, according to the advice of a famous French *chef*, to be tied in a little bag: without this precaution, the colour of the stock is liable to be clouded.

All the bones which were separated from the meat, and any which were left from the roast meat of the day before, should be chopped, remembering, as was before pointed out, that the more these are broken, the more gelatine you will have. The best way to break them up is to pound them roughly in an iron mortar, adding, from time to time, a little water to prevent them getting heated. It is a great saving thus to make use of the bones of meat, which, in too many English families, we fear, are entirely wasted; for it is certain, as previously stated, that two ounces of bone contain as much gelatine (which is the nutritive portion of stock) as one pound of meat. In their broken state tie them up in a bag, and put them in the stock-pot; adding the gristly parts of cold meat, and trimmings which can be used for no other purpose. If, to make up the weight, a piece of mutton or veal has been received from the butcher, broil it slightly over a clear fire before putting it in the stock-pot, and be very careful that it does not contract the least taste of being smoked or burnt.

Add now the vegetables, which, to a certain extent, will stop the boiling of the stock. Wait, therefore, till it simmers well up again, then draw it to the side of the fire, and keep it gently simmering till it is served, preserving, as before said, your fire always the same. Cover the stock-pot well to prevent evaporation; do not fill it up, even if a little stock be taken out, unless the meat is exposed; in which case a little boiling water may be added, but only enough to cover it. After six hours' slow and gentle simmering, the stock is done; and it should not be continued on the fire longer than is necessary, or it will tend to insipidity.

Note.—It is on a good stock, or first good broth and sauce, that excellence in cookery depends. If the preparation of this basis of the culinary art is intrusted to negligent or ignorant persons, and the stock is not well skimmed, but indifferent results will be obtained. The stock will never be clear, and when it is obliged to be clarified, it is deteriorated both in quality and flavour. In the proper management of the stock-pot an immense deal of trouble is saved, inasmuch as one stock, in a small dinner, serves for all purposes. Above all things, the greatest economy, consistent with excellence, should be practised, and the price of everything which enters the kitchen correctly ascertained.

Soup, Baked. — INGREDIENTS for

soup for 12 persons.—1 lb. of any kind of meat, any trimmings or old pieces; 2 onions, 2 carrots, 2 oz. of rice, 1 pint of split peas, pepper and salt to taste, 4 quarts of water. AVERAGE COST, 1s.

Cut the meat and vegetables in slices, add to them the rice and peas, season with pepper and salt. Put the whole in a jar, fill up with the water, cover very closely, and bake for 4 hours

TIME.—4 hours.

SEASONABLE at any time.

Note.—This will be found a very cheap and wholesome soup, and will be convenient in those cases where baking is more easily performed than boiling.

Soup à la Cantatrice. (An Excellent Soup; very Beneficial for the Voice.) — INGREDIENTS for soup for 6

persons.—3 oz. of sago, ½ pint of cream, the yolks of 3 eggs, 1 lump of sugar, and seasoning to taste, 1 bay-leaf (if liked), 2 quarts of medium stock. AVERAGE COST, 2s. 6d.

Having washed the sago in boiling water, let it be gradually added to the nearly boiling stock. Simmer for ½ hour, when it should be well dissolved. Beat up the yolks of the eggs, add to them the boiling cream; stir these quickly in the soup, and serve immediately. Do not let the soup boil, or the eggs will curdle.

TIME.—40 minutes.

SEASONABLE all the year.

Note.—This is a soup the principal ingredients of which, sago and eggs, have always been deemed very beneficial to the chest and throat. In various quantities, and in different preparations, these have been partaken of by the principal singers of the day.

Soup à la Crecy. — INGREDIENTS

for soup for 8 persons.—4 carrots, 2 sliced onions, 1 cut lettuce and chervil, 2 oz. of butter, 1 pint of lentils, the crumbs of 2 French rolls, half a teacupful of rice, 2 quarts of medium stock. AVERAGE COST, 2s.

Put the vegetables, with the butter, in the stewpan, and let them simmer 5 minutes; then add the lentils and 1 pint of the stock, and stew gently for half an hour. Now fill it up with the remainder of the stock, let it boil another hour, and put in the crumbs of the rolls. When well soaked, rub all through a tammy. Have ready the rice boiled; pour the soup over this, and serve.

TIME.—1¾ hour.

SEASONABLE all the year.

Soup à la Flamande. (Flemish). —INGREDIENTS for soup for 8 persons.—1

turnip, 1 small carrot, ½ head of celery, 6 green onions shred very fine, 1 lettuce, cut small, chervil, ¼ pint of asparagus, cut small, ¼ pint of peas, 2 oz. of butter, the yolks of 4 eggs, ½ pint of cream, salt to taste, 1 lump of sugar, 2 quarts of medium stock. AVERAGE COST, 3s. 6d.

Put the vegetables in the butter to stew gently for an hour with a teacupful of stock; then add the remainder of the stock, and simmer for another hour. Now beat the yolks of the eggs well, mix with the cream (previously boiled), and strain through a hair sieve. Take the soup off the fire, put the eggs, &c., to it, and keep stirring it well. Bring it almost to boiling point, but do not leave off stirring, or the eggs will curdle. Season with salt, and add the sugar.

TIME.—2½ hours.

SEASONABLE from May to August.

Soup à la Flamande. (Flemish). — INGREDIENTS. — 5 onions, 5 heads of

celery, 10 moderate-sized potatoes, 3 oz. of butter, ½ pint of water, ½ pint of cream, 2 quarts of stock.

Slice the onions, celery and potatoes, and put them, with the butter and water, into a stewpan, and simmer for an hour. Then fill up the stewpan with stock, and boil gently till the potatoes are done, which will be in about an hour. Rub all through a tammy, and add the cream (previously boiled). Do not let it boil after the cream is put in.

TIME.—2½ hours.

SEASONABLE from September to May.

Note.—This soup can be made with water instead of stock.

Soup, A Good Family.—INGREDIENTS for soup for 12 or 14 persons.—

Remains of a cold tongue, 2 lbs. of shin of beef, any cold pieces of meat or beef-bones, 2 turnips, 2 carrots, 2 onions, 1 parsnip, 1 head of celery, 4 quarts of water, ½ teacupful of rice; salt and pepper to taste. AVERAGE COST, 1s. 8d.

Put all the ingredients in a stewpan, and simmer gently for 4 hours, or until all the goodness is drawn from the meat. Strain off the soup, and let it stand to get cold. The kernels and soft parts of the tongue must be saved. When the soup is wanted for use, skim off all the fat, put in the kernels and soft parts of the tongue, slice in a small quantity of fresh carrot, turnip and onion; stew till the vegetables are tender, and serve with toasted bread.

TIME.—5 hours.

SEASONABLE at any time.

Soup à la Reine.—INGREDIENTS for soup for 8 persons.—1 large fowl, 1 oz. of sweet almonds, the crumb of 1½ French roll, ½ pint of cream, salt to taste, 1 small lump of sugar, 2 quarts of good white veal stock. AVERAGE COST, 5s. 6d.

Boil the fowl gently in the stock till quite tender, which will be in about an hour, or rather more; take out the fowl, pull the meat from the bones, and put it into a mortar with the almonds, and pound very fine. When beaten enough, put the meat

back in the stock, with the crumb of the rolls, and let it simmer for an hour; rub it through a tammy, add the sugar, ½ pint of cream that has boiled, and, if you prefer, cut the crust of the roll into small round pieces, and pour the soup over it, when you serve.

TIME.—2 hours, or rather more.

SEASONABLE all the year.

Note.—All white soups should be warmed in a vessel placed in another of boiling water.

Soup à la Reine. (Economical.)—

INGREDIENTS for soup for 4 or 5 persons.— Any remains of roast chickens, ½ teacupful of rice, salt and pepper to taste, 1 quart of any white stock. AVERAGE COST, exclusive of the cold chicken, 6d.

Take all the white meat and pound it with the rice, which has been slightly cooked, but not too much. When it is all well pounded, dilute with the stock, and pass through a sieve. This soup should neither be too clear nor too thick.

TIME.—1 hour.

SEASONABLE all the year.

Note.—If stock is not at hand, put the chicken-bones in water, with an onion, carrot, a few sweet herbs, a blade of mace, pepper and salt, and stew for 3 hours.

Soup à la Solferino. (Sardinian Recipe.)—INGREDIENTS.—4 eggs, ½ pint of cream or milk, 2 oz. of fresh butter, salt and pepper to taste, a little flour to thicken, 2 quarts of bouillon. AVERAGE COST, with cream, exclusive of the bouillon, 1s. 3d.; with milk, 8d.

Beat the eggs, put them into a stewpan, and add the cream, butter and seasoning; stir in as much flour as will bring it to the consistency of dough; make it into balls, either round or egg-shaped, and fry them in butter; put them in the tureen, and pour the boiling bouillon over them.

TIME.—1 hour.

SEASONABLE.—All the year.

Note.—This recipe was originally the property of an English gentleman who was present at the battle of Solferino, on June 24, 1859, and who was requested by some of Victor Emmanuel's troops, on the day before the battle, to partake of a portion of their *potage*. He willingly enough consented, and found that these clever campaigners had made a palatable dish from very easily-procured materials. In sending the recipe for insertion in this work, he has, however, Anglicised, and somewhat, he thinks, improved it.

Soup, Useful for Benevolent Purposes.

INGREDIENTS.—*An ox-cheek, any pieces of trimmings of beef, which may*  *be bought very cheaply (say 4 lbs.), a few bones, any pot-liquor the larder may furnish, ¼ peck of onions, 6 leeks, a large bunch of herbs, ½ lb. of celery (the outside pieces, or green tops, do very well); ½ lb. of carrots, ½ lb. of turnips, ½ lb.*

THE BAY.

of coarse brown sugar, ½ pint of beer, 4 lbs. of common rice, or pearl barley; ½ lb. of salt, 1 oz. of black pepper, a few raspings or bread crusts, 10 gallons of water. AVERAGE COST, 1½d. per quart.

Divide the meat in small pieces, break the bones, and put them in a copper, with the 10 gallons of water, and stew for half an hour. Cut up the vegetables, put them in, with the sugar and beer, and boil for 4 hours. Two hours before the soup is wanted, add the rice and raspings, and keep stirring till they are well mixed in the soup, which simmer gently. If the liquor boils away a little, fill up with water.

TIME.—6½ *hours.*

SEASONABLE *in winter.*

Soups, Recipes for.

Directions for making the following, appear under their respective headings:—

A Good Family.	A la Flamande.
A la Cantatrice.	,, Another Mode.
A la Crecy.	A la Reine.

A la Solferino.	Onion, Cheap.
Almond.	Ox-cheek.
Artichoke.	Ox-tail.
Asparagus.	Oyster.
Baked.	,, Another Mode.
Barley.	Pan Kail.
Brilla.	Parsnip.
Cabbage.	Partridge.
Calf's-foot Broth.	Pea (inexpensive).
Carrot.	,, Green.
,, Another Mode.	,, Winter Yellow.
Celery.	
Chicken Broth.	Pheasant.
Cock-a-leekie.	Pomeranian.
Crayfish.	Portable.
Cucumber.	Potato.
Desiccated.	,, Another Mode.
Eel.	,, Cheap.
Egg.	Pot-au-feu.
Game.	Prawn.
Giblet.	Prince of Wales'.
Gravy.	Rabbit.
Hare.	Regency.
,, Another Mode.	Rice.
Hessian.	,, Another Mode.
Hodge-podge.	Sago.
,, Another Mode.	Semolina.
Julienne.	Sheep's Head.
Kale Brose.	Spinach.
Leek.	Spring.
Lentil.	Stew.
Lobster.	,, Another Mode.
Macaroni.	,, of Salt Meat.
Maigre.	Tapioca.
Milk.	Turkey.
Mock Turtle.	Turnip.
,, Another Mode.	Useful.
Mulligatawny.	Vegetable.
,, From Tinned Meat.	,, Another Mode.
	,, without Meat.
Mutton.	Vegetable-marrow.
Mutton Broth.	Vermicelli.
Onion.	White.

Spanish Sauce, Brown; or

Espagnole.— INGREDIENTS *for sauce for one entrée.—2 slices of lean ham, 1 lb. of veal, 1½ pint of stock, 2 or 3 sprigs of parsley,*

½ a bay-leaf, 2 or 3 sprigs of savoury herbs, 6 green onions, 3 shalots, 2 cloves, 1 blade of mace, 2 glasses of sherry or madeira, thickening of butter and flour. AVERAGE COST, 2s. 6d.

Cut up the ham and veal into small square pieces, and put them into a stewpan. Moisten these with ½ pint of the stock, and simmer till the bottom of the stewpan is covered with a nicely-coloured glaze, when put in a few more spoonfuls to detach it. Add the remainder of the stock, with the spices, herbs, shalots and onions, and simmer very gently for 1 hour. Strain and skim off every particle of fat, and, when required for use, thicken with butter and flour, or with a little roux. Add the wine, and, if necessary, a seasoning of cayenne, when it will be ready to serve.

TIME.—1½ hour.

Note.—The wine in this sauce may be omitted, and an onion sliced and fried of a nice brown substituted for it. This sauce or gravy is used for many dishes, and with most people is a general favourite.

Sparrows. — INGREDIENTS *for dish for 4 persons.*—½ pint of milk, the same of water, 2 oz. of butter, ½ lb. of flour, a teacupful of bread-crumbs, salt. AVERAGE COST, 4d.

Make the flour and milk into a thick batter, with salt to taste, and drop this in small spoonfuls into boiling water, and boil about 5 minutes. They are done when they float. Melt the butter in a pan, and fry in it the bread-crumbs; then pour these over the sparrows in a dish, and serve quickly.

TIME.—5 to 10 minutes.

SEASONABLE at any time.

Spinach, To Boil. (English Mode.) —INGREDIENTS *for dish for 8 persons.*—2 pailfuls of spinach, 2 heaped tablespoonfuls of salt, 1 oz. of butter, pepper to taste. AVERAGE COST, 8d.

Pick the spinach carefully, and see that no stalks or weeds are left amongst it; wash it in several waters, and, to prevent it being gritty, act in the following manner: Have ready two large pans or tubs filled with water; put the spinach into one of these, and thoroughly wash it; then *with the hands*, take out the spinach, and put it into the *other* tub of water (by this means all the grit will be left at the bottom of the tub); wash it again, and should it not be perfectly free from dirt, repeat the process,

SPINACH GARNISHED WITH CROUTONS.

Put it into a very large saucepan, with about ½ pint of water, just sufficient to keep the spinach from burning, and the above proportion of salt. Press it down frequently with a wooden spoon, that it may be done equally; and when it has boiled for rather more than 10 minutes, or until it is perfectly tender, drain it in a colander, squeeze it quite dry, and chop it finely. Put the spinach into a clean stewpan, with the butter and a seasoning of pepper; stir the whole over the fire until quite hot; then put it on a hot dish, and garnish with sippets of toasted bread.

TIME.—10 to 15 minutes to boil the spinach, 5 minutes to warm with the butter.

SEASONABLE. — Spring spinach from March to July; winter spinach from November to March.

Note. — Grated nutmeg, pounded mace, or lemon-juice may also be added to enrich the flavour; and poached eggs are also frequently

SPINACH AND EGGS.

served with spinach: they should be placed on the top of it, and it should be garnished with sippets of toasted bread.

Spinach dressed with Cream,

à la Française.—Ingredients *for dish for 8 persons.*—2 *pailfuls of spinach, 2 tablespoonfuls of salt, 2 oz. of butter, 8 tablespoonfuls of cream, 1 small teaspoonful of pounded sugar, a very little grated nutmeg.* Average Cost, 1s. 2d.

Boil and drain the spinach ; chop it fine, and put it into a stewpan with the butter ; stir it over a gentle fire, and, when the butter has dried away, add the remaining ingredients, and simmer for about 5 minutes. Previously to pouring in the cream, boil it first, in case it should curdle. Serve on a hot dish, and garnish either with sippets of toasted bread or leaves of puff-paste.

Time.—10 *to* 15 *minutes to boil the spinach ;* 10 *minutes to stew with the cream.*

Seasonable. — *Spring spinach from March to July ; winter spinach from November to March.*

Spinach, French Mode of

Dressing.—Ingredients *for dish for 8 persons.* — 2 *pailfuls of spinach,* 2 *tablespoonfuls of salt, 2 oz. of butter,* 1 *teaspoonful of flour, 8 tablespoonfuls of good gravy ; when liked, a very little grated nutmeg.* Average Cost, 9d.

Pick, wash and boil the spinach, and when tender, drain and squeeze it perfectly  dry from the water that hangs about it. Chop it very fine, put the butter into a stewpan, and lay the spinach over that ; stir it over a gentle fire, and dredge in the flour. Add the gravy, and let it boil *quickly* for a few minutes, that it may not discolour. When the flavour of

SPINACH.

nutmeg is liked, grate some to the spinach, and when thoroughly hot, and the gravy

has dried away a little, serve. Garnish the dish with sippets of toasted bread.

Time.—10 *to* 15 *minutes to boil the spinach ;* 10 *minutes to simmer in the gravy.*

Seasonable. — *Spring spinach from March to July ; winter spinach from October to February.*

Note.—Spinach dressed by the above recipe may be pressed into a hot mould ; it should then be turned out quickly, and served immediately.

Spinach - Green (for Colouring

various Dishes).—Ingredients.—2 *handfuls of spinach.*

Pick and wash the spinach free from dirt, and pound the leaves in a mortar to extract the juice ; then press it through a hair sieve, and put the juice into a small stewpan or jar. Place this in a bain marie, or saucepan of boiling water, and let it set. Watch it closely, as it should not boil ; and as soon as it is done, lay it in a sieve, so that all the water may drain from it, and the green will then be ready for colouring. If made according to this recipe, the spinach-green will be found far superior to that boiled in the ordinary way.

Spinach Pudding. (Italian Recipe.)

—Ingredients *for dish for 6 persons.*—2 *lbs. of spinach, 6 oz. of veal forcemeat, ½ pint of Béchamel, ¼ pint of stock, 2 oz. of butter, 3 eggs, 2 potatoes, 1 turnip, 1 carrot, pepper and salt.* Average Cost, 2s.

Having washed the spinach thoroughly, boil, drain, chop and set it to cool, after

SPINACH PUDDING.

which put it in a saucepan with the stock, sauce and butter, and simmer for 5 minutes.

When again cool, add the forcemeat, the yolks of eggs and a seasoning of salt and pepper, then put it into a mould and cook for ½ hour in a *bain marie*. The vegetables must meanwhile be boiled, cut into shapes and glazed, and with these the pudding, when turned out, should be garnished.

TIME.—*Altogether, to cook about ¾ hour.*
SEASONABLE *from November to July.*

Spinach Soup. (French Recipe.)

—INGREDIENTS *for soup for 8 persons.—As much spinach as, when boiled, will half fill a vegetable dish,* 2 *quarts of very clear medium stock.* AVERAGE COST, 1s. 6d.

Make the cooked spinach into balls the size of an egg, and slip them into the soup-tureen. This is a very elegant soup, the green of the spinach forming a pretty contrast to the brown gravy.

TIME.—1 *hour.*
SEASONABLE *from October to June.*

Sponge Cake.—INGREDIENTS *for large cake.*

—*The weight of* 8 *eggs in pounded loaf sugar, the weight of* 5 *in flour, the rind of* 1 *lemon,* 1 *tablespoonful of brandy.* AVERAGE COST, 1s. 2d.

Put the eggs into one side of the scale, and take the weight of 8 in pounded loaf sugar, and the weight of 5 in good *dry* flour. Separate the yolks from the whites of the eggs ; beat the former, put them into a saucepan with the sugar, and let them remain over the fire until *milk-warm*, keeping them well stirred. Then put them

SPONGE-CAKE.

into a basin, add the grated lemon-rind mixed with the brandy, and stir these well together, dredging in the flour very gradually.

Whisk the whites of the eggs to a very stiff froth, stir them to the flour, &c., and beat the cake well for ¼ hour. Put it into a buttered mould strewn with a little fine-sifted sugar, and bake the cake in a quick oven for 1½ hour. Care must be taken that it is put into the oven immediately, or it will not be light. The flavouring of this cake may be varied by adding a few drops of essence of almonds, or a little orange-flower water, instead of the grated lemon-rind.

TIME.—1½ *hour.*
SEASONABLE *at any time.*

Sponge Cake.—INGREDIENTS *for medium-sized cake.*

—½ lb. *of loaf sugar, not quite* ¼ *pint of water,* 5 *eggs,* 1 *lemon,* ½ lb. *of flour,* ¼ *teaspoonful of carbonate of soda.* AVERAGE COST, 9d.

Boil the sugar and water together until they form a thick syrup ; let it cool a little, then pour it to the eggs, which should be previously well whisked ; and after the eggs and syrup are mixed together, continue beating them for a few minutes. Grate the lemon-rind, mix the carbonate of soda with the flour, and stir these lightly to the other ingredients ; then add the lemon-juice, and, when the whole is thoroughly mixed, pour it into a buttered mould, and bake in rather a quick oven for rather more than 1 hour. The remains of sponge or Savoy cakes answer very well for trifles, light puddings, &c. ; and a very stale one (if not mouldy) makes an excellent tipsy cake.

TIME.—*Rather more than* 1 *hour.*
SEASONABLE *at any time.*

Sponge-Cakes, Small.—INGREDI-

ENTS *for* 18 *cakes.—The weight of* 8 *eggs in flour, the weight of* 8 *eggs in pounded loaf sugar ; flavouring to taste.* AVERAGE COST, 1s.

Let the flour be perfectly dry, and the sugar well pounded and sifted. Separate the whites from the yolks of the eggs, and beat the latter up with the sugar ; then whisk the whites until they become rather stiff, and mix them with the yolks, but do not stir them more than is just necessary to mingle the ingredients well together. Dredge in the flour by degrees, add the flavouring; butter the tins well, pour in the batter, sift a little sugar over the cakes, and bake them in rather a quick oven, but do not allow them to take too much colour, as they should be rather pale. Remove them from the tins before they get cold, and turn them on their faces, where let them remain until quite cold, when store them away in a closed tin canister or wide-mouthed glass bottle.

TIME.—10 to 15 minutes in a quick oven.
SEASONABLE at any time.

Sprats.—INGREDIENTS for dish for 4 persons. — 2 lbs. of sprats, a little flour. AVERAGE COST, 2d. per lb.

Sprats should be cooked very fresh, which can be ascertained by their bright and sparkling eyes. Wipe them dry; fasten

THE SPRAT.

them in rows by a skewer run through the eyes; dredge with flour, and broil them on a gridiron over a nice clear fire. The gridiron should be rubbed with suet. Serve very hot.

TIME.—3 or 4 minutes.
SEASONABLE from November to March.

To Choose Sprats. — Choose these from their silvery appearance, as the brighter they are, so are they the fresher.

Sprats, Dried.—Dried sprats should be put into a basin, and boiling water poured over them; they may then be skinned and served, and this will be found a much better way than boiling them.

Sprats, Fried in Batter.—INGREDIENTS for dish for 3 persons.—1½ lb. of sprats, 2 eggs, flour, bread-crumbs; seasoning of salt and pepper to taste. AVERAGE COST, 6d.

Wipe the sprats, and dip them in a batter made of the above ingredients. Fry of a nice brown, serve very hot, and garnish with fried parsley. Sprats may be baked like herrings.

Spring Soup, or Potage Printanière.—INGREDIENTS for soup for 8 persons.—½ pint of green peas, if in season, a little chervil, 2 shredded lettuces, 2 onions, a very small bunch of parsley, 2 oz. of butter, the yolks of 3 eggs, 1 pint of water, seasoning to taste, 2 quarts of stock. AVERAGE COST, 2s.

Put in a clean stewpan the chervil, lettuces, onions, parsley and butter, to 1 pint of water and let them simmer till tender. Season with salt and pepper; when done, strain off the vegetables, and put two-thirds of the liquor they were boiled in to the stock. Beat up the yolks of the eggs with the other third, give it a toss over the fire, and at the moment of serving, add this, with the vegetables which you strained off, to the soup.

TIME.—¾ of an hour.
SEASONABLE from May to October.

Sprouts, To Boil Young.—INGREDIENTS. — To each ½ gallon of water allow 1 heaped tablespoonful of salt; a very small piece of soda.

Pick away all the dead leaves, and wash the greens well in cold water; drain them in a colander and put them into fast-boiling water, with salt and soda in the above proportion. Keep them boiling quickly, with

SPROUTS.

the lid removed, until tender; and the moment they are done, take them up, or their colour will be spoiled; when well drained, serve. The great art in cooking greens properly, and to have them a good colour, is to put them into *plenty of fast-boiling* water, to let them boil very quickly, and to take them up the moment they become tender.

TIME.—*Broccoli sprouts*, 10 *to* 12 *minutes; young greens*, 10 *to* 12 *minutes; sprouts*, 12 *minutes, after the water boils.*

SEASONABLE.—*Sprouts of various kinds may be had all the year.*

Stew, Irish.—INGREDIENTS *for dish for* 6 *persons.*—3 *lbs. of the loin or neck of mutton*, 5 *lbs. of potatoes*, 5 *large onions, pepper and salt to taste, rather more than* 1 *pint of water.* AVERAGE COST, 2*s.* 8*d.*

Trim off some of the fat of the above quantity of loin or neck of mutton, and cut it into chops of a moderate thickness. Pare and halve the potatoes, and cut the onions into thick slices. Put a layer of potatoes in the bottom of a stewpan, then a layer of mutton and onions, and season with pepper and salt; proceed in this manner until the stewpan is full, taking care to have plenty of vegetables at the top. Pour in the water, and let it stew very gently for 2½ hours, keeping the lid of the stewpan closely shut the *whole* time, and occasionally shaking the preparation to prevent its burning.

TIME.—2½ *hours.*

SEASONABLE. — *Suitable for a winter dish.*

Stew, Irish.—INGREDIENTS *for dish for* 6 *persons.*—3 *lb. of the breast of mutton*, 1½ *pint of water, salt and pepper to taste*, 4 *lbs. of potatoes*, 4 *large onions.* AVERAGE COST, 2*s.* 6*d.*

Put the mutton into a stewpan with the water and a little salt, and let it stew gently for an hour; cut the meat into small pieces, skim the fat from the gravy, and pare and slice the potatoes and onions. Put all the ingredients into the stewpan, in layers, first a layer of vegetables, then one of meat, and sprinkle seasoning of pepper and salt between each layer; cover closely,

and let the whole stew very gently for 1 hour, or rather more, shaking it frequently to prevent its burning.

TIME.—*Rather more than* 2 *hours.*

SEASONABLE.—*Suitable for a winter dish.*

Note.—Irish stew may be prepared in the same manner as above, but baked in a jar instead of boiled. About 2 hours or rather more in a moderate oven will be sufficient time to bake it.

Stew Soup.—INGREDIENTS *for dish for* 6 *persons.*—2 *lbs. of beef*, 5 *onions*, 5 *turnips*, ¾ *lb. of rice, a large bunch of parsley, a few sweet herbs, pepper and salt*, 2 *quarts of water.* AVERAGE COST, 2*s.*

Cut the beef up in small pieces, add the other ingredients, and boil gently for 2½ hours. Oatmeal or potatoes would be a great improvement.

TIME.—2½ *hours.*

SEASONABLE *in winter.*

Stew Soup.—INGREDIENTS *for soup for* 8 *persons.*—½ *lb. of beef, mutton or pork*; ½ *pint of split peas*, 4 *turnips*, 8 *potatoes*, 2 *onions*, 2 *oz. of oatmeal or* 3 *oz. of rice*, 2 *quarts of water.* AVERAGE COST, 10*d.*

Cut the meat in small pieces, as also the vegetables, and add them, with the peas, to the water. Boil gently for 3 hours; thicken with the oatmeal, boil for another ¼ hour, stirring all the time, and season with pepper and salt.

TIME.—3¼ *hours.*

SEASONABLE *in winter.*

Note.—This soup may be made of the liquor in which tripe has been boiled, by adding vegetables, seasoning, rice, &c.

Stew Soup, of Salt Meat.—INGREDIENTS *for soup for* 8 *persons.*—*Any pieces of salt beef or pork, say* 2 *lbs.*; 4 *carrots*, 4 *turnips*, 4 *parsnips*, 4 *potatoes*, 1 *cabbage*, 2 *oz. of oatmeal or ground rice, seasoning of salt and pepper*, 2 *quarts of water.* AVERAGE COST, 1*s.* 10*d.*

Cut up the meat small, add the water, and let it simmer for 2¾ hours. Now add the vegetables, cut in thin, small slices; season and boil for 1 hour. Thicken with the oatmeal, and serve.

TIME.—2 *hours.*

SEASONABLE *in winter.*

Note.—If rice is used instead of oatmeal, put it in with the vegetables.

Stilton Cheese.—Stilton cheese is

generally preferred to all other cheeses by those whose authority few will dispute. Those made in May or June are usually served at Christmas; or, to be in prime order, should be kept from 10 to 12 months, or even longer. An artificial ripeness in Stilton cheese is sometimes produced by inserting a small piece of decayed Cheshire into an aperture at the top. From 3 weeks to a month is sufficient time to ripen the cheese. An additional flavour may also be obtained by scooping out a piece from the top, and pouring therein port, sherry,

STILTON CHEESE.

Madeira, or old ale, and letting the cheese absorb these for two or three weeks. But that cheese is the finest which is ripened without any artificial aid, in the opinion of those who are judges in these matters. In serving a Stilton cheese, the top of it should be cut off to form a lid, and a napkin or piece of white paper, with a frill at the top, pinned round. When the cheese goes from table, the lid should be replaced.

Stock from Bones.—INGREDIENTS

for 3 quarts of stock. — *4 lbs. of bones, 2 carrots, 2 onions, a few cloves, a bunch of herbs, pepper, and salt.* AVERAGE COST, *9d.*

Chop the bones and put them, with the vegetables, seasoning and herbs, in an airtight vessel, and boil for 8 hours; then strain, and when cold remove the fat. This forms a useful and cheap stock for soups and sauces.

TIME.—8 *hours.*

SEASONABLE *at any time.*

Stock (for all kinds of Soups; Rich

Strong Stock).—INGREDIENTS.—*4 lbs. of shin of beef, 4 lbs. of knuckle of veal, ¼ lb. of good lean ham; any poultry trimmings; 2 oz. of butter; 3 onions, 3 carrots, 2 turnips (the latter should be omitted in summer, lest they ferment), 1 head of celery, a few chopped mushrooms, when obtainable; 1 tomato, a bunch of savoury herbs, not forgetting parsley; 1½ oz. of salt, 3 lumps of sugar, 12 white peppercorns, 6 cloves, 3 small blades of mace, 4 quarts of water.* AVERAGE COST, *5s.*

Line a delicately clean stewpan with the ham, cut in thin broad slices, carefully trimming off all its rusty fat; cut up the beef and veal in pieces about 3 inches square, and lay them on the ham; set it on the stove, and draw it down, and stir frequently. When the meat is equally browned, put in the beef and veal bones, the poultry trimmings, and pour in the cold water. Skim well, and occasionally add a little water, to stop its boiling, until it becomes quite clear; then put in all the other ingredients, and simmer very slowly for 5 hours. Do not let it come to a brisk boil, that the stock be not wasted, and that its colour may be preserved. Strain through a very fine hair sieve, or cloth, and the stock will be fit for use.

TIME.—5 *hours.*

Stock, Economical. — INGREDI-

ENTS.—*The liquor in which a joint of meat has been boiled, say 4 quarts; trimmings of fresh meat or poultry, shank-bones, &c., roast-beef bones, any pieces the larder may furnish; vegetables, spices, and the same seasoning as in the foregoing recipe.* AVERAGE COST, 3*d. per quart.*

Let all the ingredients simmer gently for 6 hours, taking care to skim carefully at first. Strain it off, and put by for use.

TIME.—6 *hours.*

Stock, Medium. — INGREDIENTS.—

4 lbs. of shin of beef, or 4 lbs. of knuckle of veal, or 2 lbs. of each; any bones, trimmings of poultry or fresh meat ¼ *lb. of lean bacon or ham, 2 oz. of butter, 2 large onions, each stuck with 3 cloves; 1 turnip 3 carrots, 1 head of celery 3 lumps of sugar 2 oz. of salt,* ½ *teaspoonful of whole pepper 1 large blade of mace, 1 bunch of savoury herbs, 4 quarts and* ½ *pint of cold water.* AVERAGE COST, 2s. 10*d.*

Cut up the meat or bacon or ham into pieces of about 3 inches square; rub the butter on the bottom of the stewpan; put in ½ pint of water, the meat, and all the other ingredients. Cover the stewpan, and place it on a sharp fire, occasionally stirring its contents. When the bottom of the pan becomes covered with a pale, jelly-like substance, add 4 quarts of cold water, and simmer very gently for 5 hours. As we have said before, do not let it boil quickly. Remove every particle of scum whilst it is doing, and strain it through a fine hair sieve. This stock is the basis of most of the soups mentioned in this dictionary, and will be found quite strong enough for ordinary purposes.

TIME.—5½ *hours.*

Stock, To Clarify.—INGREDIENTS.

—*The whites of 2 eggs,* ½ *pint of water, 2 quarts of stock.*

Supposing that by some accident the soup is not quite clear, and that its quantity is 2 quarts, take the whites of 2 eggs, carefully separated from the yolks, whisk them well together with the water, and add gradually the 2 quarts of boiling stock,

still whisking. Place the soup on the fire, and when boiling and well skimmed, whisk the eggs with it till nearly boiling again; then draw it from the fire, and let it settle, until the whites of the eggs become separated. Pass through a fine cloth, and the soup should be clear.

Note.—The rule is, that all clear soups should be of a light straw-colour, and should not savour too strongly of the meat; and that all white or brown thick soups should have no more consistency than will enable them to adhere slightly to the spoon when hot. All *purées* should be somewhat thicker.

Stock, White (to be used in the

preparation of White Soups). — INGREDIENTS.—*4 lbs. of knuckle of veal, any poultry trimmings, 4 slices of lean ham, 3 carrots, 2 onions, 1 head of celery, 12 white peppercorns, 2 oz. of salt, 1 blade of mace, a bunch of herbs, 1 oz. of butter, 4 quarts of water.* AVERAGE COST, 3*s.*

Cut up the veal, and put it with the bones and trimmings of poultry, and the ham, into the stewpan, which has been rubbed with the butter. Moisten with ½ pint of water, and simmer till the gravy begins to flow. Then add the 4 quarts of water and the remainder of the ingredients; simmer for 5 hours. After skimming, and straining it carefully through a very fine hair sieve, it will be ready for use.

TIME.—5½ *hours.*

Note. — When stronger stock is desired, double the quantity of veal, or put in an old fowl. The liquor in which a young turkey has been boiled is an excellent addition to all white stock or soups.

Stock, Consommé, White

(for many Sauces). — Consommé is made precisely in the same manner as white stock, and, for ordinary purposes, will be found quite good enough. When, however, a stronger stock is desired, either put in half the quantity of water, or double that of the meat. This is a very good foundation for all white sauces.

Stone Cream of Tous les Mois.

—INGREDIENTS *for dish for 4 or 5 persons.*
—½ *lb. of preserve,* 1 *pint of milk,* 2 *oz. of lump sugar,* 1 *heaped tablespoonful of tous les mois,* 3 *drops of essence of cloves,* 3 *drops of almond-flavouring.* AVERAGE COST, 10*d.*

Place the preserve at the bottom of a glass dish; put the milk into a lined saucepan, with the sugar, and make it boil. Mix to a smooth batter the tous les mois with a very little cold milk; stir it briskly into the boiling milk, add the flavouring, and simmer for 2 minutes. When rather cool, but before turning solid, pour the cream over the jam, and ornament it with strips of red-currant jelly or preserved fruit.

TIME.—2 *minutes.*

SEASONABLE *at any time.*

Strawberry Drops.

— INGREDIENTS.—½ *pint of juice crushed out of the fruit,* ½ *lb. of castor sugar,* 2 *whites of eggs.* AVERAGE COST, 6*d.*

Whisk the eggs to a very stiff froth; then mix all together, and drop on tins. Bake the drops in a very cool oven.

Strawberry Ice Cream.

—INGREDIENTS *for a quart.*—½ *lb. of strawberries and the same of jam,* 1 *lemon,* ½ *lb. of sugar,* ½ *pint of cream,* 1 *pint of milk.* AVERAGE COST, 1*s.* 9*d.*

Beat the fruit, lemon-juice and sugar into a pulp, add the jam, cream and milk; well mix together, and freeze as directed in *Ices.*

TIME.—25 *minutes to freeze.*

SEASONABLE.—*When strawberries are in season.*

Strawberry Jam.

— INGREDIENTS *for 12 pots.*—12 *pounds of strawberries; to every lb. of fruit allow* ½ *pint of red-currant juice,* 1¼ *lb. of loaf sugar.* AVERAGE COST, 7*d. per lb. pot.*

Strip the currants from the stalks, put them into a jar; place this jar in a saucepan of boiling water, and simmer until the juice is well drawn from the fruit; strain the currants, measure the juice, put it into a preserving-pan, and add the sugar. Select well-ripened but sound strawberries; pick them from the stalks, and when the sugar is dissolved in the currant-juice, put in the fruit. Simmer the whole over a moderate fire from ½ to ¾ hour, carefully removing the scum as it rises. Stir the jam only enough to prevent it from burning at the bottom of the pan, as the fruit should be preserved as whole as possible. Put the jam into jars, and when cold, cover down.

TIME.—½ to ¾ *hour, reckoning from the time the jam simmers all over.*

SEASONABLE *in June and July.*

Strawberry Jelly.

—INGREDIENTS. — *Strawberries, pounded sugar; to every pint of juice allow* 1¼ *oz. of Swinborne's gelatine.* AVERAGE COST, 1*s.* 6*d. a quart mould.*

Pick the strawberries, put them into a pan, squeeze them well with a wooden spoon, add sufficient pounded sugar to sweeten them nicely, and let them remain for 1 hour, that the juice may be extracted; then add ½ pint of water to every pint of juice. Strain the strawberry-juice and water through a bag; measure it, and to every pint allow 1¼ oz. of isinglass or gelatine, melted and clarified in ¼ pint of water. Mix this with the juice; put the jelly into a mould, and set the mould in ice. A little lemon-juice added to the strawberry-juice improves the flavour of the jelly, if the fruit is very ripe; but it must be well strained before it is put to the other ingredients, or it will make the jelly muddy.

TIME.—1 *hour to draw the juice.*

SEASONABLE *in June, July and August.*

Strawberry Liqueur.

—INGREDIENTS.—*Strawberries, which should be ripe and fresh-gathered, sugar-candy, brandy or other spirit.*

Half fill a large bottle with picked strawberries, break the candy into small pieces and fill up with it. Pour over as much spirit as the bottle will hold, and let it stand (as much in the sun as possible) for a month; then filter off, and bottle for use.

TIME.—*To stand, 1 month.*

SEASONABLE.—*Make this in dry weather, when strawberries are ripe.*

Strawberries and Cream. —

INGREDIENTS *for dish for 5 or 6 persons.*— 2 lbs. *of picked strawberries,* ½ *pint of cream,* ¼ *lb. of finely-pounded sugar,* AVERAGE COST, 1s. 10d.

Pick the stalks from the fruit, place it on a glass dish, sprinkle over it pounded sugar, and slightly stir the strawberries, that they may all be equally sweetened; pour the cream over the top, and serve. Devonshire

STRAWBERRY DISH.

cream, when it can be obtained. is exceedingly delicious for this dish; and, if very thick indeed, may be diluted with a little thin cream or milk.

SEASONABLE *in June and July.*

Note.—Instead of serving the strawberries in this manner, they may be picked only, and the cream and sugar served separately. Strawberry dishes are generally used for this fruit.

Strawberries, Preserved in

Wine.—INGREDIENTS.—*To every quart bottle allow* ¼ *lb. of finely-pounded loaf sugar; sherry or Madeira.* AVERAGE COST, *in full season,* 6d. *per lb.*

Let the fruit be gathered in fine weather, and used as soon as picked. Have ready some perfectly dry glass bottles and some nice soft corks or bungs. Pick the stalks from the strawberries, drop them into the bottles, sprinkling amongst them pounded sugar in the above proportion, and when

the fruit reaches to the neck of the bottle, fill up with sherry or Madeira. Cork the bottles down with new corks, and dip them into melted resin.

SEASONABLE.—*Make this in June or July.*

Strawberries, To Preserve

Whole.—INGREDIENTS.—*To every lb. of fruit allow* 1½ *lb. of good loaf sugar,* 1 *pint of red-currant juice.* AVERAGE COST, *in full season,* 6d. *per lb.*

Choose the strawberries not too ripe, of a fine large sort and of a good colour. Pick off the stalks, lay the strawberries in a dish and sprinkle over them half the quantity of sugar, which must be finely pounded. Shake the dish gently, that the sugar may be equally distributed and touch

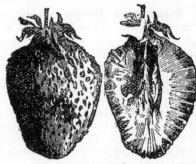

STRAWBERRY.

the under-side of the fruit, and let it remain for 1 day. Then have ready the currant-juice, drawn as for red-currant jelly; boil it with the remainder of the sugar until it forms a thin syrup, and in this simmer the strawberries and sugar until the whole is sufficiently jellied. Great care must be taken not to stir the fruit roughly, as it should be preserved as whole as possible. Strawberries prepared in this manner are very good served with thin cream.

TIME.—¼ *hour to 20 minutes to simmer the strawberries in the syrup.*

SEASONABLE *in June and July.*

Strawberry, Open Tart of, or any other kind of Preserve.

INGREDIENTS.—*Trimmings of puff-paste, any kind of jam.*

Butter a tart-pan, roll out the paste to the thickness of half an inch, and line the pan

OPEN TART.

with it; prick a few holes at the bottom with a fork, and bake the tart in a brisk oven from 10 to 15 minutes. Let the paste cool a little; then fill it with preserve,

OPEN TART MOULD.

place a few stars or leaves on it, which have been previously cut out of the paste and baked, and the tart is ready for table. By making it in this manner, both the flavour and colour of the jam are preserved, which would otherwise be lost, were it baked in the oven on the paste; and, besides, so much jam is not required.

TIME.—*10 to 15 minutes.*

SEASONABLE *at any time.*

Sturgeon, Baked.

INGREDIENTS for dish for 6 persons.—*1 small sturgeon, salt and pepper to taste, 1 small bunch of herbs, the juice of ½ lemon, ¼ lb. of butter, 1 pint of white wine.* AVERAGE COST, 1s. to 1s. 6d. per lb.

Cleanse the fish thoroughly, skin it, and split it along the belly without separating it; have ready a large baking-dish, in which lay the fish, sprinkle over the seasoning and herbs, very finely minced, and moisten it with the lemon-juice and wine.

Place the butter in small pieces over the whole of the fish, put it in the oven, and baste frequently; brown it nicely, and serve with its own gravy.

TIME.—*Nearly 1 hour.*

SEASONABLE *from August to March.*

Sturgeon, Roast.

INGREDIENTS for dish for 4 persons.—*Veal stuffing, buttered paper, the tail-end of a sturgeon.* AVERAGE COST, 1s. to 1s. 6d. per lb.

Cleanse the fish, bone and skin it; make a nice veal stuffing (*see* Forcemeats), and fill it with the part where the bones came from; roll it in buttered paper, bind it up firmly with tape, like a fillet of veal, and roast it in a Dutch oven before a clear fire. Serve with good brown gravy, or plain melted butter.

TIME.—*About 1 hour.*

SEASONABLE *from August to March.*

Note.—Sturgeon may be plainly boiled, and served with Dutch sauce. The fish is very firm, and requires long boiling.

Suet Pudding (to serve with Roast Meat).

INGREDIENTS for pudding for 6 persons.—*1 lb. of flour, 6 ozs. of finely-chopped suet, ½ saltspoonful of salt, ½ salt-spoonful of pepper, ½ pint of water.* AVERAGE COST, 5d.

Chop the suet very finely after freeing it from skin, and mix it well with the flour; add the salt and pepper (this latter ingredient may be omitted if the flavour is not liked), and make the whole into a smooth paste with the above proportion of water. Tie the pudding in a floured cloth, or put it into a buttered basin, and boil from 2½ to 3 hours. To enrich it, substitute 2 beaten eggs for some of the water; and increase the proportion of suet.

TIME.—*2½ to 3 hours.*

SEASONABLE *at any time.*

Note.—When there is a joint roasting or baking, this pudding may be boiled in a long shape, and then cut into slices a few minutes before dinner is served; these slices should be laid in the dripping pan for a minute or two and then browned before the fire. Most children like this accompaniment to roast meat.

Suet Pudding, Sweet.

INGREDIENTS *for pudding for 3 or 4 persons.*—¼ *lb. of suet, 2 oz. of raisins, a teacupful of milk, the same of golden syrup, flour, a teaspoonful of soda.* AVERAGE COST, 5*d*.

Chop the suet and mix it with the other ingredients, and flour enough to form a thick batter; put the mixture into a buttered basin, and boil or steam for 4 hours.

TIME.—4 *hours.*

SEASONABLE *at any time.*

Suet Pudding, Veal.

INGREDIENTS *for pudding for 4 or 5 persons.*—½ *lb. of veal suet, ½ lb. of bread-crumbs, ½ lb. of currants, 3 eggs, ¼ lb. of sugar, 1 quart of milk.* AVERAGE COST, 1s. 5d.

Put the suet, finely chopped, into a saucepan with the milk to get hot, but not to boil; then pour it over the bread-crumbs; add the sugar, and the currants, washed and dried, and, lastly, the eggs well beaten. Mix all together, put in a buttered pie-dish and bake 1 hour.

TIME.—1 *hour.*

SEASONABLE *at any time.*

Sugar, To Boil, to Caramel.

INGREDIENTS.—*To every lb. of lump sugar allow* 1 *gill of spring water.*

Boil the sugar and water together very quickly over a clear fire, skimming it very carefully as soon as it boils. Keep it boiling until the sugar snaps when a little of it is dropped into a pan of cold water. If it remains hard, the sugar has attained the right degree, then squeeze in a little lemon-juice, and let it remain an instant on the fire. Set the pan into another of cold water, and the caramel is then ready for use. The insides of well-oiled moulds are often ornamented with this sugar, which, with a fork, should be spread over them in fine threads or network. A dish of light pastry, tastefully arranged, or a compote of fruit,

look very pretty with this sugar spun lightly over it.

Sugar, Clarified, for Syrup.

INGREDIENTS.—*To every lb. of sugar allow* ½ *pint of water and* ½ *the white of an egg.*

Put the ingredients into a lined saucepan or preserving pan, and when the sugar has dissolved, put the pan on the fire. When it boils put in a teacupful of cold water, and bring it to the boiling point again, but do not stir after adding the water. Draw the pan to the side of the fire for the preparation to settle, carefully remove the scum, and the sugar will be ready. If the scum be put on a sieve over a basin, what sugar runs from it can be boiled up again and strained.

TIME.—20 *minutes for the sugar to dissolve, 5 minutes to boil.*

Sugar for Compotes.

INGREDIENTS.—1 *lb. of sugar,* 1½ *pint of water.*

Boil the sugar and water together for ¼ hour, and the syrup will be ready for use. This syrup is only intended for immediate use, more sugar must be used if it is required to keep.

TIME.—¼ *hour.*

Supper.

So long as late dances and receptions continue in fashion, this meal can never become a thing of the past, although the ordinary late dinner of the upper and upper middle class, and the more unpretentious "high tea," now so often served in small households, renders a guest or family supper a rarely-seen repast.

However, there are still many who, dining late six days of the week, sup on the seventh, and some few others who are old-fashioned enough to do so every day; so, for them we give a few menus for both guest and family suppers, these needing no comment save that they should be prettily and nicely served; the dishes being, generally, all upon the table at once. As at every other meal, flowers or plants should find place for their decoration, and where there is not much money or time to be spared for luxuries, the cost of a hardy fern, which can be bought for a few pence, and will last for months as a centre ornament, need not be grudged.

In the arrangement of a ball supper there is great scope for taste. Colours should be prettily contrasted, all cold meats decorated and garnished with aspic jelly, fresh parsley, glazings, ornamental skewers, &c., sweet dishes as varied as possible in colour and form; while plenty of green, given by palms or ferns, will give a softening tone to the whole.

Flowers are not absolutely needed at a ball supper, as nearly all the dishes, and specially those of fruit, give colour.

It is rarely now we see a home made supper at a ball, but we must urge a plea for these. It is so easy to order a supper to be brought in and cleared away, and many urge that it costs no more than having the dishes prepared at home, while they are made to look far more ornamental than they could be by an ordinary cook. Still, if we are content to have all our prettiest dishes made for us, there will cease to be ambition in cookery; and another and stronger argument in favour of home-made suppers may be found in the fact that it is rarely the case that they are not better in quality (especially the savoury dishes and salads) than those we buy ready made, although the latter are made to look more tempting and pretty.

Soup, at ball suppers, or served during the evening at a dance, should be white or clear, the rest of the viands may be cold ones, and in the case of a buffet supper, the poultry and game should be ready carved. For these, there are no more popular dishes than salads or mayonnaise of different kinds, such as chicken or salmon, and small fancy sweets are generally found more convenient than large ones, such as tipsy cake or trifle, although there is almost invariably one of the latter made as ornamental as possible, and placed in a prominent position.

Sandwiches, some plain, some more fanciful, in the way of *foie gras*, lobster, minced chicken and ham, &c., should always be found at a buffet supper, some people not caring to take anything more substantial.

Menus for Ball Suppers.

Summer.

Salmon Mayonnaise.
Lobster Patties.

Chicken. Tongue.
Pigeon Pie.

Lamb.
Salads of Two Kinds.
Galantine of Veal.
Foie Gras Sandwiches.
Cucumber Sandwiches,

Trifle.
Creams, Jellies.
Fancy Pastry.

Various Fruits.

Winter.

Soup.
Lobster Salad.
Oyster Patties.

Boned Turkey.
Pheasants.
Game Pie.
Chicken Salad.
Plain Salad.
Ham. Pressed Beef.
Caviare Sandwiches.

Compotes of Fruit.
Tipsy Cake. Trifle.
Jellies.
Blancmange.
Small Fancy Sweets.

MENUS FOR GUEST SUPPERS FOR TEN PERSONS.

Summer.

Cold Salmon. Cucumber.
Tartare Sauce.

Veal Pie.

Chickens. Ham.
Salad.

Fruit Tart. Cream.
Compote of Fruit.
Jelly.

Cheese Biscuits.

Winter.

Scalloped Oysters.

Game Pie.
Hashed Turkey.

Cold Beef.
Salad.

Tipsy Cake.
Vanilla Cream.
Stewed Fruit.

Cheese Soufflé.

FAMILY SUPPERS.

Summer.

Sunday.—Cold lamb, mint sauce, cucumber.—Gooseberry-fool or other stewed fruit.—Cheese, biscuits, &c.

Monday. — Rissoles of cold meat and potatoes, ham, salad.—Plain blancmange, any fresh fruit.—Cheese, biscuits, &c.

Tuesday.— Fish salad made from cold fish, ham.—Fruit puffs, rice shape, biscuits, butter, &c.

Wednesday. — Cold meat, cucumber, rissoles of cold poultry.—Compote of fruit.—Cheese, biscuits, &c.

Thursday.—Veal pies, salad.—Poached eggs.—Cold fruit tart, custard.—Cheese, butter, &c.

Friday.—Mayonnaise of cold fish, remains of cold veal pie.—Bread-and-butter pudding.—Butter, biscuits, &c.

Saturday.—Sardines on toast, any cold meat, pickles.—Plain cake, fruit.—Cheese, butter, &c.

Winter.

Sunday.—Cold roast beef, beetroot.—Any cold sweets.—Macaroni cheese.—Biscuits, butter.

Monday.—Curry of cold meat or poultry, cold tongue.—Stewed prunes and rice.—Cheese, biscuits, &c.

Tuesday.—Hashed turkey, cold tongue, pickles.—Cold pudding.—Cheese, biscuits.

Wednesday.—Kidney toast, cold meat, chutney.—Baked rice pudding.—Butter, cheese, &c.

Thursday. — Salmi of game. — Brawn, beetroot.—Jam tartlets.—Cheese, butter, &c.

Friday. — Cold meat, pickles. — Cake. — Welsh rarebit.—Biscuits, butter, &c.

Saturday. — Rissoles of cold fish, beef collops with mashed potatoes.—Cold milk pudding.—Cheese, butter, &c.

Sweetbreads, Baked.

—INGREDIENTS *for a good-sized entrée.*—3 *sweetbreads, eggs and bread-crumbs, oiled butter, 3 slices of toast, brown gravy.* AVERAGE COST, 3s. 6d.

Choose large white sweetbreads; put them into warm water to draw out the blood, and to improve their colour; let them

SWEETBREADS.

remain for rather more than 1 hour; then put them into boiling water, and allow them to simmer for about 10 minutes, which renders them firm. Take them up, drain them, brush over with egg, sprinkle with

Mayonaise of Salmon.

Raised Pie.

Lobster Salad.

Cherry Tartlets.

Game Pie.

Fancy Pastry.

Open Tart.

Tomato and Cucumber Salad.

Ratafia Pudding.

Pigeon Pie.

Meat Pie.

Supper Dishes.

Supper Dishes.

bread-crumbs; dip them in egg again, and then into more bread-crumbs. Drop on them a little oiled butter, and put the sweetbreads into a moderately-heated oven, and let them bake for nearly ¾ hour. Make 3 pieces of toast; place the sweetbreads on the toast; and pour round, but not over them, a good brown gravy.

TIME.—*To soak 1 hour, to be boiled 10 minutes, baked 40 minutes.*

SEASONABLE.—*In full season from May to August.*

Sweetbreads en Caisse.—INGRE-
DIENTS *for entrée for 6 or 8 persons.*—3 *sweetbreads, 1 oz. of bacon fat chopped fine, 1 oz. of butter, 1 teaspoonful of olive oil, 2 dessertspoonfuls of chopped mushrooms, a small teaspoonful of chopped shalot, a little finely-chopped parsley, bread-crumbs, salt, pepper and grated nutmeg.* AVERAGE COST, 3s. 6d.

Soak the sweetbreads in warm water for an hour, boil them 10 minutes, take them out and put them in cold water for a few minutes; then cut them into small pieces. Make a forcemeat of the other ingredients with the exception of the seasoning and parsley, and put this over the fire for 5 minutes; add to it the parsley and seasoning, and hold over the fire for 2 minutes more, then let it cool. Butter some paper cases, lay a little forcemeat in, then some of the sweetbread, and, over that, some more forcemeat and bread-crumbs. Bake very gently for ¼ hour, then brown over the top with a salamander or before the fire.

TIME.—¼ *hour to bake.*

SEASONABLE.—*May to August.*

Sweetbreads, Fried, à la
Maitre d'Hotel.—INGREDIENTS *for good-sized entrée.*— 3 *sweetbreads, egg and bread-crumbs, ¼ lb. of butter, salt and pepper to taste, rather more than ½ pint of maître-d'hôtel sauce.* AVERAGE COST, 4s.

Soak the sweetbreads in warm water for an hour; then boil them for 10 minutes;

cut them in slices, egg-and-bread-crumb them, season with pepper and salt, and put them into a frying-pan with the above proportion of butter. Keep turning them until done, which will be in about 10 minutes; dish them, and pour over them maître-d'hôtel sauce. The dish may be garnished with slices of cut lemon.

TIME.—*To soak 1 hour, to be boiled 10 minutes, to be fried about 10 minutes.*

SEASONABLE.—*In full season from May to August.*

Note. — The egg and bread-crumb may be omitted, and the slices of sweetbread dredged with a little flour instead, and a good gravy may be substituted for the maître-d'hôtel sauce. This is a very simple method of dressing them.

Sweetbreads, Stewed.—INGRE-
DIENTS *for dish for 6 persons.*—3 *sweetbreads, 1 pint of white stock, thickening of butter and flour, 6 tablespoonfuls of cream, 1 tablespoonful of lemon-juice, 1 blade of pounded mace, white pepper and salt to taste.* AVERAGE COST, 4s.

Soak the sweetbreads in warm water for 1 hour, and boil them for 10 minutes; take them out, put them into cold water for a few minutes; lay them in a stewpan with the stock, and simmer them gently for rather more than ½ hour. Dish them; thicken the gravy with a little butter and flour; let it boil up, add the remaining ingredients, allow the sauce to get quite hot, but *not boil*, and pour it over the sweetbreads.

TIME.—*To soak 1 hour, to be boiled 10 minutes, stewed rather more than ½ hour.*

SEASONABLE.—*In full season from May to August.*

Note.—A few mushrooms added to this dish, and stewed with the sweetbreads, will be found an improvement.

Sweetbreads, Lambs', Larded,
and Asparagus. (An Entrée.)—INGREDI-
ENTS.—2 *or 3 sweetbreads, ½ pint of veal stock, white pepper and salt to taste, a small bunch of green onions, 1 blade of*

pounded mace, thickening of butter and flour, 2 eggs, nearly ½ pint of cream, 1 teaspoonful of minced parsley, a very little grated nutmeg, asparagus-tops, bacon for larding. AVERAGE COST, 4s. 6d.

Soak the sweetbreads in lukewarm water, and put them into a saucepan with sufficient boiling water to cover them, and let them simmer for 10 minutes; then take them out and put them into cold water. Now lard them, lay them in a stewpan, add the stock, seasoning, onions, mace and a thickening of butter and flour, and stew gently for ¼ hour or 20 minutes. Beat up the egg with the cream, to which add the minced parsley and a very little grated nutmeg. Put this to the other ingredients; stir it well till quite hot, but do not let it boil after the cream is added, or it will curdle. Have ready some asparagus-tops, boiled, add these to the sweetbreads, and serve.

TIME.—Altogether, 1 hour.

SEASONABLE from Easter to Michaelmas.

Sweetbreads, Another Way

to Dress. (An Entrée.)—INGREDIENTS for dish for 5 or 6 persons.—2 sweetbreads, egg and bread-crumbs, ½ pint of gravy, ½ glass of sherry. AVERAGE COST, 3s. 6d.

Soak the sweetbreads in warm water for an hour, and throw them into boiling water to render them firm. Let them stew gently for about ¼ hour, take them out and put them into a cloth to drain all the water from them. Brush them over with egg, sprinkle them with bread-crumbs, and either brown them in the oven or before the fire. Have ready the above quantity of gravy, to which add ½ glass of sherry; dish the sweetbreads, pour the gravy under them, and garnish with watercresses.

TIME.—Rather more than ½ hour.

SEASONABLE from Easter to Michaelmas.

Swiss Cream.—INGREDIENTS for

dish for 6 persons.—¼ lb. of macaroons or 6 small sponge-cakes, sherry, 1 pint of cream, 5 oz. of lump sugar, 2 large tablespoonfuls of arrowroot, the rind of 1 lemon, the juice of ½ lemon, 3 tablespoonfuls of milk. AVERAGE COST, 2s. 6d.

Lay the macaroons or sponge-cakes in a glass dish, and pour over them as much sherry as will cover them, or sufficient to soak them well. Put the cream into a lined saucepan, with the sugar and lemon-rind, and let it remain by the side of the fire until the cream is well flavoured, when take out the lemon-rind. Mix the arrowroot smoothly with the cold milk; add this to the cream, and let it boil gently for about 3 minutes, keeping it well stirred. Take it off the fire, stir till nearly cold, when add the lemon-juice, and pour the whole over the cakes. Garnish the cream with strips of angelica or candied citron, cut thin, or bright-coloured jelly or preserve. This cream is exceedingly good, flavoured with vanilla instead of lemon; when this flavouring is used the sherry may be omitted, and the mixture poured over the dry cakes.

TIME.—About ½ hour to infuse the lemon-rind; 5 minutes to boil the cream.

SEASONABLE at any time.

Swiss Cream. (More Economical.)

—INGREDIENTS for dish for 6 persons.—A few slices of stale sponge-cake, 2 glasses of orange wine, 1 pint of milk, 3 eggs, ¼ lb. of sugar, flavouring of lemon or vanilla. AVERAGE COST, 1s.

Slice the cake into a glass dish and let it soak in the orange wine. Make a custard with the milk and eggs, flavouring it with vanilla or lemon. When cold pour it over the sponge-cake and garnish with a few crystallised cherries or a little red currant jelly.

SEASONABLE at any time.

Note.—A plain tipsy cake may be made in the same way, and an improvement may be made by spreading the slices of sponge-cake with preserve.

Syllabub.—INGREDIENTS *for syllabub for 6 persons.*—*1 pint of sherry or white wine, ½ grated nutmeg, sugar to taste, 1½ pint of milk.* AVERAGE COST, 1s. 9d.

Put the wine into a bowl, with the grated nutmeg and plenty of pounded sugar, and milk into it the above proportion of milk from the cow. Clouted cream may be laid on the top, with pounded cinnamon or nutmeg and sugar; and a little brandy may be added to the wine before the milk is put in. In some counties, cider is substituted for the wine: when this is used, brandy must always be added. Warm milk may be poured on from a spouted jug or teapot; but it must be held very high.

SEASONABLE *at any time.*

Syllabubs, Whipped.—INGREDIENTS *for 8 glasses.*—*½ pint of cream, ¼ pint of sherry, half that quantity of brandy, the juice of ½ lemon, a little grated nutmeg, 3 oz. of pounded sugar, whipped cream the same as for trifle.* AVERAGE COST, 1s. 9d.

Mix all the ingredients together, put the syllabub into glasses, and over the top of them heap a little whipped cream, made in the same manner as for trifle. Solid syllabub is made by whisking or milling the mixture to a stiff froth, and putting it in the glasses, without the whipped cream at the top.

SEASONABLE *at any time.*

Syrup for Compôtes. — INGREDIENTS *for syrup for good-sized dish.*—*1 lb. of sugar, 1½ pint of water.* AVERAGE COST. 3d.

Boil the water and sugar together for 15 minutes, carefully removing the scum as it rises. Boil the fruit intended for the compôte in this syrup till sufficiently done, and serve the dish when cold, or iced in summer.

TIME.—*15 minutes to boil the syrup.*

Syrup for Jellies, To Clarify. —INGREDIENTS.—*To every quart of water allow 2 lbs. of loaf sugar; the white of 1 egg.*

Put the sugar and water into a stewpan; set it on the fire, and, when the sugar is dissolved, add the white of the egg, whipped up with a little water. Whisk the whole well together, and simmer very gently until it has thrown up all the scum. Take this off as it rises, strain the syrup through a fine sieve or cloth into a basin, and keep it for use.

SALMON.

"The dinner waits and we are tired."

Cowper.

TAMARIND Sauce. (Indian Recipe.)—Ingredients. — *Tamarind, pounded loaf sugar.*

Fill a stone jar with the fruit when thoroughly ripe, and stew in a cool oven till tender, adding enough pounded loaf sugar to take off some of the acidity of the fruit, but not enough to destroy the flavour, as this should be an acid sauce. When quite soft, rub through a sieve.

Tapioca and Apple Pudding. —Ingredients *for pudding for* 6 *persons.* —*A cupful of tapioca,* 2 *lbs. of cooking apples,* 1 *lemon, sugar to taste.* Average Cost, 9d.

Soak the tapioca over-night in cold water, and in the morning pour over it a pint of boiling water, and cook slowly for 20 minutes. Pare and core the apples, and cover the bottom of a pudding-dish with them, with their cavities filled with sugar. Squeeze over some lemon juice, sweeten the tapioca, and pour it over the apples, and bake one hour in a slow oven.

Time.—1 *hour and twenty minutes.*
Seasonable *in autumn and winter.*

Tapioca Pudding. — Ingredients *for pudding for* 6 *persons.*—3 *oz. of tapioca,* 1 *quart of milk,* 2 *oz. of butter,* ¼ *lb. of sugar,* 3 *eggs, flavouring of vanilla, grated lemon-rind, or bitter almonds.* Average Cost, 11d.

Wash the tapioca, and let it stew gently in the milk by the side of the fire for ½ hour, occasionally stirring it; then let it cool a little; mix with it the butter, sugar, and eggs, which should be well beaten, and flavour with either of the above ingredients, putting in about 12 drops of the essence of almonds or vanilla, whichever is preferred. Butter a pie-dish, and line the edges with puff-paste; put in the pudding, and bake in a moderate oven for an hour. If the pudding is to be boiled, add a little more tapioca, and boil it in a buttered basin 1½ hour.

Time.—1 *hour to bake,* 1½ *hour to boil.*
Seasonable *at any time.*

Tapioca Soup.—INGREDIENTS *for soup for 6 persons.*—5 *oz. of tapioca,* 2 *quarts of medium stock.* AVERAGE COST, 1*s.* 8*d.*

Put the tapioca into cold stock, and bring it gradually to a boil. Simmer gently till tender, and serve.

TIME.—*Rather more than* 1 *hour.*

SEASONABLE *all the year.*

Tartare Sauce.—INGREDIENTS *for sauce for good-sized dish.*—*The yolks of* 4 *eggs,* 1 *teaspoonful of mustard,* ½ *teaspoonful of salt,* 2 *dessertspoonfuls of chopped pickled onions and gherkins,* 1 *teaspoonful of chopped parsley, olive oil, tarragon and plain vinegar, a little cayenne.* AVERAGE COST, 9*d.*

Break the yolks into a basin, with the salt and mustard, then stir in a tablespoonful of oil, then one of mixed vinegar, and so on, till the sauce is of the right consistency. This must be done very gradually, and the oil must preponderate. Then add the chopped onion and gherkin, and a little cayenne if liked.

SEASONABLE *at any time.*

Tartlets.—INGREDIENTS *for* 12 *tartlets.*—*Trimmings of puff-paste about* ½ *lb., any jam or marmalade that may be preferred.* AVERAGE COST, 9*d.*

Roll out the paste to the thickness of about ½ inch; butter some small round patty-pans, line them with it, and cut off the superfluous paste close to the edge of the pan. Put a small piece of bread into each tartlet (this is to keep them in shape),

HOME-MADE TARTLETS.

and bake in a brisk oven for 10 minutes or rather longer. When they are done, and are of a nice brown colour, take the pieces of bread out carefully, and replace them by a spoonful of jam or marmalade.

TIME.—10 *to* 15 *minutes.*

SEASONABLE *at any time.*

Tartlets, Cream.—INGREDIENTS *for* 6 *tartlets.*—2 *eggs,* 1 *oz. of butter,* 1 *oz. of sugar, flour, a pinch of salt, jam, whipped cream.* AVERAGE COST, 8*d.*

Make a paste with the eggs, the butter, and flour enough to make it smooth, working the paste as lightly as possible. Roll out this, and line some patty-pans, putting in some rice to preserve the hollows. Bake in a moderate oven, then take out the rice, and fill with jam, and put a spoonful of whipped cream on each.

TIME.—15 *minutes to bake.*

SEASONABLE *at any time.*

Tartlets, Polish.—INGREDIENTS *for* 8 *tartlets.*—½ *lb. of puff-paste, preserve, the white of an egg, pounded sugar.* AVERAGE COST, 9*d.*

Roll some good puff-paste out thin, and cut it into 2½-inch squares; brush each square over with the white of an egg, then fold down the corners, so that they all meet in the middle of each piece of paste; slightly press the two pieces together, brush them over with the egg, sift over sugar, and bake in a nice quick oven for about ¼ hour. When they are done, make a little hole in the middle of the paste, and fill it up with apricot jam, marmalade, or red-currant jelly.

TIME.—¼ *hour or* 20 *minutes.*

SEASONABLE *at any time.*

Note.—It should be borne in mind that for all dishes of small pastry, such as the preceding, trimmings of puff-paste, left from larger tarts, answer as well as making the paste expressly.

Tea.—Tea as a meal, or more often, an apology for one, is one of the most useful of all as an easy form of entertainment.

At an "At Home" tea almost any number of people may be invited, the hostess knowing that they will not all assemble at the same time; and, whereas at a luncheon or dinner a good deal of expense must be incurred, and comparatively few guests invited, a great many may be welcomed to an afternoon tea at a cost that can scarcely be reckoned.

At the regular At Home, one held on a certain day every week or month, to which only one invitation is given, by card or on a visiting one, nothing more is expected than some tea or tea and coffee, thin bread-and-butter and cakes; but at an "At Home," where one is invited only on one certain day, there is a different kind of meal needed. Here we have, in addition to the above, such things as ices, claret and champagne cup (if in season), sandwiches, small fancy ones as a rule, such as *foie gras* or cucumber, a great variety of small sweets, and, in fact, just the same kind of light refreshments usually served at a dance.

High tea may be a meal, it being really worthy to come under the category. It can be served more easily in small households, where service is lacking, than a dinner or luncheon.

It is specially convenient in the summer, when out-of-door amusements are going on, and guests may be bidden to one without formality.

We give menus for two high teas, one for summer and one for winter, as well as two for afternoons; also some plain family ones.

Menus for "At Home" Teas.

Summer.

Salmon Sandwiches.
Cucumber Sandwiches.
Salad Sandwiches.
Bread and Butter.
Madeira Cake.
Sponge Cake.
Small Almond Cakes.
Petits Fours.
Small Fancy Cakes.
Strawberries and Cream.   Ices.
Tea, Coffee, Lemonade.
Claret Cup.

Winter.

Sardine Sandwiches.
Chicken and Ham Sandwiches.
Foie Gras Sandwiches.
Bread and Butter.
Pound Cake.
Sponge Cake.
Macaroons, Ratafias.
Petits Fours.
Fancy Biscuits.
Tea, Coffee, Wine.

Menus for High Tea.

Summer.

Mayonnaise of Salmon.
Cold Chicken.
Tongue.
Galantine of Veal.
Salad.   Cucumber.
Compote of Fruit.
Jelly.
Pound Cake.
Strawberries and Cream.
Tea, Coffee, &c.

Winter.

Fish Rissoles.
Mutton Cutlets.
Cold Game.
Hashed Turkey.
Sponge Cake Pudding.
Lemon Cream.
Madeira Cake.
Stewed Prunes.
Tea, Coffee, &c.

Plain Family Teas.

Sunday.—Bread-and-butter, bread, toast, jam, potted meat, seed cake, tea, milk, sugar.

Monday.—Buttered toast, bread and bread-and-butter, sardines, marmalade, tea, coffee, &c.

Tuesday.—Bread and bread-and-butter, dry toast, currant cake, scrambled eggs, tea, &c.

Wednesday.—Hot buttered scones, bread and bread-and-butter, shrimps, fruit, jam, tea, coffee, &c.

Thursday.—Bread and bread-and-butter, dry toast, cake, marmalade, anchovy toast, fruit, tea, coffee, &c.

Friday.—Hot buttered toast, bread and bread-and-butter, jam, potted fish, cresses or radishes, tea, &c.

Saturday.—Bread and bread-and-butter, dry toast, hot cakes, marmalade, fruit, tea, coffee, &c.

Tea, To Make.—There is very little art in making good tea; if the water is boiling, and there is no sparing of the fragrant leaf, the beverage will almost invariably be good. The old-fashioned plan of allowing a teaspoonful to each person and one over, is still practised.

TEA.

Warm the teapot with boiling water; let it remain for two or three minutes for the vessel to become thoroughly hot, then pour it away. Put in the tea, pour in from ½ to ¾ pint of *boiling* water, close the lid, and let it stand for the tea to draw from 5 to 10 minutes; then fill up the pot with water. The tea will be quite spoiled unless made with water that is actually *boiling*, as the leaves will not open, and the flavour not be extracted from them; the beverage will consequently be colourless and tasteless—in fact, nothing but tepid water. Where there is a large party to make tea for, it is a good plan to have two teapots, instead of putting a large quantity of tea into one pot; the tea, besides, will go farther. When the infusion has been once completed, the addition of fresh tea adds very little to the strength; so, when more is required, have the pot emptied of the old leaves, scalded, and fresh tea made in the usual manner. Economists say that a few grains of carbonate of soda, added before the boiling water is poured on the tea, assist to draw out the goodness; if the water is very hard, perhaps it is a good plan, as the soda softens it; but care must be taken to use this ingredient sparingly, as it is liable to give the tea a soapy taste if added in too large a quantity. For mixed tea, the usual proportion is four spoonfuls of black to one of green; more of the latter when the flavour is very much liked; but strong green tea is highly pernicious, and should never be partaken of too freely.

Time.—2 *minutes to warm the teapot*, 5 *to* 10 *minutes to draw the strength from the tea.*

Sufficient.— *Allow* 1 *teaspoonful to each person.*

Tea-Cakes.—Ingredients *for* 8 *tea-cakes.*—2 *lbs. of flour*, ½ *teaspoonful of salt*, ¼ *lb. of butter or lard*, 1 *egg, a piece of German yeast the size of a walnut, warm milk.* Average Cost, 8*d.*

Put the flour (which should be perfectly dry) into a basin; mix with it the salt, and rub in the butter or lard; then beat the egg well, stir to it the yeast, and add these to the flour with as much warm milk as will make the whole into a smooth paste, and knead it well. Let it rise near the fire, and, when well risen, form it into cakes; place them on tins, let them rise again for a few minutes before putting them into the oven, and bake from ¼ to ½ hour in a moderate oven. These are very nice with a few currants and a little sugar added to the other ingredients; they should be put in after the butter is rubbed in. These cakes should be buttered, and eaten hot as soon as baked; but, when stale, they are very nice split and toasted; or, if dipped in milk, or even water, and covered with a basin in the oven till hot, they will be almost equal to new.

TIME.—¼ to ½ hour.

SEASONABLE at any time.

Tea-Cakes, Small.—INGREDIENTS for 12 cakes.—2 teacupfuls of flour, one of ground rice, one of moist sugar, 2 oz. of lard, 2 oz. of butter, 2 eggs, lemon flavouring. AVERAGE COST, 8d.

Melt the lard and butter, beat them well, and add to the flour and rice ; next add the eggs and sugar, beating all well together, with a flavouring of essence of lemon, and bake in cakes on a tin in a quick oven.

TIME.—15 minutes.

SEASONABLE at any time.

Tea-Cakes, To Toast.—Cut each tea-cake into three or four slices, according to its thickness ; toast them on both sides before a nice clear fire, and as each slice

TEA-CAKES.

is done, spread it with butter on both sides. When a cake is toasted, pile the slices one on the top of the other, cut them into quarters, put them on a very hot plate, and send the cakes immediately to table. As they are wanted, send them in hot, one or two at a time, as, if allowed to stand, they spoil, unless kept in a muffin-plate over a basin of boiling water.

Teal, Roast.—INGREDIENTS.—Teal, butter, a little flour. AVERAGE COST, 1s. 3d. each.

Choose fat, plump birds, after the frost has set in, as they are generally better flavoured ; truss them in the same manner as wild duck ; roast them before a brisk fire, and keep them well basted. Serve with brown or orange gravy, watercresses and a cut lemon. The remains of teal make excellent hash.

TIME.—From 9 to 15 minutes.

SEASONABLE from October to February.

Teal, To Carve.—Teal being of the same character as widgeon and wild duck, may be treated, in carving, in the same manner.

Tench, Matelote of. — INGREDIENTS for large dish.—½ pint of stock, ½ pint of port wine, 1 dozen button onions, a few mushrooms, 1 faggot of herbs, 2 blades of mace, 1 oz. of butter, 1 teaspoonful of minced parsley, thyme, 1 shalot, 2 anchovies, 1 tea-cupful of stock, flour, 1 dozen oysters, the juice of ½ lemon ; the number of tench, according to size.

Scale and clean the tench, cut them into pieces, and lay them in a stewpan ; add the stock, wine, onions, mushrooms, herbs and mace, and simmer gently for ½ hour. Put into another stewpan all the remaining ingredients but the oysters and lemon juice, and boil slowly for 10 minutes, when add the strained liquor from the tench, and keep stirring it over the fire until somewhat reduced. Rub it through a sieve, pour it over the tench with the oysters, which must be previously scalded in their own liquor, squeeze in the lemon-juice, and serve. Garnish with croûtons.

TIME.—¾ hour.

SEASONABLE from October to June.

Tench Stewed with Wine.—INGREDIENTS.—Tench, ½ pint of stock, ⅓ pint of Madeira or sherry, salt and pepper to taste, 1 bay-leaf, thickening of butter and flour.

Clean and crimp the tench, carefully lay it in a stewpan with the stock, wine, salt and pepper, and bay-leaf, let it stew gently for ½ hour ; then take it out, put it on a dish, and keep hot. Strain the liquor, and thicken it with butter and flour kneaded together, and stew for 5 minutes. If not perfectly smooth, squeeze it through a tammy, add a very little cayenne, and pour over the fish. Garnish with balls of veal forcemeat.

TIME.—Rather more than ½ hour.

SEASONABLE from October to June.

Tendrons de Veau, Stewed.—

INGREDIENTS *for good-sized entrée.— The gristles from 2 breasts of veal, white stock, 1 faggot of savoury herbs, 2 blades of pounded mace, 4 cloves, 2 carrots, 2 onions, a strip of lemon-peel.*

The *tendrons*, or gristles, which are found round the front of a breast of veal, are frequently served as an entrée, and when well dressed, make a nice and favourite dish. Detach the gristles from the bone, and cut them neatly out, so as not to spoil the joint for roasting or stewing. Put them into a stewpan, with sufficient stock to cover them ; add the herbs, mace, cloves, carrots, onions, and lemon, and simmer these for nearly, or quite, 4 hours. They should be stewed until a fork will enter the meat easily. Take them up, drain them, strain the gravy and boil it down to a glaze, with which glaze the meat. Dish the *tendrons* in a circle, with croûtons fried of a nice colour placed between them ; and put mushroom sauce, or a purée of green peas or tomatoes, in the middle.

TIME.—4 *hours.*

SEASONABLE.—*With peas, from June to August.*

Tendrons de Veau. —INGREDI-

ENTS *for good-sized entrée. — The gristles from 2 breasts of veal, white stock, 1 faggot of savoury herbs, 1 blade of pounded mace, 4 cloves, 2 carrots, 2 onions, a strip of lemon-peel, egg and bread-crumbs, 2 tablespoonfuls of chopped mushrooms, salt and pepper to taste, 2 tablespoonfuls of sherry, the yolk of 1 egg, 3 tablespoonfuls of cream.*

After removing the gristles from a breast of veal, stew them for 4 hours, as in the preceding recipe, with stock, herbs, mace, cloves, carrots, onions and lemon-peel. When perfectly tender, lift them out, and remove any bones or hard parts remaining. Put them between two dishes, with a weight on the top, and when cold, cut them into slices. Brush these over with egg,

sprinkle with bread-crumbs, and fry a pale brown. Take ½ pint of the gravy they were boiled in, add 2 tablespoonfuls of chopped mushrooms, a seasoning of salt and pepper, the sherry, and the yolk of an egg beaten with 3 tablespoonfuls of cream. Stir the sauce over the fire until it thickens ; when it is on the *point of boiling*, dish the tendrons in a circle, and pour the sauce in the middle. Tendrons are dressed in a variety of ways—with sauce à l'Espagnole, vegetables of all kinds : when they are served with a purée, they should always be glazed.

TIME.—4½ *hours.*

SEASONABLE *from March to October.*

Tête de Veau en Tortue. —

INGREDIENTS.—*Half a calf's head, or the remains of a cold boiled one; rather more than 1 pint of good white stock, 1 glass of sherry or Madeira, cayenne and salt to taste, about 12 mushroom-buttons (when obtainable), 6 hard-boiled eggs, 4 gherkins, 8 quenelles, or forcemeat balls, 12 crayfish, 12 croûtons.* AVERAGE COST, *without the meat,* 2s. 9d.

Half a calf's head is sufficient to make a good large entrée, and if there are any remains of a cold one left from the preceding day it will answer very well for this dish. After boiling the head until tender, remove the bones, and cut the meat into neat pieces; put the stock into a stewpan, add the wine, and a seasoning of salt and cayenne; fry the mushrooms in butter for 2 or 3 minutes, and add these to the gravy. Boil this quickly until somewhat reduced ; then put in the yolks of the hard-boiled eggs *whole*, and the whites cut in small pieces, and the gherkins chopped. Have ready a few veal quenelles, add these, with the slices of head, to the other ingredients, and let the whole get thoroughly hot *without boiling.* Arrange the pieces of head as high in the centre of the dish as possible; pour over them the ragoût, and garnish with the crayfish and croûtons placed alternately. A little of the gravy should also be served in a tureen.

TIME. — *About ½ an hour to reduce the stock.*

SEASONABLE *from March to October.*

Thanksgiving Cake.— INGREDI-
ENTS *for large cake.*—1 lb. each of butter, flour and sifted sugar, ½ lb. of currants, 2 oz. of candied-peel, 8 eggs, 2 oz. of almonds, blanched and chopped, flavouring of nutmeg and spice, a little salt. AVERAGE COST, 2s. 9d.

Beat the butter and sugar to a cream; add the eggs well beaten, mix in the flour, and add the other ingredients. Beat all thoroughly together, and bake 2 hours in a moderate oven.

TIME.—2 hours.

SEASONABLE *at any time.*

Tinned Meats.—The prejudice that some people entertained against these have now almost ceased to exist; and so many nice dishes can be made from them, at a small cost, that we should be grateful for the facility with which they are brought to us from afar. Tinned beef, that of the Ramornie brand, is excellent; and it is well worth while to try it for mulligatawny soup (for which a recipe will be found in this book), or for a meat-pudding, when there is not time to give the long boiling fresh meat requires. It is also nice eaten cold with a salad.

Tipsy Cake.—INGREDIENTS *for* 1 large dish.—1 moulded sponge or Savoy cake, sufficient sweet wine or sherry to soak it, 6 tablespoonfuls of brandy, 2 oz. of sweet almonds, 1 pint of rich custard. AVERAGE COST, 3s. 6d.

Procure a cake that is three or four days old—either sponge, Savoy, or rice answering for the purpose of a tipsy cake. Cut the bottom of the cake level, to make it stand firm in the dish; make a small hole

in the centre, and pour in and over the cake sufficient sweet wine or sherry, mixed with the above proportion of brandy, to soak it nicely. When the cake is well soaked, blanch and cut the almonds into strips, stick them all over the cake, and pour round it a good custard, made by our recipe,

TIPSY CAKE.

allowing 5 eggs to the pint of milk. The cakes are sometimes crumbled and soaked, and a whipped cream heaped over them, the same as for trifles.

TIME.—*About 2 hours to soak the cake.*

SEASONABLE *at any time.*

Tipsy Cake, or Sponge Cake
Pudding.—INGREDIENTS *for large dish.*— 12 stale small sponge-cakes, raisin wine, ½ lb. of jam, 1 pint of custard (see CUSTARD). AVERAGE COST, 2s.

Soak the sponge cakes, which should be stale (on this account they should be cheaper), in a little raisin wine; arrange them on a deep glass dish in four layers, putting some jam between the layers, and pour round them a pint of custard, made by recipe, decorating the top with cut preserved fruit.

TIME.— 2 hours to soak the cakes.

SEASONABLE *at any time.*

Toad-in-the-Hole.   (Cold Meat Cookery.) — INGREDIENTS *for good-sized dish.*—6 oz. of flour, 1 pint of milk, 3 eggs, butter, a few slices of cold mutton, pepper and salt to taste, 2 kidneys. AVERAGE COST, *exclusive of the cold meat,* 1s.

Make a smooth batter of flour, milk and eggs in the above proportion; butter a

Preserved Meats, etc.

a. Side of Bacon; *b.* York Ham; *c.* Irish Ham; *d.* Canadian Ham in bag; *e.* Bath Chaps; *f.* Hung Beef; *g.* Salt Beef; *h.* Pressed Beef; *i.* Ox Tongue; *k.* Russian Tongue; *l.* Pickled Tongue; *m.* Smoked Tongue; *n.* Reindeer Tongue; *o.* Sheep's Tongue; *p.* German Sausage; *q.* Bologna Sausage; *r.* Turtle (dried); *s.* Kippered Salmon; *t.* Kippered Herring; *u.* Smoked Herring; *v.* Yarmouth Bloater; *w.* Salt Cod; *x.* Finnan Haddock; *y.* Ringed Dish.

baking-dish, and pour in the batter. Into this place a few slices of cold mutton, previously well seasoned, and the kidneys, which should be cut into rather small pieces ; bake about 1 hour, or rather longer, and send it to table in the dish it was baked in. Oysters or mushrooms may be substituted for the kidneys, and will be found exceedingly good.

TIME.—*Rather more than* 1 *hour.*

SEASONABLE *at any time.*

Toad-in-the-Hole. (A Homely but Savoury Dish)—INGREDIENTS *for dish for* 6 *persons.*—1½ *lb. of rump-steak,* 1 *sheep's kidney, pepper and salt to taste. For the batter,* 3 *eggs,* 1 *pint of milk,* 4 *tablespoonfuls of flour,* ½ *saltspoonful of salt.* AVERAGE COST, 2*s.* 6*d.*

Cut up the steak and kidney into convenient-sized pieces, and put them into a pie-dish, with a good seasoning of salt and pepper ; mix the flour with a small quantity of milk at first, to prevent its being lumpy ; add the remainder, and the 3 eggs, which should be well beaten ; put in the salt, stir the batter for about 5 minutes, and pour it over the steak. Place it in a tolerably brisk oven immediately, and bake for 1½ hour.

TIME.—1½ *hour.*

SEASONABLE *at any time.*

Note.—The remains of cold beef, rather underdone, may be substituted for the steak, and, when liked, the smallest possible quantity of minced onion or shalot may be added.

Toast, To Make Dry.—To make dry toast properly, a great deal of attention is required ; much more, indeed, than people generally suppose. Never use new bread for making any kind of toast, as it renders it heavy, and, besides, is very extravagant. Procure a loaf of household bread about two days old ; cut off as many slices as may be required, not quite ¼ inch in thickness ; trim off the crusts and ragged edges, put the bread on a toasting-fork, and hold it before a very clear fire. Move it backwards and forwards until the bread is nicely coloured ; then turn it and toast the other side, and do not place it so near the fire that it blackens. Dry toast should be more gradually made than buttered toast, as its great beauty consists in its crispness, and this cannot be attained unless the process is slow and the bread is allowed gradually to colour. It should never be made long before it is wanted, as it soon becomes tough, unless placed on the fender in front of the fire. As soon as each piece is ready, it should be put into a rack, or stood upon its edges, and sent quickly to table.

Toast, To Make Hot Buttered. —A loaf of household bread about two days old answers for making toast better than cottage bread, the latter not being a good shape, and too crusty for the purpose. Cut as many nice even slices as may be required, rather more than ¼ inch in thickness, and toast them before a very bright fire, without allowing the bread to blacken, which spoils the appearance and flavour of all toast. When of a nice colour on both sides, put it on a hot plate ; divide some good butter into small pieces, place them on the toast, set this before the fire, and when the butter is just beginning to melt spread it lightly over the toast. Trim off the crust and ragged edges, divide each round into 4 pieces, and send the toast quickly to table. Some persons cut the slices of toast across from corner to corner, so making the pieces of a three-cornered shape. Soyer recommends that each slice should be cut into pieces as soon as it is buttered, and when all are ready, that they should be piled lightly on the dish they are intended to be served on. He says that by cutting through 4 or 5 slices at a time, all the butter is squeezed out of the upper ones, while the bottom one is swimming in fat liquid. It is highly essential to use good butter for making this dish.

Toast-and-Water. — INGREDIENTS.
—*A slice of bread*, 1 *quart of boiling water.*

Cut a slice from a stale loaf (a piece of hard crust is better than anything else for the purpose), toast it of a nice brown on every side, but *do not allow it to burn or blacken.* Put it into a jug, pour the boiling water over it, cover it closely, and let it remain until cold. When strained, it will be ready for use. Toast-and-water should always be made a short time before it is required, to enable it to get cold: if drunk in a tepid or lukewarm state, it is an exceedingly disagreeable beverage. If, as is sometimes the case, this drink is wanted in a hurry, put the toasted bread into a jug, and only just cover it with the boiling water; when this is cool, cold water may be added in the proportion required and the toast-and-water strained; it will then be ready for use, and is more expeditiously prepared than by the above method.

Toast Sandwiches. — INGREDIENTS.—*Thin cold toast, thin slices of bread-and-butter, pepper and salt to taste.*

Place a very thin piece of cold toast between 2 slices of thin bread-and-butter in the form of a sandwich, adding a seasoning of pepper and salt. This sandwich may be varied by adding a little pulled meat, or very fine slices of cold meat, to the toast, and in any of these forms will be found very tempting to the appetite of an invalid.

Toffee, Everton. — INGREDIENTS.—
1 *lb. of powdered loaf sugar*, 1 *teacupful of water*, ¼ *lb. of butter*, 6 *drops of essence of lemon.* AVERAGE COST, 8*d.*

Put the water and sugar into a brass pan, and beat the butter to a cream. When the sugar is dissolved, add the butter, and keep stirring the mixture over the fire until it sets when a little is poured on to a buttered dish; and, just before the toffee is done, add the essence of lemon. Butter a dish or tin, pour on the mixture, and when cool, it will easily separate from the dish.

Butter-Scotch, an excellent thing for coughs, is made with brown, instead of white sugar, omitting the water, and flavoured with ½ oz. of powdered ginger. It is made in the same manner as toffee.

TIME.—18 *to* 35 *minutes.*

Tomato Pickle.—INGREDIENTS.—
24 *small and perfectly ripe tomatoes*, 1 *quart of vinegar*, 4 *small onions*, 1 *oz. of pepper*, ½ *oz. of cloves*, ½ *oz. of celery-seed*, 2 *spoonfuls of mustard-seed, salt.* AVERAGE COST, 3*s.*

Prick the tomatoes and lay them in an earthen jar with a little salt sprinkled between the layers, and let them stand for 3 days covered, draining away the juice into another covered jar. Mince the onions, then boil them in the vinegar with the other ingredients. Wash and dry the tomatoes, put them in a jar, pour over the juice from the other jar and the vinegar and other ingredients when cold, then cover and tie down closely.

TIME.—*A fortnight, before the pickle is ready.*

SEASONABLE.—*Make this in September or October.*

Tomato Sauce (for Keeping; Excellent).—INGREDIENTS.—1 *dozen tomatoes*, 2 *teaspoonfuls of the best powdered ginger*, 1 *dessertspoonful of salt*, 1 *head of garlic chopped fine*, 2 *tablespoonfuls of vinegar*, 1 *dessertspoonful of Chili vinegar (a small quantity of cayenne may be substituted for this).*

Choose ripe tomatoes, put them into a stone jar and stand them in a cool oven until quite tender; when cold, take the skins and stalks from them, mix the pulp with the liquor which is in the jar, but do not strain it; add all the other ingredients, mix well together, and put it into bottles and seal the corks.

TIME.—4 *or* 5 *hours in a* cool oven.

SEASONABLE *from the middle of September to the end of October.*

Tomato Sauce (for Keeping; Excellent).—INGREDIENTS.—*To every quart of tomato pulp allow* 1 *pint of cayenne vinegar,* ¾ *oz. of shalots,* ¾ *oz. of garlic, peeled and cut in slices; salt to taste. To every* 6 *quarts of liquor,* 1 *pint of soy,* 1 *pint of anchovy sauce.*

Gather the tomatoes quite ripe; bake them in a slow oven till tender; rub them through a sieve, and to every quart of pulp add cayenne vinegar, shalots, garlic and salt, in the above proportion; boil the whole together till the garlic and shalots are quite soft; then rub it through a sieve, put it again into a saucepan, and, to every six quarts of the liquor, add 1 pint of soy and the same quantity of anchovy-sauce, and boil altogether for about 20 minutes; bottle off for use, and carefully seal or resin the corks. This will keep good for 2 or 3 years.

THE TOMATO.

TIME.—*Ready for use in a week.*

SEASONABLE.—*Make this from the middle of September to the end of October.*

Tomato Sauce (for Keeping; Excellent).—INGREDIENTS.—*3 dozen tomatoes; to every pound of tomato-pulp allow* 1 *pint of Chili vinegar,* 1 *oz. of garlic,* 1 *oz. of shalot,* 2 *oz. of salt,* 1 *large green capsicum,* ½ *teaspoonful of cayenne,* 2 *pickled gherkins,* 6 *pickled onions,* 1 *pint of common vinegar, and the juice of* 6 *lemons.*

Choose the tomatoes when quite ripe and red; put them in a jar with a cover to it, and bake them till tender. The better way is to put them in the oven over-night, when it will not be too hot, and examine them in the morning to see if they are tender. Do not allow them to remain in the oven long enough to break them; but they should be sufficiently soft to skin nicely and rub

through a sieve. Measure the pulp, and to each pound of pulp add the above proportion of vinegar and other ingredients, taking care to chop very fine the garlic, shalot, capsicum, onions and gherkins. Boil the whole together till everything is tender; then again rub it through a sieve, and add the lemon-juice. Now boil the whole again till it becomes as thick as cream, and keep continually stirring; bottle it when quite cold, cork well, and seal the corks.

TIME.—*In a cool oven one night.*

SEASONABLE *from the middle of September to the end of October.*

Note.—A quantity of liquor will flow from the tomatoes, which must be put through the sieve with the rest. Keep it well stirred whilst on the fire, and use a wooden spoon.

Tomato Sauce, Hot (to serve with Cutlets, Roast Meats, &c.).—INGREDIENTS *for* 1 *tureen.*—6 *tomatoes,* 2 *shalots,* 1 *clove,* 1 *blade of mace, salt and cayenne to taste,* ¼ *pint of gravy or stock.* AVERAGE COST, 1s.

Cut the tomatoes in two, and squeeze the juice and seeds out; put them in a stewpan with all the ingredients, and let them simmer *gently* until the tomatoes are tender enough to pulp; rub the whole through a sieve, boil it for a few minutes, and serve. The shalots and spices may be omitted when their flavour is objected to.

TIME.—1 *hour, or rather more, to simmer the tomatoes.*

SEASONABLE *in September and October.*

Tomatoes, Baked. (Excellent.)—INGREDIENTS *for dish for* 6 *persons.*—8 *or* 10 *tomatoes, pepper and salt to taste,* 2 *oz. of butter, bread-crumbs.* AVERAGE COST, 1s.6d.

Take off the stalks from the tomatoes; cut them into thick slices, and put them into a deep baking-dish; add a plentiful seasoning of pepper and salt, and butter in the above proportion; cover the whole with bread-crumbs; drop over these a little clarified butter; bake in a moderate oven from 20 minutes to ½ hour, and serve **very**

2 P

hot. This vegetable, dressed as above, is an exceedingly nice accompaniment to all kinds of roast meat. The tomatoes, instead of being cut in slices, may be baked whole; but they will take a longer time to cook.

TIME.—20 *minutes to ½ hour*

SEASONABLE *in August, September and October; may be had, forced, much earlier.*

Tomatoes, Baked. (Another Mode.)
—INGREDIENTS. — *Some bread-crumbs, a little butter, onion, cayenne and salt.*

Bake the tomatoes whole, then scoop out a small hole at the top; fry the breadcrumbs, onion, &c , and fill the holes with this as high up as possible : then brown the tomatoes with a salamander, or in an oven, and take care the skin does not break.

Tomatoes and Onions.—INGREDIENTS.—*1 dozen ripe tomatoes, their weight in onions, a quart of vinegar, a teaspoonful of allspice, 2 oz. of black pepper.* AVERAGE COST, 3s.

Wipe the tomatoes dry, and take off the skin of the onions, put them in a stewpan with the other ingredients, and let them gently simmer for 8 hours. When cold, bottle and tie over with a bladder.

TIME.—8 *hours.*

SEASONABLE. — *Make this in autumn.*

Tomatoes, Stewed. — INGREDIENTS *for dish for 4 or 5 persons.—8 tomatoes, pepper and salt to taste, 2 oz. of butter, 2 tablespoonfuls of vinegar.* AVERAGE COST, 1s. 6d.

Slice the tomatoes into a *lined* saucepan ; season them with pepper and salt, and place small pieces of butter on them. Cover the lid down closely, and stew from 20 to 25 minutes, or until the tomatoes are perfectly tender ; add the vinegar, stir two or three times, and serve with any kind of roast meat, with which they will be found a nice accompaniment.

TIME.—20 *minutes.*

SEASONABLE *in autumn.*

Tomatoes, Stewed. — INGREDIENTS *for dish for 4 or 5 persons.—8 tomatoes, about ½ pint of good gravy, thickening of butter and flour, cayenne and salt to taste.* AVERAGE COST, 1s. 6d.

Take out the stalks of the tomatoes; put them into a wide stewpan, pour over them the above proportion of good brown gravy and stew gently until they are tender, occasionally *carefully* turning them, that they may be equally done. Thicken the gravy with a little butter and flour worked together on a plate ; let it just boil up after the thickening is added, and serve. If it be at hand, these should be served on a silver or plated dish.

TIME.—20 *to* 25 *minutes very gentle stewing.*

SEASONABLE *in August, September and October; but may be had, forced, much earlier.*

Tomatoes, Stuffed. — INGREDIENTS *for dish for 6 persons.—6 tomatoes of fair and even size, about 2 oz. of good forcemeat, 2 dessertspoonfuls of salad oil.* AVERAGE COST, 1s. 4d.

Plunge the tomatoes for one minute in boiling water, take them out, remove the thin skin and season with pepper and salt. Cut off a round piece at the stalk end, and with an egg-spoon, scoop out the pips.

STUFFED TOMATOES.

Fill up the space with the forcemeat, and spread the remainder thinly over the tomatoes. Over the forcemeat scatter fine raspings, and fry in the oil for about 8 minutes, or bake for 12, and brown with a salamander.

TIME.—8 *to* 12 *minutes.*

SEASONABLE *in autumn.*

Tongue, Boiled.—Ingredients.—

1 *tongue, a bunch of savoury herbs, water.* Average Cost, *one of moderate size, 3s. 6d.*

In choosing a tongue, ascertain how long it has been dried or pickled, and select one with a smooth skin, which denotes its being young and tender. If a dried one, and rather hard, soak it at least for 12 hours previous to cooking it; if, however, it is fresh from the pickle, 2 or 3 hours will be sufficient for it to remain in soak. Put the tongue into a stewpan with plenty of cold water and a bunch of savoury herbs; let it gradually come to a boil, skim well, and simmer very gently until tender. Peel off the skin, garnish with tufts of cauliflowers or Brussels sprouts, and serve. Boiled tongue is frequently sent to table with boiled poultry, instead of ham, and is, by many persons, preferred. If to serve cold, peel it, fasten it down to a piece of board by sticking a fork through the root, and another through the top, to straighten it. When cold, glaze it, and put a paper ruche round the root, and garnish with tufts of parsley.

Time.—*A large smoked tongue, 4 to 4½ hours; a small one, 2½ to 3 hours. A large unsmoked tongue, 3 to 3½ hours; a small one, 2 to 2½ hours.*

Seasonable *at any time.*

Tongue, To Carve.—Cut a fairly

thin slice by passing the knife through in the direction from A to B, as shown in illustration, and continue to cut slices in

TONGUE.

this way until the best portions of the upper side are served. The fat which lies about the root of the tongue is carved by turning the tongue and cutting in the direction from C to D.

Tongue, To Pickle and Dress

a, to Eat Cold.—Ingredients.—6 *oz. of salt, 2 oz. of baysalt, 1 oz. of saltpetre. 3 oz. of coarse sugar; cloves, mace and allspice to taste; butter, common crust of flour and water.* Average Cost, *medium-sized tongue, 2s. 6d.*

Lay the tongue for a fortnight in the above pickle, turn it every day, and be particular that the spices are well pounded; put it into a small pan just large enough to hold it, place some pieces of butter on it, and cover with a common crust. Bake in a slow oven until so tender that a straw would penetrate it, take off the skin, fasten it down to a piece of board by running a fork through the root, and another through the tip, at the same time straightening it and putting it into shape. When cold, glaze it, put a paper ruche round the root, which is generally very unsightly, and garnish with tufts of parsley.

Time.—*From 3 to 4 hours in a slow oven, according to size.*

Seasonable *at any time.*

Tongues alla Nivernese. (Italian

Recipe.) — Ingredients *for dish for 6 persons.*—6 *sheep's tongues, 1 pint of stock, 6 small lettuces, 6 carrots, chopped parsley, salt, pepper and nutmeg.* Average Cost, *4s.*

Cleanse the tongues thoroughly, and boil them gently for 2 hours in water with the seasoning and chopped parsley. Take off the skin and let them cool, being careful to preserve their shape, then lay them in a stewpan with reduced stock, and, shortly before serving, bring them to a boil and glaze. Place them in a dish so as to form a crown, and between them, a lettuce stuffed with forcemeat, and a carrot cut in the shape of a heart, all separately cooked. Fill up the centre space with any vegetable preferred, stewed in a little stock and butter.

Time.—*2½ hours.*

Seasonable *at any time.*

Tongues, To Cure. — INGREDI- ENTS.—*For a tongue of 7 lbs., 1 oz. of salt- petre, ½ oz. of black pepper, 4 oz. of sugar, 3 oz. of juniper berries, 6 oz. of salt.* AVER- AGE COST, *of medium-sized tongue, 2s. 6d.*

Rub the above ingredients well into the tongue, and let it remain in the pickle for 10 days or a fortnight : then drain it, tie it up in brown paper, and have it smoked for about 20 days over a wood fire ; or it may be boiled out of this pickle.

TIME.—*From 10 to 14 days to remain in the pickle; to be smoked 24 days.*

SEASONABLE *at any time.*

Note.—If not wanted immediately, the tongue will keep 3 or 4 weeks without being too salt; then it must not be rubbed, but only turned in the pickle.

Transparent Pudding.—INGRE- DIENTS *for pudding for 6 persons.—6 eggs, ½ lb. of pounded sugar, 6 oz. of butter, grated nutmeg or lemon flavouring, puff paste.* AVERAGE COST, 1s. 2d.

Beat the eggs well, and mix with the other ingredients in a stewpan. Line a dish with puff-paste, pour in the mixture, and bake in a moderate oven.

TIME.—*About 20 minutes to bake the pudding.*

SEASONABLE *at any time.*

Treacle Pudding, Rolled.—IN- GREDIENTS.—1 *lb. of suet crust, ¼ lb. of treacle, ½ teaspoonful of grated ginger.*

Make, with 1 lb. of flour, a suet crust by our given recipe, roll it out to the thick- ness of ½ inch, and spread the treacle equally over it, leaving a small margin where the paste joins; roll it up, close the ends securely, tie the pudding in a floured cloth, plunge it into boiling water, and boil for 2 hours. This pudding is economical, and a favourite one with children ; but it is, of course, only suitable for a nursery, or very plain family dinner. Made with a lard instead of a suet crust, it would be

very nice baked, and would be sufficiently done in from 1½ to 2 hours.

TIME.—*Boiled pudding, 2 hours; baked pudding, 1½ to 2 hours.*

SEASONABLE *at any time.*

Trifle, Indian. — INGREDIENTS *for good-sized dish.*—1 *quart of milk, the rind of ½ large lemon, sugar to taste, 5 heaped tablespoonfuls of rice flour, 1 oz. of sweet almonds, ½ pint of custard.* AVERAGE COST, 1s.

Boil the milk and lemon-rind together until the former is well flavoured ; take out the lemon-rind, and stir in the rice-flour, which should first be moistened with cold milk, and add sufficient loaf sugar to sweeten it nicely. Boil gently for about 5 minutes, and keep the mixture stirred ; take it off the fire, let it cool a *little*, and pour it into a glass dish. When cold, cut the rice out in the form of a star, or any other shape that may be preferred ; take out the spare rice, and fill the space with boiled custard. Blanch and cut the al- monds into strips ; stick them over the trifle, and garnish it with pieces of bright- coloured jelly, or preserved fruits, or can- died citron.

TIME.—½ *hour to simmer the milk, 5 mi- nutes after the rice is added.*

SEASONABLE *at any time.*

Trifle, To Make a.—INGREDIENTS *for large dish.*—*For the whip, 1 pint of cream, 3 oz. of pounded sugar, the white of 2 eggs, a small glass of sherry or raisin wine. For the trifle, 1 pint of custard, made with 5 eggs to a pint of milk; 6 small sponge cakes, or 6 slices of sponge-cake; 12 macaroons, 2 dozen ratafias, 2 oz. of sweet almonds, the grated rind of 1 lemon, a layer of raspberry or strawberry jam, ½ pint of sherry or sweet wine, 6 tablespoonfuls of brandy.* AVERAGE COST, 4s. 9d.

The whip to lay over the top of the trifle should be made the day before it is required for table, as the flavour is better, and it is much more solid than when prepared the same day. Put into a large bowl the pounded sugar, the whites of the eggs, which should be beaten to a stiff froth, a glass of sherry or sweet wine and the cream. Whisk these ingredients well in a cool place, and take off the froth with a skimmer as fast as it rises, and put it on a sieve to drain; continue the whisking till there is sufficient of the whip, which must be put away in a cool place to drain. The next day, place the sponge-cakes,

TRIFLE.

macaroons and ratafias in layers in a dish; pour over them ½ pint of sherry or sweet wine, mixed with 6 tablespoonfuls of brandy, and, should this proportion of wine not be found quite sufficient, add a little more, as the cakes should be well soaked. Over the cakes put the grated lemon-rind, the sweet almonds, blanched and cut into strips, and a layer of raspberry or strawberry jam. Make a good custard, by recipe, using 8 instead of 5 eggs to the pint of milk, and let it cool a little; then pour it over the cakes, &c. The whip being made the day previously, and the trifle prepared, there remains nothing to do now but to heap the whip lightly over the top; this should stand as high as possible, and it may be garnished with strips of bright currant jelly (*see* illustration), or crystallized fruits of different kinds.

SEASONABLE *at any time.*

Tripe, To Dress.—INGREDIENTS.—

Tripe, onion sauce, milk and water. AVERAGE COST, 7*d. per pound.*

Ascertain that the tripe is quite fresh, and have it cleaned and dressed. Cut away the coarsest fat, and boil it in equal proportions of milk and water for ¾ hour.

Should the tripe be entirely undressed, more than double that time should be allowed for it. Have ready some onion sauce, made by our given recipe, dish the tripe, smother it with the sauce, and the remainder send to table in a tureen.

TIME.—¾ *hour; for undressed tripe, from* 2½ *to* 3 *hours.*

SEASONABLE *at any time.*

Note.—Tripe may be dressed in a variety of ways: it may be cut in pieces and fried in batter, stewed in gravy with mushrooms, or cut into collops, sprinkled with minced onion and savoury herbs, and fried a nice brown in clarified butter.

Trout, Stewed.—INGREDIENTS *for dish for 6 persons.*—2 *middling-sized trout,* ½ *onion cut in thin slices, a little parsley,* 2 *cloves,* 1 *blade of mace,* 2 *bay-leaves, a little thyme, salt and pepper to taste,* 1 *pint of medium stock,* 1 *glass of port wine, thickening of butter and flour.* AVERAGE COST, 3*s.*

Wash the fish very clean, and wipe it quite dry. Lay it in a stewpan, with all the ingredients but the butter and flour, and simmer gently for ½ hour, or rather more, should the fish be not quite done.

BOILED TROUT.

Take it out, strain the gravy, add the thickening and stir it over a sharp fire for 5 minutes; pour it over the trout, and serve.

TIME.—*According to size,* ½ *hour or more*

SEASONABLE *from May to September, and fatter from the middle to the end of August than at any other time.*

Note.—Trout may be served with anchovy or caper sauce, baked in buttered paper, or fried whole, like smelts. Trout dressed *à la Génévese* is extremely delicate; for this proceed the same as with salmon,

Trout, Stuffed, Fried.—Ingredi-

ents *for dish for 4 persons.—A fine trout, a little bread-crumb and butter, 2 oz. of truffles, 6 button-mushrooms, 1 teaspoonful of minced thyme, parsley and chervil; for the Court bouillon, a quart of water, a pint of white wine vinegar, 1 large carrot, onion and parsnip, a small head of celery, a little thyme, parsley, chervil and salt, 2 bay-leaves, 2 oz. of butter.* Average Cost, 3s. 6d.

Reduce the ingredients for the Court bouillon quickly over a strong fire, the vegetables being sliced up; strain, cool and preserve for cooking fish, replacing the liquid consumed each time by some good white wine. Stuff the trout with a force-meat made of the bread-crumbs, truffles, mushrooms, butter and herbs. The fish having been washed and dried, tie up the head, and simmer in the *Court bouillon* for ¼ hour. Take it out, dip it in egg and bread-crumbs, fry, and serve up with tomato sauce.

Time.—½ *hour.*

Seasonable *from May to September.*

Truffles à l'Italienne.—Ingredi-

ents *for dish for 6 persons.—5 or 6 truffles, 1 tablespoonful of minced parsley, 1 minced shalot, salt and pepper to taste, 2 oz. of butter, 2 tablespoonfuls of good brown gravy, the juice of ½ lemon, cayenne to taste.* Average Cost, 3s. 6d.

Wash the truffles and cut them into slices about the size of a penny-piece; put them into a frying-pan, with the parsley, shalot, salt, pepper and 1 oz. of butter; stir them over the fire, that they may all be equally done, which will be in about 10 minutes, and drain off some of the butter; then add a little more fresh butter, 2 tablespoonfuls of good gravy, the juice of ½ lemon and a little cayenne; stir over the fire until the whole is on the point of boiling, when serve.

Time.—*Altogether, 20 minutes.*

Seasonable *from November to March.*

Truffles au Naturel.—Ingredi-

ents.—*Truffles, buttered paper.*

Select some fine truffles; cleanse them, by washing them in several waters with a brush, until not a particle of sand or grit remains on them; wrap each truffle in buttered paper, and bake in a hot oven for quite an hour; take off the paper, wipe the truffles, and serve them in a hot napkin.

Time.—1 *hour.*

Seasonable *from November to March.*

Truffles, Italian Mode of

Dressing.—Ingredients. — 10 *truffles, ¼ pint of salad-oil, pepper and salt to taste, 1 tablespoonful of minced parsley, a very little finely-minced garlic, 2 blades of pounded mace, 1 tablespoonful of lemon-juice.*

After cleansing and brushing the truffles, cut them into thin slices, and put them in a baking-dish, on a seasoning of oil, pepper,

TRUFFLES.

salt, parsley, garlic and mace in the above proportion. Bake them for nearly an hour, and, just before serving, add the lemon-juice, and send them to table very hot.

Time.—*Nearly 1 hour.*

Seasonable *from November to March.*

Truffles, To Dress, with Cham-

pagne.—Ingredients *for large dish.—12 fine black truffles, a few slices of fat bacon, 1 carrot, 1 turnip, 2 onions, a bunch of savoury herbs, including parsley, 1 bay-leaf, 2 cloves, 1 blade of pounded mace, 2 glasses of champagne, ½ pint of stock.* Average Cost, *about 1s. each.*

Carefully select the truffles, reject those that have a musty smell, and wash them well with a brush, in cold water only, until perfectly clean. Put the bacon into a stewpan, with the truffles and the remaining ingredients ; simmer these gently for an hour, and let the whole cool in the stewpan. When to be served, re-warm them, and drain them on a clean cloth ; then arrange them on a delicately-white napkin, that it may contrast as strongly as possible with the truffles, and serve. The trimmings of truffles are used to flavour gravies, stock, sauces, &c., and are an excellent addition to ragoûts, made dishes of fowl, forcemeats, &c.

TIME.—1 *hour.*

SEASONABLE *from November to March.*

Turban of Veal. — INGREDIENTS *for entrée for 8 persons.*—3 *lbs. even-shaped tender fillet of veal, 2 slices of bacon, 3 slices of very red tongue, a few truffles, ¾ lb. of forcemeat, a few slices of toast, a bunch of herbs, an egg, a little clarified butter.* AVERAGE COST, 5s.

Cut the fillet into 12 slices about ¼ inch thick, and of equal size, a little narrower at

TURBAN OF VEAL.

one end. Lard 4 of the pieces with thin strips of the bacon, 4 with truffles and 4 with tongue. In a plate that will stand the fire, put the toast to make a round base, heap on it the forcemeat mixed with herbs and truffles, chopped fine, and, with a knife dipped in warm water, shape the mound with a hollow at the top. Salt slightly the slices of veal, and lay them in alternate colours round the mound, turning in top and bottom so as to hide the stuffing. When the turban is shaped, baste it with clarified butter, and cover it first with a thin slice of fat bacon, then with buttered

paper. Place in a hot oven, and in half-an-hour remove the bacon and paper and glaze the turban. Garnish the centre with a nice ragoût of sweetbreads, truffles and mushrooms, and put 1 glazed sweetbread on the top. Serve with Spanish sauce.

TIME.—1 *hour to bake.*

SEASONABLE *from March to October.*

Turbot.—In choosing turbot see that it is thick, and of a yellowish white ; for if of a bluish tint, it is not good. The turbot-kettle, as will be seen by our cut, is made differently from ordinary fish-kettles: it

TURBOT-KETTLE.

being less deep, whilst it is wider, and more pointed at the sides ; thus exactly answering to the shape of the fish which it is intended should be boiled in it.

Turbot à l'Italienne. (Italian Recipe.)—INGREDIENTS *for dish for 8 or 10 persons.*—A *good-sized turbot, a trout, 2 carp roes (other roes can be substituted), 12 button-mushrooms, a few truffles and prawns, 2 oz. of butter, white wine.* AVERAGE COST, 12s. *to* 14s.

Prepare the turbot as usual, and simmer it in good white wine for 2 hours. Drain,

TURBOT À L'ITALIENNE.

and put it on a dish with a garnish of fried pieces of trout and roes and glazed mushrooms, placed alternately. Stick into the fish some skewers decorated with truffles and prawns, and serve with a sauce *à la Princesse*, made as follows:—Add to 1 pint of sauce *allemande*, a tablespoonful of white stock, 2 tablespoonfuls of purée of tomatoes, 1 teaspoonful of parsley chopped fine, the juice of half a lemon and a little butter, and make all hot together.

TIME.—*2 hours.*

SEASONABLE *from May to September.*

Turbot, Boiled.—INGREDIENTS.— 6 *oz. of salt to each gallon of water.* AVERAGE COST, *from 3s. to 12s. each.*

Choose a middling-sized turbot; for they are invariably the most valuable; if very large, the meat will be tough and thready. Three or four hours before dressing, soak the fish in salt water to take off the slime; then thoroughly cleanse it, and with a knife make an incision down the middle of the back, to prevent the skin of the belly from cracking. Rub it over with lemon, and be particular not to cut off the fins. Lay the fish in a very clean turbot-kettle, with sufficient cold water to cover it, and salt in the above proportion. Let it gradually come

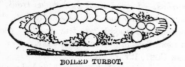

BOILED TURBOT.

to a boil, and skim very carefully; keep it gently simmering, and on no account let it boil fast, as the fish would have a very unsightly appearance. When the meat separates easily from the bone, it is done; then take it out, let it drain well, and dish it on a hot napkin. Rub a little lobster spawn through a sieve, sprinkle it over the fish, and garnish with tufts of parsley and cut lemon. Lobster or shrimp sauce, and plain melted butter, should be sent to table with it.

TIME.—*After the water boils, about ½ hour for a large turbot; middling size, about 20 minutes.*

SEASONABLE *at any time.*

Turbot, To Carve.—First run the fish-slice down the thickest part of the fish lengthwise, quite through to the bone, and then cut handsome and regular slices across the fish until all the meat on the upper side

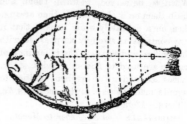

TURBOT.

is helped. When the carver has removed all the meat from the upper side of the fish, the backbone should be raised, put on one side of the dish, and the under side helped as the upper.

Turbot à la Crême.—INGREDIENTS.—*The remains of cold turbot. For sauce, 2 oz. of butter, 4 tablespoonfuls of cream; salt, cayenne and pounded mace to taste.*

Clear away all skin and bone from the flesh of the turbot, which should be done when it comes from table, as it causes less waste when trimmed hot. Cut the flesh into nice square pieces, as equally as possible; put into a stewpan the butter, let it melt, and add the cream and seasoning; let it just simmer for one minute, but not boil. Lay in the fish to warm, and serve it garnished with croûtons or a paste border.

TIME.—10 *minutes.*

SEASONABLE *at any time.*

Note.—The remains of cold salmon may be dressed in this way, and the above mixture may be served in a *vol-au vent.*

Turbot au Gratin.—INGREDIENTS. —*Remains of cold turbot, béchamel (see Sauces), bread-crumbs, butter.*

Cut the flesh of the turbot into small dice, carefully freeing it from all skin and bone

Put them into a stewpan, and moisten with 4 or 5 tablespoonfuls of béchamel. Let it get thoroughly hot, but do not allow it to boil. Spread the mixture on a dish, cover with finely-grated bread-crumbs, and place small pieces of butter over the top. Brown it in the oven, or with a sala-mander.

TIME.—*Altogether,* ½ *hour.*

SEASONABLE *at any time.*

Turbot à l'Italienne, Fillets of.

—INGREDIENTS.—*The remains of cold turbot, Italian sauce.*

Clear the flesh carefully from the bone, and take away all skin, which gives an un-pleasant flavour to the sauce. Make the sauce hot, lay in the fish to warm through, but do not let it boil. Garnish with croû-tons.

TIME.—5 *minutes.*

SEASONABLE *all the year.*

Turbot, Baked Fillets of.

—IN-GREDIENTS.—*The remains of cold turbot, lobster sauce left from the preceding day, egg and bread-crumbs ; cayenne and salt to taste ; minced parsley, nutmeg, lemon-juice.*

After having cleared the fish from all skin and bone, divide it into square pieces of an equal size ; brush them over with egg, sprinkle with bread-crumbs mixed with a little minced parsley and seasoning. Lay the fillets in a baking-dish, with suffi-cient butter to baste with. Bake for ¼ hour, and do not forget to keep them well moistened with the butter. Put a little lemon-juice and grated nutmeg to the cold lobster sauce ; make it hot, and pour over the fish, which must be well drained from the butter. Garnish with parsley and cut lemon.

TIME.—*Altogether,* ½ *hour.*

SEASONABLE *at any time.*

Note. — Cold turbot thus warmed in the remains of lobster sauce will be found much nicer than putting the fish again in water.

Turbot, or other Large Fish, Garnish for.

—Take the crumb of a stale loaf, cut it into small pyramids with flat tops, and on the top of each pyramid put rather more than a tablespoonful of white of egg beaten to a stiff froth. Over this sprinkle finely-chopped parsley and fine raspings of a dark colour. Arrange these on the napkin round the fish, one green and one brown alternately.

Turkey, Baked. (Italian Recipe.)

—INGREDIENTS *for dish for 8 persons.*—*A medium-sized turkey,* ¼ *lb. of sausage, 8 French prunes, 4 pears,* ½ *pint of boiled and peeled chestnuts, a glass of Marsala or sherry, butter, salt, a few slices of bacon and a little rosemary.* AVERAGE COST, 7s. *to* 8s.

Blanch and cut the sausage into thin long pieces, blanch and stone the prunes, peel and quarter the pears ; fry them with the chestnuts in a little butter for a minute or two ; chop the liver of the turkey fine, and add it, then mix with the wine and make a forcemeat. Salt the inside of the turkey slightly and stuff with the force-meat, and put it in the pan with the bacon, some butter, rosemary and a little salt. Place in a slow oven, basting occa-sionally, till of a good colour. Serve with its own gravy.

TIME.—*About 2 hours.*

SEASONABLE *all the year, except March to May.*

Turkey, Boiled.

—INGREDIENTS.— *Turkey ; forcemeat.* AVERAGE COST, 10d. *per lb., but often more expensive at Christ-mas.*

Choosing and Trussing.—Hen turkeys are preferable for boiling, on account of their whiteness and tenderness ; and one of moderate size should be selected, as a large one is not suitable for this mode of cook-ing. They should not be dressed until they have been killed 3 or 4 days, as they will neither look white, nor will they be tender. Pluck the bird, carefully draw, and singe it with a piece of white paper; wash it inside and out, and wipe it thoroughly dry with a cloth. Cut off the head and neck, draw the strings or sinews of the thighs, and cut off the legs at the first oint; draw the legs into the body, fill the breast with forcemeat; run a skewer through the wing and the middle joint of the leg, quite into the leg and wing on the opposite side; break the breastbone, and make the bird look as round and as compact as possible.

Put the turkey into sufficient *hot* water to cover it; let it come to a boil, then carefully remove all the scum. If this is attended to, there is no occasion to boil the bird in a floured cloth; but it should be well covered with the water. Let it simmer very gently for about 1½ hour to 1¾ hour, according to the size, and serve with either white, celery, oyster or mushroom sauce, or parsley-and-butter, a little of which should be poured over the turkey.

BOILED TURKEY.

Boiled ham, bacon, tongue, or pickled pork, should always accompany this dish; and when oyster sauce is served, the turkey should be stuffed with oyster forcemeat.

TIME.—*A small turkey, 1½ hour; a large one, 1¾ hour.*

SEASONABLE *from December to February.*

Turkey, Croquettes of. (Cold Meat Cookery.)—INGREDIENTS.—*The remains of cold turkey; to every ½ lb. of meat allow 2 oz. of ham or bacon, 2 shalots, 1 oz. of butter, 1 tablespoonful of flour, the yolks of 2 eggs, egg and bread-crumbs.*

The smaller pieces, that will not do for a fricassée or hash, answer very well for this dish. Mince the meat finely with ham or

bacon in the above proportion; make a gravy of the bones and trimmings, well seasoning it: mince the shalots, put them into a stewpan with the butter, add the flour; mix well, then put in the mince, and about ½ pint of the gravy made from the bones. (The proportion of the butter must be increased or diminished according to the quantity of mince.) When just boiled, add the yolks of 2 eggs; put the mixture out to cool, and then shape it in a wineglass. Cover the croquettes with egg and bread-crumbs, and fry them a delicate brown. Put small pieces of parsley-stems for stalks, and serve with rolled bacon cut very thin.

TIME.—*8 minutes to fry the croquettes.*

SEASONABLE *from December to February.*

Turkey, Devilled.—INGREDIENTS *for dish for 4 or 5 persons.*—*2 turkeys' legs, made mustard, pepper, salt and cayenne.*

Score the legs in regular lines in deep gashes, both along and across, pepper and salt them, adding cayenne, if liked very hot; cover them with made mustard, and leave till the following morning, if for a breakfast dish. Grill the legs over a clear, bright fire till the outside is crisp and brown. Place small pieces of butter over, and serve quickly.

TIME.—*7 minutes to grill.*

SEASONABLE *in winter.*

Turkey, Fricasséed. (Cold Meat Cookery.)—INGREDIENTS.—*The remains of cold roast or boiled turkey; a strip of lemon-peel, a bunch of savoury herbs, 1 onion, pepper and salt to taste, 1 pint of water, 4 tablespoonfuls of cream, the yolk of an egg. AVERAGE COST, exclusive of the cold turkey, 6d.*

Cut some nice slices from the remains of a cold turkey, and put the bones and trimmings into a stewpan, with the lemon-peel, herbs, onion, pepper, salt and the water; stew for an hour, strain the gravy and lay in the pieces of turkey. When warm through, add the cream and the yolk of an egg; stir it well round, and, when getting thick, take out the pieces, lay them on a hot dish and pour the sauce over. Garnish the fricassée with sippets of toasted bread. Celery or cucumbers, cut into small pieces, may be put into the sauce; if the former, it must be boiled first.

TIME.—1 *hour to make the gravy.*

SEASONABLE *from December to February.*

Turkey, Hashed.—INGREDIENTS.

—*The remains of cold roast turkey,* 1 *onion, pepper and salt to taste, rather more than* 1 *pint of water,* 1 *carrot,* 1 *turnip,* 1 *blade of mace, a bunch of savoury herbs,* 1 *tablespoonful of mushroom ketchup,* 1 *tablespoonful of port wine, thickening of butter and flour.*

Cut the turkey into neat joints; the best pieces reserve for the hash, the inferior joints and trimmings put into a stewpan with an onion cut in slices, pepper and salt, a carrot, turnip, mace, herbs and water in the above proportion; simmer these for an hour, then strain the gravy, thicken it with butter and flour, flavour with ketchup and port wine and lay in the pieces of turkey to warm through; if there is any stuffing left, put that in also, as it so much improves the flavour of the gravy. When it boils, serve, and garnish the dish with sippets of toasted bread.

TIME.—1 *hour to make the gravy.*

SEASONABLE *from December to February.*

Turkey, Roast.—INGREDIENTS.—

Turkey; forcemeat.

Choosing and Trussing.—Choose cock turkeys by their short spurs and black legs, in which case they are young; if the spurs are long, and the legs pale and rough, they are old. If the bird has been long killed, the eyes will appear sunk and the feet very dry; but, if fresh, the contrary will be the case. Middling-sized fleshy turkeys are by many persons considered superior to those

of an immense growth, as they are, generally speaking, much more tender. They should never be dressed the same day they are killed; but, in cold weather, should hang at least 8 days; if the weather is mild, 4 or 5 days will be found sufficient. Carefully pluck the bird, singe it with white paper and wipe it thoroughly with a cloth; draw it, preserve the liver and gizzard and be particular not to break the gall-bag, as no washing will remove the bitter taste it imparts where it once touches. Wash it *inside* well, and wipe it thoroughly dry with a cloth; the *outside* merely requires nicely wiping, as we have just stated. Cut off the neck close to the back, but leave enough of the crop-skin to turn over; break the leg-bone close below the knee, draw out the strings from the thighs, and flatten the breastbone to make it look plump. Have ready a forcemeat; fill the breast with this,

ROAST TURKEY.

and, if a trussing-needle is used, sew the neck over to the back; if a needle is not at hand, a skewer will answer the purpose. Run a skewer through the pinion and thigh into the body to the pinion and thigh on the other side, and press the legs as much as possible between the breast and the side-bones, and put the liver under one pinion and the gizzard under the other. Pass a string across the back of the bird, catch it over the points of the skewer, tie it in the centre of the back, and be particular that the turkey is very firmly trussed. This may be more easily accomplished with a needle and twine than with skewers.

Fasten a sheet of buttered paper on to the breast of the bird, put it down to a bright fire, at some little distance *at first.* (afterwards draw it nearer), and keep it well basted the whole of the time it is cooking. About ¼ hour before serving, remove the paper, dredge the turkey lightly with flour, and put a piece of butter into the basting-ladle; as the butter melts, baste the bird with it. When of a nice brown and well frothed, serve with a tureen of good brown gravy and one of bread sauce. Fried sausages are a favourite addition to roast turkey; they make a garnish, besides adding very much to the flavour. When these are not at hand, a few forcemeat balls should be placed round the dish as a garnish. Turkey may also be stuffed with sausage-meat, and a chestnut forcemeat with the chestnut sauce is, by many persons, very much esteemed as an accompaniment to this favourite dish.

TIME.—*Small turkey, 1½ hour; moderate-sized one, about 10 lbs., 2 hours; large turkey, 2½ hours, or longer.*

SEASONABLE *from December to February.*

Turkey, Roast, To Carve.—

A noble dish is a turkey, roast or boiled. A Christmas dinner with the middle-classes of this empire, would scarcely be a Christmas dinner without its turkey; and we can hardly imagine an object of greater envy than is presented by a respected portly

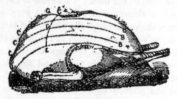

ROAST TURKEY.

paterfamilias carving, at the season devoted to good cheer and genial charity, his own fat turkey, and carving it well. The only art consists, as in the carving of a goose, in getting from the breast as many fine slices as possible; and all must have remarked the very great difference in the large number of people whom a good carver will find slices for, and a comparatively few that a bad carver will succeed in serving.

As we have stated in both the carving of a duck and goose, the carver should commence cutting slices to the wing, from B to C, and then proceed upwards towards the ridge of the breastbone: this is not the usual plan, but, in practice, will be found the best. The breast is the only part which is looked on as fine in a turkey, the legs being very seldom cut off and eaten at table: they are usually removed to the kitchen, where they are taken off, as here marked, to appear only in a form which seems to have a special attraction at a bachelor's supper table, or as a breakfast dish—we mean devilled: served in this way they are especially liked and relished. A boiled turkey is carved in the same manner as when roasted.

Turkey Poult, Roast.—INGRE-

DIENTS.—*Turkey poult; butter.* AVERAGE COST, 7s. *to* 8s. *each.*

Choosing and Trussing.—Choose a plump bird, and truss it in the following manner. After it has been carefully plucked, drawn and singed, skin the neck, and fasten the head under the wing; turn the legs at the first joint, and bring the feet close to the thighs, as a woodcock should be trussed, *and do not stuff it.*

Put it down to a bright fire, keep it well basted, and at first place a piece of paper on the breast to prevent its taking too much colour. About 10 minutes before serving, dredge it lightly with flour, and baste well; when nicely frothed, send it to table immediately, with a little gravy in the dish, and some in a tureen. If at hand, a few watercresses may be placed round the turkey as a garnish, or it may be larded.

TIME.—*About 1 hour.*

SEASONABLE.—*In full season from June to October.*

Turkey Soup. (A Seasonable dish

at Christmas.)—INGREDIENTS *for soup for 8 or 10 persons.*—2 *quarts of medium stock, the remains of a cold roast turkey, 2 oz. of rice-flour or arrowroot, salt and pepper to taste,* 1 *tablespoonful of Harvey's sauce or mushroom ketchup.* AVERAGE COST, 9*d. per quart.*

Cut up the turkey in small pieces, and put it in the stock; let it simmer slowly until the bones are quite clean. Take the bones out, and work the soup through a sieve; when cool, skim well. Mix the rice-flour or arrowroot to a batter with a little of the soup; add it with the seasoning and sauce, or ketchup. Give one boil, and serve.

TIME.—4 *hours.*

SEASONABLE.—*At Christmas.*

Note.—Instead of thickening this soup, vermicelli or macaroni may be served in it.

Turkey Stew. INGREDIENTS *for plain supper dish for* 6 *persons.*—*The carcass and inferior parts of a cold turkey,* ¾ *lb. of macaroni, salt and pepper, water.* AVERAGE COST, *exclusive of the cold turkey,* 5*d.*

Chop up the carcass of the turkey, and put it—with plenty of water to cover it—and the macaroni in a stewpan. Add the seasoning and a little pounded mace, if liked, and stew all gently for an hour, adding more water if the macaroni absorbs it. Shake the pan occasionally to prevent it sticking to the bottom of the stewpan. Before serving take out the turkey bones, cut off any meat upon them, and put it back in small pieces to the stew to get hot through.

TIME.—1½ to 1¾ *hour.*

SEASONABLE *in winter.*

Note. – This is a cheap and nice dish for a supper in winter, and if liked, grated cheese may be added and will be considered by most people an improvement.

Turkish Sweetmeat.—INGREDIENTS.—2 *lbs. of sugar,* 2 *eggs,* 1 *lemon,* ¼ *lb. of finest wheat starch,* 2¼ *pints of water, flavouring of rose.*

Make a syrup with a quart of water and the sugar, and clear it with the juice of the

lemon and the whites of the eggs. Dissolve the starch in ½ pint of cold water, strain, and add it to the syrup when boiling, and continue to boil until the mixture is stringy and thick then add the flavouring. Have ready two large dishes, one oiled, the other covered with sifted sugar, pour the mixture on the oiled one, and let it stand for a minute or two to cool, then turn on to the sugared one, soak up any oil that remains, cut into squares, and cover with sugar, so that, in putting away, the squares do not stick together.

Turnip Soup.—INGREDIENTS *for soup for* 8 *or* 10 *persons.*—3 *oz. of butter,* 9 *good-sized turnips,* 4 *onions,* 2 *quarts of cheap stock, seasoning to taste.* AVERAGE COST, 1*s.* 6*d.*

Melt the butter in the stewpan, but do not let it boil; wash, drain and slice the turnips and onions very thin; put them in the butter with a teacupful of stock, and stew very gently for an hour. Then add the remainder of the stock, and simmer for another hour. Rub it through a tammy, put it back into the stewpan, but do not let it boil. Serve very hot.

TIME.—2½ *hours.*

SEASONABLE *from October to March.*

Note.—By adding a little cream, this soup will be much improved.

Turnips, Boiled.—INGREDIENTS.—*Turnips; to each* ½ *gallon of water allow* 1 *heaped tablespoonful of salt.* AVERAGE COST, 6*d. a large bunch.*

Pare the turnips, and, should they be very large, divide them into quarters; but, unless this is the case, let them be cooked whole. Put them into a saucepan of boiling water, salted in the above proportion, and let them boil gently until tender. Try them with a fork, and, when done, take them up in a colander: let them thoroughly drain, and serve. Boiled turnips are usually sent to table with boiled mutton, but are infinitely nicer when mashed than served whole; unless nice and young, they are scarcely worth the trouble of dressing plainly as above.

TIME.—*Old turnips, ¾ to 1¼ hour; young ones, about 18 to 20 minutes.*

SEASONABLE.—*May be had all the year; but in spring only useful for flavouring gravies, &c.*

Turnips, German Mode of Cooking.

INGREDIENTS *for dish for 4 or 5 persons.*—*8 large turnips, 3 oz. of butter, pepper and salt to taste, rather more than ½ pint of weak stock or broth, 1 tablespoonful of flour.* AVERAGE COST, 10d.

Make the butter hot in a stewpan, lay in the turnips, after having pared and cut them into dice, and season them with pepper and salt. Toss them over the fire for a few minutes, then add the broth, and simmer the whole gently till the turnips are tender. Brown the above proportion of flour with a little butter; add this to the turnips, let them simmer another 5 minutes, and serve. Boiled mutton is usually sent to table with this vegetable, and may be cooked with the turnips by placing it in the midst of them; the meat would then be very delicious, as, there being so little liquid with the turnips, it would almost be steamed, and, consequently, very tender.

TIME.—*20 minutes.*

SEASONABLE.—*May be had all the year.*

Turnips, Mashed.

INGREDIENTS *for dish for 6 persons.* — *10 or 12 large turnips, to each ½ gallon of water allow 1 heaped tablespoonful of salt, 2 oz. of butter, cayenne or white pepper to taste.* AVERAGE COST, 6d.

Pare the turnips, quarter them, and put them into boiling water, salted in the above proportion: boil them until tender; then drain them in a colander, and squeeze them as dry as possible by pressing them with the back of a large plate. When quite

free from water, rub the turnips with a wooden spoon through the colander, and put them into a very clean saucepan; add the butter, white pepper or cayenne, and, if necessary, a little salt. Keep stirring them over the fire until the butter is well mixed with them, and the turnips are thoroughly hot; dish, and serve. A little cream or milk, added after the turnips are pressed through the colander, is an improvement to both the colour and flavour of this vegetable.

TIME.—*From ½ to ¾ hour to boil the turnips; 10 minutes to warm them through.*

SEASONABLE.—*May be had all the year; but in early spring only good for flavouring gravies.*

Turnips in White Sauce.

INGREDIENTS *for dish for 4 or 5 persons.*—*7 or 8 turnips, 1 oz. of butter, ½ pint of white sauce.* AVERAGE COST, 8d.

Peel and cut the turnips in the shape of pears or marbles; boil them in salt and

TURNIPS.

water, to which has been added a little butter, until tender; then take them out, drain, arrange them on a dish, and pour over the white sauce made by either of the recipes, and to which has been added a small lump of sugar. In winter, when other vegetables are scarce, this will be found a very good and pretty-looking dish; when approved, a little mustard may be added to the sauce.

TIME.—*About ¾ hour to boil the turnips.*

SEASONABLE.—*in winter.*

"Vain effort 'tis to try and feed the brain,
Unless a healthy body's nurtured too."—OLD WRITER.

ANILLA Cream.—INGREDIENTS *for 1 quart.*—1 *pint of milk, the yolks of 6 eggs, 6 oz. of sugar, 1 oz. of isinglass or Swinborne's gelatine, flavouring to taste of essence of vanilla.* AVERAGE COST, *with gelatine.* 1s. 3d.

Put the milk and sugar into a saucepan, and let it get hot over a slow fire; beat up the yolks of the eggs, to which add gradually the sweetened milk; flavour the whole with essence of vanilla, put the mixture into a jug, and place this jug in a saucepan of boiling water. Stir the contents with a wooden spoon one way until the mixture thickens, but do not allow it to boil, or it will be full of lumps. Take it off the fire; stir in the isinglass or gelatine, which should be previously dissolved in about ¼ pint of water, and boiled for 2 or 3 minutes; pour the cream into an oiled mould, put it in a cool place to set, and turn it out carefully on a dish. Instead of using the

essence of vanilla, a pod may be boiled in the milk until the flavour is well extracted. A pod, or a pod and a half, will be found

VANILLA CREAM.

sufficient for the above proportion of ingredients.

TIME.—*About* 10 *minutes to stir the mixture.*

SEASONABLE *at any time.*

Vanilla Custard Sauce, to Serve with Puddings.—INGREDIENTS *for sauce for medium-sized pudding.*—½ *pint of milk, 2 eggs, 2 oz. of sugar, 10 drops of Bush's essence of vanilla.* AVERAGE COST, 4d.

Beat the eggs, sweeten the milk; stir these ingredients well together, and flavour them with the essence of vanilla, regulating the proportion of this latter ingredient by the strength of the essence, the size of the eggs, &c. Put the mixture into a small jug, place this jug in a saucepan of boiling water, and stir the sauce *one way* until it thickens; but do not allow it to boil, or it will instantly curdle. Serve in a boat or tureen separately, with plum, bread, or any kind of dry pudding. Essence of bitter almonds or lemon-rind may be substituted for the vanilla, when they are more in accordance with the flavouring of the pudding with which the sauce is intended to be served.

TIME.—*To be stirred in the jug from 8 to 10 minutes.*

SEASONABLE *at any time.*

Vanilla Ice Cream. — INGREDIENTS *for 1 quart.*—1 *pint of cream,* ½ *pint of milk,* 1 *pod of vanilla,* ¼ *lb. of sugar, juice of* 1 *lemon, yolks of* 2 *eggs.* AVERAGE COST, 2s.

Pound the pod in a mortar, with the sugar, press it through a sieve, then place in a stewpan, with the milk and eggs, and stir over a gentle fire till the mixture thickens like custard; add the cream and lemon-juice, then strain and freeze.

TIME.—*25 minutes to freeze.*

SEASONABLE *at any time.*

Veal, Baked. (Cold Meat Cookery.) —INGREDIENTS *for dish for 3 persons.*—½ *lb. of cold roast veal, a few slices of bacon,* 1 *pint of bread-crumbs,* ½ *pint of good veal gravy,* ½ *teaspoonful of minced lemon-peel,* 1 *blade of pounded mace, cayenne and salt to taste,* 4 *eggs.* AVERAGE COST, *exclusive of the cold veal and gravy,* 9d.

Mince finely the veal and bacon; add the bread-crumbs, gravy and seasoning, and stir these ingredients well together. Beat up the eggs thoroughly; add these, mix the whole well together, put in a dish, and bake from ¾ to 1 hour. When liked, a little good gravy may be served in a tureen as an accompaniment.

TIME.—*From ¾ to 1 hour.*

SEASONABLE *from March to October.*

Veal, Roast Breast of.—INGREDIENTS.—*Veal; a little flour.* AVERAGE COST, 8d. *per lb.*

Wash the veal, well wipe it, and dredge it with flour; put it down to a bright fire, not too near, as it should not be scorched. Baste it plentifully until done; dish it, pour over the meat some good melted butter, and send to table with a piece of boiled bacon and a cut lemon.

TIME.—*From* 1½ *to 2 hours.*

SEASONABLE *from March to October.*

Veal, Breast of, To Carve.—

The carving of a breast of veal is not dissimilar to that of a fore-quarter of lamb, when the shoulder has been taken off. The breast of veal consists of two parts—the rib-bones and the gristly brisket. These two parts should first be separated by sharply passing the knife in the direction of the lines A, B; when they are entirely divided, the rib-bones should be carved in

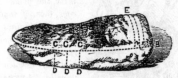

BREAST OF VEAL.

the direction of the lines E to F; and the brisket can be helped by cutting pieces in the direction C to D. The carver should ask the guests whether they have a preference for the brisket or ribs; and if there be a sweetbread served with the dish, as it often is with roast breast of veal, each person should receive a piece.

Veal, Stewed Breast of, and Peas.—INGREDIENTS *for dish for 6 persons. —Breast of veal,* 2 *oz. of butter, a bunch of savoury herbs, including parsley;* 2 *blades of pounded mace,* 2 *cloves,* 5 *or 6 young onions,* 1 *strip of lemon-peel,* 6 *allspice,* ¼ *teaspoonful of pepper,* 1 *teaspoonful of salt, thickening of butter and flour,* 2 *tablespoonfuls of sherry,* 2 *tablespoonfuls of tomato*

sauce, 1 *tablespoonful of lemon-juice*, 2 *tablespoonfuls of mushroom ketchup, green peas.* AVERAGE COST, 3s. 6d.

Cut the breast in half, after removing the bone underneath, and divide the meat into convenient-sized pieces. Put the butter into a frying-pan, lay in the pieces of veal, and fry until of a nice brown colour. Now place these in a stewpan with the herbs, mace, cloves, onions, lemon-peel, allspice and seasoning ; pour over them just sufficient boiling water to cover the meat ; well close the lid, and let the whole simmer very gently for about 2 hours. Strain off as much gravy as is required, thicken it with butter and flour, add the remaining ingredients, skim well, let it simmer for about 10 minutes, then pour it over the meat. Have ready some green peas, boiled separately ; sprinkle these over the veal, and serve. It may be garnished with forcemeat balls, or rashers of bacon curled and fried. Instead of cutting up the meat, many persons prefer it dressed whole ; in that case it should be half-roasted before the water, &c., are put to it.

TIME.—2¼ *hours.*

SEASONABLE *from March to October.*

Veal à la Bourgeoise. (Excellent.) INGREDIENTS *for dish for 6 persons.*— 2 *to* 3 *lbs. of the loin or neck of veal,* 10 *or* 12 *young carrots,* 1 *bunch of green onions,* 2 *slices of lean bacon,* 2 *blades of pounded mace,* 1 *bunch of savoury herbs, pepper and salt to taste, a few new potatoes,* 1 *pint of green peas.* AVERAGE COST, 3s. 6d.

Cut the veal into cutlets, trim them, and put the trimmings into a stewpan with a little butter ; lay in the cutlets and fry them a nice brown colour on both sides. Add the bacon, carrots, onions, spice, herbs and seasoning ; pour in about a pint of boiling water, and stew gently for 2 hours on a very slow fire. When done, skim off the fat, take out the herbs, and flavour the gravy with a little tomato sauce and ketchup. Have ready the peas and

potatoes, boiled *separately ;* put them with the veal, and serve.

TIME.—2 *hours.*

SEASONABLE *from June to August with peas ; rather earlier when these are omitted.*

Veal Cake. (A Convenient Dish for a Picnic.)—INGREDIENTS *for moderate-sized dish.*—*A few slices of cold roast veal, a few slices of cold ham,* 2 *hard-boiled eggs,* 2 *tablespoonfuls of minced parsley, a little pepper, good gravy.* AVERAGE COST, *exclusive of the cold meat,* 4d.

Cut off all the brown outside from the veal, and cut the eggs into slices. Procure a pretty mould ; lay veal, ham, eggs and parsley in layers, with a little pepper between them, and when the mould is full, get some *strong stock,* and fill up the shape. Bake for ½ hour, and, when cold, turn out.

TIME.—½ *hour.*

SEASONABLE *at any time.*

Veal Collops or Olives.—INGREDIENTS *for entrée for 6 persons.* — *About* 1½ *lb. of the prime part of the leg of veal, a few slices of bacon, forcemeat, egg and breadcrumbs, any wine to taste, gravy.* AVERAGE COST, 3s.

Cut the veal into long thin collops, flatten them, and lay on each a piece of bacon cut thin, of the same size ; have ready some forcemeat, which spread over the bacon, sprinkle with cayenne ; then roll each piece tightly up. They should not be more than 2 to 3 inches long. Skewer each one firmly, egg-and-bread-crumb them, and fry a nice brown in butter, turning them often and shaking the pan about. When done, place them in a dish before the fire, put a small piece of butter in the pan, dredge in a little flour, add about ¼ pint of water, 2 tablespoonfuls of lemon-juice, a seasoning of salt, pepper and pounded mace ; let the whole boil up, then pour it over the collops.

TIME.—10 *to* 15 *minutes.*

SEASONABLE *from March to October.*

Veal, Curried. (Cold Meat Cookery.)

—INGREDIENTS.—*The remains of cold roast eal, 4 onions, 2 apples sliced, 1 tablespoon-ful of curry-powder, 1 dessertspoonful of flour, ½ pint of broth or water, 1 tablespoonful of lemon-juice.* AVERAGE COST, *exclusive of the cold meat,* 4d.

Slice the onions and apples, and fry them in a little butter; then take them out, cut the meat into neat cutlets, and fry these of a pale brown; add the curry-powder and flour, put in the onions, apples and a little broth or water, and stew gently till quite tender; add the lemon-juice, and serve with an edging of boiled rice. The curry may be ornamented with pickles, capsicums and gherkins, arranged prettily on the top.

TIME.—¾ *hour.*

SEASONABLE *from March to October.*

Veal Cutlets. — INGREDIENTS *for dish for 8 persons.—About* 3 lbs. *of the prime part of the leg of veal, egg and bread-crumbs, 3 tablespoonfuls of minced savoury herbs, salt and pepper to taste, a small piece of butter.* AVERAGE COST, 3s. 6d.

Have the veal cut into slices about ¾ of an inch in thickness, and, if not cut perfectly even, level the meat with a cutlet-bat or

VEAL CUTLETS.

rolling-pin. Shape and trim the cutlets, and brush them over with egg. Sprinkle with bread-crumbs, with which have been mixed minced herbs and a sea-soning of pepper and salt, and press the crumbs down. Fry them of a delicate brown in fresh lard or butter, and be care-ful not to burn them. They should be very thoroughly done, but not dry. If the cutlets be thick, keep the pan covered for a few minutes at a good distance from the fire, after they have acquired a good colour: by this means, the meat will be done through. Lay the cutlets in a dish, keep them hot

and make a gravy in the pan as follows;—Dredge in a little flour, add a piece of butter the size of a walnut, brown it, then pour as much boiling water as is required over it, season with pepper and salt, add a little lemon-juice, give one boil and pour it over the cutlets. They should be garnished with slices of broiled bacon, and a few forcemeat ballswill be found a very excellent addition to this dish.

TIME.—*For cutlets of moderate thickness, about* 12 *minutes; if very thick, allow more time.*

SEASONABLE *from March to October.*

Note.—Veal cutlets may be merely floured and fried of a nice brown: the gravy and gar-nishing should be the same as in the preceding recipe. They may also be cut from the loin or neck, as shown in the engraving.

Veal Cutlets, Broiled, à l'Itali-enne.—INGREDIENTS.—*Neck of veal, salt and pepper to taste, the yolk of 1 egg, bread-crumbs,* ½ *pint of Italian sauce.* AVERAGE COST, 10d. per lb.

Cut the veal into cutlets, flatten and trim them nicely; powder over them a little salt and pepper; brush them over with the yolk of an egg, dip them into bread-crumbs, then into clarified butter, and, afterwards, in the bread-crumbs again; boil or fry them over a clear fire, that they may acquire a good brown colour. Arrange them in the dish alter-nately with rashers of broiled ham, and pour the sauce (made by recipe for Italian sauce) in the middle.

TIME.—10 *to* 15 *minutes, according to the thickness of the cutlets.*

SEASONABLE *from March to October.*

Veal Cutlets à la Maintenon.

—INGREDIENTS.—2 *or* 3 lbs. *of veal cutlets, cut from the leg, egg and bread-crumbs,* 2 *tablespoonfuls of minced savoury herbs, salt and pepper to taste, a little grated nutmeg.* AVERAGE COST, 1s. 2d. per lb.

Cut the cutlets about ¾ inch in thickness,

flatten them and brush them over with the yolk of an egg; dip them into bread-crumbs and minced herbs, season with pepper and salt and grated nutmeg, and fold each cutlet in a piece of buttered paper. Broil them, and send them to table with melted butter or a good gravy.

TIME.—*From 15 to 18 minutes.*

SEASONABLE *from March to October.*

Veal, Fillet of, au Béchamel.

(Cold Meat Cookery.)—INGREDIENTS.—*A small fillet of veal, 1 pint of béchamel sauce, a few bread-crumbs, clarified butter.*

A fillet of veal that has been roasted the preceding day will answer very well for this dish. Cut the middle out rather deep, leaving a good margin round, from which to cut nice slices; and if there should be any cracks in the veal, fill them up with forcemeat. Mince finely the meat that was taken out, mixing with it a little of the forcemeat to flavour, and stir to it sufficient béchamel to make it of a proper consistency. Warm the veal in the oven for about an hour, taking care to baste it well, that it may not be dry; put the mince in the place where the meat was taken out, sprinkle a few bread-crumbs over it, and drop a little clarified butter on the bread-crumbs; put it into the oven for ¼ hour to brown, and pour béchamel round the sides of the dish.

TIME.—*Altogether, 1½ hour.*

SEASONABLE *from March to October.*

Veal, Roast Fillet of.—INGREDI-

ENTS. — *Veal, forcemeat, melted butter.* AVERAGE COST, 1s. *per lb.*

Have the fillet cut according to the size required; take out the bone, and after raising the skin from the meat, put under the flap a nice forcemeat. Prepare sufficient of this, as there should be some left to eat cold, and to season and flavour a mince if required. Skewer and bind the veal up in a round form; dredge well with flour, put it down at some distance from the fire at first, and baste continually. About ½ hour before serving, draw it nearer the fire, that it may acquire more colour, as the outside should be of a rich brown, but not burnt. Dish it, remove the skewers, which replace by a silver one;

FILLET OF VEAL.

pour over the joint some good melted butter, and serve with either boiled ham, bacon, or pickled pork. Never omit to send a cut lemon to table with roast veal.

TIME.—*A fillet of veal weighing 12 lbs., about 4 hours.*

SEASONABLE *from March to October.*

Veal, Fillet of.—The carving of

this joint is similar to that of a round of beef. Slices, not too thick, in the direction of the line A to B are cut; and the only point to be careful about is, that the veal be *evenly* carved. Between the flap and

FILLET OF VEAL.

the meat the stuffing is inserted, and a small portion of this should be served to every guest. The persons whom the host wishes most to honour should be asked if they like the delicious brown outside slice, as this, by many, is exceedingly relished.

Veal, Stewed Fillet of.—INGRE-

DIENTS.—*A small fillet of veal, forcemeat, thickening of butter and flour, a few mush-*

rooms, white pepper to taste, 2 tablespoonfuls of lemon-juice, 2 blades of pounded mace, ½ glass of sherry. AVERAGE COST, 1s. per lb.

If the whole of the leg is purchased, take off the knuckle to stew, and also the square end, which will serve for cutlets or pies. Remove the bone and fill the space with a forcemeat. Roll and skewer it up firmly; place a few skewers at the bottom of a stewpan to prevent the meat from sticking, and cover the veal with a little weak stock. Let it simmer very *gently* until tender, as the more slowly veal is stewed, the better. Strain and thicken the sauce, flavour it with lemon-juice, mace, sherry, and white pepper; give one boil, and pour it over the meat. The skewers should be removed, and replaced by a silver one, and the dish garnished with slices of cut lemon.

TIME.—*A fillet of veal weighing 6 lbs., 3 hours' very gentle stewing.*

SEASONABLE *from March to October.*

Veal, Fricandeau of. (An Entrée.)

—INGREDIENTS *for entrée for 6 or 8 persons.—A piece of the fat side of a leg of veal (about 3 lbs.), lardoons, 2 carrots, 2 large onions, a faggot of savoury herbs, 2 blades of pounded mace, 6 whole allspice, 2 bay-leaves, pepper to taste, a few slices of fat bacon, 1 pint of stock.* AVERAGE COST, 3s. 6d.

The veal for a fricandeau should be of the best quality, or it will not be good. It may be known by the meat being white and not thready. Take off the skin, flatten the veal on the table, then at one stroke of the knife, cut off as much as is required, for a fricandeau with an uneven surface never looks well. Trim it, and with a sharp knife make two or three slits in the middle, that it may taste more of the seasoning. Now lard it thickly with fat bacon, as lean gives a red colour to the fricandeau. Slice the vegetables, and put these, with the herbs and spices, in the *middle* of a stewpan, with a few slices of bacon on the top:

these should form a sort of mound in the centre for the veal to rest upon. Lay the fricandeau over the bacon, sprinkle over it a little salt, and pour in just sufficient stock to cover the bacon, &c., without touching the veal. Let it gradually come to a boil; then put it over a slow and equal fire, and let it *simmer very* gently for about 2½ hours, or longer should it be very large. Baste it

FRICANDEAU OF VEAL.

frequently with the liquor, and a short time before serving, put it into a brisk oven, to make the bacon firm, which otherwise would break when it was glazed. Dish the fricandeau, keep it hot, skim off the fat from the liquor, and reduce it quickly to a glaze, with which glaze the fricandeau, and serve with a purée of whatever vegetable happens to be in season—spinach, sorrel, asparagus, cucumbers, peas, &c.

TIME.—2½ *hours. If very large, allow more time.*

SEASONABLE *from March to October.*

Veal, Fricandeau of. (More Economical.)

—INGREDIENTS *for entrée for 6 persons.—The best end of a neck of veal (about 2½ lbs.), lardoons, 2 carrots, 2 onions, a faggot of savoury herbs, 2 blades of mace, 2 bay-leaves, a little whole white pepper, a few slices of fat bacon.* AVERAGE COST, 2s. 6d.

Cut away the lean part of the best end of a neck of veal with a sharp knife, scooping it from the bones. Put the bones in a little water, which will serve to moisten the fricandeau: they should stew about 1½ hour. Lard the veal, proceed in the same way as in the preceding recipe, and be careful that the gravy does not touch the fricandeau. Stew very gently for 3 hours,

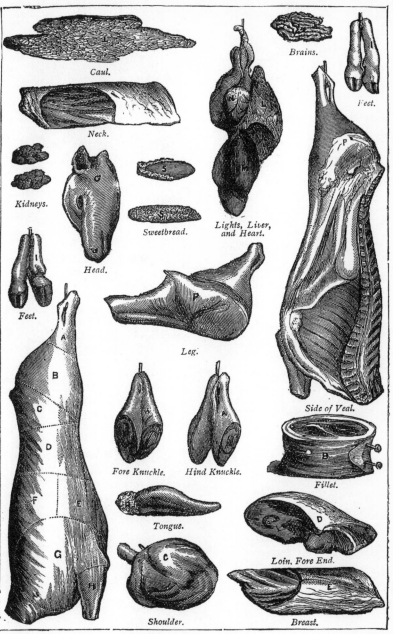

Caul.

Neck.

Brains.

Feet.

Kidneys.

Head.

Sweetbread.

Lights, Liver,
and Heart.

Feet.

Leg.

Side of Veal.

Fore Knuckle.

Hind Knuckle.

Fillet.

Tongue.

Loin, Fore End.

Shoulder.

Breast.

Various Parts of Veal.

Various Parts of Veal.

glaze, and serve it on sorrel, spinach, or with a little gravy in the dish.

TIME.—3 *hours.*

SEASONABLE *from March to October.*

Note.—When the prime part of the leg is cut off, it spoils the whole; consequently, to use this for a fricandeau is rather extravagant. The best end of the neck answers the purpose nearly or quite as well.

Veal Galantine.

INGREDIENTS *for good-sized galantine.—A small breast of veal, 2 lbs. of sausage-meat, highly flavoured with herbs, ½ lb. of cooked tongue, some truffles, mushrooms, pistachio nuts and gherkins.* AVERAGE COST, *from 4s. 6d. to 5s.*

Bone the meat and flatten it well out, and spread over a thick layer of sausage-meat; next a layer of small dice cut from tongue, truffles, mushrooms and gherkins,

VEAL GALANTINE.

over which scatter a few chopped pistachio nuts, and over this spread another layer of sausage-meat. Roll in a cloth, as a jam pudding, and boil for 6 hours. When half cold, tie up tight and press with heavy weights upon the top, and, when wanted, glaze, and serve garnished with some bright aspic jelly (which may be made from the stock in which the veal was boiled) and parsley. Cut off the outside slice before serving, that the pretty marbled appearance of the inside of the galantine may be shown.

TIME.—6 *hours to boil.*

SEASONABLE *form March to October.*

Veal, To Carve a Knuckle of.

—The engraving, showing the dotted line from A to B, sufficiently indicates the direction which should be given to the knife in carving this dish. The best slices

KNUCKLE OF VEAL.

are those from the thickest part of the knuckle, that is, outside the line A to B.

Veal, To Ragoût a Knuckle of.

—INGREDIENTS *for dish for 4 or 5 persons. —Knuckle of veal, pepper and salt to taste, flour, 1 onion, 1 head of celery, or a little celery-seed, 1 faggot of savoury herbs, 2 blades of pounded mace, thickening of butter and flour, a few young carrots, 1 table-spoonful of tomato sauce, 3 tablespoonfuls of sherry, the juice of ½ lemon.* AVERAGE COST, 2s. 6d.

Cut the meat from a knuckle of veal into neat slices, season with pepper and salt, and dredge them with flour. Fry them in a little butter of a pale brown, and put them into a stewpan with the bone (which should be chopped in several places); add the celery, herbs, mace and carrots; pour over all about 1 pint of hot water, and let it simmer very gently for 2 hours over a slow but clear fire. Take out the slices of meat and carrots, strain and thicken the gravy with a little butter rolled in flour; add the remaining ingredients, give one boil, put back the meat and carrots, let these get hot through, and serve. When in season, a few green peas, *boiled separately* and added to this dish at the moment of serving, would be found a very agreeable addition.

TIME.—2 *hours.*

Veal, Stewed Knuckle of, and

Rice.—INGREDIENTS.—*Knuckle of veal, 1 onion, 2 blades of mace, 1 teaspoonful of salt, ½ lb. of rice.* AVERAGE COST, 6d. *per lb.*

Have the knuckle cut small, or cut some cutlets from it, that it may be just large enough to be eaten the same day it is dressed, as cold boiled veal is not a particularly tempting dish. Break the shankbone, wash it clean, and put the meat into a stewpan with sufficient water to cover it. Let it gradually come to a boil, put in the salt, and remove the scum as fast as it rises.

KNUCKLE OF VEAL.

When it has simmered gently for about ¾ hour, add the remaining ingredients, and stew the whole gently for 2¼ hours. Put the meat into a deep dish, pour over it the rice, &c., and send boiled bacon and a tureen of parsley-and-butter to table with it.

TIME.—*A knuckle of veal weighing 6 lbs., 3 hours' gentle stewing.*

SEASONABLE *from March to October.*

Note.—Macaroni, instead of rice, boiled with the veal, will be found good; or the rice and macaroni may be omitted, and the veal sent to table smothered in parsley-and-butter.

Veal, Roast Loin of.—INGREDIENTS.—*Veal; melted butter.* AVERAGE COST, 10d. per lb.

Paper the kidney fat; roll in and skewer the flap, which makes the joint a good

LOIN OF VEAL.

shape; dredge it well with flour, and put it down to a bright fire. Should the loin be very large, skewer the kidney back for a time to roast thoroughly. Keep it well

basted, and, a short time before serving, remove the paper from the kidney, and allow it to acquire a nice brown colour, but it should not be burnt. Have ready some melted butter, put it into the dripping-pan after it is emptied of its contents, pour it over the veal, and serve. Garnish the dish with slices of lemon and forcemeat balls, and send to table with it boiled bacon, ham, pickled pork, or pig's cheek.

TIME.—*A large loin, 3 hours.*

SEASONABLE *from March to October.*

Note.—A piece of toast should be placed under the kidney when the veal is dished.

Veal, Loin of, au Béchamel.
(Cold Meat Cookery.)—INGREDIENTS.—*Loin of veal, ½ teaspoonful of minced lemonpeel, rather more than ½ pint of béchamel or white sauce.* AVERAGE COST, 10d. *per lb.*

A loin of veal which has come from table with very little taken off, answers well for this dish. Cut off the meat from the inside, mince it, and mix with it some minced lemon-peel; put it into sufficient béchamel to warm it through. In the mean time, wrap the joint in buttered paper, and place it in the oven to warm. When thoroughly hot, dish the mince, place the loin above it, and pour over the remainder of the béchamel.

TIME.—1½ *hour to warm the meat in the oven.*

SEASONABLE *from March to October.*

Veal, Loin of, à la Daube.—
INGREDIENTS.—*The chump end of a loin of veal, forcemeat, a few slices of bacon, a bunch of savoury herbs, 2 blades of mace, ½ teaspoonful of whole white pepper, 1 pint of veal stock or water, 5 or 6 green onions.* AVERAGE COST, 10d. *per lb.*

Cut off the chump from a loin of veal, and take out the bone; fill the cavity with forcemeat, tie it up tightly, and lay it in a stewpan with the bones and trimmings, and cover the veal with a few slices of bacon. Add the herbs, mace, pepper and onions, and stock or water ; cover the pan with a closely-fitting lid, and simmer for 2 hours, shaking the stewpan occasionally. Take out the bacon, herbs and onions ; reduce the gravy, if not already thick enough, to a glaze, with which glaze the meat, and serve with tomato, mushroom, or sorrel sauce.

TIME.—2 *hours.*

SEASONABLE *from March to October.*

Veal, To Carve Loin of.

—As is the case with a loin of mutton, the careful jointing of a loin of veal is more than half the battle in carving it. If the butcher be negligent in this matter, he should be admonished ; for there is nothing more annoying or irritating to an inexperienced carver than to be obliged to turn his knife

LOIN OF VEAL.

in all directions to find the exact place where it should be inserted in order to divide the bones. When the jointing is properly performed, there is little difficulty in carrying the knife down in the direction of the line A to B. To each guest should be given a piece of the kidney and kidney fat, which lie underneath, and are considerered great delicacies.

Veal, Minced, with Béchamel Sauce.

(Cold Meat Cookery ; very good.) —INGREDIENTS *for dish for 5 or 6 persons.* —*The remains of a fillet of veal,* 1 *pint of béchamel sauce,* ½ *teaspoonful of minced lemon-peel, forcemeat balls.* AVERAGE COST, *exclusive of the cold veal,* 1s.

Cut—but do not *chop*—a few slices of cold roast veal as finely as possible, sufficient to make rather more than 1 lb., weighed after being minced. Make the above proportion of béchamel, by recipe ; add the lemon-peel, put in the veal, and let the whole gradually warm through. When it is at the point of simmering, dish it, and garnish with forcemeat balls and fried sippets of bread.

TIME.—1 *minute to simmer.*

SEASONABLE *from March to October.*

Veal, Minced.

(More Economical.) —INGREDIENTS *for dish for 5 or 6 persons.* —*The remains of cold roast fillet or loin of veal, rather more than* 1 *pint of water,* 1 *onion,* ½ *teaspoonful of minced lemon-peel, salt and white pepper to taste,* 1 *blade of pounded mace,* 2 *or* 3 *young carrots,* 1 *faggot of sweet herbs, thickening of butter and flour,* 1 *tablespoonful of lemon-juice,* 3 *tablespoonfuls of cream or milk.* AVERAGE COST, *exclusive of the cold veal,* 5d.

Take about 1 lb. of veal, and should there be any bones, dredge them with flour, and put them into a stewpan with the brown outside, and a few meat trimmings ; add rather more than a pint of water, the onion cut in slices, lemon-peel, seasoning, mace, carrots and herbs ; simmer these well for rather more than 1 hour, and strain the liquor. Rub a little flour into some butter ; add this to the gravy, set it on the fire, and, when it boils, skim well. Mince the veal finely by *cutting,* and not chopping it ; put it in the gravy ; let it get warmed through gradually ; add the lemon-juice and cream, and, when it is on the point of boiling, serve. Garnish the dish with sippets of toasted bread and slices of bacon rolled and toasted. Forcemeat balls may also be added. If more lemon-peel is liked than is stated above, put a little very finely-minced to the veal, after it is warmed in the gravy.

TIME.—1 *hour to make the gravy.*

SEASONABLE *from March to October.*

Veal, Minced, and Macaroni.

—INGREDIENTS *for dish for 3 persons.*—¾ *lb. of minced cold roast veal,* 3 *oz. of ham,* 1 *tablespoonful of gravy, pepper and salt to taste,* ¼ *teaspoonful of grated nutmeg,* ¼ *lb. of bread-crumbs,* ¼ *lb. of macaroni,* 1 *or* 2 *eggs to bind, a small piece of butter.* AVERAGE COST, *exclusive of the cold meat,* 8*d.*

Cut some nice slices from a cold fillet of veal, trim off the brown outside, and mince the meat finely with the above proportion of ham : should the meat be very dry, add a spoonful of good gravy. Season highly with pepper and salt, add the grated nutmeg and bread-crumbs, and mix these ingredients with 1 or 2 eggs, well beaten, which should bind the mixture and make it like a forcemeat. In the meantime, boil the macaroni in salt and water, and drain it ; butter a mould, put some of the macaroni at the bottom and sides of it, in whatever form is liked ; mix the remainder with the forcemeat, fill the mould up to the top, put a plate or small dish on it and steam for ½ hour. Turn it out carefully, and serve, with good gravy poured round, but not over, the meat.

TIME.—½ *hour.*

SEASONABLE *from March to October.*

Note.—To make a variety, boil some carrots and turnips separately in a little salt and water; when done, cut them into pieces about ⅛ inch in thickness; butter an oval mould, and place these in it, in white and red stripes alternately at the bottom and sides. Proceed as in the foregoing recipe, and be very careful in turning it out of the mould.

Veal, Moulded Minced. (Cold

Meat Cookery.) — INGREDIENTS *for dish for 3 persons.*—¾ *lb. of cold roast veal, a small slice of bacon,* ¾ *teaspoonful of minced lemon-peel,* ½ *onion chopped fine, salt, pepper and pounded mace to taste,* 1 *slice of toast soaked in milk,* 1 *egg.* AVERAGE COST, *exclusive of the cold veal,* 4*d.*

Mince the meat very fine, after removing from it all skin and outside pieces, and chop the bacon ; mix these well together, adding the lemon-peel, onion, seasoning, mace and toast. When all the ingredients are thoroughly incorporated, beat up an egg, with which bind the mixture. Butter a shape, put in the meat and bake for ¾ hour.; turn it out of the mould carefully, and pour round it a good brown gravy. A sheep's head dressed in this manner is an economical and savoury dish.

TIME.—¾ *hour.*

SEASONABLE *from March to October.*

Veal, Braised Neck of.— INGRE-

DIENTS *for dish for* 8 *persons.*—*The best end of the neck of veal (from* 3 *to* 4 *lbs.), bacon,* 1 *tablespoonful of minced parsley, salt, pepper and grated nutmeg to taste ;* 1 *onion,* 2 *carrots, a little celery (when this is not obtainable, use the seed),* ½ *glass of sherry, thickening of butter and flour, lemon-juice,* 1 *blade of pounded mace.* AVERAGE COST, 3*s.* 6*d.*

Prepare the bacon for larding, and roll it in minced parsley, salt, pepper and grated nutmeg ; lard the veal, put it into a stewpan with a few slices of lean bacon or ham, an onion, carrots and celery ; and do not quite cover it with water. Stew it gently for 2 hours, or until it is quite tender ; strain off the liquor ; stir together over the fire, in a stewpan, a little flour and butter until brown ; lay the veal in this, the upper side to the bottom of the pan, and let it remain till it is a nice brown colour. Place it in the dish ; pour into the stewpan as much gravy as is required, boil it up, skim well, add the wine, pounded mace and lemon-juice ; simmer for 3 minutes, pour it over the meat, and serve.

TIME.—*Rather more than* 2 *hours.*

SEASONABLE *from March to October.*

Veal, Roast Neck of.—INGRE-

DIENTS.—*Veal, melted butter, forcemeat balls.* AVERAGE COST, 10*d. per lb.*

Have the veal cut from the best end of

the neck; dredge it with flour, and put it down to a bright clear fire; keep it well basted; dish it, pour over it some melted butter and garnish the dish with fried forcemeat balls; send to table with a cut lemon. The scrag may be boiled or stewed in various ways, with rice, onion-sauce, or parsley and butter.

TIME.—*About 2 hours.*

SEASONABLE *from March to October.*

Veal Olive Pie (Cold Meat Cookery).—INGREDIENTS *for small pie.—A few thin slices of cold fillet of veal, a few thin slices of bacon, forcemeat, a cupful of gravy, 4 tablespoonfuls of cream, puff-crust.* AVERAGE COST, *exclusive of the cold veal,* 1s.

Cut thin slices from a fillet of veal, place on them thin slices of bacon, and over them a layer of forcemeat, made by recipe, with an additional seasoning of shalot and cayenne; roll them tightly, and fill up a pie-dish with them; add the gravy and cream, cover with a puff-crust and bake for 1 to 1½ hour; should the pie be very large, allow 2 hours. The pieces of rolled veal should be about 3 inches in length and about 3 inches round.

TIME.—*Moderate-sized pie, 1 to 1½ hour.*

SEASONABLE *from March to October.*

Veal Pie.—INGREDIENTS *for good-sized pie.—2 lbs. of veal cutlets, 2 slices of lean bacon or ham, pepper and salt to taste, 2 tablespoonfuls of minced savoury herbs, 2 blades of pounded mace, crust, 1 teacupful of gravy.* AVERAGE COST, 3s.

Cut the cutlets into square pieces, and season them with pepper, salt and pounded mace; put them in a pie-dish with the savoury herbs sprinkled over, and 1 or 2 slices of lean bacon or ham placed at the top: if possible, this should be previously cooked, as undressed bacon makes the veal red and spoils its appearance. Pour in a little water, cover with crust, ornament it in any way that is approved; brush it over

with the yolk of an egg, and bake in a well-heated oven for about 1½ hour. Pour in a

VEAL PIE.

good gravy after baking, which is done by removing the top ornament, and replacing it after the gravy is added.

TIME.—*About 1½ hour.*

SEASONABLE *from March to October.*

Veal-and-Ham Pie.—INGREDIENTS *for good-sized pie.—2 lbs. of veal cutlets, ½ lb. of boiled ham, 2 tablespoonfuls of minced savoury herbs, ¼ teaspoonful of grated nutmeg, 2 blades of pounded mace, pepper and salt to taste, a strip of lemon-peel finely minced, 3 hard-boiled eggs, ½ pint of water, nearly ½ pint of good strong gravy, puff-crust.* AVERAGE COST, 4s.

Cut the veal into nice square pieces, and put a layer of them at the bottom of a pie-dish; sprinkle over these a portion of the herbs, spices, seasoning, lemon-peel and the yolks of the eggs cut in slices; cut the ham very thin, and put a layer of this in. Proceed in this manner until the dish is full, so arranging it that the ham comes at the top. Lay a puff-paste on the edge of the dish, and pour in about ½ pint of water; cover with crust, ornament it with leaves, brush it over with the yolk of an egg and bake in a well-heated oven for 1 to 1½ hour, or longer should the pie be very large. When it is taken out of the oven, pour in at the top, through a funnel, nearly ½ pint of strong gravy: this should be made sufficiently good that, when cold, it may cut in a firm jelly. This pie may be very much enriched by adding a few mushrooms, oysters or sweetbreads; but it will be found very good without any of the last-named additions.

TIME.—1½ hour, or longer should the pie be very large.

SEASONABLE from March to October.

Veal Potted (for Breakfast).—INGREDIENTS.—To every lb. of veal allow ¼ lb. of ham, cayenne and pounded mace to taste, 6 oz. of fresh butter; clarified butter, salt.

Mince the veal and ham together as finely as possible, and pound well in a mortar, with cayenne, salt, pounded mace and fresh butter in the above proportion. When reduced to a perfectly smooth paste, press it into potting-pots, and cover with clarified butter. If kept in a cool place, it will remain good some days.

SEASONABLE from March to October.

Veal, Ragoût of Cold. (Cold Meat Cookery).—INGREDIENTS.—The remains of cold veal, 1 oz. of butter, ½ pint of gravy, thickening of butter and flour, pepper and salt to taste, 1 blade of pounded mace, 1 tablespoonful of mushroom ketchup, 1 tablespoonful of sherry, 1 dessertspoonful of lemon-juice, forcemeat balls. AVERAGE COST, exclusive of the cold meat, 9d.

Any part of veal will make this dish. Cut the meat into nice-looking pieces, put them in a stewpan with 1 oz. of butter, and fry a light brown; add the gravy (hot water may be substituted for this), thicken with a little butter and flour and stew gently about ¼ hour; season with pepper, salt and pounded mace; add the ketchup, sherry and lemon-juice; give one boil, and serve.

Garnish the dish with forcemeat balls and fried rashers of bacon.

TIME.—Altogether ½ hour.

SEASONABLE from March to October.

Note.—The above recipe may be varied by adding vegetables, such as peas, cucumbers, lettuces, green onions cut in slices, a dozen or two of green gooseberries (not seedy), all of which should be fried a little with the meat, and then stewed in the gravy.

Veal Rissoles. (Cold Meat Cookery.)—INGREDIENTS.—A few slices of cold roast veal, a few slices of ham or bacon, 1 tablespoonful of minced parsley, 1 tablespoonful of minced savoury herbs, 1 blade of pounded mace, a very little grated nutmeg, cayenne and salt to taste, 2 eggs, well-beaten, bread-crumbs.

Mince the veal very finely, with a little ham or bacon; add the parsley, herbs, spices and seasoning; mix into a paste with an egg; form into balls or cones; brush these over with egg, sprinkle with bread-crumbs and fry a rich brown. Serve with brown gravy, and garnish the dish with fried parsley.

TIME.—About 10 minutes to fry the rissoles.

SEASONABLE from March to October.

Veal Rolls. (Cold Meat Cookery.)—INGREDIENTS.—The remains of a cold fillet of veal, egg and bread-crumbs, a few slices of fat bacon, forcemeat.

Cut a few slices from a cold fillet of veal ½ inch thick; rub them over with egg; lay a thin slice of fat bacon over each piece of veal; brush these with the egg, and over this spread the forcemeat thinly; roll up each piece tightly, egg-and-bread-crumb them, and fry them a rich brown. Serve with mushroom sauce or brown gravy.

TIME.—10 to 15 minutes to fry the rolls.

SEASONABLE from March to October.

Veal, Stuffed and Stewed Shoulder of.—INGREDIENTS for dish for 10-to 12 persons.—A shoulder of veal, a few slices of ham or bacon, forcemeat, 3 carrots, 2 onions, salt and pepper to taste, a faggot of savoury herbs, 3 blades of pounded mace, water; a thickening of butter and flour AVERAGE COST, 8d. per lb.

Bone the joint by carefully detaching the meat from the blade bone on one side, and then on the other, being particular not to pierce the skin; then cut the bone from the knuckle and take it out. Fill the cavity whence the bone was taken with a forcemeat. Roll and bind the veal up tightly; put it into a stewpan with the carrots, onions, seasoning, herbs and mace; pour in just sufficient water to cover it, and let it stew *very gently* for about 5 hours. Before taking it up, try if it is properly done by thrusting a larding-needle in it; if it penetrates easily, it is sufficiently cooked. Strain and skim the gravy, thicken with butter and flour, give one boil, and pour it round the meat. A few young carrots may be boiled and placed round the dish as a garnish, and, when in season, green peas should always be served with this dish.

TIME.—5 *hours.*

SEASONABLE *from March to October.*

Veal, Stewed, with Peas, Young Carrots and New Potatoes.—INGREDI-ENTS *for dish for 6 or 7 persons.*—3 *or* 4 *lbs. of the loin or neck of veal,* 15 *young carrots, a few green onions,* 1 *pint of green peas,* 12 *new potatoes,* 1 *bunch of savoury herbs, pepper and salt to taste,* 1 *tablespoonful of lemon-juice,* 2 *tablespoonfuls of tomato sauce,* 2 *tablespoonfuls of mushroom ketchup.* AVERAGE COST, 3s. 6d.

Dredge the meat with flour, and roast or bake it for about ¾ hour; it should acquire a nice brown colour. Put the meat into a stewpan with the carrots, onions, potatoes, herbs, pepper and salt; pour over it sufficient boiling water to cover it, and stew gently for 2 hours. Take out the meat and herbs, put it in a deep dish, skim off all the fat from the gravy, and flavour it with lemon-juice, tomato sauce and mushroom ketchup, in the above proportion. Have ready a pint of green peas boiled *separately;* put these with the meat, pour over it the gravy, and serve. The dish may be garnished with a few forcemeat balls. The meat, when preferred, may be cut into chops, and floured and fried, instead of being roasted; and any part of veal

dressed in this way will be found extremely savoury and good.

TIME.—3 *hours.*

SEASONABLE, *with peas, from June to August.*

Vegetable Goose.—INGREDIENTS *for small dish.*—½ *lb. of bread-crumbs,* 1 *onion,* 1 *teaspoonful of parsley and herbs, chopped,* 1 *oz. of butter, pepper and salt.* AVERAGE COST, 3d.

Soak the bread-crumbs in cold water, and squeeze them nearly dry, then mash them. Mix in the other ingredients, the onion chopped small; butter a Yorkshire pudding dish, put the mixture in and bake in a good oven for about an hour. Serve hot.

TIME.—1 *hour.*

SEASONABLE *at any time.*

Note.—This is a vegetarian recipe, but the pudding is nice served with hot meat.

Vegetable Marrow, Boiled.—INGREDIENTS.—To each ½ *gallon of water, allow* 1 *heaped tablespoonful of salt; vegetable marrows.* AVERAGE COST, 2d. *to* 4d. *each.*

Have ready a saucepan of boiling water,

VEGETABLE MARROW.

salted in the above proportion; put in the marrows after peeling them, and boil them until quite tender. Take them up with a slice, halve, and, should they be very large, quarter them. Dish them on toast, and send to table with them a tureen of melted butter, or, in lieu of this, put small pieces of salt butter over them. Large vegetable marrows may be preserved throughout the winter by storing them in a dry place, or hanging them from a kitchen-ceiling by their stalks; when wanted for use, a few slices should be cut and boiled in the same manner as above; but,

VEGETABLE MARROW ON TOAST.

when once begun, the marrow must be eaten quickly, as it keeps but a short time after it is cut. Vegetable marrows are also very delicious mashed: they should be boiled, drained, and mashed smoothly with a wooden spoon. Heat them in a saucepan, add a seasoning of salt and pepper and a small piece of butter, and dish with a few sippets of toasted bread placed round as a garnish.

TIME.—*Young vegetable marrows*, 10 to 20 *minutes; old ones*, ½ to ¾ *hour*.

SEASONABLE *in July, August and September; but may be preserved all the winter.*

Vegetable Marrow, Fried. —

INGREDIENTS *for dish for 6 persons.— 3 medium-sized vegetable marrows, egg and bread-crumbs, hot lard.* AVERAGE COST, 2*d.* to 4*d. each.*

Peel, and boil the marrows until tender in salt and water; then drain them and cut them in quarters, and take out the seeds. When thoroughly drained, brush the marrows over with egg, and sprinkle with bread-crumbs; have ready some hot lard, fry the marrow in this, and, when of a nice brown, dish; sprinkle over a little salt and pepper, and serve.

TIME.—*About ½ hour to boil the marrow,* 7 *minutes to fry it.*

SEASONABLE *in July, August and September.*

Vegetable Marrows in White Sauce.—INGREDIENTS *for dish for 6 persons.—3 moderate-sized marrows, ½ pint of white sauce.* AVERAGE COST, 2*d.* to 4*d. each.*

Pare the marrows, cut them in halves, and shape each half at the top in a point, leaving the bottom end flat for it to stand upright in the dish. Boil the marrows in salt and water

VEGETABLE MARROW IN WHITE SAUCE.

until tender; take them up very carefully, and arrange them on a hot dish. Have ready ½ pint of white sauce; pour this over the marrows, and serve.

TIME.—*From 15 to 20 minutes to boil the marrows.*

SEASONABLE *in July, August and September.*

Vegetable Marrow Soup. —

INGREDIENTS *for soup for 10 persons.—4 young vegetable marrows, or more, if very small, ½ pint of cream, salt and white pepper to taste, 2 quarts of white stock.* AVERAGE COST, 3*s.*

Pare and slice the marrows, and put them in the stock boiling. When done almost to a mash, press them through a sieve, and, at the moment of serving, add the boiling cream and seasoning.

TIME.—1 *hour.*

SEASONABLE *in summer.*

Vegetable Pie. — INGREDIENTS *for small pie.—1 onion, 1 carrot, 1 turnip, 1 stick of celery, a handful of green peas, if in season, ½ oz. of sago, 1 oz. of butter, pepper and salt, paste to cover the pie.* AVERAGE COST, 10*d.*

Cut all the vegetables small, and stew them with the sago, butter and seasoning, with a very little water till nearly cooked. Then put them in a pie-dish, and cover with paste made from butter, if for a vegetarian dish, and bake till the crust is done; any other

Asparagus.

Sea Kale.

Salad.

Artichokes.

Spinach & Eggs.

Salad in Jelly.

Stuffed Tomatoes.

Baked Potatoes.

Russian Salad.

Brussels Sprouts.

Cauliflowers.

Spanish Onions.

Vegetable Fritters.

Potato — Croquettes.

VEGETABLES.

vegetables may be used, and a few mushrooms are always an improvement.

TIME.—*About ½ hour to bake the pie.*

SEASONABLE *at any time.*

Vegetable Soup. — INGREDIENTS

for soup for 8 or 10 persons.—7 oz. of carrot, 10 oz. of parsnip, 10 oz. of potato, cut into thin slices; 1¼ oz. of butter, 5 teaspoonfuls of flour, 1 teaspoonful of made mustard, salt and pepper to taste, the yolks of 2 eggs, rather more than 2 quarts of water. AVERAGE COST, 8d.

Boil the vegetables in the water 2¼ hours; stir them often, and if the water boils away too quickly, add more, as there should be 2 quarts of soup when done. Mix up in a basin the butter and flour, mustard, salt and pepper, with a teacupful of cold water; stir in the soup, and boil 10 minutes. Have ready the yolks of the eggs in the tureen; pour on, stir well, and serve.

TIME.—3 *hours.*

SEASONABLE *in winter.*

Vegetable Soup. — INGREDIENTS

for soup for 8 or 10 persons.—Equal quantities of onions, carrots, turnips; ¼ lb. of butter, a crust of toasted bread, 1 head of celery, 1 faggot of herbs, salt and pepper to taste, 1 teaspoonful of powdered sugar, 2 quarts of common stock or boiling water. Allow ¾ lb. of vegetables to 2 quarts of stock. AVERAGE COST, 6d. per quart.

Cut up the onions, carrots and turnips; wash and drain them well, and put them in the stewpan with the butter and powdered sugar. Toss the whole over a sharp fire for 10 minutes, but do not let them brown, or you will spoil the flavour of the soup. When done, pour the stock or boiling water on them; add the bread, celery, herbs and seasoning; stew for 3 hours; skim well and strain it off. When ready to serve, add a little sliced carrot, celery and turnip, and flavour with a spoonful of Harvey's sauce, or a little ketchup.

TIME.—3½ *hours.*

SEASONABLE *all the year.*

Vegetable Soup. (Good and Cheap, made without Meat.)— INGREDIENTS *for large quantity of soup.*—6 potatoes, 4 turnips, or 2 if very large; 2 carrots, 2 onions; if obtainable, 2 mushrooms; 1 head of celery, 1 large slice of bread, 1 small saltspoonful of salt, ¼ saltspoonful of ground black pepper, 2 teaspoonfuls of Harvey's sauce, 6 quarts of water. AVERAGE COST, about 1d. per quart.

Peel the vegetables, and cut them up into small pieces; toast the bread rather brown, and put all into a stewpan with the water and seasoning. Simmer gently for 3 hours, or until all is reduced to a pulp, and pass it through a sieve in the same way as pea-soup, which it should resemble in consistence; but it should be a dark brown colour. Warm it up again when required; put in the Harvey's sauce, and, if necessary, add to the flavouring.

TIME.—3 *hours, or rather more.*

SEASONABLE *at any time.*

Vegetables, Cut, for Soups, &c.

The annexed engraving represents a cutter for shaping vegetables for soups, ragoûts, stews, &c.; carrots and turnips being the usual vegetables for which this utensil is used. Cut the vegetables into slices about ¼ inch in thickness, stamp them out with the cutter, and boil them for a few minutes in salt and water, until tender. Turnips should be cut in rather thicker slices than carrots, on account of the former boiling more quickly to a pulp than the latter.

VEGETABLE-CUTTER

Note.—Cut vegetables for soup can be bought dried and in a small compass. They are prepared by Chollet and Co.

Venison, Hashed.—INGREDIENTS.
—*The remains of roast venison, its own or mutton gravy, thickening of butter and flour.*

Cut the meat from the bones in neat slices, and, if there be sufficient of its own gravy left, put the meat into this, as it is preferable to any other. Should there not be enough, put the bones and trimmings into a stewpan, with about a pint of mutton gravy; let them stew gently for an hour, and strain the gravy. Put a little flour and butter into the stewpan, keep stirring until brown, then add the strained gravy, and give it a boil up; skim and strain again, and, when a little cool, put in the slices of venison. Place the stewpan by the side of the fire, and, when on the point of simmering, serve; do not allow it to boil, or the meat will be hard. Send red-currant jelly to table with it.

TIME.—*Altogether 1½ hour.*

SEASONABLE.—*Buck venison, from June to Michaelmas; doe venison, from November to the end of January.*

Note.—A small quantity of Harvey's sauce, ketchup, or port wine, may be added to enrich the gravy: these ingredients must, however, be used very sparingly, or they will overpower the flavour of the venison.

Venison, Roast Haunch of.—
INGREDIENTS.—*Venison, coarse flour-and-water paste, a little flour.* AVERAGE COST, 1s. 2d. to 1s. 6d. per lb.

Choose a haunch with clear, bright and thick fat, and the cleft of the hoof smooth and close; the greater quantity of fat there is, the better quality will the meat be. As many people object to venison when it is too high, ascertain how long it has been kept, by running a sharp skewer into the meat close to the bone: when this is withdrawn, its sweetness can be judged of. With care and attention, it will keep good a fortnight, unless the weather is very mild. Keep it perfectly dry by wiping it with clean cloths till not the least damp remains,

and sprinkle over powdered ginger or pepper, as a preventive against the fly. When required for use, wash it in warm water, and *dry* it *well* with a cloth; butter a sheet of white paper, put it over the fat, lay a coarse paste, about ½ inch in thickness, over this, and then a sheet or two of strong paper. Tie the whole firmly on to the haunch with twine, and put the joint down to a strong close fire; baste the venison immediately, to prevent the paper and string from burning, and continue this operation, without intermission, the whole of the time it is cooking. About 20 minutes before it is done, carefully remove the paste and paper, dredge the joint with flour, and baste well with *butter* until it is nicely frothed, and of a nice pale-brown

ROAST HAUNCH OF VENISON.

colour; garnish the knuckle-bone with a frill of white paper, and serve with a good, strong, but unflavoured gravy, in a tureen, and currant jelly; or melt the jelly with a little port wine, and serve that also in a tureen. As the principal object in roasting venison is to preserve the fat, the above is the best mode of doing so where expense is not objected to; but, in ordinary cases, the paste may be dispensed with, and a double paper placed over the roast instead: it will not require so long cooking without the paste. Do not omit to send very hot plates to table, as the venison fat so soon becomes cold: to be thoroughly enjoyed by epicures, it should be eaten on hot-water plates. The neck and shoulder may be roasted in the same manner.

TIME.—*A large haunch of buck venison with the paste, 4 to 5 hours; haunch of doe venison, 3¼ to 3¾ hours. Allow less time without the paste.*

Venison, To Carve Haunch of.

—Here is a grand dish for a knight of the carving-knife to exercise his skill upon, and, what will be pleasant for many to know, there is but little difficulty in the performance. An incision being made completely down to the bone, in the direction of the line 1 and 2, the gravy will then be able easily to flow; when slices, not too thick, should be cut along the haunch, as indicated by the line 4 to 3; that end of the joint marked 3 having been turned towards the carver, so that he may have a more complete command over the joint.

HAUNCH OF VENISON.

Although some epicures affect to believe that some parts of the haunch are superior to others, yet we doubt if there is any difference between the slices cut above and below the line. It should be borne in mind to serve each guest with a portion of fat; and the most expeditious carver will be the best carver, as, like mutton, venison soon begins to chill, when it loses much of its charm.

Venison, Potted.—INGREDIENTS.—

2 lbs. of venison, paste of flour and water, ¾ lb. of butter, ½ pint of port wine, salt, cayenne and pounded mace. AVERAGE COST, 4s. 6d.

Slice the venison into a buttered tin baking dish, pour the wine over, lay over the butter and cover with a paste. Bake an hour in a moderate oven, take off the paste and pound the meat with the butter and the seasoning and put it into pots. Put these in the oven for a quarter of an hour, then pour clarified butter over the top and store in a dry place.

TIME.—1¼ hour.

SEASONABLE.—*Buck venison from June to Michaelmas; doe venison from November to end of January.*

Venison, Stewed.—INGREDIENTS

for dish for 12 or 14 persons.—A shoulder of venison, a few slices of mutton fat, 2 glasses of port wine, pepper and allspice to taste, 1½ pint of weak stock or gravy, ½ teaspoonful of whole pepper, ½ teaspoonful of whole all-spice. AVERAGE COST, 1s. 2d. to 1s. 6d. per lb.

Hang the venison till tender; take out the bone, flatten the meat with a rolling-pin, and place over it a few slices of mutton fat, which have been previously soaked for 2 or 3 hours in port wine; sprinkle these with a little allspice and pepper, roll the meat up, and bind and tie it securely. Put it into a stewpan with the bone and the above proportion of weak stock or gravy, whole allspice, black pepper and port wine; cover the lid down closely, and simmer very gently from 3½ to 4 hours, When quite tender, take off the tape, and dish the meat; strain the gravy over it, and send it to table with red-currant jelly. Unless the joint is very fat, the above is the best mode of cooking it.

TIME.—3½ to 4 hours.

SEASONABLE.—*Buck venison, from June to Michaelmas; doe venison form November to the end of January.*

Vermicelli Pudding.—INGREDI-

ENTS *for pudding for 6 persons.*—4 oz. of vermicelli, 1½ pint of milk, ½ pint of cream, 3 oz. of butter, 3 oz. of sugar, 4 eggs. AVERAGE COST, *without cream*, 1s.

Boil the vermicelli in the milk until it is tender; then stir in the remaining ingredients, omitting the cream, if not obtainable. Flavour the mixture with grated lemon-rind, essence of bitter almonds, or vanilla; butter a pie-dish; line the edges with puff-paste, put in the pudding, and bake in a moderate oven for about ¾ hour.

TIME.—¾ hour.

SEASONABLE at any time.

Vermicelli Pudding. (More Economical.)

—INGREDIENTS for pudding for 6 persons.—¼ lb. of vermicelli, 1½ pint of milk, 2 oz. of butter, 3 oz. of sugar, 2 eggs. AVERAGE COST, 9d.

Put the vermicelli in the milk in a saucepan with a flavouring of lemon-peel or any other that is preferred, and boil till tender. If lemon-peel is used take it out before adding the other ingredients. Butter a pie-dish, pour in the mixture and bake in a moderate oven.

TIME.—To bake ¾ hour.

SEASONABLE at any time.

Vermicelli Soup.

—INGREDIENTS.—1½ lb. of bacon, stuck with cloves; ½ oz. of butter, worked up in flour; 1 small fowl, trussed for boiling; 2 oz. of vermicelli, 2 quarts of white stock.

VERMICELLI.

Put the stock, bacon, butter and fowl into the stewpan, and stew for ¾ of an hour. Take the vermicelli, add to it a little of the stock, and set it on the fire, till it is quite tender. When the soup is ready, take out the fowl and bacon, and put the bacon on a dish. Skim the soup as clear as possible; pour it, with the vermicelli, over the fowl. Cut some bread thin, put in the soup, and serve.

TIME.—2 hours.

SEASONABLE in winter.

Vermicelli Soup.

—INGREDIENTS for soup for 8 to 10 persons.—¼ lb of vermicelli, 2 quarts of clear gravy stock. AVERAGE COST, 2s.

Put the vermicelli in the soup, boiling; simmer very gently for ½ an hour, and stir frequently.

TIME.—½ an hour.

SEASONABLE all the year.

Vol-au-Vent.

—INGREDIENTS.—¾ to 1 lb. of puff-paste, fricasseed chickens, rabbits, ragoûts, or the remains of cold fish, flaked and warmed in thick white sauce. AVERAGE COST, exclusive of the ragoût or fricassee, 1s. 3d.

Make from ¾ to 1 lb. of puff-paste, taking care that it is very evenly rolled out each time, to ensure its rising properly; and if the paste is not extremely light, and put into a good hot oven, this cannot be accomplished, and the vol-au-vent will look very badly. Roll out the paste to the thickness of about 1½ inch, and, with a fluted cutter, stamp it out to the desired shape, either round or oval, and, with the point of a small knife, make a slight incision in the paste all round the top, about an inch from the edge, which, when baked, forms

VOL-AU-VENT.

the lid. Put the vol-au-vent into a good brisk oven, and keep the door shut for a few minutes after it is put in. Particular attention should be paid to the heating of the oven, for the paste cannot rise without a tolerable degree of heat. When of a nice colour, without being scorched, withdraw it from the oven, instantly remove the cover where it was marked, and detach all the soft crumb from the centre; in doing this, be careful not to break the edges of the vol-au-vent; but should they look thin in places, stop them with small flakes of the inside paste, stuck on with the white of an egg. This precaution is necessary to prevent the fricassee or ragoût from bursting the case, and so spoiling the appearance of the dish. Fill the *vol-au-vent* with a rich mince, or fricassee, or ragoût, or the remains of cold fish, flaked and warmed in a good white sauce, and do not make them very liquid, for fear of the gravy bursting the crust; replace the lid,

SMALL VOL-AU-VENTS.

and serve. To improve the appearance of the crust, brush it over with the yolk of an egg *after* it has risen properly.

TIME.—¾ *hour to bake the vol-au-vent.*

SEASONABLE *at any time.*

Note.—Small *vol-au-vents* may be made like those shown in the engraving, and filled with minced veal, chicken, &c. They should be made of the same paste as the larger ones, and stamped out with a small fluted cutter.

Vol-au-Vent of Fresh Strawberries, with Whipped Cream.

—INGREDIENTS *for dish for 6 persons.*—¾ lb. of puff-paste, 1 pint of freshly gathered strawberries, sugar to taste, a plateful of whipped cream.

Make a *vol-au-vent* case, only not quite so large nor so high as for a savoury one. When nearly done, brush the paste over with the white of an egg, then sprinkle on it some pounded sugar, and put it back in the oven to set the glaze. Remove the interior, or soft crumb, and, at the moment of serving, fill it with the strawberries, which should be picked, and broken up with sufficient sugar to sweeten them nicely. Place a few spoonfuls of whipped cream on the top, and serve.

TIME.—½ *hour to 40 minutes to bake the vol-au-vent.*

SEASONABLE *in June and July.*

Vol-au-Vent, Sweet, of Plums, Apples, or any other Fresh Fruit.

—INGREDIENTS *for good-sized dish.*—¾ lb. of puff-paste, about 1 pint of fruit compote. AVERAGE COST, 1s. 9d.

Make ¾ lb. of puff-paste, taking care to bake it in a good brisk oven, to draw it up nicely and make it look light. Have ready sufficient stewed fruit, the syrup of which must be boiled down until very thick; fill the *vol-au-vent* with this, and pile it high in the centre; powder a little sugar over it, and put it back in the oven to glaze, or use a salamander for the purpose; the *vol-au-vent* is then ready to serve. It may be made with any fruit that is in season, such as rhubarb, oranges, gooseberries, currants, cherries, apples, &c.; but care must be taken not to have the syrup too thin, for fear of its breaking through the crust.

TIME.—½ *hour to 40 minutes to bake the vol-au-vent.*

VEAL COLLOPS.

"We may live without poetry, music and art,
  We may live without conscience and live without heart;
  We may live without friends; we may live without books,
  But civilized man cannot live without cooks."

                  OWEN MEREDITH (" Lucile ").

WAFERS, GENEVA.

WAFERS, Geneva.—INGREDIENTS *for good-sized dish.* — 2 *eggs, 3 oz. of butter, 3 oz. of flour, 3 oz. of pounded sugar.* AVERAGE COST, *exclusive of the preserve and cream,* 6*d.*

Well whisk the eggs; put them into a basin, and stir to them the butter, which should be beaten to a cream; add the flour and sifted sugar gradually, and then mix all well together. Butter a baking-sheet, and drop on it a teaspoonful of the mixture at a time, leaving a space between each. Bake in a cool oven; watch the pieces of paste, and, when half done, roll them up like wafers, and put in a small wedge of bread or piece of wood, to keep them in shape. Return them to the oven until crisp. Before serving, remove the bread, put a spoonful of preserve in the widest end, and

WALNUT KETCHUP.

fill up with whipped cream. This is a very pretty and ornamental dish for the supper-table, and is very nice and easily made.

TIME.—*Altogether from 20 to 25 minutes.*
SEASONABLE *at any time.*

Walnut Ketchup.—INGREDIENTS.
—100 *walnuts,* 1 *handful of salt,* 1 *quart of vinegar,* ¼ *oz. of mace,* ¼ *oz. of nutmeg,* ¼ *oz. of cloves,* ¼ *oz. of ginger,* ¼ *oz. of whole black pepper, a small piece of horseradish,* 20 *shalots,* ¼ *lb. of anchovies,* 1 *pint of port wine.*

Procure the walnuts at the time you can run a pin through them, slightly bruise, and put them into a jar with the salt and vinegar; let them stand 8 days, stirring every day; then drain the liquor from them, and boil, with the above ingredients, for about ½ hour. It may be strained or not, as preferred, and, if required, a little more vinegar or wine can be added, according to taste. When bottled, well seal the corks.

SEASONABLE.—*Make this from the beginning to the middle of July, when walnuts are in perfection for pickling purposes.*

Walnut Ketchup.—INGREDIENTS.
—½ sieve of walnut-shells, 2 quarts of water, salt, ½ lb. of shalots, 1 oz. of cloves, 1 oz. of mace, 1 oz. of whole pepper, 1 oz. of garlic.

Put the walnut-shells into a pan with the water and a large quantity of salt; let them stand for 10 days, then break the shells up in the water, and let it drain through a sieve, putting a heavy weight on the top to express the juice; place it on the fire, and remove all the scum that may arise. Now boil the liquor with the shalots, cloves, mace, pepper and garlic, and let all simmer till the shalots sink; then put the liquor into a pan, and, when cold, bottle and cork closely. It should stand 6 months before using: should it ferment during that time, it must be again boiled and skimmed.

TIME.—*About ¾ hour.*

SEASONABLE *in September, when the walnut-shells are obtainable.*

Walnuts, Candied.—INGREDIENTS.
—*Walnuts, clarified sugar, lemon, liqueur.*

Skin the nuts after putting them in boiling water for a minute or so; after this, throw them into another pan of boiling water and boil till tender. Squeeze the juice of a lemon into a basin of lukewarm water, and put the walnuts in this. When cool, dry them, dip them in clarified sugar flavoured with a little liqueur, and lay them on a slab to dry.

Walnuts, to have Fresh throughout the Season.—INGREDIENTS.
—*To every pint of water allow 1 teaspoonful of salt.*

Place the walnuts in the salt and water for 24 hours at least; then take them out, and rub them dry. Old nuts may be freshened in this manner; or walnuts, when first picked, may be put nto an earthen pan with salt sprinkled amongst them, and with damped hay placed on the top of them, and then covered down with a lid. They must be well wiped before they are put on the table.

SEASONABLE.—*Should be stored away in September or October.*

Walnuts, Pickled. (Very Good.)
—INGREDIENTS.—100 *walnuts, salt and water. To each quart of vinegar allow 2 oz. of whole black pepper, 1 oz. of allspice, 1 oz. of bruised ginger.*

Procure the walnuts while young; be careful they are not woody, and prick them well with a fork; prepare a strong brine of salt and water (4 lbs. of salt to each gallon of water), into which put the walnuts, letting them remain 9 days, and changing the brine every third day; drain them off, put them on a dish, place it in the sun until they become perfectly black,

THE WALNUT.

which will be in 2 or 3 days; have ready dry jars, into which place the walnuts, and do not quite fill the jars. Boil sufficient vinegar to cover them, for 10 minutes, with spices in the above proportion, and pour it hot over the walnuts, which must be quite covered with the pickle; tie down with bladder, and keep in a dry place. They will be fit for use in a month, and will keep good 2 or 3 years.

TIME.—10 *minutes.*

SEASONABLE.—*Make this from the beginning to the middle of July, before the walnuts harden.*

Note.—When liked, a few shalots may be added to the vinegar, and boiled with it.

Water Souchy.

—Perch, tench, soles, eels and flounders are considered the best fish for this dish For the souchy, put some water into a stewpan with a bunch of chopped parsley, some roots, and sufficient salt to make it brackish. Let these simmer for 1 hour, and then stew the fish in this water. When they are done, take them out to drain, have ready some finely-chopped parsley, and a few roots cut into slices of about 1 inch thick and 1 inch in length. Put the fish in a tureen or deep dish, strain the liquor over them, and add the minced parsley and roots. Serve with brown bread and butter.

Wheatears, To Dress.

—INGREDI-ENTS.—*Wheatears; fresh butter.*

After the birds are picked, gutted and cleaned, truss them like larks, put them down to a quick fire, and baste them well with fresh butter. When done, which will be in about 20 minutes, dish them on fried bread-crumbs, and garnish the dish with slices of lemon.

TIME.—*20 minutes.*

SEASONABLE *from July to October.*

Wheaten Flour.

—Wheaten flour varies in quality according to the process

to which the grain is subjected, and in the ordinary milling the meal produced in one grinding is separated into several different products.

Wheaten flour makes the best of all breads. Whole-meal is thought by some to be more nutritious than white, but the rough bran in the former so hurries the process of digestion that the absorption of its nutri-WHEAT. tive qualities is not so complete as with the white. It is also calculated that there is more sustaining power in a loaf of good unadulterated white bread than in any other food which could be bought at the same cost.

CONSTITUENTS OF 1 LB. OF WHEATEN FLOUR.

				oz.	grs.
Water	...	...	...	2	34
Albumenoids	...	...	...	1	297
Starch, &c. ...	...	...	...	11	0
Fat ...	...	...	...	0	57
Mineral Matter	...	...	...	0	49
				16	0

Whiskey Cordial.

—INGREDIENTS. —*1 lb. of ripe white currants, the rind of 2 lemons, ¼ oz. of grated ginger, 1 quart of whiskey, 1 lb. of lump sugar.*

Strip the currants from the stalks; put them in a large jug; add the lemon-rind, ginger and whiskey; cover the jug closely, and let it remain covered for 24 hours. Strain through a hair-sieve, add the lump sugar, and let it stand 12 hours longer; then bottle and cork well.

TIME.—*To stand 24 hours before being strained; 12 hours after the sugar is added.*

SEASONABLE.—*Make this in July.*

Whitebait, To Dress.

—INGREDI-ENTS.— *Whitebait, a little flour, hot lard, seasoning of salt.*

This fish should be put into iced water as soon as bought, unless they are cooked

WHITEBAIT.

immediately. Drain them from the water in a colander, and have ready a nice clean dry cloth, over which put 2 good handfuls of flour. Toss in the whitebait, shake them lightly in the cloth, and put them in a wicker-sieve to take away the superfluous flour. Throw them into a pan of boiling lard, very few at a time, and let them fry till of a whitey-brown colour. Directly they are done, they must be taken out and laid before the fire for a minute or two on a sieve reversed, covered with blotting-paper to absorb the fat. Dish them on a

WHITEBAIT.

hot napkin, arrange the fish very high in the centre, and sprinkle a little salt over the whole.

TIME.—3 *minutes.*

SEASONABLE *from April to August.*

Whitebait, Devilled. — INGRE-DIENTS *for dish for 3 or 4 persons.*—1 *pint of whitebait, some flour, lard for frying, salt, cayenne.* AVERAGE COST, 2s. 6d.

Put some flour in a cloth and shake the whitebait in this ; then get rid of the super-fluous flour by putting them in a sieve and shaking well. Have ready a pan of boiling lard, into which put them in a frying basket. Fry and drain as in preceding recipe, but in addition to the salt, add a full seasoning of cayenne. Serve as hot as possible with cut lemon and very thin slices of brown bread and butter. The dryer and crisper the whitebait is when fried the better.

TIME.—*About* 3 *minutes.*

SEASONABLE *from April to August.*

White Sauce. (Good.)—INGREDI-ENTS *for sauce for a pair of fowls or a turkey.*—½ *pint of white stock,* ½ *pint of cream,* 1 *dessertspoonful of flour, salt to taste.* AVERAGE COST, 1s.

Have ready a delicately-clean saucepan, into which put the stock, which should be well flavoured with vegetables, and rather savoury ; mix the flour smoothly with the cream, add it to the stock, season with a little salt, and boil all these ingredients very gently for about 10 minutes, keeping

them well stirred the whole time, as this sauce is very liable to burn.

TIME.—10 *minutes.*

SEASONABLE *at any time.*

White Sauce. (Made without Meat.)—INGREDIENTS *for sauce for pair of fowls.*—2 *oz. of butter,* 2 *small onions,* 1 *carrot,* ½ *a small teacupful of flour,*1 *pint of new milk, salt and cayenne to taste.* AVER-AGE COST, 5d.

Cut up the onions and carrot very small, and put them into a stewpan with the butter; simmer them till the butter is nearly dried up ; then stir in the flour, and add the milk ; boil the whole gently until it thickens, strain it, season with salt and cayenne, and it will be ready to serve.

TIME.—¼ *hour.*

SEASONABLE *at any time.*

White Sauce. (A very Simple and Inexpensive Method.)—INGREDIENTS *for sauce for a medium-sized dish.*—1½ *pint of milk,* 1½ *oz. of rice,* 1 *strip of lemon-peel,* 1 *small blade of pounded mace, salt and cayenne to taste.* AVERAGE COST, 4d.

Boil the milk with the lemon-peel and rice until the latter is perfectly tender, then take out the lemon-peel and pound the milk and rice together ; put it back into the stewpan to warm, add the mace and seasoning, give it one boil, and serve. This sauce should be of the consistency of thick cream.

TIME.—*About* 1½ *hour to boil the rice.*

SEASONABLE *at any time.*

White Soup. — INGREDIENTS *for soup for 8 to 10 persons.*—¼ *lb. of sweet almonds,* ¼ *lb. of cold veal or poultry,* 1 *thick slice of stale bread, a little lemon-peel,* 1 *blade of mace, pounded,* ¾ *pint of cream, the yolks of* 2 *hard-boiled eggs,* 2 *quarts of white stock.* AVERAGE COST, 5d. *per quart.*

Reduce the almonds in a mortar to a paste, with a spoonful of water, and add to them the meat, which should be previously pounded with the bread. Beat all together, and add the lemon-peel, very finely chopped, and the mace. Pour the boiling stock on the whole, and simmer for an hour. Rub the eggs in the cream, put in the soup, bring it to a boil, and serve immediately.

TIME.—1½ hour.

SEASONABLE all the year.

Note.—A more economical white soup may be made by using common veal stock, and thickening with rice, flour and milk ; vermicelli may be served with it.

Whiting, Boiled.—INGREDIENTS.—
¼ lb. of salt to each gallon of water. AVERAGE COST, 4d. to 8d. each.

Cleanse the fish, but do not skin them ; lay them in a fish-kettle, with sufficient cold water to cover them and salt in the above proportion. Bring them gradually to

WHITING.

a boil, and simmer gently for about 5 minutes, or rather more should the fish be very large. Dish them on a hot napkin, and garnish with tufts of parsley. Serve with anchovy or caper sauce, and plain melted butter.

TIME.—*After the water boils, 5 minutes.*

SEASONABLE all the year, but best from October to March.

To Choose Whiting. — Choose for the firmness of its flesh, and the silvery hue of its appearance.

Whiting, Broiled.—INGREDIENTS.
—Salt and water; flour. AVERAGE COST, 4d. to 8d. each.

Wash the whiting in salt and water, wipe them thoroughly, and let them remain in the cloth to absorb all moisture. Flour them well, and broil over a very clear fire. Serve with *maître d'hôtel* sauce, or plain melted butter (*see* Sauces). Be careful to

preserve the liver, as by some it is considered to be very delicate.

TIME.—*5 minutes for a small whiting.*

SEASONABLE all the year, but best from October to March.

Whiting, &c., Carving of. —
Whiting, pike, haddock and other fish, when of large size, may be carved in the same manner as salmon. When of medium size, they may be cut through, bone and all, and helped in nice pieces, a middling-sized whiting serving for two slices, and when small, a fish is given to each person.

Whiting, Fried.—INGREDIENTS.—
Egg and bread-crumbs, a little flour, hot lard, or clarified dripping. AVERAGE COST, 4d. to 6d. each.

Take off the skins, clean, and thoroughly wipe the fish free from all moisture, as this is most essential, in order that the egg and bread-crumbs may properly adhere. Fasten the tail in the mouth by means of a small skewer, brush the fish over with egg, dredge with a little flour, and cover with bread-crumbs. Fry them in hot lard or clarified dripping of a nice colour, and serve them on a napkin, garnished with fried parsley. Send them to table with shrimp sauce and plain melted butter.

TIME.—*About 6 minutes.*

SEASONABLE all the year, but best from October to March.

Note.—Large whitings may be filleted, rolled and served as fried filleted soles. Small fried whitings are frequently used for garnishing large boiled fish, such as turbot, cod, &c.

Whiting au Gratin (Baked Whiting).—INGREDIENTS for dish for 4 to 6 persons.—4 whiting, butter, 1 tablespoonful of minced parsley, a few chopped mushrooms when obtainable; pepper, salt and grated nutmeg to taste, butter, 2 glasses of sherry or Madeira, bread-crumbs. AVERAGE COST, 2s. 3d.

Grease the bottom of a baking-dish with butter, and over it strew some mince parsley and mushrooms. Scale, empty and wash the whitings, and wipe them thoroughly dry, carefully preserving the livers. Lay them in the dish, sprinkle them with bread-crumbs and seasoning, adding a little grated nutmeg, and also a little more minced parsley and mushrooms. Place small pieces of butter over the whiting, moisten with the wine, and bake for 20 minutes in a hot oven. If there should be too much sauce, reduce it by boiling over a sharp fire for a few minutes, and pour under the fish. Serve with a cut lemon, and no other sauce.

TIME.—20 *minutes.*

SEASONABLE *all the year, but best from October to March.*

Whiting aux Fines Herbes.—

INGREDIENTS.—*Whiting,* 1 *bunch of sweet herbs, chopped very fine; butter.* AVERAGE COST, 4*d.* to 6*d. each.*

Clean and skin the fish, fasten the tails in the mouths, and lay them in a baking-dish. Mince the herbs very fine, strew them over the fish, and place small pieces of butter over; cover with another dish, and let them simmer in a Dutch oven for ¼ hour or 20 minutes. Turn the fish once or twice, and serve with the sauce poured over.

TIME.— ¼ *hour or 20 minutes.*

SEASONABLE *all the year, but best from October to March.*

Widgeon, Roast.—INGREDIENTS.—

Widgeons, a little flour, butter. AVERAGE COST, 1*s. each.*

These are trussed in the same manner as wild duck, but must not be kept so long before they are dressed. Put them down to a brisk fire; flour, and baste them continually with butter, and, when browned and nicely frothed, send them to table hot and quickly. Serve with brown gravy, or orange gravy, and a cut lemon.

TIME.—¼ *hour; if liked well done,* 20 *minutes.*

SEASONABLE *from October to February.*

Widgeon, To Carve.—Widgeon

may be carved in the same way as described in regard to wild duck.

Wine or Brandy Sauce (for

Puddings). — INGREDIENTS *for sauce for pudding for* 7 *or* 8 *persons.*—1 *pint of melted butter,* 3 *heaped teaspoonfuls of pounded sugar,* 1 *large wineglassful of port or sherry, or* ¾ *of a small glassful of brandy.* AVERAGE COST, 9*d.*

Make ½ pint of melted butter, omitting the salt; then stir in the sugar and wine or spirit in the above proportion, and bring the sauce to the point of boiling. Serve in a boat or tureen separately, and, if liked, pour a little of it over the pudding. To convert this into punch sauce, add to the sherry or brandy a small wineglassful of rum and the juice and grated rind of ½ lemon. Liqueurs, such as Maraschino or Curaçoa, substituted for the brandy, make excellent sauces.

TIME.—*Altogether,* 15 *minutes.*

Wine Sauce (for Puddings).—IN-

GREDIENTS *for sauce for large pudding.*—½ *pint of sherry,* ¼ *pint of water, the yolks of* 5 *eggs,* 2 *oz. of pounded sugar,* ½ *teaspoonful of minced lemon-peel, a few pieces of candied citron, cut thin.* AVERAGE COST, 1*s. 2d.*

Separate the yolks from the whites of 5 eggs; beat them, and put them into a very clean saucepan (if at hand, a lined one is best); add all the other ingredients, place them over a sharp fire, and keep stirring until the sauce begins to thicken; then take it off, and serve. If it is allowed to boil, it will be spoiled, as it will immediately curdle.

TIME.—*To be stirred over the fire* 3 *or* 4 *minutes; but it must not boil.*

SEASONABLE *at any time.*

Wine Sauce (for Puddings; Excel-

lent).—INGREDIENTS *for sauce for good-sized pudding.*—*The yolks of* 4 *eggs,* 1 *tea-*

spoonful of flour, 2 oz. of pounded sugar, 2 oz. of fresh butter, ¼ saltspoonful of salt, ½ pint of sherry or Madeira. AVERAGE COST, 1s. 3d.

Put the butter and flour into a saucepan, and stir them over the fire until the former thickens; then add the sugar, salt and wine, and mix these ingredients well together. Separate the yolks from the whites of 4 eggs; beat up the former, and stir them briskly to the sauce; let it remain over the fire until it is on the point of simmering; but do not allow it to boil, or it will instantly curdle. This sauce is delicious with plums, marrow, or bread puddings; but should be served separately, and not poured over the pudding.

TIME.—*From 5 to 7 minutes to thicken the butter; about 5 minutes to stir the sauce over the fire.*

Wine, To Mull.—INGREDIENTS.—
To every pint of wine allow 1 large cupful of water, sugar and spice to taste.

In making preparations like the above, it is very difficult to give the exact proportions of ingredients like sugar and spice, as what quantity might suit one person would be to another quite distasteful. Boil the spice in the water until the

MULL.

flavour is extracted, then add the wine and sugar, and bring the whole to the boiling-point, when serve with strips of crisp dry toast, or with biscuits. The spices usually used for mulled wine are cloves, grated nutmeg and cinnamon or mace. Any kind of wine may be mulled, but port and claret are those usually selected for the purpose; and the latter requires a very large proportion of sugar. The vessel that the wine is boiled in must be delicately clean, and should be kept exclusively for the purpose. Small tin

warmers or mulls may be purchased for a trifle, which are more suitable than saucepans, as, if the latter are not scrupulously clean, they will spoil the wine, by

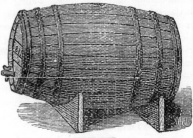

WINE CASK.

imparting to it a very disagreeable flavour. These warmers should be used for no other purpose.

Woodcock, Roast.—INGREDIENTS.
Woodcocks; butter, flour, toast.

Woodcocks should not be drawn, as the trails are, by epicures, considered a great delicacy. Pluck, and wipe them well outside; truss them with the legs close to the body, and the feet pressing upon the thighs; skin the neck and head, and bring

ROAST WOODCOCK.

the beak round under the wing. Place some slices of toast in the dripping-pan to catch the trails, allowing a piece of toast for each bird. Roast before a clear fire from 15 to 25 minutes; keep them well basted, and flour and froth them nicely. When done, dish the pieces of toast with the birds upon them, and pour round a very little gravy; send some more to table in a tureen. These are most delicious birds when well cooked; but they should not be kept too long: when the feathers drop, or easily come out, they are fit for table.

TIME.—*When liked underdone, 15 to 20 minutes; if liked well done, allow an extra 5 minutes.*

SEASONABLE *from November to February.*

Woodcock.—This bird, like partridge, may be carved by cutting it exactly into two like portions, or made into three helpings, as described in carving partridge. The backbone is considered the tit-bit of a woodcock, and by many the thigh is also thought a great delicacy. This bird is

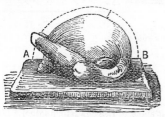

WOODCOCK.

served in the manner advised by Brillat Savarin, in connection with the pheasant, viz., on toast which has received its drippings whilst roasting; and a piece of this toast should invariably accompany each plate.

Woodcock, Salmi of. — INGREDIENTS *for Entrée.*—Remains of cold roast woodcock, a little stock or gravy, port wine, a bouquet of herbs, a small truffle, if obtainable, seasoning of cayenne and salt, ½ a lemon. AVERAGE COST, *exclusive of the cold woodcock,* 1s.

Cut as many small, neat pieces as the remains of the birds will yield, then put the remainder with all bones and any trimmings into the stock with the herbs and truffle cut up. Simmer till all the meat comes off the bones, and remove them and the herbs; put in the pieces saved of the birds, add a glass of port wine and a full seasoning, and serve when all is quite hot with a squeeze of lemon the last thing. Serve this salmi or hash in a deep entrée dish, as there should be plenty of good gravy. A few fried croûtons may be put round.

TIME.—*About ½ hour to simmer.*

SEASONABLE *from November to February.*

Woodcock, Scotch. — INGREDIENTS.—*A few slices of hot buttered toast; allow 1 anchovy to each slice. For the sauce—¼ pint of cream, the yolks of 3 eggs.* AVERAGE COST, 1s. 2d.

Separate the yolks from the whites of the eggs; beat the former, stir to them the cream, and bring the sauce to the boiling-point, but do not allow it to boil, or it will curdle. Have ready some hot buttered toast, spread with anchovies pounded to a paste; pour a little of the hot sauce on the top, and serve very hot and very quickly.

TIME.—*5 minutes to make the sauce hot.*

SEASONABLE *at any time.*

Woodcock, Scotch. (Another Way of Making.—INGREDIENTS *for dish for 3 persons.*—3 eggs, 3 sardines, 3 slices of buttered toast, ¼ pint of milk, salt, cayenne. AVERAGE COST, 9d.

Bone the sardines, pound them in a mortar with a seasoning of cayenne. Make 3 slices of toast, well butter them, spread them with the sardine paste and put them to keep hot while the sauce is being made. Make this as in preceding recipe, using, however, the whole eggs and substituting milk for the cream. Pour the sauce over the sardine toast, and serve as quickly as possible.

TIME.—*5 or 6 minutes to make the sauce.*

SEASONABLE *at any time.*

"Yet we must eat and drink, as you say."
CLOUGH.

YEAST-CAKE.

INGREDIENTS *for 2 moderate sized cakes.* — 1½ *lb. of flour,* ½ *lb. of butter,* ½ *pint of milk,* 1 *tablespoonful of good yeast,* 3 *eggs,* ¾ *lb. of currants,* ½ *lb. of white moist sugar,* 2 *oz. of candied-peel.* AVERAGE COST, 1s. 9d.

Put the milk and butter into a saucepan, and shake it round over a fire until the butter is melted, but do not allow the milk to get very hot. Put the flour into a basin, stir to it the milk and butter, the yeast and eggs, which should be well beaten, and form the whole into a smooth dough. Let it stand in a warm place, covered with a cloth, to rise, and, when sufficiently risen, add the currants, sugar and candied-peel cut into thin slices. When all the ingredients are thoroughly mixed, line 2 moderate-sized cake-tins with buttered paper, which should be about six inches higher than the tin; pour in the mixture, let it stand to rise again for another ½ hour, and then bake the cakes in a brisk oven for about 1½ hour. If the tops of them become too brown, cover them with paper until they are done through. A few drops of essence of lemon, or a little grated nutmeg may be added when the flavour is liked.

TIME.—*From* 1¼ *to* 1½ *hour.*

SEASONABLE *at any time.*

Yeast-Cake. (From Bakers' Dough.) INGREDIENTS *for 2* ½-*quartern cakes.*—1 *quartern of bakers' dough,* 1 *lb. of sultanas,* ½ *lb. of sugar (more if the cake is liked very sweet),* ¾ *lb. of butter or dripping, a flavouring of spice.* AVERAGE COST, 2s.

Have the other ingredients ready before the dough arrives; well work them in, then put the cake into well-buttered tins or tins lined with buttered paper, and bake the cakes in a quick oven from 1½ to 1¾ hour. Cakes made in this way, though plain, are nice for children, and may be baked in small tins as buns.

TIME.—1½ *to* 1¾ *hour to bake the cake.*

SEASONABLE *at any time.*

Yeast-Dumplings.— INGREDIENTS

for dumplings for 6 to 8 persons.—½ quartern of dough, boiling water. AVERAGE COST, 4*d.*

Make a very light dough as for bread, using to mix it, milk, instead of water; divide it into 7 or 8 dumplings; plunge them into boiling water, and boil them for 20 minutes. Serve the instant they are taken up, as they spoil directly, by falling and becoming heavy; and in eating them do not touch them with a knife, but tear them apart with two forks. They may be eaten with meat gravy, or cold butter and sugar; and if not convenient to make the dough at home, a little from the baker's answers as well, only it must be placed for a few minutes near the fire, in a basin with a cloth over it, to let it rise again before it is made into dumplings.

TIME.—20 *minutes.*

SEASONABLE *at any time.*

Yeast, To Make (for Bread).—

INGREDIENTS.—1½ *oz. of hops, 3 quarts of water, 1 lb. of bruised malt, ½ pint of yeast.*

Boil the hops in the water for 20 minutes; let it stand for about 5 minutes, then add to it 1 lb. of bruised malt prepared as for brewing. Let the mixture stand covered until about lukewarm; then put in not quite ½ pint of yeast; keep it warm, and let it work 3 or 4 hours; then put it into small ½-pint bottles (ginger-beer bottles are the best for the purpose), cork them well, and tie them down. The yeast is now ready for use; it will keep good for a few weeks, and 1 bottle will be found sufficient for 18 lbs. of flour. When required for use, boil 3 lbs. of potatoes without salt, mash them in the same water in which they were boiled, and rub them through a colander. Stir in about ½ lb. of flour, then put in the yeast; pour it in the middle of the flour, and let it stand warm on the hearth all night, and in the morning let it be quite warm when it is kneaded. The bottles of

yeast require very careful opening, as it is generally exceedingly ripe.

TIME.—20 *minutes to boil the hops and water, the yeast to work 3 or 4 hours.*

Yeast, Kirkleatham.—INGREDI-

ENTS.—*2 oz. of hops, 4 quarts of water, ½ lb. of flour, ½ pint of yeast.*

Boil the hops and water for 20 minutes; strain, and mix with the liquid ½ lb. of flour and not quite ½ pint of yeast. Bottle it up, and tie the corks down. When wanted for use, boil potatoes according to the quantity of bread to be made (about 3 lbs. are sufficient for about a peck of flour); mash them, add to them ½ lb. of flour, and mix about ½ pint of the yeast with them; let this mixture stand all day, and lay the bread to rise the night before it is wanted.

TIME.—20 *minutes to boil the hops and water.*

SUFFICIENT.—*½ pint of this yeast sufficient for a peck of flour, or rather more.*

Yorkshire Pudding. (To Serve

with Hot Roast Beef.)—INGREDIENTS *for pudding for 6 persons.—1½ pint of milk, 6 large tablespoonfuls of flour, 3 eggs, 1 saltspoonful of salt.* AVERAGE COST, 7*d.*

But the flour into a basin with the salt, and stir gradually to this enough milk to make it into a stiff batter. When this is perfectly smooth, and all the lumps are well rubbed down, add the remainder of the

YORKSHIRE PUDDING.

milk and the eggs, which should be well beaten. Beat the mixture for a few minutes, and pour it into a shallow tin, which has been previously well rubbed with beef dripping. Put the pudding into the oven, and bake it for an hour; then, for another ½ hour place it under the meat, to catch a little of the gravy that flows from it. Cut the pudding into small square pieces, put them on a hot dish, and serve. If the meat is baked, the pudding may be placed under it, after the meat has cooked some time and the dripping has been poured off, resting the meat on a small three cornered stand.

TIME.—1½ hour.

SEASONABLE *at any time.*

Yorkshire Pudding. (An Economical Way of Making.) — INGREDIENTS *for pudding for 6 persons.*—2 *breakfastcupfuls of flour, a teaspoonful of salt, rather more than 1 pint of water, 2 eggs.* AVERAGE COST, 4*d.*

Put the flour in a basin with the salt, and mix them well together. Make a hole in the centre and break into it the eggs, then gradually add the water, beating it well in and being careful not to leave lumps. When a fairly stiff batter, it is ready. Take the meat tin from the oven, where the meat should have quite half cooked, pour off the dripping and raise the meat, after basting well, on a trivet. Pour in the pudding and put back in the oven with as little delay as possible. Serve cut in squares on a hot dish.

TIME.—1 *to* 1½ *hour.*

SEASONABLE *at any time.*

Zwetschen Sauce. (A Nice Sauce for Puddings.)—INGREDIENTS *for sauce for good-sized pudding.*—¼ *lb. of French prunes, a glass of sherry or other white wine, the juice of a lemon,* ½ *the rind, a pinch of powdered cinnamon and sugar to taste.* AVERAGE COST, 1*s.*

Put the prunes in a stewpan with just enough water to cover them, and simmer till they are soft. Take them out, remove the stones, crack them and save the kernels, and put back the fruit. Add the other ingredients, simmer for 10 minutes and strain through a coarse sieve. Should the sauce be too thick, dilute it with a little more water.

TIME.—*About* ½ *hour.*

SEASONABLE *at any time.*

ZANTE CURRANTS.

THE COOK. THE NURSE. THE HOUSEMAID.

HOUSEHOLD WORK.

MISTRESS AND SERVANTS.

ONE of the greatest difficulties in house-keeping experienced by the beginners is the difficulty of engaging servants.

If a lady will reflect upon the importance of engaging a good servant, she will hesitate before taking a written character, unless under very exceptional circumstances. There are four ways of obtaining servants: enquiring of trades-persons; advertising for servants; answering advertisements; and applying at servants' offices.

Advertising for servants costs from three to five shillings, according to the length of advertisement, and entails remaining at home during the hours stated. This, where practicable, is an excellent plan, for when the lady sees a servant whose appearance pleases her, whose recommendations are apparently good, and whose " character " is not " short," she can enter into details of the work, show the servant the house, the rooms, and ascertain whether the arrangements, if carried out, are likely to be permanent. The servant, on her side, can judge of the kind of place and mistress, and decide for or against it at once, instead of in a " month's time."

Answering advertisements is by no means a certain way of obtaining servants, and should not be resorted to when time is an object.

Applying at servants' offices and homes is one of the best plans; and at some of these ladies can comfortably see and engage servants. The characters are all inspected by the managers; but as, with so large a number, the minute points which so particularly affect the comfort of a household cannot be determined, a mistress should never think any trouble too great which allows a personal interview with the late mistress of the proposed maid.

It is well, when engaging servants, to mention all the rules that a mistress considers best for the happiness of her household, and these details cannot be too much studied by those who hold the reins. A day's holiday every month is usual for each servant, and where two only are kept, by turns they should be allowed to go out on Sunday evenings. Some families can manage to allow one maid the Sunday morning, the other the Sunday evening, but this cannot always be done. The wages should be paid regularly upon quarter-day—the 25th March, 21st June, 29th September, and 25th December—or monthly by arrangement. It is best to provide beer and washing, unless washing is done at home, when, of course, it is done by the maids and laundress. If servants work hard they generally require some beer, and by providing a cask of good ale, and putting it in the cook's charge, they have sufficient. The ale should be computed to last a certain time, and the brewer be ordered to call at regular intervals. Women servants are usually allowed a pint, and men servants a quart per diem, and a gallon over should be allowed in small households for waste in constant drawing.

It is well at the time of hiring to state distinctly the exact nature of the service required. For example, if a cook is wanted to undertake the dining-room, hall and passages, it should be distinctly stated that such is her work. If the housemaid is to wait on the lady, it should be named, and so on through all the duties of each place.

And at the time of hiring, it is important to specify the holidays, time allowed on Sundays and the following particulars, so that a servant clearly understands what she is to expect, and enters upon her duties clearly understanding the kind of situation she accepts. The wages should be increased yearly, and every encouragement given to good servants.

In engaging servants, state the wages given now, and what rise may be expected. The time on Sunday allowed for Church or Chapel, the holidays given, etc. Inquiries to be made of the lady who gives the character as to "honesty, sobriety, cleanliness, also if she is industrious, neat, tidy in person and in work, regular and systematic." If a cook, ask particulars of soups, roasting, boiling and frying, pastry-making and general care and economy. If a nurse, temper, kindness and watchful care and experience. If a house-maid, care of stoves, ornaments, careful and neat. If a parlour-maid, if able to wait well at table. If a lady's-maid, clever hairdresser and dressmaker, discreet and quiet; and so on through the various classes of servants required. Also, number of years in place, from whom taken, reason for leaving and any particular fault or peculiarity.

By the style of house, and the class of lady from whom one is seeking a servant's character, one can judge of what it should be, whether the lady gives a true character or not. High praise is often accorded by a mistress who does not know what a good servant is, and this applies particularly to cooks, for here taste and style of serving differ essentially. As a rule, a lady is safe in taking a servant who has lived over two years in a family in the same position as her own, neither above nor below it, of whom the mistress distinctly and clearly states that she is honest, sober, clean and industrious ; the mistress's appearance being quiet, lady-like and tidy ; the house well-cared for and neat. It is a great advantage to know something of the past history of one's servants, and inquiries should be made respecting the other places held by the servant.

A mistress is often shy about telling a new servant her ways and wishes, allows herself to be as indulgent at first as she is strict and fault-finding when used to her new maid. Now, if this plan were reversed, and a lady had the courage to be strict and particular when the maid is at her best, and in her most pains-taking humour, a servant would naturally fall into the right way of pleasing by being useful to her mistress.

Gentleness, kindness and firmness are the qualities required in a mistress, with a thorough practical knowledge of what are her servants' duties. We may here remark that those households are best conducted where the mistress never converses with her servants ; never speaks but to gently give an order, ask a question, or say good morning and evening to her maids. Of course, this does not apply in times of sorrow for the servants, or with a general servant, who is depending on her mistress for all occasions of speaking, or to old, well-tried servants, but it is a safe rule for the mistress.

When servants first enter a service they naturally try their best to please, and require only teaching the "ways" of the family. They soon see if their mistress is "particular" or no, and whether they are ruled by a careful, clever hand, or by a careless, idle mistress, and will act accordingly.

What has passed into a proverb respecting the master's eye equally applies to the mistress of a household. Her observant glance ought to take in, and the mind note, every detail of housewifery. She should in herself be an example to her maids of neatness, cleanliness and order. " So particular," should be the verdict of her handmaidens. A woman who does her duty to her husband and household must be particular, must be strict and watchful. At the same time, this care and strictness does not preclude her being gentle in manner and word, kind and sympathizing with her servants in illness or trouble, tending them and helping them when such assistance is needed.

And this kindness, this help, can be given only by a careful, watchful mistress—a woman whose life is regulated by strong principles, and by love of order.

If waste is allowed to run riot in a household—if articles of daily food are wasted, badly bought, badly cooked, badly carved and made the least of— there will be no funds left in the mistress's hands with which to pay for the doctor her kindness would call in to her sick servant. Care and thrift mean power to help others; economy in daily life permits good actions in life's trials. Good housewifery comprises the duty of woman. Pages might be written upon this subject, but a few hints will suffice to prove this to a thoughtful woman.

The washing of a family should be put out where one servant alone is kept,

WASHING TUB AND BOARD.

but many clever managers find time to do all the family washing at home, and yet are not "in a muddle," as it is expressively termed, upon washing-day; the damping, folding and ironing being often done by the mistress, the hard labour by the maids. With the help of one of Bradford's washing-machines this labour is much reduced, and the wringer and mangle are equally handy.

But unless it is absolutely necessary, no lady should attempt to have the whole of the washing done at home when one servant alone is kept.

Warnings on either side are usually for that day month on which the warning was given, and it is well for a mistress to begin at once to look out for a good maid to replace the going-out servant.

After warning has been given on either side, the mistress, even if annoyed with her maid, should behave with quiet courtesy towards her; not, as we have remarked some mistresses do, treat her as if she had committed a crime. A change may be desirable for many reasons, although it is not possible to over-estimate a quiet, well-conducted servant, who is attacded to her mistress, and who will not leave her even for fairer prospects and a more luxurious home.

There is a great dissimilarity of opinion as to the amount of help given to servants, some mistresses working *with* the servant or servants unnecessarily, others expecting one or two to perform the work of four. Only a good housekeeper knows the right amount of help to give. She has a perfect knowledge of the daily work, and how long it takes to perform the various tasks, and can, therefore, easily estimate what can be properly done by her maids; and if this does not comprise the whole of the work, she will take upon herself such of the lighter duties as can be most easily done by her in the morning.

More help is given by *saving labour* than by taking the work upon one's own shoulders, and method and good management will make heavy work comparatively light.

Care and economy without meanness, on the part of a mistress, will do more to correct the extravagance of servants than any precept. If a maid sees her mistress carefully throw up the ashes, put out unnecessary candles or gaslights and economise properly, she will try also to save her mistress's property.

We think that by laying aside all pretence, and being open and honest with servants, we make them careful and exact too. Where the mistress is given to changing her servants, complaining of them, &c., the fault is *usually* her own. The fault is with the driver, not with the horses, who, in light but firm hands, would run well together, and do their work well and quickly.

Servants should never be reproved before each other or before anyone. If there is occasion for more than a word of direction, a lady should ring for her servant and speak kindly and seriously to her, showing a willingness to help her, though by no means slighting over the subject in question, or allowing any timidity of demeanour to appear.

Domestic quarrels often embitter the peace of households and cause dismissals ; these can be quelled by gentle firmness and the following rules:— Never listen to what one servant says of another ; never ask a question about a new comer of the old trusted servant ; if angry voices and loud talk reach your ear, ring for the delinquents, and before *both* say, " I have no wish to interfere with your quarrels; say and do what you please; but *I* must never hear a sound of dispute or anger in this house." The utter absurdity of being *allowed* to quarrel will, in most cases, prevent a repetition of the offence ; and as this is a *tried* recipe for domestic *broils*, we give it verbatim.

But it is only a gentlewoman who *can* say this—one who never is betrayed into an angry word or cross retort; example and precept must go hand in hand. Our experience is, that in life what we believe people to be, *we make them.* " I believe you to be honest," has kept many a poor tempted soul from evil, and it is the duty of mistresses to guard their *household* as they would their children from opportunities of doing wrong. Young girls should not be sent out late at night to post letters or to fetch beer; should be advised to put by a little of each quarter's money in the post-office savings-bank ; should be counselled as to what is nice to buv in the way of dress ; should never be given old finery ; should be lent nice books, not only religious but amusing works ; should be led to take an interest in the garden, or in the growing flowers, the birds or animals of the house; and in the children, for if the children are not utterly spoiled, and the maids not utterly bad, they cannot help taking an interest in the nursery.

If "suspicion haunts " the mistress's mind (we are supposing her to be a sensible, kind-hearted person), her best plan is to change her servants ; she cannot be comfortable with them, and there is usually more or less ground for these doubts. A mistress cannot follow her stores into the kitchen and *see* that every ounce is carefully used, but she can resist the continued petty larceny which destroys all her attempts at economy and heavily burdens her purse.

DAILY HOUSE-WORK.

The daily duties of the house servants, where there are three kept, namely, nurse, cook and housemaid, are as follows :—

The beds are stripped, and slops emptied in all the rooms. Then bed-making follows; then the sitting-room not used for breakfast must be swept, dusted and arranged; and then the routine cleaning of the day must follow. Every household has good reason for each day's work. The following regulation has been thought to be a good guide:—

Monday—One bedroom; washing for a house of moderate size, if any be done at home.

Tuesday—Spare room and library.

Wednesday—Dining-room, servants' bed-room; ironing.

Thursday—Mistress's bed and dressing rooms.

Friday—Drawing-room and one bed-room.

Saturday—Plate, stairs and sundries.

The nurse cleans her own nursery, night nursery and her own bed-room. The cook undertakes steps and hall, passages, kitchen, larder, scullery and wash-house, and downstairs closets, and, *by arrangement* with the mistress at the time of hiring, cleans the dining-room and helps to make the beds.

Window-cleaning is also a matter of special arrangement. The cook "answers the door" until twelve o'clock, after which hour the housemaid is supposed to be dressed, and should be, if she is quick and clever at her work. The cook should clean her own bed-room, even if shared by the housemaid; and the housemaid is bound, by kitchen etiquette, the unspoken tradition of the spit, to make the tea at breakfast, to arrange and make tea at the afternoon meal and to lay the cloth for the kitchen supper. This rule has originated, no doubt, in the kindly feeling which prompts those who have no cooking to do to prepare the meals for those whose work is almost entirely cooking, and who are, therefore, little disposed to do so for themselves.

DIVISION OF LABOUR BETWEEN THE SERVANTS— WORK BEFORE BREAKFAST.

To get through the work in a regular and orderly manner, such as will give satisfaction to the mistress, it is necessary that the cook and housemaid should divide it judiciously between them—certain duties being taken entirely by the one, and certain other duties by the other; so that when anything is to be done, it may always be definitely understood who is to do it.

To show how it may best be divided, the following outline of one day's work in a house assigns to each servant the share of the duties that it is usually most convenient she should take.

They should both rise at six o'clock. On coming downstairs the cook should go to the kitchen and lower offices; the housemaid to the sitting-rooms, to open all the shutters, and, if the weather be fine, the windows of the various apartments.

She then arranges the breakfast-room, and gets it ready for the family; for this she brings upstairs a carpet-broom, dustpan and some damp tea-leaves.

She should first remove the fender and fire-irons, and roll up and remove the rug; take off the table-cloth, shake and fold it; also shake and fold any antimacassars that may be in the room, and place altogether on the table, which she should cover with a dusting-sheet. She should also cover the sofa, if there be one in the room, and the easy chair, and place the other chairs one seat upon the other, and get all the furniture as much together and into the middle of the room as possible. She should then, having sprinkled the carpet all over with the tea-leaves—sweep the room, beginning at the door, going into all the corners; when it is swept all round, moving the furniture and sweeping where that stood, and bringing all the dust to the hearthstone, where she should collect it in the dustpan and remove it.

She should then shut the door, and while the dust is settling sweep out the hall and down the doorsteps, using for this not the carpet-broom, but the common house-sweeping brush. She should also take out the hall mats and shake them.

LONG HAIR BRUSH.

She should then return to the breakfast-room, bringing with her the housemaid's box, well supplied with brushes, blacklead, emery paper and leathers. The cinder-pail, a small pail of hot water, a house-flannel, a piece of hearthstone, a large coarse cloth, and paper, firewood, coals and matches to light the fire. She should then, first laying down the cloth before the fireplace to save the carpet; clean the grate, fender and fire-irons.

She should first clear out of the grate all the remains of the fire of the day before, placing the cinders and ashes in the cinder-box.

Then blacklead the grate, laying on the blacklead with a soft brush, rubbing it off vigorously with a harder one and finishing it off with a polishing brush. Then rub with a leather all the polished steel portion of the grate, which should not be touched at all with the blacklead or brushes; where any spots appear, rubbing first with the emery paper, and afterwards with the leather. The fender the same way; any portion that is of polished steel being cleaned with emery paper and leather. The fire-irons always with emery paper and leather only.

She will then light the fire, proceeding in exactly the same manner as the cook does with the kitchen fire. Then wash the hearthstone, washing it very thoroughly, rinsing it quite free from all dirt and black; then, while wet, she should rub it well over with the hearthstone, but in doing this she must be very careful to let none of the water or stone touch the grate, fender, or fire-irons.

She should then remove to the scullery all the tools and utensils she used for the grate and fire, and, bringing up a clean duster, she should thoroughly dust the breakfast-parlour. In doing this, she should go over every article carefully, not flapping the duster about, but *wiping* the dust off with it. She should go over the backs and legs of the various pieces of furniture, and should lift every small article from chimney-piece and sideboard and dust under them. She should also dust round the cornice of the room, dust the door and the window-panes, sills and ledges.

She should then re-arrange the furniture all in its proper place, and everything being in order, she should leave the room, shutting the door after her.

Next should come the cleaning the ladies' boots and shoes. Except in the case of very stout common leather boots, which some ladies use in the country in bad weather, or very old kid boots, ladies' boots must not be touched with blacking. If the soles are very muddy, they must be scraped round with an old knife, great care being taken not to touch the uppers, nor to do more to the soles than take the mud off, the leather itself must not be scraped. The mud off the uppers should be removed with a sponge dipped in milk. When boots are not actually muddy, it will be sufficient to go round the edges of the soles with a very soft brush, and to wipe the uppers gently with a flannel. When the boots become old and discoloured, the " Kid Reviver" that most bootmakers sell is better to use than common blacking. It is laid on with a sponge and left to dry, no brushing or polishing is necessary. Their morning's "dirty work" being then concluded, the servants should go to their own room, wash their faces and hands, arrange their hair and put on clean caps and aprons. Having washed her hands, the housemaid will then go upstairs and knock at the different chamber doors to arouse the family, supplying each room with warm water, and leaving the boots and shoes outside the doors of their wearers. Then she lays the breakfast-table.

The laying of the breakfast-table will vary according to the number of the family. In the present instance we will suppose it to be four, therefore she will first collect on her tray and take upstairs :—

The tablecloth.	4 Forks.
4 Napkins.	1 Large carving knife and fork.
4 Breakfast cups and saucers.	1 Smaller carving knife and fork.
4 Large plates.	4 Teaspoons.
4 Smaller plates.	1 Dessert-spoon.
The teapot-stand.	The cruet-stand.
4 Large knives.	2 Salt-cellars.
4 Small knives.	2 Pairs of knife-rests.
The bread-knife.	The slop-basin.
The butter-knife.	

In placing these on the tray, she should be careful to let the tablecloth and the napkins intervene between the china and the other things. She should place the tray on the stand outside the parlour-door, putting it in a convenient position so that she can easily pass in and out. She should first spread the cloth, doing it very carefully so as to avoid creasing it, keeping it quite straight and an equal length hanging down at each end and at the sides.

She should then place at the head of the table—the mistress's place—the teapot or coffee-pot-stand. In front of that the cups and saucers, arranged in a double row, room being left between them and the edge of the table for the mistress's plate. Then the slop-basin at the left-hand side of the cups and saucers. The smaller plates should then be put round the table, one at each person's left hand, a napkin on each; they should be near the edge, but not near enough to be in danger of falling off.

PLATE-BASKET.

One large and one small knife should be put at the right-hand side of each plate, a fork at the left-hand side. The small carving knife and fork should be put at the foot of the table—the master's place; next his own knife and fork; one pair of rests in front of them. The large carving knife and fork should be put on the sideboard with the other rests; the four large plates should be put there also. The breakfast cruet-stand should be placed in one corner of the table; the bread-knife at one side, the butter-knife at the other; one salt-cellar at the right-hand top corner, the other at the right-hand bottom corner; the dessert-spoon should be placed on the plate with the marmalade or honey when it is taken from the cellaret. A table-mat should be placed before the master's place. A vase of flowers or a plant in a pretty receptacle should be placed in the centre of the table.

All these things should be scrupulously clean and free from dust; the mustard-pot should be half-filled with fresh mustard, and the salt-cellars supplied with fine table-salt.

Having put all these things on, she should fetch up from the pantry the cold meat, ham, or pie—on a clean dish, garnished with parsley; the bread on the bread-plate or in the bread-basket; the butter in the butter-dish; the milk in the milk-jug; the cream in the cream-ewer.

The bread-basket should be free from crusts and crumbs, and there should not be less than a loaf; 3 oz. of butter, nicely rolled in pats, will be sufficient, and half-a-pint of milk.

The milk and cream should be placed at the right-hand side of the breakfast-cups, where the sugar-basin will be placed also when it is taken from the cellaret. The bread should be at the side of the table where the bread-knife was placed, the butter where the butter-knife. The cold meat should be put on the sideboard.

Whilst the housemaid is thus engaged, the cook lights the kitchen fire. She should first clean out of the fireplace the remains of the fire of the night before, then thoroughly brush all the range. For lighting the fire she will require some paper, firewood, a few lumps of round coal, some good cinders and a few matches. She should first place the paper at the bottom of the grate, but to the front near the bars ; then most of the firewood, the sticks placed lengthways, one resting on the second bar, the other at the back of the bottom of the grate, leaving a little space between them. She should then strike a match and set fire to the paper, and as it blazes up and the wood catches, she should put on the coals and cinders lightly, and the rest of the sticks among them. If the paper burns away before the sticks have caught, she should replace it with some more paper; but when the sticks have caught with a few of the coals and cinders, then as the fire lights up it will not sink.

The fire being lighted, the cook should clear away all the ashes and cinders, rub up with a leather the bright parts of the range and wash the hearth; when washed quite clean, but while it is still wet, she should rub it with a piece of hearthstone to whiten it, and place the kettle, filled with water, on the fire to boil. She should then thoroughly dust the kitchen, and put everything straight and in order ; and having removed to the scullery the brushes, the leather, the blacklead, the pail, the flannel, brick and whatever else she may have used with the fireplace, she should clean the gentlemen's boots and shoes. For this she will require some blacking and three brushes—one hard, one soft and one medium. She should first, with the hard brush, brush off the mud— but if the boots be very muddy she must scrape it off with an old knife round the edges of the soles, being very careful, however, not to touch the upper leather—then with the soft brush lay on the blacking, and when that has dried on the boot polish it off with the medium brush. Each of the brushes should be used for its own particular purpose only. The cook then washes her hands and proceeds to the hall, where she fastens the front door open, removes all coats, hats, umbrellas, and sweeps down the hall, collecting all the dust and dirt into her pan with the banister-broom. If the hall be dirty, she removes all marks with a piece of flannel wrung out in warm water and polishes with another piece dipped in milk. Twice a week the hall is washed down as follows :—

She should thoroughly wash off the dirt with flannel and warm, not hot, water ; rub dry with a cloth as she goes; and, when all is finished, rub lightly with milk and brighten it.

Having cleaned the hall, she will dust the chairs and hat-stand and pegs, and return the coats and hats to their places, receiving them from the house-maid who will have brushed them carefully downstairs. The cook beats the mat in the garden or street, and returns it to its place. She will next clean the steps, this not as a rule being necessary every day.

A scrubbing-brush, clean warm water, flannel and hearthstone will be needed. She should first scrub the steps down, then dry off with the flannel, and while wet rub in the hearthstone. Some steps are whitened by a composition of pipeclay and water made into a thin paste, and laid on with a brush. This is an admirable white, but has the disadvantages of marking dresses, &c.

The scraper in country houses is taken indoors and cleaned, but when a fixture, as in London houses, the dirt must be removed daily and the scraper washed and kept bright. After the steps, hall-door, &c., are cleaned, the cook gets the breakfast ready, and as a rule she and the housemaid will prepare and take their breakfast before that of the family.

When the kettle boils, she should move it aside, to make room for the pan or gridiron, still keeping it boiling, however. If she have an omelette to make, or fish, or cutlets to be prepared with eggs and bread-crumbs, they will have her first attention. If both fried fish and fried meat are wanted for breakfast, the fish should be done first, then covered close and kept warm while the meat is being cooked, not using the same pan. However, if the meat were only for one—such as a chop or a rasher of bacon—it might be done in a gridiron in front of the fire, while the fish or omelette was being fried on the top.

While the cooking is going on, she should put four plates to warm. She should also make some pieces of nice thin toast, and place them in the toast-rack.

When the pan is removed from the fire, she should boil the eggs; she should also make the tea or coffee—if that be done in the kitchen ; if an urn is used, she should fill that and send it up to the breakfast parlour by the housemaid, when the mistress will make it herself.

She will then place on a tray the hot dish, the eggs in the egg-cups on a dish with four egg-spoons, the toast and the teapot, and give it to the housemaid, who will take it to the breakfast-parlour.

The housemaid will wait a few moments in the parlour to hand the plates, &c. ; after that, the cook attends the breakfast-parlour, while the housemaid goes to the bedrooms, to open all the windows and turn down the beds.

She should open out and separate all the bedclothes, placing them over the ends of the bedsteads and the backs of the chairs to air. Breakfast being concluded, the cook will remove the breakfast things. After which she should bring up a hand-brush and dust-pan, and sweep up the crumbs. She should also arrange the fire, sweep up the hearth and put the chairs in their places.

MORNING WORK.

Washing up the breakfast things will begin the work. For this she will require a pail of hot water, two tea-towels and a coarse dish-cloth. These latter should be all quite clean and dry. She should first remove the tea-leaves from the teapot, and put them aside carefully for sweeping. She should then rinse out the teapot, if it be of metal, and put it aside to be rubbed up with the rest of the plate ; if it be china, it should be rinsed both outside and inside, and left to drain. Then wash the cups and saucers and all the rest of the ware, except the greasy plates and dishes, and leave them to drain. Then wash the greasy plates and dishes, adding some fresh hot water to the pail. Then the knives. These should not be dipped entirely into the water. The blades should be held down in it for a short time ; the handles should not touch it at all. They should be immediately wiped in the coarse cloth, and laid aside to be cleaned. It is best to use an old jug for this purpose.

She should then wipe thoroughly dry all the china and ware, using for the cups and saucers the tea-towels only ; but the dishes and plates must be wiped first with a coarse towel, and finished off afterwards with the finer one. The silver should be washed in a separate bowl. It should be wiped thoroughly dry, and afterwards be rubbed up with a clean leather. The teapot, if of silver or Britannia metal, should be rubbed up also.

All the things being clean, they should be immediately put by—the china and ware in their appointed places on the dresser or in the cupboard, the knives in the knife-box, the silver in the silver-basket, the salt-cellars and cruet-stand wherever they are usually kept, but the sideboard cellaret is the best place. It is a good thing, also, to take the silver up and put it in the sideboard immediately. Then the pails should be emptied and wiped out, and the cloths rinsed and hung up to dry.

The cook should then tidy up her kitchen and scullery, in readiness for her mistress when she comes down to inspect and give her orders for the day.

Whilst the cook has been removing the breakfast things and washing them up, the housemaid empties the slops. For this she should take upstairs a slop-pail, a can of boiling water and two slop-cloths. As she empties each vessel, she should scald it out, then wipe it perfectly dry. She should empty the tin baths, wipe them very dry and turn them up on end against the wall. Empty any water that may remain in the water-jugs, bottles and tumblers, and rinse them out—the bottles and tumblers with tepid water. Rinse out and wipe the soap-dish and the brush-dish ; wipe down the tops of the stands, and replace all the things in their proper position. In doing this she must be very particular to use one of the cloths with the washing apparatus only. Having finished this work in one room, she should go to another, and so through them all. She should then take downstairs her slop-pail, water-can, cloths and hot-water jugs and chamber candlesticks ; and then, being joined by the cook, who will have washed her hands and put on a large clean apron for the purpose, they will both make the beds. Feather-beds and mattresses should be turned every day ; the former, also, will require to be well beaten and shaken. The bed makers should first seize it firmly by the top corners, and shake the feathers to the bottom. Then take it by the bottom corners and shake the feathers to the top. Then shake them down equally through it all, taking care to break up any lumps. Then, when the feathers are evenly distributed throughout the whole, it should be smoothed down, and the mattress, if it be used, placed on gently and quite evenly. The under blanket comes next. It should come quite down to the bottom of the bed, and be spread smoothly without wrinkles. Then the under sheet. It should be spread quite equally and evenly over the bed, without wrinkles, and should be tucked firmly in all round. Then the bolster. They should first hold it, one at each end, and shake it well; then beat the feathers out equally through the whole, and if the strings or buttons of the case have become undone, re-fasten them. Then the pillows. They should be well shaken and smoothed, and the buttons or strings fastened. Then the upper sheet. This should be drawn up quite to the top of the bed. It should be put on quite evenly, and should be firmly tucked in at the bottom. Then the blankets, one by one. They should be put on—first, at the top, not coming up quite as high as the sheet. They should be spread gently down, taking care not to draw the sheet, and should be tucked in at the bottom and sides of the bed. Then the counterpane should be spread over all very evenly and smoothly. It should not be tucked in, but allowed to hang down on either side. When one bed is done they should go to the next, and so through them all. When finished, the cook should retire to her downstairs work, while the housemaid sweeps and dusts the bed-rooms. It is not necessary to give a thorough sweeping to a bed-room every day. It is enough to lightly brush over the carpets with a hand-broom, collecting the dust as she goes in the dust-pan; but she should particularly do so under the beds, where fluff collects the most. Having swept one bed-room, she should now dust it and finish it off before going to another. She should dust every article in the room carefully. She should remove the looking-glass, bottles, boxes, &c., from the dressing-table, and dust it thoroughly; and she should carefully dust the looking-glass and other things before replacing them. She should dust each of the chairs, the wardrobe and chest of drawers, removing any article that may be on the top of the latter, and dusting under them; the same with the chimney-piece. She must also dust the door and the sills and ledges of the windows. She should then fill all the jugs and bottles with clean cold water, and, having shut all the bed-room doors, she should sweep down the stairs, which should be done with a hand-broom and dust-pan, collecting the dust as she goes. When the stairs and closets are swept down she should dust down the banisters, rubbing the handrail well; also the lobby windows, frames, sills and ledges; and the outsides of all the doors, going thoroughly over all the panels.

Besides this daily "doing up," every bed-room in a house should get a thorough cleaning once a week; and, if not carpeted all over, should be scoured once every three weeks.

This in a house with four bed-rooms—two large and two small—would give one large bed-room to be done on Tuesday, one on Wednesday and two small on Thursday. The housemaid would then have Friday for the drawing-room, and Saturday for plate-cleaning, lamp-cleaning, &c. If any washing be done at home, Monday is the best day for it, and no other extra work should be done on that day.

CLEANING OF BED-ROOMS.

Before a bed-room is thoroughly cleaned, the slops will have been emptied, of course, but no other work done in it previously.

Having brought up a furniture-dusting-brush and a duster, the maid will begin by removing the bed, mattress and palliasse from the bedstead. She will then dust the bedstead thoroughly, going into all the joints and crevices; then brush the mattress. She will then remove the sheets and pillows and bolster-cases, and place them in the soiled-clothes basket, and having replaced the bed, mattresses, bolster, pillows, blankets and counterpane on the bedstead, but without making the bed, she will cover all with a large dusting-sheet. She

BANISTER-BRUSH.

will then fold and pin up as high as she can the bed and window-curtains, and remove the soiled muslin blinds and toilet-cover, and place them in the soiled-clothes basket. She will then remove

from the bed-room the towel-stand, all clothes that may be hanging on pegs, the looking-glass and all small ornamental articles from the dressing-table and chimney-piece. She will also roll up and remove the strips of carpeting and hearthrug, the fender and fire-irons and any small portable articles of furniture.

Then, having brought up a sweeping-brush, dust-pan and some damp tea-leaves, she will sweep the room, beginning at the door, going into all the corners, and bringing the dust to the hearthstone, from which she will collect and remove it. She should also remove the dust-pan and sweeping-brush, and shut the room door.

Although on ordinary days the staircase is not swept down until all the bed-rooms are done, on these " thorough cleaning " days, it is best to do it immediately after this sweeping, because, whilst the dust is settling there, nothing else can be done in the room.

The dust having settled, she should return, bring with her the housemaid's box, a small pail of hot water, a house flannel and a piece of Bath-brick. She should then clean the grate, proceeding in the same manner as with the breakfast-parlour grate, and wash and whiten the hearthstone. She should then thoroughly dust the room, wiping every article of furniture carefully, wiping down the walls with a clean duster tied over a sweeping-brush, going all round the cornice and over the door. She should also dust the window-panes, sills and ledges.

The dusting being done, she should take downstairs the housemaid's box, the sweeping-brush and dusters, the house-flannel and Bath-brick, and bring up a large clean bowl, a can of hot water, a piece of soap, some washing soda, a piece of clean flannel, a sponge, a clean basin-cloth and a clean linen glass-cloth. She should then thoroughly wash, with soap, soda and warm water, all the washing-table apparatus, and wipe them thoroughly dry; the water-bottle and tumbler should be wiped with the glass-cloth. She should also wash down the marble top of the washstand with warm soap and water and the flannel. She should then clean the windows. Two leathers and two pails of cold water are needed. Rub the windows up and down with a leather dipped in cold water, until all dirt, dust and stains have disappeared; then, with a clean leather and fresh water, rub down one way only, and leave the glass to dry. The window-panes being washed, she should wash the sills and ledges. She should also wash the china plates and handles of the door, and any part of the paint that may be dirty; but this, as also the paint of the window-sills and ledges, should be done with *cold* water and soap, and very carefully, or the paint will be injured.

In doing all this work, she should frequently empty her bowl into the pail, and refill it with clean water.

Her next work, having removed the bowl, cloths, &c., will be to scour the room. Boards that are scoured regularly once every three weeks require nothing more than plenty of clean cold soft water and hard scrubbing with a good scrubbing-brush, to make and keep them a good colour; but if they have been allowed to get very dirty, hot water, soda and a little soap will be necessary. The housemaid should bring up a good large pail of water, a scrubbing-brush and a clean house-flannel. She should begin to scour at the end of the room farthest from the door and work towards it. She should first scrub well a portion as far as she can reach kneeling, using plenty of water; then wipe it off dry with the flannel, move a little, and do the next portion; but she should take care to leave not the smallest bit of board unscrubbed or less scrubbed than the rest. If she use soap she

SCRUBBING-BRUSHES.

must be careful to wash it off well again with the flannel, else the boards will blacken. She should empty her pail and refill it with fresh water very frequently; it will save trouble in the end, for it is impossible to wash anything clean with dirty water.

As soon as the room is all scoured out she should open the windows and the door, to allow a thorough draught to pass through the room and dry it. In winter a fire should be lighted. But a bed-room should never be scoured in wet or even damp weather. As soon as the room is dry, the cook will come up and assist her to make the bed, on which she will put clean sheets, bolster and pillow-cases.

She will then bring back and lay down the carpets; if possible they should first be shaken. Bring back the fender and fire-irons and all the furniture ornaments and clothes which she had removed, and re-arrange them in their proper places. She should put up clean blinds, put on a clean toilet-cover and polish the looking-glass ; then, having filled the jug and bottle with fresh cold water, the room will be quite finished.

CLEANING OF THE DRAWING-ROOM.

First remove all furniture to the centre of the room, packing it up carefully and placing all ornaments, pictures, &c., upon the centre table. Cover all with the dusting-sheets. Strew the carpet with well-washed tea-leaves, and

HOUSEMAID'S STEPS.

sweep as directed on page 554 ; dust walls and cornices with the brushes for that purpose ; hen clean the grate, hearth, &c., mantelpiece, looking-glasses and windows ; dust and replace the pictures, washing the frames with *gin*, and rubbing the cords well with a duster. Replace the furniture after well dusting and rubbing it with furniture polish. Carefully wash or rub the ornaments, and replace them. A large room with much furniture can be cleaned in this manner in from three to four hours by two persons.

The cook also, in her department, should have particular days for "thorough cleanings." Thus, Mondays she too gives to the washing. Tuesdays she washes the hall. Wednesday, thoroughly cleans the dining-room. Thursday, cleans the front kitchen and scours all the tins. Friday the back kitchen and pantries ; and Saturday, the hall, the kitchen stairs and basement passage. Steps every day.

Therefore, on Tuesday, while the housemaid is engaged with the bed-rooms, the cook cleans the hall and steps.

CLEANING OF THE DINING-ROOM.

The cook should first roll up the rug and remove the fender and fire-irons. Then gather together the furniture in the middle of the room, the chairs turned one upon the other, and cover them all with dusting-sheets. She should remove all the plate, &c., from the top of the sideboard, and either put it into the sideboard or remove it from the room. She should then, having first sprinkled the carpet with damp tea-leaves, sweep the room, beginning at the door, going into all the corners, and bringing the dust to the hearthstone, where she should collect it in the dust-pan and remove it.

She should then clean the grate and hearthstone, bringing up for the purpose the housemaid's box, a pail of hot water, the house-flannel and hearthstone. She should first lay down a coarse cloth over the carpet in front of the fireplace, and place her utensils upon it. If there are the remains of a fire in the grate, that must be first cleared away and placed in the cinder-box. She should then blacklead the grate, laying it on with a soft brush, rubbing it off with a harder and finishing it off with a polishing-brush. All the bright polished steel part should be rubbed with emery paper, and afterwards with a leather, as should also be the fire-irons and the steel portion of the fender. In washing the hearthstone she should be very careful not to let any of the water touch the grate ; if a fire is to be lighted, that should be done before the washing of the hearthstone.

She should then remove all these utensils, and, having provided herself with a clean duster and a cornice-broom, she should dust all the room carefully, wiping down the walls, going over all the cornices, and the doors, the window-panes, sills and ledges. If there are any pictures in the room they should be dusted with a light feather-brush, as should the frame of the chimney-glass ; the plate should be polished with a clean dry linen cloth. She should then dust all the furniture, and replace the several articles in their proper positions.

Her morning's occupation of washing or house-cleaning being over, the cook will probably have to occupy herself with some work in the culinary depart-ment, the making of soup, or preparing sweet dishes for the late dinner ; or, if there be children in the family who dine early, she will have to get their dinner. At from one to two o'clock, luncheon is usually served.

The children's dinner will probably be at the same time. The things to be taken up will depend entirely on the nature of the meal, but for whatever is served there must be a sufficient supply of knives, forks, spoons, plates, glasses, &c., for the number of persons who are to partake of it. The housemaid lays the luncheon, and while the family are at luncheon the servants will take their dinner.

AFTERNOON WORK.

After luncheon, the cook washes up the things, proceeding the same as she did with the breakfast things, while the housemaid goes to her room, changes her morning print dress for a neat stuff, and puts on a clean white apron, cap, collar and cuffs. She is then ready to open the door for visitors.

The afternoon the housemaid will employ, on some days, in starching, sprinkling, or ironing the fine things ; on others she may have some house needlework, such as hemming dusters and glass-cloths, or mending stockings, sheets, &c., to do.

Before or at four o'clock, the cook will have set about getting the dinner ready. If the dinner-hour be half-past six or seven, five will be time enough for the housemaid to begin her preparations.

She should first clean the knives ; this, if done in the patent knife-cleaner, will be very little trouble, but they should be carefully dusted afterwards. She will then take up the stand, and place it in the hall in a convenient position, then collect on her tray all the things she will require for laying the table.

This will, of course, depend upon the nature of the meal and the number of persons to partake of it. Supposing, then, the dinner to consist of soup, fish, a roast joint, potatoes, vegetables and a sweet dish, that sherry and claret are to be served, and, as at breakfast, four persons to sit down to table, she will require :—

4 Knives.	4 Dessert-spoons.
4 Small knives.	4 Table-spoons.
4 Fish knives.	1 Gravy-spoon.
4 Forks.	1 Soup-ladle.
4 Small forks.	4 Plates.
4 Fish forks.	4 Napkins.
1 Carving knife and fork.	2 Salt-cellars.
1 Small knife and fork for cut-	The cruet-stand.
ing the tart.	The tablecloth.
1 Pair of fish carvers.	4 Tumblers.
1 Pair of knife-rests.	4 Sherry glasses.
4 Soup-spoons.	4 Claret glasses.

She should place the tray on the stand in the hall, or, if the dining-room be large, the stand and tray may be put in a convenient position there, and then proceed to lay the cloth.

PREPARATION OF DINNER.

To send a dinner to table all in nice order and thoroughly well cooked, depends not only on the cook's skill in preparing each particular dish nicely itself, but on her knowledge of how to prepare them all with regard to each other; many people quite capable of frying a dish of fish, or roasting a joint very well, *by themselves*, would yet make a complete muddle of a dinner of four courses.

The first and most important thing is to set about it in time; nothing can be properly done unless sufficient time is taken to do it in. The next is to understand what things in the dinner will bear to be cooked some little time before they are to be eaten, without spoiling, and to get them ready first.

And as the difficulty of cooking a dinner consists, not so much in the number of dishes as in the way they are to be cooked, if the cook be at all consulted by her mistress in the ordering of the dinner, she should take care, above all things, not to have several things to be cooked in the same manner, as, for instance, with soup and boiled fish not to have a boiled joint, and a boiled pudding; or with fried fish, not to have fried cutlets and a fried omelette. With a small range it is impossible to boil many things at once, and boiled things—particularly fish and puddings—spoil completely by being cooked sooner than required: if left in the water they get sodden, if dished they get flabby.

Supposing a dinner to consist of soup, boiled fish requiring 20 minutes to cook, a piece of roast beef, a baked pudding, potatoes and broccoli. The puddings hould be made in the morning; the soup, except the thickening and add-ing of wine, sauce, &c., should also be made in the morning.

The beef should be put down in time to allow a quarter of an hour to every pound, and a quarter of an hour over; if the dinner-time be half-past six she may calculate to have it done at a quarter to seven; the fish she should calculate to have done at twenty-five minutes to seven; the potatoes and broccoli should not be ready until the beef is to be served; the soup may be drawn aside on the range to let the fish-kettle go on, but the potatoes and broccoli, when once they are put down and have begun to simmer, must be kept so or else they will be spoiled.

The soup should be served punctually at half-past six. The cook should have previously warmed four plates, she should also warm the soup tureen by rinsing it out with boiling water; and some toasted or fried bread cut up into dice should be served with it if it be brown soup. In dishing it she should be very careful to pour it boldly from the digester or pan into the tureen, so that none may drip over the side of the tureen and carry blacks into it.

As soon as the soup is served, the cook should prepare the melted butter for the fish, taking care to have four hot plates and a hot dish ready for it also.

The fish being served, she should dish the beef and vegetables, having ready hot plates and dishes for them also.

This course will be the longest of any, and, while the family are partaking of it, the cook can employ herself washing up the soup and fish plates.

The pudding should then be served, it will also require a hot dish and four hot plates.

If the housemaid's attendance is required continually in the dining-room, the cook will have to carry up all the dishes and plates to the hall for her. The cook should also carry down the plates and dishes as each course is ended.

Dinner being concluded, the housemaid removes the dinner things. She should do all as quickly as possible, but at the same time gently and carefully; not crashing the glasses together, placing the knives and forks together in the knife-box, piling the plates one over another, but never with the knives, forks, or spoons left between. When the things are all removed, she should sweep the crumbs from the tablecloth with a crumb-brush, and, as soon as the cloth is removed, she should rub the table quickly all over with a soft cloth.

DRIED PLATE PAIL.

When the things are taken down, the tablecloth should be immediately shaken and folded, and placed in the linen-press.

The next work is to wash up the dinner things. In this the housemaid should assist the cook; she should do the glass and the plate, leaving the plates and dishes and knives to the cook.

The plates and dishes should be washed in the dish-tub, in very hot water, to get off the grease; they should be allowed to drain, and then wiped very dry with a clean cloth.

The water should not be so hot for the knives. The blades should be held down in the water for a little time, the handles should not touch at all. They should be wiped very dry and perfectly free from grease, and then laid aside to be cleaned.

For the glasses the water should be only tepid. They should be rinsed very thoroughly and left to drain; then wiped dry, and well rubbed, to brighten them, with a clean fine linen cloth.

The silver will require hotter water. They should not be mixed with the glasses at all in the washing, as many of them will be greasy. They should be first wiped dry with a linen cloth, and then rubbed with a leather.

When all the things are washed, they should be put in their proper places.

The cook should then clean up all her cooking-utensils, and the housemaid should clean the knives.

The cook now takes out a sufficient supply of coals to last until the next forenoon. This concludes her work for the day.

About eight o'clock, the housemaid takes up the tea and coffee, or whatever else the family may be in the habit of taking in the evening. When removed, she will wash them up and put them all by in their places; and then the housemaid should go up to the bed-rooms, taking the slop-pail with her. She should empty all slops, close the bed-room windows (in winter these must be shut by three o'clock), and, when desired, the shutters, and draw the curtains. She should also let down the curtains of the beds, and neatly fold back the bedclothes from the bolster. In doing this, she should first draw up and fold back the portion of sheet that comes up higher than the rest of the clothes, then fold them all down together. She should also refill with clean cold water any of the water-bottles and jugs that may have been emptied during the day.

Before going to bed, the housemaid should bring up all the plate to her mistress, having counted to see if it be all right. If anything is short, an instant search should be made ; and, if not found, the mistress should be at once told of the missing article.

The cook will lock all the doors, turn off the kitchen gas and take up the keys.

We have thus given the whole day's work, dividing it as we went ; but, to make it still clearer, we will now make a division of the different departments of work.

The Kitchens—and all the cleaning appertaining to them, and *all* cooking, except making toast for afternoon or evening tea, belong to the cook.

The Bed-rooms—and all work appertaining to them, with the exception of assistance in bed-making, belong to the housemaid.

The Dining-room—that is, the weekly cleaning of it, falls to the cook's share.

The Drawing-room—to the housemaid.

The Breakfast-parlour—to the housemaid.

All attendance, except the waiting at breakfast, which the cook does while the housemaid is engaged with the bed-rooms, falls to the housemaid. Answering door before twelve, the cook ; afterwards the housemaid.

The Glass and the Plate are exclusively the housemaid's care.

The knives are washed by the cook when she washes the other things, but cleaned by the housemaid.

The table-linen is also the housemaid's care, as is the mending of linen going to and returning from the wash, if this be not done by the mistress.

The boots and shoes—The cook does the gentlemen's, the housemaid the ladies' boots and shoes.

The Washing—If this is done at home it is divided ; generally the housemaid does all the finer things, the cook the coarser and heavier, the housemaid having all the starching and ironing. But if the cook were a very good ironer, it would be better for her to take that, and the housemaid to do more at the wash-tub. But it is almost impossible to lay down any definite rules for this department of work, as it must depend entirely on the extent of the washing done at home and the abilities of the servants. One general rule for all the work— both the cook and housemaid should be obliging to each other, and endeavour always to facilitate each other in their several duties. And though it is desirable that they adhere as much as possible each to her own department of work, yet neither should

WRINGING MACHINE.

object, in case of her fellow-servant being ill, or getting leave to go out, to perform her duties for her.

THE GENERAL SERVANT.

The general servant will practically have to do alone what is accomplished by housemaid and cook ; therefore to detail her work would be superfluous.

We may, however, say that she would in most families require assistance, such as help with the bed-making, dusting, &c. This, of course, varying according to the size of the house, the number of inmates and many other things. She should not, however, be expected to wait at table, or to be dressed for the afternoon before luncheon.

In many houses where there is not a great deal to do, for the children a nurse housemaid is now kept, and she takes the lighter part of the general servant's duties. Also in a still larger number of households a boy is engaged to clean boots and knives, fill scuttles, &c., thus saving one servant a great deal of work, and that when time is the most precious, namely, in the morning.

SPRING CLEANING.

In spring and autumn more extended cleaning operations go on, and the time for these periodical cleanings is usually May and October. All white-washing, painting and general repairs, should be done in the spring, and during the cleaning, carpets should be taken up, well beaten, mended, and turned so as to bring the worn pieces out of sight. Care must be taken to match the design of the carpet. All ornaments should be carefully washed, cleaned, or relacquered. Curtain-poles taken down, washed with vinegar and rubbed bright with furniture-polish. Looking-glasses cleaned. Chairs and sofas re-covered or invested with loose chintz covers. Paper rubbed down with the clean crumb of stale quartern loaves. Ornaments placed in fire-stoves, and white curtains hung up in the place of the damask or chintz, which should be well shaken, folded in large folds, with a couple of handfuls of dry bran laid between each fold, and a piece of camphor placed in the drawer or box in which they are kept.

When carpets are re-laid, the colours are greatly revived by adding a small quantity of ox-gall to warm water and washing them over with the mixture : plenty of air must be admitted after this, as the smell is very strong.

Locks should now be taken off, cleaned and oiled, bell wires adjusted, and bell-handles tightened, if necessary.

The chimney of each room should be swept, and care taken to see that the brush is sent up through the top of the chimney.

In olden days, all fires, save the kitchen, were left off on the twenty-fifth of March and the house-cleaning began as soon after as possible. Now, in these days, it is not until May that many among us begin to turn the house out of windows. The first fine week after May 1st is a good rule, but a fine hot April will sometimes tempt us to begin before the sun gains much power. At the end of March all the blankets that can be spared should be washed and hung out in the brisk wind to dry, then thoroughly aired by a good fire for twelve hours and stored in a dry place.

The first thing to be done when beginning a "spring clean," whether in March, April, or May, is to ascertain what pieces of furniture want renovating; and if any require to be taken from home, they should be sent off at once. Then the sweep must be consulted and ordered to come on the most convenient days. If the family are away, all the rooms can be swept in one day ; but if not, the arrangements must be altered by circumstances. To "begin with the top floor and go down" is not a bad rule. Before the sweep's arrival all carpets must come up and go away, or out to be beaten ; all ornaments must be removed, pictures taken down and looking-glasses covered. All furniture should be covered with sheets or with dusting-sheets.

After the sweep's necessary but grimy labours, all traces of his presence must be got rid of and the room swept *towards* the fireplace and all dirt taken up and the stove cleaned. The walls, if panelled, are washed down; if papered, either rubbed down with stale bread or cleaned by passing a clean cloth down them, taking care to remove all cobwebs from corners. In cleaning with bread, act as follows :—

First blow off the dust with the bellows. Divide a stale loaf of white bread into eight pieces. Take the crust into your hand and, beginning at the top of the paper, wipe it *downwards* in the lightest manner with the crumb; do not cross or go upwards ; wipe about half a yard at a stroke and when all the upper part is done, go round again, beginning a little above where you left off. It must be done with great lightness, or the dirt will adhere to the paper, but if properly done the paper looks like new. Then the floor is scrubbed with sand and hot water—*no soap, no soda*—and allowed to dry. The furniture is thoroughly cleansed while the floor is drying.

Those articles which are French-polished should be washed with weak vinegar and water and the following polish used to them :—3 oz. of common beeswax, 1 oz. of white wax, 1 oz. of curd soap, 1 pint of turpentine, 1 pint of *boiled* soft water ; mix these, adding the water when cold, shake well and keep for 48 hours. Apply with a flannel, and polish first with a duster and then with a silk handkerchief.

The furniture should be replaced in position, or changed to suit the altered room, which looks differently with white curtains and dressed-up fireplace. There are many ways of filling the fireplace. The blank space filled by looking-glass, with ferns and pot plants in front, is pretty but expensive ; but the trellis basket-work screen and fender is within the reach of all. The price, to begin with, is moderate, and the trellis is soon covered with creepers, nasturtium, jasmine, or clematis. The front or fender may be filled with green moss and cut flowers, or by pots containing growing plants.

Winter curtains must be put away carefully, after hanging out in the air for three or four days if in fine weather, bringing them in at night. On the day you intend to pack them away, beat them lightly with a thin stick and fold them carefully in as large folds as your store-place will allow, scatter a handful of bran (bone-dry) between each fold and, if placed in a large drawer or chest, add a big lump of camphor.

Lined chintz curtains should be treated in a similar way, but do not require the camphor. The bran cleans both chintz and damask curtains in a wonderful manner ; and there is but one thing to remember, that you must carefully shake out the bran when you draw them out again. The nicely-washed and mended muslin curtains should hang in their due place, the pictures be replaced in position. And now we turn to the blinds, a vexed subject in many households. If venetian blinds are in question, they want simply washing, perhaps repainting, the tapes renovating, not a long business in willing hands; but if the blinds be white holland, on rollers, it is sad work. First to get the blinds from the rollers, then to wash them and iron them straight, then to replace them, and then to find that no one in the house can pull them up straight. Roller-blinds that go up with a gentle spring and come down with a gentle click-click are best ; but if they are not quite clean and new, they should be taken down and made into nice glass-cloths, for which they are well adapted, and new ones placed upon the rollers.

The outside of a house, both back and front, is an index to the character of its mistress. Every room should have a window neatly dressed with curtains and blinds, clean, neat and hanging straight. The steps should rival the snow in whiteness and be fresh whitened *daily*.

The bed-rooms require a few words. The bedding should be taken out of doors if possible and well beaten and brushed, the bedstead taken to pieces, whether of wood or of iron, and well washed with hot water and soap. When quite dry the bedding should be replaced and the summer bed-curtains be arranged with the bed-furniture. An opportunity should be taken of sending all japanned goods to be repaired, as cans, baths, hot-water cans, &c.; or these may be done with enamel at home. All the glass and extra china should be washed or dusted in the china closet, the list gone over and all missing articles accounted for and replaced as soon as possible.

A few items of housewifery may be jotted down here. Have the pianos tuned as soon as the house-cleaning is over ; oil all the door-locks, keys and bolts once every month. Oil all door and window hinges. Have every trifling repair seen to at once and paid for at once; this saves much trouble and is considerably cheaper than having carpenter's and glazing jobs booked.

Turn out every box, cupboard and corner in the house-cleaning. Separate all stores required for or likely to be useful in needlework, and keep these in tiny rolls or parcels in a drawer known as the work-drawer. Wash out and fill up inkstands once a week. Few writers like much ink in the inkstand ; half an inch deep is quite enough for ordinary writing for a week, and more than enough to spill if there is an accident with the inkstand.

THE NURSERY.

The first point to be considered with regard to the children is their health. Where it is possible, large airy rooms at the top of the house should be given up to the babies. A day and night nursery are required and the night nursery should be the larger of the two. It should contain single iron beds or cots, placed upon well-scrubbed boards ; a strip of carpet or long rug should be placed at each bedside, to enable the little feet to alight from bed safely. Slippers should be kept under each little bed ; and the children taught never to go a step without them. The bed should consist of a hard mattress covered with two folds of blanket and a pillow, the ordinary bolster being dispensed with ; of course a pair of sheets and one, two, or three blankets, according to the season. A chair for each child, a wash-stand and a hip-bath should constitute the rest of the furniture, though in large rooms a wardrobe and chest of drawers may be placed. Every room occupied by children should have a fireplace and chimney, to allow of ventilation during the night. A large window is also requisite. In winter it is well to carpet the bedroom, but this should be removed at the spring cleaning. Once a week at least the bed-room fire should be lighted during the winter. If bed-rooms, whether for children or adults, are scrubbed in the winter time, it should be done early in the morning, a good fire lit and the room be perfectly dry before being slept in. No flowers of any kind or growing plants should be placed in the bed-rooms of children at night.

BERCEAUNETTE.

The children's day nursery should also be airy, well ventilated and kept perfectly clean. It is well to have as little furniture as possible: a round table and chairs are all that is really wanted, if there are good deep cupboards in the room; if not, an *armoire* of some kind must be provided for children's toys and nurse's tea and breakfast service and sundries, that should always stand in order under a good nurse's care in large families. On a high shelf, or, better still, locked up, but handy, should be a few simple medicines for children — castor-oil, rhubarb and magnesia and a pot of jam to help these down; then a box should contain lint, strapping-plaster and court-plaster; a pair of scissors should be kept in this box, and never used for other purposes: a neat roll of old linen, a roll of new flannel and some bandage strips

BABY'S BASKET.

should also be placed close at hand.   Nurse should be provided with two enamelled saucepans, with a block-tin kettle, with neat jars, containing sugar, pearl barley, Embden grits, mustard, linseed and linseed-meal.   She should keep a bottle of camphorated spirits and of ipecacuanha wine: also among her medicines she should have a store of night-lights, a food warmer and some candles; a tin of plain biscuits may also be placed in her charge.

Both nurse and mother should inspect the stores once a week and see that nothing is wanting at any time that would be required at night in a hurry. An old worn knife or a palette-knife and some spoons are required for plasters and poultices and should be at hand.

Children require to run and skip, dance and jump, and to take good walks. Children's nursery hours should be as follows :—All out of bed at seven, all dressed and sitting down to breakfast at eight, nine o'clock should see the little troop out of doors in garden, in park, or on country roads.   A walk in the morning and the afternoon is necessary in fine weather.   After the 20th of October all children under six should be indoors after three o'clock: this rule should be continued until spring days again come round.   Dinner at 1, tea at 4.30, bed at 6 or 7, according to the ages of the children.   A glass of cold water, morning and night, is the best medicine they can take.

The morning bath for healthy children of four or five years of age should be of cold water in summer and tepid in winter.   It is an excellent plan to fill a large brown pickle-jar with bay salt and Tidman's sea salt in equal parts and to fill up with soft water and tie a muslin cap over the jar ; pour off the water every morning into the bath, adding fresh until all the salt is melted, when we must begin again.   A hip-bath should be used for the morning bath, and the child rapidly sluiced all over and then enveloped in a large well-aired sheet of fine huckaback, not less than two yards square ; rub quickly but not roughly, and see that the little limbs glow before you part with them.   Then quickly dress the child in well-aired clothes and brush the hair, clean the teeth and hear the morning prayer before setting him to table.

Breakfast should be *ready*, for many children are so constituted as to be cross, because they feel ill, before breakfast: such children cannot bear the sinking feeling caused by want of food.   If such there be in a family and the number of little ones prevents the breakfast being ready for all directly, give the child a crust of bread or a biscuit and it will play happily until summoned to its breakfast.

HOW TO KEEP A LINEN-PRESS.

Sheets should be wider and longer than the bed they are used on and should be marked in pairs, with date of the year.   The ends are stronger sewn, not hemmed, with linen thread.   They should be folded in pairs and sorted according to size.   This enables a new servant, or entire stranger, to select sheets required in a hurry; for it should be the chief aim of the mistress so to arrange her house that even in her absence all should go on with regularity and order and that, in case of illness, everything may be found without her assistance.

The best pillow-cases should be of fine linen, the cases to fit easily the pillows and made with a double hem, in which button-holes are placed. Finely-frilled pillow-cases look very nice, but, unless expense is of little object, should be kept for the use of the best rooms.

Tablecloths should be folded carefully and sorted according to size. By this plan trouble and loss of time in unfolding and re-folding is avoided.

Table-napkins should not be marked in ink, but the monogram worked in raised embroidery. They should also be arranged according to size and quality.

Towels should be arranged in the same way as the other linen ; they should be arranged in half-dozens, whether rough, bath, fine, or of medium quality.

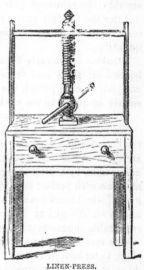

Servants' sheets, pillow-cases, towels, &c., should be all arranged in the same manner and attended to with equal care; they should be given out when required, by the mistress, who should have all changes of bed-linen made with exact regularity. The old-fashioned plan was to change the upper-sheet every week, giving a clean upper sheet and taking the upper-sheet in place of the lower. This plan insures regularity of wear in the sheets.

Glass-cloths should be of good linen ; that sold for white roller blinds answers admirably, as it is soft, without fluff and is not expensive.

LINEN-PRESS.

Tea-cloths are of coarser linen, but very coarse cloths are not economical, as they are clumsy and often cause breakages.

Kitchen-cloths.—Round towels are made of coarse linen and what is called "Crash," respectively. A good supply of these is required in every house.

Dusters are sold at prices varying from 3d. to 1s. each, but are far more effective when made of old chintz, old linings, &c., being softer and taking up the dust far better than the dressed stiff linen. Ugly, old-fashioned chintz is often sold at threepence and fourpence a yard, and, when washed, makes admirable dusters at this low price.

The following list of household linen is intended for the guidance of those whose income is moderate. Fewer articles of each kind may comfortably answer where strict economy is an object in starting; but the numbers here given have been found by experience to suit a household of medium income, keeping two servants :—Best sheets, six pairs ; servants', four pairs ; pillow-cases, six best, twelve good, six common ; towels, twelve rough, twelve coarse, twenty-four fine, twelve servants' ; bath sheets, four ; tablecloths, four breakfast, four dinner, two best, four servants'; table-napkins, twelve dinner, twelve best, six breakfast; glass-cloths, twelve; tea-cloths, eighteen ; dusters, twelve ; round towels, six. Kitchen-cloths, twenty-four; chamber-cloths, six; pudding-cloths, six. A list of all the contents of the linen-press should be neatly entered in a book, with the marks carefully copied and a space left for remarks in time to come. Example : six pairs sheets, 1888; 1 pair turned, 1890 ; 1 pair cut up into glass-cloths, 1890.

At the periodical counting of the linen, the mistress should carefully examine each article, opening sheets, darning thin places with *flax*, not cotton ; and should endeavour each year to add some article to her stock.

After the first six years, a pair of sheets and a tablecloth should be bought each year, at least, as these are very expensive articles to purchase in quantity.

Blankets are usually kept in the linen-press when out of use. They should be tied in pairs and sewn up in an old linen pillow-case, with a lump of camphor in each parcel, the name of the room or bed to which they belong should be added to the card sewn to the case.

Coloured tablecloths, when out of use, should be kept in the linen-press.

We prefer the good old-fashioned plan of the mistress herself counting over the clean linen, examining it for repairs and re-placing it in the linen-press. By these means she sees exactly what is wanted to be repaired or renewed and is able, by taking things in time, to get a great deal of needlework done at home with perfect ease to herself and maids ; and by looking over the linen herself, she knows exactly what mending is to be done each week and neither allows an idle girl to impose upon her, nor, on the other hand, makes unreasonable demands on her housemaiden's industry. At certain seasons a week's rest from all needlework should be given to servants; this is to enable them to make a dress, or turn or alter their clothes to advantage, as they can do more in a week's steady work than in a hundred odds and ends of stolen time.

Of course, the house and body-linen is regularly mended every week, but every housewife knows that there are times when linen should undergo a more " thorough repairing " than it receives weekly. The linen list should be examined, the linen counted, the list corrected and any new linen carefully made and marked. Sheets should be turned sides and middle and re-hemmed, or rather re-sewn, for the hems of all house linen should be sewn, not hemmed. Old tablecloths may be cut up into tray or lunch-cloths, old finger-napkins be darned and fringed out into d'oyleys for vegetables or for placing under pie-dishes.

WARD, LOCK AND CO., LIMITED, LONDON, NEW YORK, AND MELBOURNE.

WHO WAS MRS BEETON?

Just about everyone knows the name Mrs Beeton, but most people are not quite sure why. Was she an ancient Victorian personage? they ask. Something perhaps like Queen Victoria herself; in her dotage, humourless and dour?

The lively facts tell quite a different story. Isabella Mary Beeton was born in London in 1835 into a lower middle class family. Her father died when she was five leaving four children. Her mother soon remarried and the family ended up with 21 children altogether. As the eldest, even in this family that was to become quite well-to-do, Isabella had no choice but to grow up very quickly into a practical, no-nonsense hard-worker.

At 20, the elegant, auburn-haired Isabella married the charismatic 25-year-old publisher Sam Beeton. As a partner in Clarke, Beeton & Co his big success had been publishing the first edition of Harriet Beecher Stowe's *Uncle Tom's Cabin*, as well as a range of successful magazines, one of them being *The Englishwoman's Domestic Magazine*. This was one of the publications he took with him when he started up as an independent publisher in the year of his marriage. Sam Beeton was obviously a man before his time, and he believed in independence for women. From the start, Isabella worked on the magazines, as a compiler, editor, journalist and translator.

They were a perfect match, but it was hard work, even for this energetic and determined young woman. The rigours of running a publishing house and a home made Isabella wonder why no-one had ever written a good book for brides. In time, the numerous recipes sent in from readers and tested in Isabella's kitchen – with the unique attribution of having ingredients placed before the recipe along with the number of servings and the cost – resulted in over one thousand pages that included 900 recipes. Combined with observations on everything from servant's wages to the rearing and management of children, this tome went on to become *Beeton's Book of Household Management*, first published in a single volume form in 1861. It was a bestseller, selling over 60,000 copies at 7s 6d in the first year.

Sam's company went on to have considerable success until 1866 when a bank failure led to Sam being unable to pay his debts and he had no choice but to sell out to a larger publisher, Ward, Lock & Co. They continued to bring out *Beeton's Household Management* in a variety of formats and under different titles, including, in 1893, this revised, enlarged edition entitled *Mrs Beeton's Everyday Cookery and Housekeeping Book*, which has rearranged the recipes alphabetically – the adoption of which means 'all cross reference and that very disagreeable parenthesis is avoided'. With offices in Melbourne and New York, Ward, Lock & Co. ensured that the name 'Mrs Beeton' grew in the public consciousness until it became one of the biggest brand names in British culinary history. Today in the back of many a cupboard a dusty copy of this much loved book can still be found.

Unfortunately, Isabella herself was long gone. In 1865, she died from fever, shortly after the birth of her fourth child. She was 28.

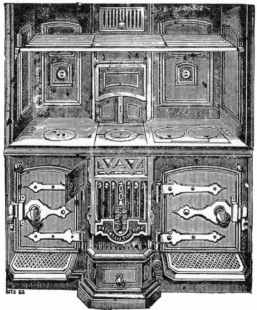